Microsoft®

Microsoft® Office Outlook® 2003 Inside Out

Jim Boyce

PUBLISHED BY
Microsoft Press
A Division of Microsoft Corporation
One Microsoft Way
Redmond, Washington 98052-6399

Library of Congress Cataloging-in-Publication Data pending.

Printed and bound in the United States of America.

1 2 3 4 5 6 7 8 9 QWT 8 7 6 5 4 3

Distributed in Canada by H.B. Fenn and Company Ltd.

A CIP catalogue record for this book is available from the British Library.

Microsoft Press books are available through booksellers and distributors worldwide. For further information about international editions, contact your local Microsoft Corporation office or contact Microsoft Press International directly at fax (425) 936-7329. Visit our Web site at www.microsoft.com/mspress. Send comments to *mspinput@microsoft.com.*

Acquisitions Editor: Alex Blanton
Project Editors: Sandra Haynes and Kristine Haugseth
Technical Editor: Thomas Keegan

Body Part No. X10-08598

For David and Austin, who have Grandpa wrapped around their fingers

Contents At A Glance

Content on the CD

Table of Contents

Chapter 29
Delegating Responsibilities to an Assistant 735

Chapter 30
Managing Folders, Data, and Archiving 751

Chapter 34
Configuring the Exchange Server Client 855

Chapter 35
Messaging with Exchange Server 869

Chapter 36
Supporting Outlook Under Exchange Server 885

Chapter 40 Collaboration with Outlook and Windows SharePoint Services 1009

Chapter 41 Accessing Messages Through a Web Browser 1027

Content on the CD

Article 1
Programming Forms with VBScript A1

Article 2
Using VBA in Outlook A17

Acknowledgments

I've authored and contributed to more than 50 books, and each project has been much the same in terms of compressed schedules and tight deadlines. This book was no different in that respect, but what made it one of the most enjoyable writing experiences of my career and eased the deadline woes was the phenomenal dedication to the project shown by all of the Microsoft Press staff.

I offer sincere thanks to Sandra Haynes and Kristine Haugseth, who served as project editors and helped mold the content and kept the project and people all moving forward as a team. My sincere thanks also go to Alex Blanton, acquisitions editor, for the opportunity to do the project and for his graciousness. David Fugate, my agent at Waterside Productions, gets a well-deserved thanks for not only bringing me this opportunity but also being my sounding board and keeping me focused.

Thanks also go to Tom Keegan, who had the difficult task of not only verifying the accuracy of a wide range of information but also trying to do that with a moving target during the beta process. I thank Teresa Horton, who served as copy editor and did a great job tightening up and clarifying the manuscript. Thanks also to Beth Lew, proofreader, for checking everyone's work and catching those errors that always seem to sneak by somehow.

My appreciation to the personnel at nSight for their outstanding project management and production work. Thanks to desktop publisher Patty Fagan, for putting together a layout that is as attractive as it is functional, and for her efforts in cleaning up and processing the screen shots and other artwork. Thanks also to editorial assistant Katie O'Connell for tracking the hundreds of components that make up a project of this size, and to project manager Mark Corsey for coordinating the overall effort.

Many thanks go to the other authors who contributed to this book: Blair Rampling and Rob Tidrow for the Outlook 2003 edition; and Deanna Maio, Tyler and Rima Regas, Dan Newland, John Durant, Matthew Nunn, and KC Lemson for their contributions to the previous edition. All of them poured heart and soul into their contributions. I offer an extra bit of thanks to Blair and Rob for making time in their schedules to take on some extra material yet again and help us make our deadlines.

Thanks also go to Bill Zumwalde, who helped with this and other projects to enable me to stay on schedule. Bill's attention to detail is phenomenal. I also express sincere thanks to Westley Annis, who took the rough script code I developed for the CustomContactPrint and CustomMessagePrint scripts in Chapter 26, and performed a major overhaul of the code to make the scripts functional and presentable.

I offer my appreciation and admiration to the Outlook development team for their efforts in making a great program even better!

Last, but not least, I extend my deepest love and appreciation to my wife, Julie, for tolerance of my obsessive work habits and understanding of my myriad other annoying character traits and bad habits.

We'd Like to Hear from You!

Our goal at Microsoft Press is to create books that help you find the information you need to get the most out of your software.

The INSIDE OUT series was created with you in mind. As part of an effort to ensure that we're creating the best, most useful books we can, we talked to our customers and asked them to tell us what they need from a Microsoft Press series. Help us continue to help you. Let us know what you like about this book and what we can do to make it better. When you write, please include the title and author of this book in your e-mail, as well as your name and contact information. We look forward to hearing from you.

How to Reach Us

E-mail: nsideout@microsoft.com
Mail: Inside Out Series Editor
Microsoft Press
One Microsoft Way
Redmond, WA 98052

Note: Unfortunately, we can't provide support for any software problems you might experience. Please go to http://support.microsoft.com *for help with any software issues.*

Introduction

Ten years ago the average computer user spent most of his or her time using productivity applications such as Microsoft Word or Microsoft Excel. In the ensuing decade, users have become more sophisticated, network implementations have become the rule rather than the exception, and collaboration has become a key facet of a successful business strategy. Perhaps the most significant change of all has been the explosive growth of the Internet. All these factors have led to a subtle but significant shift in the way people work. Today most users of Microsoft Office spend a majority of their time in Microsoft Outlook. That change alone signifies a shift toward information management as an increasingly important everyday task. Getting a handle on daily information management can be critical to your productivity, success, and sanity.

Outlook is an extremely versatile program. Most of the other applications in the Office suite have a fairly specific purpose. Outlook, however, serves as personal information manager (PIM), e-mail application, fax machine, task manager, and much more. With so much power and flexibility at your fingertips, you need to have a good understanding of Outlook's features. Understanding the ins and outs will not only help you get the most from this program, but will also have a positive impact on your workday.

Who This Book Is For

Understanding all of Outlook's features and putting them to work is the focus of *Microsoft Office Outlook 2003 Inside Out*. Most Outlook books act mainly as how-to guides for users who want to learn about the software. This approach leaves out workgroup managers and administrators when it comes to deployment, collaboration, server-side issues, and administration. *Microsoft Office Outlook 2003 Inside Out* offers a comprehensive look at the features most people will use in Outlook and serves as an excellent reference for users who need to understand how to accomplish what they need to do. In addition, this book goes a step or two further, providing useful information to advanced users and IT professionals who need to understand the bigger picture. Whether you want to learn Outlook for your own use, need to support Outlook on a peer-to-peer network, or are in charge of supporting Outlook under Microsoft Exchange Server, you'll find the information and answers you need between the covers of *Microsoft Office Outlook 2003 Inside Out*.

This book makes some assumptions about the reader. You should be familiar with your client operating system, whether it's Microsoft Windows XP or Microsoft Windows 2000. You should be comfortable working with a computer and have a good understanding of how to work with menus, dialog boxes, and other aspects of the user interface. In short, *Microsoft Office Outlook 2003 Inside Out* assumes you're an experienced computer user who might or might not have an understanding of Outlook and what it can do. The purpose of this book is to give you a comprehensive look at what Outlook can do, how to put Outlook to work, and how to manage Outlook at the user, workgroup, and server levels.

How This Book Is Organized

Microsoft Office Outlook 2003 Inside Out offers a structured, logical approach to all aspects of using and managing Outlook. Each of the 10 parts of the book focuses on a specific aspect of Outlook use or management.

Part 1—Working with Outlook

Part 1 starts with the basics. Chapter 1 takes a look at Outlook's architecture, setup, and startup options to help you understand how Outlook stores its data. In Chapter 2 you'll learn how to perform advanced setup and configuration tasks such as setting up e-mail accounts, using profiles, making Outlook work with other e-mail services, configuring receipt and delivery options, and using add-ins that extend Outlook's functionality. Chapter 3 gets you up to speed using Outlook to send and receive messages, manage your workday, locate information on the Internet, and perform other common tasks. Chapter 4 rounds out Part 1 with a detailed look at how you can use categories and types to organize your data in Outlook.

Part 2—Messaging

Part 2 delves deeper into Outlook's e-mail and fax messaging components and features. In Chapter 5 you'll learn how to manage address books and distribution lists. Chapter 6 explains how to send and receive Internet-based messages through Outlook. Chapter 7 will make you comfortable with the range of features Outlook has for creating messages both simple and complex. In Chapter 8 you'll learn how to organize your messages, apply filters and rules to process messages automatically, exclude junk and spam e-mail senders, and generate automatic responses to incoming messages. Chapter 9 gives you a detailed look at Outlook's capabilities for sending and receiving faxes.

Because security is an increasingly important topic, Chapter 10 will help you secure your system and your data, send messages securely, and prevent others from impersonating you to send messages. Chapter 11 offers a comprehensive look at how Outlook's remote mail features can be indispensable for managing your mail online and offline. Because Outlook isn't the only option available for messaging, in Chapter 12 you'll also learn how to integrate Outlook with Outlook Express and move messages, accounts, and addresses between the two applications. Outlook relies on Outlook Express as its default newsgroup reader, so you'll learn in Chapter 13 how to send, receive, and manage newsgroup messages with Outlook Express.

Part 3—Contact Management

Part 3 explores Outlook's features for managing your contacts. Chapter 14 starts with a look at how to manage contact information, including addresses, phone numbers, e-mail addresses, fax numbers, and a wealth of other information. You'll also learn how to sort, filter, and categorize your contacts, as well as share contact data with others. Chapter 15 looks at a Microsoft add-on product for Outlook called Business Contact Manager, which you can use to track business contacts, sales leads, products, and other business-related items. Chapter 16 provides a look at Lightweight Directory Access Protocol (LDAP) directory services. You'll learn how to use Outlook to query an LDAP service to obtain addresses and other information about contacts and other objects in the directory.

Chapter 17 takes a look at Notes, a useful feature in Outlook that will help you get rid of those little slips of paper cluttering your desk and the sticky notes taking over your monitor. You'll learn how to create notes, assign categories to them, change their color, move them to other applications, put them on your desktop, and much more. Chapter 18 completes Part 3 with a look at journaling, an important feature in Outlook that allows you to keep track of time spent on projects and documents and to track contacts and other items of interest.

Part 4—Scheduling

Part 4 covers scheduling, one of the most widely used features in Outlook. Chapter 19 provides an in-depth look at Outlook's appointment-scheduling capabilities. You'll learn how scheduling works, and how to schedule appointments, create recurring appointments, use color effectively to manage your schedule, allow others to access your schedule, and publish your schedule to the Web. Chapter 20 takes a look at scheduling meetings and resources using Outlook and explains the subtle differences between scheduling appointments and scheduling meetings. Chapter 21 examines all aspects of managing tasks with Outlook. You can use the Outlook Tasks folder to keep track of your own tasks as well as assign tasks to others. Integrating your tasks in Outlook can help you ensure that your tasks get done on time and are allocated to the appropriate person to complete them. Chapter 22 rounds out the coverage of scheduling with a look at integrating Outlook with another scheduling and time-management application from Microsoft called Microsoft Project. You should turn to Microsoft Project when you need advanced project scheduling features. Understanding how to integrate Outlook with Project will help you provide a seamless transition between the two.

Part 5—Customizing Outlook

Customizing an application or the user interface for your operating system isn't just a matter of picking and choosing your personal preferences. Your ability to customize the way an application functions or appears can have a profound impact on its usefulness to you and to others. In short, the ability to customize an application allows you to make that application do what you want it to do in the way that makes the most sense to you. Chapter 23 starts the coverage of customization with a look at templates and how they can simplify the creation of e-mail messages, appointments, events, and other Outlook objects. You'll learn not only how to create and edit templates, but also how to share those templates with others.

Chapter 24 takes a look at creating and using custom forms for a variety of tasks. Chapter 25 provides the detailed information you need to customize the Navigation Pane, the toolbar that appears by default to the left of the Outlook window and gives you quick access to Outlook's components. Chapter 25 also helps you customize the other aspects of the Outlook interface including command bars, the Outlook Today view, and folders. Chapter 26 explains how to create custom views and print styles for organizing and displaying your Outlook data. Chapter 27 gives you a look at a host of ways you can automate tasks in Outlook.

Part 6—Managing and Securing Outlook

Part 6 begins the transition to more advanced topics of interest to users, administrators, and IT professionals. In Chapter 28 you'll learn how to integrate Outlook with other Office applications, such as performing a mail merge in Microsoft Word based on contacts stored in Outlook or moving contact data between Outlook and Microsoft Access. Chapter 29 will help you simplify your life by teaching you how to delegate many of your responsibilities—including managing your schedule—to an assistant. In Chapter 30 you'll learn how Outlook uses folders to store your data and how to manage those folders. Chapter 30 also offers in-depth coverage of how to organize and archive your important data. Chapter 31 extends the look at data management with an examination of how to find and organize data in Outlook. Chapter 32 concludes the discussion of management topics with a look at some important issues: backing up your data, exporting data, and importing data from other sources into Outlook. The chapter not only covers the importance of a sound backup and recovery strategy, but will also help you develop and implement your own strategy that takes into account the unique requirements of Outlook and Exchange Server. Chapter 32 also includes a detailed analysis of the importance of virus protection and how to guard against virus infections and outbreaks. You'll read about both client-side and server-side solutions, covering a range of platforms in addition to Exchange Server 5.5, Exchange 2000 Server, and Exchange Server 2003. Because up-to-date virus definitions are the key to successful prevention, Chapter 32 also takes a close look at developing a virus definition update strategy. You'll also find a detailed discussion of how to configure attachment blocking at the server as well as in Outlook itself.

Part 7—Using Outlook with Exchange Server

Outlook can be an effective information management tool all by itself, whether you use it on a stand-alone computer or on a network in collaboration with other users. Where Outlook really shines, however, is in its integration with and as a client for Microsoft Exchange Server. Part 7 steps up to a more advanced level to explain a broad range of Outlook/Exchange integration topics. Chapter 33 offers information and support for network, platform, and deployment considerations. Chapter 34 turns the focus to the client, explaining how to configure Outlook as an Exchange Server client. Chapter 35 explores the wealth of features in Outlook specifically geared toward messaging with Exchange Server, such as the ability to recall sent messages before they are read, prioritize messages, and much more. This chapter also contains a detailed look at voting, an interesting feature in Outlook. You can use Outlook as a tool to solicit input from others on any issue or topic, receiving and tallying their votes quite easily. Chapter 36 is targeted toward anyone who needs to support Outlook clients under Exchange Server, including coverage of client options, mailbox management, configuring alternate recipients, message forwarding, and message journaling (archival). This chapter also includes topics that will help you to support collaboration and group scheduling. Chapter 37 helps you continue working when you're away from the office or when your server is offline, covering how to use remote features to access and manage your Outlook data.

Part 8—Collaboration and Mobility

Life isn't just about working in the confines of your office, and Part 8 takes that into account. Chapter 38 takes a detailed look at features in Outlook and Exchange Server that allow you to share data with others, including how to set up and use public folders, share personal folders, set up a message board, manage public folders, and even use the Network News Transfer Protocol (NNTP) service included with Windows 2000 Server and Windows Server 2003 to set up a newsgroup server for intranet or Internet users. Chapters 39 and 40 provide an in-depth look at Windows SharePoint Services and how you can set it up and use it to collaborate with others. Chapter 41 takes remote access one step further, explaining how to configure Exchange Server to allow users to access their data through a Web browser, and offering tips on security, site considerations, and other important issues. Chapter 42 completes this part of the book with a look at the mobility-related features in Outlook 2003 and Exchange Server 2003 that you can use to take your Outlook data on the road.

Companion CD

The Microsoft Office suite offers an impressive ability to customize and integrate applications, and Outlook is no exception. Whether you need to create a few custom forms or develop full-blown interactive applications with Outlook and other Office applications, the first three articles provide the solutions you need. In Article 1 you'll expand on the topics covered in Chapter 24 and begin to delve into Outlook programming with a look at programming forms using Microsoft Visual Basic, Scripting Edition (VBScript). Article 2 continues the coverage of programming and development with a look at using Microsoft Visual Basic for Applications (VBA) to develop Outlook applications. Article 3 completes the discussion with a detailed look at integrating Outlook and other applications through VBA. Articles 4 through 10 cover topics, such as the *Microsoft Office 2003 Resource Kit*, registry keys, add-ins, symbols, and shortcuts.

See the section "Conventions and Features Used in This Book" (page liii) for a list of some of the features you will find used throughout the book.

What's New in Outlook 2003

The first step to getting a handle on Outlook is to understand what it can do. Chances are you're familiar with Outlook or with similar programs. Throughout *Microsoft Office Outlook 2003 Inside Out* you'll find information on Outlook's features. Whether or not you're experienced with a previous version of Outlook, the following section will bring you up to speed on the new features in Outlook 2003.

A New Interface

Outlook 2003 sports a completely new interface. The Outlook Bar has been replaced by the Navigation Pane, which integrates more features into the same amount of space previously used by the Outlook Bar. The Reading Pane replaces the preview pane, giving you more options for previewing Outlook items without opening them. Several other interface changes give Outlook a new, sharper look, but most of all, these changes make Outlook easier to use.

Search Folders

Search folders are not really folders, but instead are a special type of view that displays the results of a search. You can create search folders to display the headers of messages from various folders in a single location. The messages displayed in the search folder depend on the search condition you specify for the search folder. For example, you might create a search folder to display all messages from a particular contact. Outlook includes a handful of predefined search folders and you can create as many custom search folders as you need. Search folders are an excellent new tool for organizing and finding messages in Outlook.

Cached Exchange Mode

If you use an Exchange Server account, you can use Cached Exchange Mode to improve offline use. Cached Exchange Mode creates a cached copy of your Exchange Server mailbox on your local computer. Outlook works from the local cache in much the same way it does when you configure Outlook to use an offline file (in fact, Cached Exchange Mode uses an offline file as the cache). However, with Cached Exchange Mode, Outlook automatically handles online/offline detection and performs synchronization automatically.

Junk Mail Blocking and External Content Filtering

Outlook completely revamps its junk mail filtering to add a Blocked Senders list (blacklist), Safe Senders list (whitelist), and Safe Recipients list. You can use the Blocked Senders list to identify senders whose messages should always be treated as junk mail. Use the Safe Senders list to identify senders whose messages you want to receive, regardless of the content. Use the Safe Recipients list with mailing lists and in other situations when you want to accept messages that are sent to specific addresses, such as a mailing list.

In addition to considerably improved junk mail filtering, Outlook also blocks external content in Hypertext Markup Language (HTML) messages. This prevents spammers from using Web beacons to identify valid e-mail addresses and can further cut down on spam. It also improves virus protection in Outlook 2003.

Windows SharePoint Services

Outlook 2003 provides good integration with Windows SharePoint Services, formerly known as SharePoint Team Services. With Windows SharePoint Services you can create workgroup sites that enable users to collaborate on documents, share information such as contacts and messages, and collaborate in many other ways. SharePoint Portal Server provides a step up from Windows SharePoint Services by adding support for multiple sites and several other features.

Information Rights Management

Outlook 2003 incorporates information rights management features to enable you to specify that a message you send cannot be forwarded, copied, or printed. Outlook 2003 users who receive a restricted message can view it but the features for copying, forwarding, and printing the message are disabled. Users who don't have Outlook 2003 can use the Information Rights Management add-on for Microsoft Internet Explorer to view the message in Internet Explorer. This add-on prevents the recipient from copying, forwarding, or printing the message.

Business Contact Manager

Business Contact Manager is an add-on from Microsoft that enables you to keep track of business contacts, sales opportunities, products, and other business-related items. Business Contact Manager stores these items in a database separate from your Outlook data, but does provide integration between your Outlook information store and the Business Contact Manager database. Business Contact Manager in this first release is a single-user product and provides limited database customization, but it can nevertheless be a very useful tool for individuals and small businesses to get a handle on their sales efforts.

Outlook Web Access

Although it is a feature of Exchange Server 2003 rather than Outlook 2003, the latest revision of Outlook Web Access is worth mentioning here because it offers many more features to enable users to access their Exchange Server mailboxes from a Web browser. Microsoft has added the capability to create additional Outlook item types through Outlook Web Access, more control over mailbox options, an improved interface, and the capability to manage rules through Outlook Web Access.

About the CD

The companion CD that ships with this book contains many tools and resources to help you get the most out of your *Inside Out* book.

What's On the CD

Your *Inside Out* CD includes the following:

- **Complete eBook** In this section you'll find the an electronic version of *Microsoft Office Outook 2003 Inside Out*. The eBook is in PDF format.
- ***Computer Dictionary, Fifth Edition* eBook** Here you'll find the full electronic version of the *Microsoft Computer Dictionary, Fifth Edition*. Suitable for home and office, the dictionary contains more than 10,000 entries.
- **Insider Extras** This section includes sample files referenced in the book. Use these files to follow along with the examples in the book; you can also use them to form the basis for your own work.
- **Bonus Content** This section contains three articles about developing custom forms and applications and seven articles about topics such as the Microsoft Office 2003 Resource Kit, registry keys, add-ins, symbols, and shortcuts.
- **Microsoft Resources** In this section, you'll find information about additional resources from Microsoft that will help you get the most out of the Microsoft Office System. Building on the familiar tools that many people already know, the Microsoft Office System includes servers, services, and desktop programs to help address a broad array of business needs.
- **Extending Outlook** In this section, you'll find great information about third-party utilities and tools you use to further enhance your experience with Outlook 2003.

The companion CD provides detailed information about the files on this CD and links to Microsoft and third-party sites on the Internet.

> **Note** Please note that the links to third-party sites are not under the control of Microsoft Corporation, and Microsoft is therefore not responsible for their content, nor should their inclusion on this CD be construed as an endorsement of the product or the site.
>
> Software provided on this CD is in English language only and may be incompatible with non-English language operating systems and software.

Using the CD

To use this companion CD, insert it into your CD-ROM. Accept the license agreement that is presented to access the starting menu. If AutoRun is not enabled on your system, run StartCD.exe in the root of the CD or refer to the Readme.txt file.

System Requirements

Following are the minimum system requirements necessary to run the CD:

- Microsoft Windows XP or later or Windows 2000 Professional with Service Pack 3 or later.
- 266-MHz or higher Pentium-compatible CPU
- 64 megabytes (MB) RAM
- 8X CD-ROM drive or faster
- Microsoft Windows–compatible sound card and speakers
- Microsoft Internet Explorer 5.01 or higher
- Microsoft Mouse or compatible pointing device

Note System requirements may be higher for the add-ins available on the CD. Individual add-in system requirements are specified on the CD. An Internet connection is necessary to access the some of the hyperlinks. Connect time charges may apply.

Support Information

Every effort has been made to ensure the accuracy of the book and the contents of this companion CD. For feedback on the book content or this companion CD, please contact us by using any of the addresses listed in the "We'd Like to Hear From You" section (page xli).

Microsoft Press provides corrections for books through the World Wide Web at *http://www.microsoft.com/mspress/support/*. To connect directly to the Microsoft Press Knowledge Base and enter a query regarding a question or issue that you may have, go to *http://www.microsoft.com/mspress/support/search.asp*.

For support information regarding Office 2003, you can connect to Microsoft Technical Support on the Web at *http://support.microsoft.com/*.

Conventions and Features Used in This Book

This book uses special text and design conventions to make it easier for you to find the information you need.

Text Conventions

Convention	Meaning
Abbreviated menu commands	For your convenience, this book uses abbreviated menu commands. For example, "Choose Tools, Track Changes, Highlight Changes" means that you should click the Tools menu, point to Track Changes, and select the Highlight Changes command.
Boldface type	**Boldface** type is used to indicate text that you enter or type.
Initial Capital Letters	The first letters of the names of menus, dialog boxes, dialog box elements, and commands are capitalized. Example: the Save As dialog box.
Italicized type	*Italicized* type is used to indicate new terms.
Plus sign (+) in text	Keyboard shortcuts are indicated by a plus sign (+) separating two key names. For example, Ctrl+Alt+Delete means that you press the Ctrl, Alt, and Delete keys at the same time.

Design Conventions

This text identifies a new or significantly updated feature in this version of the software.

Tip Tips provide helpful hints, timesaving tricks, or alternative procedures related to the task being discussed.

Cross-references point you to other locations in the book that offer additional information on the topic being discussed.

This icon indicates sample files or text found on the companion CD.

Caution Cautions identify potential problems that you should look out for when you're completing a task or problems that you must address before you can complete a task.

Note Notes offer additional information related to the task being discussed.

Inside Out

This statement illustrates an example of an "Inside Out" problem statement

These are the book's signature tips. In these tips, you'll get the straight scoop on what's going on with the software—inside information on why a feature works the way it does. You'll also find handy workarounds to different software problems.

Troubleshooting

This statement illustrates an example of a "Troubleshooting" problem statement

Look for these sidebars to find solutions to common problems you might encounter. Troubleshooting sidebars appear next to related information in the chapters. You can also use the Troubleshooting Topics index at the back of the book to look up problems by topic.

Sidebar

The sidebars sprinkled throughout these chapters provide ancillary information on the topic being discussed. Go to sidebars to learn more about the technology or a feature.

Part 1

Working With Outlook

Chapter 1

Outlook Architecture, Setup, and Startup

This chapter provides an overview of the architecture in Microsoft Office Outlook 2003 to help you learn not only how Outlook works but also how it stores data. Having that knowledge, particularly if you're charged with administering or supporting Outlook for other users, will help you use the application more effectively and address issues related to data storage and security, archiving, working offline, and moving data between installations.

This chapter also explains the different options you have for connecting to e-mail servers through Outlook and the protocols (Post Office Protocol version 3 [POP3] and Internet Message Access Protocol [IMAP], for example) that support those connections. In addition to learning about client support and the various platforms on which you can use Outlook, you'll also learn about the options that are available for starting and using the program.

If you're anxious to get started using Outlook, you could skip this chapter and move straight to Chapter 2, "Advanced Setup Tasks," to learn how to configure your e-mail accounts and begin working with Outlook. However, this chapter provides the foundation on which many subsequent chapters are based, and reading it will help you gain a deeper understanding of what Outlook can do so that you can use it effectively and efficiently.

Overview of Outlook

In many respects, Outlook is a personal information manager (PIM). A traditional PIM lets you maintain information about your contacts, such as your customers, coworkers, and clients. Traditional PIMs also let you keep track of your daily schedule, tasks to complete, and other personal or work-related information. Outlook does all that, but it goes well beyond the features of most PIMs to provide e-mail and fax support, group scheduling capability, and task management.

Outlook provides a broad range of capabilities to help you manage your entire work day. In fact, a growing number of Microsoft Office System users work in Outlook more than 60 percent of the time. An understanding of Outlook's capabilities and features is important not only to using Office effectively but also to managing your time and projects. The following sections will help you learn to use the features in Outlook to simplify your work day and enhance your productivity.

Messaging

One of the key features Outlook offers is messaging. You can use Outlook as a client to send and receive e-mail through a variety of services. Outlook offers integrated support for the e-mail services covered in the sections that follow.

> **Note** A *client application* is one that uses a service provided by another computer, typically a server.

Exchange Server

Outlook provides full support for Microsoft Exchange Server, which means you can take advantage of workgroup scheduling, collaboration, instant messaging, and other features offered through Exchange Server that aren't available with other clients. For example, you can use any POP3 e-mail client, such as Microsoft Outlook Express, to connect to an Exchange Server (assuming the Exchange Server administrator has configured the server to allow POP), but you're limited to e-mail only. Advanced workgroup and other special features—being able to recall a message before it is read, use public folders, and vote, for example—require Outlook.

Internet E-Mail

Outlook provides full support for Internet e-mail servers, which means you can use Outlook to send and receive e-mail through mail servers that support Internet-based standards, such as POP3 and IMAP. What's more, you can integrate Internet mail accounts with other accounts, such as an Exchange Server account, to send and receive messages through multiple servers. For example, you might maintain an account on Exchange Server for interoffice correspondence and use a local Internet service provider (ISP), CompuServe, Bigfoot, or other Internet-based e-mail service for messages outside your network. Or, perhaps you want to monitor your personal e-mail along with your work-related e-mail. In that situation, you would simply add your personal e-mail account to your Outlook profile and work with both simultaneously. You can use rules and custom folders to help separate your messages.

For more information about messaging protocols such as POP3 and IMAP, see "Understanding Messaging Protocols," page 16.

HTTP-Based E-Mail

Outlook 2003 supports HTTP-based e-mail services, such as Microsoft Hotmail. HTTP is the protocol used to request and transmit Web pages. This means you can use Outlook to send and receive e-mail through Hotmail and other HTTP-based mail servers that would otherwise require you to use a Web browser to access your e-mail (see Figure 1-1). In addition, you can download your messages to your local inbox and process them offline, rather than remaining connected to your ISP while you process messages. Another advantage is that you can keep your messages as long as you want—most HTTP-based messaging services, including Hotmail, purge read messages after a given period of time. Plus, HTTP support in Outlook lets you keep all your e-mail in a single application. Currently, Outlook 2003 directly supports Hotmail. Check with your e-mail service to determine whether your mail server is Outlook-compatible.

Figure 1-1. HTTP-based mail servers such as Hotmail have traditionally required access through a Web browser.

Fax Send and Receive

Outlook 2003 includes a Fax Mail Transport provider, which allows you to send faxes from Outlook using a fax modem. In addition, third-party developers can provide MAPI integration with their fax applications, allowing you to use Outlook as the front end for those applications to send and receive faxes. Symantec's WinFax is a good example of such an application. Both Microsoft Windows 2000 and Microsoft Windows XP include built-in fax services that support sending and receiving faxes. The Fax Service in Windows 2000 also supports MAPI and Inbox integration with Outlook and is the only Microsoft-supplied fax service supported by Microsoft for Outlook. The Windows 2000 Fax Service can deliver incoming faxes to an Outlook Inbox, as well as print them and deliver a copy to a file folder. The Windows XP Fax Service can deliver incoming faxes to a file folder or print them, but does not support delivery to an Outlook Inbox.

Windows 2000 Fax Service is now the only fax support offered for Windows. Windows XP users need to purchase a third-party fax application such as WinFax.

For a detailed explanation of how to use Outlook to send and receive faxes (complete with cover pages and other details), see Chapter 9, "Sending and Receiving Faxes."

Extensible E-Mail Support

Outlook's design allows developers to support third-party e-mail services in Outlook, such as cc:Mail and Lotus Notes. This support doesn't guarantee the availability of these third-party tools, however. For example, although earlier versions of Outlook included support for cc:Mail, Microsoft no longer offers its own service provider for support of cc:Mail.

Outlook 2003 does not include the Microsoft Mail service provider. Microsoft dropped support for Microsoft Mail in Outlook 2002, and companies that used this service will need to find another service provider.

Whatever your e-mail server type, Outlook provides a comprehensive set of tools for composing, receiving, and replying to messages. Outlook provides support for rich-text and HTML formatting, which allows you to create and receive messages that contain much more than just text (see Figure 1-2). For example, you can send a Web page as a mail message or integrate sound, video, and graphics in mail messages. Outlook's support for multiple address books, multiple e-mail accounts, and even multiple e-mail services makes it an excellent messaging client, even if you forgo the application's many other features and capabilities.

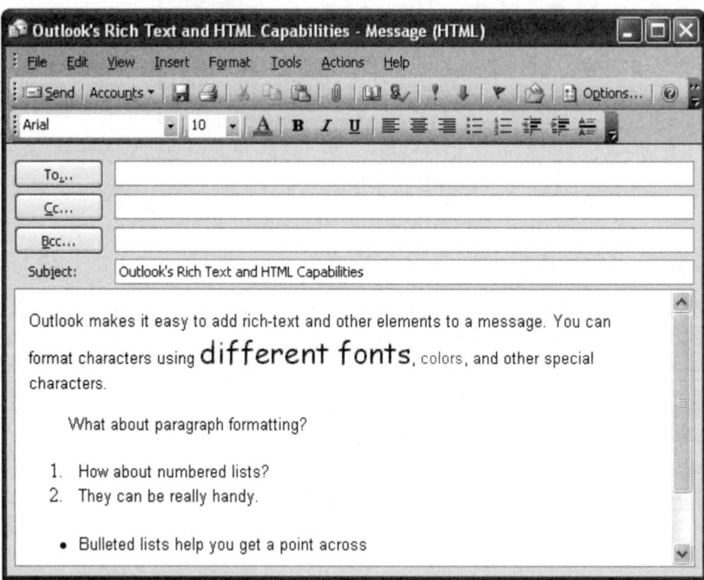

Figure 1-2. Use Outlook to create rich-text and multimedia messages.

Scheduling

Scheduling is another important feature in Outlook. You can use Outlook to track both personal and work-related meetings and appointments (see Figure 1-3), whether at home or in the office, a useful feature even on a stand-alone computer.

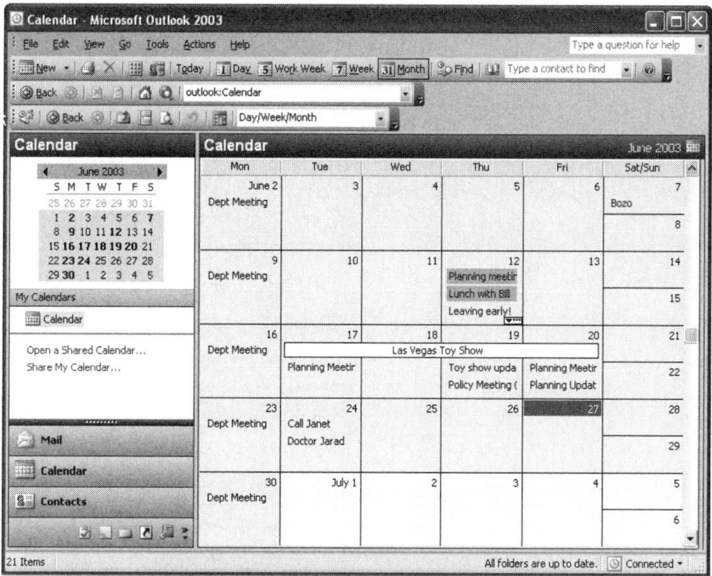

Figure 1-3. Track your personal and work schedules with Outlook.

Where Outlook's scheduling capabilities really shine, however, is in group scheduling. When you use Outlook to set up meetings and appointments with others, you can view the schedules of your invitees, which makes it easy to find a time when everyone can attend. You can schedule both one-time and recurring appointments. All appointments and meetings can include a reminder with a lead time that you specify, and Outlook will notify you of the event at the specified time. A new feature in Outlook 2003 lets you process multiple reminders at one time, a useful feature if you've been out of the office for a while.

Organizing your schedule is also one of Outlook's strong suits. You can use categories and types to categorize appointments, events, and meetings; to control the way they appear in Outlook; and to perform automatic processing. Color labels allow you to identify quickly and visually different types of events on your calendar.

In addition to managing your own schedule, you can delegate control of the schedule to someone else, such as your assistant. The assistant can modify your schedule, request meetings, respond to meeting invitations, and otherwise act on your behalf regarding your calendar. Not only can others view your schedule to plan meetings and appointments (with the exception of items marked personal), but you can also publish your schedule to the Web to allow others to view it over an intranet or the Internet (see Figure 1-4).

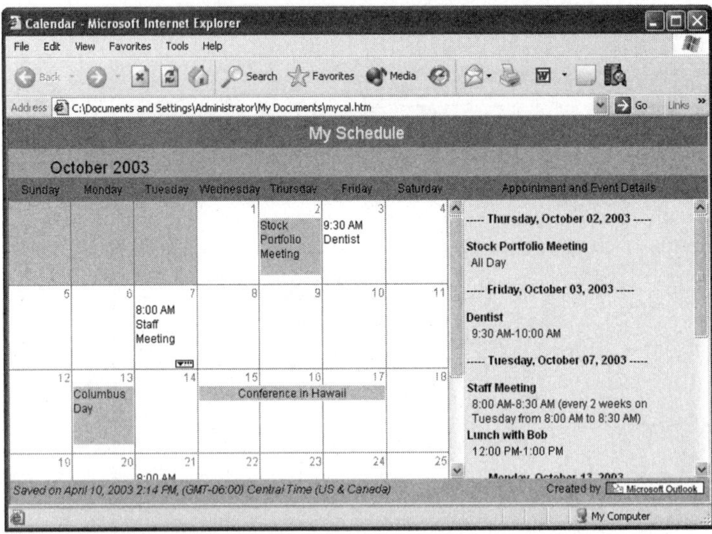

Figure 1-4. You can easily publish your schedule to the Web.

Contact Management

Being able to manage contact information—names, addresses, and phone numbers—is critical to other aspects of Outlook, such as scheduling and messaging. Outlook makes it easy to manage contacts and offers flexibility in the type of information you maintain. In addition to basic information, you can also store a contact's fax number, cell phone number, pager number, Web page URL, and more (see Figure 1-5). You can even include a picture of the person.

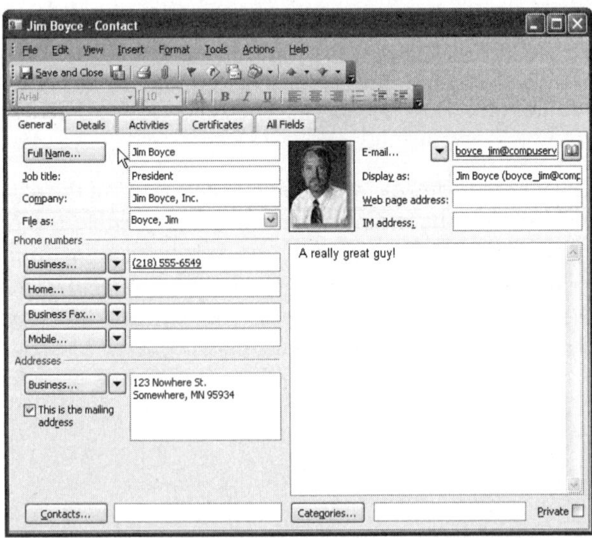

Figure 1-5. You can manage a wealth of information about each contact with Outlook.

Besides using contact information to address e-mail messages, you can initiate phone calls using the contacts list, track calls to contacts in the journal, add notes for each contact, use the contacts list to create mail merge documents, and perform other tasks. The Contacts folder also provides a means for storing a contact's digital certificate, which you can use to exchange encrypted messages for security. Adding a contact's certificate is easy—just receive a digitally signed message from the contact and Outlook adds the certificate to the contact's entry. You can also import a certificate from a file provided by the contact.

For details about digital signatures and encryption, see "Message Encryption," page 24. For additional information on the journal, see "Tracking with Outlook's Journal," page 10. For complete details on how to use the journal, see Chapter 18, "Keeping a Journal."

Task Management

Managing your work day usually includes keeping track of the tasks you need to perform and assigning tasks to others. Outlook makes it easy to manage your task list. You assign a due date, start date, priority, category, and other properties to each task, which makes it easier for you to manage those tasks (see Figure 1-6). As with meetings and appointments, Outlook keeps you informed and on track by issuing reminders for each task. You control whether the reminder is used and the time and date it's generated, along with an optional, audible notification. You can designate a task as personal, preventing others from viewing the task in your schedule—just as you can with meetings and appointments. Tasks can be one-time or recurring events.

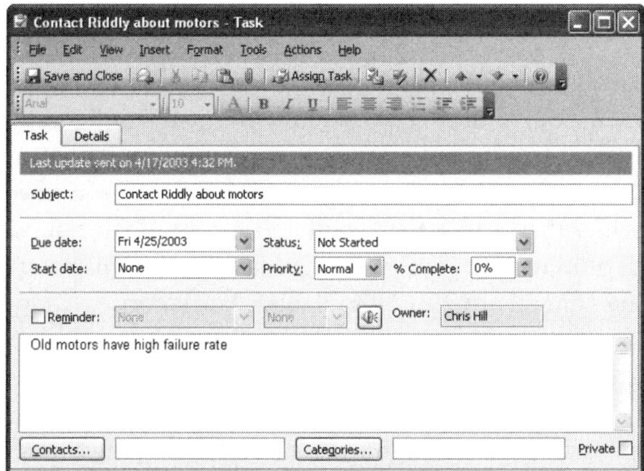

Figure 1-6. Use Outlook to manage tasks.

If you manage other people, Outlook makes it easy to assign tasks to other Outlook users. When you create a task, simply click Assign Task, and Outlook prompts you for the assignee's e-mail address. You can choose to keep a copy of the updated task in your own task list and receive a status report when the task is complete.

Tracking with Outlook's Journal

Keeping track of events is an important part of managing your work day, and Outlook's journal makes it simple. The Journal folder allows you to keep track of the contacts you make (phone calls, e-mails, and so on), meeting actions, task requests and responses, and other actions for selected contacts (see Figure 1-7). You can also use the journal to track your work in other Microsoft Office applications, giving you a way to track the time you spend on various documents and their associated projects. You can have Outlook journal items automatically based on settings that you specify, and you can also add items manually to your journal.

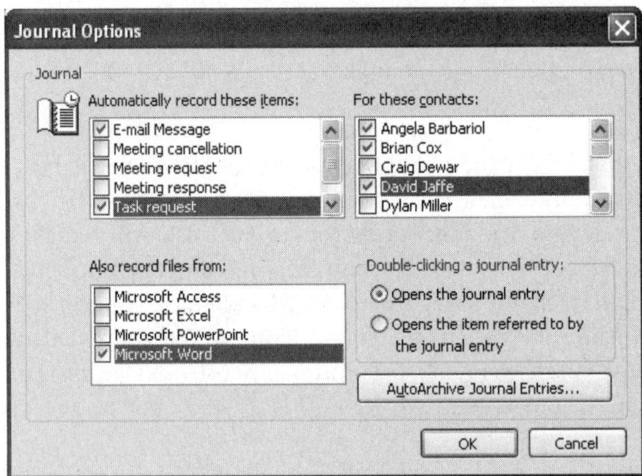

Figure 1-7. Configure your journal using Outlook's options.

When you view the journal, you can double-click a journal entry to either open the entry or open the items referred to by the entry, depending on how you have configured the journal. You can also configure the journal to automatically archive items to the default archive folder or a folder you choose, or you can have Outlook regularly delete items from the journal, cleaning out items that are older than a specified length of time. Outlook can use group policies to control the retention of journal entries, allowing a system administrator to manage journaling and data retention consistently throughout an organization.

Organizing Your Thoughts with Notes

With Outlook, you can keep track of your thoughts and tasks by using the Notes folder. Each note can function as a stand-alone window, allowing you to view notes on your desktop outside Outlook (see Figure 1-8). Notes exist as individual message files, so you can copy or move them to other folders, including your desktop, or easily share them with others through network sharing or e-mail. You can also incorporate the contents of notes into other applications or other Outlook folders by using the clipboard. For example, you might copy a note regarding a contact to that person's contact entry. As you can with other Outlook items, you can assign categories to notes to help you organize and view them.

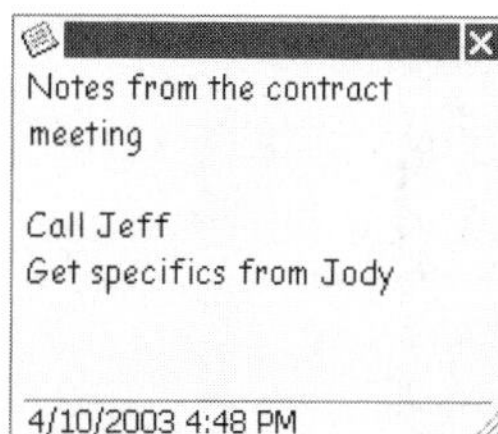

Figure 1-8. Use notes to keep track of miscellaneous information.

How Outlook Stores Data

If you work with Outlook primarily as a user, understanding how the program stores data helps you use it effectively to organize and manage your data on a daily basis, including storing and archiving Outlook items as needed. If you're charged with supporting other Outlook users, understanding how Outlook stores data allows you to help others create and manage their folders and ensure the security and integrity of their data. Finally, because data storage is the foundation of all of Outlook's features, understanding where and how the program stores data is critical if you're creating Outlook-based applications—for example, a data entry form that uses Outlook as the mechanism for posting the data to a public folder.

For information on building Outlook-based applications, see Chapter 23, "Using Templates," and Articles 1 through 3 on the companion CD, which cover programming Outlook using Microsoft Visual Basic and VBScript to create custom forms and applications.

You're probably familiar with folders (directories) in the file system. You use these folders to organize applications and documents. For example, the Program Files folder in the Microsoft Windows operating system is the default location for most applications that you install on the system, and the My Documents folder serves as the default location for document files. You create these types of folders in Windows Explorer.

Outlook also uses folders to organize data, but these folders are different from your file system folders. Rather than existing individually on your system's hard disk, these folders exist within Outlook's file structure. You view and manage these folders within Outlook's interface, not in Windows Explorer. Think of Outlook's folders as windows into your Outlook data rather than as individual elements that exist on disk. By default, Outlook includes several folders, as shown in Figure 1-9.

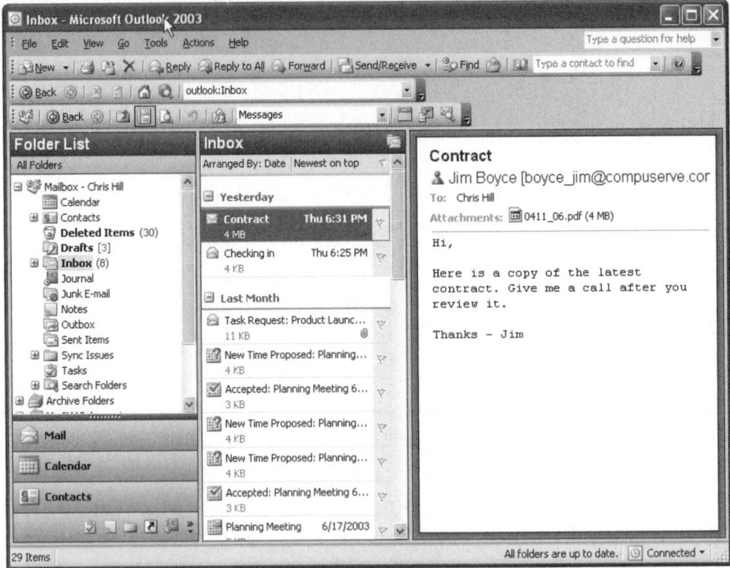

Figure 1-9. Folders organize your data in Outlook.

Personal Folders—PST Files

If your Outlook folders aren't stored as individual folders on your system's hard disk, where are they? The answer to that question depends on how you configure Outlook. As in earlier versions of Outlook, you can use a personal folders file to store your Outlook data. Outlook uses the PST file extension for a personal folders file, but you specify the file's name when you configure Outlook. For example, you might use your name as the file name to help you easily identify the file. The default PST file contains your Contacts, Calendar, Tasks, and other folders.

You can use multiple PST files, adding additional personal folders to your Outlook configuration (see Figure 1-10). For example, you might want to create another set of folders to separate your personal information from work-related data. As you'll learn in Chapter 2, "Advanced Setup Tasks," you can add personal folders to your Outlook configuration simply by adding another PST file to your profile.

> **Note** If you use Outlook as an Exchange Server client, you probably store your data in the Exchange Server mailbox rather than in a local PST file. If that's the case, you have two options to enable you to work offline. One method is to use an offline folder (OST) file, which provides an offline copy of the mailbox. OST files are covered in the following section. Another method is to use Cached Exchange Mode, which is similar to using an OST but provides automatic synchronization. Cached Exchange Mode is discussed in the following section.

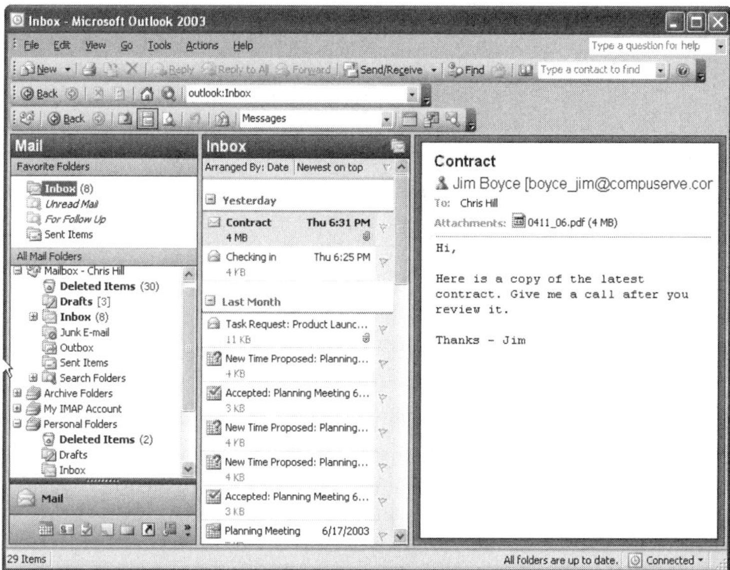

Figure 1-10. You can add multiple sets of folders to your Outlook configuration.

Options for Working Offline

If you use Outlook as an Exchange Server client and do not use PST files to store your data (instead storing your data on the Exchange Server), you have two options for working with your mailbox data offline, and these methods differ only in the way synchronization occurs.

An offline store (OST) file allows you to work offline. The OST file acts essentially as an offline copy of your data store on the Exchange Server. When you're working offline, changes you make to contacts, messages, and other Outlook items and folders occur in the offline store. When you go online again, Outlook synchronizes the changes between the offline store and your Exchange Server store when you perform a send/receive for the account. For example, if you've deleted messages from your offline store, Outlook deletes those same messages from your online store when you synchronize the folders. Any new messages in your Inbox on the server are added to your offline store. Synchronization is a two-way process, providing the most up-to-date copy of your data in both locations, ensuring that changes made in each are reflected in the other.

> **Note** For detailed information on important offline and remote access topics, see Chapter 37, "Working Offline and Remotely." For a discussion of the differences between remote mail and offline use, see Chapter 11, "Processing Messages Selectively."

Outlook 2003 adds a new feature called Cached Exchange Mode. This mode works much the same as offline synchronization with an OST. In fact, Outlook uses an OST for cached mode. The main difference is that with cached mode, Outlook always works from the copy of your mailbox that is cached locally on your computer. Outlook then automatically handles synchronization between your offline cache mailbox and the mailbox stored on the server. With cached mode, you don't need to worry about synchronizing the two—Outlook detects when the server is available and updates your locally cached copy automatically.

When you create an Outlook storage file, Outlook defaults to a specific location for the file. The default location is \Documents And Settings\<*user*>\Local Settings\Application Data\Microsoft\Outlook. On systems that were upgraded from Microsoft Windows NT to Windows 2000 or Windows XP, the user profiles still reside in the \Winnt\Profiles folder. On these systems, therefore, Outlook places the storage files by default in \%systemroot%\Profiles\<*user*>\Local Settings\Application Data\Microsoft\Outlook. As with Windows NT, %systemroot% defaults to \Winnt.

Tip **Find your data store**

If you're having trouble locating your existing storage files, choose File, Data File Management. In the Outlook Data Files dialog box (see Figure 1-11), select the file you want to locate and then determine the file location from the Filename column. If you can't see the entire path, drag the column border to expand the column. Alternatively, to go straight to the folder containing the file, select the file and click Open Folder. In the folder window, choose Tools, Folder Options. On the View tab of the Folder Options dialog box, select Display The Full Path In The Title Bar to view the absolute, full path to the file. You can also use your operating system's Find/Search command to search for all files with a PST or OST file extension.

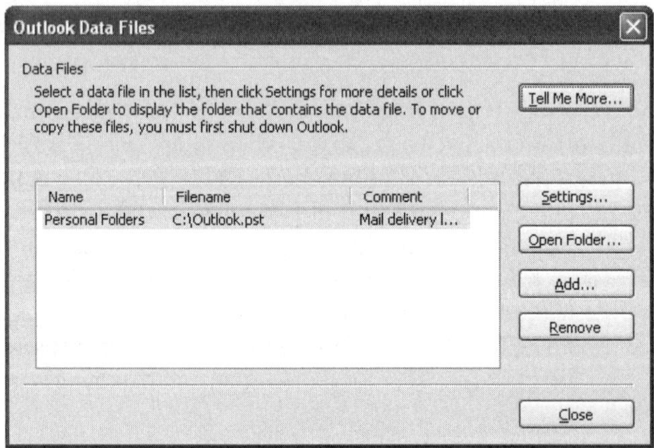

Figure 1-11. Locate your data files by using the Outlook Data Files dialog box.

If you use the same computer all the time, it's generally best to store your Outlook files on your system's local hard disk. In some situations, however, you will probably want to store them on a network share. For example, you might connect from different computers on the network and use a roaming profile to provide a consistent desktop and user interface regardless of your logon location. (A *roaming profile* allows your desktop configuration, documents, and other elements of your desktop environment to be duplicated wherever you log on.) In this situation, you (or the network administrator) would configure your profile to place your home folder on a network server that is available to you from all logon locations.Your Outlook files would then be stored on that network share, making them available to you on whichever computer you use to log on to the network. Placing your Outlook files on a server gives you the added potential benefit of incorporating your Outlook data files in the server's backup strategy.

For a detailed discussion of using roaming profiles to provide seamless access to Outlook, see Chapter 33, "Deploying and Managing Outlook in a Network." To learn how to move your Outlook files from one location to another (such as from a local drive to a network share), see "Changing Your Data Storage Location," page 52.

Troubleshooting

You use a roaming profile and logon time is increasing

If you use Outlook as a client for Exchange Server, your best option is to use your Exchange Server mailbox as the store location for your data rather than using a PST file. However, if you use a roaming profile for consistent logon from multiple locations on the local area network (LAN), consider including the OST file in the roaming profile so that you'll always have access to it. If the Exchange Server is unavailable, you'll still be able to work with your Outlook data through the OST file; and placing the OST file in your roaming profile allows you to use it regardless of your logon location. This recommendation applies whether you use an OST with or without Cached Exchange Mode.

Keep in mind, however, that the OST file can become quite large if you have a lot of data in your Exchange Server mailbox. The size of the profile affects logon time, and a large profile can cause an excessive amount of network traffic as the files are copied from the server to your workstation. Use aggressive archiving and other housecleaning methods to keep your Outlook data to a minimum, and monitor your roaming profile size as often as possible.

Sharing Storage Files

Outlook provides excellent functionality for sharing information with others. Toward that end, you can share your data using a couple of different methods. Exchange Server users can configure permissions for individual folders to allow specific users to connect to those folders and view the data contained in them. You can also configure delegate access to your folders to allow an assistant to manage items for you in the folders. For example, you might have your assistant manage your schedule but not your tasks. In that case, you would configure delegate access for the Calendar folder but not for the Tasks folder.

For a detailed discussion of delegation, see Chapter 29, "Delegating Responsibilities to an Assistant." To learn how to configure sharing permissions for individual folders and additional methods for sharing data with or without Exchange Server, see Chapter 38, "Sharing Information with Others."

Understanding Messaging Protocols

A *messaging protocol* is a mechanism that messaging servers and applications use to transfer messages. Being able to use a specific e-mail service requires that your application support the same protocols the server uses. To configure Outlook as a messaging client, you need to understand the various protocols supported by Outlook and the types of servers that employ each type. The following sections provide an overview of these protocols.

SMTP/POP3

Simple Mail Transport Protocol (SMTP) is a standards-based protocol used for transferring messages and is the primary mechanism that Internet-based and intranet-based e-mail servers use to transfer messages. It's also the mechanism that Outlook uses to connect to a mail server to send messages for an Internet account. Therefore, SMTP is the protocol used by an Internet e-mail account for outgoing messages.

SMTP operates by default on TCP port 25. When you configure an Internet-based e-mail account, the port on which the server is listening for SMTP determines the outgoing mail server setting. Unless your e-mail server uses a different port (unlikely), you can use the default port value of 25.

Post Office Protocol 3 (POP3) is a standards-based protocol that clients can use to access messages from any mail server that supports POP3. This is the protocol that Outlook uses when retrieving messages from an Internet-based or intranet-based mail server that supports POP3 mailboxes. ISP-based mail servers invariably use POP3, as do other mail servers. For example, CompuServe Classic provides POP3 support, allowing you to retrieve your CompuServe mail through Outlook. Exchange Server also supports the use of POP3 for retrieving mail.

POP3 operates on TCP port 110 by default. Unless your server uses a nonstandard port configuration, you can leave the port setting as is when defining a POP3 mail account. Figure 1-12 shows the Internet E-Mail Settings page, which you use to configure the incoming and outgoing mail server settings for an Internet mail account. Click More Settings if you need to change port settings for the account.

To learn how to set up an Internet e-mail account for an SMTP/POP3 server, see "Using Internet POP3 E-Mail Accounts," page 147. To learn how to add the account and configure advanced properties, such as SMTP or POP3 port assignments, see "Configuring Advanced Settings for Internet Accounts," page 153.

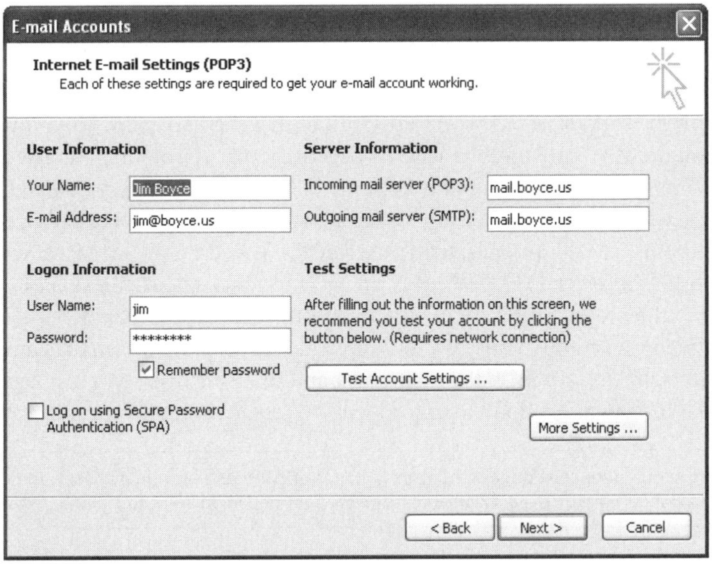

Figure 1-12. Use the E-Mail Accounts Wizard's Internet E-Mail Settings page to configure incoming and outgoing mail server settings.

IMAP

Like POP3, Internet Message Access Protocol (IMAP) is a standards-based protocol that enables message transfer. However, IMAP offers some significant differences from POP3. For example, POP3 is primarily designed as an offline protocol, which means you retrieve your messages from a server and download them to your local message store (such as your local Outlook folders). IMAP is designed primarily as an online protocol, which allows a remote user to manipulate messages and message folders on the server without downloading them. This is particularly helpful for users who need to access the same remote mailbox from multiple locations, such as home and work, using different computers. Because the messages remain on the server, IMAP eliminates the need for message synchronization.

Tip **Keep messages on the server**

You can configure a POP3 account in Outlook to leave a copy of messages on the server, allowing you to retrieve those messages later from another computer. To learn how to configure a POP3 account, see "Using Internet POP3 E-Mail Accounts," page 147. IMAP offers other advantages over POP3. For example, with IMAP, you can search for messages on the server using a variety of message attributes, such as sender, message size, or message header. IMAP also offers better support for attachments, because it can separate attachments from the header and text portion of a message. This is particularly useful with multipart Multipurpose Internet Mail Extensions (MIME) messages, allowing you to read a message without downloading the attachments so that you can decide which attachments you want to retrieve. With POP3, the entire message must be downloaded.

Security is another advantage of IMAP, because IMAP uses a challenge-response mechanism to authenticate the user for mailbox access. This prevents the user's password from being transmitted as clear text across the network, as it is with POP3.

IMAP support in Outlook allows you to use Outlook as a client to an IMAP-compliant e-mail server. Although IMAP provides for server-side storage and the ability to create additional mail folders on the server, it does not offer some of the same features as Exchange Server or even POP3. For example, you can't store nonmail folders on the server. Also, special folders such as Sent Items, Drafts, and Deleted Items can't be stored on the IMAP server. Even with these limitations, however, IMAP serves as a flexible protocol and surpasses POP3 in capability. Unless a competing standard appears in the future, it is possible that IMAP will eventually replace POP3. However, ISPs generally like POP3 because the users' e-mail is moved to their own computers, freeing space on the mail server and reducing disk space management problems. For that reason alone, don't look for IMAP to replace POP3 in the near future.

For information about other advantages and disadvantages of IMAP and how they affect Outlook, see "Using IMAP Accounts," page 155. For additional technical information on IMAP, to go *http://www.imap.org*.

MAPI

Messaging Application Programming Interface (MAPI) is a Microsoft-developed application programming interface (API) that facilitates communication between mail-enabled applications. MAPI support makes it possible for other applications to send and receive messages using Outlook. For example, third-party fax applications, such as Symantec's WinFax, can place incoming faxes in your Inbox through MAPI. As another example, a third-party MAPI-aware application could read and write to your Outlook Address Book through MAPI calls. MAPI is not a message protocol, but understanding its function in Outlook helps you install, configure, and use MAPI-aware applications to integrate Outlook.

LDAP

Lightweight Directory Access Protocol (LDAP) was designed to serve with less overhead and fewer resource requirements than its precursor, the Directory Access Protocol, which was developed for X.500. LDAP is a standards-based protocol that allows clients to query data in a directory service over a TCP connection. For example, Windows 2000 uses LDAP as the primary means for querying Active Directory directory service. Exchange Server supports LDAP queries, allowing clients to look up address information for subscribers on the server. Other directory services on the Internet, such as Bigfoot, InfoSpace, Yahoo!, and others, employ LDAP to implement searches of their databases.

Like Outlook Express, Outlook 2003 allows you to add directory service accounts that use LDAP as their protocol to query directory services for e-mail addresses, phone numbers, and other information regarding subscribers.

To learn how to add and configure an LDAP directory service in Outlook, see "Configuring a Directory Service Account in Outlook," page 453. For additional information regarding LDAP, refer to "MS Strategy for Lightweight Directory Access Protocol (LDAP)," available in the NT Server Technical Notes section of Microsoft TechNet or on the Web at *http://www.microsoft.com/TechNet/winnt/Winntas/technote/ldapcmr.asp*.

NNTP

Network News Transfer Protocol (NNTP) is the standards-based protocol for server-to-server and client-to-server transfer of news messages, or the underlying protocol that makes possible public and private newsgroups. Outlook does not directly support the creation of accounts to access newsgroup servers, but instead relies on Outlook Express as its default newsreader (see Figure 1-13).

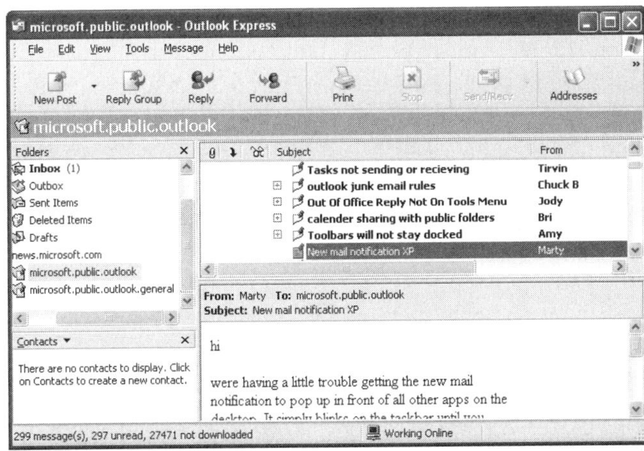

Figure 1-13. Outlook relies on Outlook Express for reading and posting to public and private newsgroups.

Note Microsoft Windows 2000 Server and Windows Server 2003 both include an NNTP service that lets a network administrator set up a news server to host newsgroups that can be accessed by local intranet or remote Internet users. Exchange Server allows the NNTP service to interface with other public or private news servers to pull newsgroups and messages via newsfeeds. Therefore, Windows 2000 Server or Windows Server 2003 by themselves let you set up your own newsgroup server to host your own newsgroups, and Exchange Server lets you host public Internet newsgroups.

Using Outlook Express, you can download newsgroups, read messages, post messages, and perform other news-related tasks. Other third-party news applications, such as Forte's Agent, offer extended capabilities. Forte's Web site is located at *http://www.forteinc.com*.

Note For a detailed explanation of setting up Outlook Express as a newsreader, see Chapter 13, "Using Outlook Express for Public and Private Newsgroups."

HTML

Hypertext Markup Language (HTML) is the protocol used most commonly to define and transmit Web pages. Several e-mail services, including Hotmail and Yahoo!, provide access to client mailboxes through Web pages and therefore make use of HTML as their message transfer protocol. You connect to the Web site and use the features and commands found there to view messages, send messages, and download attachments.

Outlook provides enhanced HTML support, which means you can configure Outlook as a client for HTML-based mail services. As mentioned earlier in the chapter, Outlook includes built-in support for Hotmail. HTML support is purely a server-side issue, so HTML-based mail services other than Hotmail have to provide Outlook support on their own sites. Hotmail accomplishes this support programmatically by means of Active Server Pages (ASP).

Tip **Find Hotmail's Outlook-Based Access**
The URL for Hotmail's Outlook-based access is *http://services.msn.com/svcs/hotmail/httpmail.asp*. Outlook configures the URL automatically when you set up a Hotmail account in Outlook (see Figure 1-14). You can't browse to this URL through your Web browser to retrieve your e-mail, however.

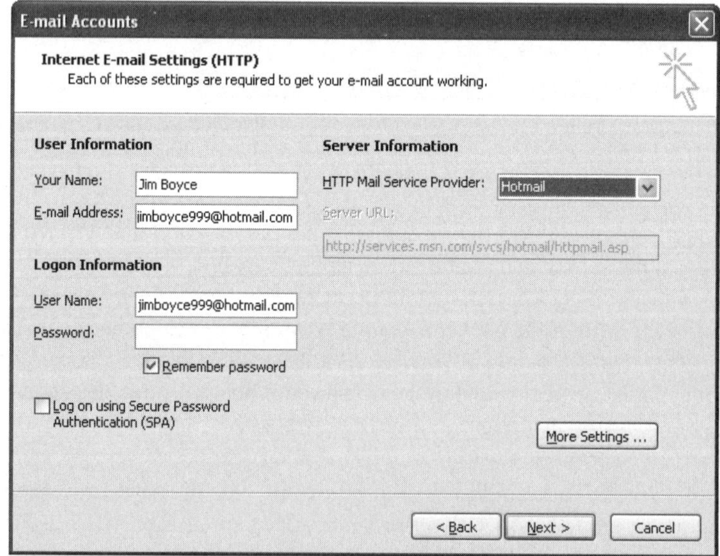

Figure 1-14. Outlook configures the URL automatically for Hotmail, but you must enter the URL manually for other HTTP-based e-mail services.

> **Tip** **Access Exchange Server 2003 with HTTP**
> Outlook 2003 can connect to an Exchange Server 2003 mailbox using HTTP as the protocol, expanding connection possibilities for users and decreasing firewall configuration and management headaches for administrators.

MIME

Multipurpose Internet Mail Extensions (MIME) is a standard specification for defining file formats used to exchange e-mail, files, and other documents across the Internet or an intranet. Each of the many MIME types defines the content type of the data contained in the attachment. MIME maps the content to a specific file type and extension, allowing the e-mail client to pass the MIME attachment to an external application for processing. For example, if you receive a message containing a WAV file attachment, Outlook passes the file to the default WAV file player on your system.

S/MIME

Secure/Multipurpose Internet Mail Extensions (S/MIME) is a standard that allows e-mail applications to send digitally signed and encrypted messages. S/MIME is therefore a mechanism through which Outlook permits you to include digital signatures with messages to ensure their authenticity and to encrypt messages to prevent unauthorized access to them.

> **Note** For a detailed discussion of using Outlook to send digitally signed and encrypted messages, as well as other security-related issues such as virus protection and security zones, see Chapter 10, "Securing Your System, Messages, and Identity."

MHTML

MIME HTML (MHTML) represents MIME encapsulation of HTML documents. MHTML allows you to send and receive Web pages and other HTML-based documents and to embed images directly in the body of a message rather than attaching them to the message. See the preceding sections for an explanation of MIME.

iCalendar, vCalendar, and vCard

iCalendar, vCalendar, and vCard are Internet-based standards that provide a means for people to share calendar free/busy information and contact information across the Internet. The iCalendar standard allows calendar and scheduling applications to share free/busy information with other applications that support iCalendar. The vCalendar standard provides a mechanism for vCalendar-compliant applications to exchange meeting requests across the Internet. The vCard standard allows applications to share contact information as Internet vCards (electronic business cards). Outlook supports these standards to share information and interact with other messaging and scheduling applications across the Internet.

Security Provisions in Outlook

Outlook 2003 provides several features for ensuring the security of your data, messages, and identity. This section of the chapter presents a brief overview of security features in Outlook to give you a basic understanding of the issues involved, with references to other locations in the book that offer more detailed information on these topics.

Support for Security Zones

Like Microsoft Internet Explorer, Outlook supports the use of security zones. In Internet Explorer, security zones allow you to specify the types of actions that scripts can take on your system, based on the zone from which they were accessed. This prevents a malicious script from surreptitiously gathering information from your system and sending it to a Web site or doing local damage such as deleting files. In Internet Explorer, you can configure four zones, each with different security settings that define the tasks scripts can perform. For example, you can disable download of signed and unsigned ActiveX controls, specify how cookies are stored on your system, or disable scripting of Java applets.

Because Outlook can receive HTML-based messages, your computer is exposed to the same security risks posed by Internet browsing with Internet Explorer. The risk is actually worse with e-mail, considering that you generally make a conscious effort to visit a Web page—e-mail messages, in contrast, come at you unbidden, making your system subject to a more active form of attack. By supporting Internet Explorer's security zones, Outlook allows you to specify the zone from which e-mail messages should be considered to have originated, letting you guard against HTML-based security risks.

To learn how to apply security zones to protect your system, see "Using Security Zones," page 288.

Protection Against Web Beacons

Many spammers (people who send unsolicited e-mail) have begun using *Web beacons* to validate e-mail addresses. They send HTML-based e-mail messages that contain links to external content on a Web site, and when the recipient's e-mail client automatically opens the remote content from the Web site to display the message, the site validates the e-mail address. The spammer then knows that the address is a "live" one and continues to send messages to it.

Outlook 2003 blocks these Web beacons, displaying a red X instead of the external image. You can selectively view external content for a message by clicking the message header and then clicking the InfoBar. You can also turn off Web beacon blocking, if you want, and control external HTML content in other ways.

Note See Chapter 10, "Securing Your System, Messages, and Identity," for an explanation of how to configure HTML message-handling options.

Attachment and Virus Security

You probably are aware that a *virus* is an application that infects your system and typically causes some type of damage. The action caused by a virus can be as innocuous as displaying a message or as damaging as deleting data from your hard disk. One especially insidious form of virus, called a *worm*, spreads itself automatically, often by mailing itself to every contact in the infected system's address book. Guarding against such viruses, then, is a critical issue.

Outlook offers two levels of attachment security to guard against virus and worm infections: Level 1 and Level 2. Outlook automatically blocks Level 1 attachments, a category that includes almost 40 file types with the potential to allow a virus to cause damage to your system—for example, EXE and VBS files. If you receive a Level 1 attachment, Outlook displays a paper clip icon beside the message but does not allow you to open or save the attachment. When you send a Level 1 attachment, Outlook displays a reminder that other Outlook users might not be able to receive the attachment, giving you the option of converting it to a different file type (such as a ZIP file) before sending it. If you receive a Level 2 attachment, Outlook allows you to save the attachment to disk but not open it directly. You can then process the file with your virus checker before opening it.

> **Note** **Update Your Virus Definitions Often**
> Your virus scanner is only as good as its definition file. New viruses crop up every day, so it's critical that you have an up-to-date virus definition file and put in place a strategy to ensure that your virus definitions are always current.

If you use Exchange Server to host your mailbox, the Exchange Server administrator can configure Level 1 and Level 2 attachments, adding or removing attachment types for each level. In addition, Outlook allows all users to control the security-level assignments for attachments.

For a detailed discussion of Outlook's virus protection, see "Protecting Against Viruses in Attachments," page 320.

Macro Viruses

Although viruses were once found almost exclusively in executable files, viruses embedded in document macros have become very common, and Office documents are as subject to them as any other files. However, Outlook and other Office applications provide a means for you to guard against macro viruses. In Outlook, you can select one of three macro security levels, as shown in Figure 1-15. These security levels let you configure Outlook to run only signed macros from trusted sources (High), prompt you to choose whether to let the macro execute (Medium), or allow all macros to execute (Low). You can also specify which sources are trusted.

To learn how to configure and use macro virus protection, see "Protecting Against Office Macro Viruses," page 324.

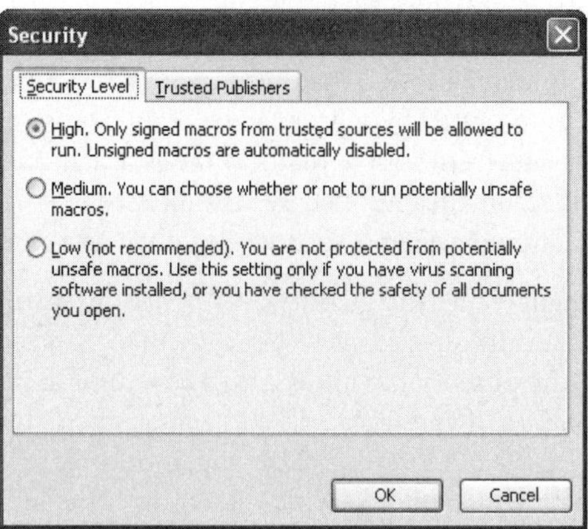

Figure 1-15. Use macro security to prevent macro-borne viruses from affecting your system.

Digital Signatures

Outlook allows you to add a certificate-based digital signature to a message to validate your identity to the message recipient. Because the signature is derived from a certificate that is issued to you and that you share with the recipient, the recipient can be guaranteed that the message originated with you, rather than with someone trying to impersonate your identity.

For information about how to obtain a certificate and use it to digitally sign your outgoing messages, see "Protecting Messages with Digital Signatures," page 293.

In addition to signing your outgoing messages, you can also use secure message receipts that notify you that your message has been verified by the recipient's system. The lack of a return receipt indicates that the recipient's system did not validate your identity. In such a case, you can contact the recipient to make sure that he or she has a copy of your digital signature.

Note Although you can configure Outlook to send a digital signature to a recipient, there is no guarantee that the recipient will add the digital signature to his or her contacts list. Until the recipient adds the signature, digitally signed messages are not validated, and the recipient cannot read encrypted messages from you.

Message Encryption

Where the possibility of interception exists (whether someone intercepts your message before it reaches the intended recipient or someone else at the recipient's end tries to read the message), Outlook message encryption can help you keep prying eyes away from sensitive messages. This feature also relies on your digital signature to encrypt the message and to allow the recipient to decrypt and read the message. Someone who receives the message without first having the public key portion of your certificate installed on his or her system sees a garbled message.

To learn how to obtain a certificate and use it to encrypt your outgoing messages, as well as how to read encrypted messages you receive from others, see "Encrypting Messages," page 315.

Security Labels

The security labels feature in this version of Outlook relies on security policies in Windows 2000 Server and Microsoft Windows Server 2003, and is supported only on clients running Windows 2000, Windows Server 2003, or Windows XP. Security labels let you add additional security information, such as message sensitivity, to a message header. You can also use security labels to restrict which recipients can open, forward, or send a specific message. Security labels therefore provide a quick indicator of a message's sensitivity and control over the actions that others can take with a message.

Understanding Outlook Service Options

If you've been using a version of Outlook prior to Microsoft Outlook 2002, you're probably familiar with Outlook's service options. Earlier versions of Outlook supported three service options: No Mail, Internet Mail Only (IMO), and Corporate/Workgroup (C/W). Outlook 2003, like Outlook 2002, uses a *unified mode*. Outlook unified mode integrates mail services in Outlook, which allows you to configure and use multiple services in a single profile. This means that you can use Exchange Server, POP3, IMAP, and Hotmail accounts all in one profile and at the same time.

To learn how to work with profiles and add multiple accounts to a profile, see "Understanding User Profiles," page 42. Although Outlook makes a great e-mail client for a wide range of mail services, you might prefer to use only its contact management, scheduling, and other nonmessaging features and to use a different application (such as Outlook Express) for your messaging needs. There is no downside to using Outlook in this configuration, although you should keep in mind that certain features, such as integrated scheduling, rely on Outlook's messaging features. If you need to take advantage of these features, you should use Outlook as your primary messaging application.

Options for Starting Outlook

Office offers several options to control startup, either through command-line switches or other methods. You can choose to have Outlook open forms, turn off the Preview pane (now called the Reading Pane), select a profile, and perform other tasks automatically when the program starts. The following sections describe some of the options you can specify.

Normal Startup

When you install Outlook, Setup places a Microsoft Outlook icon on the Start menu. You can start Outlook normally by clicking the icon. You also can start Outlook by using the Programs menu (choose Start, Programs, Microsoft Outlook).

When Outlook starts normally and without command-line switches, it prompts you for the profile to use (see Figure 1-16) if more than one exists. The profile contains your account settings and configures Outlook for your e-mail servers, directory services, data files, and other Outlook settings.

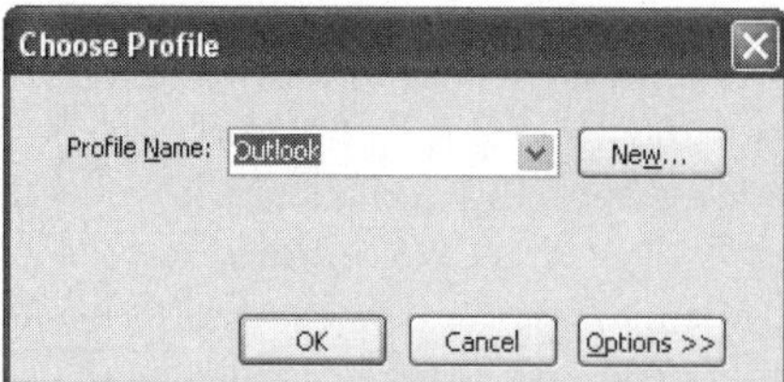

Figure 1-16. Outlook prompts you to choose a profile at startup.

You can use multiple profiles to maintain multiple identities in Outlook. For example, you might use one profile for your work-related items and a second one for your personal items. To use an existing profile, simply choose it from the drop-down list in the Choose Profile dialog box and click OK. Click New to create a new profile (covered in Chapter 2, "Advanced Setup Tasks"). Click Options to expand the Choose Profile dialog box, shown in Figure 1-16, to include this option:

- **Set As Default Profile** Select this option to specify the selected profile as the default profile, which will appear in the drop-down list by default in subsequent Outlook sessions. For example, if you maintain separate personal and work profiles, and your personal profile always appears in the drop-down list, select your work profile and choose this option to make the work profile the default.

For an in-depth discussion of creating and configuring profiles, see "Understanding User Profiles," page 42. The details of configuring service providers (such as for Exchange Server) are covered in various chapters where appropriate—for example, Chapter 6, "Using Internet Mail," explains how to configure POP3 and IMAP accounts; and Chapter 34, "Configuring the Exchange Server Client," explains how to configure Exchange Server accounts.

Safe Mode Startup

Safe mode is a startup mode available in Outlook 2003 and the other Microsoft Office 2003 applications. Safe mode makes it possible for Office applications to automatically recover from specific errors during startup, such as a problem with an add-in or a corrupt registry. Safe mode allows Outlook to detect the problem and either correct it or bypass it by isolating the source.

When Outlook starts automatically in safe mode, you see a dialog box that displays the source of the problem and asks whether you want to continue to open the program, bypassing the problem source, or try to restart the program again. If you direct Outlook to continue starting, the problem items are disabled, and you can view them in the Disabled Items dialog box (see Figure 1-17). To open this dialog box, choose Help, About Microsoft Outlook, and click Disabled Items. To enable a disabled item, select the item and click Enable.

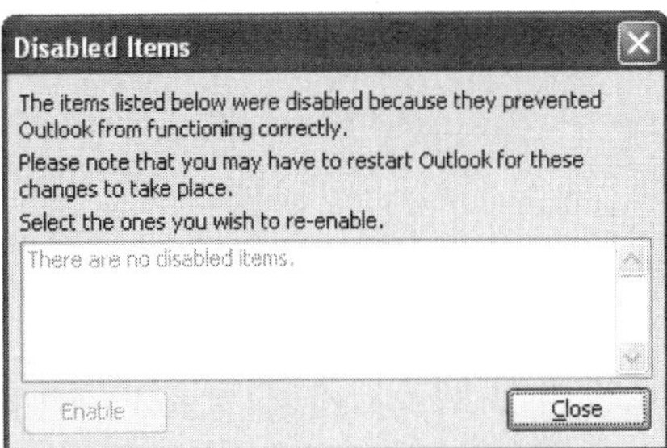

Figure 1-17. Disabled Items dialog box to review and enable items.

In certain situations, you might want to force Outlook into safe mode when it would otherwise start normally—for example, if you want to prevent add-ins from loading or prevent customized toolbars or command bars from loading. To start Outlook (or any other Office application) in safe mode, hold down the Ctrl key and start the program. Outlook detects the Ctrl key and asks whether you want to start Outlook in safe mode. Click Yes to start in safe mode or No to start normally.

If you start an application in safe mode, you cannot perform certain actions in the application. The following is a summary (not all of which apply to Outlook):

- Templates can't be saved.
- The last used Web page is not loaded (Microsoft FrontPage).
- Customized toolbars and command bars are not opened. Customizations that you make in safe mode can't be changed.
- The AutoCorrect list isn't loaded, nor can changes you make to AutoCorrect in safe mode be saved.
- Recovered documents are not opened automatically.
- No smart tags are loaded, and new smart tags can't be saved.
- Command-line options other than /a and /n are ignored.
- You can't save files to the Alternate Startup Directory.
- You can't save preferences.
- Additional features and programs (such as add-ins) do not load automatically.

To start Outlook normally, simply shut down the program and start it again without pressing the Ctrl key.

Starting Outlook Automatically

If you're like most Office users, you work in Outlook a majority of the time. Because Outlook is such an important aspect of your work day, you probably want it to start automatically when you log on to your computer, saving you the trouble of starting it later. Although you have a few options for starting Outlook automatically, the best solution is to place a shortcut to Outlook in your Startup folder.

Follow these steps to start Outlook automatically in Windows XP, or Windows 2000.

1. Close or minimize all windows on the desktop.
2. Locate the Microsoft Outlook icon on the desktop, and drag it to the Start button. Don't release the mouse button.
3. Hold the pointer over the Start menu until it opens. While continuing to hold down the mouse button, open the Programs menu and then the Startup menu.
4. Place the cursor on the Startup menu and release the mouse button. Windows informs you that you can't move the item and asks whether you want to create a shortcut. Click Yes.

> **Tip** **Create a new Outlook shortcut**
> If you don't have a Microsoft Outlook icon on the desktop, you can use the Outlook executable to create a shortcut. Open Windows Explorer and browse to the folder \Program Files\Microsoft Office\Office11. Create a shortcut to the executable Outlook.exe. Note that the default syntax for the standard Microsoft Outlook shortcut is C:\Program Files\Microsoft Office\ Office11\Outlook.exe /recycle. For an explanation of the /recycle switch and other Outlook startup options, see "Startup Switches," page 32.

> **Tip** **Change Outlook's shortcut properties**
> If you want to change the way Outlook starts from the shortcut in your Startup folder (for example, you might want to add command switches), you need only change the shortcut's properties. For details, see "Changing the Outlook Shortcut," later in this chapter.

Adding Outlook to the Quick Launch Bar

The Quick Launch bar appears on the taskbar just to the right of the Start menu. Quick Launch, as its name implies, gives you a way to easily and quickly start applications—just click the application's icon. By default, the Quick Launch bar includes the Show Desktop icon, as well as the Internet Explorer and Outlook Express icons (if Outlook Express is installed). Quick Launch offers easier application launching because you don't have to navigate the Start menu to start an application.

> **Note** If you don't see the Quick Launch toolbar, right-click the taskbar and verify that Lock The Taskbar is not selected on the shortcut menu. If it is, select Lock The Taskbar to remove the check. Then, right-click the taskbar and choose Toolbars, Quick Launch to add the Quick Launch toolbar to the taskbar.

Adding a shortcut to the Quick Launch toolbar is easy:

1 Minimize all windows so that you can see the desktop.
2 Using the right mouse button, drag the Microsoft Outlook icon to the Quick Launch area of the taskbar and then release it.
3 Choose Create Shortcut(s) Here.

Note You can also left-drag the Microsoft Outlook icon to the Quick Launch bar. Windows informs you that you can't copy or move the item to that location and asks whether you want to create a shortcut instead. Click Yes to create the shortcut or No to cancel.

Changing the Outlook Shortcut

Let's assume that you've created a shortcut to Outlook on your Quick Launch bar or in another location so that you can start Outlook quickly. Why change the shortcut? By adding switches to the command that starts Outlook, you can customize the way the application starts and functions for the current session. You can also control Outlook's startup window state (normal, minimized, maximized) through the shortcut's properties. For example, you might want Outlook to start automatically when you log on, but you want it to start minimized. In this situation, you would create a shortcut to Outlook in your Startup folder and then modify the shortcut so that Outlook starts minimized.

To change the properties for a shortcut, first locate the shortcut, right-click its icon, and choose Properties. You should see a dialog box similar to the one shown in Figure 1-18.

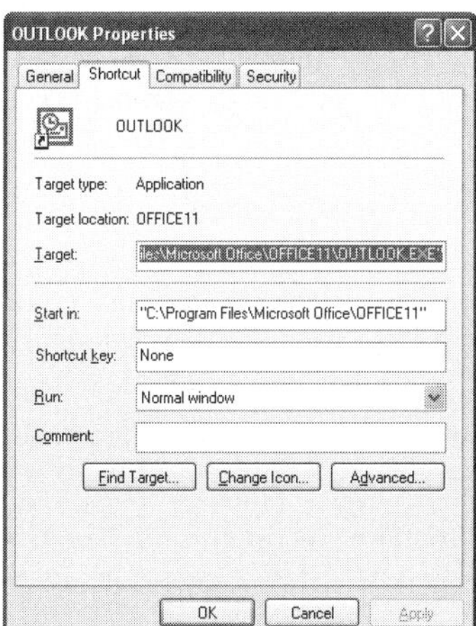

Figure 1-18. A typical Properties dialog box for an Outlook shortcut in Windows 2000.

The following list summarizes the options on the Shortcut tab of the Properties dialog box:

> **Note** These options exist on Windows 2000 systems and are similar for Windows XP systems, although some of the options have slightly different names. Click Advanced on the Shortcut tab in Windows XP to view additional settings.

- **Target Type** This read-only property specifies the type for the shortcut's target, which in the example shown in Figure 1-18 is Application.
- **Target Location** This read-only property specifies the directory location of the target executable.
- **Target** This property specifies the command to execute when the shortcut is executed. The default Outlook command is "C:\Program Files\Microsoft Office\Office11\Outlook.exe" /recycle. The path could vary if you have installed Office in a different folder. The path to the executable must be enclosed in quotes, and any additional switches must be added to the right, outside the quotes. See "Startup Switches," page 32, to learn about additional switches you can use to start Outlook.
- **Start In** This property specifies the startup directory for the application.
- **Shortcut Key** Use this property to assign a shortcut key to the shortcut, which allows you to start Outlook by pressing the key combination. Simply click in the Shortcut Key box and press the keystroke to assign it to the shortcut.
- **Run** Use this property to specify the startup window state for Outlook. You can choose Normal Window, Minimized, or Maximized.
- **Comment** Use this property to specify an optional comment. The comment appears in the shortcut's ToolTip when you rest the pointer over the shortcut's icon. For example, if you use the Run As Different User option, you might include mention of that in the Comment box to help you distinguish this shortcut from another that launches Outlook in the default context.
- **Find Target** Click this button to open the folder containing the Outlook.exe executable file.
- **Change Icon** Click this button to change the icon assigned to the shortcut. By default, the icon comes from the Outlook.exe executable, which contains other icons you can assign to the shortcut. You also can use other ICO, EXE, and DLL files to assign icons. You'll find several additional icons in Moricons.dll and Shell32.dll, both located in the %systemroot%\System32 folder.
- **Advanced** Click this button to access the two following options for Windows XP (these two options are directly available on the Shortcut tab for Windows 2000 users).
- **Run In Separate Memory Space** This option is selected by default and can't be changed for Outlook. All 32-bit applications run in a separate memory space. This provides crash protection for other applications and for the operating system.

- **Run with Different Credentials** Select this option to run Outlook in a different user context, which lets you start Outlook with a different user account from the one you used to log on to the computer. Windows prompts you for the user name and password when you execute the shortcut. This option is named Run as a Different User in Windows 2000.

> **Tip** You also can use the RUNAS command from a command console to start an application in a different user context. For additional information, see the following section, "Use RUNAS to Change User Context."

When you're satisfied with the shortcut's properties, click OK to close the dialog box.

Use RUNAS to Change User Context

As explained in the preceding section, you can use the option Run As Different User in a shortcut's Properties dialog box to run the target application in a different user context from the one you used to log on to the system. This option is applicable on systems running Windows 2000 or later.

You can also use the RUNAS command from a command console in Windows 2000 or Windows XP to run a command—including Outlook—in a different user context. The syntax for RUNAS is

```
RUNAS [/profile] [/env] [/netonly] /user:<UserName> program
```

The parameters for RUNAS can be summarized as follows:

- **/profile** Use this parameter to indicate the profile for the specified user if that profile needs to be loaded.
- **/env** Use the current user environment instead of the one specified by the user's profile.
- **/netonly** Use this parameter if the specified user credentials are for remote access only.
- **/user:**<*UserName*> Use this parameter to specify the user account under which you want the application to be run.
- **Program** This parameter specifies the application to execute.

Following is an example of the RUNAS command used to start Outlook in the Administrator context of the domain ADMIN (note that the command should be on one line on your screen):

```
RUNAS /profile /user:admin\administrator
""C:\Program Files\Microsoft Office
\Office11\Outlook.exe" /recycle"
```

It might seem like a lot of trouble to type all that at the command prompt, and that's usually the case. Although you can use RUNAS from the command console to run Outlook in a specific user context, it's generally more useful to use RUNAS in a batch file to start Outlook in a given, predetermined user context. For example, you might create a batch file containing the sample RUNAS syntax just noted and then create a shortcut to that batch file so that you can execute it easily without typing the command each time.

Startup Switches

Microsoft Outlook supports a number of command-line switches that modify the way the program starts and functions. Although you can issue the Outlook.exe command with switches from a command prompt, it's generally more useful to specify switches through a shortcut, particularly if you want to use the same set of switches more than once. Table 1-1 lists the startup switches you can use to modify the way Outlook starts and functions.

For an explanation of how to modify a shortcut to add command-line switches, see "Changing the Outlook Shortcut," page 29.

Table 1-1. Startup switches and their purposes

Switch	Purpose
/a *<filename>*	Open a message form with the attachment specified by *<filename>*
/c ipm.activity	Open the journal entry form by itself
/c ipm.appointment	Open the appointment form by itself
/c ipm.contact	Open the contact form by itself
/c ipm.note	Open the message form by itself
/c ipm.post	Open the discussion form by itself
/c ipm.stickynote	Open the note form by itself
/c ipm.task	Open the task form by itself
/c *<class>*	Create an item using the message class specified by *<class>*
/CheckClient	Perform a check to see whether Outlook is the default application for e-mail, news, and contacts
/CleanFreeBusy	Regenerate free/busy schedule data
/CleanReminders	Regenerate reminders
/CleanSchedPlus	Delete Schedule+ data from the server and enable free/busy data from the Outlook calendar to be used by Schedule+ users
/CleanViews	Restore the default Outlook views
/Folder	Hide the Outlook Bar and folder list if displayed in the previous session
/NoPreview	Hide the Preview pane and remove Preview Pane from the View menu
/Profiles	Display the Choose Profile dialog box even if Always Use This Profile is selected in profile options

Table 1-1. Startup switches and their purposes

Switch	Purpose
/Profile *<name>*	Automatically use the profile specified by *<name>*
/Recycle	Start Outlook using an existing Outlook window if one exists
/ResetFolders	Restore missing folders in the default message store
/ResetOutlookBar	Rebuild the Outlook Bar
/select *<folder>*	Display the folder specified by *<folder>*

Choosing a Startup View

When you start Outlook, it defaults to using the Inbox view (see Figure 1-19), but you might prefer to use a different view or folder as the initial view. For example, if you use Outlook primarily for scheduling, you'll probably want Outlook to start in the Calendar folder. If you use Outlook mainly to manage contacts, you'll probably want it to start in the Contacts folder.

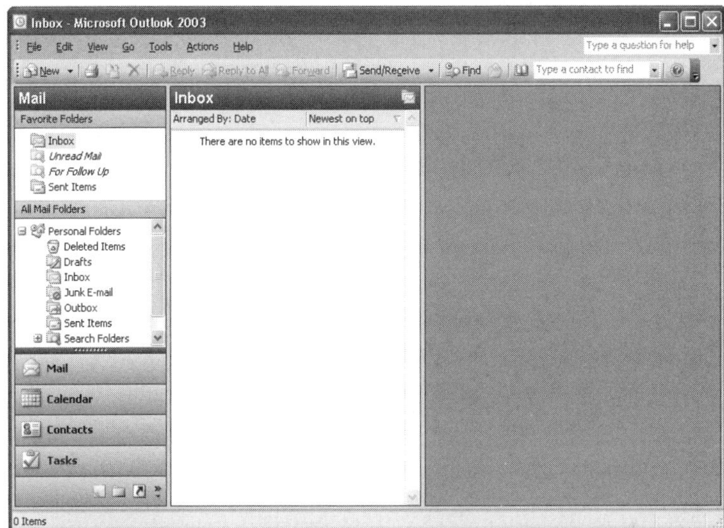

Figure 1-19. Inbox is the default view.

To specify the view that should appear when Outlook first starts, follow these steps:

1. Open Outlook and choose Tools, Options.
2. Click the Other tab and then click Advanced Options (see Figure 1-20).
3. From the Startup In This Folder drop-down list, choose the folder you want Outlook to open at startup.
4. Click OK and then close the dialog box.

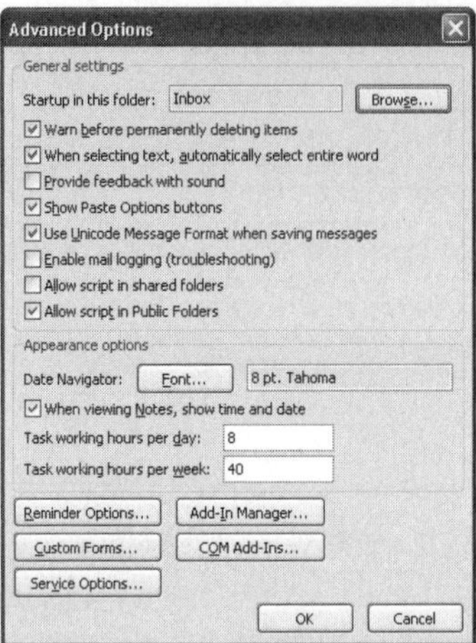

Figure 1-20. Use the Advanced Options dialog box to specify the Startup view.

If you switch Outlook to a different default folder and then want to restore Outlook Today as your default view, you can follow the previous steps to restore Outlook Today as the default.

Simply select Outlook Today from the drop-down list or follow these steps with the Outlook Today window open:

1. Open Outlook and open Outlook Today view.
2. Click Customize Outlook Today at the top of the Outlook Today window.
3. On the resulting page, select When Starting Go Directly To Outlook Today and then click Save Changes.

Creating Shortcuts to Start New Outlook Items

In some cases you might want icons on the desktop or your Quick Start toolbar that start new Outlook items. For example, perhaps you would like an icon that starts a new e-mail message and another icon that starts a new appointment item.

Sometimes you need to dash off a quick message and have to open Outlook, wait for it to load, compose the message, then close it when you are finished. You can simplify the task of sending a new e-mail for these users by creating a shortcut to a mailto: item on the desktop or in the Quick Start menu by following these steps:

1. Right-click the desktop and choose New, Shortcut.
2. In the Create Shortcut dialog box, enter **mailto:** as the item to launch and click Next.
3. Type **New Mail Message** as the shortcut name and click Finish.
4. Drag the shortcut to the Quick Start toolbar to make it quickly accessible without minimizing all applications.

When you double-click the shortcut, Outlook actually launches and prompts you for a profile unless one is set as the default profile. However, only the new message form appears—the rest of Outlook stays hidden, running in the background.

You can use the Target property of an Outlook shortcut to create other types of Outlook items. Refer to the section "Changing the Outlook Shortcut" earlier in this chapter to learn how to create an Outlook shortcut. See Table 1-1 for the switches that open specific Outlook forms. For example, the following two shortcuts start a new message and a new appointment, respectively:*

```
"C:\Program Files\Microsoft Office\Office11\Outlook.exe" /c ipm.note

"C:\Program Files\Microsoft Office\Office11\Outlook.exe" /c ipm.appointment
```

> **Tip** You can use the /a switch to open a new message form with an attachment. The following example starts a new message and attaches the file named Picture.jpg:
>
> "C:\Program Files\Microsoft Office\Office11\Outlook.exe" /a Picture.jpg.

Chapter 2

Advanced Setup Tasks

Because Microsoft Outlook has so many features, configuring the program—particularly for first-time or inexperienced users—can be a real challenge. However, after you master the basic concepts and experiment with the configuration process, it quickly becomes second nature.

This chapter examines Outlook setup issues, including what you see the first time you start Outlook and how to use the E-Mail Accounts Wizard to create, modify, and test e-mail accounts. You'll also learn about user profiles, including how to create and modify them, how to use multiple profiles for different identities, how to copy profiles, and how to configure profile properties.

After you have a solid understanding of profiles, you're ready to tackle configuring the many e-mail and data file services Outlook offers. This chapter discusses configuring both online and offline storage and will help you add, modify, and remove personal message stores (personal folders) for a profile.

In addition, the chapter explains how to configure Outlook to maintain an offline copy of your Microsoft Exchange Server mailbox and folders so that you can work with your account while disconnected from the network. You'll also learn how to change the storage location for your data and how to set options to control mail delivery.

Starting Outlook for the First Time

The first time you run Outlook after a fresh installation (as opposed to an upgrade of an earlier version of Outlook), Outlook runs the Outlook 2003 Startup Wizard. The wizard steps you through the process of setting up e-mail accounts and *data stores* (the files used to store your Outlook data). When you've completed all the steps, Outlook opens, as shown in Figure 2-1. Outlook configures the Navigation pane based on the selections you made in the wizard.

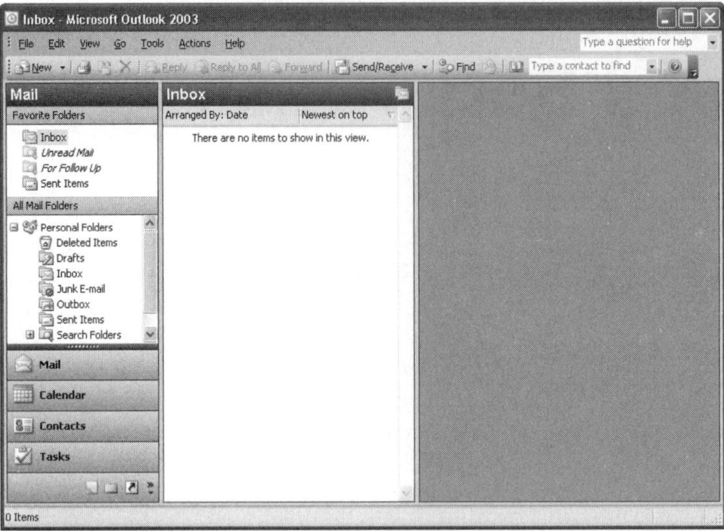

Figure 2-1. Here's what you'll see at first startup after a clean installation.

The Startup Wizard is the same wizard you use to configure e-mail accounts after Outlook is installed. For that reason, you'll encounter this wizard again in the following section.

If you upgraded Outlook over a previous version, Outlook automatically migrates your accounts, preferences, and data the first time you run it. This means you don't have to perform any other tasks before working with Outlook 2003, unless you want to add other accounts or take advantage of features not provided by your current profile settings. In the following section, you'll learn how to add other services and accounts to your current Outlook profile.

Configuring Accounts and Services

Outlook 2003 provides a wizard to help simplify setup and configuration of e-mail accounts, data stores, and directory services. You use the same Startup Wizard that installs Outlook to add new e-mail accounts. When you start Outlook for the first time after a clean installation (that is, not an upgrade), Outlook runs the wizard automatically.

Follow these steps to get started in setting up e-mail accounts:

1. Start Outlook. When the Outlook 2003 Startup Wizard appears, click Next.
2. On the E-Mail Accounts page, click Yes, indicating that you want to set up an e-mail account, and then click Next. The wizard displays the Server Type page (see Figure 2-2).

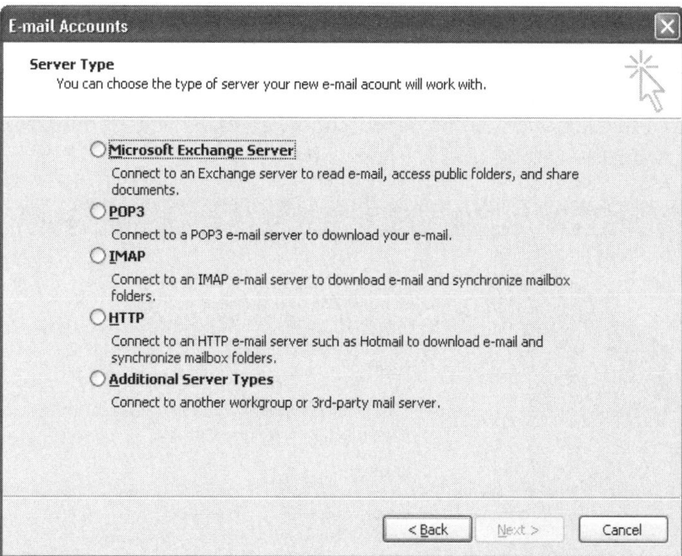

Figure 2-2. Select the type of server for the e-mail account you want to add.

3 Select the type of e-mail service for which you want to add an account and click Next.

For a discussion of user profiles and how Outlook uses them to store your account settings, see "Understanding User Profiles," page 42.

The action the wizard takes at this point depends on the type of account you select. Rather than cover account configuration here, outside the context of using each type of account, this book covers the specifics of each account type in the associated chapter. The following list helps you locate the appropriate chapter and section:

- **Exchange Server** See Chapter 34, "Configuring the Exchange Server Client."
- **Internet Mail (POP3)** See "Using Internet POP3 E-Mail Accounts," page 147.
- **IMAP** See "Using IMAP Accounts," page 155.
- **HTTP (including Hotmail and others)** See "Using Hotmail and Other HTTP-Based Services," page 158.
- **CompuServe** See "Using Outlook with CompuServe," page 156 (includes CompuServe Classic and CompuServe 2000).
- **Fax Transport** See "The Native Windows Fax Service," page 261.

You can easily add an e-mail account to your Outlook profile after Outlook is installed. Follow these steps:

1 Right-click the Outlook icon on the desktop, choose Properties, and then click E-Mail Accounts. Or, with Outlook open, choose Tools, E-Mail Accounts to display the E-Mail Accounts Wizard, shown in Figure 2-3.

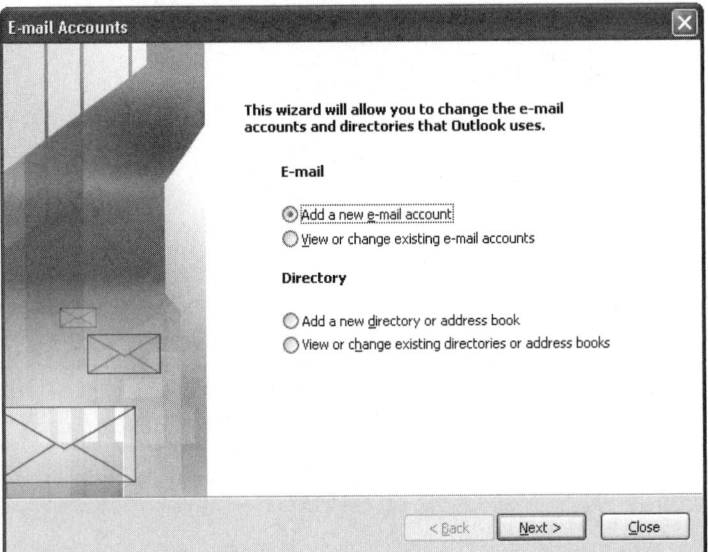

Figure 2-3. Outlook provides a wizard for adding and modifying accounts.

Note If your system includes multiple profiles, select the one to which you want to add accounts. Right-click the Outlook icon on the Start menu and choose Properties. Click Show Profiles, locate and select your profile, and click Properties. Then select E-Mail Accounts.

2 Select Add A New E-Mail Account and click Next if you want to add an account. Select View Or Change Existing E-Mail Accounts to modify existing accounts.

3 Select the type of e-mail service to add and click Next. (As noted earlier, you can refer to other chapters for information about configuring specific account types.)

Testing Your E-Mail Account

Outlook offers a new feature to help you set up your e-mail account. You can now test the new account while you create it, rather than setting it up first and testing it later. This helps you quickly identify problems with the account settings, such as an incorrect password or the wrong Domain Name System (DNS) name specified for the incoming or outgoing server.

When you run the E-Mail Accounts Wizard, enter the settings for the account on the Settings page (see Figure 2-4). Then click Test Account Settings. Outlook locates the incoming and outgoing mail servers, logs on to the incoming mail server, and sends a test message (see Figure 2-5). If all steps are completed successfully, your account settings are correct. Difficulty with a particular step can help you identify problems with your settings, a connectivity problem, and so on. Although Outlook doesn't start a troubleshooter for you or recommend a fix, specific types of difficulties point to certain common problems. For example, if Outlook indicates that it can't find your e-mail server, the most likely problem is that you have specified the wrong DNS name (assuming that your Internet or intranet connection is working).

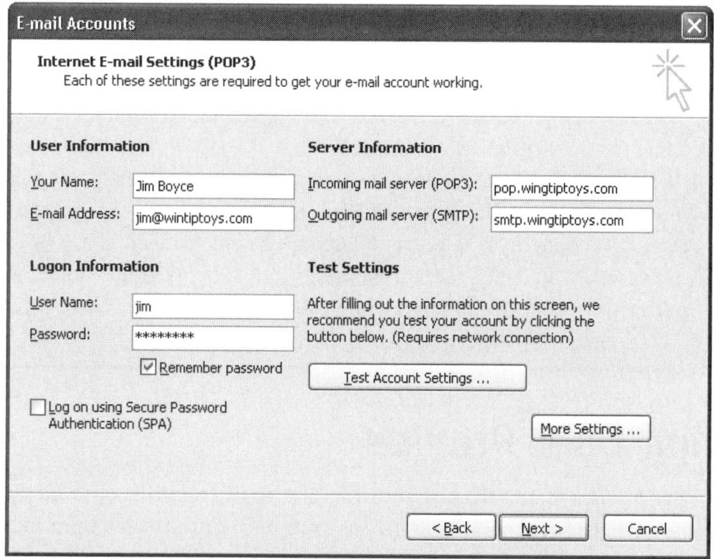

Figure 2-4. Click Test Account Settings when setting up a new account to test the account.

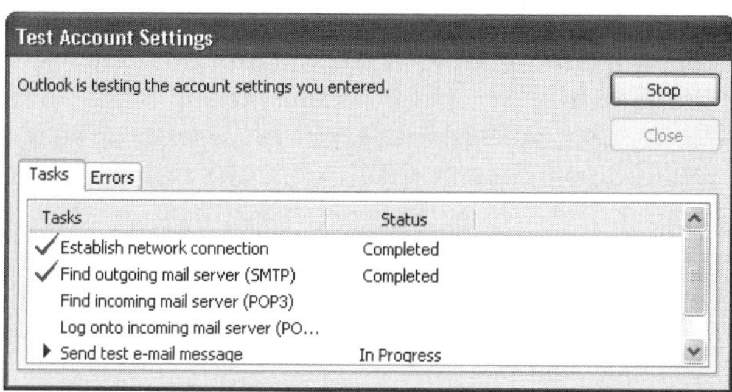

Figure 2-5. Outlook performs several tasks to check your account settings.

Troubleshooting

Outlook can't find your e-mail server

If Outlook can't seem to locate your e-mail server, you can check a handful of settings to determine the problem. First, make sure your computer is connected to the network or the Internet, depending on where the server is located. If you're specifying a server on the Internet, make sure you have specified the correct, fully qualified domain name (FQDN) of the server, such as *mail.wingtiptoys.com*. If you specify the correct name but Outlook still can't find the server, try pinging the server by name. Open a command console and type the following command where *<server>* is the FQDN of the server:

PING *<server>*

If this results in an unknown host error, it's likely that DNS is not configured or working properly on your computer. Check the DNS settings for your TCP/IP protocol to make sure you are specifying the correct DNS server. If you know the IP address of the server, ping the address. If you are able to ping, you definitely have a DNS problem or are specifying the wrong DNS name. If the ping fails, you have a network connectivity or TCP/IP stack problem. At this point, it would be best to consult your network support staff. Your configuration needs to be verified (and changed, if an incorrect value has been specified). If you have faulty hardware, it needs to be replaced.

Understanding User Profiles

In Outlook, *user profiles* store the configuration of e-mail accounts, data files, and other settings you use in a given Outlook session. For example, your profile might include an Exchange Server account, an Internet mail account, and a set of personal folders. Outlook either prompts you to select a profile at startup or selects one automatically, depending on how you've configured it.

In most cases, you'll probably use only one profile and will configure Outlook to select it automatically. In some situations, however, multiple profiles can be useful. For example, you might prefer to keep your work and personal data completely separate on your notebook computer because of privacy concerns or office policies. In this situation, you maintain two profiles: one for your work data and a second for your personal data.You then configure Outlook to prompt you to choose a profile at startup. The profile controls which set of data files and configuration settings are used for that specific session. For example, when you're working at the office, you use the office profile—and when you're using the computer at home, you use the personal profile.

It's important to understand that Outlook profiles have no relationship to the other types of profiles you'll find in a Microsoft Windows operating system, which include hardware profiles and user profiles. *Hardware profiles* store hardware settings and allow you to switch between different hardware configurations without reconfiguring your system. *User profiles* store the unique working environment (Desktop, My Documents, and so on) that you see when you log on to your computer. Outlook profiles, in contrast, apply only to Outlook.

Note Unless otherwise noted, the term *profile* in this book refers to an Outlook profile.

Each profile can contain multiple accounts and services, which means you can work with different e-mail servers at one time and use multiple sets of data files (such as a set of personal folders, or PST file). The following list describes the items stored in an Outlook profile:

- **Services** These include e-mail accounts and data files, along with their settings. For example, your profile might include an Exchange Server account, two Internet e-mail accounts, a PST file, and a directory service account. When these accounts are in a single profile, you can use all of them in the same Outlook session.
- **Delivery settings** The profile specifies the store to which Outlook should deliver new mail when it arrives. With the exception of IMAP accounts, which use their own PST files, all accounts use the same store location. You also can specify the order in which Outlook processes accounts.

To learn how to configure these delivery properties for a given profile, see "Setting Delivery Options," page 53.

- **Address settings** You can specify which address book Outlook displays first, where Outlook should store personal addresses, and the order of the address books Outlook uses to check e-mail addresses when the profile includes multiple address books. In earlier versions of Outlook, you accessed these settings through the profile properties, but in Outlook 2003 you configure addressing in the Address Book window.

For detailed information on configuring and using address books in Outlook, see Chapter 5, "Managing Address Books and Distribution Lists."

The first time you run Outlook, it creates a profile called Outlook if you don't add any e-mail accounts to the profile. If you do add an e-mail account, Outlook uses the name you specify in the account settings as the name for the profile.

As explained previously, you can use multiple profiles. The following sections explain how to create new profiles, copy existing profiles to new profiles, and perform related operations.

Creating Profiles

You don't have to be in Outlook to create a profile; in fact, you can't create one in Outlook. You create profiles from the Start menu or through Control Panel. In addition to specifying a profile name, you can also (optionally) add e-mail and other services to the profile. You can create a profile from scratch or copy an existing profile to create a new one.

Creating a Profile from Scratch

When you have no existing Outlook profile or no profile that contains the accounts or settings you need, you must create a profile from scratch.

Follow these steps to create a new profile:

1. On the Start menu, right-click the Outlook icon and choose Properties. Alternatively, open Control Panel and double-click the Mail icon. If you are using Category view in the Windows XP Control Panel, the Mail icon is located in the User Accounts category.
2. In the Mail Setup dialog box (shown in Figure 2-6), click Show Profiles.

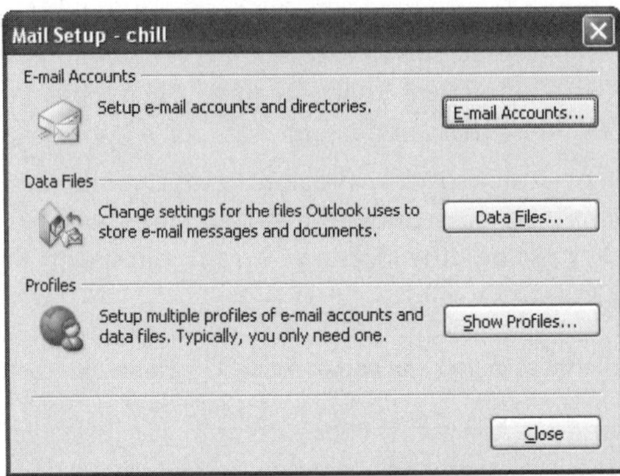

Figure 2-6. You access the current profile's settings as well as other profiles through the Mail Setup dialog box.

3. Click Add, specify a name for the profile in the New Profile dialog box, and click OK.
4. The E-Mail Accounts Wizard starts. Add accounts and other services to the profile. To create a new profile without adding any services (useful if you are not using Outlook for e-mail), click Close. In this situation, Outlook automatically creates a set of personal folders (a PST file) to store your Outlook data.

Copying a Profile

In addition to creating profiles from scratch, you can also copy an existing profile to create a new one. When you copy a profile, Outlook copies all the settings from the existing profile to the new one, including accounts and data files.

Follow these steps to copy an existing profile:

1. On the Start menu, right-click the Outlook icon and choose Properties. Alternatively, open Control Panel and double-click the Mail icon.
2. In the Mail Setup dialog box, click Show Profiles.
3. Select the existing profile that you want to use as the basis for the new profile and then click Copy.
4. In the Copy Profile dialog box, specify a name for the new profile and click OK.

Modifying or Removing a Profile

You can modify a profile at any time to add or remove services. You can also remove a profile altogether if you no longer need it.

Follow these steps to modify or remove an existing profile:

1. On the desktop, right-click the Outlook icon and choose Properties. Alternatively, open Control Panel and double-click the Mail icon.
2. In the Mail Setup dialog box, click Show Profiles.
3. Select the profile to be modified or removed.
4. Click Remove if you want to remove the profile, or click Properties to modify its settings.

Creating Multiple Profiles

For situations in which you need to create many profiles, such as when you are installing Office 2003 for multiple users or setting up a server to allow users to install Office automatically, you can turn to the Office 2003 Resource Kit for some helpful tools. One of these tools is the Custom Installation Wizard, which helps you customize the Office setup process, apply security settings for Office deployment, and provide the means to create and deploy preconfigured Outlook profiles.

Chapter 33, "Deploying and Managing Outlook in a Network," and Article 4 on the companion CD, "Office 2003 Resource Kit," cover the Custom Installation Wizard and Office 2003 Resource Kit, respectively. Chapter 33 also covers other tools in the Resource Kit for deploying Outlook and controlling Outlook with group policy.

Switching Profiles

You can configure Outlook either to use a specific profile automatically or to prompt you to select a profile at startup. If you want to change profiles, you need to exit Outlook and restart, selecting the appropriate profile.

Follow these steps to specify the default profile and use it automatically when Outlook starts:

1. On the desktop, right-click the Outlook icon and choose Properties. Alternatively, open Control Panel and double-click the Mail icon.
2. In the Mail Setup dialog box, click Show Profiles.
3. On the General tab (shown in Figure 2-7), select Always Use This Profile. In the drop-down list, select the default profile you want Outlook to use.

Figure 2-7. You can specify a default profile on the General tab.

4. Click OK.

Specifying the Startup Profile

If you work with multiple profiles and switch relatively often, you'll probably want to configure Outlook to prompt you to choose a profile at startup. This saves you the trouble of changing the default profile each time you want to switch. For example, assume that you use one profile for your personal accounts and another for your work accounts. Have Outlook prompt you for the profile when the program starts, rather than configuring the settings each time to specify the default profile.

Follow these steps to configure Outlook to prompt you to choose a profile:

1. On the desktop, right-click the Outlook icon and choose Properties. Alternatively, open Control Panel and double-click the Mail icon.
2. In the Mail Setup dialog box, click Show Profiles.
3. Select Always Use This Profile, select the profile you want Outlook to display as the initial selection in the list, and then select Prompt For A Profile To Be Used.
4. Click OK.

> **Tip** **Set the initial profile**
> You probably noticed in step 3 that you enabled an option and then immediately disabled it by selecting Prompt For A Profile To Be Used. In effect, you're accomplishing two tasks: setting the default profile and also configuring Outlook to prompt you for a profile. In the drop-down list, select the profile you use most often, which saves you the effort of selecting it when prompted at startup.

Configuring Online and Offline Data Storage

The previous section explained how to add e-mail account services and discussed data stores. This section provides a more detailed look at storage options in Outlook and how to configure those options.

Like earlier versions of Outlook, Outlook 2003 offers three options for storing data: your Exchange Server mailbox, PST files, and Offline Folder (OST) files. Outlook 2003 adds a new twist, however. Outlook 2003 can use Cached Exchange Mode in conjunction with an OST file to create a local copy of an Exchange Server mailbox. With Cached Exchange Mode, Outlook works from the cached local copy of the mailbox and automatically handles synchronization between the local cache and the server. Your mailbox is therefore always available, even when the server is not. When you connect to the network, Outlook automatically detects server connection status and synchronizes the Outlook folders.

See Chapter 34 to learn how to configure an Exchange Server client, including enabling and disabling Cached Exchange Mode.

Regardless of its location, a store holds your Outlook data, including your Contacts, Calendar, and other folders. You can have only one default store. This means your e-mail, contacts, schedule, tasks, and other information are all stored in the same set of folders. Outlook directs all incoming e-mail to your default store. The single exception to this is an IMAP account, which stores its e-mail folders and messages separately from your other data.

For detailed information on configuring and using IMAP accounts and how Outlook stores IMAP folders and messages, see "Using IMAP Accounts," page 155.

Although you can have only one default store, you can add other store files to a profile. You can use the other stores to organize or archive your data. For example, if you have a profile with an Exchange Server account and a POP3 account, the profile might be configured to deliver all mail to the Exchange Server mailbox. You might want to add another set of folders that you can use to separate your Internet mail from your workgroup mail, or perhaps you want to use a different store to separate your personal messages from your work-related messages. Another use for a second store file is to share data with others without exposing your default store. Whatever the situation, you need to decide which type of store is most appropriate for your default store as well as for your additional stores.

Personal Folders and Offline Folders

A PST file in Outlook 2003 is essentially the same as the default store type in Microsoft Outlook 97, Outlook 98, and Outlook 2000, although the native PST format of Outlook 2003 is not compatible with previous versions of Outlook. The native Outlook 2003 PST format provides better support for multilingual Unicode data and eliminates the 2-GB file size limit imposed by the previous PST format.

You can password-protect PST files for greater security, although utilities available on the Web can bypass the password security. PST files offer encryption, providing an additional level of security. PST files do not have a built-in capability for synchronization with an Exchange Server mailbox, although you can work offline if the PST rather than the Exchange Server mailbox is configured as the default store location. If the Exchange Server mailbox is your default store, however (which is recommended), you must use an OST file to work offline, whether in normal offline mode or Cached Exchange Mode.

Tip **Make your PST available when you're roaming**

If you use a roaming Windows profile to provide a common desktop configuration regardless of the computer from which you log on, consider placing the PST (if you use one) on a network share that is available from all your logon locations. This eliminates the need to copy your PST across the network each time you log on, reducing network utilization and speeding logon time. Microsoft doesn't recommend placing PSTs on a network share because of performance issues, but it has been my experience that this is a workable solution that offers enough advantages to overshadow any performance issues. Naturally, performance depends on the size of a user's mailbox and available network bandwidth.

As already mentioned, the format for PST files in this version of Outlook is different from the format in Outlook 97, Outlook 98, Outlook 2000, and Outlook 2002, which means those systems cannot share a PST file created with Outlook 2003. This is a significant consideration if you need to share a local data file with other Outlook users who have not yet upgraded to Outlook 2003. However, Outlook 2003 can use PSTs created with earlier versions of Outlook.

You can choose the format of a PST file only when you create the PST—you can't convert an existing PST to the new format. You can, however, simply export all of the items in an existing PST to a new PST that does use the new format. Open Outlook and choose File, Import and Export, then follow the wizard's prompts to export to a PST. The wizard creates an Outlook 2003 native format PST by default.

To decide which PST format you should use, consider whether you need to use the PST with an earlier version of Outlook. If not, the Outlook 2003 native format is the best choice. If you need to export items from an Outlook 2003 PST to an earlier version, simply export the items to a PST that you created with a previous version of Outlook.

Adding Other Data Stores

Outlook uses a particular store as your default store to contain your Outlook data and e-mail, but you can add other store files to help you organize, separate, or archive your data.

Adding another store is easy. Just follow these steps:

1. Right-click the Outlook icon on the desktop, choose Properties, and then click Data Files. (Select the profile first, if necessary.) Or, if Outlook is running, choose Tools, Data File Management. The current storage files are listed in the Outlook Data Files dialog box.
2. Click Add, select the type of Personal Folders file to create, and then click OK.

3 Outlook prompts for the name and location of the file. You can specify a new file or select an existing file to add it to your current profile. Click OK after you specify the file and path.

4 Outlook next displays the Create Microsoft Personal Folders dialog box, shown in Figure 2-8. Configure settings as necessary based on the following list:

- **Name** Specify the name by which you want the folders to be known in Outlook. This is not the file name for the store file, but you can use the same name for both if you want.
- **Encryption Setting** Specify the encryption level for the folder file. Choose No Encryption if you don't want Outlook to encrypt your PST file. Choose Compressible Encryption if you want Outlook to encrypt the file with a format that allows compression to conserve space. Outlook does not compress the file. Instead, you must use the compression capabilities offered by your operating system (such as NTFS compression) or by a third-party application. Choose High Encryption for highest security. PST files formatted using High Encryption can be compressed, but not as efficiently as those that use Compressible Encryption.
- **Password** Specify an optional password to protect your PST file from access by others.
- **Save This Password In Your Password List** Select this check box to have Outlook save the password for your PST file in your local password cache. This eliminates the need for you to enter the password each time you open the PST file. Clear this check box if you want Outlook to prompt you each time (providing greater security).

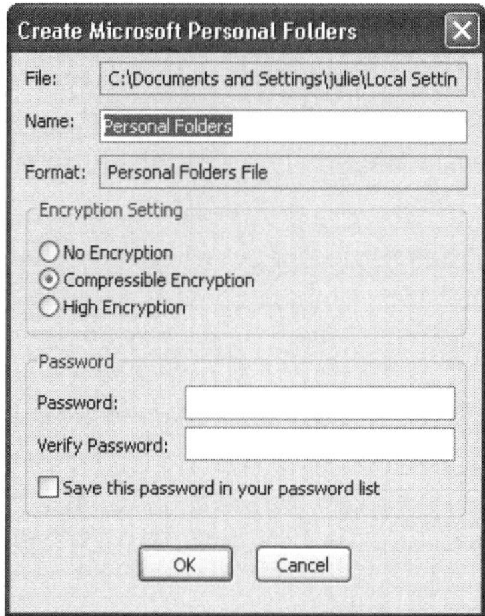

Figure 2-8. Use the Create Microsoft Personal Folders dialog box to add a PST file.

5 Click OK to close the Create Microsoft Personal Folders dialog box.

Note It's possible for others to gain access to your PST file and bypass the password, even if you use a compression option. For best security, keep your sensitive data on the Exchange Server rather than in a PST file. You can also employ NTFS permissions to secure the folder where your PST file is located, granting applicable permissions only to those users who need access to that folder or your PST file.

Inside Out

Add an existing PST to a profile

You can easily add an existing PST to a profile so you can work with its contents in Outlook, either permanently or temporarily. For example, you might want to open an archive PST to find an old message or two, then "disconnect" the PST when you have finished using it. Just open Outlook and choose File, Open, Outlook Data File, and choose the PST. When you have finished using it, right-click its root in the folder list and choose Close to remove the PST from the folder list.

Removing Data Stores

Occasionally, you might want to remove a data store from a profile—perhaps you've been using a PST file as your primary store and are now moving to Exchange Server with an OST file for offline use.

To remove a data store from a profile, you use steps similar to those you followed to add a store:

1. Right-click the Outlook icon on the Start menu, choose Properties, and then click Data Files. (Select the profile first if necessary.) Or, if Outlook is running, choose Tools, Data File Management. The current storage files are listed in the Outlook Data Files dialog box.
2. Select the data file to remove from the profile and click Remove, then click Yes to verify the action.
3. Click Close and then close the remaining dialog boxes.

When you remove a data file from a profile, Outlook does not delete the file itself. This means you can later add the file back to a profile if you need to access its contents. If you don't need the data stored in the file or if you've already copied the data to a different store, you can delete the file. Open the folder where the file is located and delete it as you would any other file.

Configuring Offline Storage

Configuring an offline store allows you to continue working with data stored in your Exchange Server mailbox when the server is not available (if your computer is disconnected from the network, for example). As soon as the server becomes available again, Outlook synchronizes the data either automatically or manually—according to the way in which you have configured Outlook.

For a detailed explanation of folder synchronization, see "Controlling Synchronization and Send/Receive Times," page 184.

As in earlier versions of Outlook, Outlook 2003 supports the use of an OST file to serve as an offline cache for Exchange Server. This method is compatible with all versions of Exchange Server, including Exchange Server 2000 and Exchange Server 2003.

Using an OST File

You can use an OST file to provide offline capability for your Exchange Server mailbox. You do not need to use a PST file in conjunction with the OST file—the OST file can be your only local store file, if you want. However, you can use other PST store files in addition to your OST file.

This section assumes you are working with an Exchange Server account that has not been configured to use Cached Exchange Mode. When you add an Exchange Server account in Outlook 2003, the wizard enables Cached Exchange Mode by default. This section helps you create and enable an offline store for a profile that has not had Cached Exchange Mode enabled previously.

Note The OST file does not appear as a separate set of folders in Outlook. In effect, the OST file is hidden and Outlook uses it transparently when your computer is offline. For more information, see "Working Offline and Remotely," page 917.

Follow these steps to configure offline storage with an OST file:

1. Right-click the Outlook icon on the Start menu, choose Properties, and then click E-Mail Accounts. If Outlook is running, choose Tools, E-Mail Accounts.
2. Select View Or Change Existing E-Mail Accounts and click Next, and then select the Exchange Server account and click Change.
3. Click More Settings to display the Microsoft Exchange Server dialog box. Click the Advanced tab, and then click Offline Folder File Settings to open the dialog box shown in Figure 2-9.

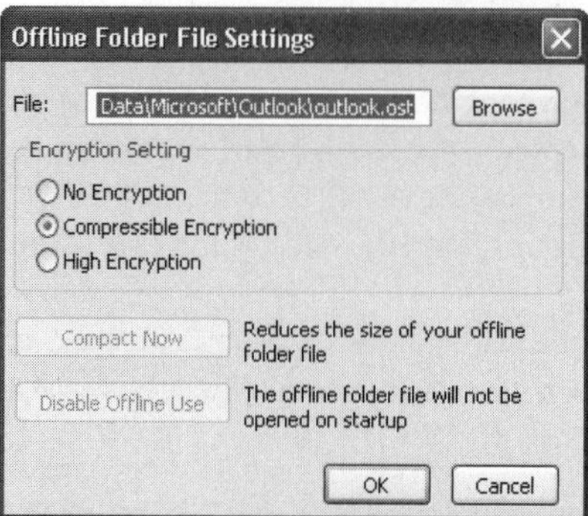

Figure 2-9. Specify the file name and other settings for the OST file.

4. Specify a path and name for the OST file in the File box, select the encryption setting, and click OK.
5. Click OK to close the Offline Folder File Settings dialog box.
6. Click Next and then click Finish.

Configuring Cached Exchange Mode

When you add an Exchange Server account to a profile in Outlook 2003, Outlook enables Cached Exchange Mode by default and creates the OST file that Cached Exchange Mode will use to store the local copy of the mailbox. If you originally added the Exchange Server account without Cached Exchange Mode, you can still enable it by following these steps:

1. Close Outlook and double-click the Mail icon in Control Panel.
2. Click Mail Accounts in the Mail Setup dialog box.
3. Choose View Or Change Existing E-Mail Accounts and click Next.
4. Select the Exchange Server account and click Change.
5. Select Use Cached Exchange Mode and click Next, then click Finish.

Outlook 2003 creates the OST file the next time you start Outlook and begins the synchronization process if the server is available.

Changing Your Data Storage Location

On occasion, you might need to move a data file from one location to another. For example, perhaps you've been using a local PST file and now want to place that file on a network share for use with a roaming profile, so that you can access the file from any computer on the network.

Moving a PST file is a manual process. You must shut down Outlook, move the file, and then reconfigure the profile accordingly.

Follow these steps to move a PST file:

1. Shut down Outlook, right-click the Outlook icon on the Start menu, and choose Properties.
2. Select a profile if necessary, and then click Data Files to display the Outlook Data Files dialog box (see Figure 2-10).

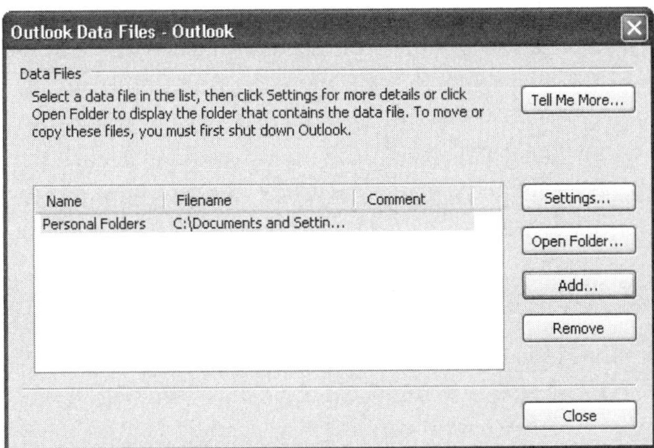

Figure 2-10. Use the Outlook Data Files dialog box to locate the existing PST.

3. Select the PST you want to move and click Open Folder. Outlook opens the folder where the PST is located and highlights the file's icon.
4. Drag the file or use the clipboard to move the file to the desired location; then close the folder.
5. Back in the Outlook Data Files dialog box, click Settings. Click OK at the error message.
6. Browse to the new location of the PST, select it, and click Open; then click OK.
7. Click Close to close the Outlook Data Files dialog box; then click Close again to close the Mail Setup dialog box.

Setting Delivery Options

Outlook uses one data store location as the default location for delivering messages and storing your other Outlook items. You can change the store location if needed. You also can specify the order in which Outlook processes e-mail accounts, which determines the server Outlook uses (where multiple servers are available) to process outgoing messages. The order also determines the order in which Outlook checks the servers for new messages.

For example, assume that you have an Exchange Server account and a POP3 account for your personal Internet mail. If the Exchange Server account is listed first, Outlook sends messages destined for Internet addresses through Exchange Server. In many cases, however, this might not be what you want. For example, you might want all personal mail to go through your POP3 account and work-related mail to go through your Exchange Server account.

You have two ways to change the e-mail service that Outlook uses to send a message: you can configure the service order or you can specify the account to use when you create the message.

Follow these steps to configure the service order for your e-mail:

1. Right-click the Outlook icon on the Start menu and choose Properties. Alternatively, with Outlook open, choose Tools, E-Mail Accounts to display the E-Mail Accounts Wizard.
2. If your system includes multiple profiles, select the one to which you want to add accounts. Click Show Profiles, locate and select your profile, and click Properties. Then select E-Mail Accounts.
3. Click View Or Change Existing E-Mail Accounts and then click Next.
4. Select accounts and use the Move Up and Move Down buttons to change the order of the accounts in the list (see Figure 2-11).

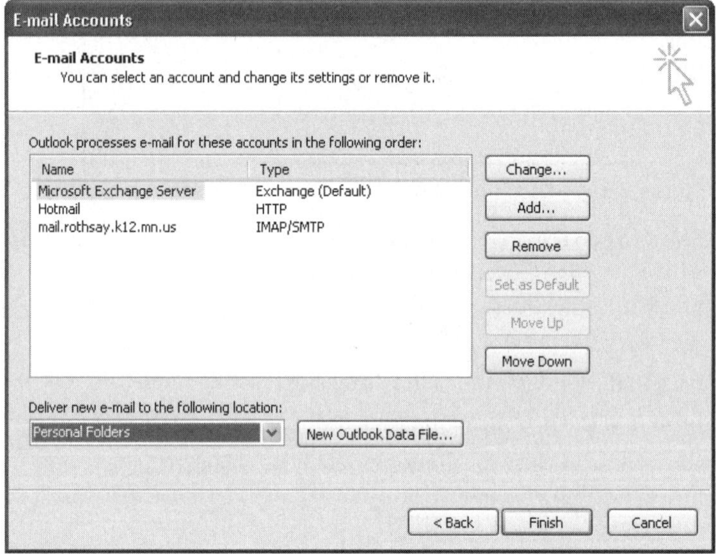

Figure 2-11. Use Move Up and Move Down to configure account order.

5. Click Finish.

When you compose a message, you can override the default e-mail service that Outlook uses to send messages simply by selecting the account before sending the message.

To select the account, follow these steps:

1. Compose the message. Before sending it, click the Accounts button on the toolbar.
2. Select the account you want to use to send the message, make any other changes to options as needed, and click Send.

Chapter 3

Working in and Configuring Outlook

If you've used earlier versions of Microsoft Outlook, you'll find that the interface in Microsoft Outlook 2003 hasn't changed that much, and you should have no problem getting started. There are, however, some new features and interface enhancements that you will probably like quite a bit. If you're new to Outlook entirely, you need to become familiar with its interface, which is the main focus of this chapter.

Outlook presents your data using different views, and this chapter shows you how to customize the way those views look. The chapter also examines other standard elements of the interface, including toolbars, the Navigation Pane, the folder list, and the Reading Pane. You'll also learn how to use multiple Outlook windows and views and navigate your way through the Outlook interface.

This chapter looks at the various ways you can configure Outlook, explaining settings that control a broad range of options, from e-mail and spelling to security. In addition, you'll learn about settings in your operating system that affect how Outlook functions. Where appropriate, the text refers you to other chapters where configuration information is discussed in detail in the context of a particular feature or function.

Web access has been expanded and improved in Outlook, and this chapter examines that Web integration. You'll learn about browsing the Web with Outlook, using the desktop conferencing options available in Outlook, and accessing your Microsoft Exchange Server e-mail through a Web browser. The chapter finishes with a discussion of add-ins, which can enhance Outlook's functionality.

Understanding the Outlook Folders

Outlook uses a standard set of folders to organize your data. Once you're comfortable working with these standard folders, you'll be able to change their location, customize their appearance, or even create additional folders, as you'll learn throughout this book.

The following list describes the default Outlook folders:

- **Calendar** This folder contains your schedule, including appointments, meetings, and events.
- **Contacts** This folder stores information about people, such as name, address, phone number, and a wealth of other data.
- **Deleted Items** This folder stores deleted Outlook items and can contain items of various types (contacts, messages, and tasks, for example). You can recover items from the Deleted Items folder, giving you a way to "undelete" an item if you've made a mistake or changed your mind. If you delete an item from this folder, however, the item is deleted permanently.
- **Drafts** Use this folder to store unfinished drafts of messages and other items. For example, you can use the Drafts folder to store a lengthy e-mail message you haven't had a chance to finish yet. Or, you might start a message, have second thoughts about sending it, and place it in the Drafts folder until you decide whether to send it.
- **Inbox** Outlook delivers your e-mail to this folder. Keep in mind that, depending on the types of e-mail accounts in your profile, you might have more than one Inbox in locations other than your default information store. For example, if you have an IMAP account and an Exchange Server account, you'll have an Inbox folder for each.
- **Journal** The Journal folder stores your journal items, allowing you to keep track of phone calls, time spent on a project, important e-mail messages, and other events and tasks.
- **Notes** The Notes folder stores and organizes notes. You can move or copy notes to other folders in Outlook as well as to folders on disk (such as your desktop). You can also create shortcuts to notes.
- **Outbox** The Outbox stores outgoing messages until they are delivered to their destination servers. You can configure Outlook to deliver messages immediately after you send them or have the messages wait in your Outbox until you process them (by synchronizing with the Exchange Server or performing a send/receive operation through your POP3 account, for example).
- **Sent Items** The Sent Items folder stores a copy of messages you have sent. You can configure Outlook to automatically store a copy of each sent item in this folder.
- **Tasks** The Tasks folder lists tasks that have been assigned to you or that you have assigned to either yourself or others.

Working with the Standard Outlook Views

Before you can become proficient at using Outlook, you need to be familiar with its standard views and other elements of its interface. This section introduces you to Outlook's standard views, including information on how to work with them and customize them to meet your needs.

Outlook Today

Outlook provides default views of its standard folders as well as one additional view that is a summary of your schedule, tasks, and e-mail for the current day—Outlook Today. To switch to the Outlook Today view if you are working in another folder, click the root folder of your mail store on the Navigation Pane (under Outlook Shortcuts). For example, click Personal Folders if your Outlook data is stored in a personal folders (PST) file, or click Mailbox if it is stored in an Exchange Server mailbox. Figure 3-1 shows a typical Outlook Today view. In the Calendar section on the left, Outlook summarizes your schedule for the current day, showing each appointment with time and title. You can easily view the details of a particular appointment by clicking the appointment time or title to open it.

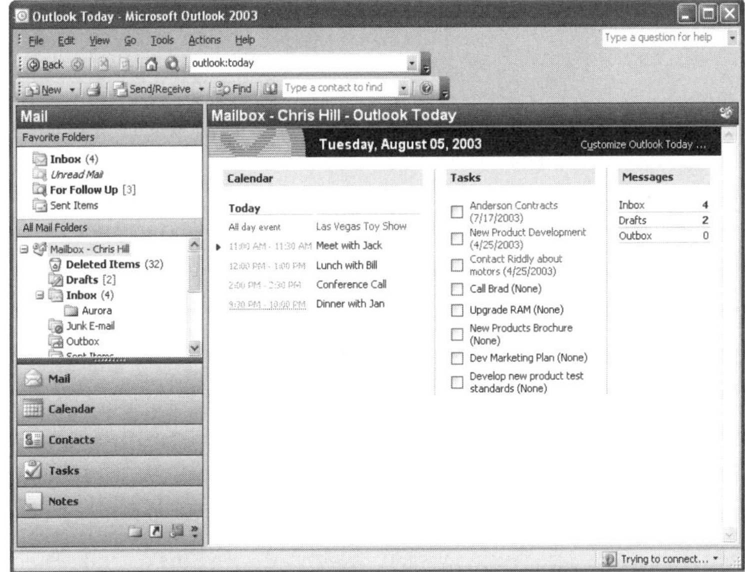

Figure 3-1. Outlook Today lets you see your day at a glance.

In the middle column, Outlook Today lists your tasks for the current day, including overlapping tasks with a duration of more than one day. The list includes a title and completion date for each task, along with a check box. You can mark the task as completed by selecting the check box; doing so crosses out the task in the list. If the check box is cleared, the task is incomplete.

The third column in Outlook Today lists the number of messages in your Inbox, Drafts, and Outbox folders. If the number appears in bold, the associated folder contains unread messages.

For details on customizing the Outlook Today view to display additional information (including the use of HTML code in such customization), see "Customizing the Outlook Interface," page 657.

Inbox

The Inbox displays your default message store (see Figure 3-2). For example, if you use an Exchange Server account and store your data on the Exchange Server, the Inbox view shows the Inbox folder on the Exchange Server. If you've configured Outlook to deliver messages to a local store (such as a PST file), the Inbox view shows the contents of the Inbox folder in that store.

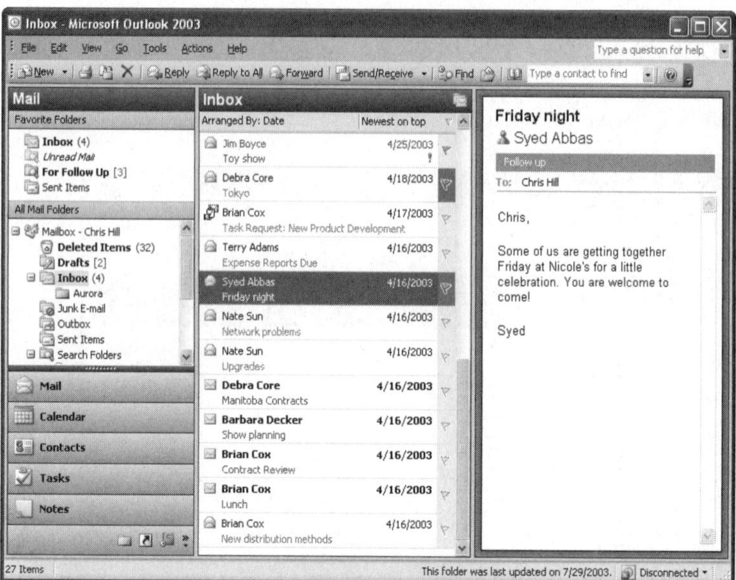

Figure 3-2. The Inbox view shows the contents of the Inbox folder of your default store.

As you can see in Figure 3-2, the Inbox view shows the message header for each message, including such information as sender, subject, and date and time received in various columns. These columns are not always visible, however, because the default configuration includes the Reading Pane at the right edge of the Outlook window, which hides many of the columns on a typical display. If you turn off the Reading Pane or move it to the bottom of the window, you can view the message header columns.

You can easily sort messages by clicking on the column header for the column you want to use as the sort criterion. For example, to quickly locate messages from a specific sender, you can click the From column header to sort the list alphabetically by sender. To switch between ascending and descending sort, simply click the column header again. An up arrow beside the column name indicates an ascending sort (such as A to Z), and a down arrow indicates a descending sort (such as Z to A).

To learn how to add and remove columns and change their appearance and order, see "Customizing the Inbox View," page 61.

By default, Outlook shows the following columns in the Inbox view:

- **Importance** This column indicates the level of importance, or priority, the sender has assigned to a message—Low, Normal, or High. A high-priority message is accompanied by an exclamation mark, whereas a down arrow marks a low-priority message. No icon is displayed for a message of normal importance.

> **Tip** After you've received a message, you can change its priority status by right-clicking the message, choosing Options, and specifying a new importance level.

- **Icon** The icon column indicates the type of message and its status. For example, unopened messages are accompanied by a closed envelope icon, and read messages are accompanied by an open envelope icon.
- **Flag Status** In this column, you can flag messages for follow-up action. For example, you can flag a message that requires you to place a call, to forward the message, or to respond at a particular time. You specify the action, date, and time for follow-up. Outlook displays a reminder for flagged items based on the flag settings you specify. To flag a message, right-click the message header and choose Follow Up. To mark the follow-up task as completed and change the flag icon, right-click the flagged message and choose Flag Complete. Choose Clear Flag to remove the follow-up.

> **For detailed information on flagging messages for follow-up and other ways to manage and process messages, see "Flagging and Monitoring Messages and Contacts," page 218.**

- **Attachment** The Attachment column displays a Paper Clip icon if the message includes one or more attachments. Right-click a message and choose View Attachments to view the attachments, or simply double-click an attachment in the Reading Pane.

> **Caution** Although Outlook provides protection against viruses and worms by preventing you from opening certain types of attachments, this is no guarantee against infection. Your network administrator might have modified the blocked attachments lists, or you might have modified your blocked attachments list locally, to allow a specific attachment type susceptible to infection to come through. So you should still exercise caution when viewing attachments, particularly from unknown sources. It's a good practice to save attachments to disk and run a virus scan on them before opening them.

- **From** This column shows the name or address of the sender.
- **Subject** This column shows the subject, if any, assigned by the sender to the message.
- **Received** This column indicates the date and time the message was received.
- **Size** This column indicates the overall size of the message, including attachments.

Inside Out

Time is Relative

The date and time displayed in the Inbox's Received column can be a little deceiving. This data reflects the time the message was placed in your message store. If you're working online with an Exchange Server account, for example, Outlook shows the time the message was placed in the Inbox folder for your mailbox on the Exchange Server. If the time on your computer isn't coordinated with the time on the server, the time you actually receive the message could be different from the time reflected in the message header. For sent messages (in the Sent Items folder), the time indicated is the time the message was placed in your Outbox. If you're working offline, that time could differ from the time the message is actually sent.

Previewing Messages

Another part of the Inbox view is the Reading Pane, which appears at the right of the view. You can use the Reading Pane to preview messages without opening them in a separate window. The scroll bar on the right of the Reading Pane lets you scroll through the message. The top of the Reading Pane presents information about the message, such as sender, recipient, subject, and attachments.

Tip Right-click any blank area of the Reading Pane and choose Header Information to turn on or off the Reading Pane header. You must click outside the white area where the message is displayed.

You can double-click most of the items in the Reading Pane header to see detailed information about the item. For example, you can double-click the name in the From field to display information about the sender (see Figure 3-3). Use this method to quickly copy contact information about the sender from the message to your Personal Address Book. You can also double-click attachments to open them. Right-clicking an item opens its shortcut menu, from which you can choose a variety of actions to perform on the item—for instance, you can right-click an attachment and choose Save As to save the attachment to disk. Experiment by right-clicking items in the Reading Pane to see which actions you can take for specific items.

Tip If a message has been flagged for follow-up, information about the follow-up (the specific action, the date due, and so on) also appears in the Reading Pane header.

Note To turn the Reading Pane on or off, choose View, Reading Pane, and choose On or Off.

For detailed information on using and customizing the Reading Pane in various folders, see "Using the Reading Pane," page 84.

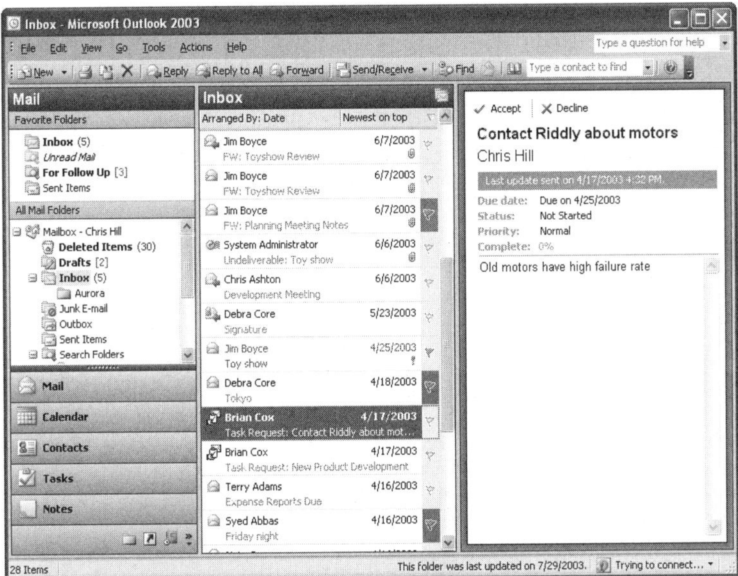

Figure 3-3. Double-click an item in the Reading Pane header to view detailed information about the item.

The AutoPreview feature also allows you to preview your messages. With message folders such as the Inbox, AutoPreview displays the first few lines of a message below its message header in the main folder window. This leaves you free to preview the first few lines of a message without opening the message or even selecting it. You can use AutoPreview in conjunction with or instead of the Reading Pane.

For additional information on configuring and using AutoPreview, see "Using AutoPreview," page 85.

Customizing the Inbox View

Outlook offers a wealth of settings that you can use to control messaging. In addition, you also have quite a bit of control over the appearance of the Inbox and other message folders. For example, you can change the column headings included in the Inbox or add and remove columns. The following sections explore specific ways to customize the Inbox (which apply to other message folders as well).

For detailed information on configuring messaging and other options, see "Configuring Outlook Options," page 86.

Adding and Removing Columns By default, Outlook displays only a small subset of the available fields for messages. You can add columns for other fields, such as CC or Sensitivity, to show additional information. However, the Inbox behaves differently depending on the location of the Reading Pane. When the Reading Pane is configured for the right side of the window, the Inbox only includes two columns in most cases. The first is the Subject, which specifies the message subject. The second is the Received date.

Outlook also provides two column headers above these columns that you can use to change views or change sort order. For example, the default view is Arranged By: Date. You can click this header to choose a different property by which to group the view.

The other column reads either Newest On Top or Oldest On Top, depending on whether the folder is sorted in ascending or descending order. You can click this column to switch between the two.

The number of columns depends on the amount of space available in the window. The more space available, the more columns Outlook displays. For example, continue to drag the left edge of the Reading Pane to the right, and Outlook eventually shows additional columns other than the Arranged By and sort order columns. You have to experiment with the size of the Reading Pane to find a layout that suits you, because the amount of available space depends on your system's display resolution.

To add and remove columns, follow these steps:

1 Open the folder you want to modify, turn off the Reading Pane or move it to the bottom, right-click the column header bar, and choose Field Chooser to display the Field Chooser dialog box, shown in Figure 3-4.

Figure 3-4. Add or remove columns by using the Field Chooser dialog box.

Note The Field Chooser command is not available if the Reading Pane is configured for the right side of the window and the window is only showing the Arrange By and sort order columns. Field Chooser is available only if the Reading Pane is turned off or located at the bottom of the window, or resized to make additional room for message header columns.

2 Locate the name of the field you want to add, and then drag the field to the desired location on the column header bar. Outlook displays arrows on the top and bottom of the column header bar to indicate where the column will be inserted.

3 Add other fields if necessary.

4 To remove a field, drag the field from the column header bar to the Field Chooser dialog box.

5 Close the Field Chooser dialog box.

You can choose other types of fields by selecting a type from the drop-down list at the top of the Field Chooser dialog box. You can also use this dialog box to create custom fields.

Outlook also provides another method for adding and removing columns in message folders:

1 Choose View, Arrange By, Current View, Customize Current View, and then click Fields to display the Show Fields dialog box (see Figure 3-5).

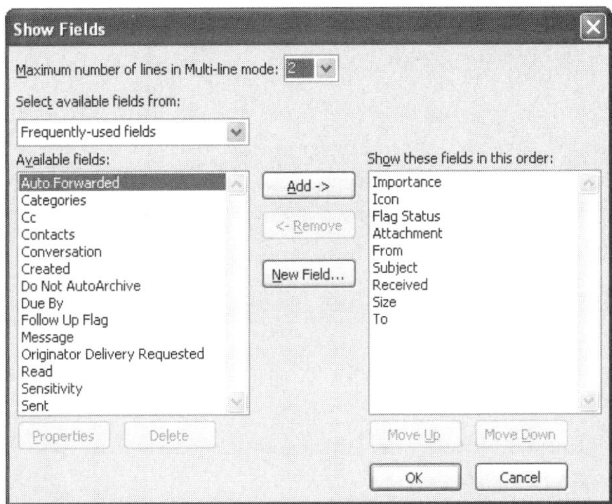

Figure 3-5. You can also use the Show Fields dialog box to add or remove columns.

2 To add a column, select the field from the Available Fields list and click Add.

3 To remove a column from the folder view, select the field from the Show These Fields In This Order list and click Remove.

4 Click OK to have your changes take effect.

Changing Column Order In a message folder, Outlook defaults to displaying columns in a specific order, but you can easily change the order. The simplest way is to drag a column header to the desired location. You also can right-click the column header bar, choose Customize Current View, click Fields to display the Show Fields dialog box (shown in Figure 3-5), and use the Move Up and Move Down buttons to change the column order.

Changing Column Names Outlook uses a default set of names for the columns it displays in message folders. However, you can change those column names—for example, you might want to rename the From column to Sender.

To change a column name, follow these steps:

1. Right-click the column header bar and choose Format Columns to display the Format Columns dialog box, shown in Figure 3-6. If the Format Columns command is not available because of the Reading Pane's location and width, choose View, Arrange By, Custom, and then click Format Columns.

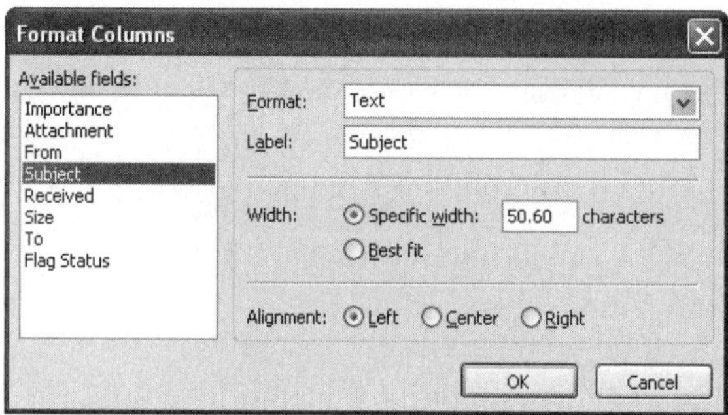

Figure 3-6. You can change several column characteristics, including column header name.

2. From the Available Fields list, select the field for which you want to change the column header.
3. In the Label box, type the label you want displayed in the column header for the selected field.
4. Repeat steps 2 and 3 for other fields you want to change.
5. Click OK to apply the changes.

Note You can't change the name of the Importance, Flag Status, or Attachment columns. However, you can switch between using a symbol or text in the Importance and Flag Status columns. You can change the Attachment column to display either the Paper Clip icon or the text True/False, On/Off, or Yes/No, depending on whether the message has an attachment.

Changing Column Width If a column isn't wide enough to show all the information for the field or if you need to make room for more columns, you might want to change the column width. The easiest way to change the width of a column is to drag the edge of the column header in the column header bar to resize it. Alternatively, you can right-click the column header bar, choose Format Columns, and specify a column width in the Format Columns dialog box (see Figure 3-6).

Tip **Automatically size columns**
Use the Best Fit option in the Format Columns dialog box to automatically size the selected column, based on the amount of data it needs to display. Outlook examines the data for the field in the existing messages and resizes the column accordingly.

Changing Column Alignment By default, all the columns are left-aligned in message folders, including the Inbox. You can, however, justify the columns to display to the left, right, or center. For example, you might want to change the format for the Size column to show only numbers and then display it right-justified. Simply right-click the column header bar and choose Format Columns, or choose View, Arrange By, Custom, and then click Format Columns. In the Format Columns dialog box (shown earlier in Figure 3-6), select the column to change and select Left, Center, or Right, depending on the type of justification you want.

Changing Column Data Format Each default column in a message folder displays its data using a particular format. For example, the From column shows only the sender, not the recipient. Although in most cases the specified recipient is you, that isn't the case when the message you've received is a carbon copy. You might, then, want to change the data format of the From column to also display the person specified in the To field of the message. Other columns also offer different formats. For example, you can change the data format used by time and date fields such as Received or Sent to show only the date rather than date and time.

To change the data format used for a particular column, right-click the column header bar and choose Format Columns, or choose View, Arrange By, Custom, and then click Format Columns. In the Format Columns dialog box (shown in Figure 3-6), select the column for which you want to change the format and then select the format from the Format drop-down list. The available formats vary according to the field selected.

Grouping Messages Outlook offers many ways to organize and display your data. A good example of this flexibility is the option of grouping messages based on a hierarchy of criteria. For example, you might want to group messages in your Inbox first by subject, and then by sender, and then by date received, as shown in Figure 3-7.

Figure 3-7. These messages are organized by three fields.

Chapter 3

To organize your messages based on a particular column, you can simply right-click the column and choose Group By This Field. If the folder is showing the Arranged By column, click this column and choose the field by which you want to group the messages.

For more complex groupings, follow these steps:

1. Right-click the column header bar and choose Group By Box to display the Group By box above the column header bar.
2. To set up a grouping, drag a column header from the column header bar to the Group By box.
3. To set up an additional level of grouping, drag another column header to the Group By box. Repeat this process until you have as many levels of grouping as you need.

To hide or show the Group By box, right-click the column header bar and choose Group By Box again. To expand or collapse your view of a group of messages, click the plus sign (+) or minus sign (–) icons next to the group or message.

For a detailed explanation of grouping and sorting, along with several other topics that will help you organize your data, see "Grouping Messages by Customizing the Folder View" page 223.

Calendar

In the Calendar folder, you can look at your schedule in several different ways. By default, the Calendar view shows the current day's schedule as well as the Date Navigator (a monthly calendar) in the upper-left corner of the Navigation Pane. You can also turn on the TaskPad, which displays tasks that overlap or fall on the current day (see Figure 3-8). You can configure the TaskPad to show other tasks, as well.

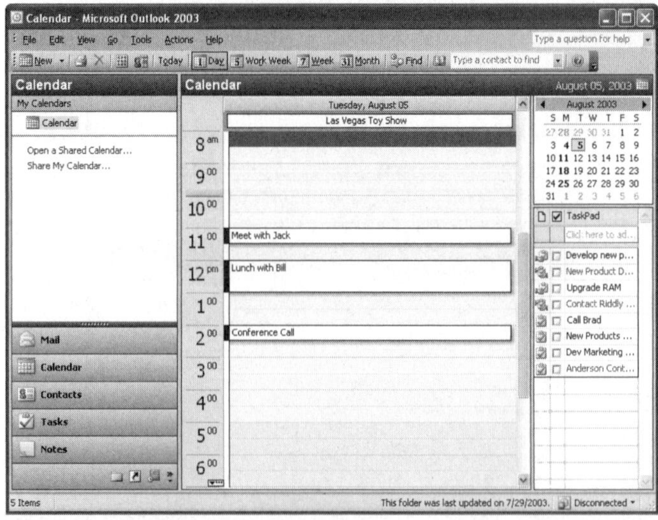

Figure 3-8. The default Calendar view shows your schedule and Date Navigator, but you can also view tasks as shown here.

Your schedule shows the subject for each scheduled item—a brief description of a meeting or an appointment, for example—beside its time slot, blocking out the time assigned to the item. Items that overlap in the schedule are displayed side by side, as shown in Figure 3-9.

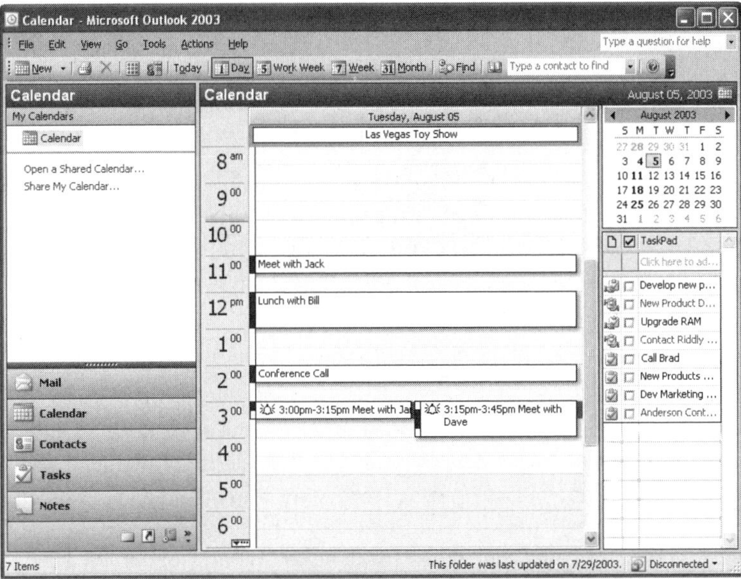

Figure 3-9. Overlapping items appear side by side in your schedule.

Working with the Schedule

The calendar view by default shows only the subject for each item scheduled in the period displayed. You can open the item to modify it or view details about it by double-clicking the item, which opens its form, shown in Figure 3-10.

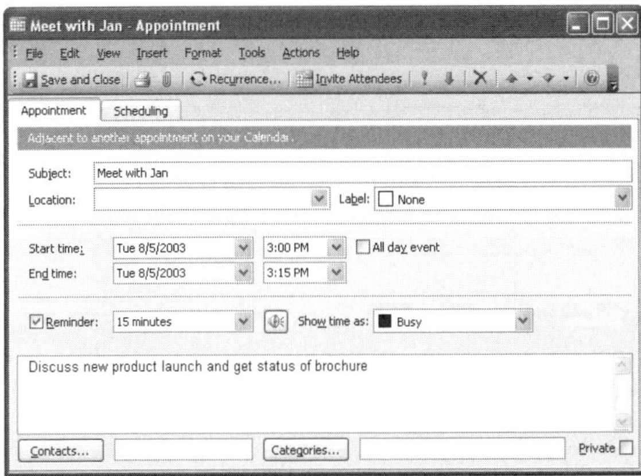

Figure 3-10. A sample appointment form showing details for a selected appointment.

You can add an item to your schedule using one of these methods:

- Double-click the time slot of the start time you want to assign to the item.
- Right-click a time slot and choose the type of item to create (an appointment, a meeting, or an event).
- Select a time slot and then choose File, New to select the item type.
- Click the down arrow beside New on the Standard toolbar and select the item type.

The first method opens an appointment form. The form opened by the other three methods depends on the type of item you select.

It is also easy to change the start or end time for an item in the schedule. To move an item to a different time without changing its duration, simply drag the item to the new time slot. To change start or end time only, place the pointer over the top or bottom edge of the item and drag it to the desired time.

Using the Calendar's Reading Pane

Like the Inbox and other message views, the Calendar view has a Reading Pane that lets you preview appointments and other items in your schedule without opening them. Just click the item to have it appear in the Reading Pane (see Figure 3-11). To turn the Reading Pane on or off, choose View, Reading Pane, then choose either On or Off. You can also locate the Reading Pane at the bottom or right side of the window. To display more or less information in the pane, drag the edge of the Reading Pane to resize it. You can also make other changes to the displayed item—such as subject and times—through the Reading Pane.

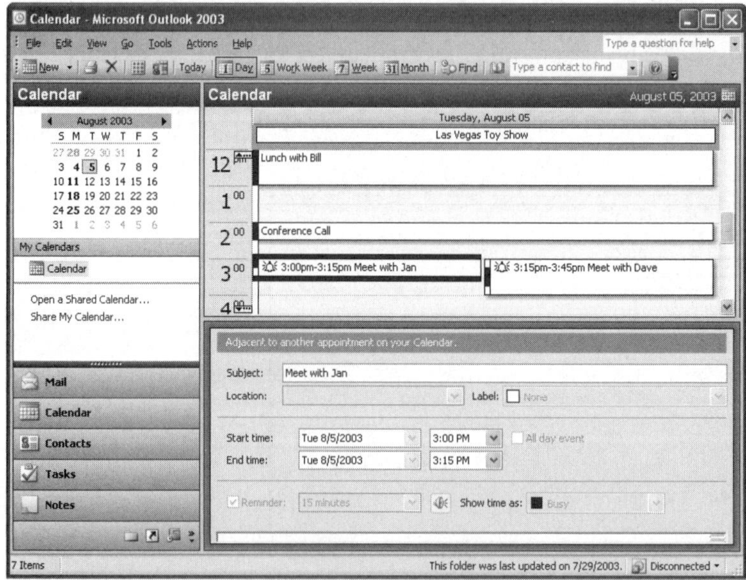

Figure 3-11. Use the Reading Pane in the Calendar view to preview scheduled items.

Using the TaskPad

The TaskPad displays a list of your tasks. You can turn the TaskPad on or off for any Calendar view. By default, the TaskPad shows the tasks for the current day. However, you can change the types of tasks displayed by choosing View, TaskPad View and then selecting the types of tasks you want Outlook to show, such as overdue tasks, tasks for the following week, or all tasks. You can mark a task as completed by selecting the check box beside the task name. As you can in the Inbox and other views, you can change the format of the columns displayed in the TaskPad: right-click the TaskPad column header bar and choose Format Columns.

For more information about the TaskPad and the features Outlook provides for working with and assigning tasks, see Chapter 21, "Managing Your Tasks."

Using the Date Navigator

The monthly calendars in the upper right area of the TaskPad are collectively called the Date Navigator. When the TaskPad is hidden, the Date Navigator appears at the top of the Navigation Pane.

The Date Navigator is useful not only as a calendar but also as a way to provide a fast glance at how heavily scheduled your time is. Days with a scheduled item appear in bold, and those without scheduled items appear in a normal font. You can view a particular day by clicking it. Click the arrow at the left or right of the Date Navigator to change which months are displayed. You can also click and hold on the column header bar above either month to choose from a shortcut menu which month to view.

Tip **Specify the Date Navigator's font**

You can configure the Date Navigator to display all dates in normal text rather than using bold for days that contain items. Choose View, Arrange By, Current View, Customize Current View and then click Other Settings. Clear the Bolded Dates In Date Navigator Represent Days Containing Items check box and then click OK.

You can change the number of months displayed by the Date Navigator by resizing the display, resizing the Calendar folder's window, or changing the font used by the Date Navigator. Assign a smaller font to show more months. (For details on how to change the Date Navigator's font, see "Setting Advanced Options," page 95.)

Customizing the Calendar View

Although the default Calendar view shows only the subject for a scheduled item, you can configure the view to show additional detail—or you can change the view completely. For example, you can switch from a daily view to one that shows the work week, the calendar week, or the month. You can see an example of Work Week view in Figure 3-12, Week view in Figure 3-13, and Month view in Figure 3-14. To select a particular view, choose View and then choose Day, Work Week, Week, or Month, according to the type of view you want.

Tip Click the Day, Work Week, Week, or Month button on the toolbar to quickly choose a Calendar view.

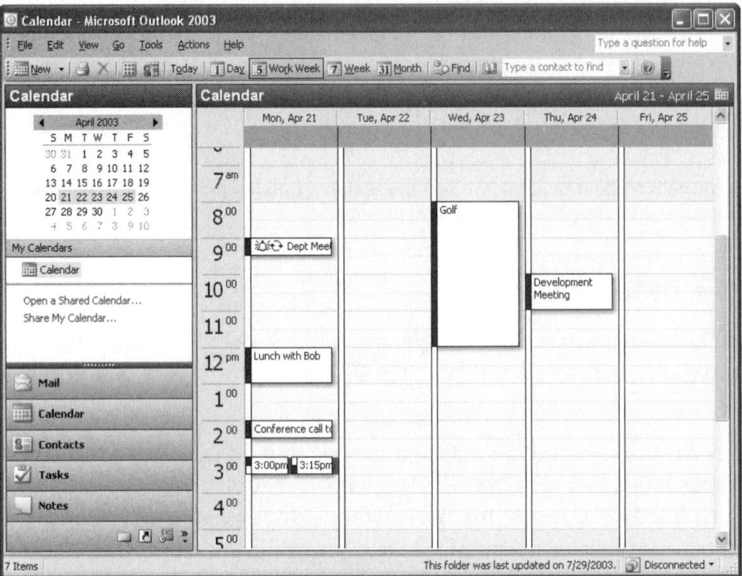

Figure 3-12. Use Work Week view to organize your work schedule.

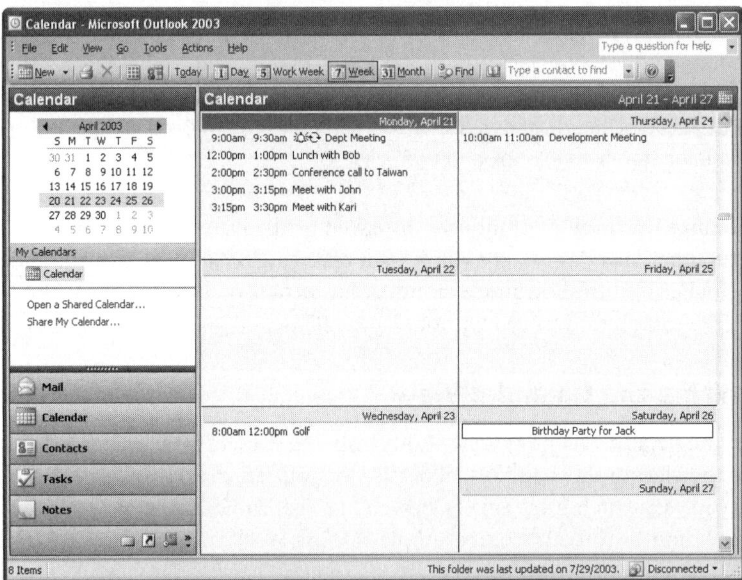

Figure 3-13. Week view can help you plan your entire week, both personal and work time.

Figure 3-14. Use Month view to plan a broader range of time.

You have additional options for viewing your schedule in the Calendar folder. Choose View, Arrange By, Current View and then one of the following to change the view:

- **Day/Week/Month** Shows the item title only in each view (Day, Work Week, Week, or Month).
- **Day/Week/Month With AutoPreview** Includes AutoPreview in Day and Work Week views. With AutoPreview, Outlook displays as much of the data for the item as possible in the current view.
- **Active Appointments** Shows only active appointments.
- **Events** Shows only events.
- **Annual Events** Shows only annual events.
- **Recurring Appointments** Displays recurring appointments.
- **By Category** Displays scheduled items grouped according to their assigned categories.

> **Note** For additional information on customizing the way Outlook displays information in the various calendar views, see Chapter 19, "Scheduling Appointments."

Contacts

The Contacts folder stores all your contact information. By default, the Contacts folder displays the Address Cards view (see Figure 3-15), which shows the name for each contact along with other selected fields (address and phone number, for example). You can view the details for a contact by double-clicking the contact's address card, which opens the contact form, shown in Figure 3-16. Using this form, you can view or make changes to the contact's data or perform other tasks, such as calling the contact, generating a meeting request, or viewing a map of the contact's address. If you have a large number of contact entries stored in the Contacts folder, you can click the buttons at the right edge of the view to select which portion of the contacts list to show.

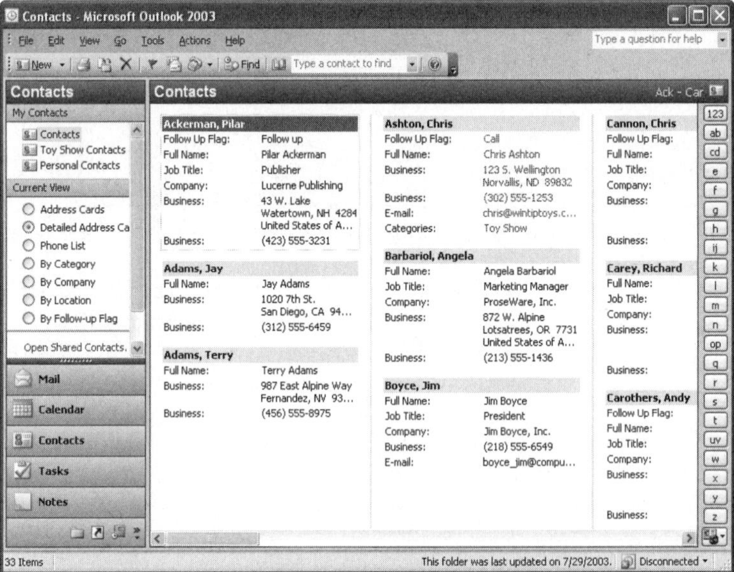

Figure 3-15. By default, the Contacts folder displays Address Cards view.

For a detailed discussion of working with contacts, including the actions you can take with the contact form, see Chapter 14, "Managing Your Contacts."

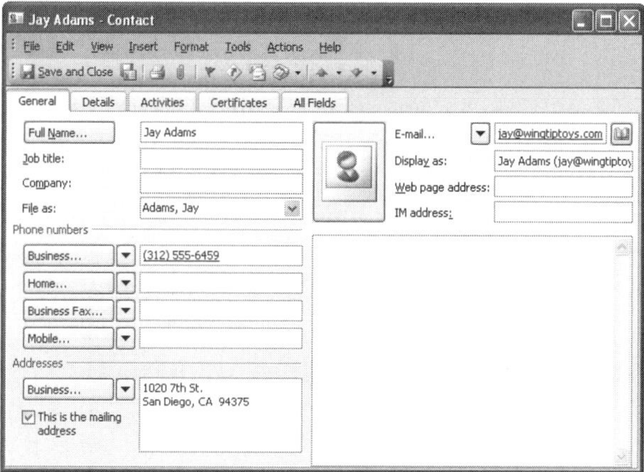

Figure 3-16. When you double-click a contact entry, you can view the contact form for that person.

Outlook offers several other ways to view the contents of your Contacts folder. Choose View, Arrange By, Current View and then one of the following commands to change the view:

- **Address Cards** Displays the name of each contact along with other selected data.
- **Detailed Address Cards** Shows additional detailed information for each contact, including the person's title, the company the person works for, personal notes, and more.
- **Phone List** Displays the contacts as a phone list.
- **By Category** Groups contacts by their assigned categories.
- **By Company** Groups contacts by the company with which they're affiliated.
- **By Location** Groups contacts by country or region.
- **By Follow-Up Flag** Groups contacts by the status of follow-up flags on their entries.

Adding contact entries to your Contacts folder is easy: Just right-click in the Contacts view and choose New Contact, or click New on the toolbar. Either action opens the contact form, in which you enter the contact's data.

Customizing the Contacts View

Like other views in other folders, the view in the Contacts folder can be customized to suit your needs and preferences. For example, you can adjust the view to display additional fields of information or to remove fields you don't need. You can sort the view based on specific contact criteria or group like items together based on multiple criteria. For details about customizing the Contacts folder view, see Chapter 14, "Managing Your Contacts."

Tasks

The Tasks folder contains your task list. The default Tasks view (see Figure 3-17) lists each task in a simple list with subject, due date, and status. Double-click an existing task to open the task form, which displays detailed information about the task, including due date, start date, status, notes, and so on (see Figure 3-18). To add a new task to the list, double-click a blank list entry to open a new task form, where you can enter all the details about the task.

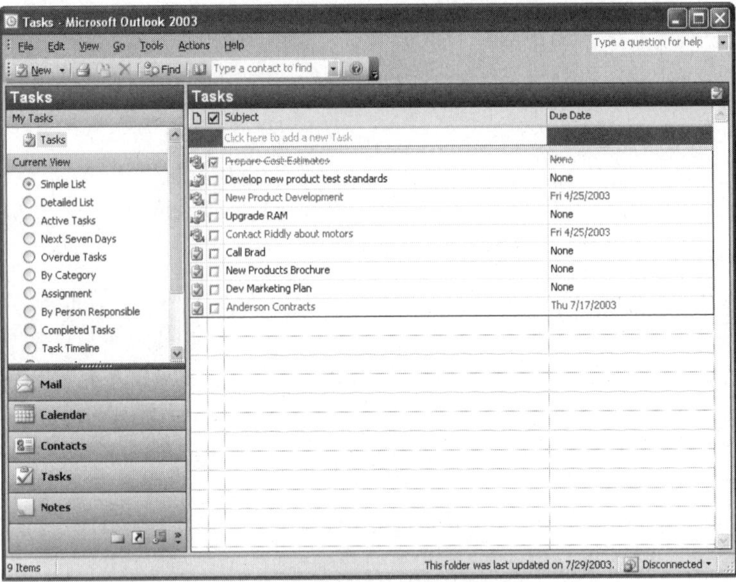

Figure 3-17. By default, the Tasks folder displays this view.

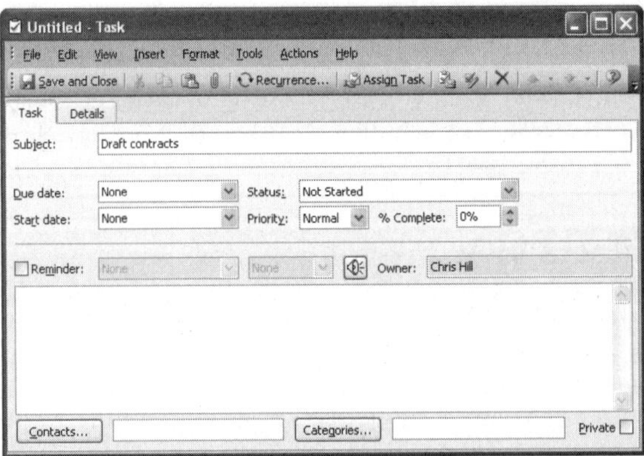

Figure 3-18. Use a task form to create a new task.

The task list shows tasks you've assigned to others as well as those tasks assigned to you (by yourself or by others). These assignments can be one-time or recurring, and the list shows both in-progress and completed tasks.

Chapter 3

Like other Outlook views, the Tasks view provides a Reading Pane you can use to view details for a task without opening the task item. To turn on the Reading Pane, choose View, Reading Pane, then the location (either Right or Bottom). AutoPreview is also available in the Tasks folder; it displays notes about the task below the task name (see Figure 3-19).

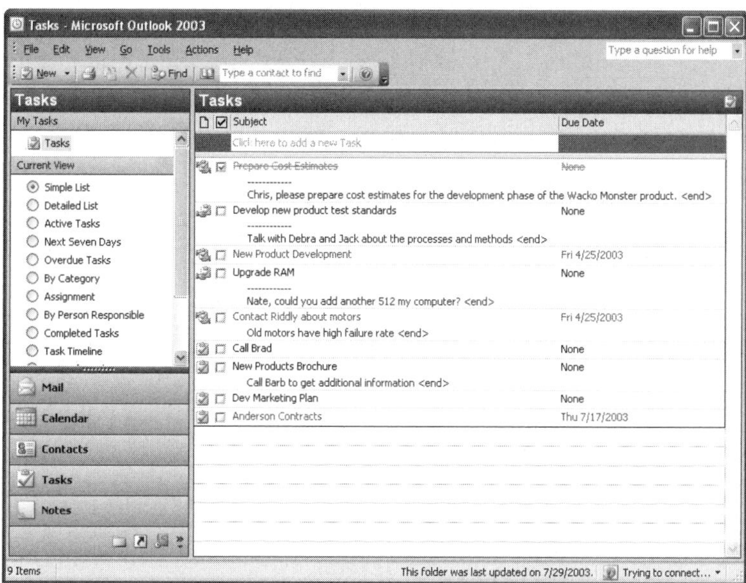

Figure 3-19. AutoPreview displays additional information about a task below the task name in the list.

Customizing the Tasks View

You can customize the view in the Tasks folder in a variety of ways—adding and removing columns, changing column names, or organizing tasks by category or other properties, to list a few. To customize the columns, right-click the column header bar and choose Format Columns. The resulting dialog box allows you to select the format for each column, change the name, apply justification, and so on. To change the order of columns in the view, simply drag the column headers into the desired positions, resizing as needed.

You can also organize your task list in various ways. You can click column headers to sort the columns in ascending or descending order, and you can group the columns based on a particular field or group of fields, just as you can in the Inbox and other Outlook folders.

You can also choose View, Arrange By, Current View and then one of the following commands to change the Tasks Folder view:

- **Simple List** Shows whether the task has been completed, the task name, and the due date.
- **Detailed List** Shows status, percent complete, and categories in addition to the information displayed in Simple List view.

- **Active Tasks** Displays tasks that are active.
- **Next Seven Days** Displays tasks for the next seven days.
- **Overdue Tasks** Displays incomplete tasks with due dates that have passed.
- **By Category** Organizes the task list by the categories assigned to tasks.
- **Assignment** Shows the tasks assigned to specific people.
- **By Person Responsible** Groups the view according to the person responsible for the various tasks.
- **Completed Tasks** Shows only completed tasks.
- **Task Timeline** Displays a timeline of all tasks.

> **Note** For more information on customizing the view in the Tasks folder, see "Viewing and Customizing the Tasks Folder," page 597.

Notes

With its Notes feature, Outlook helps you organize your thoughts and tasks. Each note can function as a stand-alone window, allowing you to view notes on your desktop outside Outlook. The Notes view provides a look into your Notes folder, where your notes are initially stored. From there, you can copy or move them to other locations (such as the desktop) or create shortcuts to them. By default, the initial Notes view displays the notes as icons, with the first line of the note serving as the title under the note's icon (see Figure 3-20).

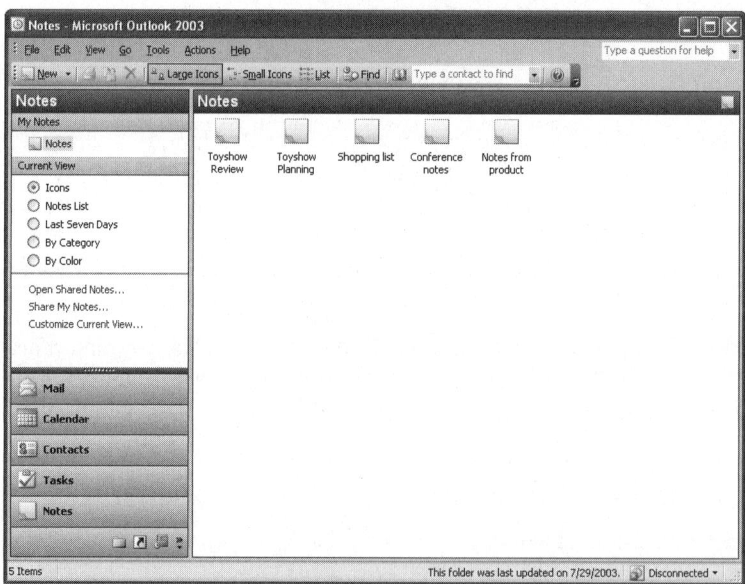

Figure 3-20. The standard Notes view displays notes as icons.

As it does for other folders, Outlook offers several other ways to view the Notes folder. Choose View, Arrange By, Current View, and then one of the following:

- **Icons** Displays an icon for each note, with the first line of the note serving as the icon's description (the default view).
- **Notes List** Displays the notes as a line-by-line list.
- **Last Seven Days** Resembles Notes List view, but restricts the display to only the past seven days, based on the current date.
- **By Category** Groups the notes by their assigned categories.
- **By Color** Groups the notes by their assigned color.

Tip You can assign different colors to notes to serve as visual cues for the note's purpose, importance, or content.

You can use a Reading Pane in the Notes folder, displaying the text of a note when you click it in the list. You can also use AutoPreview in Notes List and Last Seven Days views to automatically display the contents of each note.

You can customize the views in the Notes folder the same way you can in other folders. You can, for example, drag columns to rearrange them, resize them, change column name and other properties, add other fields, and group notes based on various criteria.

For a detailed explanation of how to work with the Notes folder, see Chapter 17, "Making Notes."

Deleted Items

The Deleted Items folder contains Outlook items that you've deleted, and it can include all the Outlook item types (such as messages, contacts, and appointments). The Deleted Items folder offers a way for you to recover items you've deleted, because the items remain in the folder until you manually delete them from that location or allow Outlook to clean out the folder. When you delete an item from the Deleted Items folder, that item is deleted permanently.

You can configure Outlook to automatically delete all items from the Deleted Items folder when you exit Outlook. To do so, choose Tools, Options and then click Other. Select the Empty The Deleted Items Folder Upon Exiting check box and click OK.

Choosing the Startup View

You might want to change the default Outlook view based on your type of work and the Outlook folders you use most. Or, you might want to use a particular view as the initial view because it presents the information you need right away each morning to start your work day.

You can designate any of the Outlook folders as your startup view. To do so, follow these steps:

1. In Outlook, choose Tools, Options.
2. Click the Other tab and then click Advanced Options.
3. Beside the Startup In This Folder text box, click Browse and select the folder you want to see by default when Outlook starts. Click the Mailbox or Personal Folders branch to choose Outlook Today as the default view.
4. Click OK, and then click OK again to close the Options dialog box.

Using Other Outlook Features

In addition to the various folders and views described in this chapter, Outlook incorporates several other standard components in its interface. The following sections explain these features and how to use them effectively.

> **Note** This book assumes that you're familiar with your operating system and comfortable using menus. Therefore, neither the Outlook menu bar nor its individual menus are discussed in this chapter. Specific menus and commands are covered where applicable.

Outlook uses personalized menus, displaying only those menu items you've used most recently. You can click the double arrow at the bottom of a menu to see all of its commands. Although personalized menus unclutter the interface, they can be annoying if you prefer to see all available commands or are searching for a specific command that isn't displayed. To display all menu commands on a specific menu, right-click the menu or a toolbar and choose Customize. On the Options tab, select Always Show Full Menus.

Using the Navigation Pane

The Navigation Pane, called the Outlook Bar in previous versions of Outlook, appears at the left edge of the Outlook window and contains shortcuts to the standard Outlook folders as well as shortcuts to folders you've created and other important data folders (see Figure 3-21). For example, the Shortcuts group includes shortcuts to the Outlook Today view and Outlook Update Web site. Just click an icon in the Navigation Pane to open that folder or item. The Navigation Pane therefore gives you quick access not only to Outlook folders but also to all your data.

Figure 3-21. The Navigation Pane provides quick access to all Outlook data and other frequently used resources and folders.

For a detailed discussion of the Navigation Pane, including how to create your own groups and shortcuts, see "Customizing the Navigation Pane," page 657.

For information about obtaining updates and finding troubleshooting resources for both Outlook and Microsoft Office, see Article 5, "Update and Troubleshooting Resources" on the companion CD.

Note You can create new shortcuts in any of the existing Shortcuts groups in the Navigation Pane, and you can also create your own groups.

Depending on your monitor's resolution and the number of shortcuts in each group, you might not be able to see all the icons in a group. If that's the case, you can use the scroll bar on the right edge of the Navigation Pane to scroll through the icons in the selected group.

Using Objects on the Navigation Pane

Most of the time, you'll probably just click an icon in the Navigation Pane to open its associated folder. However, you can also right-click an icon and use the resulting shortcut menu to perform various tasks with the selected object. For example, you might right-click the Calendar icon and choose Open In New Window to open a second window showing the calendar's contents. To view a different group, simply click the group's button in the Navigation Pane. The contents of the upper portion of the Navigation Pane change according to the folder you select. For example, the Navigation Pane shows the folder list if you click the Mail icon.

Controlling the Navigation Pane's Appearance

Outlook shows a selection of icons for standard folders in the Navigation Pane. If you don't use certain folders very often, however, you might prefer to remove them from the Navigation Pane to make room for other icons. For example, if you never use the Journal or Notes folders, you can remove those icons from the Navigation Pane and use the folder list to access those folders when needed.

To change the icons displayed in the Navigation Pane, click Configure Buttons at the bottom right of the Navigation Pane and then choose Add Or Remove Buttons to open the shortcut menu shown in Figure 3-22. Click a folder in the list to either add or remove it from the Navigation Pane. Those that are highlighted in the list appear in the pane.

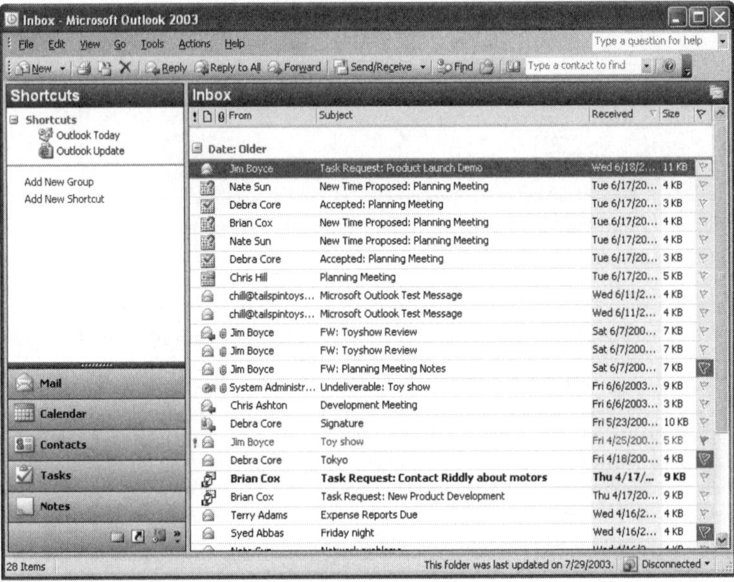

Figure 3-22. You can add or remove standard icons from the Navigation Pane.

If you need to add or remove more than one folder, click Configure Buttons and then choose Navigation Pane Options to open the Navigation Pane Options dialog box. Select each folder you want included in the Navigation Pane and then click OK.

> **Tip** Use the Move Up and Move Down buttons in the Navigation Pane Options dialog box to control the order of buttons in the Navigation Pane.

If you seldom use the Navigation Pane, you can turn it off to make room on the screen for the folder list or other data. Simply choose View, Navigation Pane to turn the display off or on.

Using the Standard Outlook Toolbars

Outlook provides a Standard toolbar for the current folder that offers quick access to the tasks and functions you perform most frequently in that folder. Thus, the contents of the Standard toolbar change depending on the folder you have open. Certain items that appear on the toolbar for all folders work in specific ways in the context of the selected folder. For example, when you're working in the Inbox folder, clicking the New toolbar button starts a new e-mail message. With the Contacts folder open, clicking New opens a new contact form. You don't have to accept the default contextual action for these types of toolbar buttons; however, you can click the small down arrow next to a button to choose a specific command instead (see Figure 3-23). To display the Standard toolbar in a folder, choose View, Toolbars, Standard. Use the same process to turn off the toolbar display.

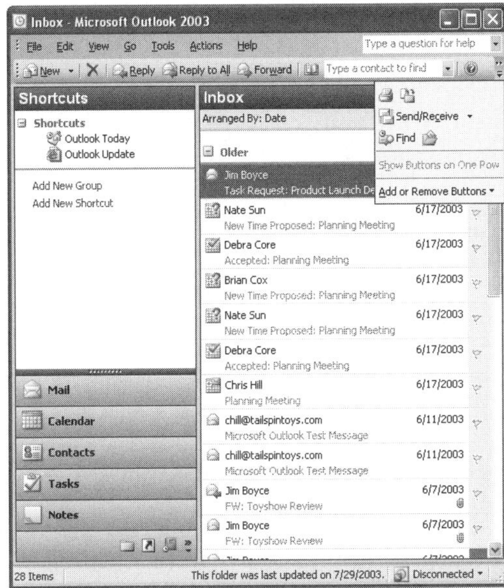

Figure 3-23. Click the down arrow beside a toolbar button to view additional command options.

> **Note** Outlook 2003 and other Microsoft Office 2003 applications refer to both menus and toolbars as *command bars*. However, Outlook still refers to the individual bars as *toolbars*. This book uses the two terms synonymously.

> **Tip** If you're not sure what function a toolbar button performs, rest the pointer over the button to have Outlook display a ScreenTip explaining the button's purpose.

If your display isn't wide enough to accommodate the entire toolbar, Outlook displays a double right arrow icon on the right edge of the toolbar. Click this icon to view the remaining toolbar buttons and add or remove buttons from the toolbar.

For more information on customizing the Standard toolbar and other toolbars, see "Customizing Command Bars," page 663.

The Advanced toolbar, shown in Figure 3-24, provides additional commands and also works in the context of the current folder. In addition to navigation buttons, the Advanced toolbar contains buttons for opening and closing the Reading Pane and the folders list, printing, setting up rules, selecting the current view, and more. Turn the Advanced toolbar on or off by choosing View, Toolbars, Advanced.

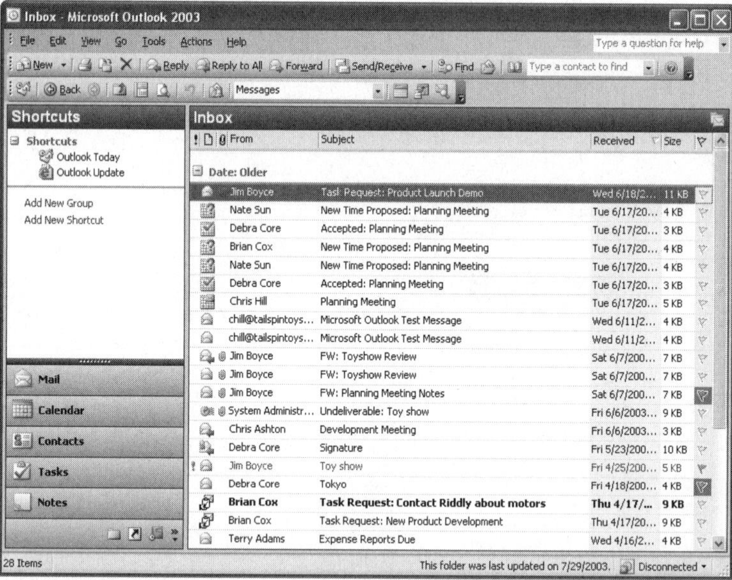

Figure 3-24. The Advanced toolbar lets you change views quickly.

The Web toolbar functions much as the navigation toolbar does in Microsoft Internet Explorer. It includes Web navigation buttons, a URL address box, buttons for stopping and refreshing the current page, and so on. Choose View, Toolbars, Web to show or hide the Web toolbar.

You can also turn on the Task pane, shown in Figure 3-25, by choosing View, Toolbars, Task Pane. The Task pane actually serves three purposes in Outlook. You can perform a search, view Help content, or perform research using several sources. With the Task pane displayed, click the down arrow at the top of the pane to choose Search Results, Help, or Research to perform a particular task. Click the Close button to close the Task pane, or choose View, Toolbars, Task Pane to turn it off.

Tip If you can't find Task Pane in the Toolbars menu, choose Help, Microsoft Office Outlook Help to turn on the Task pane.

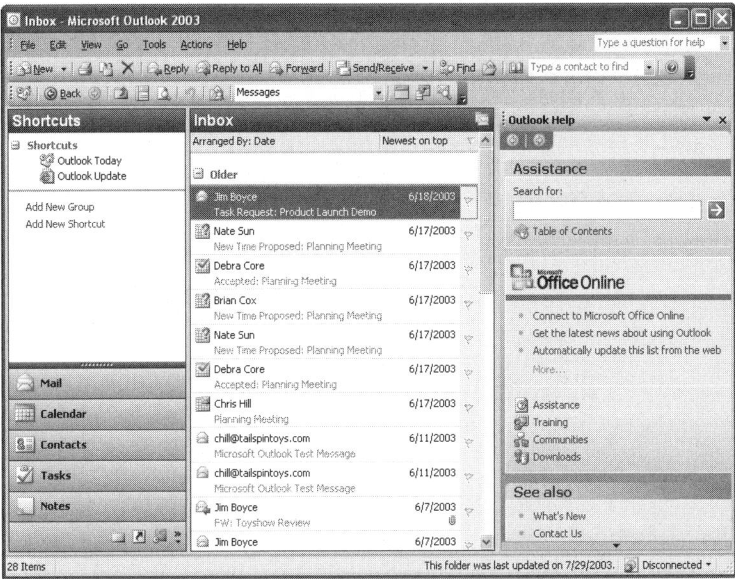

Figure 3-25. Use the Task pane to search, view Help content, or access research sources.

Using Multiple Outlook Windows

Although Outlook opens in a single window, it supports the use of multiple windows, which can be extremely useful. For example, you might want to keep your Inbox open while you browse through your schedule. Or perhaps you want to copy items from one folder to another by dragging them. Whatever the case, it's easy to use multiple windows in Outlook.

When you right-click a folder in the Navigation Pane, the shortcut menu for that folder contains the Open In New Window command. Choose this command to open the selected folder in a new window, keeping the existing folder open in the current window. You also can open a folder from the folder list (discussed next) in a new window. Simply right-click a folder and choose Open In New Window to open that folder in a new window.

Using the Folder List

When you need to switch between folders, you'll probably use the Navigation Pane most of the time. But the Navigation Pane doesn't include shortcuts to all your folders by default, and adding those shortcuts can clutter the pane, especially if you have multiple data stores. Fortunately, Outlook provides another quick way to navigate your folders: the folder list.

Click the Folder List button in the Navigation Pane to display the folder list, as shown in Figure 3-26. In the list, click the folder you want to open. Outlook hides the folder list again after you select the folder.

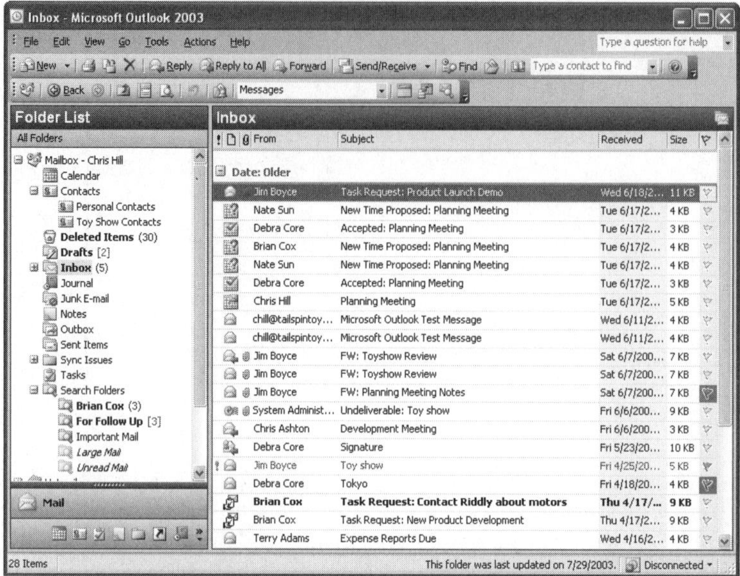

Figure 3-26. Use the folder list to browse and select other folders.

Using the Status Bar

The status bar appears at the bottom of the Outlook window (see Figure 3-27) and presents information about the current folder and selected items, such as the number of items in the folder. It can also include other status information, such as the progress of folder synchronization. If you don't need the information in the status bar, you can turn it off to gain a little more space for the current folder's display. To turn the status bar on or off, choose View, Status Bar.

Figure 3-27. The status bar provides useful information, such as the number of items in the selected folder.

Using the Reading Pane

In earlier sections of this chapter, you read about the Reading Pane, which allows you to preview Outlook items without opening them. For example, you can preview an e-mail message in the Reading Pane simply by clicking the message header. To turn the Reading Pane on or off, choose View, Reading Pane, then choose Right, Bottom, or Off. You can also click the Reading Pane button on the Advanced toolbar to turn the pane on or off.

To some degree, the way the Reading Pane functions depends on how you configure it. For example, you can set up the Reading Pane to mark messages as read after they've been previewed for a specified length of time. To configure the Reading Pane, choose Tools, Options, click the Other tab, and click Reading Pane. Select options based on the following list:

- **Mark Items As Read When Viewed in the Reading Pane** Select this option to have messages marked as read when they've been previewed for the time specified by the following option.
- **Wait *n* Seconds Before Marking Item As Read** Specify the number of seconds a message must be displayed in the Reading Pane before it is marked as read.
- **Mark Item As Read When Selection Changes** Select this option to have the message in the Reading Pane marked as read when you select another message.
- **Single Key Reading Using Spacebar** Selecting this option allows you to use the Spacebar to move through your list of messages to preview them. Press Shift+Spacebar to move up the list. You also can use the up and down arrow keys to move up and down the message list.

The Reading Pane in Outlook 2003 offers some new functionality, which includes the following:

- In a message folder, you can double-click an address in the Reading Pane to view details for the address.
- The InfoBar (discussed later in this section) now appears in the Reading Pane, giving you additional information about the selected item.
- The Reading Pane header displays the message's attachments. You can double-click an attachment to open it or right-click the attachment and choose other tasks from the shortcut menu (such as saving the attachment).
- The Reading Pane displays Accept and Decline buttons so that you can accept or decline a meeting request in the Reading Pane without opening the request.

Using AutoPreview

AutoPreview, which is available in the Inbox, Notes, and Tasks folders, allows you to preview Outlook items without opening the Reading Pane. For example, with AutoPreview turned on in the Inbox folder, the first three lines of each message appear under the message header. To turn AutoPreview on or off for the current folder, choose View, AutoPreview. The AutoPreview state (on or off) is saved on a folder-by-folder basis, so you can have AutoPreview turned on for the Inbox and turned off for Notes and Tasks.

Using the InfoBar

In versions of Outlook prior to Outlook 2002, the InfoBar appeared only in message and appointment forms, giving you additional information about the selected item. The InfoBar in a message form, for example, displays the From, To, Cc, and other fields. In Outlook 2002 the InfoBar also appeared in the Preview pane. In Outlook 2003, however, the InfoBar moves to the Reading Pane, as shown in Figure 3-28.

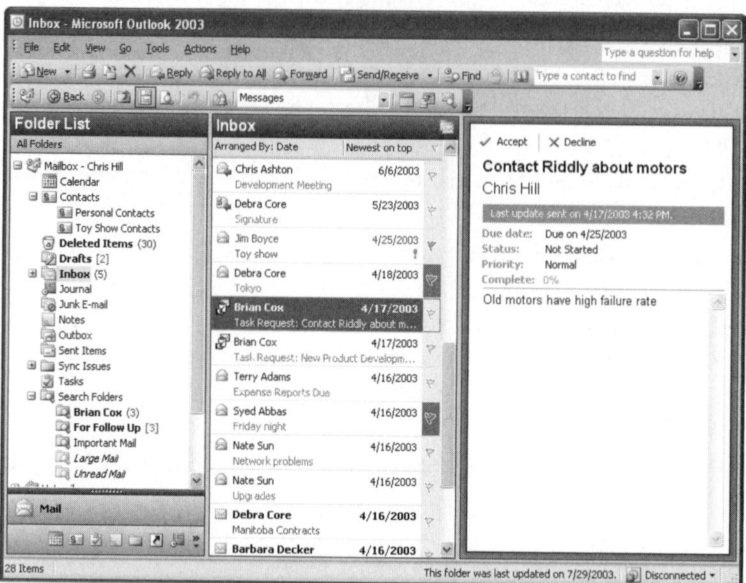

Figure 3-28. The InfoBar now appears in the Reading Pane as well as in message and appointment forms.

Some of the fields in the InfoBar simply display information, but others lead to more details. For example, you can double-click a name in the InfoBar to view the associated address and other contact information, or you can double-click attachments to open them.

Configuring Outlook Options

Because Outlook is a complex application with a broad range of capabilities, you have a good many options for controlling the way it looks and functions. This portion of the chapter is designed to help you configure Outlook to perform the way you need it to.

Each of the following sections describes a tab in Outlook's Options dialog box, providing an overview of the features listed on that tab. Because many of the options in this dialog box are best understood in the context of the feature they control, you'll find more detail about individual options in chapters that focus on a particular Outlook feature (messaging or scheduling, for example); be sure to consult the cross-references to the applicable chapters for more information.

To open the Options dialog box described here, open Outlook and choose Tools, Options.

Preferences

The Preferences tab of the Options dialog box, shown in Figure 3-29, lets you configure general settings for all of Outlook's primary functions, from e-mail to scheduling to contact management.

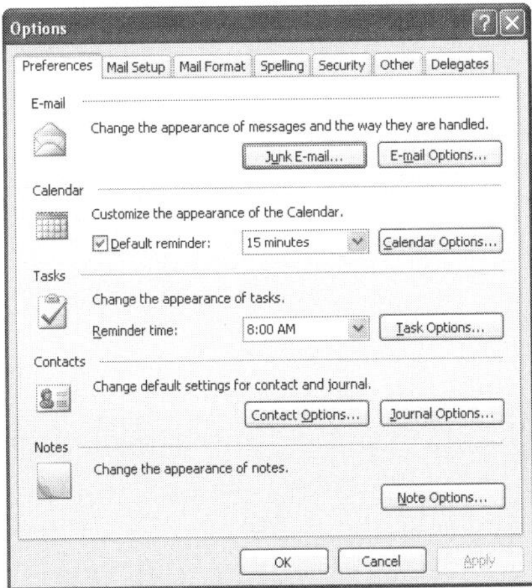

Figure 3-29. Use the Preferences tab of the Options dialog box to configure a broad range of general options.

Each of the option groups on the Preferences tab controls how a specific Outlook component works. The following list helps you locate specific settings:

- **E-Mail** You can specify how Outlook handles messages—for example, whether Outlook keeps a copy of sent items, saves unsent messages, or includes original message content in replies and forwards. You can also configure Outlook's junk e-mail filter settings. Chapter 7, "Sending and Receiving Messages," provides extensive coverage of e-mail configuration options. Chapter 8, "Filtering, Organizing, and Using Automatic Responses," explains how to block junk e-mail and filter and sort messages in other ways.
- **Calendar** You can control the look of Outlook's calendar by, for example, defining the work week, changing the workday start and end time, changing the appearance of the Date Navigator, or setting background color. See Chapter 19, "Scheduling Appointments," for a discussion of options for the Calendar folder.
- **Tasks** You can set the color for completed and overdue tasks, set up reminders for tasks with due dates, and configure other task-related settings. Chapter 21, "Managing Your Tasks," covers task options in detail.
- **Contacts** You can control the way names are displayed in the Contacts folder, check for duplicate contact entries, configure journal options, and set other options for storing and managing your contact information. See Chapter 15, "Using Microsoft Business Contact Manager," for a complete explanation.
- **Notes** You can, for example, set the color, size, and font used for notes. Chapter 17, "Making Notes," covers options for notes.

Mail Setup

On the Mail Setup tab (see Figure 3-30), you'll find additional settings that control e-mail accounts and Outlook's messaging functions. For example, you can use the Mail Setup tab to create or modify e-mail accounts and configure how and when Outlook sends and receives messages.

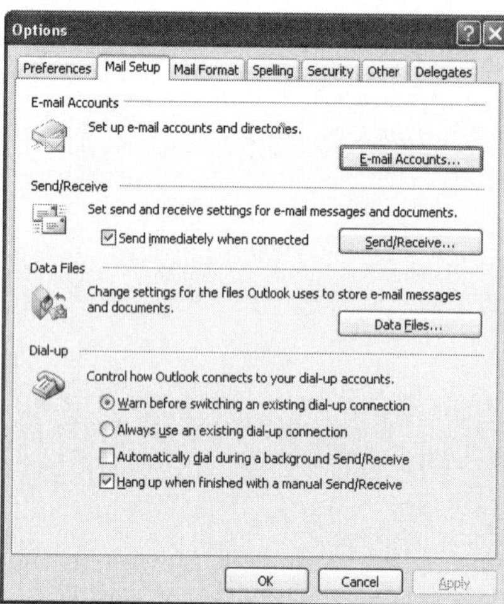

Figure 3-30. Use the Mail Setup tab to configure e-mail accounts and general messaging properties.

The following list describes the major sections of the Mail Setup tab and directs you to the chapter in which those settings are discussed:

- **E-Mail Accounts** These settings allow you to add, remove, or configure e-mail accounts. See Chapter 2, "Advanced Setup Tasks," and Chapter 6, "Using Internet Mail," to learn how to configure e-mail accounts.
- **Send/Receive** You can define groups of accounts, which Outlook then uses to determine when to process messages for specific accounts. You can configure settings separately for each group, providing a high degree of control over when and how Outlook processes messages. See Chapter 7, "Sending and Receiving Messages," for information about send/receive groups and send/receive options.
- **Data Files** These settings let you add, remove, and configure information stores (data files) for Outlook, including setting up offline access. See Chapter 1, "Outlook Architecture, Setup, and Startup," to learn how to manage data files.
- **Dial-Up** Here you can configure a handful of settings that determine how Outlook handles dial-up connections for sending and receiving messages. See Chapter 6, "Using Internet Mail," to learn about dial-up connection options.

Mail Format

Use the Mail Format tab (see Figure 3-31) to control the way your messages look and how you compose those messages. For example, you can use the Mail Format tab to specify either Microsoft Word or Outlook as the default e-mail editor, to choose between plain-text and rich-text options, and to set international formatting options.

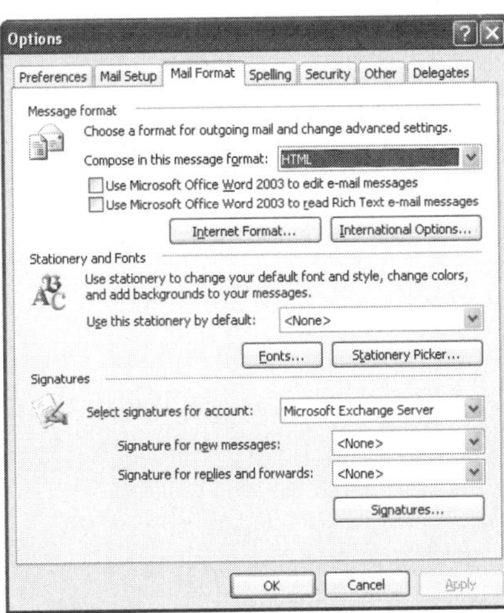

Figure 3-31. Use the Mail Format tab to select the default e-mail editor, mail format, and other properties.

The following list summarizes the option groups on the Mail Format tab. For details about the various settings in each group, consult Chapter 7, "Sending and Receiving Messages."

- **Message Format** With these settings, you can choose among HTML, plain text, and rich text for outgoing messages; specify the default e-mail editor; specify the default e-mail viewer for rich-text messages; configure Internet and international options for messages; and set up other messaging features.
- **Stationery And Fonts** You can set default stationery (background) for messages, manage stationery, and specify font settings.

- **Signature** These settings direct Outlook to add a text signature to all new messages and to replies and forwards. You can configure the two categories of messages separately. (Note that these signatures are different from digital signatures, which allow you to validate the authenticity of and encrypt messages.) New in Outlook 2003 is the ability to assign specific signatures to each e-mail account.

Spelling

The Spelling tab (see Figure 3-32) lets you specify how spelling should be checked in Outlook. The following sections summarize by function the settings available on this tab.

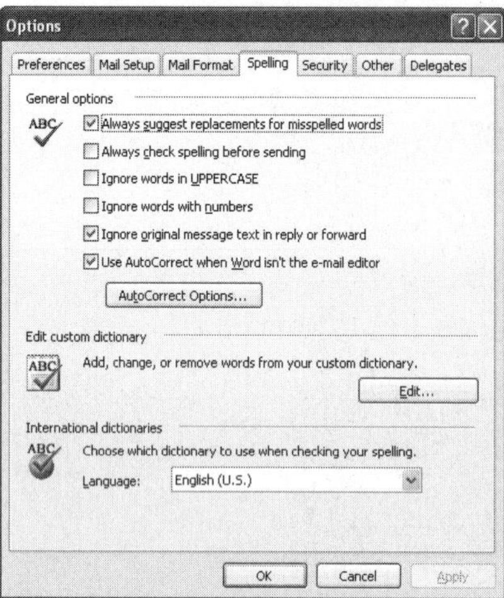

Figure 3-32. Use the Spelling tab to set options for checking spelling.

Checking Spelling

The General Options section of the Spelling tab allows you to set general guidelines for the spell checker. The options include the following:

- **Always Suggest Replacements For Misspelled Words** When you select this option, the spell checker will display suggested changes for any misspelled words it finds.
- **Always Check Spelling Before Sending** Select this option to have Outlook automatically check spelling before you send a message. You also can check spelling manually.
- **Ignore Words In UPPERCASE** You can instruct the spell checker to skip words that appear in all uppercase letters. This option is useful, for example, if your document contains numerous acronyms and you don't want the spell checker to waste time checking them.
- **Ignore Words With Numbers** When you select this option, the spell checker will not attempt to check the spelling of words that include numbers, such as *some342*.
- **Ignore Original Message Text In Reply Or Forward** Selecting this option specifies that Outlook will check spelling only in your message text, not in the original message text included in a reply or forward.
- **Use AutoCorrect When Word Isn't The E-Mail Editor** Selecting this option allows Outlook to use AutoCorrect in rich-text and plain-text messages to automatically correct certain common errors. See the following section for details.

Using AutoCorrect

Outlook, like other Office applications, supports AutoCorrect, a feature that allows Outlook to correct common spelling and typing errors and to replace characters with symbols. You also can use AutoCorrect as a shortcut, which means you can type a small string of characters and have those characters replaced by a longer string. For example, if you frequently type the words **Windows XP**, you might set up AutoCorrect to replace your shorthand typed phrase **wxp** with **Windows XP**. See the tip in the "Setting Advanced Options" section on page 95 for a handy use for smart tags and AutoCorrect entries.

Clicking AutoCorrect Options on the Spelling tab displays the AutoCorrect dialog box, shown in Figure 3-33. You can use this dialog box to add new AutoCorrect entries or change existing entries. Click Exceptions to specify exceptions to AutoCorrect rules.

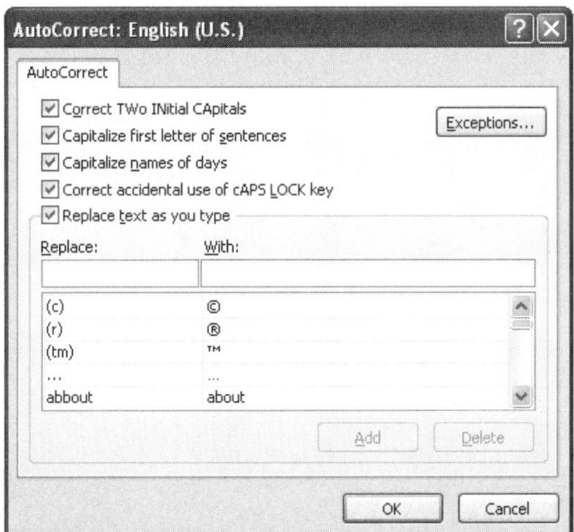

Figure 3-33. Use the AutoCorrect dialog box to add and modify AutoCorrect entries.

Editing a Custom Spelling Dictionary

When Outlook is checking spelling in a document and finds a word it considers misspelled, the program gives you the option of adding the word to a custom dictionary. This option lets you specify the correct spelling of words not found in Outlook's standard dictionary. For example, you might want to add your name to the custom dictionary if Outlook doesn't recognize its spelling. You can also add the correct spelling of special words or terms you use often to the custom dictionary.

Tip **Use custom dictionaries throughout Office**

All Office applications use the same spelling features, including the custom dictionary. Words you add to the dictionary from other applications are available in Outlook, and vice versa. This is also true for new dictionaries that you create: if you add another dictionary to Outlook, that new dictionary is available in other Office applications.

Click Edit on the Spelling tab to open the custom dictionary (Custom.dic) in Notepad to change or add entries. Enter one word per line. The custom dictionary file is stored in the Application Data\Microsoft\Proof folder of your profile folder (which varies according to your operating system).

You can add other dictionaries to Outlook. To add a new dictionary, follow these steps:

1. Open Microsoft Word and choose Tools, Spelling And Grammar.
2. Click Options in the Spelling And Grammar dialog box and then click Custom Dictionaries.
3. In the Custom Dictionaries dialog box (see Figure 3-34), select the dictionary files you want to add and click OK.

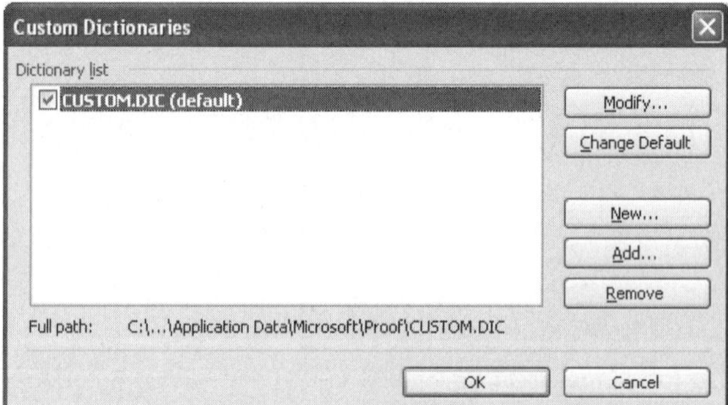

Figure 3-34. Add dictionaries using the Custom Dictionaries dialog box.

Using International Dictionaries

The International Dictionaries section on the Spelling tab allows you to specify the language that Outlook uses when checking spelling. Simply select the appropriate language from the drop-down list and click OK.

Security

The Security tab (see Figure 3-35) lets you configure a range of options that help you secure your messages, validate your identity to others, and protect your system against viruses and worms.

Figure 3-35. Use the Security tab to configure digital signatures and other security properties.

The Security tab includes the following groups of options.

For details about the specific options on the Security tab, see Chapter 10, "Securing Your System, Messages, and Identity."

- **Encrypted E-mail** You can choose to encrypt outgoing messages, add digital signatures to outgoing messages, and configure other options for digital signatures and encryption.
- **Security Zones** These options help you define security zones, which determine how Outlook handles HTML messages.
- **Download Pictures** Click Settings in this group to set options that control how Outlook handles external content in HTML messages. See Chapter 8, "Filtering, Organizing, and Using Automatic Responses," to learn more about rules and filters to block junk mail.
- **Digital IDs (Certificates)** The settings accessed through this area help you manage digital certificates and signatures, which allow you to share encrypted messages and validate your identity to message recipients.

Other

The Other tab (see Figure 3-36) provides a selection of settings that apply to various aspects of Outlook. The following sections explain how to configure specific features and behavior using this tab.

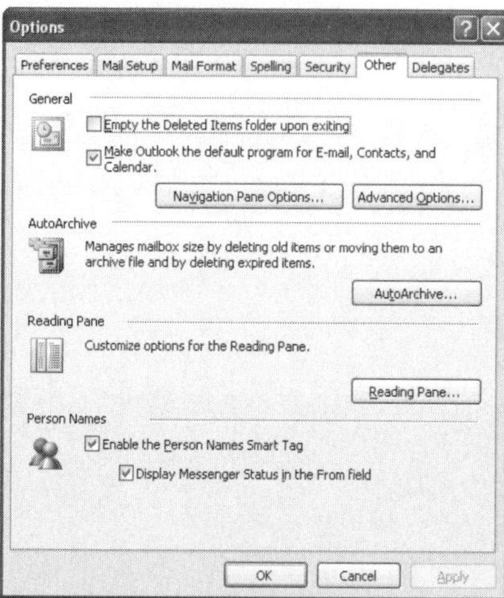

Figure 3-36. The Other tab gives you access to properties for several features.

Defining the Default Program for E-Mail, Contacts, and Calendar

One setting on the Other tab lets you specify that Outlook is the default application for creating and viewing e-mail, contacts, and calendar items. Select the Make Outlook The Default Program For E-Mail, Contacts, And Calendar check box if you want Outlook to open when you open e-mail messages, contact entries, or calendar data from other sources.

Processing Deleted Items

You can use the Other tab to determine how Outlook processes deleted items. The first of the following two options is located on the Other tab; click Advanced Options to access the second.

- **Empty The Deleted Items Folder Upon Exiting** Select this check box to have Outlook automatically delete all items from the Deleted Items folder when you exit the program. This action permanently deletes the items.
- **Warn Before Permanently Deleting Items** Click Advanced Options and select this option if you want Outlook to warn you before it permanently deletes items from the Deleted Items folder.

Setting Up AutoArchive

The options accessed by clicking AutoArchive on the Other tab let you control how Outlook archives data, processes deleted and expired items, and implements other backup properties, such as the retention policy. See Chapter 30, "Managing Folders, Data, and Archiving," for more information on backup and archival options and procedures for Outlook.

Customizing the Reading Pane

Clicking Reading Pane on the Other tab provides access to options that determine the way the Reading Pane functions. These options are explained in detail earlier in this chapter; see "Using the Reading Pane," page 84.

Setting Up Person Names

Use the Person Names area on the Other tab to enable and configure MSN Messenger and use instant messaging (sending or receiving pop-up messages in communication with other users). See "Using Instant Messaging," page 208, for more information on instant messaging.

Delegates

The Delegates tab of the Options dialog box lets you specify other persons who have delegate access to your folders and can send items on your behalf (meeting requests, for example). See Chapter 29, "Delegating Responsibilities to an Assistant," for detailed information on using delegation and specifying delegates.

Setting Advanced Options

The Other tab of the Options dialog box lets you access a set of special advanced options for configuring Outlook. Click Advanced Options on the Other tab to display the Advanced Options dialog box, shown in Figure 3-37. You can use the options in this dialog box to configure various aspects of Outlook's behavior and appearance, as described in the following list:

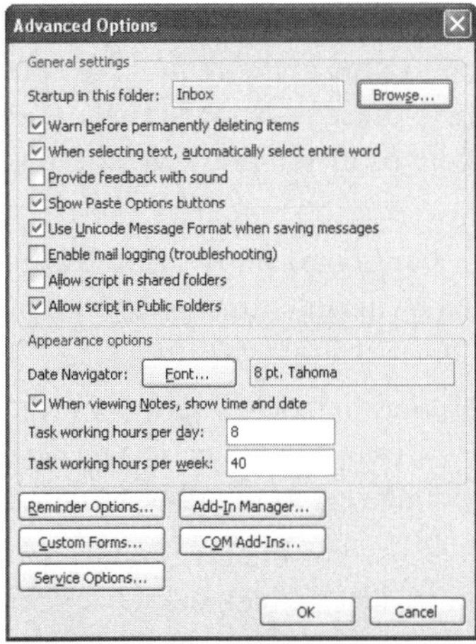

Figure 3-37. The Advanced Options dialog box controls several advanced features.

- **Startup In This Folder** This option lets you specify which folder Outlook opens by default when you start the program. Click Browse to select the folder.
- **Warn Before Permanently Deleting Items** Enable this option to have Outlook display a warning before it permanently deletes items.
- **When Selecting Text, Automatically Select Entire Word** Select this option to have Outlook automatically select the entire word and the following space when you highlight any portion of a word. This behavior simplifies selecting words and blocks of text. This option is unavailable if you have configured Word as your default e-mail editor.
- **Provide Feedback With Sound** You can direct Outlook to play a sound when you perform actions such as opening a file or deleting a message.
- **Show Paste Options Buttons** When this option is selected, Outlook displays a smart tag when you paste data from the clipboard, allowing you to change the paste format and other paste options. This method of changing these options is faster than using the Edit menu.

> **Tip** **Use smart tags to get quick access to features**
> Smart tags are controls embedded in documents to provide quick access to commands and features without forcing you to navigate the application's menu. When you paste data from the clipboard, for example, Office adds a smart tag beside the pasted data. You can select other paste formats and fine-tune the data without repasting or using the Edit menu. Smart tags also come in handy with AutoCorrect entries. If you type some text referenced by an AutoCorrect entry, Office changes the text automatically but adds a smart tag beside the modified text so you can select other changes or undo the correction. Other types of smart tags provide similar quick access to document data and editing.

- **Use Unicode Message Format When Saving Messages** Use Unicode character set when saving messages to disk.
- **Enable Mail Logging (Troubleshooting)** This option allows Outlook to log e-mail event status to the OPMLog.log file, which is located in the Temp folder of your profile folder (for example, \Documents And Settings\<*user*>\Local Settings\Temp on a system running Microsoft Windows 2000 or Microsoft Windows XP not upgraded from Microsoft Windows NT).
- **Allow Script In Shared Folders** Enable this option to allow scripts to run when you access shared folders. This option is disabled by default. Enable this option only if you are not concerned about malicious scripts in shared folders.
- **Allow Script In Public Folders** Enable this option to allow scripts to run when you access public folders on an Exchange Server. This option is enabled by default. Disable this option if you are concerned about malicious scripts in public folders.
- **Date Navigator** Click Font to select the font used by the Date Navigator (the two-month calendar that appears in the Calendar folder). Changing the font changes not only the appearance of the Date Navigator but also the number of months displayed. Make the font smaller to show more months or larger to show fewer months.

- **When Viewing Notes, Show Time And Date** You can have Outlook display the time and date a note was created or last modified at the bottom of the note.
- **Task Working Hours Per Day and Task Working Hours Per Week** These two options define your work week for managing tasks. The default settings are 8 hours and 40 hours, respectively.

Note The Advanced Options dialog box includes five buttons at the bottom that let you configure a variety of options. Some of these buttons and their options are covered in the following sections. See the section "Using Add-Ins," page 103 for more information on Add-In Manager and COM Add-Ins buttons and options. See Chapter 24, "Designing and Using Forms," for information on configuring custom forms.

Configuring Reminder Options

The Reminder Options button in the Advanced Options dialog box opens a simple Reminder Options dialog box that offers two options for configuring Outlook reminders:

- **Display the Reminder** Choose this option to have Outlook display reminders in the Reminders window when they come due.
- **Play Reminder Sound** Choose this option to have Outlook play a sound when a reminder comes due, and choose the sound file you want Outlook to use.

Setting Service Options

Clicking Service Options in the Advanced Options dialog box displays the Service Options dialog box shown in Figure 3-38. This dialog box provides access to three configuration areas.

Customer Feedback Options The Customer Feedback Options page allows you to enable or disable participation in Microsoft's Customer Experience Improvement Program. When this option is enabled, Office applications submit information about your system and the way you use your Office applications to Microsoft over the Web, along with information about errors you encounter. Participation is disabled by default. Participating can provide Microsoft with useful information that could ultimately lead to better software, but you can leave this option disable if you don't want your usage information shared, or if providing this information isn't practical because you use a dial-up Internet connection. You can also disable this function in networks with widespread Office deployment to reduce network traffic and reduce data outflow.

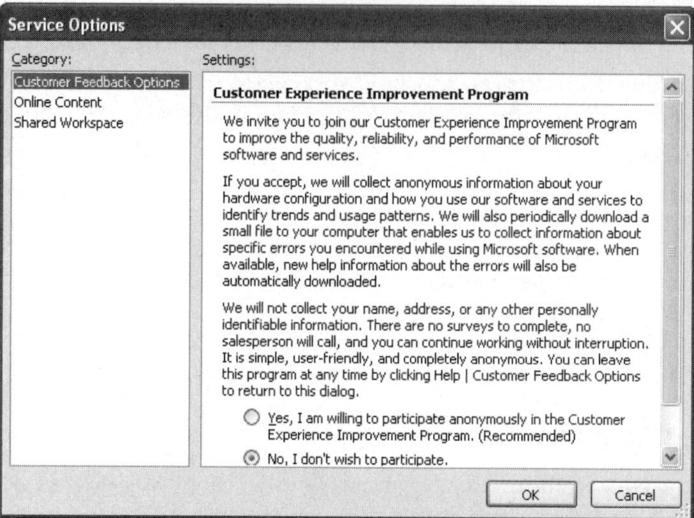

Figure 3-38. Use Customer Feedback Options to enable or disable participation in collection of usage data by Microsoft.

Chapter 3

Configuring Online Help Content By default, Outlook displays links and content from the Microsoft Office Web site when you open the Assistance pane (Help), as shown in Figure 3-39. This online content can provide very up-to-date technical information on Outlook and links to frequently asked questions and other Help topics.

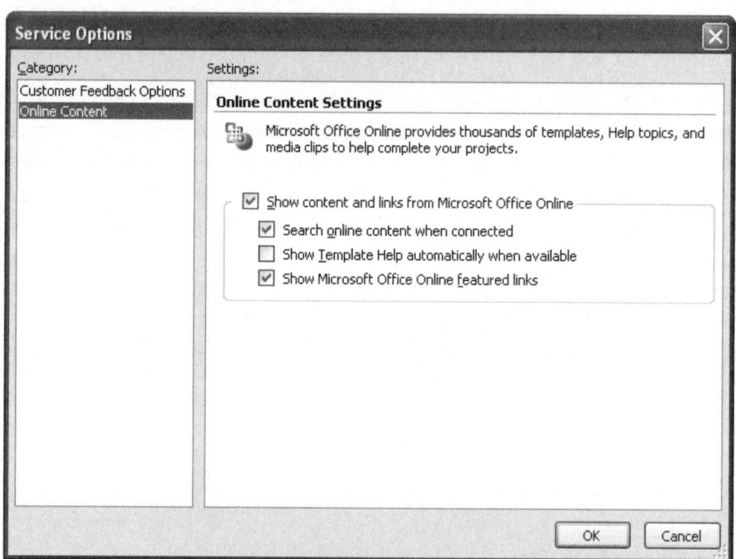

Figure 3-39. Help displays links to Web-based content on Outlook by default.

In some cases you might want to turn off this external content, such as when you use a slow link to the Internet, want to reduce network traffic, or use your own Help content developed in-house. To configure online content, click Service Options in the Advanced Options dialog box and then click Online Content to access the following options:

- **Show Content And Links From Microsoft Office Online** Use this option to globally enable or disable all online content.
- **Search Online Content When Connected** Enable this option to have Outlook search the Office Online site for Help content when your computer is connected to the Internet.
- **Show Template Help Automatically When Available** Enable this option to have Outlook display suggestions and tips for using a template when you open the template.
- **Show Microsoft Office Online Featured Links** Enable this option to have Outlook include links to information about training, assistance, user communities, and other information in the Assistance pane.

Using Outlook on the Web

Outlook includes several features that integrate its functionality with the Internet. This section explores these features, including a look at browsing the Web with Outlook, using Microsoft NetMeeting and Microsoft NetShow to facilitate desktop conferencing and collaboration, and connecting to Exchange Server through HTTP.

Browsing the Web with Outlook

Outlook's integration with Internet Explorer allows you to browse the Internet without leaving Outlook. This feature is handy when you need to retrieve a file, view online documents, or otherwise access data on the Web but don't want to open Internet Explorer. Outlook's ability to browse the Web allows you to continue working in a single interface and avoid switching between open applications.

The Web toolbar includes an Address box in which you can enter the URL for a Web-related resource, such as a Web site or an FTP site (see Figure 3-40). To view a site in Outlook, type the URL in the Address box and press Enter. Alternatively, you can click the drop-down button beside the Address box to select a URL that you've visited previously. The Stop and Refresh buttons on the toolbar perform the same function they do in Internet Explorer. When you want to go back to working with your Outlook folders, simply select the folder you need from the Navigation Pane or the folder list.

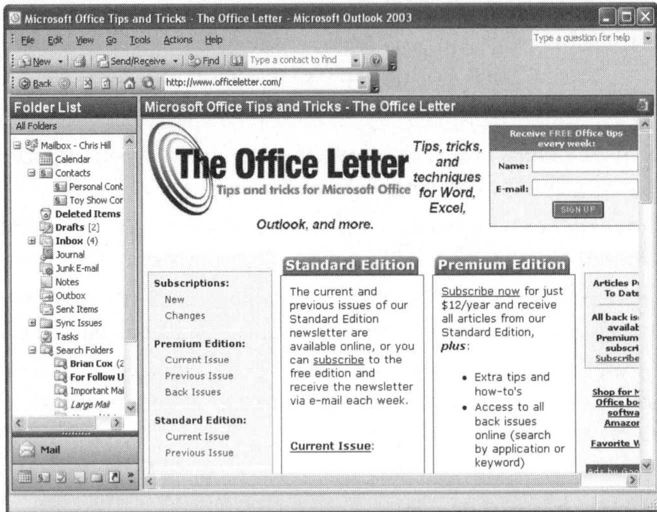

Figure 3-40. You can use Outlook to browse Web sites and other Web resources.

Connecting to Exchange Server with HTTP

Outlook 2003 adds support for connecting to Exchange Server with HTTP, the standard protocol used to access Web sites. HTTP access to Exchange Server in Outlook 2003 is not the same as using Microsoft Outlook Web Access to view your mailbox from a Web browser. Instead, Outlook itself can use HTTP to send and receive messages and interact with your Exchange Server mailbox in other ways.

Using HTTP for access to an Exchange Server provides greater flexibility for remote access with Outlook and simplifies network security configuration for Exchange Server and network administrators. Remote access and the use of HTTP in Outlook is covered in Chapter 37, "Working Offline and Remotely."

Using NetMeeting

Microsoft NetMeeting is a desktop conferencing application included with Internet Explorer that allows an unlimited number of people to participate in a virtual meeting across the Internet or an intranet. With NetMeeting, participants can speak with one another, exchange messages, view one another through video, share applications and files, and collaborate on documents using an electronic whiteboard. Some of the available features depend on the participants' system configurations. For example, video conferencing requires a video camera, and audio conferencing requires a sound card and microphone. Some features of NetMeeting are useful over dial-up connections, but effective conferencing—particularly with a larger number of participants—requires a higher speed connection, such as Digital Subscriber Line (DSL), Integrated Services Digital Network (ISDN), or dedicated T1.

NetMeeting is not a component of Outlook. Rather, NetMeeting is a separate application included with Internet Explorer. You can obtain NetMeeting and Internet Explorer from Microsoft's Web site at *http://www.microsoft.com/windows/ie/default.asp.*

For a detailed discussion of NetMeeting, including installation and configuration, see "Holding an Online Meeting," page 571.

Using NetShow

Microsoft NetShow is a client/server desktop conferencing platform for broadcasting live and on-demand audio, video, and multimedia presentations across the Internet or an intranet. NetShow is a great tool to provide not only live presentations to remote participants but also streaming multimedia across the Web.

Inside Out

Alternatives to Microsoft NetShow

Microsoft's NetShow is a complex system that is beyond the scope of this book. Chapter 20, "Scheduling Meetings and Resources," explains how to use NetShow from the client side to participate in presentations. The *Microsoft Internet Explorer Resource Kit*, available from Microsoft and other retailers, provides a detailed technical explanation of the NetShow platform from both the client and server perspectives. It also offers detailed information regarding NetShow deployment, presentation development, and related topics.

If you don't need the whiteboard or document collaboration features offered by NetMeeting but instead primarily use only video and audio chat, consider using the latest version of Microsoft Messenger. Also check out Eyeball Chat from Eyeball Networks at *http://www.eyeball.com*. Eyeball Chat provides great video performance and the application is free, as is access to the Eyeball Chat server.

Accessing Your Mail Through a Browser

Outlook serves as a great client application for e-mail, but on occasion you might want to use a simpler method of accessing your messages. For example, you might be out of town unexpectedly, without your computer, and realize that you need to read an important message. Or, perhaps you'd like to check your office e-mail from home but don't have your Outlook configuration installed on your home computer. Whatever the case, Exchange Server supports access to your Exchange Server mailbox through Outlook Web Access, a server-side feature of Exchange Server.

Using Outlook Web Access to access your mailbox on Exchange Server doesn't require extensive configuration. You simply point your Web browser to the URL on the server that provides access to your mailbox. The URL varies according to how Outlook Web Access is configured on the server, in addition to a few other considerations. For a detailed look at using Outlook Web Access to access your Exchange Server mailbox, see Chapter 41, "Accessing Messages Through a Web Browser."

Configuring Windows Settings for Outlook

Although most of the settings you'll need to configure for Outlook are configured through the program itself, some settings in the underlying operating system have an impact on the way Outlook functions and displays your data. This section offers an overview of the settings you might consider reviewing or modifying for use with Outlook.

Display Settings

Because Outlook packs a lot of information into a relatively small amount of space, your display resolution has some impact on Outlook's usefulness. You should configure your system for at least an 800 × 600 desktop, preferably larger, depending on the size of your monitor. This is particularly important if you're using multiple Outlook windows at one time.

To configure properties for the display, you use the Display icon in Windows Control Panel. You can also right-click the desktop and choose Properties to open the Display dialog box.

Tip A handful of freeware and shareware applications are available that let you create multiple virtual desktops to expand your available desktop space. A search of your favorite shareware site should turn up at least one or two such utilities. An application I particularly like for managing multiple monitors is UltraMon, from *www.ultramon.com*.

Regional Settings

The regional settings on your computer determine how the operating system displays time, dates, currency, and other localized data. Because Outlook uses these types of data extensively, configuring your regional settings properly is an important step in setting up for Outlook. This step is especially important for your calendar if you use multiple time zones. To configure regional settings, use the Regional Settings or Regional Options icon in Control Panel.

Time Synchronization

Much of your Outlook data is time-sensitive. For example, e-mail messages have sent and received times, and meetings are scheduled for specific periods. If your system's clock isn't accurate, some of that data won't be accurate. You should make sure that your clock is set correctly and that the system maintains the accurate time.You can set the time either by using the Date/Time icon in Control Panel or by double-clicking the clock in the system tray.

You also can use synchronization tools to synchronize your computer with a time server. Such tools are available as third-party utilities for use with all Microsoft Windows platforms, and a search of your favorite download site should turn up a few. In addition, Windows 2000 and Windows XP clients can take advantage of the Windows Time Service (W32Time) that allows client computers to synchronize their time with domain controllers on their network.

If you're not familiar with W32Time, check with your system administrator for help in setting it up.

> **Tip** **Synchronizing time in Windows NT domains**
> When Windows 2000 and Windows XP clients update their time on Windows NT domains, some compatibility issues can arise. If your Windows NT domain controllers use the Timeserv service, you need to upgrade to the W32Time service to allow these clients to participate. In addition, you need to make a few registry modifications on the Windows NT domain controller functioning as the time server to allow Windows 2000 clients to synchronize their times. See Microsoft Knowledge Base article 258059 for more information.

Using Add-Ins

Outlook provides tremendous functionality right out of the box and could well serve all your needs. However, if you need additional features not provided directly by Outlook, *add-ins* can help to extend Outlook's functionality. Outlook includes a handful of such add-ins, and third-party developers can produce others.

Outlook supports two types of add-ins: application-specific (standard) add-ins and COM add-ins. Standard add-ins are the type supported by earlier versions of Outlook, which allow a developer to add features to one Office application. Standard add-ins are not portable between Office applications. These add-ins are integrated into Outlook through dynamic-link libraries (DLLs).

COM add-ins use the Microsoft Component Object Model to allow shared functionality between the various Office applications. COM add-ins were added as new features in Office 2000 and are also available in Office 2003. These add-ins are integrated into Office applications, including Outlook, through either DLLs or ActiveX controls.

You install add-ins when you install Office; the list of available add-ins depends on which options you select during installation. To view the installed add-ins, choose Tools, Options and click the Other tab. Click Advanced Options to open the Advanced Options dialog box. Click Add-In Manager to view, install, and enable or disable standard Outlook add-ins and click COM Add-Ins to view, install, and enable or disable COM add-ins and control their load behavior.

For more information on different add-ins available for use with Outlook, see Article 7, "Outlook Add-Ins," on the companion CD.

Chapter 4

Using Categories and Types

One of the primary functions of Microsoft Outlook is to help you organize your data, whether that data is a collection of contacts, a task list, your schedule, or a month's worth of messages. To make this easier, you can use Outlook's *categories*, which are words or phrases you assign to Outlook items as a means of organizing the items. For example, you might assign the category Personal to a message from a family member, to differentiate it from your work-related messages, and then customize the view to exclude personal items.

This chapter explains how categories work in Outlook and shows you how to manage a Master Category List, add new categories, assign them to Outlook items, and use categories to arrange, display, and search Outlook data. You'll also learn about entry types, which work in concert with categories to give you even more flexibility in organizing your data.

Understanding Categories

If you've used a personal finance or checkbook program such as Microsoft Money or Intuit's Quicken, you're probably familiar with categories. In these programs, you can assign a category to each check, deposit, or other transaction and then view all transactions for a specific category, perhaps printing them on a report for tax purposes. For example, you might use categories to keep track of business expenses and separate them by certain criteria, such as reimbursement policy or tax deductions.

Outlook's categories perform essentially the same function: you can place data into categories and manipulate the data based on those categories. For example, you might use categories to assign Outlook items such as messages and tasks to a specific project. You could then quickly locate all items related to that project. Or, you might use categories to differentiate personal contacts from business contacts. Whatever your need for organization, categories offer a handy and efficient way to achieve your goal.

What can you do with categories? After you assign a category to each relevant Outlook item, you can sort, search, and organize your data according to the category. Figure 4-1, for example, shows the Advanced Find dialog box after a search for all Outlook items assigned to the category Toy Show. Figure 4-2 shows the Contacts folder organized by category, displaying all contacts who are involved in the toy show. The ability to search by category makes it easy to find all the items associated with a specific project, contract, issue, or general category.

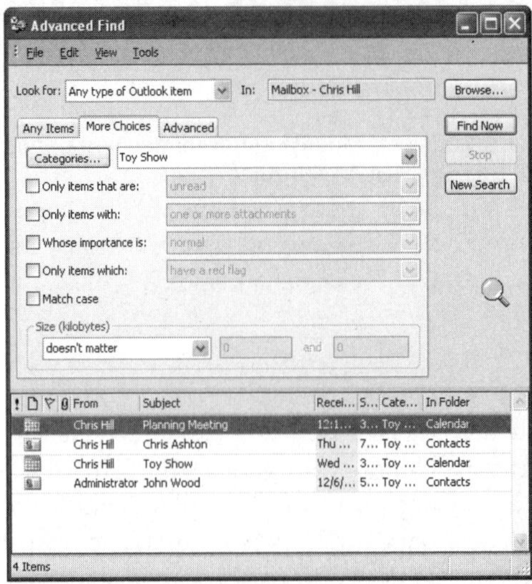

Figure 4-1. The Advanced Find dialog box displays the results of a search for all Toy Show items.

Figure 4-2. You can group contacts by category to list all contacts involved in a particular event or project.

Categories are useful only if you apply them consistently. After you become disciplined in using categories and begin to assign them out of habit, you'll wonder how you ever organized your day without them.

The Master Category List

Outlook maintains a Master Category List that contains the default categories created by Setup when you install Outlook. The Master Category List is hard-coded and can't be changed. You can, however, modify your personal copy of the Master Category List, which is stored in the registry key

HKEY_CURRENT_USER\Software\Microsoft\Office\11.0\Outlook\Categories

> **Note** The Categories key does not exist until you modify your own Master Category List. When you do, Outlook creates the registry key and stores in it your custom Master Category List.

The Master Category List serves as the basis for customizing your personal category list. The Master Category List contains several predefined categories that are useful in many situations, but your business or organization might need special categories not included with Outlook. You can customize the Master Category List to create your own category list with as many additional categories as you want, as the following section explains.

Customizing Your Personal Master Category List

Before you assign categories to Outlook items, you should go through the category list and add the categories you need. To determine which ones to add, spend some time thinking about how you intend to use them. Although you can always add categories later, creating the majority up front not only saves time but also helps you organize your thoughts and plan the use of categories more effectively.

Follow these steps when you're ready to create categories:

1. Open the Categories dialog box by choosing Edit, Categories or right-click an item and choose Categories from the shortcut menu.
2. Click Master Category List to display the Master Category List dialog box, shown in Figure 4-3.

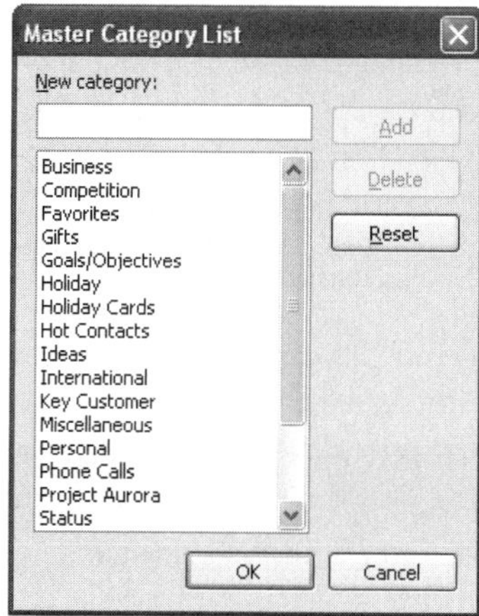

Figure 4-3. You can add a new category in the Master Category List dialog box.

3. Type the new category name in the New Category box, and click Add. Repeat this step to add other categories as needed.
4. Click OK when you've finished adding categories, and then click OK to close the Categories dialog box.

For information about creating new categories while you are assigning categories to an item, see the following section, "Assigning Categories to New Items."

The categories you add to your personal Master Category List depend entirely on the types of tasks you perform with Outlook, your type of business or organization, and your preferences. The following list suggests ways to categorize business-related data:

- Track items by project type or project name.
- Organize contacts by their type (for example, managers, assistants, technical experts, and financial advisors).
- Keep track of departmental assignments.
- Track different types of documents (for example, drafts, works in progress, and final versions).
- Track contacts by sales potential (for example, 30-day or 60-day).

Organize items by priority. The following list offers suggestions for categorizing personal data:

- Organize personal contacts by type (friends, family, insurance agents, legal advisors, and medical contacts, for starters).
- Track items by area of interest.
- Organize items for hobbies.
- Track items related to vacation or other activities.

Assigning Categories to New Items

Assigning categories to items is easy. You can assign multiple categories to each item if needed. For example, a particular contact might be involved in more than one project, so you might assign a category for each project to that contact. If you have a task that must be performed for multiple projects, you might assign those project categories to the task.

To learn how to assign categories to existing items, see "Changing Category Assignments," page 111.

Follow these steps to assign categories to a new item:

1. Open the form to create the item. (Click New with the folder open, for example.)
2. Use one of the following methods to display the Categories dialog box, depending on the type of item you're creating:
   - **Message** Click Options on the toolbar, and then click Categories.
   - **Calendar, contact, or task item** Click Categories at the bottom of the form.

> **Note** Depending on your screen resolution you might need to maximize the form to see the Categories button.

- **Note** You can't assign a category initially. Instead, add the note, right-click it, and choose Categories; or select the note and choose Edit, Categories.

3. In the Categories dialog box, select all the categories that pertain to the item. If you need to add a category, just click in the Item(s) Belong To These Categories box, type the category name, and click Add To List. This adds the category to your personal Master Category List.
4. Click OK to close the dialog box and continue creating the item.

As you can see in step 3, you don't have to open the Master Category List to create new categories. Instead, you can create a category on the fly when you're assigning categories to an item. Outlook adds the new category to your personal Master Category List. However, a drawback to creating categories on the fly is that you might not enter the category names consistently. As a result, you could end up with more than one version of a given category. As you might expect, Outlook treats category names literally, so any difference between two names, however minor, makes those categories different. Searching for one won't turn up items assigned to the other. For this reason, it's a good idea to always select categories from the Master Category List rather than creating them on the fly.

Assigning Categories Automatically

You can easily assign categories when you create an item, but you might prefer to simplify the process for items that will be assigned to the same category (or set of categories). For example, if you frequently create e-mail messages that have specific category assignments, you could bypass the steps involved in adding the categories to each new message. You can accomplish this by using an e-mail template.

> **For a detailed discussion of templates, see Chapter 23, "Using Templates."**

You can use templates for other Outlook items as well. Simply create the template, assign categories to it as needed, and then save it with a name that will help you easily identify the category assignments or the function of the template. When you need to create a message with that specific set of category assignments, you can create it from the template rather than from scratch. Because the category assignments are stored in the template, new items created from the template are assigned those categories. Using templates to assign categories not only saves you the time involved in adding categories individually but also ensures that the category assignments are consistent. (For example, you won't misspell a name or forget to add a category.)

Modifying Categories and Category Assignments

At some point, you'll want to recategorize Outlook items—that is, you'll want to add, remove, or modify their category assignments. For example, when one project ends and another begins, some of your contacts will move to a different project, and you'll want to change the categories assigned to the contact items. Perhaps you've added some new categories to further organize your data and want to assign them to existing items. Or, perhaps you made a mistake when you created an item or assigned categories to it, and now you need to make changes. Whatever the case, changing categories and category assignments is easy.

Changing Existing Categories

For one reason or another, you might need to change a category. For example, you might have misspelled the category when you created it, or you might want to change the wording a little. You can't edit an existing category, but you can remove the category and re-create it with modifications. For example, you might delete the category Foes and create a new one named Friends to replace it (assuming that your friends are not really foes).

Inside Out

View by Category to Change Categories

You'll find that one method works well when you want to make the same change to multiple items, such as changing the categories assigned to contacts. That method is to view the items organized by category. For example, assume you want to view all of the contacts that have the Foes category and add the Friends category. Choose View, Arrange By, Categories. Find the Foes group, open one contact in the group, and add the Friends category (simply change Foes to Friends). The item now appears under the Friends category group. Click on the category heading for Foes and drag it to the category heading for Friends. Outlook adds the Friends category to the contacts. You then have to remove the items in the Foes category one by one.

If you need to change a category globally rather than add one, see the section, "Changing Category Assignments of Multiple Items at One Time," page 112.

Before you start changing categories, however, it's important to understand the ramifications. Changing a category doesn't modify the category for items to which it has already been assigned. If you remove the Foes category from your Master Category List and replace it with Friends, any items previously assigned the Foes category still have that category assignment—Outlook won't automatically change them to the new category. However, Outlook also doesn't delete the category assignments of items with categories that are no longer in your Master Category List. Because the old categories remain associated with the item, you can still search based on the old category names. Therefore, when you change a category, you should search for all items using the old category and then change those items to assign the new category.

> **Note** Think of the Master Category List as a list that simplifies the assignment of categories by allowing you to pick preset categories from the list rather than entering them manually each time. The category text itself is associated with the item, so changes to the Master Category List don't affect the items to which categories have been assigned.

An earlier section, "Customizing Your Personal Master Category List" (page 107), explained how to create new categories. Because you can't edit a category but instead must replace it, changing a category is much like adding a new one.

Follow these steps to replace one category with another:

1. In Outlook, select any item and choose Edit, Categories.
2. Click Master Category List to display the Master Category List dialog box.
3. Enter the new category in the New Category box and click Add.
4. Scan through the category list to find the old category, select it, and click Delete.
5. Click OK to close the dialog box.

Resetting the Master Category List to Its Default Version

Assume that you've made substantial changes to your personal Master Category List, modifying or removing most of the original categories, and now you want to restore them. Resetting the Master Category List to its default version copies the default Master Category List to your personal list, causing all your custom categories to be removed. (Keep in mind that although this removes the categories from your personal Master Category List, it doesn't remove them from the items to which they are assigned.) You can then re-create the custom categories as needed in your personal Master Category List. Follow these steps to reset your personal Master Category List to the default copy:

1. In Outlook, choose Edit, Categories.
2. Click Master Category List.
3. Click Reset, and then click OK when prompted.
4. Click OK to close the Master Category List.

Changing Category Assignments

You can assign categories to an item at any time, adding and removing the ones you want.

To change the categories assigned to a specific item, follow these steps:

1. In Outlook, locate the item for which you want to change the category assignment.
2. Select the item and choose Edit, Categories; or right-click the item and choose Categories from the shortcut menu.
3. In the Categories dialog box, add and remove categories as needed and click OK.

Changing Category Assignments of Multiple Items at One Time

In some cases, you'll want to change the category assignments of several items at one time. For example, assume that you've replaced a misspelled category name with the correct spelling. After you change the category list, any items to which you had assigned the old category will still have the incorrect spelling. You'll probably want to search for all items with the old category and assign the new one to them.

To do so, follow these steps:

1. In Outlook, choose Tools, Advanced Find.
2. In the Look For drop-down list, select the type of Outlook item for which you want to search.
3. In the Advanced Find dialog box, click the More Choices tab.
4. Type the old category name in the box beside the Categories button, and click Find Now.
5. In the search results area, select all the items for which you want to change categories. (Use Shift+Click or Ctrl+Click to select them.) Then click Edit, Categories.
6. In the Item(s) Belong To These Categories list, highlight the portion of the category you want to change, retype it, and click OK. Outlook reassigns the categories accordingly.

Tip **Change a single category**
If an item is assigned multiple categories, Outlook doesn't make changes to any categories that don't appear in the Item(s) Belong To These Categories list. You can change a single category without changing others.

Organizing Data with Categories

Now that you've created your personal Master Category List and faithfully assigned categories to all your data in Outlook, how do you put those categories to work for you? The previous section, which explained how to search for items with given categories, is a good example of how you can use categories to organize and sort your data: by specifying the categories in question in the Advanced Find dialog box, you can compile a list of items to which those categories have been assigned.

You also can sort items by category. To do so, follow these steps:

1. Open the folder containing the items you want to sort. If the Categories field isn't displayed, right-click the column bar and choose Field Chooser.
2. Drag the Categories field to the column bar.
3. Right-click the Categories column and choose Group By This Field.

As an alternative to this method, you can use the predefined Categories view. With the folder open, choose View, Arrange By, Categories to display a tabular view sorted by categories.

Sharing a Personal Category List

If you work in a department, or if you share similar tasks and responsibilities with others, it's helpful to be able to share the same set of categories with those other users. Doing so helps to ensure that everyone is using the same categories, an important point when you're sharing items or receiving items from others that have categories assigned to them. For example, assume that your department is working on a handful of projects. Having everyone use the same project category names helps you organize your Outlook items and ensures that searches or sorts based on a given project display all items related to the project, including those you've received from others.

Exporting Your Personal Master Category List

As mentioned earlier, Outlook stores your personal Master Category List in the registry rather than as a file. This means you can't simply share a file to share your categories. Instead, you must use one of two methods to share your category list:

- You can export the registry key containing the categories and have all other users import that key into their registries.
- You can use an e-mail to copy categories. For details on this method, see "An Alternative to the Registry Solution," page 115.

The following steps outline the registry method, which copies the entire Master Category List:

1. Choose Start, Run. Type **regedit** in the Run dialog box, and then click OK.
2. Locate and select the key HKEY_CURRENT_USER\Software\Microsoft \Office\11.0\Outlook\Categories (see Figure 4-4).

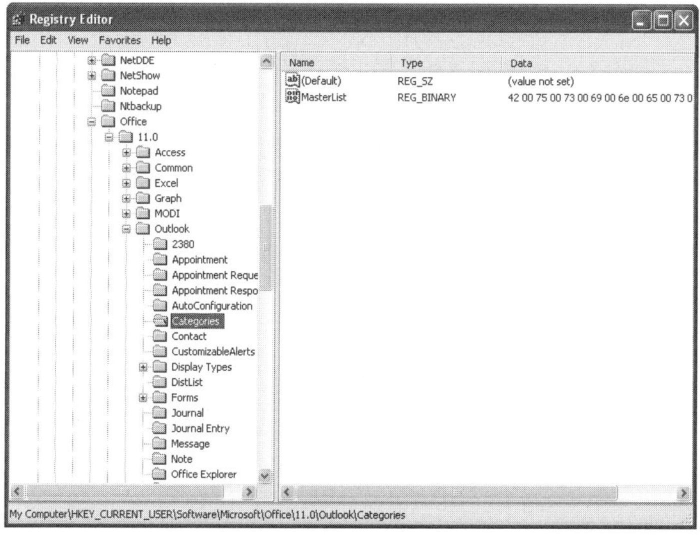

Figure 4-4. Copy the Master Category List from the Registry Editor.

3. Start the Registry Editor in the Run dialog box. Choose Registry, Export Registry File.
4. Specify a path and file name to save the file, verify that the Selected Branch option is selected, and click Save.

At this point you have a registry file that other users can use to import the Master Category List to their systems, as explained in the next section.

> **Caution** It's important to exercise care when working with the registry. Incorrect changes could cause problems ranging from minor data loss to application crashes or the inability to boot your computer.

Importing Categories

Exporting a registry key to a file creates a text file with a REG file extension. Others can then import the Categories key into their systems by double-clicking the registry file containing the Categories key or by using the import function in the Registry Editor. However, the specific process for importing the categories depends on the version of Outlook used to create the registry file and the version into which the file is being imported.

If you view the registry file in a text editor such as Notepad or WordPad, you'll find that the file contains the registry key where the categories should be stored. For Outlook 2003, this key is

HKEY_CURRENT_USER\Software\Microsoft\Office\11.0\Outlook\Categories

For earlier versions of Outlook, the key is slightly different, distinguished by the value that immediately follows the Office value. For example, Outlook 2000 uses the registry key HKEY_CURRENT_USER\Software\Microsoft\Office\9.0\Outlook\Categories to store category entries.

Before you import a registry key containing categories into your own system, verify the Outlook version you're using and the key into which the categories need to be imported. For example, if you're importing categories from an earlier version of Outlook into Outlook 2003, you need to modify the registry file to place the information in the 11.0 key. If you're copying categories from Outlook 2003 into an earlier version, you need to change 11.0 to the version being imported.

To make the change before you import, open the registry file in Notepad or WordPad. As you can see in Figure 4-5, the registry key is specified near the beginning of the file. Change the key name to reflect the appropriate destination key, save the file, and then import it into the target system. You can import the key by double-clicking it, or you can open the Registry Editor as explained previously and choose Registry, Import Registry File.

Figure 4-5. You can open a registry script in Notepad.

> **Caution** When you import the registry file, your existing categories are lost. See the following section for an alternative method if you want to retain your existing custom categories while also adding others from another user.

An Alternative to the Registry Solution

When you import a registry file, the existing categories in your Master Category List are replaced, not supplemented. This means you'll lose any custom categories you had added to your Master Category List before the import. To get around this problem, the person who originates the shared categories can create an e-mail message, assign all categories to the message, and then send it to others for import into their Master Category Lists.

To use this method of sharing categories, follow these steps:

1. On the source system for the categories, create a new mail message addressed to all users who need a copy of the categories.
2. In the message form, click Options and assign all custom categories (or only those to be shared) to the message.
3. Send the message.
4. On a receiving system, select the message and choose Edit, Categories; or right-click the message and choose Categories.
5. In the Categories dialog box, highlight all the categories in the Item(s) Belong To These Categories list and press Ctrl+C to copy them to the clipboard (see Figure 4-6).

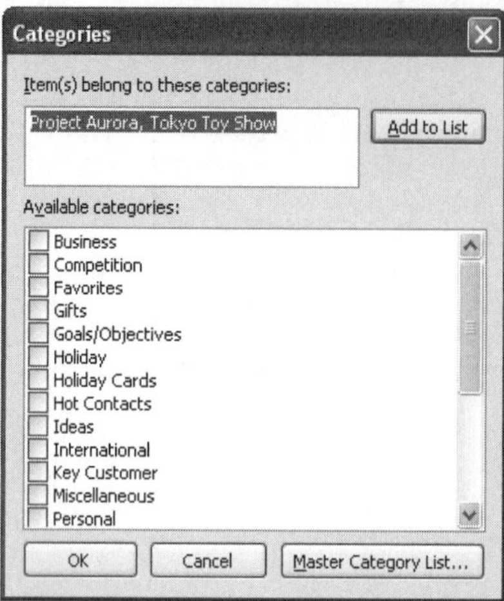

Figure 4-6. The selected categories are from a message being imported to the local Master Category List.

6 Click Master Category List, click in the New Category box, and press Ctrl+V to copy the categories to the box. Click Add to add them to the Master Category List.

> **Tip** To make sure everyone can import the categories successfully, include instructions in the body of the e-mail message explaining how to import the categories.

> **Note** As shown in Figure 4-6, Outlook identifies categories for the selected e-mail message that are not stored in the local Master Category List.

Using Entry Types

You can assign categories to all Outlook items to provide a means of sorting and organizing those items. The journal is no exception: each journal item can have multiple categories assigned to it. Journal items, however, can also be classified by *entry type*, which defines the purpose of the journal item. In many respects, entry types are like categories, because you can use them to sort and search for journal items.

When you create a journal item manually, Outlook assumes that you're creating a phone call journal entry and automatically selects Phone Call as the entry type. However, you can select a different entry type from the Entry Type drop-down list. Figure 4-7 shows the majority of the available entry types.

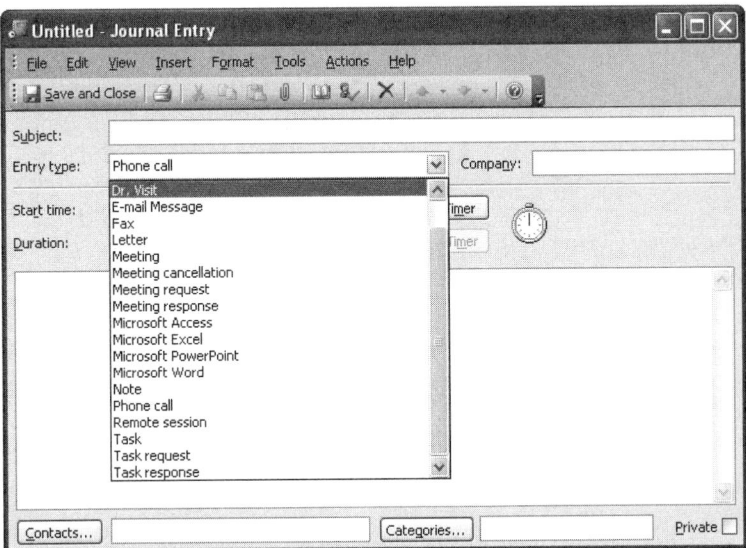

Figure 4-7. You can select entry types only from a predefined list.

Unlike categories, which you can create on the fly, journal entry types are limited to those types found in Outlook's predefined list. Although the default entry types cover a lot of bases, they don't offer much flexibility. For example, you might want to use the journal to track your activity in an application that isn't included on the list, or you might need to keep track of trips to the doctor, school programs, or other events. Although you don't have the ability to add entry types directly when you create a journal entry, you can modify the registry to add journal entry types.

Here's how:

1. Open the Registry Editor. (Choose Start, Run; type **regedit**; and click Open.)
2. Open the key HKEY_CURRENT_USER\Software\Microsoft\Shared Tools\Outlook\Journaling.
3. Right-click Journaling and choose New, Key.
4. Rename the key based on what the new entry type will be. For example, you might name it Dr. Visit.
5. Right-click the key you just created and choose New, String Value. Rename the string value Description.
6. Double-click the Description value just created, and set its value to the text you want to appear in the Entry Types drop-down list, such as Dr. Visit.
7. Close the Registry Editor.

After you have edited the registry to add the new entry type, it should appear on the journal entry form in the Entry Type drop-down list.

Part 2

Messaging

Chapter 5

Managing Address Books and Distribution Lists

An e-mail program isn't very useful without the ability to store addresses. Microsoft Outlook, like other e-mail–enabled applications, has this storage ability. In fact, Outlook offers multiple address books that can help make sending messages easy and efficient.

This chapter explores how Outlook stores addresses and explains how Outlook interacts with Microsoft Exchange Server (which has its own address lists) to provide addressing services. You'll learn how to store addresses in Outlook's Contacts folder and use them to address messages, meeting requests, appointments, and more. You'll also learn how to create distribution lists to broadcast messages and other items to groups of users and how to hide the details of the distribution list from recipients. The chapter concludes with a look at how you can share your address books with others.

Although this chapter discusses the Outlook Contacts folder in the context of address lists, it doesn't cover this folder in detail. For a detailed discussion of using and managing the Contacts folder, see Chapter 14, "Managing Your Contacts."

Understanding Address Books

As you begin working with addresses in Outlook, you'll find that you can store them in multiple locations. For example, if you're using an Exchange Server account, you have a couple of locations from which to select addresses. Understanding where these address books reside is an important first step in putting them to work for you. The following sections describe the various address books in Outlook and how you can use them.

Outlook Address Book

On all installations, including those with no e-mail accounts, Outlook creates a default Outlook Address Book (OAB). This address book consolidates all your Outlook contacts folders. With a new installation of Outlook, the OAB shows only one location for storing addresses: the default Contacts folder. As you add other contacts folders, those additional folders appear in the OAB, as shown in Figure 5-1. As you'll learn in "Removing Contacts Folders from the OAB," page 127, you can configure additional contacts folders so that they don't appear in the OAB.

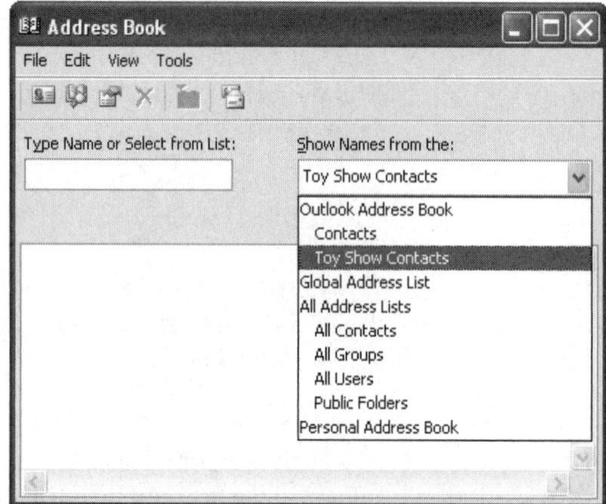

Figure 5-1. The OAB shows all contacts folders for your profile.

For detailed information on creating and using additional contacts folders, see "Creating Other Contacts Folders," page 390.

The OAB functions as a virtual address book rather than as a physical one because Outlook doesn't store the OAB as a file separate from your data store. Rather, the OAB provides a view into your contacts folders. When you add contact entries to the OAB, you're actually adding them to the Outlook Contacts folder. Because of this, you have all the same options for creating contact entries in the OAB as you do in the folder—the OAB and the Contacts folder are essentially one and the same.

Personal Address Book

You can add one Personal Address Book (PAB) to a profile and use the PAB to store additional contact information. Unlike the OAB, the PAB is a physical address book that Outlook stores on disk separate from your data store. The PAB uses a PAB file extension, and Outlook creates the file when you add the PAB to your profile.

To learn how to add a PAB to a profile, see "Adding a PAB," page 125.

The PAB doesn't function as a hook into your Contacts folder, so you don't have the same options for creating an entry in the PAB that you do in the Contacts folder. Figure 5-2 shows the New Internet Address Properties dialog box, which Outlook provides for creating new entries in the PAB. As you can see, you can't save the same amount of data for a contact in the PAB as you can in the Contacts folder.

For more information on creating contacts and their available options, see "Creating a Contact Entry," page 387.

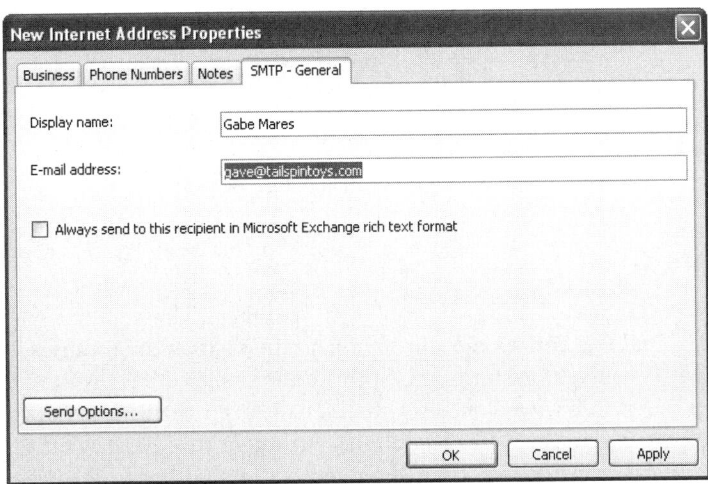

Figure 5-2. The form for creating a PAB entry doesn't include the same information as a form in the Contacts folder.

Even though the PAB doesn't store the same amount of information as an item in the Contacts folder, it's still a useful feature. You can use the PAB to store personal addresses or other contact information that you want to keep separate from your other Outlook data. Plus, you can use the PAB to share addresses with other users.

Global Address List

When you use a profile that contains an Exchange Server account, you'll find one other address list in addition to the OAB and PAB: the Global Address List (GAL). This address list resides on the Exchange Server and presents the list of mailboxes on the server as well as other address items created on the server, including distribution groups and external addresses (see Figure 5-3). You can't create address information in the GAL, as you can in the other types of address books, however; only the Exchange Server system administrator can do this.

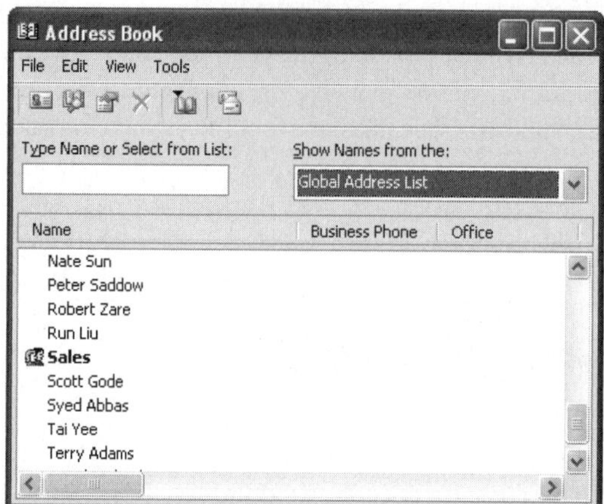

Figure 5-3. The GAL shows addresses on the Exchange Server.

Other Address Lists

In addition to the OAB, PAB, and GAL, you might see other address sources when you look for addresses in Outlook. For example, in an organization with a large address list, the Exchange Server system administrator might create additional address lists to filter the view to show only a selection, such as contacts with last names starting with the letter A or contacts external to the organization (see Figure 5-4). You might also see a list named All Address Lists. This list, which comes from Exchange Server, can be modified by the Exchange Server administrator to include additional address lists.

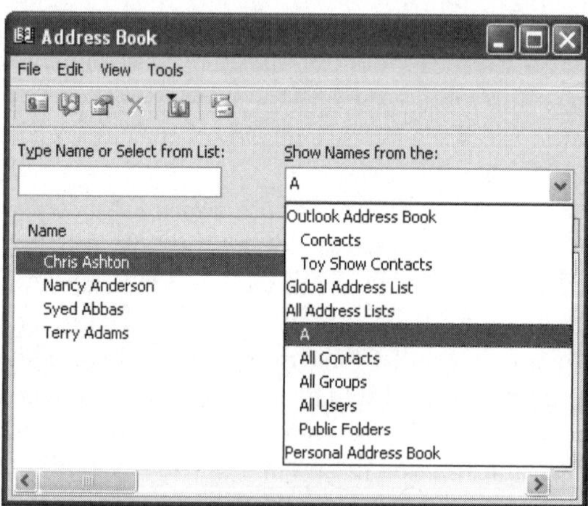

Figure 5-4. Additional address lists can display filtered lists of contacts.

Configuring Address Books and Addressing Options

Outlook offers a handful of settings you can use to configure the way your address books display contacts and address information. You also can add personal address books and choose which address book Outlook uses by default for opening and storing addresses and processing messages.

Adding a PAB

You might decide to add a PAB to store addresses outside your Contacts folder. For example, you might use the PAB to store personal addresses separately from work addresses. Follow these steps to add a PAB to your profile:

1. Close Outlook, right-click the Outlook icon on the desktop, and choose Properties. (Alternatively, you can use the Mail icon in Control Panel.)
2. Click E-Mail Accounts to start the E-Mail Accounts Wizard.
3. Select Add A New Directory Or Address Book and click Next.
4. Select Additional Address Books and click Next.
5. Select Personal Address Book and click Next.
6. Set properties for the new address book and click OK.
7. Click Close to close the Mail Setup dialog box.
8. Restart Outlook to use the new address book.

Setting Options for the OAB

You can set only one option for the OAB. This setting controls the order in which Outlook displays names from the OAB—either First Name Last Name or Last Name, First Name.

Follow these steps to set this display option:

1. If Outlook is open, choose Tools, E-Mail Accounts to start the E-Mail Accounts Wizard. If Outlook is not open, right-click the Outlook icon on the desktop, choose Properties, and then click E-Mail Accounts.
2. Select View Or Change Existing Directories Or Address Books and click Next.

3 Select Outlook Address Book and click Change to display the Microsoft Outlook Address Book dialog box, shown in Figure 5-5.

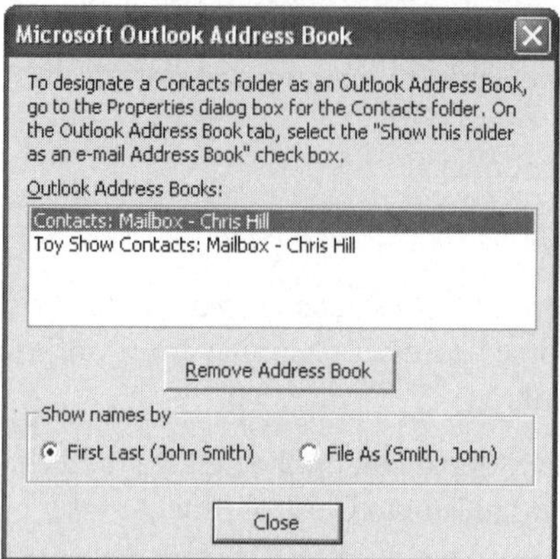

Figure 5-5. Select the format for OAB entries in the Microsoft Outlook Address Book dialog box.

4 In the Show Names By box, select the display format you prefer. Click Close, and then click Finish.

Setting Options for the PAB

For the PAB, you can select a format for displaying names, change the display name for the address book, specify a path to a different file, or include optional notes with the address book.

> **Tip** **Specifying a different path**
> When you need to place the PAB on a network share to make it available when you log on from other locations, and the file is not located in your Microsoft Windows profile folders, you might want to specify a path other than the default for the PAB. You might also change paths to select an existing PAB.

Follow these steps to configure the PAB:

1 If Outlook is open, choose Tools, E-Mail Accounts to start the E-Mail Accounts Wizard. If Outlook is not open, right-click the Outlook icon on the desktop, choose Properties, and then click E-Mail Accounts.

2 Select View Or Change Existing Directories Or Address Books and click Next.

3 Select Personal Address Book and click Change to display the Personal Address Book dialog box, shown in Figure 5-6.

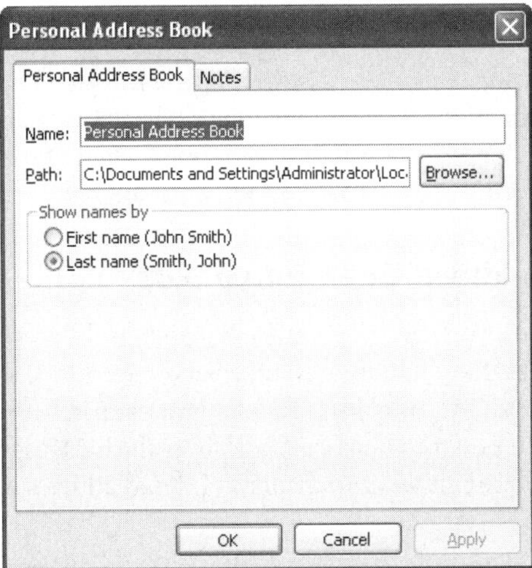

Figure 5-6. The Personal Address Book dialog box offers several configuration choices.

4. To change the name of the address book that appears in Outlook, type the name you want to use in the Name box on the Personal Address Book tab.
5. In the Path box, type a path name or click Browse to specify the path to the PAB file.
6. Choose one of the Show Names By options to specify how you want the names displayed in the PAB.
7. Click the Notes tab. Add optional notes here to be stored with the PAB. These notes are visible only in the Personal Address Book dialog box.

Removing Contacts Folders from the OAB

In most cases, you'll want all your contacts folders to appear in the OAB. If you have several contacts folders, however, you might prefer to limit how many folders appear in the OAB, or you might simply want to restrict the folders to ensure that specific addresses are used.

You can set the folder's properties to determine whether it appears in the OAB by following these steps:

1. Open Outlook and open the folders list. Then right-click the contacts folder in question and choose Properties.
2. Click the Outlook Address Book tab and clear the Show This Folder As An E-Mail Address Book option to prevent the folder from appearing in the OAB.
3. Change the folder name, if necessary, and then click OK.

Setting Other Addressing Options

You can configure other addressing options to determine which address book Outlook displays by default for selecting addresses, which address book is used by default for storing new addresses, and the order in which address books are processed when Outlook checks names for sending messages. The following sections explain these options in detail.

Selecting the Default Address Book for Lookup

To suit your needs or preferences, you can have Outlook display a different address list by default. For example, for profiles that include Exchange Server accounts, Outlook displays the GAL by default. If you use the GAL only infrequently and primarily use your contacts folders for addressing, you might prefer to have Outlook show the OAB as the default address list rather than the GAL. Or, you might want to display a filtered address list other than the GAL on the server.

Follow these steps to specify the default address list:

1 In Outlook, choose Tools, Address Book or click the Address Book icon on the toolbar. Outlook displays the Address Book dialog box (see Figure 5-7).

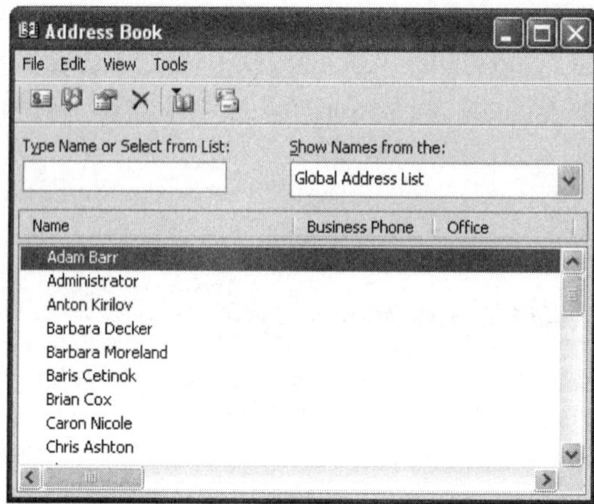

Figure 5-7. You can specify the default address list in the Address Book dialog box.

2 Choose Tools, Options.

3 In the Addressing dialog box, select the default address list from the Show This Address List First drop-down list.

4 Click OK.

Specifying the Default Address Book for New Entries

You can choose which address book you want to use for personal addresses. Although you can't store these addresses in the GAL or other server address books, you can store them in either your OAB or PAB. When you create a new address in the New Entry dialog box, Outlook suggests storing the entry in the address book you have chosen as the default. If you want to store a particular address in a different address book, you can do so by clicking the Put This Entry In The option and selecting the address book from the drop-down list (see Figure 5-8).

Note The OAB is the default location for storing personal addresses because the profile does not include a PAB unless you add one. Keep in mind, however, that you don't actually store addresses in the OAB itself. Rather, you store addresses in your Contacts folder, which appears as your OAB.

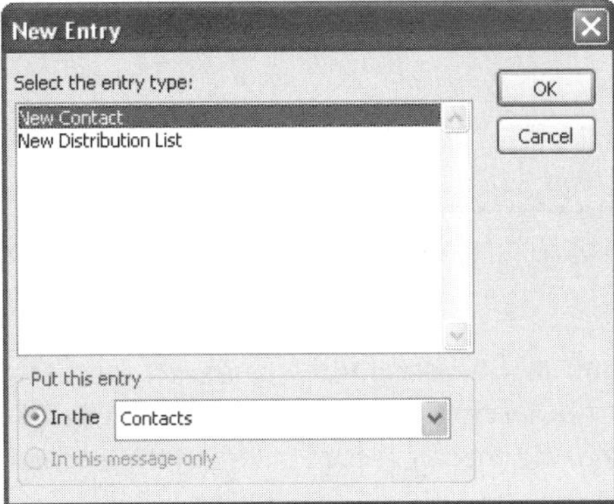

Figure 5-8. Use the New Entry dialog box to determine where to store addresses.

Follow these steps to specify the default location for storing new personal addresses:

1. Open the Address Book window and choose Tools, Options.
2. Select the default address location for personal addresses from the Keep Personal Address In drop-down list.
3. Click OK.

Specifying How Names Are Checked

When you create a message, you can specify the recipient's name rather than specifying the address. Rather than typing **jim@boyce.us**, for example, you might type **Jim Boyce** and let Outlook convert the name to an address for you. This saves you the time of opening the address book to look for the entry if you know the name under which it's stored.

When you click Send to process the message, Outlook checks the address books to determine the correct address based on the name you entered. Outlook checks names from multiple address books if they are defined in the current profile. For example, Outlook might process the address through the GAL first, then through your OAB, and then through the PAB (assuming that all three are in the profile). If Outlook finds a match, it replaces the name in the message with the appropriate address. If it doesn't find a match or finds more than one, it displays the Check Names dialog box, shown in Figure 5-9, where you can select the correct address, create a new one, or open the address book to display more names and then select an address.

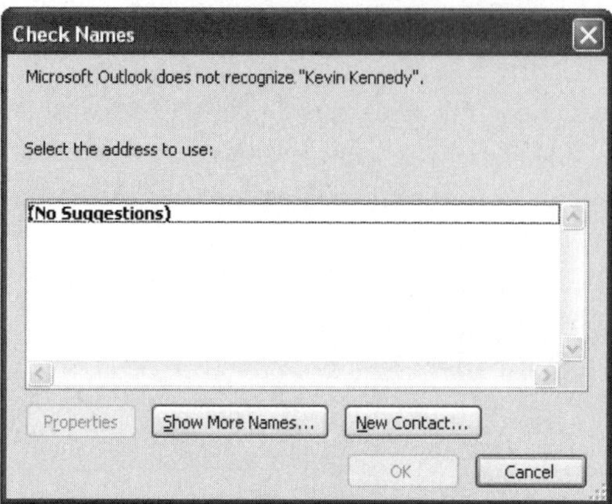

Figure 5-9. The Check Names dialog box helps you resolve address problems before you send a message.

Why change the order in which Outlook checks your address books? If most of your addresses are stored in an address book other than the one Outlook is currently checking first, changing the order can speed up name checking, particularly if the address book contains numerous entries.

Here's how to change the address book order:

1. In Outlook, open the Address Book window and choose Tools, Options.
2. Click the up and down arrow buttons that appear with the When Sending Mail list to rearrange the address book order in the list.
3. Click OK to close the dialog box.

Managing Contacts in the Personal Address Book

You can add entries for people and their corresponding addresses either in your contacts folders or in the PAB. You can add the address when you're creating a message, or you can work directly in the address book without opening or starting a message. This section of the chapter explains how to create address book entries in the PAB.

To learn how to create contact entries in your contacts folders, see "Creating a Contact Entry," page 387.

Creating Address Book Entries

To create an entry while you're composing a message, click To, Cc, or Bcc beside the corresponding box in the message form to display the Select Names dialog box (see Figure 5-10). Then click Advanced, New to display the New Entry dialog box. You can also open the New

Entry dialog box directly from the PAB. To do this, open the address book and click the New Entry button on the toolbar or choose File, New Entry.

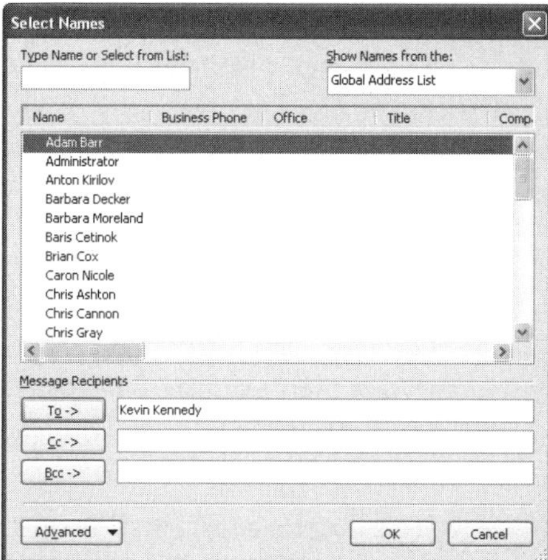

Figure 5-10. The Select Names dialog box leads you to the New Entry dialog box.

In the New Entry dialog box, select the type of address you want to create and click OK. The resulting dialog box depends on the type of address you selected. Figure 5-11 shows the dialog box for an Internet address.

> **Note** If you don't have the PAB set as the default location for new addresses, you won't be able to select an address type. You can change the default address location, create the entries, and then change the default location back if necessary.

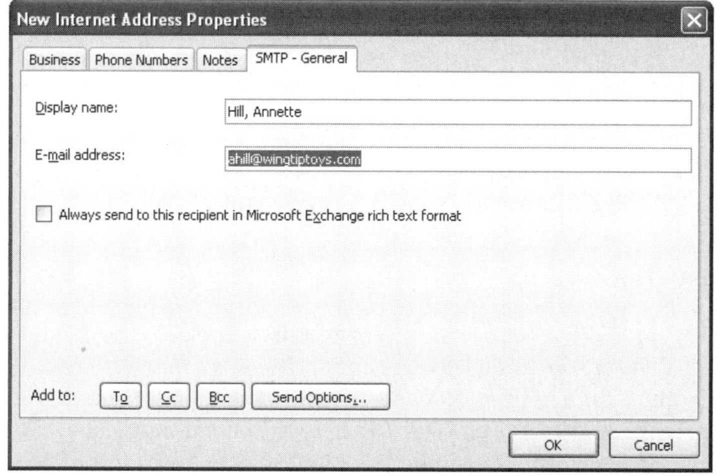

Figure 5-11. Use the New Internet Address Properties dialog box to enter information and set the format for a new Internet address.

Most of the address fields in Figure 5-11, such as name and phone number, are self-explanatory. After you enter the basic information, you can also set options for Internet address types that define how Outlook should send the message. On the SMTP-General tab, click Send Options to display the Send Options For This Recipient Properties dialog box shown in Figure 5-12. Select I Want To Specify The Format For Messages To This Recipient, and then set options from the following list:

- **MIME** Select this option to send the message using Multipurpose Internet Mail Extensions (MIME). This is the default option and should work for most recipients.
- **Plain Text** Select this option to always send the message body as plain text.
- **Include Both Plain Text And HTML** Select this option to send the message body as both plain text and HTML.
- **HMTL** Select this option to send the message body using only HTML.
- **Plain Text/UUEncode** Select this option to send the message using plain text and encoding for attachments rather than MIME.
- **BINHEX** Select this option to use BINHEX for Macintosh attachments.

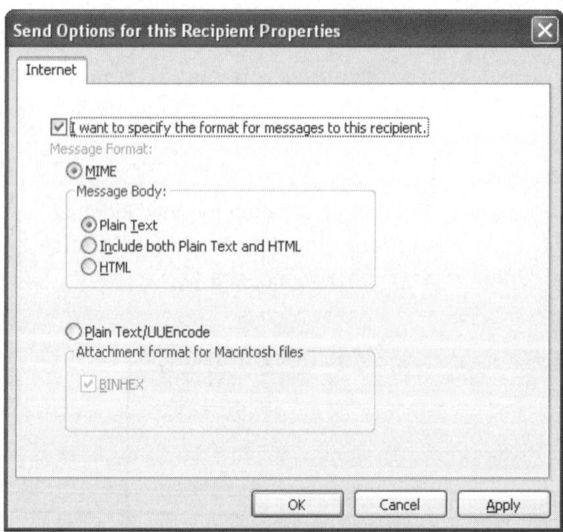

Figure 5-12. You can select sending options for Internet addresses.

Modifying Addresses

You can modify any addresses stored in your own address books, as well as in the address books of other users for which you have the appropriate access. You can modify an address while working with a form or while working directly in the address book. If you're using a message form, click To, Cc, or Bcc. Select the address you want to change and click Advanced, Properties. If you're working in the address book instead, select the address and click Properties on the toolbar. You can also choose File, Properties or right-click the address and choose Properties. Outlook displays the same form you used to create the contact. Make the changes you want and click OK.

Removing Addresses

Removing a contact from the PAB is much easier than creating one. Open the address book, select the address you want to delete, and click the Delete button on the toolbar or press the Delete key.

Finding People in the Address Book

If your address book contains numerous addresses, as might be the case in a very large organization, it can be a chore to locate an address if you don't use it often. Outlook provides a search capability in the address book to overcome that problem, making it relatively easy to locate addresses based on several criteria.

Follow these steps to locate an address in any address book:

1. Click the Address Book button on the toolbar to open the address book.
2. In the Show Names drop-down list, select the address book you want to search.
3. Click the Find Items button on the toolbar or choose Tools, Find to display the Find dialog box, shown in Figure 5-13 (for Exchange Server address lists) or Figure 5-14 (for the OAB and PAB).

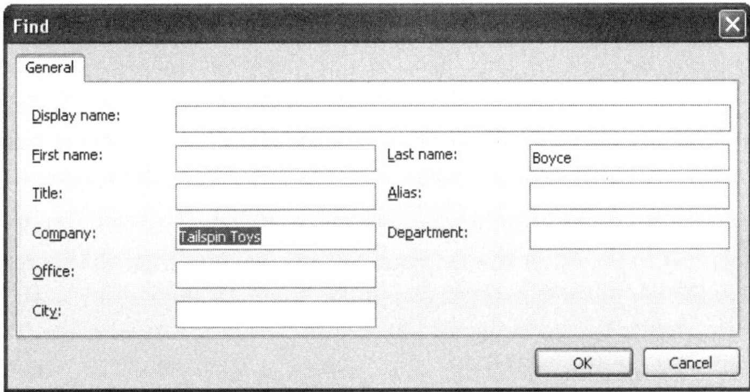

Figure 5-13. Use the Find dialog box to locate people in the address book.

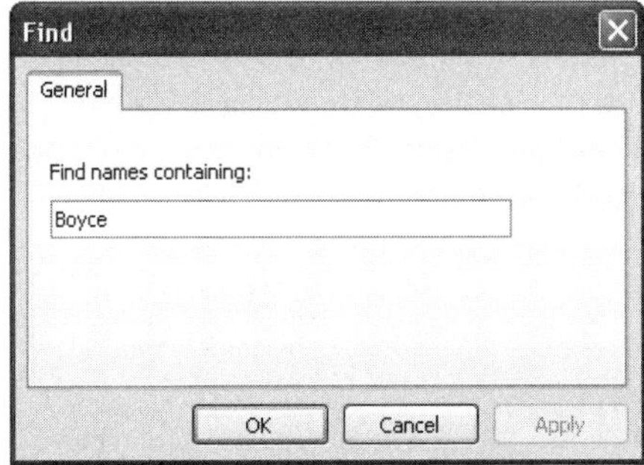

Figure 5-14. The Find dialog box offers only a single search field for OAB and PAB searches.

4 If you're searching an address list on the Exchange Server, decide what criteria you want to use and enter data in the fields to define the search. If you're searching an OAB or your PAB, specify the text to search for, which must be contained in the contact's name.

5 Click OK to perform the search.

When you click OK, Outlook performs a search in the selected address book based on your search criteria and displays the results in the Address Book window. You can revert to the full address book list by selecting the address book from the Show Names drop-down list. Select Search Results from the Show Names drop-down list to view the results of the last search.

Tip **Using a directory service**
In addition to searching your address books, you also can search a *directory service* for information about contacts. A directory service is a server that answers queries about data (typically contact information) stored on the server. For detailed information on setting up and using directory services in Outlook, see "Configuring a Directory Service Account in Outlook," page 453.

Using AutoComplete for Addresses

Outlook automatically keeps track of addresses that you enter in the address fields and stores them in an AutoComplete cache file in your profile folder. When you type an address in the To, Cc, or Bcc fields, Outlook adds the address to the cache. The cache file has the file name *profile*.nk2, where *profile* is your Outlook profile name. The default location for the file is the \Documents and Settings*user*\Application Data\Microsoft\Outlook folder.

When you begin typing in any of these address fields, Outlook begins matching the typed characters against the AutoComplete cache. If it finds a match, it automatically completes the address. If there is more than one match in the cache, Outlook displays a drop-down list that contains the names for all of the matching entries (see Figure 5-15). Use the arrow keys or mouse to select a name from the list and then press Enter or Tab to add the address to the field.

Note AutoComplete doesn't check to see if a particular contact has more than one e-mail address. Instead, it uses whatever address it finds in the cache. If Outlook has cached one address but you prefer that it cache a different one, delete the existing cache entry as explained in the next section. Then, address a new message to the contact using the desired e-mail address to cache that address.

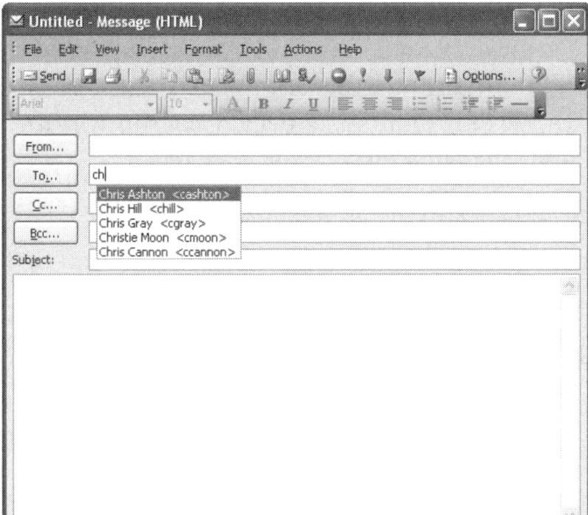

Figure 5-15. Select a name from the AutoComplete cache list offered by Outlook.

You can turn AutoComplete on or off to suit your needs by following these steps:

1. Choose Tools, Options, and click E-Mail Options on the Preferences tab.
2. Click Advanced E-Mail Options.
3. Select or deselect the Suggest Names While Completing To, Cc, And Bcc Fields option to turn AutoComplete on or off, respectively.

> **Tip** You can move your AutoComplete cache file from one computer to another. You can also back it up so you can restore it in the event your computer crashes. See "Backing Up Additional Outlook Data," page 799, for details.

Deleting a Name from the Cache

You don't have any control over which addresses Outlook stores in the AutoComplete cache. Outlook caches all entries, at least up to a point. The cache is limited to 1000 entries, and Outlook stops caching when it reaches that number.

You probably won't run up against the 1000-entry limit, but if you do, you can delete entries from the cache to make more room. There is another more common reason to delete a name from the cache—you either don't use it very often or you want to use a different e-mail address for that contact.

It's easy to delete a name from the cache using these steps:

1. Start a new e-mail message and type the first few letters of the name.
2. When Outlook displays the shortcut menu with the matching entries, select the one you want to delete and press Del on the keyboard.
3. Repeat this process for any other cached addresses you want to delete.

This method works fine if there is more than one entry with the same first few letters. However, you can't delete an entry if it's the only matching one because Outlook doesn't display the shortcut menu—it simply adds the address to the field. The trick in this situation is to add another entry that does match, causing Outlook to display the shortcut menu. This enables you to delete both entries by following these steps:

1. Start a new e-mail message and click in the To field.
2. Type another entry with the same first few letters as the one you want to delete (or a correct entry, if the other is incorrect).
3. Tab to the Cc field and type the first few characters. Outlook should display the shortcut menu, enabling you to select and delete the cached entry.

Deleting the Entire Cache

It's possible, although not common, for the AutoComplete cache to become corrupted, preventing if from working or causing it to offer incorrect addresses. If you experience this problem, close Outlook and locate the .NK2 file for your profile as explained at the beginning of this section. Rename or delete the file and restart Outlook to create a new AutoComplete cache file (Outlook creates the file automatically).

Using Distribution Lists

If you often send messages to groups of people, adding all their addresses to a message one at a time can be a real chore, particularly if you're sending the message to many recipients. As in other e-mail applications, *distribution lists* in Outlook help simplify the process, allowing you to send a message to a single address and have it broadcast to all recipients in the group. Rather than addressing a message to each individual user in the sales department, for example, you could address it to the sales distribution group. Outlook (or Exchange Server) takes care of sending the message to all the members of the group.

You can create distribution lists in either the OAB or your PAB. You also can use distribution lists that reside in the Exchange Server address lists, although you can't create distribution lists in the GAL or other Exchange Server address lists—only the Exchange Server system administrator can create the distribution lists on the server. However, you can modify distribution lists on the Exchange Server if you're designated as the owner of the list.

For a discussion of server-side distribution lists and how to create them, see "Creating Distribution Lists," page 911.

Creating Distribution Lists

Setting up a distribution list in your PAB or OAB is a relatively simple procedure. You can create a distribution list using addresses from multiple address books, which means, for example, that you might include addresses from the GAL on the Exchange Server as well as personal addresses stored in your Contacts folder and PAB. You can also include addresses of different types (for example, Exchange Server addresses, Internet addresses, and X.400 addresses). In general, it's easiest to set up a distribution list if all the addresses to be included already exist, but you can enter addresses on the fly if needed.

Follow these steps to create a distribution list:

1. Open the address book.
2. Click New Entry or choose File, New Entry.
3. In the drop-down list, select the address book in which you want to store the distribution list.
4. In the Select The Entry Type list, select Personal Distribution List or New Distribution List (the option that is displayed varies according to address book type), and then click OK.
5. If you are creating the distribution list in the PAB, Outlook displays the dialog box shown in Figure 5-16. If you are creating the distribution list in one of your contacts folders, you'll see a dialog box that is somewhat different, as shown in Figure 5-17.

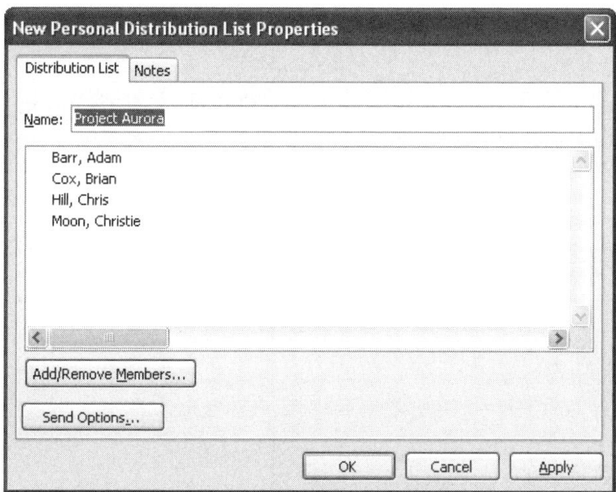

Figure 5-16. Use the Distribution List tab to set up a PAB distribution list.

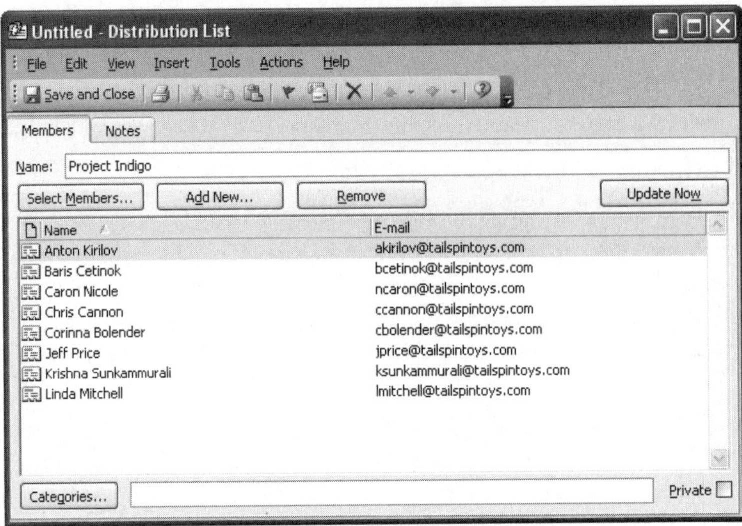

Figure 5-17. Use the Distribution List dialog box for a distribution list in the Contacts folder.

6 In the Name box, specify a name for the list. This is the distribution list name that will appear in your address book.

7 For a PAB distribution list, click Add/Remove Members. For an OAB list, click Select Members. Either action opens the Select Members dialog box (see Figure 5-18).

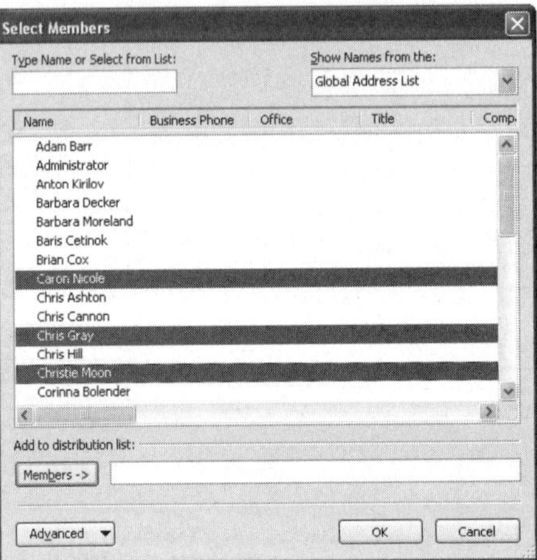

Figure 5-18. Add members to the distribution list using the Select Members dialog box.

8 Add members as needed, or click Add New in the Distribution List dialog box to enter new addresses if the addresses don't already exist in one of your address books. Click OK when you've finished adding members to the list.

9 Set other options as needed for the distribution list—for example, you can assign categories to the list.

10 For a PAB list, click OK on the Distribution List tab; for an OAB list, click Save And Close in the Distribution List dialog box.

> **Note** You can't assign categories to a personal distribution group created in the PAB. However, you can assign certain other per-recipient properties depending on the address type for PAB entries.

Distribution lists appear in the address book with a group icon and a boldface name to differentiate them from individual addresses (see Figure 5-19).

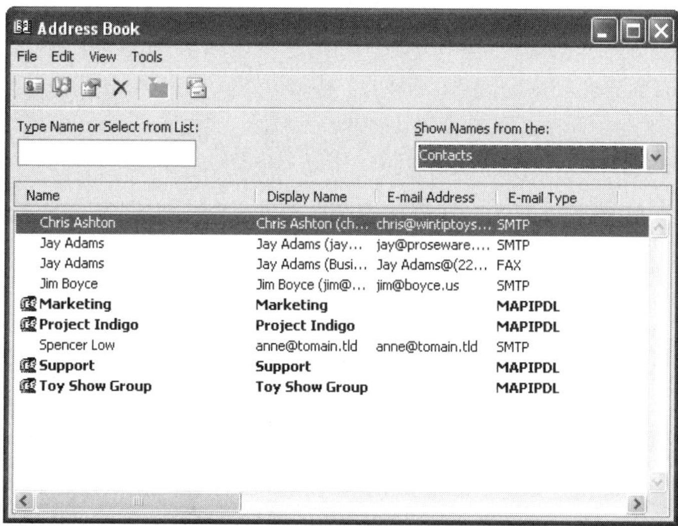

Figure 5-19. Outlook differentiates between addresses and distribution lists in the address book.

Inside Out

Hooray! Address types identified!

I'd like to take credit for this one, but I'm sure I wasn't the only one who suggested that the Outlook team differentiate addresses in the Select Names dialog box as well as the Address Book. Now when you address an e-mail message, you can tell which address is a fax number and which is an e-mail address. You can also easily differentiate personal addresses from work address in both the Select Names and Address Book dialog boxes.

Creating a Contacts Distribution List

You can use the procedure just described to create a distribution list in your Contacts folder using addresses from the Contacts folder, your PAB, or Exchange Server address lists. You also can create distribution lists within the Contacts folder rather than creating them through the address book.

To do so, open the Contacts folder, right-click any area of the folder other than a contact entry, and choose New Distribution List. Alternatively, with the Contacts folder open, click New, Distribution List on the toolbar or choose File, New, Distribution List. Any of these actions opens the Distribution List dialog box. Then continue by following the procedure described in the previous section.

Note In a contacts folder, distribution lists look just like addresses, although Outlook displays a distribution list in the address list with a group icon and with the distribution list name in bold. The distribution list also shows less information than a contact in Address Cards views.

Modifying a Distribution List

Your distribution lists will probably be dynamic rather than static, meaning you'll need to add or remove names on an ongoing basis. To modify the contents of a list, locate the distribution list in the address book or in your Contacts folder, open the list, and then use the Select Members button (for an OAB list) or the Add/Remove Members button (for a PAB list).

Renaming a Distribution List

You can change the name of a distribution list any time after you create it to reflect changes in the way you use the list, to correct spelling, or for any other reason. To rename a distribution list, locate the list in the address book, open it, and then change the name in the Name box. Close the distribution list to apply the change.

Deleting a Distribution List

You can delete a distribution list the same way you delete an address. Locate the distribution list in the address book or contacts folder, select it, and then click the Delete button on the toolbar or press Delete. Alternatively, you can right-click the list and choose Delete from its shortcut menu.

Note Deleting a distribution list doesn't delete the addresses associated with the list.

Hiding Addresses When Using a Distribution List

If you include a distribution list in the To or Cc field of a message, all the recipients of your message—whether members of the distribution list or not—can see the addresses of individuals in the list. Outlook doesn't retain the list name in the address field of the message but instead replaces it with the actual addresses from the list.

In some cases, the members of a distribution list might not want to have their addresses made public, even to other members of the list. In these situations, address the message using the Bcc field rather than the To or Cc field. To display the Bcc field in the message form, click the arrow beside Options on the toolbar and choose Bcc. Then enter in the Bcc field all addresses and distribution lists that should remain hidden.

Distribution Lists for Multiple Address Fields

Regardless of where you create a distribution list, you can't allocate some addresses in the list to the To field and other addresses to the Cc or Bcc fields. You can, however, place the distribution list address in either the Cc or Bcc fields, if needed. As I explained in the previous section, placing it in the Bcc field prevents recipients from seeing the addresses of others in the group.

If you often need to separate addresses from distribution lists into different address fields, you can use a couple of techniques to simplify the process. First, consider splitting the distribution list into two or three separate lists. This approach works well if the To, Cc, and Bcc fields generally receive the same addresses each time. A second approach is to create a custom form, by following these steps, with the address fields already filled in with the appropriate individual addresses:

1. Choose Tools, Forms, Design A Form.
2. Select the Message form and click Open.
3. If you need the Bcc field in the form, in the Field Chooser, select All Mail Fields from the drop-down list, then drag the Bcc field to the form. Resize and reposition controls as needed to allow it to fit.
4. Double-click the text field for each and add the addresses as needed.
5. Choose Tools, Forms, Publish Form, select a location available to the users, and click Publish.
6. Click Yes when prompted to save the form definition.

When you need to send a message using the form, choose Tools, Forms, Choose A Form, and select the form. Add any additional addresses, text, or attachments, and send the message as usual.

> **Tip** Setting up a form or multiple distribution lists like this makes it easier for users to send messages to multiple recipients, but perhaps more important, it helps ensure that the right recipients are listed in each field.

Granting Delegate Permission to a Distribution List

Many companies use a single common mailbox to send and receive messages for an entire department. For example, a sales department might use a common mailbox to send out sale notices. Outlook's send-on-behalf-of permission allows a user to send a message through another user's account. This send-on-behalf-of permission—also called *delegate permission*—is available only to Exchange Server users.

You can grant delegate permissions to users individually, but if you're delegating permissions for an entire group or department, it's more efficient to grant permissions using a distribution list. You can then control delegate access by adding or removing users from the distribution list.

Here's how to delegate access to a distribution list:

1. On a system running Microsoft Windows 2000 Server or Microsoft Windows Server 2003, open the Active Directory Users And Computers console and create the distribution list. Add users to the distribution list as needed.
2. Open Outlook and log on to the mailbox for which you need to grant delegate access.
3. Choose Tools, Options, and click the Delegates tab.
4. Click Add, select the distribution list, click Add, and then click OK.
5. The Delegate Permissions dialog box opens automatically. Configure permissions for the Inbox if you need to enable users in the list to view, create, or modify messages in the mailbox's Inbox. None of these permissions is needed to allow the list users to send outgoing messages.
6. Click OK.

Here's how users can send messages through the delegated mailbox:

1. Open Outlook and start a new message.
2. Choose View, From Field.
3. Click From, choose the delegated account, and click OK.
4. Compose and send the message.

Note If you're using Microsoft Exchange Server 5.5 and distribution list members receive an error message claiming that they don't have delegate permission for the mailbox, install Exchange Server 5.5 Service Pack 3 or later to fix the problem.

Using Distribution Lists on a Server

You can use distribution lists on Exchange Server—which are set up by the system administrator—the same way you use local distribution lists to simplify broadcasting messages to multiple recipients. (As mentioned earlier, you can't create distribution lists in the GAL or other Exchange Server address lists from Outlook, although you can modify such a list if you are designated as the list owner.)

You can use a server-side distribution list the same way you use a local distribution list. Select the list from the appropriate address list on the server. The list name is converted to addresses when you send the message, just as a local distribution list is.

Differences Between Exchange Server 5.5 and Exchange 2000 Server and Exchange Server 2003

Distribution lists in Microsoft Exchange 2000 Server and Microsoft Exchange Server 2003 are different from those in Exchange Server 5.5. Exchange Server 5.5 uses a dedicated directory structure and a distribution list object that is separate from security groups. Exchange 2000 Server and Exchange Server 2003 use Active Directory and automatically use security groups as distribution lists. With Windows 2000 Server and Windows Server 2003, you can also create distribution groups that function solely for the purpose of e-mail distribution (the equivalent of Exchange Server 5.5 distribution lists). Distribution groups in Windows 2000 Server and Windows Server 2003 cannot be used as security groups.

For more information on Exchange 2000 Server, refer to *Microsoft Exchange 2000 Server Administrator's Companion* (Microsoft Press, 2000).

Modifying a Server-Side Distribution List

If you are the designated manager of a distribution list on Exchange Server, you can modify (but not create) the list through Outlook. To make changes, first open the address book and double-click the list. You will see a dialog box similar to the Marketing Properties dialog box shown in Figure 5-20.

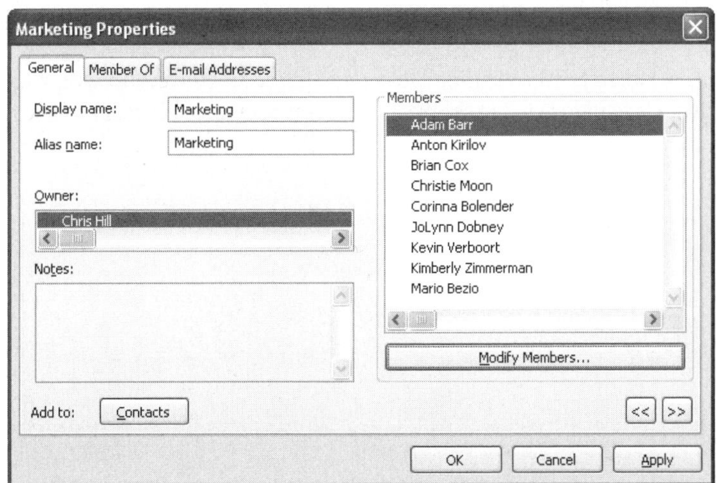

Figure 5-20. Modify a server-side distribution list using the General tab.

The three tabs of this dialog box allow you to view information about the selected list and its individual members:

- **General** This tab displays general read-only information about the list, such as display name, alias, and owner.
- **Member Of** This tab lists the other distribution groups of which the selected list is a member.
- **E-Mail Addresses** This tab shows the e-mail addresses for the selected distribution list in all its available formats (SMTP and X.400, for example).

To modify the distribution list, click Modify Members on the General tab of the dialog box. You can add and remove members in the resulting Distribution List Membership dialog box.

Tip Use the arrow buttons at the lower right corner of the dialog box's General tab to display the next and previous items in the address book.

Note In Exchange 2000 Server and Exchange Server 2003, you don't grant ownership of a distribution group as you do over other objects such as files or folders. Rather, the user or group designated as the manager for the distribution group is considered the owner for the purposes of allowing modifications. You specify the manager on the Managed By tab of the group's dialog box in the Active Directory Users And Computers console.

Adding a Server-Side Distribution List to Contacts

If you prefer working through your local address books rather than the server address lists, you might want to add a server-side distribution list to your local Contacts folder. You can easily do so through the address book or the list's dialog box. Open the address book, locate the distribution list, and choose File, Add To Contacts. If you have the list's dialog box open, click Contacts on the General tab. Outlook then adds the list to your Contacts folder.

Outlook displays a form for the list that you can use to modify the group, assign categories, or mark it as private (see Figure 5-21). Make any necessary changes and click Save And Close.

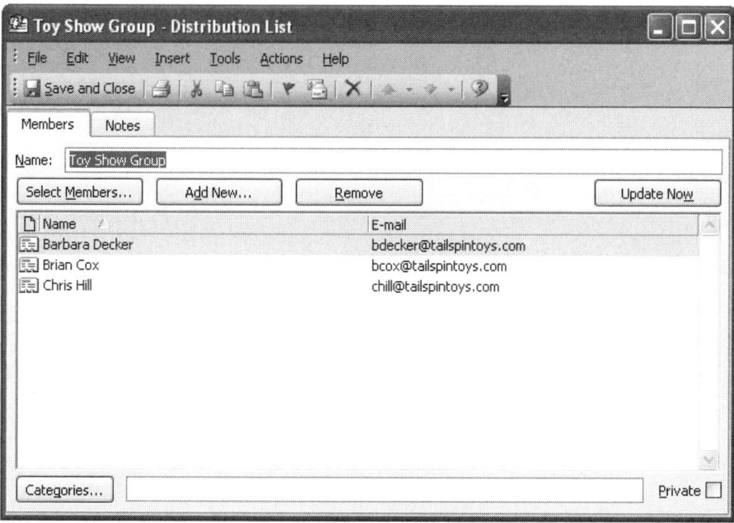

Figure 5-21. You can select various options for lists you store in the Contacts folder.

Automatically Adding Addresses to the Address Book

When you receive a message from a sender whose address you want to save in your local Contacts folder, you can add the address manually. Outlook also provides an easier method, however. With the message open, double-click the sender's address on the InfoBar. In the Properties dialog box, click Contacts. Outlook adds the address to your Contacts folder.

Chapter 6

Using Internet Mail

Not too many years ago, a person with an Internet e-mail address was the exception rather than the rule. Today, however, it seems as though everyone is using Internet e-mail. So it's a pretty good bet you'll want to use Microsoft Outlook to send and receive messages through at least one Internet e-mail account.

This chapter focuses on setting up Outlook to access Internet mail servers and accounts. The chapter also covers topics related to sending and receiving Internet e-mail. You'll learn how to create Internet e-mail accounts, use multiple accounts, and work with e-mail accounts for services such as Hotmail and CompuServe. You'll also learn how to ensure that your messages are available from different locations, what to do if your e-mail service won't accept outgoing mail from your dial-up location, and how to view full message headers in Internet e-mail.

Note This chapter assumes your system is already set up to connect to the Internet, either on a broadband connection such as local area network (LAN), Digital Subscriber Line (DSL), cable modem, or by a dial-up connection. Whatever the situation, your Internet service provider (ISP) or network administrator has likely set up the connection for you. This chapter instead focuses on configuring Outlook to use the existing connection and setting up specific types of accounts.

For help in creating e-mail accounts and assigning the dial-up connection, see "Configuring Accounts and Services," page 38.

Using Internet POP3 E-Mail Accounts

Most Internet-based e-mail servers use Simple Mail Transfer Protocol (SMTP) and Post Office Protocol 3 (POP3) to allow subscribers to send and receive messages across the Internet. (A few exceptions, such as CompuServe 2000, use IMAP; still other services, such as Hotmail and Yahoo!, use HTTP. These other protocols are covered in subsequent sections of this chapter.) If you have an account with a local ISP or other service provider that offers POP3 accounts, or if your office server is a non–Microsoft Exchange Server system that supports only POP3, you can add an Internet e-mail account to Outlook to access that server.

Tip **Configure multiple accounts in one profile**
You can configure multiple Internet e-mail accounts in a single Outlook profile, giving you access to multiple servers to send and receive messages. For additional information, see "Using Multiple Accounts," page 160.

Follow these steps to add an Internet e-mail account to Outlook:

1. In the Outlook 2003 Startup Wizard (which starts automatically the first time you start Outlook), navigate to the Server Type page. To reach this page if your profile already includes a mail account, start the Mail applet in the Control Panel, and then click E-Mail Accounts. Choose Add A New E-Mail Account and click Next. You also can choose Tools, E-Mail Accounts in Outlook to add an e-mail account.
2. Select POP3 and click Next.
3. On the Internet E-Mail Settings (POP3) page (see Figure 6-1), specify the following information:

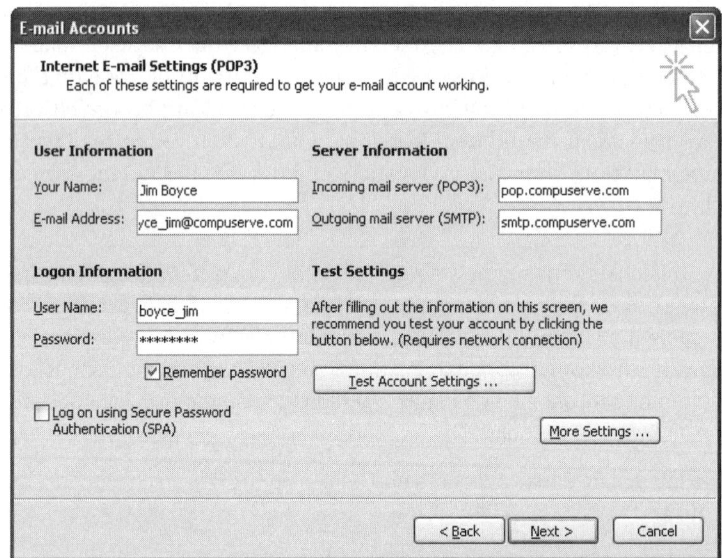

Figure 6-1. Use the Internet E-Mail Settings (POP3) page to configure the account settings.

- **Your Name** Specify your name as you want it to appear in the From box of messages that others receive from you.

- **E-Mail Address** Specify the e-mail address for your account in the form *<account>@<domain>*—for example, *Jim@wingtiptoys.com*.
- **Incoming Mail Server (POP3)** Specify the IP address or Domain Name System (DNS) name of the mail server that processes your incoming mail. This is the server where your POP3 mailbox is located and from which your incoming mail is downloaded. Often, your mail server will use the host name *mail* and your mail server's domain name. So, an example of a mail server DNS name might be mail.wingtiptoys.com. However, this isn't a given, so check with your ISP or network administrator for the correct mail server host name.
- **Outgoing Mail Server (SMTP)** Specify the IP address or DNS name of the mail server that you use to send outgoing mail. In many cases, this is the same server as the one specified for incoming mail; but it can be different if your account requires it. Some organizations separate incoming and outgoing mail services onto different servers for load balancing, security, or other reasons.

Note Many servers don't support outgoing mail unless you connect to the server's network. To learn how to overcome that problem, see "My Mail Server Won't Accept Outgoing Messages," page 163.

- **User Name** Specify the user account on the server that you must use to log on to your mailbox to retrieve your messages. Do not include the domain portion of your e-mail address. For example, if your address is *jimb@wingtiptoys.com*, your user name is jimb.
- **Password** Specify the password for the user account entered in the User Name box.
- **Remember Password** Select this option to have Outlook maintain the password for this account in your local password cache, eliminating the need for you to enter the password each time you want to retrieve your mail. Clear this check box to prevent other users from downloading your mail while you are away from your computer. If the check box is cleared, Outlook prompts you for the password for each session.
- **Log On Using Secure Password Authentication (SPA)** Select this option if your server uses SPA to authenticate your access to the server.

4 Click More Settings to display the Internet E-Mail Settings dialog box, shown in Figure 6-2. You can configure these settings based on the information in the following sections.

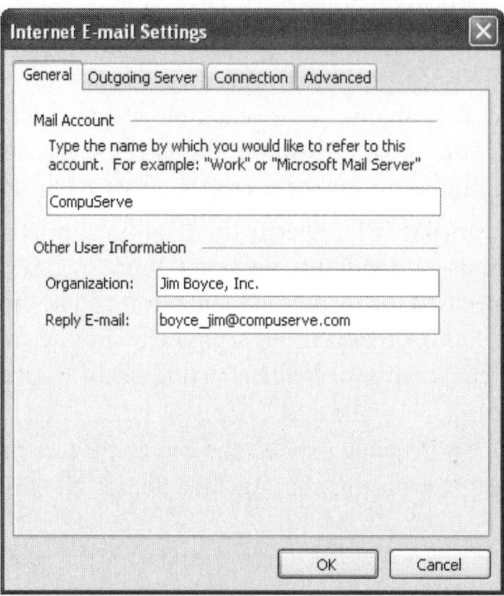

Figure 6-2. Use the Internet E-Mail Settings dialog box to configure additional Internet account settings.

Configuring General Settings for Internet Accounts

Use the General tab of the Internet E-Mail Settings dialog box (see Figure 6-2) to change the account name that is displayed in Outlook and to specify organization and reply address information:

- **Mail Account** Specify the name of the account as you want it to appear in Outlook's account list. This name has no bearing on the server name or your account name. Use the name to differentiate one account from another—for example, you might have various accounts named CompuServe, Work, and Personal.
- **Organization** Specify the group or organization name you want to associate with the account.
- **Reply E-Mail** Specify an e-mail address that you want others to use when replying to messages that you send with this account. For example, you might redirect replies to another mail server if you are in the process of changing ISPs or mail servers. Enter the address in its full form—*jenny@tailspintoys.com*, for example. Leave this option blank if you want users to reply to the e-mail address you specified in the E-Mail Address box for the account.

Configuring Outgoing Server Settings for Internet Accounts

Use the Outgoing Server tab (see Figure 6-3) to configure a handful of settings for the SMTP server that handles the account's outgoing messages. Although in most cases you won't need to modify these settings, you will have to do so if your server requires you to authenticate to send outgoing messages. Some ISPs use authentication as a means of allowing mail relay from their clients outside their local subnets. This allows authorized users to relay mail and prevents unauthorized relay, or unauthorized users from sending spam through the server.

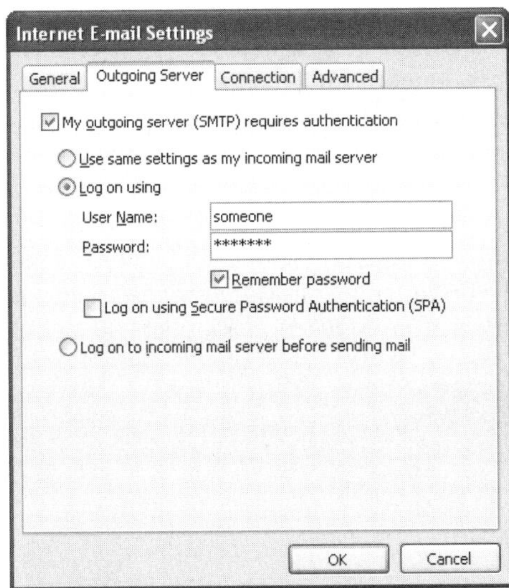

Figure 6-3. Use the Outgoing Server tab to configure authentication and other options for your SMTP server.

The Outgoing Server tab contains the following options:

- **My Outgoing Server (SMTP) Requires Authentication** Select this option if the SMTP mail server that processes your outgoing mail requires your client session to authenticate. Connections that don't provide valid credentials are rejected. Selecting this option makes several other options on the tab available.
- **Use Same Settings As My Incoming Mail Server** Select this option if the SMTP server credentials are the same as your POP3 (incoming) server credentials.
- **Log On Using** Select this option if the SMTP server requires a different set of credentials from those required by your POP3 server. You should specify a valid account name on the SMTP server in the User Name box as well as a password for that account. In general, you should have to change this setting only if your SMTP and POP3 servers are separate physical servers.
- **Remember Password** Select this check box to have Outlook save your password from session to session. Clear it if you want Outlook to prompt you for a password each time.

- **Log On Using Secure Password Authentication (SPA)** Select this check box if your server uses SPA to authenticate your access to the server.
- **Log On To Incoming Mail Server Before Sending Mail** Select this option to have Outlook log on to the POP3 server before sending outgoing messages. Use this option if the outgoing and incoming mail servers are the same server and if the server is configured to require authentication to send messages.

Configuring Connection Settings for Internet Accounts

Use the Connection tab (see Figure 6-4) to specify how Outlook should connect to the mail server for this Internet account. You can connect using the LAN (which includes DSL and cable modem broadband connections), a dial-up connection, or a third-party dialer such as the one included with Microsoft Internet Explorer. Select the LAN option if your computer is hard-wired to the Internet (LAN, DSL, cable modem, or other persistent connection) or if you use a shared dial-up connection to access the Internet. Select the Connect Via Modem When Outlook Is Offline check box if you want Outlook to attempt a LAN connection first, followed by a dial-up connection if the first attempt fails (for example, when your notebook PC is disconnected from the LAN but a dial-up connection is available).

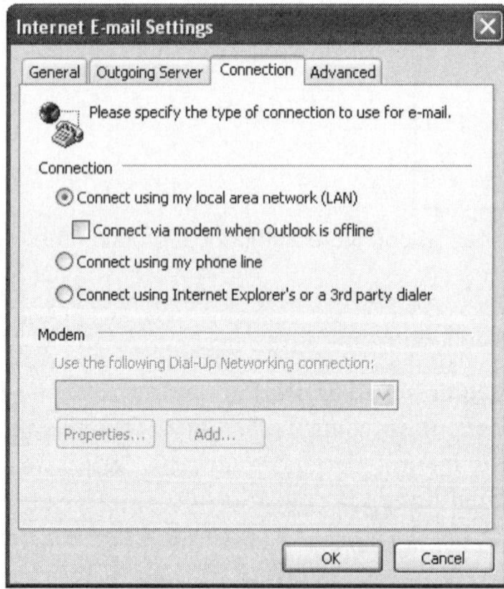

Figure 6-4. Use the Connection tab to specify how Outlook should connect to the server.

Select the Connect Using My Phone Line option to use an existing dial-up networking connection or create a new dial-up connection. Select the connection from the drop-down list, and then click Properties if you need to modify the dial-up connection. Click Add if you need to add a dial-up connection.

If you want to connect to the Internet or to your remote network using the dialer that is included with Internet Explorer or a dialer that is included with a third-party dial-up client, select the Connect Using Internet Explorer's Or A 3rd Party Dialer option.

Configuring Advanced Settings for Internet Accounts

Although you won't normally need to configure settings on the Advanced tab (see Figure 6-5) for an Internet account, the settings can be useful in some situations. You can use the options on this tab to specify the SMTP and POP3 ports for the server, along with timeouts and these other settings:

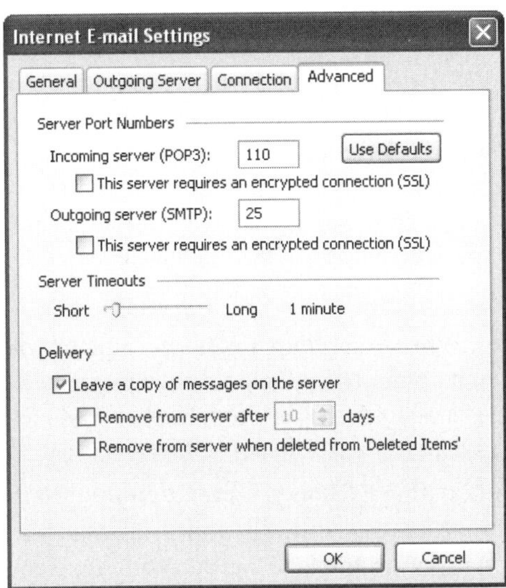

Figure 6-5. Use the Advanced tab to specify nonstandard TCP ports for the server.

- **Incoming Server (POP3)** Specify the TCP port used by the POP3 server. The default port is 110. Specifying a nonstandard port works only if the server is listening for POP3 traffic on the specified port.
- **Outgoing Server (SMTP)** Specify the TCP port used by the SMTP server for outgoing mail. The default port is 25. Specifying a nonstandard port works only if the server is listening for SMTP traffic on the specified port.
- **Use Defaults** Click this to restore the default port settings for POP3 and SMTP.
- **This Server Requires An Encrypted Connection (SSL)** Select this check box if the server requires the use of a Secure Sockets Layer (SSL) connection. With rare exceptions, public POP3 and SMTP mail servers do not require SSL connections.
- **Server Timeouts** Use this control to change the period of time Outlook will wait for a connection to the server.
- **Leave A Copy Of Messages On The Server** Select this check box to retain a copy of all messages on the server, downloading a copy of the message to Outlook. This is a useful feature if you want to access the same POP3 account from different computers and want to be able to access your messages from each one. Clear this check box if you want Outlook to download your messages and then delete them from the server. Some servers impose a storage limit, making it impractical to leave all your messages on the server.

- **Remove From Server After *n* Days** Select this check box to have Outlook delete messages from the server a specified number of days after they are downloaded to your system.
- **Remove From Server When Deleted From 'Deleted Items'** Select this option to have Outlook delete messages from the server when you delete their downloaded copies from your local Deleted Items folder.

Controlling Where Outlook Stores POP3 Messages

When you create a POP3 account, Outlook needs to know where to store your mail folders. By default, Outlook stores your POP3 mail folders in whatever location is currently specified as the default delivery location for new mail. For example, if you already have an Exchange Server account with the Exchange Server mailbox designated as the location for e-mail delivery, Outlook uses the same mailbox location for POP3 mail. Where Outlook stores the folders also depends on the other services, if any, you're using with Outlook. The following list summarizes the possibilities:

- **POP3 only or as a first account** When you set up a POP3 account as your only Outlook e-mail account or as your first account, Outlook creates a personal folders (PST) file in which to store your POP3 e-mail folders. Outlook uses the same PST file to store your other Outlook data, such as contacts and calendar information.
- **POP3 added to a profile with an existing Exchange Server account** In this scenario, Outlook uses the e-mail delivery location specified for your Exchange Server account as the location to deliver POP3 mail. For example, if you currently store your Exchange Server data in your Exchange Server mailbox on the server, your POP3 messages will be placed in your Exchange Server mailbox. In effect, this means your POP3 messages are downloaded to your computer from your Internet mail account and then uploaded to your Exchange Server mailbox. If you specify a local folder for Exchange Server instead, Outlook places your POP3 messages in that same local folder.
- **POP3 added after an IMAP account** IMAP accounts are stored only in PST files, and Outlook automatically creates a PST file for the IMAP account. (The file is created when you first open Outlook using the profile that contains the IMAP account.) Outlook also creates a PST file for storing your other Outlook data, keeping your IMAP data and other Outlook data separate. Outlook designates the PST file as the default location for new mail, even though messages from your IMAP account are delivered to your IMAP PST file. If you later create a POP3 account, Outlook uses the same PST file for your POP3 account by default. This means your IMAP folders and mail are kept separate from your POP3 and Exchange Server mail. You can change the settings afterward if you want to designate a different file for storing your POP3 messages, but doing so also changes the location of your Contacts folder, Calendar folder, and other Outlook folders.

Using IMAP Accounts

IMAP is becoming more common on Internet-based e-mail servers because it offers several advantages over POP3. Outlook's support for IMAP means that you can use Outlook to send and receive messages through IMAP servers as well as through Exchange Server, POP3, and the other mail server types that Outlook supports.

For more information on IMAP and its differences from POP3, see "IMAP," page 17.

Configuring an IMAP account is a lot like configuring a POP3 account. The only real difference is that you select IMAP as the account type rather than POP3 when you add the account. You can refer to the previous section on creating POP3 accounts for a description of the procedure to follow when adding an IMAP account. The one setting you might want to review or change for an IMAP account as opposed to a POP3 account is the root folder path. This setting is located on the Advanced tab of the account's Properties dialog box. Open this dialog box, click More Settings, and click Advanced. Specify the path to the specific folder in your mailbox folder structure that you want to use as the root for your mailbox. If you aren't sure what path to enter, leave this option blank to use the default path provided by the account.

Controlling Where Outlook Stores IMAP Messages

When you create an IMAP account in an Outlook profile, Outlook doesn't prompt you to specify the storage location for the IMAP folders. Instead, Outlook automatically creates a PST file in which to store the messages. The folder branch for the account appears in Outlook with the name of the IMAP account as the branch name (see Figure 6-6). Each IMAP account in a profile uses a different PST file, so all your IMAP accounts are separate from one another and each appears under its own branch in the folders list.

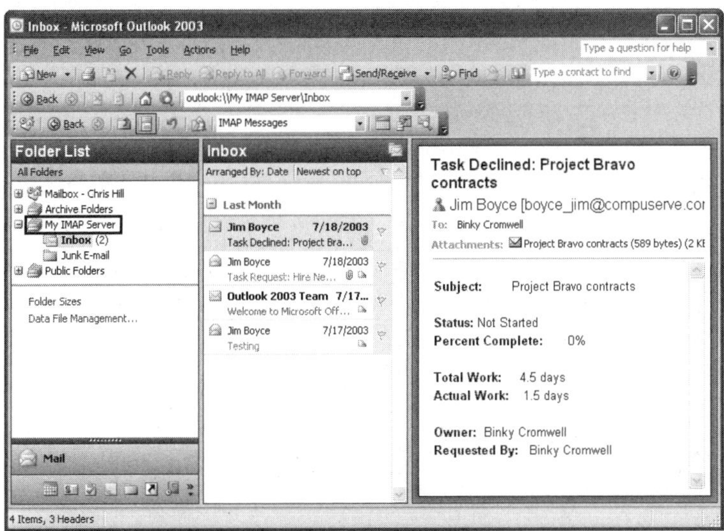

Figure 6-6. An IMAP account uses its own PST file and appears as a separate folder branch.

How accounts are treated depends on the types of accounts you add to the profile. The following list summarizes the possibilities:

- **IMAP as the first or only account in the profile** Outlook automatically creates a PST file to contain the IMAP folder set and a second PST file (which, for clarity, I'll call a *global PST file*) to contain your other Outlook data such as contacts and calendar information.
- **Multiple IMAP accounts in the profile** Each IMAP account uses a separate PST file created by Outlook. Outlook also adds a separate global PST file to contain your other Outlook data.
- **IMAP first, followed by non-IMAP accounts** The non-IMAP accounts default to storing their data in the global PST that is created when you add the IMAP account. The global PST is defined as the location where new mail is delivered. You can change the location after you set up the accounts, if you prefer. For example, if you add an Exchange Server account, you'll probably want to change the profile's properties to deliver mail to your Exchange Server mailbox instead of to the global PST file. IMAP mail is unaffected by the setting and is still delivered to the IMAP account's PST file.
- **Non-IMAP accounts followed by IMAP accounts** The existing accounts maintain their default store location as defined by the settings in the profile. Added IMAP accounts each receive their own PST.

Using Outlook with CompuServe

You can use Outlook to send and receive CompuServe mail through either Classic CompuServe or CompuServe 2000 accounts. The following sections explain the differences between the two and how to configure Outlook to accommodate them.

Configuring Outlook for Classic CompuServe Accounts

Classic CompuServe accounts use e-mail addresses that end in @compuserve.com or @csi.com. Classic CompuServe accounts function as POP3 accounts, so configuring them in Outlook is much the same as configuring other POP3 accounts. However, you need to understand that the logon password you use for your POP3 account is not necessarily the same as the password you use to connect to CompuServe. Your connection password is associated with your user ID, which takes the form *nnnnn,nnnn*—for example, 76516,3403. Your POP3 password is associated with your CompuServe POP3 account name, which is the first part of your CompuServe address (without the domain). In the address *boyce_jim@csi.com*, for example, boyce_jim is the user name. Although you can set the two passwords to be the same, they do not have to match.

Before you can begin managing your CompuServe Classic e-mail account through Outlook, you must set your POP3 password. You can do this only by connecting to CompuServe through the CompuServe software. Click Go, enter **POPMAIL** as the destination, and press Enter to access the POPMAIL area, where you can set your POP3 password.

For details on configuring POP3 accounts, see "Using Internet POP3 E-Mail Accounts," page 147.

After you set the password, create a POP3 account in Outlook using the settings described in the following list:

- **Your Name** Specify your name as you want it to appear in the From box of messages you send.
- **E-Mail Address** Enter your CompuServe e-mail address in the form <*user*>@compuserve.com or <*user*>@csi.com, where <*user*> is your user account number in dotted format or your POP3 alias. The compuserve.com and csi.com domains are synonymous—you should be able to use either one.
- **Incoming Mail Server** Enter **pop.compuserve.com** as the incoming mail server.
- **Outgoing Mail Server** Enter **smtp.compuserve.com** as the outgoing mail server if you dial a CompuServe access number, or specify the SMTP server name for your local ISP account or for a server on your network that allows mail relay from your computer. The smtp.compuserve.com server does not support mail relay from outside the CompuServe network to reduce spamming.
- **User Name** Specify your CompuServe account.
- **Password** Specify the password for your CompuServe account.
- **Log On Using Secure Password Authentication (SPA)** Do not select this option (leave it cleared).

Configure the remaining settings as you would for any other POP3 account.

Note If you use CompuServe only for e-mail, you might not have the CompuServe software installed on your system. You can't use CompuServe 2000 software to configure your POP3 e-mail password because CompuServe Classic and CompuServe 2000 are separate services. You can download the necessary software from *ftp.csi.com/software/windows/cs402/without_ie/cs495bn.exe*. The download is nearly 18 MB, however, so be prepared for a long download if you connect through dial-up.

Configuring Outlook for CompuServe 2000 Accounts

CompuServe 2000 accounts use addresses that end in @cs.com and use IMAP rather than POP3. Configure an Outlook account for CompuServe 2000 by using the following settings in the E-Mail Accounts Wizard when you create the account:

- **Your Name** Specify your name as you want it to appear in the From box of messages you send.
- **E-Mail Address** Enter your CompuServe e-mail address in the form <*user*>@cs.com, where <*user*> is your user account screen name.
- **Incoming Mail Server** Enter **imap.cs.com** as the incoming mail server.

- **Outgoing Mail Server** Enter **smtp.cs.com** as the outgoing mail server if you dial a CompuServe access number, or specify the SMTP server name for your local ISP account or for a server on your network that allows mail relay from your computer. The smtp.compuserve.com server does not support mail relay from outside the CompuServe network to reduce spamming.
- **User Name** Specify your CompuServe account.
- **Password** Specify the password for your CompuServe account.

Configure the remaining settings as you would for any other IMAP account.

Using Hotmail and Other HTTP-Based Services

Because Outlook supports the HTTP protocol, you can access your HTTP-based mail services (such as Hotmail) through Outlook rather than using a Web browser to send and receive messages. Using Outlook gives you the ability to compose and reply to messages offline, potentially saving you connect charges if you use metered Internet access. HTTP-based mail support also gives you the advantages of Outlook's composition, filtering, and other features you might not otherwise have when managing your mail with a Web browser.

The following section explains how to set up an account in Outlook to process your Hotmail account. You can use the same information for almost any HTTP-based account, changing the settings as needed to point to the appropriate URL for the server. Although the following assumes that you're setting up the account for Hotmail, it also provides additional information on configuring other HTTP-based accounts.

Using Outlook with Hotmail Accounts

Because Hotmail is a service owned and operated by Microsoft, it's no surprise that Outlook includes built-in support for sending and receiving messages through Hotmail.

Follow these steps to configure a Hotmail account in Outlook:

1. In the Outlook 2003 Startup Wizard, navigate to the Server Type page. To reach this page, if your profile already includes a mail account, open the Mail applet in the Control Panel, and then click E-Mail Accounts. Choose Add A New E-Mail Account and click Next.

If you want to use multiple profiles and want to learn how to configure settings and accounts for a specific profile, see "Understanding User Profiles," page 42.

2. Select HTTP and click Next.
3. On the Internet E-Mail Settings (HTTP) page, specify the following information:
   - **Your Name** Specify your name as you want it to appear in the From box of messages that others receive from you.
   - **E-Mail Address** Specify the e-mail address for your account in the form *<account>*@*<domain>*—for example, *someone@domain.tld*. For a Hotmail

account, specify <*account*>@hotmail.com, where <*account*> is your Hotmail account name.

- **User Name** Specify the user account on the server that you must use to log on to your mailbox to retrieve your messages. For a Hotmail account, specify your e-mail address, including the @hotmail.com part of the address, such as *jimboyce999@hotmail.com*.
- **Password** Specify the password for the user account entered in the User Name box.
- **Log On Using Secure Password Authentication (SPA)** Select this option if your HTTP-based e-mail server uses SPA to authenticate your access to the server. Hotmail does not use SPA, so you can leave this option cleared for Hotmail accounts.
- **HTTP Mail Service Provider** Select Hotmail from this drop-down list if you're setting up a Hotmail account, or choose Other if you're configuring Outlook for a different HTTP-based mail service. If you choose Hotmail, Outlook fills in the Server URL option with the appropriate URL for accessing Hotmail through Outlook.
- **Server URL** If you are setting up an account for an HTTP-based service other than Hotmail, specify the URL for the server's Web page that provides access to your mail account. This is not necessarily the same URL you would use when accessing your account by using a browser.

4 Click More Settings to access the settings shown in Figure 6-7 and described in the following sections.

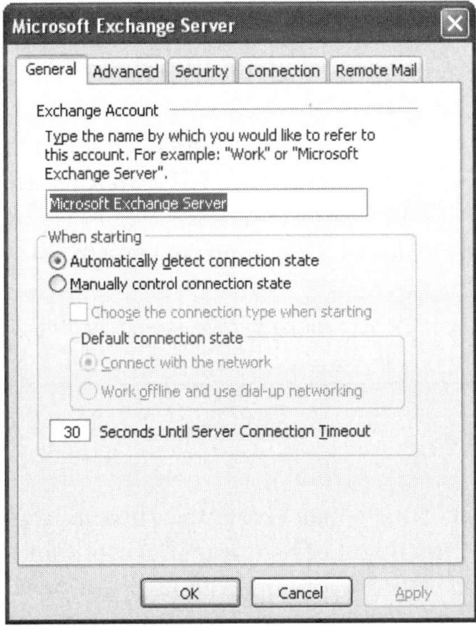

Figure 6-7. Use the General tab to configure more settings for the HTTP account.

Chapter 6

For more information on configuring properties for HTTP-based accounts, see "Using Internet POP3 E-Mail Accounts," page 147. Most of the settings for HTTP and POP3 are the same.

Understanding Where Outlook Stores HTTP Messages

Outlook stores mail messages for Hotmail and other HTTP e-mail accounts locally, just as it does for POP3. When you add a Hotmail or other HTTP account to a profile, Outlook creates a PST specifically for that account, regardless of whether the profile already includes other accounts. Outlook delivers new messages to that PST, even if the default delivery location is elsewhere. For example, assume that you create a profile with an Exchange Server account as the default delivery location for new mail. You add a POP3 account, and your mail is delivered to your Exchange Server mailbox. You then add a Hotmail account and an IMAP account. Each of these last two accounts gets its own PST file, and Outlook delivers new messages for each account to its respective PST file.

Using Outlook with Prodigy

The Prodigy e-mail service functions as a standard POP3 server. You therefore can use Outlook to send and receive e-mail through your Prodigy account. Configure the account for pop.prodigy.net as the incoming mail server and smtp.prodigy.net as the outgoing mail server. Specify your Prodigy account and password for authentication, add a PST if you don't want to use the default delivery location (such as an Exchange Server mailbox), and configure other settings as you would for any other POP3 account.

Using Outlook with MSN

Although MSN mail accounts are available through the Hotmail Web site, you must configure Outlook with a different URL (not the Hotmail URL) to retrieve your MSN mail. Start the E-Mail Accounts Wizard and select HTTP as the account type. When the wizard prompts you for the account information, select MSN from the HTTP Mail Service Provider drop-down list, and specify your MSN account name and password in the Logon Information section of the dialog box. Outlook creates a PST in which to store the messages.

For additional information on configuring HTTP account properties, see "Using Outlook with Hotmail Accounts," page 158.

Using Multiple Accounts

Although many people still have only one e-mail account, it's becoming much more common to have several. For example, you might have an e-mail account for work, a personal POP3 account with your ISP, and a Hotmail account. Although versions of Outlook before Outlook 2002 sometimes made it difficult to use multiple accounts, Outlook 2003 accommodates multiple accounts with ease, all in the same profile, which means that you don't need to switch profiles as you use different accounts.

Setting up for multiple accounts is easy—just add the accounts, as needed, to your profile. However, working with multiple accounts in a single profile requires a few considerations, as explained here.

Sending Messages Using a Specific Account

When you send a message, Outlook uses the account specified as the default (see Figure 6-8). This can sometimes be a problem when you have multiple accounts in your profile. For example, you might want to send a personal message through your personal POP3 account, but if your Exchange Server account is designated as the default, your personal message will go through your office mail server. This might violate company policies or expose your personal messages to review by a system administrator. Additionally, the reply address comes from the account Outlook uses to send the message, which means replies will come back to that account. You might want to check your POP3 mail from home, for example, but you find that replies have been directed to your office account because the original messages were sent under that account.

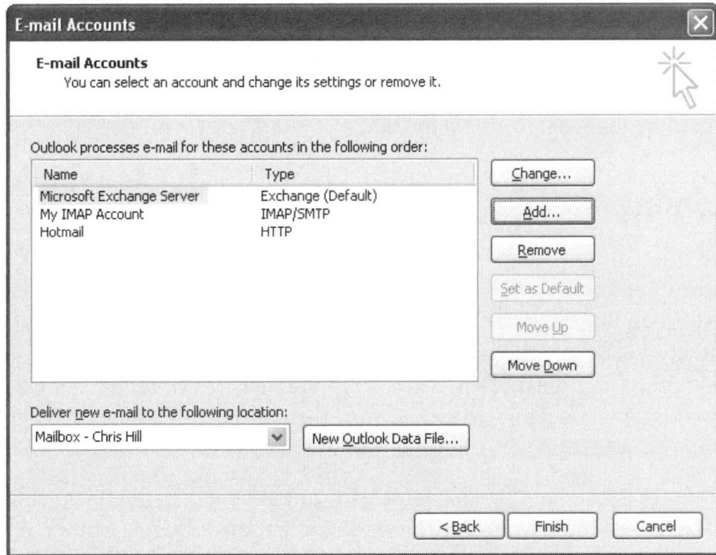

Figure 6-8. Outlook uses one of your e-mail accounts as the default account for outgoing messages.

Sending messages with a specific account is simple in Outlook. When you compose the message, click the down arrow beside Accounts on the message form toolbar (see Figure 6-9), and select the account you want Outlook to use to send the current message. Outlook then uses the reply address and other settings for the selected account for that message.

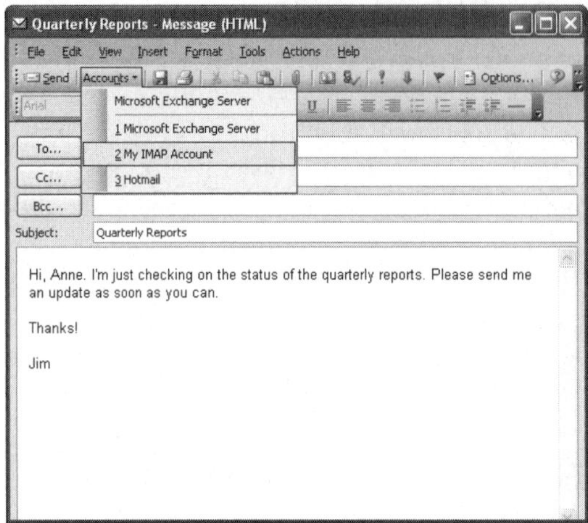

Figure 6-9. Select the account from which you want to send the message using the Accounts button on the message form toolbar.

Separating Incoming Messages by Account

With the exception of mail for IMAP and HTTP accounts, Outlook delivers all mail to the default message store. (Outlook delivers IMAP and HTTP mail to the store associated with the respective accounts.) This can be a problem or an annoyance because all your e-mail could potentially wind up in the same Inbox, regardless of which account it came through. If you manage multiple accounts, it's useful to keep the messages separate. For example, you might want to keep personal messages that come through your POP3 account separate from those that come to your Exchange Server account.

You can separate messages into specific folders or stores using message rules, which allow you to specify actions Outlook should take for messages that meet specific criteria, including the account to which they were delivered. For a complete discussion of rules and automatic message processing, see "Processing Messages Automatically," page 224.

Tip **Keep messages separate on a shared computer**

If you share a computer with other users, you probably want to keep your messages separate from those of the other users. Although you could use the same logon account and create separate profiles or even use the same profile and set up message rules to separate the incoming messages, neither method is a very good solution. Instead, use different logon accounts on the computer, which keeps your Outlook profiles separate and therefore keeps your messages separate.

Keeping a Copy of Your Mail on the Server

If you want to be able to retrieve your mail from different computers, you might want to keep a copy of your messages on the mail server. This makes all messages available no matter where you are or which computer you use to retrieve them. For example, if your computer at the office is configured to retrieve messages from your POP3 account every hour and you don't leave a copy of the messages on the server, you'll be able to see only the last hour's worth of messages if you connect from a different computer.

IMAP stores messages on the server by default. POP3 accounts, however, work differently. By default, Outlook retrieves the messages from the POP3 server and deletes them from the server. If you want the messages to remain on the server, you need to configure Outlook specifically to do so.

Here's how:

1. If Outlook is open, choose Tools, E-Mail Accounts. Alternatively, open the Mail applet in the Control Panel, and then click E-Mail Accounts.
2. Select View Or Change Existing E-Mail Accounts and click Next.
3. Select the POP3 account and click Change.
4. Click More Settings and then click the Advanced tab.
5. Select Leave A Copy Of Messages On The Server, and then use the two associated options if you want Outlook to remove the messages after a specific time or after they have been deleted from your local Deleted Items folder.
6. Click OK, click Next, and then click Finish.

Troubleshooting

My mail server won't accept outgoing messages

Your mail service might not accept mail relay (outgoing messages) unless you connect to the server's network. For example, POP3 Classic CompuServe accounts do not support mail relay from other servers. You must dial up a CompuServe point-of-presence to place your computer on CompuServe's network and establish a connection to CompuServe's outgoing mail server.

Connecting through the server's network isn't always practical, however. For example, if you live in a rural area, you might not have a local access number for your service. In this situation, you might use a local ISP account to connect to the Internet to retrieve your messages from other mail servers. Your ISP then invariably allows mail relay from your subnet, which lets you send messages through your own account on the ISP's mail server.

To make this work, simply specify your ISP's outgoing mail server instead of the mail server for the remote network; or, if you connect through your LAN and your organization provides a mail server with relay capability, specify that server for outgoing mail.

You specify the outgoing mail server through the e-mail account's dialog box by following these steps:

1. If Outlook is open, choose Tools, E-Mail Accounts. Alternatively, right-click the Outlook icon on the Start menu and choose Properties, and then click E-Mail Accounts.
2. Select View Or Change Existing E-Mail Accounts and click Next.
3. Select the POP3 account and click Change.
4. Specify the server in the Outgoing Mail Server (SMTP) box and click Next. Then click Finish.

Another option is to use the SMTP service included with Microsoft Windows 2000 and Microsoft Windows XP to send outgoing mail. See the following section for details.

Tip **Synchronization With IMAP**
Accessing a POP account from more than one computer can cause some real synchronization headaches. Rather than configuring the POP server to leave messages on the server so you can access them from other computers, switch to using IMAP instead of POP3 if the server supports IMAP. The messages remain on the server by default, eliminating the need for you to worry about synchronization at all.

Set Your Own Computer as the Outgoing Mail Server

In some situations, such as the one described in the previous section, you won't have access to an outgoing mail server for a particular account. Most ISPs, large or small, prevent users from sending mail through their server unless the users are connected to the ISP's network. Dialing in to the ISP provides this connection.

In situations when it isn't practical for you to send outgoing mail through another e-mail server, you can often use your own computer to send the mail. Outlook isn't capable of this, but the SMTP service included with Windows 2000 and Windows XP Professional is designed for just that purpose. (The SMTP service is not included with Windows XP Home Edition.)

Note Some mail servers do not accept mail from unrecognized servers, so in some instances you might have problems using your own computer to send mail to certain domains. Even so, the SMTP service can be a very handy tool that handles the majority of your outgoing mail. However, if your computer is connected to a network, check with your network administrator before installing the SMTP service as explained in this section. Adding the service entails some risk, which I identify later in this section.

First, check to see if the SMTP service is already installed on your computer. The SMTP service requires Microsoft Internet Information Services (IIS), so you need to add IIS, as well:

1. Open Control Panel and launch Add Or Remove Programs.
2. Click Add/Remove Windows Components.
3. Scroll down and select Internet Information Services, then click Details.
4. Select the SMTP service and click OK.
5. Click Next and follow the prompts to complete the IIS/SMTP installation.
6. After IIS is installed, open the Internet Information Services console from the Administrative Tools folder, right-click the Default Web Site, and choose Properties.
7. Click the Directory Security tab, click Edit in the Anonymous Access and Authentication Control group, clear the Anonymous Access option, and then click OK. Click OK again to close the properties for the Web site.
8. Right-click the SMTP virtual server and choose Properties, then click the Access tab. Click Authentication, clear the Anonymous Access option, select the Integrated Windows Authentication option, and click OK.
9. Click Relay, click Only The List Below, click Allow All Computers Which Successfully Authenticate to Relay, Regardless of the List Above, and click OK. Click OK to close the properties for the SMTP server.
10. In Outlook, open the Properties dialog box for the account for which you need to specify the outgoing mail server and enter **localhost** (if you are using the SMTP service on a different computer on your network, enter that IP address instead).
11. Click More Settings to open the Internet E-mail Settings dialog box, then click the Outgoing Server tab. Select the option My Outgoing Server (SMTP) Requires Authentication, select the Log On Using option, and enter valid credentials (such as your own local logon account) in the User Name and Password fields, and click OK. Click Next, then Finish to complete the changes to the account settings.

> **Note** If other users on the network will be using the SMTP service on your computer to send outgoing mail, or you are sending through the SMTP service on another computer, select the Log On Using Secure Password Authentication (SPA) option on the Outgoing Server tab in the Outlook account settings.

In step 7, you disabled anonymous access to the Default Web Site, which will help prevent infections by Web-borne viruses and worms. In steps 8 and 9, you restricted access to the SMTP service to only those clients who authenticate on the server, which should prevent spam relay through your computer.

Viewing Full Message Headers

Internet messages include routing information in their headers that specifies the sending address and server, the route the message took to get to you, and other data. In most cases, the header offers more information than you need, particularly if all you're interested in is the body of the message. However, if you're trying to troubleshoot a mail problem or identify a sender who is spamming you, the headers can be useful.

> **Tip** **Track down spammers**
> You can't always assume that the information in a message header is accurate. Spammers often spoof or impersonate another user or server—or relay mail through another server—to hide the true origin of the message. The header helps you identify where the mail came from so you can inform the server's administrator that the server is being used to relay spam. To notify the administrator, you can send a message to *postmaster@<domain>* where *<domain>* is the relaying mail server's domain, such as *postmaster@wingtiptoys.com*. Most ISPs also recognize an abuse mailbox, such as *abuse@compuserve.com*.

To view the full message header, right-click the message and choose Options to display the Message Options dialog box, shown in Figure 6-10. The message header appears in the Internet Headers box. You can highlight the text and press Ctrl+C to copy the text to the clipboard for inclusion in a note or other message.

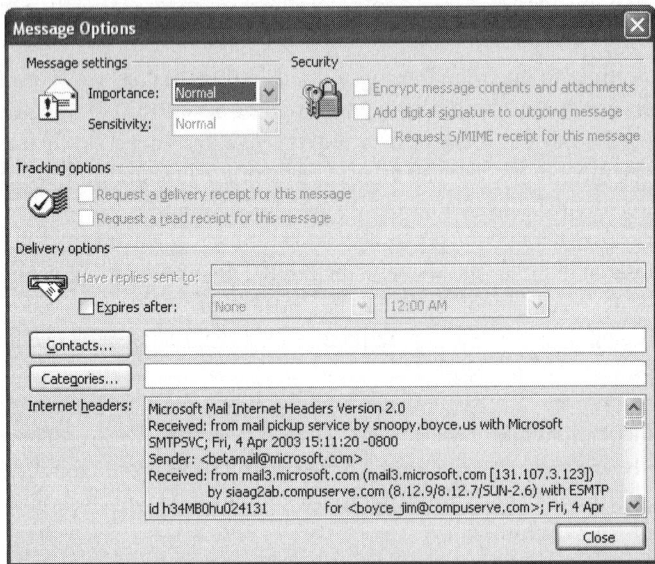

Figure 6-10. View the full message header in the Message Options dialog box.

> **Tip** You can take several steps to reduce the amount of unsolicited e-mail you receive. See Chapter 8, "Filtering, Organizing, and Using Automatic Responses," for details on blocking spam and filtering messages.

Chapter 7

Sending and Receiving Messages

Of all the features in Microsoft Outlook, messaging is probably the most frequently used. Even if you use Outlook primarily for contact management or scheduling, chances are good that you also rely heavily on Outlook's e-mail and other messaging capabilities. Because many of Outlook's key features make extensive use of messaging for workgroup collaboration and scheduling, understanding messaging is critical to using the program effectively.

This chapter provides an in-depth look at a wide range of topics related to sending and receiving messages with Outlook. You'll learn the fundamentals—working with message forms, addressing, replying, and forwarding—but you'll also explore other more advanced topics. For example, this chapter explains how to control when your messages are sent, how to save a copy of sent messages in specific folders, and how to work with attachments.

You'll discover how to add more than just plain text to your messages by working with graphics, hyperlinks, files, attachments, and electronic business cards. As this chapter explains, you can also spruce up your messages by using stationery, which allows you to assign a theme to your messages. Outlook provides a choice of stationery, or you can create your own. You'll also learn how to automatically attach a text signature or an electronic business card to each message you send.

Working with Messages

This section of the chapter offers a primer to bring you up to speed on Outlook's basic messaging capabilities. It focuses on topics that relate to all types of e-mail accounts. The Inbox is the place to start learning about Outlook, so launch the program and open the Inbox folder. The next section explains how to work with message forms.

> **Note** If you haven't added e-mail accounts to your profile, see the appropriate chapter for details. Chapter 6, "Using Internet Mail," explains how to configure POP3, IMAP, and HTTP accounts; Chapter 34, "Configuring the Exchange Server Client," explains how to configure the Microsoft Exchange Server client.

Opening a Standard Message Form

You can begin a new message in Outlook using any one of these methods:

- Choose File, New, Mail Message.
- With the Inbox open, click New on the message form toolbar.
- Click the down arrow beside the New button on the message form toolbar and choose Mail Message.
- With the Inbox open, press Ctrl+N.

Outlook uses Microsoft Word as the default e-mail editor. When you begin a new message, Word starts and displays the Untitled Message form shown in Figure 7-1. If you've chosen Outlook as your default message editor instead of Word, Outlook displays the message form shown in Figure 7-2.

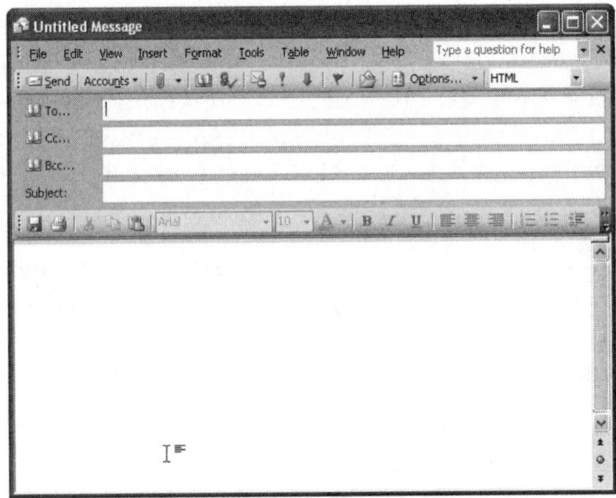

Figure 7-1. You use this standard message form when Word is the default editor.

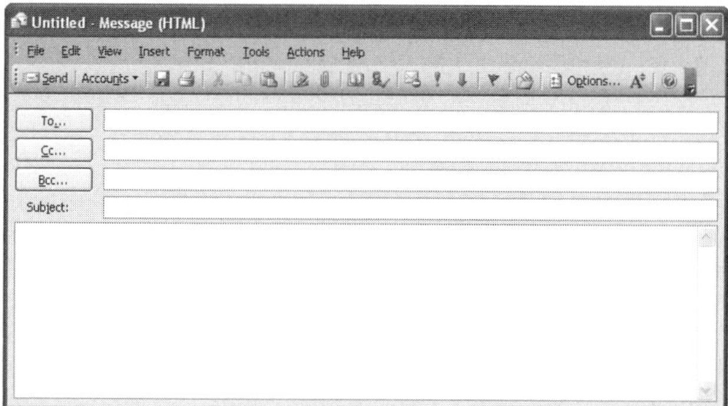

Figure 7-2. You use this standard message form when Outlook is the default editor.

Configuring Your E-Mail Editor and Viewer

You can specify the application you want to use for creating, editing, and viewing messages. To locate these settings, choose Tools, Options and click the Mail Format tab. By default, Outlook uses Word as the e-mail editor for creating and editing messages. If you prefer, however, you can use Outlook as your editor. It takes slightly longer to begin composing a message when Word is the editor, because Outlook must start Word if it is not already running. If you work primarily with plain-text messages and don't use text formatting or graphics in messages, using Outlook as your default e-mail editor speeds up the process. You can also specify whether to use Word or Outlook for reading rich-text messages.

For an explanation of plain-text and rich-text formats, see "Formatting Text in Messages," page 194.

On the Mail Format tab of the Options dialog box, you can adjust the following settings:

- **Use Microsoft Office Word 2003 To Edit E-Mail Messages** Select this option to specify Word as the default e-mail editor. Clear the option to use Outlook as the editor.
- **Use Microsoft Office Word 2003 To Read Rich Text E-Mail Messages** Select this option to use Word to read rich-text messages. Clear the option to use Outlook instead.

Addressing Messages

Outlook's address books make it easy to address messages. When you want to send a message to someone whose address is stored in one of your local address books or an address list on the server, you can click in the To box on the message form and type the recipient's name—you don't have to enter the entire address. When you send the message, Outlook checks the name, locates the correct address, and adds it to the message. If multiple addresses match the name you specify, Outlook shows all the matches and prompts you to select the appropriate one. If you want to send a message to someone whose address isn't in any of your address books, you need to type the full address in the To box. Alternatively, you can open a personal address book (PAB), add the address so that it will be available in the future, and then select it from there.

For more information about Outlook address books, see Chapter 5, "Managing Address Books and Distribution Lists."

Tip Outlook can check the names and addresses of message recipients before you send the message. Enter the names in the To box and click the Check Names button on the message form toolbar to perform this action.

To open the address book (see Figure 7-3), click an Address Book icon (To, Cc, or Bcc) beside an address box on the message form. Outlook opens the Select Names dialog box, which you can use to address the message.

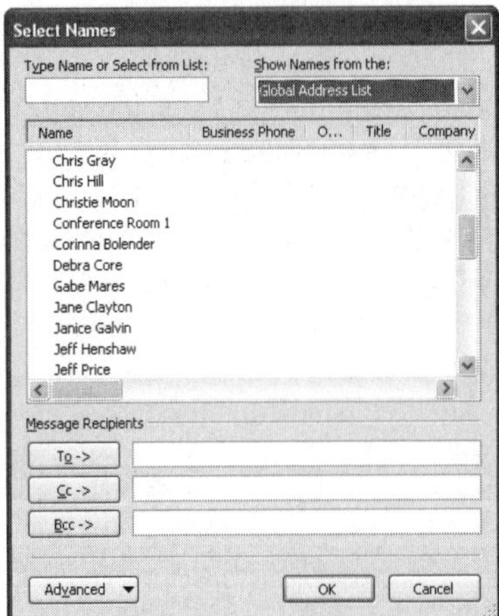

Figure 7-3. In the Select Names dialog box, you can select addresses from the address book.

Follow these steps to select addresses in this dialog box and add them to your message:

1. In the Show Names From The drop-down list, select the address list you want to view.
2. Select a name from the list, and click To, Cc, or Bcc to add the selected address to the specified address box.
3. Continue this process to add more recipients if necessary. Click OK when you're satisfied with the list.

Tip You can include multiple recipients in each address box on the message form. If you're typing the addresses yourself, separate them with a semicolon.

Including Carbon Copies and Blind Carbon Copies

You can direct a single message to multiple recipients either by including multiple addresses in the To box on the message form or by using the Cc (Carbon Copy) and Bcc (Blind Carbon Copy) boxes. The Cc box appears by default on message forms, but the Bcc box does not. To display the Bcc box, in Word click the down arrow beside Options on the message form toolbar and choose Bcc, or choose View, Bcc in Outlook. You use the Cc and Bcc boxes the same way you use the To box: type a name or address in the box, or click the Address Book icon beside the box to open the address book.

Tip **Hide addresses when necessary**
The names contained in the To and Cc boxes of your message are visible to all recipients of the message. If you're using a distribution list, Outlook converts the names on the list to individual addresses, exposing those addresses to the recipients. If you want to hide the names of one or more recipients or don't want distribution lists exposed, place those names in the Bcc box.

Copying Someone on All Messages

In some situations you might want every outgoing message to be copied to a particular person. For example, maybe you manage a small staff and want all of their outgoing messages copied to you. Or, perhaps you want to send a copy of all of your outgoing messages to yourself at a separate e-mail account.

Rules you create with Outlook's Rules Wizard can process outgoing messages as well as incoming ones. One way to ensure a recipient is copied on all outgoing messages is to add a rule that automatically adds the recipient to the message's Cc field. Follow these steps to do so:

1. Choose Tools, Rules Wizard to begin creating the rule.
2. Click New, choose Start From A Blank Rule, choose Check Messages After Sending, and click Next.
3. Click Next again without choosing any conditions to cause the rule to be used for all messages.
4. Select the action Cc The Message To People Or Distribution List, then click the underlined link in the Rule Description box and enter the Cc recipient's address.
5. Click Next and set exceptions as needed, and then click Finish.

Unfortunately, Outlook doesn't offer a Bcc action for the rule. The add-on Always BCC for Outlook, available at *http://www.sperrysoftware.com/jcAlwaysBCC.asp*, lets you automatically add a Bcc recipient and is designed to work with the Outlook E-Mail Security Update for Outlook 2000, and the same features built into Microsoft Outlook 2002 and Outlook 2003.

Use Templates and Custom Forms for Addressing

A rule is handy for copying all messages—or only certain messages—to one or more people, as explained in the previous section. Distribution lists are handy for addressing a message to a group of people without entering the address for each person.

If you regularly send the same message to the same people, but want to specify some on the To field, others in the Cc field, and still others in the Bcc field, distribution lists and rules won't do the trick. Instead, you can use a template or a custom form to send the message. You create the form or template ahead of time with the addresses in the desired fields, then open that item, complete it, and send it on its way. Use the following steps to create and use a template for this purpose:

1. In Outlook, start a new message.
2. Enter the e-mail or distribution list addresses as needed in the To, Cc, and Bcc fields.
3. Enter any other information that remains the same each time you send the message, such as subject or boilerplate text in the body of the message.
4. Choose File, Save As.
5. In the Save As dialog box, choose Outlook Template (OFT) from the Save As Type drop-down list.
6. Enter a name in the File Name field, and if you want to use a location other than your Templates folder, choose a path for the template.
7. Click Save to save the template.
8. Close the message form and click No when prompted to save changes.
9. When it's time to create the message, choose Tools, Forms, Choose A Form to open the Choose Form dialog box (see Figure 7-4).

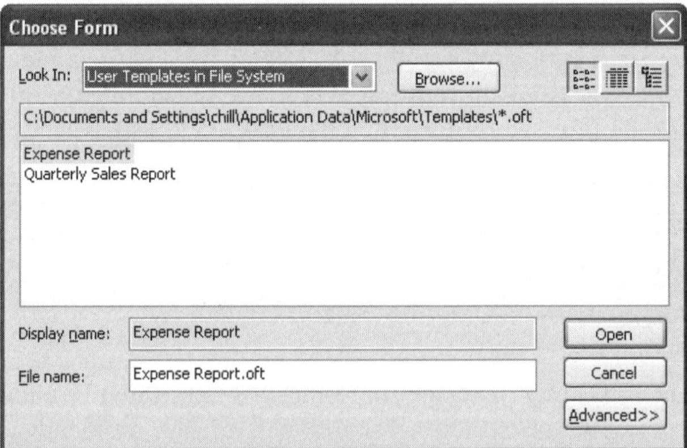

Figure 7-4. Open the template from the Choose Form dialog box.

10. Choose User Templates In File System from the Look In drop-down list, choose the template you created in step 7, and click Open.
11. Add any other recipients of message content and click Send to send it.

> **Tip** If you use the default Template folder for your templates, you won't have to browse for them when you choose the User Templates In File System option.

See Chapter 23, "Using Templates," for more information on using templates in Outlook, and Chapter 24, "Designing and Using Forms," for details on creating and using custom forms.

Using Word to Compose Messages

Using Word as the default e-mail editor means you can take advantage of all Word's formatting, graphics, and other capabilities to create rich-text, multimedia messages. For example, you can use character and paragraph formatting, bulleted lists, automatic numbered lists, animated text, graphics, and other Word features to create dynamic messages (see Figure 7-5). If Outlook is set up to use Word as your default editor, simply open a new message form and begin creating the message, using any Word features you need.

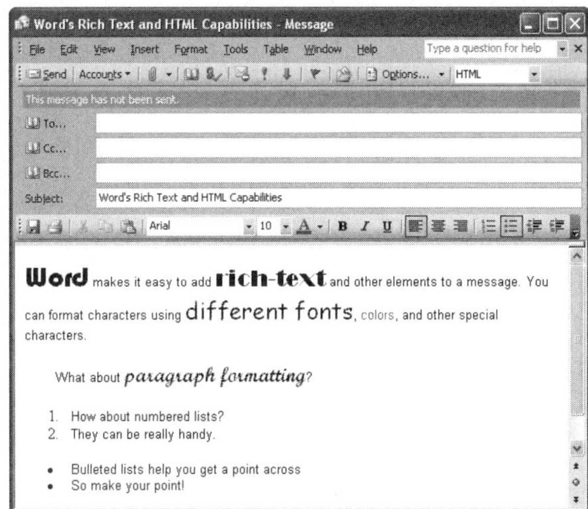

Figure 7-5. With Word as your editor, you have additional options for creating rich-text messages.

For information on specifying Word as the default e-mail editor, see the sidebar "Configuring Your E-Mail Editor and Viewer," page 169.

You can also create messages when you start Word outside Outlook by following these steps:

1. With Word open, create the message in the body of the document.
2. Choose File, Send To, Mail Recipient. Word displays a message form with To, Cc, and Subject boxes.
3. Address the message and click Send when the message is complete.

Troubleshooting

The e-mail headers won't go away in Word

When you're working in Word and you choose File, Send To, Mail Recipient, Word displays an e-mail toolbar with From, To, Cc, Bcc, and Subject headers. This lets you address a message and send the current document as the body of the message. If you decide not to send the message after all and want to continue editing the document, you could make the headers go away by shutting down Word, restarting, and reopening the document. However, there is a much easier way: just choose File, Send To, Mail Recipient again. This command acts like a toggle to turn the e-mail toolbar on and off.

Specifying Message Priority and Sensitivity

By default, new messages that you create in either Outlook or Word have their priority set to Normal. You might want to change the priority to High for important or time-sensitive messages or to Low for nonwork mail or other messages that have relatively less importance. Outlook displays an icon in the Importance column of the recipient's Inbox to indicate High or Low priority. (For messages with Normal priority, no icon is displayed.)

The easiest way to set message priority is by using the toolbar in the message form. Click the High Priority button (which has an exclamation point icon) to specify High priority. Click the Low Priority button (which has a down arrow icon) to specify Low priority. To set the priority back to Normal, click the selected priority again to remove the highlight around the button (see Figure 7-6). You can also click Options on the toolbar and set the message priority in the Message Options dialog box. In the Message Settings section of the dialog box, choose the priority level from the Importance drop-down list.

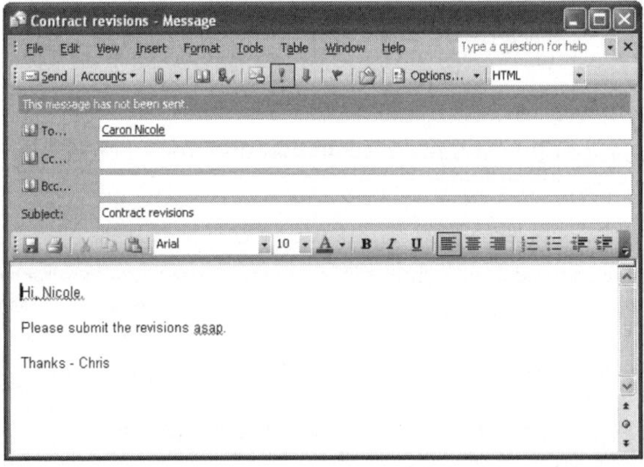

Figure 7-6. Outlook highlights the appropriate priority button to provide a visual indicator of the message's priority.

You also can specify a message's sensitivity, choosing a Normal (the default), Personal, Private, or Confidential sensitivity level. Setting sensitivity adds a tag to the message that displays the sensitivity level you've selected. This helps the recipient see at a glance how you want the message to be treated. To set sensitivity, click Options on the message form toolbar and select the sensitivity level from the Sensitivity drop-down list.

Saving a Message to Send Later

Although you can create some messages in a matter of seconds, others can take considerably longer—particularly if you're using formatting or special features or if you're composing a lengthy message. If you're interrupted while composing a message, or if you simply want to leave the message to finish later, you can save the message in your Drafts folder. Later, when you have time, you can reopen the message, complete it, and send it. Choose File, Save in the message form to have Outlook save the message to the Drafts folder (see Figure 7-7). When you're ready to work on the message again, open the Drafts folder and double-click the message to open it.

To learn how to configure Outlook to automatically save a copy of messages you send, see "Saving Messages Automatically," page 190.

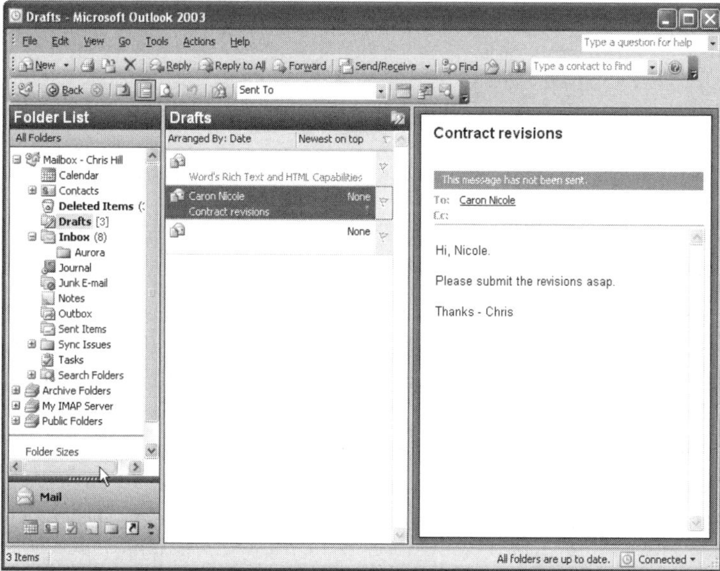

Figure 7-7. Messages in progress are kept in the Drafts folder.

Tip You also can choose File, Save As to save a message as a Word document (or in another document format) outside your Outlook folders.

Setting Sending Options

In the Advanced E-Mail Options dialog box (see Figure 7-8), you can configure various options that affect how Outlook sends e-mail messages. To open this dialog box, choose Tools, Options and click E-Mail Options on the Preferences tab. In the E-Mail Options dialog box, click Advanced E-Mail Options.

For details on specifying which account is used to send a message, see "Sending Messages Using a Specific Account," page 161.

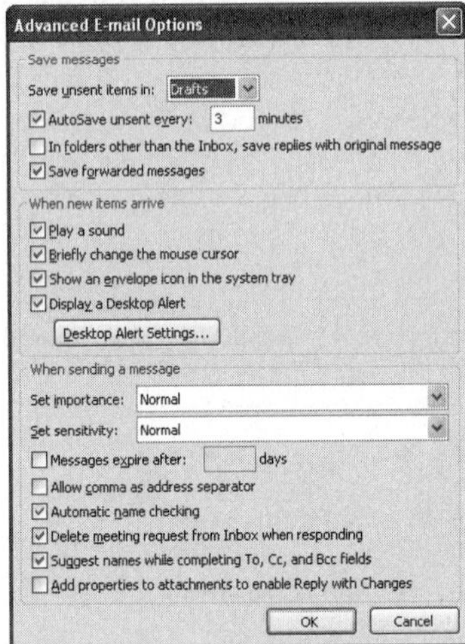

Figure 7-8. You can choose options for sending messages in the Advanced E-Mail Options dialog box.

In the Advanced E-Mail Options dialog box, you can modify the following settings:

- **Set Importance** This option sets the default importance, or priority level for all new messages. When you compose a message, you can override this setting by clicking the High Priority button or the Low Priority button on the toolbar in the message form or by clicking Options on the toolbar and setting the priority in the Message Options dialog box. The default setting is Normal.
- **Set Sensitivity** This option sets the default sensitivity level for all new messages. When you compose a message, you can override this setting by clicking Options on the toolbar and setting the sensitivity level in the Message Options dialog box.
- **Message Expires After n Days** This option causes the messages to expire after the specified number of days. The message appears in strikethrough in the recipient's mailbox at that time.
- **Allow Comma As Address Separator** If this check box is selected, you can use commas as well as semicolons in the To, Cc, and Bcc boxes of a message form to separate addresses.

- **Automatic Name Checking** Select this check box to have Outlook attempt to match names to e-mail addresses. Verified addresses are underlined, and those for which Outlook finds multiple matches are underscored by a red wavy line. When multiple matches exist and you've used a particular address before, Outlook underscores the name with a green dashed line to indicate that other choices are available.
- **Delete Meeting Request From Inbox When Responding** Select this check box to have Outlook delete a meeting request from your Inbox when you respond to the request. If you accept the meeting, Outlook enters the meeting in your calendar. Clear this check box if you want to retain the meeting request in your Inbox.
- **Suggest Names While Completing To, Cc, And Bcc Fields** When this check box is selected, Outlook completes addresses as you type them in the To, Cc, and Bcc boxes of the message form. Clear this check box to turn off this automatic completion. See Chapter 5, "Managing Address Books and Distribution Lists," for more information on the address nickname cache and how to work with it.
- **Add Properties To Attachments To Enable Reply With Changes** When this check box is selected, Outlook adds properties to the attached documents of outgoing messages that allow the recipient to reply to the message with changes.

Note Other options in the Advanced E-Mail Options dialog box are explained in other locations in this book, including in the following sections.

Controlling When Messages Are Sent

To specify when Outlook should send messages, choose Tools, Options and click Mail Setup to locate the Send Immediately When Connected option. With this option selected, Outlook sends messages as soon as you click Send, provided Outlook is online. If Outlook is offline, the messages go into the Outbox until you process them with a send/receive operation (which is also what happens if you do not select this option).

Requesting Delivery and Read Receipts

Regardless of which e-mail editor you use, you can request a *delivery receipt* or a *read receipt* for any message. Both types of receipts are messages that are delivered back to you after you send your message. A delivery receipt indicates the date and time your message was delivered to the recipient's mail server. A read receipt indicates the date and time the recipient opened the message.

Specifying that you want a delivery receipt or read receipt for a message doesn't guarantee that you're going to get one. The recipient's mail server or mail client might not support delivery and read receipts. The recipient might have configured his or her e-mail client to automatically reject requests for receipts, or the recipient might answer No when prompted to send a receipt. If you receive a receipt, it's a good indication that the message was delivered or read. If you don't receive a receipt, however, don't assume that the message wasn't delivered or read. A message receipt serves only as a positive notification, not a negative one.

To request receipts for a message you're composing, click the Options button on the message form toolbar to display the Message Options dialog box (see Figure 7-9). You'll find the delivery and read receipt options in the Voting And Tracking Options group.

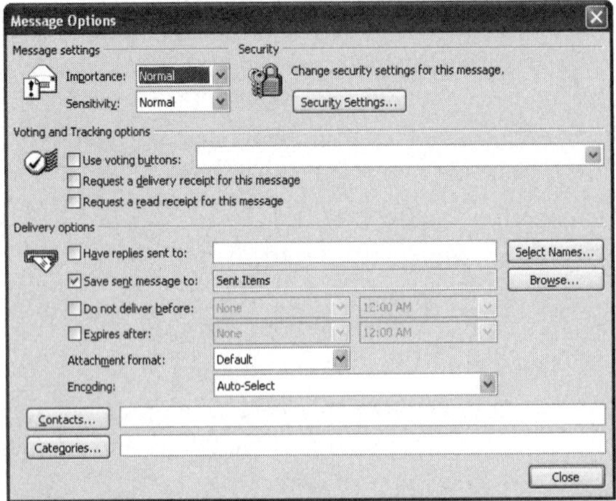

Figure 7-9. Use the Message Options dialog box to request a delivery receipt, a read receipt, or both.

Using Message Tracking and Receipts Options

You can set options to determine how Outlook handles delivery and read receipts by default. Choose Tools, Options and click E-Mail Options on the Preferences tab. In the E-Mail Options dialog box, click Tracking Options to display the Tracking Options dialog box, shown in Figure 7-10, where you'll find the options discussed in this section.

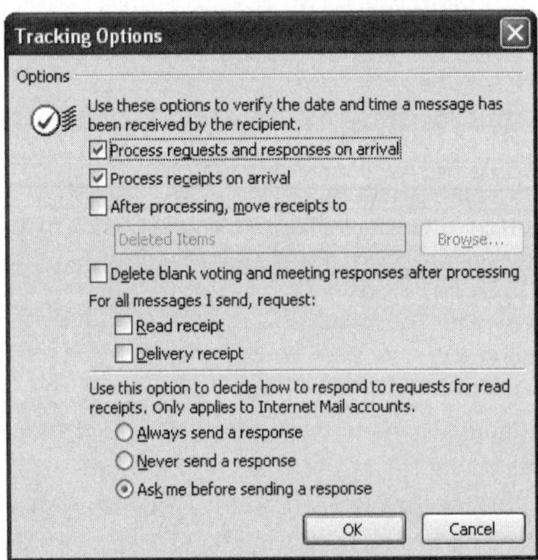

Figure 7-10. Process receipts and responses in the Tracking Options dialog box.

The following options control how Outlook requests read receipts and how the receipts are processed after they are received:

- **Process Requests And Responses On Arrival** Select this check box to have Outlook process all message receipt requests and responses when they arrive.
- **Process Receipts On Arrival** Select this check box to have Outlook generate received/read receipts when messages come in requesting them. Clear this check box to have Outlook prompt you for each receipt.
- **After Processing, Move Receipts To** Select this check box to have Outlook move receipts from the Inbox to the specified folder.
- **For All Messages I Send, Request Read Receipt** Select this check box to have Outlook request a read receipt for each message you send. When you compose a message, you can override this setting; to do so, click the Options button on the message form toolbar.
- **For All Messages I Send, Request Delivery Receipt** Select this check box to have Outlook request a delivery receipt for each message you send. (Note that this option is not available for messages that are sent through Internet e-mail accounts.)

These three options in the Tracking Options dialog box let you control how Outlook responds to requests from others for read receipts on messages you receive, and they apply to Internet mail accounts only:

- **Always Send A Response** When this option is selected, Outlook always sends a read receipt to any senders who request one. Outlook generates the read receipt when you open the message.
- **Never Send A Response** Select this option to prevent Outlook from sending read receipts to senders who request them. Outlook will not prompt you regarding receipts.
- **Ask Me Before Sending A Response** Selecting this option lets you control, on a message-by-message basis, whether Outlook sends read receipts. When you open a message for which the sender has requested a read receipt, Outlook prompts you to authorize the receipt. If you click Yes, Outlook generates and sends the receipt. If you click No, Outlook doesn't create or send a receipt.

Note The Delete Blank Voting And Meeting Responses After Processing check box, if selected, causes Outlook to delete voting and meeting requests that contain no comments. Instead, Outlook processes these automatically. See Chapter 35, "Messaging with Exchange Server," to learn more about voting, and Chapter 19, "Scheduling Appointments," to learn about the Calendar and scheduling meetings.

Sending a Message for Review

If you compose a message from Word (that is, you started Word outside Outlook), you have the ability to send the message as a document for review. You might use this feature if you're collaborating on a document with others or incorporating their comments into the final draft. Recipients can review the document and add comments, which they send back to you.

They also can incorporate the changes directly in the document, which lets them take advantage of Word's revision marks feature. To send a document for review, open the document in Word and choose File, Send To, Mail Recipient (For Review).

For more detailed information on sending documents for review, see *Microsoft Office Word 2003 Inside Out*, by Mary Millhollon and Katherine Murray (Microsoft Press, 2003).

Sending a Message as an Attachment

If you compose a message using Word as the e-mail editor, you can send the message as an attachment rather than the body of the message. For example, you might be working on a long document that you would prefer to send as an intact DOC file. If that's the case, with the document open in Word, choose File, Send To, Mail Recipient (As Attachment).

Sending to a Routing Recipient

Another option that's available when you use Word as your e-mail editor is routing a document to a group of users, either one at a time or all at the same time. For example, you might need to send a document to three recipients for each person's approval. Or you might want to route a document to all the members of a group in a specific sequence, giving each member a chance to review both the document and the comments of earlier reviewers. Routing slips allow you to accomplish either of these tasks.

Follow these steps to use a routing slip:

1. In Word, compose the message and choose File, Send To, Routing Recipient.
2. Outlook displays a message indicating that another program (Word) is attempting to access addresses you have stored in Outlook. When you click Yes to allow Word to read your addresses, the Routing Slip dialog box is displayed (see Figure 7-11).

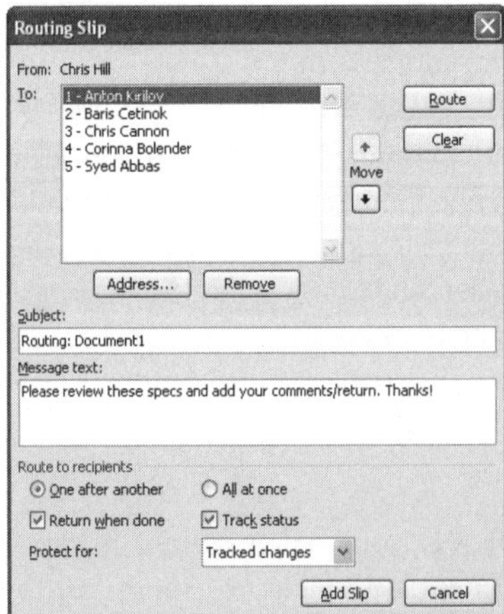

Figure 7-11. Use the Routing Slip dialog box to route a message to multiple recipients.

3. Click Address and add the addresses of all recipients to whom you want to send the message. If you want the message to be routed to the recipients in sequence (the One After Another option at the bottom of the dialog box), select the addresses in the order in which you want the recipients to receive the message.

> **Tip** If you prefer, you can add the addresses to the Routing Slip dialog box in any order. Then you can use the Move arrow buttons to change the routing order, as indicated in Figure 7-11.

4. Specify the subject and the message text for the routing slip, and then select from the following options:
   - **One After Another** Outlook sends the message only to the first recipient on the list. That recipient then uses the routing slip to route the message to the next person on the list.
   - **All At Once** Outlook sends the message to all recipients on the routing list at the same time.
   - **Return When Done** Outlook automatically returns the routed document to you when the last recipient closes it.
   - **Track Status** Outlook delivers an e-mail message to you each time a recipient sends the document to another person on the routing list.
   - **Protect For** In the drop-down list, select Comments to allow recipients to insert comments but not to modify the document. Select Tracked Changes to turn on revision marks and allow recipients to insert changes using revision marks. Select Forms if you're routing a form that you want recipients to fill out, but you don't want them to modify the form itself. Select None if you don't want to track any changes.
5. Click Add Slip to add the routing slip, and then click Send to send the document.

You'll probably find that Outlook displays a security warning dialog box indicating that a program is trying to access your e-mail addresses. That program is Word. Just click Yes to allow Word to access your Address Book. If you use Exchange Server, see "Enabling Applications to Send E-Mail with Outlook," page 825, to learn how to configure security options on the server to bypass this warning.

> **To learn more about sending documents using a routing slip, see *Microsoft Office Word 2003 Inside Out*, by Mary Millhollon and Katherine Murray (Microsoft Press, 2003).**

Replying to Messages

When you reply to a message, Outlook sends your reply to the person who sent you the message. Replying to a message is simple: select the message in the Inbox, and then click the Reply button on the Standard toolbar; choose Actions, Reply; or press Ctrl+R. Outlook opens a message form and, depending on how you have configured Outlook for replies, can also include the original message content in various formats.

If the message to which you're replying was originally sent to multiple recipients and you want to send your reply to all of them, click Reply All; choose Actions, Reply To All; or press Ctrl+Shift+R.

For more information about message replies, see "Using Other Reply and Forwarding Options," below.

Tip **Hide the recipients list**
When you use Reply All, Outlook places all the addresses in the To box. If you don't want the recipients list to be visible, use the Bcc box to send blind carbon copies. To do this, click Reply All, highlight the addresses in the To box, and cut them. Then click in the Bcc box and paste the addresses there.

Forwarding Messages

In addition to replying to a message, you can forward the message to one or more recipients. To forward a message, select the message header in the message folder (Inbox or other), and then click Forward on the message form toolbar; choose Actions, Forward; or press Ctrl+F. Outlook opens a new message form and either incorporates the original message in the body of the current one or attaches it to the new message.

If you forward a single message, Outlook by default forwards the original message in the body of your new message, and you can add your own comments. If you prefer, however, you can configure Outlook to forward messages as attachments rather than including them in the body of your messages.

For information about options for forwarding, see "Using Other Reply and Forwarding Options," below.

Note If you select multiple messages and click Forward, Outlook sends the messages as attachments rather than including them in the body of your message.

Using Other Reply and Forwarding Options

You can change how Outlook handles and formats message replies and forwarded messages. These options are found in the E-Mail Options dialog box, shown in Figure 7-12.

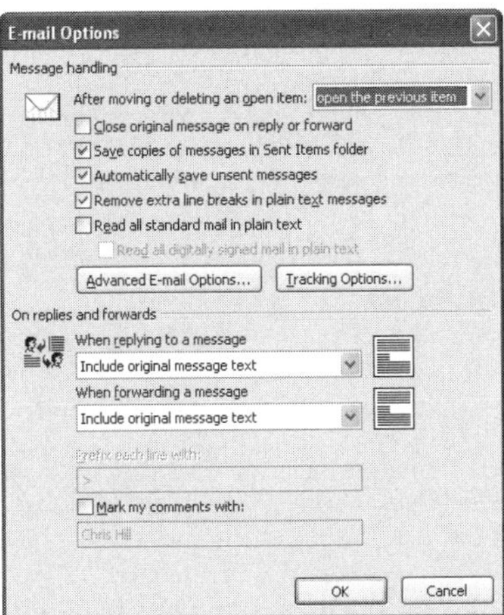

Figure 7-12. You can set options for message replies and forwarded messages in the E-Mail Options dialog box.

To open this dialog box, choose Tools, Options and click E-Mail Options on the Preferences tab. You can then view or set the following options that affect replies and forwards:

- **Close Original Message On Reply Or Forward** Select this check box to have Outlook close the message form when you click Reply or Forward. Clear this check box to have Outlook leave the message form open. If you frequently forward the same message with different comments to different recipients, it's useful to have Outlook leave the message open so that you don't have to open it again to perform the next forward.
- **When Replying To A Message** Use this drop-down list to specify how Outlook handles the original message text when you reply to a message. You can choose to have Outlook generate a clean reply without the current message text, include the text without changes, or include but indent the text, for example. Note that you can either include the original message text in the body of your reply or add it to the message as an attachment.
- **When Forwarding A Message** Use this drop-down list to specify how Outlook handles the original message text when you forward a message. You can, for example, include the message in the body of the forwarded message or add it as an attachment.
- **Prefix Each Line With** If you select Prefix Each Line Of The Original Message in the When Replying To A Message drop-down list or the When Forwarding A Message drop-down list, you can use this box to specify the character Outlook uses to prefix each line of the original message in the body of the reply or forwarded message. The default is an angle bracket (>) and a space, but you can use one or more characters of your choice.
- **Mark My Comments With** Select this check box and enter a name or other text in the associated box. Outlook will add the specified text to mark your typed comments in the body of a message that you are replying to or forwarding. This option has no effect if you're using Word as your e-mail editor, because Word uses revision marks for document annotation.

For more details on replying to and forwarding messages, see "Replying to Messages" and "Forwarding Messages," page 182.

Troubleshooting

You can't forward a single message as an attachment

In Outlook 2003, you can send documents from other Microsoft Office applications as attachments, and you can forward multiple messages in Outlook as attachments. However, sending a single message as an attachment rather than including it in the body of the message in Outlook requires that you either reconfigure Outlook's default behavior before forwarding the message or use a workaround.

To change Outlook's default behavior so that it sends a single message as an attachment when you forward it, choose Tools, Options, E-Mail Options. In the When Forwarding A Message drop-down list, select Attach Original Message and click OK. This setting now applies to all messages you forward, not just the current one.

If you want to override Outlook's default behavior for the current message only, use one of these two workarounds. One method is to select *two* messages to forward and then, in the message form, delete the attached message that you don't want to include. A second method is to compose a new message and choose Insert, Item to insert the message (or any other Outlook item).

Controlling Synchronization and Send/Receive Times

Outlook uses *send and receive groups* (or *send/receive groups*) to control when messages are sent and received for specific e-mail accounts. You can also use send/receive groups to define the types of items that Outlook synchronizes. *Synchronization* is the process in which Outlook synchronizes the local copy of your folders with your Exchange Server message store. For example, assume that while you've been working offline you have created several new e-mail messages and scheduled a few events. You connect to the Exchange Server and perform a synchronization. Outlook uploads to your Exchange Server the changes you made locally and also downloads changes from the server to your local store, such as downloading messages that have been delivered to your Inbox on the server.

Send/receive groups allow you to be flexible in controlling which functions Outlook performs for synchronization. For example, you can set up a send/receive group for your Exchange Server account that synchronizes only your Inbox and not your other folders, for those times when you simply want to perform a quick check of your mail.

Send/receive groups also are handy for helping you manage different types of accounts. For example, if you integrate your personal and work e-mail into a single profile, you can use send/receive groups to control when each type of mail is processed. You might create one send/receive group for your personal accounts and another for your work accounts. You can also use send/receive groups to limit network traffic to certain times of the day. For example, if your organization limits Internet connectivity to specific times, you could use send/receive groups to schedule your Internet accounts to synchronize during the allowed times.

Think of send/receive groups as a way to collect various accounts into groups and assign to each group specific send/receive and synchronization behavior. You can create multiple send/receive groups, and you can include the same account in multiple groups if needed.

Setting Up Send/Receive Groups

To set up or modify send/receive groups in Outlook, choose Tools, Send/Receive, Send/Receive Settings, Define Send/Receive Groups. Outlook displays the Send/Receive Groups dialog box, shown in Figure 7-13. By default, Outlook sets up one group named All Accounts and configures it to send and receive when online and offline. You can modify or remove that group, add others, and configure other send/receive behavior in the Send/Receive Groups dialog box.

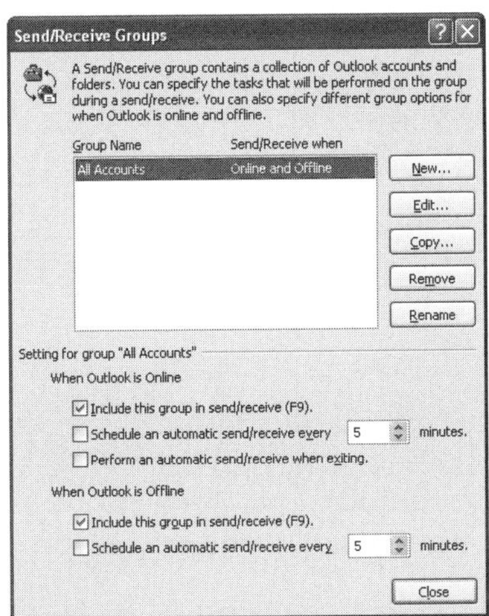

Figure 7-13. You can specify send/receive actions in the Send/Receive Groups dialog box.

When you select a group from the Group Name list, Outlook displays the associated settings in the Setting For Group area of the dialog box:

- **Include This Group In Send/Receive (F9)** Select this check box to have Outlook process accounts in the selected group when you click Send/Receive on the message form toolbar or press F9. Outlook provides this option for both online and offline behavior.
- **Schedule An Automatic Send/Receive Every *n* Minutes** Select this check box to have Outlook check the accounts in the selected group every n minutes. The default is 5 minutes. Outlook provides this option for both online and offline behavior.

- **Perform An Automatic Send/Receive When Exiting** Select this check box to have Outlook process the accounts in the selected group when you exit Outlook from an online session.

Creating New Groups

Although you could modify the All Accounts group to process only selected accounts, it's better to create other groups as needed and leave All Accounts "as is" for those times when you do want to process all your e-mail accounts together.

Follow these steps to create a new group:

1. In Outlook, choose Tools, Send/Receive Settings, Define Send/Receive Groups.
2. Click New, type the name for the group as you want it to appear on the Send/Receive submenu, and click OK. Outlook displays the Send/Receive Settings dialog box, shown in Figure 7-14.

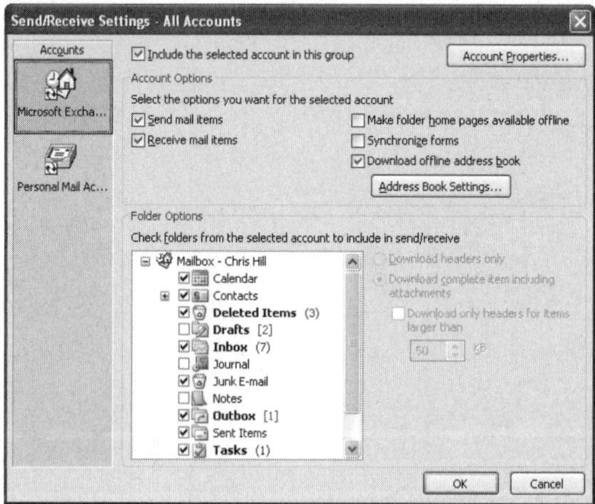

Figure 7-14. You can configure account processing in the Send/Receive Settings dialog box.

3. In the Accounts bar on the left, click the account you want to configure. By default, all accounts in the group are excluded from synchronization, indicated by the red X on the account icon.
4. Select the Include The Selected Account In This Group check box to activate the remaining options in the dialog box and to have the account included when you process messages for the selected group.
5. In the Check Folders From The Selected Account To Include In Send/Receive list, select the check box beside each folder that you want Outlook to synchronize when processing this group.

6 Select other settings, using the following list as a guide:

- **Send Mail Items** Select this check box to have Outlook send outgoing mail for this account when a send/receive action occurs for the group.
- **Receive Mail Items** Select this check box to have Outlook retrieve incoming mail for this account when a send/receive action occurs for the group.
- **Make Folder Home Pages Available Offline** This check box has Outlook cache folder home pages offline so that they are available to you any time.
- **Synchronize Forms** Select this check box to have Outlook synchronize changes to forms that have been made locally as well as changes that have been made on the server.
- **Download Offline Address Book** When this check box is selected, Outlook updates the offline address book when a send/receive action occurs for the group.
- **Get Folder Unread Count** For IMAP accounts only, you can select this option to have Outlook get the number of unread messages from the server.

7 If you need to apply filters or message size limits, do so. Otherwise, click OK and then click Close to close the Send/Receive Groups dialog box.

For information on how to apply message size limits, see "Limiting Message Size," below.

Note Other options for the send/receive group are explained in the following sections.

Modifying Existing Groups

You can modify existing send/receive groups in much the same way you create new ones. Choose Tools, Send/Receive Settings, Define Send/Receive Groups. Select the group you want to modify and click Edit. The settings you can modify are the same as those discussed in the preceding section.

Limiting Message Size

You can also use the Send/Receive Settings dialog box to specify a limit on message size for messages downloaded from the Inbox of the selected Exchange Server 2003 account. This provides an easy way to control large messages that arrive in your Exchange Server account. Rather than downloading messages that are larger than the specified limit, Outlook downloads only the headers. You can then mark the messages for download or deletion, or simply double-click the message to download and open it.

Note Specifying a message size limit in the Send/Receive Settings dialog box doesn't affect the size of messages that you can receive on the server. It simply directs Outlook to proccess them differently.

Follow these steps to specify a message size limit for an Exchange Server 2003 account:

1. Choose Tools, Send/Receive, Send/Receive Settings, Define Send/Receive Groups.
2. Select a group to modify and click Edit.
3. From the Accounts bar, select the Exchange Server account containing the folder for which you want to set a message size limit.
4. Select a folder as shown in Figure 7-15.

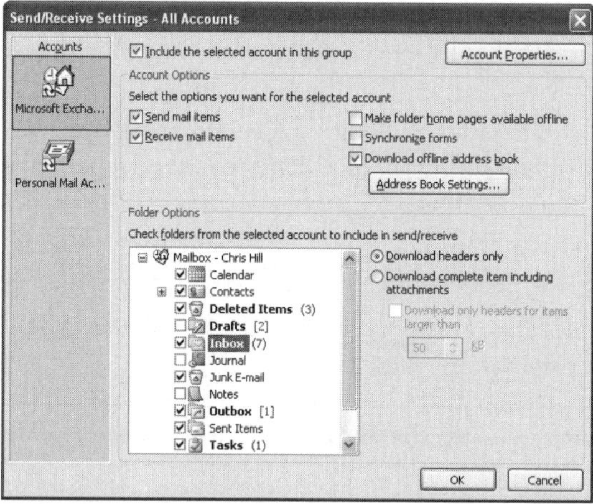

Figure 7-15. Select a folder and then set its parameters in the Send/Receive Settings dialog box.

5. Specify the criteria you want to use to limit message download based on the following option list, and click OK:
   - **Download Headers Only** Download only the message header and not the message body or attachments.
   - **Download Complete Item Including Attachments** Download the entire message including body and attachments.
   - **Download Only Headers For Items Larger Than** Download only headers for messages over the specified size.

If you need to configure more advanced options or exercise a finer degree of control over the size limit criteria, choose Tools, Rules Wizard. The Rules Wizard allows you to create a custom large message rule to suit your requirements.

For more details about working with message rules, see "Processing Messages Automatically," page 224. To learn how to control message size with Exchange 2000 Server and Exchange Server 5.5 accounts, see, "Configuring Header Processing for Exchange 2000 or Earlier Versions," page 935.

You can use a similar mechanism to control downloading of large messages from POP3 accounts. In this case, you can choose to download only message headers for messages larger than a specified size.

Follow these steps to configure POP3 message size filtering:

1. Choose Tools, Send/Receive Settings, Define Send/Receive Groups.
2. Select a group to modify and click Edit.
3. From the Accounts bar, select the POP3 account for which you want to set a message size limit.
4. Select the Download Only Headers For Items Larger Than *nn* KB check box, specify the size limit, and click OK.

To retrieve a message with a large attachment from a POP3 server, mark the message to be downloaded.

For details on using remote mail with POP3 accounts, see "Working with Message Headers," page 331.

Scheduling Send/Receive Synchronization

You can schedule synchronization for each send/receive group separately, giving you quite a bit of control over when Outlook processes your Inbox, Outbox, and other folders for synchronization. You can configure Outlook to process each send/receive group on a periodic basis and to process specific groups when you exit Outlook. For example, you might schedule the All Accounts group to synchronize only when you exit Outlook, even though you've scheduled a handful of other groups to process messages more frequently during the day. Because you can create as many groups as needed and can place the same account in multiple groups, you have a good deal of flexibility in determining when each account is processed.

Tip **Simplify with Cached Exchange Mode**
If you use an Exchange Server account, configure the account to use Cached Exchange Mode (keep a local copy of the mailbox) and avoid the issue of synchronization altogether. With Cached Exchange Mode enabled, Outlook handles synchronization on the fly, adjusting to online or offline status as needed. See Chapter 1, "Outlook Architecture, Setup, and Startup," and Chapter 34, "Configuring the Exchange Server Client," for discussion of Cached Exchange Mode.

Configuring Send/Receive Schedules

Follow these steps to configure synchronization for each send/receive group:

1. Choose Tools, Send/Receive, Send/Receive Settings, Define Send/Receive Groups.
2. In the Send/Receive Groups dialog box, select the group for which you want to modify the schedule.
3. In the Setting For Group area, select Schedule An Automatic Send/Receive Every *n* Minutes, and then specify the number of minutes that should elapse between send/receive events for the selected group. Set this option for both online and offline behavior.

4. If you want the group to be processed when you exit Outlook, select Perform An Automatic Send/Receive When Exiting.

You can use a combination of scheduled and manually initiated send/receive events to process messages and accounts. For example, you can specify in the Send/Receive Group dialog box that a given group (such as All Accounts) must be included when you click Send/Receive or press F9 and then configure other accounts to process as scheduled. Thus some accounts might process only when you manually initiate the send/receive event, and others might process only by automatic execution. In addition, you can provide an overlap so that a specific account processes manually as well as by schedule—simply include the account in multiple groups with the appropriate settings for each group.

Disabling Scheduled Send/Receive Processing

On occasion, you might want to disable scheduled send/receive events altogether. For example, assume that you're working offline and don't have a connection through which you can check your accounts. In that situation, you can turn off scheduled send/receive processing until a connection can be reestablished.

To disable scheduled send/receive processing, choose Tools, Send/Receive, Send/Receive Settings, Disable Scheduled Send/Receive. Select this command again to enable the scheduled processing.

Managing Messages and Attachments

Using Outlook's e-mail features effectively requires more than understanding how to send and receive messages. This section of the chapter helps you get your messages and attachments under control.

Saving Messages Automatically

You can configure Outlook to save messages automatically in several ways—for example, saving the current message periodically or saving a copy of forwarded messages. You'll find most of the following options in the E-Mail Options dialog box (shown earlier in Figure 7-12) and in the Advanced E-Mail Options dialog box (shown earlier in Figure 7-8).

- **Automatically Save Unsent Messages (in the E-Mail Options dialog box)** Use this check box to have Outlook save unsent messages in the Drafts folder. Outlook by default saves unsent messages to the Drafts folder every 3 minutes. Clear this check box if you don't want unsent messages saved in this folder.
- **Save Unsent Items In (in the Advanced E-Mail Options dialog box)** Specify the folder in which you want Outlook to save unsent items. The default location is the Drafts folder.
- **AutoSave Unsent Every *n* Minutes (in the Advanced E-Mail Options dialog box)** Specify the frequency at which Outlook automatically saves unsent items to the folder specified by the Save Unsent Items In setting. The default is 3 minutes.

- **In Folders Other Than The Inbox, Save Replies With Original Message (in the Advanced E-Mail Options dialog box)** With this check box selected, Outlook saves a copy of sent items to the Sent Items folder if the message originates from the Inbox (new message, reply, or forward). If the message originates from a folder other than the Inbox—such as a reply to a message stored in a different folder—Outlook saves the reply in the same folder as the original. If this option is cleared, Outlook saves all sent items in the Sent Items folder.

Note You can also use rules to control where Outlook places messages. For more information on creating and using rules, see Chapter 8, "Filtering, Organizing, and Using Automatic Responses."

- **Save Forwarded Messages (in the Advanced E-Mail Options dialog box)** Select this check box to save a copy of all messages that you forward. Messages are saved in either the Sent Items folder or the originating folder, depending on how you set the previous option.

Retaining a Copy of Sent Messages

Keeping track of the messages you send can often be critical, particularly in a work setting. Fortunately, with Outlook, you can automatically retain a copy of each message you send, providing a record of when and to whom you sent the message.

By default, Outlook stores a copy of each sent message in the Sent Items folder. You can open this folder and sort the items to locate messages based on any message criteria. You can view, forward, move, and otherwise manage the contents of Sent Items just as you can with other folders.

If you allow Outlook to save a copy of messages in the Sent Items folder, over time the sheer volume of messages can overwhelm your system. You should therefore implement a means—whether manual or automatic—to archive or clear out the contents of the Sent Items folder. With the manual method, all you need to do is move or delete messages from the folder as your needs dictate. If you want to automate the archival process, you can do so; for details on how to automatically archive messages from any folder, see "Configuring the Automatic Archiving of Items," page 775. Follow these steps to specify whether Outlook retains a copy of sent messages in the Sent Items folder:

1. Choose Tools, Options and click E-Mail Options on the Preferences tab.

2 In the E-Mail Options dialog box (see Figure 7-16), select the Save Copies Of Messages In Sent Items Folder check box to have Outlook retain sent messages. If you want to prevent Outlook from keeping a copy of sent messages, clear this check box. Click OK.

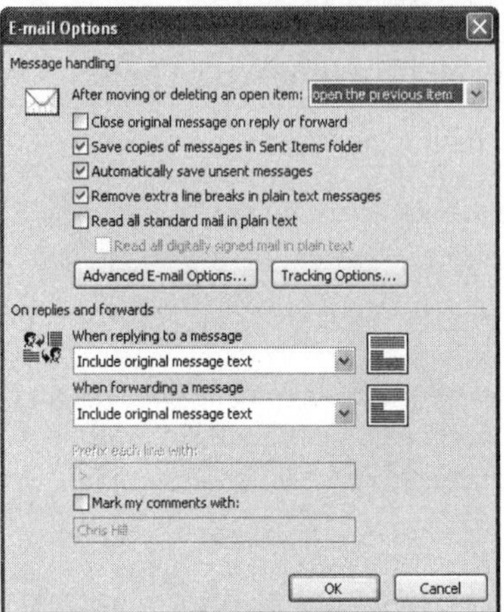

Figure 7-16. In the E-Mail Options dialog box, you can choose whether Outlook saves copies of sent messages.

> **Tip** If you need to change Outlook's behavior for a single message, you can override the setting. With the message form open, choose File, Properties and then select the action you want Outlook to take.

Saving Attachments to a Disk

It's a sure bet that some of the messages you receive include attachments such as documents, pictures, or applications. In general, you can work with these attachments in Outlook without saving them separately to disk. For example, you can double-click an attachment in the InfoBar to open the attachment. The next step then depends on the attachment's extension and the application with which that extension is registered on your system.

In many instances, however, it's necessary to save attachments to disk. For example, you might receive a self-extracting executable containing a program you need to install. In that case, the best option is to save the file to disk and install it from there.

You can save attachments using either of these methods:

- If you're using the Reading Pane, right-click the attachment in the InfoBar and choose Save As.
- Choose File, Save Attachments if you want to save one or more attachments or if the Reading Pane is not available. This option is handy when you want to save all attachments.

Saving Messages to a File

Although Outlook maintains your messages in your store folders, occasionally you might need to save a message to a file. For example, you might want to archive a single message or a selection of messages outside Outlook or save a message to include as an attachment in another document. You can save a single message to a file or combine several messages into a single file. When you save a single message, Outlook gives you the option of saving it in one of the following formats:

- **Text Only** Save the message as a text file, losing any formatting in the original message.
- **Rich Text Format** Save the message in RTF format, retaining the original message formatting.
- **Outlook Template** Save the message as an Outlook template that you can use to create other messages.
- **Outlook Message Format** Save the message in MSG format, retaining all formatting and attachments within the message file.
- **Outlook Message Format – Unicode** Save the message in MSG format with Unicode character set.

When you save a selection of messages, you can store the messages only in a text file, and Outlook combines the body of the selected messages in that text file. This then allows you to concatenate the various messages (that is, join them sequentially) into a single text file. You might use this capability, for example, to create a message thread from a selection of messages.

To save one or more messages, open the Outlook folder where the messages reside and select the message headers. Choose File, Save As and specify the path, file name, and file format.

Configuring Message Handling

Outlook provides several options that let you control how Outlook handles and displays messages. In the E-Mail Options dialog box (shown earlier in Figure 7-16), you can change either of these two settings:

- **After Moving Or Deleting An Open Item** Use this option to control what action Outlook takes when you move or delete an open item, such as a message. You can set Outlook to open the previous message, open the next message, or return to the Inbox without opening other messages.
- **Remove Extra Line Breaks In Plain Text Messages** Select this check box to have Outlook automatically remove extra line breaks from plain-text messages that you receive. Clear the check box to leave the messages as they are.

Moving and Copying Messages Between Folders

Managing your messages often includes moving them to other folders. For example, if you're working on multiple projects, you might want to store the messages related to each specific project in the folder created for that project. The easiest method for moving a message between folders is to drag the message from its current location to the new location. If you want to copy a message rather than move it, right-click the message, drag it to the folder, and then choose Copy.

If you can't see both the source and destination folders in the folder list, or if you prefer not to drag the message, you can use a different method of moving or copying. Select the message in the source folder and choose Edit, Move To Folder or Copy To Folder, depending on which action you need. Outlook displays a dialog box in which you select the destination folder.

> **Tip** You can use the shortcut menu to move a message to a specified folder by right-clicking the message and choosing Move To Folder.

Deleting Messages

When you delete messages from any folder other than the Deleted Items folder, the messages are moved to the Deleted Items folder. You can then recover the messages by moving them to other folders, if needed. When Outlook deletes messages from the Deleted Items folder, however, those messages are deleted permanently.

You can set Outlook to automatically delete all messages from the Deleted Items folder whenever you exit the program, which helps keep the size of your message store manageable. However, it also means that unless you recover a deleted message before you exit Outlook, that message is irretrievably lost. If you seldom have to recover deleted files, this might not be a problem for you.

To change what happens to items in the Deleted Items folder when you exit Outlook, choose Tools, Options and click the Other tab. Select or clear Empty The Deleted Items Folder Upon Exiting.

Including More Than Text

The majority of your messages might consist of unformatted text, but you can use formatted text and other elements to create rich-text and multimedia messages. For example, you might want to use character or paragraph formatting for emphasis, add graphics, or insert hyperlinks to Web sites or other resources. The following sections explain how to accomplish these tasks.

Formatting Text in Messages

Formatting text in messages is easy, particularly if you're comfortable with Microsoft Word. Even if you're not, you should have little trouble adding some snap to your messages with character, paragraph, and other formatting.

Your options for rich text depend in part on whether you use Word or Outlook as your e-mail editor. Outlook offers some rich-text capabilities, but Word offers many more. For example, you can apply paragraph formatting to indent some paragraphs but not others, create bulleted and numbered lists, and apply special color and font formatting. Regardless of which editor you use, the formatting options are available on the editor's Format menu. These options are simple to use. Understanding the underlying format in which your messages are sent, however, requires a little more exploration.

By default, Outlook uses Hypertext Markup Language (HTML) as the format for sending messages. HTML format lets you create multimedia messages that can be viewed directly in a Web browser and an e-mail client. Depending on the capabilities of the recipient's e-mail client, however, you might need to use a different format. Plain-text format doesn't allow any special formatting, but it offers the broadest client support—every e-mail client can read plain-text messages. Alternatively, you can use rich-text format to add paragraph and character formatting and to embed graphics and other nontext media in your message.

Note Using HTML format for messages doesn't mean that you need to understand HTML to create a multimedia message. Outlook takes care of creating the underlying HTML code for you.

You choose the format for the current message from the message form's Format menu, selecting Plain Text, Rich Text, or HTML. If Word is your editor, choose one of those options from the drop-down list on the message form toolbar. To set the default message format for all new messages, choose Tools, Options on the Outlook menu bar and click the Mail Format tab (see Figure 7-17). Select the format from the Compose In This Message Format drop-down list.

Figure 7-17. Use the Mail Format tab to set the default message format.

On the Mail Format tab of the Options dialog box, you can click Fonts to display the Fonts dialog box, shown in Figure 7-18. Use the options in this dialog box to control which fonts Outlook uses for specific tasks, such as composing new messages, replying to or forwarding a message, and composing or reading plain-text messages. You can specify the font as well as the font size, color, and other font characteristics.

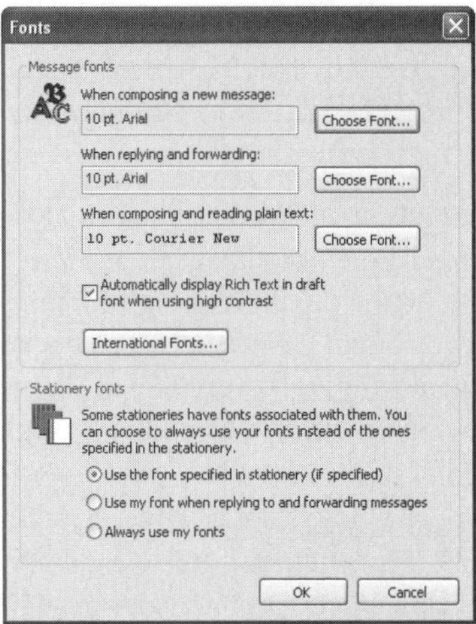

Figure 7-18. Use the Fonts dialog box to control the appearance of fonts in Outlook for specific tasks.

Including Graphics in Messages

Your ability to insert graphics in a message depends in part on which editor and message format you use. You can't insert embedded graphics in a message that uses plain-text format in either editor. If Outlook is your default editor, you can insert embedded graphics only when using HTML format. With Word as the editor, you can insert graphics using either rich-text or HTML format.

> **Note** Although you can't insert embedded graphics, you can attach graphics files to a plain-text message with either Outlook or Word as the editor.

The process you use to insert graphics and the options that are available also vary according to which editor you use. The following sections explain the differences.

Attaching Graphics Files to Plain-Text Messages

With either Outlook or Word as your editor, follow these steps to attach a graphics file to a plain-text message:

1. In the message form, choose Insert, File.
2. In the Insert File dialog box, locate the file you want to attach and click Insert.

Inserting Graphics with Outlook as the Editor

With Outlook as the default editor, follow these steps to insert a graphic in a message:

1. In the message form, choose Format, HTML to use HTML format for the message.
2. Choose Insert, Picture to display the Picture dialog box, shown in Figure 7-19.

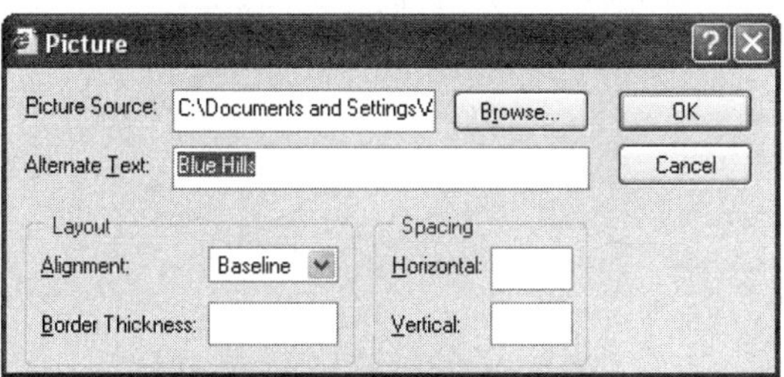

Figure 7-19. Use the Picture dialog box to specify a border and other properties for the picture you want to insert in your message.

3. In the Picture dialog box, enter the following information:
   - **Picture Source** Specify the path to the graphics file that contains the picture or click Browse to locate the file.
   - **Alternate Text** Enter optional text to appear in place of the picture for recipients whose e-mail clients don't support HTML or whose clients are configured not to show graphics.
   - **Alignment** Specify how you want the image aligned in the message and how text will flow with the graphic. For example, you would select Texttop if you wanted the top of the image to be in line with the top of the text to its right. Click the question mark on the title bar and then click this drop-down list to view explanations of the available options.
   - **Border Thickness** Add an optional border around the graphic, with a specified pixel width.
   - **Spacing** Enter the amount of spacing, in pixels, that should be added to the horizontal and vertical sides of the image.
4. Click OK to insert the graphic.

Inserting Graphics with Word as the Editor

When Word is your default editor, you have additional options for inserting a graphic in a message:

1. Begin composing a new message using HTML or rich-text format, and place the cursor in the body of the message where you want the picture placed.
2. Choose Insert, Picture and then choose one of the following commands:
   - **Clip Art** Insert a clip art image from disk.
   - **From File** Insert a graphics file from disk.

- **From Scanner Or Camera** Import a picture from your scanner or digital camera.
- **Organization Chart** Insert an organizational chart (which you can modify). Figure 7-20 shows an example.

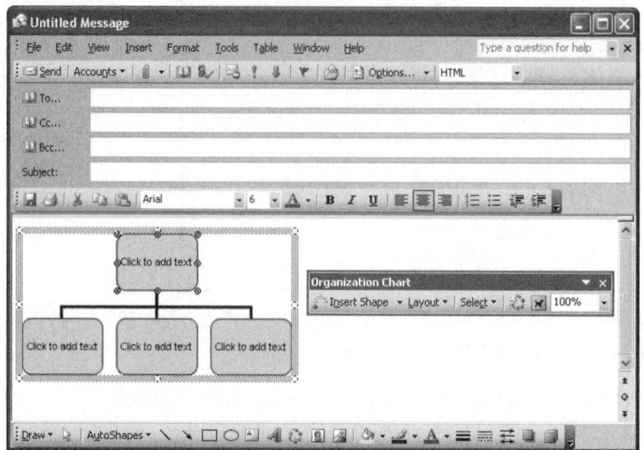

Figure 7-20. You can easily insert an organizational chart that you can modify as needed.

- **New Drawing** Insert a Drawing Canvas object in which you can draw using Word's built-in drawing tools.
- **AutoShapes** Insert a Word AutoShape symbol from Word's AutoShape library.
- **WordArt** Insert a WordArt object. WordArt provides special formatting and other text effects that allow you to create dynamic text.
- **Chart** Insert a Microsoft Graph chart object.

At this point, the next steps depend on which command you have chosen. If you need help with a particular procedure, consult theWord online Help feature or see *Microsoft Office Word 2003 Inside Out*, by Mary Millhollon and Katherine Murray (Microsoft Press, 2003).

> **Tip** You can insert various types of editable diagrams in a message by choosing Insert, Diagram.

Inserting Hyperlinks

With either Outlook or Word as your e-mail editor, you can easily insert hyperlinks to Web sites, e-mail addresses, network shares, and other items in a message. When you type certain kinds of text in a message, Outlook automatically converts the text to a hyperlink, requiring no special action from you. For example, if you type an e-mail address, an Internet URL, or a Universal Naming Convention (UNC) path to a share, Outlook converts the text to a hyperlink. To indicate the hyperlink, Outlook underlines it and changes the font color.

When the recipient of your message clicks the hyperlink, the resulting action depends on the type of hyperlink. With an Internet URL, for example, the recipient can go to the specified Web site. With a UNC path, the remote share opens when the recipient clicks the hyperlink. This is a great way to point the recipient to a shared resource on your computer or another computer on the network.

> **Tip** **Follow a hyperlink**
> You can't follow (open) a hyperlink in a message you're composing by clicking the hyperlink. This action is restricted to allow you to click the hyperlink text and edit it. To follow a hyperlink in a message you're composing, hold down the Ctrl key and click the hyperlink.

Inserting Hyperlinks with Outlook as the Editor

When Outlook is your e-mail editor, you have another option for inserting a hyperlink in a message:

1. Locate the cursor where you want to insert the hyperlink, and choose Insert, Hyperlink to display the Hyperlink dialog box, shown in Figure 7-21.

Figure 7-21. Use this dialog box to insert a hyperlink when Outlook is your e-mail editor.

2. From the Type drop-down list, select the type of hyperlink you want to insert. Outlook adds the appropriate prefix to the URL field.
3. Complete the URL and click OK.

Inserting Hyperlinks with Word as the Editor

When you use Word as your e-mail editor, you have many more options for inserting hyperlinks. Locate the cursor where you want to insert the hyperlink, and choose Insert, Hyperlink to display the Insert Hyperlink dialog box, shown in Figure 7-22.

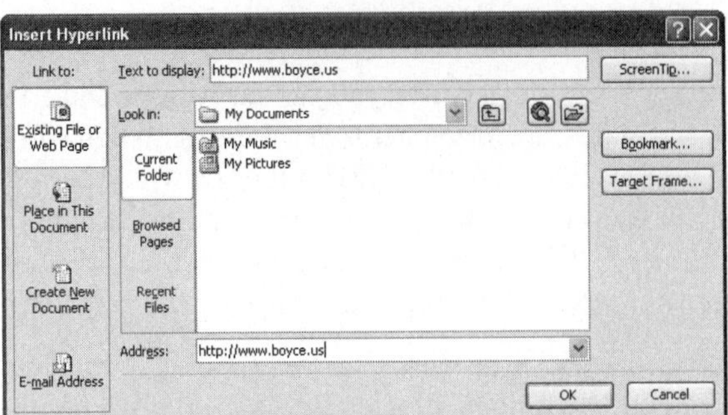

Figure 7-22. Use the Insert Hyperlink dialog box to insert a hyperlink in a message when Word is your e-mail editor.

The options displayed in the Insert Hyperlink dialog box vary according to the type of hyperlink you're inserting, as the following sections explain.

Inserting Hyperlinks to Files or Web Pages To insert a hyperlink to a file or Web page, select Existing File Or Web Page in the Link To bar. Then, provide the following information in the Insert Hyperlink dialog box:

- **Text To Display** In this box, type the text that will serve as the hyperlink in the message. Outlook underlines this text and changes its color to indicate the hyperlink.
- **Look In** If you are linking to a file, use this drop-down list to locate and select the file on the local computer or on the network. (If you want to insert a hyperlink to a file you've used recently, click Recent Files to view a list of most recently used files in the document list of the dialog box.)
- **Browse The Web** To browse for a URL to associate with the hyperlink, click the Browse The Web button to open your browser. (If you want to insert a hyperlink to a page you've recently viewed in your Web browser, click Browsed Pages. The document list in the dialog box changes to show a list of recently browsed pages.)
- **Address** Type the local path, the Internet URL, or the UNC path to the file or Web site in this box.
- **ScreenTip** Click this button to define an optional ScreenTip that appears when the recipient's pointer hovers over the hyperlink.
- **Bookmark** Click this button to select an existing bookmark in the specified document. When the recipient clicks the hyperlink, the document opens at the bookmark location.
- **Target Frame** Click this button to specify the browser frame in which you want the hyperlink to appear. For example, choose New Window if you want the hyperlink to open in a new window on the recipient's computer.

Troubleshooting

Recipients of your messages can't access linked files

If you're setting up a hyperlink to a local file, bear in mind that the recipient probably won't be able to access the file using the file's local path. For example, linking to C:\Docs\Policies.doc would cause the recipient's system to try to open that path on his or her own system. You can use this method to point the recipient to a document on his or her own computer. However, if you want to point the recipient to a document on your computer, you must either specify a UNC path to the document or specify a URL (which requires that your computer function as a Web server).

The form of the UNC path you specify depends on your operating system as well as that of the recipient. UNC paths in Microsoft Windows 95, Microsoft Windows 98, Microsoft Windows Me, and Microsoft Windows NT are limited to *<server>**<share>**<document>*, where *<server>* is the name of the computer sharing the resource, *<share>* is the share name, and *<document>* is the name of the document to open. In Microsoft Windows 2000 and later versions, you can specify a deeper UNC path, such as *<server>**<share>**<subfolder>**<sub-subfolder>**<document>*.doc. For the deep hyperlink to work properly, however, the recipient must also be using Windows 2000 or later.

Inserting a Hyperlink to a Place in the Current Message If you click Place In This Document in the Link To bar, the Insert Hyperlink dialog box changes, as shown in Figure 7-23. The Select A Place In This Document area shows the available locations in the open document: headings, bookmarks, and the top of the document. Select the location to which you want to link, provide other information as necessary (the text to display in the hyperlink, for example, or perhaps a ScreenTip), and then click OK.

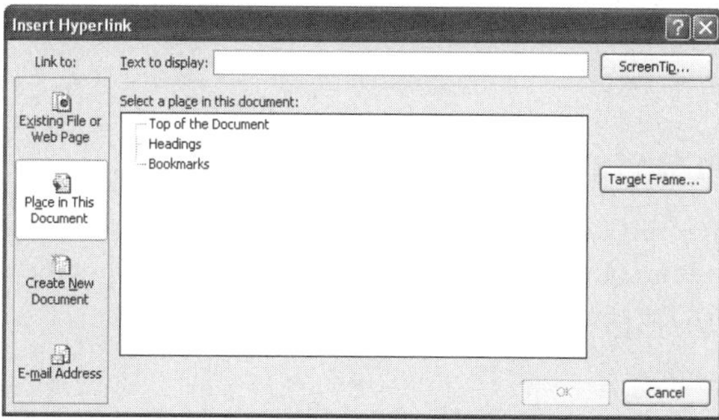

Figure 7-23. You can easily link to a location in the current document.

Note This method is most commonly used when you have opened a document in Word and are inserting a hyperlink in that document rather than in a separate e-mail message.

Inserting a Hyperlink to a New Document If you select Create New Document in the Link To bar of the Insert Hyperlink dialog box, you can specify the path to a new document and choose to either edit the document now or insert the hyperlink for later editing. You'll most often use this method for inserting hyperlinks in a Word document rather than in an e-mail message.

Inserting a Hyperlink to an E-Mail Address If you select E-Mail Address in the Link To bar, you can easily insert an e-mail address as a hyperlink in a message. When recipients click the hyperlink, their e-mail programs will open a new e-mail message addressed to the person you have specified in the hyperlink. Although you can simply type the e-mail address in the message and let Outlook convert it to a mailto: link, you might prefer to use the Insert Hyperlink dialog box instead (when Word is your e-mail editor). As Figure 7-24 shows, you can use this dialog box to select from a list of e-mail addresses you have recently used on your system and to specify the subject for the message as well as the address.

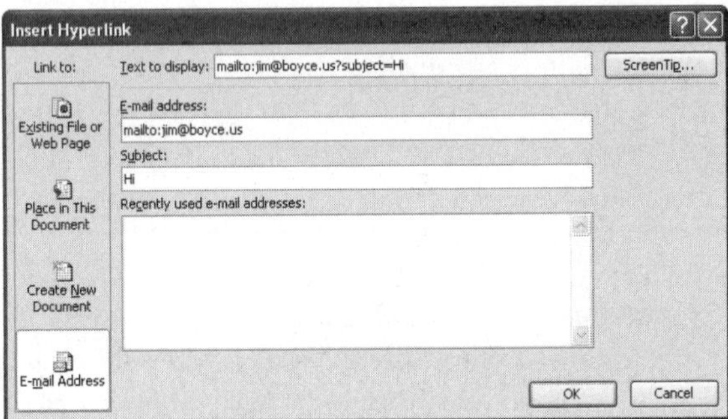

Figure 7-24. You can insert a mailto: hyperlink with extra options when Word is your e-mail editor.

Removing a Hyperlink To remove a hyperlink, right-click in the hyperlink and then choose Remove Hyperlink from the shortcut menu. Outlook retains the underlying text but removes the hyperlink.

Inserting Files in the Body of a Message

Occasionally, you'll want to insert a file in the body of a message rather than attaching it to the message. For example, you might want to include a text file, a Word document, or another document as part of the message.

Follow these steps to insert a file:

1. Place the cursor where you want to insert the file, and choose Insert, File to open the Insert File dialog box.
2. Locate and select the file to insert, and click the arrow beside the Insert button.
3. Click Insert As Text to insert the file in the body of the message.

Tip **Use the clipboard to insert a file**

In some cases, you'll find it easier to use the clipboard to insert a file in a message, particularly if the file is already open in another window. (Just select the file and copy and paste or cut and paste it into the message.) You can also use the clipboard when you need to insert only a portion of a file, such as a few paragraphs from a document.

Attaching Files

To attach a file to a message, you can use the steps described in the preceding section for inserting a file, with one difference: in step 3, click Insert rather than Insert As Text. Alternatively, you can click the paper clip icon on the toolbar to insert a file as an attachment, or you can simply drag the file into the message window.

Attaching a Business Card to a Message

With Outlook, you can send a copy of a contact item in vCard format, a standard format for exchanging contact information. This allows the recipient to import the contact data into a contact management program, assuming that the recipient's program supports the vCard standard (as most do).

Here's how to share your contact information with others using a vCard:

1. In Outlook, open the Contacts folder and select the contact item you want to send.
2. Choose Action, Forward As vCard. Outlook inserts the vCard into the message.
3. Complete the message as you normally would and click Send.

Tip **Send data as an Outlook item**

If you know that the recipient uses Outlook, you can right-click the contact and choose Forward—or select the contact and choose Action, Forward—to send the contact data as an Outlook contact item. Outlook users can also use vCard attachments.

For more details on using and sharing vCards, see "Sharing Contacts with vCards," page 420.

Customizing Your Messages with Stationery

By default, Outlook uses no background or special font characteristics for messages. However, it does support the use of stationery, so you can customize the look of your messages.

With Outlook stationery, you use a set of characteristics that define the font style, color, and background image for messages. In effect, stationery can give your messages a certain look and feel (see Figure 7-25). You can easily switch from one stationery to another—you're not locked into using the same stationery for all messages, and you don't need to change Outlook options each time you want to use a different stationery.

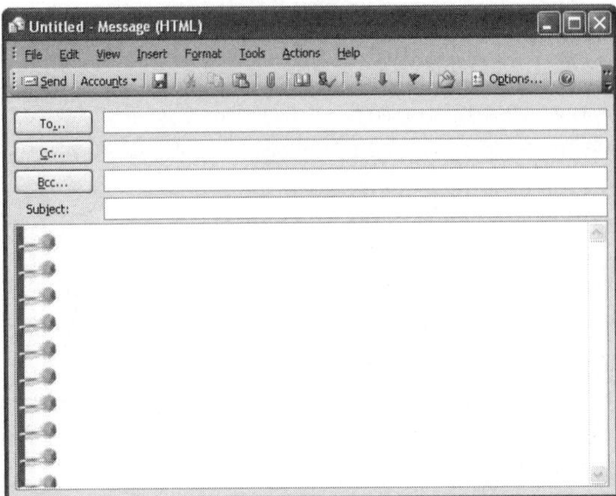

Figure 7-25. Stationery gives your messages a thematic look.

> **Note** To use stationery, you must use HTML format for the message. When you use stationery, you're actually adding HTML code to the message to control its appearance.

If you're like the majority of Outlook users, you use the program mostly for business purposes and probably won't use stationery on a regular basis. However, it's useful to know the basics about this feature, which can add creativity, personality, or even some humor to your personal mail.

Using Predefined Stationery

Outlook provides several predefined stationery themes that you can use in your messages. To view these themes, choose Tools, Options and click the Mail Format tab. Click Stationery Picker to display the Stationery Picker dialog box, shown in Figure 7-26.

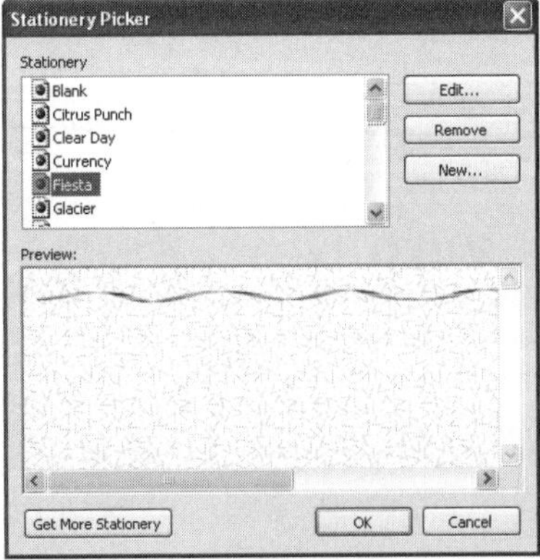

Figure 7-26. Use the Stationery Picker dialog box to preview stationery.

Note The Stationery Picker button on the Mail Format tab is unavailable if you have selected either Plain Text or Rich Text as your default message format.

You can edit most of the stationery listed in this dialog box, changing background image and font, although a few—such as Currency and Jungle—cannot be edited. To edit stationery, open the Stationery Picker dialog box, select the stationery you want to modify, and click Edit to display the Edit Stationery dialog box, where you can make changes as you like.

You can assign a default stationery to be used in all your messages. To do so, choose Tools, Options and click the Mail Format tab. Select the default stationery in the Use This Stationery By Default drop-down list and then click OK. If you don't want your messages to use stationery, or if you want to use it only infrequently, follow the same procedure but set the default stationery to None.

If Word is your e-mail editor, you can specify which stationery to use when you compose a message. This allows you to override the default stationery or to assign a stationery to that particular message, even though none of your other messages include it. To choose a stationery for a single message, open the message form, click the down arrow beside the Options button, and then choose Stationery. Outlook displays the Personal Stationery tab of the E-Mail Options dialog box, which you can use to assign a theme.

Creating Your Own Stationery

You can create your own stationery using the background image, font, and color settings of your choice. You can either use an existing stationery theme as a starting point or create one from scratch.

Follow these steps to create a new stationery theme:

1. Choose Tools, Options and click the Mail Format tab.
2. Click Stationery Picker, and then click New. Outlook provides a wizard to step you through the process of creating stationery.
3. In the wizard, specify a name for the stationery, select an existing stationery to use as a template, or start a blank one, and then click Next.
4. In the Edit Stationery dialog box, specify font characteristics and background and click OK.

After you add your new stationery, it appears in the Stationery list in the Stationery Picker dialog box. To use the stationery, simply select it and click OK.

Tip **Select additional stationery themes**
You'll find additional stationery themes at the Microsoft Office Update Web site. To find the right page, choose Tools, Options, Mail Format. Click Stationery Picker, and then click the Get More Stationery button.

Using Signatures

Outlook supports two types of signatures that you can add automatically (or manually) to outgoing messages: standard signatures and digital signatures. This chapter focuses on standard signatures, which can include text and graphics, depending on the mail format you choose.

> **Note** To learn about digital signatures, which allow you to authenticate your identity and encrypt messages, see "Protecting Messages with Digital Signatures," page 293.

Understanding Message Signatures

Outlook can add a signature automatically to your outgoing messages. You can specify different signatures for new messages and for replies or forwards. Signatures can include both text and graphics as well as vCard attachments. Both rich-text and HTML formats support vCards, but you can include graphics only if you use HTML as the message format. If your signature contains graphics and you start a new message using either plain-text or rich-text format, the graphics are removed, although any text defined by the signature remains. When you start a message using plain-text format, any vCard attachments are also removed.

Why use signatures? Many people use a signature to include their contact information in each message. Still others use a signature to include a favorite quote or other information in the message. Regardless of the type of information you want to include, creating and using the signature is easy.

> **Tip** You can create a unique signature for each e-mail account. When you send a message using an account, Outlook appends that account's signature to the outgoing message.

Defining Signatures

To define a signature, you use Outlook's Mail Format options. If you want to include a graphic, check before you start to ensure that you already have that graphic on your computer or that it's available on the network.

Follow these steps to create a signature:

1. In Outlook, choose Tools, Options and click the Mail Format tab.
2. Click Signatures to open the Signatures dialog box, and then click New to open the Create New Signature Wizard.
3. Specify a name for the signature as it will appear in Outlook. Select the option to start a new signature or select one to use as a template, and then click Next to open the Edit Signature dialog box (see Figure 7-27).

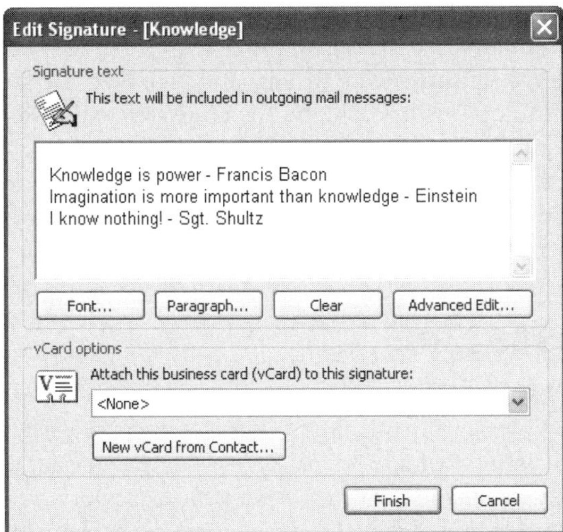

Figure 7-27. Format the text of your signature in the Edit Signature dialog box.

4 In the Signature Text box, type the text you want to include in the signature, and use the Font and Paragraph buttons to format the text. (These two buttons aren't available if you have specified Plain Text as the default format on the Mail Format tab.)

5 To attach a vCard from an Outlook contact item, click New vCard From Contact. Select the contact item, click Add, and click OK. You also can select existing vCards from the Attach This Business Card (vCard) To This Signature drop-down list.

6 Create other signatures, and then click OK in the Create Signature dialog box.

Adding Signatures to Messages

The signature Outlook adds to new messages and the signature it adds to replies and forwards don't have to be the same. To set up different signatures for these different kinds of messages, choose Tools, Options and click the Mail Format tab. Use the Signature For New Messages and the Signature For Replies And Forwards drop-down lists to select the appropriate signature for each kind of message.

> **Tip** **Specify the default message format**
> Keep in mind that the signature data Outlook adds to the message depends on the default message format specified on the Mail Format tab. Set the default format to HTML if you want to create or edit signatures that contain graphics.

Other than letting you specify the signature for new messages or for replies and forwards, Outlook does not give you a way to control which signature is attached to a given message. For example, if you want to use different signatures for personal and business messages, you must switch signatures manually. However, Outlook 2003 does store signature options separately for each account, so you can control signatures to some degree just by sending messages through a specific account.

To change the signature to be used by a specific account, choose Tools, Options, Mail Format. Select a mail account from the Select The Signatures To Use With The Following Account drop-down list; then select a signature from the Signature For New Messages and Signature For Replies And Forwards drop-down lists in the Signature area of the Mail Format tab. You also can change the signature when composing a message. If Word is your e-mail editor, click the arrow beside the Options button and choose E-Mail Signature. If Outlook is your editor, click the Signature button on the Standard toolbar and select the signature you want to use as the new default signature.

Using Instant Messaging

Outlook integrates support for Windows Messenger, referred to as *instant messaging*, which allows you to send instant messages to others across the Internet. In effect, instant messaging functions something like online chat does—you send and receive messages in real time with other online users. The latest version of Windows Messenger supports video conferencing and other features in addition to text chat. This section of the chapter explains how to configure and use Windows Messenger with Outlook.

When you use instant messaging in Outlook, Outlook checks the online status of a contact when you open the person's contact item or open an e-mail item from the contact. You can then click the online indicator for that person on the InfoBar, which opens a menu of Windows Messenger options (see Figure 7-28). In this menu, you can start a chat session, start a video chat session, and perform other Messenger-related tasks.

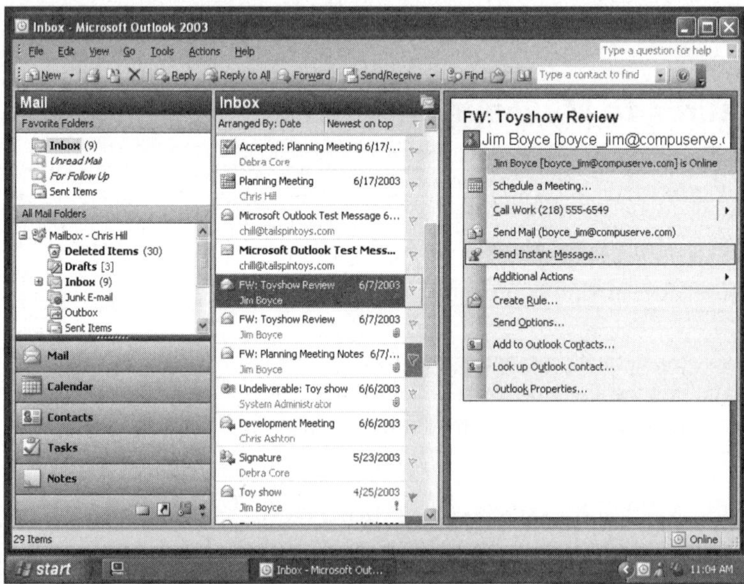

Figure 7-28. Select a Windows Messenger–related command after clicking the smart tag.

Note Outlook checks the online status of the other person only once, when you open the contact or e-mail item. It doesn't check periodically for a change in online status after the item has been opened.

Outlook by itself doesn't extend Windows Messenger functionality—rather, it hooks into the existing Windows Messenger, which you must install separately. In addition, to have others appear online in Outlook, you need to add those contacts to your Windows Messenger list of contacts.

Caution You should never give out your password, credit card information, or other personal data in an instant message conversation because instant messaging is not secure. This is particularly important if you don't really know the person with whom you're conversing.

Installing Windows Messenger

If Windows Messenger isn't installed on your system, you can download and add the latest version. Simply point your Web browser to *http://windowsupdate.microsoft.com*. Click Scan For Updates. In the Windows Update pane at the left, click Windows XP (or Windows 2000) to view the recommended system updates. Browse through the list to find Windows Messenger and click Add, then click Review and Install Updates to start the installation process.

Adding Contacts for Windows Messenger

Outlook itself doesn't check the online state of your contacts; instead, it relies on the Windows Messenger application to perform this task. Before you can start using Windows Messenger with Outlook, you need to add contacts to your Windows Messenger contact list by following these steps:

1. Double-click the Windows Messenger icon in the system tray to display the Windows Messenger window, shown in Figure 7-29.

Figure 7-29. You can add, send, call, or page by using the Windows Messenger window.

2 Click Add A Contact to start the Add A Contact Wizard (see Figure 7-30).

Figure 7-30. Use the Add A Contact Wizard to add contacts in Windows Messenger.

3 Select By E-Mail Address Or Sign-In Name and click Next.

4 Enter the contact's e-mail address and click Finish.

> **Note** If the contact doesn't have a passport from passport.com, you won't be able to add that contact in Windows Messenger.

Repeat these steps to add other contacts with whom you want to be able to communicate using Windows Messenger. The Windows Messenger window will show the online or offline status of each contact.

Setting Instant Messaging Options

Outlook has only two settings of its own related to Windows Messenger, both on the Other tab of the Options dialog box:

- **Enable The Person Names Smart Tag** Enable this option to have Outlook check the Windows Messenger online status of the sender or contact and display a small Windows Messenger icon in the Reading Pane's InfoBar.
- **Display Messenger Status In The From Field** Enable this option to have Outlook display the sender's Windows Messenger online status with a small Windows Messenger icon beside the From field in a message form when you open the message to read or reply.

You can configure several options for Windows Messenger through the Windows Messenger application. You can find these options by clicking Tools, Options in the Windows Messenger window. These options are specific to Windows Messenger, not to Outlook, so you should consult the Windows Messenger Help documentation for details about the various settings.

Sending Instant Messages in Outlook

When you click a message header in your Inbox, Outlook checks Windows Messenger to determine whether the e-mail address matches a contact defined in your Windows Messenger contact list. If it finds a match, Outlook checks the contact's online status. If the person is online, Outlook indicates that in the InfoBar (see Figure 7-31). Click the Messenger icon on the InfoBar and choose Send Instant Message to open the Windows Messenger window and begin chatting.

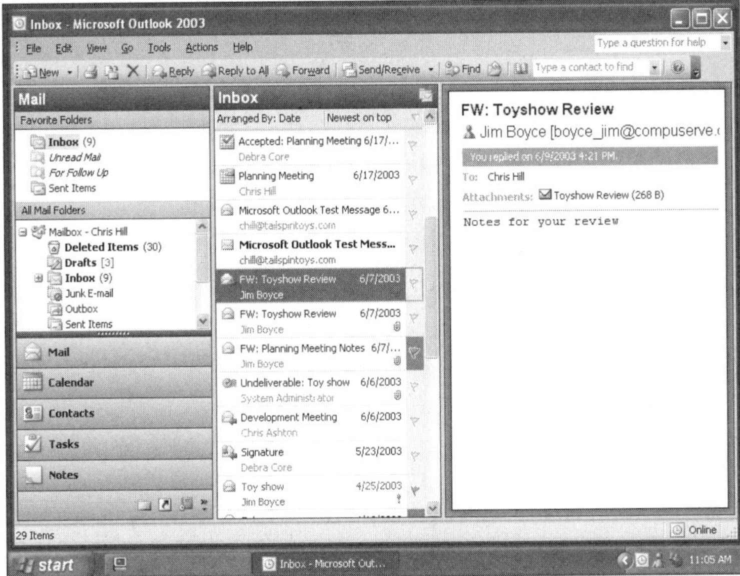

Figure 7-31. Click the online status indicator in the InfoBar to begin chatting.

Configuring Other Messaging Options

This section of the chapter provides an explanation of additional options in Outlook that control messaging features and tasks. You can specify how you want to be notified when new mail arrives, configure how Outlook connects for e-mail accounts that use dial-up networking, and control the formatting of Internet and international e-mail messages.

Setting Up Notification of New Mail

You might not spend a lot of time in Outlook during the day if you're busy working with other applications. However, you might want Outlook to notify you when you receive new messages. Outlook 2003 adds new Desktop Alert features to provide you with notification of the arrival of new messages. These options and additional notification options are located in the Advanced E-Mail Options dialog box (shown earlier in Figure 7-8):

- **Play A Sound** Select this option to have Outlook play a sound when a new message arrives. By using the Sounds icon in Control Panel, you can change the New Mail Notification sound to use a WAV file of your choosing.
- **Briefly Change The Mouse Cursor** Select this option to have Outlook briefly change the pointer to a mail symbol when a new message arrives.
- **Show An Envelope Icon In The Notification Area** Select this option to have Outlook place an envelope icon in the system tray when new mail arrives. You can double-click the envelope icon to open your mail. The icon disappears from the tray after you've read the messages.
- **Display A New Mail Desktop Alert (default Inbox only)** Enable this option to have Outlook display a pop-up window on the desktop when a new message arrives.

If you enable this last option, click Desktop Alert Settings to display the Desktop Alert Settings dialog box (Figure 7-32). In this dialog box you specify the length of time the alert remains on the desktop, the alert's transparency value, and whether you want alerts to be hidden if an application is maximized. Click Preview to preview the alert.

Figure 7-32. Configure alert settings with the Desktop Alert Settings dialog box.

Controlling Dial-Up Account Connections

The Mail Setup tab of the Options dialog box (choose Tools, Options) includes a handful of options that determine how Outlook connects when processing mail accounts that use dial-up networking:

- **Warn Before Switching An Existing Dial-Up Connection** Select this option to have Outlook warn you before it disconnects the current dial-up connection to dial another connection specified by the account about to be processed. This warning gives you the option of having Outlook use the current connection instead of dialing the other one.
- **Always Use An Existing Dial-Up Connection** Select this option to have Outlook use the active dial-up connection rather than dialing the one specified in the account settings.

- **Automatically Dial During A Background Send/Receive** When this option is selected, Outlook dials without prompting you when it needs to perform a background send/receive operation.
- **Hang Up When Finished With A Manual Send/Receive** When this option is selected, Outlook hangs up a dial-up connection when it completes a manual send/receive operation (one you initiate by clicking Send/Receive).

Formatting Internet and International Messages

The Mail Format tab of the Options dialog box (choose Tools, Options) provides access to a handful of settings that control how Outlook processes Internet and international messages.

Setting Internet Format

To control how Outlook formats messages sent to Internet recipients, click Internet Format on the Mail Format tab to open the Internet Format dialog box, shown in Figure 7-33.

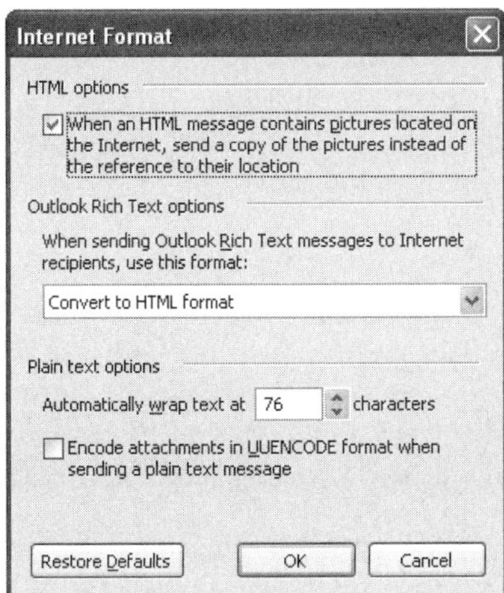

Figure 7-33. Use the Internet Format dialog box to control the format of outgoing Internet messages.

The following list explains the options in the Internet Format dialog box:

- **When An HTML Message Contains Pictures Located On The Internet, Send A Copy Of The Pictures Instead Of The Reference To Their Location** With this check box selected, Outlook inserts a copy of the pictures in the message. Clear this check box to have Outlook insert a hyperlink to the graphics instead.
- **When Sending Outlook Rich Text Messages To Internet Recipients, Use This Format** Use this drop-down list to specify how Outlook converts rich-text messages when sending those messages to Internet recipients.
- **Automatically Wrap Text At *n* Characters** In this box, enter the number of characters per line that Outlook should use for Internet messages.

- **Encode Attachments In UUENCODE Format When Sending A Plain Text Message** When this check box is selected, attachments to messages sent as plain text are encoded within the message as text rather than attached as binary Multipurpose Internet Mail Extensions (MIME) attachments. The recipient's e-mail application must be capable of decoding UUEncoded messages.
- **Restore Defaults** Click this button to restore Outlook's default settings for Internet messages.

Setting International Options

Click International Options on the Mail Format tab to display the International Options dialog box (see Figure 7-34), which lets you specify whether Outlook uses English for message headers and flags and controls the format for outgoing messages.

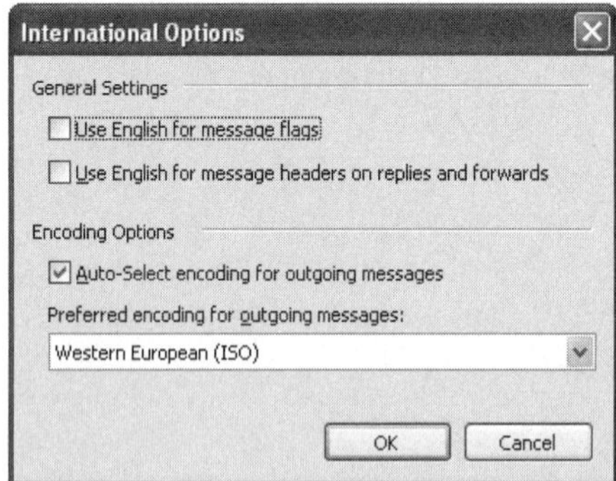

Figure 7-34. Use the International Options dialog box to configure language options for Outlook.

The International Options dialog box includes the following options:

- **Use English For Message Flags** Select this check box to use English for message flag text, such as High Priority or Flag For Follow-Up. If you use a different language and this option is not selected, message flags appear in the selected language rather than in English.
- **Use English For Message Headers On Replies And Forwards** When you're using a non-English version of Outlook, you can select this check box to display message header text—such as From, To, or Subject—in English rather than in the default language.
- **Auto-Select Encoding For Outgoing Messages** Select this check box and then choose a preferred encoding option from the drop-down list to specify the encoding character set for outgoing messages. If this check box is not selected, you can choose Format, Encoding with a message form open and select the encoding option for the message. If this option is enabled, you cannot change the default encoding for the message.
- **Preferred Encoding For Outgoing Messages** Use this drop-down list to specify the encoding character set Outlook should use for outgoing messages. Select the setting to take into account the requirements of the majority of messages you send (based on their destination and the language options you use).

Chapter 8

Filtering, Organizing, and Using Automatic Responses

Without some means of organizing and filtering e-mail, most people would be inundated with messages, many of which are absolutely useless. In addition, when you're out of the office for an extended period—on vacation, for example—and are still being bombarded with new messages, Microsoft Outlook's ability to automatically process and respond to incoming messages can be critical.

This chapter examines the features in Outlook that allow you to automatically manage messages based on a variety of factors, including sender, account, and size of message. For example, you can have Outlook move messages sent by a specific account to a specific folder, giving you an easy way to organize and separate messages from different accounts. This chapter also shows you how to customize your message folder views, which can aid you in organizing and managing your work.

Outlook helps you handle unwanted mail, such as junk and adult content messages, often referred to as *spam*. This chapter explains how to manage and filter out those types of messages. You'll also examine Outlook's ability to automatically respond to messages, which lets you generate Out Of Office replies to incoming messages.

Finding and Organizing Messages with Search Folders

Outlook 2003 introduces a new feature called Search Folders that you will find extremely useful for finding and organizing messages. A search folder isn't really a folder, but rather a special view that functions much like a separate folder. In effect, a search folder is a saved search. You specify conditions for the folder, such as all messages from a specific sender or all messages received in the last day, and Outlook displays in that search folder view those messages that meet the specified conditions.

In a way, a search folder is like a rule that moves messages to a special folder. However, although the messages seem to exist in their own folder, they continue to reside in their respective folders. For example, a search folder might show all messages in the Inbox and Sent Items folders that were sent by Jim Boyce. Even though these messages appear in the Jim Boyce search folder (for example), they are actually still located in the Inbox and Sent Items folders.

Using Search Folders

It isn't difficult at all to use a search folder. The folder list includes a Search Folders branch (see Figure 8-1) that lists all of the search folder contents. Simply click on a search folder in the folder list to view the headers for the messages it contains.

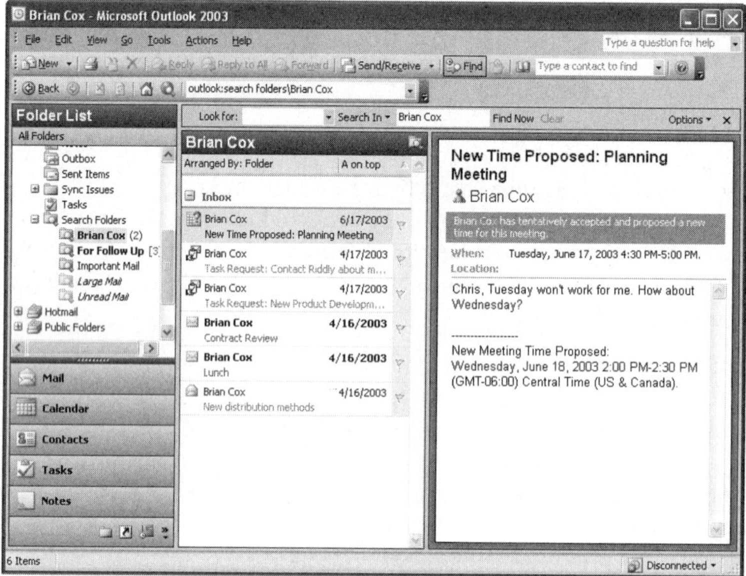

Figure 8-1. Search folders appear under their own branch in the folder list. This folder shows all messages from Brian Cox.

Customizing Search Folders

Outlook includes four search folders by default, which you can use as-is or customize to suit your needs. These folders include the following:

- **For Follow Up** This search folder shows all messages that are flagged for follow-up.
- **Important Mail** This search folder shows all messages that are marked as Important.
- **Large Mail** This search folder shows all messages that are 100 KB or higher.
- **Unread Mail** This search folders shows all messages that are unread.

You can customize these existing search folders as well as those you create yourself. For example, you might increase the value in the Large Mail search folder from 100 KB to 200 KB if you frequently receive messages larger than 100 KB that you don't want included in the Large Mail search folder.

To customize an existing search folder, open the folder list, right-click the folder, and choose Customize This Search Folder to open the Customize dialog box similar to the one shown in Figure 8-2.

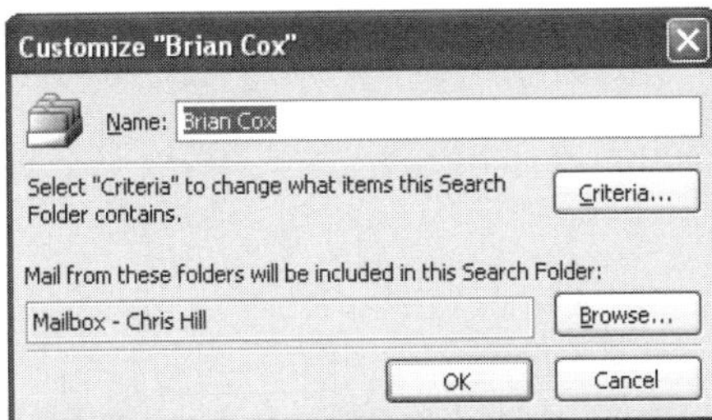

Figure 8-2. Set the criteria or folders to include for a search folder in the Customize dialog box.

You can change the name of the search folder in the Name field on the Customize dialog box. To change the criteria for the search folder, click the Criteria button to display a dialog box that enables you to change your selection. The dialog box that appears depends on the criteria you used when you created the folder. For example, if you are modifying a search folder that locates messages from a specific sender, Outlook displays the Select Names dialog box so you can choose a different person (or additional people).

Tip You can only change the criteria of one of the default search folders, the Large Mail folder. The criteria for the other three can't be changed. However, you can change the folders to be included in the search for all of the default search folders.

To change which folders are included in the search folder, click Browse in the Customize dialog box to open the Select Folder(s) dialog box (see Figure 8-3). Place a check beside each folder to include. Select the Personal Folders or Mailbox branch to include all folders in the mail store in the search. Enable the option Search Subfolders to include in the search all subfolders for a selected folder.

Creating a New Search Folder

If the default search folders don't suit your needs, you can create your own with the criteria and included folders that locate the messages you want. To create a search folder, right-click the Search Folder branch and choose New Search Folder to open the New Search Folder dialog box (see Figure 8-3).

Figure 8-3. Create a new search folder with the New Search Folder dialog box.

There are several predefined search folders, and you can easily create a custom search folder by choosing one from the list. If the search folder you select requires specifying additional criteria, click the Choose button to open a dialog box in which you specify the criteria. Then, in the New Search Folder dialog box, select an account from the Search Mail In drop-down list to search that account.

If the predefined search folders won't do the trick, choose Create a Custom Search Folder and then click Choose to open the Custom Search Folder dialog box to specify a custom criteria for the search folder, search folder name, and folders to include.

Flagging and Monitoring Messages and Contacts

Outlook allows you to *flag* a message to draw the recipient's attention to the message. Perhaps you're sending a message to an assistant, who needs to follow up on the message by a certain day the following week. In that case, you would flag the message for follow-up and specify the due date. When your assistant receives the message, the flag appears in the message header, as shown in Figure 8-4.

New in Microsoft Outlook 2003 is the addition of six flag types, compared to just one in previous versions. You can choose from one of six colored flags each time you flag an item. These different colors can represent different priorities or actions, according to whatever scheme suits you. You can use these different colors to organize your flagged items.

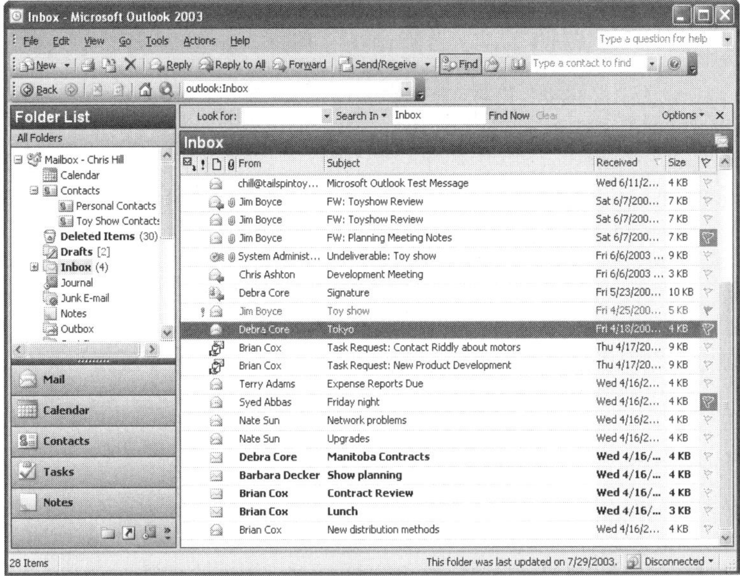

Figure 8-4. You can flag a message to highlight it or to include additional information.

Flagging Outgoing Messages

A flag gives you a means of including additional information or instructions with a message. The information stands out more if you include the flag text in the header rather than in the body of the message, where it might be overlooked. Perhaps most important, the flag can set a reminder on the recipient's system to help ensure that your instructions, whatever they are, are carried out. For example, if you want the recipient to phone you by a specific date regarding the message, the reminder will appear on the recipient's system at the appropriate time (assuming that he or she uses Outlook). Outlook provides several predefined flag messages, or you can create your own message.

Use the following steps to flag a message you send:

1. With the message form open, choose Actions, Follow Up, Add Reminder or click the Follow Up button on the form's Standard toolbar. Either action displays the Flag For Follow Up dialog box, shown in Figure 8-5.

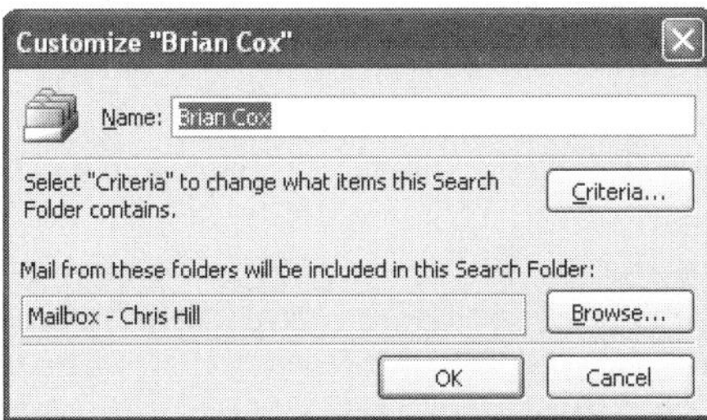

Figure 8-5. Select the flag text or type your own message in this dialog box.

Chapter 8

Note The Actions menu is unavailable in the message form if you use Word as your e-mail editor.

2 From the Flag To drop-down list, select the text you want to include with the flag, or type your own text in this box.

3 If you want to include a due date and a subsequent reminder, select the date in the Due By drop-down list, which opens a calendar you can refer to. Alternatively, you can enter a date, day, time, or other information as text in the Due By box.

4 Click OK and then send the message as you normally would.

Troubleshooting

Reminders don't work for flagged messages you have moved

Incoming messages typically go in the Inbox folder, and the same is true for flagged messages. Outlook displays reminders for flagged messages as long as those messages reside in the Inbox. However, if a flagged message is moved to another folder, either manually or by a message rule, Outlook won't display the reminder at the designated time. If you must move flagged messages, try to move them to a common folder so that they'll be easier to spot. Or you might create a rule that assigns them a High priority level, which will give you a further visual clue when you're searching for flagged messages.

Viewing and Responding to Flagged Messages

When you receive a flagged message, a flag icon appears next to the message header in the message folder. If you have configured Outlook to display the Reading Pane, the flag text appears in the Reading Pane header above the addresses (see Figure 8-6). The flag icons help you identify flagged messages when the Reading Pane is turned off. You can sort the view in the folder using the Flag column, listing all flagged messages together to make them easier to locate. To view the flag text when the Reading Pane is turned off, simply open the message. The flag text appears above the addresses.

Outlook has no special mechanism for processing flagged messages other than the reminders previously discussed. You simply call, e-mail, or otherwise respond based on the flag message. To change the flag status, right-click a flagged message and choose Flag Complete. To remove the flag from the message, right-click a flagged message and choose Clear Flag.

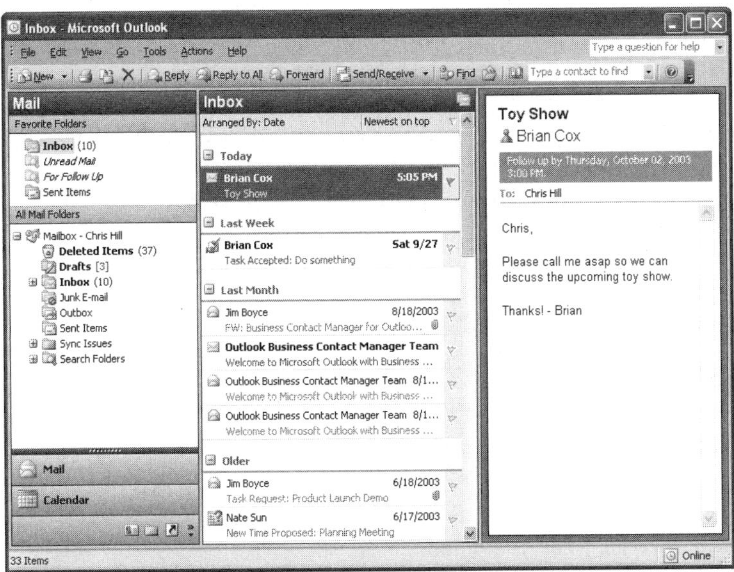

Figure 8-6. Flagged messages display a flag icon in the message folder, and the flag text appears in the Reading Pane header.

Flagging Sent and Other Messages

In addition to flagging your outgoing messages, you also can flag messages that you've already sent. Although this action can't display a flag after the fact on the recipient's system, it does give you a way to flag and follow-up messages from your end. You can flag messages in any message folder, including the Sent Items folder. You can work with these flags and flagged messages the same way you work with the flagged messages you receive from others.

> **Note** When you send a flagged message, Outlook also flags the copy of the message that it saves in the Sent Items folder (assuming that you have configured Outlook to save a copy of sent messages).

In addition to flagging items that you send, you might also want to flag messages you have received from others that didn't originally include flags. For example, you might flag a message that you need to follow up, or you might use the flag text to indicate other tasks you must perform in connection with the message or its subject.

> **Tip** **Add notes to received messages**
>
> You can use flags to add notes to messages you receive from others, giving yourself a quick reminder of pending tasks or other pertinent information. If the messages reside in your Inbox folder, Outlook can generate a reminder for you concerning the flagged item. To set up Outlook to do so, right-click the message, choose Follow Up, Add Reminder, and then set a due date and time.

Flagging Contact Items

You can flag contact items as well as messages, marking them for follow-up or adding other notations to an item. For example, you might flag a contact item to remind yourself to call the person by a certain time or date or to send documents to the contact. A flag you add to a contact item shows up in all contacts views, but it isn't always readily apparent—for instance, the flag shows up as text in Address Cards and Detailed Address Cards views (see Figure 8-7). In other views, Outlook uses a flag icon (see Figure 8-8). As you can for messages, you can use one of Outlook's predefined flags to mark a contact item, or you can specify your own flag text.

Figure 8-7. You can flag contacts as well as messages.

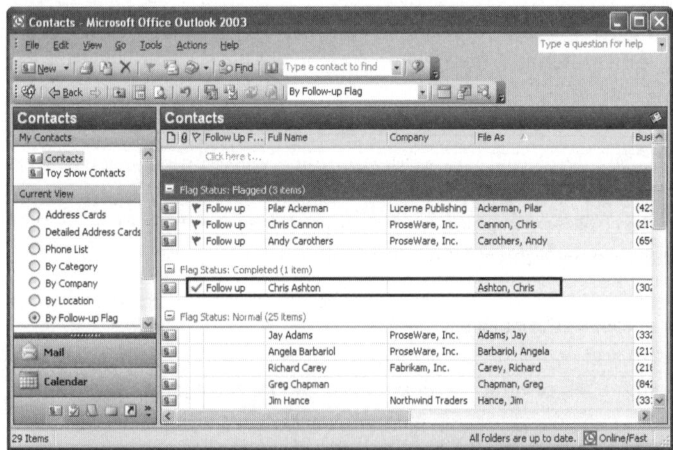

Figure 8-8. You can list items in the Contacts folder by flag.

To assign a flag to a contact item, follow these steps:

1. Right-click the contact item and choose Follow Up.
2. In the Flag For Follow Up dialog box, select the flag type in the Flag To drop-down list, or type in your own text.
3. Specify the due date and time, and then click OK.

Note You can't set the flag type (color) for a contact as you can for a message. The Contacts folder even ignores the default flag color you set in the Inbox, instead always flagging contacts with red flags.

Outlook uses the same icons for flagged contact items as it does for messages. A red flag icon indicates a pending action, and a check mark indicates a completed action. To change the flag status for a contact item, right-click the item and choose Flag Complete or Clear Flag.

You'll sometimes find it helpful to view the Contacts folder sorted by flag, so you can see at a glance which contacts are flagged and what action is required. You can group by flag in several different views, but Outlook also provides a standard view that sorts contacts by flag, as shown in Figure 8-8. To display this view of the Contacts folder, choose View, Arrange By, Current View, By Follow-Up Flag.

Grouping Messages by Customizing the Folder View

To help you organize information, Outlook allows you to customize various message folder views. By default, Outlook displays only a small selection of columns for messages, including the From, Subject, Received, Size, Flag, Attachment, and Importance columns.

For details on how to add and remove columns from a folder view to show more or less information about your messages, see "Working with the Standard Outlook Views," page 56.

You can easily sort messages using any of the column headers as your sort criterion. To view messages sorted alphabetically by sender, for example, click the column header of the From column. To sort messages by date received, click the column header of the Received column. Click the Attachment column header to view all messages with attachments.

In addition to managing your message view by controlling columns and sorting, you can *group* messages based on columns. Whereas sorting allows you to arrange messages in order using a single column as the sort criterion, grouping allows you to display the messages in groups based on one or more columns. For example, you might group messages based on sender, and then on date received, and finally on whether they have attachments. This method helps you locate messages more quickly than if you had to search through a message list sorted only by sender.

Grouping messages in a message folder is a relatively simple process:

1. In Outlook, open the folder you want to organize by grouping the messages it contains.
2. Right-click the column header and choose Group By This Field if you want to group based only on the selected field. Choose Group By Box if you want to group based on multiple columns.

> **Tip** Close the Reading Pane if you are unable to right-click a column and choose Group By This Field.

Processing Messages Automatically

If you're like most people, you are often swamped by messages that are useless or annoying, including sales pitches, announcements, and possibly adult content messages, all of which you probably didn't request. Outlook gives you the means to block those messages or process them automatically to clean out your Inbox. If you receive a lot of messages, you might want to have the messages analyzed as they come in, to perform actions on them before you read them. For example, you can have all messages from a specific account sent to a specific folder. Perhaps you want messages that come from specific senders to be assigned High priority. Whatever the case, Outlook lets you manipulate your incoming messages to accomplish the result you want. This section of the chapter shows you how, starting with an overview of message rules.

> **Tip** **Limit the number of message rules you create**
> Because of a limitation in Message Application Programming Interface (MAPI), MAPI allocates only 32 KB for storing server-side rules. Although this is fine for most users, you could reach that limit if you create too many server-side rules. However, it's unlikely that you will run out of room for client-side rules.

Understanding Message Rules

A *message rule* defines the actions Outlook takes for a sent or received message if the message meets certain conditions specified by the rule. For example, you might create a rule that tells Outlook to move all messages from a specific POP3 account into a specified folder rather than leaving them in your default Inbox. Or you might want Outlook to place a copy of all outgoing High priority messages in a special folder.

In Outlook, you use several *conditions* for defining a message rule. These conditions can include the account from which the message was received, the message size, the sender or recipient, specific words in various fields or in the message itself, the priority assigned to the message, and a variety of other conditions. In addition, you can combine multiple actions to refine the rule and further control its function. For example, you might create a rule that moves all your incoming POP3 messages to a folder other than the Inbox and also deletes any messages that contain certain words in the subject field. Although not a complete list, the following are some of the most common tasks you might perform with message rules:

- Organize messages based on sender, recipient, or subject.
- Copy or move messages from one folder to another.
- Flag messages.
- Delete messages automatically.
- Reply to, forward, or redirect messages to individuals or distribution lists.
- Respond to messages with a specific reply.
- Monitor message importance (priority).
- Print a message.
- Play a sound.
- Execute a script or start an application.

For details on how to generate automatic replies to messages, see "Creating Automatic Responses with the Out Of Office Assistant," page 252, and "Creating Automatic Responses with Custom Rules," page 256.

Whatever your message processing requirements, Outlook probably offers a solution through a message rule, based on either a single condition or multiple conditions. You also can create multiple rules that work together to process your mail. As you begin to create and use message rules, keep in mind that you can define a rule to function either when a message is received or when it is sent. When you create a rule, you specify the event to which the rule applies.

You create all message rules in the same way, regardless of the specific purpose of the rule. Rather than focusing on defining rules for specific tasks, this chapter explains the general process of creating rules. With an understanding of this process, you should have no problem setting up rules for a variety of situations. In fact, creating message rules is relatively easy, thanks to Outlook's Rules Wizard.

To start the wizard in Outlook, choose Tools, Rules And Alerts. You'll first see the Rules And Alerts dialog box, shown in Figure 8-9. The E-Mail Rules list contains all the existing rules that you have defined. Outlook applies the rules in the order in which they are listed, an important fact to consider when you're creating rules.

Note You can't open the Rules and Alerts dialog box if you are working offline with an Exchange Server account.

For more information about determining the order in which message rules execute, see "Setting Rule Order," page 236.

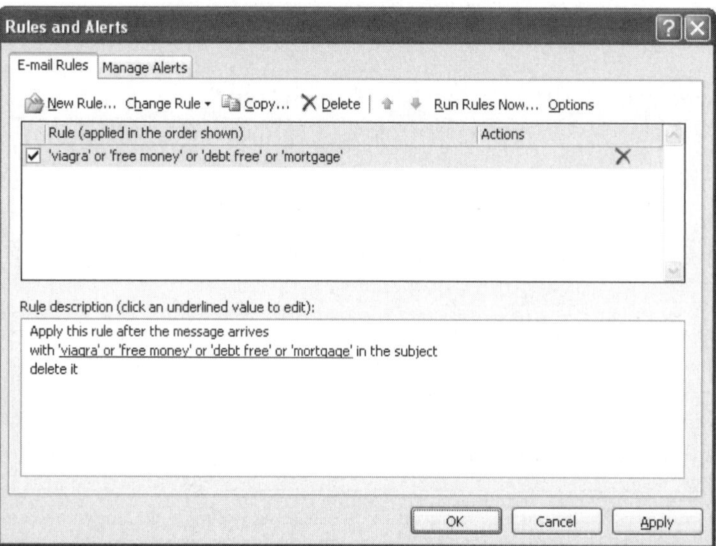

Figure 8-9. The Rules And Alerts dialog box displays existing rules and allows you to create and modify message rules.

Troubleshooting

Rules don't work for some of your accounts

If some of your rules work only for certain accounts and not for others, the problem could be that some of those accounts are HTTP-based mail accounts. Outlook's message rules do not process messages sent to or received from HTTP-based mail accounts, such as Microsoft Hotmail, nor can you manually apply rules to process messages in the Inbox sent from HTTP accounts after the messages have been received. Check with your HTTP mail service provider to determine whether it offers server-side message rules that you can use in place of Outlook's rules to process your messages.

You might use certain rules all the time but use others only at special times. Each rule includes a check box beside it. Select this check box when you want to use the rule; clear it when you want to disable the rule.

Creating Client-Side and Server-Side Rules

In Outlook, you can create either *client-side* or *server-side* rules. Outlook stores client-side rules locally on your computer and uses them to process messages that come to your local folders, although you also can use client-side rules to process messages on Microsoft Exchange Server. A client-side rule is needed when you're moving messages to a local folder rather than to a folder on Exchange Server. For example, if messages from a specific sender that arrive in your Exchange Server Inbox must be moved to one of your personal folders, the rule must function as a client-side rule, because the Exchange Server computer is not able to access your personal folders.

Server-side rules reside on the Exchange Server rather than on your local computer, and they can usually process messages in your Exchange Server mailbox whether or not you're logged on and running Outlook. The Out Of Office Assistant (discussed later in this chapter) is a good example of how server-side rules can be used. It processes messages that come into your Inbox on the server even when your computer is turned off and you're a thousand miles away. As long as Exchange Server is up and functioning, the server-side rules can perform their intended function.

When you create a rule, Outlook examines the rule's logic to determine whether it can function as a server-side rule or a client-side rule. If it can function as a server-side rule, Outlook stores the rule on the Exchange Server and treats it as a server-side rule. If the rule must function as a client-side rule, Outlook stores it locally and appends the parenthetical phrase *(client-only)* after the rule name to designate it as a client-side rule. Figure 8-10 shows a selection of rules in Outlook, some of which function as client-side rules and others that function as server-side rules.

Note If you don't use an Exchange Server account, all rules you create are client-side rules.

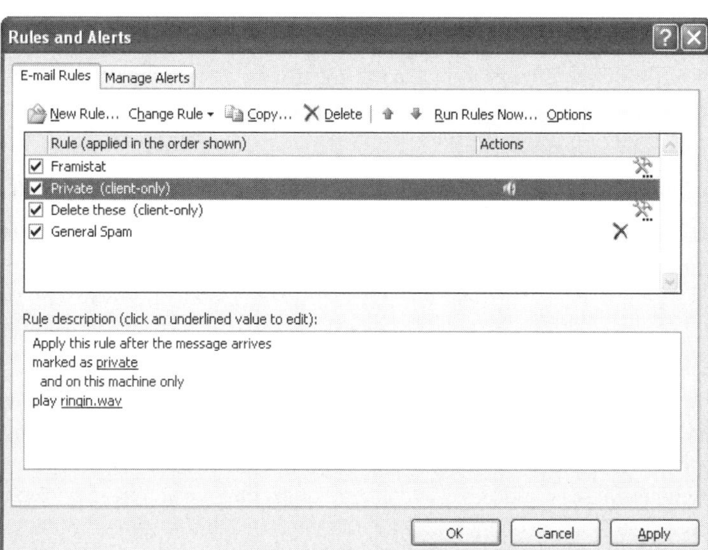

Figure 8-10. Outlook supports server-side rules as well as client-side rules.

Troubleshooting

Your server-side rules don't execute

Server-side rules, which process messages that come into your Exchange Server Inbox, usually can execute when Outlook isn't running. In some cases, however, server-side rules can't function unless Outlook is running and you're connected to the server.

When a server-side rule is unable to process a message because Outlook is offline (or for other reasons), the Exchange Server generates a deferred action message (DAM), which it uses to process the message when Outlook comes back online. When Outlook goes online, it receives the DAM, performs the action, and deletes the DAM.

For information on how to apply client-side rules to specific folders or to all accounts, see "Applying Rules to Specific Folders," page 233.

Creating New Rules

When you create a message rule, you must first specify whether you want to create the rule from a predefined template or from scratch. Because the templates address common message processing tasks, using a template can save you a few steps. When you create a rule from scratch, you set up all the conditions for the rule as you create it. You can use many different conditions to define the actions the rule performs, all of which are available in the Rules Wizard. With or without a template, you have full control over the completed rule and can modify it to suit your needs. Outlook's templates are a great way to get started, however, if you're new to using Outlook or message rules.

Let's look first at the general procedure for creating rules and then at more specific steps. The general process is as follows:

1. Select the Inbox in which the rule will apply. For example, if you have an Exchange Server account and an IMAP account, you must choose the Inbox to which the rule will apply.

Note If you have only one account, or an Exchange Server account and one or more POP3 accounts, you have only one Inbox to choose as the target for the rule. IMAP accounts, however, use their own Inbox folders, meaning you can apply rules to these accounts separately from your Exchange Server and POP3 accounts. For example, if you have an Exchange Server account, two POP3 accounts, and an IMAP account in the same profile, you'll see two Inboxes listed as possible targets for the rule: one for the Exchange Server and POP3 accounts and one for the IMAP account.

2. Specify when the rule applies—that is, when a message is received or when it is sent.

3. Specify the conditions that define which messages are processed—for example, account, sender, priority, or content.
4. Specify the action to take for messages that meet the specified conditions—for example, move, copy, or delete the message; change its priority; flag it for follow up; or generate a reply.
5. Create other message rules to accomplish other tasks as needed, including possibly working in conjunction with other rules.
6. Set the order of rules as needed.

Troubleshooting

You have conflicting message rules

Outlook's support for multiple accounts, combined with its ability to use both client-side and server-side rules, can pose certain problems. For example, assume that you have a POP3 account that delivers messages to your Exchange Server mailbox rather than to a local store. Also assume that you create a client-side rule to process certain POP3 messages but that you also have a server-side rule for processing messages. The server-side rule takes precedence because the client-side rule doesn't execute until the message arrives in the Inbox, even though the message came through your computer before it was placed in your Exchange Server mailbox. Thus the message is processed by the server-side rule, potentially bypassing the local rule. If the server-side rule deletes the message, for example, the message will never make it back to your personal folders to allow the client-side rule to act on it.

The order of rule precedence is important for the same reason—two rules, even on the same side, can perform conflicting actions. Keep this in mind when you're creating rules and working with non-Exchange accounts that store messages in your Exchange Server mailbox.

Note When you specify multiple conditions for a rule, the rule combines these conditions in a logical AND operation—that is, the message must meet all of the conditions to be considered subject to the rule. You also can create rules that use a logical OR operation, meaning that the message is subject to the rule if it meets any one of the conditions. For details, see "Creating Rules That Use OR Logic," page 235.

The following steps guide you through the more specific process of creating a message rule:

1. In Outlook, choose Tools, Rules And Alerts to display the Rules And Alerts dialog box.
2. In the Apply Changes To This Folder drop-down list, select the folder to which you want to apply the rule. If you have only one Inbox, you don't need to make a selection.

3 Click New Rule to display the wizard page shown in Figure 8-11.

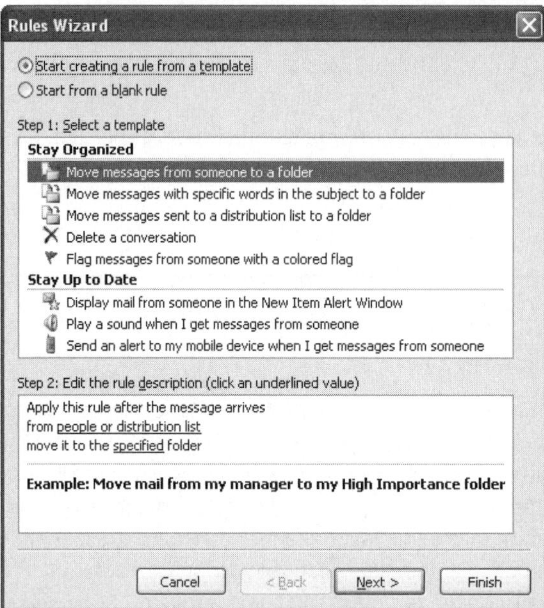

Figure 8-11. To create a rule, you can use a template or start from scratch.

4 If you want to use a template to create the rule, select the template from the list and click Next. To create a rule from scratch, choose Start From A Blank Rule and continue with step 5.

5 If you're starting a rule from scratch, Outlook prompts you to select when you want the rule to execute. Select Check Messages When They Arrive to apply the rule to incoming messages, or select Check Messages After Sending to apply the rule to sent messages. If you're creating the rule from a template, Outlook skips this step, because the processing event is already defined by the template.

6 In the conditions list in the top half of the wizard page shown in Figure 8-12, select the conditions that define the messages to which the rule should apply. For template-based rules, a condition is already selected, but you can change the condition and add others as necessary.

7 In the rule description area of the wizard page, click the underlined words that specify the data for the conditions. For example, if you're creating a rule to process messages from a specific account, click the word *specified*, which is underlined, and then select the account from the Account dialog box. Click OK and then click Next.

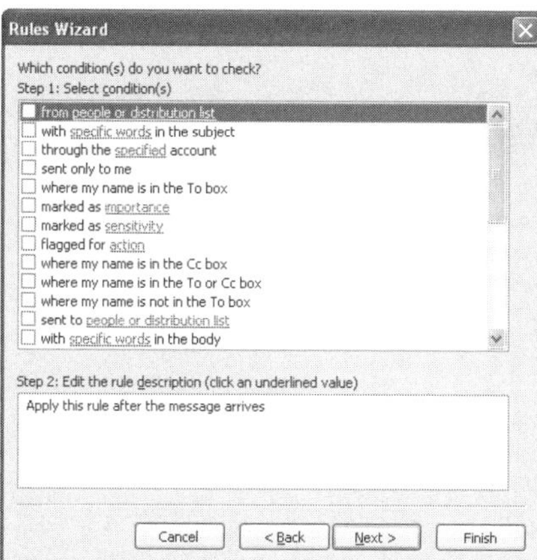

Figure 8-12. Select the conditions to define the messages to which the rule will apply.

8 In the upper half of the new wizard page, select the actions you want Outlook to apply to messages that satisfy the specified conditions (see Figure 8-13).

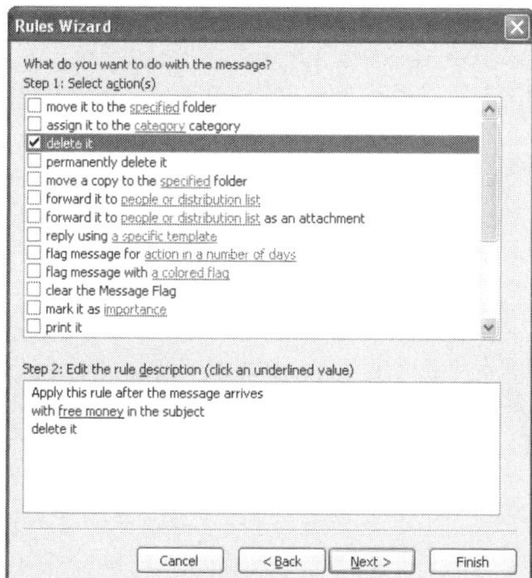

Figure 8-13. Select the actions Outlook should take for messages that meet the rule's conditions.

9 In the lower half of the wizard page, click each underlined value needed to define the action and specify the data in the resulting dialog box. Click OK to close the dialog box and then click Next.

10 Select exceptions to the rule if needed, and specify the data for exception conditions (see Figure 8-14). Click Next.

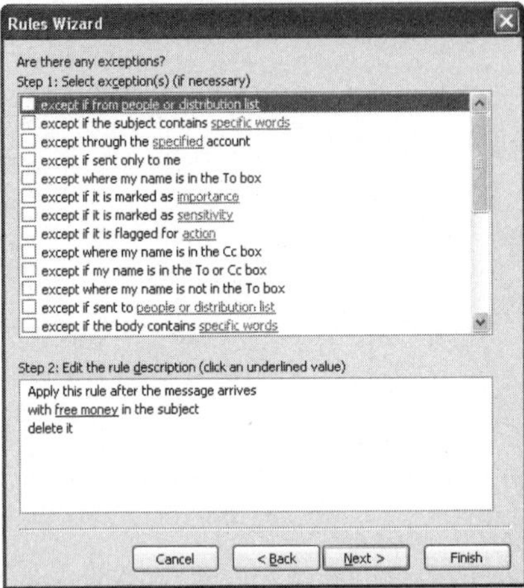

Figure 8-14. You can specify exceptions to the rule to fine-tune message processing.

11 On the final page of the Rules Wizard (see Figure 8-15), specify a name for the rule as you want it to appear in Outlook.

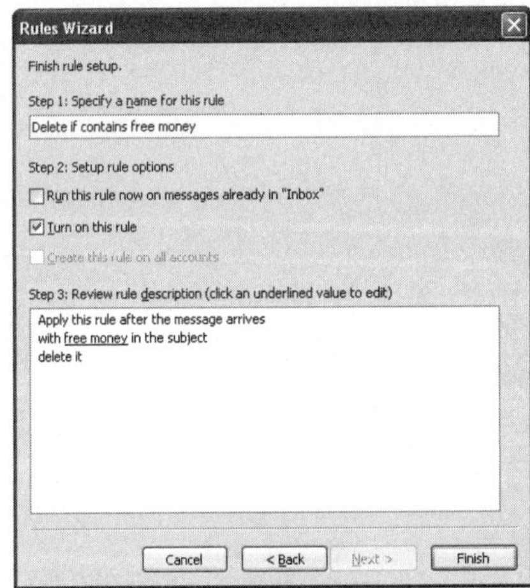

Figure 8-15. Configure a name and options for the rule.

12 Select options according to the following list, and click Finish:

- **Run This Rule Now On Messages Already In "Inbox"** Select this check box if you want Outlook to apply the rule to messages that you have already received and that currently reside in the Inbox folder in which the rule applies. For example, if you have created a rule to delete messages from a specific recipient, any existing messages from the recipient are deleted after you select this check box and click Finish to create the rule.

- **Turn On This Rule** Select this check box to begin applying the rule you have created.
- **Create This Rule On All Accounts** Select this check box to apply the rule to all applicable folders. For example, if you have three folders listed in the Apply Changes To This Folder drop-down list at the top of the initial Rules Wizard page, selecting this check box causes Outlook to apply the rule to all three folders rather than only the selected folder.

For more details about using rules in various folders, see the following section, "Applying Rules to Specific Folders."

Tip To create a rule that operates on all messages, don't specify a condition that Outlook must check. Outlook prompts you to verify that you want the rule applied to all messages.

Applying Rules to Specific Folders

When you first open the Rules Wizard, it displays the rules that have already been defined for your profile, both client-side and server-side, as shown earlier in Figure 8-7. You might recall that you use the Apply Changes To This Folder drop-down list at the top of the dialog box to select the folder for which you want to create or modify a rule.

Regardless of the folder you select, the rules list in the wizard always displays your server-side rules. The client-side rules that appear in the list depend on the folder you select. The list for a selected folder contains only the client-side rules for that particular folder, unless you've copied a rule to multiple folders or created a rule expressly for all folders.

To apply a rule to a specific folder, select that folder in the Apply Changes To This Folder drop-down list when you begin creating the rule. To apply a rule to all folders, select the Create This Rule On All Accounts option at the completion of the wizard (as explained in step 12 on page 232).

Copying Rules to Other Folders

By default, Outlook doesn't create rules for all folders; instead, it creates the rule only for the selected folder. If you have created a rule for one folder but want to use it in a different folder, you can copy the rule to the other folder.

Follow these steps to do so:

1. Choose Tools, Rules And Alerts to open the Rules And Alerts dialog box.
2. Select the rule you want to copy and click Copy.
3. When you're prompted, select the destination folder for the rule and click OK.

For details on sharing rules with other Outlook users, see "Sharing Rules with Others," page 238.

Creating Rules Based on Existing Messages

In some situations, you'll want to create rules from specific messages. For example, if you frequently receive unwanted messages from a particular sender, you might want to delete the messages without downloading them. You can specify the address when you begin to create a rule in the Rules Wizard, but in this case it would be easier to create the rule from the message instead, saving you the trouble of typing the sender's name or address. Or, perhaps the subject of a particular group of messages always contains a unique string of text, and you want to build the rule around that text. Rather than typing the text yourself, you can create the rule from one of the messages.

Here's how to create a rule from a specific message:

1. In Outlook, open the folder containing the message.
2. Right-click the message header and choose Create Rule.
3. Outlook displays a Create Rule dialog box that reflects the properties of the selected message—sender and subject, for example (see Figure 8-16). Select an action from the Do The Following group in the dialog box. Or, click Advanced Options to open the Rules Wizard to choose additional actions. Select a condition and complete the rule as you normally would if you were creating it from a template or from scratch.

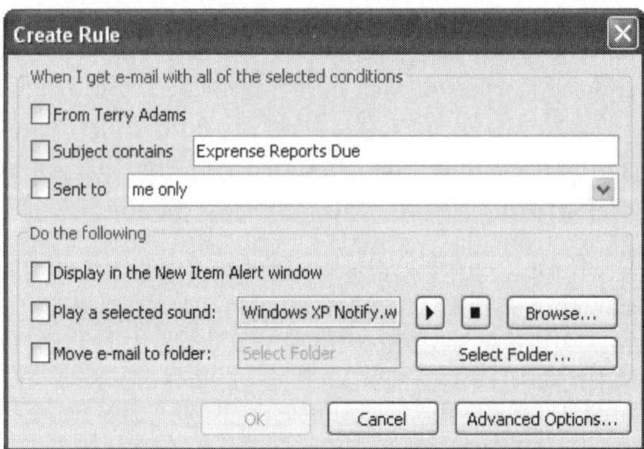

Figure 8-16. Use the Create Rule dialog box to specify basic rule conditions and actions.

> **Note** Remember that HTTP accounts don't support Outlook rules. If you right-click a message stored in a folder for an HTTP-based mail account, you'll see that the Create Rule command is not available. Also, rules are always created in the Inbox, not in other folders. You can, however, run rules manually in other folders.

Creating Rules That Use OR Logic

To this point, you've explored relatively simple rules that function based on a single condition or on multiple AND conditions. In the latter case, the rule specifies multiple conditions and applies only to messages that meet all the conditions. If a rule is defined by three AND conditions, for example, Outlook uses it only on messages that meet condition 1, condition 2, and condition 3.

You also can create rules that follow OR logic. In this case, a rule specifies a single condition, but multiple criteria for that condition. The rule will then act on any message that meets at least one of the criteria for the condition. For example, you might create a rule that deletes a message if the subject of the message contains any one of three words. If one of the conditions is met (that is, if the subject of a message contains at least one of the three words), Outlook deletes that message.

With Outlook, you can create several rules that use OR logic within a single condition, but you can't create a single rule that uses OR logic on multiple conditions. For example, you might create a rule that deletes a message if the message contains the phrase *MLM, Free Money,* or *Guaranteed Results*. However, you can't create a message rule that deletes the message if the subject of the message contains the words *Free Money* (condition 1), or if the message is from a specific sender (condition 2), or if the message is larger than a given size (condition 3). OR must operate within a single condition. When you create a rule with multiple conditions, Outlook always treats multiple conditions in the same rule using AND logic. You would have to create three separate rules to accommodate the latter example.

Inside Out

Outlook Express uses OR logic better

Microsoft Outlook Express beats Outlook hands down when it comes to creating rules that use OR logic. The interface in Outlook Express is much more intuitive, and the ability to create such rules is obvious to the user because of the way Microsoft designed the interface. It would be great if, for example, you could create a single rule with multiple OR conditions in Outlook as easily as you can in Outlook Express.

If you have a situation where you need to check for more than one piece of data in a single condition, you can do so easily enough; however, when you create the rule and define the condition, specify multiple items. For example, if you need a rule that processes messages based on four possible strings in the subject of the messages, click Specific Words in the rule description area of the Rules Wizard. In the Search Text dialog box, enter the strings separately. As you can see in Figure 8-17, the search list includes the word *or* to indicate that the rule applies if any one of the words appears in the subject.

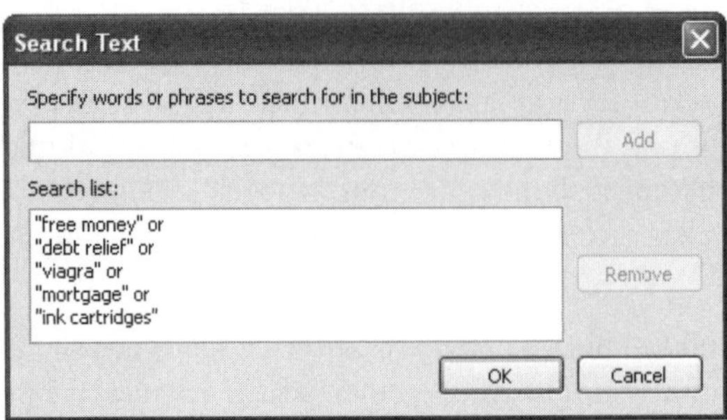

Figure 8-17. Specify data separately to create a rule that uses OR logic.

Although you can't create a single rule with OR logic operating on multiple conditions in Outlook, you can create rules that combine AND and OR logic. For example, you might create a rule that applied if the message was from a specific sender and the subject contained the words *Free Money* or *Guaranteed Results.* Keep in mind that you must specify two conditions—not one—to build the rule. The first condition would check for the sender and the second would check for the words *Free Money* or *Guaranteed Results.*

Modifying Rules

You can modify a rule at any time after you create it. Modifying a rule is much like creating one. To modify a rule, choose Tools, Rules And Alerts to open the Rules And Alerts dialog box. Select the rule you want to modify and click Change Rule to display a menu of editing options. If you select Edit Rule Settings from the menu, Outlook presents the same options you saw when you created the rule, and you can work with them the same way. Click Rename Rule to change the name of the rule, or click an action to add the selected action to the rule (retaining any existing actions).

Setting Rule Order

Outlook executes rules for incoming messages when they arrive in the Inbox, whether on the server or locally (depending on whether the rules are client-side or server-side). Outlook executes rules for outgoing messages when the messages arrive in the Sent Items folder.

As mentioned earlier, the order in which rules are listed in Outlook determines how Outlook applies them. In some situations, the sequence could be important. Perhaps you have one rule that moves high-priority messages to a separate folder and another rule that notifies you when high-priority messages arrive. For the latter rule to work properly, it needs to execute before the one that moves the messages, because the notification rule won't execute if the messages are no longer in the Inbox.

You can control the order of Outlook rules quite easily by taking the following steps:

1. In Outlook, choose Tools, Rules And Alerts to open the Rules And Alerts dialog box.
2. Select a rule to be moved.

3 Use the Move Up and Move Down buttons to change the order in the list (see Figure 8-18). Rules execute in the order listed, the one at the top executing first and the one at the bottom executing last.

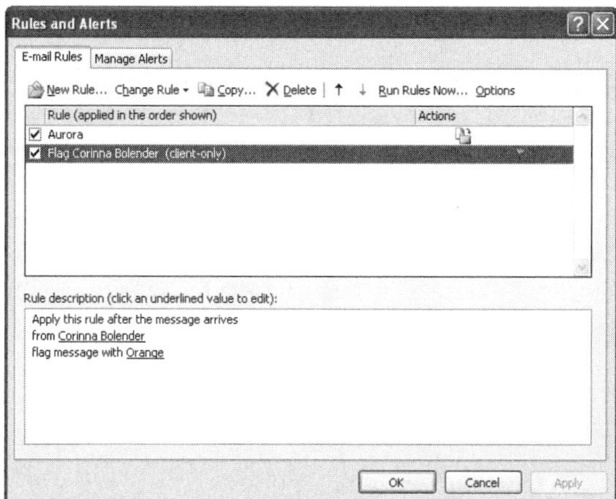

Figure 8-18. You can control execution order for rules by rearranging the rules list.

Stopping Rules from Processing

In certain cases, you might want your message rules to stop processing altogether. Perhaps someone has sent you a very large message that is causing your dial-up connection to time out or is taking a long time to download. You would like to create a rule to delete the message without downloading it, but you don't want any of your other rules to execute. In this case, you would place a new rule at the top of the list and define it so that the last action it takes is to stop processing any other rules. In effect, this allows you to bypass your other rules without going through the trouble of disabling them.

You can also use the Stop Processing More Rules action to control rule execution in other situations. To stop Outlook from executing other rules when a message meets a specific condition, include Stop Processing More Rules as the last action for the rule. You'll find this action in the What Do You Want To Do With The Message list in the wizard.

Disabling and Removing Rules

In some cases, you might want message rules to execute only at certain times. Perhaps you use a rule to do routine cleanup on your mail folders but don't want the rule to run automatically. Or perhaps you want to create a rule to use only once or twice but you would like to keep it in case you need it again later. In those cases, you can disable the rule. Choose Tools, Rules And Alerts and then clear the check box for that rule in the list. Only those rules with check boxes that are selected will apply to incoming or outgoing messages.

Because the amount of space allocated for message rules in Outlook is finite, removing unused rules can make room for additional ones, particularly if you have several complex rules. If you don't plan to use a rule again, you can remove it by choosing Tools, Rules And Alerts, selecting the rule, and clicking Delete.

Sharing Rules with Others

By default, Outlook stores server-side rules on the Exchange Server and stores client-side rules on your local system. Regardless of where your message rules are stored, you can share them with others by exporting the rules to a file. You can then send the file as an e-mail attachment or place it on a network share (or a local share) to allow other users to access it. You can also export the rules to create a backup of them for safekeeping or in the event you need to move your Outlook rules to a new computer, as explained in the next section.

Follow these steps to export your message rules to a file:

1. In Outlook, choose Tools, Rules And Alerts.
2. In the Rules And Alerts dialog box, click Options.
3. Click Export Rules (see Figure 8-19), and then select a path for the file in the resulting Save Exported Rules As dialog box (a standard file/save dialog box).

Figure 8-19. Use the Options dialog box to import and export rules.

4. To save the rules using either Microsoft Outlook 2000 or Microsoft Outlook 98 format, select a format in the Save As Type drop-down list.
5. Click Save.

You can export your rules in any of four formats, depending on the version of Outlook used by the people with whom you want to share your rules. If you need to share with various users, export using the earliest version of Outlook. Later versions will be able to import the rules because they are forward-compatible.

> **Note** See "Sharing a Common PST with the Briefcase," page 942, to learn how to share an entire personal folders file (PST) with other users. Sharing a PST in this way enables multiple users to access contacts and other items.

Backing Up and Restoring Rules

Outlook stores server-side rules in your Exchange Server mailbox, so in principle there is no reason to back up your server-side rules. I say "in principle" because that point of view assumes the Exchange Server administrator is performing adequate backups of your mailbox so you won't lose your messages or your rules. It's still a good idea to back up server-side rules just in case, using the method explained previously in the section "Sharing Rules with Others."

Outlook stores client-side rules in the default mail store—that is, the PST defined in your Outlook profile as the location for incoming mail. Storing the rules in the PST simplifies moving your rules to another computer, because you are also likely to move your PST to the other computer to retain all of your Outlook items. To make this process work, however, you need to add the PST to the second computer in a certain way.

Outlook checks the default mail store PST for the rules, but doesn't check any other PSTs you might have added to your profile. So, if you added an e-mail account to the profile and then added the PST from your old system, you won't see your rules.

One of the easiest methods for making sure things get set up right is to add the PST to your profile before you add the e-mail account. Then when you add the account, Outlook uses the existing PST as the default store. The result is that your rules will be available without any additional manipulation.

Here's how to make it happen. Copy the PST to your second computer. Then, create a new Outlook profile on the computer. In the E-mail Accounts Wizard, choose View Or Change Existing E-Mail Accounts and click Next. Click New Outlook Data File and add the PST copied from the original computer. Click Finish in the wizard and click OK when Outlook asks if you really want to create a profile with no e-mail account. Then, open the profile's properties again and add the e-mail account with the wizard. Instead of creating a new PST, Outlook uses the existing one in the profile.

When you open Outlook you should now have access to the rules stored in the PST, plus all of your existing Outlook items.

Using the Organizer Pane to Create Rules

The Rules Wizard isn't the only method you can use to manage messages in Outlook. Using the organizer pane provides an easier way to create certain types of rules, making it an attractive alternative for novice users. With this method, however, you do have fewer options and less flexibility.

When you choose Tools, Organize with the Inbox open, Outlook changes the view to include the organizer pane at the top of the view, as shown in Figure 8-20. The organizer pane includes three modes:

- **Using Folders** Use this mode to move selected messages into a specified folder.
- **Using Colors** Use this mode to apply a specified color to messages with a specific sender or recipient. Outlook changes the color of the message header in the Inbox accordingly. You can also color messages sent only to you.

- **Using Views** Use this mode to choose a view for the Inbox.

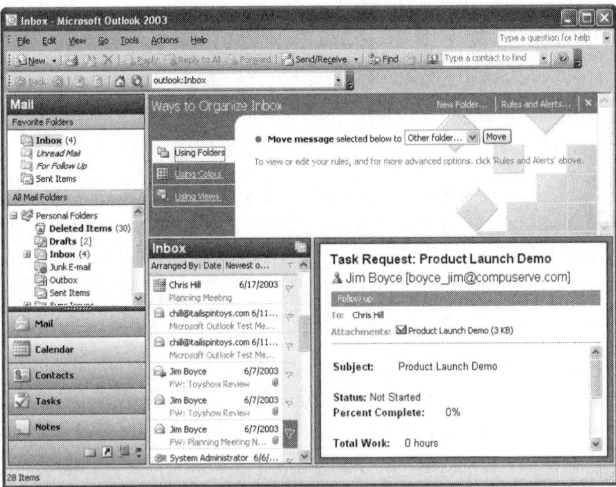

Figure 8-20. Use the organizer pane to manage messages with colors, folders, and views.

Managing messages with the organizer pane is generally self-explanatory; it's included here only to identify it as an alternative to the Rules Wizard. If you provide support for other Outlook users, you might want to recommend the organizer pane to those users you believe will have difficulty using the Rules Wizard.

Using Rules to Move Messages Between Accounts

One common task users often want to perform is to move messages between accounts. Assume that you have two accounts: an Exchange Server account for work and a POP3 account for personal messages. You have specified the Exchange Server mailbox as the delivery location for new mail, so all your POP3 messages go into your Exchange Server Inbox. However, you now want those messages to go into an Inbox in a local PST rather than your Exchange Server mailbox. In this case, it's a simple matter to move the personal messages from the Exchange Server Inbox to the POP3 Inbox. Just create a rule that moves messages that meet the specified conditions to your POP3 Inbox.

Here's how to accomplish this:

1. In Outlook, choose Tools, Rules And Alerts to open the Rules And Alerts dialog box.
2. Click New, select Start From A Blank Rule, and click Next.
3. Select Through The Specified Account. In the rule description area, click the underlined word *specified* and select your POP3 account. Then, click OK.
4. Click Next. Select Move It To The Specified Folder, and click the underlined word *specified* in the rule description area.
5. Select the folder in your PST to which the messages should be moved and click OK.

6. Click Next. Specify any exceptions to the rule and then click Next again.
7. Specify a name for the rule and other options as needed and then click Finish.

Running Rules Manually and in Specific Folders

Normally you use message rules to process messages when they arrive in your Inbox or are placed in the Sent Messages folder. However, you also can run rules manually at any time. Perhaps you have created a rule that you want to use periodically to clean out certain types of messages or move them to a specific folder. You don't want the rule to operate every time you check mail; instead, you want to execute it only when you think it's necessary. In this case, you can run the rule manually.

You might also want to run a rule manually when you need to run it in a folder other than the Inbox. For example, assume that you've deleted messages from a specific sender and now want to restore them, moving the messages from the Deleted Items folder back to your Inbox. In this situation, you could create the rule and then execute it manually in the Deleted Items folder.

It's easy to run a rule manually and in a specific folder following these steps:

1. Choose Tools, Rules And Alerts.
2. Click Run Rules Now. Outlook displays the Run Rules Now dialog box, shown in Figure 8-21.

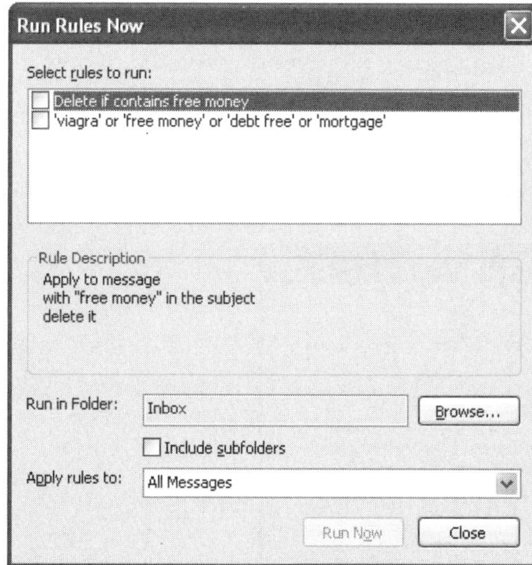

Figure 8-21. Use the Run Rules Now dialog box to run a rule manually in a specified folder.

3. Select the rule you want to run in the list. By default, Outlook will run the rule in the Inbox unless you specify otherwise. Click Browse to browse for a different folder. If you also want to run the rule in subfolders of the selected folder, select the Include Subfolders check box.

4 In the Apply Rules To drop-down list, select the type of messages on which you want to run the rule (All Messages, Read Messages, or Unread Messages).

5 Click Run Now to execute the rule, or click Close to cancel.

Managing Junk and Adult Content Mail

Tired of wading through so much junk mail? Anyone with an e-mail account these days is hard-pressed to avoid unsolicited ads, invitations to multilevel marketing schemes, or unwanted adult content messages. Fortunately, Outlook offers several features to help you deal with all the junk coming through your Inbox.

Outlook 2003 completely revamps the junk and adult content filters in the previous editions of Outlook to provide much better antispam features. Outlook 2003 offers four different levels of junk mail protection, with Safe Senders and Safe Recipients lists to help you identify valid messages. It also provides a Blocked Senders list to help you identify e-mail addresses and domains that send you junk mail, which enables you to exclude those messages from your Inbox.

How Outlook 2003 Junk Filtering Works

If you are familiar with the Junk and Adult Content filters in previous versions of Outlook, you already know a little about how Outlook filters junk mail. However, Outlook 2003 adds some new features and expands junk filtering considerably. Before you start configuring Outlook to filter your junk mail, you should have a better understanding of how it applies its filters.

Outlook 2003 provides four filter modes. To specify the filter mode, choose Tools, Options, and click Junk E-Mail on the Preferences tab to display the Junk E-Mail Options dialog box shown in Figure 8-22. The following sections explain the four filter modes.

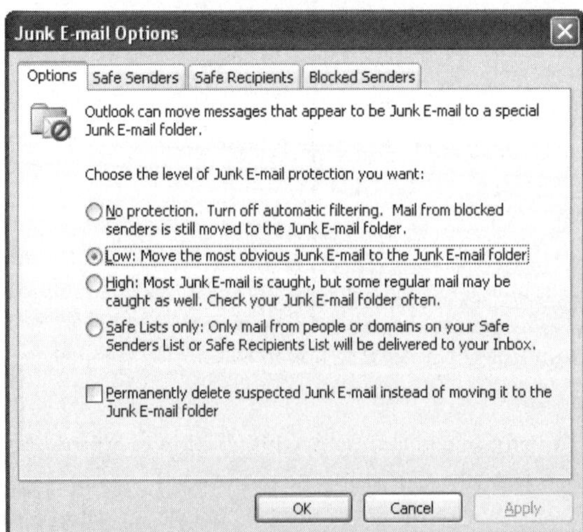

Figure 8-22. Use the Junk E-Mail Options dialog box to quickly configure Outlook to filter unwanted messages.

No Protection

The No Protection option, as its name implies, offers no protection against junk messages. Outlook does not scan the messages for sender, subject, content, or other criteria. Instead, Outlook delivers all messages to your Inbox.

Low

This option functions essentially like the Junk and Adult Content filters in previous versions of Outlook. Outlook uses a predefined filter to scan the body and subject of messages to identify likely spam.

You can't specify additional filter criteria for subject or content checking for this junk e-mail filter, although you can create your own custom junk mail rules to block messages using additional criteria.

High

This level uses the same filtering as the low level, but it also uses additional message scanning logic to determine whether a message is spam. Outlook scans the message body and message header for likely indications that the message is spam. You do not have any control over this scanning, other than to enable it by choosing the high scanning level.

If you choose the High option, you should not enable the option to delete junk messages rather than move them to the Junk E-Mail folder. Although Outlook will catch most spam, it will also generate false positives, blocking messages that you expect or want. You should review the Junk E-Mail folder periodically and mark any valid messages as not being junk mail. Marking messages in this way is explained later in this chapter.

Safe Lists Only

This level provides the most extreme message blocking. Only messages originating with senders in your Safe Senders and Safe Recipients lists are treated as valid messages, and all others are treated as junk mail. Consider this Outlook's whitelist-only mode in which it delivers messages to you only if the sender is on your whitelist.

Although this level offers the most chance of blocking all of your junk mail, it also offers the most chance of blocking wanted messages. To use this level effectively, you should allow Outlook to place messages in the Junk E-Mail folder and review them periodically for valid messages. When you find a valid message, add the sender to your Trusted Senders list.

Understanding How Outlook Uses the Filter Lists

Outlook 2003 maintains three lists: Safe Senders, Safe Recipients, and Blocked Senders. Figure 8-23 shows the Blocked Senders list, which acts as a *blacklist* for senders, blocking their messages. Messages originating from an address or domain on the list are filtered out. Entering a domain in the Blocked Senders list blocks all messages from that domain, regardless of sender. Add wingtiptoys.com to the list, for example, and Outlook would block messages from *joe@wingtiptoys.com*, *jane@wingtiptoys.com*, and all other e-mail addresses ending in *@wingtiptoys.com*.

The Safe Senders and Safe Recipients lists act as *whitelists*. A whitelist identifies senders and domains that Outlook should not filter, regardless of subject or content. Use the Safe Senders list to identify valid messages by their originating address. Use the Safe Recipients list to identify valid messages by their target address. For example, if you participate in a mailing list, messages for that list are addressed to a mailing list address rather than your own address, such as *list@wingtiptoys*.com rather than *jim@wingtiptoys.com*. Add the mailing list address to the Safe Recipients list to prevent Outlook from treating the list messages as junk mail.

Figure 8-23. Use the Blocked Senders list to block by address or domain.

You have two options for adding entries to each of the three filter lists: specify an e-mail address or specify a domain. As previously mentioned, if you specify a domain, Outlook blocks all messages from that domain, regardless of sender. However, Outlook is rather selective in blocking. Specify *@wingtiptoys.com*, for example, and Outlook will block messages from *joe@wingtiptoys.com* and *jane@wingtiptoys.com*, but will not block messages from *joe@sales.wingtiptoys.com*. You must specify the subdomain explicitly in a list to either accept or block that subdomain. For example, to block the subdomain *sales.wingtiptoys.com*, enter **sales.wingtiptoys.com** in the Blocked Senders list.

> **Note** Outlook recognizes wildcard characters, so you can simply enter ***.domain** to block all messages from a domain and its subdomains. For example, use ***.wingtiptoys.com** to block *sales.wintiptoys.com*, *support.wingtiptoys.com*, and all other subdomains of *wingtiptoys.com*.

Tip You can import and export a filter list, which enables you to move a list between computers or share it with others.

Delete Instead of Move

Outlook by default moves junk mail to the Junk E-Mail folder, which it creates by default in your mailbox. The Junk E-Mail folder gives you the capability to review your junk messages before deleting them. If you prefer you can configure Outlook to delete messages rather than place them in the Junk E-Mail folder. In general, you should configure Outlook to delete messages only after you have spent a month using the Junk E-Mail folder, adding senders to your Safe Senders list, and otherwise identifying to Outlook valid messages that have generated false positives.

Junk Filtering with Exchange Server

The junk filtering technology in Outlook works in most situations. However, to take advantage of junk filtering with an Exchange Server account hosted on Microsoft Exchange 2000 Server or earlier, you must use Cached Exchange Mode to create a locally cached copy of your mailbox. Filtering is not available with Exchange 2000 Server or earlier when working online unless you configure your Exchange Server account to deliver messages to a local PST instead of the mailbox on the server. Outlook does scan messages if they are delivered to a PST.

Note Junk filtering does work with Microsoft Exchange Server 2003 in both online and Cached Exchange Modes.

The junk e-mail filter lists are stored in your mailbox on your Exchange Server. These filters are available for all of your e-mail accounts, not just for the Exchange Server account. What's more, with Exchange Server 2003, the server scans messages before they even reach Outlook. Messages that should be blocked are moved to your Junk E-Mail folder (or deleted, depending on your configuration) right at the server.

Junk Filtering with Non-Exchange Accounts

The junk filtering features in Outlook 2003 are supported with non–Exchange Server accounts, as well. You can filter messages delivered to HTTP, POP3, and IMAP accounts. All of the filtering, however, happens locally for these types of accounts. In other words, Outlook performs the scanning, not the server, as is the case with Exchange Server 2003.

Enabling and Configuring Junk E-Mail Filtering

To start filtering out unwanted messages, open Outlook and follow these steps:

1. Choose Tools, Options, and click the Junk E-Mail button on the Preferences tab to open the Junk E-Mail Options dialog box (see Figure 8-22).
2. Choose a level of protection on the Options tab, as explained in the previous section.

3. If you want to delete messages rather than move them to the Junk E-Mail folder, select the option Permanently Delete Suspected Junk E-Mail Instead Of Moving It To The Junk E-Mail Folder.
4. Click the Safe Senders tab, then click Add and enter the e-mail address or domain of senders that you want Outlook to deliver to your Inbox, regardless of content or subject.
5. On the Safe Senders tab, select the option AlsoTrust E-Mail From My Contacts if you want Outlook to always accept e-mail from senders in your Contacts folder, regardless of content or subject.
6. Click the Safe Recipients tab (see Figure 8-24) and add the target addresses or domains for which Outlook should allow messages (used typically to accept mail sent to a mailing list).

Figure 8-24. Add allowed target addresses on the Safe Recipients list.

7. Click the Blocked Senders tab and add the addresses or domains of junk senders whose messages you want Outlook to explicitly block.
8. Click OK to apply the filter changes.

Marking and Unmarking Junk Mail

The junk e-mail filters in Outlook might not catch all of the messages you consider to be junk. You can easily mark and unmark messages as junk without opening the Junk E-Mail Options dialog box. When you receive a message that is junk but which Outlook does not place in the Junk E-Mail folder (or delete), right-click the message, choose Junk E-Mail, and then choose the list to which you want the sender added. You can add it to the Blocked Senders, Safe Senders, or Safe Recipients list, as needed according to the message's content. You can also add the sender's domain to the Safe Sender's list.

If Outlook marks a message as junk mail and moves it to the Junk E-Mail folder, but you don't want the message treated as junk, you can mark the message as not junk (essentially, unmark the message). Open the Junk E-Mail folder, right-click the message, and choose Junk E-Mail, Mark As Not Junk. Outlook displays a Mark As Not Junk dialog box. If you click OK without taking any other action, Outlook moves the message back to the Inbox. Select the Always Trust E-Mail From option to also have the sender's e-mail address added to the Trusted Senders list.

Creating Other Junk E-Mail Rules

The filtering technology built into Outlook 2003, once you configure it and make adjustments for false positives, can be an effective tool for waging your daily fight against junk e-mail. The filtering technology in Outlook isn't perfect, however, so you might need to handle junk e-mail in other ways. One is to create your own rules to handle exceptions that the built-in filters can't adequately address.

Earlier versions of Outlook included rule conditions that specifically referenced the junk and adult content filters. Outlook 2003 drops these conditions. However, you can still create rules that look explicitly for keywords or phrases in the subject or body of a message, or look for specific other criteria, and move those messages to the Junk E-Mail folder (or delete them). See the section "Processing Messages Automatically," page 224, for details on creating and working with rules.

Reply or Unsubscribe?

Although you might be tempted to have Outlook automatically send a nasty reply to every piece of spam you receive, resist the urge. In many cases, the spammer's only way of knowing whether a recipient address is valid is when a reply comes back from that address. You make your address that much more desirable to spammers when you reply, because they know there's a person at the other end of the address. The best course of action is to delete the message without looking at it.

In the past, many spammers also used unsubscribe messages to identify valid addresses, which made unsubscribing to a particular spammer a hit-or-miss proposition. In some cases the spammer would delete your address, and in others, simply add it to the good e-mail address list. With legislators starting to crack down on spammers and individuals and companies becoming more litigious with them, spammers more often heed unsubscribe requests than not. Just a few years ago I would have recommended that you not bother unsubscribing to spam. Today, you will likely have at least a little better luck unsubscribing to spam without generating a flood of new messages. However, you should still approach the problem cautiously.

Other Spam Filtering Solutions

The spam-blocking features in Outlook 2003 can help considerably in blocking unwanted messages, but there are other options you should consider in addition to Outlook's filtering technologies.

Filtering in Exchange Server

If your company or organization uses Exchange Server, you can perform some spam filtering tasks right at the server without adding third-party software. Exchange 2000 Server and Exchange Server 2003 both support domain filtering for virtual SMTP servers. Exchange Server 2003 offers some additional features not included in Exchange 2000 Server, making it potentially more effective for blocking spam.

> **Tip** Microsoft Exchange Server 5.5 also can block messages. See the Microsoft Knowledge Base article 245465 at *http://support.microsoft.com/default.aspx?scid=kb;en-us;245465* for details.

In Exchange 2000 Server, open Exchange System Manager, expand the server, and expand the Global Settings branch. Right-click Message Delivery and choose Properties to display the Message Delivery Properties dialog box. Then, click the Filtering tab (Figure 8-25).

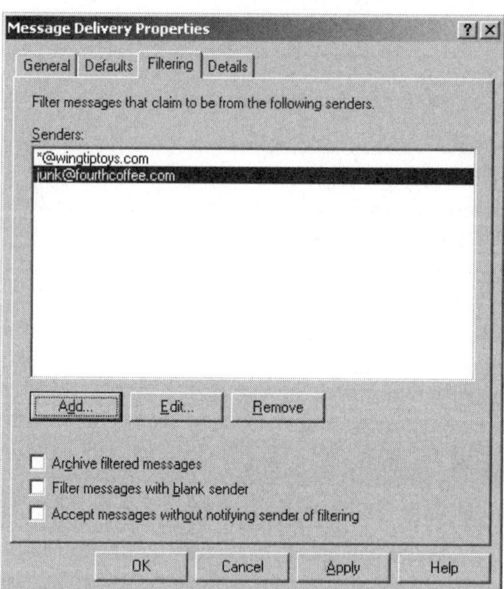

Figure 8-25. Use the Filtering tab to block spam in Exchange 2000 Server.

Click Add, then enter the e-mail address or domain you want to block. Use wildcards to block an entire domain. For example, enter ***@wingtiptoys.com** to block everything from that domain. Use ***@*.wingtiptoys.com** to block all subdomains as well.

You can also specify the following options on the Filtering tab:

- **Archive Filtered Messages** Select this check box to keep a copy of all filtered messages in Exchsrvr\Mailroot\Vsi#\Filter, where # is replaced by a number that identifies the virtual server. If you choose to archive filtered messages, scan the folder frequently to delete unwanted messages and prevent a full disk.
- **Filter Messages With Blank Sender** Block messages that do not have a sender specified in the From field. Many spammers omit a From address, but this option can also lead to some Exchange Server notification messages being filtered. Obtain the latest Exchange 2000 Server service pack to address this problem. See Microsoft Knowledge Base article 312634 at *http://support.microsoft.com/default.aspx?scid=kb;en-us;312634* for details.
- **Accept Messages Without Notifying Sender Of Filtering** Select this check box if you do not want Exchange Server to generate a nondelivery report (NDR) for each filtered message. With this option enabled, the sender of the filtered message receives no notification that the message was blocked. Clear this check box to have Exchange 2000 Server generate an NDR for each filtered message (which can cause a lot of NDRs and a potential performance drain).

In addition to configuring the filter, you must enable it for each virtual SMTP server on which you want it to function by following these steps:

1. Open Exchange System Manager and expand the Protocols\SMTP branch of the server on which you want to configure filtering.
2. Right-click the SMTP virtual server and choose Properties.
3. On the General tab, click Advanced to open the Advanced dialog box.
4. Select a server identity and click Edit.
5. Select the Apply Filter option, and click OK, then close the remaining dialog boxes.

Exchange Server 2003 offers some additional filtering options. To configure filtering options, right-click the Global Settings\Message Delivery branch and choose Properties in Exchange System Manager. The Sender Filtering tab offers the same features and capabilities as the Filtering tab in Exchange 2000 Server—explained previously—with one additional option:

- **Drop Connection If Address Matches Filter** Choose this option if you want Exchange Server to drop the connection with the remote SMTP server if the remote SMTP server resides in a domain that is specified in the filter list.

Use the Recipient Filtering tab (see Figure 8-26) to filter out messages based on the recipient address. Add the destination addresses you want Exchange Server to block. Select the Filter Recipients Who Are Not In The Directory check box to block all messages to destination addresses that do not exist in Active Directory.

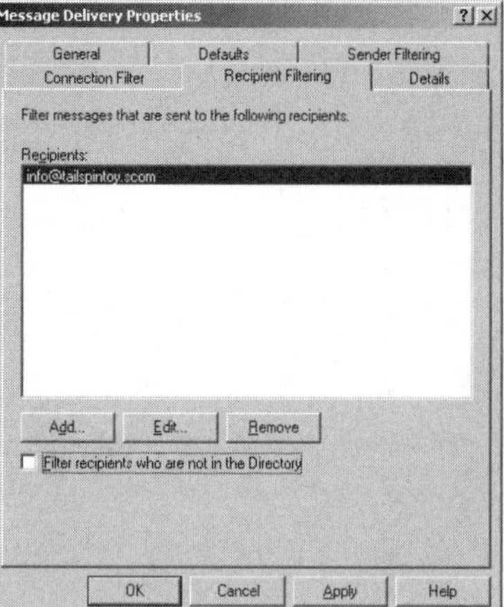

Figure 8-26. Use the Recipient Filtering tab to block spam in Exchange Server 2003.

You can use the Connection Filter tab (see Figure 8-27) to filter SMTP connections and help block spam. In the Connection Filter Rules list, you create and organize rules that enable you to block connections with specific SMTP servers. You use the lower half of the page to specify exceptions by server IP address or subnet, or by destination SMTP address.

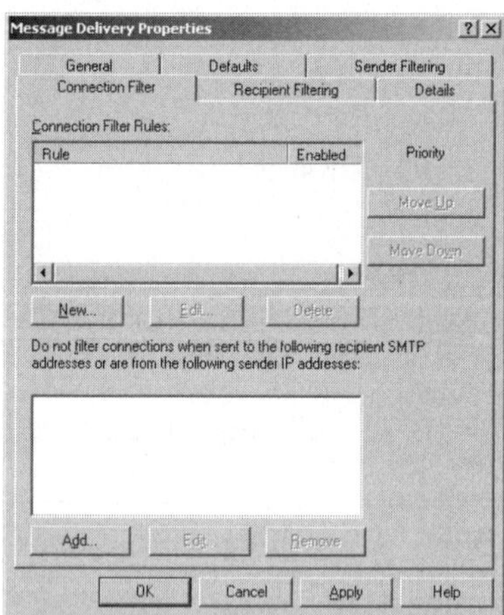

Figure 8-27. Use the Connection Filter tab in Exchange Server 2003 to filter server connections.

Third-Party Filters

There are several third-party antispam solutions that you can consider for your organization. For example, Symantec's Mail-Gear provides content scanning and filtering capabilities. Mail-Gear can function as your organization's only mail server or you can use it to filter incoming messages and forward them to your existing mail server. Mail-Gear can also filter outgoing messages. You'll find more information about Mail-Gear at *http://enterprisesecurity.symantec.com/products/products.cfm?ProductID=17&EID=0.*

Another product to consider is GFI Mail Essentials (*http://www.gfi.com/mes*). Mail Essentials provides several levels of content filtering with support for blacklists, whitelists, and additional header checking options (see Figure 8-28) that enable it to detect and block spam based on a broad range of criteria.

Mail Essentials works with Exchange 5.5 or later, Lotus Notes, and any SMTP e-mail server. In addition to spam filtering, Mail Essentials supports automatic addition of message disclaimers, mail archiving, inbound and outbound mail monitoring, automatic replies, and a POP2 Exchange service that downloads messages from POP3 servers and delivers them to Exchange Server mailboxes.

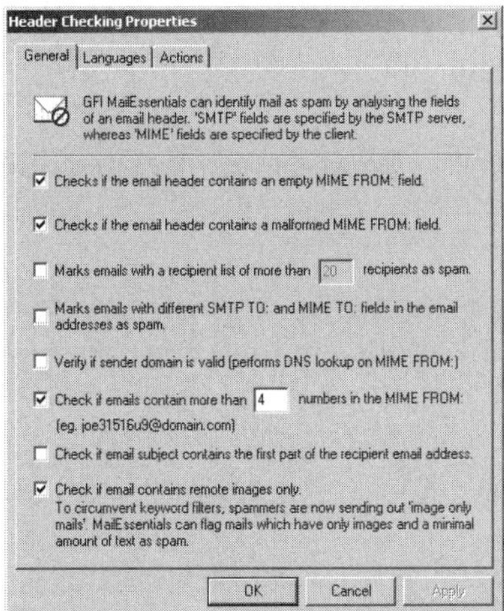

Figure 8-28. GFI Mail Essentials provides an excellent set of filtering features.

These are just two of the solutions available for filtering and managing messages. Many mail servers offer their own filtering capabilities, and many other products provide filtering services for existing mail servers.

One of the most prevalent spam filtering solutions is SpamAssassin, based on an open-source heuristic scanning application developed originally for UNIX-based servers. You can find information about open-source SpamAssassin at *http://spamassassin.org*.

Depending on your existing mail server platform and the development expertise within your organization, you might be able to implement your own filtering solution based on SpamAssassin. There are commercial implementations of SpamAssassin, as well. For example, the Network Associates suite of SpamKiller products is based on SpamAssassin. You can find more information about SpamKiller at *http://www.mcafee.com/myapps/msk/*.

Creating Automatic Responses with the Out Of Office Assistant

One of the key features in Outlook that makes it a great e-mail client is the Out Of Office Assistant, which lets you automatically generate replies to incoming messages when you aren't in the office. For example, if you're going on vacation for a couple of weeks and won't be checking your e-mail, you might want to have the Out Of Office Assistant send an automatic reply to let senders know you'll respond to their messages when you get back.

Note The Out of Office Assistant is an Exchange Server feature. To learn how to create automatic responses with custom rules for other use with other e-mail servers, see "Creating Automatic Responses with Custom Rules," page 256.

Managing Mail When You're Out

Before you start learning about the Out Of Office Assistant, take a few minutes to consider a few other issues that relate to managing e-mail when you're out of the office.

First, the Out Of Office Assistant is a server-side component for Exchange Server. This means you can use it to process your Exchange Server account but not your POP3, IMAP, HTTP, or other e-mail accounts, unless those accounts deliver incoming messages to your Exchange Server Inbox. You can create rules to process your other accounts and simulate the function of the Out Of Office Assistant, but you must do this by creating custom rules.

Second, keep in mind that because the Out Of Office Assistant functions as a server-side component, it processes your messages even when Outlook isn't running (a likely situation if you're scuba diving off the Great Barrier Reef for a couple of weeks). To process your other accounts with custom Out Of Office rules, Outlook must be running and checking your messages periodically. If you have a direct Internet connection, you can configure the rules, configure your send/receive groups to allow Outlook to periodically check messages for the non–Exchange Server accounts, and leave Outlook running. If you have a dial-up connection to these accounts, you'll have to also configure Outlook to dial when needed and disconnect after each send/receive operation.

Caution Be sure to configure your dial-up connection to disconnect after a reasonable idle period, such as 15 minutes. Otherwise, if your Internet access is metered, you might come back from two weeks of sun and fun to find that your dial-up connection has been connected continuously for the last two weeks. Most Internet service providers (ISPs) implement an idle cutoff, but any activity on the line can cause it to remain connected, so it's important to configure the behavior from your side as well. Also be sure to configure Outlook to disconnect after the send/receive operation is completed.

Using the Out Of Office Assistant

Using the Out Of Office Assistant is relatively easy. Here's the process in a nutshell:

1. Specify the text you want Outlook to use for automatic replies when you're out of the office.
2. If necessary, create custom rules for the Exchange Server to use to process incoming messages during your absence.

For information about custom Out Of Office rules, see "Creating Custom Out Of Office Rules," page 254.

3. Tell Outlook you're out of the office, which causes the Out Of Office Assistant to start responding accordingly.
4. When you get back, tell Outlook you're in the office, which turns off the Out Of Office Assistant rules processing.

Note When you start Outlook, it checks to see whether the Out Of Office Assistant is turned on. If it is, Outlook asks whether you want to turn it off. After the Out Of Office Assistant is set up and functioning, messages that arrive in your Inbox receive an Out Of Office response with the message text you've specified. Exchange Server keeps track of the send-to list and sends the Out Of Office response the first time a message comes from a given sender. Subsequent messages from that sender are sent to your Inbox without generating an Out Of Office response. This procedure cuts down on the number of messages generated and keeps the senders from becoming annoyed with numerous Out Of Office replies.

Note Exchange Server deletes the send-to list for Out Of Office responses when you close the Out Of Office Assistant from Outlook.

Setting Up the Out Of Office Assistant

Follow these steps to specify the text for automatic replies and to tell Outlook you're out of the office:

1. In Outlook, select the Exchange Server Inbox and choose Tools, Out Of Office Assistant.
2. In the Out Of Office Assistant dialog box (see Figure 8-29), type the body of your automatic message reply in the AutoReply box. While the Out Of Office Assistant is active, Exchange Server uses this message to reply to incoming messages.

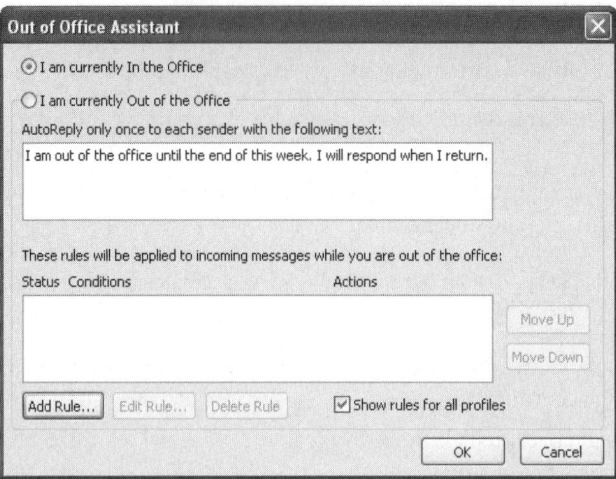

Figure 8-29. Use the Out Of Office Assistant dialog box to specify your automatic message reply.

3 Select I Am Currently Out Of The Office and click OK.

Creating Custom Out Of Office Rules

With the Out Of Office Assistant, you can create custom rules to use in addition to the basic automatic reply. To create a custom rule, open the Out Of Office Assistant and click Add Rule to display the Edit Rule dialog box, shown in Figure 8-30.

Figure 8-30. You can create custom rules to use with the Out Of Office Assistant.

The options in the Edit Rule dialog box are straightforward, particularly if you're now an old hand at creating rules. Specify the conditions the incoming messages should meet, and then specify the action Exchange Server should perform if a message meets those conditions.

When you define the conditions, keep in mind that the Out Of Office Assistant conditions can be met by either full or partial matches. For example, you could enter **yce** in the Sent To box, and the rule would apply if the address contained Joyce, Boyce, or Cayce. If you want the condition to be met only if the full string is found, enclose the text in quotation marks—for example, enter "yce".

Applying OR Logic in Out Of Office Assistant Rules

To understand how to apply OR logic in Out Of Office Assistant rules, consider two issues. First, unlike the Outlook rules discussed previously in this chapter, Out Of Office Assistant rules that contain multiple conditions using OR logic rather than AND logic can be processed by Exchange Server. For example, if you enter **free money** as a condition for the Subject box and **Nate Sun** as a condition for the From box, Exchange Server applies the rule if the message subject contains the words *free money* or if the sender is Nate Sun. This is in contrast to Outlook's rule behavior, which would apply the rule only if the subject contained the words *free money* and if the sender was Nate Sun.

Second, you can use semicolons within an Out Of Office rule to create an OR condition that addresses multiple possible matches. For example, if you want to create a rule that deletes messages containing the text *free money*, *MLM*, or *Trial Offer*, click Subject and enter the following text: **"free money"; "MLM"; "Trial Offer"**.

How Outlook evaluates the message depends on whether the condition data is enclosed in quotation marks. If you omit the quotes, partial-word matches satisfy the condition. If you enter **cat; car; amble**, for example, Outlook applies the rule to messages that include the words *cat*, *catapult*, *car*, *carpet*, *amble*, and *bramble*. If you enclose each string in quotes, Outlook matches only messages containing *cat*, *car*, and *amble*. In this example, Outlook will apply the rule to any message that has any one of those three strings in its subject.

You also can use this type of logic when addressing case sensitivity in your rules. For example, you might specify the following to allow Outlook to apply the rule to all messages that include the specified text in the subject using different case: **"No Worries"; "NO WORRIES"; "no worries"**.

When you create rules for the Out Of Office Assistant to use, you can click Advanced in the Edit Rule dialog box to specify additional conditions for the rule. Outlook displays the Advanced dialog box, shown in Figure 8-31. You can specify multiple conditions for the rule in this dialog box.

Tip Although Microsoft's documentation indicates that you need to use a semicolon to define an OR condition, commas seem to work just as well.

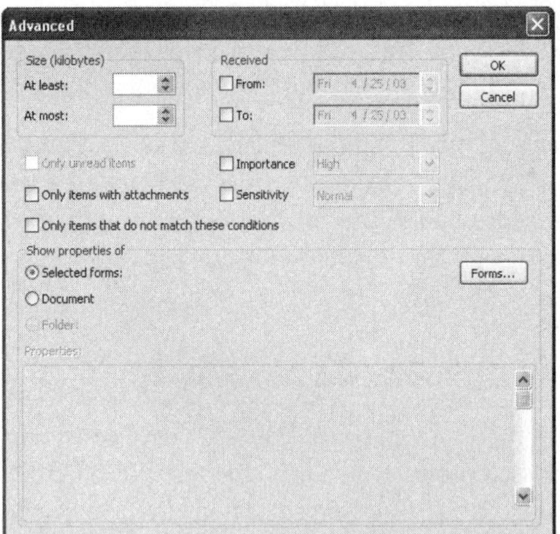

Figure 8-31. Use the Advanced dialog box to specify additional rule conditions.

Creating Automatic Responses with Custom Rules

The Out Of Office Assistant is great for generating automatic replies to messages that arrive in your Inbox when you're out of the office. However, the Out Of Office Assistant sends an Out Of Office response only the first time a message arrives from a given sender. Subsequent messages go into the Inbox without generating an automatic response (unless you set up a separate server-side rule).

In some cases, you might want Outlook to generate automatic replies to messages at any time and for other accounts—not only for messages that arrive in your Exchange Server mailbox. Perhaps you've set up an Internet e-mail account to take inquiries about a product or service you're selling. You can create a rule to automatically send a specific reply to messages that come in to that account. Or you might want people to be able to request information about specific products or topics by sending a message containing a certain keyword in the subject line. In that case, you can create a rule to generate a reply based on the subject of the message.

> **Note** In Web jargon, applications or rules that create automatic responses are often called *autoresponders*.

You create automatic responses such as these not by using the Out Of Office Assistant, but by creating custom Outlook rules with the Rules Wizard. As with other rules, you specify conditions that incoming messages must meet to receive a specific reply. For example, you might specify that an incoming message must contain the text *Framistats* in its subject to generate a reply that provides pricing on your line of gold-plated framistats.

Note You aren't limited to specifying conditions only for the subject of an incoming message. You can use any of the criteria supported by Outlook's rules to specify the conditions for an automatic response.

Setting Up the Reply

When you use a custom rule to create an automatic response, you don't define the reply text in the rule. Rather, you have two options: specifying a template on your local computer or setting up a specific message on the server. If you opt to use a template on your local computer, you create the message in Outlook and save it as a template file.

Follow these steps to create the template:

1. Configure Outlook as your default e-mail editor. To do so, choose Tools, Options and click the Mail Format tab. Clear the Use Microsoft Word To Edit E-Mail Messages option and click OK.
2. Begin a new message and enter the subject and body, but leave the address boxes blank.

Tip Include an address in the Bcc field if you want a copy of all automatic responses sent to you or to a specific address.

3. Choose File, Save As.
4. In the Save As dialog box, specify a path and name for the file, and then select Outlook Template in the Save As Type drop-down list. Click Save.

Using a template from your local system causes the rule to function as a client-side rule. As a result, Outlook can use the rule to process accounts other than your Exchange Server account (such as a POP3 account), but Exchange Server can't generate automatic responses when Outlook isn't running or is offline.

If you opt to store the message on the server, you select or create the message when you create the rule. Outlook stores the message on the server, which allows the rule to function as a server-side rule even when Outlook is offline. Outlook can continue generating automatic responses to messages that arrive in your Inbox even when Outlook isn't running. In many respects, this is the best option, because it helps ensure that the rule can function all the time. In addition, client-side responses are generated only once per session for a given sender, but server-side responses execute for all messages that meet the rule conditions.

Troubleshooting

Your autoresponse rule executes only once

When you create a rule using the Reply Using A Specific Template action, Outlook executes the rule only once for a given sender in each Outlook session. Outlook keeps track of the senders in a list and checks incoming messages against the list. For the first message from a given sender that matches the rule conditions, Outlook generates the response; for subsequent messages, Outlook doesn't generate the response. Closing and restarting Outlook refreshes the sender list, and the next message from that sender that meets the criteria generates a response. This prevents Outlook from sending repetitive responses to a person who sends you multiple messages that satisfy the rule conditions. The Out Of Office Assistant uses the same process—and this behavior is by design.

If you create a server-side rule that uses Have Server Reply Using A Specific Message, the Exchange Server creates an autoresponse for all messages that meet the specified conditions, regardless of whether the message is the first from a particular sender.

Creating Automatic Responses from Local Templates

Follow these steps to create a client-side rule that responds to incoming messages with a reply from a template stored locally on your computer:

1. Using Outlook as your e-mail editor, compose the reply message and save it as a template (OFT) file.
2. Choose Tools, Rules And Alerts to open the Rules And Alerts dialog box.
3. Select the folder where you want the rule applied and click New.
4. Select Start From A Blank Rule and click Next.
5. Specify the conditions for the rule and click Next.
6. Select Reply Using A Specific Template.
7. In the rule description area, click A Specific Template.
8. From the Select A Reply Template dialog box (see Figure 8-32), select the template you want to use for the reply and click Open.
9. Click Next and specify exceptions, if any, for the rule.
10. Click Next, specify final options for the rule, and click Finish.

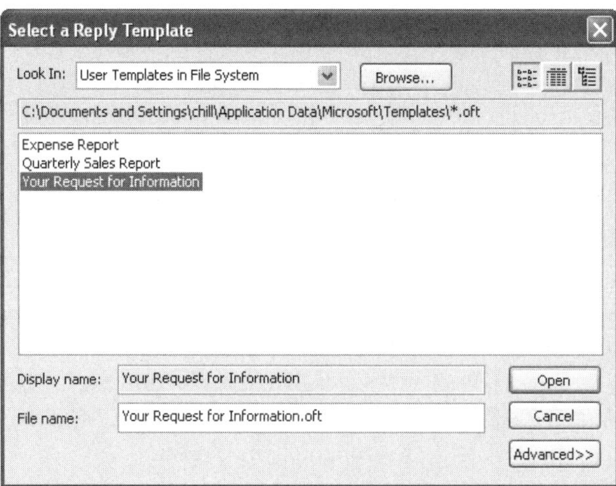

Figure 8-32. Select the message template to use as the reply.

Creating Automatic Responses from the Server

Follow these steps to create a server-side rule to generate automatic responses using a message stored on the server:

1. Choose Tools, Rules And Alerts to open the Rules And Alerts dialog box.
2. Select the folder where you want the rule applied and click New.
3. Select Start From A Blank Rule and click Next.
4. Specify the conditions for the rule and click Next.
5. Select Have Server Reply Using A Specific Message.
6. In the rule description area, click A Specific Message.
7. Create the message using the resulting message form, specifying the subject and text but no addresses (unless you want to copy the reply to a specific address), and then click Save and Close.
8. Click Next and specify exceptions, if any, for the rule.
9. Click Next, specify final options for the rule, and click Finish.

Using Message Alerts

In Chapter 7, I described the options you can set in Outlook 2003 to have Outlook notify you when a new message arrives. You can view these options by choosing Tools, Options, and clicking E-Mail Options, Advanced E-Mail Options. New in Outlook 2003 is the Display A New Mail Desktop Alert option, which causes Outlook to display a pop-up alert on the desktop when a new message arrives.

If you enable the Display A New Mail Desktop Alert option, Outlook displays the alert for each new message. In most cases that's more than you need. Instead, you probably want Outlook to alert you only when you receive certain messages, such as those from people in your Contacts folder, from a specific sender, or with certain words in the subject. So rather than enable this option globally, you might prefer to create a rule that causes the alert to be displayed when the rule fires.

There are two rule actions you can use to generate alerts:

- **Display A Desktop Alert** This action causes Outlook to display a desktop alert when the rule fires. The alert persists on the desktop for the period of time you have set for the alert in Outlook's Advanced E-Mail Options dialog box.
- **Display A Specific Message In The New Item Alerts Window** With this action you can specify a message that appears in the New Item Alerts window (see Figure 8-33). The window persists on the desktop until you close it.

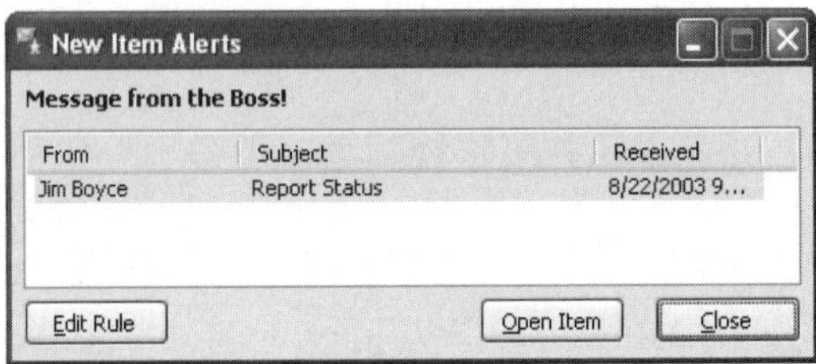

Figure 8-33. The New Item Alerts window displays text you specify.

Which action you use depends on whether you want a custom message to appear for the alert and whether you want the alert to persist until you close it or display and then go away.To create an alert rule using one (or both) of these actions, create the rule as you would any other, and select the alert action you want to use.

If you create an alert rule that uses the Display A Desktop Alert action, it's likely that you will not want Outlook to display an alert for all messages. You should choose Tools, Options, click E-Mail Options, click Advanced E-Mail Options, and clear the Display A New Mail Desktop Alert option. If you use the Display A Specific Message In The New Item Alert Window option, you might want to leave that enabled, which will cause Outlook to display a desktop alert for all messages, and to display the New Item Alerts window for those messages that fire the rule.

Chapter 9

Sending and Receiving Faxes

Although Microsoft Outlook 2003 doesn't include its own fax service, it does support faxing through third-party applications such as WinFax. This means that most MAPI-enabled fax applications can deliver incoming faxes to your Inbox. In addition, Outlook supports the fax service provided with Microsoft Windows 2000 to deliver incoming faxes to the Inbox. Unfortunately, Microsoft decided to drop support for the fax service in Microsoft Windows XP for incoming faxes. However, Outlook 2003 is quite capable of sending outgoing faxes through your fax modem, whether you use Windows 2000 or Windows XP. The program also supports additional faxing solutions, including Internet faxing.

Covering the configuration of third-party fax applications in this book isn't practical because of the number of applications available. Instead, this chapter explains how to install, configure, and use the Windows 2000 fax service in conjunction with Outlook. This chapter also explains how to use Outlook to send faxes, as well as several tasks related to managing faxes in Outlook.

The Native Windows Fax Service

Earlier versions of Outlook included the WinFax Starter Edition from Symantec (WinFax SE) for faxing in Internet-Only Mail mode and relied on the native Windows fax service for faxing from Corporate/Workgroup mode. Microsoft Outlook 2002 integrated messaging into a single mode and eliminated WinFax SE, and these changes carry over into Outlook 2003. Outlook now relies on the native Windows fax service or on third-party faxing solutions, whether they are applications you install on your computer or a network server, or Internet-based faxing solutions.

Although you can use third-party fax applications with Outlook, many users don't need the extended features these programs offer, such as fax broadcast or the extensive selection of cover pages. Instead, the ability to print to the fax printer driver to send and receive faxes in your Inbox—the limit of what the Windows fax service can do—is enough. For that reason, this chapter focuses on using the native Windows 2000 fax service with Outlook. If you need help using a third-party fax application with Outlook, check that fax application's documentation, Web site, or support center for more information.

Windows XP users, who are unable to take advantage of the native fax service, can still send outgoing faxes from Outlook. This chapter covers sending faxes in support of all users, including those running Windows XP.

> **Note** Windows Server 2003 also includes a fax service, but this chapter doesn't cover Windows 2003 because it is an unlikely platform for running Outlook for most users.

Configuring the Fax Service

Installing and configuring the Windows 2000 fax service to work with Outlook 2003 is relatively easy. This section explains how to work through that process.

Installing Under Windows 2000

Setup automatically installs Microsoft Fax when you install Windows 2000. In fact, Windows 2000 doesn't even provide a way to remove the service. The fax service is already installed on your system and ready to use with Outlook. You do, however, need to take some steps to configure your system.

Adding Microsoft Fax to Your Profile

Adding the Windows 2000 Microsoft Fax Transport provider in Outlook requires more effort than simply configuring a few fax settings. The additional security provided by Windows 2000 requires you to also modify the user account under which the fax service operates and the service's startup properties.

For Microsoft Fax to deliver faxes to Outlook in Windows 2000, the following conditions must be met:

- The user's account, whether local or domain, must be a member of the local Administrators group.
- The fax service must be configured to use the user's account to log on rather than the system account.

> **Note** If you want to only send outgoing faxes from Outlook and do not need to receive them to your Inbox, you do not need to reconfigure the fax service. You can skip to the section "Configuring Microsoft Fax in Windows 2000."

The user's account must have the right to log on as a service. Follow these steps to configure these properties on a computer that is a member of a workgroup:

1. Log on as Administrator, right-click My Computer, and choose Manage.
2. Expand the Local Users And Groups branch and select the Users node (see Figure 9-1).
3. Double-click the user account used to log on with Outlook.

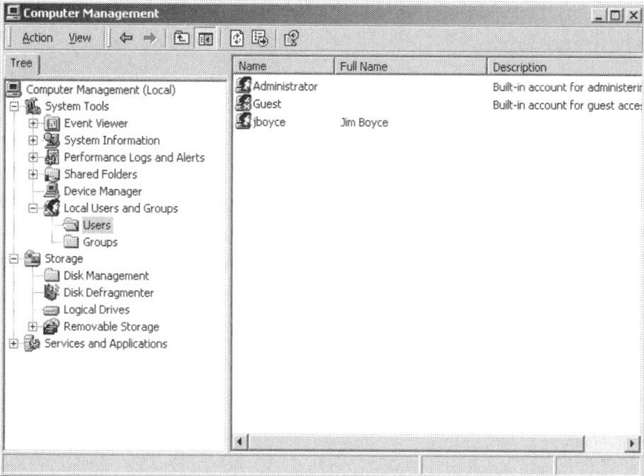

Figure 9-1. Configure group membership through the Local Users And Groups branch.

4. Click the Member Of tab. If the Administrators group isn't listed, click Add, select Administrators, click Add, and click OK.
5. Close the Computer Management console.

If the user is a member of a domain, the process is somewhat different because in this case you need to make the user's domain account a member of the local Administrators group:

1. Log on as Administrator, right-click My Computer, and choose Manage.
2. Expand the Local Users And Groups branch and select the Groups node.
3. Double-click the Administrators group.
4. In the Administrators Properties dialog box, click Add.
5. In the Select Users Or Groups dialog box, select the target domain in the Look In drop-down list.
6. Select the user's domain account in the list (see Figure 9-2), click Add, and click OK.

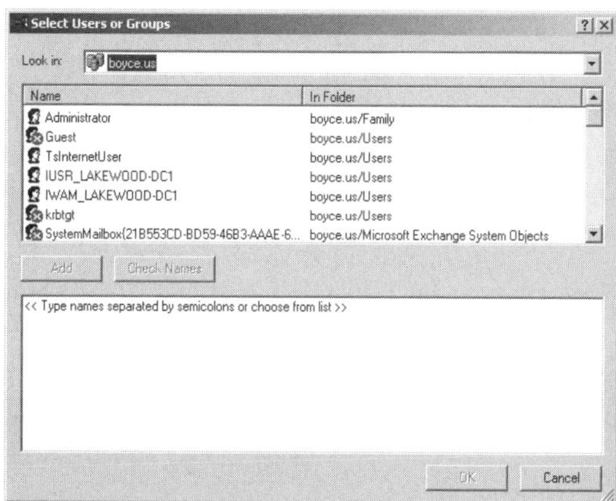

Figure 9-2. Add the user's domain account to the local Administrators group.

7 Click OK to close the Administrators Properties dialog box, and then close the Computer Management console.

Follow these steps to accomplish the next part of the task—adding the fax transport to your profile:

1 Close Outlook, right-click the Outlook icon on the desktop, choose Properties, and click E-Mail Accounts.
2 Select Add A New E-Mail Account and click Next.
3 Select Additional Server Types and click Next.
4 Select Fax Mail Transport and click Next (see Figure 9-3).

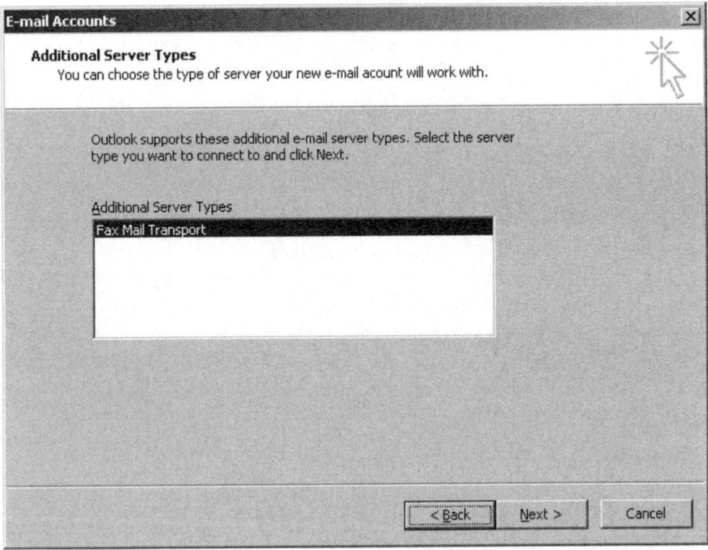

Figure 9-3. Outlook uses the Fax Mail Transport to deliver incoming faxes to your Inbox.

5 Click Close.

Next configure the fax service to log on using the user's account rather than the system account by following these steps:

1 Choose Start, Programs, Administrative Tools, Services to open the Services console. (Alternatively, open the Services branch of the Computer Management console.)
2 Locate and double-click Fax Service.
3 In the Fax Service Properties dialog box, select Automatic in the Startup Type drop-down list, as shown in Figure 9-4.

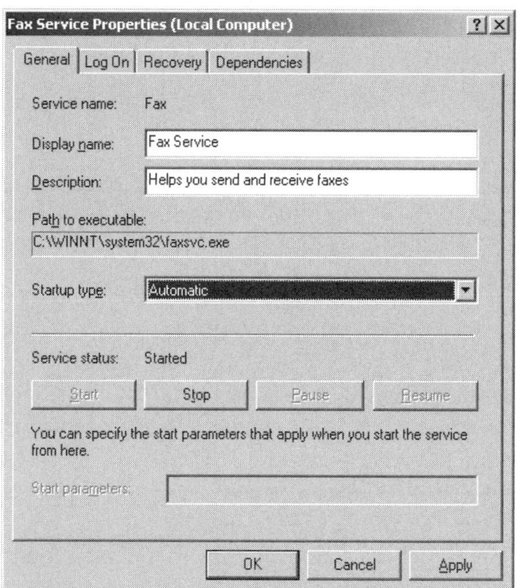

Figure 9-4. Configure the service to start automatically.

4 Click the Log On tab (see Figure 9-5). Select This Account and click Browse.

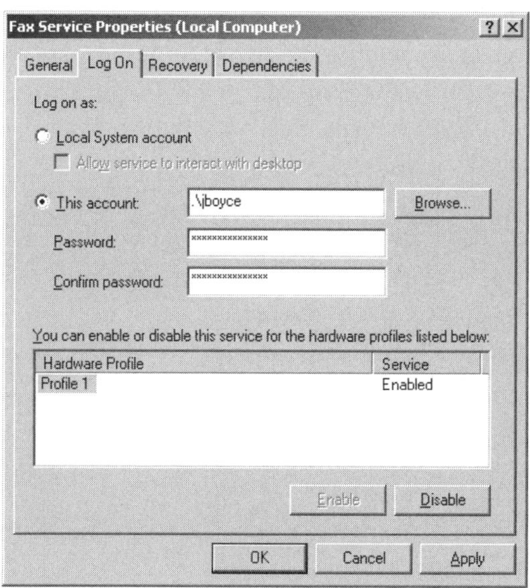

Figure 9-5. On the Log On tab, configure the fax service to use the user's account.

5 Select the user's local account or domain account in the Select User dialog box and then click OK.

6 In the Password box, type the password associated with the specified user account. Verify the password and click OK. Windows 2000 automatically grants the account the right to log on as a service.

7 Stop and restart the fax service.

Troubleshooting

Adding a user to Domain Admins doesn't work

For the fax service to deliver messages to the user's profile, the user's domain or local account must be a direct member of the local Administrators group. Adding the user's domain account to the Domain Admins group, and then adding the Domain Admins group to the local Administrators group won't work. This approach is appropriate only for domain administrators and presents a security risk, even if successful.

The last phase configures the fax service to log on using the user's account and selects the profile to which faxes should be delivered:

1 Click Start, Programs, Accessories, Communications, Fax, Fax Service Management to open the Fax Service Management console.

2 Click Devices and then double-click the fax modem.

3 Select Enable Receive, set the number of rings before answer, and click the Received Faxes tab.

4 Select Send To Local E-Mail Inbox, and then select the profile to which faxes should be delivered (see Figure 9-6).

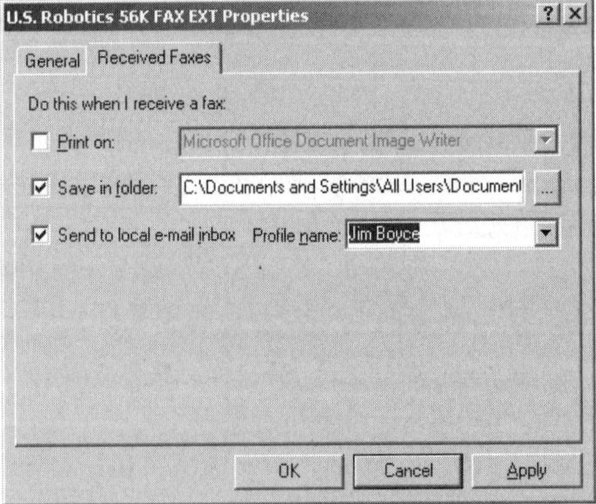

Figure 9-6. Choose the profile for fax delivery.

5 Click OK and close the Fax Service Management console.

Configuring Microsoft Fax in Windows 2000

You use the Fax Service Management console to configure the fax service settings in Windows 2000.

Follow these steps to configure Microsoft Fax in Windows 2000:

1. Log on as Administrator.
2. Click Start, Programs, Accessories, Communications, Fax, Fax Service Management to open the Fax Service Management console, shown in Figure 9-7.

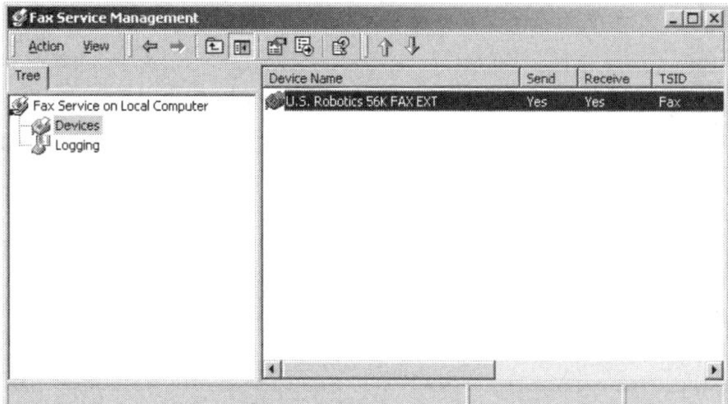

Figure 9-7. Use the Fax Service Management console to configure fax properties in Windows 2000.

3. Right-click Fax Service On Local Computer and choose Properties to display the dialog box shown in Figure 9-8.

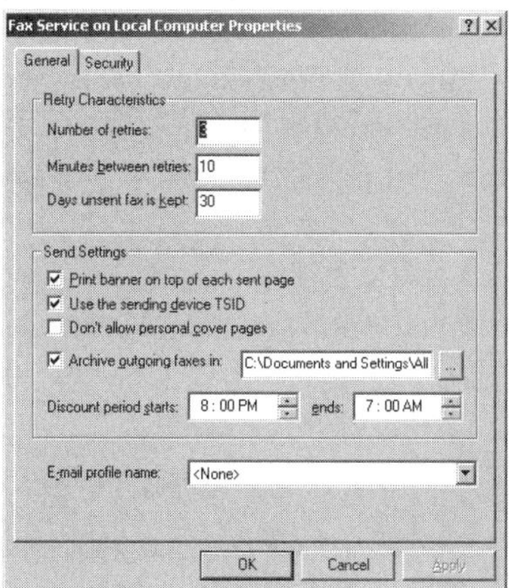

Figure 9-8. Configure general properties for Microsoft Fax on the General tab.

4. Configure options on the General tab using the following list as a guide:
   - **Retry Characteristics** Use these three settings to specify the way Microsoft Fax attempts to resend faxes after a failure.

- **Print Banner On Top Of Each Sent Page** Select this check box to include your name, fax number, and other information as a banner at the top of each outgoing fax page. You can use the Fax icon in Control Panel to configure the user properties; see "Configuring User Properties," page 269.
- **Use The Sending Device TSID** Select this check box to include on the cover page the Transmission Station Identifier (TSID) of the fax device rather than the fax number specified in your user properties. Clear this check box to use the fax number specified on the User tab.
- **Don't Allow Personal Cover Pages** Select this check box to prevent users from sending faxes with cover pages other than the default cover pages provided with Microsoft Fax. Clear this check box to allow users to use any cover page.
- **Archive Outgoing Faxes In** Use this check box to archive all outgoing faxes to a specified folder. The default location is \Documents And Settings\All Users\Documents\Faxes\My Faxes\Sent Faxes, but you can click the button beside the text box to select a different folder. Clear this check box if you don't want to save a copy of each fax.

> **Note** On systems running Windows 2000 that have been upgraded from Microsoft Windows NT, the root folder for profiles is %systemroot%\Profiles rather than \Documents And Settings.

- **Discount Period** Use these two settings to set the start and stop times that indicate a period when outgoing calls are less expensive.
- **E-Mail Profile Name** Select an Outlook profile from this drop-down list if you want the fax service to send an e-mail notification when a fax is successfully sent.

5 Click the Security tab, shown in Figure 9-9, and configure security as needed. Add accounts or groups, specifying the permissions each should have, and then click OK.

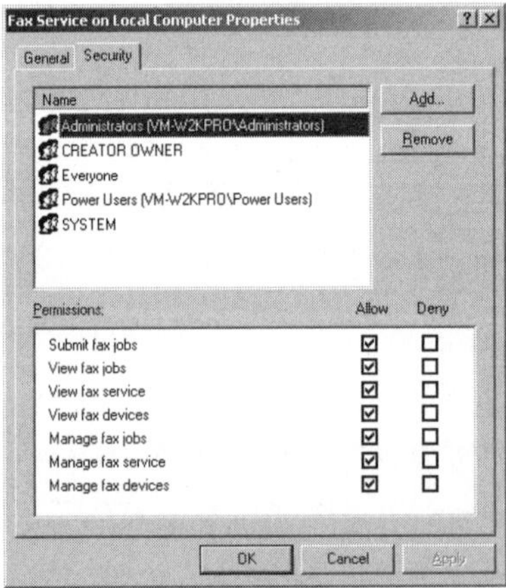

Figure 9-9. Use the Security tab to control the actions users can perform with the fax service.

6 Close the Fax Service Management console.

Configuring User Properties

You can configure additional properties for Microsoft Fax, such as user information and cover pages, through Control Panel. When you double-click the Fax icon in Control Panel, Windows 2000 opens a dialog box with four tabs. The following sections explain the options on each tab.

User Information Tab

The User Information tab (see Figure 9-10) provides spaces for name, fax number, e-mail address, and other information that Microsoft Fax can include in the banner and cover pages of outgoing faxes. You can enter details as you like, including your company and department affiliation, your job title, and a billing code for faxes.

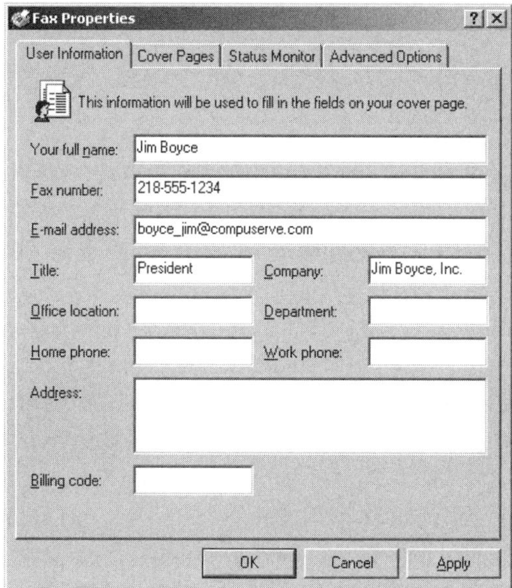

Figure 9-10. Enter information about yourself on the User Information tab.

Cover Pages Tab

You can use the Cover Pages tab of the dialog box to add and modify your own cover pages. For details about using this tab, see "Using Cover Pages," page 275.

Status Monitor Tab

The Status Monitor tab, shown in Figure 9-11, provides options that determine how the fax service notifies you of incoming faxes. The available options include the following:

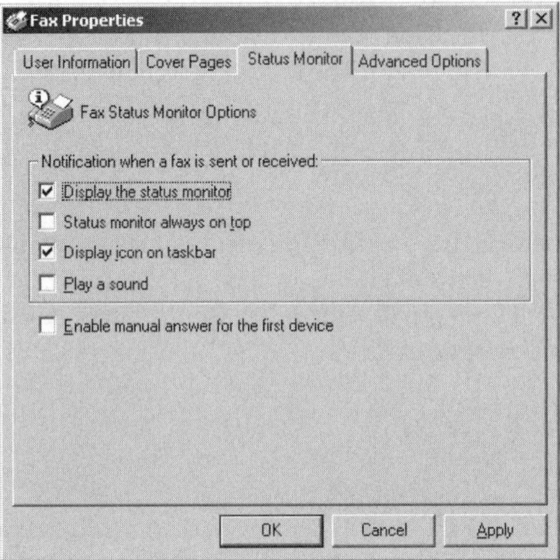

Figure 9-11. Use the Status Monitor tab to specify how the fax service notifies you of incoming faxes.

- **Display The Status Monitor** With this check box selected, Microsoft Fax displays the Status Monitor dialog box when a call comes in.
- **Status Monitor Always On Top** Select this check box to have the Status Monitor dialog box appear on top of all other application windows, even when the Status Monitor does not have focus (is not the active window).
- **Display Icon On Taskbar** Select this check box to include a Status Monitor icon on the system tray to quickly access the fax queue and other fax service properties.
- **Play A Sound** Select this check box to have Fax play a sound when a fax comes in. Use the Sounds And Multimedia icon in Control Panel to configure the WAV file used for incoming fax notification. The sound is specified by the Windows Explorer/Incoming Fax item (by default, Ringin.wav).
- **Enable Manual Answer For The First Device** Select this check box if you share a line for voice and fax calls on the fax modem and want to be able to answer calls manually rather than let Windows answer the call. When a call comes in, you can answer the call manually and, if it's a fax call, direct Microsoft Fax to pick up the call to receive the fax.

Advanced Options Tab

The Advanced Options tab provides three buttons that open the Fax Service Management console, open the Fax Service Management Help file, or add a fax printer driver.

Working with the Windows XP Fax Service

Although Windows XP's native fax service doesn't integrate with Outlook for incoming faxes, you can use it to send outgoing faxes. Configuration for the Windows XP fax service is somewhat different from the Windows 2000 service. The following section provides a brief overview of how to configure the Windows XP fax service.

Adding Fax Services in Windows XP

If the fax service is not currently installed in Windows XP, you can add it easily through Control Panel:

1. Open Add or Remove Programs in Control Panel and click Add/Remove Windows Components.
2. In the Windows Components Wizard, select Fax Services and click Next.
3. Follow the wizard's prompts to complete the installation of the fax service.

Configuring the Windows XP Fax Service

Windows XP simplifies fax configuration with a wizard. Most of the options are the same in Windows XP as in Windows 2000, so you should have little trouble following these steps to configure faxing in Windows XP:

1. Click Start and choose All Programs, Accessories, Communications, Fax, Fax Console to open the Fax Console (see Figure 9-12).

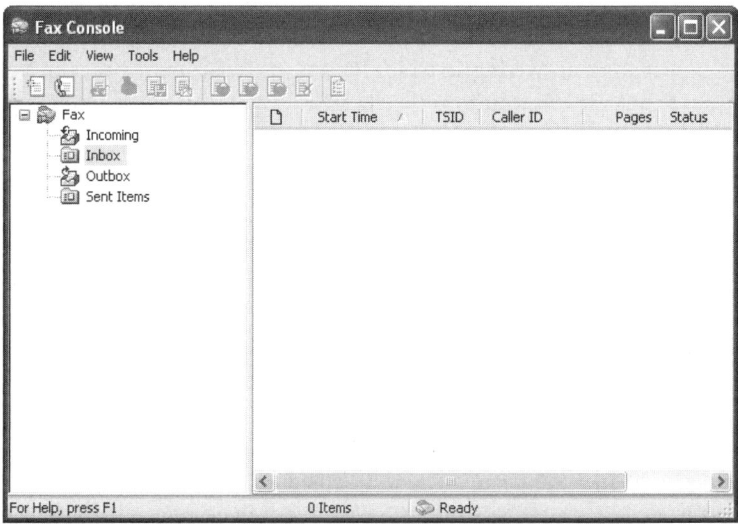

Figure 9-12. Use the Fax Console to send and receive faxes and configure the fax service.

2 Choose Tools, Configure Fax to start the Fax Configuration Wizard, and then click Next.

3 The wizard prompts for your contact- and fax-related information (see Figure 9-13). Fill in the information (which is generally self-explanatory) and click Next.

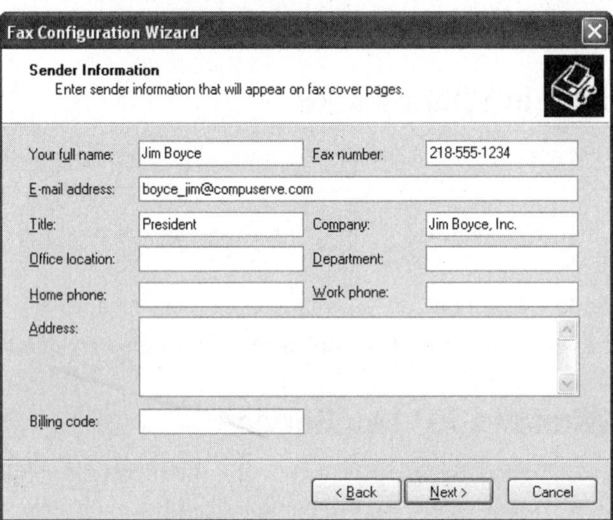

Figure 9-13. Configure options for the fax service using the Fax Configuration Wizard.

4 Choose the fax modem, and select Enable Send to allow outgoing fax messages. Select Enable Receive to allow incoming faxes. If you select the Enable Receive option, you can configure the service to answer automatically after a specified number of rings, or use manual answering, in which the fax service prompts you with a dialog box to allow it to answer an incoming call. Click Next when you finish configuring send/receive options.

5 Enter the TSID, or the identifying information sent with outgoing faxes to identify the fax source, and click Next.

6 Enter the CSID, or the identifying information sent to fax senders to identify your fax modem (name or business, for example) for incoming faxes. Click Next.

7 Specify how you want incoming faxes routed. You can choose to print the fax, store in a file system folder, or both. Click Next after you choose the desired options, then click Finish.

> **Note** Incoming faxes are delivered to the Fax Console's Inbox in Windows XP by default. The option to save the fax to a folder is separate from this Inbox. If you want to deliver incoming faxes only to the Fax Console Inbox (not to be confused with the Outlook Inbox), you need not enable the Store A Copy In A Folder option.

Sending Faxes

Regardless of which operating system you use, you can send faxes from any application because Microsoft Fax functions as a printer driver. To send a fax, just print the document to the Fax printer (see Figure 9-14). To do so, choose File, Print to open the Print dialog box. Select Fax in the Name drop-down list (which lists all available printers) and click OK.

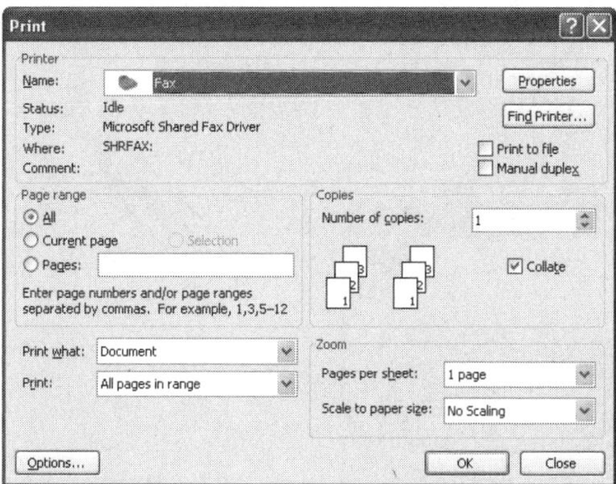

Figure 9-14. Send a fax from any application using the Fax printer.

You also can send a cover page fax outside an application when you need to send only a quick note as a fax, rather than a document.

Follow these steps to send a cover page fax in Windows XP (the process is very similar for Windows 2000):

1. Click Start, All Programs, Accessories, Communication, Fax, Send A Fax. After the Send Fax Wizard starts, click Next.
2. In the Send Fax Wizard, enter the information for the recipient (see Figure 9-15). Alternatively, click Address Book to add the recipient to the address book or select an existing recipient.

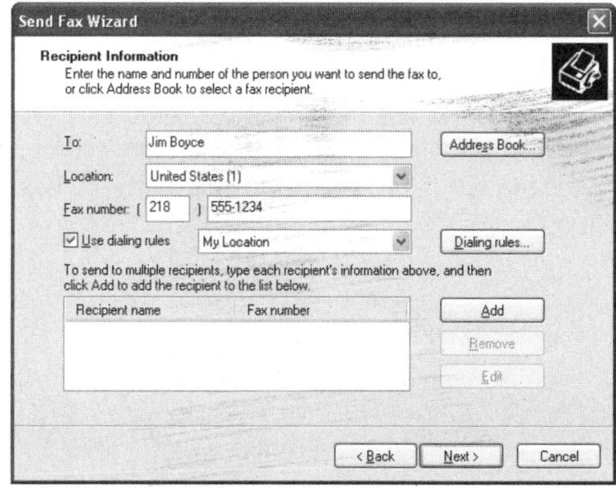

Figure 9-15. Specify recipient information for the fax.

3. Select the Use Dialing Rules check box if you want the fax service to dial the call using the dialing rules defined by the selected location. Clear this check box to dial the call as a local call (using only the number specified in the phone number portion of the Fax Number boxes).
4. Click Add to add the recipient to the list.
5. If you want to include other recipients, add them and then click Next.
6. Select the cover page to use for the fax, enter a subject, and type the body of your fax in the Note box. Click Next.
7. On the Schedule page of the wizard (see Figure 9-16), specify when you want the fax sent and its priority.

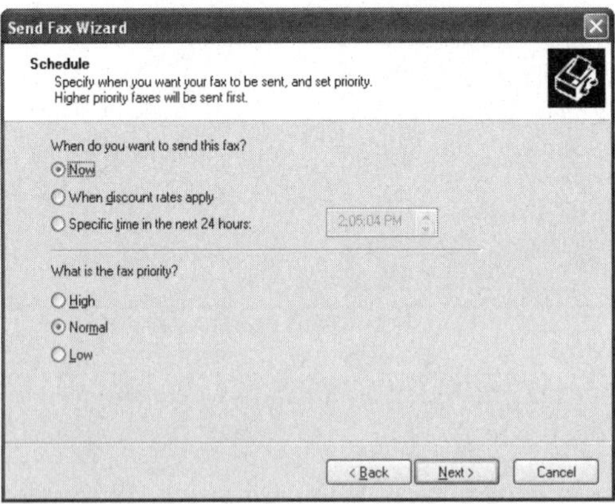

Figure 9-16. Specify send time and priority level.

> **Tip** **View fax event logs**
> You can use the Event Viewer to view the fax event logs in the Windows Application log. Look for events with Fax Service as the source. To easily locate fax events, sort the Application log view by the Source field.

8. Click Next and then click Finish to submit the fax to the queue.

In Windows 2000, you can specify a billing code for the fax to associate the fax with a project, account, or other billing mechanism. The billing code is included with fax events in the Application log. Billing codes are also included in the Application log for Windows XP, but you can only set the billing code globally in the Fax Console (with the Fax Configuration Wizard), rather than for each fax.

Using Cover Pages

As the previous steps illustrated, you can use a cover page as the only page of the fax for a simple message. The fax service can automatically include information on the cover page, such as your user information and the time the fax was sent. You can also include cover pages with other data. For example, you might need to fax a Microsoft Word document and include a cover sheet. The following section explains how.

The first step in using cover pages with Microsoft Fax under Windows 2000 or Windows XP is to add or create them. Both operating systems include four basic cover pages; you can either use them without modification or change them to suit your needs. You also can create your own cover pages from scratch.

Adding Default Cover Pages

When you first configure Microsoft Fax, none of the default cover pages appear in your list of personal cover pages.

Follow these steps to add the four default cover pages to your list in Windows 2000:

1. Double-click the Fax icon in Control Panel.
2. Click the Cover Pages tab and click Add.
3. Browse to \Documents And Settings\All Users\Documents\My Faxes\Common Coverpages.

> **Tip** The root for user profiles on systems that have been upgraded from Windows NT is %systemroot%\Profiles rather than \Documents And Settings.

4. Select a cover page and click Open to add it to the list.
5. Repeat to add other cover pages, pulling them from other locations if available on your local computer or on the network.

Follow these steps to add personal cover pages in Windows XP:

1. Click Start, All Programs, Accessories, Communications, Fax, Fax Console.
2. In the Fax Console, choose Tools, Personal Cover Pages.
3. In the Personal Cover Pages dialog box (see Figure 9-17), click Copy.

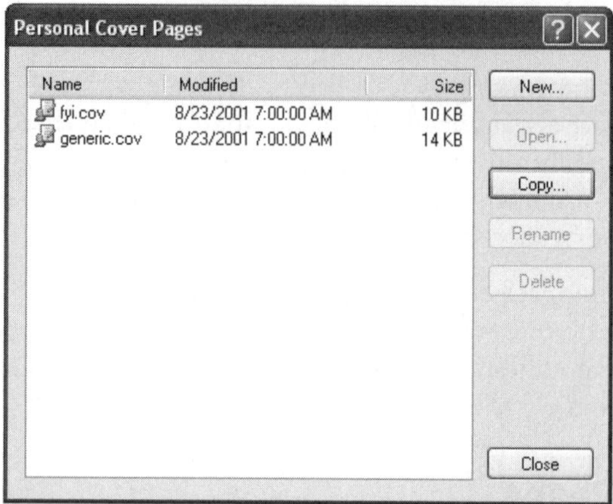

Figure 9-17. Use the Personal Cover Pages dialog box to add personal cover pages.

4 Browse to \Documents And Settings\All Users\Application Data\Microsoft\Windows NT\MSFax\Common Coverpages (the Fax Console opens this folder by default).

5 Select a cover page and click Open to copy it to your personal cover page store.

Creating New Cover Pages

Windows 2000 and Windows XP both include an application called the Fax Cover Page Editor that lets you create and save custom fax cover pages to use with the fax service. Essentially, the Fax Cover Page Editor is a lot like a page layout tool for desktop publishing. If you have experience using Word, Web site development applications, or even Microsoft Paint, you shouldn't have any trouble creating your own cover pages. Rather than explaining the Fax Cover Page Editor in detail, this section covers the main points to get you started.

First, to start the editor in Windows 2000, double-click the Fax icon in Control Panel. On the Cover Pages tab, click New to open the editor (see Figure 9-18). In Windows XP, click Start, All Programs, Accessories, Communications, Fax, Fax Cover Page Editor. Or, with the Fax Console open, choose Tools, Personal Cover Pages to open the Personal Cover Pages dialog box, then click New.

> **Tip** Although you can create cover pages from scratch, you might find it easier to modify one of the existing pages to suit your needs, saving it with a different file name.

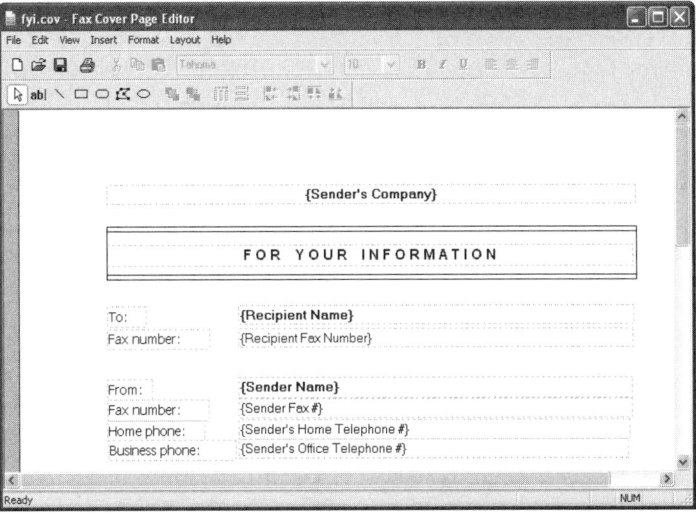

Figure 9-18. The Fax Cover Page Editor functions as a simple page layout tool.

You can insert graphics, text, and basic shapes on a cover page with the tools the editor provides. For example, you might want to include your company's logo on your fax cover pages. More important, perhaps, is your ability to insert dynamic fields on the cover page that Fax automatically fills in when you send a fax. These fields include your user name, fax number, time sent, and recipient name. Choose Insert, followed by Recipient, Sender, or Message, to view the types of fields you can insert on the cover page.

Inside Out

To insert graphics, use the clipboard

Unfortunately you can't insert a graphic from a file using the Fax Cover Page Editor's interface. This would be a handy feature to include in future versions of the Fax Cover Page Editor. You can insert graphics, but you have to use the clipboard to do so.

After you complete the layout of your cover page, save it to a disk. To do so, choose File, Save As. Then specify a path and name and click OK.

Receiving Faxes with Outlook in Windows 2000

Assuming that you've set up Microsoft Fax and Outlook properly, incoming faxes should be routed directly to your Inbox, where you can handle them just as you handle e-mail messages. Figure 9-19 shows a fax in the Inbox. Note that the message header's subject is always Received Fax, not the subject described in the fax. Because the fax comes through as a bitmap, the fax service has no way to extract the subject from the fax itself.

Figure 9-19. Faxes appear as messages with attachments in the Inbox.

If you've configured the fax service for manual reception, the service displays a dialog box when a call comes in. Click Yes to answer the call and receive the fax. As with automatic reception, the fax service delivers the fax to your Inbox.

Viewing Faxes

The fax comes through as an attachment in TIF format, which you can view with the application that is associated with TIF files on your system. To view a fax, open the attached TIF file as you would open any other attachment. By default, Outlook associates TIF files with the Microsoft Office Document Imaging application. The application is located by default in \Program Files\Common Files\Microsoft Shared\ MSPaper\Mspview.exe. If Document Imaging is the default application for TIF files, you should see something similar to Figure 9-20 when you open a fax TIF attachment.

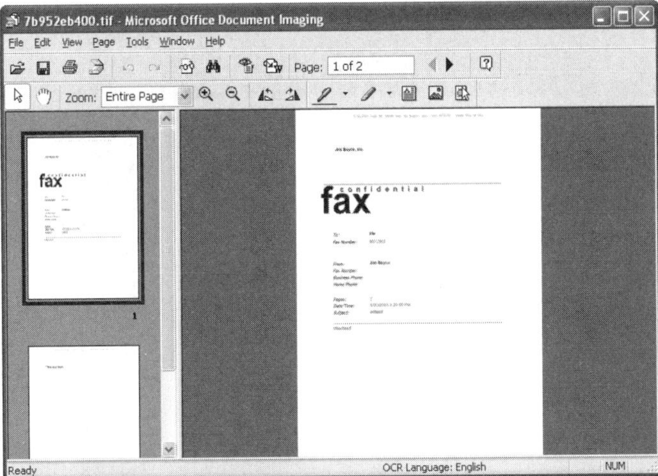

Figure 9-20. Use the Document Imaging application to view and manipulate received faxes.

You have an alternative in Windows XP

In Windows XP, the fax opens in the Document Imaging application if you open the TIF file from Outlook, but opens in the Windows Picture and File Viewer application if you save the TIF file and open it from a file system folder outside of Outlook. Each has its advantages. If you prefer this application over Document Imaging, change the file association for TIF files to point to the Windows Picture and File Viewer. See the upcoming section "Setting the Default Viewer" for details.

The Document Imaging application shows the fax pages as thumbnails in the left pane and shows the selected page in the right pane. You can rotate pages, zoom in, print, and perform a handful of other tasks that make it easier to view and print the fax. You can also move individual pages to a new file by first selecting the page and then choosing Edit, Move Pages To New File. Document Imaging is a simple application, and a few minutes exploring its interface should make you comfortable using it.

Controlling the View

The Document Imaging application supports two viewing modes: Reading view and Page view. The default is Page view, which displays the fax as shown in Figure 9-20. You also can press F11 or choose View, Reading View to switch modes. Reading view displays the fax one page at a time, as shown in Figure 9-21. Click the up or down arrows to scroll through the document and view other pages. Click the down arrow beside the fax document name, and choose Return To Page View or press Esc to return to Page view.

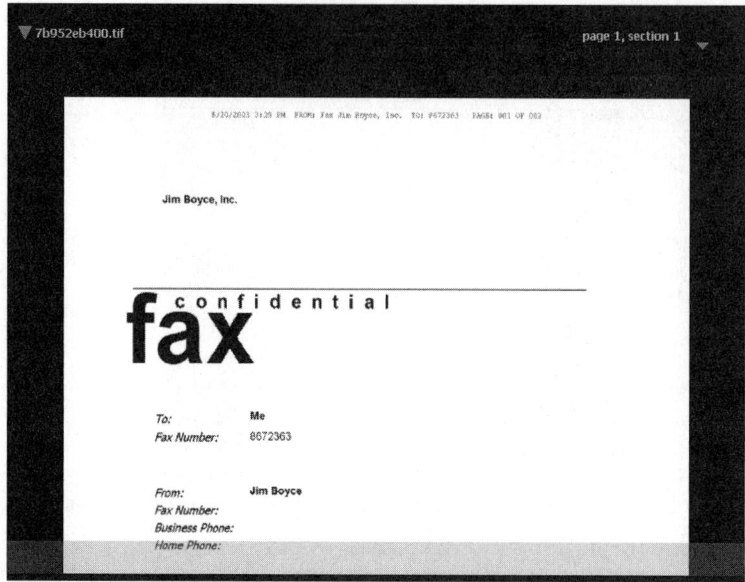

Figure 9-21. You can view the fax one page at a time in Reading view.

Troubleshooting

Fax images are displayed with a different application and show only the first page

Outlook uses the application defined by the system's TIF document association to display faxes. Your system might be configured to use a different application to view TIF files. Because not all graphics applications support viewing multipage TIF documents, you might see only the first page of a fax. If that's the case, you need to associate TIF files with an application that supports multipage TIF documents. The following section explains how to restore Document Imaging as the default viewer for TIF files.

Setting the Default Viewer

If you install other graphics applications on your system, it's a strong possibility that one of these programs might change document associations on the system and that TIF files might now be associated with the new application rather than with Document Imaging. If you're seeing only the first page of faxes or want to use Document Imaging for other reasons, you need to reassociate Document Imaging with TIF files. Or, perhaps you want to set the Windows Picture and Fax Viewer in Windows XP as the default viewer.

Follow these steps to change the application associated with TIF files:

1 Open any folder in Windows Explorer (such as My Computer).

2 Choose Tools, Folder Options and click the File Types tab, shown in Figure 9-22.

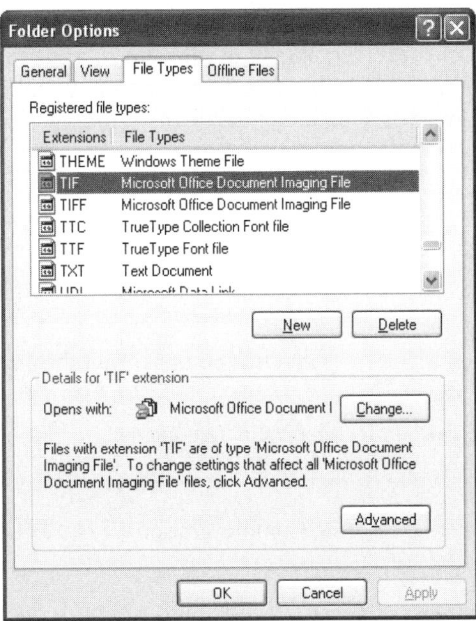

Figure 9-22. Use the File Types tab to change document association.

3 Scroll through the document list, locate TIF, select it, and click Change.

4 Select either Microsoft Office Document Imaging or Windows Picture and Fax Viewer (or another application of your choice), and click OK.

5 Click OK to close the Folder Options dialog box.

> **Tip** **Set file association manually**
>
> If you need to specify the application manually because it is located in a nonstandard folder, click Advanced on the File Types tab after you select TIF from the list. Select Open, click Edit, and enter the following in the Application box (include the quotation marks and be sure to change the path if the file is located in a different folder or volume):
>
> **"C:\Program Files\Common Files\Microsoft Shared\MSPaper\Mspview.exe" "%1"**
>
> Specify an appropriate path if you are associating a different application with TIF files.

Printing Incoming Faxes

When a fax arrives in Windows 2000, you have four options for processing the fax: print it, place it in your incoming fax queue folder, place it in your Inbox, or perform any combination of those three actions. Windows XP also offers four options: save in the Fax Console Inbox, print, save to a folder, or a combination of the three.

If you want Outlook to act like a fax machine, printing each fax as soon as it arrives, follow these steps in Windows 2000:

1. Choose Start, Programs, Accessories, Communication, Fax, Fax Service Management.
2. Click the Devices node, and then double-click the fax modem to open its Properties dialog box.
3. Click the Received Faxes tab, select Print On, and then select the printer from the drop-down list.
4. Click OK and close the Fax Service Management console.

Follow these steps in Windows XP to configure the fax service to print incoming faxes:

1. Click Start, All Programs, Accessories, Communications, Fax, Fax Console.
2. Choose Tools, Configure Fax.
3. On the Routing Options page of the Fax Configuration Wizard, enable the Print It On option and select a printer, then complete the wizard.

Note In addition to printing the fax, you also should have it delivered to your Inbox or to a folder as specified by the other options. This ensures that you have a backup copy if something goes wrong with the print job.

You can print individual faxes at any time. Simply open the fax in Document Imaging (or another application) and choose File, Print to print it just as you would print any other document.

Managing Faxes

You can manipulate faxes that have been delivered to your Inbox the same way you manipulate other messages in the Inbox. For example, you can move them from one folder to another or delete them. Having faxes delivered to your Inbox is a good way to easily recognize when new faxes come in, but you might want them delivered to another folder instead.

Note This section applies only to Windows 2000 users because Windows XP does not deliver to the Outlook Inbox, which eliminates the ability to process incoming faxes with rules.

You can do so by creating a rule, using these steps:

1. In Outlook, create the folder in which you want faxes to be stored, making sure that it's a standard message folder. Using another folder type will cause Outlook to handle the faxes differently from how it handles e-mail messages, making them more difficult to retrieve.
2. Choose Tools, Rules And Alerts to open the Rules And Alerts dialog box.
3. Click New Rule, select Start From A Blank Rule, and click Next.
4. Select With Specific Words In The Subject.
5. In the rule description area, click Specific Words, type **Received Fax** in the Specify Words box, click Add, and click OK.
6. Click Next and select Move It To The Specified Folder.
7. In the rule description area, click Specified, select the destination folder, and click OK.
8. Click Next, specify any exceptions to the rule, and click Next.
9. If you want to move existing faxes to the folder, select Run This Rule Now On Messages Already In Inbox.
10. Click Finish to create the rule.

For a detailed explanation of message rules and how to create and manage them, see "Understanding Message Rules," page 224.

Faxing Across the Internet

In some situations it's more practical to send a document not through a fax modem, but instead through an Internet fax service. With such a service, the outgoing fax is transmitted as an e-mail message across the Internet to a fax service provider. The provider then transmits the document as a fax to the recipient. You save on the cost of fax server hardware that would otherwise be required to support multiple users for outgoing faxes (or individual fax modems and associated phone lines). You can also save on costs, as the cost for the service provider to deliver the fax will be less than if the document were sent across your own phone line.

There are several Internet fax service providers that offer integration with Outlook 2003. One of these is the Venali Internet Fax Service for Microsoft Office 2003. It isn't practical to cover all of the available Internet fax services, but a brief overview of the Venali service and how it works with Outlook 2003 will help you understand how these services can simplify faxing from Outlook and other Microsoft Office applications.

The first step is to sign up for the service with the service provider. In the case of Venali, you can do that on the company's Web site at *http://www.venali.com/solutions/microsoft/office_2003.asp*. Through the sign-up process you provide your contact information, e-mail address, voice and fax phone numbers, and of course, a credit card for billing. Then, you download and install the Internet Fax Service add-in. There is no configuration required—just double-click the downloaded executable file to install the service.

The Venali Internet Fax Service for Microsoft Office 2003 only works in conjunction with Outlook if you use Word as your e-mail editor. There is no integration with the service in the Outlook message form. The service is also only available for faxing messages—you cannot fax other Outlook items (such as contacts) unless you export the data to Word or other application that supports the service, and fax from that application.

With Word as your e-mail editor, follow these steps to send a fax through the Venali Internet Fax Service for Microsoft Office 2003:

1. Open an existing message or compose a new one.
2. With the message form open, choose File, Send To, Recipient Using Internet Fax Service. The add-in converts the message to a TIF file and attaches it to a new message (see Figure 9-23).

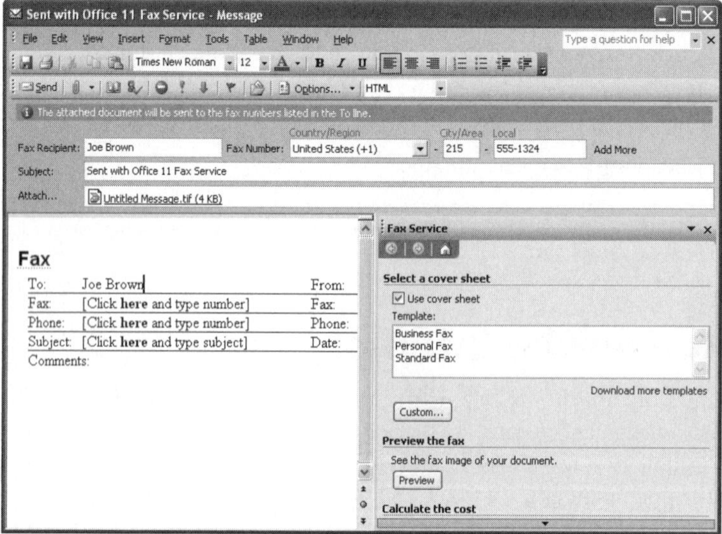

Figure 9-23. Enter cover page and recipient information for the fax.

3. Type the recipient's name in the Fax Recipient text box. If the contact exists in your Contacts folder, the name is automatically completed as you type. When you press Tab to move to the next field, the associated fax number is filled in automatically.
4. If you type a name not in your Contacts list, select the fax destination country or region from the Country/Region drop-down list. Then, enter the city or area code in the City/Area field and the fax number in the Local field.
5. Modify the Subject field if desired, then click in the fields in the cover page and complete those fields as needed. You can choose a different cover sheet from the Fax Service pane, but doing so causes any information entered in the current cover page to be lost.

6 Scroll down in the Fax Service pane to access other options (see Figure 9-24), including the ability to calculate the cost of the fax and preview the fax before you send it.

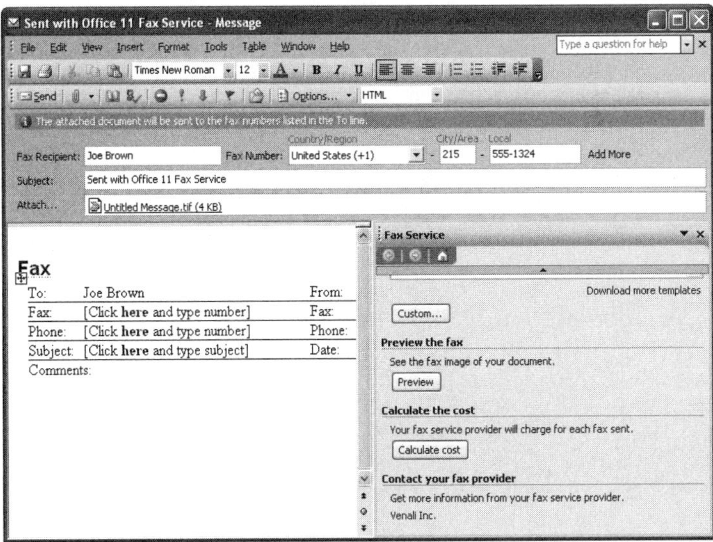

Figure 9-24. Scroll in the Fax Service pane to access additional options.

7 When you're ready to send the fax, click the Send button in the toolbar.

When you click Send, the message is transmitted over the Internet to the Venali service, where the message is queued for fax delivery.

Chapter 10

Securing Your System, Messages, and Identity

Microsoft Outlook includes features that can help protect your system from computer viruses and malicious programs, prevent others from using e-mail to impersonate you, and prevent the interception of sensitive messages. Some of these features—such as the ability to block specific types of attachments—were first introduced in Microsoft Outlook 2002. Microsoft Outlook 2003 adds some new features, including the ability to block external images in HTML-based messages. This feature enables Outlook to block HTML messages sent by spammers to identify valid recipient addresses.

This chapter begins by examining security zones, which allow you to specify how Outlook should handle HTML-based messages. Because HTML messages can contain malicious scripts or even HTML code that can easily affect your system, Outlook's ability to handle these messages is extremely important.

This chapter also discusses the use of both digital signatures and encryption. You can use a digital signature to authenticate your messages, proving to the recipient that a message indeed came from you and not from someone trying to impersonate you. Outlook allows you to encrypt outgoing messages to prevent them from being intercepted by unintended recipients; you can also read encrypted messages sent to you by others. In this chapter, you'll learn how to obtain and install certificates to send encrypted messages and how to share keys with others so that you can exchange encrypted messages.

Virus protection is another important feature in Outlook. You can configure Outlook to automatically block specific types of attachments, thus helping prevent virus infections. Outlook provides two levels of attachment protection, one for individual users and one for system administrators.

Using Security Zones

Outlook's support for HTML-based messages poses certain security risks. It's relatively easy, for example, for someone to embed in an HTML message scripts that extract data from your system, delete data, or insert a Trojan horse virus. Because of this, restricting the actions that HTML messages can perform can have a significant impact on your system's security.

Outlook uses the security zones defined by Microsoft Internet Explorer. By default, Outlook assigns HTML messages to the Restricted Sites zone. This zone prevents HTML messages from carrying out most potentially dangerous actions, such as downloading unsigned ActiveX controls or files, active scripting, or scripting of Java applets.

In most cases, you'll want to continue to use the Restricted Sites zone for Outlook. In some situations, however, you might need to use a different zone or modify the settings to create a custom zone. For example, you might want to eliminate the restrictions if you don't receive messages from outside your intranet (which, of course, implies trust of the other users on the intranet).

Tip Regardless of which zone you select for Outlook, the program deactivates ActiveX controls and does not run scripts.

To select the security zone you want Outlook to apply to HTML messages, choose Tools, Options and click Security. In the Security Zones section of the Security tab (see Figure 10-1), select a zone in the Zone drop-down list.

Figure 10-1. Use the Security tab to select the security zone you want Outlook to apply to HTML messages.

If you need to change the zone settings, click Zone Settings to display the Security dialog box, shown in Figure 10-2. Select a general security level, or click Custom Level to display the Security Settings dialog box (see Figure 10-3), in which you can specify custom settings.

Figure 10-2. Use the Security dialog box to select a zone or change its settings.

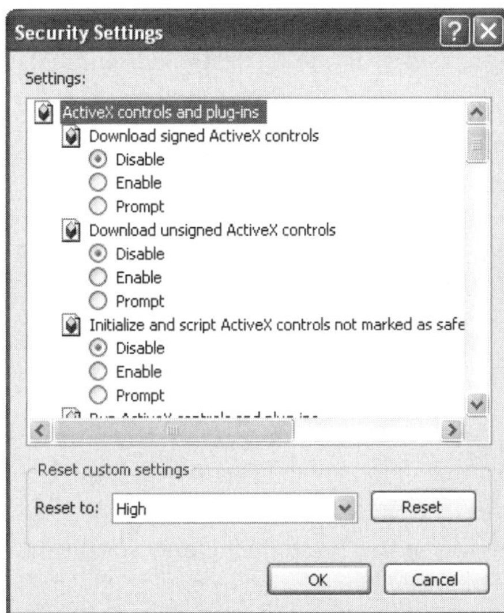

Figure 10-3. Use the Security Settings dialog box to define custom security settings.

It's important to understand that when Outlook processes messages, it uses the security settings from the security zone you've selected—it does not consider settings you might have made in other zones. For example, assume that you've specified several restricted domains in the Restricted Sites zone but have configured Outlook to use the Internet zone. When an HTML message arrives that originated in one of the domains specified in your Restricted Sites zone, Outlook applies the security settings for the Internet zone, ignoring the restriction you've placed on that domain. Because Outlook treats all HTML messages the same, adding

Chapter 10

sites to other security zones in Outlook doesn't provide additional security. Instead, you should consider the security zone you select to be the main determinant of how HTML messages are handled globally. (For that reason, this book doesn't cover the topic of adding sites to security zones.)

> **Note** Unlike Outlook, Internet Explorer does consider the settings in all zones when determining how to handle pages from specific domains and security zones. If you're using Internet Explorer, it's therefore a good idea to add domain restrictions for various zones as needed. Keep in mind, however, that Outlook considers only the zone, not the domains it might specify.

Configuring HTML Message Handling

Spammers are always looking for new methods to identify valid e-mail addresses. Knowing that a given address actually reaches someone is one step in helping spammers maintain their lists. If a particular address doesn't generate a response in some way, it's more likely to be removed from the list.

One way spammers identify valid addresses is through the use of *Web beacons*. Often, spammers send HTML messages that contain links to external content, such as pictures or sound clips. When you display the message, your mail program retrieves the remote data to display it, and the remote server then validates your address. These external elements are the Web beacons.

> **Note** Nonspammers also frequently include external content in messages to reduce the size of the message. So, external content isn't a bad thing per se; it is dependent on how it is used.

Outlook 2003 introduces a new feature that blocks external content from HTML messages by default, displaying a red X in the place of the missing content. The result is that these Web beacons no longer work because the external content is not accessed when the message is displayed. Messages that fit criteria for the Trusted Recipients and Trusted Senders lists are treated as exceptions—the external content for these messages is not blocked. Another exception is content that originates from domains in the Trusted Sites and Local Intranet security zones in Internet Explorer, which is also allowed by default.

> **Tip** You can rest the mouse pointer on a blocked image to view the descriptive alternate text (if any) for the image.

When you preview an image in the Reading Pane for which Outlook has blocked external content, Outlook displays a message in the InfoBar indicating that the blocking occurred (see Figure 10-4). You can click the InfoBar and choose Show Blocked Content to view the external content. Outlook then downloads and displays the content in the Reading Pane. The same is true if you open a message; Outlook displays an indicator in the message form that content was blocked (see Figure 10-5). You can click the warning message and choose Show Blocked Content to download and view the content. Outlook's blocking of external content for messages in this way lets you take advantage of content blocking without using the Reading Pane.

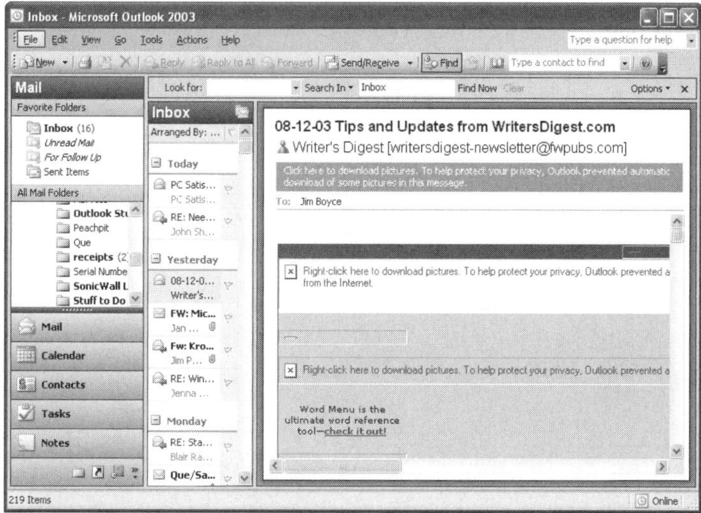

Figure 10-4. Click the InfoBar in the Reading Pane to view external content for a selected message.

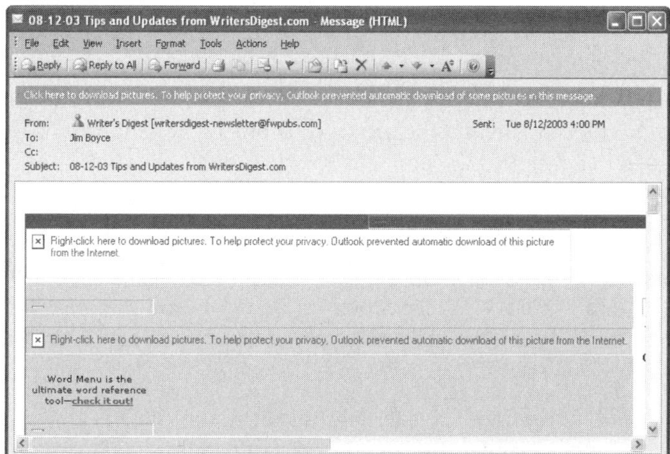

Figure 10-5. You can access blocked content when you open a message.

If you edit, forward, or reply to a message containing blocked content, Outlook displays a warning dialog box indicating that the external content will be downloaded if you continue. You can click OK to download the content and continue with the reply or forward, or click Cancel to not open the message or download the content. Therefore, you can't reply to or forward a message without downloading the external content.

Outlook provides a few options to control the way content blocking works. To configure these options, choose Tools, Options, click the Security tab, and click Change Automatic Download Settings in the Download Pictures area. Figure 10-6 shows the resulting External Content Settings dialog box.

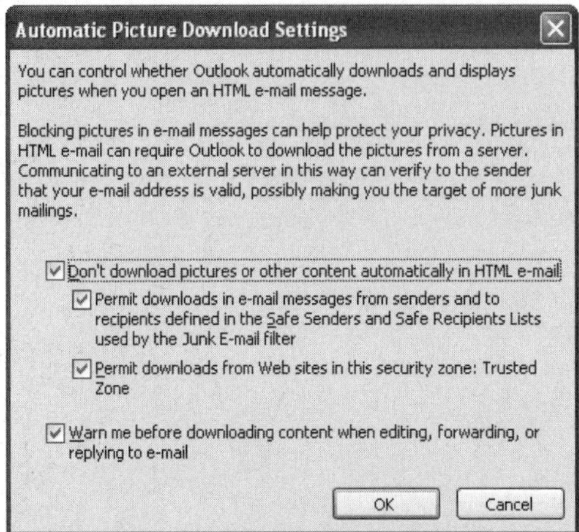

Figure 10-6. Configure content blocking with the External Content Settings dialog box.

Configure content blocking using the following options:

- **Don't Download Pictures Or Other Content Automatically in HTML E-Mail** Select this check box to allow Outlook to block external content with the exception of messages that fit theTrusted Senders andTrusted Recipients lists.
- **Permit Downloads In E-mail Messages From Senders And To Recipients Defined In The Safe Senders And Safe Recipients List Used By The Junk E-mail Filter** Allow Outlook to download content if the message is from a sender in your Safe Senders list or is addressed to a recipient in your Safe Recipients list.
- **Permit Downloads From Web Sites In This Security Zone: Trusted Zone** Select this check box to allow external content from sites in Internet Explorer's Trusted Sites zone.
- **Warn Me Before Downloading Blocked Content When Editing, Forwarding, Or Replying To E-Mail** Select this check box to receive a warning about external content when you edit, reply to, or forward a message for which external content has been blocked.

To take advantage of the exceptions for external content, you must add the message's originating address to the Trusted Senders list, add the recipient address to the Trusted Recipients list, or add the remote domain to the Trusted Sites zone in Internet Explorer. See "Enabling and Configuring Junk E-Mail Filtering," page 245, for more details on configuring the Trusted Recipients and Trusted Senders lists. See "Using Security Zones" earlier in this chapter for information on Internet Explorer security zones and how to manage them.

Protecting Messages with Digital Signatures

Outlook supports the use of *digital signatures* to sign messages and validate their authenticity. For example, you can digitally sign a sensitive message so that the recipient can know with relative certainty that the message came from you and that no one is impersonating you by using your e-mail address. This section of the chapter explains digital certificates and signatures and how to use them in Outlook.

Understanding Digital Certificates and Signatures

A *digital certificate* is the mechanism that makes digital signatures possible. Depending on its assigned purpose, you can use a digital certificate for a variety of tasks, including the following:

- Verifying your identity as the sender of an e-mail message
- Encrypting data communications between computers—between a client and a server, for example
- Encrypting e-mail messages to prevent easy interception
- Signing drivers and executable files to authenticate their origin

A digital certificate binds the identity of the certificate's owner to a pair of keys, one public and one private. At a minimum, a certificate contains the following information:

- The owner's public key
- The owner's name or alias
- A certificate expiration date
- A certificate serial number
- The name of the certificate issuer
- The digital signature of the issuer

The certificate can also include other identifying information, such as the owner's e-mail address, postal address, country, or gender.

The two keys are the aspect of the certificate that enables authentication and encryption. The private key resides on your computer and is a large unique number. The certificate contains the public key, which you must give to recipients to whom you want to send authenticated or encrypted messages. Think of the keys in a literal sense, as two keys that open a lock with two keyholes. The only way to open the lock is to have both keys.

Outlook uses slightly different methods for authenticating messages with digital signatures and for encrypting messages, as you'll see later in the chapter. Before you begin either task, however, you must first obtain a certificate.

Obtaining a Digital Certificate

Digital certificates are issued by certificate authorities (CAs). In most cases, you obtain your e-mail certificate from a public CA such as VeriSign or Thawte. However, systems based on Microsoft Windows NT Server and Microsoft Windows 2000 Server or Microsoft Windows Server 2003 running Certificate Services can function as CAs, providing certificates to clients who request them. Check with your system administrator to determine whether your enterprise includes a CA. If it doesn't, you need to obtain your certificate from a public CA, usually at a minimal cost. Certificates are typically good for one year and must be renewed at the end of that period.

If you need to obtain your certificate from a public CA, point your Web browser to the CA's Web site, such as *http://www.verisign.com* or *http://www.thawte.com*. Follow the instructions provided by the site to obtain a certificate for signing and encrypting your e-mail (see Figure 10-7, for example). The certificate might not be issued immediately; instead, the CA might send you an e-mail message containing a URL that links to a page where you can retrieve the certificate. When you connect to that page, the CA installs the certificate on your system.

> **Tip** You can click Get A Digital ID on the Security tab of the Options dialog box to display a page from Microsoft's Web site that includes links to several certificate authorities.

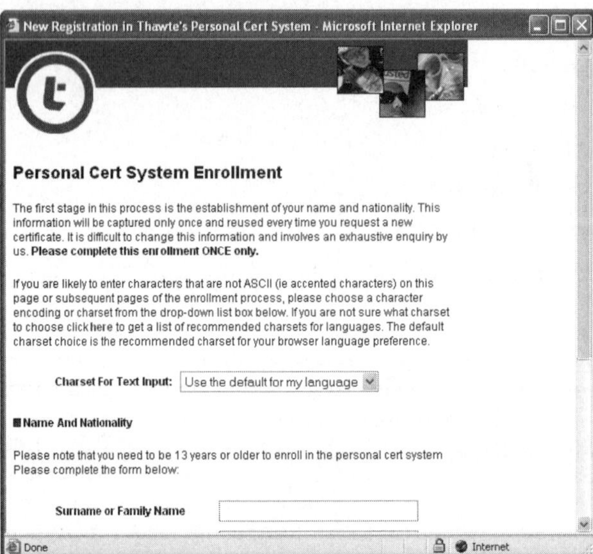

Figure 10-7. You can use the Web to request a digital certificate from a public CA.

If you're obtaining a certificate from a CA on your network, the method you use depends on whether the network includes an enterprise CA or a stand-alone CA.

If you're using Windows 2000 or Windows XP as a domain client on a network with an enterprise CA, follow these steps to request a certificate:

1. Choose Start, Run and type **MMC**. Click OK.
2. In the Microsoft Management Console (MMC), choose Console, Add/Remove Snap-In.
3. In the Add/Remove Snap-In dialog box, click Add.
4. In the Add Standalone Snap-In dialog box, select Certificates and click Add.
5. In the Certificates Snap-In dialog box, select My User Account and click Finish.
6. Click Close, and then click OK to return to the MMC.
7. Expand the Certificates–Current User branch.
8. Expand the Personal branch, right-click Certificates, and choose All Tasks, Request New Certificate. You can also right-click the Personal branch and choose All Tasks, Request New Certificate.
9. Follow the prompts provided by the Certificate Request Wizard and the enterprise CA to request your certificate. The certificate should install automatically.

To request a certificate from a stand-alone CA on your network (or if your computer is part of a workgroup), point your Web browser to *http://<server>/certsrv*, where <server> is the name or IP address of the CA. The CA provides a Web page with a form that you must fill out to request the certificate (see Figure 10-8). Follow the CA's prompts to request and obtain the certificate. The site includes a link that you can click to install the certificate.

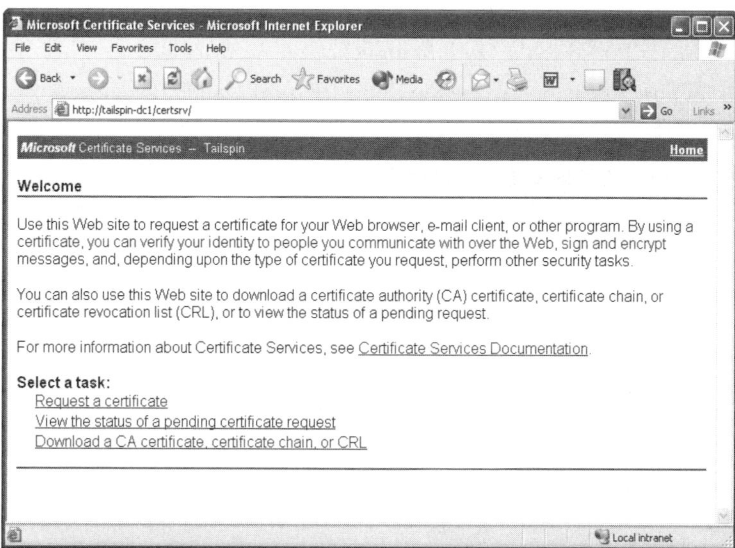

Figure 10-8. A Windows 2000 Server or Windows Server 2003 CA presents a Web form that you can use to request a certificate.

Copying a Certificate to Another Computer

You can copy your certificate from one computer to another, which means that you can use it on more than one system. The process is simple: you first export (back up) your certificate to a file and then import the certificate into the other system. The following sections explain how to export and import certificates.

Note As you use the Certificate Import Wizard and the Certificate Export Wizard (discussed in the following sections), you might discover that they don't precisely match the descriptions presented here. Their appearance and operation might vary slightly, depending on the operating system you're running and the version of Internet Explorer you're using.

Backing Up Your Certificate

Whether you obtained your certificate from a public CA or from a CA on your network, you should back it up in case your system suffers a drive failure or the certificate is lost or corrupted. You also should have a backup of the certificate so that you can export it to any other computers you use on a regular basis, such as a notebook computer or your home computer. In short, you need the certificate on every computer from which you plan to digitally sign or encrypt messages. To back up your certificate, you can use Outlook, Internet Explorer, or the Certificates console (available in both Windows 2000 and Windows XP). Each method offers the same capabilities; you can use any one of the three.

Follow these steps to use Outlook to back up your certificate to a file:

1. In Outlook, choose Tools, Options and click the Security tab.
2. Click Import/Export to display the Import/Export Digital ID dialog box, shown in Figure 10-9.

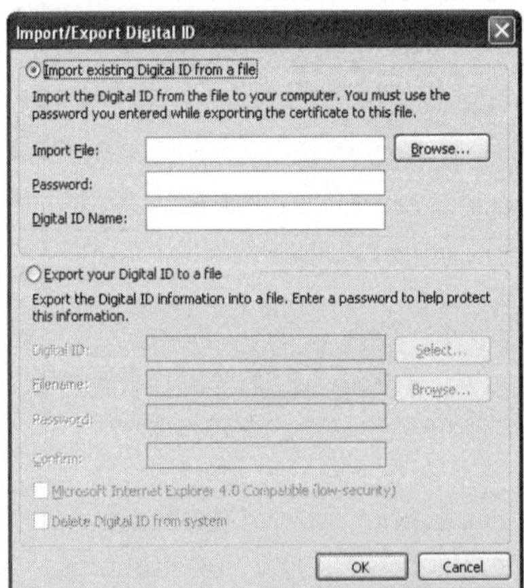

Figure 10-9. You can export certificates in the Import/Export Digital ID dialog box.

3. Select the Export Your Digital ID To A File option. Click Select and select the certificate to be exported.

4. Click Browse and specify the path and file name for the certificate file.
5. Optionally, you can enter and confirm a password.
6. If you plan to use the certificate on a system with Internet Explorer 4, select the Microsoft Internet Explorer 4.0 Compatible (Low-Security) check box. If you use Internet Explorer 5 or later, clear this check box.
7. Click OK to export the file.

If you want to use either Internet Explorer or the Certificates console to back up a certificate, use the Certificate Export Wizard, as follows:

1. If you're using Internet Explorer, begin by choosing Tools, Internet Options. Click the Content tab and then click Certificates. In the Certificates dialog box, shown in Figure 10-10, select the certificate you want to back up and click Export to start the wizard. If you're using the Certificates console, begin by opening the console and expanding Certificates–Current User/Personal/Certificates. Right-click the certificate to export, and choose All Tasks, Export to start the wizard.

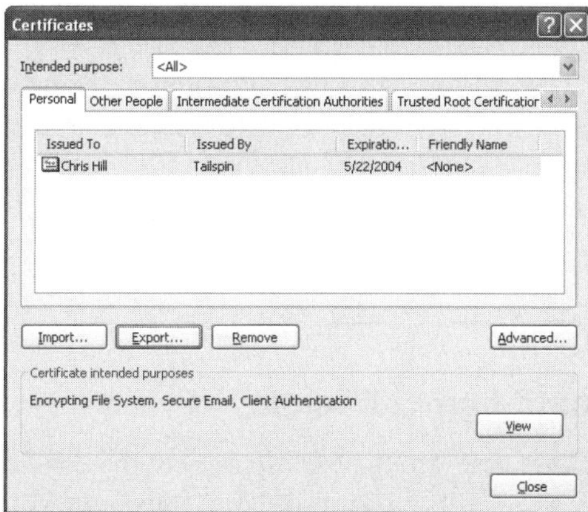

Figure 10-10. You can use the Certificates dialog box to export a certificate.

2. In the Certificate Export Wizard, click Next.
3. On the wizard page shown in Figure 10-11, select Yes, Export The Private Key and then click Next.

Figure 10-11. This wizard allows you to export the private key.

4. Select Personal Information Exchange, and then clear the Enable Strong Protection option. If other options are selected, clear them as well. Click Next.

Note If you're using Internet Explorer 5 or later, you do not need to clear the Enable Strong Protection option. You should clear the other options, however.

5. Specify and confirm a password to protect the private key and click Next.
6. Specify a path and file name for the certificate and click Next.
7. Review your selections and click Finish.

Troubleshooting

You can't export the private key

To use a certificate on a different computer, you must be able to export the private key. If the option to export the private key is unavailable when you run the Certificate Export Wizard, it means that the private key is marked as not exportable. Exportability is an option you choose when you request the certificate. If you request a certificate through a local CA, you must select the Advanced Request option to request a certificate with an exportable private key. If you imported the certificate from a file, you might not have selected the option to make the private key exportable during the import. If you still have the original certificate file, you can import it again, this time selecting the option that will allow you to export the private key.

Installing Your Certificate from a Backup

You can install (or reinstall) a certificate from a backup copy of the certificate file by using Outlook, Internet Explorer, or the Certificates console. You must import the certificate to your computer from the backup file.

The following procedure assumes that you're installing the certificate using Outlook:

1. In Outlook, choose Tools, Options and click the Security tab.
2. Click Import/Export to display the Import/Export Digital ID dialog box, shown earlier in Figure 10-9.
3. Click Browse to locate the file containing the backup of the certificate.
4. In the Password box, type the password associated with the certificate file.
5. In the Digital ID Name box, type a name by which you want the certificate to be shown. Typically, you'll enter your name, mailbox name, or e-mail address, but you can enter anything you want.
6. Click OK to import the certificate.

You can also import a certificate to your computer from a backup file using either Internet Explorer or the Certificates console, as explained here:

1. If you're using Internet Explorer, begin by choosing Tools, Internet Options. Click the Content tab, click Certificates, and then click Import to start the Certificate Import Wizard. If you're using the Certificates console, begin by opening the console. Then right-click Certificates–Current User/Personal and click All Tasks, Import to start the wizard.
2. In the Certificate Import Wizard, click Next.
3. Browse and select the file to import and then click Next.
4. Select the Automatically Select The Certificate Store Based On The Type Of Certificate option and click Next.
5. Click Finish.

Signing Messages

Now that you have a certificate on your system, you're ready to start digitally signing your outgoing messages so that recipients can verify your identity. When you send a digitally signed message, Outlook sends the original message and an encrypted copy of the message with your digital signature. The recipient's e-mail application compares the two versions of the message to determine whether they are the same. If they are, no one has tampered with the message. The digital signature also allows the recipient to verify that the message is from you.

Understanding S/MIME and Clear-Text Options

Secure/Multipurpose Internet Mail Extensions (S/MIME), an Internet standard, is the mechanism in Outlook that allows you to digitally sign and encrypt messages. The e-mail client handles the encryption and decryption required for both functions.

Users with e-mail clients that don't support S/MIME can't read digitally signed messages unless you send the message as clear text (unencrypted). Without S/MIME support, the recipient is also unable to verify the authenticity of the message or verify that the message hasn't been altered. Without S/MIME, then, digital signatures are relatively useless. However, Outlook does offer you the option of sending a digitally signed message as clear text to recipients who lack S/MIME support. If you need to send the same digitally signed message to multiple recipients—some of whom have S/MIME-capable e-mail clients and some of whom do not—digitally signing the message allows those with S/MIME support to authenticate it, and including the clear-text message allows the others to at least read it.

The following section explains how to send a digitally signed message, including how to send the message in clear text for those recipients who require it.

Adding Your Digital Signature

Follow these steps to digitally sign an outgoing message:

1. Compose the message in Outlook.
2. Click the Options button on the message form toolbar to open the Message Options dialog box.
3. Click Security Settings to open the Security Properties dialog box, shown in Figure 10-12.

Figure 10-12. You can add a digital signature using the Security Properties dialog box.

4. Select Add Digital Signature To This Message, and then select other check boxes as indicated here:
   - **Send This Message As Clear Text Signed** Select this check box to include a clear-text copy of the message for recipients who don't have S/MIME-capable e-mail applications. Clear this check box to prevent the message from being read by mail clients that don't support S/MIME.
   - **Request S/MIME Receipt For This Message** Select this check box to request a secure receipt to verify that the recipient has validated your digital signature. When the message has been received and saved and your signature verified (even if the recipient doesn't read the message), you receive a return receipt. No receipt is sent if your signature is not verified.
5. If necessary, select security settings in the Security Setting drop-down list. (If you have not yet configured your security options, you can do so by clicking Change Settings; for details, see "Creating and Using Security Profiles," page 302.)
6. Click OK to add the digital signature to the message.

> **Tip** **Speed up digital signing**
> If you send a lot of digitally signed messages, you'll want to configure your security options to include a digital signature by default; see the following section for details. In addition, you might want to add a button to the toolbar to let you quickly sign the message without using a dialog box. For details about how to add such a button, see the Troubleshooting sidebar "You need a faster way to digitally sign a message," page 304.

Setting Global Security Options

To save time, you can configure your security settings to apply globally to all messages, changing settings only as needed for certain messages. In Outlook, choose Tools, Options and then click Security. On the Security tab, shown in Figure 10-13, you can set security options using the following list as a guide.

Figure 10-13. Use the Security tab of the Options dialog box to configure options for digital signing and encryption.

- **Encrypt Contents And Attachments For Outgoing Messages** If most of the messages you send need to be encrypted, select this check box to encrypt all outgoing messages by default. You can override encryption for a specific message by changing the message's properties when you compose it. Clear this check box if the majority of your outgoing messages do not need to be encrypted.

For information about encryption, see "Encrypting Messages," page 315.

- **Add Digital Signature To Outgoing Messages** If most of your messages need to be signed, select this check box to digitally sign all outgoing messages by default. Clear this check box if most of your messages do not need to be signed; you will be able to digitally sign specific messages as needed when you compose them.
- **Send Clear Text Signed Message When Sending Signed Messages** If you need to send digitally signed messages to recipients who do not have S/MIME capability, select this check box to send clear-text digitally signed messages by default. You can override this option for individual messages when you compose them. In most cases, you can clear this check box because most e-mail clients support S/MIME.
- **Request S/MIME Receipt For All S/MIME-Signed Messages** Select this check box to request a secure receipt for all S/MIME messages by default. You can override the setting for individual messages when you compose them. A secure receipt indicates that your message has been received and the signature verified. No receipt is returned if the signature is not verified.
- **Settings** Click Settings to configure more advanced security settings and create additional security setting groups. For details, see the following section, "Creating and Using Security Profiles."
- **Publish To GAL** Click this button to publish your certificates to the Global Address List (GAL), making them available to other Exchange Server users in your organization who might need to send you encrypted messages. This is an alternative to sending the other users a copy of your certificate.

Creating and Using Security Profiles

Although in most cases you need only one set of Outlook security settings, you can create and use multiple security profiles. For example, you might send most of your secure messages to other Exchange Server users, only occasionally sending secure messages to Internet recipients. In that situation, you might maintain two sets of security settings: one that uses Exchange Server security and another that uses S/MIME, each with different certificates and hash algorithms (the method used to secure the data).

You can configure security profiles using the Change Security Settings dialog box, which you access through the Security tab of the Options dialog box. One of your security profiles acts as the default, but you can select a different security profile any time it's needed.

Follow these steps to create and manage your security profiles:

1. In Outlook, choose Tools, Options and click the Security tab.
2. Click Settings to display the Change Security Settings dialog box, shown in Figure 10-14. Set the options described on pages 303 and 304 as needed.
3. Click OK to close the Change Security Settings dialog box.

Figure 10-14. Configure your security profiles in the Change Security Settings dialog box.

4 In the Default Setting drop-down list on the Security tab, select the security profile you want to use by default and then click OK.

- **Security Settings Name** Specify the name for the security profile that should appear in the Default Setting drop-down list on the Security tab.
- **Cryptographic Message** In this drop-down list, select the secure message format for your messages. The default is S/MIME, but you also can select Exchange Server Security. Use S/MIME if you're sending secure messages to Internet recipients. You can use either S/MIME or Exchange Server security when sending secure messages to recipients on your Exchange Server.
- **Default Security Setting For This Cryptographic Message Format** Select this check box to make the specified security settings the default settings for the message format you selected in the Secure Message Format drop-down list.
- **Default Security Setting For All Cryptographic Messages** Select this check box to make the specified security settings the default settings for all secure messages for both S/MIME and Exchange Server security.
- **Security Labels** Click to configure security labels, which display security information about a specific message and restrict which recipients can open, forward, or send that message. Security labels rely on security policies implemented in Windows 2000 or later.
- **New** Click to create a new set of security settings.
- **Delete** Click to delete the currently selected group of security settings.

- **Password** Click to specify or change the password associated with the security settings.
- **Signing Certificate** This read-only information indicates the certificate being used to digitally sign your outgoing messages. Click Choose if you want to choose a different certificate.

You assign the default signing and encryption certificates through Outlook's global security settings; for information, see "Setting Global Security Options," page 301.

- **Hash Algorithm** Use this drop-down list to change the hash algorithm used to encrypt messages.
- **Encryption Certificate** This read-only information indicates the certificate being used to encrypt your outgoing messages. Click Choose if you want to specify a different certificate.
- **Encryption Algorithm** Use this drop-down list to change the encryption algorithm used to encrypt messages. The encryption algorithm is the mathematical method used to encrypt the data.
- **Send These Certificates With Signed Messages** Select this check box to include your certificate with outgoing messages. Doing so allows recipients to send encrypted messages to you.

Troubleshooting

You need a faster way to digitally sign a message

If you don't send a lot of digitally signed messages, you might not mind the steps you need to go through to get to the Security Properties dialog box to sign the message when you compose it. However, if you frequently send digitally signed messages but don't want to configure Outlook to sign all messages by default, all the clicking involved in signing the message can seem like a very long trip.

To digitally sign your messages faster, consider adding a toolbar button that lets you toggle a digital signature with a single click by following these steps:

1. Open the Inbox folder in Outlook.
2. Click New to display the message form for a new message.
3. In the message form, choose View, Toolbars, Customize and then click the Commands tab, shown in Figure 10-15. If you later want to switch security profiles, you can select the profile you want to use in the Default Setting drop-down list on the Security tab.

Figure 10-15. Use the Commands tab to add the Digitally Sign Message command to the toolbar.

4 Click Standard in the Categories list, and then drag the Digitally Sign Message command to a location on the toolbar.

> **Note** To modify the Standard toolbar, you must be using Outlook as your e-mail editor. If you switch to using Microsoft Word as the e-mail editor, changes you make to the toolbar are not carried over to Word.

5 If you frequently encrypt messages, you can also drag the Encrypt Message Contents And Attachments command to the toolbar.

6 Click Close and then close the message form.

Now whenever you need to digitally sign or encrypt a message, you can click the appropriate button on the toolbar when you compose the message. Outlook displays a blue outline around the button to indicate that the command has been selected, so you can tell at a glance whether the message will be signed, encrypted, or both.

Reading Signed Messages

When you receive a digitally signed message, Outlook displays the encrypted version of the message as an attachment. The Inbox displays a Secure Message icon in place of the standard envelope icon (see Figure 10-16) and shows a Secure Message button in the preview pane. The message form also includes a Secure Message button (see Figure 10-17). You can click the Secure Message button in either the preview pane or the form to display information about the certificate.

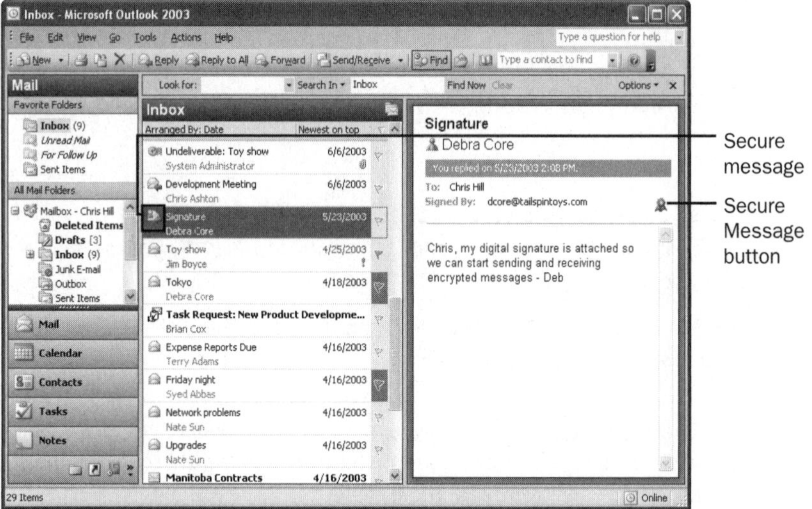

Figure 10-16. Outlook displays a different icon in the Inbox for secure messages.

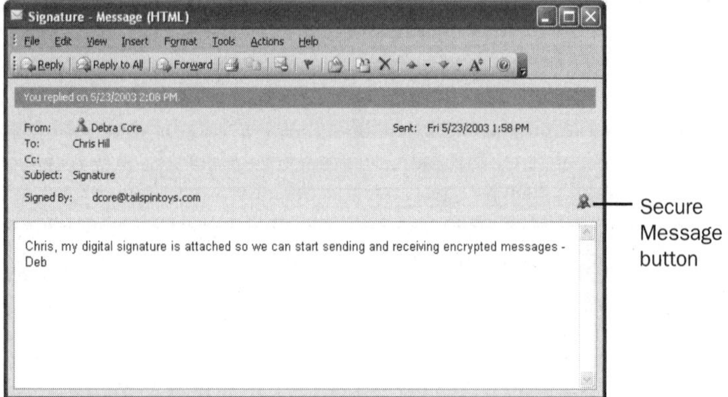

Figure 10-17. Click the Secure Message button on the message form to view information about the certificate.

Because Outlook supports S/MIME, you can view and read a digitally signed message without taking any special action. How Outlook treats the message, however, depends on the trust relationship of the associated certificate. If the certificate is not explicitly distrusted, Outlook displays the message in the Reading Pane. If the certificate is not trusted, you'll see an error message in the Reading Pane header, as shown in Figure 10-18. You can open the message, but you've been alerted that there's a problem with the sender's certificate. Outlook also displays a dialog box noting the error when you open the message (see Figure 10-19).

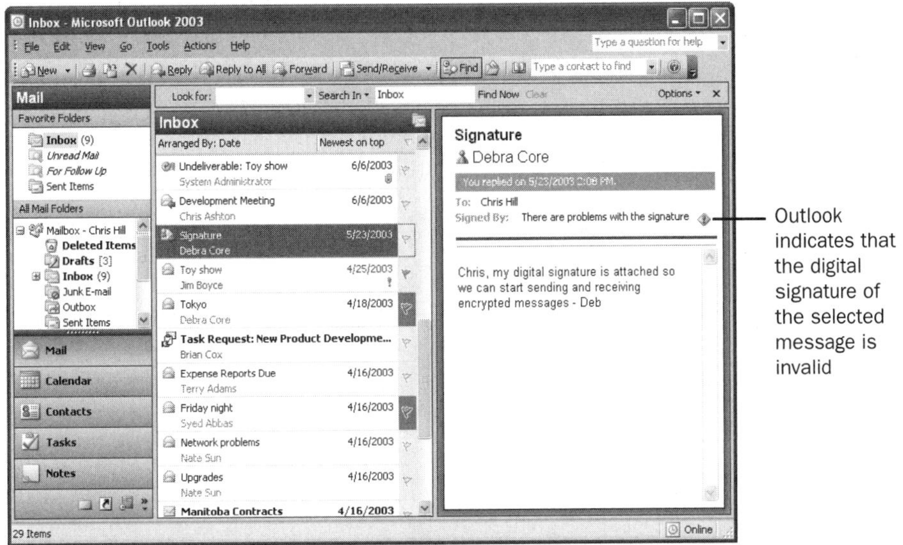

Figure 10-18. Outlook displays an error message if the digital signature of an incoming message is untrusted.

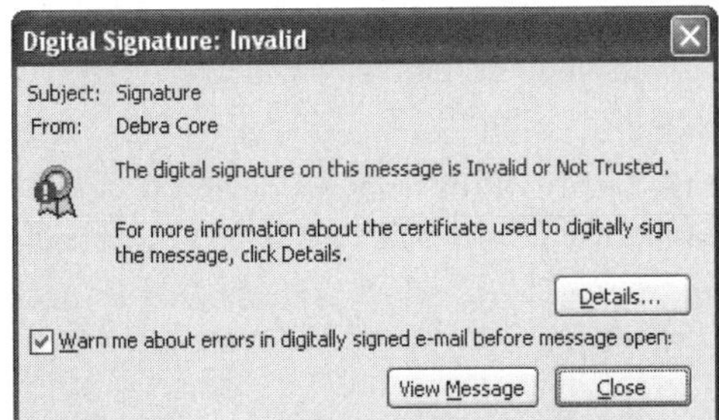

Figure 10-19. Outlook warns you when you open a message that has a certificate problem.

There is no danger in opening a message with an invalid certificate. However, you should verify that the message really came from the person listed as the sender and is not a forged message.

Changing Certificate Trust Relationships

To have Outlook authenticate a signed message and treat it as being from a trusted sender, you must add the certificate to your list of trusted certificates. An alternative is to configure Outlook to inherit trust for a certificate from the certificate's issuer. For example, assume that you have a CA in your enterprise. Rather than configuring each sender's certificate to be trusted explicitly, you can configure Outlook to inherit trust from the issuing CA—in other words, Outlook will implicitly trust all certificates issued by that CA.

Follow these steps to configure the trust relationship for a certificate:

1 In Outlook, select the signed message. If the Reading Pane displays an error message, or if you aren't using the Reading Pane, open the message and click the Secure Message button to view the Message Security Properties dialog box (see Figure 10-20). Otherwise, click the Secure Message button in the Reading Pane.

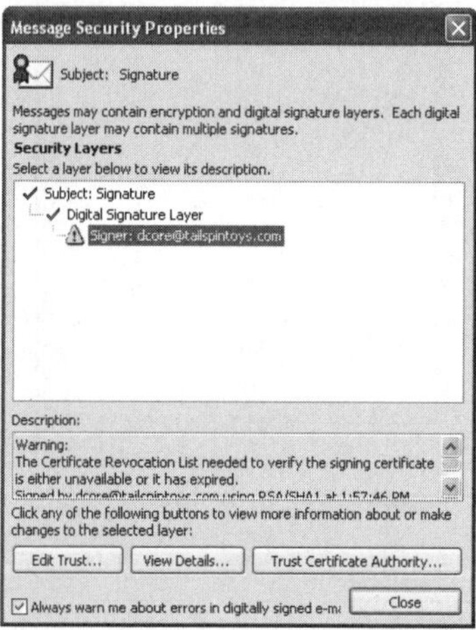

Figure 10-20. Use the Message Security Properties dialog box to view status and properties of the certificate.

2 Click Details, and in the Message Security Properties dialog box, click the Signer line, and then click Edit Trust to display the Trust tab of the View Certificate dialog box, shown in Figure 10-21.

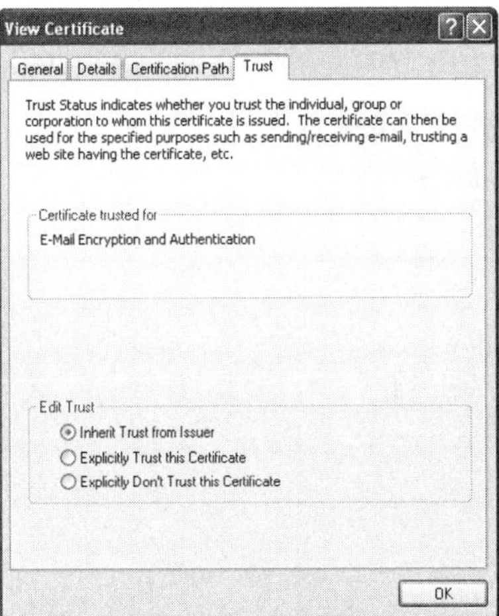

Figure 10-21. Use the Trust tab to configure the trust relationship for the certificate.

3 Select one of the following options:

- **Inherit Trust From Issuer** Select this option to inherit the trust relationship from the issuing CA. See the following section, "Configuring CA Trust," for detailed information.
- **Explicitly Trust This Certificate** Select this option to explicitly trust the certificate associated with the message if you are certain of the authenticity of the message and the validity of the sender's certificate.
- **Explicitly Don't Trust This Certificate** Select this option to explicitly distrust the certificate associated with the message. Any other messages that you receive with the same certificate will generate an error message in Outlook when you attempt to view them.

4 Click OK, and then click Close to close the Message Security Properties dialog box.

For more information on viewing a certificate's other properties and configuring Outlook to validate certificates, see "Viewing and Validating a Digital Signature," page 312.

Configuring CA Trust

Although you might not realize it, your computer system by default includes certificates from several public CAs (typically VeriSign, Thawte, Equifax, GTE, or several others), which were installed when you installed your operating system. By default, Outlook and other applications trust certificates issued by those CAs without requiring you to obtain and install each CA's certificate.

The easiest way to view these certificates is through Internet Explorer:

1 In Internet Explorer, choose Tools, Internet Options and click the Content tab.

2 Click Certificates to open the Certificates dialog box (see Figure 10-22). Click the Trusted Root Certification Authorities tab, which contains a list of the certificates.

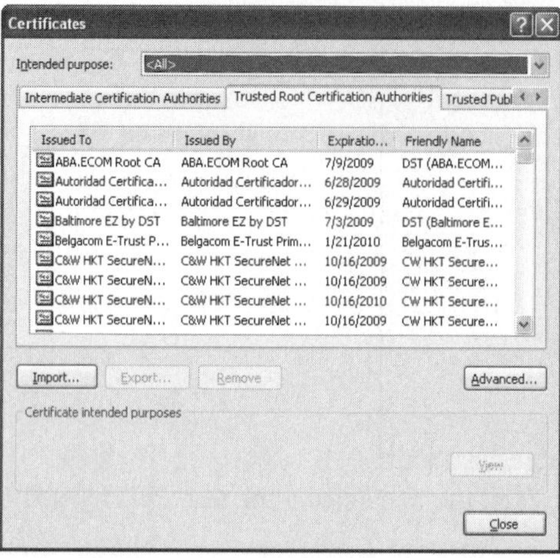

Figure 10-22. You can view a list of certificates in Internet Explorer's Certificates dialog box.

If you have a personal certificate issued by a specific CA, the issuer's certificate is installed on your computer. Messages you receive that are signed with certificates issued by the same CA inherit trust from the issuer without requiring the installation of any additional certificates. If you're working in a large enterprise with several CAs, however, you'll probably receive signed messages containing certificates issued by CAs other than the one that issued your certificate. Thus you might not have the issuing CA's certificate on your system, which prevents Outlook from trusting the certificate. In this case, you need to add that CA's certificate to your system.

If you need to connect to a Windows 2000–based, Windows Server 2003–based, or Windows NT–based enterprise CA to obtain the CA's certificate and install it on your system, follow these steps:

1 Point your Web browser to *http://*<machine>*/certsrv*, where <machine> is the name or IP address of the CA.

2 After the page loads, select Retrieve The CA Certificate Or Certificate Revocation List, and then click Next.

3 Click Install This CA Certification Path to install the CA's certificate on your system.

The procedure just outlined assumes that the CA administrator has not customized the certificate request pages for the CA. If the pages have been customized, the actual process you must follow could be slightly different from the one described here.

> **Tip** If you prefer, you can download the CA certificate rather than installing it through the browser. Use this alternative when you need to install the CA certificate on more than one computer and must have the certificate as a file.

Configuring CA Trust for Multiple Computers

The process described in the previous section is useful when configuring CA trust for a small number of computers, but can be impractical with a large number of computers. In these situations you can turn to group policy to configure CA trust in a wider area such as an organizational unit (OU), domain, or entire site.

You can create a certificate trust list (CTL), which is a signed list of root CA certificates that are considered trusted, and deploy that CTL through group policy. This solution requires that you be running Windows 2000 Server or Windows Server 2003, with Windows 2000 and/or Windows XP clients as domain members.

Follow these steps to create and deploy the CTL:

1. Log on to a domain controller and open the Active Directory Users And Computers console.
2. Create a new Group Policy Object (GPO) or edit an existing GPO at the necessary container in Active Directory, such as an OU.
3. In the Group Policy Editor, expand the branch User Configuration\Windows Settings\Security Settings\Public Key Policies\Enterprise Trust.
4. Right-click Enterprise Trust and choose New, Certificate Trust List to start the Certificate Trust List Wizard.
5. Click Next, then specify a name and valid duration for the CTL (both optional) as shown in Figure 10-23. Select one or more purposes for the CTL in the Designate Purposes list (in this example, choose Secure Email), and click Next.

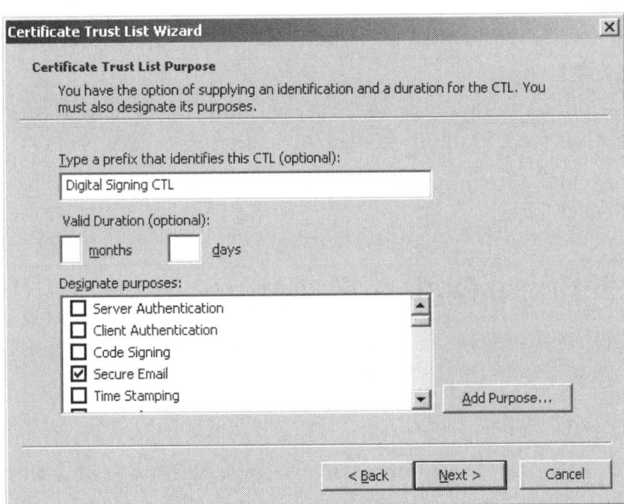

Figure 10-23. Select a purpose for the CTL and other properties, such as a friendly name for easy identification.

6. On the Certificates In The CTL page (see Figure 10-24), click Add From Store to add certificates to the list from the server's certificate store. Choose one or more certificates and click OK.

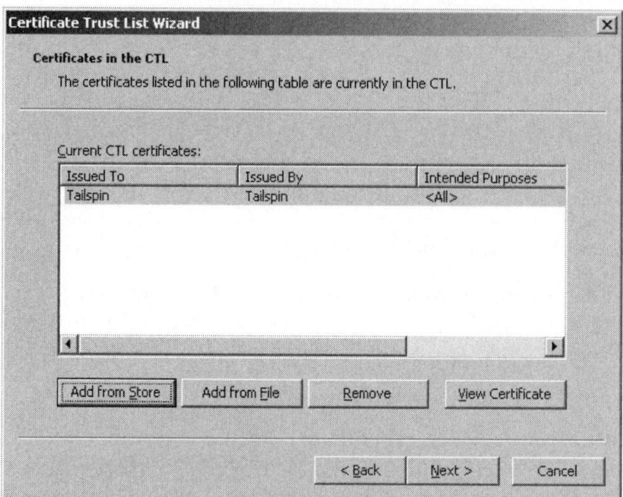

Figure 10-24. Add certificates to the CTL.

7. If the certificates are stored in an X.509 file, Microsoft Serialized Certificate Store, or PKCS #7 certificate file, click Add From File, select the file, and click Open.
8. Back on the Certificates In The CTL page, click Next. On the Signature Certificate page, select a certificate to sign the CTL. The certificate must be stored in the local computer certificate store rather than the user certificate store. Click Next after you select the certificate.
9. You can optionally choose the Add A Timestamp To The Data option and specify a timestamp service URL if one is available. Otherwise, click Next.
10. Optionally enter a friendly name and description for the CTL to help identify it, click Next, and click Finish.

Viewing and Validating a Digital Signature

You can view the certificate associated with a signed message to obtain information about the issuer, the person to whom the certificate is issued, and other matters.

To do so, follow these steps:

1. Open the message and click the Secure Message button in either the Reading Pane or the message form, then click Details to display the Message Security Properties dialog box, which provides information about the certificate's validity in the Description box.

2 Click Signer in the list to view additional signature information in the Description box, such as when the message was signed (see Figure 10-25).

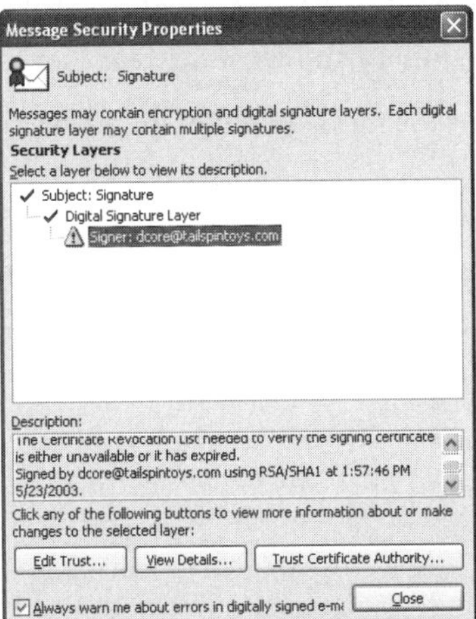

Figure 10-25. The Description box offers information about the validity of the certificate.

3 Click View Details to open the Signature dialog box, shown in Figure 10-26, which displays even more detail about the signature.

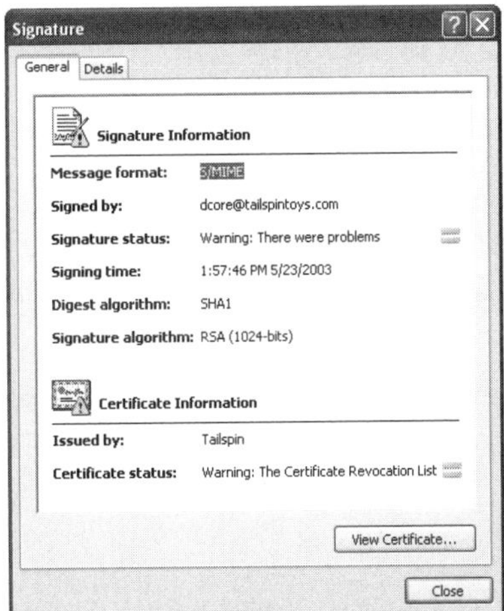

Figure 10-26. Use the Signature dialog box to view additional properties of the signature and to access the certificate.

4 On the General tab of the Signature dialog box, click View Certificate to display information about the certificate, including issuer, certification path, and trust mode.

5 Click OK and then click Close to close the Message Security Properties dialog box.

The CA uses a certificate revocation list (CRL) to indicate the validity of certificates. If you don't have a current CRL on your system, Outlook can treat the certificate as trusted but won't be able to validate the certificate and will indicate this when you view the signature.

You can locate the path to the CRL by examining the certificate's properties as follows:

1. Click the Secure Message button for the message, either in the Reading Pane or in the message form.
2. Click Signer and then click View Details.
3. On the General tab of the Signature dialog box, click View Certificate and then click the Details tab (see Figure 10-27).

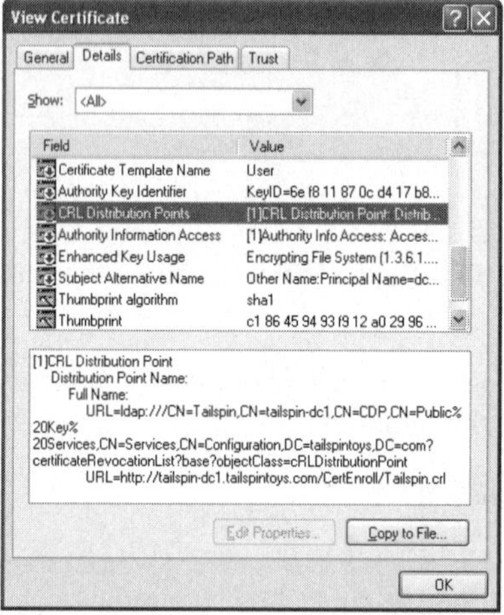

Figure 10-27. Use the Details tab to view the CRL path for the certificate.

4. Scroll through the list to find and select CRL Distribution Points.
5. Scroll through the list in the lower half of the dialog box to locate the URL for the CRL.

When you know the URL for the CRL, you can point your browser to the site to download and install the CRL. If a CA in your enterprise issued the certificate, you can obtain the CRL from the CA.

To obtain and install the CRL, follow these steps:

1. Point your browser to *http://<machine>/certsrv*, where <machine> is the name or IP address of the server.
2. Select the Retrieve The CA Certificate Or Certificate Revocation List option and click Next.
3. Click Download Latest Certificate Revocation List and save the file to disk.
4. After downloading the file, locate and right-click the file, and then choose Install CRL to install the current list.

Troubleshooting

You need a faster way to validate certificates

If you often work with digitally signed messages and frequently need to verify certificates, consider adding the Verify Digital Signature command to the toolbar to give you a one-click method of viewing the certificate properties.

To add the command to the toolbar, follow these steps:

1. Open any existing message.
2. Right-click the toolbar in the message form and choose Customize.
3. Click Standard in the Categories list, and then drag Verify Digital Signature from the Commands list to the toolbar. Note that you can do this only if Outlook—not Word—is your e-mail editor.
4. Click Close, and then close the message form.

The next time you want to validate a certificate, all you need to do is click the button on the toolbar.

Encrypting Messages

You can encrypt messages to prevent them from being read by unauthorized persons. It is, of course, true that with significant amounts of computing power and time any encryption scheme can probably be broken. However, the chances of someone investing those resources in your e-mail are pretty remote. So you can be assured that the e-mail encryption Outlook provides offers a relatively safe means of protecting sensitive messages against interception.

Before you can encrypt messages, you must have a certificate for that purpose installed on your computer. Typically, certificates issued for digital signing can also be used for encrypting e-mail messages.

For detailed information on obtaining a personal certificate from a commercial CA or from an enterprise or stand-alone CA on your network, see "Obtaining a Digital Certificate," page 294.

Getting Ready for Encryption

After you've obtained a certificate and installed it on your system, encrypting messages is a simple task. Getting to that point, however, depends in part on whether you're sending messages to an Exchange Server recipient on your network or to an Internet recipient.

Swapping Certificates

Before you can send an encrypted message to an Internet recipient, you must have a copy of the recipient's certificate. To read the message, the recipient must have a copy of your certificate, which means you first need to swap certificates.

Note When you are sending encrypted messages to an Exchange Server recipient, you don't need to swap certificates. Exchange Server takes care of the problem for you.

The easiest way to swap certificates is to send a digitally signed message to the recipient and have the recipient send you a signed message in return, as outlined here:

1. In Outlook, choose Tools, Options and click the Security tab.
2. Click Settings to display the Change Security Settings dialog box.
3. Verify that you've selected S/MIME in the Secure Message Format drop-down list.
4. Select the Send These Certificates With Signed Messages option and click OK.
5. Click OK to close the Options dialog box.
6. Compose the message and digitally sign it. Outlook will include the certificates with the message.

When you receive a signed message from someone with whom you're exchanging certificates, you must add the person to your Contacts folder to add the certificate by following these steps:

1. Open the message, right-click the sender's name, and then choose Add To Outlook Contacts. If the Reading Pane is displayed, you can right-click the sender's name in the pane and choose Add To Outlook Contacts.
2. Outlook displays the General tab of the contact form (see Figure 10-28). Fill in additional information for the contact as needed.

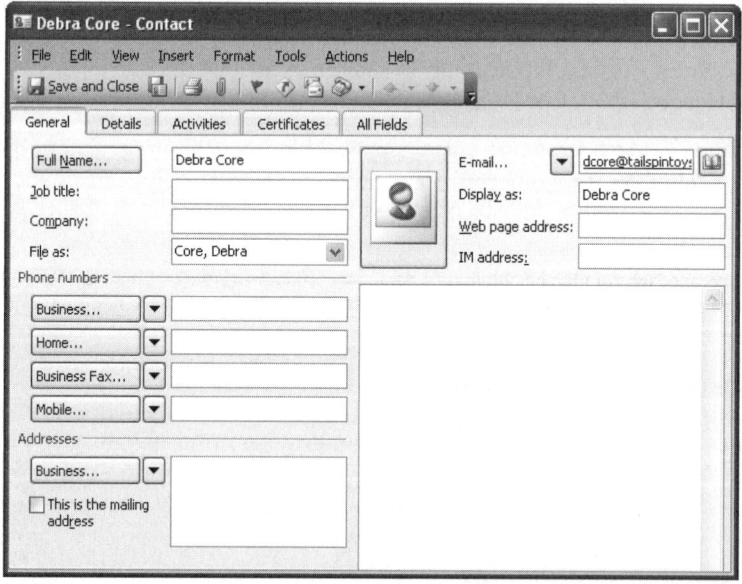

Figure 10-28. Use the contact form to add the sender's certificate to your system.

3 Click the Certificates tab. You should see the sender's certificate listed (see Figure 10-29), and you can view the certificate's properties by selecting it and clicking Properties. If no certificate is listed, contact the sender and ask for another digitally signed message.

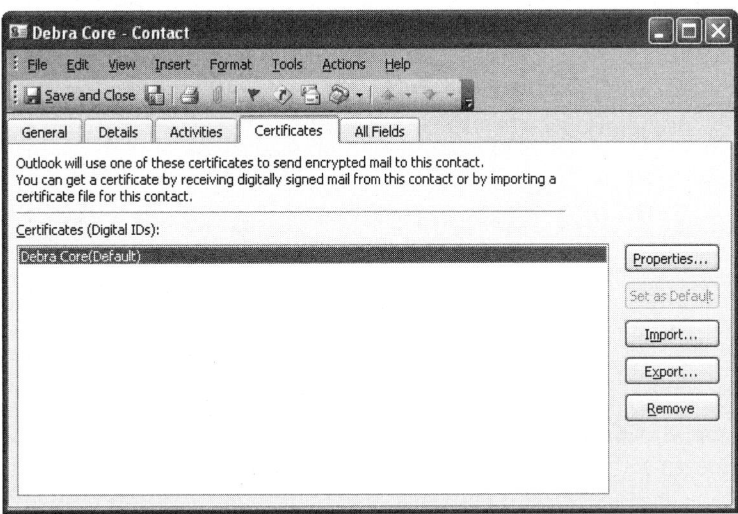

Figure 10-29. The Certificates tab of the contact form displays the sender's certificate.

4 Click Save And Close to save the contact item and the certificate.

Obtaining a Recipient's Public Key from a Public CA

As an alternative to receiving a signed message with a certificate from another person, you might be able to obtain the person's certificate from the issuing CA. For example, if you know that the person has a certificate from VeriSign, you can download that individual's public key from the VeriSign Web site. Other public CAs offer similar services. To search for and download public keys fromVeriSign (see Figure 10-30), connect to *https://digitalid.verisign.com/services/client/index.html*. Check the sites of other public CAs for similar links that allow you to download public keys from their servers.

The process for downloading a public key varies by CA. In general, however, you enter the person's e-mail address in a form to locate the certificate, and the form provides instructions for downloading the certificate. You should have no trouble obtaining the public key after you locate the certificate on the CA.

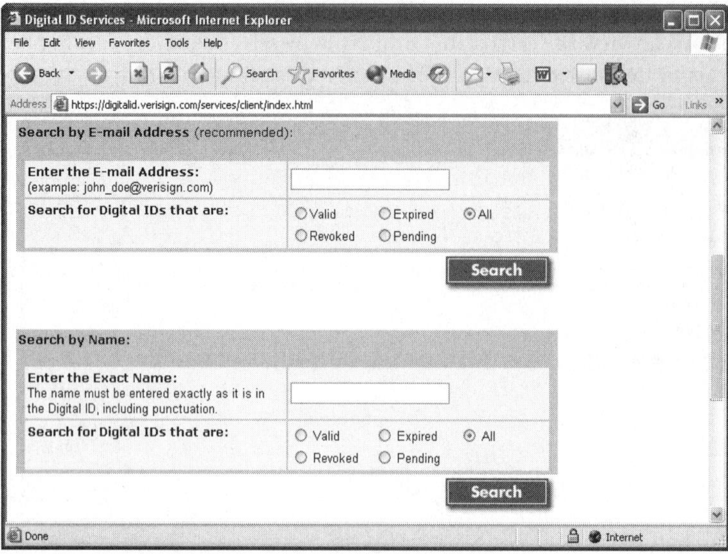

Figure 10-30. VeriSign, like other public CAs, provides a form you can use to search for and obtain public keys for certificate subscribers.

Save the public key to disk, and then follow these steps to install the key:

1. Open the Contacts folder in Outlook.
2. Locate the contact for whom you downloaded the public key.
3. Open the contact item, and click the Certificates tab.
4. Click Import. Browse to and select the certificate file obtained from the CA and click Open.
5. Click Save And Close to save the contact changes.

Sending Encrypted Messages

When you have everything set up for sending and receiving encrypted messages, it's a simple matter to send one:

1. Open Outlook and compose the message.
2. In the message form, click Options, and then click Security Settings.
3. Select Encrypt Message Contents And Attachments, and then click OK.
4. Click Close, and then send the message as you normally would.
5. If the message is protected by Exchange Server security, you can send it in one of three ways, depending on your system's security level:
   - If the security level is set to Medium (the default), Outlook displays a message informing you of your security setting. Click OK to send the message.

- If the security level is set to Low, Outlook sends the message immediately, without any special action on your part.
- If the security level is set to High, type your password to send the message.

> **Tip** **Simplify message encryption**
> To make it easier to encrypt a message, you can add the Encrypt Message Contents And Attachments command to the toolbar in the message form. For details about the process involved in doing this, see the Troubleshooting sidebar "You need a faster way to digitally sign a message," page 304.

Reading Encrypted Messages

When you receive an encrypted message, you can read it as you would read any other message, assuming that you have the sender's certificate. Double-click the message to open it. Note that Outlook uses an icon with a lock, rather than the standard envelope icon, to identify encrypted messages.

> **Tip** **Read encrypted messages**
> You can't preview encrypted messages in the Reading Pane. Also, the ability to read encrypted messages requires an S/MIME-capable mail client. Keep this in mind when sending encrypted messages to other users who might not have Outlook or another S/MIME-capable client.
>
> You can verify and modify the trust for a certificate when you read a message signed by that certificate. For information on viewing and changing the trust for a certificate, see "Changing Certificate Trust Relationships," page 308.

Importing Certificates from Outlook Express

If you have used Microsoft Outlook Express to send and receive secure messages, your Outlook Express address book contains the public keys of the recipients. You can import those certificates to use in Outlook if they are not already included in the Contacts folder. Unfortunately, Outlook Express doesn't export the certificates when you export its address book; instead, you must export the certificates one at a time.

Follow these steps to move certificates from Outlook Express to Outlook:

1. Open Outlook Express and choose Tools, Address Book.
2. In the address book, double-click the name of the person whose certificate you want to export.
3. Click the Digital IDs tab.
4. Select the certificate to export and click Export.
5. Save the certificate to a file. (Outlook Express uses the CER file extension.)

6 Open Outlook, open the Contacts folder, and open the contact item for the person who owns the certificate you're importing.
7 Click the Certificates tab, click Import, select the file created in step 5, and click Open.
8 Save and close the contact form.

Virus Protection

Outlook provides a handful of features to help protect your system against viruses and other malicious system attacks. For example, Outlook 2003 supports attachment virus protection, which helps protect against viruses you might receive through infected e-mail attachments. Outlook also offers protection against Microsoft Office macro viruses.

For information about protecting against malicious HTML-based messages, see "Using Security Zones," page 288.

This section examines two client-side antivirus technologies: attachment blocking and macro security. The discussion of attachment blocking focuses on how Outlook sends and receives messages with specific types of attachments.

For information on server-side antivirus technologies, including how to configure attachment blocking at the server, see Chapter 32, "Data Security and Virus Protection."

Protecting Against Viruses in Attachments

In the "old days," infected boot floppy disks were the most common way computer viruses were spread. Today, e-mail is by far the most common infection mechanism. Viruses range from mostly harmless (but irritating) to severe, sometimes causing irreparable damage to your system. Worms are a more recent variation, spreading across the Internet primarily through e-mail and by exploited operating system flaws. Worms can bog down a system by consuming the majority of the system's resources, and they can cause the same types of damage as viruses.

Outlook provides protection against viruses and worms by letting you block certain types of attachments that are susceptible to infection. Executable programs (EXE, COM, and BAT files) are good examples of attachments that are primary delivery mechanisms for viruses. Many other document types are equally susceptible—HTML documents and scripts, for instance, have rapidly become favorite delivery tools for virus terrorists. Outlook provides two levels of protection for attachments, Level 1 and Level 2. The following sections explain these two levels, the file types assigned to each, and how to work with attachments.

Level 1 Attachments

When you receive a message containing an attachment in the Level 1 group, Outlook displays the paper clip icon beside the message header, indicating that the message has an attachment, just as it does for other messages with attachments. When you click the message header, Outlook displays a message in the InfoBar informing you that it has blocked the attachment (see Figure 10-31). Table 10-1 lists the Level 1 file types.

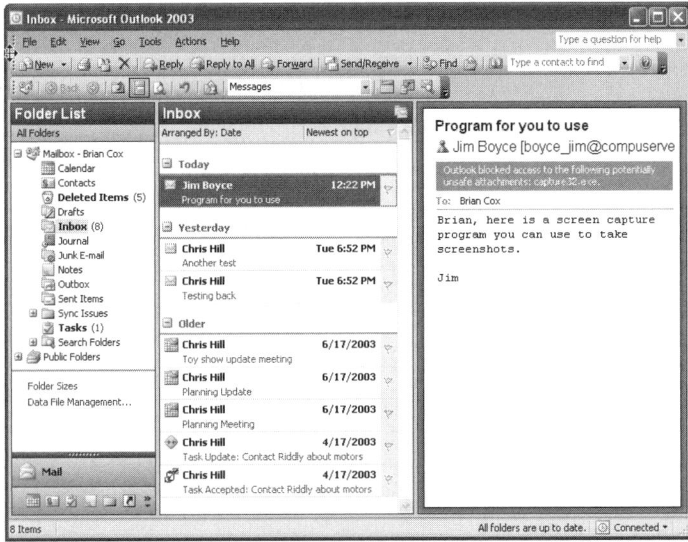

Figure 10-31. Outlook displays a message informing you that it has blocked the attachment.

Table 10-1. Level 1 Attachments

File Extension	Description
ADE	Microsoft Access project extension
ADP	Microsoft Access project
BAS	Microsoft Visual Basic class module
BAT	Batch file
CHM	Compiled HTML Help file
CMD	Microsoft Windows NT/Windows 2000 command script
COM	Microsoft MS-DOS program
CPL	Control Panel extension
CRT	Security certificate
EXE	Program
HLP	Help file
HTA	HTML program
INF	Setup Information File
INS	Internet Naming Service
ISP	Internet Communication settings
JS	Microsoft JScript file

Table 10-1. Level 1 Attachments

File Extension	Description
JSE	Microsoft JScript-Encoded Script file
LNK	Shortcut
MDA	Microsoft Access add-in program
MDB	Microsoft Access program
MDE	Microsoft Access MDE database
MDZ	Microsoft Access wizard program
MSC	Microsoft Common Console document
MSI	Microsoft Windows Installer package
MSP	Microsoft Windows Installer patch
MST	Microsoft Visual Test source files
PCD	Photo CD image or Microsoft Visual Test compiled script
PIF	Shortcut to MS-DOS program
REG	Registration entries
SCR	Screen saver
SCT	Microsoft Windows Script Component
SHS	Shell Scrap Object
URL	Internet shortcut
VB	Microsoft VBScript file
VBE	Microsoft VBScript-Encoded script file
VBS	Microsoft VBScript file
WSC	Microsoft Windows Script Component
WSF	Microsoft Windows Script file
WSH	Microsoft Windows Script Host settings file

You cannot open Level 1 attachments that are blocked by Outlook. You can open and view the messages, but Outlook disables the interface elements that otherwise would allow you to open or save the attachments. If you forward a message with a blocked attachment, Outlook strips the attachment from the forwarded message.

Note If you use Exchange Server, the Exchange Server administrator can configure attachment blocking at the server. In addition, you can configure Outlook to allow certain Level 1 attachments (essentially removing them from the Level 1 list) by modifying the registry. For details on virus protection in Exchange Server and how to have Outlook open blocked attachments, see "Configuring Blocked Attachments," page 811.

You have another option for accessing blocked attachments if your Exchange Server has Outlook Web Access OWA. Outlook Web Access doesn't provide any attachment blocking, which makes it possible to retrieve the messages—with attachments—through your Web browser. Point your browser to *http://<server>/Exchange*, where <server> is the IP address or name of your server. Use your Exchange Server account to log on and open the message with the attachment, and then save the attachment to disk.

Note Your server might use a different URL for Outlook Web Access depending on how your administrator has configured the server. For coverage of Outlook Web Access, see Chapter 41, "Accessing Messages Through a Web Browser."

If Outlook Express is installed on your computer, you have an additional method for opening blocked attachments. Outlook doesn't strip out the attachments—rather, it simply prevents you from opening or saving them. You can, then, import the messages into Outlook Express and open the attachments there.

Here's how to import an attachment for opening:

1. Create a new folder in Outlook, and move the message with the blocked attachment to that folder. You could leave the message in the Inbox, but that would require you to import all messages from the Inbox to Outlook Express. Moving the message to a different folder lets you import only one message.
2. Open Outlook Express and choose File, Import, Messages.
3. Choose Microsoft Outlook in the Outlook Express Import Wizard and click Next.
4. Select the folder from step 1 and click Next to begin the import.
5. Click Finish when the messages have been imported.

Level 2 Attachments

Outlook also supports a second level of attachment blocking. Level 2 attachments are defined by the administrator at the server level (and therefore apply to Exchange Server accounts). You can't open Level 2 attachments directly in Outlook; but Outlook does allow you to save them to disk, and you can open them from there. To open a Level 2 attachment this way, follow these steps:

1. Open the message and choose File, Save Attachments. Select the attachment you want to save.
2. In the Save Attachment dialog box, specify the folder in which you want to save the file and click Save.
3. Outside Outlook, browse to the folder and open the file.

Because the Level 2 list is empty by default, no attachments are blocked as Level 2 attachments unless the Exchange Server administrator has modified the Level 2 list.

For detailed information on configuring attachment blocking under Exchange Server, see "Configuring Blocked Attachments," page 811.

Protecting Against Office Macro Viruses

Like other Office applications, Outlook allows you to use macros to automate common tasks. Macros have become an increasingly popular infection mechanism for viruses because most inexperienced users don't expect to have their systems infected by common Office documents. However, Office macros can contain viruses that cause just as much damage as any other virus. Protecting yourself against macro viruses is an important step in safeguarding your system overall.

You can guard against macro viruses by implementing a virus scanner on your system that checks your documents for macro viruses, by installing a virus scrubber on your e-mail server, or by using both methods. Another line of protection is to control how and when macros are allowed to run. Outlook provides three security levels for macros that determine which macros can run on the system. To set the level, choose Tools, Macro, Security and select one of these three levels:

- **High** Only signed macros from sources you've designated as trusted will run. Outlook disables unsigned macros, preventing them from running.
- **Medium** For each macro, Outlook prompts you to decide whether to run the macro.
- **Low** All macros are allowed to run.

For additional information on configuring macro security and specifying trusted sources, see "Setting Macro Security," page 716.

Protecting Data with Information Rights Management

In response to market demands for a system with which companies can protect proprietary and sensitive information, Microsoft has developed an umbrella of technologies called Information Rights Management (IRM). Outlook 2003 incorporates IRM, enabling you to send messages that prevent the recipient from forwarding, copying from, or printing the message. The recipient can view the message, but the features for accomplishing these other tasks are unavailable.

Note IRM is an extension for Office applications of Windows Rights Management. For information on using IRM with other Office applications, see *Microsoft Office 2003 Inside Out*, from Microsoft Press.

There are two paths to implementing IRM with Office 2003. Microsoft offers an IRM service that, as of this writing, is free. This path requires that you have a Microsoft Passport to send or view IRM-protected messages. You must log in to the service with your Passport credentials to download a certificate, which Outlook uses to verify your identity and enable the IRM features. The second path is to install Microsoft Windows Server 2003 running the Rights Management Service (RMS) on Windows Server 2003. With this path, users authenticate on the server with NTLM or Passport authentication and download their IRM certificates.

The first path provides simplicity because it does not require that organizations deploy an RMS server. The second path provides more flexibility because the RMS administrator can configure company-specific IRM policies, which are then available to users. For example, you might create a policy template that requires that only users within the company domain can open all e-mail messages protected by the policy. You can create any number of templates to suit the company's data rights needs for the range of Office applications and document types.

Not everyone who receives an IRM-protected message will be running Outlook 2003, so Microsoft has developed the Rights Management Add-On for Internet Explorer, which enables these users to view the messages in Internet Explorer. Without this add-on, recipients are unable to view IRM-protected messages. With the add-on, recipients can view the messages, but the capability to forward, copy, or print the message is disabled, just as it is in Outlook 2003.

This chapter explains how to configure and use IRM in Outlook 2003 with the Microsoft IRM service. As of this writing, RMS is not available for Windows Server 2003. Check *www.boyce.us* and *www.microsoft.com/windowsserver2003/technologies/rightsmgmt/default.mspx* periodically for additional information on RMS when it becomes available.

Using Microsoft's IRM Service

To configure Outlook to use the IRM service and send IRM-protected messages, follow these steps:

1. Open Outlook and start a new message. With the message form open, choose File, Permission, Do Not Forward.
2. If you do not have the IRM add-on installed, Outlook displays the dialog box shown in Figure 10-32. Choose Yes and click Next.

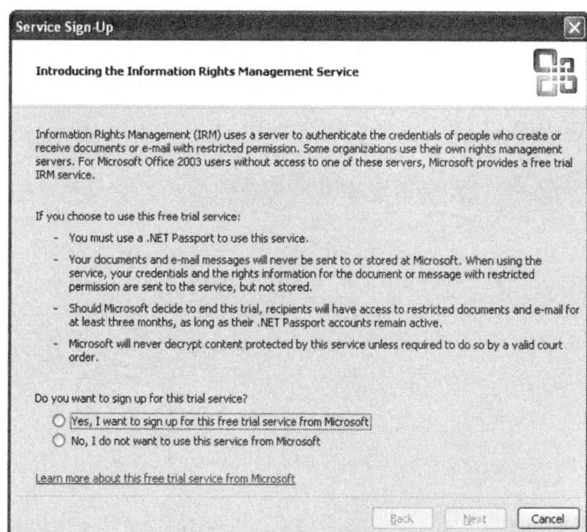

Figure 10-32. Choose Yes and click Next to start the enrollment process.

3 The wizard asks if you already have a Microsoft Passport. If so, choose Yes and click Next to open a sign-in dialog box and enter your Passport credentials. If not, choose No and click Next, then follow the prompts to obtain a Microsoft Passport.

4 After you obtain a Passport and click Next, Outlook displays the page shown in Figure 10-33. Choose Standard to obtain a certificate that you can use on your own computer. Choose Temporary if you need a certificate only for a limited time, such as when you are working from a public computer. Then click Next, Finish to complete the process.

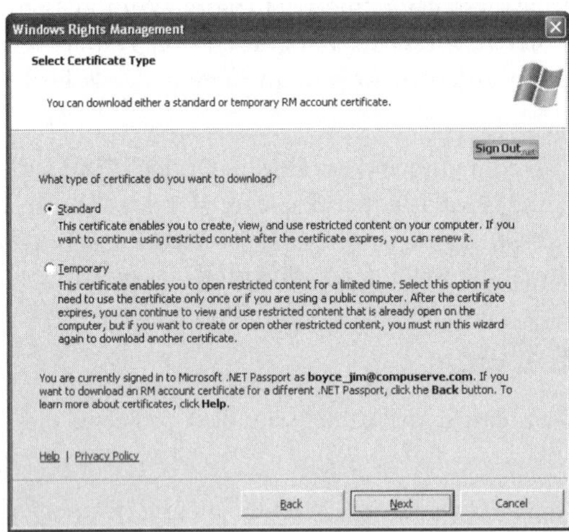

Figure 10-33. You can choose between a standard certificate and a temporary one.

Note You can download a certificate for a given Passport 25 times, or to 25 computers.

5 After the IRM certificate is installed on your computer, Outlook returns you to the message form. The InfoBar in the form displays a Do Not Forward message as shown in Figure 10-34, indicating that the message is protected by IRM.

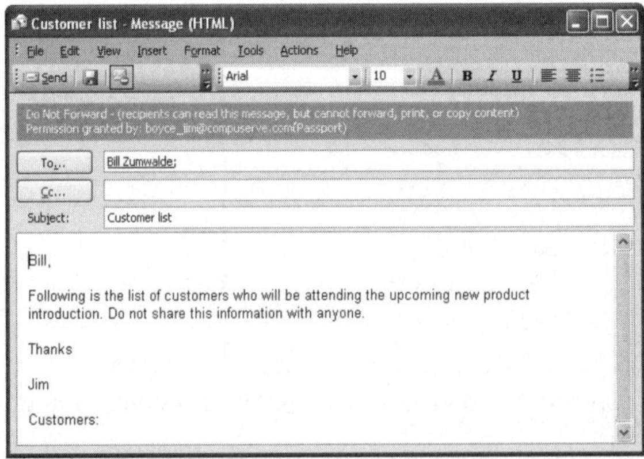

Figure 10-34. The InfoBar indicates when a message is protected by IRM.

6 Address the message and add the message body and attachments, if any, as you would for any other message. Then send the message.

Viewing IRM-Protected Messages

If you attempt to view an IRM-protected message without first obtaining a certificate, Outlook gives you the option of connecting to Microsoft's service to obtain one. After the certificate is installed, you can view the message, but Outlook indicates in the InfoBar (both Reading Pane and message form) that the message is restricted (see Figure 10-35). The commands for forwarding, copying, and printing the message are disabled.

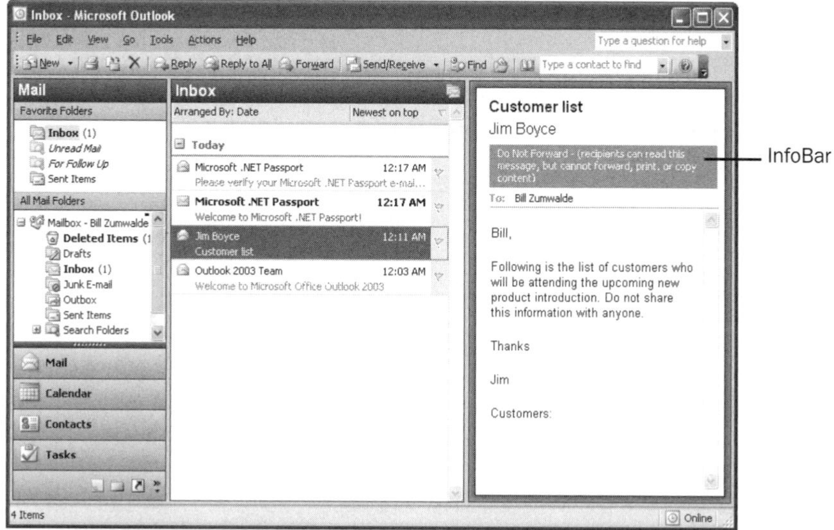

Figure 10-35. The InfoBar in the Reading Pane indicates that a message is restricted.

Working with Multiple Accounts

It's possible that you use more than one Microsoft Passport. If you have more than one Passport and need to choose between them when you send or view an IRM-protected message, open the message form for sending or viewing and choose File, Permission, Restrict Permission As to open the Select User dialog box shown in Figure 10-36. Choose an account and click OK to use that account for the current message.

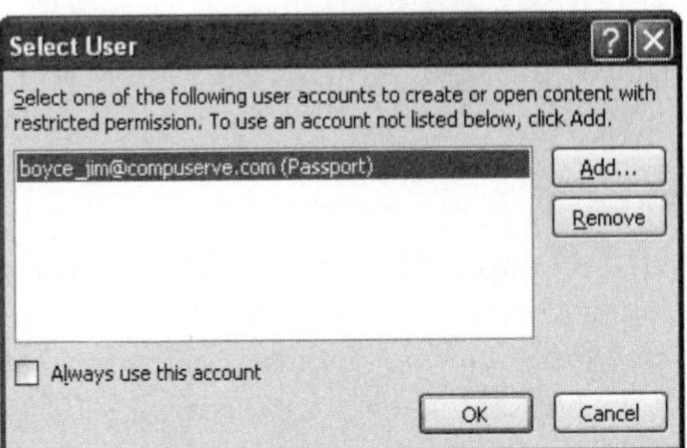

Figure 10-36. You can select from multiple accounts to restrict messages or view restricted messages.

If you have only one account configured on the computer and want to add another account, click Add to start the Service Sign-Up Wizard and download a certificate for another e-mail address and corresponding Microsoft Passport.

Chapter 11

Processing Messages Selectively

Like previous versions of the program, Microsoft Outlook 2003 includes a feature called *remote mail* that allows you to manage your e-mail messages without downloading them from the server. Although you might not believe that you need yet another way to retrieve your messages, remote mail offers advantages that you'll come to appreciate over time.

Although remote mail was primarily a feature for Microsoft Exchange Server originally, other e-mail accounts can take advantage of similar capabilities (which, for the sake of simplicity, this chapter refers to generically as remote mail). For example, with POP3, IMAP, and HTTP accounts, you can download message headers only to review your messages before downloading the message bodies and attachments. The process is similar for all these types of accounts, although POP3 and Exchange Server accounts offer additional options.

This chapter focuses specifically on using remote mail for non–Exchange Server accounts. It explains how to set up your system to use remote mail for IMAP, HTTP, and POP3 accounts; how to manage your messages through remote mail; and how to use alternatives to remote mail, such as send/receive groups.

For detailed information on configuring and using the remote mail feature for Exchange Server accounts, see "Using Remote Mail," page 930.

Understanding Remote Mail Options

The primary advantage of using remote mail is the ability to work with message headers of waiting messages without downloading the messages themselves. You can simply connect to the e-mail server, download the headers for new messages, and disconnect. You can then take your time reviewing the message headers to decide which messages to download, which ones to delete without reading, and which ones to leave on the server to handle later. After you've made your decisions and marked the headers accordingly, you can connect again and download those messages you've marked to retrieve, either leaving the others on the server or deleting them.

Remote mail is extremely useful when you're pressed for time but have a message with a large attachment waiting on the server. You might want to retrieve only your most critical messages without spending the time or connect charges to download that message and its attachment. To accomplish this, you can connect with remote mail and select the messages you want to download, leaving the one with the large attachment on the server until a less busy time when you can download it across the network or through a broadband Internet connection.

Remote mail is also useful when you discover a corrupt message in your mailbox that might otherwise prevent Outlook from downloading your messages. You can connect with remote mail, delete the offending message without downloading it, and then continue working normally.

> **Note** With the exception of Hotmail accounts, remote mail works only for the Inbox; you can't use it to synchronize other folders. With a Hotmail account you can download headers for the Inbox, Deleted Items, Junk Mail, and Sent Items folders.

Remote Mail in a Nutshell

Outlook 2003 offers remote mail for several types of accounts, with differing capabilities. All of the following accounts allow you to download and mark message headers without downloading the messages themselves:

- **Exchange Server** By marking the message headers, you can indicate which messages to download and which to delete from the server. In addition, you can specify conditions that determine which messages are downloaded—for example, those with particular subjects, those from certain senders, those smaller than a specified size, or those without attachments. You can mark messages offline.
- **POP3** By marking the message headers, you can indicate which messages should be moved from the server to your system, which messages should be downloaded with a copy left on the server, and which messages should be deleted from the server without being downloaded. You also can specify a size limit and download only messages that are smaller than the specified size; for messages that exceed the size limit, you can download headers only. You can mark messages offline.
- **IMAP and HTTP** By marking the message headers, you can indicate which messages to download and which to delete from the server. Both types of accounts store mail on the server, so marking to download a copy isn't relevant (as it is for a POP3 account) because a copy of the message stays on the server anyway. With an HTTP account, you must be online to mark message headers for deletion; IMAP accounts allow you to mark for deletion while offline. You don't have any special options for selective or conditional processing with either type of account.

Using Remote Mail with Hotmail

Remote mail is a good choice for managing your POP3, IMAP, or Exchange Server mailbox remotely. With Microsoft Hotmail accounts, remote mail doesn't offer any real advantage because Hotmail accounts download the headers without the full messages anyway; the message bodies are downloaded only when you view the messages. However, you can't delete messages from Hotmail without being online, although you can delete unread messages without downloading them as long as you don't have the Reading Pane turned on. You also can connect through your Web browser to Hotmail to delete messages without downloading them.

Setting Up for Remote Mail

Non–Exchange Server accounts generally deliver messages to a personal folders (PST) file, although you can configure POP3 accounts to deliver messages to your Exchange Server mailbox. If your POP3 account delivers mail to your Exchange Server mailbox, you can use remote mail with the account as long as you're connected to the Exchange Server while you're using remote mail on the POP3 account. For example, assume that you connect over the local area network (LAN) to the Exchange Server but connect to a POP3 account by modem. In that scenario, you'd be able to use remote mail for the POP3 account.

In another scenario, assume that you dial into your LAN to work with your Exchange Server account, and the remote access server also provides connectivity to the Internet. Your POP3 account delivers mail to your Exchange Server mailbox. In this case, you can use remote mail for both accounts because you have access to your mail store. The key is that to use remote mail, you must have access to your mail store so that Outlook has a place to deliver the downloaded message headers.

If you don't use Exchange Server, you don't need to do anything special to configure your system to use remote mail. Because your mail store is local, you have access to it all the time (unless the server is down or offline).

To use remote mail, you naturally need a connection to the remote server. Generally this takes the form of a dial-up connection, either to the server's network or to the Internet. If you haven't already done so, you'll need to set up a dial-up connection to the appropriate point.

Working with Message Headers

The following sections explain the specific steps to follow as you perform various tasks with message headers through remote mail. You'll learn how to download the headers, how to selectively mark them, and how to process them.

Downloading Message Headers

When you want to process messages selectively, you first download the message headers and then decide what action you want to perform with each message, based on its header. Downloading message headers for an account is easy. In Outlook, choose Tools, Send/Receive, *Account* Only, Download Inbox Headers, where *Account* is the name of the account whose headers you want to process.

After you select the Download Inbox Headers command, Outlook performs a send/receive operation but downloads only message headers from the specified account . If you want to save on connect charges, you can then disconnect from the server to review the headers and decide what to do with each message.

Outlook displays the downloaded message headers in the Inbox. The icon for a message header with an associated message that has not been downloaded is slightly different from the standard envelope icon. In addition, Outlook displays an icon in the Header Status column to indicate that the message has not yet been downloaded (see Figure 11-1).

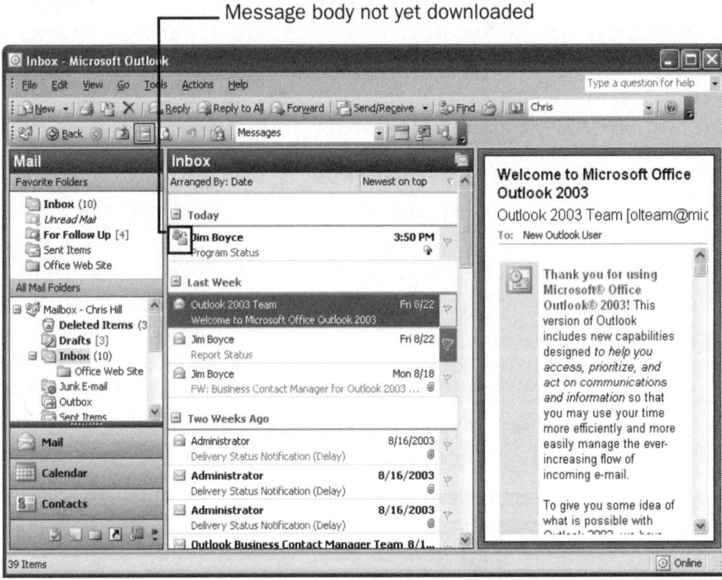

Figure 11-1. Outlook places an icon in the Header Status column to indicate that the message itself has yet to be downloaded.

Marking and Unmarking Message Headers

After you download the headers, you can decide what to do with each message: retrieve it, download a copy, or delete it.

Marking to Retrieve a Message

With a POP3 account, you can mark a message header to have Outlook retrieve the message, remove it from the server, and store it in your local store. With IMAP or HTTP mail accounts, you can mark a message header to have Outlook download the message, but those accounts continue to store the message on the server until you delete it.

To mark a message to be downloaded from the server to your local store, select the message header, right-click it, and choose Mark To Download Message(s). Alternatively, you can choose Tools, Send/Receive, Mark To Download Message(s).

> **Tip** To select multiple message headers quickly, hold down the Ctrl or Shift key while you click the message headers.

Marking to Retrieve a Copy

In some cases, you might want to download a copy of a message but also leave the message on the server—for example, you might need to retrieve the same message from a different computer. To mark a message header to have Outlook retrieve a copy, select the message header, right-click it, and choose Mark To Download Message Copy. Alternatively, you can select the message header and choose Tools, Send/Receive, Mark To Download Message Copy. Outlook indicates in the Header Status column of the Inbox that the message is marked for download and changes the message icon accordingly (see Figure 11-2).

> **Note** As explained earlier, it isn't necessary to download a copy from an IMAP or HTTP server, as those servers continue to store a copy of the message on the server. Downloading a copy is applicable only to POP3 and Exchange Server accounts.

Figure 11-2. This message is marked to have Outlook retrieve a copy.

> **Tip** So that you can easily identify the pending action, Outlook displays different icons in the Header Status column of the Inbox for messages marked to download and messages marked to download a copy.

Marking to Delete a Message

You also can mark messages to be deleted from the server without downloading. You might do this for junk mail or messages with large attachments that you don't need and don't want choking your download session.

To mark a message for deletion, select the message header, right-click it, and choose Delete or press the Delete key. Outlook strikes through the message header and changes the download icon to indicate that the message will be deleted the next time you process messages (see Figure 11-3).

Figure 11-3. Strikethrough indicates that the message will be deleted without downloading.

Unmarking a Message

As you work with message headers, you'll occasionally change your mind after you've marked a message. In that case, you can unmark the message. Select the message header, right-click it, and choose Unmark Selected Headers. Alternatively, you can choose Tools, Send/Receive, Unmark Selected Headers.

You also can unmark all message headers, clearing all pending actions. To do so, choose Tools, Send/Receive, Unmark All Messages.

Processing Marked Headers

After you've reviewed and marked the message headers, you can process the messages to apply the actions you've chosen. When you do so, for example, messages marked for download are downloaded to your system, and messages marked for deletion are deleted from the server.

To process all marked messages, choose Tools, Send/Receive, Process All Marked Headers. You can also choose Process Marked Headers In This Folder to process only the current folder, or choose Tools, Send/Receive, *Account* Only, Process Marked Headers to process only a specific account. After you select a command, Outlook connects and performs the specified actions (see Figure 11-4).

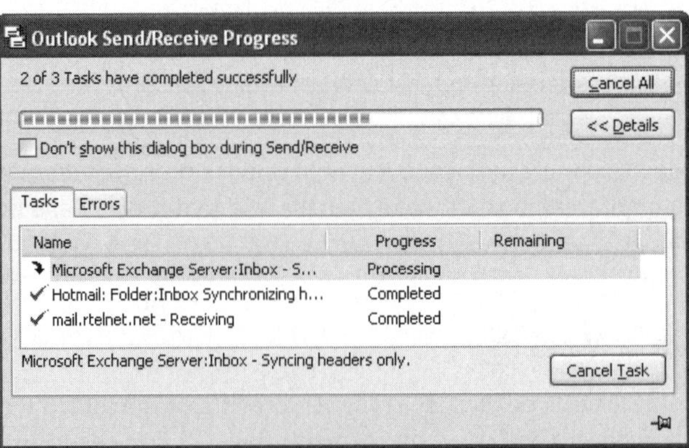

Figure 11-4. Outlook displays this dialog box to indicate progress status for remote mail, as it does for other send/receive operations.

Chapter 11

Troubleshooting

You can't find the remote mail commands

As you work with remote mail, you'll probably wish for an easier, faster way to access the remote mail commands. These commands are buried in the Tools menu, making it difficult to locate them quickly. Outlook also doesn't provide a toolbar for remote mail commands. Fortunately, you can create your own toolbar if you find remote mail useful.

Follow these steps to create your own toolbar for remote mail:

1. In Outlook, choose View, Toolbars, Customize to open the Customize dialog box. Click the Toolbars tab, shown in Figure 11-5.

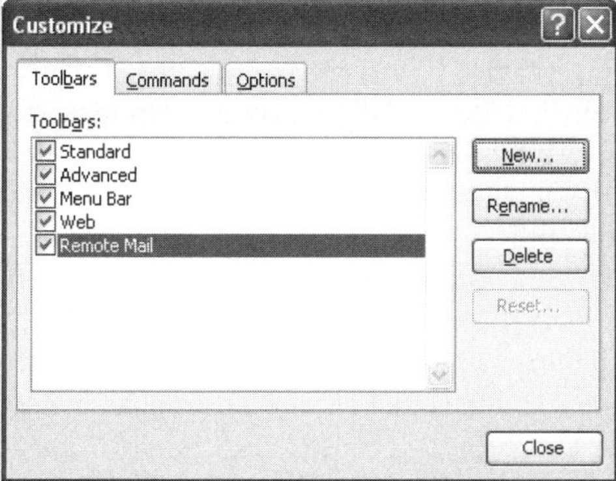

Figure 11-5. Use the Toolbars tab to create your own toolbar for remote mail.

2. Click New. Type the name **Remote Mail** in the New Toolbar dialog box and click OK. Outlook opens an empty toolbar.
3. Click the Commands tab in the Customize dialog box and select Tools from the Categories list.
4. Drag the commands you want to include on the toolbar from the Commands list to the new toolbar. At a minimum, the following commands are useful:
   - Download Headers In This Folder
   - Mark To Download Message(s)
   - Mark To Download Message Copy
   - Delete
   - Unmark Selected Headers
   - Unmark All Headers
   - Process All Marked Headers
   - Process Marked Headers In This Folder

Selective Downloading for POP3 Using Send/Receive Groups

Using send/receive groups in Outlook gives you additional options for selective message processing with POP3 accounts. You can configure a POP3 account in a send/receive group to download only headers, for example, or to download only those messages smaller than a specified size while retrieving only headers for larger messages. If you prefer to process your POP3 account selectively—perhaps because you connect over a dial-up connection, or because you want to delete unwanted messages before they arrive in your Inbox, or because you need to control which messages are downloaded—you can use a send/receive group to process the account.

For details on setting up send/receive groups, see "Controlling Synchronization and Send/Receive Times," page 184.

Let's assume that your profile includes two POP3 accounts, a Hotmail account, and an Exchange Server account. You want to process messages normally for the Hotmail and Exchange Server accounts but would like to process the POP3 accounts selectively. You can configure a send/receive group (either the default All Accounts group or another that you create) to perform a send/receive operation for the other accounts that processes all messages. You can also configure the POP3 accounts in the send/receive group to download only message headers. When you perform a send/receive operation with the group, the POP3 accounts download only headers and the other accounts download messages.

Tip You can't use send/receive groups for selective processing with Hotmail and HTTP accounts.

You can configure multiple send/receive groups, using different settings for each (although some settings, such as Exchange Server filters, apply to all send/receive groups to which the folder belongs). For example, you might configure your POP3 accounts in the All Accounts send/receive group to download message bodies and attachments but create a second send/receive group named POP3 Remote that processes only message headers for your POP3 accounts when that group is executed.

Retrieving Only Message Headers

After you decide which combination of send/receive groups makes the most sense for you, follow these steps to configure a POP3 account to retrieve only message headers and then process the headers:

1. In Outlook, choose Tools, Send/Receive, Send/Receive Settings, Define Send/Receive Groups.
2. Select the existing send/receive group in which you want to configure POP3 accounts for headers only (or create a group for that purpose) and then click Edit.
3. On the Accounts bar of the Send/Receive Settings dialog box (see Figure 11-6), click the POP3 account.

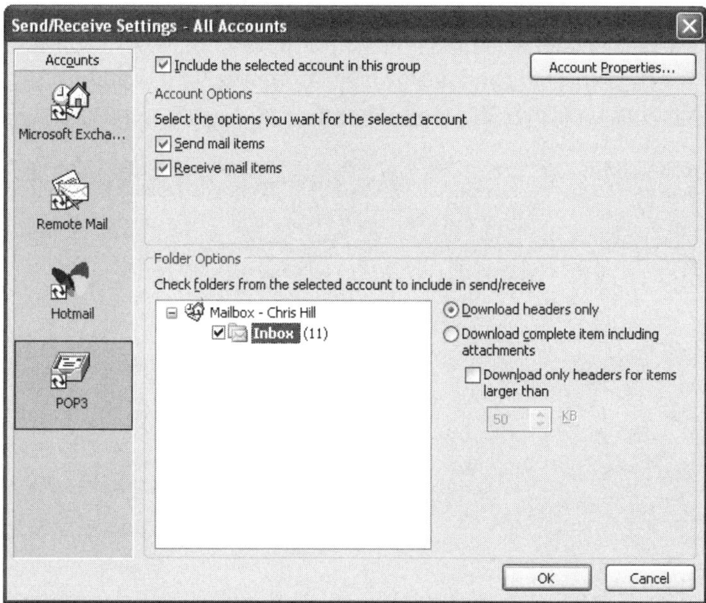

Figure 11-6. You can configure a POP3 account to download only headers.

4. Select the option Download Headers Only.
5. If you don't want the group to send messages from the selected POP3 account, clear the Send Mail Items check box.
6. Click OK and then close the Send/Receive Groups dialog box.
7. Choose Tools, Send/Receive, and select the group to have Outlook process it according to the settings you specified in the previous steps. Outlook then downloads message headers.
8. Review and mark the downloaded message headers and then process the group again. Alternatively, choose Tools, Send/Receive, Process All Marked Headers.

Retrieving Based on Message Size

You can configure a POP3 account in a send/receive group to specify a message size limit. Messages that meet or are below the specified size limit are downloaded in their entirety, complete with attachments. For messages larger than the specified size, only headers are downloaded. This is an easy way to restrict the volume of incoming POP3 mail and keep large messages from choking a low-bandwidth connection such as a dial-up.

Follow these steps to configure a POP3 account in a send/receive group to download headers only for messages over a specified size:

1. In Outlook, choose Tools, Send/Receive, Send/Receive Settings, Define Send/Receive Groups.
2. Select or create the send/receive group and click Edit.
3. Select the POP3 account on the Accounts bar of the Send/Receive Settings dialog box, and then select the option Download Complete Item Including Attachments.
4. Select Download Only Headers For Items Larger Than *n* KB, as shown in Figure 11-7.

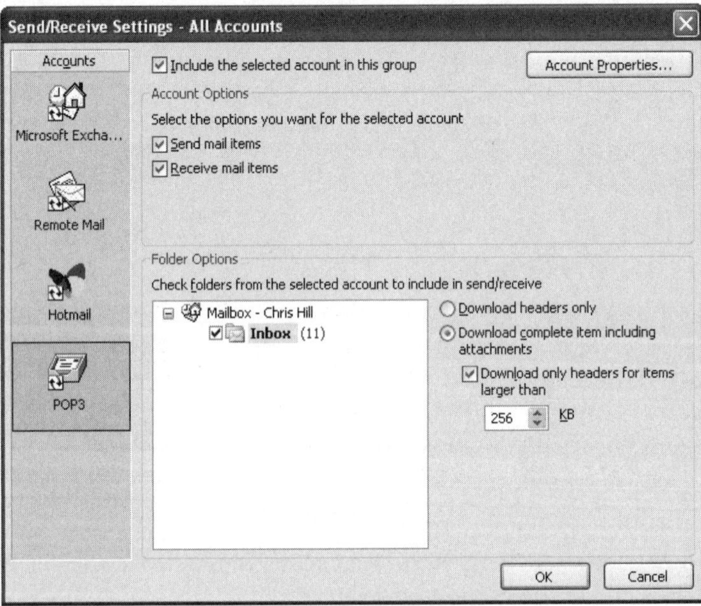

Figure 11-7. You can specify a message size limit to control connect time and mail volume.

5. Enter a value to define the message size limit and then click OK.
6. Click Close to close the Send/Receive Groups dialog box.

Keeping Messages on the Server

Often you'll want to keep a copy of your messages on the server and download a copy. For example, you might be checking your messages from the office but want to be able to retrieve them from home or from your notebook computer. Or perhaps you're using remote mail to process a few important messages and want to leave copies on the server for safekeeping. You can configure the account to leave a copy of all messages on the server, allowing you to retrieve the messages again from another system.

When you configure a POP3 account to retain messages on the server, you also can specify that the messages must be removed after they've been on the server for a designated period of time. Alternatively, you could have Outlook delete the messages from the server when you delete them from your Deleted Items folder, which prevents the messages from being downloaded again from the server after you've deleted your local copies.

Here's how to configure these options for POP3 accounts:

1. In Outlook, choose Tools, E-Mail Accounts; or right-click the Outlook icon on the Start menu, choose Properties, and click E-Mail Accounts.
2. Choose View Or Change Existing E-Mail Accounts and click Next.
3. Select the POP3 account and choose Change.
4. Click More Settings and then click the Advanced tab (see Figure 11-8).

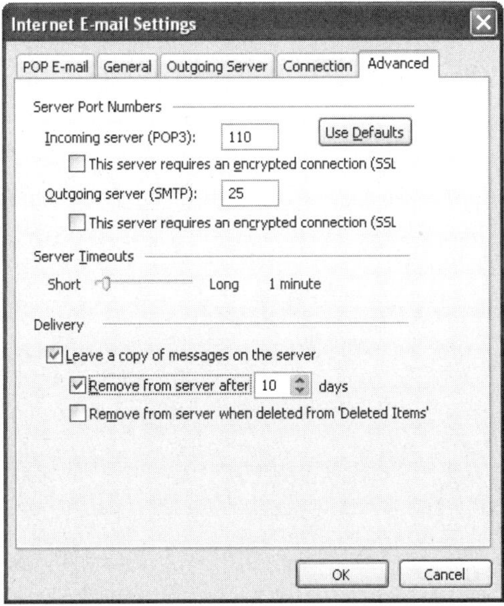

Figure 11-8. Use the Advanced tab to configure the account to leave messages on the server.

5. Select the Leave A Copy Of Messages On The Server check box, and then select one of the two associated check boxes if needed. Click OK.
6. Click Next and then click Finish.

Chapter 12

Integrating Outlook Express and Outlook

Even if you do use all of Outlook's features in your everyday work, you might still encounter times when you need an alternative to Microsoft Office Outlook 2003. You might be going out of town, for example, and want to check e-mail while you're gone but not use any of Outlook's other features. Microsoft Outlook Express is probably already on your notebook computer, has a smaller footprint than Outlook, and is a good choice as a POP3, IMAP, and HTTP client—with a few features even Outlook doesn't match.

Because this book focuses specifically on Outlook, this chapter doesn't cover all the details of how to use Outlook Express. Rather, it explains how to integrate the two programs, moving messages and addresses between them. Information about integrating the two programs can be particularly useful if you're switching from one to the other or if you need to use Outlook Express for a short period and want your addresses and selected messages on hand.

Tip **Use POP3 or IMAP with Microsoft Exchange Server**

If you have a Microsoft Exchange Server account, you can connect to it by using Outlook Express if the Exchange Server is running the POP3 connector or a virtual POP3 or IMAP server. You might also be able to access your Exchange Server account using a Web browser. Check with your system administrator for details, or see Chapter 41, "Accessing Messages Through a Web Browser," for information on accessing the Exchange Server through a browser.

Copying Messages and Addresses to Outlook

You can move messages from Outlook Express to Outlook, and vice versa. This is extremely useful if you're making a permanent switch from Outlook to Outlook Express or want to transfer messages from Outlook to Outlook Express for use out of the office. The following sections explain how to transfer messages between the two programs.

Understanding How Outlook Express Stores Messages

Outlook Express stores messages grouped in database files, not in individual files. Each database file represents an Outlook Express folder. (Outlook uses a single store file.) The Outlook Express Inbox, for example, resides in the Inbox.dbx file. Other folders have their own files.

You don't really need to know where the Outlook Express folders are stored to migrate your messages to Outlook. However, it's a good idea to know where they are in case you want to back them up or in case you need to move your messages between two Outlook Express installations or to a disk with more space. It's also important because you might need to move your Outlook Express files from one computer to another before exporting them to Outlook.

Migrating Messages Between Systems

You can move your messages from Outlook Express to Outlook, provided that the Outlook Express message store exists on the same system that holds your Outlook profile. Thus the first task is to get your Outlook Express messages on the computer where Outlook is installed, if they aren't there already. Then you can easily export them to your existing Outlook profile.

Tip Don't bother trying to place the Outlook Express store on a shared network if you're changing the location of your store or moving to another computer. The Outlook Express store must be stored locally.

You can copy individual folders to Outlook if you don't need to import all your Outlook Express folders. For example, if you're interested only in the Inbox, you can copy only the Inbox.dbx file. If you want to perform a selective copy but want to include folders other than the Inbox, however, make sure that you also copy the Folders.dbx file from your Outlook Express store folder to your Outlook system.

Follow these steps if your Outlook Express messages are not already located on the computer where Outlook is installed:

1. On the system containing your Outlook Express data, choose Tools, Options to open the Options dialog box. Click the Maintenance tab, shown in Figure 12-1.
2. Click Store Folder to display the location of your Outlook Express information store (see Figure 12-2).
3. Note the path to your store folder and click Cancel.
4. Configure Windows Explorer to show hidden files and folders. (The Outlook Express folder is by default located in a hidden folder.)

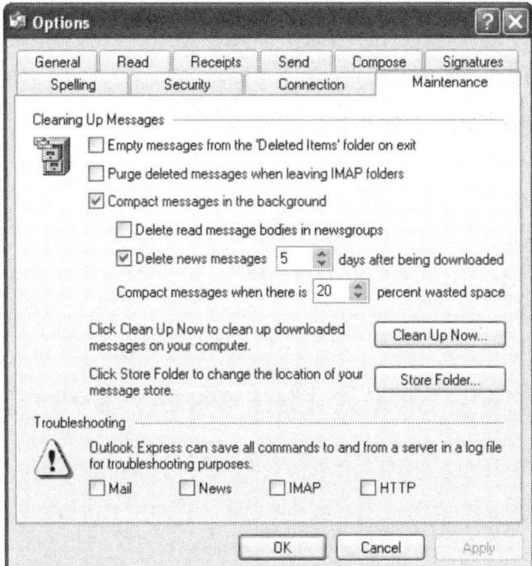

Figure 12-1. Use the Maintenance tab to locate your Outlook Express information store folder.

Figure 12-2. Each user has an information store folder based on the user profile.

5 Copy the entire Outlook Express folder to the system where Outlook is installed. You can copy across the network, use a Zip disk or CD-R, or use a direct-cable connection if the computers aren't networked. The destination really doesn't matter because you'll be using the folders only temporarily. Make sure to copy the entire folder as a whole, rather than as individual files.

6 On the system where Outlook is installed, open Outlook Express. If Outlook Express prompts you to create an e-mail account, click Cancel.

7 Choose Tools, Options and click Maintenance.

8 Click Store Folder and click Change.

9 Locate and select the folder you copied in step 5 and then click OK.

10 Click OK in the Store Location dialog box.

11 Outlook Express detects that files are present in the specified location and asks whether you want to use them or replace them with the messages from your old store location. Click Yes to switch to that store.

12 Shut down and restart Outlook Express to have the change take effect.

Note Copying the message files to the system where Outlook is installed doesn't also copy the Outlook Express Address Book, which is stored separately. See the following section if you need to move your address book from one computer to another.

Tip You can also use the Files and Settings Transfer Wizard on Microsoft Windows XP systems to move Outlook Express data to another computer.

Migrating Your Windows Address Book Between Systems

Outlook Express uses the Windows Address Book to store addresses. The address book file has the same name as your Windows logon name with a WAB file extension. The address book file is located by default in the \Documents and Settings\<*user*>\Application Data\Microsoft\Address Book folder of your profile, where <*user*> is your logon name. Outlook can't use the WAB file directly, but you can easily import the addresses from a WAB file into Outlook's Personal Address Book (PAB). Before you can import the address book, however, it must reside on the same system as Outlook.

If your Outlook Express data is located on another computer, follow these steps to copy the address book to the system where Outlook is installed:

1. On the system where your Outlook Express data resides, locate your WAB file as explained earlier. If you're not sure where to look, perform a search on *.wab to locate all WAB files on the system. Yours will be the one with a file name that matches your Windows logon name.
2. Copy the WAB file to the same location on the computer where Outlook is installed, either across the network, by disk, or other means.
3. Open Outlook Express on the target system (where Outlook is located), and verify that all your addresses are intact.

Copying Messages, Addresses, and Rules to Outlook from Outlook Express

Before you transfer addresses, you might need to perform one more advanced step. Outlook 2003 no longer includes a Personal Address Book option as the destination for imported addresses, instead placing all incoming addresses in the Contacts folder. You therefore have two options for moving addresses from Outlook Express to Outlook: from Outlook, import the addresses into your Contacts folder, or from Outlook Express, export the addresses to a PAB that already exists in your Outlook profile.

Exporting Addresses from Outlook Express

If you want to store your Outlook Express addresses in an Outlook PAB, the easiest method is to export the addresses directly from Outlook Express to thePAB. Follow these steps to export addresses from Outlook Express to your Outlook PAB:

1. Add the PAB to your Outlook profile if it isn't already there.

For details about adding the PAB to your profile, see "Configuring Address Books and Addressing Options," page 125.

2. In Outlook, choose Tools, Address Book to open the Address Book window.
3. In the Address Book window, choose Tools, Options.
4. On the Addressing tab, select Personal Address Book in the Keep Personal Addresses In drop-down list. Then click OK and close the Address Book window.
5. Open Outlook Express and choose File, Export, Address Book.
6. In the Address Book Export Tool dialog box, select Microsoft Exchange Personal Address Book and click Export.
7. If Outlook isn't running, Outlook Express prompts you to select the profile. Select the profile in which you want the addresses stored and click OK.
8. Click Close after the export is completed.
9. Open the Address Book window again and, if needed, change the location for storing personal addresses from the PAB back to the location you want.

Importing Addresses Within Outlook

If you're not using a PAB and don't want the incoming addresses mingled with your existing contacts list, you need to do a little planning. Let's first look at an overview of the process and then examine the specific steps involved. Because the addresses always import into the Outlook Contacts folder, you need to move the existing contacts temporarily, import the addresses, move them to the location you want, and then restore your original contacts. If you want the incoming messages stored in a subfolder of the Contacts folder, create two folders: one as a temporary haven for your existing contacts and a second for the incoming addresses. In this example, assume that the first is called Temp and the second is called My Addresses.

Move the existing contacts from the Contacts folder to the Temp folder. Perform the import to add the incoming addresses to the Contacts folder. Move them to the My Addresses folder. Move the contacts from the Temp folder back to the Contacts folder, and then delete the Temp folder.

Tip **Clean house before importing**
Be sure to clean out unwanted messages and folders from Outlook Express before importing the messages, especially if Outlook Express contains numerous messages. You also should clean up the names and addresses in the Outlook Express address book, adding names to any addresses that include only the e-mail address. Otherwise, Outlook uses the domain from the user's e-mail address as the name.

After you have located your Outlook Express messages and address book on the same computer as Outlook, the hard work is done, and you can quickly and easily import those items into Outlook.

Because you can copy the messages and address book at the same time in Outlook, the following steps describe this particular approach:

1. Make sure that your Outlook Express messages (and, optionally, your address book) reside on the same computer as Outlook.
2. If you need to separate incoming addresses from your existing contacts, create folders as necessary. For example, create subfolders of the Contacts folder named My Addresses and Temp.
3. Move the existing contacts to the temporary folder.
4. In Outlook, choose File, Import And Export.
5. In the Import And Export Wizard, select Import Internet Mail And Addresses and click Next.
6. Select Outlook Express 4.x, 5.x, 6.x in the list, and select the items you want to import (see Figure 12-3). Then click Next.

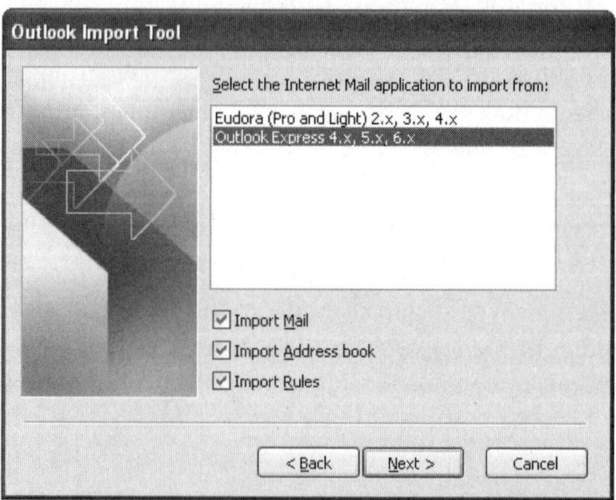

Figure 12-3. You can import mail, addresses, and rules.

7 Specify how you want duplicate items to be handled (see Figure 12-4) and click Finish.

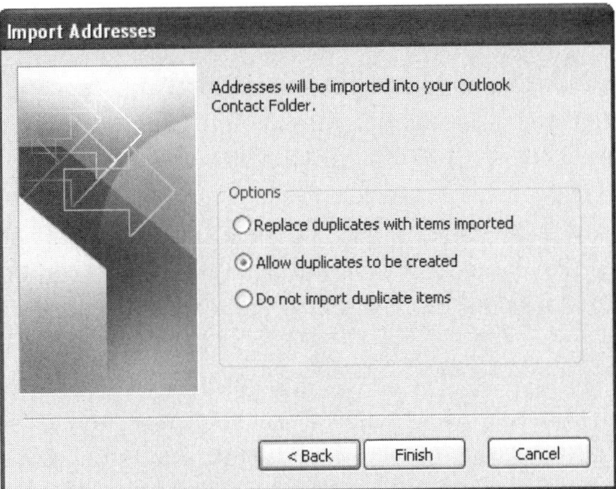

Figure 12-4. Specify how duplicates should be handled.

8 If you want to separate the incoming addresses from your existing contacts, move the newly imported addresses from the Contacts folder to the location you want to use (such as My Addresses). Then move the original contacts back to the Contacts folder.

9 Delete the Temp folder.

Depending on the number of addresses and messages you have, copying your data from Outlook Express to Outlook could take a long time. That's why it's a good idea to clean out old messages and any other unwanted items from Outlook Express before you begin importing the data in Outlook.

Tip **Copy or move addresses from a Contacts folder to a PAB**

There is no direct method for copying or moving addresses from a Contacts folder to a PAB. However, you can accomplish the same thing in a roundabout way. Export the contacts from Outlook to a comma-delimited file. Import the addresses into Outlook Express, and then export them from Outlook Express to a PAB.

Troubleshooting

Some contacts don't appear in the Outlook Address Book

You might run across a situation in which items in your Contacts folder don't appear in the Outlook Address Book, even when you select the contact items under Outlook Address Book in the Show Names drop-down list. This isn't a bug—it's by design. The Address Book shows only addresses that contain an e-mail address or a fax number. Any contact item that lacks both of those fields won't show up in the Outlook Address Book.

Copying Addresses and Messages to Outlook Express

In addition to moving addresses and messages from Outlook Express to Outlook, you also can move them the other way. You might do this if you're going to be out of the office and need to check your e-mail but don't want to install Outlook on your notebook computer.

Tip Microsoft Outlook Web Access is a much better solution than Outlook Express for accessing an Exchange Server mailbox when you don't have access to Outlook. See Chapter 41, "Accessing Messages Through a Web Browser," for details on using Outlook Web Access.

To copy addresses from Outlook to Outlook Express, you must run Outlook Express on the same system as Outlook. After copying the addresses to Outlook Express, you can copy the WAB file to another computer to make it available on that system. Then simply locate the appropriate WAB file and copy it to the appropriate location on the other computer.

For details on this method, see "Migrating Your Windows Address Book Between Systems," page 344.

Copying Addresses from an Outlook PAB to Outlook Express

You can copy addresses from an Outlook PAB to your Outlook Express address book.

Follow these steps to import addresses from Outlook into Outlook Express:

1. Open Outlook Express and choose File, Import, Other Address Book.
2. Select Microsoft Exchange Personal Address Book and click Import.
3. If Outlook isn't running, Outlook Express prompts you to select the profile from which to import addresses. Click OK to begin the import operation.
4. If the Outlook Express address book already contains an entry that is being imported, Outlook Express displays the Confirm Replace dialog box shown in Figure 12-5. Click the appropriate button to specify how you want Outlook Express to treat duplicates.

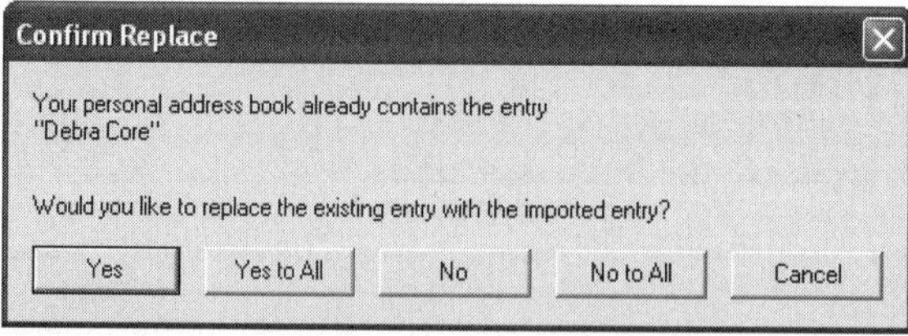

Figure 12-5. Outlook Express prompts you to specify how to handle duplicates.

5. Click Close. Then open the address book in Outlook Express to verify that your addresses were imported correctly.

Copying Outlook Contacts to Outlook Express

The previous section explained how to copy addresses from a PAB in Outlook to Outlook Express. If you store your contacts in the Contacts folder, you need to use a different method to copy messages to Outlook Express:

1. In Outlook, choose File, Import And Export to open the Import and Export Wizard.
2. Choose Export To A File and click Next.
3. Choose Comma Separated Values (Windows) and click Next.
4. Select the Contacts folder and click Next.
5. Enter a path and file name for the file, giving it a CSV file extension. Click Next and then click Finish.
6. Open Outlook Express and choose File, Import, Other Address Book.
7. Choose Text File (Comma Separated Values) and click Import.
8. Select the file you created in step 5 and click Next to open the CSV Import dialog box shown in Figure 12-6.

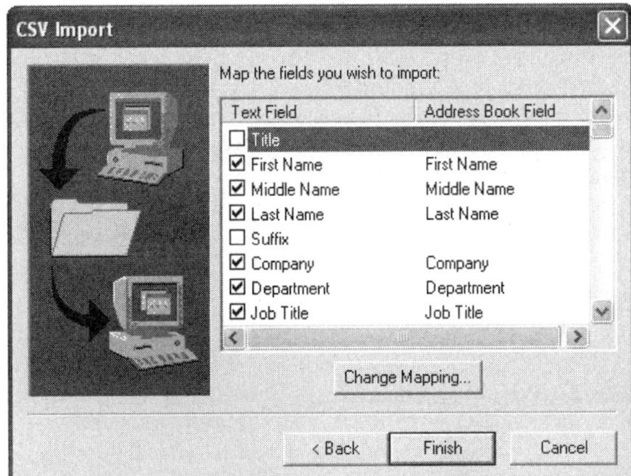

Figure 12-6. You can change field mapping, if needed, when importing to Outlook Express.

9. The default field mapping will work as is, so simply click Finish to import the contacts.

Copying Messages from Outlook to Outlook Express

You can import messages to Outlook Express from Outlook by using a wizard provided with Outlook Express for that purpose. Outlook Express imports from your default message store (that is, the store you've configured in Outlook as the location for incoming mail). This means you might need to change the default store to import messages.

For example, assume that you have an Exchange Server account and have configured Outlook to deliver mail to your Exchange Server mailbox, but you want to import messages from your personal folders to Outlook Express. In that situation, you would configure the personal folders as the default store in Outlook, import the messages into Outlook Express, and then reconfigure Outlook to use the Exchange Server mailbox as the default store.

Tip **Import from multiple message stores**
You can import from multiple stores by performing multiple imports, changing the default store in Outlook before each import. Keep in mind that Outlook Express won't differentiate between stores, however; the messages in the Inbox folders for two different Outlook stores will all show up in the same Inbox in Outlook Express.

Follow these steps to import messages into Outlook Express from Outlook:

1. If you need to import messages from a store other than your current default store, configure Outlook to use that store for new message delivery.
2. Open Outlook Express, and choose File, Import, Messages.
3. Select Microsoft Outlook in the Select Program list and click Next.
4. If Outlook isn't running, Outlook Express prompts you to select the profile from which to import the messages. Select a profile and click OK.
5. Outlook Express prompts you to specify which folders to import (see Figure 12-7). Select All Folders to import all messages, or select Selected Folders, and then select the folders to include. (You can use the Shift or Ctrl key to select multiple folders.)

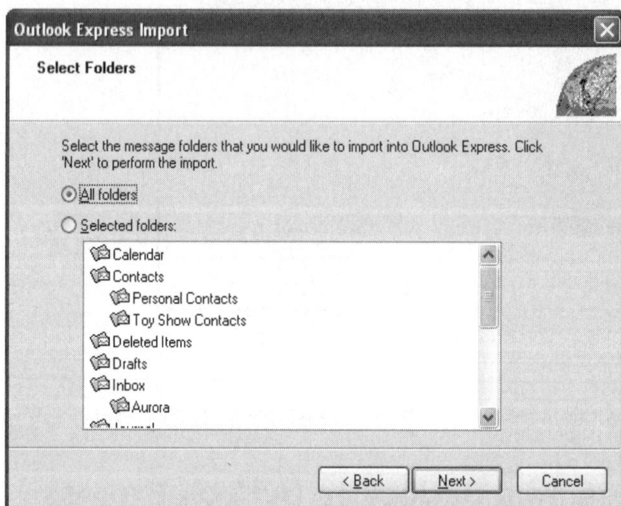

Figure 12-7. Outlook Express prompts you to specify which folders to import.

6. Click Next to start the import, and then click Finish.
7. If you changed the default Outlook store in step 1, change it back.

If you import folders other than your message folders, you might not see what you expect in Outlook Express after the import is completed. Outlook Express imports everything as messages. Contact items, tasks, and calendar items all come in as messages because Outlook

Express doesn't support these other item types. Figure 12-8 shows the results of importing the Contacts folder into Outlook Express.

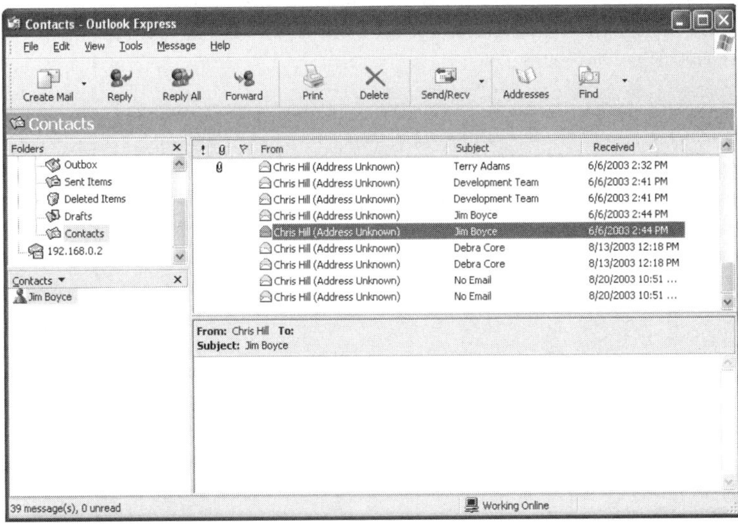

Figure 12-8. Nonmessage items are imported into Outlook Express as messages.

Copying Accounts

In most cases, it's as easy to create accounts from scratch as it is to copy them from Outlook to Outlook Express, or vice versa. If you want to save yourself a little typing, however, importing the account is the way to go.

> **Tip** **Import accounts automatically**
> Outlook checks for new Outlook Express accounts on startup. If one exists, Outlook asks whether you want to import the account. Outlook prompts only once, so if you click No, it won't prompt you again. Instead, you must use the procedure outlined in the following section.

Copying Accounts to Outlook

Copying accounts from Outlook Express to Outlook is simple, thanks to a wizard in Outlook:

1. In Outlook, choose File, Import And Export.
2. Select Import Internet Mail Account Settings and click Next.
3. Outlook prompts you to select the e-mail client from which to import accounts. Select Outlook Express and click Next.

4. If more than one account exists in Outlook Express, Outlook prompts you to select one (see Figure 12-9). Select the account you want to import and click Next.

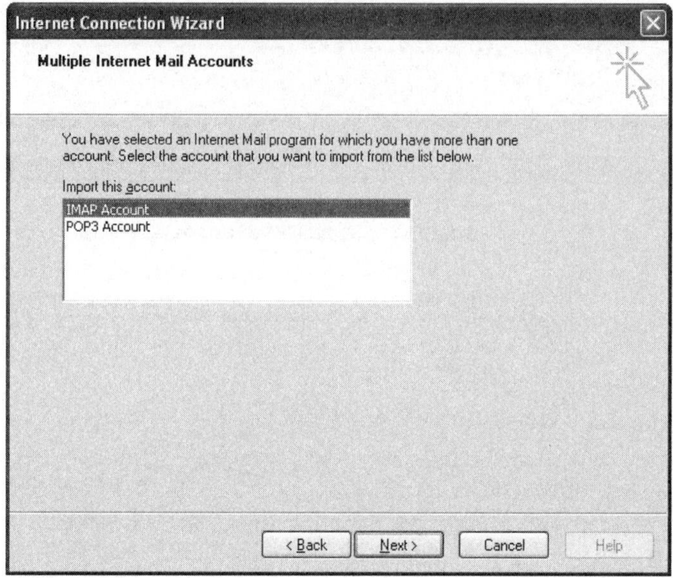

Figure 12-9. Outlook prompts you to select the account to import.

5. Outlook then presents a series of wizard pages that include the account information. Verify the information and click Next on each page, and then click Finish.

Copying Accounts to Outlook Express

The process for importing accounts from Outlook into Outlook Express is also easy, thanks to the wizard Outlook Express provides for that purpose.

Follow these steps to import Outlook accounts into Outlook Express:

1. In Outlook Express, choose File, Import, Mail Account Settings.
2. Select the option Microsoft Windows Messaging or Exchange or Outlook and click Next.
3. Select an account to import and click Next.
4. In the Confirm Settings dialog box, verify the settings for the account. If they are correct, click Next and then click Finish. If you need to make changes, select Change Settings, click Next, and modify settings as needed.

Chapter 13

Using Outlook Express for Public and Private Newsgroups

Like its predecessors, Microsoft Office Outlook 2003 doesn't include a newsgroup reader. Instead, Outlook relies on Outlook Express as its default newsgroup reader. Outlook Express is included with Microsoft Internet Explorer 4.0 and later. Although other newsgroup applications are available—most notably Forte's Agent, which offers some additional benefits—Outlook Express is a good choice for occasional forays into newsgroups and situations where you're not dealing with a large number of encoded attachments.

This chapter explores the newsgroup features in Outlook Express and shows you how to use Outlook Express to read newsgroup messages, post new messages, handle attachments, and process items automatically.

You'll find additional discussion of Outlook Express in Chapter 12, "Integrating Outlook Express and Outlook," which explains how to move messages, address books, and accounts between Outlook and Outlook Express.

Overview of Newsgroups and News Servers

Newsgroups are the Internet's equivalent of a huge bulletin board. Each newsgroup focuses on a specific area of interest, and you can post messages to a newsgroup and view other people's postings. Newsgroups are *threaded*, which means that you can easily follow a specific discussion within the group. Outlook Express organizes all messages related to a specific topic in an expandable and collapsible hierarchy. Each newsgroup has a unique name not only to help you identify its topic, but also to help you locate the group among the other newsgroups hosted by the server.

Public Internet newsgroups number in the tens of thousands, and many businesses provide their own news servers that allow customers to obtain support or provide feedback. Microsoft, for example, maintains public news servers where you can get support for various products and interact with other users. It also maintains private news servers for participation by beta testers.

In addition, many organizations implement private news servers where employees can share information and collaborate on projects. You can use Outlook Express as a newsreader for both public and private newsgroups. The only real difference between the two types of groups is access—private news servers restrict access and public news servers do not.

> **Note** News servers use a standard protocol called Network News Transfer Protocol (NNTP) to support connection from news clients such as Outlook Express. Microsoft Windows 2000 Server and Microsoft Windows Server 2003 include an NNTP service you can use to set up your own news server. If you're interested in setting up your own news server for private newsgroups, see "NNTP + Outlook = Internet Newsgroups," page 973.

Configuring Outlook Express for Newsgroups

This chapter assumes that you have some degree of familiarity with newsgroups but don't necessarily have a lot of experience working with them. This section, which focuses on setting up Outlook Express to access your news server, should help you get started.

> **Note** Before you can begin using Outlook Express to view Internet newsgroups or other public or private newsgroups outside your local area network (LAN), you need to establish an Internet connection.

Starting Outlook Express to Read Newsgroups

You can start Outlook Express to read news in two ways: either from Outlook or from the Windows desktop. Microsoft Outlook 2002 included a News command on the Go menu, but Outlook 2003 doesn't include the command by default, so you have to add it. Right-click the menu and choose Customize. Click Go in the Categories list on the Commands tab, drag the News item from the Commands list to the Go menu, and click Close. Then to start Outlook Express from Outlook, choose View, Go To, News. Outlook Express opens (if it isn't already running) but doesn't open a specific news account or newsgroup.

You also can open Outlook Express from the Windows desktop. Windows automatically places an Outlook Express icon on the Quick Start menu, just to the right of the Start menu. Alternatively, you can start the program by choosing Start, All Programs, Outlook Express.

Setting Up a News Account

Setting up a news account is the first step in using Outlook Express to access a news server. The process is simple, but it requires some preparation. In particular, you need to have the following information available:

- **News server name or IP address** You need to know the Domain Name Service (DNS) name or the Internet Protocol (IP) address of the news server so that Outlook Express can connect to it.
- **Logon information** Most public news servers don't require logon. Many private servers, however, do require that you specify valid account credentials (user name and password).
- **Port, if not standard** The default Transmission Control Protocol (TCP) port for NNTP is 119. Almost all news servers use the default, so you will rarely need to specify a nonstandard port.
- **Whether the server requires Secure Sockets Layer (SSL)** Most public servers do not require SSL, although some private servers do. If you're unable to connect without SSL, try enabling it and then retest the connection.
- **Whether Secure Password Authentication (SPA) is required** Most news servers do not require SPA. If you are unable to connect, however, enable SPA and try again.

Follow these steps when you're ready to set up your news accounts:

1. Create the Internet connection for your computer (if you don't already have one).
2. Open Outlook Express and choose Tools, Accounts to open the Accounts dialog box.
3. Click the News tab and then click Add, News to start the Internet Connection Wizard.
4. Specify your name, e-mail address, server name, and other information as prompted by the wizard and then click Finish.
5. In the Internet Accounts dialog box, double-click the account you just created or select it and click Properties.
6. Configure settings for the account, as explained in the following four sections.

General Tab

On the General tab (see Figure 13-1), you can change the account name, specify your name and e-mail addresses, and determine whether the account is included when checking for new messages.

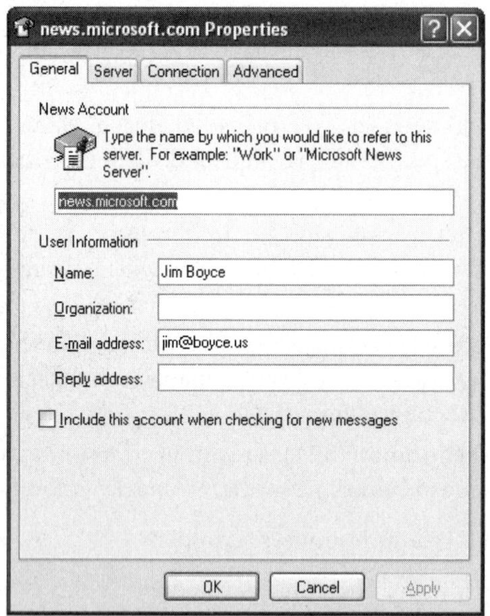

Figure 13-1. Enter user information on the General tab for a news account.

Configure settings on the General tab using the following list as a guide:

- **News Account** Specify the name for the account as you want it to appear in Outlook Express. This account name appears in the Internet Accounts dialog box and in the folder list in Outlook Express.
- **Name** Specify your name as you want it to appear in the header of messages that you post.
- **Organization** Specify an optional organization name (such as a company name).
- **E-Mail Address** Enter your e-mail address as you want it to appear in messages that you post. Leave this box blank if you don't want your e-mail address posted.
- **Reply Address** Specify the address to which replies to your posts will be sent if a reader replies directly to you rather than to the newsgroup.
- **Include This Account When Checking For New Messages** Select this option if you want Outlook Express to check the newsgroups to which you've subscribed and indicate the number of unread messages beside the group name in the folder list.

Server Tab

Use the Server tab (see Figure 13-2) to specify the server's DNS name or IP address and authentication settings, as explained in the following list:

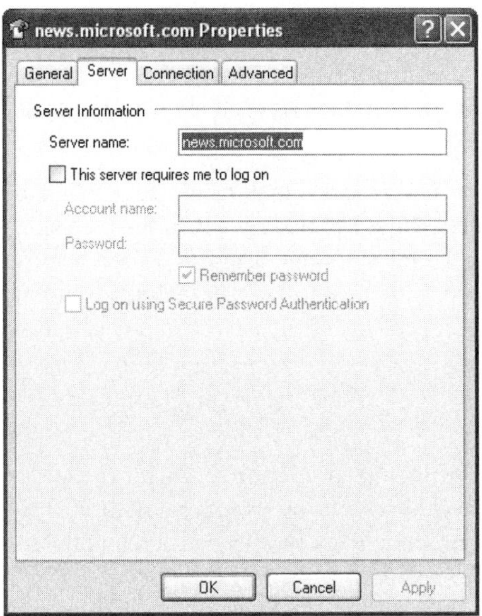

Figure 13-2. You can specify server options on the Server tab.

- **Server Name** Enter the fully qualified domain name (FQDN) of the server or enter its IP address.
- **This Server Requires Me To Log On** Select this check box if the news server requires that you provide an account name and password to access the server.
- **Account Name** Specify the account name to use if the server requires you to log on. If the server is hosted on a server in a Windows domain but uses accounts in a trusted domain for authentication, include the domain name before the user name, such as *MYDOMAIN\myusername*.
- **Password** Specify the password associated with the account specified by the Account Name setting.
- **Remember Password** Select this check box if you want Outlook Express to store the password for this news server in your password cache.
- **Log On Using Secure Password Authentication** Select this check box if the news server requires SPA for authentication.

Troubleshooting

You are unable to connect to a server that doesn't require authentication

Many news providers opt to use *subnet exclusion* rather than authentication to control access to the news server. For example, an Internet service provider (ISP) will typically allow access to the news server only by clients within the ISP's own subnets. This method, which allows the ISP to restrict access to the news server to its customers only, is easier to implement than authentication, from an administration perspective.

If you're having problems connecting to a news server that doesn't require authentication, and you know your settings are correct, subnet exclusion could be the problem. The only way around the problem is to dial into the ISP's network using its access numbers, establish a virtual private network (VPN) connection to a VPN server that resides within an allowed subnet, or connect through a broadband connection within an allowed subnet.

Connection Tab

On the Connection tab, you specify the dial-up connection to use for the selected server. Clear the Always Connect Using This Account check box if you connect through a LAN or want to connect using whichever dial-up connection is active when you attempt the connection.

Advanced Tab

Use the Advanced tab (see Figure 13-3) to specify the port for the NNTP server and other advanced settings, as described in the following list:

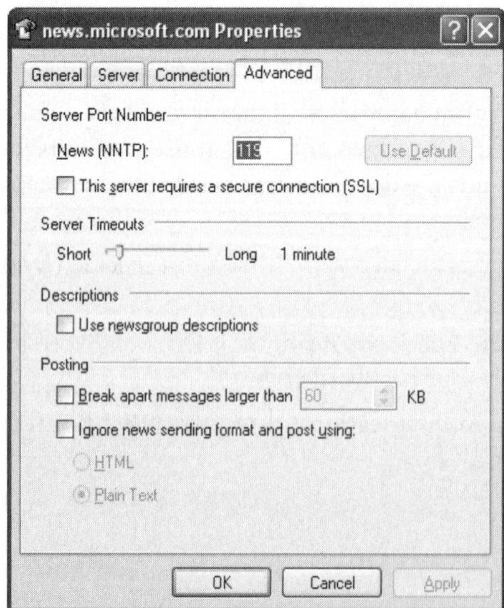

Figure 13-3. The Advanced tab includes the port setting and other newsgroup options.

- **News (NNTP)** Specify the TCP port used for the NNTP protocol on the news server. The default is 119. Most servers use the default settings, so you should not have to change this setting in most situations.
- **This Server Requires A Secure Connection (SSL)** Select this check box if the server requires SSL for the connection. SSL provides higher security, but most servers don't require it.
- **Server Timeouts** Specify the amount of time the server can be unresponsive before Outlook Express cancels the download of messages or groups. Use a shorter timeout if you have a fast Internet connection or the server is not relatively busy. Use a longer timeout for slow Internet connections and heavily used servers.
- **Use Newsgroup Descriptions** In addition to its newsgroup name, each newsgroup also can have a longer description that helps you identify it. Select this check box if you want Outlook Express to download newsgroup descriptions with the newsgroup names when you refresh the newsgroup list or download new newsgroups.
- **Break Apart Messages Larger Than *n* KB** You can use this option to break messages into multiple messages smaller than the specified size. Most servers support large messages, so you'll rarely need to use this option.
- **Ignore News Sending Format And Post Using** Select this check box and specify the format for posting to the selected newsgroup if you want to override the default setting defined in the global properties of Outlook Express. To configure the default setting, choose Tools, Options and click the Send tab.

Managing the Newsgroup List

Each server maintains a certain number of newsgroups. A typical public Internet news server hosts 40,000 or more; other public and private news servers usually host fewer. Microsoft's public news server at *news.microsoft.com*, for example, currently hosts approximately 1400 newsgroups. Other business and private news servers generally host a smaller number of groups.

When you first add a news account, Outlook Express asks whether you want to download the list of newsgroups from the server. You must download this list to be able to browse the newsgroups. This generally doesn't take very long, even when you're downloading from a public Internet news server. You can download the 40,000-plus newsgroup list in a matter of a few minutes, even on the slowest connections. Keep in mind that you're downloading only the newsgroup names (and, optionally, the group descriptions), but no message headers or messages.

Downloading and Updating the List

If you didn't let Outlook Express download the newsgroup list when you set up your account, you can download it at a later time. You also might want to reset the list if you think it might contain new newsgroups not included in your original list or if you want to download the newsgroup descriptions as well as the names.

Follow these steps to reset the newsgroup list, which downloads a new copy of the list:

1. Open Outlook Express, click the server in the folders list, and then click Newsgroups in the right pane to display the Newsgroup Subscriptions dialog box (see Figure 13-4).

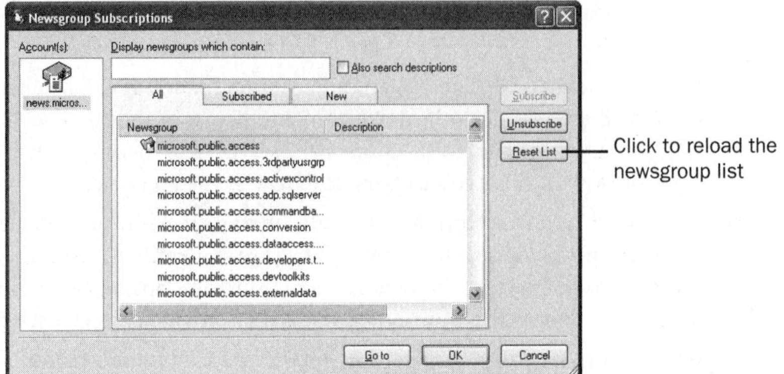

Figure 13-4. Reset the newsgroup list by using the Newsgroup Subscriptions dialog box.

2. If you want to download descriptions as well as names, select the Also Search Descriptions check box.

Note If descriptions are not currently downloaded, Outlook Express asks whether you want to reset the list. Click Yes to do so.

3. Click Reset List to download the new copy of the list.

Tip If you don't want to download descriptions, you can reset the list quickly this way: right-click the news server in the folders list and choose Reset List.

Subscribing and Unsubscribing to Groups

You can view any newsgroup without subscribing to the group, but subscribing to a group you frequently visit can simplify access because Outlook Express includes subscribed newsgroups in the folders list (see Figure 13-5). You can then quickly open a specific group by clicking it in the folders list.

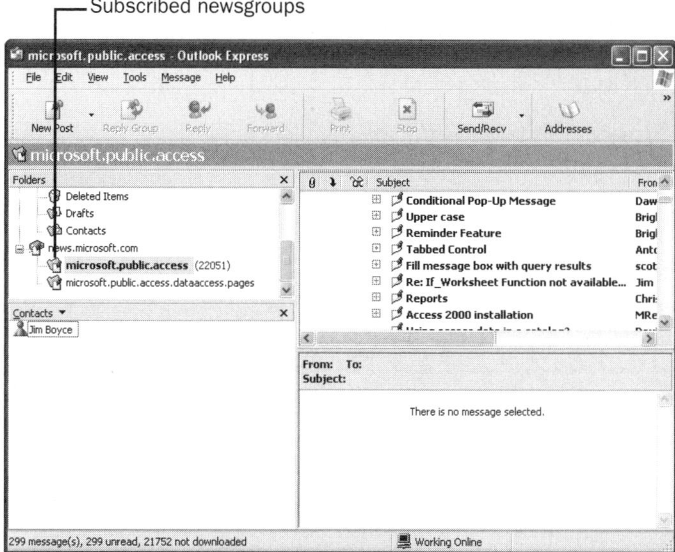

Figure 13-5. Subscribed newsgroups appear in the folders list, making them easily accessible.

Subscribing to a newsgroup has no effect on the server. You're not associating your user account, e-mail address, or any other information with any setting on the server. Nor can others who use a news server determine to which newsgroups you subscribe. Subscription is purely a client-side setting that makes it easier for you to access frequently used groups. Follow these steps to subscribe to a newsgroup and add it to your folders list:

1. Open Outlook Express, click the news server in the folders list, and then click Newsgroups in the right pane.
2. In the Newsgroup Subscriptions dialog box, click the All tab, and then locate and select the newsgroup to which you want to subscribe.
3. Click Subscribe.
4. Repeat the process to subscribe to other newsgroups.

> **Tip** To subscribe to multiple groups, hold down the Ctrl key and select multiple newsgroups.

Outlook Express displays a small icon beside each subscribed group on the All tab.You also can click the Subscribed tab in the Newsgroup Subscriptions dialog box to view a list that includes only your subscribed newsgroups, as shown in Figure 13-6. The New tab shows new newsgroups.

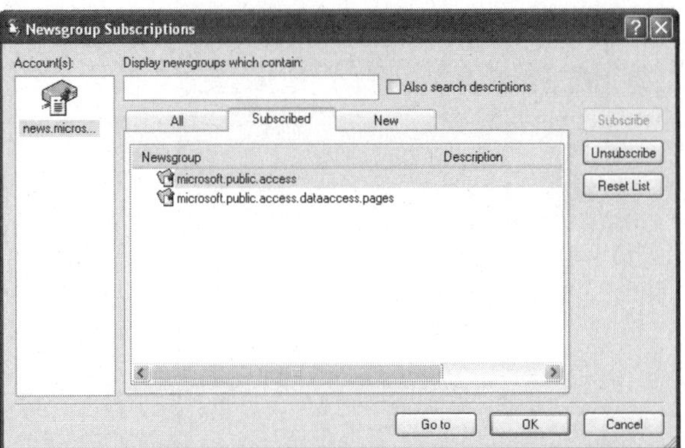

Figure 13-6. Use the Subscribed tab to view the list of newsgroups to which you have already subscribed.

Viewing a Group

You don't have to subscribe to a group to view its contents, but only those groups to which you've subscribed appear in the folder list by default.

To open other groups to read and post messages, follow these steps:

1. Click the Newsgroups button on the toolbar to open the Newsgroup Subscriptions dialog box, shown previously in Figure 13-4.
2. In the Display Newsgroups Which Contain box, enter the newsgroup name to view a specific newsgroup. To view all the newsgroups associated with a given topic, enter any portion of the newsgroup name; for example, enter **microsoft.public.access** to view all newsgroups about Microsoft Access. Enter a single word to view a list of all newsgroups that contain that word.
3. After you find the newsgroup you want, select it in the Newsgroup list and then click Go To.

Searching Descriptions

As explained previously, newsgroups can include optional descriptions that explain the content or intent of the newsgroup. When you search for a newsgroup on a particular topic, Outlook Express searches only on the newsgroup name by default. To include the description in the search, select the Also Search Descriptions check box in the Newsgroup Subscriptions dialog box. If you have not yet downloaded the descriptions, Outlook Express prompts you to reset the newsgroup list and download descriptions. Even with a full complement of Internet newsgroups, downloading generally takes only a few minutes over a dial-up connection and is considerably faster over a dedicated connection.

Reading Messages

Because of the way Outlook Express presents the newsgroup and its contents, reading messages in newsgroups is easy. Before you can read messages, however, you need to download message headers. You can then read messages, follow a discussion thread, and mark messages for offline processing.

Downloading Message Headers

After you select a newsgroup, Outlook Express downloads a certain number of message headers from the newsgroup by default. The message headers appear in the right pane, and you can sort the view based on the various columns—subject, size, or date and time posted, for example.

The number of message headers that Outlook Express downloads automatically when you open a newsgroup depends on how you've configured the program. Choose Tools, Options and click the Read tab to display the Read options shown in Figure 13-7. The Get *n* Headers At A Time check box specifies the number of headers that Outlook Express will download when you open the newsgroup and when you direct it to download message headers by choosing Tools, Get Next *n* Headers. If you clear the Get *n* Headers At A Time check box, Outlook Express downloads all headers from the newsgroup.

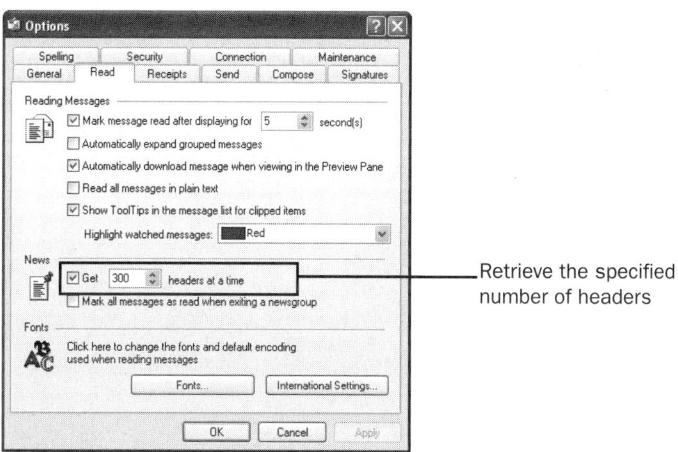

Figure 13-7. Use the Read tab to determine how Outlook Express downloads message headers.

> **Note** If you clear the Get *n* Headers At A Time check box, the command on the Tools menu changes to Get New Headers.

Troubleshooting

You can't download message headers

On occasion you might not be able to download message headers because your message store is preventing Outlook Express from properly distinguishing between existing and new message headers. If that's the case, you can clear out all headers so that Outlook Express can download them again.

To do so, follow these steps:

1. Save any newsgroup messages or attachments you don't want to lose.
2. Open Outlook Express and choose Tools, Options. Click the Maintenance tab.
3. Click Clean Up Now, click Browse, and select the subscribed newsgroup (or the news server if you haven't subscribed to any groups).
4. Click Reset to delete all message headers and bodies, and then download the message headers again.

Viewing and Reading Messages

Reading a newsgroup message is about as easy as reading an e-mail message in your Inbox. Depending on how you have configured Outlook Express, it can be as simple as opening the newsgroup and clicking the message header to download the message and view it in the preview pane. You also can double-click a message header to open it in a message window.

Choose View, Layout to display the Window Layout Properties dialog box, shown in Figure 13-8. Use the options in the Preview Pane group to turn the preview pane on or off and to specify its location and whether it includes the preview pane header.

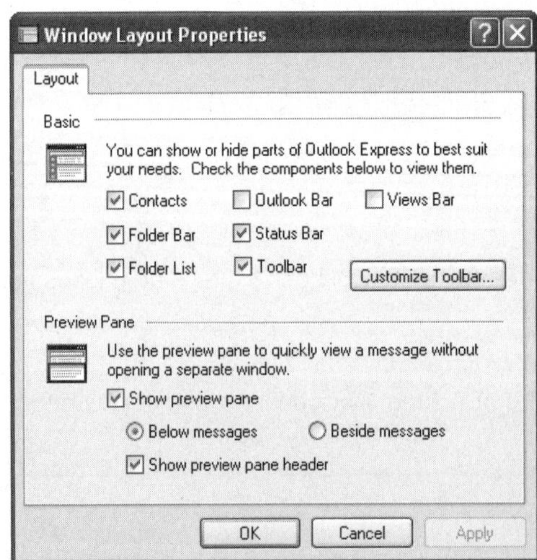

Figure 13-8. Use the Window Layout Properties dialog box to set preview pane options.

You can configure Outlook Express not to download messages when you click their headers. If a selected message hasn't been downloaded, Outlook Express tells you so in the preview pane, and you can then double-click the message to download it. (If the preview pane isn't displayed, Outlook Express takes no action.) You can select multiple message headers, open all of them, and mark them for later download.

Outlook Express displays a half-page icon beside the header of a message that hasn't been downloaded yet and shows a full-page icon beside a message that has been downloaded. The headers of unread messages appear in a bold font, and the headers of read messages appear in a normal font, giving you a quick indication of which messages have been read and which have not. If not all messages in a thread have been read, the first message in the thread retains the bold font when the thread is collapsed but not when you expand the thread. This helps you determine that the thread contains unread messages.

By default, Outlook Express marks as read any message that has been previewed for more than 5 seconds, but you can modify this behavior and set a different preview duration by following these steps:

1. In Outlook Express, choose Tools, Options and click Read.
2. On the Read tab, select the Mark Message Read After Displaying For *n* Seconds check box to have Outlook Express automatically mark as read all messages that are previewed for the specified duration. If you don't want Outlook Express to automatically mark messages as read unless you have actually opened them, clear this check box.
3. Change the preview period in the associated seconds box if you want to increase or decrease the duration of the preview.

> **Tip** Increasing the preview period allows you to read part of a message and skip to another without the first being marked as read.

4. If you want Outlook Express to mark all messages in the newsgroup as read when you exit the newsgroup, select the Mark All Messages As Read When Exiting A Newsgroup check box.
5. Click OK to close the dialog box.

Working with Message Threads

Messages in a newsgroup are organized in Outlook Express by *thread*. A thread is a group of interrelated messages, or posts and replies to those posts. Message threads are also called *conversations*. Outlook Express indicates message threads by displaying a plus sign beside the first message in the thread. You can click the plus sign to expand the thread, which changes the icon to a minus sign. Click the minus sign to collapse the thread. As Figure 13-9 shows, Outlook Express also organizes the messages in a thread by indenting them to indicate the relationship between them in the thread.

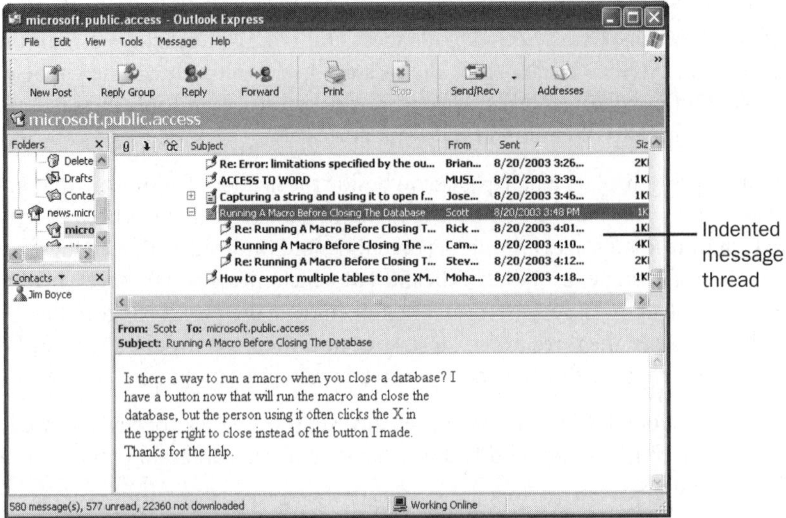

Figure 13-9. Outlook Express indents messages in a thread to make it easier to follow the conversation.

To learn how to "ungroup" messages from conversations and display them individually, see "Controlling Which Messages Are Shown," page 375.

Unscrambling Messages

Outlook Express supports a standard called ROT13 that allows you to unscramble messages. ROT13 doesn't provide actual security; it simply replaces each character in a message with a character 13 places later in the alphabet, which means that anyone can unscramble the message. However, scrambling messages can hide messages that might be considered offensive or ones the sender wants to make more difficult to read for other reasons. You can't scramble messages in Outlook Express, but you can unscramble messages that others have posted to a newsgroup. Download the message, select its header, and choose Message, Unscramble.

Posting Messages

Posting messages to a newsgroup is a lot like sending an e-mail message. You can post a message to a single newsgroup or post to several at one time.

Posting a Message to a Single Group

To compose a message to post to a newsgroup, click the New Post button on the toolbar or choose File, New, News Message. Outlook Express displays a message form, as shown in Figure 13-10, and automatically includes the name of the current newsgroup in the Newsgroups box.

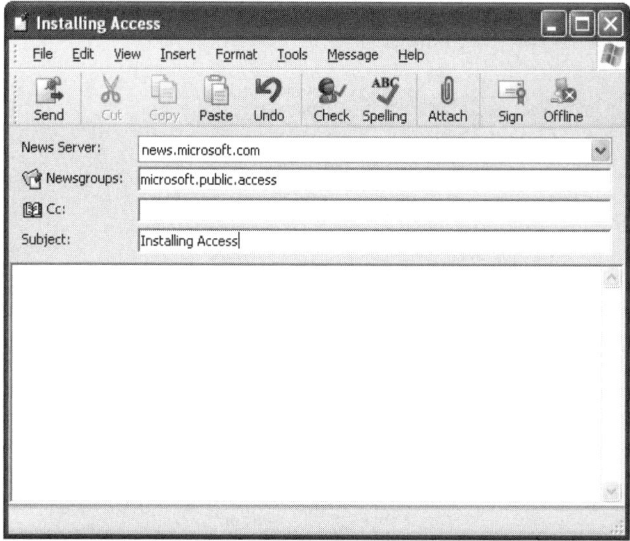

Figure 13-10. Composing a news message is much like composing an e-mail message.

Type the topic of your message in the Subject box, and then type your message in the message box. As you can also do in Outlook, you can post the message using HTML, which means you can create a rich-text message with character and paragraph formatting, bullets, and numbered lists. Click Attach if you want to attach a file to the message, and then click Send. Depending on how you've configured Outlook Express, the message is either posted immediately or sent to the Outbox until the next time you process messages. Outlook Express places a copy of the post in the Sent Items folder, if you've configured the program to do so (on the Send tab in the Options dialog box).

> **Tip** Use the Cc box on the message form to send a copy of the message post to one or more e-mail addresses.

Posting a Message to Multiple Groups

In some cases, you'll want to post the same message to more than one newsgroup. You might be looking for a particular item to buy, for example, and want to post an inquiry to several newsgroups all related to the same topic. Posting to multiple newsgroups is called *cross-posting*.

Composing the message, saving it, and then posting it separately to each newsgroup requires that you monitor each newsgroup for answers. If you cross-post the message, however, you can monitor all the replies in any one newsgroup as they appear in all. Only one instance of the message thread exists, but because you've assigned it to multiple newsgroups, it appears in each one. To cross-post a message, address it to multiple newsgroups when you compose the message, separating the newsgroup names with a comma. Click the Newsgroups button on the message form to open the Pick Newsgroups dialog box (see Figure 13-11), in which you can select the newsgroups. Use the Show Only Subscribed Newsgroups button to select groups without having to type their names.

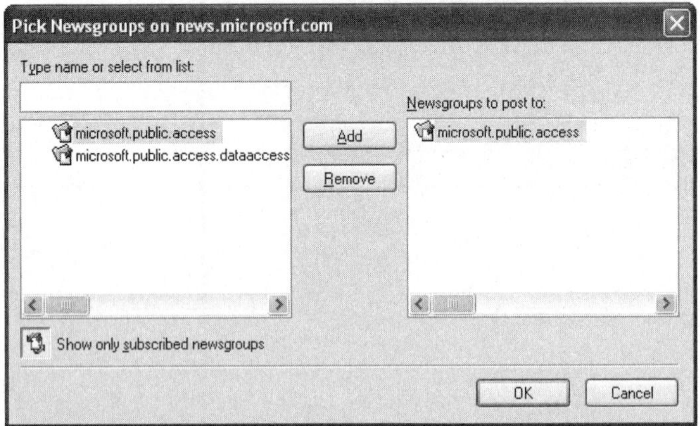

Figure 13-11. Select newsgroups from the Pick Newsgroups dialog box.

> **Note** Limit your cross-posting and the number of newsgroups to which you post a particular message. Excessive cross-posting is considered poor etiquette.

Processing Newsgroups and Working Offline

Outlook Express provides a good selection of features for automatic processing of messages and working with newsgroups offline. For example, you might want to review message headers offline—if you connect through a metered dial-up connection—and mark selected messages to be downloaded the next time you connect. The following sections explain how to process messages automatically and use Outlook Express offline.

Downloading a Selection of Messages

If you have a dedicated Internet connection, you'll probably do most of your work with Outlook Express online, downloading messages one at a time. If you want to download a large selection of messages or if you connect through a metered dial-up connection, you might prefer to mark messages for downloading and process them automatically. Handling messages this way allows you to process a large group of messages without manually downloading each one. Furthermore, you can review the message headers offline, decide which ones to download, and process them automatically the next time you go online.

> **Note** A metered dial-up connection is one for which you are charged a per-hour or per-minute connect fee rather than a flat fee. More online time therefore equates to greater expense.

Tip If you're working online and have configured Outlook Express to download messages when previewed, you can select multiple messages and Outlook Express will download them one after another.

Follow these steps to download a selection of messages:

1. Choose Tools, Options. Click the Read tab and clear the Automatically Download Message When Viewing In The Preview Pane check box. Close the Options dialog box.
2. Beside each message you want to download, click the Download column, indicated by a down arrow. By default, the Download column is the second column from the left.
3. After you select all the messages you want to download, choose Tools, Synchronize Newsgroup. Then select Get Messages Marked For Download and click OK.
4. If you're currently working offline, Outlook Express prompts you to connect (unless you've configured it to connect automatically) and then displays a download dialog box that shows the status of the download.

Note Hold down the Shift key and click the first and last messages in a range to select the range. Hold down the Ctrl key and click to select noncontiguous messages.

Selecting the first message in a thread for download automatically selects all other messages in the thread for download. If you don't want all the messages, expand the thread and cancel the selection of those messages you don't want Outlook Express to download.

Tip You also can choose Tools, Mark For Offline, Download Message Later or Download Conversation Later to mark messages for download.

Creating Messages Offline

You can compose messages offline for later posting, which is particularly useful if you connect through a metered dial-up connection. Composing your posts offline can cut your online time considerably. Outgoing messages wait in your Outbox until you connect and perform a send/receive operation.

You can compose messages offline without any special configuration. However, you'll probably want to set up Outlook Express so that it does not attempt to send messages immediately—that is, you'll want to prevent it from attempting to log on to your ISP and sending messages as soon as you click Post after you compose the message. To do this, choose Tools, Options and click the Send tab. Clear the Send Messages Immediately check box and click OK. Then compose messages as you normally would. If Outlook Express prompts you to go online, select the option to work offline. When you're ready to post the message, choose Tools, Send And Receive, Send All.

Synchronizing Individual Newsgroups

In addition to letting you mark messages for later download, Outlook Express provides other features for synchronizing newsgroups. You can direct Outlook Express to perform the following actions:

- **Retrieve All Messages From A Newsgroup** Select this option to have Outlook Express download all messages in the selected newsgroup.
- **Retrieve New Messages Only** Use this option to retrieve new messages from the server. This option retrieves the message body as well as the message header.
- **Download Headers** Select this option to download all message headers from the newsgroup.

To perform any of these actions, choose Tools, Synchronize Newsgroup. Select the appropriate option from the Synchronize Newsgroup dialog box and click OK. This action processes messages or headers only in the current newsgroup. If you have other newsgroups with messages or headers to download, you must synchronize those separately.

Note Synchronizing newsgroups helps you process them automatically, which means you'll spend less time manually reviewing message headers or marking messages for download. When you synchronize newsgroups, all messages that you have marked for download are processed and message headers for new messages are downloaded.

Synchronizing All Newsgroups and E-Mail Accounts

In addition to synchronizing selected newsgroups, you also can synchronize all newsgroups and e-mail accounts. If you choose Tools, Synchronize All, Outlook Express checks for new messages on your e-mail accounts and processes subscribed newsgroups according to their synchronization settings. For example, if a newsgroup's synchronization settings are configured to download new headers only, Outlook Express downloads marked messages in the newsgroup and any new headers. If the synchronization setting is configured to download all messages, Outlook Express downloads all messages for the newsgroup during the synchronization, regardless of whether the messages are marked for download.

To configure synchronization settings for a subscribed newsgroup, right-click the newsgroup in the folders list, choose Synchronization Settings, and then choose one of the following options:

- **Don't Synchronize** Don't include this newsgroup in the synchronization process.
- **All Messages** Download all messages from the newsgroup, regardless of whether they're marked for download.
- **New Messages Only** Download only new messages for which headers are not currently downloaded.
- **Headers Only** Download only message headers not currently downloaded.

The synchronization settings for subscribed newsgroups are the best way to perform automatic processing on a global scale. You can configure each subscribed newsgroup separately to achieve the type of synchronization you need.

Monitoring and Managing Messages

Outlook provides tools for monitoring and managing e-mail messages; Outlook Express provides similar tools for monitoring and managing newsgroup messages. This section of the chapter examines these features, starting with message flagging.

Flagging Messages

You can flag messages in Outlook Express just as you do in Outlook. Outlook Express places a flag icon beside the message header. Unlike Outlook, however, Outlook Express provides no mechanism for generating reminders for flagged messages or for assigning follow-up actions to flagged messages. However, you can sort the display to view all flagged messages together, which means you can quickly identify messages that you've flagged.

By default, Outlook Express doesn't display the Flag column, but you can turn it on to flag messages by following these steps:

1. Choose View, Columns and select Flag from the list.
2. Use the Move Up and Move Down buttons to change the column order and then click OK.
3. To flag a message, click in the Flag column beside the message header. Click again to clear a flag.

> **Tip** You can also simply drag column headers from one location to another to change the order in which the columns appear.

Watching a Conversation

With smaller newsgroups, you don't need to perform any special processing to monitor the group for messages that interest you. As the number of messages in a newsgroup grows, however, keeping track of specific messages and conversations becomes more difficult. For example, perhaps you've posted a message to a newsgroup and you want to monitor the group to determine when someone posts a reply. You can direct Outlook Express to monitor the particular conversation and notify you when new messages are added to it. This saves you the trouble of updating the message headers, scrolling through the newsgroup to locate your message, and checking it for new replies.

To direct Outlook Express to watch a conversation, click beside the message header in the Watch/Ignore column (indicated in the column bar by a pair of spectacles). Outlook Express places a similar icon beside the message to indicate that it is being watched, as shown in Figure 13-12. When you process message headers, Outlook Express colors the message thread red to indicate that it contains new replies. Outlook Express also colors the newsgroup name in the folders list red to indicate that it contains watched messages with new replies.

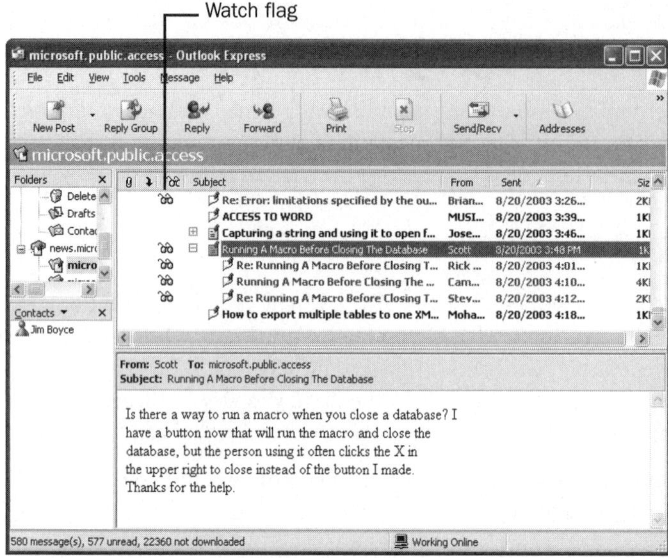

Figure 13-12. Outlook Express is watching several conversations in a newsgroup.

Ignoring a Conversation

In addition to flagging messages to be watched, you can flag messages to be ignored. Flagging a conversation to be ignored doesn't change the way Outlook Express handles it for synchronization, but it does exclude those messages from your current view. For example, you might not be interested in the majority of messages in a newsgroup and want to ignore them to focus on the rest. You can flag the conversation to be ignored and then configure Outlook Express to hide those ignored messages from the current view. This simplifies the view and lets you concentrate on those messages that interest you.

Follow these steps to ignore a conversation:

1. Click in the Watch/Ignore box beside the message header to set it to Watch. Click it again to set it to Ignore.
2. Outlook Express places a circle and slash icon beside the message header to indicate that it's being ignored (see Figure 13-13).
3. Configure the view to hide read and ignored messages by choosing View, Current View, Hide Read Or Ignored Messages.

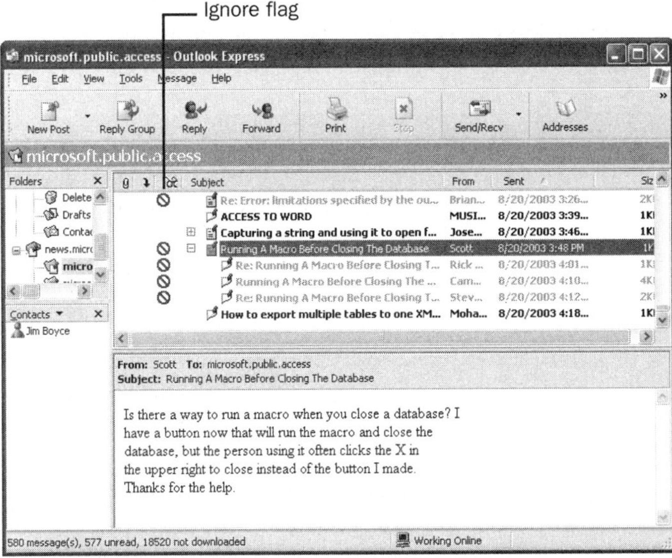

Figure 13-13. Conversations are flagged to be ignored.

Finding Messages

Outlook Express provides a search feature that finds messages based on various search criteria you specify—for example, words in the subject or the body of the message, the sender, or the date. Choose Edit, Find, Message In This Folder to display the Find dialog box, shown in Figure 13-14. Specify the text to search for in the Look For box. If you want to also search the message bodies of all downloaded messages, select the Search All The Text In Downloaded Messages check box.

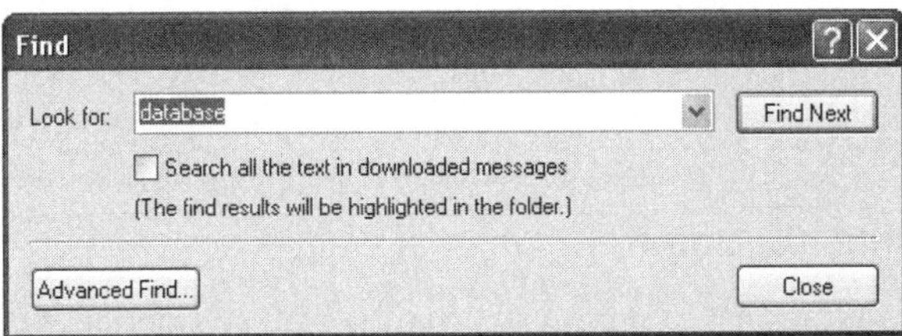

Figure 13-14. Use the Find dialog box to locate messages that fit specific search criteria.

If you need to perform a more extensive search, click Advanced Find in the Find dialog box or choose Edit, Find, Message. Outlook Express displays the Find Message dialog box, shown in Figure 13-15, which provides several additional fields you can use to refine the search. You also can click Browse to specify the root of the search location. For example, you might select the news server as the root to search all subscribed newsgroups for messages that fit your search criteria. In the Find Message dialog box, select the Include Subfolders check box to have Outlook Express search all subfolders of subscribed newsgroups within the news server.

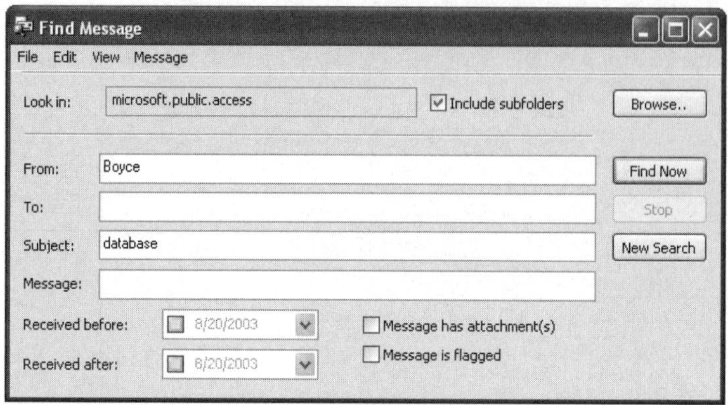

Figure 13-15. Use the Find Message dialog box to perform advanced searches.

Filtering and Controlling the Message View

With newsgroups that contain a lot of messages (typical of many Internet newsgroups and common even with many other private newsgroups), it's often useful to sort or filter the view so that you can focus on specific messages or threads. You can sort the message headers in Outlook Express based on any of the displayed columns. To do so, simply click the appropriate column header. For example, click the From column header if you're trying to locate a message from a specific sender or click the Subject header if you want to locate messages with a specific subject. Click the column header a second time to switch between ascending and descending sort order.

Note If you don't want to use the mouse, you can choose View, Sort By to sort the message headers.

Adding and Removing Columns

Outlook Express provides additional columns you can display in addition to the default set. For example, you can include a Flag column (explained earlier) to keep track of specific messages. You can also exclude certain columns if you're not interested in the information they provide. For example, if you aren't interested in the size of messages, you can turn off the Size column to make room for other columns.

To change the columns Outlook Express displays, choose View, Columns or right-click a column header and choose Columns to display the Columns dialog box. Select the columns you want to include, use the Move Up and Move Down buttons to change their display order, and then click OK. You can resize columns or change their order by dragging the column headers.

Controlling Which Messages Are Shown

By default, Outlook Express shows all messages, whether or not they've been downloaded. You can set up the view to show all messages, to show only downloaded messages, or to hide read messages. Choose View, Current View, and then one of the following commands:

- **Show All Messages** Select this option to show all message headers, whether or not the message bodies have been downloaded.
- **Hide Read Messages** Select this option to show only those messages that are marked as unread.
- **Show Downloaded Messages** Select this option to show only those messages with message bodies that have been downloaded.
- **Hide Read Or Ignored Messages** Select this option to hide messages that are marked as read or marked to be ignored.
- **Show Replies To My Messages** Select this option to show replies to messages that you have posted.
- **Group Messages By Conversation** Select this option to group messages according to thread; clear the option to display messages individually.

Using Rules

Outlook Express supports the use of rules for processing e-mail and newsgroup messages. In addition, you can use rules to create custom views to show or hide messages based on specific criteria.

Creating Custom Views

Although the views included by default with Outlook Express are useful in many situations, you might occasionally need to filter the view in other ways. For example, you might want to create a view that hides ignored messages but not read messages. You can accomplish this by creating a custom view, which applies a rule that you define to filter the newsgroup folder.

Follow these steps to create a custom view:

1. In Outlook Express, choose View, Current View, Define Views.

2 In the Define Views dialog box (see Figure 13-16), click New to display the New View dialog box (see Figure 13-17).

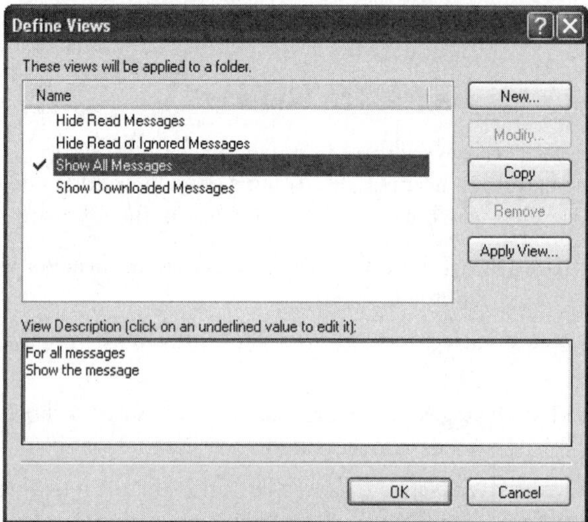

Figure 13-16. The Define Views dialog box shows currently defined views and allows you to create custom views.

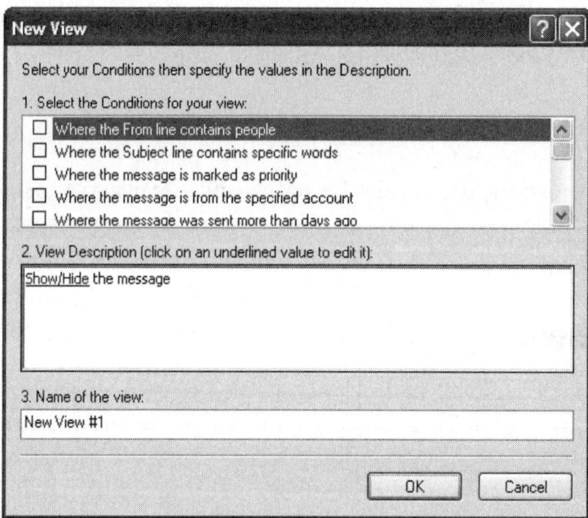

Figure 13-17. Use the New View dialog box to define a rule that filters the newsgroup folder view.

3 Select the rule condition that will apply to the new view. For example, to hide all ignored messages, select Where The Message Is Watched Or Ignored.

4 In the View Description area, click the underlined word that specifies the condition and then specify the criteria. For example, click Watched Or Ignored to specify Ignore Threads if you're creating a rule that hides ignored messages.

5. In the View Description area, click the underlined word that specifies the action to take and then select an action. For example, to hide all ignored messages, click Show/Hide and select Hide Messages.
6. Enter a name for the rule in the Name Of The View box and click OK.
7. To apply the view, select the view rule you just created, click Apply View, select either The Currently Selected Folder or All Of My Folders, and click OK. Outlook Express filters the view accordingly, and the applied view appears as a command on the Current View menu.

> **Tip** You can modify the rule that defines the current view by choosing View, Current View, Customize Current View.

Processing Messages with Rules

In addition to controlling the view through message rules, you can use rules to process messages automatically. For example, you might create a message rule that marks for download all messages from specific senders or messages containing certain words in the Subject box. Or perhaps you want to use certain colors to identify messages from specific senders.

You can either apply rules when message headers and messages are downloaded or apply them manually afterward.

In either case, the first task is to create the rule, as follows:

1. In Outlook Express, choose Tools, Message Rules, News and click New.
2. In the New News Rule dialog box, select the condition or conditions to apply to the message in the Conditions list.
3. In the Actions list, select the action or actions you want Outlook Express to take on messages that fit the conditions.
4. Click the underlined words in the Rule Description area to define the condition and the action.
5. In the Name Of The Rule box, enter a name for the rule as you want it to appear in the rules list and click OK.

News rules that you select on the News Rules tab of the Message Rules dialog box are applied automatically when Outlook Express downloads message headers and messages. You can turn off a rule by canceling the selection in the list.

You can apply a message rule manually at any time. For example, you might create a rule that deletes read messages with dates older than a given date. Rather than applying the rule automatically, you can apply it any time you want to clean out old messages.

Follow these steps to apply a rule manually:

1. Choose Tools, Message Rules, News.

2 Click Apply Now to display the Apply News Rules Now dialog box (see Figure 13-18).

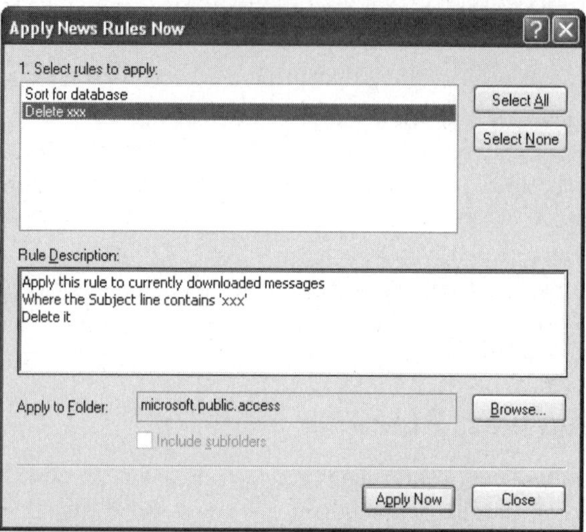

Figure 13-18. Select which rules to apply from the Apply News Rules Now dialog box.

3 Select the rules you want to apply.

4 Check the Apply To Folder box to determine whether the correct folder is displayed. If it isn't, click Browse and select it. Select the news server if you want to apply the rule to all messages that fit the conditions in all subscribed newsgroups.

5 Click Apply Now.

Working with Attachments

Internet newsgroups are a very popular means of sharing all sorts of files—from images to sound files to video clips. With Outlook Express, you can post newsgroup messages that include attachments. The following sections cover viewing, saving, and manipulating attachments to newsgroup messages.

Previewing Attachments

Outlook Express examines the attachment for a message when you preview the message and, if the file type is supported, includes the attachment in the preview pane. Click a message containing a JPEG attachment, for example, and Outlook Express shows the JPEG below the message in the preview pane. Regardless of whether Outlook Express can preview the attachment, it includes a paper clip icon in the preview pane header. Click the paper clip icon and select the attachment to open it.

Saving Attachments

To save one or more attachments to disk, you can click the paper clip icon and choose Save Attachments. You also can choose File, Save Attachments. In either case, Outlook Express prompts you for the location where the file should be saved.

Posting Messages with Attachments

Posting a message with an attachment is as easy as sending an e-mail message with an attachment. Just follow these steps:

1. Click New Post and compose your message.
2. Click the Attach button on the toolbar or choose Insert, File Attachment.
3. Locate and select the file and click Attach.
4. Post the message as you would any other.

Decoding Attachments

Most news servers impose a maximum size limit on messages, so certain types of messages—particularly those containing larger video clips—are often split into multiple messages. To read the message or view the attachment, you must recombine the multiple messages into one. To do so, select all the messages in the set after downloading them, and then choose Message, Combine And Decode.

Outlook Express displays a dialog box containing the messages and prompts you to arrange them in order. Typically, the messages' titles indicate their order. Use the Move Up and Move Down buttons to arrange them, with the first at the top of the list and the last at the bottom, and then click OK. Outlook Express combines and decodes the message and displays it in a separate window. Choose File, Save As to save the entire message to disk.

Archiving and Restoring Messages

Outlook Express doesn't provide an easy means for archiving and restoring messages, whether from newsgroups or e-mail. However, you can save messages to disk, move messages between Outlook Express installations, and retain your messages during a reinstallation of Outlook Express if it becomes necessary.

Archiving Messages

As it does with e-mail messages, Outlook Express stores messages and attachments not as individual files but collectively in folder files, one newsgroup per file. Because all messages are stored together, there is no easy way to archive groups of messages from within a newsgroup. However, you can save messages and attachments individually to keep an archive copy, which means you can save important messages and attachments outside Outlook Express.

To save a message, select the message in Outlook Express and choose File, Save As. Specify the path and file name for the message and click Save. By default, Outlook Express uses the message header name as the file name, but you can specify any name you like. To save attachments, select the message and choose File, Save Attachments. Specify a path for the attachments and click Save.

Archiving a Newsgroup

Although the Outlook Express interface doesn't provide a way to archive a newsgroup, you can archive a newsgroup manually by copying the newsgroup file to a backup location. For example, suppose that you want to archive all messages in a particular newsgroup as of the current date, clearing the newsgroup file to start with messages from that date.

Here's how to accomplish this without saving individual messages and attachments:

1. In Outlook Express, choose Tools, Options and click the Maintenance tab.
2. Click Store Folder and note the location of your Outlook Express message store (see Figure 13-19).

Figure 13-19. Note the location of your Outlook Express message store folder.

3. Click Ok to close Outlook Express.
4. Open the folder identified in step 2 and change the file extension for the newsgroup file you want to archive from DBX to something else, such as BAK.

> **Tip** You can move the file to a backup location, but you must move it back to the original folder if you want to use it later.

Start Outlook Express and open the archived newsgroup. Outlook Express re-creates the missing folder file by replacing it with an empty one and, depending on how you have configured the program, downloads the headers from the newsgroup but not the messages. How do you use the archived file? Unfortunately, it isn't an easy process. You need to change the file extension of the current newsgroup file, restore the DBX extension to the backup file, and then restart Outlook Express. When you open Outlook Express, you'll find the old message file in place, complete with downloaded messages and attachments.

> **Tip Archive newsgroup messages selectively**
> An alternative to this procedure is to copy individual newsgroup files or the entire contents of your Outlook Express store folder to a backup location and then delete messages from the current store. When you need to work with the archive copy, choose Tools, Options. Click the Maintenance tab, click Store Folder, and point Outlook Express to the archive location. Point it back to the original location when you're finished working with the archived messages.

Moving Your Message Store

You can move your Outlook Express message store, which is useful for archival purposes, as just explained; it's also useful when you want to move your newsgroups and messages from one computer to another or to a disk with more space.

Moving the message store is relatively easy:

1. Open Outlook Express and choose Tools, Options. Click the Maintenance tab and then click Store Folder to identify the current location of your store folder.
2. Close Outlook Express and copy the store folder to its new location.
3. Open Outlook Express and choose Tools, Options. Click the Maintenance tab, click Store Folder, and then click Change. (If you're moving your message store to a different computer, perform this step and step 4 on the computer to which you moved or copied your store file.)
4. Select the new location and click OK. Outlook Express informs you that the specified location already includes a store and asks whether you want to use that store. Click Yes.

Retaining Accounts and Messages During a Reinstallation

Although it doesn't happen often, you might occasionally need to reinstall Outlook Express. Or perhaps you're moving to a new computer and want to retain your accounts and messages.

Retaining Accounts

The easiest way to retain accounts during a reinstallation or move is to make a backup copy of the appropriate registry key before installation and then restore the key after you reinstall Outlook Express (or move to another computer):

1. Close Outlook Express and click Start, Run. Type **regedit** and click OK.
2. In the Registry Editor, open the branch HKEY_CURRENT_USER\Software\Microsoft\Internet Account Manager.
3. Choose Registry, Export Registry File.
4. Specify a file name and path, verify that the Selected Branch option is selected, and click Save.

5. On the system to which you are moving Outlook Express, or after performing a reinstallation, double-click the REG file created in step 4 to add the registry settings to your registry.
6. Open Outlook Express and verify that your accounts are working.

Retaining Messages

You can retain existing newsgroups and messages by copying your entire message store to the other computer or, in the case of reinstalling Outlook Express, backing it up and then restoring the message store:

1. Open Outlook Express and choose Tools, Options. Click the Maintenance tab and then click Store Folder to identify the current location of your store folder.
2. Close Outlook Express and, if you're moving to a different computer, copy the store folder to its new location. If you're preparing to reinstall Outlook Express, copy the store folder to a backup location.
3. Install or reinstall Outlook Express, and then open Outlook Express. Use the Maintenance tab to locate your current store, as you did in step 1.
4. Close Outlook Express, copy your backup store in the location determined in step 2, and then restart Outlook Express.

Part 3

Contact Management

Chapter 14

Managing Your Contacts

The Contacts folder in Microsoft Outlook 2003 is an electronic tool that can organize and store the thousands of details you need to know to communicate with people, businesses, and organizations. Use the Contacts folder to store e-mail addresses, street addresses, multiple phone numbers, and any other information that relates to a contact, such as a birthday or an anniversary date.

From a contact entry in your list of contacts, you can click a button or choose a command to have Outlook address a meeting request, an e-mail message, a letter, or a task request to the contact. If you have a modem, you can have Outlook dial the contact's phone number. You can link any Outlook item or Microsoft Office document to a contact to help you track activities associated with the contact.

Outlook allows you to customize the view in the Contacts folder to review and print your contact information. You can sort, group, or filter your contacts list to better manage the information or to quickly find entries.

Outlook 2003 integrates well with Windows SharePoint Services (WSS) and SharePoint Portal Server, both of which provide the means for users to share documents, contacts, messages, and other items through a Web-based interface. You can import contacts from Outlook to a WSS site, or vice versa.

Outlook also supports the use of vCards, the Internet standard for creating and sharing virtual business cards. You can save a contact entry as a vCard and send it in an e-mail message. You can also add a vCard to your e-mail signature.

This chapter introduces Outlook's contact management ability. Outlook's Contacts feature provides powerful tools to help you manage, organize, and find important contact information.

Working with the Contacts Folder

The Contacts folder is one of Outlook's default folders. This folder stores information such as name, physical address, phone number, and e-mail address for each contact. You can use the Contacts folder to quickly address e-mail messages, place phone calls, distribute bulk mailings through mail merge (in Microsoft Word), and perform many other communication tasks.

The Contacts folder is not, however, the same as your address book. Your Outlook Address Book (OAB) lets you access the Contacts folder for addressing messages, but the OAB also lets you access addresses stored in personal address books and Microsoft Exchange Server address lists.

For detailed information about working with address books in Outlook, see Chapter 5, "Managing Address Books and Distribution Lists."

You can open the Contacts folder either by clicking the Contacts button in the navigation pane or by opening the folder list and clicking Contacts. When you open the folder, you'll see its default view, Address Cards, which displays contact entries as address cards that show name, address, phone number, and a handful of other items for each contact (see Figure 14-1). Outlook provides seven predefined views for the Contacts folder that offer different ways to display and sort the contacts list.

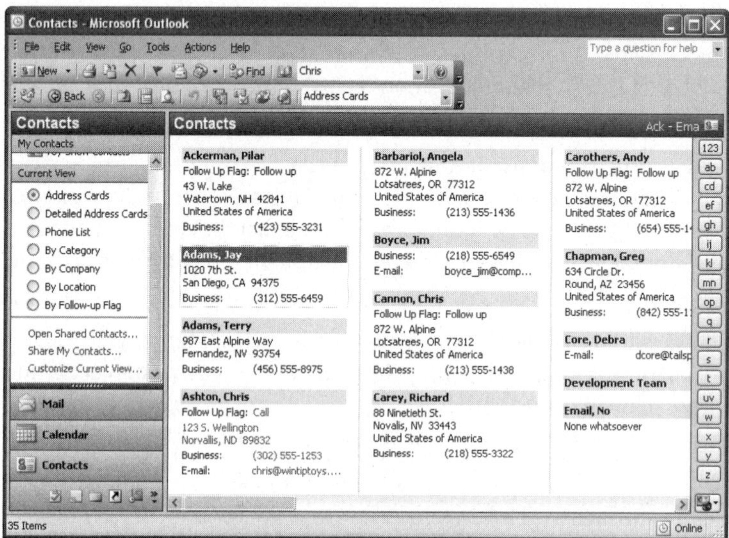

Figure 14-1. Use the Contacts folder to manage contact information such as address, phone number, and fax number for your business associates and friends.

For details about the available views in the Contacts folder and how to work with them, see "Viewing Contacts," page 407.

Tip You can use the button bar at the right of the folder (see Figure 14-1) to quickly jump to a specific area in the Contacts folder. For example, click the MN button to jump to the list of contacts whose names begin with M.

When you double-click a contact entry in the Contacts folder, Outlook opens a contact form similar to the one shown in Figure 14-2. This multitabbed form lets you view and modify a wealth of information about the person.You also can initiate actions related to the contact.

For example, you can click the AutoDialer button on the form's toolbar to dial the contact's phone number. You'll learn more about these tasks throughout the remainder of this chapter. The following section explains how to create a contact entry and also introduces the tabs on the contact form to help you understand the types of information you can store.

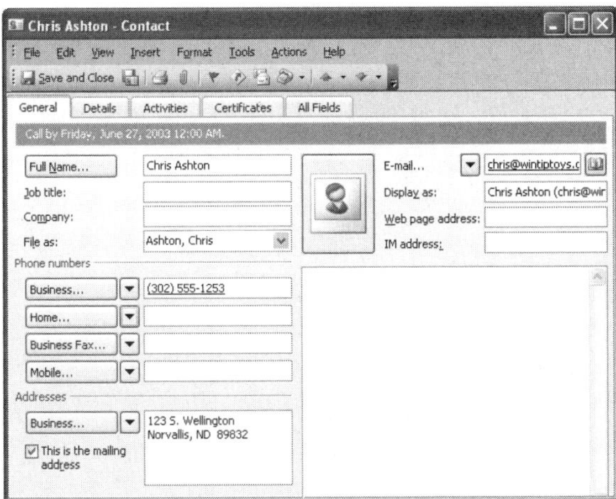

Figure 14-2. The General tab of a contact form shows address, phone, and other information about the contact.

Creating a Contact Entry

To create a contact entry, you can start from scratch, or you can base the new entry on a similar, existing entry—for example, the entry for a contact from the same company.

You can open a contact form and create a new entry from scratch in any of the following ways:

- Choose File, New, Contact.
- Right-click a blank area in the Contacts folder (not a contact entry), and choose New Contact.
- With the Contacts folder open, press Ctrl+N.
- If the Contacts folder is not open, click the arrow beside the New button on the toolbar and choose Contact.

When the contact form opens, type the contact's name in the Full Name box and enter all the other information you want to include for the contact, switching tabs as needed. To save the entry, click Save And Close.

Filling in the information on the contact form is a fairly straightforward process. You might find a few of the features especially useful. For example, the File As drop-down list allows you to specify how you want the contact to be listed in the Contacts folder. You can choose to list the contact under his or her own name in either Last Name, First Name format or First Name Last Name format; to list the contact by company name rather than personal name; or to use a combination of contact name and company name.

You can also store more phone numbers in the contact entry than the four that are displayed on the form. When you click the drop-down button by a phone number entry (see Figure 14-3), you see a list of possible phone numbers from which you can select a number to view or modify; the checked items on the list are those that currently contain information. When you select a number, Outlook shows it on the form.

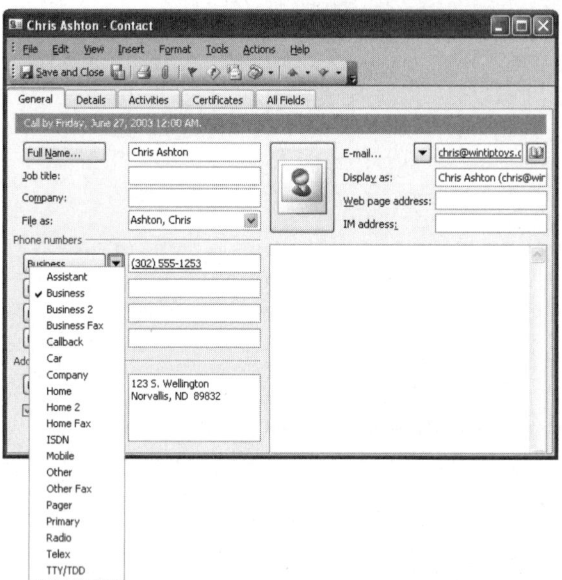

Figure 14-3. You can store multiple phone numbers for a contact, but only four appear on the form at one time.

In addition to storing multiple phone numbers for a contact, you also can store multiple physical addresses. Click the drop-down button under the Address button on the form to select a business, home, or other address. The E-Mail box can also store multiple data items; click the drop-down button to choose one of three e-mail addresses for the individual. For example, you might list both business and personal addresses as well as an HTTP-based address (such as a Microsoft Hotmail address) for the contact. The Details tab of the contact form (see Figure 14-4) lets you add other information, such as the contact's department, office number, birthday, and anniversary. The Online NetMeeting Settings area of the form lets you specify the default directory server to use when establishing a Microsoft NetMeeting session with the contact and the e-mail alias that NetMeeting uses to locate the contact. You can click Call Now to open NetMeeting and start a session with the contact.

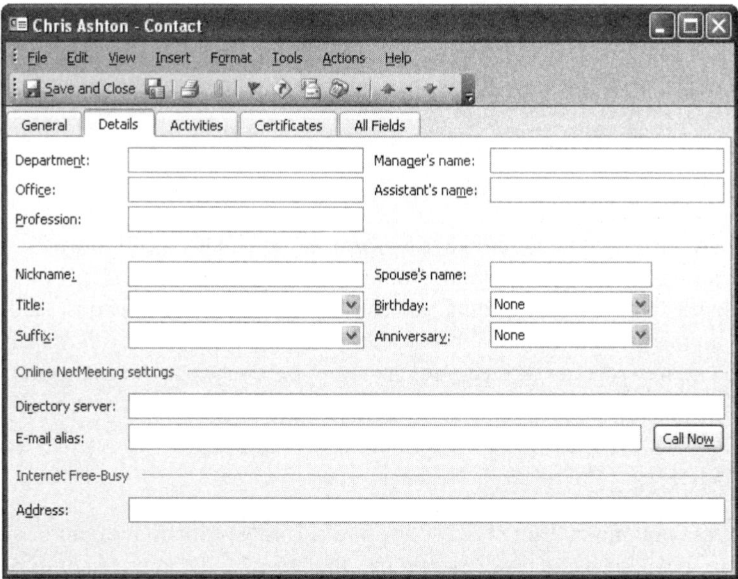

Figure 14-4. The Details tab stores additional information—both business and personal—about the contact.

For detailed information on configuring and using NetMeeting, see "Holding an Online Meeting," page 571.

The Activities tab of the contact form is useful for locating e-mail messages, logged phone calls, and other items or activities associated with a specific contact. For information about using the Activities tab, see "Associating a Contact with Other Items and Documents," page 392.

Tip **Add contacts quickly**

When you use one of the table views (such as Phone List) to display your Contacts folder, you'll see a row at the top of the list labeled Click Here To Add A New Contact. This is a handy way to enter a contact's name and phone number quickly—simply type the information directly in the row, and Outlook adds the contact entry to the folder.

Creating Contact Entries from the Same Company

If you have several contacts who work for the same company, you can use an existing contact entry to create a new entry. Simply open the existing entry and choose Actions, New Contact From Same Company. Outlook opens a new contact form with all the company information (name, address, and phone numbers) supplied—all you have to do is fill in the personal details for that individual.

Note You can also use a template to create multiple contact entries that share common data such as company affiliation. For information about working with templates in Outlook, see Chapter 23, "Using Templates."

Creating a Contact Entry from an E-Mail Message

When you receive an e-mail message from someone you'd like to add to your contacts list, you can create a contact entry directly from the message. In the From box of the message form or on the InfoBar of the reading pane, right-click the name and choose Add To Outlook Contacts on the shortcut menu. Outlook opens a new contact form with the sender's name and e-mail address already entered. Add any other necessary data for the contact, and click Save And Close to create the entry.

Copying an Existing Contact Entry

In some cases, you might want to create a copy of a contact entry. For example, although you can keep both personal and business data in a single entry, you might want to store the data separately. You can save time by copying the existing entry rather than creating a new one from scratch.

To copy a contact entry in the Contacts folder, right-drag the entry to an empty spot in the folder and choose Copy. Outlook creates a new entry containing all the same information as the original. You also can copy contact information to another folder. Open the folder where the contact entry is stored, and then locate the destination folder on the navigation pane or in the folder list. Right-drag the contact entry to the destination folder and choose Copy from the shortcut menu.

Creating Other Contacts Folders

In addition to providing its default Contacts folder, Outlook allows you to use multiple contacts folders to organize your contacts easily. For example, you might use a shared contacts folder jointly with members of your workgroup for business contacts and keep your personal contacts in a separate folder. Or you might prefer to keep contact information you use infrequently in a separate folder to reduce the clutter in your main Contacts folder. The process of creating a contact entry in any contacts folder is the same regardless of the folder's location—whether it is part of your Exchange Server account or in a personal folders (PST) file, for example.

You can create six types of folders in Outlook, each designed to hold a specific type of data. A Contact Items folder stores contacts.

To create a new folder for storing contacts, follow these steps:

1. Choose File, New, Folder. Alternatively, you can right-click the folder list and choose New Folder to open the Create New Folder dialog box (see Figure 14-5).

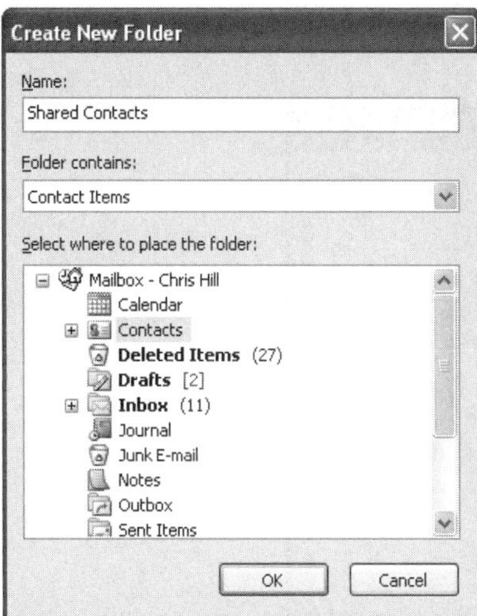

Figure 14-5. Use the Create New Folder dialog box to create new Outlook folders.

2. In the Name box, type a name for the folder. This is the folder name that will be displayed in Outlook (on the navigation pane and in the folder list, for example).
3. Select Contact Items in the Folder Contains drop-down list.
4. In the Select Where To Place The Folder list, select the location for the new folder.
5. Click OK.

When you create a new contacts folder using this method, Outlook sets up the folder using default properties for permissions, rules, description, forms, and views. If you want to create a new contacts folder that uses the same custom properties as an existing folder, you can copy the folder design, as explained in the following section.

Copying the Design of a Folder

Another way to set up a new contacts folder is to copy the design of an existing contacts folder to the new one. Folder design properties include permissions, rules, description, forms, and views.

Note You can copy a folder design as described here only for folders that are contained in an Exchange Server mailbox.

For information about various folder properties, see "Setting Folder Properties," page 760.

To copy the design of an existing contacts folder, follow these steps:

1. In the folder list, click the contacts folder to which you want to copy the folder properties.
2. Choose File, Folder, Copy Folder Design.

3. In the Copy Design From dialog box (see Figure 14-6), click the folder with the design you want to copy.

Figure 14-6. In the Copy Design From dialog box, select the folder with the design you want to copy.

4. In the Copy Design Of area, select the specific properties you want to copy.
5. Click OK. An Outlook prompt warns you that the existing properties of the current folder will be replaced with properties from the source folder. Click Yes to perform the copy or click No to cancel.

Copying a folder's properties this way does not copy the contents of the folder—it copies only the selected properties. It is also different from copying the folder itself, which copies the contents of the folder to a new location.

For more information about copying folders, see "Copying and Moving a Folder," page 758.

Working with Contacts

You can do much more with your Outlook contacts list than just viewing address and phone information. Outlook provides a set of tools that make it easy to phone, write, e-mail, or communicate with contacts in other ways. This section of the chapter explains these tools.

Associating a Contact with Other Items and Documents

As you work with contacts, it's useful to have e-mail messages, appointments, tasks, documents, or other items related to the contact at your fingertips. You can relate items to a contact by creating links. For example, if you create a task to call several of your contacts, you can use the Contacts button on the task form to link the task to those contacts: click Contacts on the task form, and then select the contacts in the resulting Select Contacts dialog box (see Figure 14-7).

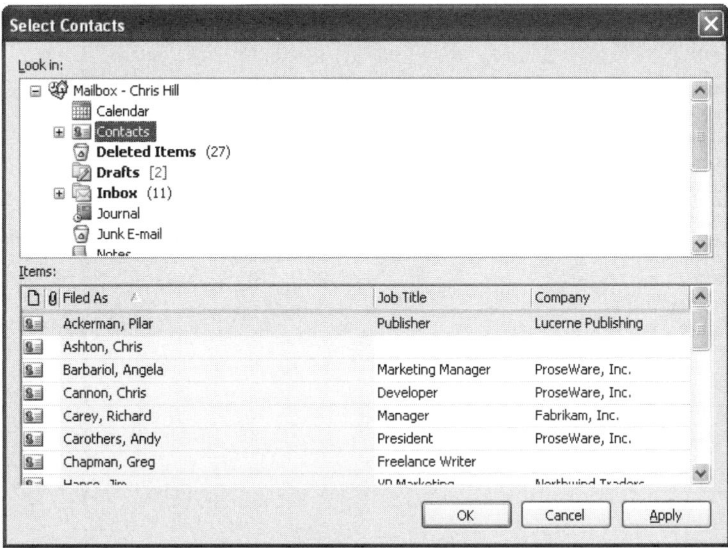

Figure 14-7. Use the Select Contacts dialog box to associate contacts with a task.

For details on setting up tasks, see "Creating a Task," page 584.

E-mail messages that you send to a contact are automatically linked to that contact and show up on the Activities tab of the contact form (discussed shortly). In addition, most items you create using the Actions menu are automatically linked to the contact entry and appear on the Activities tab. For example, if you choose Actions, New Task For Contact to create a new task for a contact, Outlook links the task to the contact.

Troubleshooting

Creating a new letter doesn't create a contact link

If you choose Actions, New Letter To Contact, Outlook starts a new letter to the contact but does not link the document to that contact item. You can work around the problem by manually linking the document and the contact item. For details on creating the link, see "Linking a Contact to a Document," page 395.

The Activities tab of any contact form displays all the items related to that contact, as shown in Figure 14-8. Outlook searches for links to items in the main Outlook folders, including Contacts, e-mail (Inbox and other message folders), Journal, Notes, Tasks, and Calendar.

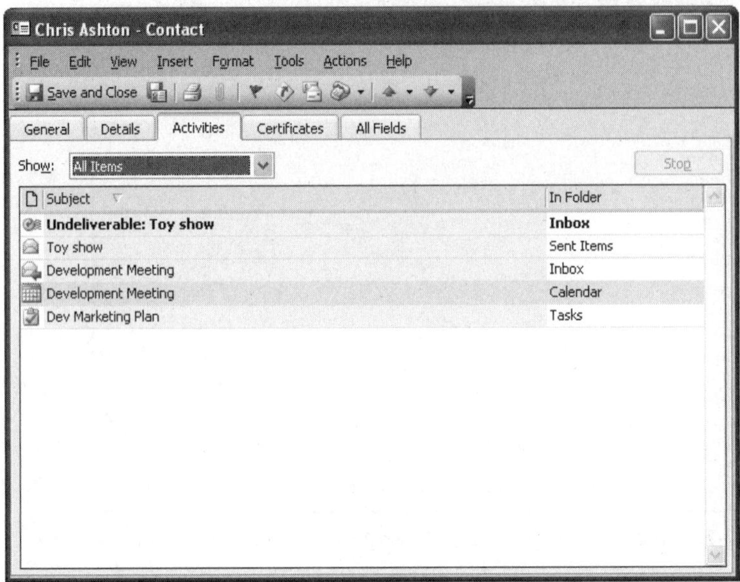

Figure 14-8. The Activities tab shows all items linked to the contact.

> **Tip** **Open linked contacts**
> You can open a contact item from within another item linked to it by double-clicking the contact name in the Contacts box on the other item's form. For example, if you have linked an appointment to a contact, you can open the contact item by double-clicking the contact name shown on the appointment form.

What good is the Activities tab? It's extremely useful for finding items associated with a specific contact. For example, you could sort the Inbox by sender to locate an e-mail message from a particular person, or you could use the Activities tab in his or her contact form to achieve the same result. You could also view a list of the tasks assigned to an individual by checking the Activities tab. Although you can view these associations in other folders, the Activities tab not only offers an easier way to view the links but also lets you see all linked items, not just specific types of items.

Linking a Contact to Existing Outlook Items

As mentioned previously, Outlook automatically links contacts to most Outlook items if you create the item using the Actions menu. For those items that aren't linked automatically, you can create the link manually. For example, you might want to create a link from a contact entry to a message that did not come from the contact.

To link a contact entry to an existing Outlook item, such as a task or an appointment, follow these steps:

1. Select or open the contact entry.
2. Choose Actions, Link, Items to display the Link Items To Contact dialog box (see Figure 14-9).

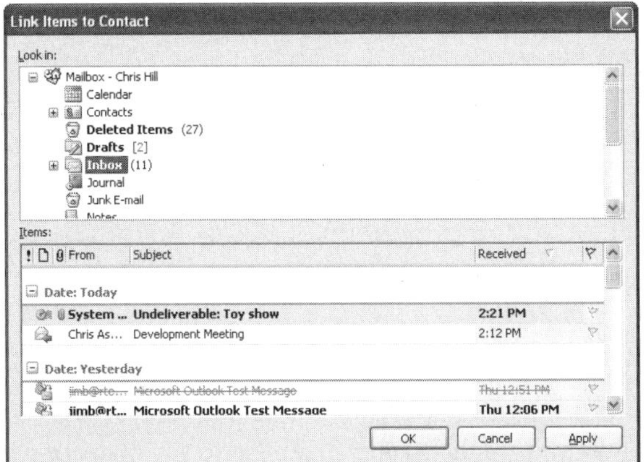

Figure 14-9. Use the Link Items To Contact dialog box to set up a link.

3. In the Look In list, select the folder that contains the item you want to link to the contact.
4. In the Items list, select the specific items you want to link to the contact.
5. Click OK to create the links.

Linking a Contact to a Document

In many cases, you might want to create a link between a contact and one or more documents. For example, assume that you manage contracts for several individuals or companies. You can create a link from a contract document to the contact covered by the contract to make it easier to open the document from the contact form. With this link, you don't need to remember the document name if you know the name of the contact with whom it is associated. Follow these steps to create a link between a document and a contact:

1. Open the Contacts folder, right-click the contact item, and choose Link, File to display the Choose A File dialog box (a standard file selection dialog box).
2. Locate the files you want to associate with the contact and click Insert.
3. Outlook opens a new journal entry form with a link to the document inserted in the item. Click Save And Close to create the link.

When you want to open the document, open the contact form and click the Activities tab. Locate the linked document and double-click it to open the journal entry. Then double-click the document shortcut to open the document.

Linking a Contact to a New Message

When you send an e-mail message to a contact, Outlook automatically links that message to the contact. However, you can also link a message to a contact even if that person is not one of the recipients of the message. For example, every time you send a message regarding a particular client to your sales staff, you can associate the message with the client's contact entry.

Here's how to establish the link:

1. Create a new e-mail message.
2. Click Options on the message form, and then click Contacts to display the Select Contacts dialog box.
3. Select the name of the person to whom the message should be linked and click OK.
4. Click Close to return to the message form.
5. Complete the message and send it.

Removing a Link

Occasionally you'll want to remove a link between a contact and another item. For example, perhaps you've accidentally linked the wrong document to a contact, or perhaps the contact who had been associated with a particular project has taken a different job.

To remove a link from a contact to an item, follow these steps:

1. Open the contact item and click the Activities tab.
2. Double-click the link to the item you want to remove.
   - If the linked item is an e-mail message, choose View, Options. In the Contacts box, select the linked contact and press Delete.
   - For any other type of linked item, open the item and delete the contact name from the Contacts box at the bottom of the form.

Note Although you can remove the contact association in a task, doing so removes the task from the contact's Activities tab only if the task is assigned to someone other than the linked contact. If the contact owns the task, the task continues to be listed on the Activities tab even after the task is marked as completed.

Assigning Categories to Contacts

A *category* is a keyword or a phrase that helps you keep track of items so that you can easily find, sort, filter, or group them. Use categories to keep track of different types of items that are related but stored in different folders. For example, you can keep track of all the meetings, contacts, and messages for a specific project when you create a category named after the project and assign items to it.

Categories also give you a way to keep track of contacts without putting them in separate folders. For example, you can keep business and personal contacts in the same contacts folder and use the Business and Personal categories to sort the two sets of contacts into separate groups.

One quick way to assign categories to a contact is to right-click the contact item and choose Categories. Then, in the Categories dialog box, you can select the check boxes next to the categories you want to assign to the contact. Alternatively, you can open the contact item and click the Categories button on the contact form to open the Categories dialog box. This dialog box is useful not only for assigning categories but also for reviewing the categories you've already assigned to an item.

For more information about how to assign a category to a contact; how to use categories to sort, filter, and group contact items; and how to create your own categories, see Chapter 4, "Using Categories and Types."

Resolving Duplicate Contacts

If you create a contact entry using the same name or e-mail address as an entry that already exists in your Contacts folder, Outlook displays a dialog box in which you can choose to either add the new contact entry or update your existing entry with the new information (see Figure 14-10).

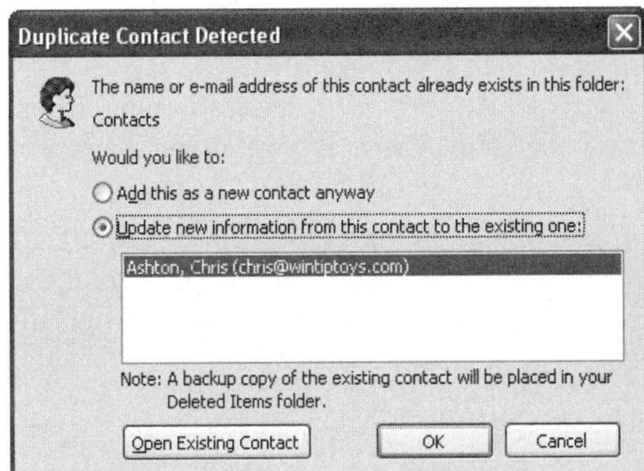

Figure 14-10. Use the Duplicate Contact Detected dialog box to tell Outlook how to handle a duplicate contact.

If you select the first option, Outlook adds the new contact to your Contacts folder, and you'll now have two entries listed under the same name or e-mail address. In that case, you'll probably want to add some additional information to the contact forms—perhaps company affiliation or a middle initial—to distinguish the two entries.

If you select the second option, to update the existing entry with information from the new one, Outlook compares the fields containing data in both entries and copies the data from the new entry into any fields that have conflicting data. For example, if you have a contact named Chris Ashton whose phone number is 555-5655, and you create a new contact entry for Chris Ashton with a new phone number, Outlook copies the new number into the existing entry and leaves the other fields the same.

Not all data is simply copied, however. Outlook does not copy any categories you've assigned to the new entry or any text that appears in the message box of the new entry. If you want to copy data from these fields from a new entry into an existing entry, you must copy that data manually. Likewise, if you've added links to items other than contacts on the Activities tab of the new contact form (links to tasks or appointments, for example), Outlook does not copy them. Certificates and links to contacts on the Activities tab are copied from the new entry and added to the existing entry without replacing the original information.

In case you need to revert to the information in the original contact entry, a copy of the original entry is stored in your Deleted Items folder whenever Outlook copies new data.

Note If you are adding many contacts, Outlook can save the information faster if you do not require the program to detect duplicates. To turn off duplicate detection, choose Tools, Options. Click Contact Options, and clear the Check For Duplicate Contacts check box.

Phoning a Contact

If you have a modem, you can use Outlook to dial any phone number you specify, including phone numbers for contacts in your contacts list. Before Outlook can make phone calls for you, however, you must set up your computer and a modem for automatic phone dialing.

To set up automatic dialing, follow these steps:

1. Install a modem through Control Panel, and verify that the modem works. (Dial your Internet service provider or use the Phone Dialer application on the Accessories menu to dial a number.)
2. Open the Phone And Modem Options icon in Control Panel, and use the Dialing Rules tab to specify your area code and other dialing properties so that Outlook will know how to dial the phone numbers (what number to dial for an outside line, whether to use a credit card to dial, and other dialing properties).

To make a phone call to a contact using Outlook, follow these steps:

1. Open the Contacts folder.
2. Right-click a contact item and choose Call Contact to open the New Call dialog box with the contact's phone number already entered (see Figure 14-11).

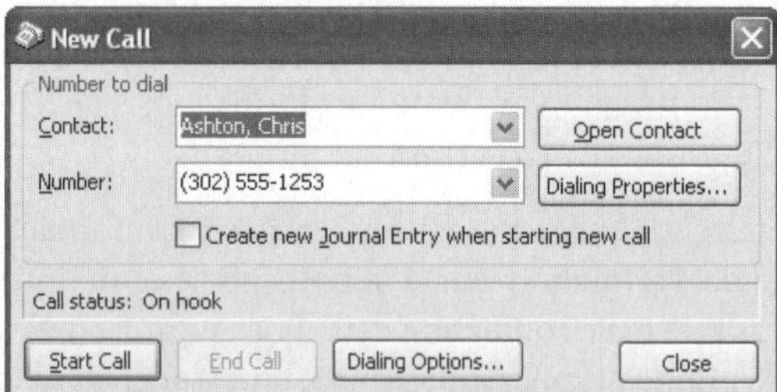

Figure 14-11. Select the number to call and other options in the New Call dialog box.

- If you want Outlook to use a phone number associated with a different contact, type the contact's name in the Contact box and press Tab or click in the Number box. Alternatively, you can simply enter the phone number in the Number box.
- If the contact entry for the person you're calling already includes phone numbers, select the phone number in the Number box. If the contact entry doesn't specify a phone number, type the number in the Number box.

3 To keep a record of the call in the journal, select the Create New Journal Entry When Starting New Call check box. If you select this check box, a journal entry opens with the timer running after you start the call.You can type notes in the text box of the journal entry while you talk.

4 Click Start Call.

5 Pick up the phone handset and click Talk.

6 If you created a journal entry for the call, click Pause Timer to stop the clock when you've finished the call. Then click Save And Close.

7 Click End Call and hang up the phone.

Tip **Keep track of phone calls**
If you want to time a call and type notes in Outlook while you talk, you can create a journal entry for the call as you dial. The journal entry form contains a timer that you can start and stop and also provides space to type notes. For example, you might want to use this option if you bill clients for time spent on phone conversations. For more information about using the journal for phone calls, see Chapter 18, "Keeping a Journal."

Note If you omit the country code and area code from a phone number, the automatic phone dialer uses settings from the Dialing Properties dialog box, which you can access through the Phone And Modem icon in Control Panel or by clicking Dialing Properties in the New Call dialog box. If you include letters in the phone number, the automatic phone dialer does not recognize them.

Setting Up Speed Dial Entries

If you make frequent calls to particular phone numbers, you can create a speed dial list of those phone numbers and quickly make calls from the list. Before you become enamored with the idea of Outlook's speed dialing feature, however, you should understand that it suffers from a bug that renders it only moderately useful. Although you can add names and numbers to the speed dial list, Outlook keeps only the numbers and loses the names. If you remember who a particular number belongs to, this isn't a problem. However, if you have more than a few numbers on the list, the speed dial feature won't do you much good.

Follow these steps to create entries in the speed dial list:

1 Open the Contacts folder and choose Actions, Call Contact, New Call to open the New Call dialog box.

2 Click Dialing Options to display the Dialing Options dialog box (see Figure 14-12).

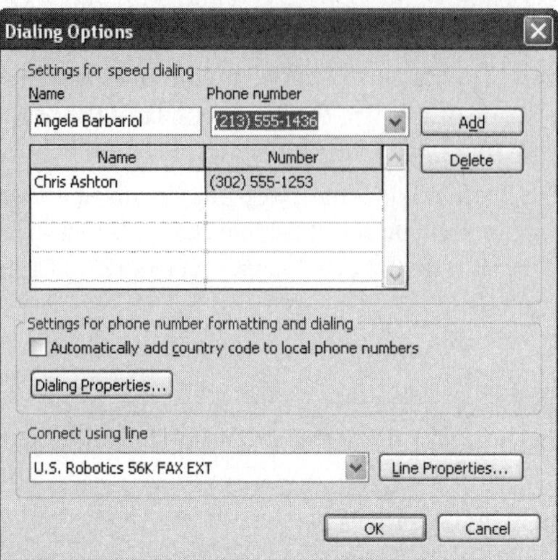

Figure 14-12. Use the Dialing Options dialog box to add speed dial numbers.

3 If the person's contact information is stored in the Contacts folder, type the name in the Name box and press Tab to move to the Phone Number box, where Outlook automatically fills in the phone number from the contact entry. If you need to use a different number, select it from the drop-down list or type the number in the Phone Number box.

4 Click Add to add the entry to the speed dial list.

5 Repeat these steps to add other numbers as needed and then click OK.

6 Click Close to close the New Call dialog box.

Redialing Recently Dialed Numbers

In addition to using the speed dial list, you also can select a phone number from a list of numbers you've recently dialed. To do so, choose Actions, Call Contact, Redial and select the number you want to dial from the menu.

Sending an E-Mail Message to a Contact

If you're working in the Contacts folder, you can send an e-mail message to one of your contacts without switching to the Inbox folder. This is a handy feature that can save a lot of time in an average work day.

Here's how to send a message from the Contacts folder:

1 In the Contacts folder, select the contact item and choose Actions, New Message To Contact. Or simply right-click the contact and choose New Message To Contact.

2 In the Subject box, type the subject of the message.

3. In the message body, type the message.
4. Click Send.

Sending a Letter to a Contact

Although it's a digital world, you still occasionally need to send a paper letter through the mail. However, you can use Outlook technology to make it easier. Rather than retyping a contact's information in a Word document when you need to write a letter, use the data from the Contacts folder and let Outlook enter that data for you.

Follow these steps to use contact information in a Word letter:

1. Open the Contacts folder.
2. Select the contact item for the person to whom you're writing the letter.
3. Choose Actions, New Letter To Contact.
4. Follow the instructions in the Letter Wizard in Word to create the letter.

Connecting to a Contact's Web Site

It seems everyone has a Web site these days, whether it's a company's site or a collection of family photos. If you have the URL for a contact's Web page recorded in the contact entry, you can connect to that site directly from Outlook. This is particularly handy for linking to business sites from a company contact entry—for example, you might create a link to the company's support or sales page. Associating Web sites with contacts is often more meaningful than simply storing a URL in your Favorites folder.

With the Contacts folder and the contact item open, you can connect to the contact's Web site by performing one of the following actions:

- Choose Actions, Explore Web Page.
- Press Ctrl+Shift+X.
- Click the hyperlink that appears in the Web Page Address box in the contact entry.

Scheduling Appointments and Meetings with Contacts

Many Outlook users believe that the Calendar folder is the only place you can easily schedule a new appointment or meeting, but that's not the case. You can schedule an appointment or a meeting in any Outlook folder. The Contacts folder, however, is a logical place to create new appointments and meetings because those events are often associated with one or more contacts stored in the Contacts folder.

Scheduling an Appointment with a Contact

In Outlook, an appointment involves only your schedule and time, whereas a meeting involves inviting others and coordinating their schedules. Also, when you set up a meeting,

Outlook generates a meeting request, which it doesn't do for an appointment. In most other respects, appointments and meetings are the same.

Although you can schedule an appointment in the Calendar folder, you might prefer to schedule it from the Contacts folder instead. The primary advantage is that you don't have to leave the Contacts folder to create the appointment. Outlook automatically adds the contact to the Contacts box on the appointment form.

To schedule an appointment with one of your contacts, follow these steps:

1. In the Contacts folder, open the contact item for the person with whom you want to schedule the appointment and choose Actions, New Appointment With Contact. Or simply right-click the contact and choose New Appointment With Contact.
2. Enter any applicable information on the appointment form, such as subject, location, or time.
3. Click Save And Close to create the appointment.

Note Using this method to schedule an appointment with a contact places the appointment on your calendar. It does not notify the contact of the appointment.

For details about setting up appointments, see Chapter 19, "Scheduling Appointments."

Scheduling a Meeting with a Contact

As mentioned previously, meetings differ from appointments in that they are collaborative efforts that involve the schedules of all the attendees. When you set up a meeting, Outlook creates and sends meeting requests to the individuals you want to invite. You can create meeting requests for any number of contacts through the Contacts folder, saving the time of switching folders.

To send a meeting request to one or more of your contacts from the Contacts folder, follow these steps:

1. Open the Contacts folder and select the contact entries for those people you want to invite to the meeting. (To select multiple entries, hold down the Ctrl key and click the entries.)
2. Choose Actions, New Meeting Request To Contact.
3. In the Subject box, type a description of the proposed meeting.
4. In the Location box, enter the location.
5. Enter the proposed start and end times for the meeting.
6. Select any other options you want.
7. Click Send.

For details about setting up meetings and sending meeting requests, see Chapter 20, "Scheduling Meetings and Resources."

Assigning a Task to a Contact

The Tasks folder in Outlook offers a handy way to keep track of your work and the work you delegate to others. For example, if you manage a group of people, you probably use the Tasks folder to assign tasks to the people who work for you. However, if you need to assign a job to one of your contacts, you can do this directly from the Contacts folder. Doing so adds the contact's name to the Contacts box in the task request.

Follow these steps to assign a task to a contact:

1. In the Contacts folder, open the contact item and then choose Actions, New Task For Contact. Or simply right-click the contact and choose New Task For Contact.
2. Outlook opens a new task form. Enter the subject and other information about the task and then click Assign Task. Outlook adds the contact's e-mail address in the To box.
3. Click Send to send the task request.

Flagging a Contact for Follow-Up

You can flag a contact item for follow-up to have Outlook remind you to call or e-mail the contact. For example, suppose that you want to make a note to yourself to call a colleague at 10:00 A.M. tomorrow to ask about the status of a project. You could create a note in the Notes folder, create a task, or add an appointment to your schedule—but an easy way to create the reminder is to add a follow-up flag to the contact entry in the Contacts folder. Flagging a contact item adds an additional field to the contact data. The flag appears in the contacts list (see Figure 14-13) and shows up as a message on the contact form (see Figure 14-14). You can also organize the view in the Contacts folder to show contacts sorted by flag: choose View, Current View, By Follow-Up Flag.

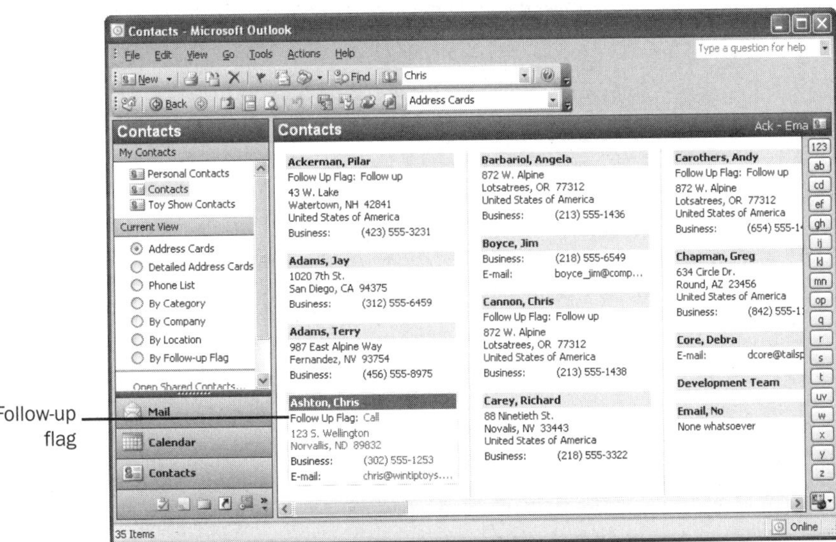

Figure 14-13. The follow-up flag appears in the contacts list.

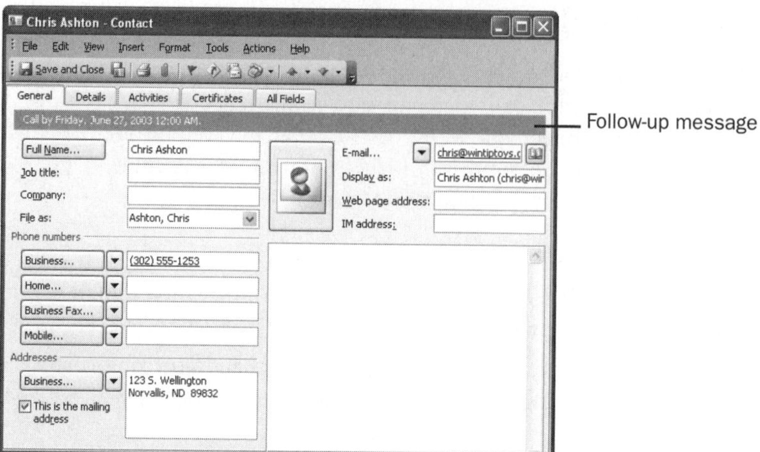

Figure 14-14. Outlook displays a message on the contact form indicating that a follow-up is needed for the contact.

If you specify a particular date and time for follow-up when you add the flag, Outlook generates a reminder at the appointed time. Adding a reminder helps ensure that you don't forget to follow up with the contact at the appropriate time.

Follow these steps to flag a contact for follow-up:

1. In the Contacts folder, select the contact item you want to flag and choose Actions, Follow Up. Or right-click the contact and choose Follow Up.
2. In the Flag To box of the Flag For Follow Up dialog box (see Figure 14-15), select the type of flag you want Outlook to use or type your own.

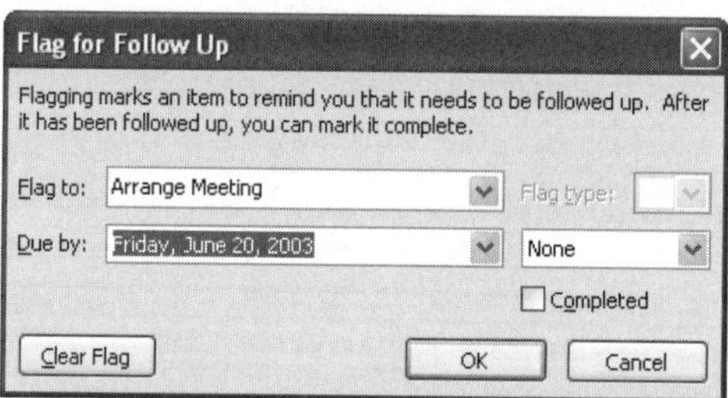

Figure 14-15. Use the Flag For Follow Up dialog box to specify the flag text and set an optional reminder.

3. Enter a date in the Due By box, and select a time in the drop-down list if you want Outlook to generate a reminder for the follow-up.
4. Click OK. Outlook adds the flag text to the contact item, as shown in Figure 14-13.

> **Tip** You can flag a contact item in any view by right-clicking it and choosing Follow Up.

When you have completed your follow-up action, you can remove the flag from the contact item (clear the flag) or mark the follow-up as completed. If you clear the flag, Outlook removes it from the contact item. If you prefer to have the flag remain, you can mark the follow-up as completed. In this case, the flag remains but the contact form includes a message indicating that the follow-up was accomplished (and the date). When you choose View, Arrange By, Current View, By Follow-Up Flag to view the Contacts folder sorted by flag, the completed items are grouped together. Use one of the following methods to mark a follow-up flag as completed:

- Select the flagged contact item, choose Actions, Follow Up, and select the Completed check box.
- Right-click the contact item and choose Flag Complete.

Use one of the following methods to clear a flag, which removes it from the contact item:

- Right-click the contact item in the Contacts folder and choose Clear Flag.
- Select the contact item, choose Actions, Follow Up, and click Clear Flag in the Flag For Follow Up dialog box.

Finding Contacts

If you store only a small list of contacts, finding a particular one is usually not a problem. As the number of contacts grows, however, it becomes more and more difficult to locate information, especially if you aren't sure about a name. For example, you might remember that a person works for a certain company but can't recall the person's name. Outlook provides a handful of features to help you quickly and easily locate contact information.

Perhaps the easiest method of locating a contact if you know the name is to type the name in the Find A Contact box on Outlook's Standard toolbar and then press Enter. Outlook locates the contact and displays the contact form. If more than one contact matches the data you've entered, Outlook displays a dialog box listing all the matches to allow you to select the appropriate one (see Figure 14-16).

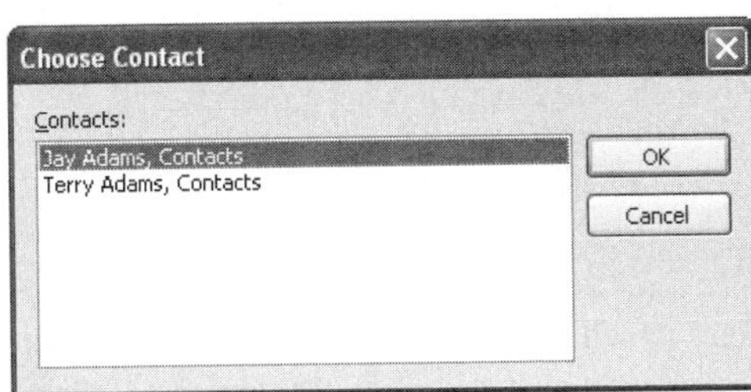

Figure 14-16. Use the Choose Contact dialog box to select the correct contact after a search.

You also can choose Tools, Find, Find to open a Find Bar above the Contacts folder, as shown in Figure 14-17. You can use this Find Bar to locate other information in addition to contacts (such as e-mail messages or tasks).

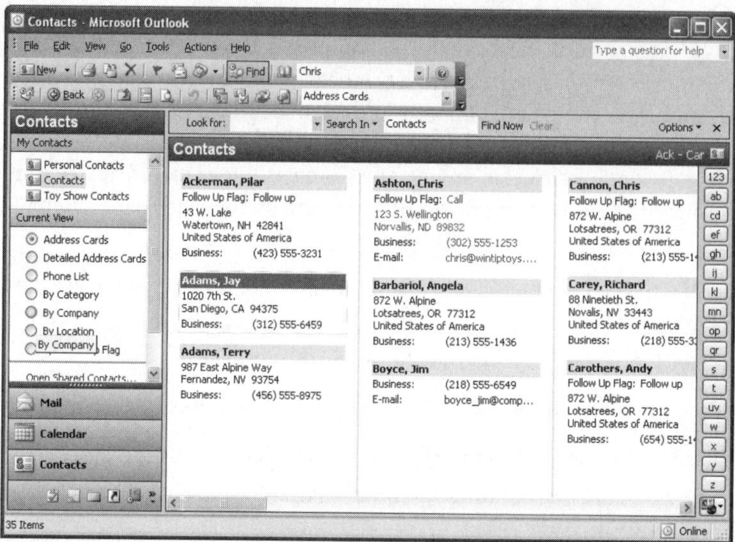

Figure 14-17. Use the Find Bar to locate contacts and other information in Outlook.

> **Tip** Choose Tools, Find a second time to close the Find Bar.

Finally, if you need to perform an advanced search, choose Tools, Advanced Find to open the Advanced Find dialog box (see Figure 14-18). You can use this dialog box to perform more complex searches based on multiple conditions, such as searching for both name and company.

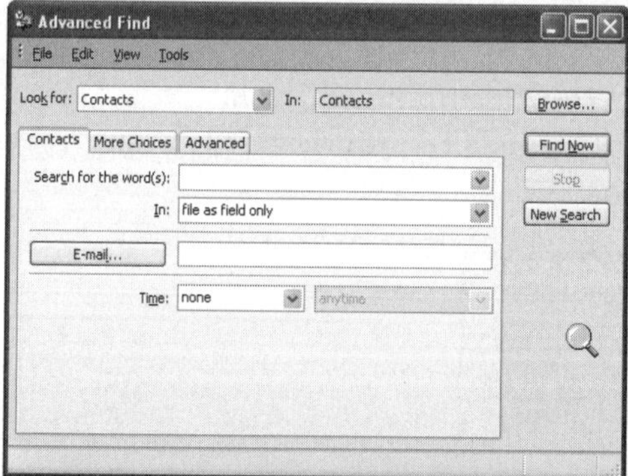

Figure 14-18. Use the Advanced Find dialog box to perform more complex searches using multiple conditions.

For a detailed discussion of how to perform both simple and complex searches in Outlook, see Chapter 31, "Finding and Organizing Data."

Making a Common Change to Multiple Contacts

Making changes to a single contact doesn't take long, but making the same change to several contacts can take a lot of time. You can relieve some of that time drain by propagating a change to a single contact to multiple contacts.

For example, let's say that your Contacts folder includes contacts for several people who work for the same organization. The organization's fax number has changed, and now you need to make that change for each contact. Propagating the change to other contacts is a simple drag-and-drop action with Outlook's ability to group items in the Contacts folder view.

Here's how to make it happen:

1. Open the folder containing the contacts to be changed.
2. Click View, Arrange By, Current View and choose a table view that best displays the information you need to change. In this example, choose Group By Company because its table view includes the fax number. Then, choose View, Arrange By, Current View, Customize Current View.
3. Click Group By and then click Clear All. From the Group Items By list, choose the item you want to change (in this example, Business Fax).
4. From the Expand/Collapse Defaults drop-down list, choose All Collapsed. Click OK twice to return to the view you just created.
5. Expand the group that includes the item you want to change.
6. Open one of the contacts and make the needed change, then save and close the contact. This contact now appears by itself under a different group.
7. To propagate the change, drag the gray grouping bar for the unchanged contacts and drop it on the grouping bar for the modified contact. Outlook makes the change to the other contacts automatically.

Changing multiple items at one time is easy as long as you remember that you need to first display a table view and then group it by the item you want to change. You can either customize an existing view or create a new one. If you customize an existing standard view, you can restore it to its default condition by clicking View, Arrange By, Current View, Define Views, selecting the view, and clicking Reset.

Viewing Contacts

Outlook provides predefined views for reviewing your contacts list in the Contacts folder. For example, Address Cards view displays names and addresses of contacts in blocks that look like address labels. This view is a convenient way to look up a contact's mailing address. In Phone List view, Outlook displays contact entries in table rows with details such as phone, job title, and department name in columns. This view is helpful for quickly finding a contact's phone number or job title. You can customize the various standard views to control the amount of detail or to help you organize and analyze information.

Using Standard Views in the Contacts Folder

The Contacts folder offers seven standard formats for viewing contacts. To change views, choose View, Arrange By, Current View and select the view you want to use. Two of the standard formats are card views and five are table views, as described in the following list:

- **Address Cards** This view (the default) displays contact entries as individual cards with name, one mailing address, and business and home phone numbers.
- **Detailed Address Cards** This view also displays individual cards, which show name, business and home addresses, phone numbers, and additional details such as job title, company, and Web address.
- **Phone List** This table view displays a list with the contact's name, the company name, business phone number, business fax number, home phone number, mobile phone number, categories, and a check box to enable or disable journaling for the contact.
- **By Category** This view groups contacts by their assigned categories.
- **By Company** This view groups contacts by company, which is helpful when you're trying to find a contact who works for a particular company.
- **By Location** This view groups contacts by country or region.
- **By Follow-Up Flag** In this view, you can easily locate all the contact entries that are flagged for follow-up. Outlook groups them together and also shows the due date for follow-up action.

Tip You can easily resize address cards by dragging the vertical dividing line between cards, which changes the width of all card columns.

Customizing the Contacts View

The methods of customizing the view in Outlook folders are generally the same for all folders. This section examines a handful of specific ways you might customize the Contacts folder to make it easier to locate and work with contacts. For example, you might have Outlook use a specific color for contacts who work for a particular company. You can also change the fonts used for the card headings and body, specify card width and height, and have Outlook automatically format contact entries based on rules.

For more details about customizing views (applicable to the Contacts folder), see "Customizing the Inbox View," page 61. In addition, Chapter 26, "Creating Custom Views and Print Styles," covers additional ways to customize views.

Filtering the Contacts View

You can filter the view in the Contacts folder to show only those contacts that meet the conditions you specify in the filter. For example, you can use a filter to view only those contacts who work for a particular company or who live in a particular city.

Follow these steps to set up a view filter in the Contacts folder:

1. Open the Contacts folder and choose View, Arrange By, Current View, Customize Current View.
2. Click Filter in the Customize View dialog box.
3. In the Filter dialog box, specify the conditions for the filter. If you don't see the items you need to specify for the condition, use the Field drop-down list on the Advanced tab to select the necessary field.
4. Click OK to close the Filter dialog box, and then click OK in the Customize View dialog box to apply the filter.

When you want to view the entire contents of the folder again, you can remove the filter, as detailed here:

1. Choose View, Arrange By, Current View, Customize Current View.
2. Click Filter.
3. In the Filter dialog box, click Clear All and then click OK.
4. Click OK to close the View Summary dialog box.

Configuring Fonts and Card Dimensions

You can change the font Outlook uses for card headings and the card body text in the card views (Address Cards view and Detailed Address Cards view). You can also change the font style, size, and script, but not the color.

Follow these steps to change the font for card headings and body text:

1. Choose View, Arrange By, Current View, Customize Current View.
2. In the Customize View dialog box, click Other Settings to display the Format Card View dialog box (see Figure 14-19).

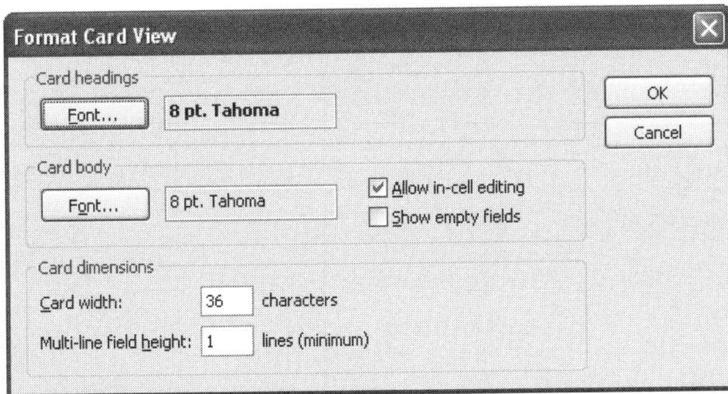

Figure 14-19. Use the Format Card View dialog box to specify the font for card headings and body text.

3. Click Font in the Card Headings or Card Body areas of the dialog box to open a standard Font dialog box in which you can select font characteristics.
4. Make your font selections and click OK in the Font dialog box.

5. Specify options according to the following list and then click OK:
   - **Allow In-Cell Editing** Selecting this check box allows you to modify contact data by clicking a field in the view without opening the contact form.
   - **Show Empty Fields** Select this check box if you want Outlook to show all fields for all contacts, even if the fields are empty. Clear this check box to simplify the view of your Contacts folder. Note that when this check box is selected, Outlook displays all fields defined for the view, not all contact fields.
   - **Card Width** Set the card width (in number of characters) using this option.
   - **Multi-Line Field Height** Use this option to specify the number of lines you want Outlook to display on the card for multiline fields.
6. Click OK to close the Customize View dialog box.

Using Automatic Formatting

Outlook performs some limited automatic formatting of data in the Contacts folder. For example, it uses bold for distribution list items, regular font for unread contacts, and red for overdue contacts (contact entries with an overdue follow-up flag). You can make changes to these automatic formatting rules, and you can even create your own rules. For example, you might want to display overdue contacts in blue rather than in red, or you might want to use a particular color for all contacts who work for a certain company.

Follow these steps to modify an existing rule or create a new one:

1. In Outlook, open the Contacts folder and choose View, Arrange By, Current View, Customize Current View.
2. Click Automatic Formatting in the Customize View dialog box to display the Automatic Formatting dialog box, shown in Figure 14-20.

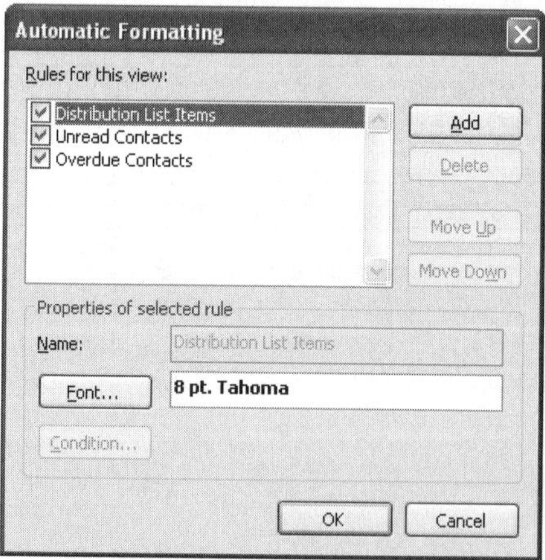

Figure 14-20. Use the Automatic Formatting dialog box to create custom rules that control how Outlook displays contacts.

3 If you want to modify an existing rule, select the rule and click Font to change the font characteristics or click Condition to modify the condition for the rule (see step 5).

Note You can modify a rule condition only for rules that you have created. You cannot change the condition for the three predefined rules.

4 Click Add if you want to add a new rule. Outlook creates a new rule named Untitled.

5 Type a new name in the Name field, click Font and specify font characteristics, and then click Condition to open the Filter dialog box, shown in Figure 14-21.

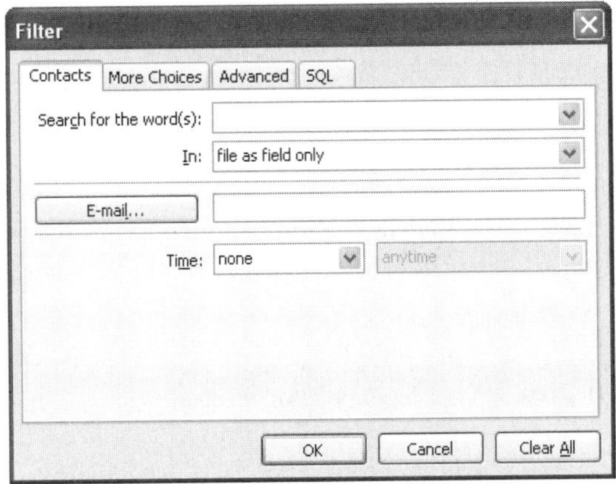

Figure 14-21. You can specify complex conditions using the Filter dialog box.

6 Specify the criteria to define the rule condition. For example, click Advanced, click Field, click Frequently Used Fields, and click Company. Then, select Contains in the Condition drop-down list and type a company name in the Value box. This causes Outlook to automatically format all contacts from the specified company using the font properties you specify in the next step.

7 Click OK to close the Filter dialog box, click Font in the Automatic Formatting dialog box, specify the font properties, and click OK.

8 Close the Automatic Formatting and Customize View dialog boxes to view the effects of the new rule.

Note Automatic formatting rules follow the hierarchy in the list shown in the Automatic Formatting dialog box. Use the Move Up and Move Down buttons to change the order of rules in the lists and thereby change the order in which they are applied.

Printing Contacts

As an experienced user of Microsoft Windows, you probably need little if any explanation of how to print. So rather than focusing on basic printing commands, this section offers some insight into why you might print from the Contacts folder and what your options are when you do print.

Why print? If you're like most people, you probably try to work from your computer as much as possible and reduce the amount of paper you generate. The completely paperless office is still a distant goal for most people, however, and there will be times when you want to print your contacts list. For example, you might need to take a copy of your contacts with you on a business trip, but you don't have a notebook computer. A hard copy of your contacts is the solution.

Outlook supports several predefined paper types that allow you to print contact information using various formats, including preprinted sheets for several popular day planners. You can print a single contact entry, a selection of entries, or all entries. To print a selection (one or more), first select the contact entries to print by holding down the Ctrl key and clicking each one. If you want to print all contacts, choose Edit, Select All. Then choose File, Print to open the Print dialog box (see Figure 14-22).

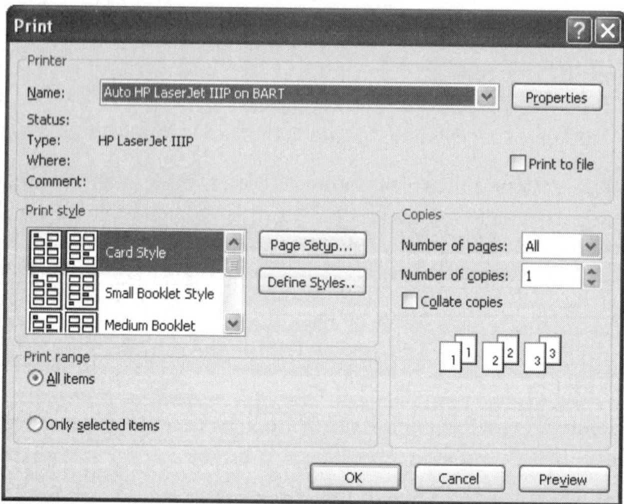

Figure 14-22. You can select several predefined styles from the Print dialog box.

In the Print Style area of the Print dialog box, you can select one of five print styles, each of which results in a different printed layout. You can use the styles as listed, modify them, or create new styles. To modify an existing style, select the style and click Page Setup to display the Page Setup dialog box, which resembles the one shown in Figure 14-23.

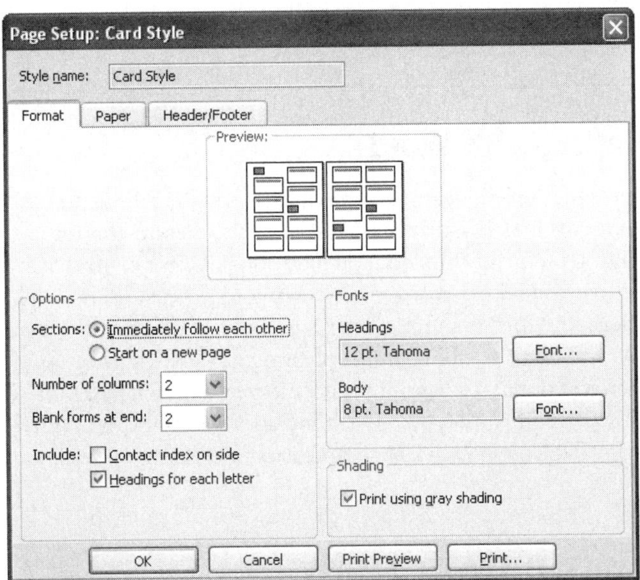

Figure 14-23. Modify a print style in the Page Setup dialog box.

Use the Format tab of this dialog box to specify fonts and shading and to set options such as printing a contact index on the side of each page, adding headings for each letter, and setting the number of columns. Use the Paper tab to select the type of paper, such as a preprinted sheet for your day planner, as well as to set up margins, paper source, and orientation. Use the Header/Footer tab to add a header, a footer, or both to the printout.

If you need a custom layout but don't want to modify the existing styles, you can create your own style. In the Print dialog box, click Define Styles to display the Define Print Styles dialog box (see Figure 14-24). Select a style to use as the basis for your new style, and click Copy to open the Page Setup dialog box. Modify settings as needed and click OK to save the new style. Outlook uses the same name but prefixes the name with Copy Of (Copy Of Card Style, for example). You can change the name in the Style Name box in the Page Setup dialog box.

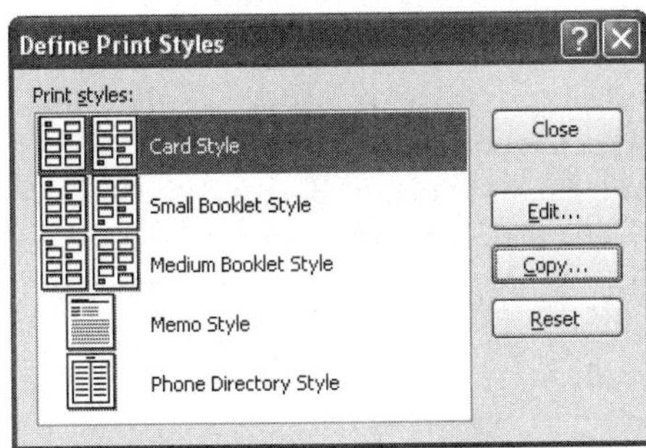

Figure 14-24. Select a style to copy in the Define Print Styles dialog box.

For a detailed discussion of printing in Outlook and creating custom print styles, see "Printing in Outlook," page 694.

Custom Contact Printing with Word

Although Outlook provides several features for printing, your capability to customize the way the printed documents look is rather limited. You can overcome this limitation by using Word rather than Outlook to print contacts. You have considerable control over how a Word document looks and prints, making Word an excellent tool for custom printing. You can copy data from Outlook to Word manually, but it's much more efficient to use a macro to automate the process and make custom contact printing a one-click process. Because the process requires macros and macros haven't yet been covered in detail, refer to Chapter 26, "Creating Custom Views and Print Styles," which includes a section that explains how to print contacts using Word. It also includes sample macro code that you can tailor to your specific needs.

Working with Distribution Lists

A distribution list is a collection of contacts. It provides an easy way to send messages to a group of people. For example, if you frequently send messages to the marketing team, you can create a distribution list called Marketing Team that contains the names of all members of this team. A message sent to this distribution list goes to all recipients who belong to the list. Outlook converts the address list to individual addresses, so recipients see their own names and the names of all other recipients in the To box of the message instead of seeing the name of the distribution list. You can use distribution lists in messages, task requests, and meeting requests.

Tip **Use nested distribution lists**
Distribution lists can contain other distribution lists as well as individual addresses. For example, you might create a distribution list for each of seven departments and then create one distribution list containing those seven others. You could use this second list when you need to send messages to all seven departments.

You can create distribution lists in your Contacts folder using your contacts list. You also can create distribution lists in a personal address book (PAB), which is separate from your Contacts folder and stored in a PAB file. You can have one PAB per profile but any number of contacts folders. There is essentially no difference between distribution lists in PABs and contacts folders. You can store addresses from any available source (the Global Address List, a personal address book, contacts list, and so on). In general, you should create your distribution lists in the location where you store the majority of your addresses. This chapter assumes that you're creating distribution lists in your Contacts folder.

For details on creating distribution lists in a PAB and working with address books, see "Using Distribution Lists," page 136.

Creating a Personal Distribution List

As mentioned previously, you can create a distribution list either in a PAB or in your Contacts folder.

Follow these steps to create a new distribution list in the Contacts folder:

1. In Outlook, choose File, New, Distribution List to open a distribution list form similar to the one shown in Figure 14-25.

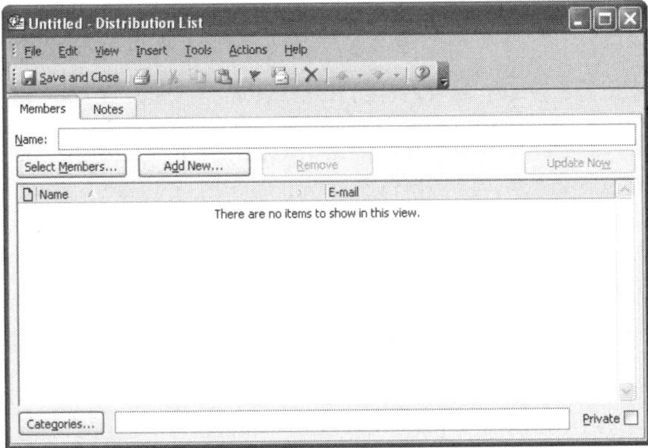

Figure 14-25. Add and remove members for a distribution list on the distribution list form.

2. Type the name of the list in the Name box. This is the name by which the list will appear in your Contacts folder. If you're creating a distribution list for the marketing department, for example, use the name Marketing.
3. Click Select Members to open the Select Members dialog box (see Figure 14-26).

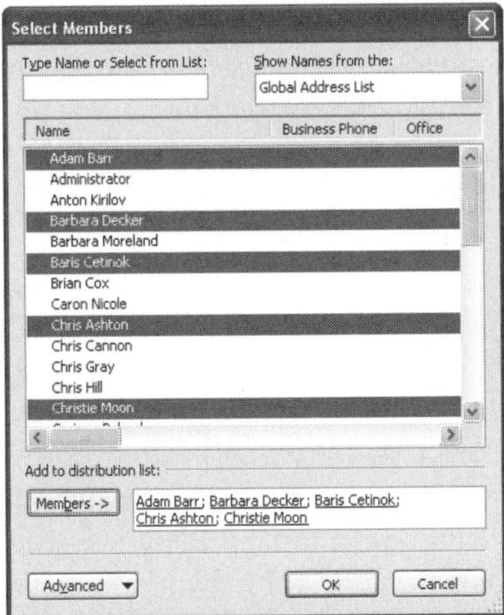

Figure 14-26. Use the Select Members dialog box to select addresses to include in the list.

4. In the Show Names From The drop-down list, select the location from which you want to select addresses (the Global Address List or the Contacts folder, for example).
5. In the Type Name Or Select From List box, type a name you want to include, which locates the name in the list. Or select the name in the Name list. Then click Members.
6. Repeat step 4 to add all addresses to the list and click OK when finished.
7. If you want to add a longer description of the distribution list, click the Notes tab and type the text.
8. Click Save And Close.

Adding or Deleting Names in a Distribution List

You can easily add and delete names in a distribution list. For example, perhaps your department has added a few new employees and you need to add their addresses to the department distribution list.

Follow these steps to add or remove names in a distribution list:

1. In your Contacts folder, open the distribution list to display the distribution list form.
2. Perform one or more of the following actions:
   - To add an address from an address book or a contacts folder, click Select Members.
   - To add an address that is not in a contacts folder or an address book, click Add New.
   - To delete a name, click the name and then click Remove.
3. Click Save And Close.

> **Tip** **Fine-tuning distribution lists**
> You can assign categories to a distribution list, mark it as private, or add notes to it by using the distribution list form. You can also update addresses in a distribution list if their source addresses have changed. For example, if you've changed a colleague's e-mail address in the contact entry and now want to update the corresponding address in the distribution list, you can open the distribution list, select the address, and click Update Now on the distribution list form.

Sharing Contacts

Outlook lets you share contacts with others by sending vCards through e-mail or by sharing a contacts folder. The former method lets you share contacts with people who don't use Outlook or who don't have access to your network or Exchange Server to be able to share your Contacts folder. The latter method—sharing your Contacts folder—is a good solution when you need to provide access to contacts for others on your network. This chapter explains how to share contacts through vCards, offers a brief overview of sharing the Contacts folder, and explains how to share contacts from a public folder.

> **Note** For a complete discussion of sharing Outlook folders, using public folders, and other methods of sharing data with other Outlook users, see Chapter 38, "Sharing Information with Others." Chapter 38 also explains how to share a PST with other users by copying it to the Windows Briefcase. You can use this method to share contacts with others who don't have Exchange Server.
>
> You can also use WSS to share contacts and even integrate those contacts within Outlook. See Chapter 40, "Collaboration with Outlook and Windows SharePoint Services," to learn how to work with and share contacts from a WSS site.

Sharing Your Contacts Folders

If you are running Outlook with Exchange Server, you can assign permissions to a folder stored in your Exchange Server mailbox to give other users access to that folder. You can grant permissions on a group basis or a per-user basis. Outlook provides two groups by default—Anonymous and Default—that you can use to assign permissions on a global basis. You also can add individual users to the permissions list and use distribution lists to assign permissions.

Follow these steps to set permissions on your Contacts folder to allow other users access to your contacts:

1. Open the folder list, right-click the Contacts folder, and choose Properties on the shortcut menu to display the Contacts Properties dialog box for the folder.
2. Click the Permissions tab (see Figure 14-27).

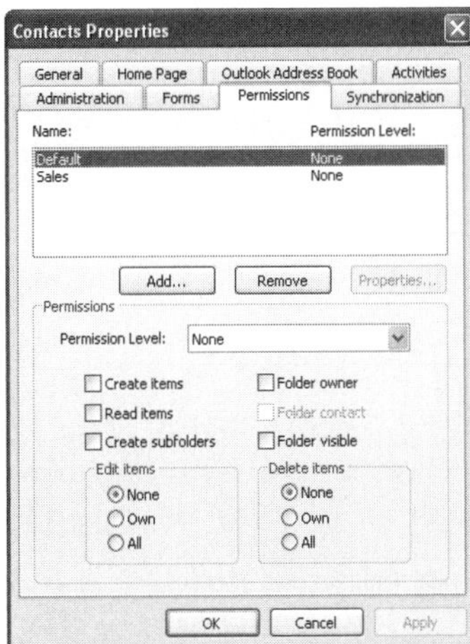

Figure 14-27. Configure permissions on the Permissions tab.

3. Click Add to display the Add Users dialog box.
4. Select the person for whom you want to configure permissions and click Add. Click OK to return to the Permissions tab.
5. In the Name box, select the name of the person you just added.

6. In the Permission Level drop-down list, select a level of permission according to the tasks the user should be able to do with your Contacts folder. When you select a permission level, Outlook selects one or more individual permissions in the Permissions area. You also can select or clear individual permissions as needed.
7. Click OK to save the permission changes.

You can grant several permissions for a folder, and you can assign them in any combination you need. For example, you should select the Folder Visible and Read Items permissions if you want someone to be able to view the contacts but not modify them or add new ones. Add the Create Items permission if you want the user to be able to add new contact items. Use the Edit Items and Delete Items groups of options to specify whether the user can edit or delete existing items.

For a complete explanation of permissions and folder sharing, see "Granting Access to Folders," page 741.

Sharing Contacts with a Public Folder

If all the users who need to access the shared address book use Exchange Server, the easiest solution is to create a folder on the server and configure it to allow other users to access it. This method offers the benefit of providing access to remote users as well as local users.

Note It's possible for remote users to access a shared PAB file. However, the network must provide remote access, and the computer or share where the address book file is located must be available to remote users.

Use the following method to share a folder containing contact information on the server:

1. Open the Public Folders branch and select All Public Folders.
2. In Outlook, choose File, Folder, New Folder or right-click All Public Folders and choose New Folder.
3. In the Create New Folder dialog box (see Figure 14-28), type a name for the new folder in the Name box.

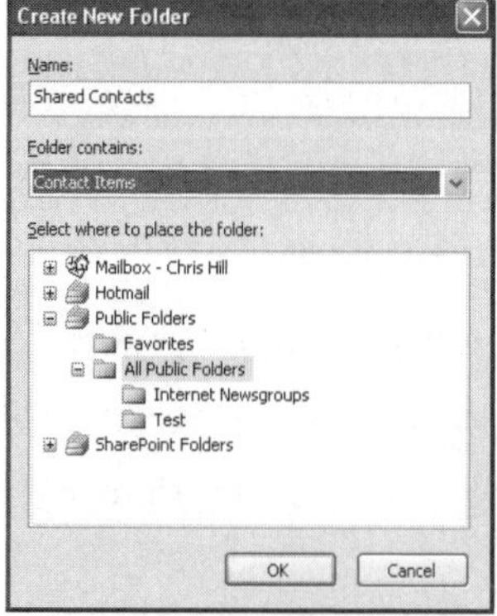

Figure 14-28. Use the Create New Folder dialog box to create a folder.

4 Choose Contact Items from the Folder Contains drop-down list and click OK to create the folder as a root public folder.

Note You can create root-level public folders only if you've been given that right by the Exchange Server administrator.

5 Right-click the folder you just created and choose Properties, and then click Permissions to display the Permissions tab (see Figure 12-29).

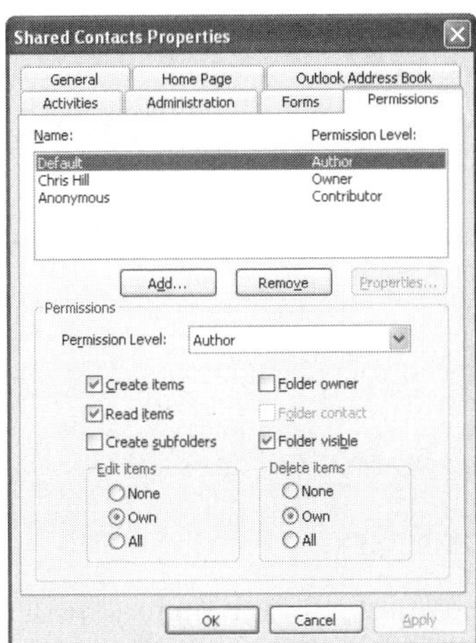

Figure 14-29. Use the Permissions tab to configure access to a public folder.

6 Configure the permissions based on the following explanation, and then click OK.

On the Permissions tab, you can specify the types of access that other users will have to the folder. Initially, in the Name box, the Default permission is set to None, making the folder visible but allowing no other access. When Anonymous is set to Contributor, all other users can create and read items in the folder, allowing them to create new contact entries and edit only those items they own (the ones they create).

You can configure permissions to grant individual users specific types of access. To do so, click Add, add the user, and then specify permissions as needed. However, you can use the Default and Anonymous settings to control access by most users and add individual users only if they need permissions that are more or less restrictive than those defined by Default and Anonymous.

Outlook gives you other ways to control permissions as well. For example, you can control the ability to edit and delete items separately from the ability to create items. You configure these permissions depending on what actions you want other users to be able to perform in the folder. You can also configure groups of permissions using the Permission Level drop-down list or by specifying them individually.

For a detailed discussion of creating and using public folders, see Chapter 38, "Sharing Information with Others."

Sharing Contacts with vCards

A vCard presents contact information as an electronic business card that can be sent through e-mail. vCards are based on an open standard, allowing any application that supports vCards to share contact information. In addition to sending a vCard as an attachment, you also can include it with your message signature.

When you receive a message with a vCard attached, a paper clip icon appears in the Reading Pane to indicate the attachment. Use one of the following methods to add the data in the vCard as a contact entry:

- From the Reading Pane, select the paper clip icon and click the file name that appears.
- If you've opened the message, right-click the business card icon in the message and click Open.

After you can view the information sent in the vCard, click Save And Close to add the information to your contacts list.

Tip You can drag a vCard from a message to your Contacts folder to add the contact information.

Creating a vCard from a Contact Entry

As mentioned previously, one way to send contact information to someone else is to attach the contact entry to a message as a vCard. You can use this method to share your own contact information or to share one or more other contact entries with another person.

Follow these steps to attach a vCard to a message:

1. In the Contacts folder, select the contact item you want to send as a vCard.
2. Choose Actions, Forward As vCard. Outlook opens a new message form with the contact entry attached as a vCard.
3. Specify an address, complete the message as you would any other, and then click Send to send it.

Including a vCard with Your Signature

The second method of sharing a contact is useful when you want to share your own contact information. Rather than attaching it to a message, you can have Outlook send it along with your message signature. This ensures that the vCard is sent with all outgoing messages.

Note You can attach text (such as a favorite quote) and graphics to each outgoing message as part of your signature. For complete details on using signatures with Outlook, see "Using Signatures," page 206.

Follow these steps to add your contact information as a vCard to your message signature:

1 Create your own contact entry if you have not already done so.
2 Choose Tools, Options.
3 On the Mail Format tab, click Signatures.
4 Click New.
5 Enter a name for your signature.
6 Select Start With A Blank Signature.
7 Click Next.
8 In the Edit Signature dialog box (see Figure 14-30), click New vCard From Contact.

Figure 14-30. Use the Edit Signature dialog box to add text, graphics, and a vCard to your outgoing messages automatically.

9 In the Select Contacts To Export As vCards dialog box, select your name from the contact list, click Add, and then click OK.
10 Click Finish and then click OK twice.

From now on, your contact information will be attached to outgoing messages.

> **Tip** To prevent signatures from being added to your outgoing messages, choose Tools, Options and click the Mail Format tab. Select None in the Signature For New Messages drop-down list.

Saving a Contact Entry as a vCard

In addition to sending vCards as e-mail attachments, Outlook allows you to save a contact entry to a file as a vCard. You might do this if you want to link to vCards on a Web site so that others can download the vCards directly rather than receiving a message with the vCards attached. Or perhaps you want to save a large number of contacts as vCards and send them to someone on a Zip disk or other removable media rather than through e-mail.

Follow these steps to save a contact item as a vCard file:

1. In Outlook, open the contact item you want to save as a vCard.
2. Choose File, Export To vCard File.
3. Type a name in the File Name box and then click Save.

Saving a vCard Attachment to Your Contacts Folder

When you receive a message containing a vCard attachment, you'll probably want to save the vCard as a contact item in your Contacts folder. Follow these steps to do so:

1. Open the message containing the attached vCard.
2. Double-click the attachment to open it.
3. In the open contact form, click Save And Close. The information in the vCard is saved to your Contacts folder by default.

Setting Contact Options

Outlook provides a handful of options that control how it stores and displays contacts. To view these options, choose Tools, Options and click Contact Options on the Preferences tab. In the Contact Options dialog box (see Figure 14-31), configure the options on the facing page.

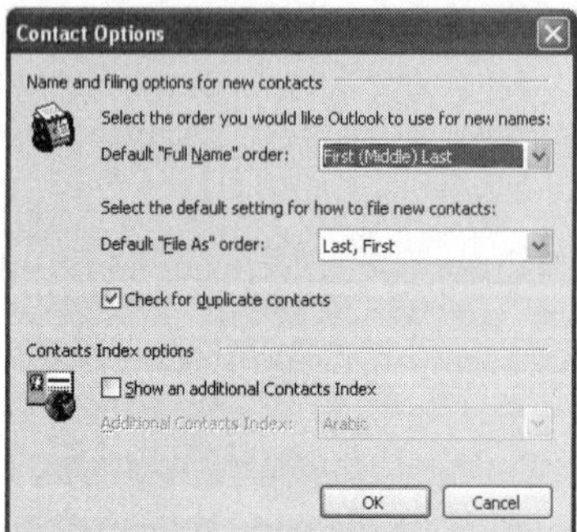

Figure 14-31. Configure options for contacts in the Contact Options dialog box.

- **Default "Full Name" Order** This option specifies how Outlook creates the Full Name field when you click Full Name in the new contact form and enter the contact's first, middle, and last names, along with suffix and title.
- **Default "File As" Order** This option specifies the name Outlook creates in the card title. Outlook uses the information you specify for first, middle, and last name—as well as company—to create the card title based on how this option is set.
- **Check For Duplicate Contacts** Select this check box if you want Outlook to check for duplicate contacts when you create new contacts.

Chapter 15

Using Microsoft Business Contact Manager

Microsoft Business Contact Manager is an add-on for Microsoft Outlook 2003 that builds on the customer management features already in Outlook to create a system for managing clients, sales opportunities, and other business data. Business Contact Manager doesn't replace Outlook, but rather adds new item types, additional folders, and features for managing these items to help you keep track of accounts, customers, and business opportunities more efficiently.

This chapter explores Business Contact Manager and explains how to install the software, create accounts and contacts, generate reports, and use its other features. By the end of this chapter you'll have a solid background in using Business Contact Manager and can begin taking advantage of it to manage your business contacts and accounts.

Note Business Contact Manager is disabled if your profile includes an Exchange Server account. You cannot use Business Contact Manager in conjunction with Exchange Server, although you can create a separate profile without Exchange Server and use Business Contact Manager with that profile. You can export contacts and other data from your Exchange Server account to a PST to import into Business Contact Manager.

Understanding What Business Contact Manager Can Do

Business Contact Manager is a customer resource management (CRM) tool that integrates with Outlook 2003. By itself, Outlook lets you manage contacts, e-mail, a calendar, and tasks. Business Contact Manager extends those capabilities to add accounts, business contacts, and business opportunities (such as sales) to your Outlook data. These items appear under their own Business Contact Manager branch in the folder list, as shown in Figure 15-1.

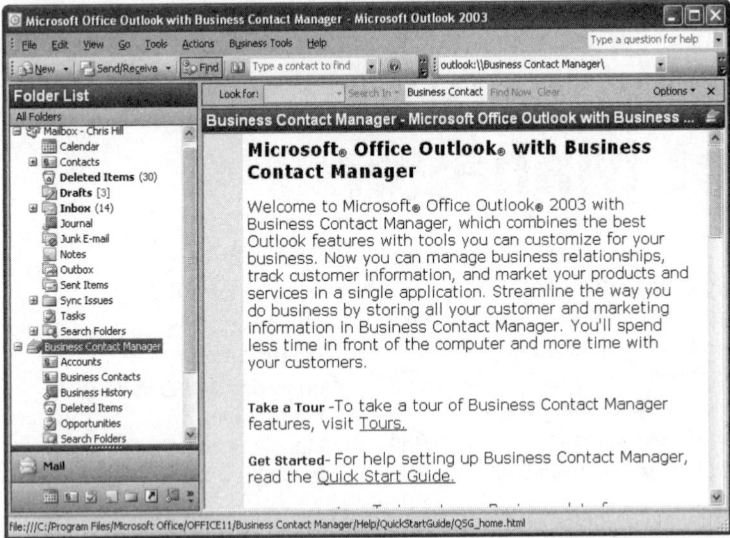

Figure 15-1. Business Contact Manager adds additional folders and item types to Outlook.

The main benefit of using Business Contact Manager is that it gives you the means to easily integrate all information about a customer account in one place (see Figure 15-2). You can easily link e-mail, contacts, notes, documents, and other items related to an account and view and manage those items from a single point. The result is the capability to organize all account data in one location, quickly find information, and improve customer response, which ultimately should mean both a cost savings and potentially more revenue.

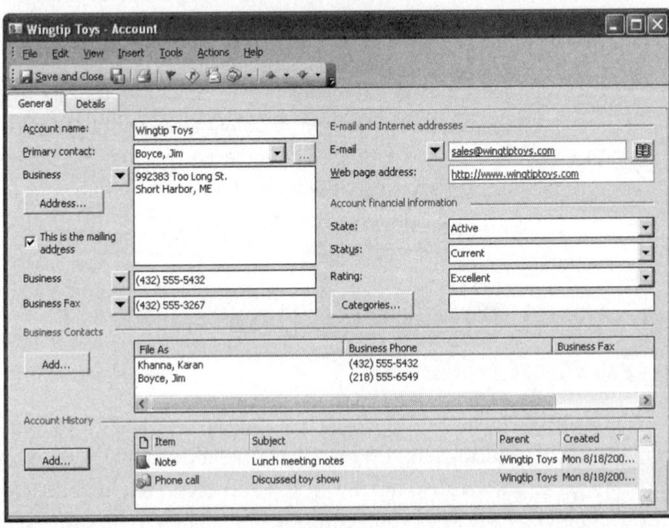

Figure 15-2. Account items give you a means to manage information about a customer account.

Using Microsoft Business Contact Manager

Business Contact Manager also enables you to keep track of sales opportunities and the product information associated with those sales from initial contact through aftersale customer support. The Opportunity item type, shown in Figure 15-3, stores information about a sales contact, potential or actual order, product items, and other details related to the potential sale.

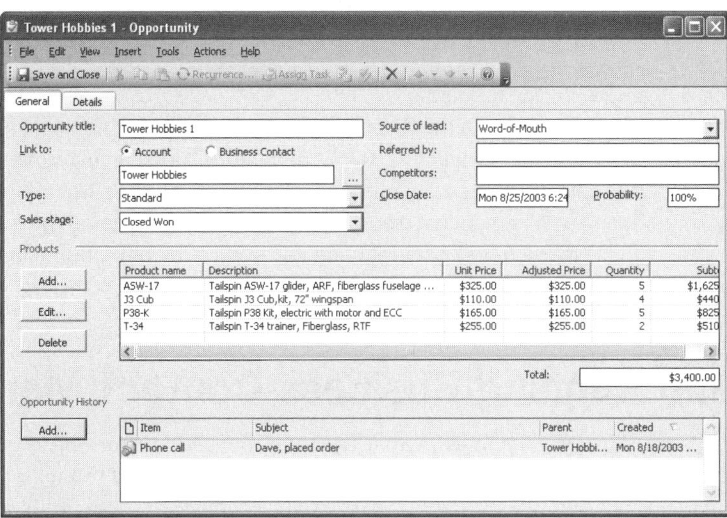

Figure 15-3. Use Opportunity items to record potential or actual sales and related information.

The Business History folder (see Figure 15-4) is a Journal folder that keeps track of events associated with each contact, account, or opportunity. By automatically journaling items, the Business History folder makes it relatively easy to search for and locate these items.

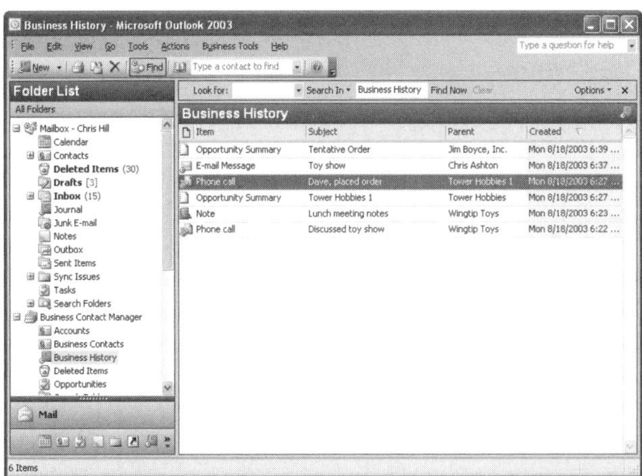

Figure 15-4. Use the Business History folder to quickly locate items.

In addition to these special-purpose folders, Business Contact Manager also adds reporting capabilities to Outlook to help you manage and analyze the information you've stored about your accounts, contacts, and sales. These include several predefined reports for each item type, which you can use as is or modify to suit your needs.

Chapter 15

This section has provided a brief overview of what Business Contact Manager can do. In a nutshell, the program adds new item types and folders to Outlook to give you a set of tools for managing your business accounts, contacts, and sales opportunities. As you begin to experiment with Business Contact Manager through the remaining chapters, you'll develop a better understanding of how Business Contact Manager can fit in with your business practices. Before you can start, however, you need to get Business Contact Manager installed.

Tip **Organizing and searching for data**
You can assign categories to each of the Business Contact Manager item types, just as you can for standard Outlook items. Categories help you organize and search for data. This chapter doesn't cover categories. See Chapter 4, "Using Categories and Types," for details on creating and working with categories. See Chapter 8, "Filtering, Organizing, and Using Automatic Responses," to learn how to create and use search folders with Business Contact Manager to organize and locate items.

Installing and Running Business Contact Manager

Business Contact Manager is included with Microsoft Office Professional Enterprise Edition 2003, Microsoft Office Professional Edition 2003, and Microsoft Office Small Business Edition 2003. The installation process for Business Contact Manager is straightforward.

When you run Setup from the Business Contact Manager CD, Setup first determines if the Microsoft .NET Framework, which is required to run Business Contact Manager, is installed on the computer. If not, Setup launches the .NET Framework installation. You'll see a handful of dialog boxes that track the .NET Framework installation progress. The only input you need to provide during this phase is to accept the .NET Framework license agreement, as shown in Figure 15-5.

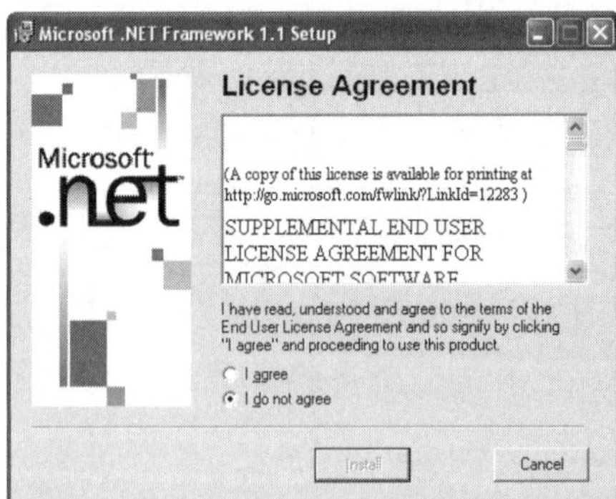

Figure 15-5. Accept the .NET Framework license agreement to complete its installation.

After the .NET Framework installation is finished, Setup starts the installation process for Business Contact Manager, displaying the Setup Wizard for Business Contact Manager for Outlook 2003. After you accept the license agreement in the wizard, Setup prompts you for the location in which to install Business Contact Manager, as displayed in Figure 15-6. This is the only option you can configure for the installation. Set the installation location, click Next, and click Install to complete the installation.

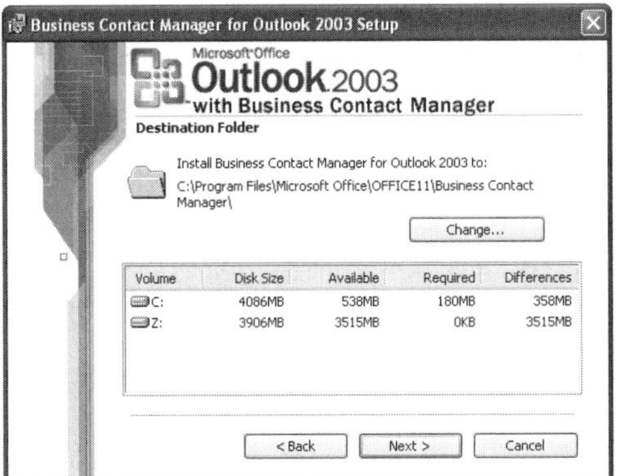

Figure 15-6. Select the location in which to install Business Contact Manager.

Note You must install Business Contact Manager on a local hard disk for this release. Installation on a network share is not supported.

The first time you run Outlook after installing Business Contact Manager, you'll see the startup dialog box shown in Figure 15-7. Click Yes to begin using the software with your current Outlook profile. After you click Yes, Business Contact Manager automatically creates a new database in which to store your Business Contact Manager data if one does not already exist. If Business Contact Manager detects a database, it gives you the option of selecting an existing database or creating a new one (see Figure 15-8). To create a new database, choose Create A New Database and click Next. To use an existing database, such as one you copied from another computer, choose Use An Existing Database, select the database from the drop-down list, and click Next. Specify a unique name for the database (such as MyBCMData), and click Next. After the database is created, click Finish and you're ready to start setting up your business items, as explained in the section "Working with Business Contacts," on page 430. First, however, you might want to know more about how to control Business Contact Manager.

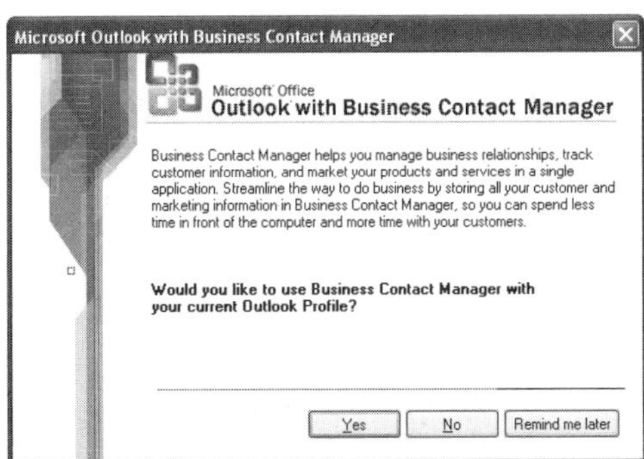

Figure 15-7. Business Contact Manager asks if you want to use it with your current Outlook profile.

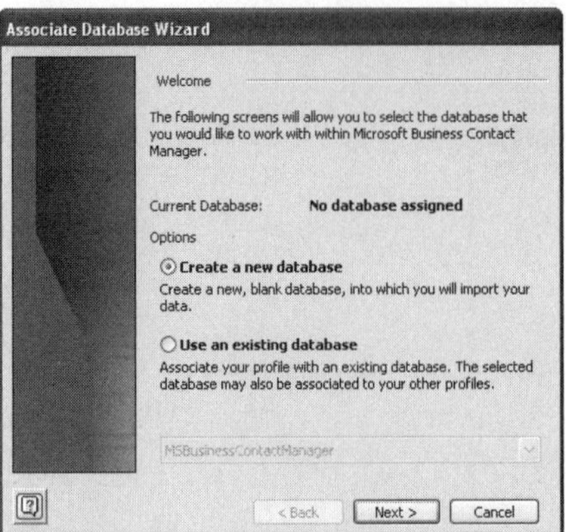

Figure 15-8. You have the option of creating a new database or using an existing one.

Note Business Contact Manager uses the Microsoft SQL Server Desktop Engine (MSDE), a run-time database engine that provides the core features of SQL Server without the expense or installation of SQL Server. Business Contact Manager Setup installs its own copy of MSDE, even if you have an existing installation already on the computer. If you remove Business Contact Manager, Setup removes this copy of MSDE as well, but leaves any other versions installed on the computer.

Where Is Business Contact Manager?

As you first start to use Business Contact Manager, you might not need to know where it's located on your computer, but as time goes on and you need to perform other tasks such as backing up your database, you'll want to know where its files are located.

Setup installs Business Contact Manager by default into the \Program Files\Microsoft Office\Office11\Business Contact Manager folder. This main folder stores the Business Contact Manager core executables and dynamic-link libraries (DLLs), as well as support files such as templates, scripts, icons, and documentation. The following subfolders contain additional items:

- **DB** This folder contains your Business Contact Manager database files.
- **Help** This folder contains the Business Contact Manager Help documentation and related files.
- **IM** This folder stores files that support import and export functions between Business Contact Manager and other business management applications such as Act!.
- **Reports** This folder stores report templates and by default includes several report types.

Adding and Removing Business Contact Manager for a Profile

When Business Contact Manager is installed on a computer, you receive a prompt asking if you want to enable it (see Figure 15-7) the first time you open Outlook with a profile that doesn't include Business Contact Manager. Simply click Yes and follow the prompts as explained in the section "Installing and Running Business Contact Manager," on page 426.

If you decide you don't want to use Business Contact Manager with a particular profile after it is enabled, you can close Business Contact Manager easily enough. Open the folder list, right-click the Business Contact Manager branch, and choose Close Business Contact Manager. Outlook removes the folders from the folder list and removes the Business Contact Manager–related commands from the Outlook menu. This method affects only the current profile; it does not remove Business Contact Manager entirely from the computer, nor does it affect other profiles.

Perhaps you are creating a new Outlook profile and want to explicitly add a Business Contact Manager database to the profile. Or, after you remove Business Contact Manager from a profile, you might decide you want it back again.

You can add a Business Contact Manager database to a new profile or to an existing one. If you choose the former approach, simply create a new Outlook profile that contains your existing Outlook data. When you start Outlook with that profile, Outlook asks if you want to use Business Contact Manager. Click Yes to add it to the profile.

If you click No, Outlook will not add a database to the profile. However, you can add one manually. To add or restore a Business Contact Manager database to an existing profile, follow these steps:

1. Open the Mail tool from Control Panel or right-click the Outlook icon on the Start menu and choose Properties.
2. Click Show Profiles and select the profile to which you want to add Business Contact Manager, then click Properties.
3. Click Data Files and in the Outlook Data Files dialog box, click Add.
4. Select Business Contact Manager Database and click OK.
5. To add an existing database, select Use An Existing Database, and select the database previously used with the profile. To create a new database, choose the Create A New Database option. Then click Next, Finish.
6. Click Close, Close, OK to close the remaining dialog boxes, then start Outlook and verify that your Business Contact Manager data and folders are now available in Outlook.

Working with Business Contacts

One of the first tasks you will likely want to accomplish after installing Business Contact Manager is to add business contacts. It makes sense to add contacts before you add accounts, because each account will likely have at least one contact associated with it. If the contact is already created, you can simply assign it to an account when you create the account.

Note Business Contact Manager can import data from several different sources. If you currently use another contact management application and want to move its data to Business Contact Manager, see the section "Importing and Exporting Information," page 446, for details.

Copying Existing Contacts

You can copy existing contacts from your Contacts folder (or other contacts folders) to the Business Contacts folder. To do so, simply open the Contacts folder and open the folder list, then scroll down to locate the Business Contacts folder under the Business Contact Manager branch. Right-click a contact from the Contacts folder and drag and drop it on the Business Contacts folder, then choose Copy from the shortcut menu. To move the contact instead of copying it, choose Move from the menu or simply drag the contact to the Business Contacts folder.

A Business Contact item includes additional fields not found in a standard Outlook Contact item. After you copy or move the item to the Business Contacts folder, you will likely want to edit the contact to include additional information. Double-click the contact to open it, then add or edit information in it according to the information provided in the following section.

Export Your Outlook Contacts to Business Contact Manager

If you have many contacts in your Outlook Contacts folder that you want to copy to your Business Contacts folder, you can simply select multiple contacts and drag them to the Business Contacts folder. An alternative is to export your contacts from Outlook to a Microsoft Access database and then import them into Business Contact Manager. When exporting or copying contacts, keep in mind that contacts that include file attachments will generate an error message because business contacts don't include a picture field, but the rest of the contact information will come through. Exporting and importing through Access bypasses this potential problem because Outlook does not export attachments when you export your contacts to Access. See "Importing Contacts or Accounts," page 446, for details on how to import contacts into Business Contact Manager.

Creating New Business Contacts

You create a new Business Contact item in much the same way you create a standard Outlook Contact item. Double-click a blank area of the Business Contacts folder or open the folder and click New on the toolbar (or choose File, New, Business Contact). Figure 15-9 shows a Business Contact item with many of its fields filled in.

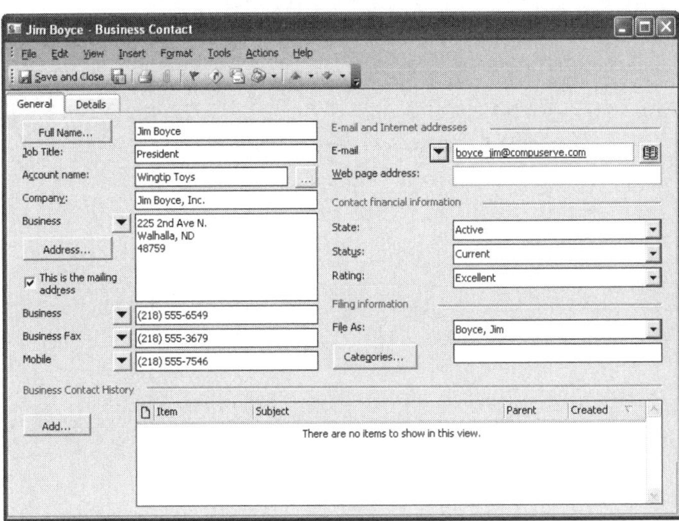

Figure 15-9. A Business Contact item includes several fields not found in a standard Contact item.

Most of the fields on the General tab are the same as those found in a standard Outlook Contact item. See Chapter 14, "Managing Your Contacts," if you need more information on working with contacts and these standard fields.

Two groups of fields on the General tab for a Business Contact item are new: Contact Financial Information and Business Contact History. The first of these two groups provides three drop-down lists that let you specify information about the contact's financial status:

- **State** Use this option to specify whether the contact is active or inactive. You can use this field in reports to separate active from inactive contacts.
- **Status** Choose between Current and Overdue for the contact's account status.
- **Rating** Select an overall financial rating for the contact from this drop-down list.

The Business Contact History group shows all of the items that are linked to the contact, including e-mail messages, notes, opportunities, tasks, appointments, phone logs, and files. Some of these items you must link yourself through the contact item, whereas others are linked automatically. For example, if you send an e-mail to a business contact, Business Contact Manager automatically links the e-mail to the contact and includes it in the Business Contact History list.

This section of the chapter focuses on creating and working with Business Contact items. See the section "Attaching Items," page 440, for details on linking items to your contacts.

The Details tab for a Business Contact item, shown in Figure 15-10, provides several additional fields you can use to track various items of information about a business contact.

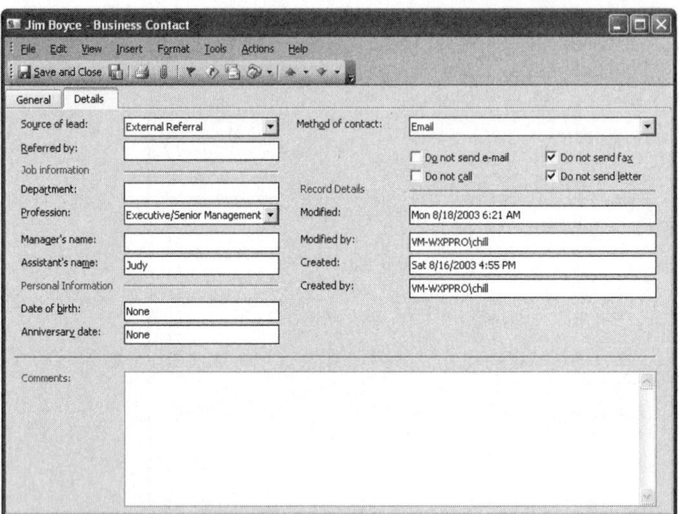

Figure 15-10. Use the Details tab to add more information to the contact.

The fields on the Details tab are generally self-explanatory. Note that the four check boxes under the Method Of Contact field (Do Not Send E-Mail, Do Not Call, Do Not Send Fax, and Do Not Send Letter) are informational fields only and do not actually prevent these actions. For example, if you select the Do Not Send E-Mail check box for the contact, Outlook does not honor that setting if you attempt to send an e-mail. The message will go through without any prompts to the contrary.

Use Views to Honor Contact Settings

If you want to honor these fields (for example, not calling someone if Do Not Call is selected for their contact item), you should make it a habit of checking them before taking the actions specified by them. An alternative is to create a custom view that filters the items based on the pertinent field. Chapter 26, "Creating Custom Views and Print Styles," discusses how to create custom views, but I touch on it here because these fields are user-defined fields, which are not specifically mentioned in Chapter 26.

The following example shows how to create a view that shows only those contacts whose Do Not Call check box is cleared:

1. Open the Business Contacts folder and choose View, Arrange By, Current View, Define Views.

2 In the Custom View Organizer dialog box, click New. Enter the name **OK To Call**, choose Table from the Type Of View list, and click OK.

3 In the Customize View dialog box, click Filter, then click Advanced to show the Advanced tab shown in Figure 15-11.

Figure 15-11. Add filter criteria for the view on the Advanced tab.

4 Click Field, choose User-Defined Fields In Folder, and choose Do Not Call. Choose a different field if you want to filter based on that field instead.

5 Make sure the Condition drop-down list is set to Equals, and choose No from the Value drop-down list. Then click Add To List.

6 Click OK, OK, and Apply View to show the view you just created.

Currently, Business Contact Manager does not properly initialize the values of these settings for imported contacts, so you should select, then clear the values to set them to No (selected indicates Yes). Business Contact Manager does properly initialize these fields for newly-created contacts.

Using Contacts

There are several actions you might take with a business contact, including sending an e-mail, calling, faxing, sending a letter, or adding a note. When you perform many of these tasks, Business Contact Manager adds the item to the contact's history. For example, send an e-mail to a contact, and Business Contact Manager links that e-mail to the contact. This linking happens automatically in most cases. In the case of an e-mail, you don't even have to go through the Business Contact folder to have the e-mail linked to the contact. With the Inbox folder open, simply send the contact a message. Outlook checks the recipient; if it is one of your business contacts, Outlook automatically links the e-mail to that contact.

You can initiate actions for a business contact in different ways. For example, select a contact in the Business Contacts folder and then choose Actions, followed by the action you want to perform, such as New Letter To Contact. You can also right-click a contact in the folder and choose an action from the resulting shortcut menu. Each of the actions you can perform for a business contact are detailed elsewhere in this book where applicable. For example, "Working with Contacts," page 392, explains several actions such as sending e-mail, calling, and sending a letter. Chapter 19, "Scheduling Appointments," and Chapter 20, "Scheduling Meetings and Resources," explain how to schedule appointments and meetings with contacts.

Creating and Using Accounts

Business Contact Manager also adds *accounts* as a new type of Outlook item. An account is generally synonymous with a customer, but you might have different accounts for a single customer. To create a new account, simply double-click in an empty area of the Accounts folder. You can also click New on the toolbar with the Accounts folder open, or choose File, New, Account.

As Figure 15-12 shows, the General tab for an account includes a name to identify the account, the name of the primary contact for the account, address, phone numbers, and several other items that are no doubt familiar to you. An account also includes the same financial status information as a contact. It also enables you to associate multiple contacts with the account. Finally, the General tab includes an Account History area that lists all of the items (e-mail, tasks, notes, and so on) that are linked to the account.

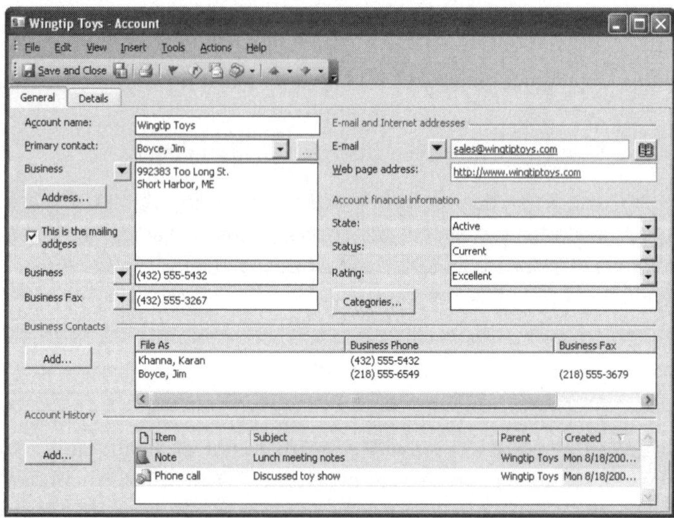

Figure 15-12. Use the General tab to set account name, primary contact, and other general fields.

> **Note** When you send an e-mail to any contact associated with an account, Business Contact Manager links the e-mail to the contact. The Account History list shows all items linked to all of the account's contacts, not just for the primary contact. This automatic tracking is one of Business Contact Manager's most useful features.

The Details tab, shown in Figure 15-13, provides additional fields to track other information about the account such as Type Of Business and Territory, and provides a comments field in which you can record comments about the account.

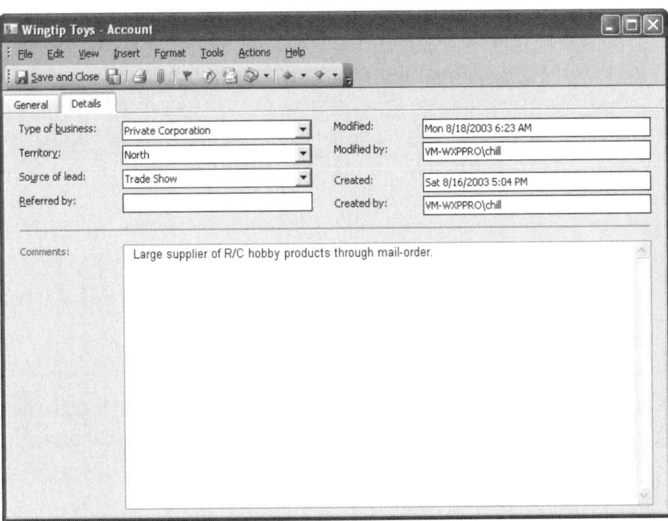

Figure 15-13. Specify additional information and comments on the Details tab.

Many of the fields are the same for an account as they are for a contact. For example, contacts and accounts both have address fields, phone number fields, and financial status fields. However, the fields are unique. For example, the Phone Number field for an account can be different from the Phone Number field of the contact assigned as the primary contact for the account. Keep this in mind when creating accounts and contacts.

Performing Actions with Accounts

You can also perform many of the same actions for an account as you can for a contact. For example, you can right-click an account and choose Call Contact to open the New Call dialog box with the account phone number displayed. Or, you might choose New Message To Contact to start a new e-mail message to the address specified in the account's E-Mail field.

As with a contact, you can access these actions from the Actions menu or by right-clicking an account and choosing the desired action. However, understand that Business Contact Manager performs the action using the information associated with the account, not with the contacts that are linked to the account. For example, if you right-click an account and choose Call Contact, Business Contact Manager shows the account's phone number in the New Call dialog box, not the phone number assigned in the Primary Contact field. The same is true for an e-mail message—Business Contact Manager addresses the e-mail to the address specified in the account's E-Mail field, not the primary contact's e-mail address. If you need to work with a contact's information instead, either open the contact directly from the Business Contacts folder or double-click the contact in the Business Contacts area on the account's form and then use the Actions menu in the resulting contact form to perform the action.

Creating and Using Opportunities

Business Contact Manager is geared primarily to people in sales, and the inclusion of the Opportunity item type illustrates that focus. You can use opportunities to track sales leads at various stages, from the initial inquiry through to the placement of the order.

To create a new opportunity, open the Opportunities folder and click New on the toolbar or chose File, New, Opportunity. As Figure 15-14 illustrates, the General tab for an opportunity item includes a name for the opportunity, source for the lead, stage of the sale, and product list, among other sales-related fields. The Details tab includes a handful of additional fields and a place to add comments.

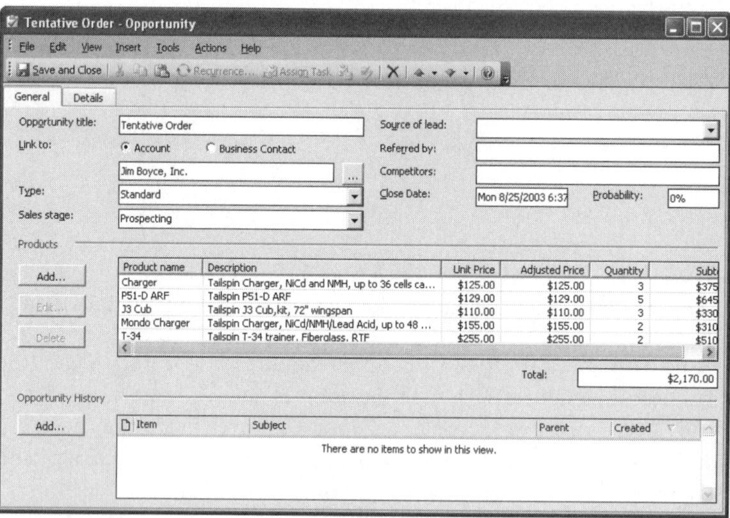

Figure 15-14. An Opportunity item defines a sale or a potential sale.

Each opportunity must be associated with an account or a business contact by the Link To options on the opportunity's General tab, just under the opportunity's title. Select either Account or Business Contact, then click the ellipses button beside the text box and choose Add Existing Account (or Contact) or Create New Account (or Contact). If you choose to add an existing item, Business Contact Manager displays either the Accounts or Business Contacts dialog box (see Figure 15-15), which you use to select the account or contact. Choose the item and click OK to add it to the opportunity.

If you choose the command to create a new account or contact, Business Contact Manager prompts you to enter the name for the account or contact. After you enter the name and click OK, Business Contact Manager creates a new item of the selected type and associates it with the opportunity. However, it does not prompt you to complete the other fields for the new item. Therefore, after you add the item to the opportunity and save the opportunity, you should open the newly created account or business contact and enter the other information for the new item.

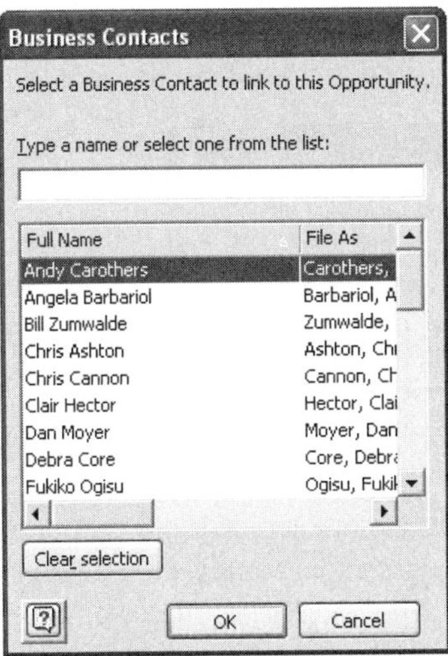

Figure 15-15. Use the Business Contacts dialog box to choose a contact to associate with the opportunity.

Creating and Managing Products

In addition to the general information included in an opportunity, you can also track specific sale-related information including products. Business Contact Manager creates a product database in which you maintain your company's product line, and you can add items to the opportunity from this product database. You can add existing items to the opportunity or create new items in the database as needed.

To manage the product list, choose Business Tools, Product List to open the Edit Product Master List dialog box (see Figure 15-16). This dialog box lists the existing product items in the database.

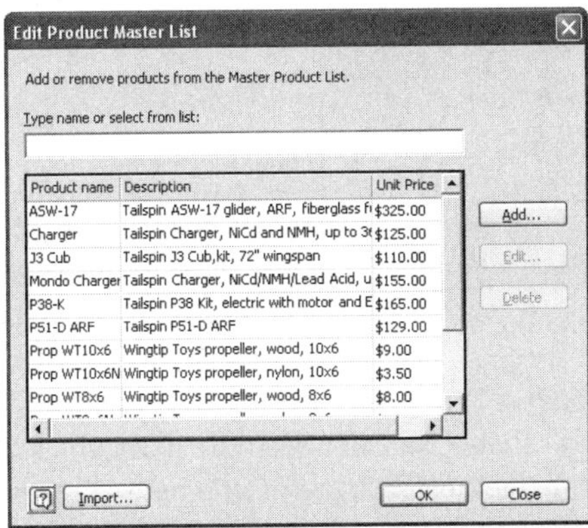

Figure 15-16. Use the Edit Product Master List to add or modify products in the database.

To add a new item, click Add to display the Add/Edit Product Properties dialog box shown in Figure 15-17. Enter information in the Product Name, Description, Unit Price, and Default

Quantity fields and click OK to add the information to the database. Repeat the process to add other items to the product database.

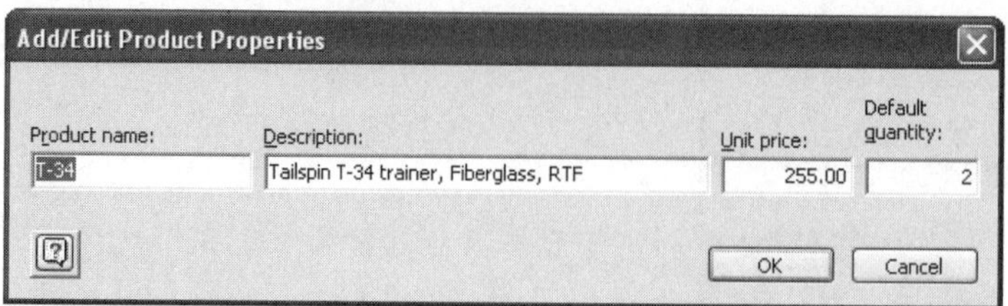

Figure 15-17. Enter a new product with the Add/Edit Product Properties dialog box.

Note You probably already have a product database outside of Business Contact Manager. If so, you can import the database to Business Contact Manager rather than re-create all of the entries and save a lot of time and effort. See "Importing Products," page 448, to learn how.

You can also manage existing products. In the Edit Product Master List dialog box, select an existing product and click Edit to open the Add/Edit Product Properties dialog box for the item and make changes. To delete a product, select the product in the master list and click Delete.

Adding Products to an Opportunity

As you learned earlier, an opportunity can include a list of products to be included in the sale. To add products, open the opportunity and on the General tab under the Products group, click Add. Business Contact Manager displays an Add/Edit Product Entry dialog box that is similar to the Add/Edit Product Properties dialog box you use to create products in the database, but as Figure 15-18 illustrates, you can enter additional information including an adjusted price, adjusted percentage, and quantity. The dialog box also shows the subtotal for the item.

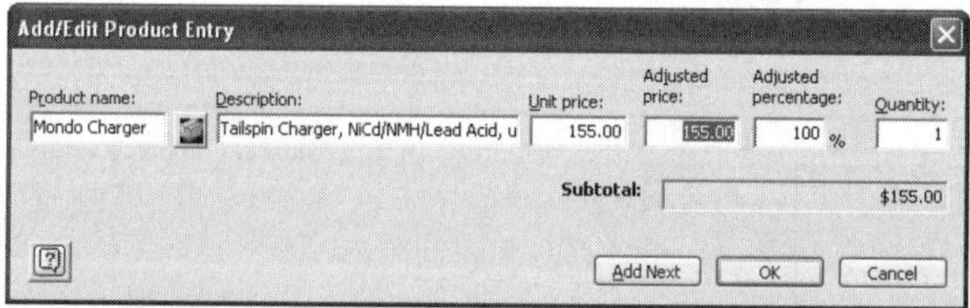

Figure 15-18. Add a product, set adjusted price, quantity, and other items with the Add/Edit Product Entry dialog box.

You can create an item on the fly with this dialog box, but it's more likely you will want to select an existing item from the product database. Click the button between the Product Name and Description fields to display the Edit Product Master List dialog box, select a product, and click OK. Business Contact Manager imports the product information from the database and you can then set the adjusted price, percentage, or quantity as needed. Click OK to close the dialog box and return to the opportunity form, or click Add Next to add the current item, clear the form, and add another item.

Tracking Item History

The Business History folder provides a place for you to view all of the events and items that are linked to accounts, business contacts, and opportunities in your Business Contact Manager database. The Business History folder is much like the Journal folder in your other Outlook folders in that it automatically tracks events such as e-mail messages and meetings.

The Business History folder shows all linked items and is useful when you need a global view of all items. As with other folders, the Business History folder provides a handful of predefined views that you can use to change the way its information is displayed. For example, you can use the Messages view, shown in Figure 15-19, to see all of the messages linked to items in your Business Contact Manager database.

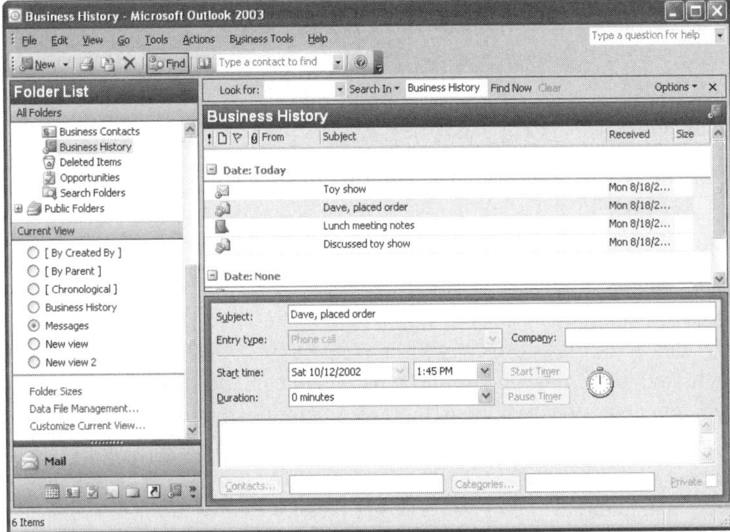

Figure 15-19. The Business History folder includes a handful of predefined views, including the Messages view.

You can also create your own views as needed to organize the folder's items in other ways. For example, you might create a custom view that shows messages only from a specific sender or that are associated with a particular account. Chapter 26, "Creating Custom Views and Print Styles," explains in detail how to create and use custom views. The following steps illustrate an example of how to create a view of the Business History folder that shows all items for a specific account:

1. Open the Business History folder and choose View, Arrange By, Current View, Define Views.
2. In the Custom View Organizer dialog box, click New.

3. Enter the name **Wingtip Toys**, choose Table, and click OK.
4. Click Filter in the Customize View dialog box, then click the Advanced tab (see Figure 15-20).

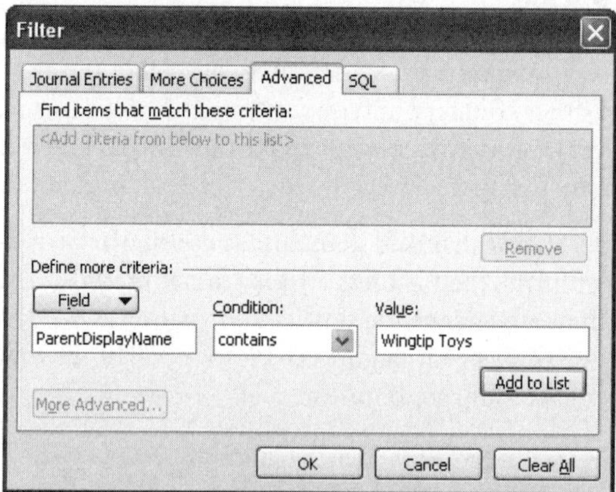

Figure 15-20. Use the Advanced tab to create a filtered view of the Business History folder.

5. Click Field, User-Defined Fields In Folder, and ParentDisplayName.
6. Click in the Value field and type **Wingtip Toys**, click Add To List, and click OK.
7. Click OK, then click Apply View to view all items associated with the Wingtip Toys account.

> **Tip** **View history of an item**
>
> Because the Business History folder shows all items by default, it's not usually the best place to go to find items associated with a particular contact, account, or opportunity. Although you can create custom views that will locate these items for you, a better approach is to simply open the account, contact, or opportunity, and view the associated items there. Viewing the links from the item's form saves you the trouble of creating a view to locate the linked items.

Attaching Items

In most cases, Business Contact Manager adds items to the Business History folder automatically. For example, send an e-mail to a business contact, and Business Contact Manager links the e-mail to the contact and it shows up in the Business History folder. Or, create a Call Contact task for a contact, and Business Contact Manager adds that to the contact.

You can also link items manually. For example, you might want to add a phone log item to an account when you receive a call from one of the account's contacts, attach a document to the account, or schedule an appointment for a contact. You can add the following to each of the Business Contact Manager item types:

- **Business Note** Add a note containing a subject, comments, and information about who created the note and when it was created.
- **Task** Add a standard Outlook task to the selected item.
- **Appointment** Add a standard Outlook appointment to the selected item.
- **Phone Log** Add to the item a phone log entry that includes call start time, duration, subject, and comments. The Business Phone Log form includes a timer you can start and pause during the call to time the call.
- **File** Add any type of file to the selected item. For example, you might add a Microsoft Word document, a Microsoft Excel worksheet, or brochure in Portable Document Format (PDF) format.

You can also add the following to contacts and accounts:

- **Mail Message** Send a mail message to the business contact or to the e-mail address specified in the account's properties.
- **Opportunity** Add a new sales opportunity item to the business contact or account.

To add an item to an account, contact, or opportunity, open that item from its folder and under the History area on the General tab, click Add. Choose from the shortcut menu the type of item to add. Business Contact Manager opens a form that varies depending on the type selected. Enter the needed information in the form and click Save And Close to associate it with the selected item. The linked item will then show up in the History list as well as in the Business History folder.

Creating Reports

What would a CRM system be without reports? Business Contact Manager includes several predefined reports that you can use as is or customize to suit specific needs. There are reports for business contacts, opportunities, and accounts, as well as two additional reports to display your business task list and sources of sales leads.

To create a report, click the Business Tools menu, choose Reports, then choose the report category and specific report you want to view. A report window opens and displays the report, as shown in Figure 15-21.

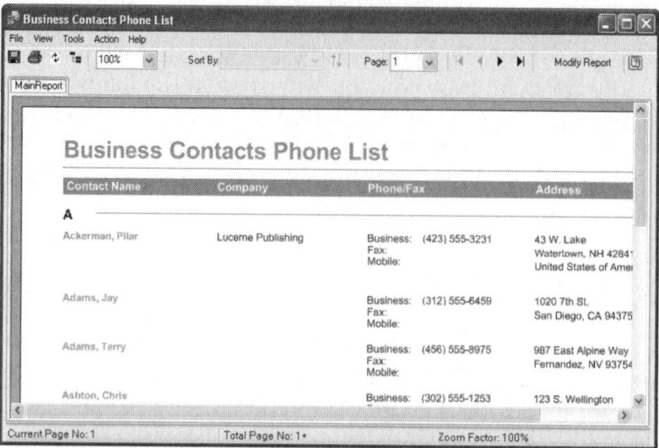

Figure 15-21. Business Contact Manager includes several reports for analyzing information in your database.

The report window shows the first page of the report. You can page through the report using the arrow buttons at the top of the window or choose a page from the Page drop-down list. You can also zoom in or out to change the amount of information you can see.

> **Tip** To go to a specific page, press Ctrl+G, enter the page number, and click OK.

Navigating Through a Report

If a report is lengthy, you can use its groupings to quickly move through the report to locate specific information. For example, assume you open the Business Contacts Phone List report and want to view the entries that start with the letter R. You could page or scroll through the report until you find the Rs, but a better way is to turn on grouping display. Click the Show/Hide Groupings button on the toolbar or choose View, Show Group to add a grouping pane to the left side of the report, as shown in Figure 15-22.

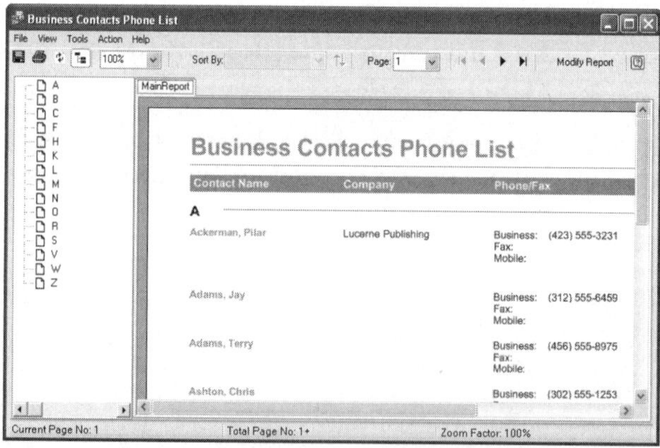

Figure 15-22. Use the grouping pane to quickly navigate through a long report.

Just click an item in the left pane to navigate to that location in the report. Click the Show/ Hide Groupings button again to turn off the grouping pane.

Modifying Reports

You can modify reports to change the way they appear or change the information displayed in them. For example, you might want to make relatively minor changes, such as changing the report title, adding other information to the header, or turning off page numbers. Or, you might want to make more extensive changes, such as filtering in only specific items, for example, including in a phone list only those contacts that begin with a certain letter.

Click the Modify Report button on the toolbar or choose Action, Modify Report to open the Modify Report dialog box shown in Figure 15-23. The General tab contains several options that control the information that appears in the report. Options that don't pertain to the selected report are dimmed and unavailable. For example, reports that don't include a date range have the Date Range group dimmed.

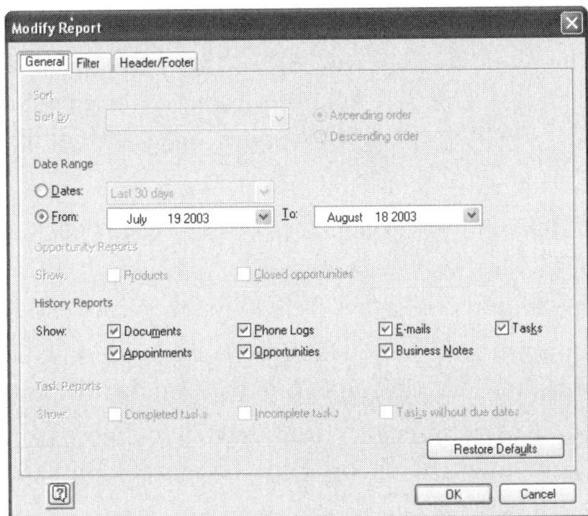

Figure 15-23. Use the General tab to control the information included on a report.

You can use the Filter tab (see Figure 15-24) to select which records are included in the report and to set up filters that include or exclude information. Under the Records group, click Select (the button name changes according to the report type) to explicitly choose the records you want included in the report. When you click Select, Business Contact Manager displays a dialog box in which you select the items to include.

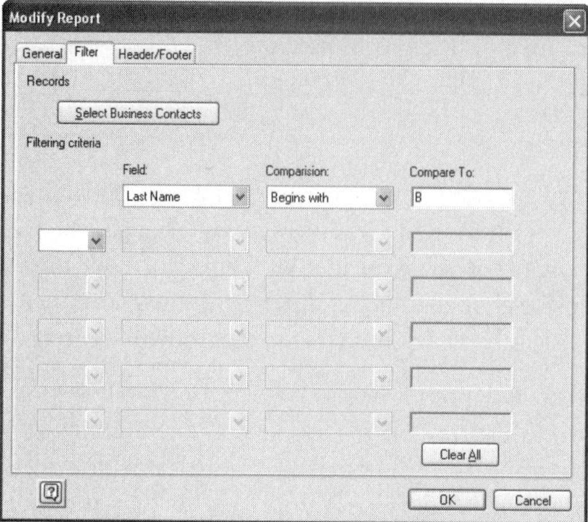

Figure 15-24. Use the Filter tab to include or exclude records in the report.

The capability to filter the report is an important tool to tailor the information included in the report. You'll find that setting filters is easy, particularly if you have used the filter capabilities in Outlook's views, which are similar. The following example filters the Business Contacts Phone List to include only those contacts with last names that start with B and a home state of TX.

1. Choose Business Tools, Reports, Business Contacts, Business Contacts Phone List to create a phone list report.
2. In the report window, click Modify Report on the toolbar, then click the Filter tab.
3. In the first row, select Last Name from the Field drop-down list, choose Begins With from the Comparison drop-down list, and enter **B** in the Compare To text box.
4. In the second row, choose AND from the first drop-down list, choose Home State/Province from the Field drop-down list, choose Equals from the Comparison drop-down list, and then enter TX in the Compare To text box.
5. Click OK to refresh the report based on the new filter criteria.

Tip **Use AND and OR logic**

You can use AND or OR logic for a filter condition. Choose AND when you want the condition to apply in addition to the previous conditions; for example, to display contacts with names that start with B and who are located in Texas. Use OR to display contacts with names that start with B or who live in Texas. In this example, a contact would appear in the report if his or her last name started with B, or he or she lived in Texas, or both, if you used the OR logic.

The Header/Footer tab, shown in Figure 15-25, gives you a place to add other information to the report's header or footer. You can also specify the font used for specific items. The options on the Header/Footer tab are self-explanatory.

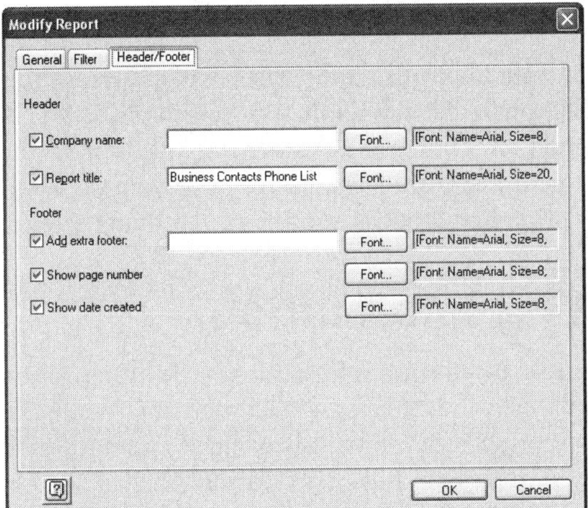

Figure 15-25. Use the Header/Footer tab to include other information in the report's header or footer, or to change fonts.

Tip You can save a report to a Word or Excel document and edit the report in those applications. The next section explains how.

Saving Reports

After you create a report you can print it, but you might also want to save the report to disk so you can edit it, send it to someone else, or put in on a Web site. Business Contact Manager can save reports in four formats:

- **Word Document** Choose this type to save the document in Microsoft Office Word 2003 format. You can then open the document in Word to edit it.
- **Rich-Text Format** Choose this type to save the document in rich-text format (RTF), which is useful for sharing the report with others who do not have Microsoft Word. The Wordpad application included with Windows can read and edit RTF files (as well as some Word files).
- **Excel Workbook** Choose this type to save the report as a Microsoft Office Excel 2003 workbook. This type is particularly useful when you need to analyze the figures included in a report.
- **Web Page** Choose this type to save the report as an HTML file that you can post on a Web site.

To save a report, open the report and modify as needed, then choose File, Save As to open the Save As dialog box. Choose the file type, choose a path, enter a name for the report, and click Save. If you want to edit the report, simply locate the saved report, double-click it, and the appropriate application will open with the report loaded into it.

Printing Reports

At some point you will probably want to print a report. Business Contact Manager gives you the capability to print reports, although the options are somewhat limited. To print a report, open the report, modify it as needed, and choose File, Print or click the Print button on the toolbar. Business Contact Manager opens a standard Print dialog box you can use to select a printer and set the number of copies to print. Just click OK to print the report to the selected printer.

Importing and Exporting Information

If you are just starting to organize your business information in electronic format, you will likely have to enter most of it manually in Business Contact Manager, creating contacts, accounts, and sales opportunities yourself. If you've been using other solutions to keep track of this information and now want to move to Business Contact Manager, you can import data from those other applications to Business Contact Manager and save quite a bit of time.

Importing Contacts or Accounts

Business Contact Manager can import data from a handful of other applications. You can import data from Act!, Microsoft Excel, Microsoft bCentral List Builder, QuickBooks, or any application that can export to a comma-separated value (.csv) file. All but the Act! 4.0, 5.0 Database option prompt you to specify a file from which to import. Importing from Act! requires that you have Act! installed on your computer.

To import data, choose File, Import And Export, Business Contact Manager to open the Business Data Import/Export Wizard. Click Import A File and click Next. Choose the data source (see Figure 15-26) and click Next.

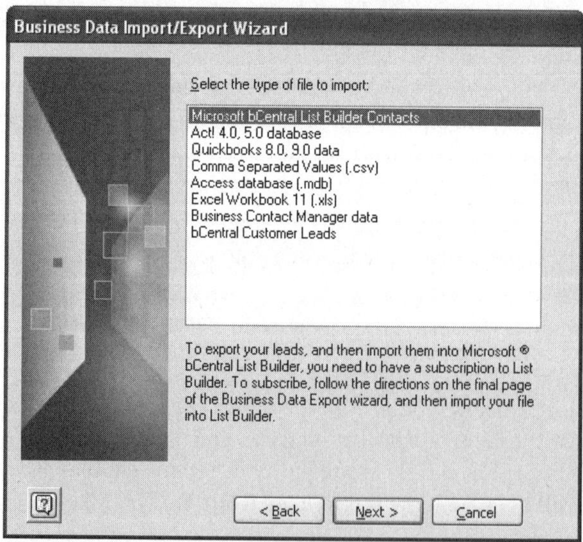

Figure 15-26. Choose the source for importing data to Business Contact Manager.

The following example imports contacts from an Access database:

1. Choose File, Import And Export, Business Contact Manager to open the Business Data Import/Export Wizard.
2. Choose Access Database and click Next, then click Browse to locate and select the .mdb file containing your contact list. Specify how you want duplicates handled, and then click OK.
3. In the Business Data Import/Export Wizard page shown in Figure 15-27, select Business Contacts as the destination to import the contacts as business contacts, or choose Accounts to import the contacts as accounts.

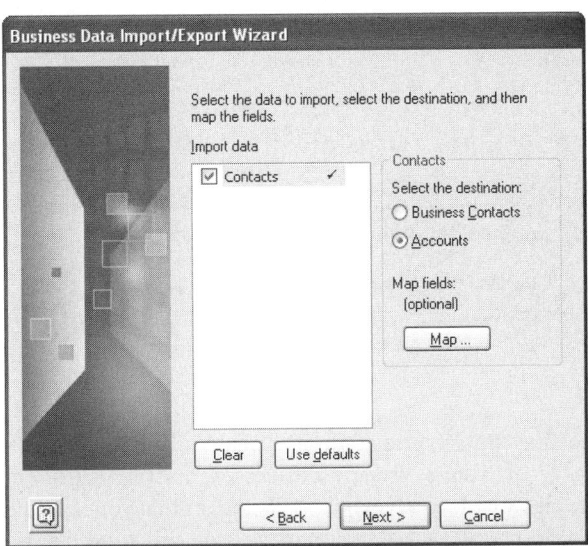

Figure 15-27. Select the destination for the incoming data.

4. Click Map to open the Map Fields dialog box, shown in Figure 15-28. Drag fields from the left pane to the right pane, dropping them on the fields to which you want them mapped. For example, drag the LastName field in the left pane to the Last Name field in the right pane for a contact, or map the Company field to the Account Name field for an account. Ignore (do not map) those fields that you do not want imported into Business Contact Manager.

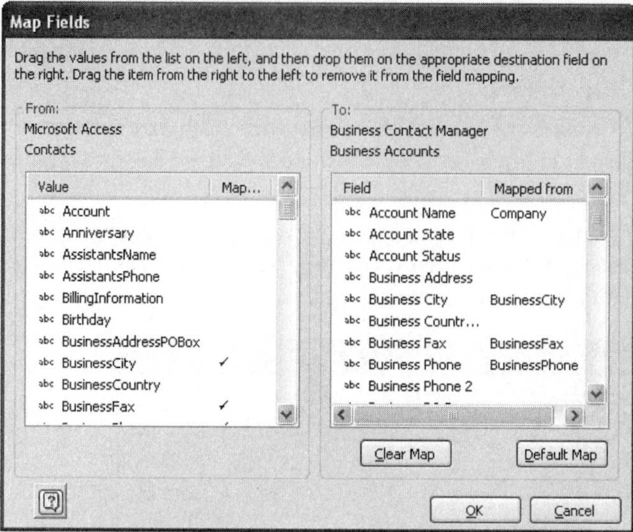

Figure 15-28. Map fields from the source to the destination.

5 After you have mapped all of the desired fields, click Next, then click Next again to start the import process.

Importing Products

In addition to importing contacts and accounts, you can also import a product list into Business Contact Manager. In this first version, Business Contact Manager will import products only from a comma-delimited (.csv) text file. This means that you must first export the data from its current location to a CSV file. It also means you might need to tweak the existing database format before you export the data to make sure it is in the right format. Business Contact Manager requires four fields in this sequence: Product Name, Description, Unit Price, and Default Quantity. The database can include additional fields, but when you export the data, you must export it so these four fields (or the ones that correspond to them in your existing product database) are exported as the first four fields and in the sequence specified.

> **Tip** To change field order in an Access table, open the table in design view, place the cursor at the left edge of a row and when the cursor changes to a right-facing arrow, click and drag the row into the desired position in the table.

> **Note** The Edit Product Master List dialog box does not show the Default Quantity field, but it is included in the Business Contact Manager Products database.

The following steps explain how to export a table from a Microsoft Access database to a CSV file. For details on exporting from other applications, check the application's Help documentation.

1 Open Access and click Tables in the Objects pane, then right-click the table and choose Copy.

2 Right-click in the right pane and choose Paste to open the Paste Table As dialog box (see Figure 15-29). Enter a unique name for the table, choose Structure And Data, and click OK.

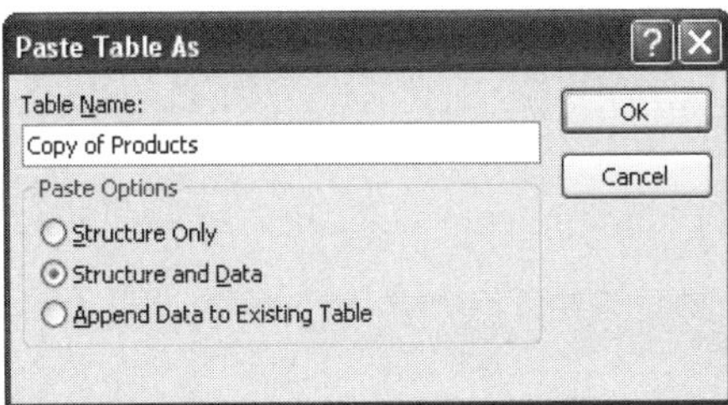

Figure 15-29. Paste the table into the database as a copy.

3 Open the copy of the table you created in step 2 in design view and adjust the order of the fields so that from top to bottom the fields are product name, description, cost, and unit quantity. Close the table and save changes to its layout.

4 Choose File, Export to open the Export Table dialog box. From the Save As Type drop-down list, choose Text Files, and enter the file name **MyProducts.csv** (or another unique file name that does not already exist).

5 Click Export to open the Export Text Wizard (see Figure 15-30) and verify that the fields are listed in the correct order without any additional fields in front of the product name field. Click Finish to accomplish the export.

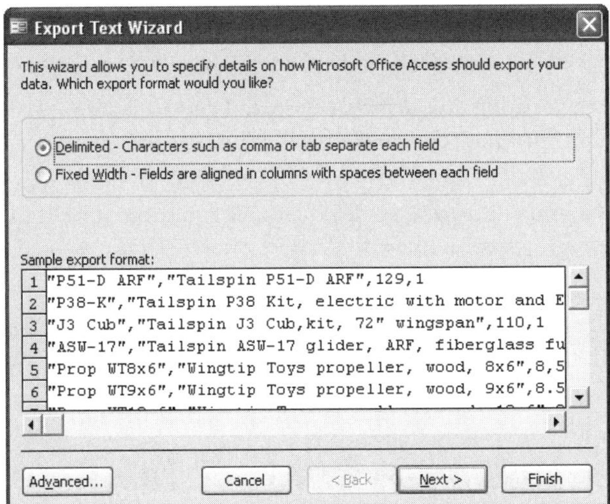

Figure 15-30. Use the Export Text Wizard to export from Access to a CSV file.

Note The default settings in Access for exporting to a CSV file are correct for exporting to Business Contact Manager. These include a " character as the text qualifier and a comma as the field separator.

With the table exported to a CSV file, you're ready to import the product list into Business Contact Manager by following these steps:

1. In Outlook, choose Business Tools, Product List to open the Edit Product Master List dialog box.
2. Click Import to open the Products Import dialog box, shown in Figure 15-31.

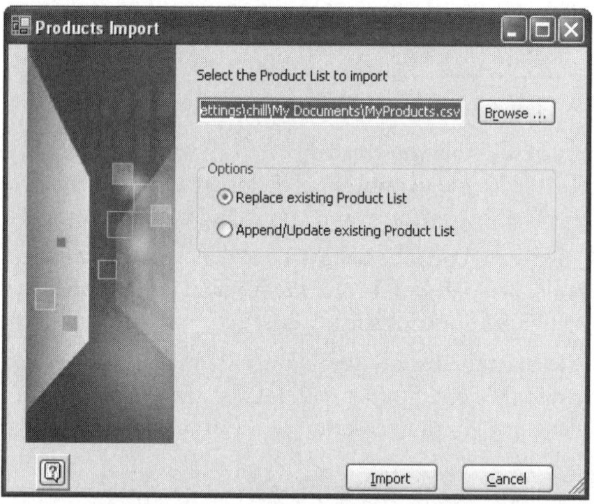

Figure 15-31. Import product items in the Products Import dialog box.

3. To replace any existing product list, choose the Replace Existing Product List option. To append the incoming data to your existing Business Contact Manager product list, choose the Append/Update Existing Product List option.
4. Click Browse and select the CSV file, then click Import to import the data. The products should now appear in the Edit Product Master List dialog box. Click OK to close the dialog box.

With your product list now imported into Business Contact Manager, you can begin associating products with opportunities as explained previously in the section "Adding Products to an Opportunity," page 438.

Managing Your Business Contact Manager Data

After you go through the time and trouble of setting up accounts, contacts, opportunities, and your product list, you certainly don't want to have to go through it all again if your system crashes. So, you should regularly back up your Business Contact Manager database. If your system does crash or the database is lost for some other reason, you can recover the database from the backup copy.

Business Contact Manager adds a handful of database management tasks to Outlook's File menu, as explained in the next few sections.

Cleaning Up the Database

One of the tasks you should perform regularly is to defragment the database to improve performance and check the database for errors. You accomplish both of these tasks in one operation. Choose File, Business Database, Maintenance to open the Database Maintenance dialog box. Click Start to start the process. Business Contact Manager displays the progress in the dialog box. Click Close when the process is finished.

Backing Up the Database

As a precaution against a lost or corrupted database, you should frequently back up your Business Contact Manager databases. To back up a database, choose File, Business Database, Backup to display the Database Backup dialog box, shown in Figure 15-32. Click Browse and specify the location and file name for the database, then click Save. Optionally, enter a password to protect the database and then click OK. Business Contact Manager creates a compressed backup of the database file. When Business Contact Manager displays its completion message, click OK.

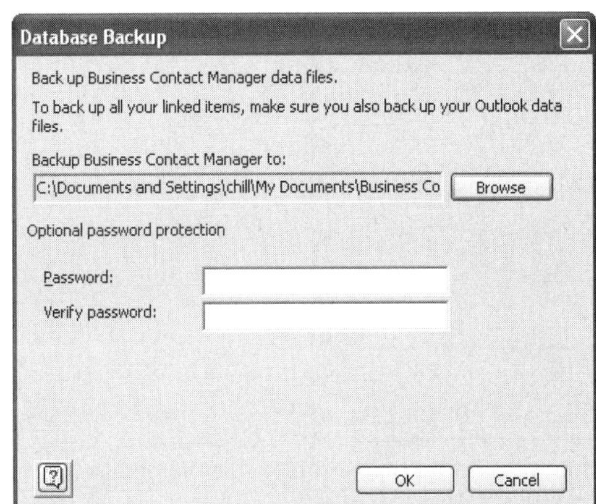

Figure 15-32. Click Browse to specify the backup location and file name.

Tip For best recoverability, place backup copies of your database on a network server or copy them to a CD. This will enable you to recover the files if your local hard disk fails.

Restoring the Database

To restore a database, open Outlook and choose File, Business Database, Restore to open the Database Restore dialog box. Click Browse to locate and select the backup file and then click Open. Enter a password if the backup is password-protected and then click OK to start the restore.

Deleting Databases

You can delete a Business Contact Manager database if you no longer need it. A typical database can take up a lot of space, so deleting those you no longer need can help you conserve disk space.

To delete a database, first make sure you don't need it and know specifically which ones (by name) can be deleted. As a precaution, you should back up the database and copy it to CD before deleting it. When you're ready to delete it, choose File, Business Database, Properties to open the Database Properties dialog box, shown in Figure 15-33. Select a database from the list and click Delete.

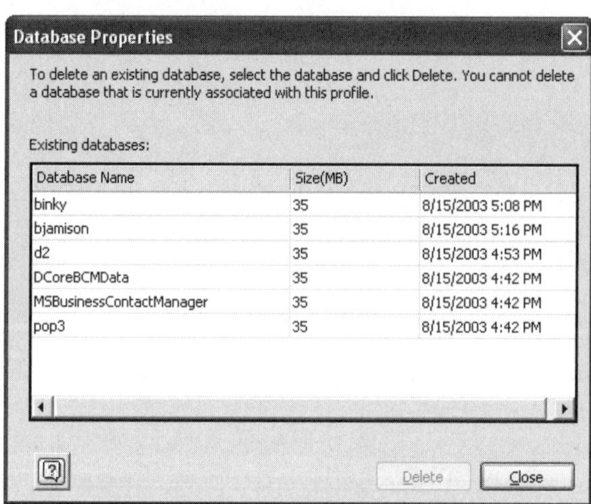

Figure 15-33. Delete a database with the Database Properties dialog box.

Tip **Remove a database associated with the current profile**

You can't delete a database that is associated with the current profile. To remove it from the profile, right-click the Business Contact Manager branch in the folder list and click Close Business Contact Manager. You can also choose File, Data File Management to open the Outlook Data Files dialog box and remove the file. If you share your computer with someone else, make sure you aren't deleting someone else's Business Contact Manager data.

Chapter 16

Using LDAP Directory Services

Lightweight Directory Access Protocol (LDAP) is a standard for querying directory services. For example, you can query LDAP servers for the address, phone number, or other information associated with an entry in the directory. Microsoft Windows 2000 Server and Windows Server 2003 use LDAP as the primary mechanism for accessing the Active Directory directory service. Servers running Microsoft Exchange Server can also act as LDAP servers, allowing users to look up addresses and associated information in the directory.

This chapter explores LDAP and explains how to configure LDAP directory service accounts in Microsoft Outlook and Microsoft Outlook Express. The last section of the chapter explains how to configure your own LDAP server using Microsoft Exchange Server 5.*x*, Microsoft Exchange 2000 Server, and Microsoft Exchange Server 2003.

Overview of LDAP Services

LDAP was designed to serve with less overhead and fewer resource requirements than its predecessor, the Directory Access Protocol, which was developed for X.500. LDAP is a standards-based protocol that allows clients to query data in a directory service over a TCP connection. Microsoft's Active Directory and other directory services on the Internet such as Bigfoot, InfoSpace, and Yahoo! employ LDAP to implement searches of their databases.

> For additional information regarding LDAP, refer to "MS Strategy for Lightweight Directory Access Protocol (LDAP)," available in the NT Server Technical Notes section of Microsoft TechNet or on the Web at *http://www.microsoft.com/TechNet/winnt/Winntas/technote/ldapcmr.asp.*

Configuring a Directory Service Account in Outlook

In addition to supporting e-mail accounts, Microsoft Outlook 2003 also allows you to add LDAP-based directory service accounts to query for subscriber information in the remote server's directory. The LDAP server might be internal to your organization, might be hosted by another company, or might be one of several LDAP directories located on the Internet. With an LDAP account in your profile, you can look up names, addresses, and other information stored in the directory.

To set up and configure an LDAP account in Outlook, follow these steps:

1. Right-click the Outlook icon on the desktop and choose Properties. Then click E-Mail Settings (and select the profile if necessary). Alternatively, if Outlook is already open, choose Tools, E-Mail Accounts.
2. Select Add A New Directory Or Address Book in the E-Mail Accounts Wizard and click Next.
3. Select Internet Directory Service (LDAP) and click Next.
4. On the Directory Service (LDAP) Settings page of the wizard (see Figure 16-1), type the server name or the IP address in the Server Name box.

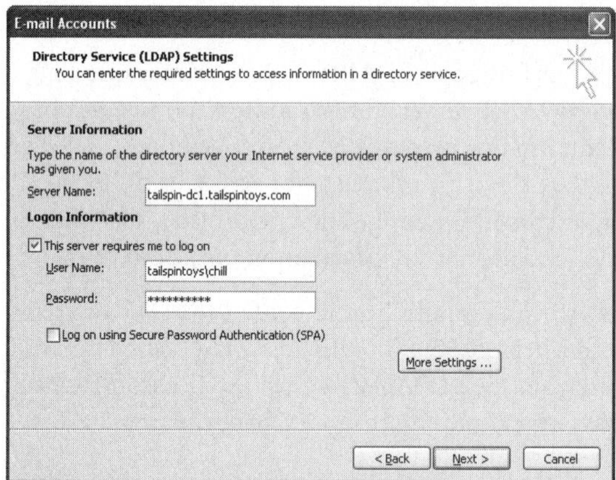

Figure 16-1. Specify the server name, and supply logon credentials if the server requires authentication.

5. If the server requires authentication, select the This Server Requires Me To Log On check box. Specify the logon credentials in the User Name and Password boxes. If you're authenticating on a Windows NT, Windows 2000 Server, or Windows Server 2003 domain controller, include the domain by entering *<domain>**<user>* in the User Name box, where *<domain>* is the domain name and *<user>* is the user account.

> **Tip** **Add the domain for LDAP authentication**
>
> Failing to include the domain in the authentication string will result in the authentication error message, "Failed to connect to *<server>* due to invalid authentication." If you clear the This Server Requires Me To Log On check box and the server requires authentication, you'll receive the error message, "No entries were found. You may need to supply authentication information in order to be able to access the directory." Clear this check box only if the server allows anonymous LDAP queries.

6 Click More Settings to open the Microsoft LDAP Directory dialog box, shown in Figure 16-2.

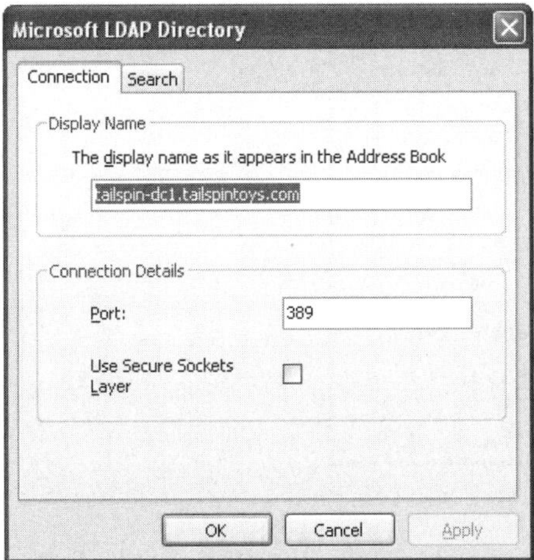

Figure 16-2. Change the display name, port, and other properties as needed.

7 Change the name in the Display Name box to the name you want Outlook to display in the address book for the directory service.

8 In the Port box, type the port number required by the LDAP server. The default port is 389, although you can use 3268 for most searches in an Active Directory's global catalog (GC).

Tip **Use two ports**
Port 3268 is the default port for the Active Directory GC. Certain types of data are available through one specific port, whereas other types of data are accessed through the other. For example, read-only copies of data from other domains are available only through the GC port. For that reason, you might create two directory services, one for each port. For details, see "Configuring an LDAP Server," page 462.

9 You can select the Use Secure Sockets Layer (SSL) check box to connect to the LDAP server through SSL. In most cases, SSL won't be required. This option works only if the server allows an SSL connection.

10 In the Microsoft LDAP Directory dialog box, click the Search tab, shown in Figure 16-3.

Figure 16-3. Use the Search tab to configure timeout, number of hits to return, and the search base.

11 Specify the search timeout and the maximum number of entries you want returned in a search. In the Search Base box, type the root for your search in the directory. If you're searching Active Directory, for example, you might enter **dc=<*domain*>,dc=<*suffix*>**, where <*domain*> is your domain name (without the domain suffix). Specify the domain suffix (net, com, org, or us, for example) as the last data item. See "Setting the Search Base" in the next section for more details.

12 Click OK to close the dialog box. Then click Next and click Finish to complete the account setup.

> **Note** Queries to the Active Directory using SSL should be directed to port 636. GC queries using SSL should be directed to port 3269.

You can use the directory service accounts created in Outlook to perform LDAP queries from within Outlook. Outlook Express accounts can also be used for these types of searches. However, you can't use these accounts from the search/find feature of your operating system.

> **Tip** You can make changes to a directory service account in Outlook and query using the new settings without restarting Outlook.

Setting the Search Base

The search base for an LDAP query specifies the container in the directory service where the query will be performed. When querying against Active Directory on a Windows server, specifying no search base causes Outlook to return all items in the directory that have an e-mail address. Often, this means you see many system-level objects, as shown in Figure 16-4. These additional objects often confuse casual users, and even users familiar with Active Directory generally don't want to see these system-level objects. You can set the search base to more closely target the information you're trying to find, but to do so, you must understand what the search base really is.

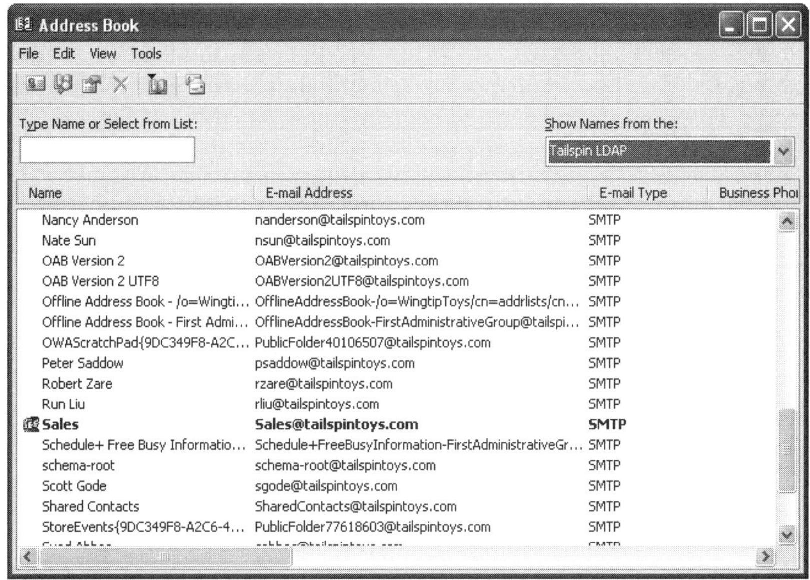

Figure 16-4. A query with no search base returns all objects with e-mail addresses.

Each entry in the directory has a distinguished name, which is a fully qualified name that identifies that specific object. Relative distinguished names (RDNs) are concatenated to form the DN, which uniquely identifies the object in the directory. RDNs include the following:

- cn=common name
- ou=organizational unit
- o=organization
- c=country
- dc=domain

> **Tip** Active Directory drops the c= attribute and adds the dc= attribute.

For example, assume you want to search the users container in the domain boyce.us. The search base would be as follows:

cn=users,dc=boyce,dc=us

Notice that the domain is represented by two dc attributes. If the domain you are searching is microsoft.com, you would use dc=microsoft,dc=com instead. Or, if your domain does not use a Domain Name System (DNS)-compliant domain name (as in a Windows NT domain), you would simply specify a single dc attribute for the domain name.

In some cases the part of the directory you want to search will be in a specific organizational unit (OU). Or, you might be setting up multiple LDAP accounts in Outlook, each configured to search a specific OU. For example, perhaps your company has Sales, Marketing, Support, External Contacts, and a handful of other OUs, and you want to configure an LDAP query for each one. One solution is to add an LDAP service for each and configure the search base accordingly. For example, let's say we're configuring an LDAP service account to query the Support OU in the boyce.us domain. The search base would be as follows:

ou=support,dc=boyce,dc=us

Keep the following points in mind when deciding on a search base:

- Specifying no search bases causes Outlook to retrieve objects from the entire directory.
- Specifying a search base sets the branch of the directory to search in the directory tree.

If you decide to include a search base, determine the common name for the object or OU, then add the domain. You can't specify just the ou or cn attributes without the domain, but you can specify the domain by itself to perform a top-down search of the domain.

Tip If you need to search different branches of the directory tree, you can add multiple LDAP service accounts to your profile, each with the appropriate search base. Or, add only one LDAP service account, then simply change its search base when you need to query a different branch.

Troubleshooting

Your LDAP query returns this error message: There Are No Entries In The Directory Service That Match Your Search Criteria

Sooner or later, you'll attempt to query an LDAP server that you know contains at least one item meeting your search criteria—but you'll receive an error message telling you that no entries in the directory service match your criteria. One possible cause of this problem is that the search option specified at the LDAP server might be preventing the query from completing successfully. For example, you might be issuing an "any" query, but the server is configured to treat such queries as initial queries.

For a detailed discussion of query types and how to configure the search option, see "Configuring Exchange Server 5.*x* LDAP Properties," page 464.

You might also receive this error message if you've incorrectly set LDAP directory service account properties—for example, you might have configured the account to use port 389 when the server requires SSL. Check your directory service account settings to ensure that you have specified the proper server name or address, port, and search base.

Configuring a Directory Service Account in Outlook Express

You can use Outlook Express as well as Outlook to perform LDAP searches. This capability can be handy when you're working on a system that does not have Outlook installed, such as a notebook computer that you use infrequently. You can access LDAP queries by using the Outlook Express address book or by using the search/find feature of your operating system.

For an explanation of how to perform LDAP queries through your operating system, see "Searching from Windows," page 462.

To configure Outlook Express LDAP directory services, follow these steps:

1. In Outlook Express, choose Tools, Accounts.
2. In the Internet Accounts dialog box, click Directory Service to display the Directory Service tab (see Figure 16-5).

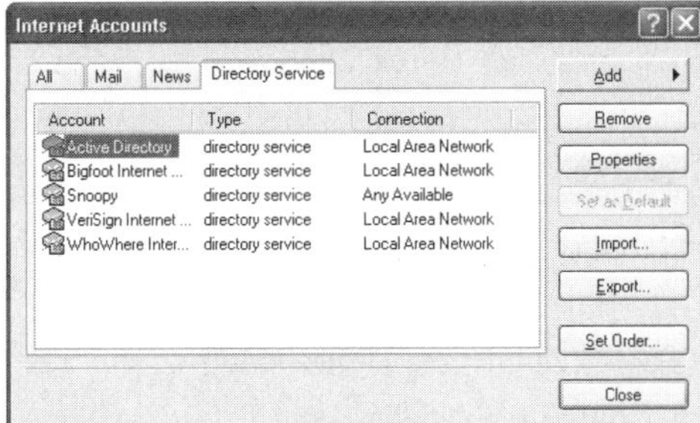

Figure 16-5. Use the Directory Service tab to view, add, and change directory service accounts.

3. Choose Add, Directory Service to start the Internet Connection Wizard.
4. In the Internet Directory (LDAP) Server box, type the DNS name or the IP address of the LDAP server. If the server requires authentication, select the My LDAP Server Requires Me To Log On option and click Next.
5. If you selected authentication, specify the account name and password for the directory server. If you're authenticating using a domain account outside your current domain, enter the account in the form <*domain*>\<*account*>. Specify the password and, if you're using Secure Password Authentication, select the Log On Using Secure Password Authentication (SPA) option and click Next.
6. The wizard asks whether you want to check addresses using this directory service. Choose Yes and click Next.
7. Click Finish to complete the account's setup.

8 On the Directory Service tab of the Internet Accounts dialog box, select the account you just created and click Properties to display the Properties dialog box for the account (see Figure 16-6).

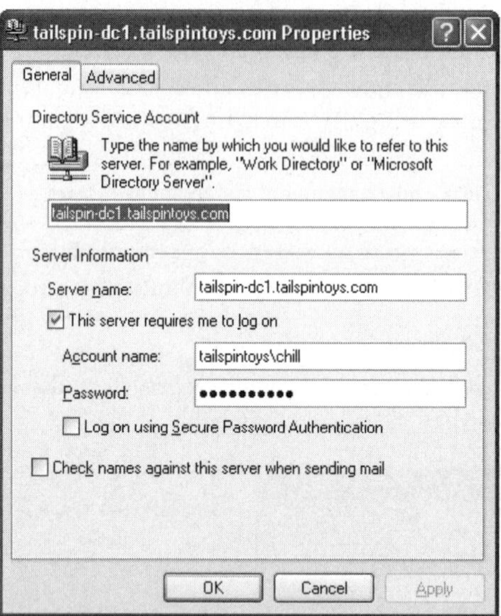

Figure 16-6. Use the General tab to specify name, server location, and other LDAP server properties.

9 Click Advanced. On the Advanced tab (see Figure 16-7), specify the port you want to use, the search timeout, and other properties. Click OK.

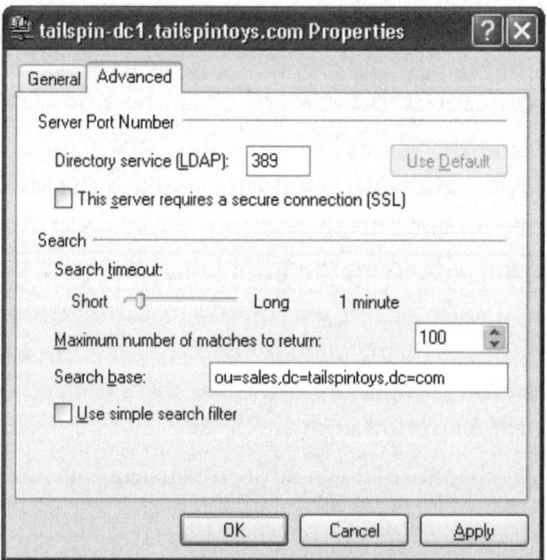

Figure 16-7. Use the Advanced tab to configure the port and other search properties.

10 Close the Internet Accounts dialog box.

Using LDAP to Find People

LDAP directory services that you create within Outlook can be searched through the Outlook Address Book only. Outlook Express comes preconfigured with several LDAP directory service accounts. You can query these directory services using the Outlook Express address book or using your operating system's search/find feature. The following sections explain the different ways you can perform LDAP queries through directory service accounts.

Searching from Outlook

You can perform LDAP queries in Outlook by using directory service accounts you add to Outlook. You can't search these directory service accounts outside Outlook, as you can with Outlook Express.

Follow these steps to perform an LDAP query with an LDAP server in Outlook:

1. In Outlook, click the Address Book icon to open the Address Book window. Alternatively, you can choose Tools, Address Book.
2. In the Outlook Address Book, choose the directory service from the Show Names drop-down list. Depending on how the directory service account is configured, Outlook might display the contents of the directory immediately in the address book.
3. To search using specific criteria, click the Find Items button on the toolbar or choose Tools, Find. Either action opens the Find dialog box (see Figure 16-8).

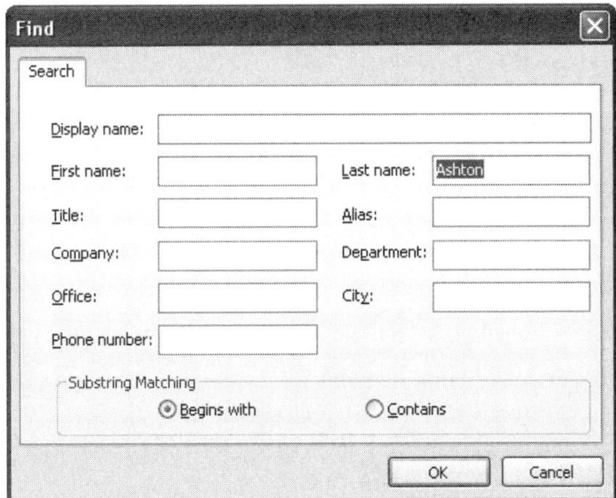

Figure 16-8. Use the Find dialog box to specify the criteria for the LDAP query.

4. Specify the criteria for the search and click OK.

Searching from Outlook Express

You can perform queries from within Outlook Express using LDAP directory service accounts you create in Outlook Express.

Follow these steps to do so:

1. In Outlook Express, click the Addresses icon on the toolbar or choose Tools, Address Book to open the address book.
2. In the address book, click the Find People button on the toolbar or choose Edit, Find People to display the Find People dialog box (see Figure 16-9).

Figure 16-9. Use the Find People dialog box to perform LDAP queries in Outlook Express.

3. In the Look In drop-down list, select the directory service account to use.
4. Specify the criteria for the search (such as name or e-mail address), click Advanced to specify additional parameters if needed, and click Find Now.

Searching from Windows

You can perform LDAP queries from Microsoft Windows using directory service accounts you create in Outlook Express. Follow these steps to do so:

1. In Windows 2000, click Start, Search, For People. In Microsoft Windows XP, choose Start, Search, Computers Or People, People In Your Address Book. These actions open the Find People dialog box.
2. In the Look In drop-down list, select the directory service to query.
3. Enter the search criteria and click Find Now.

Configuring an LDAP Server

As you read the previous sections about directory services, you might have come to the conclusion that you'd like to enable LDAP queries on your own directory service. This section of the chapter isn't intended as an in-depth explanation of the LDAP services offered by Exchange Server or the Windows 2000 Active Directory, but it does discuss the most common configuration issues you'll encounter as you get your LDAP service online and configure its primary settings.

Adding Global Catalog Servers

When you promote a computer running Windows 2000 Server to a domain controller (DC), Windows 2000 automatically installs Active Directory on the server. The same is true for Windows Server 2003. Active Directory uses LDAP as its primary lookup mechanism, listening on the standard port 389 for LDAP queries and on port 636 for secure queries through SSL. Thus, to enable LDAP lookups, you need only install a Windows DC. However, you should consider whether you need to add another GC.

The GC is an important part of Active Directory's structure. The GC is the mechanism through which searches occur in Active Directory and therefore is critical to all Active Directory functions, including authentication. In the simplest terms, the GC functions much like a key database does, simplifying searches of Active Directory. The GC contains a full writable replica of all objects in Active Directory for its host domain. It also contains a partial read-only replica of the other domains in the forest. This read-only replica contains a copy of all objects in the domain forest, minus all but the attributes useful for searching. In essence, the GC serves as a flat database of the objects in the forest that allows quick location of any object in the directory—in other words, it's the directory's directory. The GC is built automatically by Active Directory's replication mechanisms. By default, the first DC in a domain forest is designated as the GC server. Status as a DC does not equate to being a GC server—the only DC that functions by default as a GC server is the first one in the domain forest. Other DCs that come online do not function as GC servers unless you configure them as such. Why configure a DC to act as a GC server? Redundancy is a primary reason, and availability is a close second. Because a GC server is necessary for authenticated logon, it's good design practice to include a GC server at each site, particularly when the domain spans a wide area with links susceptible to failure. Having a local copy of the GC allows users to log on through Active Directory if the link to the other GC servers is down. If the GC is unavailable, Windows uses cached credentials for logon.

A network segment that is subject to disconnection from the site where the GC is hosted should have its own GC server. If the network connection is down and no GC server is available, clients will have difficulty logging on. Native-mode DCs require access to the GC to determine complete group membership access levels for each user, and if the GC is unavailable, the DC denies logon. Having spare GC servers is therefore crucial.

To configure a computer as a GC server, you must first install it as a DC and then follow these steps:

1. Open Active Directory Sites And Services, expand the target site to locate the DC in the Servers node, and then expand the server.
2. Right-click NTDS Settings and choose Properties.
3. Select the Global Catalog check box and click OK.

Note You can use ports 3268 and 3269 (SSL) only after Active Directory is installed successfully, the server becomes a DC, and the Global Catalog option is set. DCs that do not host a copy of the GC will respond only to ports 389 and 636 (SSL).

Configuring Exchange Server 5.*x* LDAP Properties

When you install Exchange Server 5.*x*, Setup installs the LDAP protocol. If Exchange Server 5.*x* is installed on a Windows 2000 domain controller, or if Site Server is also installed on the same server, you'll experience problems because Active Directory and Site Server both use the default ports 389 and 636 (SSL) for LDAP queries. In either situation, you need to change the ports used by Exchange Server. You might want to change LDAP properties in other situations as well—for example, if your Exchange Server resides on the Internet, you might want to prevent anonymous LDAP queries and require users to authenticate. You can configure the LDAP protocol at the site level and at the server level. By default, all servers in a site use the site's LDAP protocol settings. You can, however, modify individual servers to configure their LDAP properties differently. For example, you might allow anonymous queries on one but not another, require SSL on one but not another, and so on. In general, you'll want to configure global settings at the site level and then apply server-specific settings at the server level.

Follow these steps to configure LDAP settings at the site level for Exchange Server 5.*x*:

1. Open the Exchange Administrator and expand the site. Click Protocols in the left pane (see Figure 16-10).

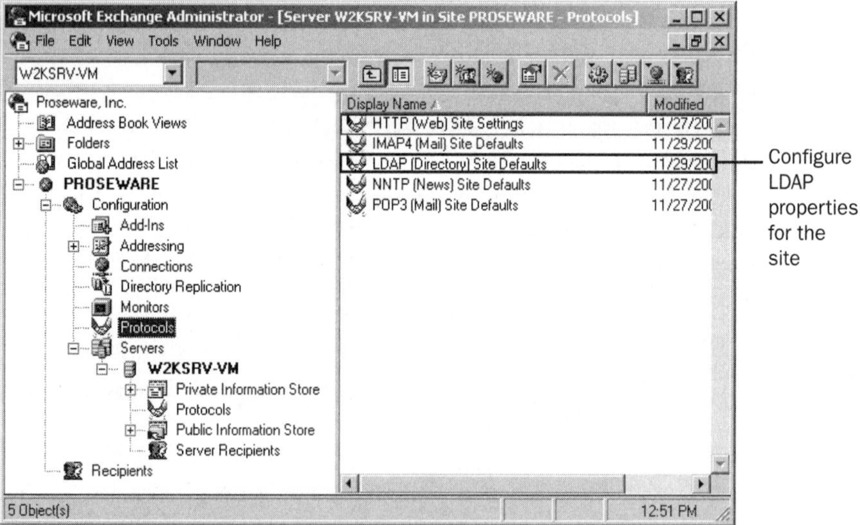

Figure 16-10. You can configure LDAP at the site level to define defaults for all servers in the site.

2 Double-click LDAP (Directory) Site Defaults in the right pane to open the dialog box shown in Figure 16-11.

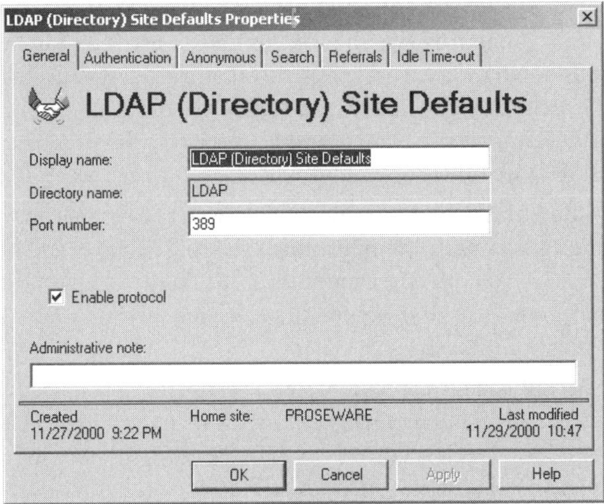

Figure 16-11. Use the LDAP (Directory) Site Defaults Properties dialog box to configure sitewide LDAP properties.

3 To enable LDAP, select the Enable Protocol check box. (To disable LDAP, clear this check box.)

4 In the Port Number box, specify the default port number for non-SSL queries.

5 Click Authentication. On the Authentication tab (see Figure 16-12), select the authentication methods that will be allowed.

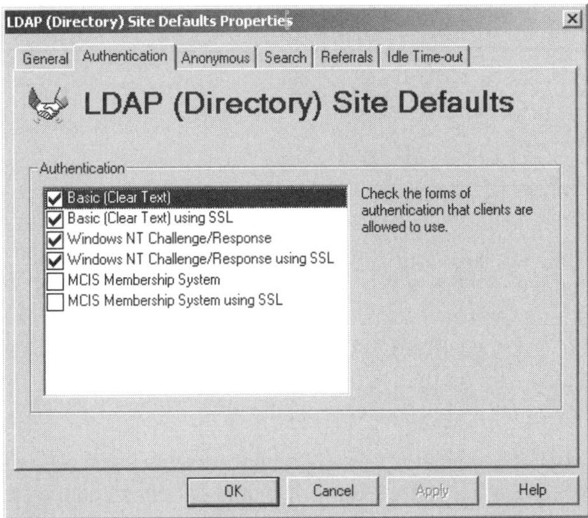

Figure 16-12. Use the Authentication tab to specify authentication methods used by servers in the site.

6 To allow anonymous LDAP queries, click the Anonymous tab and select the Allow Anonymous Access check box. To prevent anonymous queries, clear this check box.

7 Click the Search tab and select one of the following options:

- **Treat "Any" Substring Searches As "Initial" Substring Searches (Fast)** Select this option to have Exchange Server treat all partial string searches as initial substring searches. (See the sidebar "Using Substring Searches" later in this chapter for further explanation.) For example, specifying the substring Bo would return the results Boyce and Boris but would not return the result Placebo or Hobo.
- **Allow Only Initial Substring Searches (Fast)** Select this option to have Exchange Server perform only initial substring searches and not final substring searches. For example, Exchange Server would perform a substring search for Bo and return Boyce but would not perform a substring search of ce that would return the result Boyce.
- **Allow All Substring Searches (Slow)** Select this option to allow Exchange Server to perform initial, final, and any substring searches. This option generally provides slower performance than the other two, so use it judiciously if you're running Exchange Server on a slow server or one that receives a significant number of LDAP queries.

8 For the Maximum Number Of Search Results Returned option, specify the largest number of search results that should be returned for a given query.

9 Click Referrals. Use the Referrals tab to create LDAP referral entries. (See the following section, "Setting Up Referrals," for details.)

10 Click the Idle Time-Out tab to specify whether Exchange Server closes idle LDAP connections and to specify the timeout period.

11 Click OK to apply the changes and close the dialog box.

Inside Out

Using substring searches

LDAP clients can perform three types of substring searches: initial, final, and any. With an initial substring search, the LDAP server attempts to match the string provided in the query against the beginning of entries in the directory. For example, an initial substring query for Ji would return Jim, Jill, and Jiggle. With a final substring search, the LDAP server attempts to match the string provided against the end of the entries in the directory. For example, a final substring search for st would return Last, Best, and Most. With an any substring query, the LDAP server attempts to match the string against any characters in the attributes. Such a search for re would return Rebrovich, Bare, and Arena.

You can perform substring searches by using the Advanced tab of the Find People dialog box in Outlook Express or by using the Begins With and Contains options in the Find dialog box in Outlook.

Querying LDAP servers is an area where Outlook Express bests Outlook. Outlook Express provides several additional options for performing queries, including Is, Contains, Starts With, Ends With, and Sounds Like. Outlook provides only the Contains and Begins With options. This means it's much easier to perform complex LDAP queries with Outlook Express than with Outlook.

You can also configure individual servers in a site with nondefault settings, as follows:

1. Open the Exchange Administrator and expand the Servers branch. Expand the server you want to modify and select the Protocols branch in the left pane.
2. In the right pane, double-click LDAP (Directory) Settings.
3. Clear the Use Site Defaults For All Properties option.
4. Configure settings for the server as needed. The options are the same as those discussed for the site level earlier in this section.

Setting Up Referrals

You can configure Microsoft Exchange Server 5.5 to use up to 350 LDAP referral servers to perform LDAP queries on behalf of clients for information not found (or for additional information) in response to a client query. For example, a client might query the server for Jim Boyce, but no items in the directory match that name. However, the server can then submit the query to a referral server to obtain information about the queried data.

Follow these steps to set up LDAP referral servers in Exchange Server 5.*x*:

1. Open the Exchange Administrator.
2. Open the Protocols branch at the site level to specify a referral server at the site level. To specify a referral server at the server's level, open the Protocols branch of a specific server.
3. Click Referrals in the LDAP (Directory) Site Defaults Properties dialog box to open the Referrals tab, and then click New.
4. In the Referral Details dialog box (see Figure 16-13), specify the name or the IP address of the LDAP server, the directory name (search base), and the port number. If the server requires SSL, select the Connect Over SSL check box.

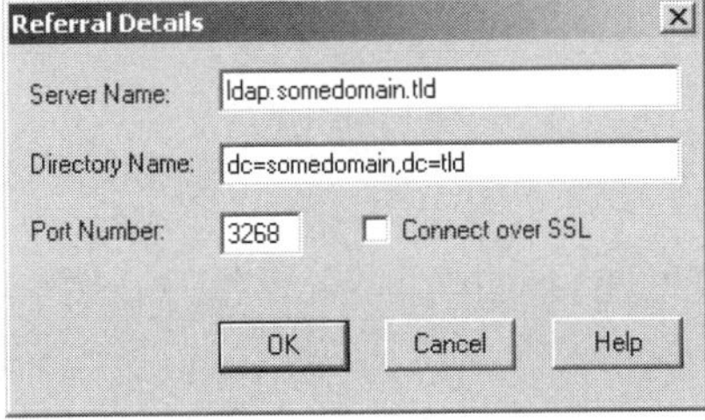

Figure 16-13. Use the Referral Details dialog box to specify the server properties for the LDAP referral server.

5 Click OK and then add any other referral servers you need.

6 Close the LDAP dialog box, and then close the Exchange Administrator.

Configuring Windows 2000 Server and Windows Server 2003 LDAP Properties

Unlike Exchange Server 5.*x*, Exchange 2000 Server and Exchange Server 2003 integrate with Active Directory rather than provide their own directory services. For that reason, you don't need to configure Exchange Server LDAP separately from Active Directory, nor will you encounter the conflicts that are possible with Exchange Server 5.*x* (discussed in the preceding section). A few other common issues might affect you, however. The following sections explain these issues and how to address them with Windows 2000 Server and Windows Server 2003 Active Directory.

Creating External Referrals

Like Exchange Server 5.*x*, Active Directory can use LDAP referrals to help clients locate queried information. References for referrals within the Active Directory forest are created automatically and replicated across the directory, allowing DCs to offer referrals for directory partitions in the forest that the DCs don't hold (partitions located on other DCs.) These cross-reference objects are created automatically when the DCs are promoted, and they are replicated across the directory.

If you need to have Active Directory provide query referrals to external directory services, you can add external cross-references. For clients to be able to use the referrals, they must support *chase referrals*, which allow a client to receive a referral to an external service and follow that referral to complete the query. Both the Windows Address Book (Outlook Express) and Outlook support chase referrals.

Unlike Exchange Server 5.*x*, Windows 2000 Server and Windows Server 2003 don't by default provide an easy means of adding external cross-references. However, you can use the ADSI Edit console, one of the optional support tools included with Windows 2000 Server and Windows Server 2003. To install the support tools from a Windows 2000 Server CD, run Setup.exe from the \Support\Tools folder. Run Suptools.msi from a Windows Server 2003 CD to install ADSI Edit.

Note ADSI Edit is powerful and can be a dangerous tool if you don't know what you're doing.

Then follow these steps to use the ADSI Edit console to add a cross-reference to an external LDAP service:

1 After installing the support tools, click Start, Run and start the Microsoft Management Console (MMC).

2 In the MMC, choose Console, Add/Remove Snap-In. Click Add, select ADSI Edit, click Add, click Close, and click OK.

3 Click the ADSI Edit branch and choose Action, Connect To.

4 In the Connection dialog box (see Figure 16-14), select the Select A Well Known Naming Context option, and then select Configuration from the associated drop-down list.

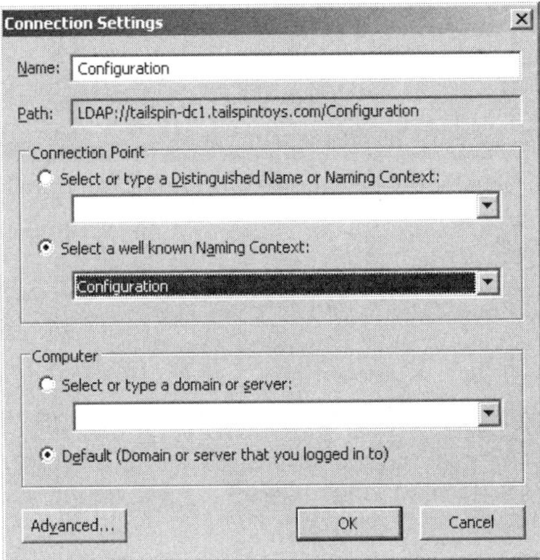

Figure 16-14. Use the Connection dialog box to specify how to connect to the directory.

5 If you're connecting to the DC to which you're logged on, select Default. Otherwise, select the Select Or Type A Domain Or Server option, and then select the appropriate domain or server. Click OK.

6 Expand the Configuration Container branch, and then expand the CN= Configuration branch.

7 Right-click CN=Partitions and click New, Object.

8 By default, crossRef is selected, so click Next.

9 In the Value box, type a name to describe the location and click Next.

10 In the Value box, type the DN for the external domain and click Next.

> **Note** For an external LDAP server, you must specify a value for the external domain's DN that matches the actual external directory name.

11 In the Value box, type the DNS name for the server hosting the directory partition or type the domain name, and then click Next.

12 Click Finish when you're satisfied with the settings.

Securing Global Address Lists

In some situations, you might want to apply access control lists (ACLs) to certain address lists to prevent LDAP queries for those address lists. For example, you might host multiple organizations on your Exchange Server and want to prevent users in one from browsing the addresses in another.

You can control access to address lists by setting ACLs on the list to restrict access, as explained here:

1. Open Exchange System Manager, and expand the branch containing the address list in question.
2. Right-click the list and choose Properties. Then click Security.
3. On the Security tab, configure the permissions as needed (see Figure 16-15), and then click OK to close the dialog box.

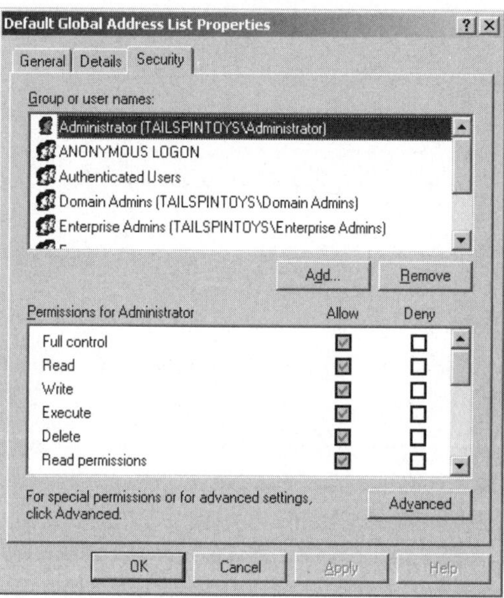

Figure 16-15. Use the Security tab to configure permissions for an address list and control access to it.

Chapter 17

Making Notes

If you're like most people, there's at least one note stuck to your monitor, lying on your desk, or tucked in a drawer, keeping some critical piece of information relatively safe until you need it again—safe, that is, until you lose the note. If you're looking for a better way to keep track of all the small bits of information you receive every day, you can use Microsoft Outlook 2003 to create electronic notes for quick to-do lists, phone numbers, shopping lists—you name it. Notes reside in the Notes folder by default, but you can copy or move notes to other Outlook folders, use them in documents, place them on the desktop, or place them in your other file system folders.

This chapter examines notes and explores how to use them effectively in Outlook as well as how to integrate them in your other applications.

Understanding Outlook Notes

You can use Outlook notes to keep track of any kind of text-based information. For example, you might make a note as a reminder to call someone, to pick up a few things from the store on the way home, or to jot down a phone number. Outlook notes are really just simple text files, which you can create and view in the Outlook Notes folder (see Figure 17-1).

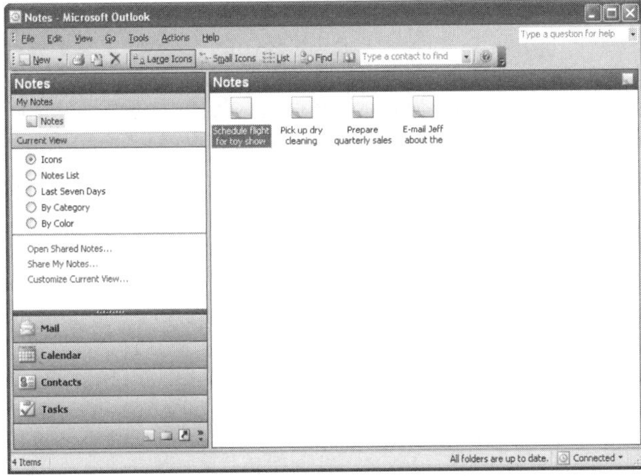

Figure 17-1. You can create and view your notes in the Notes folder.

When you create a new note, Outlook opens a window similar to the one shown in Figure 17-2. The note window is essentially a text box. As you type, the text wraps, and the window scrolls to accommodate the text. At the bottom of the note window, Outlook displays the date and time you created the note.

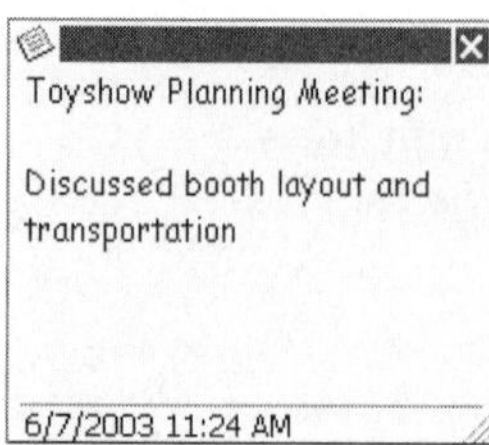

Figure 17-2. To create a new note, type in a note window.

You don't have to save the note explicitly—just close the note window and Outlook adds the note you've created to the Notes folder. You can copy or move a note to another Outlook folder or to a file system folder (such as your desktop), copy the text to the clipboard for inclusion in another document, or save the note to a text file. The following sections explain not only how to perform these actions, but also how to use notes in other ways.

Inside Out

Choose the best feature for the job

Although you can use notes in Outlook to keep track of just about any kind of information, a note is not always the best approach. Be sure you're not using the note in place of a more effective Outlook feature. For example, if you need to remind yourself to make a casual phone call at some time during the day, a note might suffice. However, if you need to set up an important conference call, it's better to create a task and have Outlook provide a reminder at the appropriate time. Likewise, the Contacts folder is the best place to keep track of contact information, rather than recording it on scattered notes. Notes are great when you need speed and convenience, but when another Outlook feature is suitable, you should view a note as a stopgap. For example, you might create a note for a quick to-do list now, and then add each item as a task in your Tasks folder later on when you have the time. As you become more familiar with notes, take a look at how you use them to make sure you're working effectively.

Configuring Note Options

Before you start creating notes, you might want to take a few minutes to configure the options that control the default appearance of notes.

To set these options, follow these steps:

1 Open Outlook and choose Tools, Options.

Making Notes

2 Click Note Options to display the Notes Options dialog box, shown in Figure 17-3.

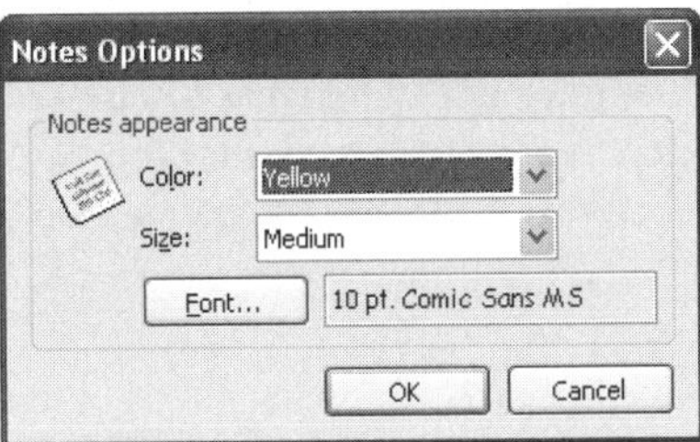

Figure 17-3. Use the Notes Options dialog box to control the size and color of the note window and the font used for notes.

3 Set the various options in this dialog box to determine the default color for notes (the color of the note window), the default size of the window, and the font used for the note text.

You can change the window size of any individual note by dragging the note window's border. You also can change the color of an existing note at any time (as explained in the following section).

> **Tip** Because Outlook stores the date and time created for each note, you should check to make sure that your system time is accurate.

Working with Notes

Of all Outlook's features, notes are by far the easiest to use. The following sections explain how to create notes, change their color, copy them to other folders, and more.

Adding a Note

You create notes in the Notes folder. To open this folder, click the Notes icon on the Outlook Bar.

After you've opened the folder, follow these steps to create a note:

1 Right-click in the Notes folder and choose New Note or simply double-click in the folder window. Either action opens a blank note window.

2 Type your note directly in the window.

3 Click the Close button in the upper-right corner of the note window to close and save it.

Outlook uses the first few dozen characters in the note as the title and displays it under the note's icon in the Notes folder.

> **Tip** When you click a note to select it in the Notes folder, Outlook displays the entire note contents under the icon so that you don't have to open the note to read it.

Reading and Editing a Note

To read a note, you can double-click it to open the note window or click the note and read the text under the icon. To change the content of a note, open it as just described and edit it the same way you would edit a text file. Keep in mind, however, that you have no formatting options, so your notes are limited to plain text. To save your changes, simply close the note window.

Forwarding a Note

Although you'll probably create notes mainly for your own use, you might need to forward a note to someone. For example, a colleague might request a phone number or other contact information you've stored in a note. The easiest way to share the information is to forward the note as a message. Because Outlook sends the note as an attachment, the recipient can easily copy the note to his or her own Notes folder, place it on the desktop, or use the clipboard to copy the data to a new contact entry.

To forward a note, follow these steps:

1 Open the Notes folder, right-click the note, and choose Forward from the shortcut menu. Outlook opens a standard message form. If you are using Outlook as your e-mail editor, the note is shown as an attachment to the message (see Figure 17-4). If Microsoft Word is your e-mail editor, Word embeds the note as an icon in the body of the message.

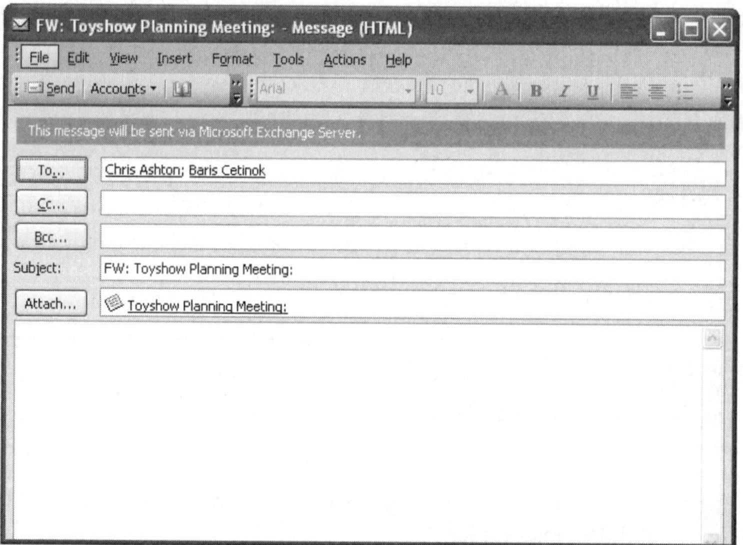

Figure 17-4. When you forward a note, Outlook attaches it to the message.

2 Complete and send the message as you would any other message.

Chapter 17

You can send notes in e-mail messages using other methods, too—you're not limited to embedding the note in the message or attaching it. For example, you can open the Notes folder and right-drag a note to the Inbox. The resulting shortcut menu allows you to create a message with the note as text in the body of the message, as a shortcut, or as an attachment.

Adding a Note Sent to You

When someone else sends you a note in an e-mail message, you can work with the note directly in the message. The note appears as an attachment to the message, as shown in Figure 17-5. You can open the message and double-click the note to open it in a note window, but you'll probably prefer to copy the note to your own Notes folder.

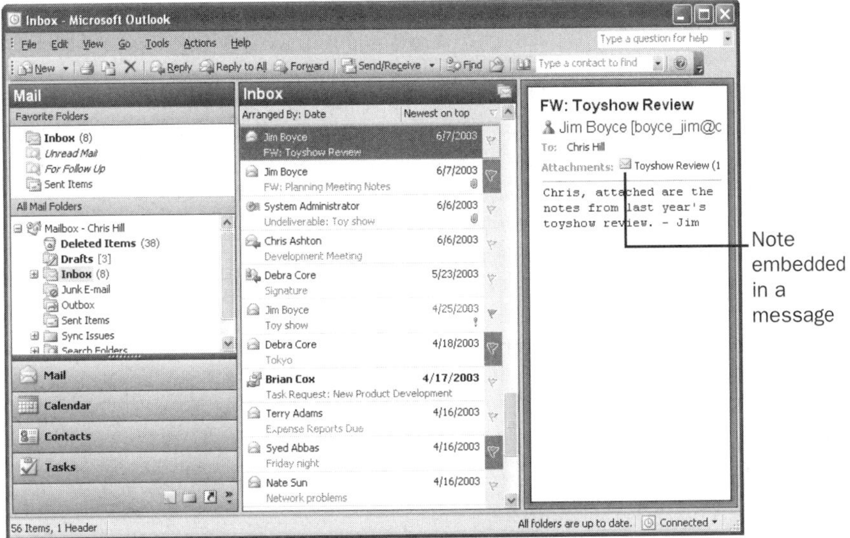

Figure 17-5. When a note is embedded in an e-mail message, you can open the note by double-clicking it.

To copy a note you've received to your Notes folder, follow these steps:

1. Open the Navigation Pane (if it is not already open) and scroll down so that the Notes icon is visible.
2. Open your Inbox, locate the note, and drag it to the Notes icon on the Navigation Pane. If the Reading Pane in the Inbox is open, you can drag the note from there; otherwise, open the message and drag the note.
3. When Outlook opens the Note form, type a title for the note as you want it to appear in the Notes folder.

Using a Note to Create a Task or an Appointment

If you've made a note about a task you must perform or an appointment you must keep, you can easily create an Outlook task or an appointment directly from the note. To do so, drag the note to the Tasks icon or the Calendar icon on the Navigation Pane, as appropriate. Outlook opens a new task form or a new appointment form with the note contents as the subject and contents of the task or appointment.

Moving and Copying Notes

You can move and copy notes to other folders. How Outlook treats the note depends on the destination folder itself. For example, if you copy a note to another notes folder, Outlook treats it as a note. But if you copy a note to the Calendar or Tasks folder, Outlook uses the note to create a new appointment or a new task.

If you right-drag a note to the Contacts icon on the Navigation Pane, Outlook creates a new contact and gives you several options for how to handle the note text. Outlook can add the text to the contact, add it as an attachment, or add it as a shortcut, depending on your selection. You can also copy the note as a journal entry by right-dragging it to the Journal icon on the Navigation Pane. You can choose to create the journal item with the note as an attachment or as a shortcut.

Tip Copying a note within the Notes folder is easy. Just right-drag the note to a new location in the folder, release the mouse button, and choose Copy.

You can move or copy notes by dragging. To move a note to another notes folder, drag the note's icon to the destination folder. To copy a note instead of moving it, hold down the Ctrl key while dragging the note.

Note Dragging a note to a non-notes folder always copies the note rather than moving it—the original note remains in the Notes folder.

Copying a Note to the Clipboard

If you'd like to use the text of a note in another application or another Outlook folder, you can copy the note text to the clipboard. For example, you might copy a phone number from a note to a contact entry in the Contacts folder. To copy the entire contents of a note to the clipboard, right-click the note and choose Copy. If you're working with the note in the Notes folder, you can select the note (or part of its text, such as a phone number) and choose Edit, Copy or press Ctrl+C. Then open the application or form where you want to use the note text and choose Edit, Paste or press Ctrl+V to paste the data from the clipboard.

Note If you copy a note from an e-mail message and then paste the note into another message, Outlook copies the note as an embedded object linking and embedding (OLE) object rather than as text.

Copying a Note to the Desktop or Other Folder

In addition to moving and copying notes inside Outlook, you also can move or copy notes to your desktop or to another file system folder. Outlook creates an MSG file (an Outlook message file) to contain the note when you copy or move it outside Outlook. After you have copied or moved the note, you can double-click the file to open it.

To copy a note to the desktop or a file system folder, you need only drag it from the Notes folder to the desired destination. To move the note instead of copying it, hold down the Shift key while dragging.

Tip You can also move or copy a note from the desktop or a file system folder to your Notes folder. Just drag the note from its current location to the Notes folder.

Changing Note Color

By default, Outlook notes are yellow (unless you've changed the default color in the Notes Options dialog box). However, you can change the color of an individual note at any time. Open the Notes folder, right-click the note you want to change, and choose Color, followed by one of the five available colors: blue, green, pink, yellow, or white.

Why change color? Using a specific color for a specific type of note provides a visual cue about the purpose of the note. For example, you might use pink for notes with more urgent contents or for notes that have pending tasks associated with them. Perhaps you could use green to indicate personal notes and yellow for business-related notes.

For information about the Notes Options dialog box, see "Configuring Note Options," page 472.

Assigning Categories to Notes

You can assign categories to notes, just as you can to any other Outlook item. Categorizing helps you organize your notes, particularly if you choose to view your Notes folder by category. You can assign multiple categories to each note. For example, you might assign a project category to a note as well as an Urgent category.

For information on By Category view, see "Viewing Notes," page 479. To assign categories to a note, follow these steps:

1. Right-click the note and choose Categories, or select the note and choose Edit, Categories.
2. In the Categories dialog box (see Figure 17-6), select the applicable categories.

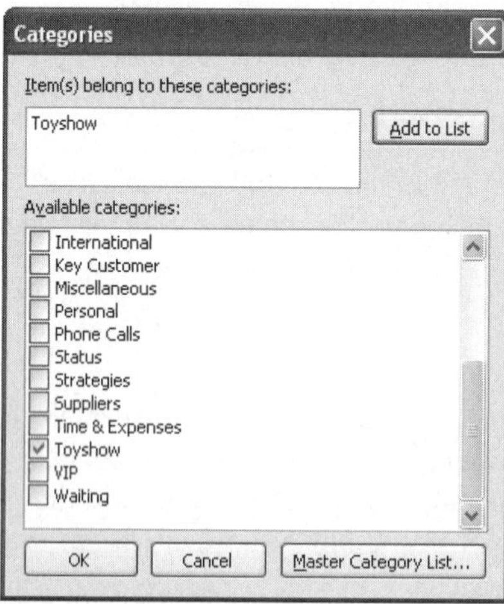

Figure 17-6. Use the Categories dialog box to assign categories to notes.

3. If you don't see the categories you need, click Master Category List, create the required categories, and click OK.

> **Tip** You can't directly edit an existing category, but you can achieve the same result by removing the existing category and replacing it with a new one.

4. Click OK in the Categories dialog box to close it and assign the selected categories.

You can view the categories assigned to a note using any one of several methods. For example, you can choose View, Arrange By, Current View, By Category to view the Notes folder organized by category. Or, you can select a note and choose File, Print Preview—the printout contains the note's categories.

For detailed information on working with categories, see Chapter 4, "Using Categories and Types."

Printing a Note

To print a note, select the note and choose File, Print. Alternatively, you can right-click the note and choose Print from the note's shortcut menu. Outlook prints your name at the top of the page, followed by the date the note was created or last modified, the categories assigned to the note (if any), and the body of the note text. You also can choose File, Print Preview to preview the note.

Date and Time Stamping Notes

Outlook stamps each note with the date and time you created it and displays this information at the bottom of the note window. This date and time remain until you modify the note by adding or removing text. Then Outlook replaces the original date and time with the date and time you modified the text and stores this information with the note.

> **Tip** **Change a note's time stamp**
> Simply opening and reading a note does not change its timestamp. If you need to modify the note but retain the original timestamp, create a copy of the note and modify the copy. Drag the note to another location in the Notes folder to create the copy.

Deleting a Note

If you no longer need a note, you can delete it. Deleting a note moves it to the Deleted Items folder. What happens to it from there depends on how you have configured Outlook to process deleted items. If Outlook clears out the Deleted Items folder each time you exit the program, for example, the note is permanently deleted at that time. You can delete a note in any of the following ways:

- Right-click the note and choose Delete.
- Select the note and press the Delete key.
- Select the note and choose Edit, Delete.
- Drag the note to the Deleted Items folder on the Navigation Pane.

Viewing Notes

Outlook provides five predefined views for the Notes folder. To switch to a different view, choose Views, Arrange By, Current View. You can use any of the following predefined views:

- **Icons** This default view displays an icon for each note with the first line of the note text serving as the icon's description.
- **Notes List** This view displays the notes as a line-by-line list.
- **Last Seven Days** This view is similar to Notes List view, but it displays only those notes created or modified within the past seven days, based on the current date.

- **By Category** This view groups the notes as a list by their assigned categories. If more than one category is assigned to a single note, the note appears in each category group.
- **By Color** This view groups the notes as a list by their assigned color.

You can use a preview pane in the Notes folder to display the text of a note when you click the note. When you use Notes List view or Last Seven Days view in the Notes folder, you can also use AutoPreview, which automatically displays the contents of each note in the list.

You can customize any of the views in the Notes folder the same way you customize the standard views in other folders. You can, for example, drag columns to rearrange them, resize columns, change column names and other properties, add other fields, and group notes based on various criteria.

For information about customizing folder views, see "Customizing the Inbox View," page 61. For details about creating your own custom views, see Chapter 26, "Creating Custom Views and Print Styles."

Chapter 18

Keeping a Journal

Remembering everything you've done during the course of a busy day—e-mail messages sent, phone calls made, appointments set up—can be difficult. However, the journal feature in Microsoft Outlook 2003, which records your daily activities, can help you keep track of it all. In addition to tracking Outlook items such as e-mail messages and appointments automatically, you can use the journal to monitor every Microsoft Office document you create or modify. You can also manually record an activity that occurs away from your computer—a phone conversation, for example, or a handwritten letter you mailed or received.

The Journal folder provides a single place to track all your work and your daily interactions. For example, you can use the journal to list all items related to a specific contact: e-mail messages sent and received, meetings attended, and tasks assigned. You can track all the hours you've spent on activities related to a particular project. Or you can use the journal to retrieve detailed information based on when you performed an action—for example, if you know that you worked on a Microsoft Excel document last Tuesday but can't remember the path to the file, you can quickly look up the document if you've configured the journal to automatically record work on Excel files.

This chapter shows you how to record your work in the journal both automatically and manually. You'll also learn how to view and print your journal in standard and customized views.

Understanding the Outlook Journal

The Journal folder (see Figure 18-1) provides you with tools to track and record daily activities. Journal entries can range in complexity from a manually created record of a phone call to an automatic entry generated every time an e-mail message is sent to a specific contact or each time you work on a specific document. In addition to tracking Outlook items and Office documents, the journal also allows you to track a handwritten letter or the receipt of a courier package as well as any other event you choose to add to the journal manually, such as a conversation, a trip, or something you saw on the way to work.

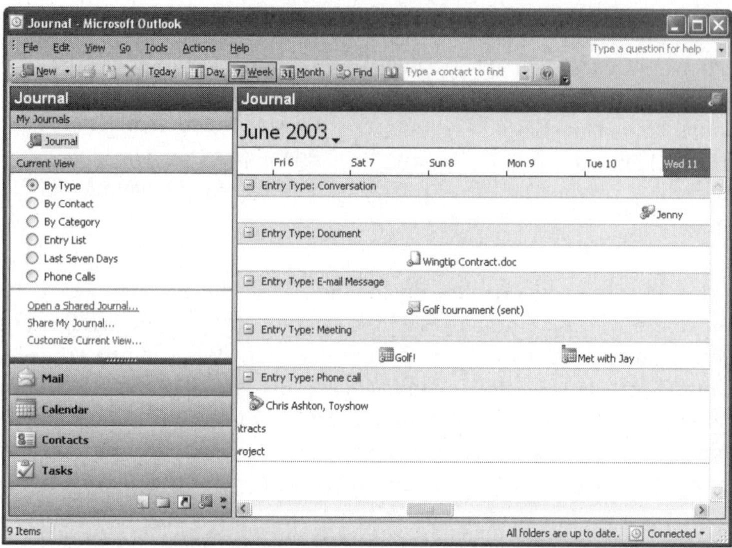

Figure 18-1. Use the Journal folder as an electronic diary of events, phone calls, tasks, and other daily items.

Although other components of Outlook provide similar note-keeping abilities, only the journal provides a full (and optionally automatic) means to date and timestamp an activity, log the entry type (for example, a phone call or a meeting request), and even track the time spent on an activity for billing purposes.

Outlook records entries in your Journal folder based on when an action occurs. For example, a Microsoft Word document is recorded on the journal timeline when you create or modify the document. You can organize journal entries on the timeline into logical groups—such as e-mail messages, meetings, phone calls, or any items related to a specific project. You also can assign categories to journal items and organize the folder view by category. For example, you could assign a project name as a category to all journal items associated with that project, which would allow you to easily group journal entries by project.

You can open a journal entry form (see Figure 18-2) and review details about an activity, or you can use the journal entry as a shortcut to go directly to the Outlook item or the file referred to in the journal entry. For example, if you created a contract as a Word document that is associated with a journal entry, you could open the contract through that entry rather than locating it in the My Computer or My Documents folder.

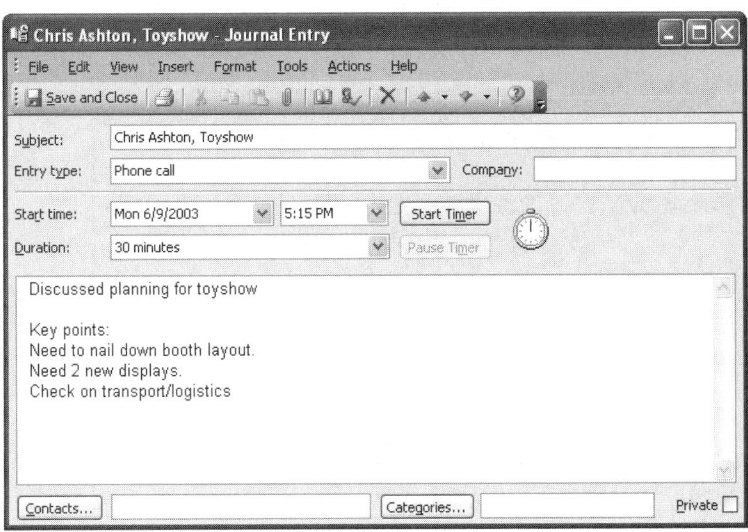

Figure 18-2. The journal entry form contains many fields to help you organize, store, and find your journal entries.

Outlook's journal is an electronic diary. Everything that you normally write on your calendar or day planner (what you did, when you did it, and all the details you want to remember) you can record in the journal. The journal is better than a paper diary, though, because it can automatically record activities such as e-mail messages you send to your boss, work you do on a Microsoft Access database, contracts you review or edit, and other items you work with in Office applications. Some activities, such as a conversation in a trade show parking lot or a shopping excursion to find a new printer, can't be recorded automatically, but you can record anything manually. For example, you can record a phone call (not the voices, just the activity) and use the journal's timer to record the duration of the phone call in your journal entry. Or you could enter details about a conversation you had with a colleague during an impromptu lunch at which you discussed a project on which you are collaborating.

To open the Journal folder, click the Journal icon on the Navigation Pane. If you're new to Outlook, you'll probably find a few entries in your journal already, because the journal records some items automatically by default. Figure 18-1 showed the journal's default view, which you see the first time you open the journal. Figure 18-3 shows Entry List view, another way of organizing your Journal folder.

For information about the views available to organize your Journal folder, see "Viewing the Journal," page 496.

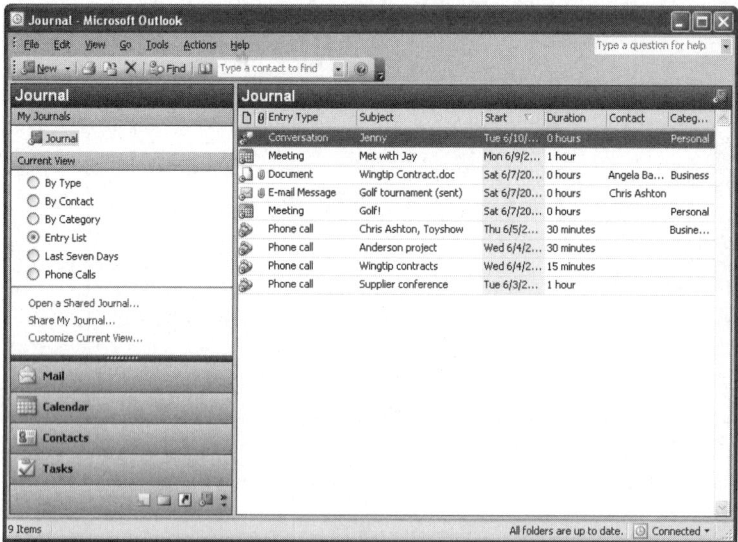

Figure 18-3. You can switch to the Entry List view of the Journal folder.

Using Automatic Journaling

You can have Outlook create automatic journal entries for a wide range of items, including e-mail messages (both sent and received), task requests, and files you create or open in other Office applications. In fact, you can use automatic journaling to record activities based on any contact, Office document, or Outlook item you select.

For example, suppose that you routinely exchange important e-mail messages with a business associate, and you want to track all exchanges for reference. Incoming messages from this associate arrive in your Inbox. You read them, reply to them, and then archive the incoming messages to another folder. Now, however, your associate's messages are stored in one folder and your replies are in another. (By default, replies are stored in Outlook's Sent Items folder.) Configuring the journal to automatically track all of your e-mail exchanges with your associate places a record of all messages relating to this contact (both received and sent) in one convenient location. Instead of hunting for your response to your associate's question from two weeks ago, you can open the journal and find the entry associated with the message. Double-click the link embedded in the journal entry, and Outlook takes you to the message containing your response. Figure 18-4 shows a journal entry automatically added from an e-mail message.

Figure 18-4. The journal can automatically note when you send or receive e-mail messages to or from specific contacts.

Tip **Organize messages using search folders**
Search folders are another useful tool for organizing messages. You might set up a search folder that lists all of the messages to or from a specific contact to help you quickly find those messages. See Chapter 8, "Filtering, Organizing, and Using Automatic Responses," for a complete discussion of search folders.

Tip **Find e-mail items quickly**
To find e-mail items in the journal more quickly, select Entry List view and then click the Contact column to sort the view according to contact. This helps you see all journal items associated with a specific contact, including those items created automatically from e-mail messages.

Troubleshooting

E-mail messages are missing from the journal

If you've set up automatic tracking for a contact who has more than one e-mail address, the journal will track only messages sent and received using the contact's default address—that is, the entry shown in the E-Mail box on the contact form, not an alternative e-mail address that might be entered in the E-Mail 2 or E-Mail 3 field. If you send a message to a contact using one of the alternative e-mail addresses in the E-Mail 2 or E-Mail 3 field, Outlook will not journal those messages. If you need to use one of these alternative addresses and want Outlook to journal the message, you must include the default address in the Cc line of the message form. This results in Outlook sending a duplicate message to the contact's default address, but it allows the item to be recorded.

As another example, consider a writer who uses Word every day to make a living. Turning on automatic document tracking for this application could provide some interesting insight into how the writer allocates his or her work day and which documents are the most demanding. The same holds true for other Office applications you use frequently.

If you use document tracking in such a scenario, however, you should be aware of the distinction between how Outlook tracks a document and how Word itself records editing time. (In Word, you can choose File, Properties and click the Statistics tab to locate the Total Editing Time field.) Outlook tracks the time a document is open, whereas Word tracks the time spent physically editing a document (that is, pressing keys). The Outlook journal automatically records the entire span of time a document is open, even if you are away from your desk tending to other matters.

If a record of the actual time spent working on a document is important to you (whether mulling a paragraph, reading a lengthy section, editing, or entering new text), the journal offers a more realistic record. However, if you fail to close the document when you move on to other things, you'll end up adding time to the document's journal entry that wasn't really spent on the document. It's best to use a combination of Word's editing time field and the Outlook journal's tracking to get a realistic picture of how you spend your time.

Overall, the best choice is usually to use automatic tracking for your critical contacts and for specific applications that benefit from an automatic audit trail. You can place other items in the journal manually as required.

Note After you set it up, the journal's automatic tracking is always on. A piece of Outlook code runs in the background and monitors the Office applications you've selected to track—even if Outlook itself is closed.

Another issue to consider in relation to journaling is latency. When you use automatic tracking for documents, you'll often notice a significant lag between the time you close a document and the time the entry appears (or is updated) in the journal. Also keep in mind that if you've opened the document previously, the most recent tracking entry doesn't appear at the top of the list. By default, journal entries are ordered according to start date, which in this case would be the first time the document was opened or created, not the most recent.

Note Using automatic journaling can have a significantly negative impact on the performance of your applications because of the added overhead involved in journaling. This might not be apparent on your system, depending on its capabilities and the types of documents you use. However, if you see a significant decrease in performance after turning on automatic journaling and can't afford the performance drop, you'll need to stop automatic journaling and resort to adding journal entries manually.

Setting Journal Options

The journal has many options that allow you to control what is recorded, how it is recorded, and when it is recorded. To set journal options, choose Tools, Options. On the Preferences tab, click Journal Options to open the Journal Options dialog box, shown in Figure 18-5. The choices you make in this dialog box determine how your journal is set up and what it tracks.

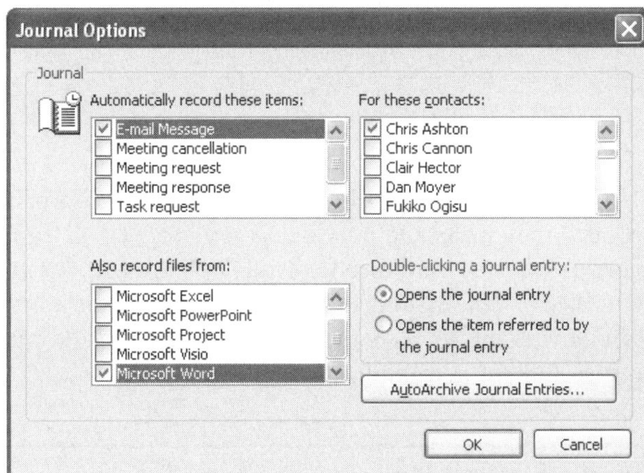

Figure 18-5. The Journal Options dialog box contains customization choices for the journal.

The following list summarizes the options in the Journal Options dialog box:

- **Automatically Record These Items** Select from a list of Outlook items that can be tracked as journal entries. All options here involve three forms of messaging: regular e-mail, meeting notifications, and task delegation. Item types selected from this list are tracked for the contacts you choose in the For These Contacts list. Selecting an item to track without choosing an associated contact has no effect for that tracking option.
- **For These Contacts** Here you link items you want to track with those contacts you want to track them for—task requests from your boss, for example. Outlook then automatically creates journal entries for the selected contacts and related items. Only contacts in your main Contacts folder can be selected for automatic journaling. You'll need to move (or copy) contact entries from subfolders to the main Contacts folder if you want to track items for them.

- **Also Record Files From** Outlook creates an automatic journal entry every time an Office application selected in this list creates or accesses a document. The selections available depend on which Office applications are installed on your system. Documents from Access, Excel, Microsoft PowerPoint, Word, and Microsoft Project can be tracked.

Caution When you set up automatic tracking for a particular document type (for example, Word documents), this setting applies to all documents you create, open, close, or save with the selected application. Thus it can also create many journal entries filled with information you might not need to preserve. Make this selection with care.

- **Double-Clicking A Journal Entry** Double-clicking a journal entry can open either the entry itself or the item referred to by the entry, depending on your selection in this portion of the dialog box. Use this option to specify which action you prefer as the default. You can later override this setting by right-clicking the journal entry in any journal view.
- **AutoArchive Journal Entries** Click to open the Journal folder's Properties dialog box and configure archive settings for the Journal folder.

For details on archiving Outlook items, see Chapter 30, "Managing Folders, Data, and Archiving."

Turning Off Automatic Journaling

You won't find a one-click solution when you want to turn off automatic journaling. To turn this feature off, you must open the Journal Options dialog box and clear all the check boxes in the Automatically Record These Items and Also Record Files From lists. It's not necessary to clear contacts selected in the For These Contacts list. Because automatic journaling consists of tracking specific Outlook events for a contact as well as when specific types of Office files are accessed, breaking the link for items to track is enough.

Troubleshooting

Automatic journaling is causing delays

Automatic journaling can cause very long delays during manual or automatic timed saves as well as when you exit the application. Although it might appear that the application has hung, in fact it is simply saving the journal information. If you experience apparent lock-ups during these procedures, check Outlook to see whether automatic journaling is turned on for the specific application involved. If so, wait a minute or two to give the application a chance to save your data, and then turn off automatic journaling if it has become too onerous to use. You can continue to add journal items manually for the application, if needed.

Automatically Recording E-Mail Messages

Recording e-mail to and from colleagues in the journal is a great way to keep track of discussions and decisions concerning a project, and it's easy to locate those messages later.

To record e-mail messages exchanged with a specific contact, follow these steps:

1. In Outlook, choose Tools, Options and then click Journal Options on the Preferences tab to open the Journal Options dialog box.
2. In the Automatically Record These Items list, select the E-Mail Message check box.
3. In the For These Contacts list, select the contact whose e-mail you want to record.
4. Click OK twice to close both dialog boxes.

Automatically Recording Contact Information

You can configure your journal to automatically keep track of your interactions with any one of your contacts. If you're working with a colleague on a specific project, for example, you might want to monitor your progress by recording every e-mail message, meeting, and task that involves this colleague.

To set up your journal to keep such a record based on the name of the contact, follow these steps:

1. In Outlook, choose Tools, Options and then click Journal Options on the Preferences tab to open the Journal Options dialog box.
2. In the Automatically Record These Items list, select the types of Outlook items you want to record in the journal.
3. In the For These Contacts list, select the relevant contact. (You can select more than one.)
4. Click OK twice to close both dialog boxes.

Tip **Set up automatic journaling for a new contact**

When you create a new contact entry in your Outlook Contacts folder, click the All Fields tab on the contact form. In the Select From drop-down list, select All Contact Fields and then set the Journal field to Yes. Any activity related to the contact (meetings, appointments, phone calls, and so on) will now be recorded in the journal.

Automatically Recording Document Activity

Suppose you create and maintain custom Excel spreadsheets for the different divisions in your corporate enterprise. In the course of a busy day, it's easy to forget to write down which files you worked on and for how long. There's a better way than keeping track on paper: you can have the journal automatically record every Office file you open, including when and how long you had each file open. Outlook can monitor your files and create a journal entry for every document you open and work on from Word, Excel, Access, PowerPoint, Microsoft Visio, and Microsoft Project.

Note Although the journal can automatically record work only in the Microsoft Office programs Word, Excel, Access, PowerPoint, Microsoft Visio, and Microsoft Project, you can enter your work from other programs manually.

Follow these steps to automatically record files you create or open:

1. In Outlook, choose Tools, Options and then click Journal Options on the Preferences tab to open the Journal Options dialog box.
2. In the Also Record Files From list, select the programs for which you want to automatically record files in your journal. The journal will record a new entry for each document from the selected programs when it is created, opened, closed, or saved.
3. By default, double-clicking an icon on the journal timeline opens the journal entry. If you'd rather be able to open the associated file when you double-click the icon, select the Opens The Item Referred To By The Journal Entry option.

Tip Regardless of which option you choose to be the default in the Journal Options dialog box, you can always right-click an icon on the journal timeline and then choose either Open Journal Entry or Open Items Referred To from the shortcut menu.

4. Click OK twice to close both dialog boxes.

Inside Out

Manually adding items

If you've set up automatic journaling for all entries created by an application (Excel, for example), every document you create in that application generates a journal entry. If you right-click an entry and choose Open Item Referred To, Outlook opens the document that created the journal entry. However, this behavior can change. If you add a document item manually to the entry, and the icon for that item appears before the original document's icon in the entry, Outlook opens the manually added document. In other words, Outlook always opens the first document referenced in the entry when you choose Open Item Referred To from the entry's shortcut menu. This can be confusing because the subject continues to reference the original document. In addition, the manually added document does not appear in the View Attachments list on the entry's shortcut menu unless you inserted it as a file rather than as a shortcut. So, when you add entries manually, make sure to place the icon for the document added manually after the original document's icon and insert the document as a file.

Note Because journal entries contain links to your documents rather than copies of the actual documents, the entries might reference documents that no longer exist on your system. The journal has no way to record the deletion, moving, or renaming of files.

Adding Journal Items Manually

Automatic journaling can be tremendously useful, but what if some of the work you need to track is done in applications other than Office applications? You can't record the files automatically in your journal, but you can record them manually. Or what if you want to track your work only in a specific Word file rather than in every Word document? Instead of turning on automatic recording for all Word files, you can manually record your work in only specified files.

Likewise, if you want to record a nonelectronic event in your journal—a chat at the water cooler, a box of chocolates sent to a client, or your approval of a printed proposal—you can add a journal entry manually. You can also use this method if you'd prefer to pick and choose which documents, messages, meetings, and task requests are entered in the journal rather than having Outlook routinely record all such items.

Recording Work in a File Manually

To keep a record of when and how long you worked in a file (along with any extraneous notes to yourself), follow these steps:

1. Locate the file you want to work in. You can navigate to the folder that contains the file using any technique you like, such as browsing My Computer or My Documents.
2. Drag the file icon in the folder window to the Journal icon on the Navigation Pane. It's easiest to drag the file if you resize both Outlook and the folder window so that you can clearly see both.
3. Click Start Timer to begin recording your working hours (see Figure 18-6), and then double-click the file shortcut icon to open the file. At any time, you can enter notes to yourself in the box where the shortcut icon is located.

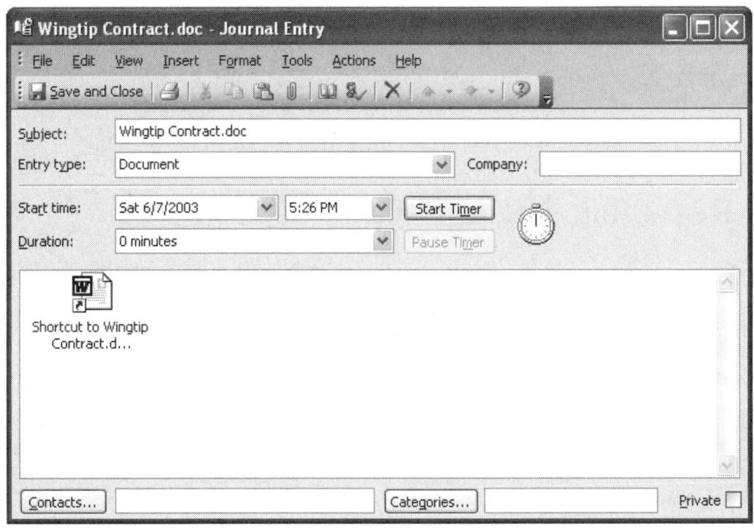

Figure 18-6. Click Start Timer to start recording time spent on a document.

4 When you finish working in the file, remember to stop the journal timer by clicking Pause Timer and then clicking Save And Close.

> **Tip** If you need to take a temporary break in your work, click Pause Timer. When you return to work on the file, click Start Timer to continue recording your working hours.

Recording Outlook Items Manually

Recording an Outlook item such as a task in the journal is even easier than recording a file: open the Outlook window where the item is listed and drag it to the Journal icon on the Navigation Pane. For example, suppose that you want to record how much time you spend cleaning out your filing cabinets, a task you've entered in the Tasks folder. Open the Tasks folder and drag the task item to the Journal icon on the Navigation Pane. Click Start Timer and go to work. Then click Pause Timer to take a break. When you finish, click Save And Close.

Recording Other Activities Manually

Any activity you want to record can be entered in your journal. For example, you can monitor the time you spend on the Internet (which can be considerable) as well as recording any Web page addresses you want to save and other notes you need to jot down.

Follow these steps:

1. Double-click a blank area in your Journal folder. A new journal entry form opens.
2. In the Subject box, type a description of your activity.
3. In the Entry Type box, select an appropriate entry type for the activity. You can't create your own entry type, but you can choose among several available types. For example, you could classify an Internet search as Remote Session. Type any notes, including hyperlinks, in the large text box.
4. Click Start Timer to begin recording your activity.
5. When you're finished with your activity, click Pause Timer to stop the timer. Then click Save And Close to close the journal entry.

Manually Recording Phone Calls

When you use automatic dialing to call a contact, you can time the phone call, type notes in Outlook while you talk, and create a journal entry for the call. This feature can come in handy if, for example, you bill clients for your time spent on phone conversations.

Follow these steps to keep a record of an outgoing call in Journal:

1. Open the Contacts folder and select the contact entry for the person you want to call.
2. Click the Dial button on the Standard toolbar to open the New Call dialog box (see Figure 18-7).

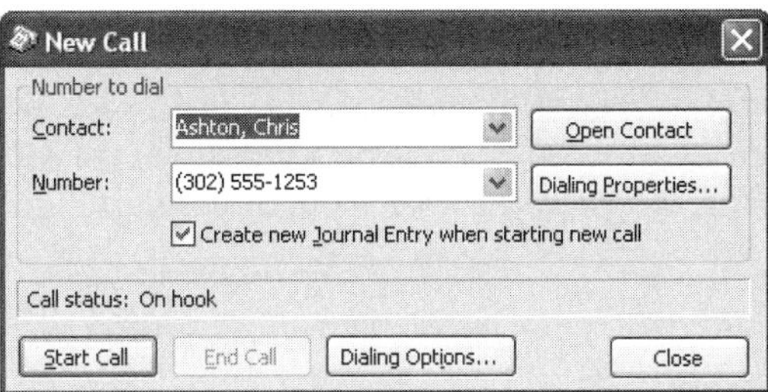

Figure 18-7. You can automatically start a new journal entry from the New Call dialog box.

3. Select the Create New Journal Entry When Starting New Call check box, and then click Start Call. A journal entry opens with the timer running. You can type notes in the body of the journal entry while you talk.
4. When you're finished with the call, click Pause Timer to stop the clock. Then click Save And Close.

You also can create journal entries for incoming calls, although Outlook currently offers no means of automatically creating the journal entries when you pick up the phone and start talking. Instead, when you answer the call and realize that you want to track it, you can open the journal as you begin the conversation, start a new journal item, and click Start Timer. Make notes as needed, and click Pause Timer when you hang up. Add any necessary details to the journal entry form, and then click Save And Close to create the item.

Tip **Use the journal as an inexpensive stopwatch**
You can start a new journal item and use the timer to time any activity, assuming that you don't need to-the-second timing. Just stop the timer and close the form without saving it unless you actually want to save the information in the journal.

For information about setting up automatic phone dialing and making calls from the Contacts folder, see "Phoning a Contact," page 398.

Changing Journal Entries

You can modify any details of a journal entry—for example, adding more notes to yourself, adding a contact's names or categories, or changing the duration of your activity. You can also move the entry to a different position on the journal timeline if you entered the wrong start date or time when you began recording the activity.

For information about timeline views in the Journal folder, see "Viewing the Journal," page 496.

Modifying an Entry

Suppose that in the middle of your department budget meeting, you realize that you didn't stop the journal timer when you stopped working on a spreadsheet to come to the meeting. You know that you worked on the spreadsheet for about three hours, however, so you can change the journal entry to reflect your actual work time.

To change the duration or any other property of an existing journal entry, follow these steps:

1. Open the Journal folder, and double-click the entry to open it.
2. Select the information you want to change and enter the correct data. For example, to change an incorrect record of how long you spent on an activity, double-click in the Duration box, change the value, and press Enter.
3. Make other changes as needed in the journal entry form.
4. Click Save And Close.

Moving an Entry on the Timeline

Suppose that you belatedly created a journal entry for a phone call you made yesterday and inadvertently entered the wrong date. When you later notice that the journal entry is in the wrong spot on the timeline, you can move the entry to the correct date.

Follow these steps to do so:

1. Open the Journal folder and double-click the entry to open it.
2. Click the arrow next to the Start Time box, and select the correct date.
3. Click Save And Close. Outlook then moves the entry to the correct spot on the timeline.

Deleting an Entry

Deleting a single entry from your journal timeline is easy: either click the entry's icon to select it and then press Delete, or right-click the entry's icon and choose Delete from the shortcut menu.

What if you've been automatically recording your work in Excel workbooks but have also been experimenting with Excel, creating several test workbooks that you don't want to save or track? Now you have numerous useless entries cluttering up your Journal folder. You can delete them one at a time, but it's faster to switch to a table view of your entries, sort them so that all the useless entries are in one group, and delete them all at once.

For information about the various views in the Journal folder, including table views and timeline views, see "Viewing the Journal," page 496.

Follow these steps to delete a group of entries:

1. In the Journal folder, choose View, Arrange By, Current View, Entry List. The view switches to a table view of all your journal entries.

2 To sort the entries so that all the ones you want to delete appear together, click the Entry Type column header. To sort specific entries by subject within a group of entry types, hold down the Shift key while you click the Subject column header.

Tip You can sort by as many as four categories using this method of holding down the Shift key while you click column headers.

3 To select and delete multiple journal entries, press Shift or Ctrl while you select the entries you want to delete and then click the Delete button on the toolbar. (Alternatively, you can press the Delete key to delete selected entries or right-click any of the selected entries and choose Delete from the shortcut menu.)

4 When you finish deleting the journal entries that you don't want, you can choose View, Arrange By, Current View and select the view you were using previously.

Connecting Journal Activities to Individual Contacts

If you work on a project with a colleague, you can associate your journal entries for the project with that colleague's contact entry. All the journal entries that are associated with the contact will appear on the Activities tab of the contact form.

For example, Figure 18-8 shows a journal entry for a Word letter to an associate. To connect a journal entry and document to a contact, click Contacts at the bottom of the journal entry form. In the resulting Select Contacts dialog box, click the names of the contacts with whom the journal entry should be associated and then click OK. The selected names appear in the Contacts box at the bottom of the journal entry form.

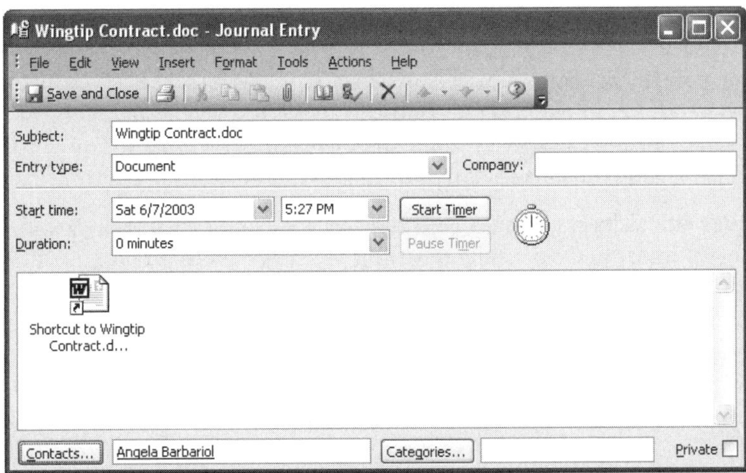

Figure 18-8. This journal entry shows a Word document associated with a contact.

So what does this do for you? When you open the contact entry for an associated contact and click the Activities tab (see Figure 18-9), you'll see a list of every Outlook item associated with that contact. You can open any of these items by double-clicking it. This is just one more way Outlook keeps all your information interconnected.

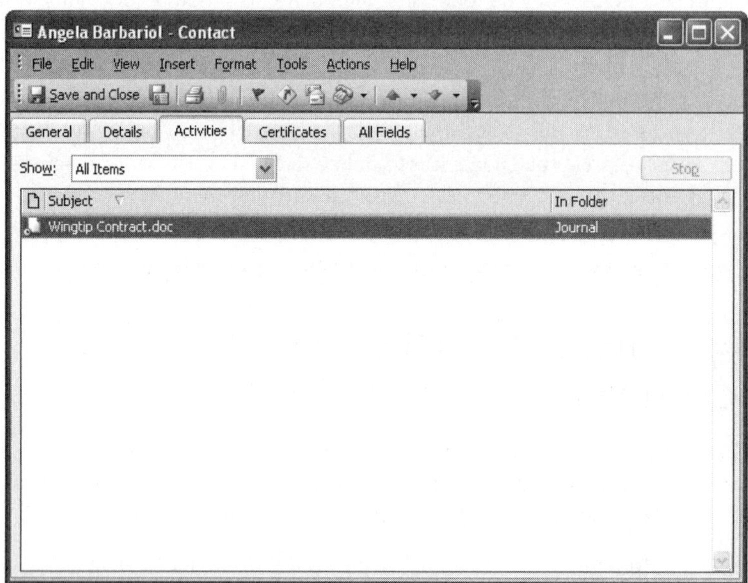

Figure 18-9. The Activities tab shows all items associated with the selected contact.

Viewing the Journal

When you look at the Journal folder in a monthly timeline view, you get a good overall picture of your recorded activities, but you must point to an individual icon to identify the activity. (When you point to an icon, a subject label appears.) You can make a few changes to a journal timeline view—for example, you can choose to always display the subject labels for icons in a monthly view, or you can specify a more useful length for the labels.You can also show week numbers in the timeline heading, which is useful for planning in some industries.

Because the Outlook journal creates a record of your activities, the six standard views available in the Journal folder differ considerably from the views in other types of Outlook folders. The following sections introduce you to each of the Journal folder views.

> **Tip** You can choose whether to view a timeline in a journal view in day, week, or month increments by clicking the Day, Week, or Month button on the toolbar. These buttons are available only in the journal views that show a timeline and are not available in list views.

Using By Type View

The default view for the Journal folder is By Type view (see Figure 18-10). In this view, the journal entries are arranged in a timeline and are categorized by the entry type. To select the By Type view, choose View, Arrange By, Current View, By Type.

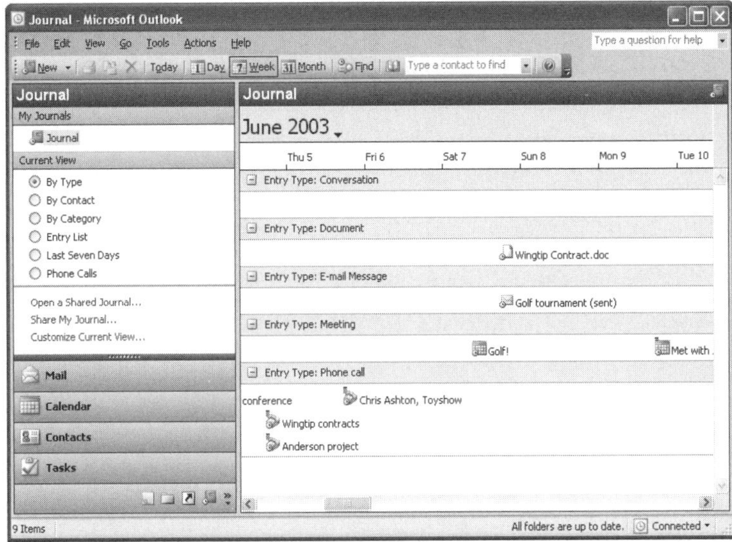

Figure 18-10. By Type view is the default Journal folder view.

Each entry type is indicated on a title bar. You can click the small box on the left edge of the title bar to expand or contract the type. A plus sign (+) in the box means that the type is collapsed, whereas a minus sign (–) indicates that the type is expanded. You might need to use the vertical scroll bar to see the complete list. When you expand a type, you can view any journal entries for that type in the area below the title bar.

> **Tip** If you are surprised to find no entries when you expand a particular type, it's because Outlook displays the entries as a timeline. If no entries for the selected type were created recently, you might need to use the horizontal scroll bar to find the most recent entries.

By Type view is most useful if you want to find out which documents you worked on during a specific period. This view is not particularly useful for locating documents based on any other criteria. For example, you wouldn't want to use By Type view to locate all documents relating to a particular contact.

Using By Contact View

In By Contact view (see Figure 18-11), journal entries are also arranged in a timeline and are categorized by the contact associated with the entries.

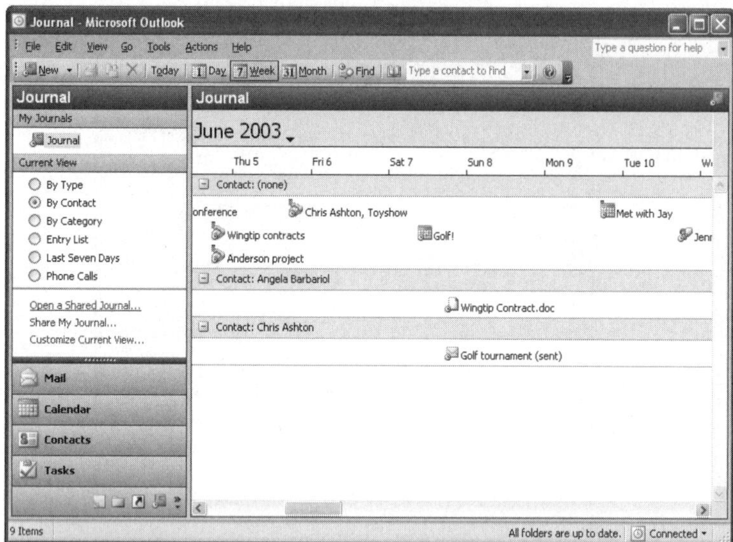

Figure 18-11. Use By Contact view to organize the journal by the contacts associated with each journal entry.

Each contact is indicated by a title bar that shows the contact's name. Click the small box to expand or collapse the contact. You might also need to use the horizontal scroll bar to view all items from a given contact.

By Contact view makes it easy to find all documents and other journal items related to a specific contact. Any type of document can appear in the list, as can phone calls and other items associated with specific contacts.

Inside Out

Correctly link documents and contacts

Journal entries will appear in the correct category in By Contact view only if the entry is linked to the correct contact. Outlook does this automatically for items such as e-mail messages, but you must take care to see that Office documents are linked correctly. One way to ensure that documents are correctly linked is to select the contact in the Contacts folder and then choose File, New Office Document to create the file.

Using By Category View

In By Category view (see Figure 18-12), journal entries are also arranged in a timeline and are organized by the categories you've assigned to them.

Tip A journal item will appear in more than one location in the list if your assign multiple categories to it.

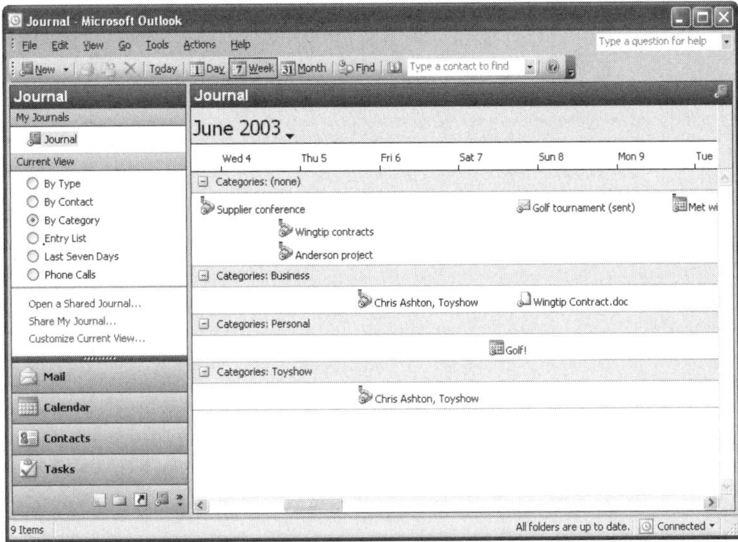

Figure 18-12. Use By Category view to organize the Journal folder based on the categories assigned to each journal item.

By Category view can be handy if you create categories that break down journal entries by project. This view can be almost useless, however, unless you take the time to assign categories when you create documents. Outlook doesn't assign any categories by default. You can assign categories using Outlook's standard list, or you can create your own categories.

For information about assigning categories and creating custom categories, see Chapter 4, "Using Categories and Types."

Tip **Assign categories to multiple entries**
You can access the Categories dialog box by right-clicking the journal entry and choosing Categories. To assign a category to multiple journal entries, select them all (by holding down the Shift or Ctrl key as you select), right-click the selection, and choose Categories.

Using Entry List View

Entry List view (see Figure 18-13) might be the most useful view of all. This view dispenses with the timeline and instead displays all journal entries in a table.

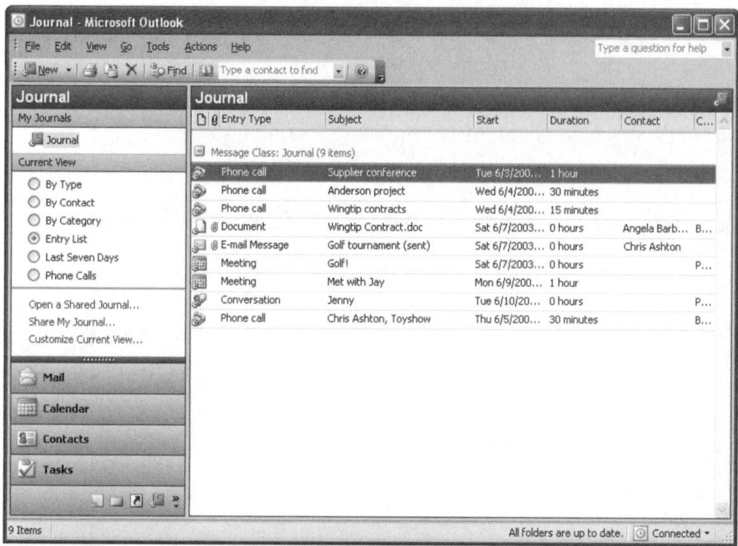

Figure 18-13. Entry List view displays journal entries in a table rather than on a timeline.

Because Entry List view does not use the timeline to display entries, it's much easier to view the list of entries—you don't have to use the horizontal scroll bar to locate the items. By default, this view is sorted in descending order based on the start date, but you can quickly sort the list using any of the column headers. Simply click a column header to sort the list; click the header a second time to reverse the sort order.

The paper clip icon in the second column of Entry List view indicates that an entry is a document. If this icon isn't displayed, the entry is a log of an activity that occurred within Outlook, such as an e-mail message.

Using Last Seven Days View

Last Seven Days view resembles Entry List view. This view is useful when you need to locate items you've worked on recently—especially if you can't quite remember the file name, contact, or category.

When you look closely at Last Seven Days view, you might notice that something doesn't look quite right: the dates shown for the journal entries clearly span much more than a week. The explanation is that the dates shown are the start dates for the journal entries, not the dates when the items were last accessed. Outlook is displaying the journal entries that have been created, accessed, or modified within the past week. Each entry shown in this view was accessed in some way during the past week, although the original entries might have been created quite some time ago.

> **Tip** **Change the period of time shown in Last Seven Days view**
> You can customize Last Seven Days view to specify a different time period, such as the past month. To do so, choose View, Arrange By, Current View, Customize Current View. Click Filter in the Customize View dialog box and select the new time duration in the Time drop-down list.

Using Phone Calls View

Phone Calls view (see Figure 18-14) displays only journal items that are associated with phone calls. Tracking phone calls and viewing them in the Journal folder can be extremely helpful. You can, for example, monitor the time you spend on billable calls. Even if you don't bill for your time, you'll find that phone call journal entries make it easier to recall phone conversations.

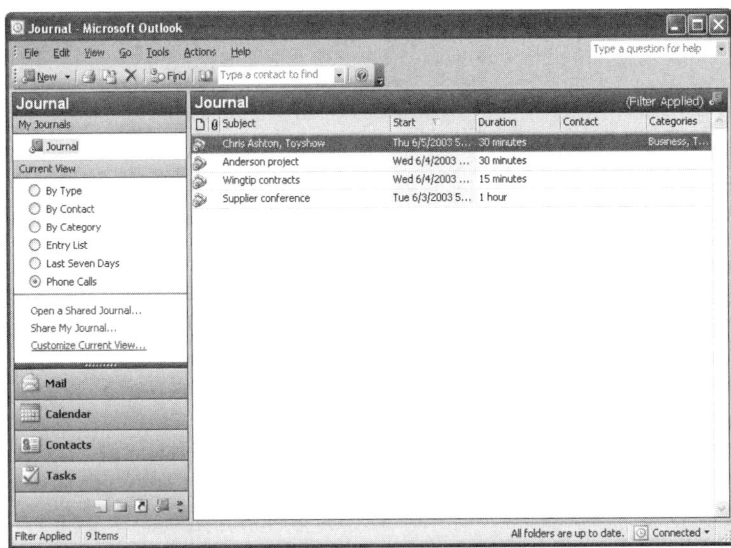

Figure 18-14. Use Phone Calls view to organize the Journal folder according to journal items associated with phone calls.

Outlook creates journal entries for phone calls automatically only if you use the AutoDialer to begin the call. You must specify the duration yourself by entering the appropriate time on the phone call journal entry form. You can do so by actually entering a time.

> **Note** Remember to link your phone call journal entries to the appropriate contacts so that it will be easier to find all entries relating to specific contacts.

Customizing Journal Views

All the standard views in the Journal folder are customizable in a variety of ways. The changes you make to these views are persistent, however, so proceed with care. If you end up mangling a standard view beyond repair, it can be restored to its default by using the Reset button in the Define Views dialog box, which you can open by choosing View, Arrange By, Current View, Define Views. (No such option exists for custom views.)

For information about creating custom views in Outlook, see Chapter 26, "Creating Custom Views and Print Styles."

Displaying Item Labels in the Monthly Timeline

A journal entry's label for a Journal entry designates where the file the journal entry references is located on your computer.

To display item labels on a monthly timeline, follow these steps:

1. In By Type view, right-click in an empty area of the Journal folder, and choose Other Settings on the shortcut menu.
2. In the Format Timeline View dialog box, select the Show Label When Viewing By Month check box.

Note By default, the label width is 25 characters, but if you find that your labels are too short or too long, return to this dialog box and change the number in the Maximum Label Width box. The label width applies to the labels in the day and week timeline as well as the month timeline. To also hide the display of week numbers, you can clear the Show Week Numbers check box.

3. Click OK to close the dialog box.

Showing Week Numbers

In some industries, it's important to know schedules based on weeks of the year.

You can show week numbers in your timeline view by following these steps:

1. Right-click in an empty area of the Journal folder, and choose Other Settings on the shortcut menu.
2. In the Format Timeline View dialog box, select the ShowWeek Numbers check box.
3. Click OK to close the dialog box. In a monthly timeline, week numbers replace dates. In week and day views, both the week number and dates are displayed in the timeline header.

Printing Journal Items

The options available when you print from the Journal folder depend on whether a timeline view or a table (list) view is currently open. In a table view, you can open and print individual items, print the entire list, or print only selected rows. Printing the list is useful if you want a snapshot of the journal for a specific period of time. You can print table views using either Table or Memo print styles (explained shortly).

> **Tip** You don't have to open an item to print it. Simply right-click the item and choose Print from the shortcut menu.

In a timeline view, you can only open and print individual journal items. You can print individual items only in Memo style, but you can print attached files along with the journal entry details. To print the attached files, select the Print Attached Files check box in the Print dialog box.

> **For more information about printing views in Outlook and creating custom print styles, see Chapter 24, "Designing and Using Forms."**

Table print style (see Figure 18-15) is available from any table view. It prints the selected view just as you see it in Outlook: each item on a separate row, with the fields displayed as columns. Table print styles have limited configuration options.

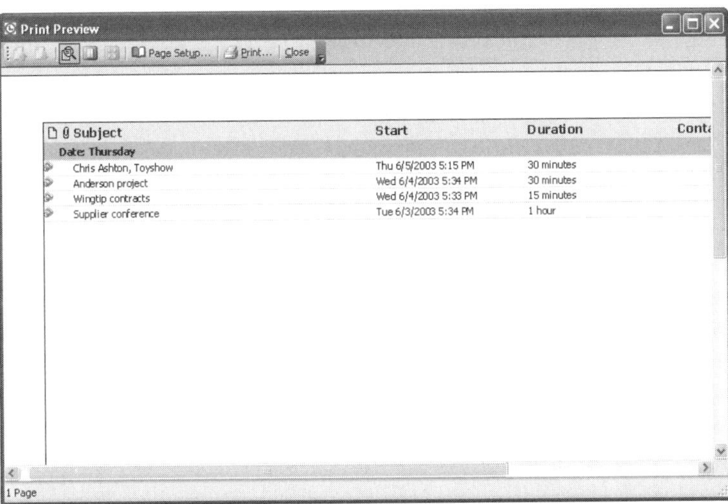

Figure 18-15. The Table print style prints journal entries in a table.

Memo style (see Figure 18-16) prints one item per page, with your name as the title and the details of the record following. Memo is a simple and quick, one-item-at-a-time print style. You can specify the title and field fonts, paper options, and the contents and fonts used by the header and footer.

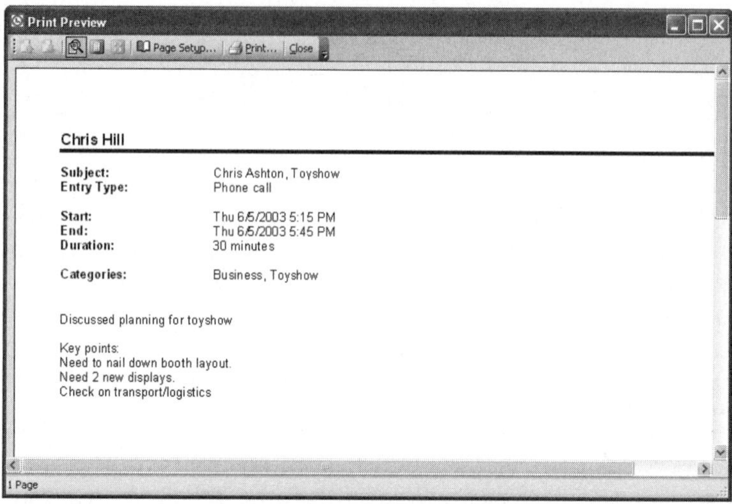

Figure 18-16. Memo style prints a single journal item per page.

Printing from the Journal folder is not a particularly difficult task for anyone who has used and printed from any Microsoft Windows–based application. However, you might be wondering how you can print just a selection of a table view. For example, you might need to print only the items that fall within a specific range or those associated with a particular contact.

Follow these steps to print a selection of a table view:

1. Open the table view.
2. Click columns as needed to sort the data to help you locate the items you want to print. For example, click the Start column header to locate items that fall within a certain time range or click the Contact column header to locate items associated with a specific contact.
3. Select the first item in the range, hold down the Shift key, and select the last item in the range.
4. Choose File, Print to open the Print dialog box.
5. Select Table Style from the Print Style area and then select the Only Selected Rows option.
6. Set other print options as needed and click OK.

Sharing Journal Information

Because the Outlook journal keeps track of activities using a timeline, you might find that it is one of the most useful of Outlook's folders to share. If you're working on a project with several people, a shared Outlook Journal folder might be just what you need to make certain everyone is on track.

If you and all the people with whom you want to share the Journal folder use Microsoft Exchange Server, you can share the Journal folder as a public folder on the Exchange server.

Follow these steps to share a personal Journal folder:

1. In Outlook, open the folders list and click the push pin to keep the list open.
2. Right-click the Journal folder and choose Properties to open the Journal Properties dialog box. Click the Permissions tab (see Figure 18-17).

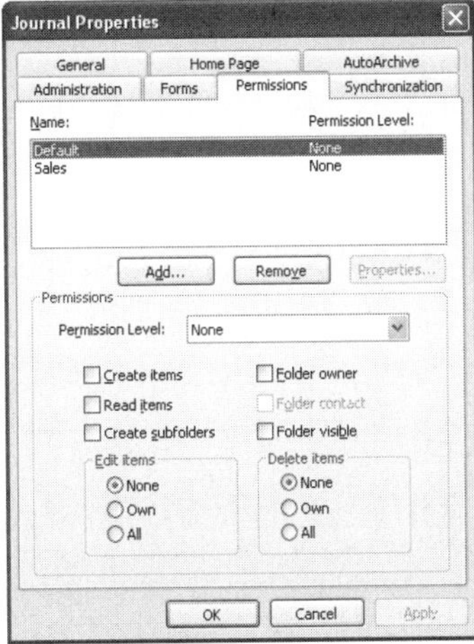

Figure 18-17. Share a folder by using the folder's Permissions tab in its Properties dialog box.

3. Click Default and select options in the Permissions area to specify the types of tasks all users can perform if they have no explicit permissions set (explained next).
4. Click Add to open the Add Users dialog box, select a user (or more than one), and click OK to return to the Permissions tab.
5. With the user selected in the Name list, select permissions in the Permissions area to specify the tasks that the user can perform.
6. Click OK to apply the permissions.

For details about sharing folders, see "Granting Access to Folders," page 741.

If everyone you want to share the folder with is using Exchange Server, you might find it more efficient to create a public Journal folder on the server and grant permissions as needed in that folder, rather than share your own Journal folder. This allows you to keep your Journal folder private and inaccessible to others but allows everyone (assuming they are given the necessary permissions) to create and view items in the shared folder.

Follow these steps to create a shared public Journal folder:

1. In Outlook, open the folders list and click the push pin to keep the list open.
2. Expand the Public Folders branch, right-click the All Public Folders branch, and choose New Folder to open the Create New Folder dialog box (see Figure 18-18).

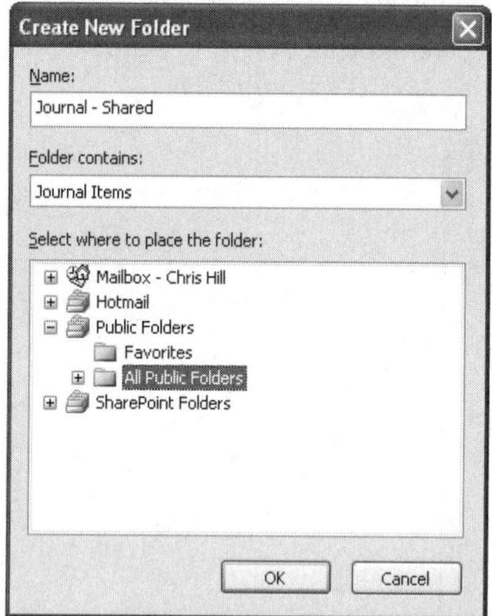

Figure 18-18. Use the Create New Folder dialog box to create a public Journal folder.

3. Specify a name for the new folder in the Name box.
4. Select Journal Items in the Folder Contains drop-down list.
5. Verify that All Public Folders is selected in Select Where To Place The Folder (or select a different location if needed) and click OK.
6. Right-click the newly created folder, choose Properties to open its Properties dialog box, and then click the Permissions tab. This tab is similar to the one shown previously in Figure 18-17.
7. Set permissions for the Default user to apply permissions for all users who won't have explicit permissions for the folder. Add users and set permissions for those who do need explicit permissions, and click OK to apply the permissions.

Note For a detailed discussion of creating public folders, see "Setting Up Public Folders," page 943.

Part 4

Scheduling

Chapter 19

Scheduling Appointments

For most of us, a calendar is a basic tool for organizing our lives, both at work and at home. With the calendar in Microsoft Outlook 2003, you can schedule regular appointments, all-day and multiday events, and meetings. You can view your schedule almost any way you want. In addition, you can share your calendar with others, which is a big help when scheduling organizational activities.

This chapter first describes the calendar and explains how to work with the basic Calendar folder view. Then you'll learn how to schedule and work with appointments and events. You'll also find information about the more advanced view options for the calendar and about how to share your calendar and free/busy information and view different time zones.

Both this chapter and the next focus on the features available in the Outlook Calendar folder. This chapter covers appointments and events; the following chapter discusses meetings and resources.

Calendar Basics

The Outlook Calendar folder provides a central location for storing vast amounts of information about your schedule. Figure 19-1 shows a basic one-day view of a calendar. You see this view when you first click the Calendar icon on the Navigation Pane to open the folder. This calendar contains no appointments yet, and no tasks are listed on the TaskPad.

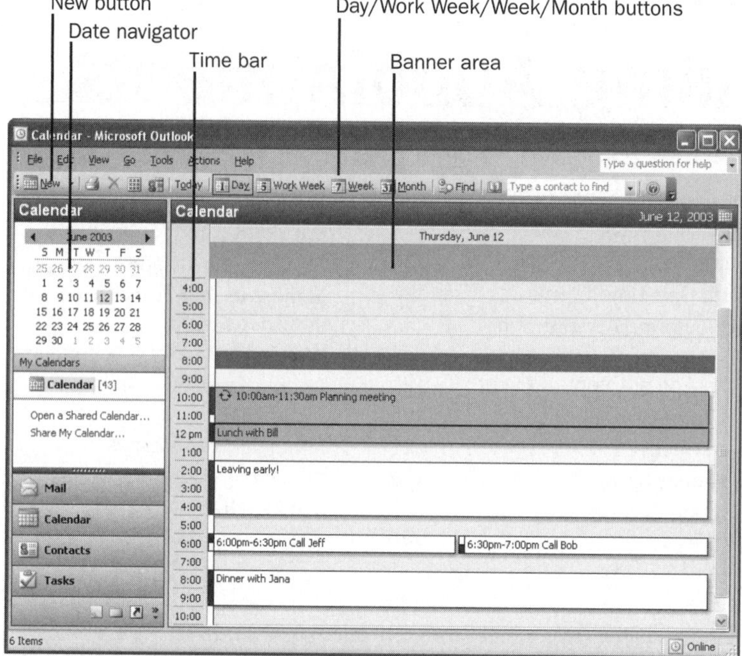

Figure 19-1. This is the default one-day view of the Outlook calendar.

Understanding Calendar Items

Outlook's calendar can contain three types of items: appointments, events, and meetings.

- An *appointment*, which is the default calendar item, involves only your schedule and time and does not require other attendees or resources. The calendar shows appointments in the time slots corresponding to their start and end times.
- When an appointment lasts longer than 24 hours, it becomes an *event*. An event is marked on the calendar not in a time slot, but in a banner at the top of the day on which it occurs.
- An appointment becomes a *meeting* when you invite other people, which requires coordinating their schedules, or when you must schedule resources. Meetings can be in person or set up online using Microsoft NetMeeting, Microsoft Windows Media Services, or Microsoft Exchange Conferencing.

For in-depth information about meetings, see Chapter 20, "Scheduling Meetings and Resources." For information about online meetings, see "Holding an Online Meeting," page 571.

You can create an appointment in any of these ways:

- Choose File, New, Appointment.
- When the Calendar folder is open, click the New toolbar button.
- When any other Outlook folder is open, click the arrow beside the New toolbar button and choose Appointment.
- Click a time slot on the calendar, and simply type the subject of the appointment in the time slot.

For detailed information about creating appointments and using the appointment form, see "Working with One-Time Appointments," page 516.

Using the Time Bar

When you choose a calendar display of six days or less, the Time Bar appears, displaying 30-minute time increments by default. Figure 19-2 shows the Time Bar set to 30-minute increments, with a 30-minute appointment on the calendar.

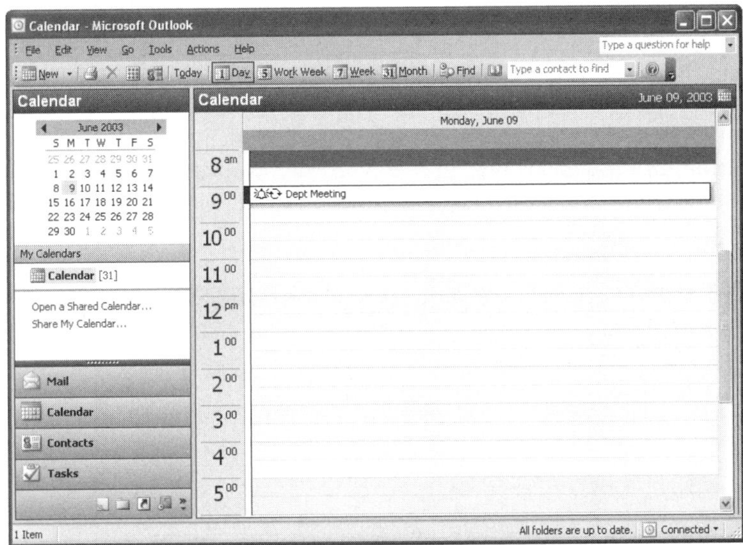

Figure 19-2. By default, the Time Bar is set to display 30-minute increments.

You can set the Time Bar to display different time increments. To do so, begin by right-clicking the Time Bar to display the menu shown in Figure 19-3.

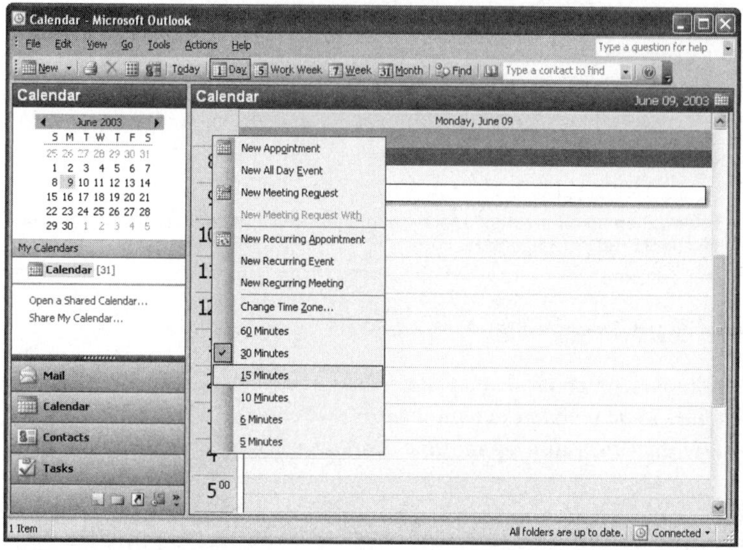

Figure 19-3. Use this menu to change the time increment.

If you want to change the time scale to 10 minutes, click Other Settings to display the Format Day/Week/Month View dialog box. In the Time Scale drop-down list, choose 10 Minutes; the 30-minute appointment then takes up three time intervals instead of one, as shown in Figure 19-4.

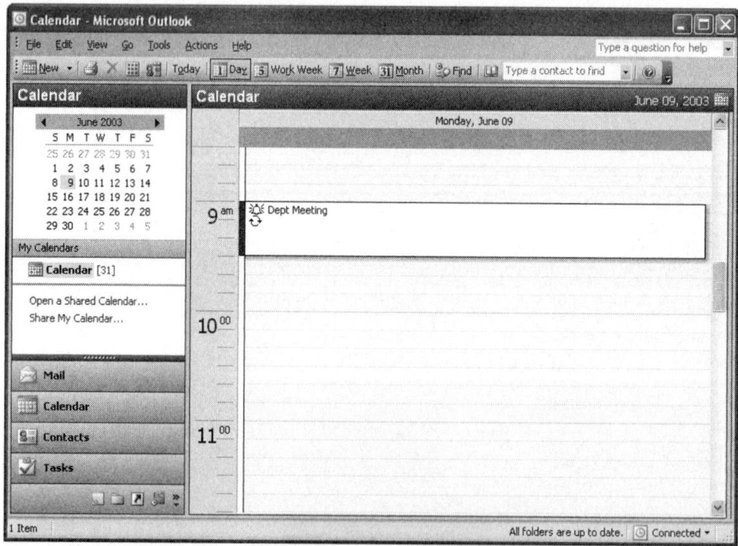

Figure 19-4. The Time Bar has been changed to display 10-minute increments.

Now choose 60 Minutes from the drop-down list; Figure 19-5 shows the result. Note that when an appointment takes up less than a full Time Bar increment, as in this example, the scheduled time of the appointment is displayed with the appointment subject on the calendar.

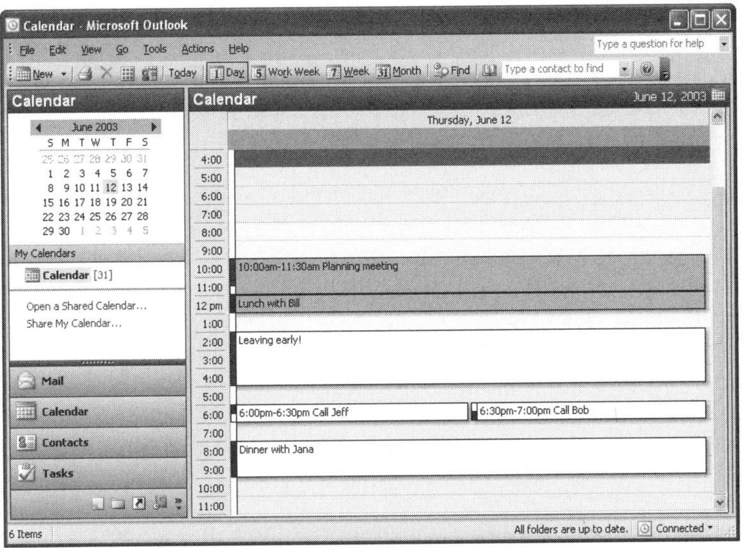

Figure 19-5. The Time Bar is set to 60-minute intervals.

If a time interval is not completely filled by an appointment, only the portion of the interval that is filled is highlighted to the left of the appointment on the calendar. Also, as shown in Figure 19-5, Outlook places appointments side-by-side on the calendar when they are scheduled in the same time interval.

Using the Date Navigator

The Date Navigator has several important uses. For example, you can use it to select the day to view on the calendar—in effect, jumping from one date to another. When you click a day in the Date Navigator, Outlook displays that day according to how you have set the view (by using the Day, Work Week, or Week toolbar buttons):

- In Day view, the selected day is displayed.
- In Work Week view (five days), Outlook displays the week containing the day you clicked in the Date Navigator.
- In Week view (seven days), the calendar switches to a one-day view for the date you click.

> **Tip** When the TaskPad is displayed, the Date Navigator appears at the top of the TaskPad. When you close the TaskPad, the Date Navigator moves to the top of the Navigation Pane.

By clicking the right and left arrows next to the month names in the Date Navigator, you can scroll forward and backward through the months.

For information about Day, Work Week, and Week views, see "Setting the Number of Days Displayed," page 515.

Another use of the Date Navigator is to denote days that contain scheduled items. Those days appear in bold type; days with no scheduled items appear as regular text. This allows you to assess your monthly schedule at a glance.

Finally, you can use the Date Navigator to view multiple days on the calendar. In the Date Navigator, simply drag across the range of days you want to view; those days will all appear on the calendar. For example, Figure 19-6 shows what happens when you drag across three days in the Date Navigator. You can also view multiple consecutive days by clicking the first day and then holding down the Shift key and clicking the last day. To view multiple nonconsecutive days, click the first day you want to view and then hold down the Ctrl key and click each day that you want to add to the view.

For more information on the Tasks folder and working with tasks, see Chapter 21, "Managing Your Tasks."

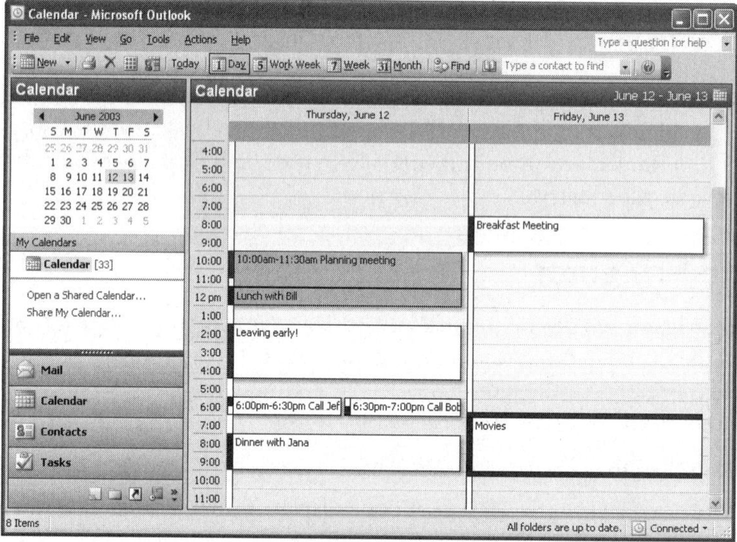

Figure 19-6. You can view multiple days by selecting them in the Date Navigator.

Using the TaskPad

The TaskPad offers an easy way of working with tasks from the Calendar folder. The TaskPad displays existing tasks from the Tasks folder and also allows you to add new tasks. Adding a new task is as simple as clicking in the TaskPad and typing the task subject. Double-click the task item to open the task form if you'd like to add more details. When you create a task on the TaskPad, Outlook automatically adds it to the Tasks folder.

One of the main advantages of having the TaskPad in the Calendar folder is that it gives you the ability to assess your schedule and fit tasks in where appropriate. When you drag a task from the TaskPad to the calendar, the appointment form appears, with the task information filled in. You need only set the schedule information for the appointment and save it to the calendar (as explained later in the chapter).

Setting the Number of Days Displayed

You can set the number of days displayed in the calendar in several ways. One way is to use the Date Navigator, as discussed earlier. The easiest way, however, is to use the appropriate toolbar button. To select the number of days to view, click Day, Work Week, Week, or Month on the toolbar.

When the calendar displays six days or less, the days are shown side by side with the Time Bar (refer back to Figure 19-6, for example). Figure 19-7 shows the calendar with seven days displayed.

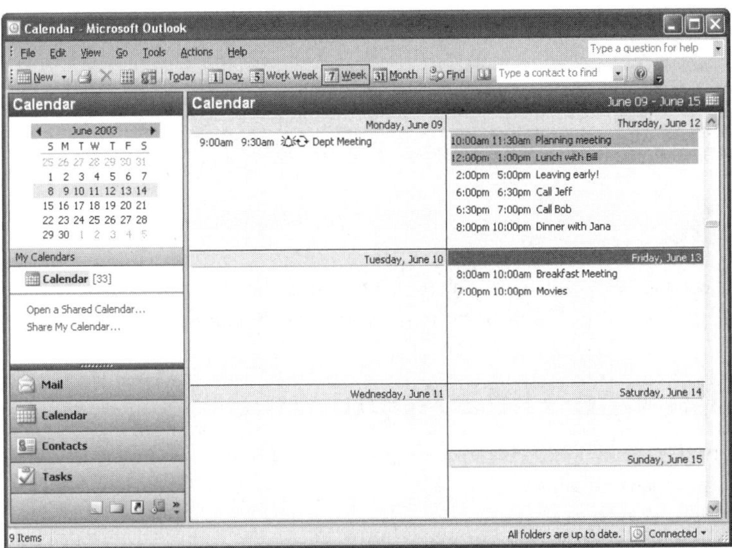

Figure 19-7. The calendar display changes depending on the number of days you are viewing.

When you click the Month button on the toolbar, the view is slightly different from the view you see when you choose more than seven days in the Date Navigator. However, the Date Navigator and the TaskPad can optionally appear in Month view, as shown in Figure 19-8. This behavior is different from previous versions of Outlook, which do not include the Date Navigator or TaskPad in Month view.

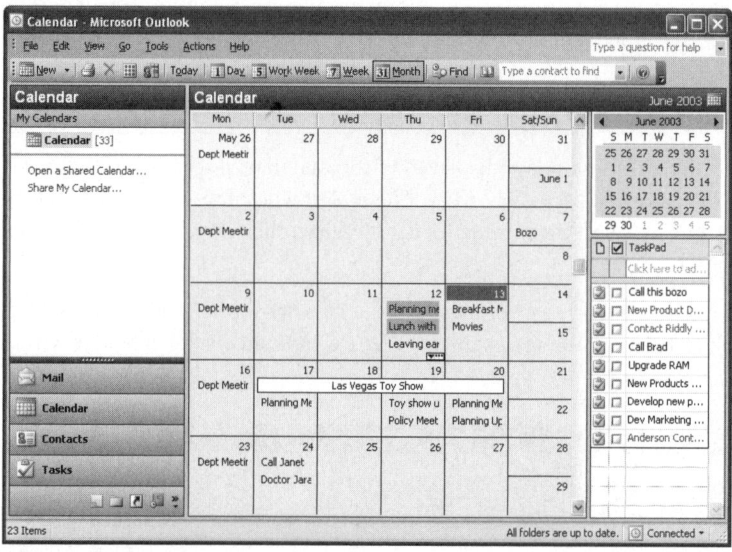

Figure 19-8. Month view can include the Date Navigator and the TaskPad.

Selecting a Date

You can select a date in two ways. The first is by using the Date Navigator. The second way to select a date is to click the Today button on the toolbar; this action takes you to the current day.

Working with One-Time Appointments

The most basic calendar item is the one-time appointment. You can create a one-time appointment in several ways:

- If the Calendar folder is not open, choose File, New, Appointment or click the down arrow next to the New toolbar button and choose Appointment. The appointment defaults to the next full 30 minutes (that is, if it's 1:50, the appointment is listed with a start time of 2:00 and an end time of 2:30).
- If the Calendar folder is open, click the New toolbar button or right-click the calendar and choose New Appointment. The appointment is scheduled for the time selected in the calendar.
- Right-click a date in the Month view and choose New Appointment. The appointment defaults to your specified start-of-workday time and runs for 30 minutes.

When you take any of these actions, Outlook opens an appointment form, shown in Figure 19-9, where you can specify information for the new item.

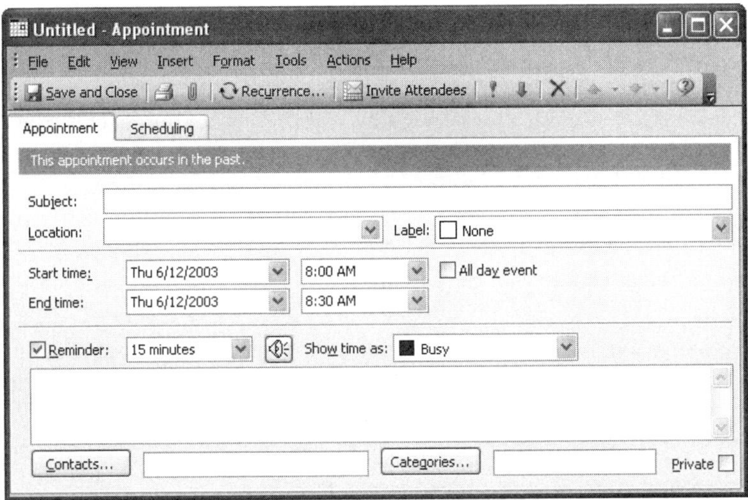

Figure 19-9. Use the appointment form to create a new appointment.

> **Tip** Create an appointment quickly
> To quickly create an appointment, you can click a blank time slot on the calendar and type the subject of the appointment. When you use this method, however, Outlook doesn't automatically open a new appointment form. To add details to the appointment, you must double-click the new appointment to open the form. Note that if you click a blank date in the Month view and type a subject, Outlook creates an all-day event rather than an appointment.

Specifying the Subject and Location

Type the subject of an appointment in the Subject box at the top of the appointment form. Make the subject as descriptive as possible because it will appear on the calendar.

If you want, you can type a location for the appointment in the Location box. To view a list of all previously typed locations, click the drop-down arrow beside the Location box; rather than typing the location, you can select from this list. Outlook displays the location you specify in parentheses next to the appointment subject.

Specifying Start and End Times

You set the start and end times of the appointment by typing the date and time in the Start Time and End Time boxes or by clicking the drop-down arrows beside each box. If you click a drop-down arrow for a date, a calendar appears. Click a drop-down arrow for time, and a list of potential start and end times in 30-minute increments appears. The End Time drop-down list shows how long the appointment will be for each given end time. You can also click in these fields and type a value. For example, you might use this method when you want to create a 15-minute appointment when Outlook is set to use a 30-minute default appointment duration.

Setting a Reminder

You can set a reminder for an appointment by selecting the Reminder check box on the appointment form. In the accompanying drop-down list, you can specify when the reminder should appear; the default is 15 minutes before the appointment. By default, a reminder both plays a sound and displays a reminder window, as shown in Figure 19-10. If you don't want the reminder to play a sound, or if you want to use a different sound, click the Sound button on the appointment form to change the settings.

Note To change the default behavior of appointment reminders, choose Tools, Options and click Preferences. In the Calendar section of the Preferences tab, you can select (or clear) the default reminder and set the default reminder time.

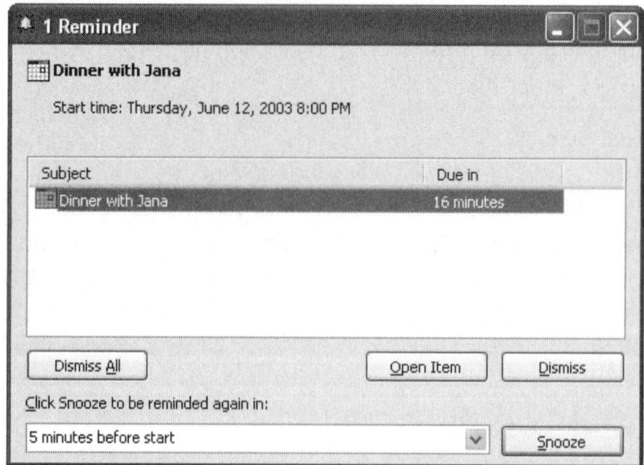

Figure 19-10. You can dismiss a reminder by clicking Dismiss or postpone it by clicking Snooze.

Classifying an Appointment

When you schedule an appointment on the calendar, it's displayed with one of four indicators:

- Busy (shaded black)
- Free (not shaded)
- Tentative (shaded with diagonal lines)
- Out Of Office (shaded gray)

The indicator appears on your local calendar and is also displayed when other users view the free/busy times of that calendar. By default, the time occupied by an appointment is classified as Busy. To reclassify an appointment, select the indicator from the Show Time As drop-down list, as shown in Figure 19-11.

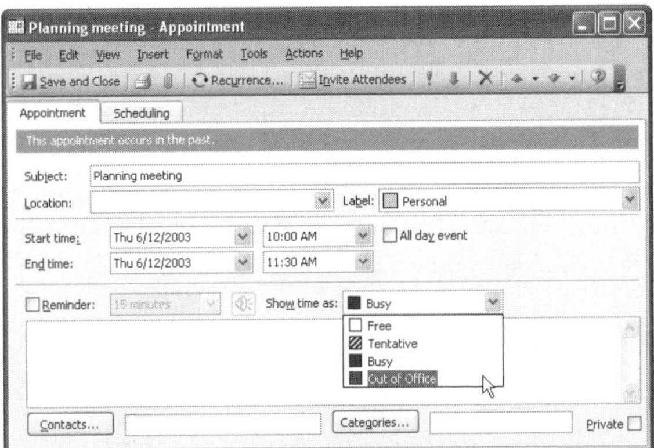

Figure 19-11. Use this drop-down list to select a classification for your appointment, which determines how it is displayed on your calendar.

Adding a Note

Sometimes an appointment requires more detail. You might need to remind yourself about documents you need to bring to the appointment, or perhaps you need to write down directions to an unfamiliar location. When that's the case, you can add a note by typing your text in the large text area of the form, as shown in Figure 19-12.

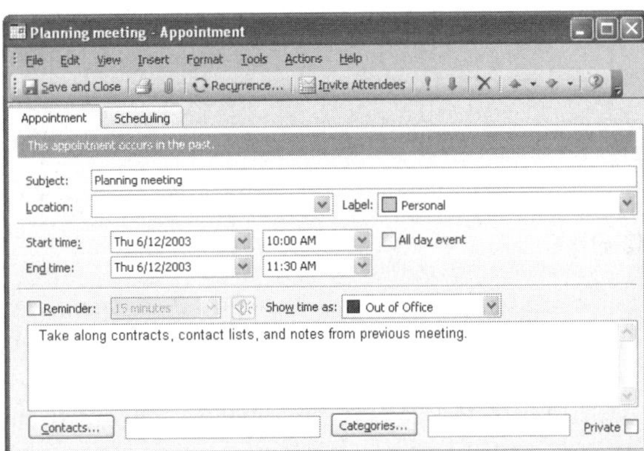

Figure 19-12. You can write a note on the appointment form.

Assigning a Contact

After you create an appointment, you might decide that it would be helpful to include contact information. For example, if you scheduled a veterinary appointment, you might want to include the phone number and address. Rather than typing that information as a note, you can link to it (assuming that the data is stored in your Contacts folder).

For more information about working with the Contacts folder, see Chapter 14, "Managing Your Contacts."

To assign a contact to an appointment, click Contacts at the bottom of the appointment form. This opens the Select Contacts dialog box, shown in Figure 19-13. Then select a folder, select a contact, and click OK to assign the contact to the appointment.

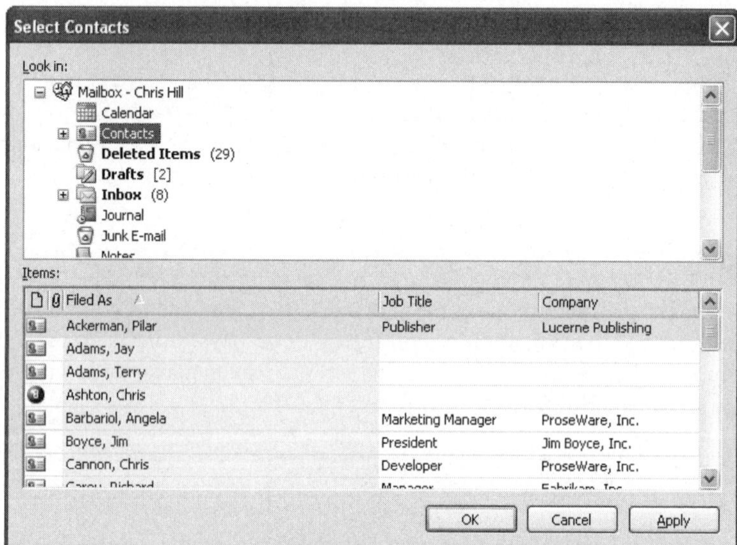

Figure 19-13. You can assign a contact to your appointment.

Categorizing an Appointment

Assigning an appointment to a category is simply another method of organizing your information. Outlook provides a number of categories by default (Business, Goals, and Ideas, for example), and you can add your own custom categories. Outlook allows you to categorize your appointments so that you can then filter or sort them before viewing. In this way, you can get an overview of all Outlook items based on a particular category. For example, you could view all appointments, meetings, messages, contacts, and tasks that have been assigned the same category—perhaps all the items related to a specific work project or objective.

For more information on working with categories in Outlook, see Chapter 4, "Using Categories and Types."

To assign a category to an appointment, click Categories at the bottom of the appointment form. In the Categories dialog box (see Figure 19-14), you can select one or more categories; click OK to assign them to the appointment.

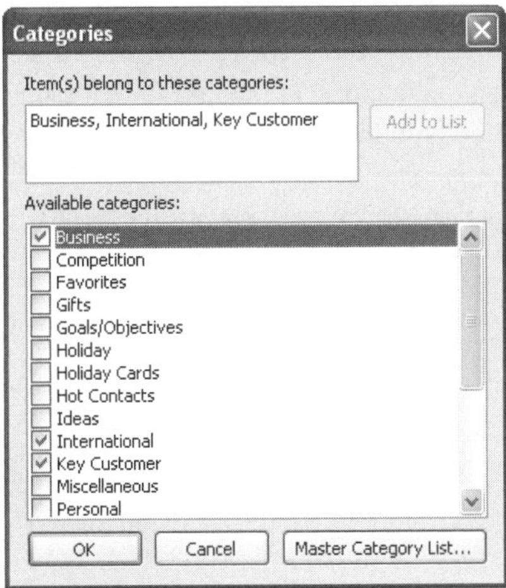

Figure 19-14. You can assign one or more categories to your appointment.

Saving an Appointment

You can save an appointment in several ways. The most basic method is to click the Save And Close button on the toolbar of the appointment form. This saves the appointment to the Calendar folder and closes the appointment form. If you want to save the appointment but keep the form open, choose File, Save.

A more complex way to save appointments allows them to be transferred to other users (who might or might not use Outlook) and opened in other applications. To save your appointments in any of a number of file formats, choose File, Save As to display the Save As dialog box (see Figure 19-15).

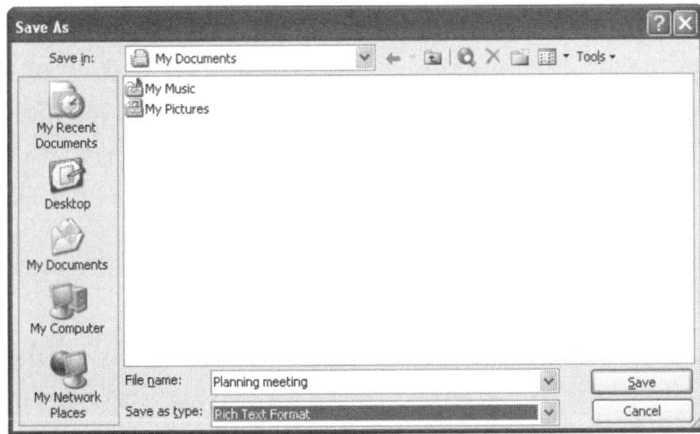

Figure 19-15. You can save your appointment in any of several formats so that the appointment can be opened with another application.

The following formats are available:

- **Text Only and Rich Text Format** These formats save the appointment in a file that text editors can read. Figure 19-16 shows an example of an appointment saved in Rich Text Format and then opened in WordPad.

> **Tip** You can create a new appointment from an Outlook Template file by choosing File, New, Choose Form and selecting User Templates In File System from the Look In list.

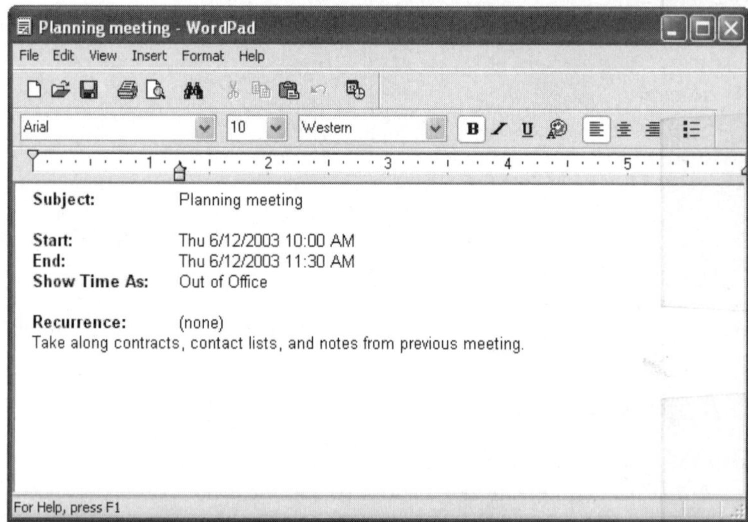

Figure 19-16. An appointment saved in Rich Text or Text Only format can be displayed in any application that supports those file types.

- **Outlook Template** This format allows you to save an appointment and use it later to create new appointments.
- **Message Format** Saving an appointment in this format is almost the same as saving an appointment to the calendar, except that the appointment is saved to a file in case you want to archive it or move it to another copy of Outlook. You can view the file in Outlook, and the data appears as it would if you had opened the item from the calendar.
- **iCalendar and vCalendar Format** These formats are used to share schedule items with people who use applications other than Outlook. iCalendar is a newer version of the standard (maintained by the Internet Mail Consortium) and should be used if possible.

Changing an Appointment to an Event

To change an appointment to an event, select the All Day Event check box on the appointment form. When an appointment is converted to an event, the start and end times are removed and only the start and end dates are left because events by definition last all day. The event appears in the banner area of the calendar.

Working with One-Time Events

An event is an appointment that lasts for one or more entire days. You can create an event by right-clicking the calendar and selecting New All Day Event. Unlike appointments, events are not shown in time slots on the calendar. Instead, events are displayed as banners at the top of the calendar day. Figure 19-17 shows the calendar with a scheduled event—in this case, a trade show.

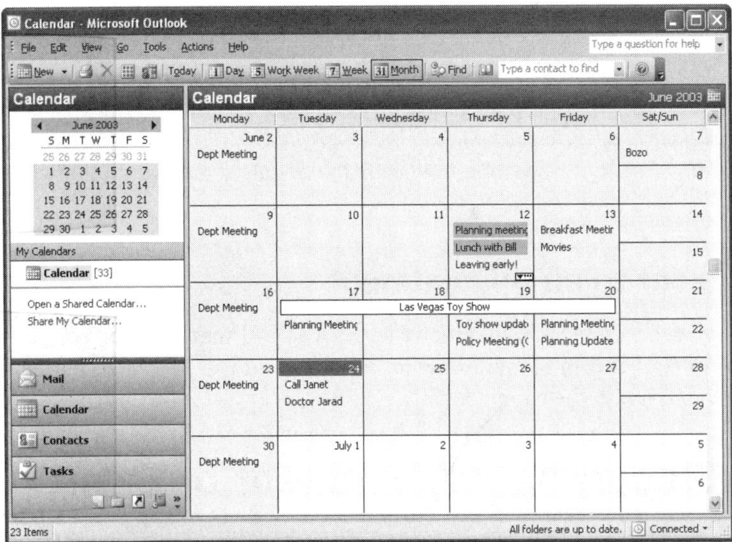

Figure 19-17. Outlook displays events as banners on the calendar.

> **Tip** **Create an event quickly**
>
> A simple way to add an event is to click the banner area of the calendar and start typing the subject of the event. When you add an event this way, the event is automatically set to last for only the selected day. Or, in Month view, click on a date and type the subject to create a one-time event on that date. To add details and change the duration of the event, you must use the event form.

Using the Event Form

You can use an event form in much the same way you use an appointment form, with a few exceptions: you can set the start and end times only as dates, not times; the default reminder is set to 18 hours; and the time is shown by default as Free, as opposed to Busy. The event form and the appointment form look the same except that the All Day Event check box is selected on the event form. You open an event form the same way you open an appointment form.

To create an event using the event form, type the subject, specify the start and end dates, add any optional information, and then click Save And Close on the toolbar. Figure 19-18 shows the event form for a trade show event.

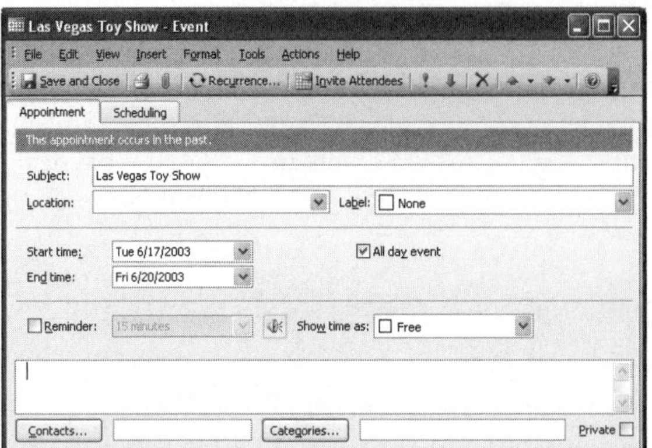

Figure 19-18. Use the event form to specify the details of an event to be added to your calendar.

Changing an Event to an Appointment

To change an event to an appointment, clear the All Day Event check box on the event form. The boxes for start and end times reappear, and the event will now be displayed in time slots on the calendar, not in the banner area.

Creating a Recurring Appointment or Event

When you create a *recurring appointment* or a *recurring event*, Outlook automatically displays the recurrences in the calendar. A recurring appointment could be something as simple as a reminder to feed your fish every day or pay your mortgage every month. You can create a recurring calendar item by right-clicking the calendar and choosing New Recurring Appointment or New Recurring Event. Alternatively, you can open a normal (nonrecurring) item and click the Recurrence button on the toolbar. Either method displays the Appointment Recurrence dialog box, shown in Figure 19-19.

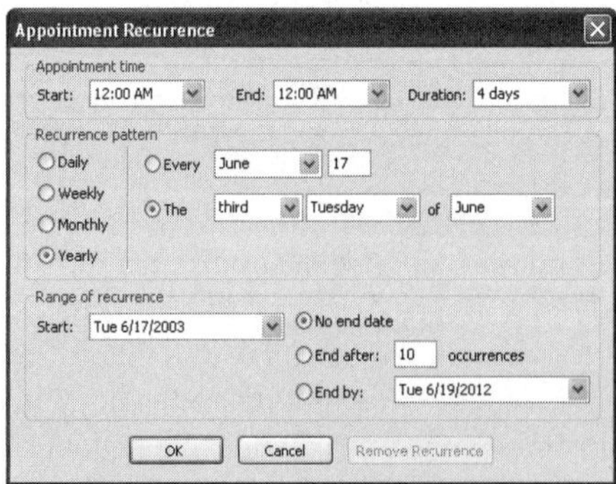

Figure 19-19. You can specify criteria that direct Outlook to display an appointment or event multiple times in the calendar.

In the Appointment Time area, you set the appointment time and duration. If you're creating the recurrence from an existing nonrecurring appointment, the time of that appointment is listed by default.

The Recurrence Pattern area changes depending on whether you select the Daily, Weekly, Monthly, or Yearly option, as follows:

- **Daily** Specify the number of days or every weekday.
- **Weekly** Specify the number of weeks and the day (or days) of the week.
- **Monthly** Specify the number of months as well as the day of the month (such as the 27th) or the day and week of the month (such as the fourth Wednesday).
- **Yearly** Specify the date (such as December 27th) or the day and week of the month (such as the fourth Wednesday of each December).

The last part of the Appointment Recurrence dialog box is the Range Of Recurrence area. By default, the start date is the current day, and the recurrence is set to never end. You can choose to have the appointment recur a specified number of times and then stop, or you can set it up to recur until a specified date and then stop—either method has the same effect. For example, to set up a recurring appointment that starts on the first Monday of a month and continues for four Mondays in that month, you could either set it to occur four times or set it to occur until the last day of the month.

Modifying an Appointment or Event

Changing an appointment or event is easy. First, open the appointment or event by locating it in the calendar and either double-clicking or right-clicking it and choosing Open. Make the necessary changes in the form and then click Save And Close on the toolbar. The updated appointment or event is saved to the Calendar folder.

Deleting an Appointment or Event

You can delete an appointment or event in several ways. To send the item to the Deleted Items folder, right-click the item and choose Delete, or select the item and press the Delete key. To permanently delete the item, hold down Shift while choosing Delete or pressing the Delete key.

> **Caution** You cannot recover an item that has been deleted using the Shift key unless you are using Microsoft Exchange Server and your administrator has configured the server for a retention period.

Using Color Effectively

You can use color as a tool to identify appointments and events. The easiest way to assign color to an appointment is to use the Label drop-down list in the appointment form. You can also create rules that direct Outlook to assign color labels automatically.

Assigning Color to an Appointment Manually

The Label drop-down list on the appointment form shows the different color labels you can assign to an appointment as a visual cue to indicate the purpose of the appointment, its importance, or its requirements. Simply select a color in the drop-down list when you fill in the appointment form. In Figure 19-20, the appointment is a personal one, and it will be displayed on the calendar in the specified color.

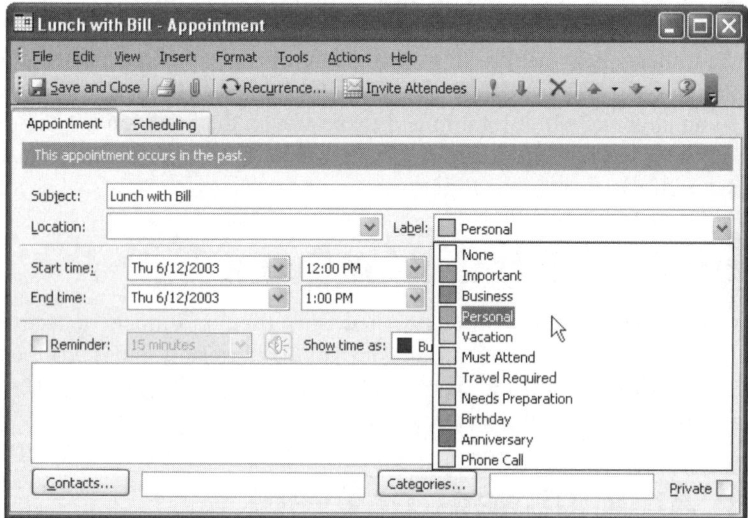

Figure 19-20. You can assign a color label to your appointment.

Assigning Color to an Appointment Automatically

To have Outlook automatically assign a color label to an appointment, you can create automatic formatting rules.

To create a Color rule, do the following:

1. Choose View, Arrange By, Current View, Customize Current View to open the Customize View dialog box.
2. Click Automatic Formatting to display the Automatic Formatting dialog box.
3. Click Add to add a new rule.

4 Type a name and assign a label to the new rule. Figure 19-21 shows a rule to automatically color all birthdays with the default Birthday label.

Figure 19-21. This new rule automatically assigns a Birthday label to all birthdays.

5 Click Condition to open the Filter dialog box (see Figure 19-22).

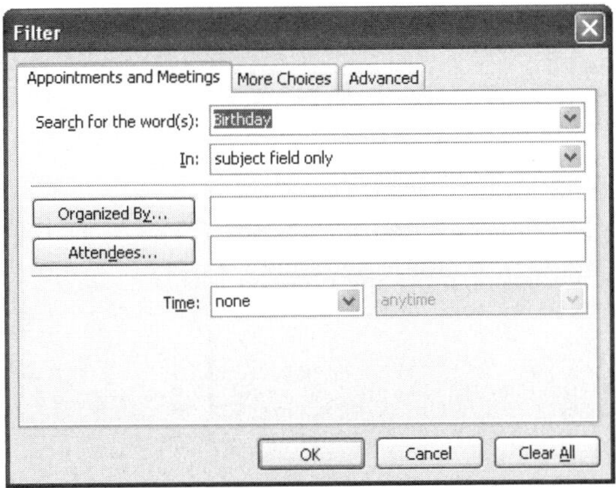

Figure 19-22. The Filter dialog box lets you set a filter that defines the condition on which the automatic color rule works.

For details about using filters, see "Customizing the Current Calendar View," page 528.

6 In this dialog box, assign a condition to the rule. For example, you might use the most basic type of filter and look for the word *birthday* in the subject line of all appointments.

7 Click OK to assign the condition to the new rule.

8 Click OK twice, once to close the Automatic Formatting dialog box and again to close the Customize View dialog box. A rule is now in effect that all appointments with the word *birthday* in their subject will be assigned the yellow Birthday label.

Printing Calendar Items

You can print calendar items in two ways. The simplest method is to right-click the item and choose Print from the shortcut menu. This method prints the item using the default settings.

The other way to print an item is to first open it by double-clicking it or by right-clicking it and choosing Open. You can then click the Print button on the toolbar to print using the default settings, or you can choose File, Print to display the Print dialog box.

You can make selections in the Print dialog box to change the target printer, the number of copies, and the print style, if necessary. The print style defines how the printed item will look. Click Page Setup to change the options for the selected style. Use the Format tab to set fonts and shading; the Paper tab to change the paper size, orientation, and margin settings; and the Header/Footer tab to add information to be printed at the top and bottom of the page.

Customizing the Current Calendar View

Besides setting the number of days displayed, configuring the Time Bar, and color-coding your appointments, you can customize the standard view of the Calendar folder in other ways. You can redefine fields, set up filters that determine which items are displayed on your calendar, and control fonts and other view settings. To configure the view, begin by choosing View, Arrange By, Current View, Customize Current View to open the Customize View dialog box, shown in Figure 19-23.

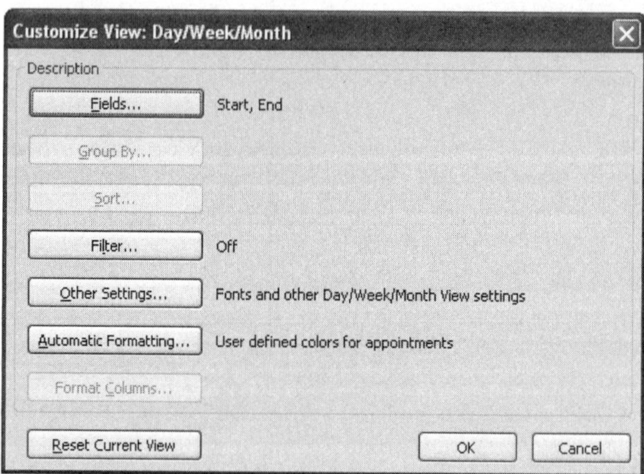

Figure 19-23. Use the Customize View dialog box to change view settings.

> **Tip** **Customize additional views**
> You can also customize views other than the current one. To do so, choose View, Arrange By, Current View, Define Views. Then select the view in the Custom View Organizer dialog box, and click Modify. This displays the Customize View dialog box, where you can change the options for the selected view.

Redefining Fields

Only two of the fields used for calendar items can be redefined: the Start and End fields. The values in these fields determine an item's precise location on the calendar—that is, where it is displayed. By default, the value contained in the Start field is the start time of the appointment, and the value contained in the End field is the end time of the appointment, which means that the item is displayed on the calendar in the time interval defined by the item's Start and End values.

To redefine either of the Start or End values, click Fields in the Customize View dialog box to open the Date/Time Fields dialog box. In the Available Date/Time Fields list, select the field that you want to use for the Start field and click Start. Use the End button to change the End field. For example, if you redefine the Start field to Recurrence Range Start and the End field to Recurrence Range End, all recurring calendar items will display as a single item that starts on the date of the first occurrence and ends on the date of the last occurrence. This can be handy if you want to view the entire recurrence range for a given item graphically.

Filtering Calendar Items

You can filter calendar items based on their content, their assigned category, or other criteria. By filtering the current view, you can determine which calendar items are displayed on your calendar—for example, all items related to one of your work projects, all items that involve a specific coworker, or items with a particular importance level.

To filter calendar items, follow these steps:

1. Choose View, Arrange By, Current View, Customize Current View to open the Customize View dialog box.
2. Click Filter to open the Filter dialog box.
3. If the Appointments And Meetings tab isn't displayed (see Figure 19-24), click it to bring it to the front.

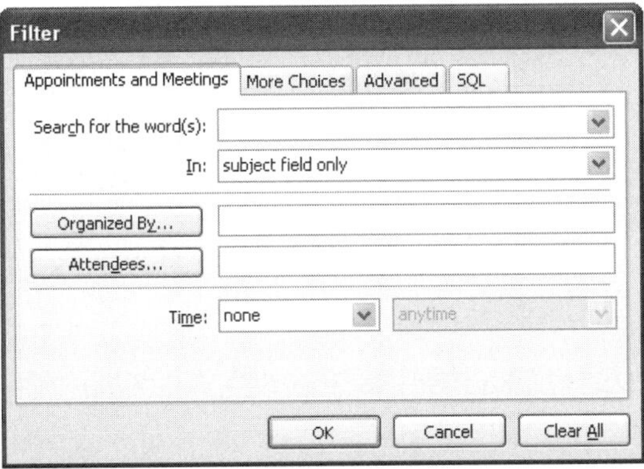

Figure 19-24. You can filter calendar items based on a specified word or phrase.

4 In the Search For The Word(s) box, type the word or phrase you want to use as the filter.

5 In the In drop-down list, select which areas of the calendar item to search—for example, you might have Outlook look only in the Subject field of your appointments.

6 When you click OK, Outlook displays on your calendar only those calendar items that contain the specified word or phrase.

To set additional criteria, you can use the three other tabs in the Filter dialog box—More Choices, Advanced, and SQL—as follows:

- **More Choices** On this tab you can click Categories to select any number of categories. After you click OK, only calendar items belonging to the selected categories are displayed on the calendar. Using the check boxes on the More Choices tab, you can filter items based on whether they are read or unread, whether they have or do not have attachments, or their importance setting. The final check box on the tab enables or disables case matching for the word or phrase specified on the Appointments And Meetings tab. You can also filter items depending on size.
- **Advanced** This tab allows an even wider range of filter criteria.You can specify any field, adding a condition such as Contains or Is Not Empty or a value for conditions that require one. Clicking Add To List adds the criteria to the list of filters.
- **SQL** This tab has two purposes. In most cases, it displays the SQL code for the filter, based on the filter criteria you select on the other three tabs. If the Edit The Filter Directly check box is selected, however, you can manually type the SQL code for filtering calendar items directly on the SQL tab. This flexibility allows you to fine-tune your filters with a great degree of precision.

Controlling Fonts and Other View Settings

You can use the Customize View dialog box (see Figure 19-23) to make additional changes to the current view. In the Customize View dialog box, click Other Settings, which displays the Format Day/Week/Month View dialog box, shown in Figure 19-25.

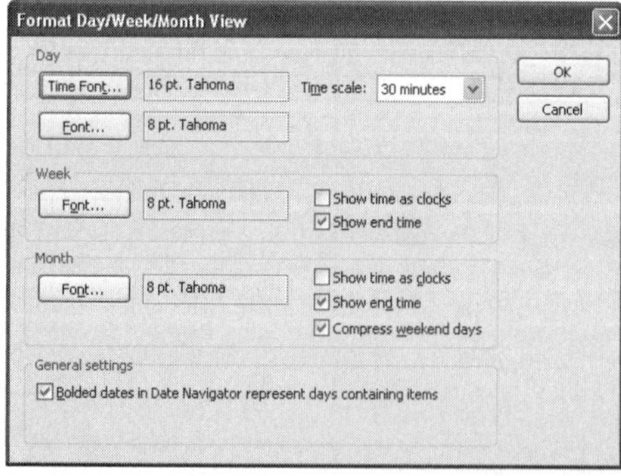

Figure 19-25. You can use the Format Day/Week/Month View dialog box to set font preferences for the Calendar folder as well as other options.

In the Format Day/Week/Month View dialog box, you can do the following:

- Set the fonts used in the calendar view.
- Set the calendar's time increments by selecting an option in the Time Scale drop-down list. This sets the amount of time represented by each interval in the Time Bar.
- Display weekend days in the calendar's Month view as smaller than week days by selecting the Compress Weekend Days check box.
- Determine whether days with scheduled items should appear in bold in the Date Navigator.

Creating a Custom View

Until now, this chapter has discussed only the customization of existing views, but you can also create completely new views and copy and modify views. If your current view is one you use often but nevertheless must change frequently to filter calendar items or modify fields, you might find it easier to create a new view.

To create a view or to see a list of already defined views, choose View, Arrange By, Current View, Define Views to open the Custom View Organizer dialog box, shown in Figure 19-26.

> **Note** To work with Outlook's calendar views, you must open the Calendar folder.

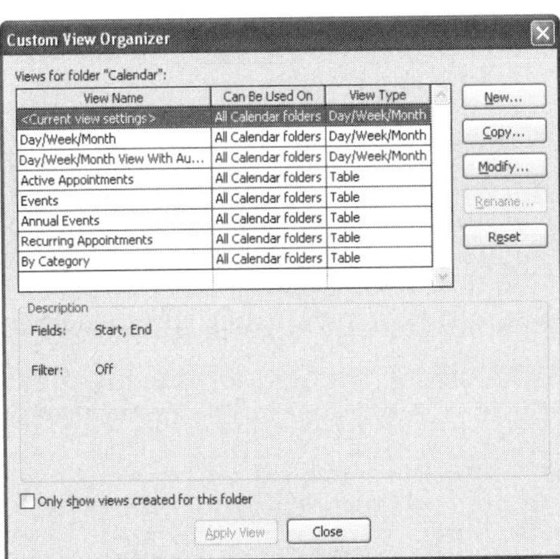

Figure 19-26. The Custom View Organizer dialog box allows you to see and work with the currently defined views as well as create new ones.

Creating a New View

To create a view, follow these steps:

1. Click New in the Custom View Organizer dialog box to open the Create A New View dialog box, shown in Figure 19-27.

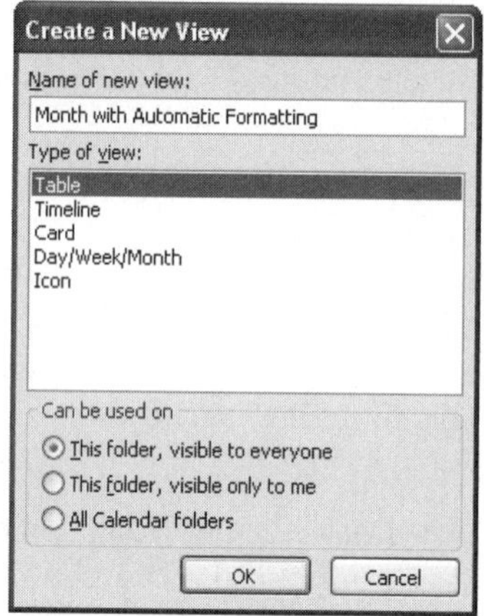

Figure 19-27. You can use the Create A New View dialog box to specify a name, a view type, the folder to which the view applies, and who is allowed to see the view.

2. Name the new view and select a view type. In the Can Be Used On section, specify the folder to which the view applies and who is allowed to see the view. You can select one of the following options:
   - **This Folder, Visible To Everyone** Limits the view to the current folder and makes it available to any user.
   - **This Folder, Visible Only To Me** Limits the view to the current folder but makes it available only to the current user.
   - **All Calendar Folders** Allows the view to be used in any calendar folder by any user.
3. When you click OK to create the new view, the Customize View dialog box appears, in which you can set the options for the new view.

> **Tip** **Change the availability of an existing view**
>
> To change the availability of an existing view or who is allowed to see a view, first copy the view and assign a name to the copy. (See "Copying a View," the next section, for more information about copying views.) Then select a new option in the Can Be Used On area. Finally, delete the original view and rename the new view using the name of the deleted view.

For information about setting view options in the Customize View dialog box, see "Customizing the Current Calendar View," page 528.

Copying a View

If you want to modify an existing view but also want to keep the original, you can make a copy of the view. To copy a view, select it in the Custom View Organizer dialog box and click Copy. In the Copy View dialog box, you can specify the name of the new view, the folder to which the view will apply, and who is allowed to see the view. Click OK to create the copy, which is added to the list in the Custom View Organizer dialog box and the list on the View, Arrange By, Current View menu.

Backing Up Your Schedule

To back up items in your Calendar folder, you must export the data to a personal folders (PST) file. To do so, follow these steps:

1. Choose File, Import And Export to start the Import And Export Wizard.
2. Choose Export To A File, as shown in Figure 19-28, and click Next.

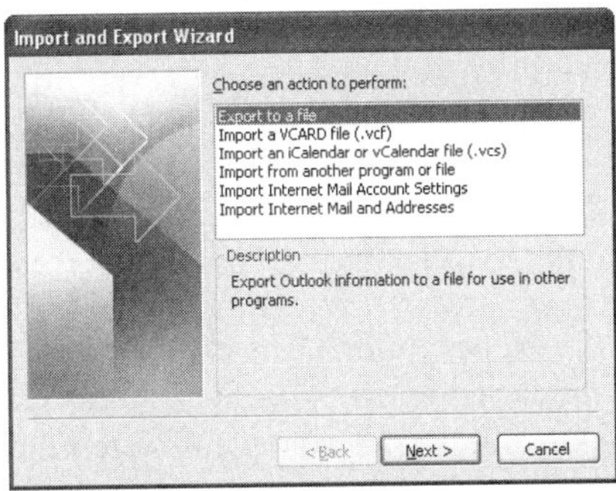

Figure 19-28. To back up calendar items, first open the Import And Export Wizard and select Export To A File.

3. On the Export To A File page (see Figure 19-29), select Personal Folder File (.pst) and then click Next.

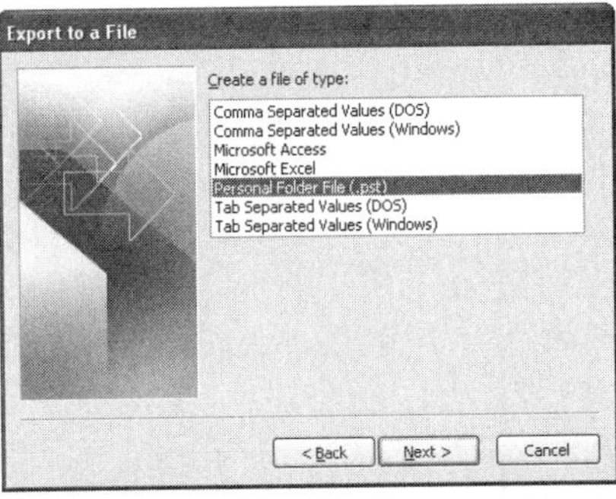

Figure 19-29. Calendar items should be backed up to a personal folders file.

4 On the Export Personal Folders page, select the folder to export (the Calendar folder, in the example shown in Figure 19-30). If you select the Include Subfolders check box, any subfolders of the selected folder are exported as well.

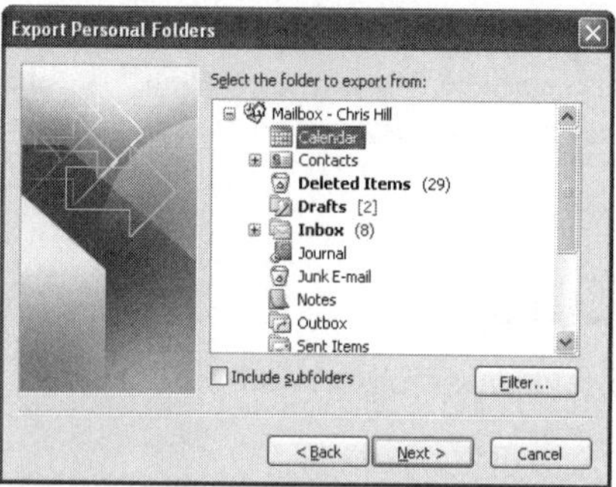

Figure 19-30. You use the Export Personal Folders page to specify the folder to export to a file.

5 Click Filter to open the Filter dialog box, in which you can specify the items to be exported. You can use the Filter dialog box if you want to export only specific items from your Calendar folder. If you choose not to use the Filter dialog box, all items will be exported.

For details about using the Filter dialog box, see "Filtering Calendar Items," page 529.

6 Specify the exported file and the export options. The export options control how Outlook handles items that have duplicates in the target file. You can choose to overwrite duplicates, create duplicates in the file, or not export duplicate items.

7 Click Finish. The Create Microsoft Personal Folders dialog box (see Figure 19-31) displays the selected file name.

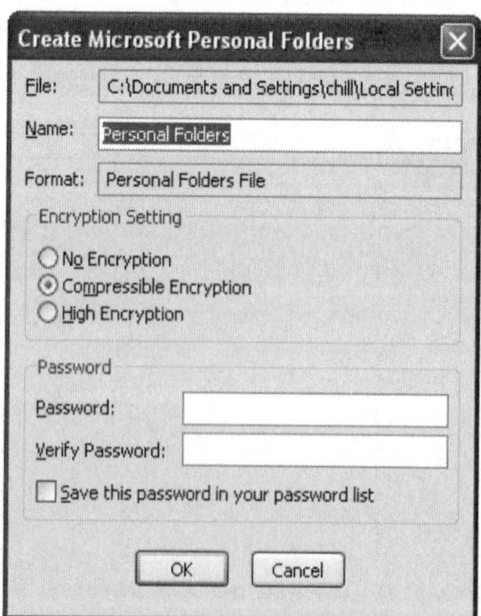

Figure 19-31. Type a password and choose encryption options before creating the PST file.

8. Specify a descriptive name for the personal folders file. You can also set encryption levels and a password for the file.
9. Click OK to create the file.

To restore data backed up to the PST file, follow these steps:

1. Choose File, Import And Export to start the Import And Export Wizard.
2. Choose Import From Another Program Or File and then click Next.
3. Select Personal Folder File (.pst) and click Next.
4. On the Import Personal Folders page, specify the backup file and how Outlook should handle duplicate items. You can choose to overwrite duplicates, create duplicate items, or not import duplicates. Then click Next.
5. Select the folder within the PST to be imported (the Calendar folder in this case), decide whether to include subfolders, and select the target folder. (By default, the target folder is the folder with the same name in the current mailbox, as shown in Figure 19-32.) You can also click Filter to specify in the Filter dialog box which items are to be imported.
6. Click Finish to complete the import process.

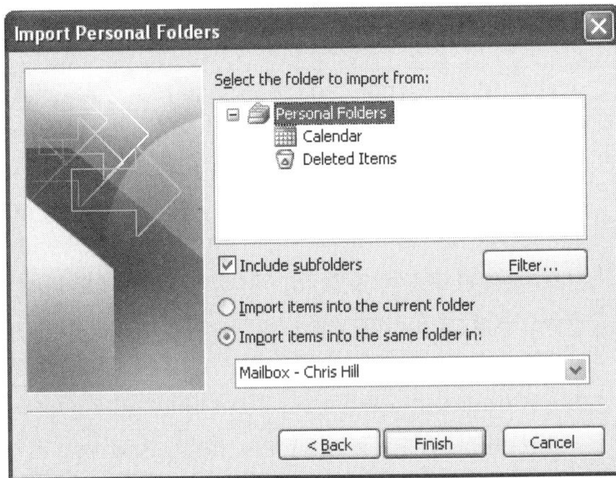

Figure 19-32. When you're importing items, you must select the folder to be imported from the personal folders file, whether to include subfolders, and the target folder.

Sharing Your Calendar

If you use Exchange Server, you can allow other users to access your entire calendar or selected calendar items. To share your calendar and its items, you must set permission levels for various users. In most cases, permissions are set by using built-in roles, as indicated in Table 19-1, but you can also set custom permissions for the rare cases when the built-in role does not fit the situation. Some permissions allow users to view your calendar; others allow users to add or even edit items. Table 19-1 explains these permissions.

Table 19-1. Folder Permissions

Permission	Description
Owner	The Owner role gives full control of the folder. An Owner can create, modify, delete, and read folder items; create subfolders; and change permissions on the folder.
Publishing Editor	The Publishing Editor role has all rights granted to an Owner, except the right to change permissions. A Publishing Editor can create, modify, delete, and read folder items and create subfolders.
Editor	The Editor role has all rights granted to a Publishing Editor, except the right to create subfolders. An Editor can create, modify, delete, and read folder items.
Publishing Author	A Publishing Author can create and read folder items and create subfolders but can modify and delete only folder items that he or she creates, not items created by other users.
Author	An Author has all rights granted to a Publishing Author but cannot create subfolders. An Author can create and read folder items and modify and delete items that he or she creates.
Nonediting Author	A Nonediting Author can create and read folder items but cannot modify or delete any items, including those that he or she creates.
Reviewer	A Reviewer can read folder items but nothing else.
Contributor	A Contributor can create folder items and cannot read items.
None	The None role has no access to the folder.

The first step in sharing the Calendar folder is to right-click it in the folder list on the Navigation Pane and choose Properties. Then click the Permissions tab to view the current permissions for the folder. Figure 19-33 shows the Permissions tab with the Calendar folder's default permissions.

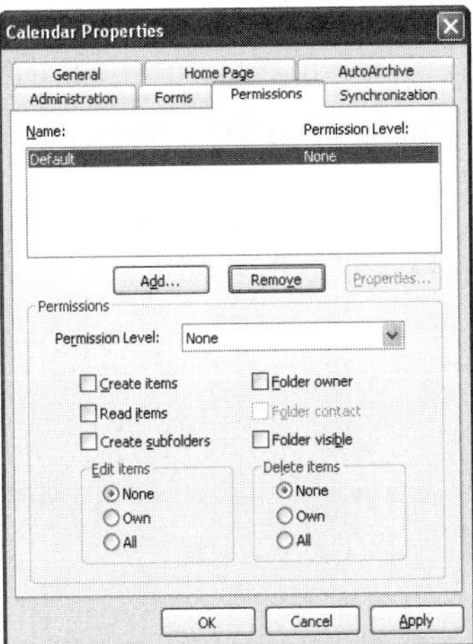

Figure 19-33. The default permissions for a folder are set to None.

To allow all users to view the calendar, you need to assign Reviewer permission to the default user. A *default user* is any user who is logged in. (An *anonymous user* is any user, whether he or she is logged in or not. Default users are a subgroup of anonymous users.) Select Default in the Name column and then change the permission level by selecting Reviewer in the Permission Level drop-down list.

You might assign a permission of Publishing Editor to users if they are colleagues who need to be able to schedule items for you as well as view and edit your calendar.

To give users Publishing Editor access to the calendar, follow these steps:

1. On the Permissions tab of the Folder Properties dialog box, click Add to open the Add Users dialog box, shown in Figure 19-34.

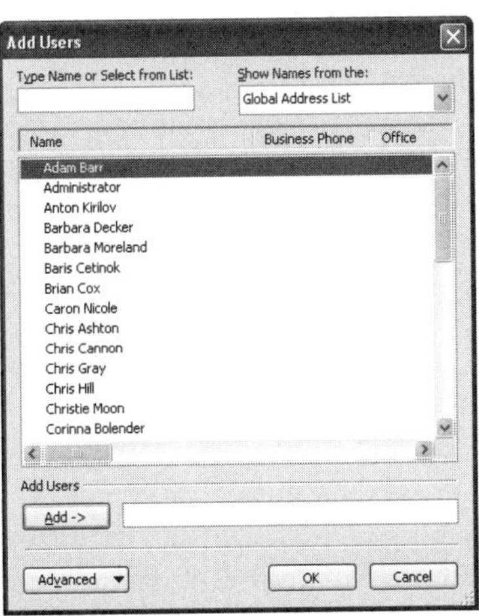

Figure 19-34. Add users to the Permissions tab so that you can specify their permissions for folder sharing.

2. Select a user from the list on the left and then click Add.
3. Repeat step 2 until you have selected all the users you want to add. Click OK.
4. By default, Outlook adds users to the Permissions tab with Reviewer permission. To change the permission of a newly added user to Publishing Editor, select the user's name and then select the permission in the Permission Level drop-down list. Figure 19-35 shows the Permissions tab after these changes have been made.

As you can see in Figure 19-35, the permissions granted to a user can be configured manually using the check boxes on the bottom half of the Permissions tab. However, this is usually unnecessary because you can set most combinations of settings using the Permission Level drop-down list.

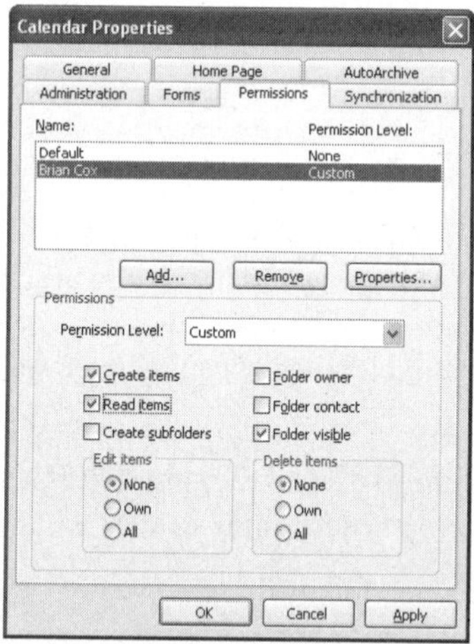

Figure 19-35. The default user's permission has been changed to None, and a user has been added and given custom permissions.

> **Tip** **Permissions and delegation are different**
> Giving someone else permissions in you Calendar folder is not the same as assigning them as a delegate. Delegate permission gives the person send-on-behalf permission, as well. See Chapter 29, "Delegating Responsibilities to an Assistant," for details on assigning delegate permissions.

Managing Your Free/Busy Information

By default, if you're using Exchange Server, your free/busy information is shared automatically with all other users on that server. If you want users who are not on your server to be able to view that information, or you do not use Exchange Server at all, you can still share your free/busy information. One option is to share the free/busy information using the Microsoft Office Internet Free/Busy Service, a free service offered by Microsoft to enable Office users to share their free/busy information. You can also post the information to other free/busy servers through FTP, HTTP, or file URLs. For example, your company might set up its own free/busy server to enable users to share their free/busy information with others, whether within the company (for example, if you don't use Exchange Server) or outside of the company.

Note This section of the chapter focuses on how to publish your free/busy information and configure Outlook to search for free/busy information. See the section "Working with Group Schedules," later in this chapter to learn how to view others' free/busy information.

Troubleshooting

Other users don't see your schedule changes

When you make changes to your schedule, those changes might not be visible right away to other users who need to see your free/busy times. By default, Outlook updates your free/busy information every 15 minutes. To change the frequency of these updates, choose Tools, Options and click Calendar Options. Then click Free/Busy Options to locate the Update Free/Busy Information On The Server Every *n* Minutes option, which you can use to set the frequency of updates.

Publishing your free/busy information makes it possible for others to see your free/busy times in Outlook when they need to schedule meetings with you or view or manage your calendar. Likewise, the free/busy times of people who publish their free/busy information, and who give you access to that information, are visible to you in Outlook. The ability to publish free/busy information therefore brings group scheduling capabilities to Outlook users who do not have access to Exchange Server.

Understanding What Status Is Available

Exchange Server provides four free/busy states for a given time period: Free, Busy, Tentative, and Out of Office. The Microsoft Office Internet Free/Busy Service, however, only provides status as Busy or Unknown. Therefore, if you view someone's free/busy information that is published to the Microsoft Office Internet Free/Busy Service, all time the user has marked as Tentative or Out of Office appears as Busy when you view his or her schedule in Outlook or from the Microsoft Office Internet Free/Busy Web site. This same behavior holds true when you post your free/busy information from Outlook to FTP, HTTP, or file URL, as explained in the following section. Therefore, the only way to see Tentative and Out of Office status is to pull that information directly from Exchange Server.

Inside Out

Prevent free/busy publishing

You can avoid publishing your free/busy information to any servers if you prefer. Choose Tools, Options and click Calendar Options. Then click Free/Busy Options. You can set the Publish *n* Months Of Calendar Free/Busy Information On The Server option to specify how much of your free/busy information is published. By setting this value to 0, no free/busy information is published, and your free/busy information will appear blank to other users.

Publishing Your Schedule

The Microsoft Office Internet Free/Busy Service is a central place on the Internet where you can publish your schedule. Publishing your schedule allows anyone (or only those you specify) to access your free/busy information from anywhere on the Internet. This free Microsoft service is useful if you don't use Exchange Server but still want to share your free/busy information with others, whether inside or outside of your company. You can also use Microsoft's service in conjunction with Exchange Server, publishing your free/busy information to the service to allow users outside of your Exchange Server organization to view schedule status.

Inside Out

Viewing free/busy data from an Outlook profile

The current iteration of the Microsoft Office Internet Free/Busy Service apparently has problems with free/busy data published from an Outlook profile that contains an Exchange Server account. Although others can see the information from Outlook, they will not be able to view it from Microsoft's Web interface to the Free/Busy Service (which is rather limited anyway). Free/busy data published from an Outlook profile without an Exchange Server account is visible from both Outlook and the Web interface.

The following sections explain how to publish to the different types of free/busy servers. Later in this chapter you also learn how to set up your own free/busy server.

Publishing to the Microsoft Office Internet Free/Busy Service

To publish the schedule of your free/busy times using the Microsoft Office Internet Free/Busy Service, follow these steps:

1 Choose Tools, Options and click Calendar Options. Then click Free/Busy Options to open the Free/Busy Options dialog box (see Figure 19-36).

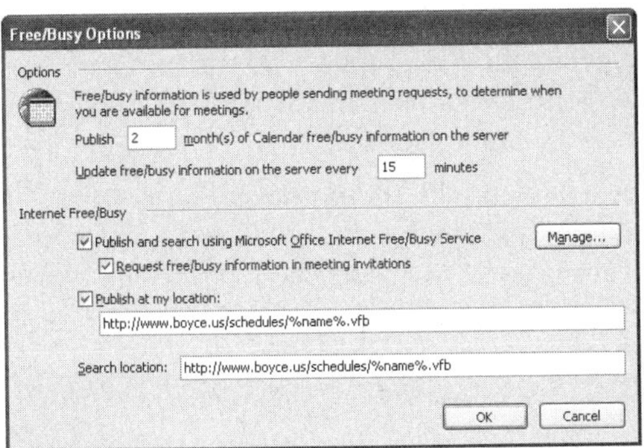

Figure 19-36. Configure the free/busy options and the location for publishing free/busy information.

2 Specify how much free/busy information you want to have published (two months is the default) and how often the free/busy information should be updated on the server (every 15 minutes is the default).

3 Select the Publish And Search Using Microsoft Office Internet Free/Busy Service check box.

4 To configure the service, click Manage. You must have an Internet connection to use the service. Figure 19-37 shows the sign-in page for the Microsoft Office Internet Free/Busy Service.

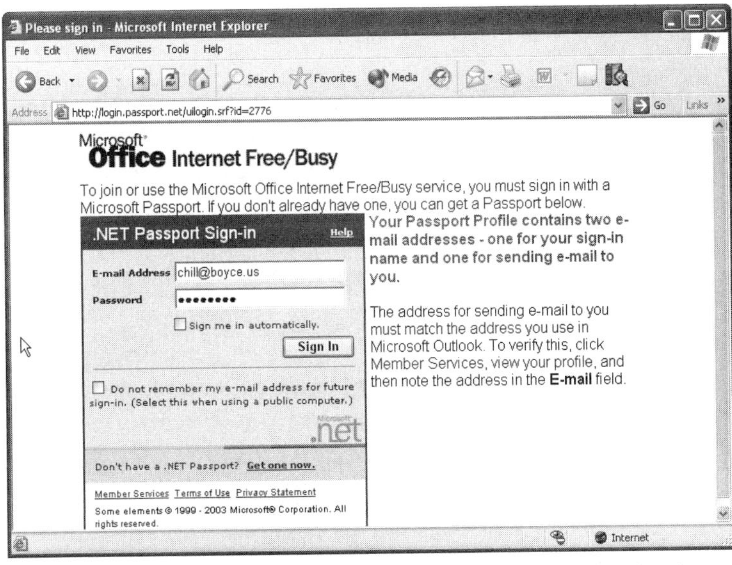

Figure 19-37. To use the Microsoft Office Internet Free/Busy Service, you must sign in using a Microsoft Passport login.

5 If you need to get a Microsoft Passport login, click Get One Now on the sign-in page. Fill out the form, including the e-mail address you are using with Outlook, and click Sign Up. You can then continue to the Free/Busy Service. After you sign up, the service tells you how to configure Outlook for use.

6 From the screen shown in Figure 19-38, you can authorize other users to view your free/busy information by typing their e-mail addresses. Or select the All Microsoft Office Internet Free/Busy Service Members check box to allow all users to see your information.

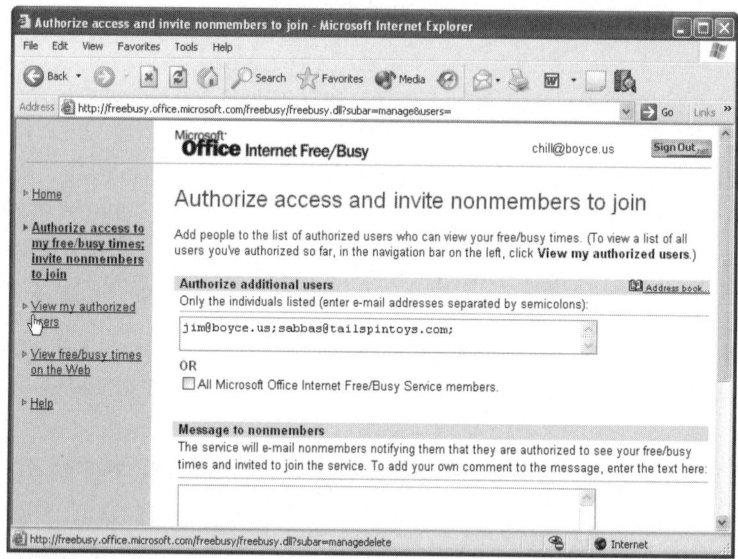

Figure 19-38. Specify the users who are allowed to access your free/busy information or select the check box to allow all users access.

7 If you want, type a personalized message to include in the e-mail sent by the Free/Busy Service. (The service sends an e-mail to all users who are not members of the service to notify them that they can view your free/busy information—and to invite them to join the service.)

8 Click OK to save your changes.

9 Continue clicking OK to close the Free/Busy Options, Calendar Options, and Options dialog boxes.

Your free/busy information is now shared using the Microsoft Office Internet Free/Busy Service, and other users who have joined the service can see that information.

Publishing to FTP, HTTP, and File Servers

You can also publish your free/busy schedule to another server using FTP, HTTP, or file URLs. For example, if you don't use Exchange Server in your company, you might set up a Web server on your network to enable users to publish and share their free/busy information. Using your own server eliminates the need to use Microsoft's free service or for users to have Microsoft Passports (which are required to use the Microsoft service).

You can publish to local or remote FTP or HTTP servers, making it easy to publish free/busy information to servers outside of your organization. For example, you might work at a division that doesn't have its own Web server, but the corporate office does have a server that you can use to publish your free/busy information. Publishing to a file URL, however, requires a local file server. However, that doesn't mean that users who need to access that free/busy information must be located on the local network. You might publish to a local Web server using a file URL, for example, but remote users access that free/busy information through the Web server's HTTP-based URL.

You must know the correct URL for the server to configure the free/busy URL in Outlook. The following are three examples:

- *http://www.tailspintoys.com/schedules/chill.vfb*
- *ftp://ftp.tailspintoys.com/schedules/chill.vfb*
- f:\Schedules\Chill.vfb

Note that schedule files use a VFB file extension. Also, the first two examples assume a virtual or physical folder named Schedules under the root of the specified server URL.

In addition to specifying the URL string explicitly, you can also use two replaceable parameters in the URL string:

- %*server*% This parameter represents the server portion of the e-mail address. For example, with the address *chill@tailspintoys.com*, %*server*% would resolve to tailspintoys.com. If you specified the URL *http://%server%/schedules/chill.vfb*, Outlook would resolve the server domain, and the resulting URL would be *http://tailspintoys.com/schedules/chill.vfb*.
- %*name*% This parameter represents the account portion of the e-mail address. Using the *chill@tailspintoys.com* example, %*name*% would resolve to chill. If you specified the URL *http://%server%/schedules/%user%.vfb*, for example, Outlook would resolve the URL to *http://tailspintoys.com/schedules/chill.vfb*.

Tip **Specifying the URL**

If you need to include *www* in the URL, add it like this: *http://www.%server%/schedules/%name%.vfb*.

If your profile includes an Exchange Server account, specifying %*name*% in the URL string will result in Outlook trying to use the X.400 address from your Exchange Server account. Instead of using the variable, specify an explicit name.

Why provide replaceable parameters if you can just type in the correct URL? You can use group policies to control Outlook's configuration, and one of the policies controls the free/busy publish and search URLs. You can specify the URL with replaceable parameters in the group policy, and those parameters are then replaced when the user logs on, resulting in the correct URL for the user based on his or her e-mail address.

See the section "Group Policy Considerations for Outlook and Office," page 850, for details on applying Outlook-specific group policies.

Configuring Outlook to publish to an FTP, HTTP, or file URL is easy. Follow these steps to configure Outlook to publish your free/busy information:

1. In the Free/Busy Options dialog box, select Publish At My Location.
2. In the text box, specify the fully qualified path to the server on which your free/busy information is to be published.
3. In the Search Location text box, specify the server to search. This server will be used to view other users' free/busy information. (See the following section for additional details on configuring search locations.)
4. Click OK to close the Free/Busy Options dialog box.

Setting the Search Location for Free/Busy Information

The Free/Busy Options dialog box includes two options that determine where Outlook will search for free/busy information when you create group schedules or meeting requests:

- **Publish And Search Using Microsoft Office Internet Free/Busy Service** With this option enabled, Outlook publishes your free/busy information to the Microsoft service, and also searches the service for free/busy information of others.
- **Search Location** You can specify a URL here and Outlook will search the specified URL for free/busy information.

Both of these global settings work in conjunction with Exchange Server, if present, providing a search location for addresses not stored in Exchange Server. In addition to these global settings, you can also specify a search URL for individual contacts. You would specify the search URL in the contact if the contact's free/busy information is not stored on the Microsoft service or the other server specified by the Search Location field.

Follow these steps to set the free/busy search URL for a contact:

1. Open the contact and click the Details tab.
2. Click in the Address field in the Internet Free/Busy area and type the URL as an HTTP, FTP, or file URL.
3. Click Save And Close.

Configuring Authentication for Free/Busy Searches

If you publish to an HTTP or file URL that requires authentication, your Web browser or Microsoft Windows itself will prompt you for a user name and password when Outlook attempts to connect. If you are publishing to an FTP site, however, you need to use a different method to specify the user name and password for the free/busy server. You cannot simply embed the user name and password in the publish/search string as you would when connecting to an FTP site from Microsoft Internet Explorer.

Follow these steps to add authentication information for an FTP site in Outlook:

1. In Outlook, choose File, Open, Outlook Data File.
2. In the Open Outlook Data File dialog box, click the Look In drop-down list and choose Add/Modify FTP Locations. Outlook displays the Add/Modify FTP Locations dialog box shown in Figure 19-39.

Figure 19-39. Specify FTP settings in the Add/Modify FTP Locations dialog box.

3. Enter the FTP server name or IP address in the Name Of FTP Site field.
4. Select the User option and enter a user name in the User field, then enter the password in the Password field.
5. Click Add and then click OK. Click Cancel to close the Open Outlook Data File dialog box.

Refreshing Your Schedule

Free/busy information is refreshed automatically at the intervals set in the Free/Busy Options dialog box. (Choose Tools, Options, click Calendar Options, and then click Free/Busy Options to access this dialog box.)

You can refresh free/busy information manually as well. First, make sure that the Calendar folder is open. Then choose Tools, Send/Receive, Free/Busy Information.

Sending Your Free/Busy Information Through E-Mail

To e-mail your free/busy information to others, you must first link that information to a vCard as follows:

1. Open a contact item containing your own contact information.
2. Click the Details tab of the contact form, shown in Figure 19-40.

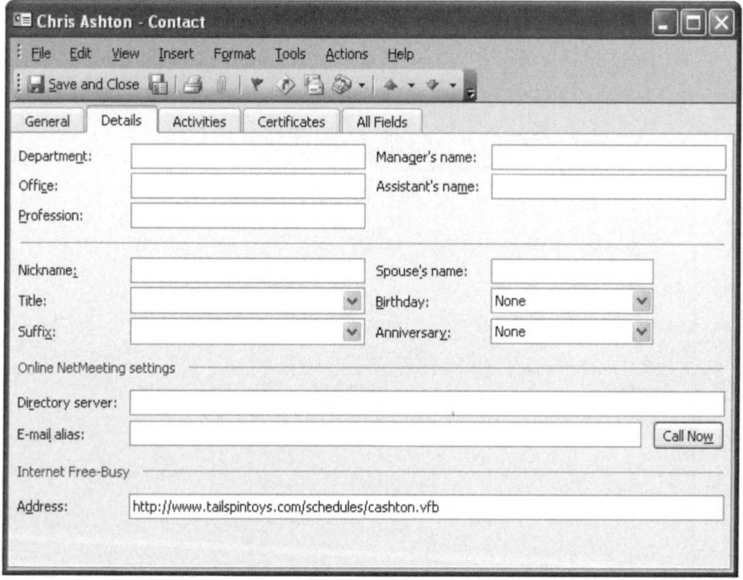

Figure 19-40. On the Details tab of a contact form, you can specify the Internet Free/Busy server.

3. In the Address box in the Internet Free-Busy area, type the address of the server containing your free/busy information.
4. Choose File, Save As and select vCard Files from the Save As Type drop-down list to save the contact information as a vCard.
5. Click OK to create the vCard.

You can now send the vCard to other users, and they can reference your free/busy information.

For details about using vCards, see "Sharing Contacts with vCards," page 420.

Changing the Free/Busy Status of an Item

You can change the free/busy status of an item easily. One method is to right-click the item and choose Show Time As, Free/Busy. The second method is to open the item (double-click or right-click it and choose Open), and choose Free/Busy from the Show Time As drop-down list.

Working with Group Schedules

Group scheduling is another very useful and important feature made possible by Outlook. This section offers an overview of group scheduling to help you implement and manage it in your organization. Through the group scheduling features in Outlook, managers and those who allocate resource in an organization can have easy access to schedule and contact information for all members of the organization. Managers can get an overview of what their teams are doing by viewing the team members' joint schedules. A receptionist who needs to locate employees can check the database for Outlook schedules, which can serve as an in–out board. Anyone who needs to plan a meeting can create and save a list of invitees to streamline the process. Scheduling is simplified because you can view free/busy information for all invitees in a single place.

As this section explains, you can use Outlook's group scheduling feature in three ways: by using your organization's internal Exchange Server database, by using your own free/busy server (or a third-party server), or by using the Microsoft Office Internet Free/Busy Service. You can use any of these in combination as needed.

Creating a Group Schedule

To see how the group scheduling feature can work in your organization, open Outlook's Calendar folder. Choose Actions, View Group Schedules to display the Group Schedules dialog box, shown in Figure 19-41.

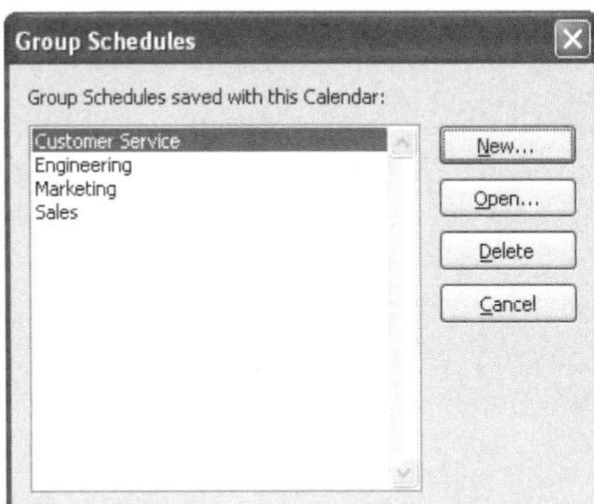

Figure 19-41. As you create custom group schedules, they're listed here.

To create a new schedule, click New. In the Create New Group Schedule dialog box, shown in Figure 19-42, type a name for the new group schedule.

Figure 19-42. When naming schedules, use simple but descriptive names.

Use a name that is descriptive and easily identifiable (Figure 19-42). After you've entered a name, click OK. The group scheduling window is displayed for the new group, as shown in Figure 19-43.

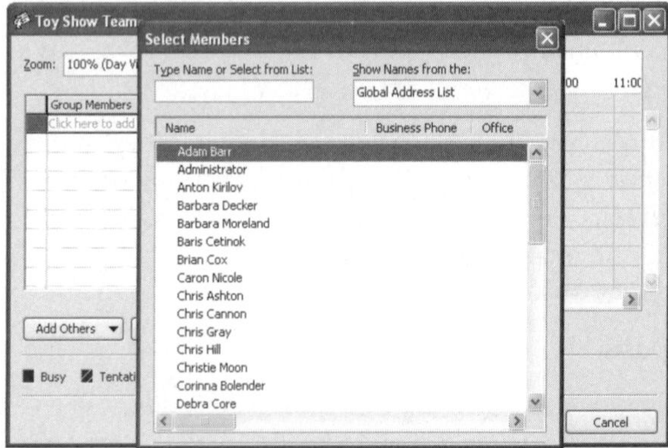

Figure 19-43. The group scheduling window is displayed for the Toy Show Team group.

Adding Members to the Group

Next you must create a list of group members. In the group scheduling window, click Add Others. You can either add members from an address book or from a public folder. When you click Add From Address Book, Outlook opens the Select Members dialog box, shown in Figure 19-44.

> **Tip** You can simply type, in the Group Members column, the e-mail address of the person you want to add. You don't have to click Add Others to add addresses.

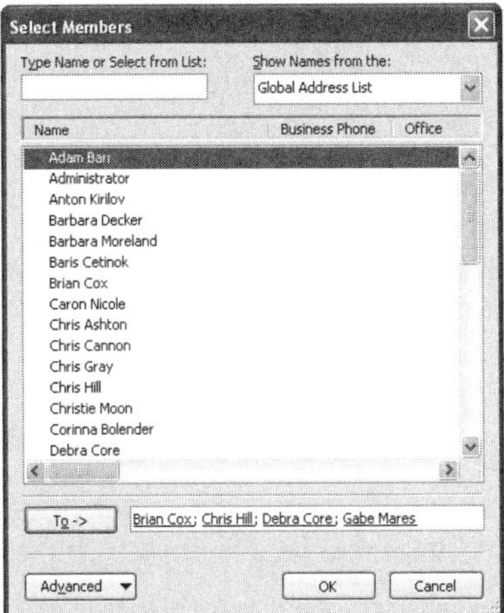

Figure 19-44. Use this dialog box to add users to the group schedule.

This dialog box lists users who can be added to the group schedule list. Select each member in the Name list and click To to add that person to the list. You can use the Exchange Server Global Address List or other address lists to which you have scheduling information access. (Additionally, any resources that need to be monitored can be added to this list.) After you've added all the people who need to be included in this group, click OK to close the dialog box.

For information about how to schedule a resource, see "Scheduling Resources," page 565.

Viewing a Group Schedule

In the group scheduling window, you'll now see a list of the group members you selected, with each individual's schedule information displayed to the right, as shown in Figure 19-45. Note the legend in the lower left that indicates what the color coding represents.

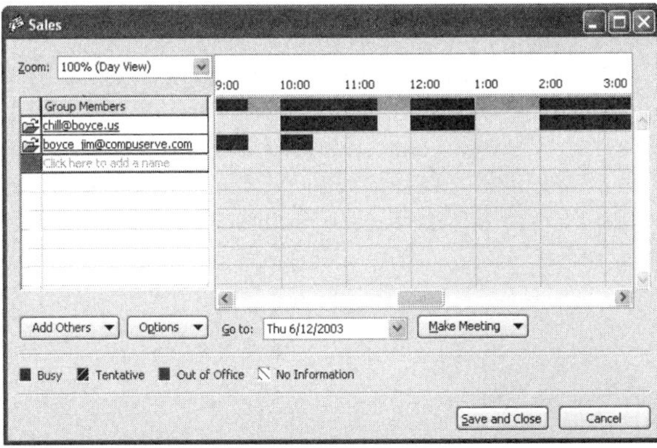

Figure 19-45. Scheduling information for each user in the group schedule is shown on a different line.

Each schedule shows blocks of time that are designated as follows:

- **Busy** The member is not available. You cannot schedule over this block of time. These appointments are shown in solid blue.
- **Tentative** The block of time is tentatively scheduled—perhaps an appointment for that time has not yet been confirmed, or a meeting at that time is not a priority for the member. If you schedule over a tentative appointment, the member will need to decide which appointment to attend. Tentative appointments are colored with diagonal blue and white stripes.
- **Out Of Office** The member is on vacation, at a conference, or otherwise unavailable. These times are shown in purple.
- **Open** Open time is indicated by gray areas. The member has no appointments or meetings on the calendar, and this block of time can be scheduled.
- **No Information** Exchange Server has no information about the member's schedule. Such blocks of time are shown as white areas with diagonal black lines (not included in Figure 19-45). This might indicate that the member does not use Outlook, that the account is new, or that the account has problems.

Note If you have been given the appropriate permissions, you can view specific listings of meetings and appointments on a group member's schedule, rather than seeing only color-coded blocks of time. Thus a manager or a receptionist could know not only that someone is out of the office but also where that person has gone. For privacy reasons, only users who are specifically given permission can view the details of other people's calendar entries. For information about giving other users permission to view your Calendar folder, see "Sharing Your Calendar," page 536.

In Figure 19-45, the top bar of the group schedule is a composite of the individual schedules. This allows you to see at a glance which times are open for all group members. By scrolling left or right, you can check on previous or future times. You can also change views by using the Zoom drop-down list.

Note that you can add members to the group even if they are not part of your organization. Just add them from your Contacts folder or whatever address book location in which their contact information is stored. As long as you have configured the appropriate free/busy search paths as explained previously in this chapter, Outlook should be able to locate their free/busy information. However, keep in mind that only Exchange Server users' Tentative and Out of Office times will appear as such in the group schedule. Members whose information is pulled from other free/busy servers will have their Tentative and Out of Office time shown simply as Busy.

Setting Up a Meeting or Sending E-Mail

You can use group schedules as a starting point for setting up a meeting or sending an e-mail message. Figure 19-46 shows some of the available options. When you choose one of these options, Outlook opens a new meeting request form or a message form, and you can create the meeting request or the message just as you normally would in Outlook.

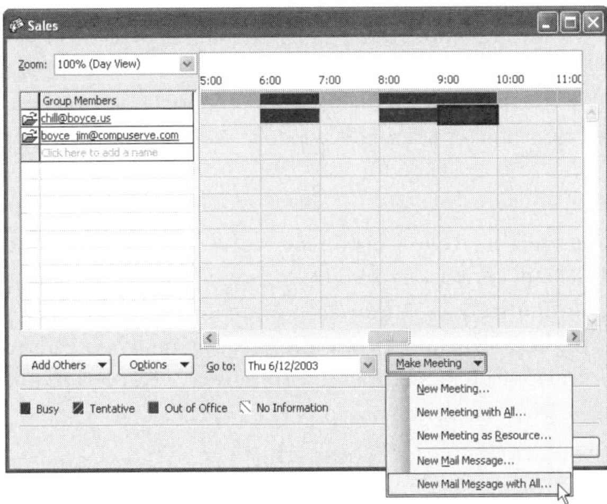

Figure 19-46. You can take a variety of actions based on the group schedule information.

Creating Your Own Free/Busy Server

If you don't have Exchange Server in your organization, you can still publish your free/busy information to enable others, whether inside your organization or outside of it, to view that information for scheduling purposes. As explained earlier in this chapter, Outlook can publish to FTP, HTTP, or file URLs. Which type you choose depends on the availability of such servers in your network, whether outside users need access to the free/busy information, and firewall and security issues for incoming access to the servers. For example, if your network does not allow FTP traffic through its firewalls but does allow HTTP, then HTTP would be the choice for your free/busy server. However, keep in mind that publishing and searching are two different tasks that can use two different methods. You might have users internal to the network publish using a file URL to a shared network folder, but outside users would access the information by HTTP. Naturally, this means that the target folder for publishing the free/busy information must also be a physical or virtual directory of the Web URL that outsiders use to view free/busy information. If your free/busy server must be located on the other side of a firewall from your users, FTP or HTTP would be a logical choice for publishing.

After you decide the type of access methods you need to provide for publishing and viewing free/busy information, it's a simple matter of setting up the appropriate type of server. There are no requirements specific to free/busy data for the server, so any FTP, HTTP, or file server will do the trick. Following are some points to keep in mind as you begin planning and deploying your free/busy server.

Tip **Host free/busy FTP or HTTP virtual servers**
You can use Microsoft Internet Information Services (IIS) running on Microsoft Windows 2000 Server or Microsoft Windows Server 2003 to host free/busy FTP or HTTP virtual servers. If you need no more than a maximum of 10 concurrent connections, you can use Microsoft Windows 2000 Professional or Microsoft Windows XP Professional to host the site.

- FTP Set up the virtual server to allow both read and write permissions for the physical or virtual folder that will contain the free/busy data. For the best security, configure the server to require authentication and disallow anonymous access. However, you then need to provide authentication information to everyone who needs to access the server for free/busy information. Remember to configure NTFS permissions as needed to control access if the directory resides on an NTFS partition.
- HTTP The physical or virtual directory containing the free/busy data must be configured for both read and write permissions. If the directory resides on an NTFS partition, configure NTFS permissions as necessary to allow access to the directory as needed. You can disallow anonymous access if desired for greater security. Users who attempt to access the free/busy data are then required to provide a user name and password when publishing or searching.
- File Configure folder and file permissions as needed to allow users to access the shared directory. For better security, place the folder on an NTFS partition and use NTFS permissions to restrict access to the folder and its contents as needed.

Managing Time Zones

Outlook gives you a great deal of flexibility when it comes to time zones on your calendar. You can change time zones easily and even add a second time zone to the calendar. If you work for a corporation that has multiple offices in different time zones, being able to quickly reference your calendar with various zones can make scheduling simpler.

Changing the Time Zone

To work with time zones, use the Time Zone dialog box (see Figure 19-47). To open this dialog box, right-click the Time Bar and choose Change Time Zone. (Alternatively, choose Tools, Options and click Calendar Options. Then click Time Zone.)

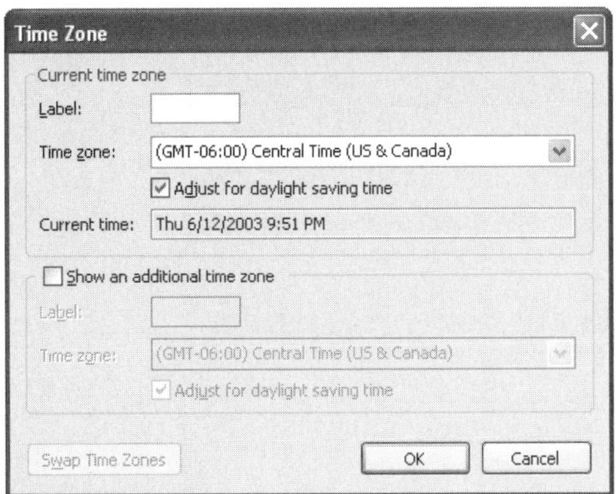

Figure 19-47. You can set the current time zone and display a second time zone.

In the Time Zone dialog box, you can specify a label for the current time zone, which is displayed above the Time Bar on your calendar. You can also set the time zone you want to use by selecting it from the Time Zone drop-down list, and you can choose whether to automatically adjust for daylight saving time.

> **Note** Changing the time zone in the Time Zone dialog box has the same effect as changing the time zone by using the Date/Time icon in Control Panel.

When you change the time zone, the time of your appointments adjusts as well. Your appointments stay at their scheduled time in the original time zone but move to the appropriate time in the new time zone. For example, an appointment scheduled for 10:00 A.M. in the GMT+2 time zone will move to 8:00 A.M. if the time zone is changed to GMT (Greenwich Mean Time). Appointments are scheduled in absolute time, regardless of the time zone.

Using Two Time Zones

To add a second time zone to your calendar, follow these steps:

1. In the Time Zone dialog box, select the Show An Additional Time Zone check box.
2. Assign a label to the second time zone. This step is not necessary, but it can help to avoid confusion later on. (If your first time zone does not already have a label, adding one now will allow you to easily distinguish between the two.)
3. In the second Time Zone drop-down list, select the second time zone.
4. Select the Adjust For Daylight Saving Time check box if you want Outlook to make this adjustment.
5. You can click Swap Time Zones to swap the current time zone with the second time zone. This feature is useful if you travel between corporate offices in different time zones.

Figure 19-48 shows the calendar after these changes have been applied.

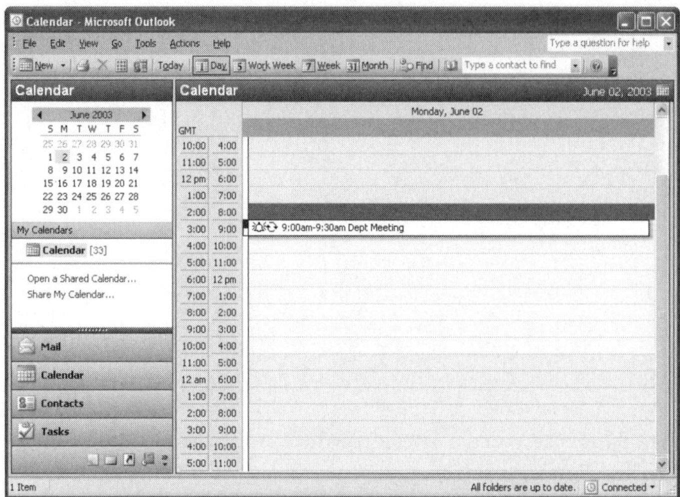

Figure 19-48. The calendar displays both time zones in the Time Bar under their respective labels.

Publishing Your Calendar as a Web Page

If you want individuals who are not running Outlook or another scheduling program to be able to view your calendar, you can save it to a Web page. You can save the calendar to any Web server using FTP and to some using HTTP. For an example of a calendar saved as a Web page, see Figure 19-49.

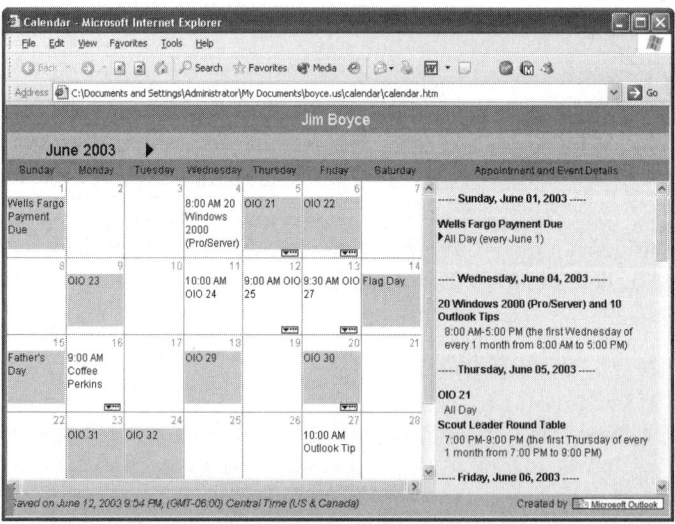

Figure 19-49. This is an example of a calendar published as a Web page.

To save a calendar to a Web page, follow these steps:

1. Ensure that the Calendar folder is open.
2. Choose File, Save As Web Page to open the Save As Web Page dialog box.
3. Specify the start and end dates of the schedule you want to publish.
4. Choose whether to include appointment details.
5. If you want, specify a background graphic in the text box.
6. Specify a title for the Web page and the location for saving the page. You can save the page to a file on the local drive or to an FTP or HTTP server specified by the URL.
7. Click Save to display the saved Web page by default. (If you do not want the Web page displayed by default, clear the Open Saved Web Page In Browser check box.)

Chapter 20

Scheduling Meetings and Resources

Before the introduction of workgroup software such as Microsoft Exchange and Microsoft Outlook, scheduling a meeting could be a difficult task. Now all it takes is a few simple steps to avoid those endless e-mail exchanges trying to find a suitable meeting time for all invitees. Outlook provides you with a single place to schedule both people and resources for meetings. You can take advantage of these features whether or not you use Exchange Server.

Chapter 19, "Scheduling Appointments," tells you all about scheduling appointments. Meetings and appointments are similar, of course: both types of items appear on your calendar, and you can create, view, and store them in your Outlook Calendar folder. An appointment, however, involves only your schedule and time, whereas a meeting involves inviting others and coordinating their schedules. Another difference is that a meeting often requires you to schedule resources, such as a conference room or an overhead projector.

You can schedule meetings with other Outlook users as well as those who use any e-mail or collaboration application that supports the vCal or iCal standards. This chapter takes you through the process of scheduling meetings and lining up resources. It also introduces online meetings, which can be set up through applications such as Microsoft NetMeeting, and another form of online collaborative communication, the broadcast of Microsoft PowerPoint presentations.

Sending a Meeting Request

To schedule a meeting, you begin by sending a meeting request. Choose File, New, Meeting Request or click the arrow beside the New button on the toolbar and choose Meeting Request. The meeting form opens, as shown in Figure 20-1.

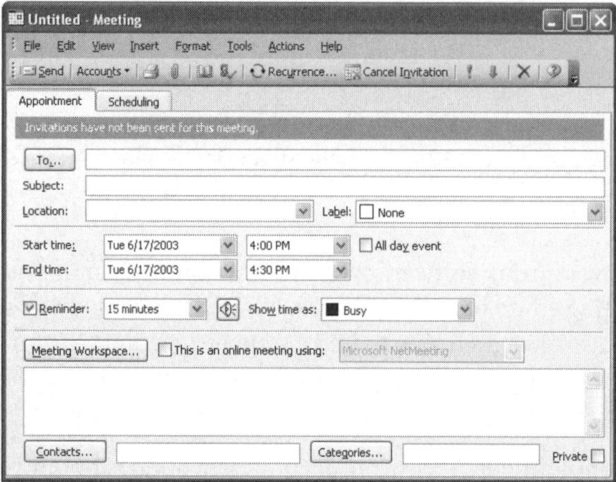

Figure 20-1. You use the meeting form to schedule meetings and send meeting requests.

A meeting request is like an appointment item, but with a few additional details—and you can work with it in much the same way you work with an appointment. This chapter describes only the parts of a meeting request that differ from an appointment.

For details about creating and working with appointments in Outlook's Calendar folder, see Chapter 19, "Scheduling Appointments."

Selecting Attendees

To invite people to your meeting, start by selecting their names on either the Appointment tab or the Scheduling tab of the meeting form. To select them on the Appointment tab, you can type each name in the To box, separating them with a semicolon. When you enter the names manually, Outlook considers each person a required attendee. Alternatively, you can click To to open the Select Attendees And Resources dialog box (see Figure 20-2). In this dialog box, select a name in the Name list and click Required or Optional to designate whether or not that person's attendance is critical. (This choice will be reflected in the meeting request you send to these individuals.) After you have finished adding names, click OK to close the dialog box.

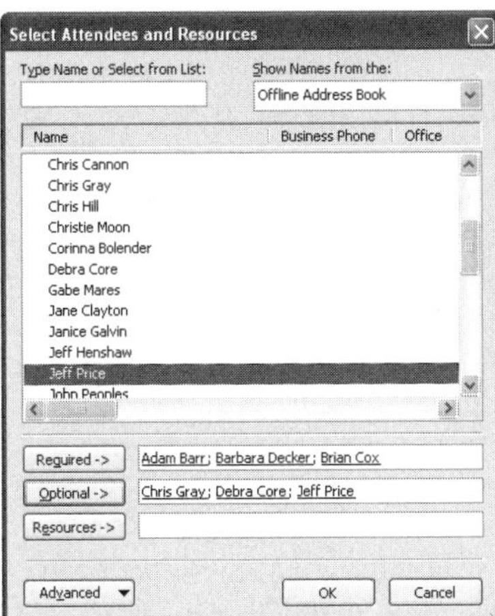

Figure 20-2. In the Select Attendees And Resources dialog box, you can add the names of the individuals you're inviting to your meeting.

To add names using the Scheduling tab, shown in Figure 20-3, you can click in the designated box in the All Attendees column and type a name or an e-mail address. Alternatively, you can click Add Others and select the location from which you want to add the names. For example, if you want to add individuals from the Global Address List, click Add Others and then select Add From Address Book to open the Select Attendees And Resources dialog box. As before, select a name, click Required or Optional, and then click OK.

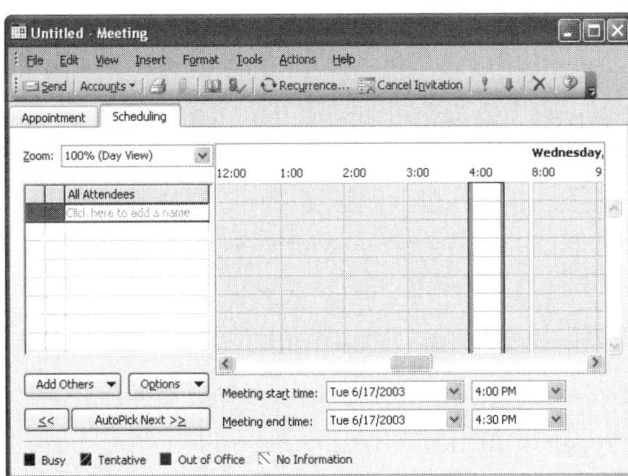

Figure 20-3. You can use the Scheduling tab to add meeting attendees and view their schedules.

Inside Out

Select the correct address list

Can't find the attendee you're looking for and you know that attendee is in the address book? Make sure that the correct address list is selected in the Show Names From The drop-down list. By default, the Global Address List, which shows all names from your Exchange Server organization, is selected (if you're running Outlook with Exchange Server). It is possible to change the default address list, however, and yours could be set to something else.

Scheduling a Meeting

After you have added the names of the individuals you want to invite, you can schedule the meeting on the Scheduling tab of the meeting form, which now displays free/busy information for all the people you selected. In Figure 20-4, the Scheduling tab shows information for the meeting organizer (you), required attendees, and optional attendees.

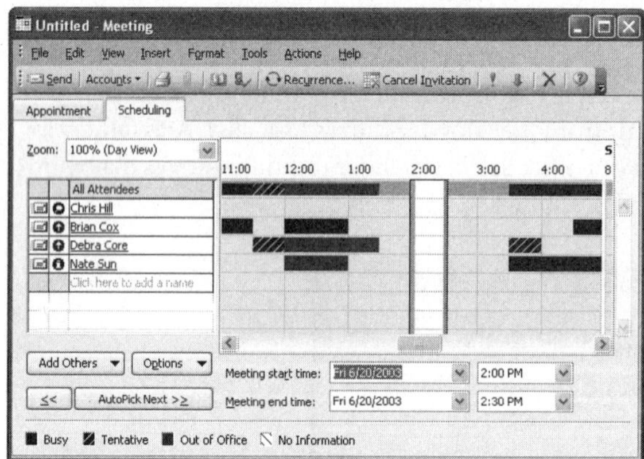

Figure 20-4. The Scheduling tab shows the attendees you selected along with their free/busy times.

The icons you see beside each name mean the following:

- The magnifying glass icon indicates the meeting organizer.
- The arrow indicates a required attendee.
- The icon containing the letter *i* indicates an optional attendee.

Tip **Specify free/busy server location**
Outlook queries the free/busy time of each attendee based on the settings you have configured for that purpose. As Chapter 19 explains, you can configure Outlook to check the Microsoft Office Internet Free/Busy Service, another globally specified free/busy server, and individual servers specified with each contact. These all work in conjunction with Exchange Server, if present.

After you have identified a time slot that fits everyone's schedules, you can schedule the meeting for a particular time slot using the Meeting Start Time and Meeting End Time drop-down lists.

If you want Outlook to fit the meeting into the next available time slot, click AutoPick Next. By default, AutoPick selects the next time slot in which all attendees and at least one resource are free.

Tip Configure the AutoPick feature
To change the default actions of AutoPick, click Options on the Scheduling tab and make your choices on the AutoPick menu. You can set AutoPick to select the next time slot in which all attendees and all resources are free, the next time slot in which all attendees and at least one resource are free (the default), a slot in which only required attendees are free, or a slot in which required attendees and at least one resource are free.

You can decide whether the Scheduling tab's display of free/busy information should show only working hours (the default) or the entire day. To define working hours, choose Tools, Options in Outlook and click Calendar Options. Working hours are a way of displaying your time in the Calendar folder and controlling which hours are displayed on the Scheduling tab. In most cases, including nonworking hours on the Scheduling tab would become unmanageable.

After you have selected all the attendees, found an available time slot, and filled in all the necessary details on the message form, click Send on the form to send the meeting request to the attendees.

Scheduling a Meeting from the Contacts Folder

If it's more convenient, you can initiate meeting requests from the Contacts folder rather than the Calendar folder. Right-click the contact entry for the person you want to invite to a meeting and choose New Meeting Request To Contact. The meeting form opens, with the contact's name in the To box. From here, you can select more attendees and enter meeting details such as subject and location.

If the contact entry contains an address for an Internet free/busy server, you can download the contact's free/busy information by clicking Options on the Scheduling tab and selecting Refresh Free/Busy Information. You can also download the contact's free/busy information from the Microsoft Office Internet Free/Busy Service, if the contact uses that service, or from another free/busy server if specified in the Outlook Free/Busy Options dialog box, explained in detail in Chapter 19.

For details about the Microsoft Office Internet Free/Busy Service, see "Managing Your Free/Busy Information," page 538.

Changing a Meeting

To change any part of a meeting request, including attendees, times, or other information, first double-click the meeting item in the Calendar folder to open it and then make your changes. Click Save And Close to save the changes to the Calendar folder, or click Send Update to send an updated meeting request to the attendees. If you make changes that affect the other attendees, such as adding or removing attendees or changing the time or location, you should click Send Update so that the attendees get the new information.

Responding to a Meeting Request

When you click Send on a meeting form, a meeting request e-mail message is sent to the invited attendees. This message allows the attendees to accept, tentatively accept, or reject the meeting invitation; propose a new time for the meeting; and include a message in the reply.

Receiving a Request for a Meeting

The attendees you've invited to your meeting will receive a meeting request message similar to the one shown in Figure 20-5. When an attendee clicks Calendar, a copy of his or her calendar opens, showing the meeting tentatively scheduled.

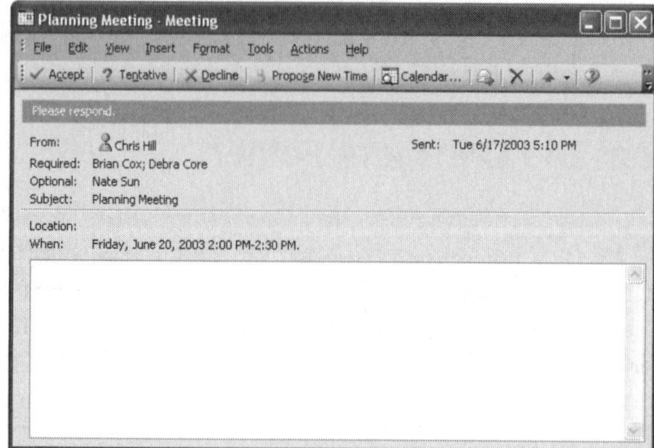

Figure 20-5. This meeting request has been received by an attendee.

An invited attendee has four options when replying to a meeting request:

- Accept the meeting outright.
- Tentatively accept the meeting.
- Decline the meeting.
- Propose a new time for the meeting.

When an attendee accepts, tentatively accepts, or declines the meeting, he or she can send the response immediately (which sends the default response), edit the response before sending (which allows the attendee to send a message with the response), or send no response.

To propose a new meeting time, the attendee can click Propose New Time. A dialog box appears that is essentially the same as the Scheduling tab of the meeting form. From here, the attendee can select a new time for the meeting and propose it to the meeting organizer by clicking Propose Time.

Troubleshooting

You have lost a meeting request

When you respond to a meeting request, it is automatically deleted from your Inbox. If you accepted or tentatively accepted the meeting request, Outlook adds the meeting information to your Calendar folder. If you need to retrieve any of the data, check your Deleted Items folder for the meeting request itself and your Calendar folder for the meeting information.

To have Outlook keep meeting request messages in your Inbox even after you've responded, follow these steps:

1. Choose Tools, Options and click E-Mail Options.
2. Click Advanced E-Mail Options.
3. Clear the Delete Meeting Request From Inbox When Responding option.

Receiving a Response to Your Request

When an invited attendee responds to a meeting request, a message is returned to you, the meeting organizer. This message contains the response, including any message the attendee chose to include. In the meeting request response shown in Figure 20-6, the attendee has accepted the meeting and included a message. Note that the response also lists the attendees who have accepted, tentatively accepted, and declined up to this point.

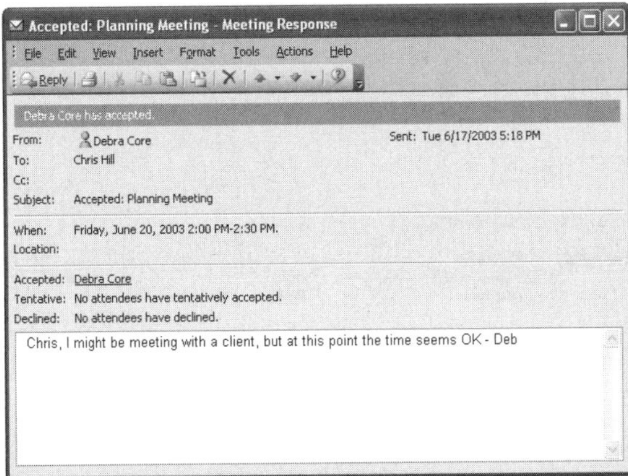

Figure 20-6. A response to a meeting request shows the acceptance status of the request and any message from the attendee.

Figure 20-7 shows a response in which the attendee has selected the Propose A New Time option on the meeting request.

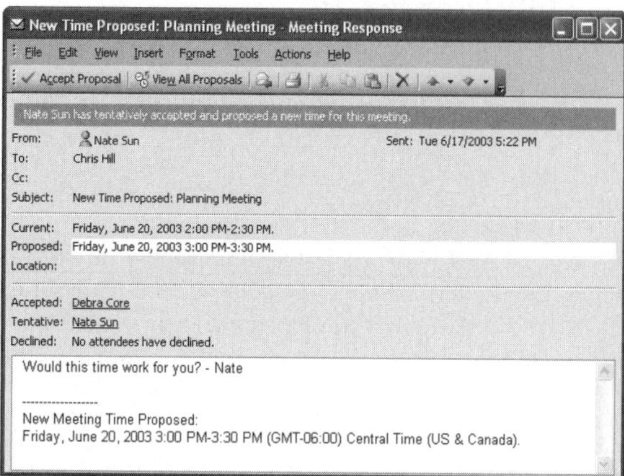

Figure 20-7. When an invited attendee proposes a new time for the meeting, the response to the meeting organizer looks like this.

When you receive a response proposing a new meeting time, you have two choices:

- Click Accept Proposal to accept the new time and open the meeting form. Verify any changes and then click Send Update to send the new proposed time to the attendees.
- Click View All Proposals to open the Scheduling tab of the meeting form, which displays a list of all proposed new times for the meeting suggested by any of the attendees (see Figure 20-8). You can select a new time from the list of proposed times and click Send Update to send the new time to the meeting attendees.

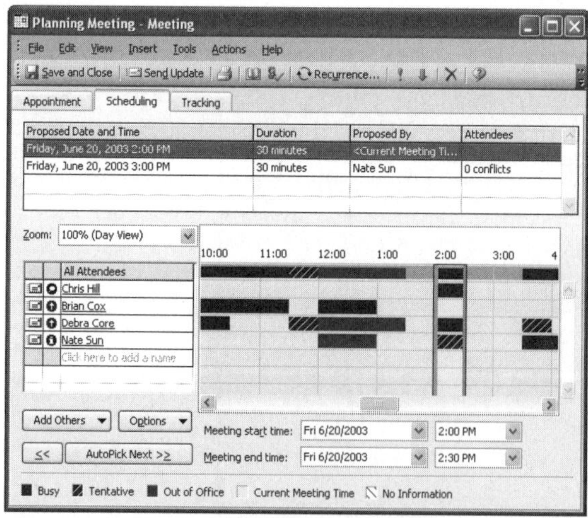

Figure 20-8. You can view the meeting times proposed by all attendees.

Checking Attendees

After you send a meeting request, you can check which attendees have accepted or declined by opening the meeting form in the Calendar folder and clicking the form's Tracking tab (see Figure 20-9). (The Tracking tab is not displayed on the initial meeting form; Outlook adds it after the meeting request has been sent.) The Tracking tab shows each invited attendee, along with whether their attendance is required or optional and the status of their response. The meeting organizer is the only person who can view the status of attendees.

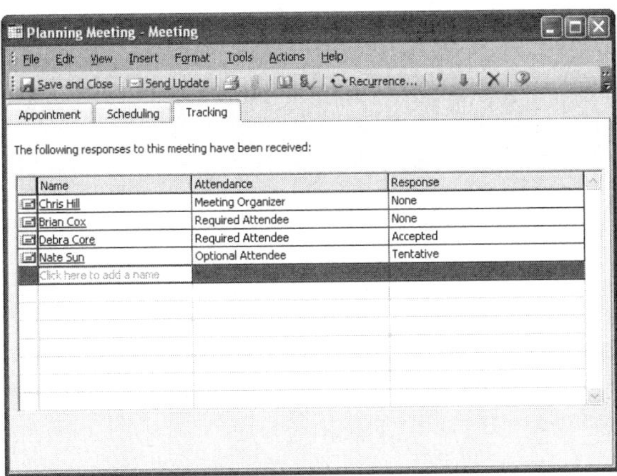

Figure 20-9. Only the person who scheduled the meeting can view the status of the attendees.

Scheduling Resources

To successfully plan and carry out a meeting, you'll usually need to schedule resources as well as people. *Resources* are items (such as computers and projectors) or locations (such as a meeting room) that are required for a meeting. You select resources in much the same way you select attendees.

The ability to schedule resources is typically most useful when you need to set up a meeting, but you might find other occasions when this capability comes in handy. For example, you might want to schedule laptop computers for employees to take home for the weekend or schedule digital cameras to take to building sites.

Setting Up Resources for Scheduling

You schedule a resource by sending a meeting request, adding the resource as a third type of attendee. (The other two types of attendees are Required and Optional, as previously mentioned; see "Selecting Attendees," page 558.) Because a resource is scheduled as a type of attendee, it must have a mailbox and a method of accepting or rejecting meeting requests. When you use Outlook and Exchange Server, a resource is almost identical to any other Exchange Server user except that it is configured to allow another user (the resource administrator) full access to its mailbox.

Note To use the process described here, you must be running Microsoft Outlook 2000 or a later version.

The first step in setting up a resource for scheduling is to create (or have your system administrator create) a mailbox and an account for the resource. In many cases, resource account names are preceded by a symbol, such as # or &, so that the names, when alphabetized, appear as a group at the top or bottom of the Global Address List.

After creating the mailbox, you must grant permission for the user who will be the resource administrator to access that mailbox, as described here:

1. Choose Start, Programs, Administrative Tools In Windows and then select Active Directory Users And Computers.
2. Choose View, Advanced Features.
3. Click Users in the left pane and double-click the resource in the right pane.
4. On the Exchange Advanced tab, click Mailbox Rights and assign Full Mailbox Access to the resource administrator.

The resource administrator must now be able to log on to the resource's mailbox to set its resource scheduling options. The simplest way to approach this is to create a new Outlook profile for the resource's mailbox.

To create this profile, follow these steps:

1. In Control Panel, double-click Mail and then click Show Profiles.
2. Click Add to create a new profile, specify a name, and then click OK to continue.
3. Click E-mail Accounts. On the E-Mail Accounts Wizard page, select Add A New E-Mail Account (see Figure 20-10).

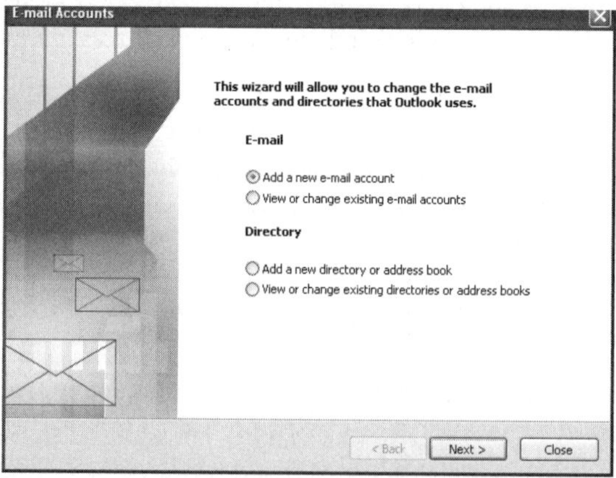

Figure 20-10. Add a new e-mail account to the newly created profile.

4. For the server type, select Microsoft Exchange Server and then click Next.

5 On the next page of the wizard, shown in Figure 20-11, type the name of your Exchange Server and the name of the resource's mailbox, and then click Check Name to verify the resource name. After the name and the server have been verified, Outlook underlines them and the Check Names button becomes unavailable.

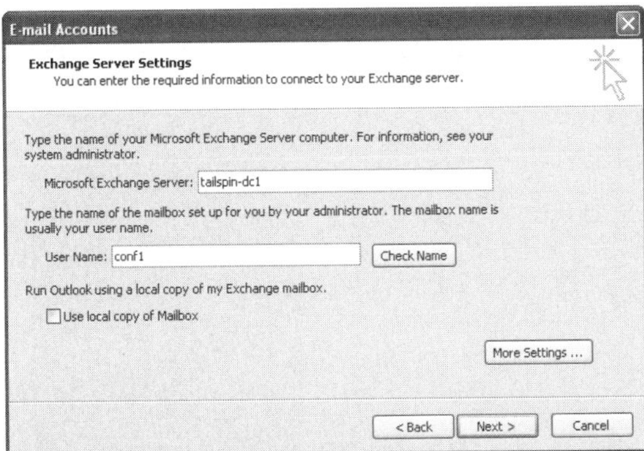

Figure 20-11. Specify the name of your Exchange Server and the name of the resource's mailbox, and then click Check Name to verify.

6 Click Next to save the new e-mail account settings, and then click Finish to save the profile. Figure 20-12 shows the new profile added to the list.

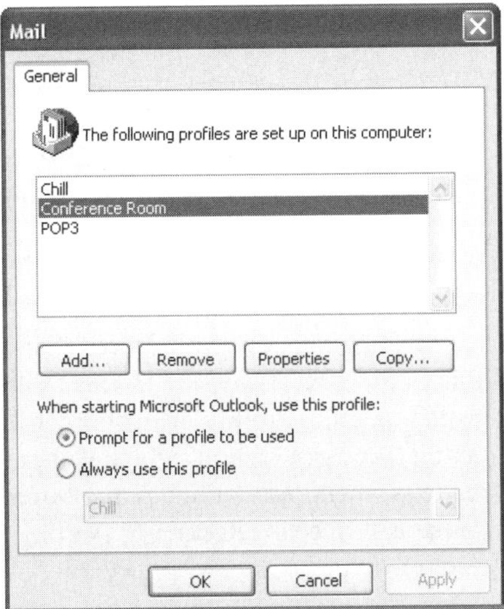

Figure 20-12. A new profile for resources has been added.

7 Because you will probably open this profile only once, to set the resource scheduling options, select the Always Use This Profile option. Then select the newly created profile from the drop-down list and click OK. (If you foresee having to open the resource's mailbox frequently to make changes, however, you can select Prompt For A Profile To Be Used. Each time you open Outlook, you will be prompted to select a profile.)

When you next open Outlook, you should see the resource's new mailbox in the folder list, as shown in Figure 20-13.

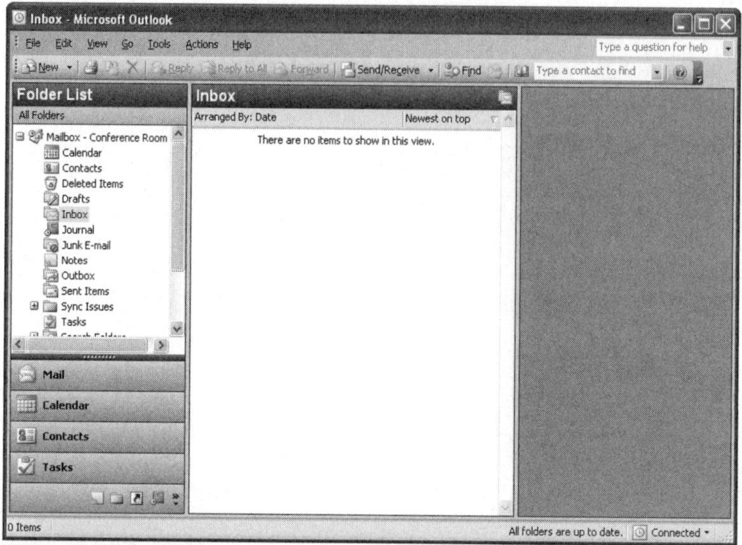

Figure 20-13. The new profile has opened the mailbox you specified for the resource when you created the profile.

> **Tip** If you want to configure more than one resource mailbox, each resource must have its own profile.

Now the resource administrator is able to configure the resource by following these steps:

1. In Outlook, choose Tools, Options and click Calendar Options.
2. Click Resource Scheduling to open the Resource Scheduling dialog box.
3. Select the Automatically Accept Meeting Requests And Process Cancellations option, which permits resource scheduling to work. (If you fail to select this option, you cannot schedule resources.) To avoid schedule conflicts, it's also a good idea to select Automatically Decline Conflicting Meeting Requests, which will cause the resource's mailbox to decline meeting requests when a scheduling request overlaps with another meeting. The last option, Automatically Decline Recurring Meeting Requests, is useful if you don't want to allow a resource to be booked with recurring meetings.

> **Tip** **Allow others to book a resource**
> The Set Permissions button in the Resource Scheduling dialog box allows you to configure the permissions of the resource's Calendar folder so that users can book resources offline. In the steps outlined here, however, the actions in step 5 automatically configure the permissions.

4. Click OK to continue.
5. If resource permissions are not already set, the dialog box shown in Figure 20-14 opens, asking whether you want to automatically set permissions for all users for offline booking. Selecting this option gives users permission to view and edit the resource's calendar directly, which can get out of hand if you have a large user base. Set these permissions only if you think you can manage a situation in which users have the ability to directly edit the calendar.To set the permissions, click OK. Otherwise, click Cancel.

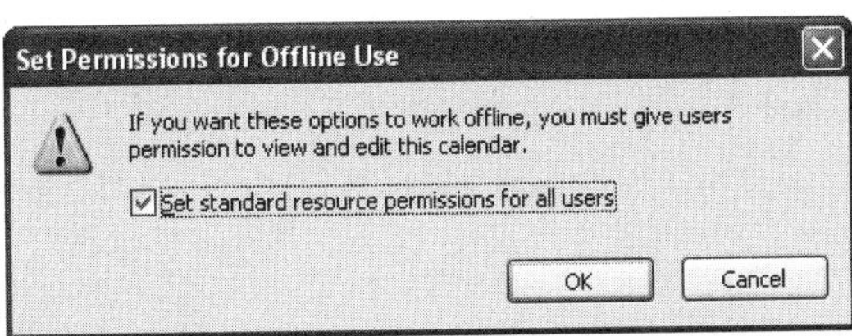

Figure 20-14. This dialog box automatically sets permissions so that users can view and edit the resource's calendar directly.

6. Click OK to close the Calendar Options dialog box, and click OK again to close the Options dialog box.
7. Close Outlook.
8. To change the profile back to the default, double-click Mail in Control Panel, and then click Show Profiles. Select the original profile from the drop-down list and click OK.

Using the Configured Resources

To schedule a resource after you have configured it, create a meeting request and fill in the details. When you add attendees to the meeting request using the Select Attendees And Resources dialog box, select the resource you want to add from the list and then click Resources (see Figure 20-15). Resources are added to the Resources box instead of to the Required or Optional box. When you have finished adding resources, click OK. Then complete and send the meeting request as you normally would.

> **Note** For details about creating and sending meeting requests, see "Sending a Meeting Request," page 558.

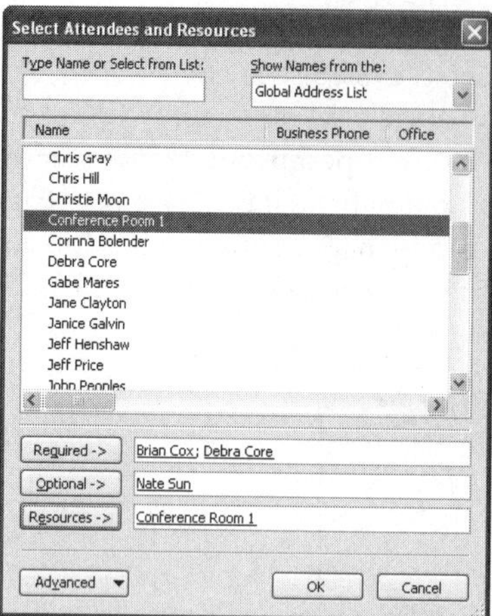

Figure 20-15. Add a resource by selecting it from the list and clicking Resources.

After you send the meeting request, Outlook responds with a message about the resource's availability. If the resource is available during the time slot proposed for the meeting, Outlook notifies you that the resource has been booked successfully (see Figure 20-16).

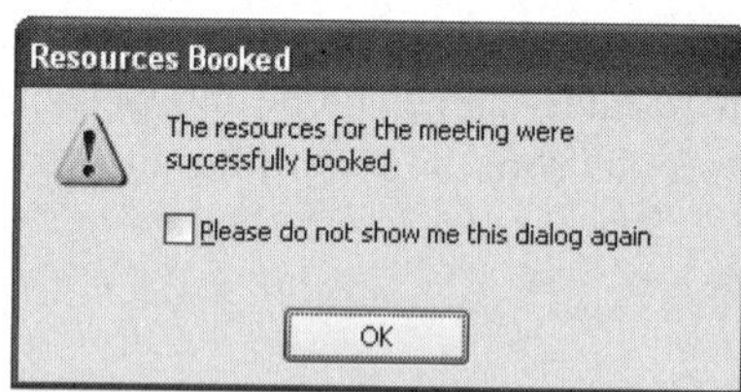

Figure 20-16. Outlook notifies you if the resource was successfully booked.

Figure 20-17 shows the message that appears when you try to book a resource in a time that overlaps with an existing meeting in that resource's calendar. Click OK to return to the meeting form, where you must reschedule the meeting or choose a different resource.

Figure 20-17. When resources are already booked, you must change the meeting time or choose another resource.

Figure 20-18 shows the calendar for the resource being scheduled in the previous examples. The meetings shown have been scheduled automatically.

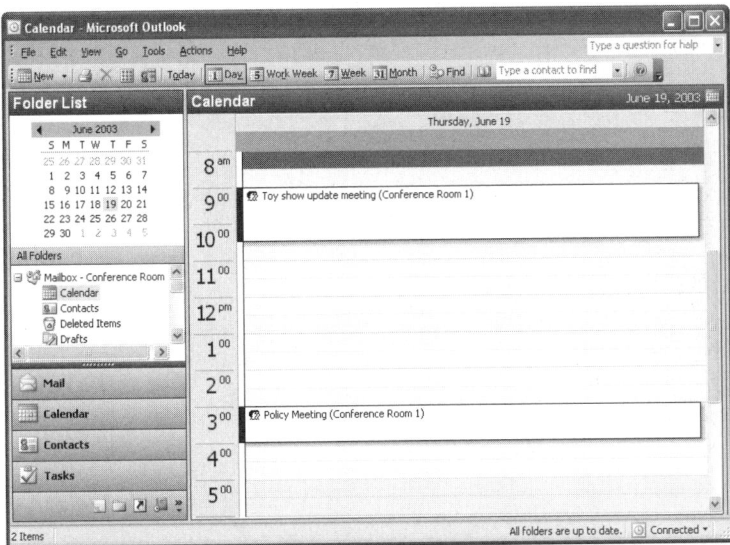

Figure 20-18. The meetings shown on the resource's calendar were booked automatically.

Holding an Online Meeting

So far in this chapter, you've seen how to schedule a face-to-face meeting in Outlook. You can also use Outlook to schedule online meetings using NetMeeting, a multimedia collaboration application.

Setting Up NetMeeting

NetMeeting is installed with Microsoft Windows 2000 and Microsoft Windows XP by default. If you want additional information about NetMeeting not listed here, you will find it at *http://www.microsoft.com/windows/netmeeting.*

> **Tip** **Add a NetMeeting icon**
> Windows XP does not add NetMeeting to the All Programs\Accessories\Communications menu. You will find the NetMeeting application in \Program Files\Netmeeting\ Conf.exe. Double-click this file to start NetMeeting, or right-drag it to the desktop to create a shortcut to it.

To set up NetMeeting for the first time, follow these steps:

1. In Windows 2000, start the program by clicking Start, Programs, Accessories, Communications, NetMeeting. In Windows XP, double-click \Program Files\Netmeeting\ Conf.exe.
2. Click Next on the first NetMeeting Wizard page (an overview of NetMeeting's features).
3. Type your name and e-mail address information and then click Next.

4 Choose whether you want to log on to the NetMeeting directory server automatically each time NetMeeting starts (see Figure 20-19).

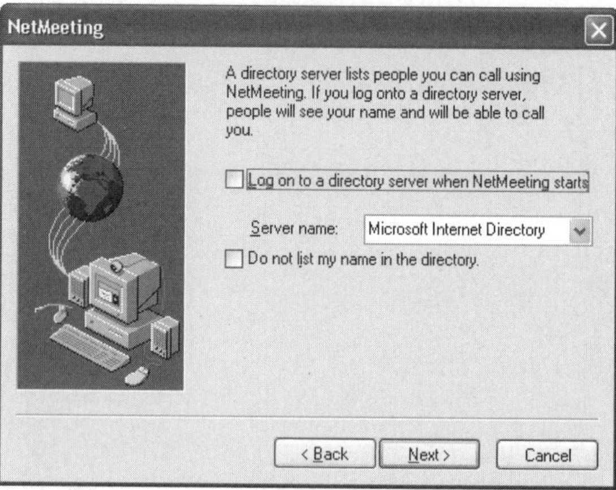

Figure 20-19. You can specify whether you want to log on to the NetMeeting directory server automatically and whether you want your name listed in the directory.

5 Choose whether you want your name advertised in the directory and click Next.

6 Select your connection speed in the list and then click Next to continue.

7 Choose whether to put a NetMeeting shortcut on your desktop and on the Quick Launch bar. Click Next to continue. The final page indicates the status of the NetMeeting setup. If you don't have a sound card, NetMeeting tells you that you can't use its audio features.

8 Click Finish to complete the NetMeeting configuration. NetMeeting opens, using its new configuration settings.

Scheduling a NetMeeting Conference

Scheduling a NetMeeting conference is similar to scheduling a face-to-face meeting: choose File, New, Meeting Request. Fill in the details of the meeting, including at least the start and end dates and times and the subject. Next select the This Is An Online Meeting Using check box, and then select Microsoft NetMeeting in the drop-down list. When you select the check box, more options become available (see Figure 20-20).

In the Directory Server box, you can specify the NetMeeting directory server to use for the scheduled online meeting. Outlook adds your e-mail address to the Organizer's E-Mail box. If you select the Automatically Start NetMeeting With Reminder check box, NetMeeting will start when the appointment reminder is displayed. The Office Document box allows you to specify a Microsoft Office document to be shared with the other meeting attendees.

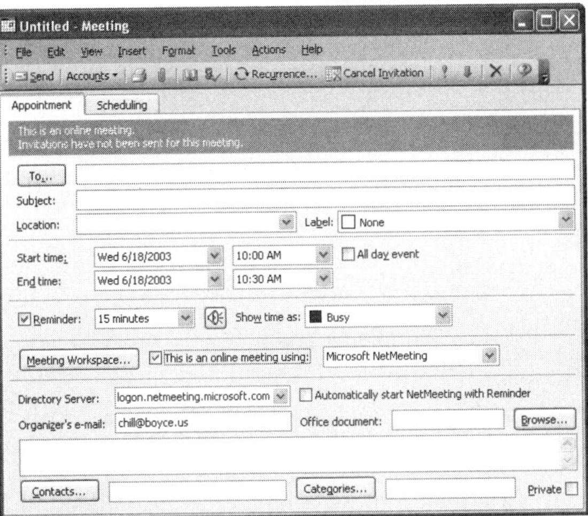

Figure 20-20. More options become available for online meetings that use NetMeeting.

Using NetMeeting

If the meeting has been set up to begin when Outlook displays the reminder, NetMeeting starts automatically when the reminder appears. Otherwise, you can open NetMeeting manually or by clicking Meeting Services in the reminder window and choosing Start Net-Meeting. Figure 20-21 shows the initial NetMeeting screen.

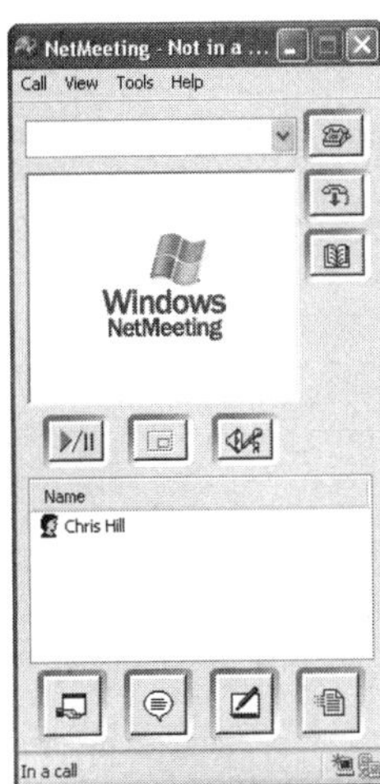

Figure 20-21. When the online meeting starts, you see the initial NetMeeting screen.

After NetMeeting starts, you must place a call to the other meeting participant. To place a call, choose Call, New Call or click the telephone icon to open the Place A Call dialog box (see Figure 20-22).

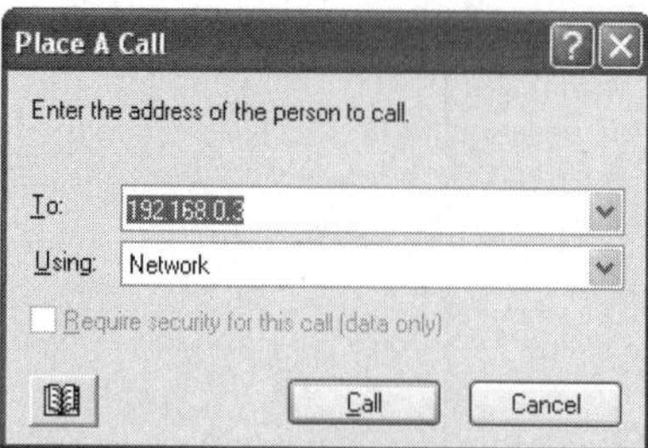

Figure 20-22. From this dialog box, you can connect to another NetMeeting user.

In the dialog box, type or select the e-mail address, computer name, or IP address of the user to call and then click Call. While NetMeeting is calling the other party, you'll see the status of the call in a window (see Figure 20-23).

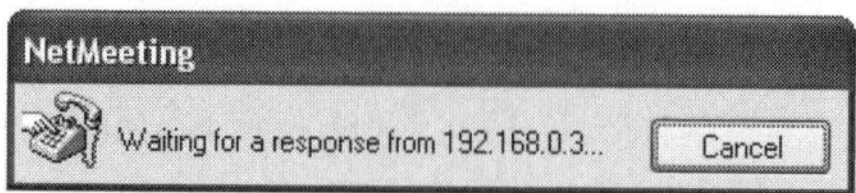

Figure 20-23. NetMeeting displays the call status.

The receiving party's computer "rings" (the actual sound depends on how the user set the incoming call sound in Control Panel), and a window appears on the receiving party's screen (see Figure 20-24). This window shows who is calling and allows the receiver to accept or decline the call. If the receiver fails to make a choice within a short amount of time, your computer ends the call.

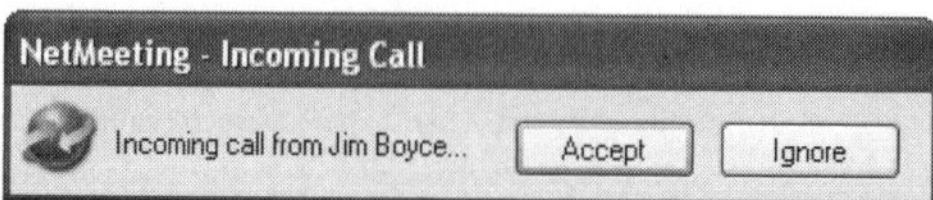

Figure 20-24. You can accept or decline a NetMeeting call.

When the call is established, you can speak to the other participant if both of you have sound cards, speakers, and microphones. You can also see each other if you have video capture devices. If only one party has any of these devices, they can still be used—but only one way.

> **For in-depth information about using NetMeeting, see *http://www.microsoft.com/windows/netmeeting*.**

NetMeeting gives you the tools to communicate with other people over the Internet. The four tools provided by NetMeeting are as follows:

- Share Program
- Chat

- Whiteboard
- File Transfer

With the Share Program tool, you can share a program with the other parties in the meeting by following these steps:

1. Make sure the program you want to share is open on your desktop.
2. Click Share Program in NetMeeting to open the Sharing dialog box (see Figure 20-25).

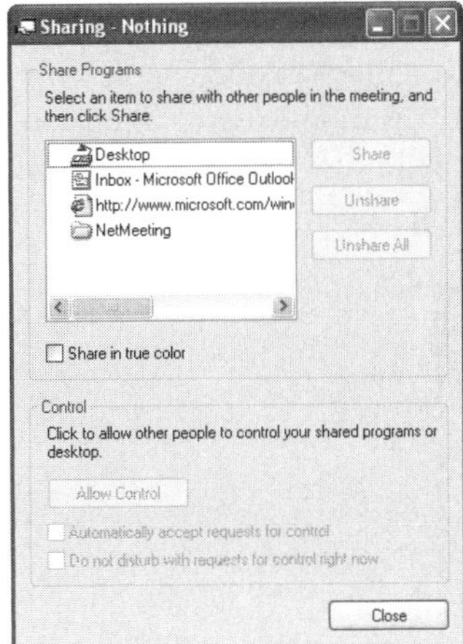

Figure 20-25. You can share programs on your computer with other NetMeeting users.

3. Select the program to share in the list of open programs and then click Share. The shared program opens in a window on the desktop of the other parties (see Figure 20-26).

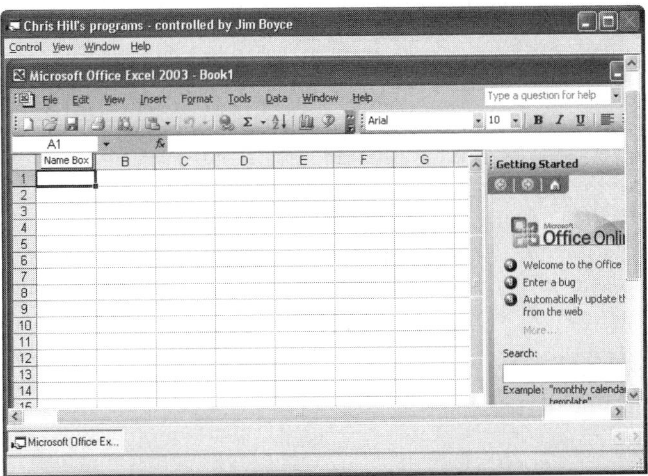

Figure 20-26. A program shared by another user is displayed in a window on the local desktop.

4 Using the options in the Sharing dialog box, shown in Figure 20-25, you can allow other users to control the application as follows:

- Clicking Allow Control allows other users to request control of the application; you can then choose to grant or deny that control.
- Selecting the Automatically Accept Requests For Control check box automatically grants control to users who request it.
- Selecting the Do Not Disturb With Requests For Control Right Now check box prevents control requests.

The Chat tool is a basic text chat in which those in a NetMeeting can chat by typing instead of by using audio and video capture devices. This can be useful when you're holding a NetMeeting with users who don't have sound or video devices. To open the Chat window (see Figure 20-27), simply click Chat in NetMeeting.

Figure 20-27. Use the NetMeeting Chat window to have text chat sessions with other parties in a call.

The Whiteboard tool is essentially a shared version of the Microsoft Paint accessory with a few extra features. Click Whiteboard in NetMeeting to open this feature. All users can draw on the whiteboard, and all other users see those changes unless one of them clicks Lock Contents, in which case only that user can make changes. The Remote Pointer button places on the whiteboard a hand icon that can be used to point out specific items during a meeting. The Select Area and Select Window buttons are used to paste the next area selected or the next window clicked, respectively, from your computer to the whiteboard. Figure 20-28 shows a whiteboard in use by two NetMeeting users.

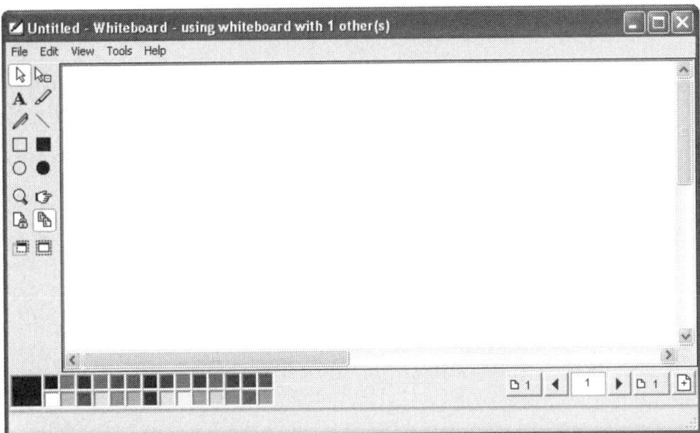

Figure 20-28. The NetMeeting Whiteboard is essentially a shared version of Paint with extra collaboration features.

To send one or more files, you can use NetMeeting's File Transfer tool as follows:

1. Open the File Transfer tool by clicking File Transfer in NetMeeting.
2. Click Add Files in the File Transfer dialog box to browse for the file you want to transfer.
3. Select the file to be transferred and click Add. The selected file appears in the File Transfer dialog box (see Figure 20-29). To remove a file in the list, select the file and click the Remove Files button.

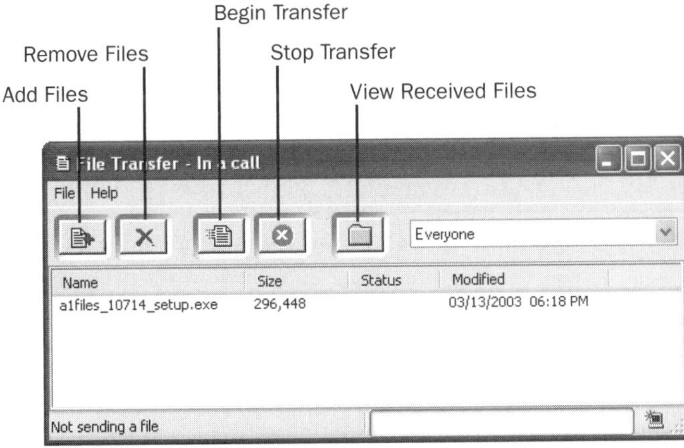

Figure 20-29. Use NetMeeting's File Transfer dialog box to send files to meeting participants.

4. In the drop-down list, select the user to whom you want to send the file (the default is Everyone).
5. Click the Send All button to send the file.

Meeting Through Exchange Conferencing Server

Microsoft Exchange Conferencing Server provides a tool through which companies can host online meetings and provide multicast real-time conferencing. To the user, the process is much like that for using NetMeeting to participate in an online meeting, as explained in the previous sections.

To invite others to participate in a meeting through Exchange Conferencing Server, follow these steps:

1. Open Outlook and start a new meeting request.
2. In the meeting form, enter information in the fields as necessary, then select the This Is An Online Meeting Using option.
3. From the drop-down list, choose Microsoft Exchange Conferencing. Outlook changes the meeting form slightly as shown in Figure 20-30.

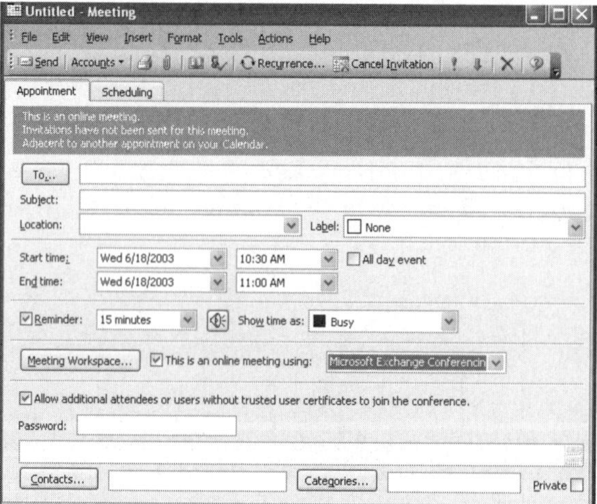

Figure 20-30. Choose Microsoft Exchange Conferencing from the drop-down list.

4. If all of the attendees are using Exchange Conferencing Server, clear the Allow Additional Attendees Or Users Without Trusted User Certificates To Join The Conference check box. To include external users in the meeting, select this check box and then enter the password for the conference in the Password field.
5. Make sure you add all of the attendees to the To field, then click Send to send the meeting request.

For more information on using NetMeeting to participate in the meeting, see the previous sections.

Meeting Through Windows Media Services

Microsoft Windows Media Services is included with Microsoft Windows 2000 Server and Microsoft Windows Server 2003 to add streaming capabilities to those server platforms. Windows Media Services can stream on-demand and scheduled streams from existing content, and can also deliver live streams. Therefore, organizations can use Windows Media Services to deliver canned or live conferencing feeds. For example, an organization might use Media Services to deliver a live keynote address by a corporate officer to different divisions within the company.

Note Windows Media Services does not provide a mechanism for whiteboard or application sharing. However, you can certainly use a combination of Windows Media Services to provide a canned or live stream and a separate NetMeeting event to provide collaboration capabilities. However, bandwidth will certainly become an issue if you are streaming a feed and trying to collaborate with NetMeeting at the same time.

Outlook includes the capability to schedule these online feeds. Users access streams hosted by a Windows Media Services server through the stream's URL. The same is true for online meetings hosted through Windows Media Services. The server, depending on its configuration, can stream through HTTP, Microsoft Media Service (MMS) protocol, or both. When you specify the URL, you include the protocol at the beginning of the string, just as you do with a Web URL such as *http://www.microsoft.com*. The URL for an online meeting takes the following form:

<protocol>://<server>/<PublishingPointAlias>

The *<protocol>* portion of the URL is replaced by http if the meeting is streamed using HTTP and mms if streamed using the MMS protocol. The *<server>* portion references the IP address or fully qualified domain name (FQDN) of the Windows Media Services server hosting the publishing point. *<PublishingPointAlias>* is the alias that the Windows Media Services administrator has configured for the stream on the server.

Follow these steps to initiate a meeting that includes a Windows Media Services stream:

1. In Outlook, start a new meeting request.
2. On the Appointment tab of the meeting form, select the This Is An Online Meeting Using option, then choose Windows Media Services from the drop-down list.

3 In the Event Address field (see Figure 20-31), enter the URL for the stream.

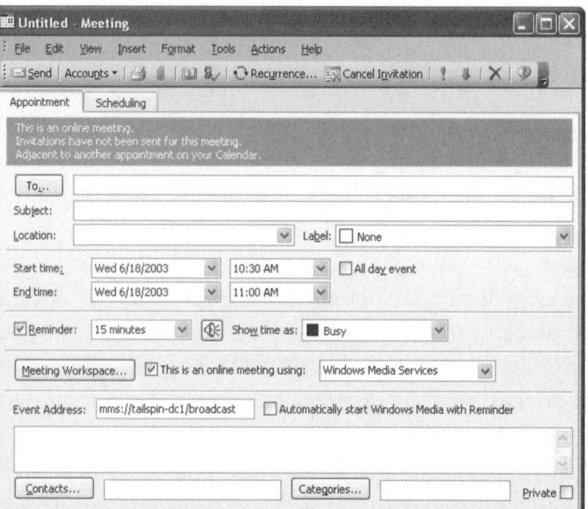

Figure 20-31. Enter the URL for the Windows Media Services stream.

4 If you want Windows Media Player to open automatically and Outlook to remind you about the meeting five minutes prior to its start, select the Automatically Start Windows Media With Reminder check box.

5 Enter additional fields as necessary, including the recipients in the To field, then click Send.

Chapter 21

Managing Your Tasks

Microsoft Outlook 2003 offers a broad selection of tools to help you manage your work day, including e-mail; a way to manage appointments, meetings, and events; a handy method of creating quick notes; and a journal for tracking projects, calls, and other items. All these tools are often related to creating and completing tasks. For example, writing this book was a long string of tasks to be completed: drawing up the outline, writing each chapter, and reviewing edits, for starters.

In your job, your tasks during the average day are no doubt different. Perhaps they include completing contracts, making sales calls, writing or reviewing documents, completing reports, developing Web sites, or developing program code. Some tasks take only a little time to complete, whereas others can take days, weeks, or even months.

Outlook provides the means not only to track your own tasks, but also to manage those tasks you need to assign to others. This feature is a much more efficient and effective way to manage tasks than using a notebook, sticky notes, or just your memory. You can set reminders and sort tasks according to category, priority, or status to help you view and manage them.

This chapter examines the Tasks folder and its related features. In addition to learning how to manage your own tasks, you'll also learn to assign and manage tasks for others.

Working with Tasks in the Tasks Folder

Outlook provides several ways for you to create and manage tasks. You can create one-time tasks or recurring tasks, set up reminders for tasks, and assign tasks to others. In this section, you'll see how to create tasks for yourself and how to use Outlook to manage those tasks effectively.

The default view in the Tasks folder, shown in Figure 21-1, offers a simple list that shows four columns—Icon, Complete, Subject, and Due Date—that are summarized here:

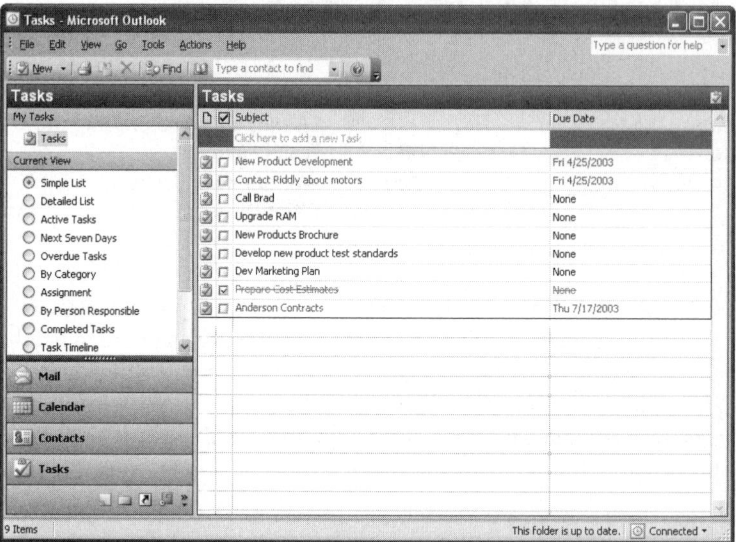

Figure 21-1. Outlook uses a simple list as the default Tasks folder view.

- **Icon** The Icon column indicates one of two states: either that the task is yours or that it's assigned to another person. The clipboard icon with a check mark indicates that the task is your own. A hand under the icon indicates that the task is assigned to someone else.
- **Complete** Use this check box to indicate that a task has been completed. A check in the box indicates a completed task. Outlook crosses through the task's subject and due date when you mark the task as completed, offering another visual cue to help you distinguish completed tasks from those that are still outstanding.
- **Subject** You can enter any text in the Subject column, but generally it should describe the task to be performed. You can also add notes to each task to further identify the purpose or goal of the task.
- **Due Date** This column indicates the due date for the task and by default shows the day and date.You can specify different date formats if you want.

For details on customizing the Tasks folder view, see "Viewing and Customizing the Tasks Folder," page 597. For additional information about features in Outlook that can help you use and manage views, see "Using Other Outlook Features," page 78.

You can view all the details of a task by double-clicking the task item. Doing so opens the task form, the format of which varies, depending on whether the task is yours or is assigned to someone else. Figure 21-2 shows the form for a task that belongs to you. Figure 21-3 shows the Task tab of a form for a task assigned to someone else.

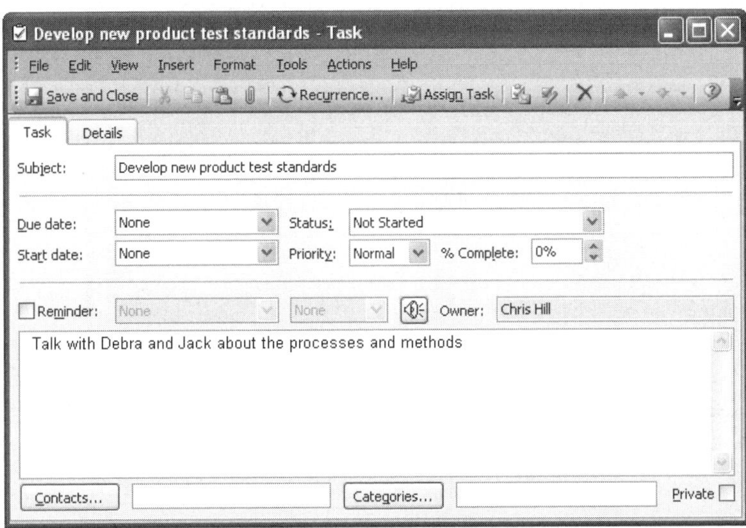

Figure 21-2. Create a new task with this standard task form.

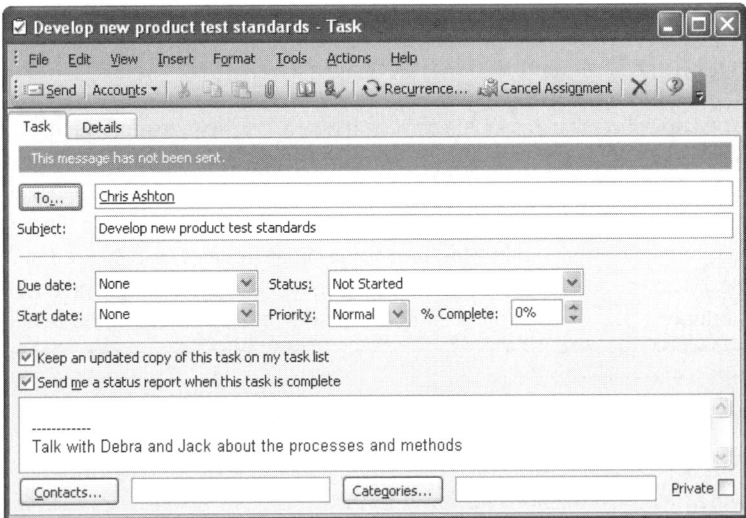

Figure 21-3. The task form for a task assigned to someone else shows less information than the task form for one of your own tasks.

The Details tab of the task form (see Figure 21-4) shows additional information about the task such as date completed, total work required, actual work performed, and related background information.

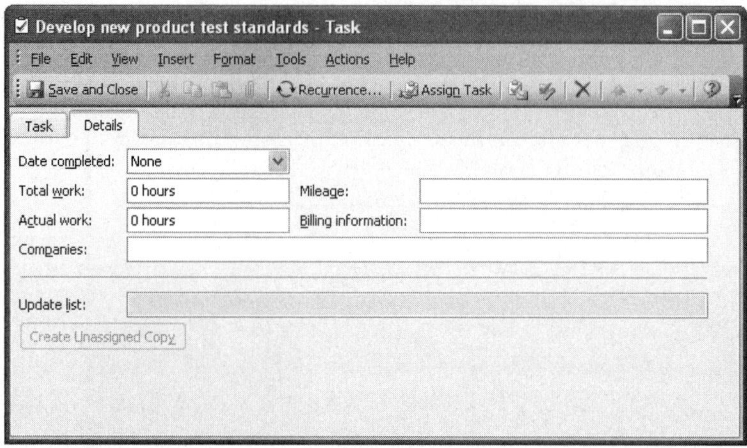

Figure 21-4. Use the Details tab to view additional information about the task.

Tip Press Ctrl+Tab to switch between tabs in any multitabbed dialog box or form, including the task form.

Navigating Tasks Quickly

Although you can open tasks by double-clicking them in the Tasks folder, you might prefer to cycle through your tasks right in the task form. For example, when you want to review several tasks, opening and closing them from the task list one after another is a waste of clicks and effort. Instead, you can use the Next Item and Previous Item buttons on the form's Standard toolbar to display tasks in forward or reverse order (relative to the listed order in the Tasks folder). The list doesn't cycle from end to beginning or beginning to end, however, so clicking a button when you're at either of those points in the list closes the task form.

Creating a Task

Creating a task is mechanically much the same as creating any item in Outlook. Use any of the following methods to open a new task form:

- Between the column header bar and the first task in the list is a new task entry line labeled Click Here To Add A New Task. Click the line and start typing if you want to specify only the subject for the task, without initially adding details or selecting options. You can open the task at any time afterward to add other information.
- Double-click in an empty area of the task list.

- Right-click in an empty area of the task list and choose New Task.
- With the Tasks folder open, click New on the Standard toolbar.
- With any Outlook folder open, click the arrow beside the New button on the Standard toolbar and choose Task. This allows you to create a new task when another folder such as the Inbox or the Calendar folder is displayed.

The options on the task form are straightforward. Simply select the options you want and set the task properties (such as start date and due date). Opening the Due Date or Start Date drop-down list displays a calendar you can use to select the month and date for the task. If no specific date is required for the task, you can leave the default value None selected. If you currently have a date selected and want to set it to None, select None in the drop-down list.

Inside Out

Specifying Total Work and Actual Work

As you'll learn a little later in this section, you can specify values for Total Work and Actual Work on the Details tab of the task form. Total Work indicates the total number of hours (days, weeks, and so on) required for the task; Actual Work lets you record the amount of work performed to date on the task. Unfortunately, the Percent Complete value on the Task tab is not tied to either of these numbers. Thus, if Total Work is set to 40 hours and Actual Work is set to 20 hours, the Percent Complete box doesn't show 50 percent complete. Instead, you must manually specify the value for Percent Complete.

Note The Percent Complete value is tied to the Status field on the Task tab. If you set Percent Complete to 100, Outlook sets the status to Completed. If you set Percent Complete to 0, Outlook sets the status to Not Started. Any value between 0 and 100 results in a status of In Progress. Selecting a value in the Status drop-down list has a similar effect on Percent Complete. Select Not Started, for example, and Outlook sets the Percent Complete value to 0.

In addition to entering information such as the percentage of work that's completed, the priority, and the status, you can also set a reminder for the task. As it does for other Outlook items, such as appointments, Outlook can display a reminder window and play a sound as a reminder to start or complete the task. You can set only one reminder to a task, so it's up to you to decide when you want Outlook to remind you about the task. Click the speaker button on the task form to select the audio file you want Outlook to use for the reminder.

One key task setting on the Task tab is the Owner setting. When you create a task, you own that task initially. Only the owner can modify a task.Task ownership is relevant only to assigned tasks—that is, tasks you assign to others to perform.

For details about task ownership, see "Assigning Tasks to Others," page 590.

Other information you can specify on the Task tab includes contacts, categories, and the private or nonprivate status of the task. Assigning contacts to a task helps you to quickly access contact information for people associated with a task. For example, you might need to send an e-mail or make a call to someone who's working on a task with you. In that case, you can open the task item and double-click the name in the text box beside the Contacts button. This opens the contact entry, from which you can initiate a call, open the person's Web site, quickly create a new e-mail message, or perform any of the other actions available through the contact form. The ability to assign categories to tasks can help you organize your tasks. You can assign multiple categories to each task as needed and view the Tasks folder sorted by category. For example, you might assign project categories to tasks to help you sort the tasks according to project, allowing you to focus on the tasks for a specific project.

For details on working with categories, see "Assigning Categories to New Items," page 108.

The private or nonprivate status of a task allows you to control whether others who have delegate access to your folders can see a specific task. Tasks marked as private aren't visible unless you explicitly grant permission to the delegate to view private items. To control the visibility of private items, choose Tools, Options and click the Delegates tab. Double-click a delegate, and in the Delegate Permissions dialog box (see Figure 21-5) select or clear the Delegate Can See My Private Items check box. Repeat the process for any other delegates as needed.

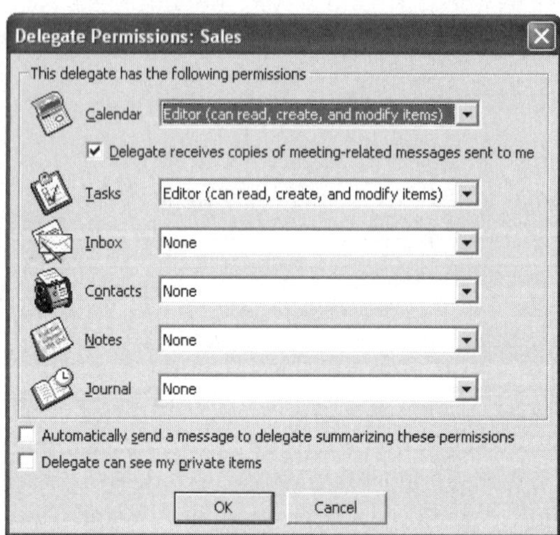

Figure 21-5. Use the Delegate Permissions dialog box to control the visibility of private items.

Note The Delegates option is available only if you're using Microsoft Exchange Server and only if the Delegates add-in (Dlgsetp.ecf) is installed. Click Tools, Options, Other, Advanced Options, and click Add-In Manager to add or remove the Delegates add-in.

The Details tab of the task form (shown earlier in Figure 21-4) allows you to specify additional information about the task. The options on the Details tab include the following:

- **Date Completed** Use this calendar to record the date the task is completed. This is the actual completion date, not the projected completion date.
- **Total Work** Specify the total amount of work required for the task. You can enter a value in minutes, hours, days, or weeks by entering a value followed by the unit, such as 3 days.
- **Actual Work** Record the total amount of work performed on the task to date. You can enter the data using the same units as in the Total Work box.
- **Companies** List any companies associated with the task such as suppliers, customers, or clients.
- **Mileage** Record mileage associated with the task if mileage is reimbursable or a tax-deductible expense.
- **Billing Information** Record information related to billing for the task, such as rate, person to bill, and billing address.
- **Update List** This option applies to tasks assigned to others. It shows the person who originally sent the task request and the names of all others who received the task request, reassigned the task to someone else, or elected to keep an updated copy of the task on their task list. When you send a task status message, Outlook adds these people as recipients of the status message.
- **Create Unassigned Copy** Use this button to create a copy of an assigned task that you can send to another person.

For details on working with the update list, assigned tasks, and unassigned copies, see "Assigning Tasks to Others," page 590.

Troubleshooting

Others can't see your tasks

For others to see your tasks, you must share your Tasks folder. If you're using Exchange Server as your mail server, you can also allow others to see your tasks by granting them delegate access to your Tasks folder. The two methods are similar with one major difference: granting delegate access to others allows them to send messages on your behalf. Sharing a folder simply gives others access to it without granting send-on-behalf-of permission.

To share your Tasks folder without granting send-on-behalf-of permission, right-click the Tasks folder icon on the folder list in the Navigation Pane and choose Properties. Click the Permissions tab and add or remove users and permissions as needed.

For additional details on sharing folders and setting permissions, see "Granting Access to Folders," page 741. To learn how to set up delegate access to your folders, see Chapter 29, "Delegating Responsibilities to an Assistant."

Copying an Existing Task

You can quickly create a new task from an existing one by copying it through the clipboard. The new task has all the same information as the original task, but you can change any of the information as needed.

Follow these steps to copy a task:

1. Select the task by clicking the icon in the Icon column in the task list. The icon shows a clipboard with a check mark on it.
2. Choose Edit, Copy or press Ctrl+C to copy the task to the clipboard.
3. Choose Edit, Paste or press Ctrl+V to paste the contents of the clipboard as a new task.

Creating a Recurring Task

Earlier in the chapter, you learned several different ways to create a task that occurs once. You can also use Outlook to create recurring tasks. For example, you might create a recurring task for reports you have to submit on a weekly, monthly, or quarterly basis. Perhaps you perform backup operations once a week and want Outlook to remind you to do this.

You create a recurring task much the same way you create a single-instance task, except that when the task form is open, you click the Recurrence button on the form's toolbar to display the Task Recurrence dialog box (see Figure 21-6).

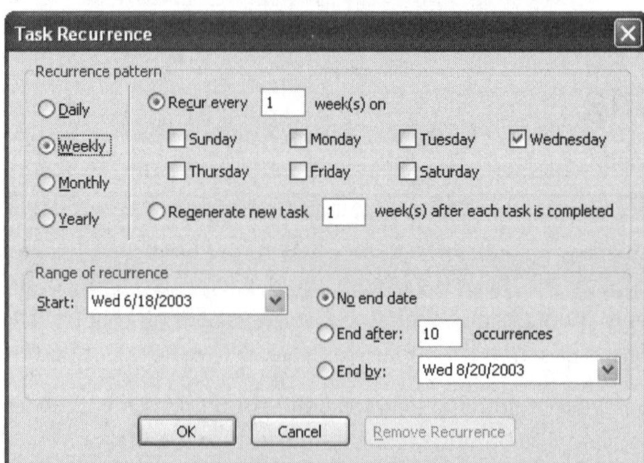

Figure 21-6. Create recurring tasks by using the Task Recurrence dialog box.

You can select daily, weekly, monthly, or yearly recurrence. Selecting one of these four options in the dialog box changes the options available in the dialog box, allowing you to select the recurrence pattern. For example, select Weekly and then select the days of the week on which you want the task to occur.

When you create a recurring task, one of the decisions you must make is whether you want the task to recur at a specified period regardless of the task's completion status. You can also choose to regenerate a new task after the existing task is completed. For example, you can create a task that recurs every Friday. The task will recur whether or not you marked the previous instance as completed. If you need to complete the previous task before the next task is generated, however, you should configure the recurrence so that the new task is created only after the previous one is completed. For example, perhaps you run a series of reports, but each relies on the previous report being completed. In this situation, you would probably want to set up the task to regenerate only after the preceding one was completed.

The Regenerate New Task option in the Task Recurrence dialog box allows you to configure the recurrence so that the new task is generated a specified period of time after the previous task is completed. Select the Regenerate New Task option and then specify the period of time that should pass after completion of the task before the task is regenerated.

Other options for a recurring task are the same as those for a one-time task. Specify subject, details, contacts, categories, and other information as needed. Remember to set up a reminder for the task if you want Outlook to remind you before the task's assigned completion time.

Adding a Reminder

You can add a reminder to a task when you create the task or after you create it. As with reminders for appointments, you specify the date and time for the reminder as well as an optional sound Outlook can play along with the reminder.

To add a reminder, follow these steps:

1. Open the task and select Reminder on the Task tab.
2. Use the calendar in the drop-down list beside the Reminder check box to select the date, and then select a time for the reminder. You can select a time in half-hour increments in the drop-down list or specify your own value by typing it in the box.
3. Click the Speaker icon to open the Reminder Sound dialog box, in which you select a WAV file to assign to the reminder.
4. Click OK and close the task form.

> **Note** Outlook uses a default time of 8:00 A.M. for the reminder. You can change this default value by choosing Tools, Options and setting the Reminder Time option on the Preferences tab.

Setting a Task Estimate

When you create a task, you might also want to estimate the time it will take to complete it. You can enter this estimate in the Total Work box on the Details tab of the task form. As the task progresses, you can change the Total Work value to reflect your changing estimate or leave it at the original value to track time overruns for the task. For example, assume that you propose a 40-hour task to a client. As you work through the task, you continue to update the Actual Work box to reflect the number of hours you've worked on the task. You reach 40 hours of work on the task and haven't completed it. You then have to make a decision: do you update the Total Work value to show a new estimate for completion and bill the client accordingly, or do you leave it as is and absorb the cost overrun?

Unfortunately, the Total Work and Actual Work fields are simple, nonreactive data fields. Outlook provides no interaction between the two to determine an actual Percent Complete value for the task. For that reason—and because Outlook can't calculate job costs based on charge rates and the amount of work completed—Outlook by itself generally isn't a complete job tracking or billing application. You should investigate third-party applications to perform that task or develop your own applications using the Microsoft Office 2003 suite as a development platform.

For details on how to get started developing your own Office applications, see Articles 1, 2, and 3 on the companion CD.

Marking a Task as Completed

Logically, the goal for most tasks is completion. At some point, therefore, you'll want to mark tasks as completed. When you mark a task as completed, Outlook strikes through the task in the task list to provide a visual cue that the task is finished. The easiest way to mark a task as completed is to place a check in the Complete column, which by default is the second column in the task list. You can also mark a task as completed on the Task tab. Simply select Completed in the Status drop-down list or set the Percent Complete box to 100.

Outlook by default sorts the task list by completion status. If you've changed the list to sort based on a different column, simply click that column header. For example, clicking the Complete column header sorts the task list by completion status. If you want to view only completed tasks, choose View, Arrange By, Current View, Completed Tasks. Viewing only incomplete tasks is just as easy: choose View, Arrange By, Current View, Active Tasks.

For additional details on customizing the Tasks folder view, see "Viewing and Customizing the Tasks Folder," page 597.

Assigning Tasks to Others

In addition to creating tasks for yourself in Outlook, you can also assign them to others. For example, you might manage a staff of several people and frequently need to assign them projects or certain tasks in a project. The main benefit of using Outlook to assign those tasks is that you can receive status reports on assigned tasks and view these status reports in your

Tasks folder. Outlook automates the process of sending task requests and processing responses to those requests. You'll learn more about assigning tasks in the sections that follow. First, however, you need to understand task ownership.

About Task Ownership

When you create a task, you initially own that task. Only a task's owner can make changes to it. This means that you can modify the properties (the percent complete, the status, the start date, and so on) of all tasks that you create and own. When you assign a task to someone else and that person accepts the task, the assignee becomes the owner of the task. You can then view the task's properties but can no longer change them. Similarly, you become the owner of tasks assigned to you when you accept them, and you can then make changes to those tasks.

A task's Owner property is a read-only value, which appears in the Owner box of the Task tab. The value has a gray background to indicate that it's read-only. You can click the value, but you can't change it directly. The only way to change owners is to assign the task and have the assignee accept it.

Making or Accepting an Assignment

Assigning a task to someone else is a simple process. In general, you create the task, add details, and specify options for the task. Then you tell Outlook to whom you want to assign the task, and Outlook takes care of generating the task request and sending it to the assignee.

Follow these steps to assign a task to someone else:

1. In Outlook, open the Tasks folder and create a new task.
2. Add information and set options for the task such as start date, due date, status, and priority.
3. Click Assign Task on the form's toolbar. Outlook changes the form to include additional options, as shown in Figure 21-7.

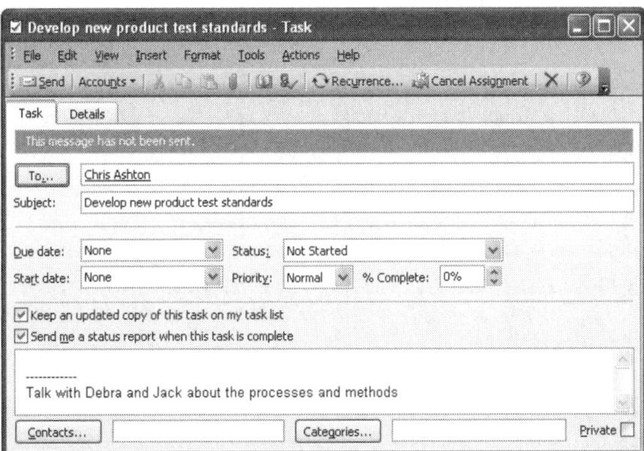

Figure 21-7. Outlook offers additional options when you assign a form to someone else.

4 In the To box, enter the address of the person to whom you're assigning the task, or click To to browse the address book for the person's address.

5 Outlook automatically selects the following two check boxes. Set them as you want and click Send to send the task request to the assignee.

- **Keep An Updated Copy Of This Task On My Task List** Select this check box if you want to keep a copy of the task in your own task list. You'll receive updates when the assignee makes changes to the task, such as a change in the Percent Complete status. If you clear this check box, you won't receive updates, nor will the task appear in your task list.
- **Send Me A Status Report When This Task Is Complete** Select this check box if you want to receive a status report on completion. The status report comes in the form of an e-mail message that Outlook generates automatically on the assignee's system when the assignee marks the task as completed.

For information about task updates and status reports, see "Tracking the Progress of a Task," page 595.

Tip Click Cancel Assignment in the task form to cancel an assignment and restore the original task form.

When you click Send, Outlook creates a task request message and sends it to the assignee. If you open the task, you'll see a status message indicating that Outlook is waiting for a response from the assignee (see Figure 21-8). This message changes after you receive a response and indicates whether the assignee accepted the task.

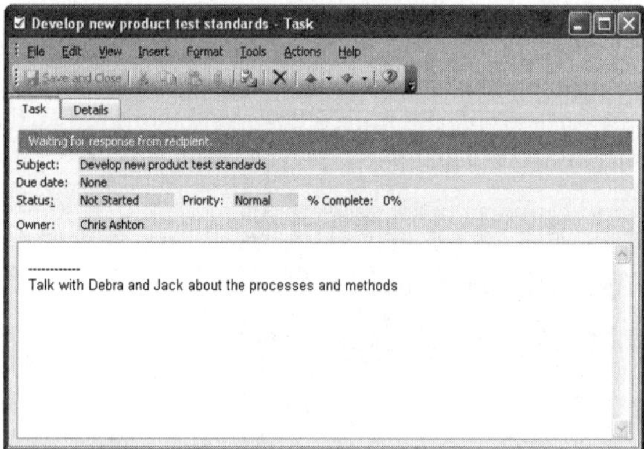

Figure 21-8. Outlook indicates that it is waiting for a response to a task request for a selected task.

When you receive a task request from someone who wants to assign a task to you, the message includes buttons that allow you to accept or decline the task. Figure 21-9 shows the buttons on the InfoBar when the Reading Pane is displayed.

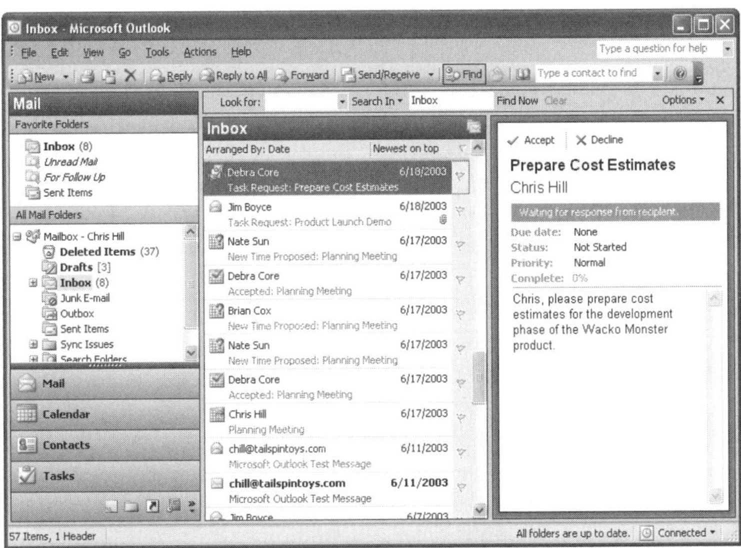

Figure 21-9. You can easily accept or decline a task request by using the Accept or Decline button on the Reading Pane's InfoBar.

You can click either Accept or Decline to respond to the request. If the Reading Pane isn't open, you can open the message and click Accept or Decline on the message form toolbar. When you do so, Outlook displays a dialog box giving you the option of sending the message as is or editing it. For example, you might want to add a note to the message that you'll have to change the due date for the task or that you need additional information about the task. Choose Edit The Response Before Sending in the dialog box if you want to add your own comments; select Send The Response Now if you don't want to add comments. Then click OK to generate the message. The next time you synchronize your Outbox with the server, the message will be sent.

You have one additional option besides accepting or declining a task request that's waiting for your response—you can "pass the buck" and assign the task to someone else. For example, assume that you manage a small group of people. Your supervisor assigns a task to you, and you want to assign it to one of the people under you. When you receive the task request, open it, click Assign Task, and then select the person to whom you want to assign it. Outlook creates a task request and sends it to the assignee. When the assignee accepts the task, his or her copy of Outlook sends an acceptance notice to you and adds both the originator's address and your address to the update list on the Details tab of the task form. This means that changes to the task by the assignee are updated to your copy of the task and to the originator's copy.

Troubleshooting

Task requests keep disappearing

After you accept or decline a task, Outlook automatically deletes the task request from your Inbox. Unlike meeting requests, task requests are always deleted—Outlook doesn't provide an option that allows you to control this behavior. Outlook does, however, keep a copy of the task request in the Sent Items folder. Outlook also deletes task update messages after you read them. These messages are generated automatically when someone modifies an assigned task. Outlook sends the task update message to the people listed in the update list on the Details tab of the task form. Although you can manually move these update messages out of the Deleted Items folder, Outlook provides no way to prevent them from being deleted.

When a response to a task assignment reaches you, Outlook doesn't automatically act on the response. For example, if someone accepts a task that you assigned, Outlook doesn't consider the task accepted until you open the response. Until that point, the InfoBar in the Reading Pane still indicates that Outlook is waiting for a response. When you open the response, the InfoBar in the message form indicates whether the task has been accepted or declined, depending on the assignee's action. Outlook deletes the response when you close the message. You have no options for controlling this behavior—Outlook always deletes the response.

If an assignee declines your task request, you can easily assign the task to someone else (or reassign it to the same individual). Open the response, and click Assign Task in the form's toolbar just as you would when assigning a new task.

Reclaiming Ownership of a Declined Task

Your tasks won't always be accepted—you're bound to receive a rejection now and then. When you do, you have two choices: assign the task to someone else or reclaim ownership so that you can modify or complete the task yourself. To reclaim a task, open the message containing the declined task request and choose Actions, Return To Task List.

Note When you assign a task, the assignee becomes the temporary owner until he or she accepts or rejects the task. Reclaiming the task restores your ownership so you can modify the task.

Assigning Tasks to Multiple People

In some situations, you'll no doubt want to assign a task to more than one person. As a department manager, for example, you might need to assign a project to the people in your department or at least to a small group. Outlook is somewhat limited in task management: it can't track task status when you assign a task to more than one person. You can certainly assign the task, but you won't receive status reports.

What's the solution? You must change the way you assign tasks, if only slightly. Rather than assigning the whole project as a single task, for example, break the project into separate tasks and assign each one individually, or break a specific task into multiple tasks. Use a similar name for each task to help you recognize that each one is really part of the same task. For example, you might use the names Quarterly Report: Joe and Quarterly Report: Jane to assign the preparation of a quarterly report to both Joe and Jane.

Inside Out

Working around limitations

Although Outlook's task management features are certainly useful, a more comprehensive set of tools for distributing and managing tasks within a project would be a great addition to the program. For example, the ability to subdivide a task automatically would be helpful, as would the ability to assign a task to multiple people and still receive updates without having to subdivide the task. You can, however, work around this by adjusting the way you assign and manage tasks.

Assigning Multiple Tasks Through an Assistant or a Group Leader

If you manage more than one group, task assignment becomes a little more complex because you probably have more than one group or department leader under you. Ideally, you would assign a task to a group leader and the group leader would delegate portions of the task to members of his or her group. How you accomplish that delegation depends on whether you want to receive status updates directly from group members or only from the group leader.

If you want to receive updates from group members, divide the overall task into subtasks and assign them to the group leader. The leader can then assign the tasks as needed to individuals in the group. Task updates are then sent to both you and the group leader. If you prefer to receive updates only from the group leader, create a single all-encompassing task and assign it to the group leader, who can then divvy up the project into individual tasks to assign to group members as needed.

Tracking the Progress of a Task

When you assign a task, you can choose to keep an updated copy of the task in your task list. This copy allows you to track the status of the task. As the assignee adds or changes task information—such as changing the Total Work value—that assignee's copy of Outlook generates an update and sends it to the addresses listed in the task's update list (on the Details tab of the task form). Typically, the update list includes only one name—the name of the person who assigned the task. If the task was delegated (passed on from one person to another), the update list shows all persons in the assignment chain.

> **Note** If you assign a task to multiple people, Outlook can no longer track task status. This limitation is one reason to subdivide a task, as explained in the previous section.

As mentioned, Outlook sends task status messages to the update list addresses when an assignee makes changes to a task. When you receive a status message, Outlook updates your copy of the task when you read the status message. Outlook then deletes the status message, with one exception: when the assignee marks the task as completed, Outlook sends a task completed message to the update list addresses. When you receive and read the message, Outlook marks your copy of the task as completed but does not delete the task completed message. Figure 21-10 shows a task completed message.

Chapter 21

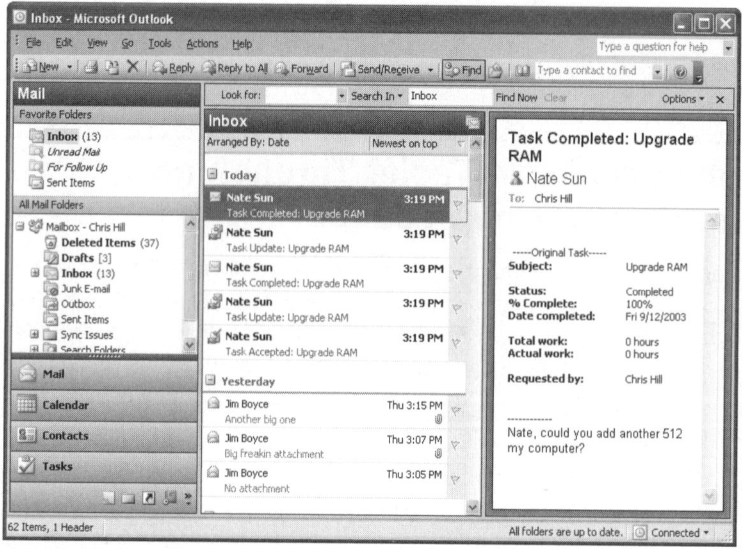

Figure 21-10. Outlook generates a task completed message when an assignee marks a task as completed.

Sending a Task Status Report

As you work on an assigned task, you'll probably want to send status updates to the person who assigned the task to you. Sending task status reports is more than easy—it's automatic. Outlook generates the updates each time you modify the task, such as when you change the Percent Complete value. Because you can't force another update without changing the task, you might want to make a small change in one of the task's properties—for example, increasing the Percent Complete value by 1 percent—to generate an update.

Creating an Unassigned Copy of an Assigned Task

Outlook allows you to create an unassigned copy of a task that you have assigned to someone else. This unassigned copy goes into your task list with you as the owner. You can then work on the task yourself or assign it to someone else. For example, suppose that you assigned a task to someone but you want to work on it, too. You can create a copy and then work on the copy, changing its dates, completion status, and other information as you go.

Creating an unassigned copy has one drawback, however: you will no longer receive updates for the assigned task. This makes it more difficult to track the other person's progress on the assigned task.

Follow these steps to create an unassigned copy of a task:

1. In Outlook, open the Tasks folder and then open the assigned task.
2. Click the Details tab, and then click Create Unassigned Copy.
3. Outlook displays a warning that creating the copy will prevent you from receiving updates to the assigned task. Click OK to create the copy or Cancel to cancel the process.
4. Outlook replaces the existing task with a new one. The new task has the same name except that the word *copy* is appended to the name in the Subject box. Make changes as needed to the task and then choose Save And Close to save the changes.

Viewing and Customizing the Tasks Folder

As mentioned at the beginning of this chapter, Outlook uses a simple list as the default Tasks folder view. Several other predefined views are also available, including those described in the following list. To use any of these views, choose View, Arrange By, Current View, and select the view you want.

- **Simple List** Shows the task name, the due date, and whether the task is completed. This is the default view for the Tasks folder.
- **Detailed List** Shows not only the information in a simple list but also status, percent complete, and categories.
- **Active Tasks** Shows tasks that are active (incomplete).
- **Next Seven Days** Shows tasks for the next seven days.
- **Overdue Tasks** Shows incomplete tasks with due dates that have passed.
- **By Category** Organizes the task list by the categories assigned to tasks.
- **Assignment** Shows tasks assigned to specific people.
- **By Person Responsible** Groups the view according to the person responsible for a task.
- **Completed Tasks** Shows only completed tasks.
- **Task Timeline** Shows a timeline of all tasks.

Outlook provides several ways to customize the view of theTasks folder. These methods are the same as those for other Outlook folders. For details on sorting, grouping by various columns, adding and removing columns, and customizing the folder view in other ways, see "Customizing the Inbox View," page 61.

For information on using filters to locate and display specific tasks, such as those with certain text, dates, or other properties, see "Using Advanced Find," page 783.

In addition to using the customizing methods described in Chapter 3, "Working In and Configuring Outlook," you might also want to change the way Outlook displays certain items in the Tasks folder. For example, you could change the font or character size for the column names or change the color that Outlook uses to display overdue tasks (red by default). The following sections explain how to make these types of changes in the Tasks folder.

Changing Fonts and Table View Settings

Outlook by default uses an 8-point Tahoma font for column headings, rows, and AutoPreview text. You can select a different font or different font characteristics (point size, italic, color, and so on). You also can change the style and color for the grid lines on list views and specify whether to show the Reading Pane.

Follow these steps to customize your view settings:

1. Right-click the column header bar and choose Customize Current View, or choose View, Arrange By, Current View, Customize Current View.
2. In the Customize View dialog box, click Other Settings to display the Other Settings dialog box, shown in Figure 21-11.

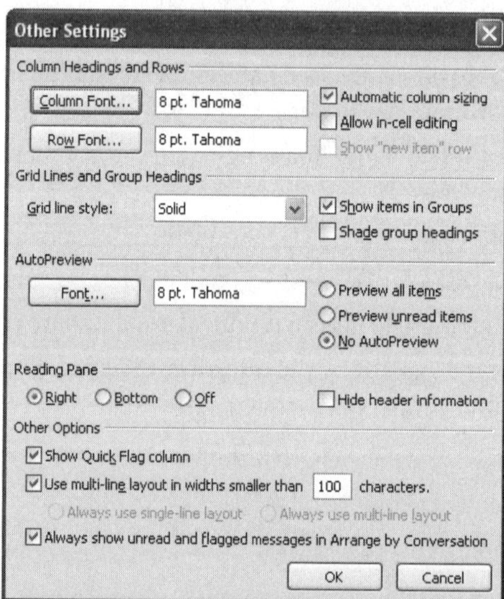

Figure 21-11. Configure font properties for the Tasks folder in the Other Settings dialog box.

3 Click Font in the Column Headings And Rows or AutoPreview area of the dialog box to open a standard Font dialog box you can use to select font, size, and other settings for the specified text.

Note You can change color only for the AutoPreview text. Row and column text is displayed in a fixed color.

4 Use the options in the Grid Lines And Group Headings group to specify the line type and color you want Outlook to use for list views.

5 Set other options (use the following list as a guide), click OK to close the Other Settings dialog box, and then click OK to close the Customize View dialog box.

- **Automatic Column Sizing** Sizes columns automatically and fits them to the display's width. Clear this check box to specify your own column width (by dragging each column's header), and use a scroll bar to view columns that don't fit the display.
- **Allow In-Cell Editing** Allows you to click in a cell and modify the contents. If this check box is cleared, you must open the task to make changes.
- **Show "New Item" Row** Displays a row at the top of the list for adding new tasks. The New Item row appears only if in-cell editing is selected.
- **Preview All Items** Turns on AutoPreview and causes Outlook to display the first three lines of the contents of all items.
- **Preview Unread Items** Turns on AutoPreview and causes Outlook to display the first three lines of the contents of unread items only.
- **No AutoPreview** Displays only the headings for items and does not display AutoPreview text.
- **Shade Group Headings** Adds shading to headings when you view items in a grouped table view (where items are grouped by column value, such as all tasks with the same due date).
- **Reading Pane** The options in this group control the location of the Reading Pane. Choose the Off radio button to hide it. You also can choose View, Reading Pane to select the location or turn the Reading Pane on or off.
- **Hide Header Information** Shows or hides the From, To, Cc, and Subject boxes in the InfoBar in the Inbox folder. However, this option has no effect in the Tasks folder.

Using Automatic Formatting

Outlook can perform automatic text formatting in the Task folder just as it can for other folders. For example, Outlook displays overdue tasks in red and uses gray strikethrough for completed and read tasks. Outlook has six predefined automatic formatting rules, and you can create additional rules if you want to set up additional automatic formatting. For example, you might create a rule to show in red all tasks that haven't been started and are due within the next seven days.

To create automatic formatting rules, choose View, Arrange By, Current View, Customize Current View. Then click Automatic Formatting to display the Automatic Formatting dialog box, shown in Figure 21-12.

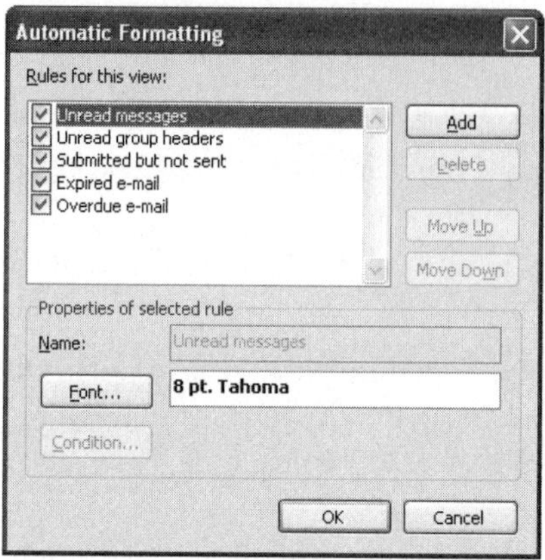

Figure 21-12. Modify or create custom automatic formatting rules in the Automatic Formatting dialog box.

Follow these steps to create a new rule:

1. In the Automatic Formatting dialog box, click Add. This creates a new rule named Untitled.
2. Type a title for the rule and click Font. Use the resulting Font dialog box to specify the font characteristics you want Outlook to use for tasks that meet the rule's conditions. Click OK to close the Font dialog box.
3. Click Condition to open the Filter dialog box (see Figure 21-13). Specify the criteria for the condition. For example, select Due in the Time drop-down list, and select In The Next 7 Days. This specifies that you want Outlook to use the font selections from step 2 to format any tasks that are due within the next seven days.

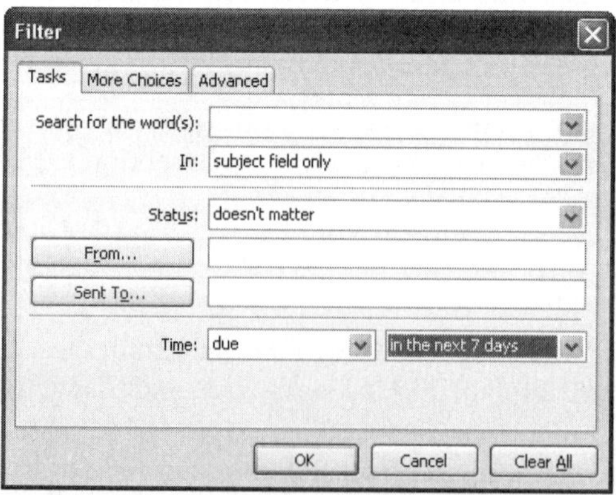

Figure 21-13. Use the Filter dialog box to specify conditions for the formatting rule.

4. Use the More Choices and Advanced tabs to set other conditions as needed, and then click OK.
5. Add other rules as needed. Click OK to close the Automatic Formatting dialog box, and then click OK to close the Customize View dialog box.

You can create fairly complex rules using the Filter dialog box, which can help you organize and identify specific types of tasks. Also note that you can change the order of the rules in the Automatic Formatting dialog box by using the Move Up and Move Down buttons. Outlook applies the rules in order from top to bottom, so it's possible for one rule to override another.

Setting General Task Options

Outlook provides a few options that control the appearance of items in the Tasks folder, reminders, and other task-related elements. To set these options, choose Tools, Options. On the Preferences tab of the Options dialog box, the Reminder Time option specifies the default reminder time for tasks. This option is set to 8:00 A.M. by default, but you can change the time if you like—perhaps you'd prefer to see reminders at 10:00 A.M. instead. Keep in mind that this setting is the default that Outlook uses for task reminders when you create a task, but you can change the reminder time for individual tasks as needed.

If you click Task Options, Outlook displays the Task Options dialog box, which includes the following options:

- **Overdue Task Color** Select the color you want Outlook to use to display overdue tasks.
- **Completed Task Color** Select the color you want Outlook to use to display completed tasks.
- **Keep Updated Copies Of Assigned Tasks On My Task List** Select this option to have Outlook keep a copy of assigned tasks in your Tasks folder and update their status when assignees make changes to the tasks.
- **Send Status Reports When Assigned Tasks Are Completed** Select this option to have Outlook send status reports to you when tasks you assigned to someone else are completed.
- **Set Reminders On Tasks With Due Dates** Select this option to have Outlook set a reminder on tasks with due dates. Outlook bases the timer on the task's due date and the reminder time specified in the Options dialog box.

Working with Tasks in Other Ways

Outlook provides a few other ways to work with tasks in addition to the Tasks folder. The following sections explain how to set up and track tasks in the TaskPad and in Outlook Today view.

Working with Tasks on the TaskPad

If you use the calendar feature of Outlook, you'll find that the TaskPad appears in the Calendar folder's Day, Work Week, and Week views. Figure 21-14 shows Day view with the TaskPad highlighted. The TaskPad appears under the Date Navigator.

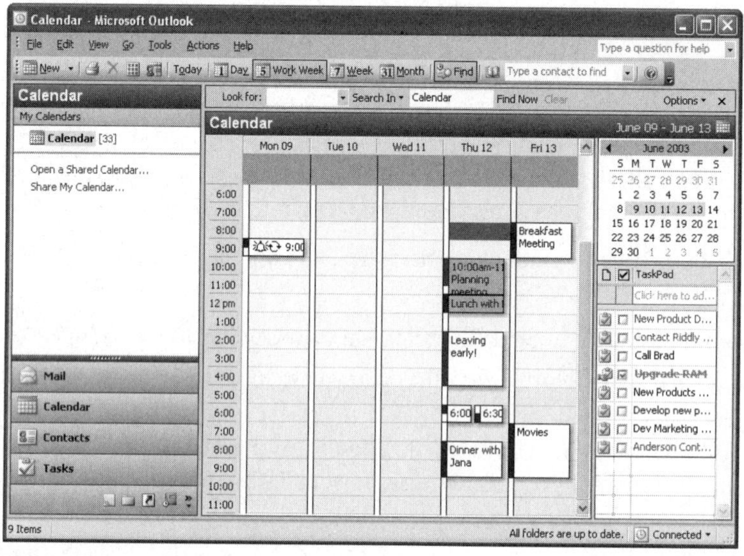

Figure 21-14. Use the TaskPad to work with tasks in your Calendar folder.

By default, Outlook shows only the Icon, Complete, and Subject columns for tasks in the TaskPad, but you can add and remove columns as needed. To do so, right-click the column header bar above the TaskPad and choose Field Chooser. Drag columns to and from the Field Chooser dialog box.

You can modify tasks directly in the TaskPad just as you can in the Tasks folder, depending on the view settings you've specified. For example, if you've turned on in-cell editing, you can make changes to a task simply by clicking it and typing the needed changes. You can mark a task as completed, change the Actual Work value, change the due date, and so on. The TaskPad is, in this respect, no different from the Tasks folder. The primary benefit of the TaskPad is that it allows you to work with your schedule and your tasks in a single window.

Tip **Showing and hiding the TaskPad**
You can drag the borders of the TaskPad to show it or hide it. If you drag the TaskPad's bottom border to the bottom of the view, the Date Navigator increases in size (and number of months displayed) to take up the space vacated by the TaskPad. Simply click in the bottom of the view and drag the mouse back up to restore the TaskPad. You also can drag the left edge of the TaskPad to the right edge of the display to hide it and the Date Navigator.

You can use the same methods that you use to create tasks in the Tasks folder to create a new task in the TaskPad. Right-click in the empty area of the TaskPad and choose New Task or New Task Request, depending on whether you're creating the task for yourself or assigning it to someone else. If both the Show New Item Row option and in-cell editing are enabled, you can click the Click Here row between the first task in the list and the column header to create a new task. Alternatively, you can click the arrow beside the New button on the toolbar and choose Task to create a new task.

Changing the TaskPad's View

Outlook offers seven options for viewing tasks in the TaskPad. In essence, these offer different TaskPad views. To select a TaskPad view, right-click in the empty area of the TaskPad and choose TaskPad View, followed by one of these selections:

- **All Tasks** Shows all tasks regardless of status or due date.
- **Today's Tasks** Shows all tasks active (incomplete) on the current date.
- **Active Tasks For Selected Days** Shows active tasks on selected days. Select one or more dates, and then select this option to see which tasks are active.
- **Tasks For Next Seven Days** Shows all tasks that are active during the next seven days from the current date.
- **Overdue Tasks** Shows all overdue tasks.
- **Tasks Completed On Selected Days** Shows completed tasks on selected days. Select one or more dates, and then select this option to see which tasks were completed.

The last option on the menu, Include Tasks With No Due Date, is not a view per se. Instead, selecting this option causes Outlook to include in the selected view those tasks that have no due date. Clear this option to hide tasks without due dates, excluding them from the list.

Setting TaskPad Options

Earlier this chapter explained how to customize the Tasks folder view by changing character formatting, column display, and more. You can make some of these same changes in the TaskPad to customize its view. For example, you can add and remove columns, group by specific fields, sort the display, and set fonts and grid style. To configure these settings, right-click the TaskPad, choose TaskPad Settings, and then select the item you want to change.

For details on modifying the Task folder view, see "Viewing and Customizing the Tasks Folder," page 597.

Working with Tasks in Outlook Today

Chapter 3, "Working In and Configuring Outlook," explained in detail how Outlook Today gives you quick access to a useful selection of data (see Figure 21-15). The Calendar area displays meetings and events scheduled for the current day (and for subsequent days, if space allows). The Messages area indicates the number of unread messages in your Inbox, messages in the Drafts folder, and unsent messages in the Outbox. The Tasks area lists your tasks.

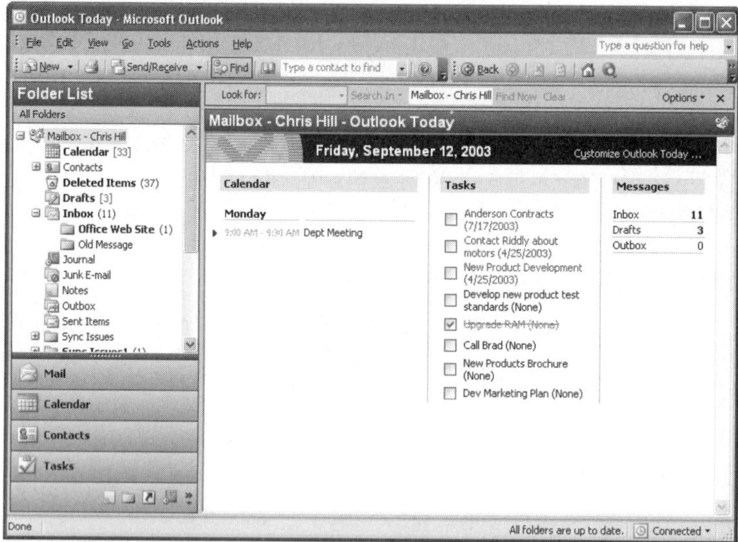

Figure 21-15. Outlook Today offers quick access to a range of information.

For detailed information on using Outlook Today, see "Outlook Today," page 57.

You can't create a task by clicking in the Tasks area of Outlook Today, but you can click the arrow beside the New button on the toolbar and choose Task to create a new task. To modify a task, click the task's name in the list to open the task form. Mark a task as completed by selecting the check box beside its name.

Chapter 22

Integrating Microsoft Outlook and Microsoft Project

Software programs are designed to handle specific tasks or sets of tasks. For instance, Microsoft Office Outlook 2003 provides tools to perform several tasks, including creating and managing e-mail, setting up to-do lists, and organizing your contacts. You can even use Outlook to assign tasks, manage meetings, and keep track of events. When you need to manage a project, however, you might want to look into a project management program such as Microsoft Office Project 2003.

This chapter focuses on integrating Microsoft Outlook and Microsoft Project. For instance, you'll learn how to set up a resource list in Microsoft Project using Outlook contacts. In addition, you can use Outlook's reminder feature to send yourself alerts about tasks during a project's lifetime.

Before you learn how to integrate Outlook and Microsoft Project, you first need to look at what Microsoft Project is and what you can do with it as a stand-alone program.

Overview of Microsoft Project

Microsoft Project is an electronic project management tool. You can use Microsoft Project to perform the following tasks:

- Create project plans
- Track projects from start to finish
- Capture important milestones during a project
- Send announcements to team contacts about the status of a project
- Point out potential and actual problems during the course of a project
- Schedule meetings with important people

These are just a few examples of how Microsoft Project makes it easy to view and manage your projects. Figure 22-1 shows one of the ways Microsoft Project displays information related to your projects.

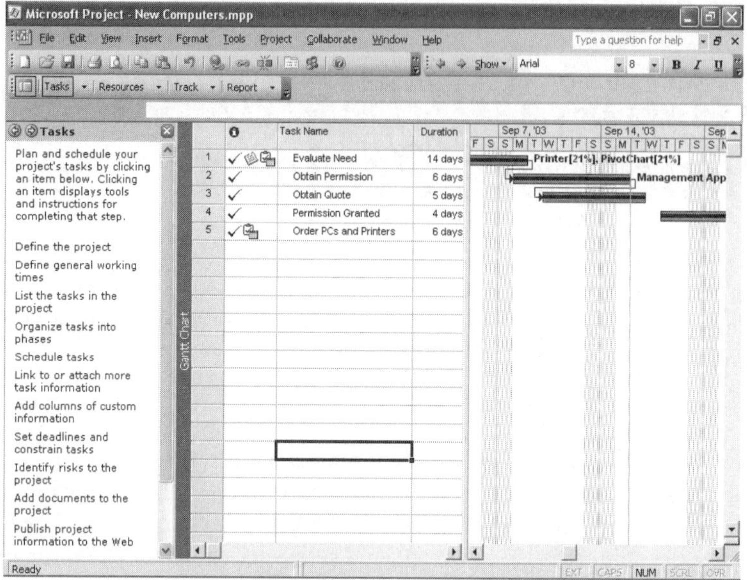

Figure 22-1. Use Microsoft Project to organize, manage, and track projects for you, your team, or your entire organization.

Now let's look at some basic project management considerations as well as Microsoft Project tasks and how to perform them.

Project Management Basics

Almost everyone—worker, homeowner, or organizational leader—works on some type of project. Some common projects include the following:

- Creating marketing material for an upcoming product launch
- Writing and publishing a book or newsletter
- Planning fundraising activities
- Renovating a room in your home
- Starting a new business
- Launching a Web site
- Managing employee training

Depending on the project you manage, you might need to keep track of a few or several hundred details. For instance, some projects are small enough that you need to keep track of only two or three employees, a few material resources (such as a load of gravel or a small shipment of computers), and start and finish dates. For larger projects, you might need to monitor not only your own employees but also the schedules of related firms' employees and include milestones to ensure that your schedule stays on track.

Some projects don't require a robust software tool such as Microsoft Project. For instance, if you're put in charge of only one small project that can be finished in less than a day, you can probably track the project more efficiently with a scratchpad and pen. You shouldn't waste time starting Microsoft Project, entering new project criteria, mapping a Gantt chart, and then starting the project. Simply get the resources you need and finish the project as quickly as you can.

On the other hand, suppose that you are assigned multiple small projects, a few medium-sized ones, and a large project that must all be completed over several months. A project management tool such as Microsoft Project can help ensure that you remember the details and maintain the schedule.

Keeping a Project in Balance

As a project gets underway and while it's in progress, you must strive to keep three things in balance: scope, schedule, and resources.

A project's *scope* is the set of tasks required to finish the project. If you are remodeling a bathroom in your home or office, for example, you must finish specific tasks before your bathroom is considered complete. Some of these tasks might include designing a new floor plan, ordering bathtub and sink fixtures, setting up a plumbing contractor, and demolishing the existing bathroom. All these tasks make up the scope of the project.

Your project's *schedule* is the time required to complete the project's tasks and the order of those tasks. The schedule includes the obvious: projected start and finish dates. However, you must also consider scheduling other resource items, such as dates for the plumbing and heating personnel, the tile contractor, the electrician, and the inspector. Schedules should also include proposed receipt dates of any materials you need, such as custom faucet fixtures, lighting tracks, and a water filtration unit.

Finally, the *resources* for a project include the materials, equipment, and people necessary to complete the project. In many instances, you include not only contact information but also wage and benefit information for the people involved. (Benefits can include time off or holidays you must schedule around.) Likewise, materials and equipment connected with your project have related costs, operating expenses, and scheduling dynamics you must consider.

Another resource is where the project will take place. You must know the availability of the space throughout the project. In our example, the project's location is a bathroom, so you might not want to plan a renovation project to start when, for example, you are also hosting a large party. Similarly, if a project involves training employees, you don't want to schedule the training sessions to coincide with vacations or company-related events when an employee or group of employees will be out of town.

Microsoft Project's Four Project Management Steps

Microsoft Project helps you with the four main project management steps:

- Defining the project
- Creating the project plan
- Tracking the project
- Finishing the project

When you define the project, you outline the goals, define the scope, determine the necessary resources, and estimate how much time is needed to complete the project. You should also add milestones and internal deadlines, such as the date you want a wall demolished.

The *project plan* is the blueprint for your project. In short, the plan specifies exactly what needs to be accomplished, who will complete each task, how much time is estimated for each task, which tasks are dependent on others to finish before they can start, and any constraints you want applied to a task or a schedule. An example of a task constraint, or *dependency*, is that you might need to hire an electrician to rough in electrical outlets before your drywall contractor puts up your walls. Completing the drywall is dependent on the completion of the electrical work. Constraints might also include starting a task on a specific date (such as not on a weekend or holiday because of higher contracting costs).

Microsoft Project's strength is that it can track your project's history from start to finish as long as you enter correct data and keep the information up-to-date. Microsoft Project can compare the actual time to complete a task with the time you estimated (and budgeted for). It also can analyze resource requirements to determine whether a resource is overloaded or whether you have scheduled a resource to complete more than one task at the same time. (Your plumber can work on only one part of the bathroom at a time, for instance.) This allows you to reformulate the plan to include additional resources, extend the project time, or redefine the scope of the project.

When a project is complete, that doesn't mean your work is finished. For instance, you might want to analyze the project so you can figure out how to manage a future project. Or you might have to gather project costs to review them with your manager or spouse. In addition, you might want to archive the project file for future reference.

Creating a Simple Project

To help you understand how Microsoft Project works, this section shows you how to create a simple project plan for publishing a departmental newsletter.

Follow these steps to create the project:

1. Start Microsoft Project 2003. If the Microsoft Project Help window appears, click Close to close it.
2. Choose File, Close to close the blank project.
3. Choose File, New.
4. In the New Project pane, click the Blank Project link (see Figure 22-2). A blank project window opens and project tasks are shown in theTasks pane.

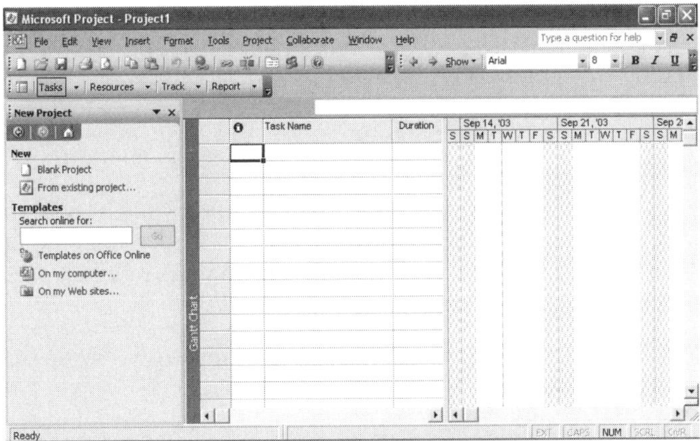

Figure 22-2. Start a new project by clicking the Blank Project link.

5 Click the Define The Project link, then enter a start or finish date. In this example, choose to start the project today.
6 Click Save And Go To Step 2.
7 Specify if you want to use Microsoft Project's new Project Server to let you collaborate with others on your project. For now we'll click No.
8 Click Save And Go To Step 3.
9 Click Save And Finish to begin adding details about your project.

The Tasks pane shows several links to wizards that will walk you through adding details to your project. We'll walk you through two more to help get your project going.

To set up working times for your project, do the following:

1 Click the Define General Working Times link in the Tasks pane (see Figure 22-3).

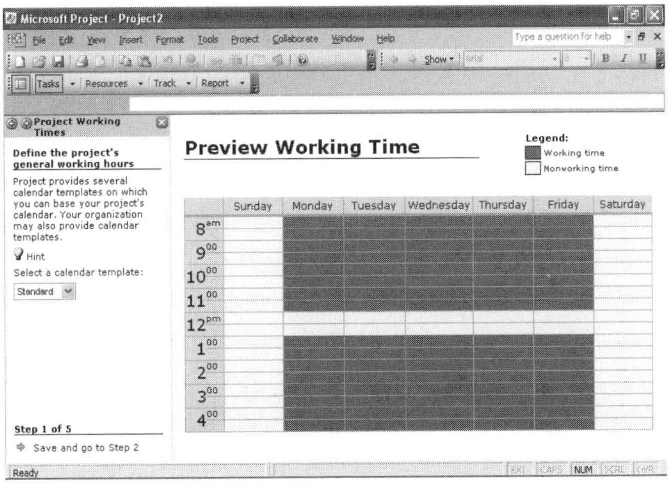

Figure 22-3. Set working times for your project here.

2. Select a calendar template from the Project Working Times pane. Choose Standard, 24 Hours, or Night Shift to specify the type of hours your project will display. Select Standard for now.
3. Click Save And Go To Step 2.
4. Select the days of the week for your project.
5. Click I Want To Adjust The Working Hours to change the times that are displayed as working and nonworking times. You can change one day at a time, or select new times and then click Apply To All Days to have your changes reflected on all days.
6. Click Save And Go To Step 3.
7. Click Change Working Time to set the holidays and days off you want to recognize during your project (see Figure 22-4).

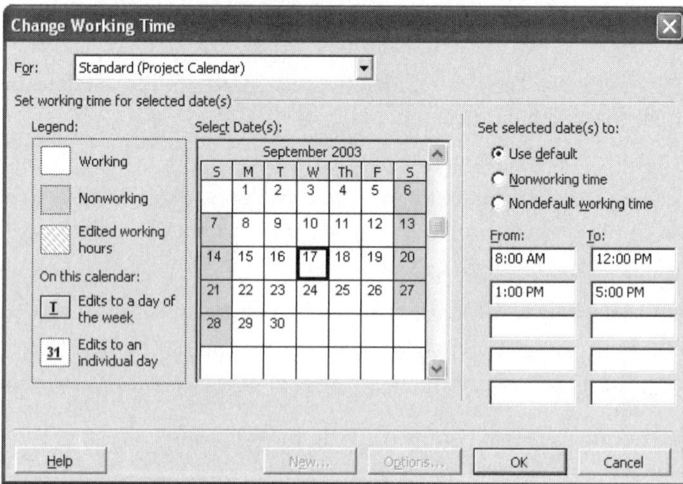

Figure 22-4. If you want to recognize holidays and days off during your project, use the Change Working Time dialog box.

8. Click OK when finished setting up these special times.
9. Click Save And Go To Step 4.
10. Specify the default time units. Microsoft Project starts you off by using the standard 8-hour days, 40 hours per week, and 20 days per month. Adjust these numbers as needed for your project.
11. Click Save And Go To Step 5.
12. Click Save and Finish to complete the Project Working Times task.

> **Note** You need to choose File, Save, type a file name in the File Name field, and click Save to actually save your new project file to disk.

Choose File, Save to save the project. Enter the project name **Issue 1** and click Save.

Now you're ready to enter your task list. The task list for this example includes the following:

- **Write each article** In this four-page newsletter, each page will include one article, named Page One Article, Page Two Article, and so on.
- **Create the author list** Each article will have a separate author.
- **Define the editor and editor dates** The newsletter will be edited by one editor.
- **Submit articles to the desktop publisher** The newsletter will be desktop published by one person.
- **Submit the newsletter to the printer** The edited and desktop published newsletter will be shipped to a printer on a specific date for printing.
- **Send out finished newsletter** The printed newsletter will be mailed to subscribers by a specific date.

As you can see from the list, a simple four-page newsletter can include many tasks, dates, and resources.

Now add these tasks to your new project using Gantt Chart view:

1. In Microsoft Project, on the View menu, click Gantt Chart.

> **Note** In Gantt Chart view, you can view your tasks as you enter them and see information that Microsoft Project provides about the task.

2. In the Task Name box, type a task name, such as **Newsletter Issue 1**. Press Enter.
3. Continue adding tasks and durations. If you're following along with the example, you can refer to Table 22-1 for the list of tasks and their duration.
4. Order the tasks in the outline by indenting them as shown in Table 22-1. (For instance, indent the Write Page One Article task two times.) To indent a task, click the Indent button on the Formatting toolbar.
5. Add predecessors as indicated in Table 22-1. To do this, double-click a task and click the Predecessor tab. Click the Task Name column and select the predecessor in the drop-down list. Click OK to apply the change.

> **Note** In Microsoft Project, a predecessor task is a task that must start or finish before another task can begin. For example, before an article can be edited, it first must be written. Thus all editing tasks have a predecessor task of writing. You can specify predecessor tasks using the Predecessors tab of the Summary Task Information dialog box.

6. Check to be sure that your entries match those shown in Figure 22-5.
7. Choose File, Save to save the project.

Table 22-1. Tasks for Newsletter Issue 1

Task Name	Duration	Indents	Predecessor
Newsletter Issue 1	22 days	None	N/A
Write Articles	11 days	One	N/A
Write Page One Article	1 day	Two	N/A
Write Page Two Article	7 days	Two	N/A
Write Page Three Article	3 days	Two	N/A
Write Page Four Article	9 days	Two	N/A
Edit Articles	10 days	One	Write Articles
Edit Article One	1 day	Two	Write Page One Article
Edit Article Two	2 days	Two	Write Page Two Article
Edit Article Three	1 day	Two	Write Page Three Article
Edit Article Four	2 days	Two	Write Page Four Article
Desktop Publish Issue 1	3 days	One	Edit Articles
Print Newsletter	8 days	One	Desktop Publish Issue 1
Send Newsletter To Printer	2 days	Two	Desktop Publish Issue 1
Review and Approve Test Prints	1 day	Two	Send Newsletter To Printer
Print Copies Of Newsletter	2 days	Two	Review and Approve Test Prints
Receive Printed Newsletters	2 days	Two	Print Copies of Newsletter
Mail Newsletter to Recipients	1 day	One	Receive Printed Newsletters

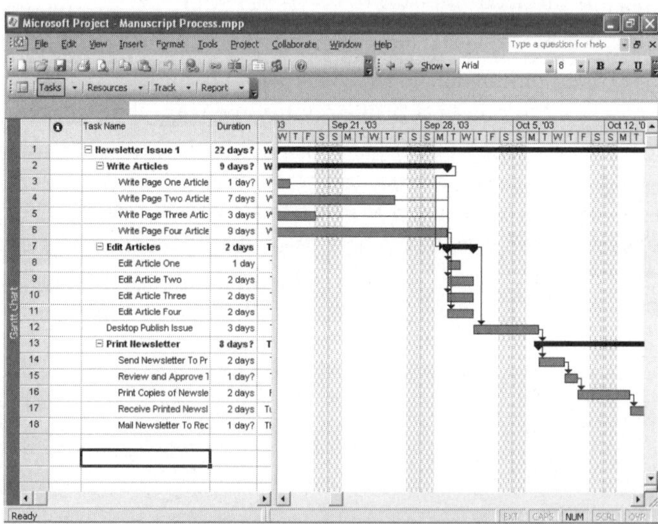

Figure 22-5. You can create a simple project plan, shown here in Microsoft Project.

After you create your project plan, you can edit it for real data. For instance, suppose that the author of the article on page four needs an extra three days to complete it. Because everything that follows the authoring stage—editing, page layout, printing, and mailing—is dependent on the article being written, you must adjust your plan accordingly. To do this, change the duration date from 9 days to 12 days. Notice how this affects everything after the authoring stage.

This example, simple as it is, shows you how Microsoft Project can manage and keep track of your projects. The next section looks at how you can integrate Microsoft Project and Outlook.

For more information on using Microsoft Project, visit the Microsoft Office Project 2003 Web site at *http://www.microsoft.com/office/project/*.

Troubleshooting

You're having trouble viewing and printing tasks and dependencies for projects

If you're starting to have difficulties working with your projects, part of the problem might be that the project has grown too large, which can happen pretty easily. In this section, you learned how to create a simple project. This small project could easily grow into a large project if you expanded it to include marketing and advertisement tasks. In general, as you're creating your projects, you might want to consider breaking large tasks into smaller multiple tasks to make them more manageable. To do this, follow these steps:

1. On the View menu, choose Gantt Chart.
2. Hold down Ctrl and click the row heading of each task you want to break out as a new project.
3. Right-click and choose Cut Task.
4. Choose File, New. Click From Existing Project, and type a new file name. Click Create New to save the project.

Integrating Your Outlook Calendar

With the Outlook calendar, you can set up, manage, view, and set reminders for important meeting dates, events, and other activities. When you're working in Microsoft Project, you can set Outlook reminders to alert you when tasks need to start or finish.

To set an alert with an Outlook reminder, do the following:

1. In Microsoft Project, on the View menu, click Gantt Chart.
2. Select the task or tasks for which you want to set up reminders. Hold down the Ctrl key to select multiple tasks.
3. Click the Set Reminder button to display the Set Reminder dialog box. If the toolbars do not display a Set Reminder button, choose View, Toolbars, Customize. Click the Commands tab and then click Tools. Drag the Set Reminder button to a toolbar. Click Close.

4 Set the reminder options you want for the tasks. For example, to get a reminder two days before a task is scheduled to finish, type **2**, select Days in the drop-down list, and then select Finish in the Before The *n* Of The Selected Tasks drop-down list.
5 Click OK.

Note Microsoft Project warns you if you try to set a Start reminder after a task is scheduled to start or try to set a Finish reminder after a task is scheduled to finish.

Integrating Your Address Book

After you create an address book in Outlook, you don't need to waste time typing resource names each time a project plan requires them. Instead, just use an Outlook address book from within Microsoft Project to add resource names, addresses, and e-mail information. This saves time and eliminates errors you might introduce when retyping resource information.

Creating a Resource List

A *resource list* is a list of names, distribution lists, or other contact information you use when assigning a task. For instance, if you want to assign a particular editor to edit your newsletter articles, you can add that editor's name to a resource list compiled from your Outlook Contacts folder and then assign that editor to the Edit Articles task.

The following steps show how to create a resource list in Microsoft Project using an Outlook address book:

1 In Microsoft Project, on the View menu, click Gantt Chart.
2 On the Standard toolbar, click Assign Resources to display the Assign Resources dialog box (see Figure 22-6).

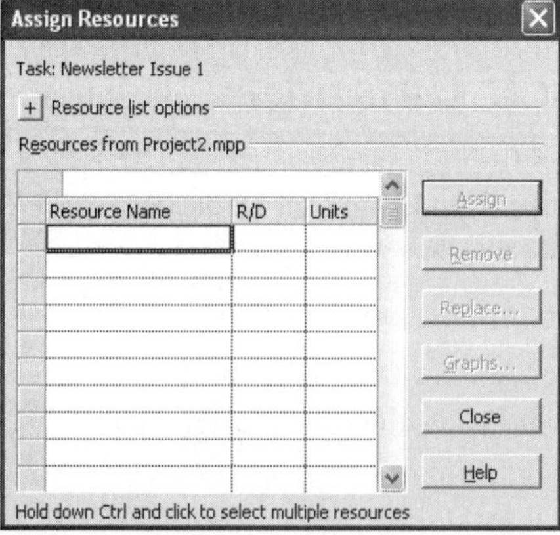

Figure 22-6. Use the Assign Resources dialog box from within Microsoft Project to assign Outlook contacts as resources.

3 Click the Plus (+)to the left of Resource List Options.

4 Click Add Resources and then click From Address Book to display your address book contacts.

5 Select the resource you want to assign to project tasks (see Figure 22-7).

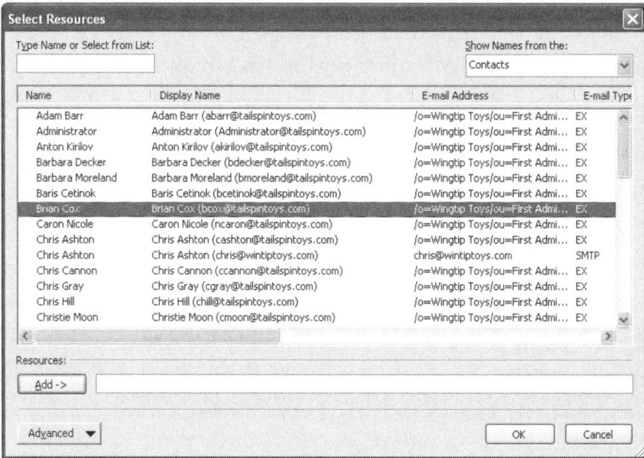

Figure 22-7. Microsoft Project's Select Resources dialog box looks similar to the Select Names dialog box you use when you're addressing an e-mail message in Outlook.

6 In the Name list, select a resource name or distribution list and click Add to add this name to the resource list. You can use this name as a resource for any task in Microsoft Project.

For a detailed discussion of distribution lists, see Chapter 5, "Managing Address Books and Distribution Lists." For more on assigning tasks to and working with contacts, see Chapter 14, "Managing Your Contacts."

7 Continue adding names as necessary.

8 When you have finished adding names, click OK. The resources you selected are now part of the Assign Resources dialog box list.

9 Click Close to close the Assign Resources dialog box.

Tip **Use a distribution list**

In Microsoft Project, you can use a distribution list as you would in Outlook to make your work easier. To use a distribution list as a resource in Microsoft Project, create the distribution list in Outlook and then select the distribution list as shown in step 5 of the preceding procedure. A distribution list is handy if you must assign a task to multiple resources, such as a task in which multiple team members must attend a training class or multiple resources must be used to finish a construction job.

Assigning a Resource to a Task

After you create your resource list, you can assign resources to any tasks in Microsoft Project. The following steps show you how:

1. In Microsoft Project, on the View menu, click Gantt Chart.
2. In the Task Name column, select a task.
3. Click the Assign Resources toolbar button to display the Assign Resources dialog box.
4. Select a resource name or distribution list and then click Assign.
5. Continue assigning resources as necessary.
6. When you've finished, click Close.

To see a list of resources assigned to a task, double-click the task in the Task Name list and then click the Resources tab (see Figure 22-8). You can also select resources here. To do so, click a row in the Resources list, click the down arrow, and then select a resource in the drop-down list. Click OK to close the dialog box and apply any changes you've made to the list.

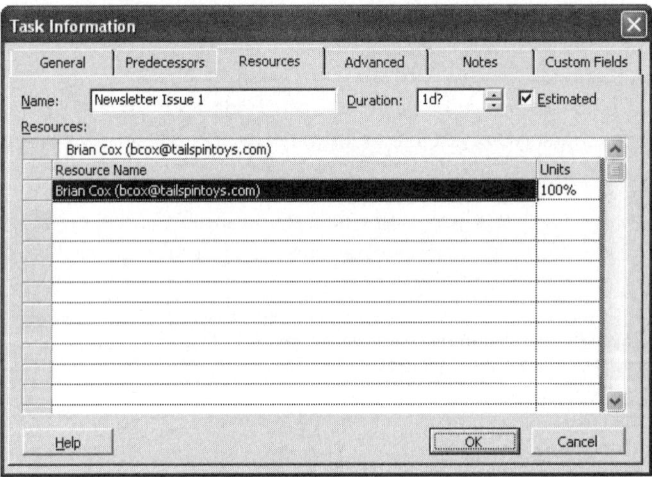

Figure 22-8. Click the Resources tab to review a list of resources assigned to a task.

Keeping Track of Your Progress

You can integrate Outlook's Journal feature with Microsoft Project to keep a record of all the work you do on a project, including when you opened, saved, and printed the project file. This feature comes in handy, for example, when you want to find out which project file you worked on yesterday or last week or which file you printed a few days ago.

To use the Outlook journal to track your project file work, do the following:

1. In Outlook, choose Tools, Options.
2. Click the Preferences tab.

3 Click Journal Options.

4 In the Also Record Files From list, select Microsoft Project (see Figure 22-9).

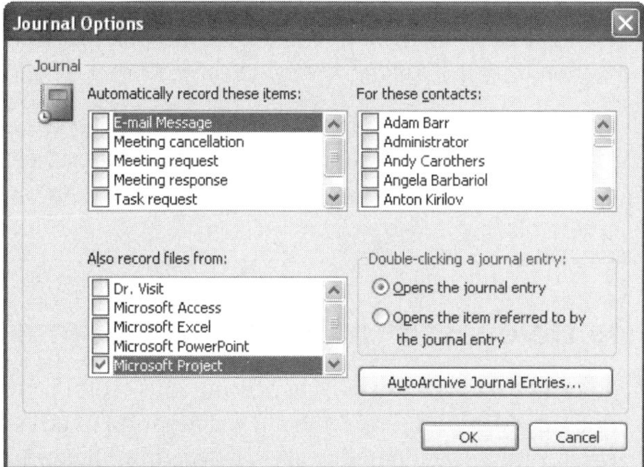

Figure 22-9. You can use Outlook's journal to keep journal information about your Microsoft Project files.

5 Click OK to close the Journal Options dialog box, and then click OK again.

Now, as you use Microsoft Project, the journal will automatically keep track of the work you do on your Microsoft Project files.

For more information about working with the Outlook journal, see Chapter 18, "Keeping a Journal."

Integrating Communication Features

One of the most difficult parts of managing a project is communicating with the people associated with a task or a set of tasks. If your company uses e-mail messages or the Internet, you can integrate Outlook's communication features with Microsoft Project to help you effectively communicate with resources about task responsibilities.

With Microsoft Office Project Server 2003, you can use Microsoft Project to send messages to workgroup system members, also called *teams*. Workgroups can then use Microsoft Project to assign tasks, send and receive task updates, accept or decline task assignments, and submit status reports. Team members can delegate tasks to other team members.

In addition to the collaborative features of Microsoft Project Server 2003, members of a team can use e-mail messages, the Web, or both to exchange Microsoft Project information. Microsoft Project files can include hyperlinks to other supporting documents so that resources can quickly and easily access related documents. These documents might include a Microsoft Word document describing the project in detail, a cost analysis worksheet in Microsoft Excel, or a related Web site you can view in Microsoft Internet Explorer.

> **Note** The following section shows how to use Outlook's e-mail features to send and receive messages concerning task assignment, reporting status, and reporting updates. It's assumed that the workgroup functionality of Microsoft Project is installed on your and your recipients' computers. To learn more about how to do this, consult the documentation that accompanies the Microsoft Project 2003 and Microsoft Office Project Server 2003 software.
>
> In addition, because e-mail systems and networks differ, the specific steps and features shown in this section might not work for your organization. Consult your network or e-mail administrator to find out whether your e-mail or local area network (LAN) system can use Microsoft Project's communication features.

Allowing Tasks to Be Delegated to Other Team Members

Before you can assign tasks to other team members using Microsoft Project's collaboration feature, you must configure Microsoft Project to allow delegation of tasks. In addition, your Microsoft Project Server must be configured to allow delegations. If you are not sure you can delegate tasks, or if you have problems after following these steps, contact your system administrator for more information about your particular organization's server. In addition to setting up the server information, your tasks must have resources assigned to them.

To allow team members (and yourself) to assign tasks to other team members, do the following:

1. Start Microsoft Project if it is not already started.
2. Choose Tools, Options to open the Options dialog box.
3. Click the Collaborate tab.
4. From the Collaborate Using drop-down list, select Microsoft Office Project Server.
5. Type the path (Uniform Resource Locator [URL]) to the Microsoft Project Server (see Figure 22-10).

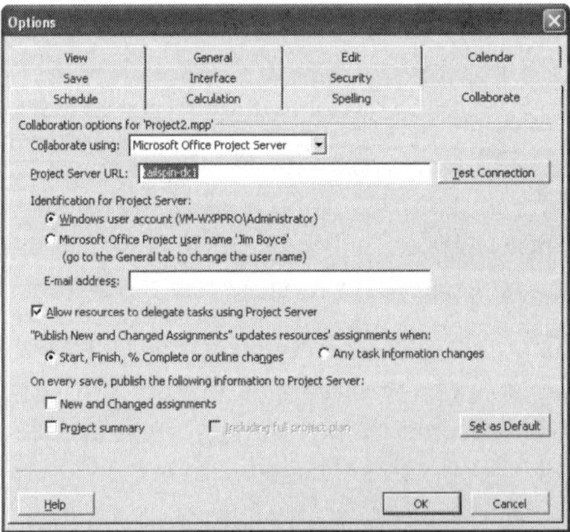

Figure 22-10. Before you can delegate tasks to other team members, configure Microsoft Project to work with your company's Microsoft Project Server.

6. Click Test Connection if you want to confirm that you've typed the correct URL and that the server is working correctly.
7. Select the Allow Resources To Delegate Tasks Using Project Server check box.
8. Configure other settings on this tab as needed. For more information see the Microsoft Project documentation.
9. Click OK to save your settings.

Publishing Tasks

To delegate, or publish, tasks to other members, do the following:

1. Select the task you want to publish.
2. Right-click and choose Publish New And Changed Assignments.
3. Click OK when prompted that your project will be saved.
4. Click Make Site Trusted if you need to specify that the server to which you are publishing is a trusted server. Note that if you are publishing to a Web site URL, you must make the Internet site trusted from within Internet Explorer before using Microsoft Project to publish tasks.

Sending an Update

After your project gets underway, you will have slips in the schedule, updates to tasks, and other events that require you to modify your Microsoft Project file. When these events occur, you need to update your team members appropriately. You can do this using the Publish New And Changed Assignments feature, as follows:

1. In your project, update the task about which you want to publish a new or changed assignment. You cannot send an update unless the task has actually been updated first.
2. Save your project.
3. Right-click a task and choose Publish New And Changed Assignments.
4. Click OK.

Importing an Outlook Task

Microsoft Project is designed to work with Outlook tasks. You can create a task in Outlook and then import that task into a project you are working on. This way you do not have "stray" tasks in Outlook that should really be part of a project file.

To import an Outlook task into a project, do the following:

1. Open Outlook and click the Task icon.
2. Create a new task and save it (see Figure 22-11).

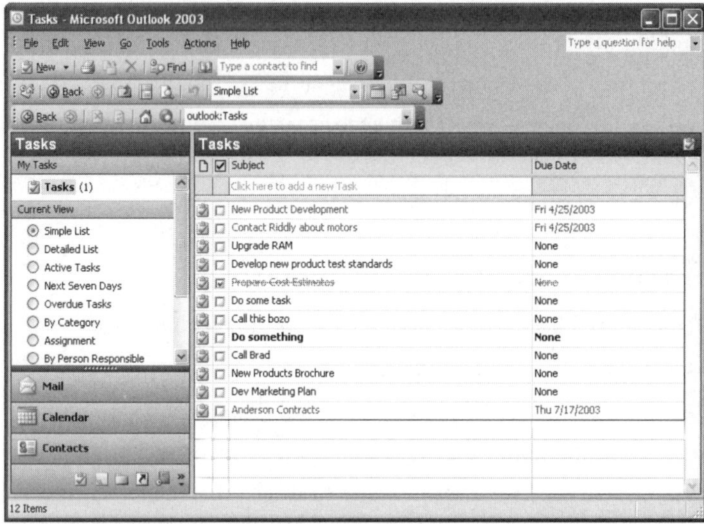

Figure 22-11. You can import an Outlook task into a project created in Microsoft Project.

3 Switch to Microsoft Project.

4 Choose Tools, Import Outlook Tasks.

5 Click Allow Access For 5 Minutes and click Yes if Outlook warns that another program is attempting to access e-mail addresses from your computer.

6 Select the check box next to the task you want to import in the Import Outlook Tasks dialog box, shown in Figure 22-12.

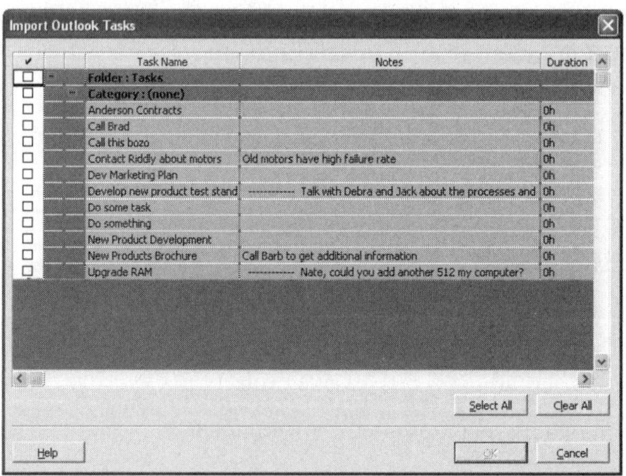

Figure 22-12. Select the task to import from this dialog box.

7 Click OK.

If necessary, you can move the task to another row and indent it under another task.

Sending a Microsoft Project File Using Outlook

One way you might want to share a Microsoft Project file is to send it as a project file using Outlook e-mail. Recipients can then save the file to disk and open it in Microsoft Project, allowing them to view, modify, or print the Microsoft Project file. Of course, each person who receives the file must have Microsoft Project 2003 installed on his or her computer.

To send a Microsoft Project file this way, do the following:

1. In Microsoft Project, choose File, Send To, Mail Recipient (As Attachment) to display the message form (see Figure 22-13).

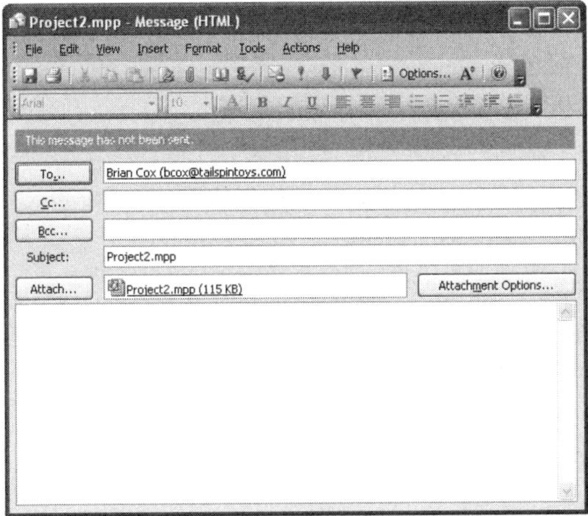

Figure 22-13. Send a Microsoft Project file from Microsoft Project using Outlook's e-mail features.

2. In the To box, type an e-mail address (or click To to access your address book). Add as many recipients as needed.
3. In the Subject box, type a subject. By default, Microsoft Project uses the file name as the subject.
4. In the message area, type a message.
5. Click Send.

Routing a Microsoft Project File Using Outlook

You can also use Outlook to route a Microsoft Project file. With routing, you send a file sequentially from one team member to the next or to all team members at one time. Use the former method if you want only one version of the file to be seen by all team members in the routing slip list. In this way, one member can review and modify the file before sending it to the next person on the routing slip. Use the latter method if you want all individuals to review and modify the file and return it directly to you.

> **Tip** **Use caution when routing sequentially**
> One downside to routing a file to a list of team members sequentially is that if someone in the routing list is out of the office for an extended time, your routed file could get stuck in that person's Inbox until they return, delaying any work you want to do on the file.

To route a Microsoft Project file, follow these steps:

1. In Microsoft Project, choose File, Send To, Routing Recipient to display the Routing Slip dialog box.
2. Click Address to display the Address Book dialog box.
3. Select the recipients and then click OK. The addresses are added to the To list, as shown in Figure 22-14.

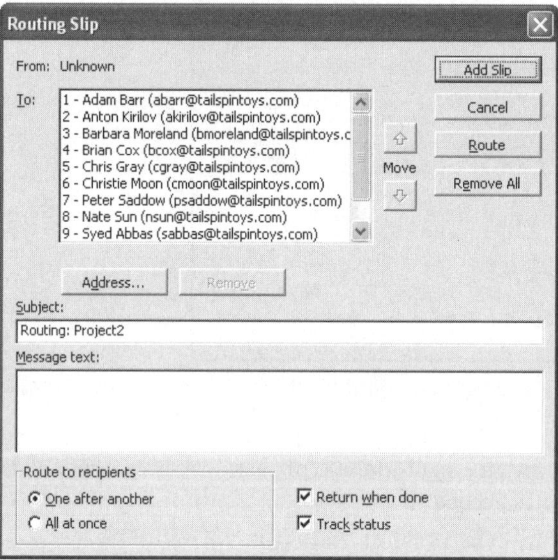

Figure 22-14. You can route a Microsoft Project file using Outlook's routing features.

4. Click the up and down Move arrows to move recipients' locations in the list, specifying the order in which you want them to receive the routing slip. If you want everyone to receive a copy simultaneously, select the All At Once option at the bottom of the dialog box.
5. In the Subject box, type a subject.
6. In the message area, type a message.
7. If you want the Microsoft Project file returned to you after all recipients have received it, select the Return When Done check box.
8. If you want Outlook to send you an e-mail notification each time the file is routed to the next recipient, select the Track Status check box. This allows you to keep track of where the file is in the routing sequence.

> **Tip** **Save the routing slip**
> You can save the routing slip with the Microsoft Project file if you are not ready to send it out yet. To do so, click Add Slip. To route the file, choose File, Send To, Next Routing Recipient, and then click OK.

9. When you're ready to start routing the file to specified recipients, click Route. If you receive a message telling you that another program is attempting to access your e-mail addresses, click Yes to continue. Outlook routes the file to the recipients.

Forwarding a Microsoft Project File Using Outlook

If a Microsoft Project file is routed to you, you must forward it to the next person in the list.

To forward a Microsoft Project file, follow these steps:

1. Open Outlook and view the routed message.
2. Double-click the Microsoft Project icon in the e-mail message to display the Microsoft Project file.
3. In Microsoft Project, view and modify the project as needed.
4. Choose File, Save to save your changes.
5. In Microsoft Project, choose File, Send To, Next Routing Recipient.
6. Click OK when prompted to send the file to the specified person.

Part 5

Customizing Outlook

Chapter 23

Using Templates

If you use Microsoft Word frequently, you're probably familiar with templates. These useful tools can help you quickly and easily create documents that share standard elements—for example, boilerplate text, special font and paragraph formatting, and paragraph styles.

You can also use templates in Microsoft Outlook 2003 to streamline a variety of tasks. There is nothing magical about these templates; they are simply Outlook items that you use to create other Outlook items. For example, you might create an e-mail template for preparing a weekly status report that you send to your staff or management. Perhaps you use e-mail messages to submit expense reports and would like to use a template to simplify the process.

This chapter not only discusses e-mail templates, but also explores the use of templates for other Outlook items. For example, you'll learn how to use templates to create appointments, contact entries, task requests, and journal entries. The chapter also suggests some ways of sharing templates with others.

Working with E-Mail Templates

An e-mail template is really nothing more than a standard e-mail message that you have saved as a template. Here are some suggested uses for e-mail templates:

- Create an expense report form.
- Send product information to potential clients.
- Create status reports for ongoing projects.
- Send messages to specific groups of recipients.
- Create a form for information requests or product registration.

When you need to send similar messages frequently, creating a message template can save you quite a bit of time, particularly if the message contains a great deal of frequently used text, graphics, or form elements. You also reduce potential errors by reusing the same message each time rather than creating multiple messages from scratch. You can use the template to provide the bulk of the message, filling in any additional information required in each particular instance.

Creating an E-Mail Template

Creating an e-mail template is as easy as creating an e-mail message. You can start by opening a new message form, just as you would if you were sending a new message to a single recipient or group.

To create an e-mail template from scratch, follow these steps:

1. Be sure that you have specified Outlook as your e-mail editor. You can't save a message as a template with Microsoft Word as your editor.
2. With the Inbox folder open, click the New toolbar button to open a new message form. Enter the boilerplate text and any information that you want to include every time you send a message based on this template. For example, you can specify the subject, address, other headings, bullets, lists, and tables.
3. Choose File, Save As in the message form.
4. In the Save As dialog box, shown in Figure 23-1, specify a path and a name for the file. Select Outlook Template in the Save As Type drop-down list. Outlook adds an OFT extension to the file name.

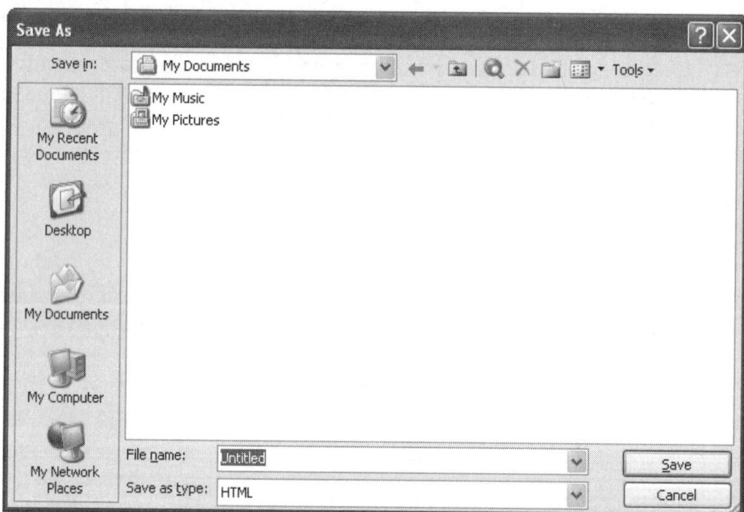

Figure 23-1. Save your newly created template as an OFT file.

Outlook opens your My Documents folder with HTML as the default file type. The default location for user templates, however, is the <*profile*>\Application Data\Microsoft\Templates folder, where <*profile*> is your user profile folder (which is Documents And Settings\<*user*> on most systems). When you select Outlook Template as the file type, Outlook automatically switches to your Templates folder.

You can create as many e-mail templates as you need, storing them on your local hard disk or on a network server. Placing templates on a network server allows other Outlook users to use them as well.

Using an E-Mail Template

After you create an e-mail template, it's a simple matter to use it to create a message, as detailed here:

1. In Outlook, click the arrow beside New on the Standard toolbar and click Choose Form. Alternatively, choose File, New, Choose Form. Outlook opens the Choose Form dialog box (see Figure 23-2).

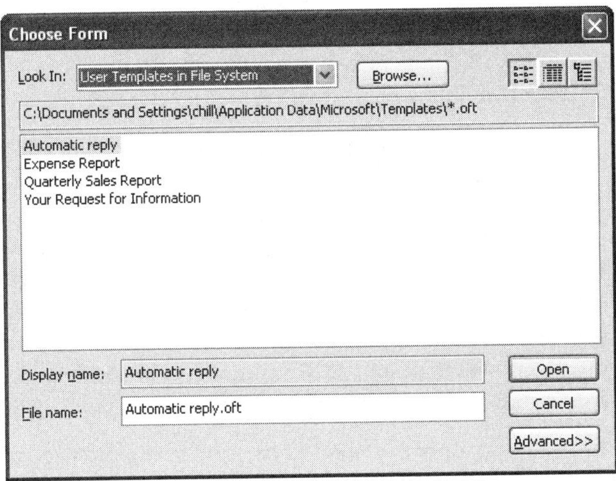

Figure 23-2. Select the template from the Choose Form dialog box.

2. In the Look In drop-down list, select the location where the template is stored.
3. Select the template from the list and click Open. This opens a message form based on the template data.
4. Fill out the message form to include any additional or modified information, and then send the message as you would any other.

Using a Template with a Distribution List

You can easily send messages to recipients in a distribution list without using a template: simply start a new message, select the distribution list from the address book, and send the message. If the messages you send to the members of the list are different each time you use it, you don't need a template. However, if the messages contain much the same information time after time, they're good candidates for templates. For example, you might need to submit weekly reports to a group of administrators or managers, send task lists to people who work for you, or broadcast regular updates about products or services.

You create a template for a distribution list the same way you create any other e-mail template. The only difference is that you store the list of recipients within the template. To do so, simply select the distribution list in the appropriate address box when you create the template. If you don't want the various members of the group to see the addresses of other members on the list, be sure to insert the distribution group in the Bcc box rather than in the To or Cc box.

For more information about working with distribution lists, see Chapter 5, "Managing Address Books and Distribution Lists."

Using Other Outlook Template Types

E-mail messages are not the only Outlook item you can create from a template. In fact, you can create a template for any type of Outlook item. This section of the chapter explores some common situations in which you might use specific types of templates.

Appointments and Meetings

You might find it useful to create templates for setting up certain types of appointments and meetings. If you prefer to use a set of appointment properties that differ from Outlook's default properties, you can use a template that contains your preferred settings and then create each new appointment or meeting from that template. For example, if you have regular meetings with the same group of people, you can set up a template in which those individuals are already selected on the Scheduling tab so that you don't have to assemble the list each time you schedule a meeting. Perhaps you prefer to have Outlook issue a reminder an hour before each appointment rather than the default of 15 minutes. Maybe the majority of your meetings are online meetings that use Microsoft NetMeeting and thus require a few specific settings.

You can create templates for appointments and meetings the same way you create e-mail templates. Open a new appointment form or meeting request and fill in all the data that will be standard each time you use the template. Then choose File, Save As and save the file as an Outlook template. When you want to use the template, choose File, New, Choose Form and follow the steps outlined earlier in "Using an E-Mail Template," page 629. You can also click the arrow beside the New button on the Standard toolbar and select Choose Form to select a form.

For more information about using appointment forms and their settings, see Chapter 19, "Scheduling Appointments." For details about meeting requests, see Chapter 20, "Scheduling Meetings and Resources."

Contacts

In your Contacts folder, you're likely to add contact entries for people who work in or belong to the same organization, business, department, or other entity. These contacts might share the same company name, address, or primary phone number. In such a case, why not create a template to save yourself the trouble of entering the information for each contact entry separately (and potentially getting it wrong)? Or, for example, you might use the same conferencing URL for all of your online meetings hosted by Windows Media Services. Why not create a template that specifies the URL, eliminating the chore of setting it each time you create a new contact?

As with other templates, you create a contact template by opening a new contact form and filling in the standard data. Then choose File, Save As and save the contact as an Outlook template.

For more information about creating contact entries and working in the Contacts folder, see Chapter 14, "Managing Your Contacts."

Tip **Create contacts from the same company**
You can create contact entries that share common company information by selecting a contact item and choosing Actions, New Contact From Same Company. However, this might not give you the results you need in all cases. For example, the New Contact From Same Company command uses the same address, company name, business phone number, business fax number, and Web page address for the new contact as for the selected one. If you also want to use the same directory server, categories, notes, or other properties for the new contacts, it's best to create a contact entry, save it as a template, and then create other contact entries from the template.

Tasks and Task Requests

If you perform the same task frequently, you can create a basic task as a template and then modify it as needed for each individual occurrence of the task. You also can create a task template with a specific set of properties and then use it to create various tasks. For example, you could create all your tasks with the status specified as In Progress rather than the default Not Started. Or perhaps you need to create many tasks with the same set of categories assigned to them.

In addition to creating task items from templates, you might also want to use templates to create task requests. A task request template is handy if you manage a group of people to whom you need to assign similar or identical tasks. Set up a template that incorporates the common elements and then create each task request from the template, filling in or modifying the unique elements, and addressing it to the specific person assigned to the task.

You use the same methods described earlier for e-mail templates to create and open templates for tasks and task requests.

For more information about creating tasks and task requests, see Chapter 21, "Managing Your Tasks."

Journal Entries

You can use the Outlook journal to keep track of activities such as phone calls, remote sessions, or other actions that you want to record. Why use journal templates? Any time you find yourself adding a manual journal entry for the same type of activity with the same or similar properties, consider creating a template for the action. Perhaps you frequently record journal entries for phone calls to a particular individual, account, or company that contain the same phone number or company name or log the same duration. Rather than creating a journal entry from scratch each time, create a template and use the template instead.

For more information about working with the Outlook journal, see Chapter 18, "Keeping a Journal."

Editing Templates

Outlook stores templates as OFT files when you save them to disk. You can modify any template to make changes as needed.

To modify a template, follow these steps:

1. Choose Tools, Forms, Choose Form.
2. Outlook displays the Choose Form dialog box (shown earlier in Figure 23-2). In the Look In drop-down list, select the location where the template is stored.
3. Select the template and click Open.
4. Make changes as needed and choose File, Save to save the changes.

> **Tip** To find templates you've created so you can edit them, choose User Templates In File System from the Look In drop-down list in the Choose Form dialog box and then browse to the folder where you saved the template.

Sharing Templates

In some situations, you might find it useful to share templates with other users. For example, assume that you're responsible for managing several people who all submit the same type of report to you on a regular basis through e-mail. In that situation, you might create an e-mail template with the appropriate boilerplate information and your address in the To box and then have the staff use that template to generate the reports. This ensures that everyone is providing comparable information. In addition, whenever you need a different set of data from these employees, you need only modify the template.

By default, Outlook stores your template files in the Application Data\Microsoft\Templates folder of your user profile. On a clean installation of Microsoft Windows 2000 or Windows XP, for example, this folder would be \Documents And Settings\<*user*>\Application Data\Microsoft\Templates, where <*user*> is your user name. On systems upgraded from Microsoft Windows NT Workstation, the folder would be located in \Winnt\Profiles\<*user*>\Application Data\Microsoft\Templates.

The easiest way to find the location where Outlook stores your templates is to save a template or at least go through the motions of saving it. Open a form, choose File, Save As, and then select User Templates In File System. Outlook displays the path to the folder just underneath the Look In drop-down list.

Why do you need to know where Outlook stores your templates? To share a template, you need to share the template file. This means placing the template in a shared network folder, sharing your template folder, or sending the template file to other users (the least desirable option). For any of these options, you need to know the location of the template file you want to share. After you locate the file, you can share the folder that contains it, copy the template to a network share, or forward it to other users as an attachment.

Inside Out

Sharing a template using a network share

The best option for sharing a template, in my opinion, is to create a network share and place the template in that share. Configure permissions for the share so that you have full control and other users have read-only access to the folder. This allows you to make changes to the template, while allowing others to use but not modify the template. If other users need to create and manage templates in the same folder, give all users the permissions necessary to create and modify files in the folder, then use file-level NTFS permissions for individual template files to control which users can modify them.

Chapter 24

Designing and Using Forms

Even without any custom programming, Microsoft Outlook 2003 provides an excellent set of features. In fact, many organizations don't need anything beyond what Outlook offers right out of the box. Others, however, have special needs that are not addressed adequately by Outlook—perhaps because of the way these organizations do business or because of specific requirements in their particular industries. In such cases, you have ample opportunity to extend the functionality of Outlook through custom design and programming.

For example, you might need to add some additional fields to your message forms or your meeting request forms. Perhaps you need an easier way for users to perform mail merge operations with Microsoft Word and Outlook contacts lists. Maybe you simply want to fine-tune your forms to add your company logo, special instructions, or warnings for users.

Whatever your situation, you can easily make changes to the existing Outlook forms, or you can even design new ones. The changes you make can be simple or complex: you might add one or two fields to the standard contact form, or you might add a considerable amount of program code to allow Outlook to perform custom tasks or interact with other Microsoft Office applications. This chapter starts you on the right path by explaining how Outlook uses forms and how you can customize them to suit your needs. If you aren't comfortable programming with Microsoft Visual Basic for Applications, don't worry—you can accomplish a lot with custom forms without ever writing a single line of program code.

Forms are such a normal part of everything we do on computers that we sometimes take them for granted. It's still true, however, that a lot of programs used all over the world can be accessed only with screens that provide monochrome text and puzzling menus with strange codes and submission sequences. With their versatility and ease of use, forms offer a revolutionary approach—and you can unlock their power with several mouse clicks and some solid planning. This chapter discusses the rationale for using Outlook forms as part of a software solution for individual computing needs. It also examines the types of forms you can modify and create and how the forms are created, published, and stored.

With Outlook, you can employ two basic strategies for form development. The first is to use or modify a standard form. The second is to create your own form from scratch. With either strategy, it's important to remember that you're programming events that are specifically associated with the item involved, not with the Outlook application generally. In other words, when you put code behind your form, you're dealing with events related to the item that's represented by the form. For example, if you were to design a form to create a custom e-mail message, you'd probably program a common event named *Item_Send*, which occurs when the item (the message) is sent.You couldn't program the form to respond to an event that fires (that is, occurs or executes) when the item is specifically shipped from the Outbox to another user's Inbox or when the user's view changes from one folder to another. This is because in form development you can access only the events associated with the item in question.

Overview of Standard Forms, Item Types, and Message Classes

Outlook uses a combination of forms, item types, and message classes as its fundamental components. Although you don't need to understand much about any of these three components to use Outlook, a developer must understand them reasonably well. Obviously, the more you know, the more powerful your Outlook-based solution will be.

Outlook Forms

Outlook provides numerous predefined forms that you can use as the foundation of your form-based solution. These standard forms include the following:

- Appointment form
- Contact form
- Journal entry form
- Meeting request form
- Message form
- Post form
- Task form
- Task request form

As this list of Outlook forms indicates, the basic item types available in a typical Outlook/ Microsoft Exchange application are each represented by a corresponding form.

Each of these forms comes with built-in user interface elements and corresponding functionality. For example, the appointment form, shown in Figure 24-1, has interface elements and functions that relate to setting appointments, such as generating reminders and controlling the calendar display. The contact form, in contrast, is designed to permit the addition or modification of contact information.

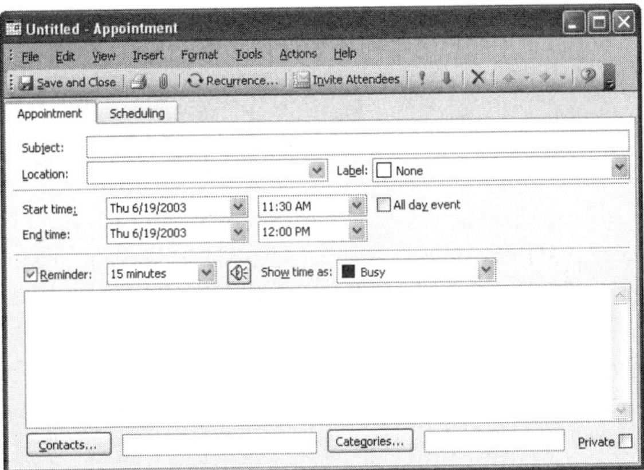

Figure 24-1. The appointment form is one of the numerous forms that Outlook provides.

Outlook Item Types

Several basic item types are part of an Outlook installation. These item types include the following:

- MailItem
- ContactItem
- TaskItem
- AppointmentItem
- PostItem
- NoteItem

Note Two other item types are also built into Outlook: JournalItem and DistributionListItem. This book does not cover these two types, but you can find information about them by consulting the Microsoft MSDN Web site at *http://msdn.microsoft.com/library/default.asp?URL=/library/officedev/vbaol10/olmscOutlookItemObjects.htm*.

These item types represent built-in functionality. If you have ever used Outlook to create an e-mail message or to add an appointment to your calendar, you have benefited from this functionality. Of particular importance, this functionality is accessible to you as you develop custom solutions with Outlook. Outlook provides corresponding forms for each of these item types, and these standard forms are designed with behaviors that directly relate to the item types they represent. You can extend the behaviors of these forms and leverage all the functions and properties of the item types, some of which are not exposed in the standard forms. In addition, you can reach beyond Outlook to incorporate the functionality of other Microsoft Office applications such as Microsoft Word, Microsoft Excel, Microsoft PowerPoint, Microsoft Project, Microsoft Visio, and any application or control that exposes a programmatic COM interface.

For a good overview of COM and COM+, take a look at *Understanding COM+* by David S. Platt (Microsoft Press, 1999).

Outlook Message Classes

Although forms and item types are the basic elements you need to understand to create a custom Outlook solution, it's helpful to know what a message class is and how it relates to Outlook form development. A message class represents to Outlook internally what an item type represents to a user or developer externally. In other words, when a user opens an e-mail message from the Inbox, that message is a MailItem. Internally, however, Outlook calls it by a different name, IPM.Note. IPM (interpersonal message) is a holdover from previous generations of Microsoft's messaging legacy. All messages in Outlook are representations of an IPM of some sort. A calendar item, for example, is an IPM.Appointment. The list of default message classes includes the following:

- IPM.Note
- IPM.Contact
- IPM.Appointment
- IPM.Task
- IPM.Post

Again, unless you're developing a fairly sophisticated collaborative solution, these message classes won't surface often. However, understanding what they mean to Outlook will help as you progress in your use of the program and in developing Outlook solutions.

Creating Custom Forms from Standard Forms

A standard form is a great point of departure for developing a custom solution. For example, have you ever sent an e-mail message with an attached document to someone and forgotten to include the attachment? In a large company, this rather common error could amount to hundreds, if not thousands, of extra e-mail messages being sent each day as users send follow-up messages containing the omitted attachments. By adding a small script to the standard mail message form, you can avoid this problem. You can programmatically assess whether an attachment has actually been added to the e-mail message and prompt the user to add one if needed.

To begin working with the standard forms, choose Tools, Forms. Then select Design A Form to display the Design Form dialog box, shown in Figure 24-2. You can simply select one of the standard forms listed in this dialog box and begin working with the form in design mode. Later sections in the chapter discuss how to save and publish the forms you modify or create.

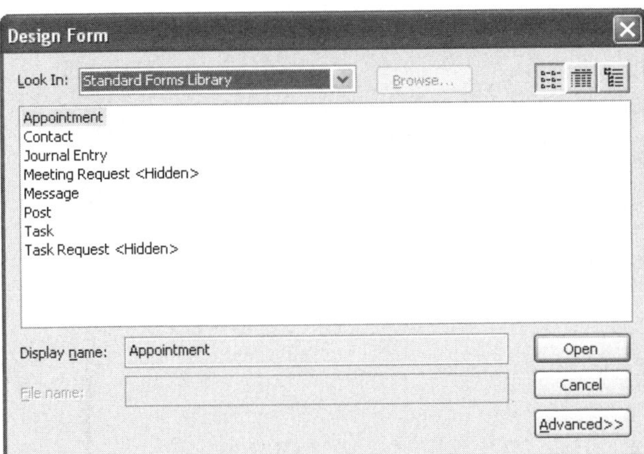

Figure 24-2. In the Design Form dialog box, you can choose the type of form you want to create.

> **Tip** **Avoid scripts when opening forms for design**
> When you choose to redesign an existing form, that form might have a script with event handlers that will fire when you open the form in design mode. Usually, however, you don't want to have code firing when you're trying to design a form. To keep this from happening, hold down the Shift key as you click the form to open it for design. The code will still be present and will run when you debug the form, but it will not run while you open, design, and save the form.

Compose vs. Read

Obviously, one of the most basic processes in Outlook is sending and receiving messages and documents. Although this is a fairly simple process, it requires a close look. In nearly all cases, the form a sender employs to compose an e-mail message is not the exact form that the receiver of that message uses to read the message. For example, although a user can edit the Subject field when composing a message, the recipient can't, under normal circumstances, edit the subject. This is because the standard forms have Compose and Read areas.

Figure 24-3 shows a message being composed; Figure 24-4 shows the same message after it has been received.

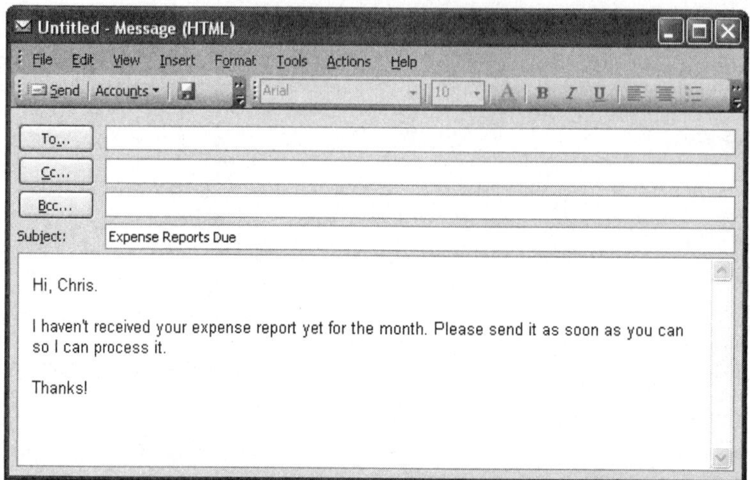

Figure 24-3. Compose a message using a standard message form.

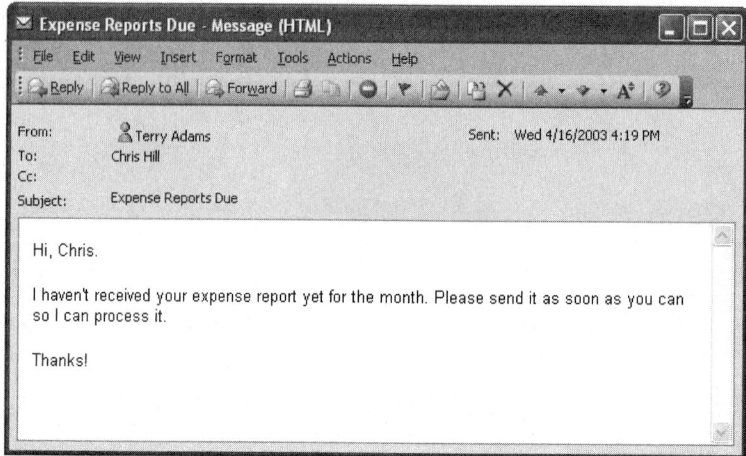

Figure 24-4. Here is the same message shown in Figure 24-3, after it has been received. Notice that some fields can no longer be modified.

Notice that some of the fields, such as Subject and To, can't be modified by the recipient in the Read version. It is, however, entirely possible to configure a form with identical Compose and Read areas. Whether this makes sense for your Outlook solution is up to you.

When you're working with a standard form in design mode, you can switch between the Compose and Read pages by clicking the Edit Compose Page and Edit Read Page buttons on the Form Design toolbar. In Figure 24-5, the Compose page of the standard message form is ready for editing. When you click Edit Read Page, the Read area of the form appears for editing, as shown in Figure 24-6.

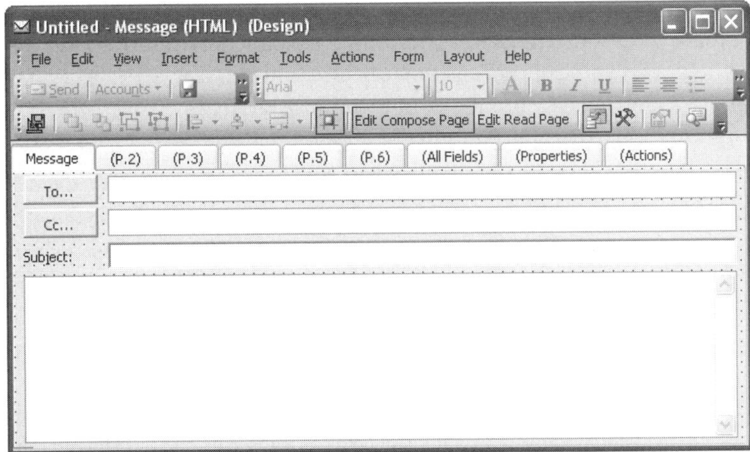

Figure 24-5. This standard Compose area is ready for editing.

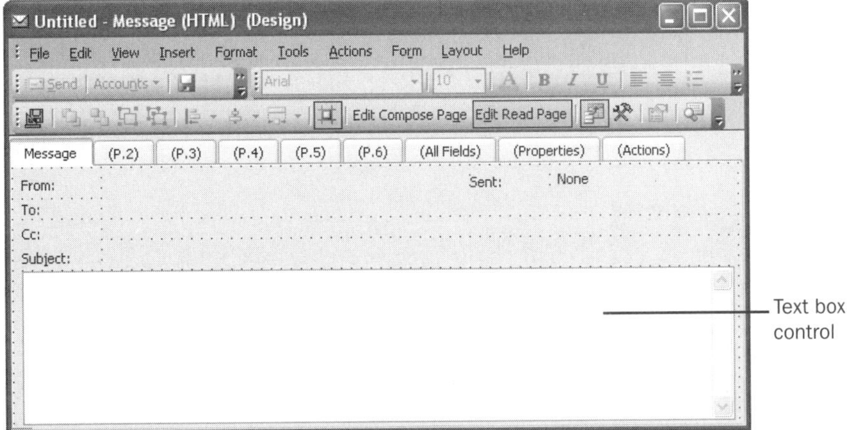

Figure 24-6. The Read area for a message item looks similar to the Compose area.

Because this is a standard form, a number of controls are already on the form. For example, the text box control for the body of the message is the largest element on the form. This control is bound to an Outlook field. The following section examines fields and what they mean to an Outlook solution; working with controls is discussed later in the chapter.

Outlook Fields

An Outlook field represents a discrete unit of information that is intelligible to Outlook, such as the Bcc and To fields in an e-mail message. You don't need to tell Outlook that e-mail messages have these fields—they are already included in the standard form. Outlook provides a number of fields that you can use, and you can also add new fields. In theory, an unlimited number of fields are available, but the most common practice is to use a generous number of the built-in fields and a judicious number of new, user-defined properties. For now, the discussion focuses on the fields already available to you.

Because it provides so many built-in fields, Outlook groups them to make it easier to find the ones you need. For example, some fields, such as To, From, Subject, Importance, Expires, Due By, Created, Size, and Attachment, are particular to e-mail messages. Other fields, such as City, Children, and Birthday, are associated with Outlook contacts. You can, however, use fields from different logical areas to suit your needs on any form you're designing—for example, Outlook doesn't prevent you from adding a Birthday field to an e-mail form.

You can also find more information on user-defined fields at Microsoft's support site at *http://support.microsoft.com*. See article ID number 290656.

When you work with a form, you can view the available fields in the Field Chooser dialog box, shown in Figure 24-7. To display this dialog box, click the button to the right of the Edit Read Page toolbar button; clicking this button shows or hides the Field Chooser. In the Field Chooser, the fields are organized by categories and displayed in a list. You can choose a category in the drop-down list and then search in the body of the Field Chooser for the fields you need.

Figure 24-7. The Field Chooser dialog box allows you to view and choose the fields available for use.

Item Types and Fields

The scrollable list of fields shown in the Field Chooser dialog box in Figure 24-7 contains all the fields available for a form published in a certain folder. The standard item types come with a number of fields already defined. For example, a mail message comes with To, Subject, Body, and Sent fields already defined. Although you have the full battery of fields available as you modify or create a form, you can speed your development time and decrease your effort by carefully selecting the standard form that most closely corresponds to the solution you're developing. This way, you can leverage as many built-in fields as possible. Later in the chapter, you'll learn how to represent these fields on your form using controls; see "Adding and Arranging Controls," page 644.

Creating Custom Forms from Scratch

Working with standard forms is great if you want to build a solution that is directly related to one of the Outlook item types. However, you might need an Outlook form that isn't based on an item type at all. For example, you might want to create a form that allows users to report their work hours or initiate a purchase order. Although you could base these examples on a standard form, they could just as easily require a completely new form, which you need to create.

The good news is that creating a completely new form sounds like more work than it actually is. In fact, Outlook doesn't really permit you to create forms completely from scratch, although you can certainly achieve the same effect.You have two ways to create a form that doesn't contain any built-in form elements:

- Modify a standard form by deleting all built-in interface elements from the form and adding your own.
- Modify a standard form by hiding the page that contains built-in interface elements and showing a new page that contains elements that you add.

You'll learn how to add pages to forms in the next section. First let's look at how to break down a standard form to a blank form by removing built-in interface controls.

The following steps show how to turn a standard post form into a blank form:

1. Choose Tools, Forms.
2. Select Design A Form.
3. Select the post form and click Open. The form opens in design mode with the Message page selected.
4. Click each control (TextBox, Label, Button, and so on) on the Message page and delete it.
5. With the Message page still selected, choose Form, Rename Page.
6. Type a new name in the dialog box, and click OK.

The form now looks like the form shown earlier in Figure 24-6. The figure shows a modified Compose area for this form, but you can also modify the Read area. Of course, you'll also want to make these pages do something, but for now you at least have a blank form to work with.

Creating Multipage Forms

A multipage form allows you to fit a great deal of information on one form while also reducing confusion for the user. For example, you could create a form on which employees could both report their time for the week and report any expenses for which they need reimbursement. By using two pages, one form can serve both needs.

Any form can be a multipage form; all possible pages are already on the form you create or modify. However, these pages are not automatically visible. If you look closely at the names on the page tabs shown previously in Figure 24-6, you'll see that, except for the first name in the list, the name of each page is enclosed in parentheses, indicating that the page is not visible. To change the Visible property of a page, click its tab and then choose Form, Display This Page.

> **Tip** You can make all pages visible, but you cannot make all pages invisible. If you try to do so, Outlook tells you that at least one page must be visible on the form.

The first (default) page of a form, which is initially visible, has Compose and Read capabilities already available, as mentioned earlier. The additional pages on a form, which are initially invisible, don't have these capabilities until you add them. To do so, select one of these pages and choose Form, Separate Read Layout, which activates the Edit Compose Page and Edit Read Page command bar buttons.

Adding and Arranging Controls

The real power of forms comes from the controls you place on them. To construct a truly robust Outlook forms solution, you need to carefully plan what the form is supposed to do; what pieces of information it will display, modify, save, or send; which controls will display these information units; and how the controls will be laid out. You can put two types of controls on a form: a control bound to an Outlook field and a control that is not bound. This section looks first at field-bound controls.

As mentioned earlier, Outlook fields represent units of information. They are also bound to specific control types, such as drop-down lists, text boxes, command buttons, labels, or check boxes.

To represent a field on your form, follow these steps:

1. Display the Field Chooser and select a field category in the drop-down list.
2. From the scrollable list in the Field Chooser, drag a field onto the form.
3. Format the control as needed.

Tip **Work with the users of the form**

You can place any number of controls on a form, but it's a good idea to plan your form with an eye toward usability. Work closely with those individuals who will be using the form to ensure that it corresponds to their real needs. Find out how the users want the forms to be laid out, and listen to their suggestions about how the information should flow. No matter how much work you put into your solution, it won't be useful unless the users embrace it.

You can resize, move, or rename a control, and you can change a number of its properties. To resize the control, select the control (by clicking it) and place your pointer over one of the control handlers, which are represented by small boxes. When a small arrow appears, you can drag the handlers in the appropriate direction to resize the control.

To move a control to a new location, simply drag it. Notice that the form canvas is covered with a grid. Each point on the grid is a possible location for a corner or other relevant point on a control. You can define the distances between the points on this grid. This is important, because the greater the scale of the grid (the greater the distance between points on the grid), the fewer places you can locate a control on your form. Conversely, the smaller the scale, the more you can refine the positioning of your controls.

To change the grid, follow these steps:

1. Choose Form, Set Grid Size.
2. Type a number for the height and width spacing.
3. Click OK.

The smaller the number you use for spacing, the smaller the scale. This means that more points on the grid will appear, and you can have more control over where your objects fit on the grid. The default is 8, but 3 is a good number to choose for greater positioning control.

Inside Out

Limiting controls on your forms

When you're using controls on forms, you can be tempted to make one form do too much. Although there's no precise limit for the number of controls that can be included on one form, the recommendation is using fewer than 300. However, experience with custom forms development suggests that even 200 is excessive. You should try to keep the number of controls down to a few dozen or so when possible. Forms that try to do too much usually become confusing to users, and they often do not perform as well. Keeping your forms focused and giving them a crisp design make them easier to code and debug, too. If you find that your form is overloaded, consider creating a COM add-in to allow a broader application context.

Properties

Controls have a number of properties that you can view and modify. To find out what these properties are, right-click a control and choose Properties from the shortcut menu to display the Properties dialog box. Figure 24-8 shows a Properties dialog box for a text box control.

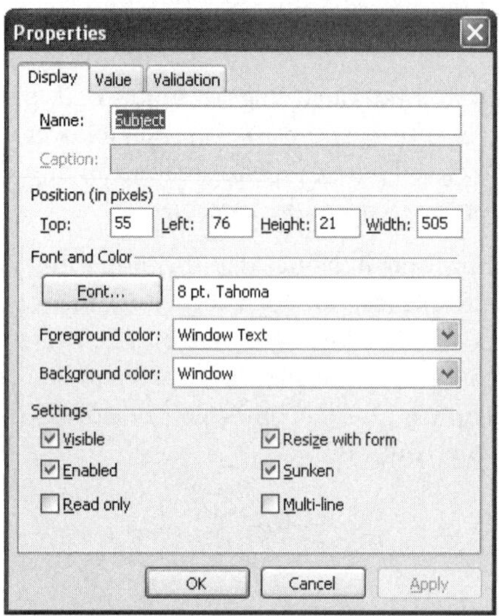

Figure 24-8. You can use the Properties dialog box to modify the properties of a control.

Display

The Display tab of a control's Properties dialog box (refer to Figure 24-8, for example) shows the most commonly used properties of the particular control. Changing the setting of a property in this dialog box enables the Apply button; clicking Apply or OK sets the value of that property for the selected control.

> **Tip** If you're unsure about the purpose of a property shown in the Properties dialog box, click the question mark button at the top of the dialog box, and then click the property to display a brief description of it.

The default names of controls are rather generic, such as TextBox1 or CheckBox1. You'll want to change these to names that are more descriptive for your solution, such as txtFirstName or chkHasVacation.

> **You can learn more about naming conventions for controls by visiting Microsoft's MSDN Web site at *http://msdn.microsoft.com/library/default.asp?URL=/library/devprods/vs6/vbasic/vbcon98/vbconcodingconventionsoverview.htm*.**

Value

The Value tab of the Properties dialog box contains a number of settings that relate to the field value that the control represents. As mentioned, each control in the Field Chooser list is bound to an Outlook field. When you modify the properties of a control, you can change the field to which that control is bound.

To change the bound-field property, click Choose Field and select the field to which you want to bind the control from the drop-down list. Make sure that the field value is bound to the correct property of your control. Normally, the field value is tied to the control's Value property; this is rarely changed. However, you can change this setting so that, for example, the value of a field is tied to your control's Enabled property. In this case, if the value of the field is True, the control is enabled; if the value is False, the control is not enabled.

You can also set the initial value of your control to display a default value. Select the Initial Value check box, and then type an initial value in the text box. This value doesn't have to be a predetermined one—you can have it correspond to a dynamic value, such as the current day or the concatenation of Subject field and the current date. To make the initial value more dynamic, click Edit to open the dialog box shown in Figure 24-9.

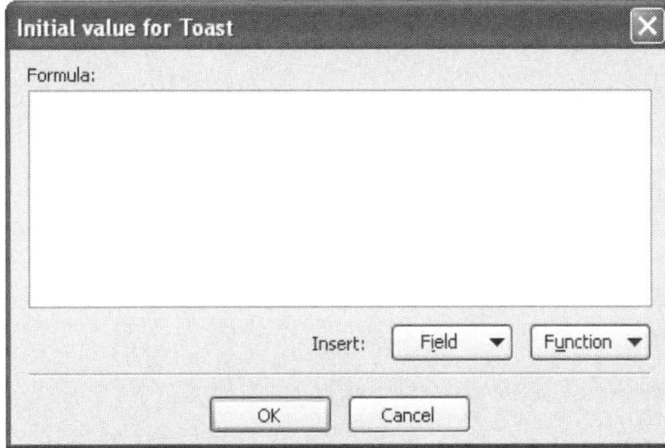

Figure 24-9. Use this dialog box to customize the initial value for a control.

In this dialog box, you establish a formula for the initial value of your control. For example, you can simply insert a built-in function, such as Date( ), for the formula.

To insert a built-in function—the Date( ) function, in this example—follow these steps:

1. Click the Function button.
2. Choose Data/Time, Date( ).
3. Verify that this function appears in the Formula text box.
4. Click OK, and then click OK to close the Properties dialog box.

When the form is run, the text box control you created will contain the current date as its value. This does not mean, however, that you can't change the value of the text box.

Validation

The Validation tab of the Properties dialog box allows you to set certain properties that relate to how (or whether) the value of the control is validated. For example, if you create a form for a purchase order, you might want to ensure that users indicate the quantity of parts they want to order. The order processing department will send you many thanks for requiring certain values before the purchase order gets to them, as it reduces the amount of information traffic and busy work needed to process an order.

Suppose that you've added a control to your form that requires a value for a text box, and that value is required to be less than or equal to 10 characters. If the user fails to enter a valid value, Outlook will display a message that prompts the user to enter a correct value.

To set the properties on the Validation tab that will be necessary for this example, follow these steps:

1. Display the Properties dialog box, and click the Validation tab.
2. Select the A Value Is Required For This Field check box.
3. Select the Validate This Field Before Closing The Form check box.
4. Click Edit (to the right of the Validation Formula text box).
5. Click Function.
6. Choose Text, Len(string) and confirm that the formula text box contains the Len(string) function.
7. After the text of this function, type **<=10** in the Formula text box.
8. Click OK.
9. In the Display This Message If The Validation Fails box, type the following text (including the quotation marks):

   "Please enter a value between 1 and 10 characters."
10. Click OK to close the Properties dialog box.

When a user works with your form, the text box for which this validation has been defined must contain a value, and the value must be less than or equal to 10 characters. If the value the user enters is 11 characters or more, Outlook will display a message box containing the validation text you provided when the user tries to send the form. The user can then make the appropriate changes to the text box value and attempt to resend the form.

Standard Controls

This chapter has thus far concentrated on controls that are bound to Outlook fields and that appear in the Field Chooser. However, these aren't the only controls you can add to a form. In fact, you can use a virtually unlimited number of controls. A thorough discussion of the nature of these controls is beyond the scope of this book, but this section takes a brief look at some of the standard controls as well as a control that comes as part of Office installation on your computer.

Controls appear on a Controls Toolbox, which is a small, resizable window made visible when you click the button just to the right of the Field Chooser toolbar button on the form. Figure 24-10 shows the Toolbox.

Figure 24-10. The Controls Toolbox allows you to add controls to your form.

As the pointer hovers over the control icons in the Toolbox, the name of each control appears. To add one of these controls to your form, simply drag the control icon onto the form. You can then resize and reposition the control or set its properties, as discussed earlier.

Refer to *Programming Microsoft Outlook and Microsoft Exchange, Second Edition,* by Thomas Rizzo (Microsoft Press, 2000), to learn more about the properties, methods, events, and possible uses of the standard controls.

These standard controls are useful but limited. As your skills in developing Outlook-based solutions progress, you'll find that you need functionality that transcends the abilities of the standard controls provided in the Toolbox. Fortunately, other controls are available and also accessible via the Toolbox window. For example, you can add an Excel PivotTable control to a form.

Follow these steps to add the PivotTable control to the Toolbox:

1. Right-click an empty area of the Toolbox window.
2. Choose Custom Controls.
3. Scroll down the Available Controls list and click the box next to the Microsoft Office PivotTable 10.
4. Click OK.

You can now add this control to a form and work with its specific properties and behaviors just as you did for the standard controls.

Custom controls can make your Outlook solution extremely robust and powerful. However, be aware that the control you're using might not exist on the computer of the person receiving the message. In other words, although you might have the PivotTable control on your computer, the person who uses your form to compose a message or receives a message composed on your form might not have the PivotTable control installed. For your solution to work well, you need to make sure that the custom controls you use are properly distributed and installed on other users' computers.

> **Note** Methods of distributing custom controls vary widely. Some controls come without an installing package, many use Microsoft Installer, and others use a third-party installation mechanism. You should read the documentation that accompanies your custom control or consult the manufacturer to determine the best method for distributing your control.

After creating your form, you can test it to see what it looks like when it is run. With the new form open, choose Form, Run This Form. This won't cause the form to close or disappear. Instead, Outlook produces a new form based on the form you've just created. The newly created form is an actual running form that you can send and read.

Adding Graphics to Forms

Although developing solutions in Outlook can require much thought and effort, users might not necessarily share your enthusiasm and excitement about the forms you've created. One way to increase acceptance and usability is to add some pleasing graphics to the forms. These graphics can come in a variety of formats, such as JPG, GIF, WMF, EMF, and ICO.

One way to add a graphic to your form is to use the image control from the Control Toolbox. Initially, the control will appear as a gray square. You can resize it, just as you can resize any of the standard controls, although it's a good idea to place the picture in the control before you resize it. Set the picture source for the image control by using the Advanced Properties dialog box, shown in Figure 24-11.

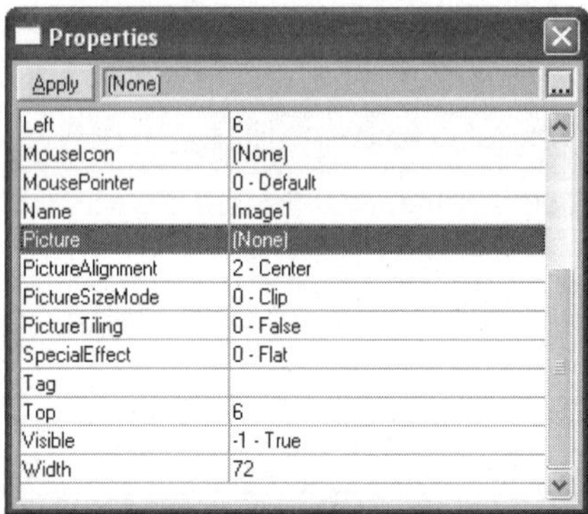

Figure 24-11. Use the Advanced Properties dialog box to select a picture to insert into the image control.

Follow these steps to insert a picture in your control:

1. Right-click the image control.
2. Choose Advanced Properties.
3. In the list of properties, scroll down to the Picture property.
4. To the far right of the Apply button, click the small button that displays ellipses points (...).

5 Use the Load Picture dialog box to navigate to the picture you want to appear in the image control, and then click Open.

6 Close the Advanced Properties dialog box and verify that the control now contains the picture you chose.

Tip **Change the source of your images at run time**
As is the case with all the controls you use on a custom form, you can change the values of many of their properties when the form is running. For example, you can create a form with an image that changes based on certain criteria. You can add code to your form that alters the setting of the control's Picture property and thus loads an image into the control that is different from the image you specified at design time.

Another way to make your forms more attractive and usable is to add an icon to buttons on the forms. You can configure the command button available in the Toolbox to display both a text caption and a graphic. For example, if your button sends a custom message to a recipient when clicked, you could add an envelope image to the button to convey the notion of sending a message. To have the button display an image, set the Picture property for the button just as you would for an image control. You can also set the Picture property for other controls, such as text boxes and labels.

In addition, you can display a custom icon in the form's title bar. Outlook always displays a default icon in the upper left corner of a form, indicating whether it is a task form, an appointment form, and so on. You can change this icon by clicking the Properties tab of your form when you're working in design mode. Click Change Large Icon or Change Small Icon and navigate to the ICO file you want to use. The Large Icon setting tells Outlook which image to display when a user displays the properties of the form. The Small Icon setting specifies the title bar image and the image that is shown when the form is displayed in an Outlook folder.

Using Office Documents to Create Outlook Forms

If you have installed Outlook, you probably also have Word, Excel, and PowerPoint installed. These other programs provide an even more powerful Outlook form solution: you can use documents, spreadsheets, and slide presentations as the form of a message. For example, suppose that you created a form that required a user to enter several values and send the form to someone else. The recipient then has to type those values into an Excel spreadsheet. Wouldn't it make more sense to have the first user type the values directly into the spreadsheet at the outset? If your company already uses an Excel spreadsheet for expense reimbursements, you can leverage this by letting employees use the spreadsheet as they always have—the only difference is that each employee will now set a recipient or a public folder as the spreadsheet's destination.

Although you could have the users open the document, make changes, and then choose File, Send To, Mail Recipient to mail the document, you might prefer to incorporate the document into a standard form. For example, perhaps you want to broadcast an Excel spreadsheet to a group of users to show sales status or other data. You can create a standard message form but in place of (or in addition to) the message body, add an Excel custom control that pulls the spreadsheet data from a server, updating the data when the user opens the form from his or her Inbox.

Covering this type of form development falls outside the scope of this chapter, but you might only need a nudge in the right direction to begin adding these custom controls to your own forms.

Here's how:

1. In Outlook, choose Tools, Forms, Design A Form to open the Design Form dialog box.
2. Select Message in the Standard Forms Library and click Open.
3. Resize the message body control to make room for the spreadsheet control.
4. Right-click the Controls Toolbox and choose Custom Controls to open the Additional Controls dialog box.
5. Scroll through the Available Controls list to locate and select the Microsoft Office Spreadsheet 11.0 control. Then click OK to add it to the Controls Toolbox.
6. Click the Spreadsheet control in the Controls Toolbox and drag it to your form. Figure 24-12 shows a Spreadsheet control added to a message form.

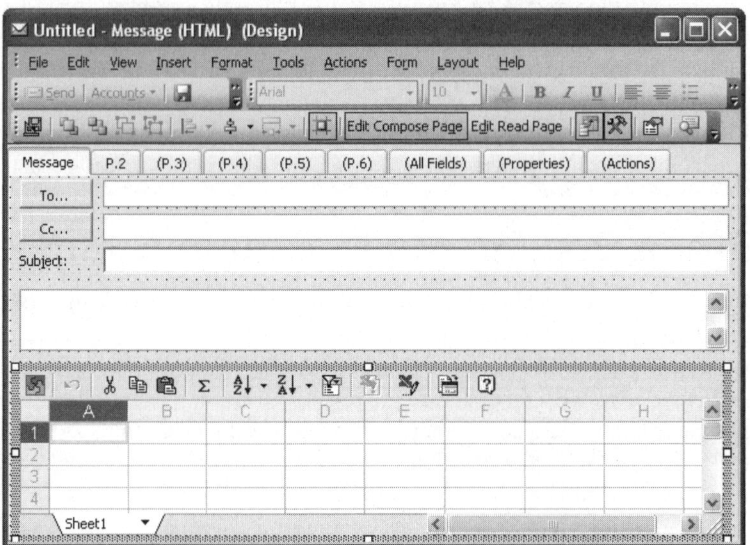

Figure 24-12. You can add custom Office controls to a form to publish or accept data input.

7. Resize the Spreadsheet control to fit the form as needed, then right-click the toolbar portion of the control and choose Advanced Properties.
8. Use the properties in the control's Properties dialog box to specify the data location and other properties to define the data.

9 Make other design changes as needed to the form and then save or publish the form.

If you browse through the Additional Controls dialog box you'll find a wide range of additional controls you can add to your forms. You can add charts, PivotTables, database forms, and many other controls to create powerful and useful forms.

Publishing and Sharing Forms

After you create your form and define its behaviors, properties, and settings, you'll want to make it available to users. First, however, you'll need to preserve your form in one of these two ways:

- Publish the form to a folder or other location.
- Save the form as a file.

Publishing Forms

Believe it or not, you don't need to explicitly save a form to retain it, allow it to be used, and make it available for later modification. This is contrary to the lesson you've learned from having to rewrite so many unsaved documents that you lost after power outages. However, publishing a form is a lot like saving the form. When you finish your form, you can publish it to a specific folder location. You can publish it to your Inbox or another folder in your mailbox, a public folder, or your Personal Forms Library.

Follow these steps to publish a form to a folder or forms library:

1. Choose Tools, Forms, Publish Form to open the Publish Form As dialog box.
2. In the Look In drop-down list, choose the folder or forms library where you want to publish the form.
3. Specify the display name and the form name.
4. Click Publish to close the dialog box.

Tip **Create a staging area for your forms**
When you're creating a form, it's a good idea to keep the production version of the form separate from the development version. Create a special production folder where you publish the forms you're working on. When you complete a form design, publish the form in this staging folder at least occasionally so you don't lose the modifications you've made to the form. Restrict your staging folder access to those who are designing forms for your organization.

After you publish a form, the folder in which you publish it contains the form itself and all the underlying information that another person's instance of Outlook needs to understand the form.

Note If you are using a version of Exchange Server earlier than Microsoft Exchange 2000 Server, you can usually publish your form to the Organizational Forms Library. For information on this, see *http://msdn.microsoft.com/library/default.asp?url=/library/en-us/off2000/html/rehowSaveFormIntoFormsLibraryPublishFormAs.asp*. You can also visit the link *http://www.microsoft.com/Exchange/en/55/help/default.asp?url=/Exchange/en/55/help/documents/server/XGS06010.HTM*. For information about using this forms library with Exchange 2000 Server, see Knowledge Base article ID 271816.

Publishing Forms Programmatically

You can also publish a form by using code. This technique can be helpful if you're creating custom forms with code and want to publish them to either a public folder or a personal folders file. The following code shows how to create a custom form and publish it when a user clicks a button on an Outlook form:

```
Dim objNS
Dim objFolder
Dim objItem
Dim objNewForm

Sub cmdCreateNewTaskForm_Click()
  Set objNS = Item.Application.GetNamespace("MAPI")
  Set objFolder = objNS.GetDefaultFolder(13)  'Publishes to Tasks
  Set objItem = Application.CreateItem(3)     'Creates a TaskItem
  Set objNewForm = objItem.FormDescription    'Get the task form
  objNewForm.Name = "Our New Form"            'Customize the
                                              'form name
  objNewForm.DisplayName = "New Form Display" 'Customize display

  objNewForm.PublishForm 4, objFolder         'Publish the form

End Sub
```

In the last line of this sample code, the constant 4 causes the form to be published to the organizational forms library. If you don't have an organizational forms library, you will receive an error when the code executes. You can use a different value to change the location to which the form is published. For example, a value of 0 publishes the form to the default location. Refer to *http://support.microsoft.com/support/kb/articles/q285/2/02.asp* for more information on other constants you can use to specify the location for publishing the form.

Sharing Forms in Public Folders

The best way to make your form available to others is to publish it in a public folder (assuming that Outlook is being used with Exchange Server). When you do this, users who connect to that public folder will have access to your form and will be able to use it just as if they had created and saved it on their own computers. Outlook takes care of all the underlying work with form definitions, so you won't need to do anything special to make sure that another user's instance of Outlook can understand the definitions.

For detailed information on using public folders in Exchange Server, see Chapter 38, "Sharing Information with Others."

If you aren't sure whether the intended users of your form will have access to the form definition where it's published, you'll want to save the form definition and make it available to these target users. Saving a form means saving the definition of the form as a file in a file system directory. Thus, while publishing a form doesn't allow a user to use the file system search tools to search for the form, saving the form does make this possible. Forms saved to a local disk have an OFT extension. There is nothing terribly mysterious about this file—it's just another file that is comprehensible to Outlook, just as a DOC file is intelligible to Word. You can even send your form definition to others as a mail attachment, and they'll be able to open the form and use it as if it were published.

Saving a form definition does make the form harder to maintain, however. If you save the form as a file with an OFT extension, distribute it to a large number of users, and then make a change to the form, all users of the form need to receive the updated file. Publishing the form to a public folder prevents this confusion. In that case, after you modify the form, you republish the form in the folder. The next time a user opens the form, he or she will be the beneficiary of the latest modifications.

Troubleshooting

Users can't access your custom form

After you've completed and published your custom form, you might hear from a user who reports receiving this message when trying to access the form: "The custom form could not be opened, and Outlook will use an Outlook form instead. The object could not be found." You should first make sure that your form is properly published. If the form is not published so that Outlook can find it, or if an OFT file is not available, Outlook won't be able to open the file.

Sometimes, however, Outlook reports this error even when the form is available. The cause might be corruption in a file named Frmcache.dat. The Frmcache.dat file contains information that Outlook uses to prevent multiple instances of the same form from being loaded. Outlook checks the cache to see whether a form using the same message class name is in the cache before attempting to display a form. Outlook copies the form definition to the cache if it does not exist, or it loads the definition already in the cache, and then displays the form. In addition, if a change has been made to a form, Outlook copies the new form definition to the cache. The file is located at Documents And Settings\<*profile name*>\Local Settings\Application Data\Microsoft\Forms on a computer running Windows 2000 or Windows XP or at Windows\Forms on computers running earlier versions of Windows.

If this file is indeed corrupted, reinstalling Outlook can solve the problem, but there is a simpler way. You could try closing Outlook and deleting the Frmcache.dat. Or, you can locate an instance of Outlook that does display the form properly and copy that profile's instance of Frmcache.dat to the profile of the offending instance, thus overwriting the file.

Publishing to local folders or to the Personal Forms Library is perfectly acceptable, but you might find that many of your solutions are destined for a wider audience, which, in an Exchange Server environment, can be reached only through public folders.

For More Information on VBScript and Outlook

This chapter has presented a brief introduction to programming Outlook solutions. Because the skills you acquire as you learn to use and extend Outlook will pay off for a long time, you'll undoubtedly want to deepen your understanding. There are numerous additional sources you can consult to do so.

Microsoft supplies a copious amount of documentation about Outlook and about building collaborative solutions around Outlook. The online documentation for Outlook and the Microsoft Office Developer Documentation are probably the best in the industry for any product. Although the MSDN Web site (*http://msdn.microsoft.com*) has an overwhelming but well-organized body of documentation, you might want to consider purchasing Microsoft Office Developer as well. Microsoft Office Developer not only offers more documentation than MSDN but also contains extremely useful code samples and other materials.

Some terrific magazines target developers of Outlook and Microsoft Office. DevX (*http://www.devx.com*) puts out a monthly periodical called *Exchange & Outlook* that covers a wide variety of topics for both the neophyte and the enterprise developer. Advisor (*http://www.advisor.com*) provides the Microsoft Exchange Outlook Advisor Zone. Informant Communications Group publishes *Microsoft OfficePRO* magazine (*http://www.msofficepro.com*), which is designed for the Office developer but features articles of great use to the Outlook developer. Informant also sponsors the Microsoft Office Deployment and Development Conference each year, a great place to meet other like-minded developers and gain in-depth exposure to the most significant technologies to emerge in the Office development arena.

The *Microsoft Office XP Resource Kit* and a wide selection of Microsoft Press books can aid you in learning about VBScript, Microsoft Office, and Microsoft Exchange development. Visit the Microsoft Press Web site (*http://mspress.microsoft.com*) to find the latest releases that discuss the most current technologies.

Chapter 25

Customizing the Outlook Interface

Microsoft Outlook 2003 has a useful interface that serves most users well right out of the box. However, you probably perform certain tasks that are not readily available through the standard Outlook interface. For example, perhaps you use remote mail frequently and want quick access to the remote mail functions rather than scrolling through menus to find them.

As all Microsoft Office applications do, Outlook provides a way to tailor the interface to your needs. You can customize the Navigation Pane to add your own shortcuts, customize Outlook Today view and other standard views, and customize the way Outlook displays your folders. You can also create custom command bars.

This chapter focuses on the various ways you can fine-tune Outlook to the way you work. Some of the changes covered are minor; others are more significant. All of them can enhance your experience with Outlook and make it a more useful tool for bringing efficiency to your work day.

Customizing the Navigation Pane

Most people navigate through Outlook folders using the Navigation Pane. This section explains how you can customize the Navigation Pane to suit your preferences.

A Quick Tour of the Navigation Pane

The Navigation Pane, which appears on the left side of the Outlook window, replaces the Outlook Bar that was a staple of the Outlook interface in previous versions. The Outlook development team has attempted to streamline the interface by removing many of the items previously found on the Outlook Bar.

The Navigation Pane contains buttons that serve as shortcuts to your Outlook folders (see Figure 25-1). The Navigation Pane also includes shortcuts to a few common items, including the Outlook Today view and the Outlook Update Web site.

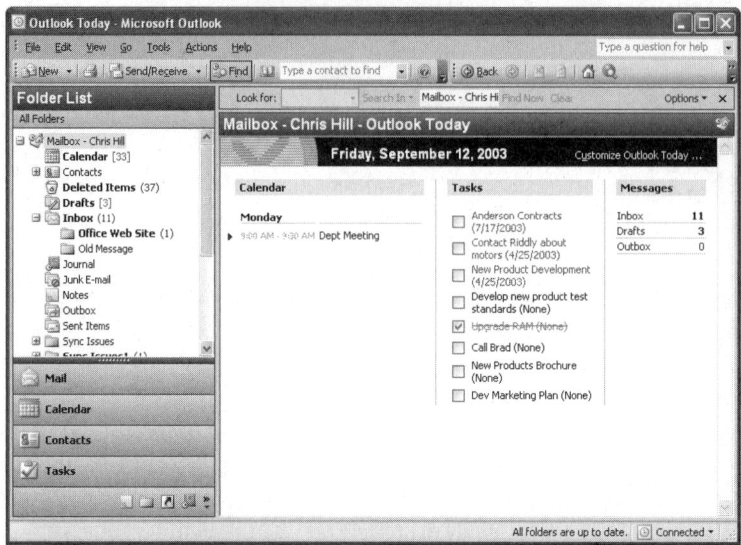

Figure 25-1. The Navigation Pane provides shortcuts to Outlook folders and other objects.

You can make several changes to the Navigation Pane, including adding and removing groups, adding and removing shortcuts, and changing the appearance of its icons. The following sections explain these changes.

Tip You can change the width of the Navigation Pane by dragging its border.

Showing and Hiding the Navigation Pane

If you use the Navigation Pane often, you'll probably want it to remain open all the time, but if you work with a particular Outlook folder most of the time, you might prefer to have the additional space for your favorite folder view or Reading Pane. To that end, Outlook allows you to hide and display the Navigation Pane as needed. Choose View, Navigation Pane to turn the Navigation Pane on and off.

Tip Press Alt+F1 to quickly show or hide the Navigation Pane.

Changing the Number of Buttons on the Navigation Pane

Outlook can display up to eight buttons on the bottom portion of the Navigation Pane, and these include a button for each of the standard Outlook folders, the Folder List, and the Shortcuts. The number of buttons displayed depends on the size of the Outlook window. If you need more space for the Folder List, for example, you can simply drag the bar above the Mail icon to resize the lower portion of the Navigation Pane, which changes the number of buttons shown. You can show or hide buttons by clicking the double arrow at the bottom of the Navigation Pane and choosing Show More Buttons or Show Fewer Buttons (see Figure 25-2).

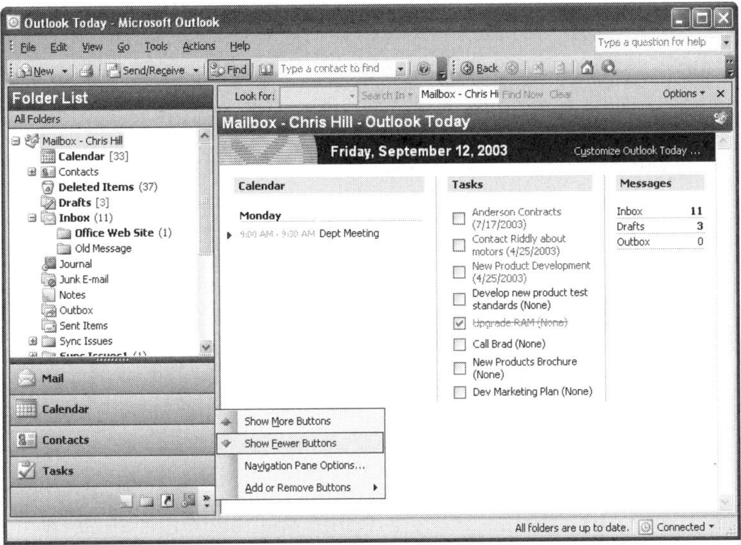

Figure 25-2. Use this menu to show or hide buttons.

Outlook does not by default show all of the available buttons on the Navigation Pane. For example, the Journal doesn't appear by default in the Navigation Pane. To add or remove buttons, click Configure Buttons (the double arrow) at the bottom of the Navigation Pane, click Add Or Remove Buttons, and select the button you want to add or remove.

> **Tip** If you want to add or remove more than one folder, right-click a folder icon on the Navigation Pane and choose Navigation Pane Options to open a dialog box you can use to add and remove buttons.

Adding a Shortcut to an Outlook or Public Folder

The Navigation Pane includes buttons for each of the common Outlook folders, and the Folder List provides quick access to all other Outlook folders and public folders (Microsoft Exchange Server only). You can easily add shortcuts to any folder by following these steps:

1. Click the Shortcuts button at the bottom of the Navigation Pane to open the Shortcuts pane.
2. Click Add New Shortcut to open the Add To Navigation Pane dialog box (see Figure 25-3).

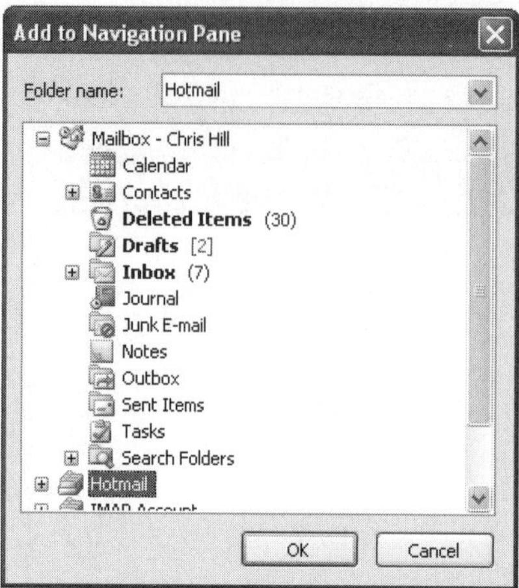

Figure 25-3. Select the folder for which you want to add a shortcut.

3. Select a folder from the list and click OK. Outlook adds the shortcut to the Shortcuts group.
4. Drag the shortcut to a different group, if desired.

Adding a File Folder or Document to the Navigation Pane

You can create shortcuts to file system folders or Outlook folders and add them to existing Navigation Pane groups or to new groups that you create. For example, if you use a particular document folder often, you might want to add that folder to one of your Navigation Pane shortcut groups.

The process is similar, regardless of the type of shortcut you're adding:

1. Open Outlook, and open the group in which you want to create the shortcut.
2. Click the Shortcuts button on the Navigation Pane to open the Shortcuts pane.
3. In Windows, open the folder containing the folder or file for which you want to create a shortcut; then position the folder and Outlook so you can see both (see Figure 25-4).
4. Drag the folder or document from the folder window and release it on the shortcut group name where you want it added.

> **Tip** **Create shortcuts to network shares you use often**
> You can specify Universal Naming Convention (UNC) paths in addition to mapped drives. A UNC path takes the form *<server>**<share>*, where *<server>* is the computer sharing the folder and *<share>* is the folder's share name. On systems running Microsoft Windows 2000 or Microsoft Windows XP, you can specify longer UNC paths, such as *<server>*\Documents\Contracts\Completed. To use network shortcuts in Outlook, first create the shortcut on the desktop and then drag it to a shortcut group on the Navigation Pane.

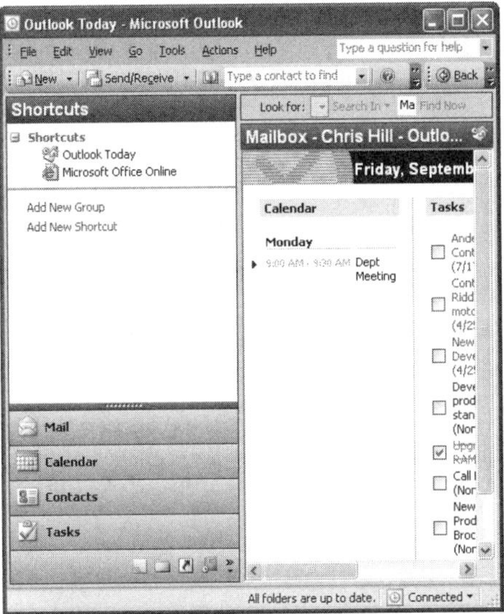

Figure 25-4. Drag a folder or document from Windows to the Navigation Pane to create a shortcut.

Adding a Web Site to the Navigation Pane

You can add shortcuts to Web sites to the Navigation Pane. This lets you quickly open a site from Outlook to do research, check stock quotes, view news, and so on.

> **Tip** Outlook does not include the Favorites menu by default, but you can add it. See the section "Customizing Command Bars" later in this chapter for details on how to add the Favorites menu to Outlook's menu bar.

Microsoft Outlook 2002 offered two ways to add Internet shortcuts to the Outlook Bar, but Outlook 2003 reduces the methods to one. Unfortunately, the remaining method isn't as easy to use as the old one, but at least you still have the opportunity to create Web shortcuts.

To add a Web site shortcut to the Navigation Pane, first create the shortcut on the desktop or other folder. Open the Navigation Pane shortcut group in which you want to place the shortcut, and then simply drag the existing shortcut to the Navigation Pane. You can also copy shortcuts from your Favorites menu easily. Position your Web browser so you can see it and the Outlook Navigation Pane. Open the Favorites menu, then drag the favorite from the browser to the shortcut group in Outlook.

> **Tip** **Create new Web shortcuts**
> You can create new Web shortcuts on the desktop or in a file system folder by right-clicking the location and choosing New, Shortcut. On the first page of the Create Shortcut Wizard, type the URL to the Web page, File Transfer Protocol (FTP) site, or other Internet resource. Use *http://* as the URL prefix for Web pages, use *ftp://* for FTP sites, or use *https://* for secure sites that use Secure Sockets Layer (SSL).

Removing an Icon from the Navigation Pane

If you decide you no longer want a particular shortcut on the Navigation Pane, you can remove it easily. Simply right-click the shortcut and choose Delete Shortcut. Click Yes to remove the shortcut or No to cancel.

Renaming a Shortcut on the Navigation Pane

In some cases, you'll want to change the name Outlook assigns to a shortcut on the Navigation Pane. For example, when you add a Web site shortcut, its name is the URL, which typically doesn't fit very well on the Navigation Pane. Perhaps you simply want to change the shortcut's name to something more descriptive.

To change the shortcut name, right-click the shortcut's icon and choose Rename Shortcut. Type the new name and press Enter.

Working with Groups on the Navigation Pane

Outlook creates one group by default on the Navigation Pane. You can also add your own groups, remove groups, and rename them. This section explains these tasks.

Adding a Group to the Navigation Pane

At some point, you might want to add your own groups of shortcuts to the Navigation Pane to help you reorganize existing shortcuts or organize new shortcuts. For example, you might want to create a group to contain all your Web shortcuts.

Adding a new group is easy. Click the Shortcuts button on the Navigation Pane, and then click Add New Group. Outlook adds a new group named New Group and highlights the group name so that you can change it (see Figure 25-5). Type the group name and press Enter. Then begin adding shortcuts or moving shortcuts to it from your other groups.

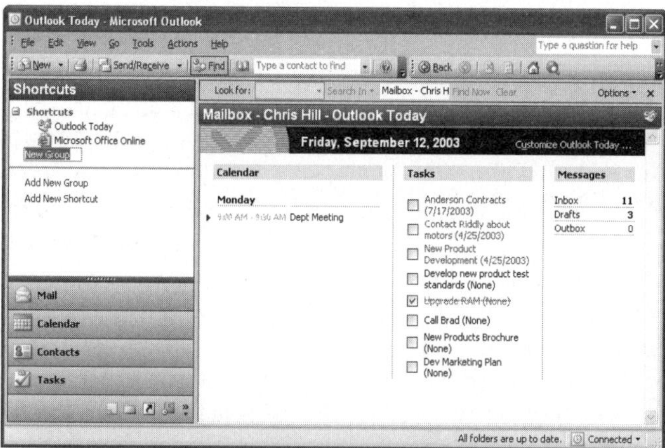

Figure 25-5. Type a name for the new group.

Tip You can copy shortcuts from one group to another. Simply hold down the Ctrl key and drag the shortcut to the group in which you want it placed.

Renaming a Group on the Navigation Pane

You can rename a group as easily as you rename a shortcut. Open Outlook, right-click the group name on the Navigation Pane, and choose Rename Group. Type a new name for the group and press Enter.

Removing a Group from the Navigation Pane

If you decide that you want to remove a group from the Navigation Pane, you can do so at any time. Simply right-click the group name on the Navigation Pane and choose Remove Group. Click Yes to remove the group or No to cancel.

Tip If the group you remove contains shortcuts you've copied from other locations (such as the desktop), removing the group does not affect those shortcuts. Only the group is removed from the Navigation Pane. Shortcuts that exist only in that group are deleted, however.

Customizing Command Bars

Microsoft refers to menus and toolbars collectively as *command bars*. You can work with command bars as they're provided by Outlook, or you can customize their location and contents to suit your preferences. This section explains how to relocate command bars, add and remove commands, and configure custom options.

Note The terms *command bar* and *toolbar* are used synonymously throughout this chapter.

Working with Toolbars

Outlook includes the menu bar and three toolbars by default: Standard, Advanced, and Web. You can also create your own toolbars or command bars (see "Creating Custom Command Bars," page 665). Outlook makes it easy to rearrange your screen by displaying or hiding toolbars. You also can move command bars to different locations in the Outlook interface.

Displaying and Hiding Toolbars

You probably use the same one or two toolbars on a regular basis but sometimes need to display or hide a particular toolbar. By default, Outlook always displays the menu command bar—you can't turn it off. Outlook also displays the Standard toolbar by default, although you can turn it off if you don't use it.

To display or hide a toolbar, choose View, Toolbars and then select the toolbar in question. A check mark beside a toolbar indicates that it is displayed; no check mark indicates that the toolbar is hidden.

Tip You can right-click the menu bar or any toolbar and turn toolbars on or off using the shortcut menu.

Moving and Docking Toolbars

All Outlook command bars—including the menu—are *dockable*. This means you can attach the command bar to any of the four sides of the Outlook window. You can also float a command bar. Figure 25-6 shows the menu bar docked at the right edge of the Outlook window. Figure 25-7 shows the menu bar floating on the desktop.

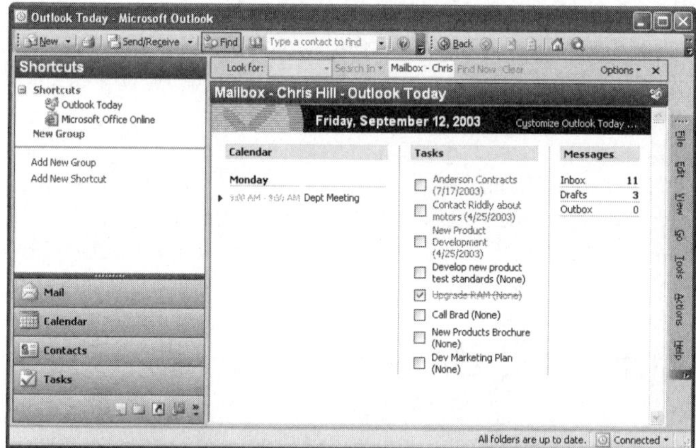

Figure 25-6. You can dock command bars at any of the four window edges.

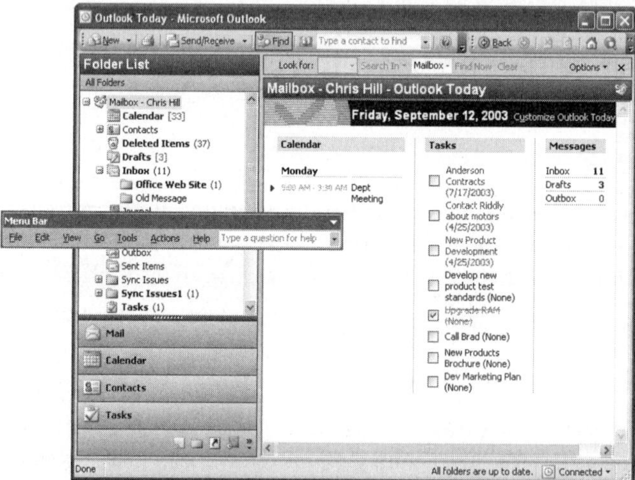

Figure 25-7. Command bars can also float on the desktop.

At the left edge of each command bar (if the bar is displayed at the top or bottom of the Outlook window) or at the top edge (if the command bar is docked at the right or left edge of the window) is an anchor you can use to move the command bar. Place the cursor over the anchor, and the cursor should change to a four-way arrow. Then drag the command bar to its new location. Drag the command bar away from a window edge to make it float. Drag it back to a window edge to dock it.

> **Tip** If you need more vertical room in your folder views and don't use the menu often, consider docking the menu and toolbars at the right or left edge of the Outlook window.

Creating Custom Command Bars

Outlook gives you considerable control over the appearance and content of the command bars. Because Microsoft has combined menus and toolbars as a single type of command bar, you use a similar process to modify menus and toolbar items. The following sections explain how to make several types of changes to your command bars, including adding new ones.

> **Tip** If you wreak havoc with the default command bars in your zeal to customize them, you can restore them with relative ease. For details, see "Recovering the Default Command Bars," page 672.

You can modify the existing command bars, but in many cases you'll probably want to create your own. For example, you might want to create a command bar for remote mail. Perhaps you use another group of commands to which you'd like quick access.

After you add a new command bar, you can add buttons and menus to it (explained in the following section). As mentioned, menus and toolbars are both considered command bars in Outlook 2003, so the process for creating a menu is the same as the one for creating a toolbar.

Follow these steps to create a command bar:

1. In Outlook, right-click any command bar and choose Customize to open the Customize dialog box. Alternatively, choose View, Toolbars, Customize.
2. In the Customize dialog box, click the Toolbars tab and then click New.
3. Type a name for the command bar and then click OK. Outlook opens a blank command bar.

Refer to the following section to add commands to your new command bar.

Adding Items

The default toolbars provided with Outlook cover the most commonly used commands, but they are not all-inclusive. Therefore, you might want to add frequently used commands to the existing toolbars or create custom toolbars.

In either case, you need to know how to add buttons to a toolbar. Just follow these steps:

1. In Outlook, right-click any toolbar and choose Customize to open the Customize dialog box. Alternatively, choose View, Toolbars, Customize.

2. Click the Commands tab (see Figure 25-8).

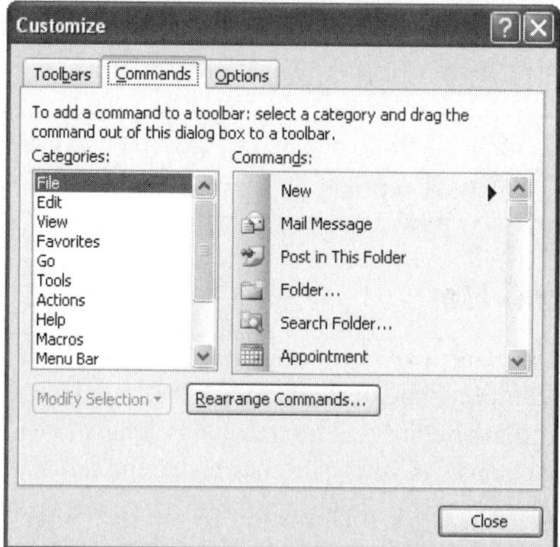

Figure 25-8. Use the Commands tab to add commands.

3. In the Categories list, select the command category containing the command you want to add.
4. In the Commands list, locate the command to add and drag it to the appropriate toolbar.
5. Repeat steps 3 and 4 to add other commands as needed.
6. Click Close to close the Customize dialog box.

> **Tip** You can add a combination of menus and buttons to any command bar.

Removing Items

If you don't use certain commands on a toolbar, you might want to remove them to make room for others or to simplify the Outlook interface.

To remove a button, follow these steps:

1. In Outlook, open the Customize dialog box.
2. With any tab of the Customize dialog box displayed, drag the button out of its toolbar. You can release the button as soon as you see a small X appear by the pointer.
3. Click Close to close the Customize dialog box.

> **Tip** **Reset toolbars to their defaults**
> You can reset any changes you made to a toolbar. Choose View, Toolbars, Customize, and then click the Toolbars tab. Select the toolbar to reset and click Reset. Click OK to reset the toolbar to its default state or Cancel to cancel the operation.

Reorganizing Items

You can reorganize the buttons on a command bar. The key point to understand is that whenever the Customize dialog box is open, any action you take on a command bar modifies that command bar. For example, if you drag a button or command out of the command bar, Outlook removes it.

Therefore, the basic method of reorganizing a command bar is to open the Customize dialog box and then simply drag the buttons or commands, as follows:

1. In Outlook, open the Customize dialog box.
2. With any tab in the Customize dialog box displayed, drag an item on a command bar from one location to another on the same command bar or on a different command bar.
3. Click Close to close the Customize dialog box.

Modifying Command Bar Items

Outlook inserts items on a command bar using a set of default characteristics. However, you can change these characteristics for any command bar item. For example, you can change the name of a menu, its shortcut key, or the icon assigned to a button. Following is a list of the modifications you can make:

- Change an item's name, reset it to its default properties, or delete the item.
- Modify the button image assigned to a command bar item by selecting a different image or editing the existing image.
- Change the style of the item so that it appears as text only, image only, or a combination of image and text.
- Assign a hyperlink to an item. When you click the item in Outlook, the document or site referenced by the link opens.

Follow these steps to modify an existing command bar item:

1. In Outlook, open the Customize dialog box.
2. Right-click the command button or menu item you want to change. Outlook presents a shortcut menu from which you can choose one of the following commands:
   - **Reset** Resets the item to its default properties (button image, name, for example).
   - **Delete** Removes the item from the command bar.
   - **Name** Changes the name of the item. Precede with the & character the key you want to use as the keyboard shortcut (the key you press instead of clicking the item). Note that some objects do not display their name by default.
   - **Copy Button Image** Copies the button image of the selected item to the clipboard for use on a different button or in another program (or for documentation).
   - **Paste Button Image** Pastes the contents of the clipboard on the item for use as the button icon.

- **Reset Button Image** Resets the button to display its default image.
- **Edit Button Image** Opens the Button Editor dialog box (see Figure 25-9) so that you can edit the button image.

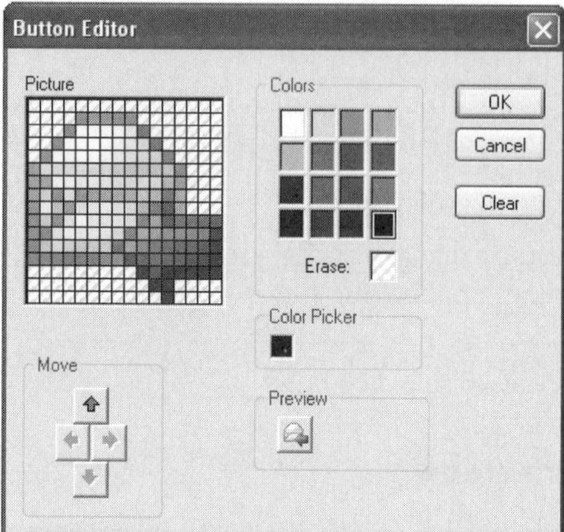

Figure 25-9. Use the Button Editor dialog box to edit the image assigned as a button's icon.

- **Change Button Image** Selects a different icon image from a set of predefined icons.
- **Default Style** Resets the button to its default style, such as image only or text only.
- **Text Only (Always)** Shows the item as text without an image regardless of whether the item is on a toolbar or a menu.
- **Text Only (In Menus)** Shows the item as text only (without an image) if it's used on a menu.
- **Image And Text** Shows the item as an icon with a text description beside it.
- **Begin A Group** Inserts a separator above a selected menu item or to the left of a selected toolbar button.
- **Edit Hyperlink** Assigns to the selected item a hyperlink that opens the linked site or document when you select the command bar item in Outlook.

3 Click Close to close the Customize dialog box.

Changing the Width of the Drop-Down List

Some Outlook command bar items use a drop-down list to display a list of information or to allow you to type information such as a search phrase or an address. If the drop-down list isn't wide enough to adequately display its information, you can widen it. You can also shrink lists that are too wide.

Here's how to change the width of a drop-down list:

1. In Outlook, open the Customize dialog box.
2. Select the drop-down list you want to modify.
3. Drag the left or right border of the drop-down list to resize it as needed.
4. Click Close to close the Customize dialog box.

Changing the Button Size

You can configure toolbars to display their buttons using either small icons (the default) or large icons. If your monitor is configured for a relatively high resolution, which can make the toolbar buttons hard to distinguish, configuring the toolbars for large icons can considerably improve their readability.

Follow these steps to configure button size:

1. In Outlook, open the Customize dialog box.
2. Click the Options tab (see Figure 25-10).

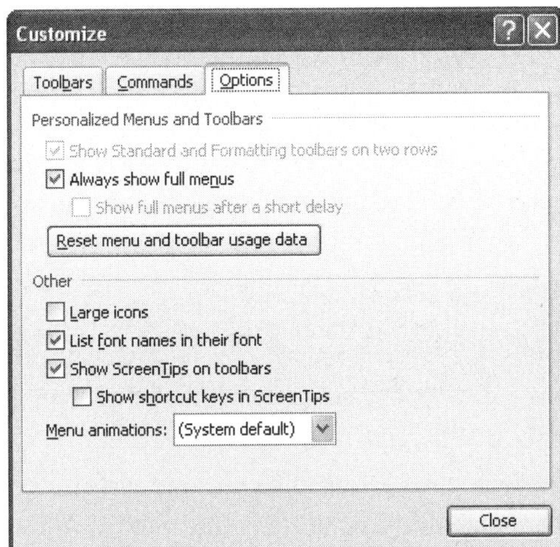

Figure 25-10. Configure icon size on the Options tab.

3. Select the Large Icons check box to turn on large icons, or clear the check box if you want to use the default small icon size. The change occurs immediately when you select or clear the option.
4. Click Close to close the Customize dialog box.

Troubleshooting

You can't add or remove separators on command bars

Command bars can include separators. On a toolbar, the separator is a vertical gray line that separates one group of commands or menus from another. On a menu, the separator is a horizontal gray line that separates one set of commands on the menu from another. Separators are purely an aesthetic element—they serve no other purpose than to provide a visual separation between items on a toolbar or menu.

The process of adding or removing separators is as far from being intuitive as you can get in Outlook. No obvious feature in the user interface gives you the ability to drag separators into position or remove them. Actually, adding and removing them is easy, but you have to know the secret.

Follow these steps to add or remove a separator on a toolbar:

1. In Outlook, open the Customize dialog box.
2. Locate the two items you want to separate. Drag the item on the right slightly to the right. Outlook inserts a separator to the left of the item you dragged.
3. To remove a separator, drag the item just to the right of the separator slightly to the left.
4. Click Close to close the Customize dialog box.

You can also add a separator to a toolbar by using an item's shortcut menu. Open the Customize dialog box, right-click an item, and choose Begin A Group. Outlook inserts a separator to the left of the item.

Follow these steps to add or remove a separator on a menu:

1. In Outlook, open the Customize dialog box.
2. Locate the two menu items you want to separate. Drag the bottom of the two items slightly downward. Outlook inserts a separator just above it.
3. To remove a separator, drag the menu item just below the separator slightly upward.
4. Click Close to close the Customize dialog box.

Restoring Default Command Bars

If you've made quite a few changes to the default command bars, the time might come when you want to reset them to their default state.

You can do so easily, as the following steps illustrate:

1. In Outlook, open the Customize dialog box.
2. Click the Toolbars tab.
3. Select the toolbar you want to reset and then click Reset. Outlook prompts you to verify that you want to reset the selected toolbar.
4. Click OK to reset the toolbar or Cancel to cancel the task.

Renaming a Custom Toolbar

Although Outlook doesn't allow you to rename the standard command bars, you can rename any custom command bars that you've created.

Follow these steps to rename a custom command bar:

1. In Outlook, open the Customize dialog box.
2. Select the command bar you want to rename and then click Rename.
3. Type a new name and click OK.
4. Click Close to close the Customize dialog box.

Deleting a Custom Command Bar

You can turn off any command bar to hide it. However, if you no longer need a custom command bar you've created, you probably want to delete it.

Follow these steps:

1. In Outlook, open the Customize dialog box.
2. Click the Toolbars tab.
3. Select the command bar to delete and then click Delete.
4. Click OK to verify that you want to delete the command bar or Cancel to cancel the task.

Sharing a Custom Command Bar

Outlook stores your command bar definitions in the Outcmd.dat file. The data stored there includes changes you make to the default command bars as well as custom command bars you create. Outlook maintains a separate Outcmd.dat file for each user. If you share your computer with others who also use Outlook, there are probably multiple Outcmd.dat files stored on the system. By default, Outlook stores the file in the \Documents And Settings\ <*user*>\Application Data\Microsoft\Outlook folder, where <*user*> is your user name.

If you've spent quite a bit of time customizing the command bars and want to share those changes with others, you can do so by sharing your Outcmd.dat file. If someone else has customized such a file for you, you can easily install it on your system.

If you've received a customized Outcmd.dat file from another user, follow these steps to install it on your system:

1. Obtain the customized Outcmd.dat file from the other user (or, if you're sharing yours, give the file to others who need its customized toolbars).
2. To install the customized file on your system, exit Outlook and locate the Outcmd.dat file in your profile folder on your system.
3. Rename the existing Outcmd.dat file as Outcmd.old.

4. Copy the other user's Outcmd.dat file to your profile folder where the original Outcmd.dat file was located.
5. Restart Outlook.

Caution If you made changes to your command bars before installing the other user's Outcmd.dat file, you'll lose those changes after installing the new file.

Recovering the Default Command Bars

As mentioned, Outlook stores command bar customization settings in the Outcmd.dat file, located in the Application Data\Microsoft\Outlook folder under your profile folder. If your Outcmd.dat file becomes corrupted, you can restore the default command bars by deleting or renaming the existing Outcmd.dat file. This process is also handy when you've made extensive changes to your command bars and want to restore them to their defaults.

Follow these steps:

1. Close Outlook.
2. Locate the Outcmd.dat file for your profile.
3. Rename the file Outcmd.old.
4. Restart Outlook. You should now see only the default command bars.

Controlling Command Bar Appearance and Behavior

Outlook lets you configure a handful of properties that control the way your command bars appear and function. To set these properties, open Outlook and choose View, Toolbars, Customize. Click the Options tab in the Customize dialog box (see Figure 25-10 on page 669).

The Options tab includes the following settings:

- **Show Standard And Formatting Toolbars On Two Rows** Shows the Standard and Formatting toolbars on two rows when both toolbars are displayed.
- **Always Show Full Menus** Turns off adaptive menus (those that show only the most frequently used commands) and shows all menu items. Clear this option to turn on adaptive menus.
- **Show Full Menus After A Short Delay** Shows all menu items after you rest the pointer on a menu for a short delay period.
- **Reset Menu And Toolbar Usage Data** Resets the usage data for adaptive menus. This command has no effect on the location of a command bar or on customized command bars (command bar modifications remain as they are).
- **Large Icons** Shows large command bar icons.
- **List Font Names In Their Font** Displays font names in their actual font to give you a sample of the font.

- **Show ScreenTips On Toolbars** Shows ScreenTips when you rest the pointer over a toolbar button.
- **Show Shortcut Keys In ScreenTips** Includes with the ScreenTip text the shortcut key (such as a function key), if any, assigned to each command bar item.
- **Menu Animations** Lists a menu on which you can select a menu animation effect for Outlook to use when you open a menu. Select the (System Default) option to use your operating system's default menu effect.

> **Tip** You can configure the operating system's menu animation effect by using the Effects tab of the Display dialog box. Right-click the desktop and choose Properties to display this dialog box. Select (System Default) and configure the system for no animation to turn off animations in Outlook.

Customizing Outlook Today View

Outlook uses Outlook Today view as its default view. Outlook Today synthesizes your most commonly used Outlook data into a single view, summarizing your schedule, tasks, and key e-mail folders for the current day. You can work with the view as is or modify it to suit your needs. This section explores how to customize Outlook Today view (see Figure 25-11).

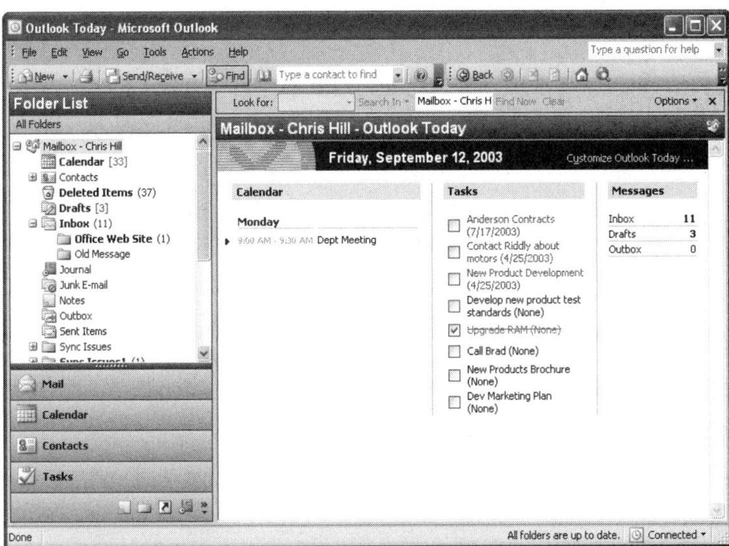

Figure 25-11. Outlook Today, which is the default Outlook view, summarizes your current day.

For a basic description of how to use Outlook Today view, see "Configuring Outlook Today," page 674.

Although Outlook Today presents useful information, it might not show all the information you want or need to really keep track of your work day. You can customize Outlook Today view to show additional information and use HTML to present a truly customized interface. The following sections explain how.

Configuring Outlook Today

You can configure several options that control how this view looks as well as the data it displays. To configure the view, click the Customize Outlook Today link in Outlook Today view (in the upper-right corner of the view). The screen shown in Figure 25-12 appears.

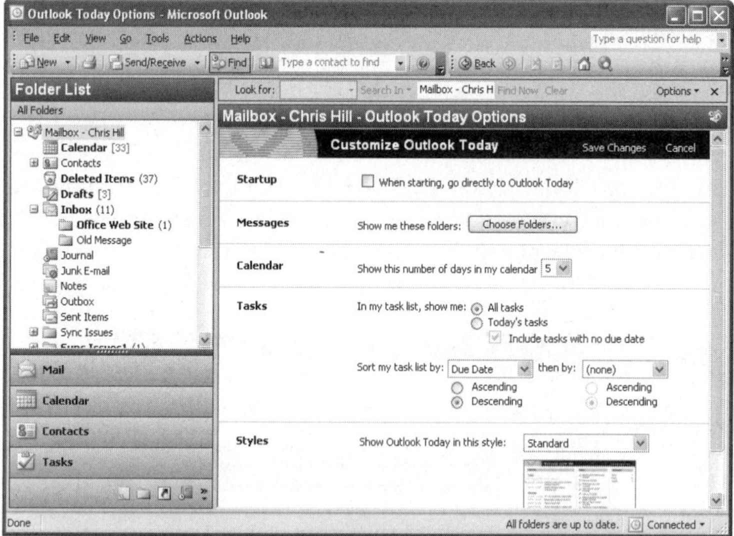

Figure 25-12. Use the settings shown here to configure Outlook Today view.

The following sections explain the changes you can make to Outlook Today view on this page. When you're satisfied with the changes, click Save Changes in the Customize Outlook Today title bar, or click Cancel to close the page without applying the changes.

Specifying the Startup Option

If you select the When Starting, Go Directly To Outlook Today check box, Outlook opens Outlook Today view when you first start the program.

You also can specify the startup folder by using Outlook's options, as explained here:

1. In Outlook, choose Tools, Options.
2. Click Other.
3. Click Advanced Options.

4. In the Startup In This Folder drop-down list, select Outlook Today.
5. Click OK twice to close the dialog boxes.

The Startup In This Folder drop-down list specifies the folder Outlook will use by default when you start Outlook. Choosing Outlook Today in the list has the same effect as choosing When Starting, Go Directly To Outlook Today.

Tip If Outlook Today is configured as the default view and you clear the When Starting, Go Directly To Outlook Today check box without specifying a different startup folder in the Options dialog box, Outlook makes your Inbox the startup folder.

Specifying Folders to Show

Outlook Today view shows the Drafts, Inbox, and Outbox folders. If you seldom use the Drafts folder, you might prefer to remove it from Outlook Today. Or perhaps you want to add other folders to the view, such as Tasks and Contacts, to give you a quick way to open those folders without using the Navigation Pane.

To configure the folders that Outlook Today displays, click Choose Folders on the Customize Outlook Today page to open the Select Folder dialog box (see Figure 25-13). Select each folder you want to display, and then click OK.

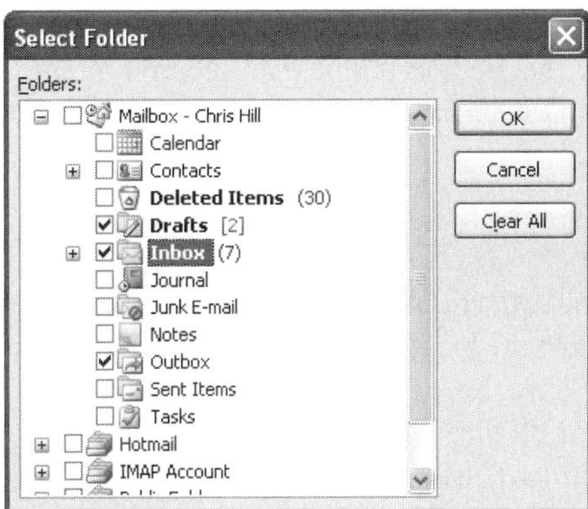

Figure 25-13. Use the Select Folder dialog box to choose the folders you want Outlook Today to display.

Setting Calendar Options

The Calendar portion of Outlook Today view displays a certain number of days from your calendar based on the current date. You can specify the number of days displayed by using the Show This Number Of Days In My Calendar option. Select a number from 1 to 7.

Setting Task Options

The Tasks area of the Customize Outlook Today page lets you configure how Outlook Today displays your tasks. The following list summarizes these options:

- **All Tasks** Shows all tasks regardless of the status or completion deadline.
- **Today's Tasks** Shows overdue tasks and incomplete tasks that are due today.
- **Include Tasks With No Due Date** Shows tasks for which you've assigned no due date.
- **Sort My Task List By *criteria* Then By *criteria*** Sort your task list according to the task's importance, due date, creation time, and start date. You can specify two sort conditions and also choose between ascending or descending sort order for both conditions.

Using Styles

By default, Outlook Today displays its information using three columns on a white background. Outlook provides additional styles you can select to change the overall appearance of Outlook Today view. Use the Show Outlook Today In This Style drop-down list to select a style. The Customize Outlook Today page shows a sample of the style after you select it.

Customizing Outlook Today with HTML

If you have any experience with HTML development, you might have surmised that Outlook Today view is driven by HTML code. Therefore, this view is extensible, allowing you to customize it by modifying the HTML code that defines it. For example, you might want to add a stock ticker, a Web site, links to a database, or other information to your Outlook Today view.

The code for Outlook Today resides in the Outlwvw.dll file, which is normally located in the \Program Files\Microsoft Office\Office11\1033 folder for an English installation. If you're not sure where the Outlwvw.dll file is located, choose Start, Find (or Start, Search) to search your system for the file. You need to know the location to extract the HTML code from the file for modification (explained shortly). You have two options for customizing Outlook Today: you can create a custom Outlwvw.dll file, which requires programming ability and a compiler, or you can use an HTML document instead of the DLL file. This chapter focuses on the second option.

> For more information on customizing Outlook Today, check the *Microsoft Outlook Deployment Kit*, which includes extensive documentation on customizing this view as well as other aspects of Outlook. The Outlook Deployment Kit is included with the Microsoft Office 2003 Resource Kit. You'll find additional information at Microsoft's Web site at *http://www.microsoft.com/office/ork/2003/default.htm*.

Extracting Outlook Today's HTML Code

Although you could write the HTML code for your Outlook Today view from scratch, doing so would take an in-depth understanding of not only HTML but also Outlook. Most people find it easier to extract the HTML code from the default Outlwvw.dll file to use as the basis for their customization work. After you have the default code, you can begin customizing it to add the features you need.

Follow these steps to extract the HTML code from the Outlwvw.dll file:

1. Close Outlook and open Microsoft Internet Explorer.
2. Locate your Outlwvw.dll file by choosing Start, Search (or Start, Find) or by browsing for the file.
3. Click in the Address field in Internet Explorer, and type the following (replace the path to the file if yours is different):
   Res://C:\Program Files\Microsoft Office\Office11\1033\Outlwvw.dll/outlook.htm
4. Internet Explorer might generate a script error, but the exact behavior depends on your version of Internet Explorer and whether you have the Script Editor installed. Just cancel the dialog box or click No if it appears.
5. In Internet Explorer, choose View, Source to open a Notepad window that displays the HTML code for Outlook Today view (see Figure 25-14).

Figure 25-14. The HTML code for the default Outlook Today view is displayed in Notepad.

6. In Notepad, choose File, Save As and save the file with an HTM file extension (for example, Outlook Today.htm).
7. Use Notepad's Replace feature to perform a global search and replace operation in the file, searching for all instances of display:none and replacing them with display:. Then save the file.

Modifying Outlook Today

At this point, you have a functional OutlookToday.htm file. You can open the file in your favorite HTML editor and modify it as needed. For example, you might open the file in Microsoft FrontPage or Macromedia Dreamweaver to make your changes. You can also make the changes right in Notepad, but doing so requires an in-depth understanding of HTML programming and is the most difficult way to modify the file.

What kind of changes can you make to Outlook Today? Almost anything is possible, depending on your skills with your Web design program and scripting know-how. For example, you might do something as simple as add a company logo to the Outlook Today view (Figure 25-15). Or, you might give your users quick access to the day's news, as shown in Figure 25-16.

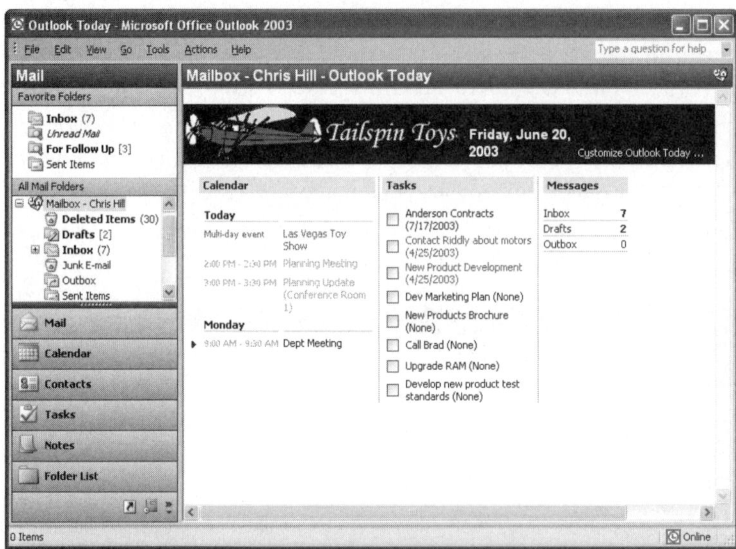

Figure 25-15. This custom Outlook Today view includes a company logo.

Figure 25-16. This custom view includes links to news sites.

When deciding what to add to your custom Outlook Today view, think about the types of resources you or your users need to access on a regular basis. For example, it might be useful to include links on the Outlook Today view to frequently used intranet sites such as a SharePoint team site where the users can share contacts, documents, and other resources. Stock tickers, news feeds, and other dynamic data sources are other good examples of information you might include in the custom Outlook Today view (see Figure 25-17).

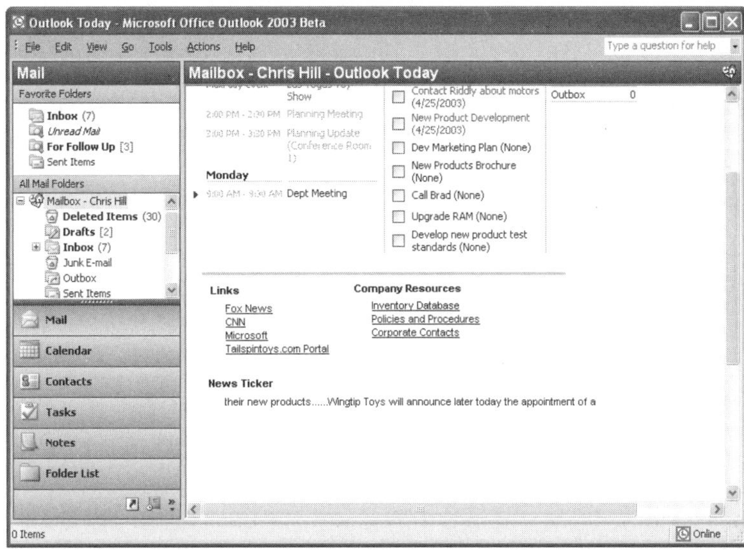

Figure 25-17. This custom view includes links to external Web sites, the company inventory database, a news ticker, and other useful resources.

> **Tip** Place custom graphics and other resources referenced by your custom Outlook Today view in the same folder as the customized HTML file. Outlook will look in this folder for referenced graphics by default, unless those graphics are referenced by an external URL.

After you modify the file, you need to make a registry change to allow Outlook to use your custom file instead of the default DLL. The next section explains how.

Specifying Your Custom Outlook Today Page

Outlook by default looks to Outlwvw.dll for the Outlook Today view. For Outlook to use your custom HTML file instead, you must make a small change in the registry. Before you make the change, however, you should back up the Outlook registry key in case you have problems making the required change. If you do experience problems, you can restore the registry key to repair the problem.

Follow these steps to back up the Outlook registry key and make the change necessary to point Outlook to your new custom HTML file:

1. Choose Start, Run.
2. In the Run dialog box, type **regedit**.
3. In the Registry Editor, select the branch HKEY_CURRENT_USER\Software\Microsoft\Office\11.0\Outlook\Today.
4. Choose Registry, Export Registry File.
5. Verify that the Selected Branch option is selected in the Export Registry File dialog box, specify a file name (such as Today.reg), and click Save. If you later have problems getting your Outlook Today view to work, double-click this file to restore the Today registry key.
6. In the Today registry key, double-click the Url value or select the value and choose Edit, Modify. The Edit String dialog box opens (see Figure 25-18).

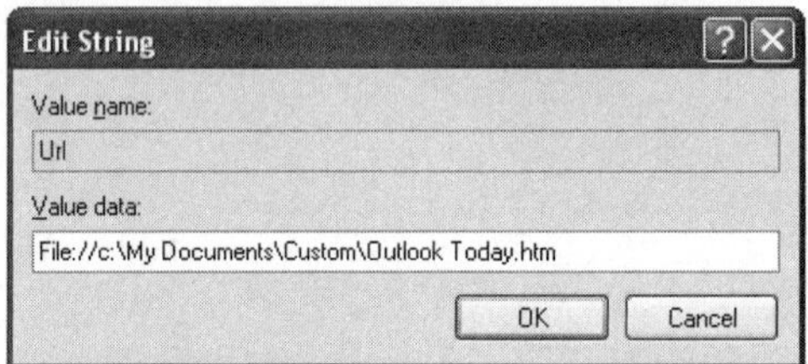

Figure 25-18. Change the registry value to point Outlook to a different Outlook Today view.

Note If the Url value doesn't exist, create it as a string value and then set its value according to the next step.

7. Type the path to your custom HTML file, preceding it with File://, as in the following example:
   File://c:\My Documents\Custom\Outlook Today.htm
8. Click OK to save the changes.
9. Close the Registry Editor.
10. Open Outlook and select Outlook Today view to verify that Outlook is using your custom file and to test the code.

Sharing an Outlook Today Page

After you've gone to the trouble to use HTML to customize Outlook Today view, you might want to share that custom file with others or use it on a different computer. Simply copy the file to the other system, and make the same modification to the other system's registry to allow it to use the file.

Chapter 26

Creating Custom Views and Print Styles

Earlier chapters discussed the standard views Microsoft Outlook 2003 provides for its many folders and data types. Those chapters also discussed customizing standard views by grouping and sorting items and by adding and removing columns, changing column order and properties, filtering the view, and so on.

In this chapter, you'll learn how to create custom views in Outlook to present the information you want in a format that suits your needs. Because generating a printout of your data is often a by-product of creating a view, this chapter also focuses on how to create custom print styles in Outlook. For those situations in which Outlook's custom views and print styles won't give you the results you need, you can turn to scripts and Microsoft Word to accomplish custom printing tasks.

For more information on customizing existing views, see "Working with the Standard Outlook Views," page 56. You'll also find information about specific views in the chapters that cover them. For example, for more information on working with and customizing views in the Contacts folder, see "Viewing Contacts," page 407.

Creating and Using Custom Views

If the options for customizing existing Outlook views don't provide the information view you need, you can create your own views. You have two options for doing so: modifying an existing view or creating a new one from scratch.

Basing a New View on an Existing View

You can create a new, custom view from an existing view if the existing one offers most of the view elements you need. This is usually the easiest method because it requires the least amount of work.

Follow these steps to create a new, custom view from an existing view:

1. Open the folder for which you want to modify the view, and then select the view to display it.

2 Choose View, Arrange By, Current View, Define Views to open the Custom View Organizer dialog box (see Figure 26-1).

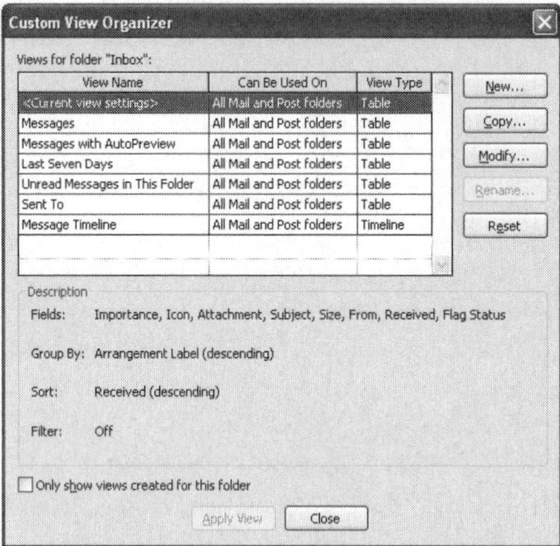

Figure 26-1. Use the Define Views dialog box to create a new view.

3 In the Views For Folder list, select the view you want to use as the basis for your new view, and then click Copy.

4 When Outlook prompts you to name the view, type a name.

5 Choose one of the following options:

- **This Folder, Visible To Everyone** Makes the view available only in the folder from which it was created. Anyone with access to the specified folder can use the view.
- **This Folder, Visible Only To Me** Makes the view available only in the folder from which it was created. Only the person who created the view can use it.
- **All *type* Folders** Makes the view available in all folders that match the specified folder type. For example, when you create a custom view based on the Inbox, this option becomes All Mail And Post Folders, and Outlook makes the view available from the Inbox, Outbox, Drafts, Sent Items, and other message folders. If you base the new view on the Contacts folder, this option becomes All Contact Folders and makes the view available from all contacts folders.

6 Click OK to create the copy. The Customize View dialog box opens (see Figure 26-2).

7 Use the options provided by the Customize View dialog box to customize the view.

For details on all the options you can configure in the Customize View dialog box, see "Customizing a View's Settings," page 686.

8 After you've modified the settings as needed, click OK to close the Customize View dialog box and apply the view changes.

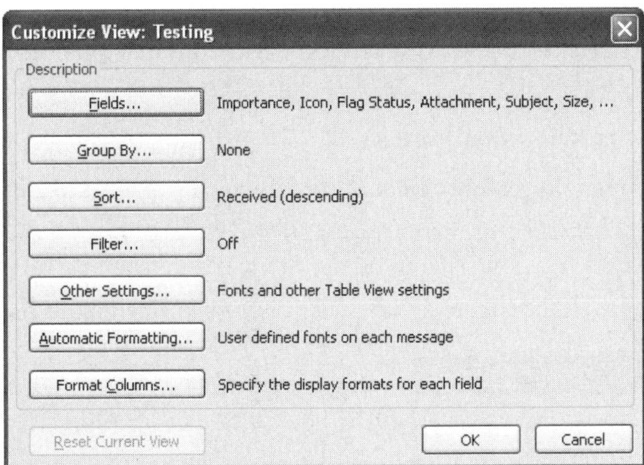

Figure 26-2. The Customize View dialog box lets you access the functions you can use to define your custom view.

Creating a New View from Scratch

You can create an Outlook view from scratch if the view you want doesn't have much in common with any of the existing views. For example, perhaps you want to create an Inbox view that displays your messages as icons rather than headers (see Figure 26-3). You can't modify a standard message view to display messages as icons, so you need to create the view from scratch.

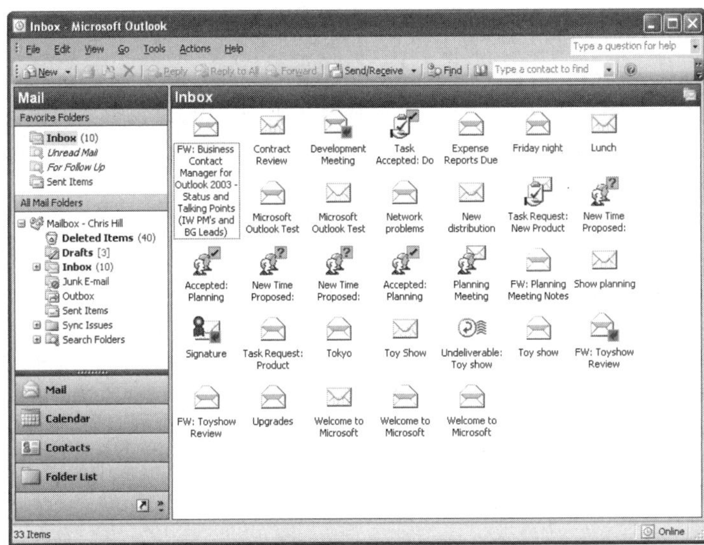

Figure 26-3. This Inbox view shows message icons rather than headers.

The process for creating a view from scratch is much like the process of modifying an existing view. When you create a new view, however, you have additional options for specifying the view.

Follow these steps to create a view from scratch:

1. In Outlook, open the folder or folder type for which you want to create a custom view.
2. Choose View, Arrange By, Current View, Define Views to open the Define Views dialog box.
3. Click New to open the Create A New View dialog box (see Figure 26-4).

Figure 26-4. You can create several types of new views.

4. In the Name Of New View box, type a name for your new view.
5. In the Type Of View list, select the type of view you want to create, as follows:
   - **Table** Presents information in tabular form with one item per row and columns according to your selections. The default Inbox view is an example of a table view.
   - **Timeline** Displays items on a timeline based on the item's creation date (such as the received date for a message or the event date for a meeting). You might find this view type most useful for the Calendar folder.
   - **Card** Displays information using cards, as in Address Cards view (the default view in the Contacts folder).
   - **Day/Week/Month** Displays days in the left half of the window and monthly calendars in the right half. The actual view depends on the type of folder for which you create the view. Figure 26-5 shows a Day/Week/Month view created for the Inbox folder.
   - **Icon** Displays the items as icons, much as a file system folder does.
6. From the Can Be Used On group, select an option as described in the preceding section, and then click OK. The Customize View dialog box opens.

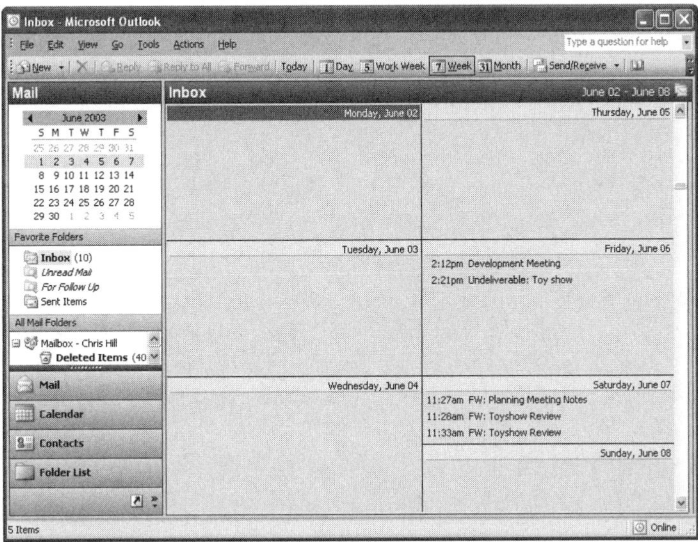

Figure 26-5. This Day/Week/Month view was created for the Inbox folder.

7 Customize the view as needed and then click OK.

8 Click Apply View to apply the view, or click Close to close the dialog box without applying the view.

For details on all the options you can configure in the Customize View dialog box, see "Customizing a View's Settings" on page 686.

Modifying, Renaming, or Deleting a View

You can easily modify, rename, and delete custom views. For example, perhaps you want to apply a filter to a view in the Contacts folder to show only those contacts who work for a particular company. Maybe you want to have Outlook apply a certain label to appointments that have specified text in the subject.

To modify, rename, or delete a view, follow these steps:

1 Choose View, Arrange By, Current View, Define Views to open the Define Views dialog box.

2 In the Views For Folder list, select the view you want to change and do one of the following:

- To modify the view, click Modify. Use the options in the Customize View dialog box to apply changes to the view (as explained in the following section).
- To rename the view, click Rename and type the new name.
- To delete the view, click Delete. The Reset button changes to Delete if you select a custom view.

3 Click Close.

Customizing a View's Settings

Outlook gives you considerable control over the appearance and contents of a view. When you define a new view or modify an existing view, you end up in the Customize View dialog box, shown earlier in Figure 26-2. You can open this dialog box in the following ways:

- Choose View, Arrange By, Current View, Customize Current View.
- Choose View, Arrange By, Current View, Define Views and then select a view and click Modify.

The options available in the Customize View dialog box change according to the folder selected. For example, the options for a contacts folder differ in some respects from the options for the Inbox. The same general concepts hold true for each type of folder, however. The following sections explain the various ways you can use these dialog box options to customize a view.

Configuring Fields

Clicking Fields in the Customize View dialog box in most cases opens the Show Fields dialog box (see Figure 26-6), which allows you to select the fields that you want to include in the view. (Exceptions to this behavior are discussed later.) For example, you might use the Show Fields dialog box to add the Cc or Sensitivity fields to the view.

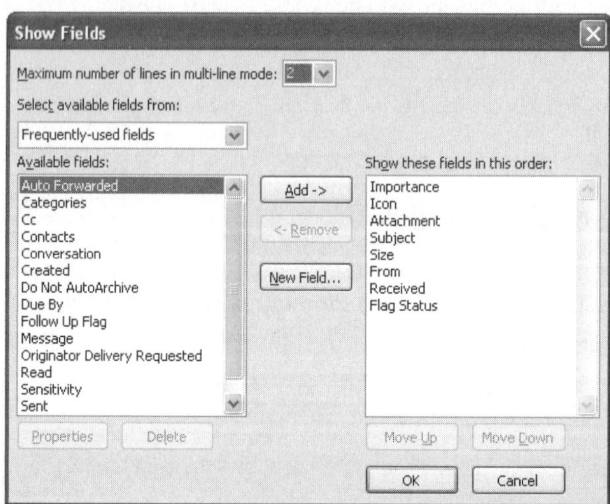

Figure 26-6. Use the Show Fields dialog box to add or remove fields in the view.

Adding fields in the Show Fields dialog box is easy. The available fields (those not already in the view) appear in the list on the left, and the fields already displayed appear in the list on the right. Select a field in the Available Fields list and click Add to add it to the view. To remove a field from the view, select the field in the Show These Fields In This Order list and click Remove. Use the Move Up and Move Down buttons to rearrange the order in which the fields are displayed in the view.

Troubleshooting

You need to restore a view to its original settings

You've customized a view, and now you've decided that you need the old view back again. For the future, remember that you can copy an existing view. Rather than modifying an existing view, you can copy a view and then modify the copy. This way you'll still have the original view if you need it.

It's easy to restore a view to its previous settings, however. Choose View, Arrange By, Current View, Define Views. Select the view you want to restore and click Reset. Click OK when prompted to confirm the action.

Tip You can rearrange the order in which fields are displayed in a table view by dragging the column header for a field to a new location on the column header bar.

You can click New Field in the Show Fields dialog box to create a custom field. For additional information on creating and using custom fields, see Chapter 24, "Designing and Using Forms," and Article 1, "Programming Forms with VBScript," on the companion CD.

In some cases, clicking Fields in the Customize View dialog box opens a Date/Time Fields dialog box similar to the one shown in Figure 26-7. This occurs when you're working with a view that shows time duration, such as Day/Week/Month view in the Calendar folder, By Type view in the Journal folder, or Task Timeline view in the Tasks folder—in effect, nontable views that show time duration graphically.

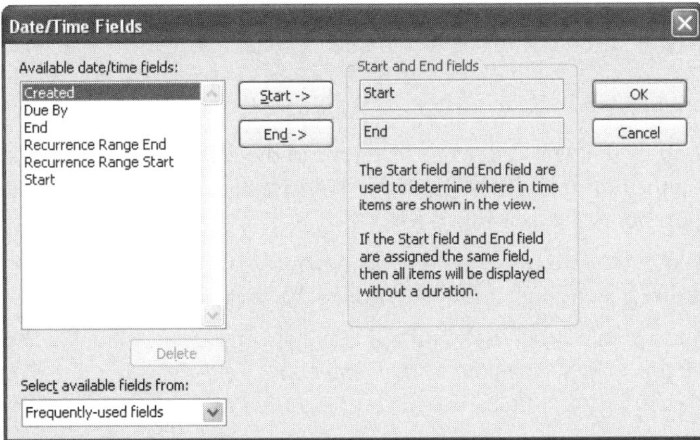

Figure 26-7. In the Date/Time Fields dialog box, specify the date fields used to show duration.

You use the Date/Time Fields dialog box to specify the fields Outlook will use to show item duration in the view. The default settings vary but are typically either Start and End or Start Date and Due Date. As an example, you might use the Date/Time Fields dialog box to change

Task Timeline view in the Tasks folder to show the Date Completed field for the task's end rather than the Due Date field.

Grouping Data

Sometimes it's helpful to be able to group items in an Outlook folder based on specific data fields. For example, you might want to group tasks by owner so that you can see at a glance the tasks assigned to specific people. Perhaps you want to organize contacts by country or region. In these and similar cases, you can modify an existing view or create a new one to organize the view based on the most pertinent data. To group data in a view, click Group By in the Customize View dialog box to open the Group By dialog box, shown in Figure 26-8.

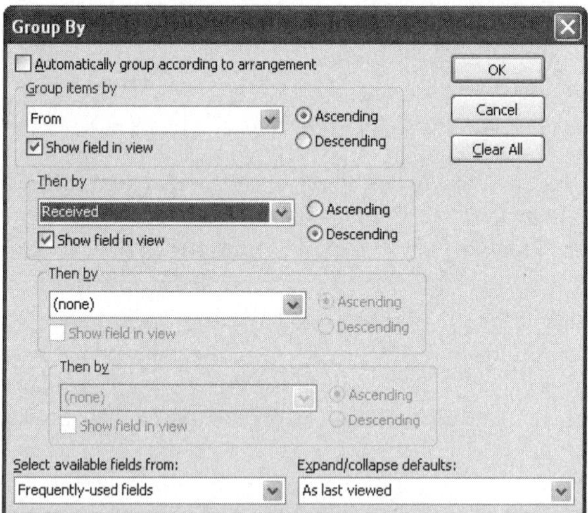

Figure 26-8. Use the Group By dialog box to specify criteria for grouping items in a view.

Follow these steps to group data in a view:

1. In the Group By dialog box, select a field type in the Select Available Fields From drop-down list at the bottom of the dialog box. This selection controls the fields that appear in the Group Items By drop-down list.
2. Select a field in the Group Items By drop-down list, and then select either Ascending or Descending depending on the sort order you want to use.
3. If you want to create subgroups under the main group, select a field in the Then By drop-down list. (The dialog box contains three such lists, providing three additional grouping levels.) For example, you might group tasks by Owner and then by Due Date.

4 After you've specified all the grouping levels you need, use the Expand/Collapse Defaults drop-down list to select how you want Outlook to treat the groups. Use the following list as a guide:

- **As Last Viewed** Collapses or expands the group according to its state in the previous session.
- **All Expanded** Expands all items in all groups.
- **All Collapsed** Collapses all items in all groups.

5 When you're satisfied with the group settings, click OK to close the Group By dialog box. Then click OK to close the Customize View dialog box.

Sorting Data

Sorting data in a view is different from grouping data. For example, you might group the Tasks folder by owner. Each group in the view then shows the tasks assigned to a particular person. You can then sort the data within the group as needed. For example, you might sort the tasks based first on due date and then on subject. Figure 26-9 shows the Tasks folder grouped by owner and sorted by subject.

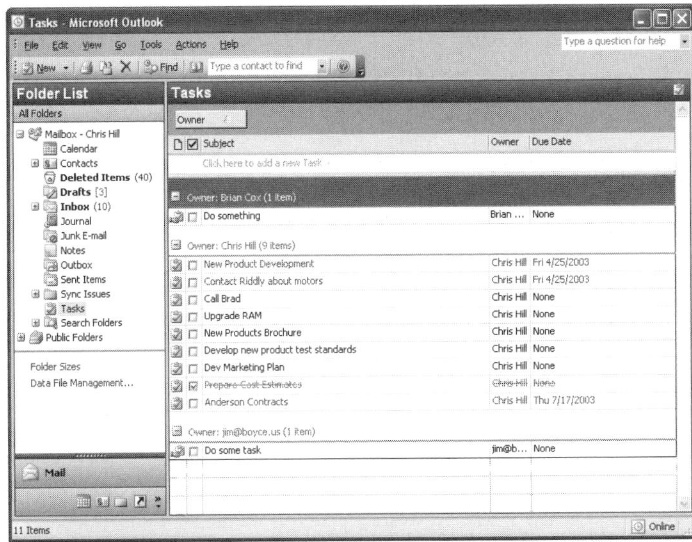

Figure 26-9. In this view, tasks are grouped by owner and sorted by subject, placing the tasks in alphabetical order by subject.

Sorting doesn't rely on grouping—you can sort a view whether it is grouped or not. For example, you might sort the Inbox based on the Received field to show messages in the order in which you received them.

> **Tip** **Sort table views quickly**
> You can quickly sort a table view by clicking the column header for the field by which you want to sort the view. Click the header again to change between ascending and descending sort order.

To create a sort order when you customize or define a view, click Sort in the Customize View dialog box to open the Sort dialog box (see Figure 26-10).

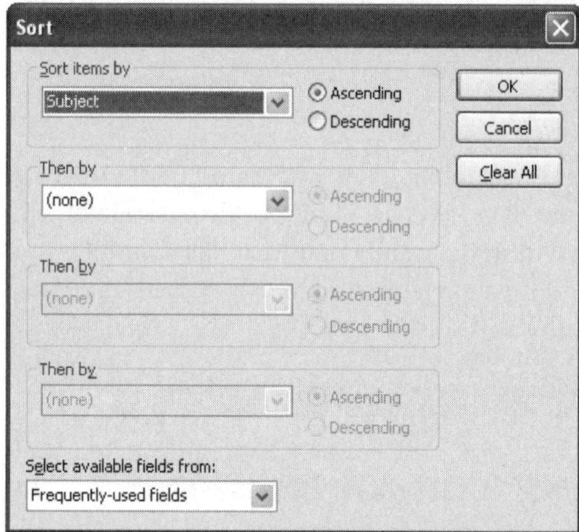

Figure 26-10. Configure sort order for the view in the Sort dialog box.

To configure sorting in the Sort dialog box, follow these steps:

1. In the Select Available Fields From drop-down list, select the type of field the sort should be based on.
2. In the Sort Items By drop-down list, select the specific field by which you want to sort the view.
3. Select Ascending or Descending, depending on the type of sort you need.
4. Use the Then By lists to specify additional sort levels, if necessary.
5. Click OK to close the Sort dialog box, and then click OK to close the Customize View dialog box.

Applying Filters to the View

Outlook's ability to filter a view is an extremely powerful feature that gives you considerable control over the data displayed in a given view. For example, you might have hundreds of messages in your Inbox and need to filter the view to show only those messages from a particular sender. You could simply sort the Inbox by the From field and scan the list of messages, but you might want to refine the search a little, perhaps viewing only messages from a specific sender that have an attachment and were sent within the previous week. Filters allow you to do just that.

To configure a filter, click Filter in the Customize View dialog box to open the Filter dialog box, shown in Figure 26-11. This multitabbed dialog box lets you specify multiple conditions to define which items will appear in the view.

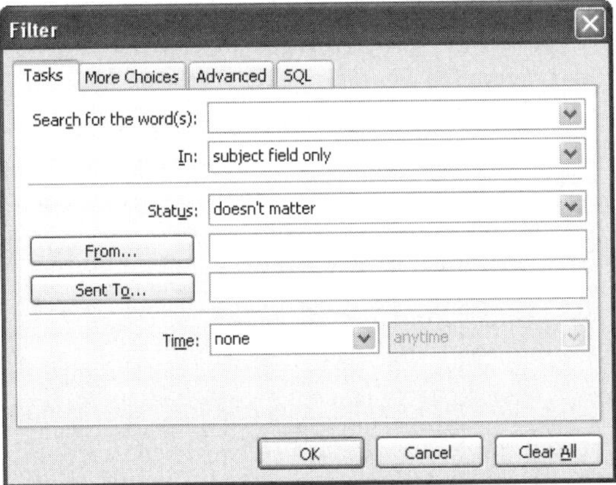

Figure 26-11. Use the Filter dialog box to specify multiple conditions that determine what data appears in the view.

The various tabs in the Filter dialog box include a broad range of options that let you specify multiple conditions for the filter. You can use conditions from more than one tab. For example, you might enter words to search for and a sender on the Messages tab, select categories on the More Choices tab, and specify a particular field and value on the Advanced tab. Note that the first tab of the dialog box varies according to the current folder type. For a contacts folder, for example, the first tab is labeled Contacts and offers options for creating filter conditions that apply to contacts. For a message folder, the first tab is labeled Messages and provides options for creating filter conditions specific to messages.

Tip **Use powerful filters**

The Advanced tab of the Filter dialog box gives you access to all available fields and several conditions (Contains, Doesn't Contain, and Is Empty, for example), making it the place to go to configure conditions not available on the other tabs. Use the SQL tab to perform Structured Query Language queries to retrieve data from the folder to show in the custom view.

Configuring Fonts and Other General Settings

When you click Other Settings in the Customize View dialog box, Outlook opens a dialog box that lets you configure some general settings for the custom view. These options vary from one folder type to another—the Contacts folder, the Inbox, and the Calendar folder, for example, all use different options. You can change such properties as the font used for column headers and row text, the grid style and shading for table views, and a handful of other general options.

Creating Rules for Automatic Formatting of Text

Click Automatic Formatting in the Customize View dialog box to display the Automatic Formatting dialog box, similar to the one shown in Figure 26-12. This dialog box lets you create rules that cause Outlook to automatically format data in the view based on the criteria you specify. For example, you might create an automatic formatting rule that has Outlook display in blue all tasks that you own and display all other tasks in black. Or perhaps you could create a rule to display in green all contacts from a specific company.

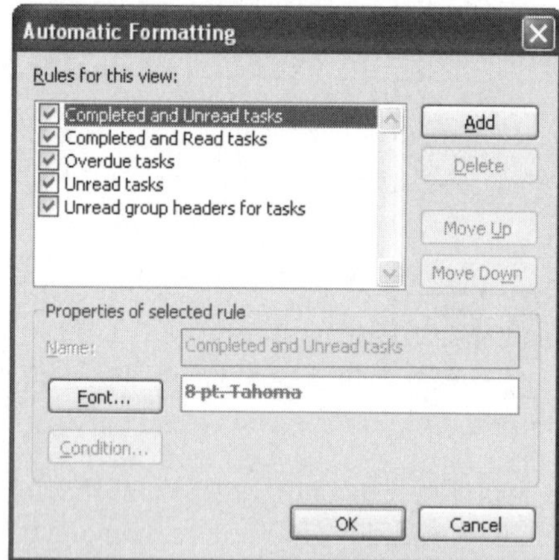

Figure 26-12. Use the Automatic Formatting dialog box to create rules that automatically format text in views based on the conditions you specify.

As you're working in the Automatic Formatting dialog box, keep in mind that you can't create task-oriented rules, as you can with the Rules Wizard. For example, you can't create a rule in this dialog box that moves messages from one folder to another. The rules you create in the Automatic Formatting dialog box control only the appearance (color, font, and font styles) of data in the view.

For information about the Rules Wizard, see "Processing Messages Automatically," page 224.

You can't modify the conditions for predefined rules, but you can specify the font characteristics to use for the rule. You can also create your own rules and change the order in which rules are applied to achieve the results you need.

To set up an automatic formatting rule for text, follow these steps:

1. Click Add in the Automatic Formatting dialog box to add a new rule named Untitled.
2. Click Font to open a standard Font dialog box in which you specify the font, font style, and color that will apply to text that meets the rule's condition.
3. Close the Font dialog box, and click Condition to open the Filter dialog box, shown in Figure 26-13. This dialog box offers three tabs you can use to specify the condition for the rule. You can specify multiple conditions from multiple tabs, if needed.

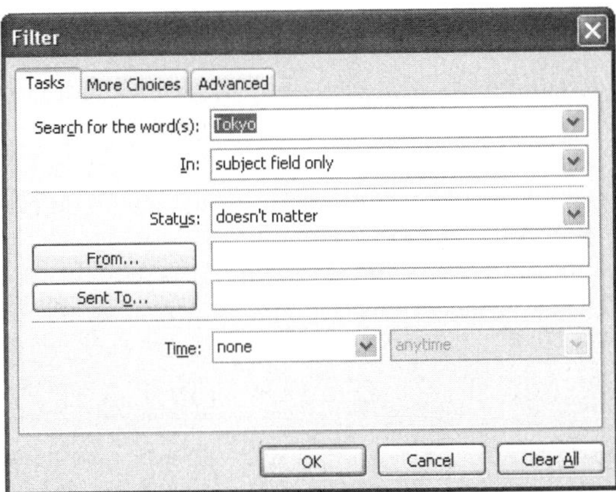

Figure 26-13. Specify conditions for the rule in the Filter dialog box.

4 Click OK when you're satisfied with the filter condition.

5 Click OK to close the Automatic Formatting dialog box, and then click OK to close the Customize View dialog box.

Troubleshooting

You need to restrict the available views

In some situations, you might want to restrict the available views to only the custom views you've created, hiding the standard views that Outlook provides. For example, perhaps you created a custom calendar view that you want all employees to use rather than the standard calendar views because your custom view includes additional information the standard views don't contain. When you restrict Outlook's views to only custom views, the standard views no longer appear on the View menu.

You must configure each folder separately. For example, you might restrict the Calendar folder views without restricting the Inbox folder views. This would give users the ability to choose one of the standard Outlook views in the Inbox folder but would limit their choices to only custom views in the Calendar folder.

Follow these steps to restrict the views Outlook provides on the View menu:

1 In Outlook, select the folder for which you want to restrict views.

2 Choose View, Arrange By, Current View, Define Views to open the Define Views dialog box.

3 Select the Only Show Views Created For This Folder check box and click Close.

4 Repeat steps 2 and 3 to restrict other folders as necessary.

Printing in Outlook

Many users work in Outlook and never print any of the items they store in the program. For other users, however, the ability to print from Outlook is important. For example, if you use a hard-copy day planner rather than a notebook computer or a personal digital assistant to keep track of your daily schedule, you might prepare the schedule in Outlook and then print it for insertion in the day planner.

This section examines the options and methods for printing your Outlook data. It also explains how to customize the print styles provided by Outlook to create custom styles that better suit your preferences or needs.

Overview of Print Styles

Outlook offers several predefined print styles you can use to print information from various Outlook folders. The most common print styles are Table and Memo, as indicated in Table 26-1, which lists the standard print styles in Outlook.

Table 26-1. Outlook print styles by folder type

Folder Type	View	Print Styles
Calendar	Day/Week/Month Day/Week/Month with AutoPreview	Daily, Weekly, Monthly, Tri-Fold, Calendar Details, Memo
	Active Appointments Events Annual Events Recurring Appointments By Category	Table, Memo
Contacts	Address Cards Detailed Address Cards	Card, Small Booklet, Medium Booklet, Memo, Phone Directory
	Phone List By Category By Company By Location By Follow Up Flag	Table, Memo
Inbox	All except Message Timeline	Table, Memo
	Message Timeline	Print individual items only
Journal	By Type By Contact By Category	Print individual items only
	Entry List Last Seven Days Phone Calls	Table, Memo

Table 26-1. Outlook print styles by folder type

Folder Type	View	Print Styles
Tasks	All except Task Timeline	Table, Memo
	Task Timeline	Print individual items only

Inside Out

Printing a timeline

As Table 26-1 indicates, you can print only individual items when you're working with a timeline view. However, if you're scheduling a major project, a printout of a timeline view would be useful. If you need that capability, consider using Microsoft Project instead of Outlook. For details about how you can use Outlook to enhance your work in Project, see Chapter 22, "Integrating Microsoft Outlook and Microsoft Project."

Printing from Outlook

Printing from Outlook is just as easy as printing from any other application. Simply select the view or item you want to print and choose File, Print to print the document or File, Print Preview to preview it.

If you choose File, Print, Outlook displays a Print dialog box similar to the one shown in Figure 26-14. The contents of the dialog box vary according to the type of view from which you're printing.

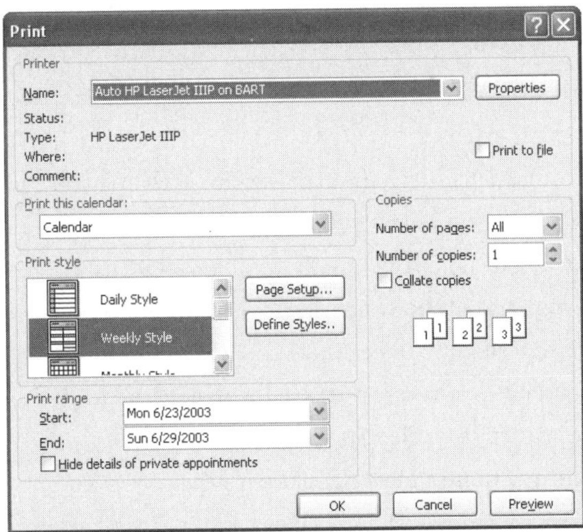

Figure 26-14. You can select an existing print style from the Print dialog box.

In the Print Style list, select a print style. For example, select the Phone Directory style for the Contacts folder to print a phone list or select one of the two booklet styles if you want to print contact entries for a day planner. If you need to fine-tune the print settings, click Page Setup. Outlook displays a Page Setup dialog box similar to the one shown in Figure 26-15.

For additional details on printing contacts and using different print styles with the Contacts folder, see "Printing Contacts," page 412.

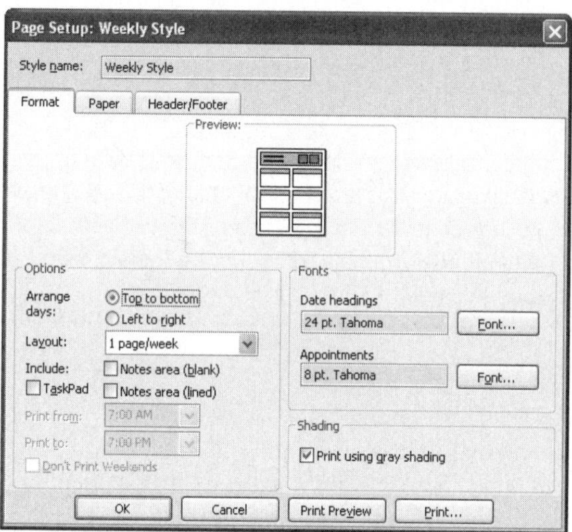

Figure 26-15. Use the Page Setup dialog box to modify print options for the selected style.

Use the Format tab of the Page Setup dialog box (see Figure 26-15) to specify the layout, fonts, and other general properties for the job. The options on the Format tab vary from one folder type to another. For example, you can use the Format tab to set the following options, some of which are specific to particular folder types:

- Whether Outlook keeps sections together or starts a new page for each section.
- The number of columns per page.
- The number of blank forms to print at the end of the job (such as blank contact forms).
- Whether Outlook prints a contact index on the page edge.
- Whether letter headings for each alphabetic section of a contact list are included.
- The font used for headings and for body text.
- Whether Outlook adds gray shading to headings.
- Whether the TaskPad and notes areas are displayed with a calendar.
- Whether weekends are printed in a calendar view.
- Whether Outlook prints one month of a calendar per page.

Use the Paper tab (see Figure 26-16) to select the page type, size, source, and other properties. For example, in the Type list on the Paper tab, you can select the type of day planner you use so that Outlook prints using that style.

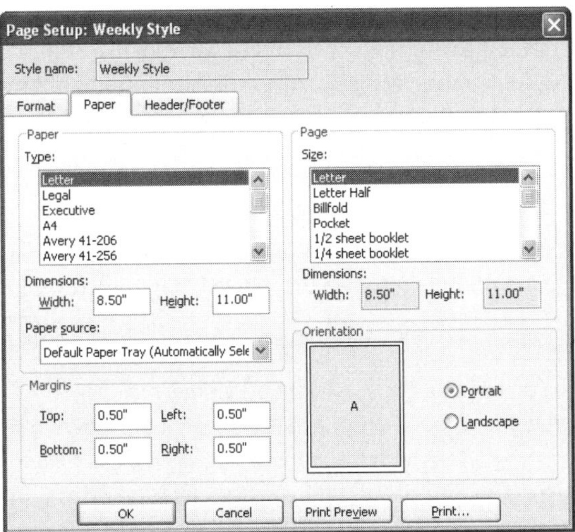

Figure 26-16. Use the Paper tab to select the paper source, size, type, and other paper settings.

Use the Header/Footer tab (see Figure 26-17) to specify the items you want printed in the header and the footer. This tab provides three boxes for the header and three for the footer. The left box specifies items that print on the left side of the page, the middle box specifies items that print on the middle of the page, and the right box specifies items that print on the right side of the page. You can enter text manually or use the buttons near the bottom to insert specific data such as page numbers, the user, the time, and other dynamic data.

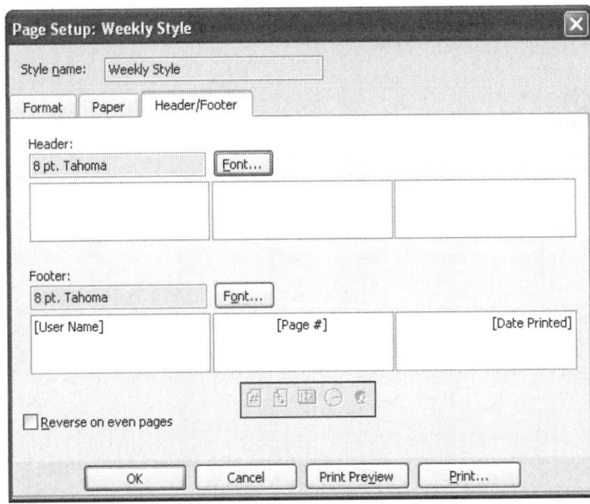

Figure 26-17. Use the Header/Footer tab to enter header and footer data.

After you select the page setup options, you can return to the Print dialog box or preview the document. The Print dialog box offers a handful of options that can help you further refine the printed data. For example, use the Start and End lists to specify a range of data to print. Select the Hide Details Of Private Appointments check box if you don't want the details of your private appointments printed. Set printer properties, the number of copies to print, and other general print settings. Then click OK to print or click Preview to preview the document.

Creating Custom Print Styles

Outlook provides a broad range of print styles, so it's likely that they will fit most of your needs. When these print styles don't quite offer what you need, however, you can create a custom print style.

Tip If you find yourself using an existing print style but frequently making the same option changes before printing, modify the existing print style to create a custom print style.

You can either modify an existing print style or copy a style and then modify it to incorporate the changes you need. If you always use the same modifications on a particular print style, you might prefer to simply modify that existing style rather than creating a new one. If you use the default style occasionally but modify its properties for most other print jobs, consider creating a custom print style based on the existing one so that both are available.

Follow these steps to modify or create a new print style:

1. Open Outlook, and then open the view for which you want to modify print style or on which you want to base your custom print style.
2. Choose File, Page Setup, Define Print Styles to open the Define Print Styles dialog box (see Figure 26-18).

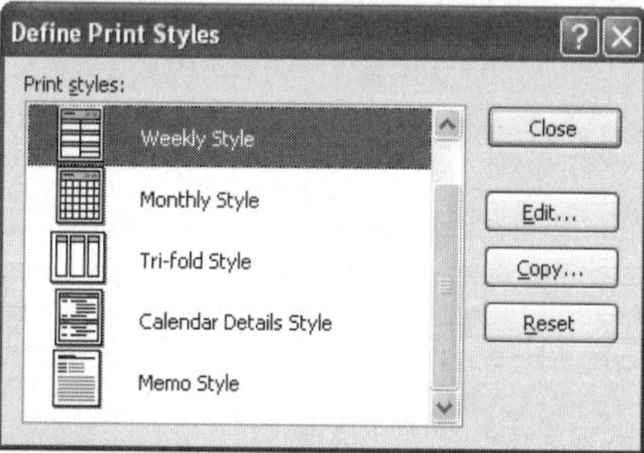

Figure 26-18. Use the Define Print Styles dialog box to modify and copy print styles.

3. If you want to create a new style, select an existing style and click Copy. Otherwise, select an existing style and click Edit. In either case, Outlook displays a Page Setup dialog box similar to the one shown in Figure 26-19.

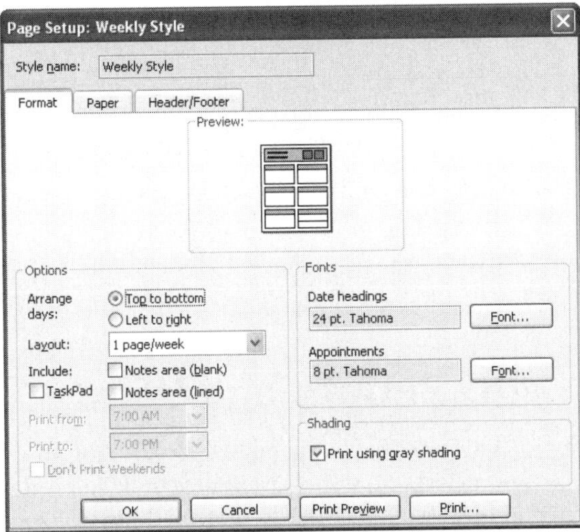

Figure 26-19. Specify properties for the print style.

4. Specify options as needed in the dialog box and then click OK to apply the changes.
5. From the Define Print Styles dialog box, click Close.

When you want to print with a particular style, open the view from which you want to print and choose File, Print. In the Print dialog box, select the style in the Print Style list, set other properties as necessary, and click OK to print.

Deleting Print Styles

If you've created some custom print styles but no longer use them, or if you've been experimenting with print styles and have a few samples you want to delete, removing them is a simple matter.

Follow these steps to remove a print style:

1. Choose File, Page Setup, Define Print Styles to open the Define Print Styles dialog box.
2. Select the style you want to remove and then click Delete.
3. When you have finished deleting print styles, click Close.

Resetting Print Styles

You can't delete the standard print styles provided by Outlook, but you can restore them to their default state. For example, suppose that you made several changes to the default Small Booklet style for the Contacts folder. Now you want to restore the print style to its default settings, but you don't remember what they are. Fortunately, Outlook remembers them for you.

To reset a print style, follow these steps:

1 Choose File, Page Setup, Define Print Styles to open the Define Print Styles dialog box.
2 Select the style you want to reset and click Reset. Outlook prompts you to verify the action.
3 Click OK to reset the style or Cancel to cancel the operation.
4 Click Close.

Custom Printing with Scripts and Word

The existing print styles in Outlook and the capability to define custom styles accommodate the needs of most users. In some situations, however, these built-in printing features are not enough. With a little custom scripting and Microsoft Word, however, you can overcome these limitations.

Word offers almost unlimited print layout capabilities, making it a great tool for laying out almost any type of document. For example, assume you're not satisfied with the way Outlook prints messages from mail folders. When you print a message, the recipient's name appears in large, bold type at the top of the page (see Figure 26-20). You are likely printing your own messages, and you know who you are, so you might want different information—such as the message subject—displayed on the first line.

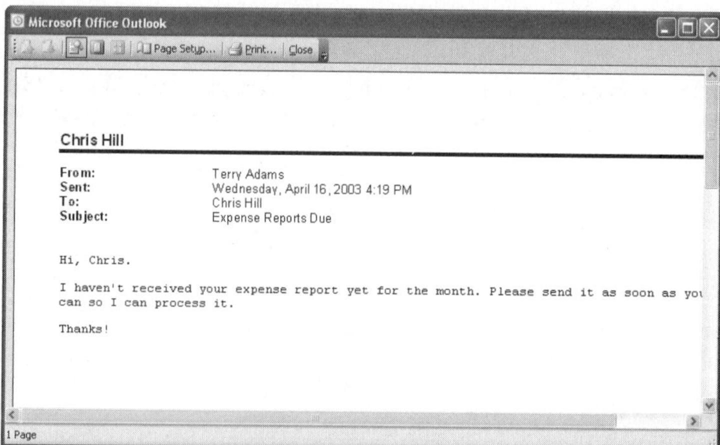

Figure 26-20. The standard message layout

Although you can make minimal changes to print layout such as adding headers or footers, you can't do much in Outlook to change the way most items print. You can, however, copy Outlook items to Word, format the document as needed, and print it (fromWord). You might think that moving the data from Outlook to Word is a time-consuming task, but you can make it happen in less than a second—provided you create a script to accomplish the task for you.

Using a Custom Contact Style

In this first example, assume you want to create a specific layout for contacts that prints the contact name in bold, places the contact's picture in the upper-right corner, and then includes selected contact information such as address, phone, e-mail, and other properties underneath. Figure 26-21 illustrates this custom print layout.

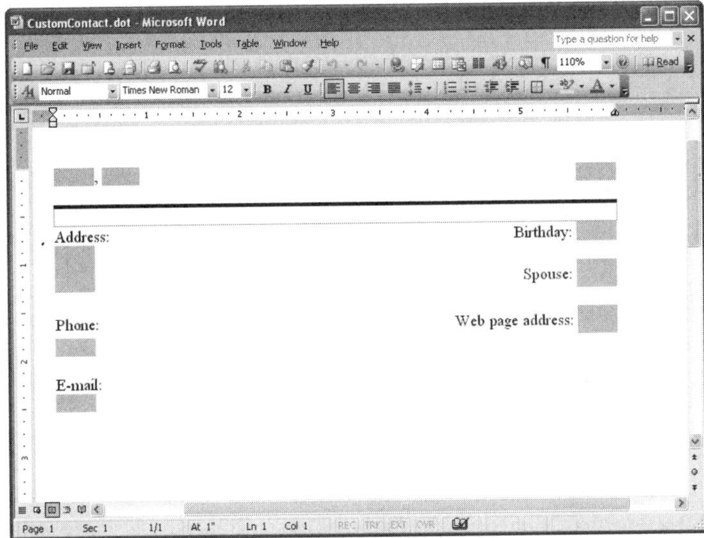

Figure 26-21. This contact style presents selected information in a specific layout.

The first step in creating this custom contact style is to create the document layout in Word. In a nutshell, this means creating a document template that contains a text form field for each contact item you want included on the printout and following these steps.

> **Note** The *Outlook 2003 Inside Out* CD contains a sample template named CustomContact.dot that you can customize to suit your needs, or simply to use as a sample for this section.

1. Open Word and start a new document, then choose View, Toolbars, Forms to display the Forms toolbar.
2. Enter labels for the fields. Then, insert a text form field from the Forms toolbar to contain the data that will come from the Outlook contact.
3. Select the first text form field and choose Insert, Bookmark. As shown in Figure 26-22, type a name for the bookmark that identifies the field (such as LastName), and click Add.

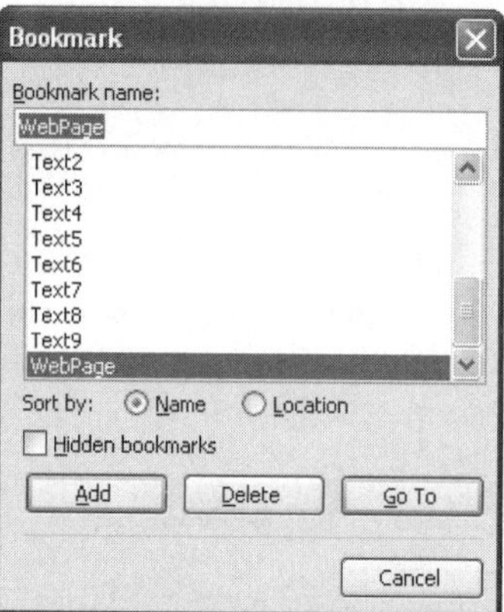

Figure 26-22. Add a bookmark for each text form field.

4 Select and add bookmarks for the remaining fields, naming them according to the information the field will contain, such as FirstName, Email, Phone, and so on.

5 Select the Title field and format it using a larger font, and add any other characteristics such as bold type.

6 Draw a line between the name and other information, if desired.

7 Choose File, Save As, choose Document Template from the Save As Type drop-down list, specify the path and name C:\CustomContact.dot, and click Save. Then, close Word.

You now have a template that is ready to be filled in by Outlook. The next step is to create a macro in Outlook that copies the desired information from the current contact item to the form, then prints the form. The following sample macro accomplishes these tasks. However, this sample does not provide extensive error checking, so consider this a starting point for your own macro. For example, you might want to add code that verifies that the current item is a contact item, and if not, displays an error message and exits.

Note The following macro is included on the *Outlook 2003 Inside Out* CD in the file CustomContactPrint.txt.

Choose Tools, Macro, Macros, enter **CustomContactPrint** in the Macro Name field, and click Create. Then enter the following code:

```
Sub CustomContactPrint()
    'Set up objects
    Dim strTemplate As String
    Dim objWord As Object
    Dim objDocs As Object
    Dim objApp As Application
    Dim objItem As Object
    Dim objAttach As Object
    Dim numAttach As Integer
    Dim objNS As NameSpace
```

```
    Dim mybklist As Object
    Dim x As Integer
    Dim pictureSaved As Boolean
    Dim myShape As Object
    'Dim ContactAddress
    'Create a Word document and current contact item object
    Set objApp = CreateObject("Outlook.Application")
    Set objNS = objApp.GetNamespace("MAPI")
    'Check to ensure Outlook item is selected
    If TypeName(objApp.ActiveInspector) = "Nothing" Then
        MsgBox "Contact not open. Exiting", vbOKOnly + vbInformation, "Outlook
Inside Out"
        Exit Sub
    End If
    Set objItem = objApp.ActiveInspector.CurrentItem
    Set objWord = CreateObject("Word.Application")
    strTemplate = "c:\CustomContact.dot"
    Set objDocs = objWord.Documents
    objDocs.Add strTemplate
    Set mybklist = objWord.activeDocument.Bookmarks
    'Fill in the form
    objWord.activeDocument.Bookmarks("LastName").Select
    objWord.Selection.TypeText CStr(objItem.LastName)
    objWord.activeDocument.Bookmarks("FirstName").Select
    objWord.Selection.TypeText CStr(objItem.FirstName)
    If objItem.HasPicture = True Then
        Set objAttach = objItem.Attachments
        numAttach = objAttach.Count
        For x = 1 To numAttach
            If objAttach.Item(x).DisplayName = "ContactPicture.jpg" Then
                objAttach.Item(x).SaveAsFile "C:\" & _
                objAttach.Item(x).DisplayName
                pictureSaved = True
            End If
        Next x
        If pictureSaved = True Then
            objWord.activeDocument.Bookmarks("Picture").Select
            Set myShape =
objWord.activeDocument.Shapes.AddPicture("c:\ContactPicture.jpg", False, True,
432, -25)
            objWord.activeDocument.Shapes(1).Left = 432 -
objWord.activeDocument.Shapes(1).Width
        End If
    End If
    objWord.activeDocument.Bookmarks("Address1").Select
    objWord.Selection.TypeText CStr(objItem.BusinessAddressStreet)
    objWord.activeDocument.Bookmarks("Address2").Select
    objWord.Selection.TypeText CStr(objItem.BusinessAddressCity)
    objWord.Selection.TypeText ", "
    objWord.Selection.TypeText CStr(objItem.BusinessAddressState)
    objWord.Selection.TypeText " "
    objWord.Selection.TypeText CStr(objItem.BusinessAddressPostalCode)
    objWord.activeDocument.Bookmarks("Spouse").Select
    objWord.Selection.TypeText CStr(objItem.Spouse)
```

```
    objWord.activeDocument.Bookmarks("Phone1").Select
    objWord.Selection.TypeText CStr(objItem.BusinessTelephoneNumber)
    objWord.activeDocument.Bookmarks("WebPage").Select
    objWord.Selection.TypeText CStr(objItem.BusinessHomePage)
    objWord.activeDocument.Bookmarks("Email1").Select
    objWord.Selection.TypeText CStr(objItem.Email1Address)
    'Print and exit
    objWord.PrintOut Background:=True

    'Process other system events until printing is finished
    While objWord.BackgroundPrintingStatus
        DoEvents
    Wend
    objWord.Quit SaveChanges:=wdvbaDoNotSaveChanges
    Set objApp = Nothing
    Set objNS = Nothing
    Set objItem = Nothing
    Set objWord = Nothing
    Set objDocs = Nothing
    Set mybklist = Nothing
End Sub
```


If you examine this macro code, you'll see that it uses named bookmarks to locate the position in the document where each contact element will be inserted. Also note that the lines in the macro that insert specific contact items reference those items by their Outlook object model names, such as Email1Address, BusinessTelephoneNumber, BusinessHomePage, and so on. If you want to modify this macro to insert other contact items, you'll need to know their names. To view contact item properties, choose Tools, Macro, Visual Basic Editor, then choose Help, Microsoft Visual Basic Help. Expand the Objects branch, expand C, and click ContactItem Object. Click the Properties link and scroll through the list of properties to locate the one you need.

This macro also determines whether the contact has a picture associated with it. If so, the macro cycles through the attachments to locate the picture (which is always named ContactPicture.jpg) and saves it to disk. The macro then inserts the picture in the Word document. It is my observation that ContactPicture.jpg is always the first attachment, regardless of the order in which they are attached or their names. However, this macro checks each attachment anyway to accommodate future changes in Outlook's behavior regarding picture attachments.

> **Note** The macro saves the picture file to the root of drive C. You can change the macro code to save and load the picture from any path. You can also change the path location for the Word document template as needed.

Using a Custom Message Style

You can use a method similar to the one in the previous section to print messages from Outlook using Word. For example, assume you want to print e-mail messages with the subject in large, bold type at the top of the page, with other message content printed below that. Figure 26-23 shows a sample form in Word. Use the same general steps detailed in the previous section to create a Word template that contains the form text fields and bookmarks needed to hold the message items.

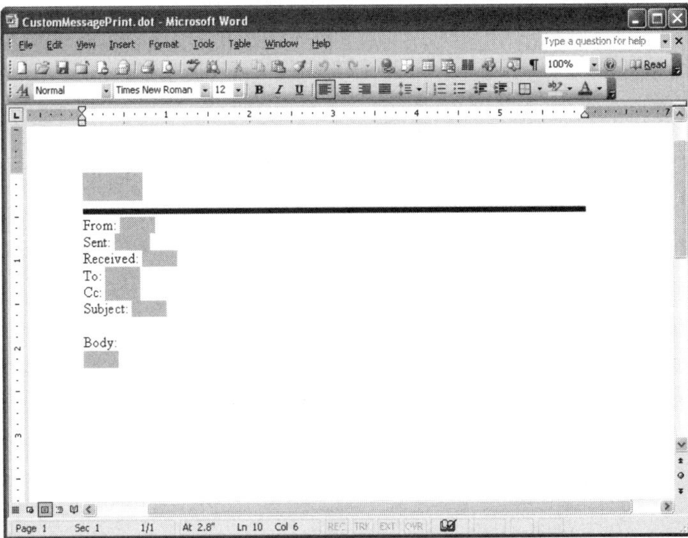

Figure 26-23. A sample form in Word for printing messages.

After you create the document template in Word and save it, open the Visual Basic Editor and create the following macro:

Note This sample macro is contained on the *Outlook 2003 Inside Out* CD as CustomMessagePrint.txt.

```
Sub CustomMessagePrint()
    'Set up objects
    Dim strTemplate As String
    Dim objWord As Object
    Dim objDocs As Object
    Dim objApp As Application
    Dim objItem As Object
    Dim objNS As NameSpace
    Dim mybklist As Object
    'Create a Word document and current message item object
    Set objApp = CreateObject("Outlook.Application")
    Set objNS = objApp.GetNamespace("MAPI")
    'Check to ensure Outlook item is selected
    If TypeName(objApp.ActiveInspector) = "Nothing" Then
        MsgBox "Message not open. Exiting", vbOKOnly + vbInformation, "Outlook
Inside Out"
        Exit Sub
    End If
    Set objItem = objApp.ActiveInspector.CurrentItem
```

Chapter 26

```
    Set objWord = CreateObject("Word.Application")
    strTemplate = "c:\prnmsg.dot"
    Set objDocs = objWord.Documents
    objDocs.Add strTemplate
    Set mybklist = objWord.activeDocument.Bookmarks
    'Fill in the form
    objWord.activeDocument.Bookmarks("Title").Select
    objWord.Selection.TypeText CStr(objItem.Subject)
    objWord.activeDocument.Bookmarks("From").Select
    objWord.Selection.TypeText CStr(objItem.SenderName)
    objWord.activeDocument.Bookmarks("Sent").Select
    objWord.Selection.TypeText CStr(objItem.SentOn)
    objWord.activeDocument.Bookmarks("Received").Select
    objWord.Selection.TypeText CStr(objItem.ReceivedTime)
    objWord.activeDocument.Bookmarks("To").Select
    objWord.Selection.TypeText CStr(objItem.To)
    objWord.activeDocument.Bookmarks("Cc").Select
    objWord.Selection.TypeText CStr(objItem.CC)
    objWord.activeDocument.Bookmarks("Subject").Select
    objWord.Selection.TypeText CStr(objItem.Subject)
    objWord.activeDocument.Bookmarks("Body").Select
    objWord.Selection.TypeText CStr(objItem.Body)
    'Print and exit

    objWord.PrintOut Background:=True
    'Process other system events until printing is finished
    While objWord.BackgroundPrintingStatus
        DoEvents
    Wend
    objWord.Quit SaveChanges:=wdvbaDoNotSaveChanges
End Sub
```

As with the Contact item macro, you can customize this macro and document template to accommodate different or additional message fields as needed.

Custom Printing with Excel

Microsoft Excel is another solution to the custom printing requirements, particularly for Outlook table views. For example, assume you want to print all of your Outlook contacts but arrange them in a different order from what the Table style offers in Outlook, and use different formatting for some of the columns. The solution is to simply copy the contacts to Excel, format and rearrange as needed, and print by following these steps:

1 Open the Outlook folder containing the items you want to print, then choose a table view. This example uses the Phone List view (see Figure 26-24).

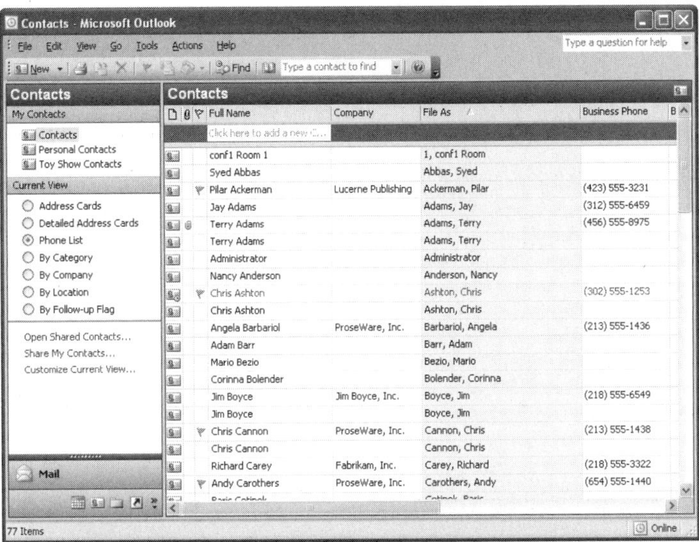

Figure 26-24. You can easily copy data from an Outlook table view to Excel.

2 Select the items you want included in the printed document, the press Ctrl+C or choose Edit, Copy to copy the items to the Clipboard.

3 Open Excel and press Ctrl+V or choose Edit, Paste to paste the data into Excel (see Figure 26-25).

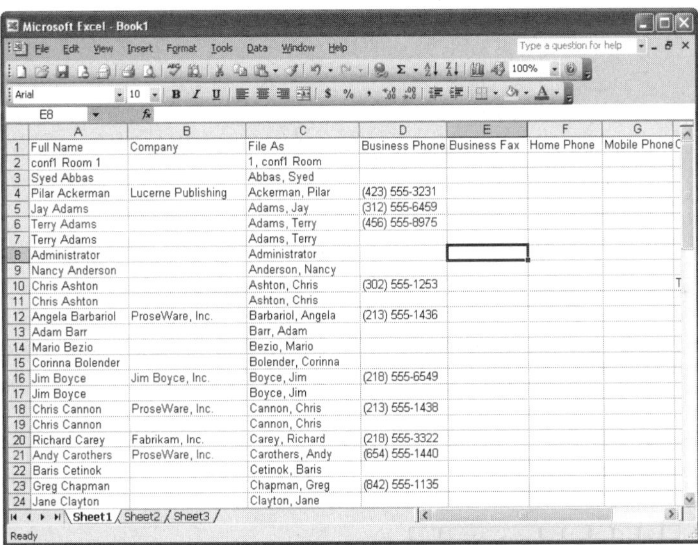

Figure 26-25. Arrange and format the data in Excel and print.

4 Rearrange columns, apply formatting, and otherwise adjust the layout as needed, then print the worksheet.

Chapter 27

Automating Common Tasks

Microsoft Office Outlook 2003 is a feature-rich product and, as such, has an option, a wizard, or a graphical tool for accomplishing nearly anything you require from a personal information manager. If something does come up that the folks at Microsoft haven't planned for, though, you also have the option of customizing Outlook by using its built-in support for Microsoft Visual Basic code additions. Through the use of flexible Visual Basic for Applications (VBA) scripting options and built-in security controls, you can easily simplify and automate common tasks.

In this chapter, you'll learn how to create and use a macro. This includes creating the macro, stepping through a macro to test it, and deleting macros you no longer need. In addition, you'll find out about implementing security options for macros.

This chapter explores macros in general. For a more complete discussion of developing custom applications and automating tasks with Visual Basic, see Articles 1 through 3 on the companion CD.

Understanding Automation Options

Outlook has a number of built-in automation options that allow the application to perform certain tasks for you. For example, the Rules Wizard automatically moves, copies, and forwards e-mail messages; and the organizer pane automatically color-codes e-mail messages and deals with junk and adult e-mail messages. The Out Of Office Assistant acts as an answering service when you're away.

For information about these examples of built-in automation options, see "Processing Messages Automatically," page 224, and "Using the Out Of Office Assistant," page 253.

If a built-in option can accomplish the automated task you require, it should be your first choice. By using a built-in option instead of a custom one, you minimize problems that can occur if you need to reinstall Outlook or use Outlook on multiple machines. Using standardized options also guards against compatibility problems with upgrades to Outlook.

If none of the automation options does the trick, however, you can accomplish just about any customization by using VBA. This chapter focuses on the use of VBA procedures known as macros to automate common tasks.

For detailed information about using VBA with Outlook, see Article 2, "Using VBA in Outlook," and Article 3, "Integrating Outlook and Other Applications with VBA," on the companion CD.

Understanding Macros

So just what is a macro? In general terms, a *macro* is a number of commands grouped together to execute a particular task. Macros are like small programs that operate within other programs. Macros have been around for a long time, and all Microsoft Office products support them at some level. In Outlook 2003, macros are implemented as VBA procedures that are not linked to a particular form and are available from anywhere in Outlook. In Outlook, you manage macros by using the Tools menu, which contains a Macro submenu.

Using Macros

Macros are most useful for tasks that must be performed repeatedly without change. Even so, because a macro contains Visual Basic code, it can be flexible and can respond to variables or user input. With the power of scripting, a macro can accomplish a task in the most efficient way in response to specific conditions.

Caution Macros can be extremely powerful. This power can be a great asset for you, but it can also mean that any problems can become serious ones. Like many other things, macros can be dangerous when used improperly. Inexperienced programmers should take great care when writing and using macros in Outlook.

Following are the three basic programming elements you can work with in an Outlook macro:

- **Object** An object is a particular part of a program, such as a button, a menu item, or a text field. Objects make up any element of Outlook that you can see or work with. An object has properties, and how you set these properties determines how the object functions.
- **Property** Any part of an object—its color, its width, and its value—is part of the set of attributes that make up its properties.
- **Method** A method is a task that an object carries out. Methods can be modified based on user input or the value of certain properties.

In general, a VBA macro either determines or modifies the value of an object's property or calls a method. Macros, then, are nothing more than simple programs that use VBA to access or modify Outlook information.

> **Note** With the Macro Recorder in Microsoft Excel and Microsoft Word, you can simply record your mouse movements and keystrokes, and the computer plays them back when you execute the macro. Outlook 2003 doesn't include a macro recorder or any other graphical device for the nonprogrammatic creation of macros. As such, users familiar with programming basics and VBA will have a head start in learning to create Outlook macros.

Creating a Macro from Scratch

The process for creating an Outlook macro is simple. The process for creating a *useful* macro, on the other hand, is more complex. Because of that, the discussion of advanced VBA is left for later chapters. In this chapter, I'll fall back on the most basic of functions, the Hello World dialog box macro. This macro creates a function that displays a message box containing the text "Hello World." Clicking OK (the only button) closes the message box and ends the macro.

To create this macro, follow these steps:

1. Choose Tools, Macro, Macros to open the Macros dialog box.
2. In the Macro Name box, type a descriptive name for your new macro (no spaces are allowed). In Figure 27-1, the macro is titled HelloWorldMsgBox.

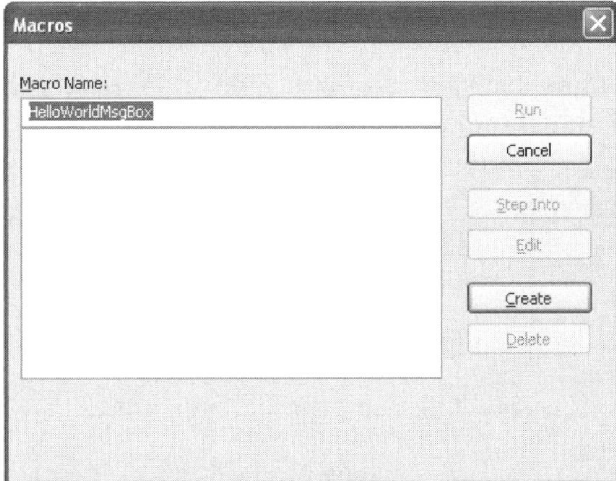

Figure 27-1. Enter the name for a new macro in the Macro Name box.

3. Click Create. The Microsoft Visual Basic Editor starts, which allows you to add functionality to your macro. For those who are not programmers, creating VBA code might seem daunting, but simple tasks are actually quite easy.

4 Type the following (see Figure 27-2): **MsgBox ("Hello World")**

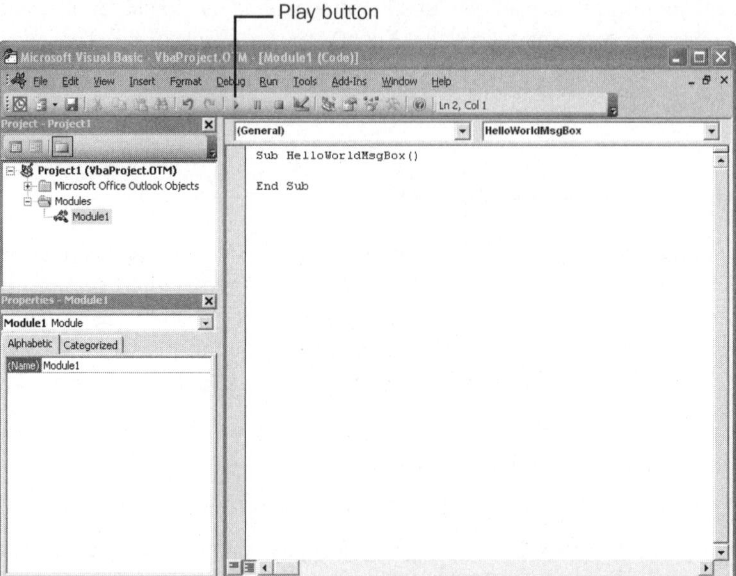

Figure 27-2. You add code between the first and last lines of a macro.

5 To test the code, choose Run, Run Sub/UserForm or click the Play button on the toolbar.

6 When you're prompted for which macro you want to run, select your macro and click Run. The message box shown in Figure 27-3 appears.

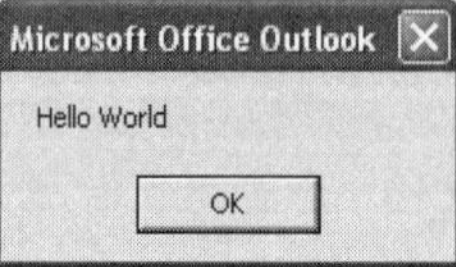

Figure 27-3. This is what you see when you run the macro.

7 Choose File, Save. The default file name is VbaProject.otm.

8 Close the Visual Basic Editor.

Running a Macro

After you save a macro, it is available for use. Choose Tools, Macro, Macros and select the HelloWorldMsgBox macro. When you click Run, the window appears as it did when you tested the macro in the Visual Basic Editor. Calling a macro this way is inconvenient, however. If you'll be using the macro often, you might want to add it as an item on your toolbar for easier access.

To add the macro to a toolbar, follow these steps:

1. Choose View, Toolbars, Customize to open the Customize dialog box.
2. Click the Commands tab.
3. In the Categories list, select Macros. The Hello World macro appears on the right (see Figure 27-4).
4. Drag the Hello World macro to a location on the toolbar. Outlook adds a button to the toolbar, and clicking it runs the macro immediately.

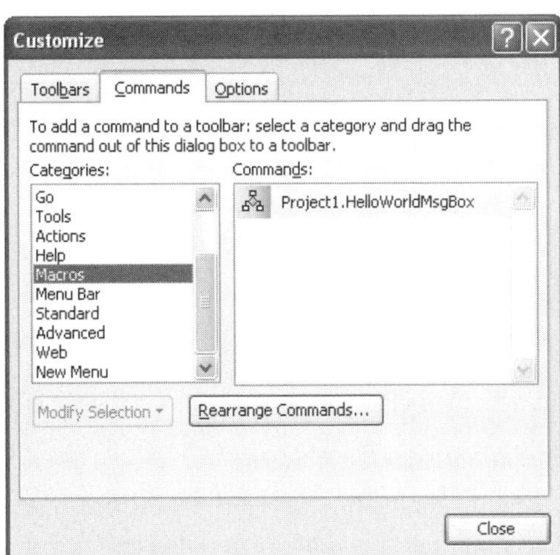

Figure 27-4. Locate the macro and add it to the toolbar.

Editing a Macro

After you create a macro, you can edit it by returning to the Macros dialog box:

1. In the Macros dialog box, select the HelloWorldMsgBox macro and then click Edit. The Visual Basic Editor starts and displays the selected macro.
2. Modify the macro so that it matches the following:

```
Sub HelloWorldMsgBox()
MsgBox ("Click OK to create a new message")
Set newMsg = Application.CreateItem(0)
    newMsg.Subject = "Sample Message from a Macro"
    newMsg.Body = "You can even add text automatically."
    newMsg.Display
End Sub
```

3 Verify that the changed macro works properly by clicking the Run Macro button on the Visual Basic Editor toolbar. Instead of just showing a simple message box as before, the macro should now present you with a new e-mail message window. The message should have information automatically filled in in the subject and body fields, as in Figure 27-5.

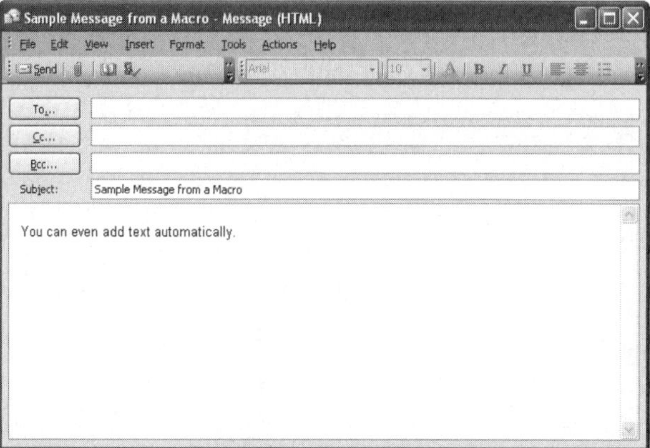

Figure 27-5. This is the new message created by running the macro.

4 Save the changes and close the Visual Basic Editor.

5 When you return to the Macros dialog box, select the modified macro and click Run. You should see the same e-mail message that you saw in step 3.

> **Tip** When you edit a macro, you'll eventually want to save it and test the changes. To ensure that you can return to the original macro in case of trouble, first export the project so that you can retrieve it later. For information about exporting, see "Sharing Macros with Others," page 715.

Stepping Through a Macro

When you're creating a macro, it's often helpful to step through the code, which allows you to watch each line as it is being processed and see problems as they occur. To do this, open the sample macro for editing (as described in the preceding section), and then press F8. The first line of the macro is highlighted, and its code is processed. To process the next line, press F8 again.

Step through the rest of the macro using the F8 key. Notice that clicking OK merely closes the message box rather than creating the e-mail message. This is because later steps are not followed automatically. The new e-mail message is created only after you press F8 through all the lines of the subprocedure.

> **Note** You can step through a macro only when it is being edited. When macros are executed from within Outlook, they automatically move through all procedures.

Troubleshooting

Your macro doesn't run properly

If you are having problems getting a macro to run properly, you can try several different approaches to determine the source of the problem. The most common problem is incorrect syntax in your code. Finding errors in code can be a vexing job, but using the step-through process generally helps to find the line that is causing you problems.

If your syntax is correct, the problem might have to do with the way you're running the macro. Among the problems you should check are the security settings on the macro and the security settings on the computer. Also, if the macro has been deleted, but a toolbar button still remains, you might be trying to run a macro that no longer exists.

Deleting a Macro

Sometimes a macro outlives its usefulness. To delete a macro you no longer need, choose Tools, Macro, Macros. In the Macros dialog box, select the macro you want to remove and click Delete. When you're prompted to verify that you want to permanently delete the macro, click Yes to remove the macro from the list, making its code unavailable to Outlook.

Note If you have created a toolbar button for a macro that you subsequently delete, you must locate the button and remove it in a separate operation.

Sharing Macros with Others

If you're creating macros for use by a group of people, or even an entire organization, the macros must be installed separately for each user. Unfortunately, although the Macros dialog box has options for creating and deleting macros, it has no option for adding macros from other places. You can't share macros the same way you share files. Instead, sharing macros with other users is generally a two-step process: the user who creates the macro must export the macro code, and the other user must import the code.To share a macro, follow these steps:

1. Choose Tools, Macro, Visual Basic Editor.
2. In the Visual Basic Editor, choose File, Export File to open the Export File dialog box (see Figure 27-6).

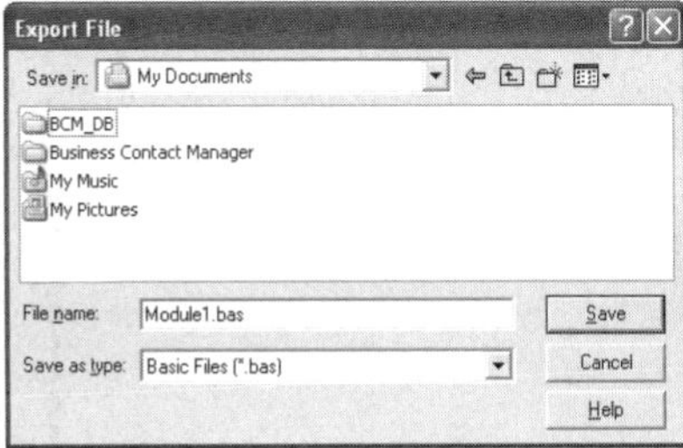

Figure 27-6. The macro file is being exported so that it can be shared.

3 In the Save As Type box, save the project as a BAS file. (By doing so, you can then e-mail the file to another user or make it available on the network.)

Once another user has access to the BAS file, that user can install the macro by following these steps:

1 Choose Tools, Macro, Visual Basic Editor.
2 In the Visual Basic Editor, choose File, Import File.
3 Browse to the file, open it, and save it to his or her machine.
4 The user can now access the macro through the Macros dialog box, as you do.

Setting Macro Security

Macros have several advantages, including their power, their flexibility, and their ability to run automatically, even without your knowledge. These advantages have a dark side, though, and poorly written or malicious macros can do significant damage to an Outlook message store. Because of the potential danger that macros pose, the Outlook Tools menu offers three security levels for Outlook macros:

- **High** Your system can run only macros that are digitally signed. This means that some macros—even benign and potentially useful ones—are not available.
- **Medium** You will be prompted as to whether you want to run untrusted macros.
- **Low** Macros run automatically, regardless of their signature. This is the most dangerous setting.

For information about digital signatures, see "Protecting Messages with Digital Signatures," page 293.

Using Security Levels

To view or change the security level, choose Tools, Macro, Security and click the Security Level tab (see Figure 27-7). The default setting is Medium, which is probably the best choice for most users.

Inside Out

Security and user-created macros

When you create your own macros, they are not controlled by the security settings. User-created macros do not need to be signed and will run regardless of the security setting you have selected. This is nice for purposes of design and editing, but it assumes that you realize exactly what a macro will do. Moreover, it means that when you want to test macro security settings, you must run Outlook under a different user account.

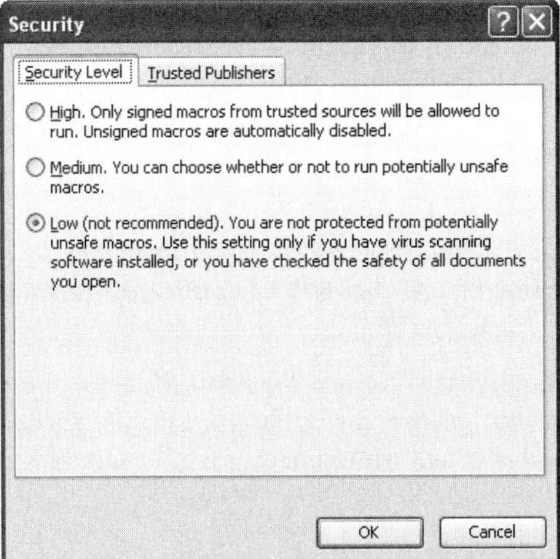

Figure 27-7. You can set the security level for macros on this tab.

Specifying Trusted Sources

To reduce the number of times you're prompted about whether to run a macro (if you've set a Medium security level) or to be able to run macros at all (if you've set a High security level), you can specify a trusted source.

When a digitally signed macro runs, Outlook displays the certificate attached to the macro. Besides choosing whether or not to run the macro, you're also given the choice of adding the certificate holder (the organization or individual who created the macro) to your list of trusted sources. Once the holder of the certificate is trusted, any macros signed with that certificate run without prompting at a Medium security setting and are among the macros that run at a High security setting.

To view the list of trusted certificates or to remove a trusted source, choose Tools, Macro, Security. Click the Trusted Publishers tab to view the sources. To remove a trusted source, select one of the sources and then click Remove.

Signing Your Macros to Avoid Security Warnings

Macro security in Outlook gives you control over when macros can run, which helps prevent malicious code from affecting an Outlook user's system. When macro security is set to High in Outlook, only digitally signed macros from trusted sources can run. A setting of Medium causes Outlook to prompt you whether to enable and allow macros to run. A setting of Low allows all macros to run, which poses significant risks from malicious code.

If you create your own macros, you probably would like to digitally sign your macros so they will run without triggering Outlook's macro security warnings. Outlook 2003, like Outlook 2000 and Outlook 2002, provides the means to sign VBA projects.

Start by searching the \Program Files\Microsoft Office\Office11 folder for the file Selfcert.exe, which enables you to create your own code-signing certificate. If the file is not on the system, run Setup and add the feature Digital Signature for VBA Projects. After you install or locate Selfcert.exe, run the program and when prompted, enter a name for the certificate, such as Outlook Code Signing Certificate.

Next, choose Tools, Macro, Macros, select a macro, and click Edit to open the Visual Basic editor. Choose Tools, Digital Signature to open the Digital Signature dialog box. Click Choose, select your code-signing certificate, and click OK. Click OK again, and then close the Visual Basic Editor.

Verify that you have configured Outlook macro security for either Medium or High settings, then attempt to run a macro. When Outlook asks if you want to trust the macro publisher, click Yes. Your custom macros should now run without triggering the Outlook security warnings.

Part 6

Managing and Securing Outlook

Chapter 28

Integrating Outlook with Other Office Applications

Microsoft Office Outlook 2003 works well as a stand-alone application, but its real strength is realized when you integrate it with other Microsoft Office applications. Most of us spend our day working in one or two main programs, such as a word processor or a database program, so most of our information is saved in files designed for those programs. For instance, you probably save letters and other correspondence in Microsoft Word files; save contact information in Outlook; and save inventory, invoices, and other data in Microsoft Access or Microsoft Excel. With Office, you can integrate all this, which lets you choose the best tool for creating your information and the best tool for sharing or producing your data.

Some of the ways you can integrate Outlook with other Office applications include the following:

- Using Outlook contacts for a Word mail merge
- Exporting Outlook contacts to Word, Excel, or Access
- Importing contacts from Word, Excel, or Access into Outlook
- Using Outlook notes in other Office applications

In this chapter, you'll learn about using Outlook and other Office applications to share information between applications. Rather than employing standard copy-and-paste or cut-and-paste techniques, you'll find out about ways to reuse your information in Outlook or another file format without retyping or re-creating the data.

Using Contacts for a Mail Merge in Word

The Outlook Contacts folder allows you to create contact entries to store information about a person, a group, or an organization. You can then use that contact data to create e-mail messages, set up meetings or appointments, or complete other tasks associated with a contact. Your contacts list can also be used as the data source to provide names, addresses, phone numbers, and other pertinent data to your mail merge documents.

You perform a *mail merge* in Word when you want to create multiple documents that are all based on the same letter or document but that have different names, addresses, or other specific information (referred to as *merge data*). For instance, you might perform a mail merge operation when you want to do a mass mailing to your customers about a new product launch.

You begin by creating and saving a standard letter. Next you place field codes where you want the recipient's address, the salutation, and other merge data to appear. *Field codes* are placeholders in documents where data will change. For instance, the name of the recipient should be a field code because it will change for each letter you send out.

You next create or assign a database to populate the field codes (that is, to insert the merge data). Word uses the database and contact information to create separate letters. You can then save these files or print each letter for your mass mailing.

> **Tip** Before starting to set up a mail merge using your Outlook contact data, review your contact entries to make sure that the data is complete and current and that you don't have duplicate entries.

To perform a mail merge using Microsoft Office Word 2003, follow these steps:

1. Start Word.
2. Choose Tools, Letters And Mailing, Mail Merge (see Figure 28-1).

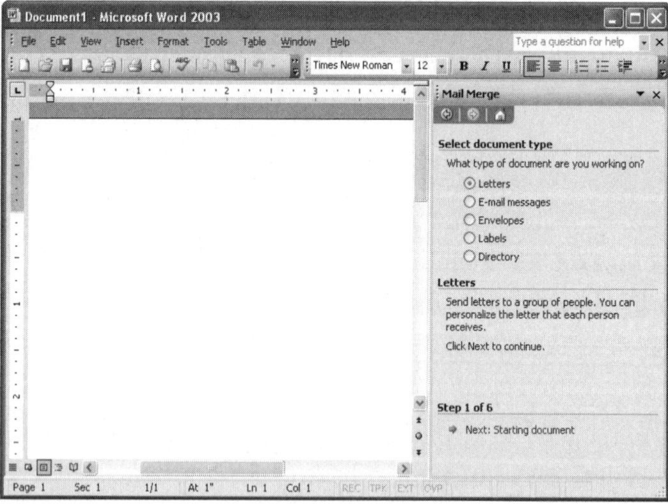

Figure 28-1. Start a mail merge by opening Word's Mail Merge Wizard, which appears in the task pane on the right.

3. In the task pane, select the type of document to create, such as Letters, and then click Next: Starting Document at the bottom of the pane.
4. Select the document to use—for example, the current document. Click Next: Select Recipients.

5 Select the Select From Outlook Contacts option.

6 Select the Choose Contacts Folder option to open the Select Contact List Folder dialog box (see Figure 28-2).

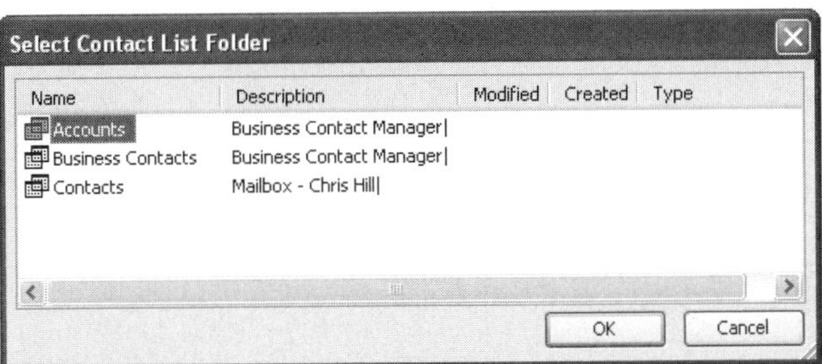

Figure 28-2. Select your Contacts folder here.

7 Select the folder that contains your contacts list and click OK to open the Mail Merge Recipients dialog box (see Figure 28-3).

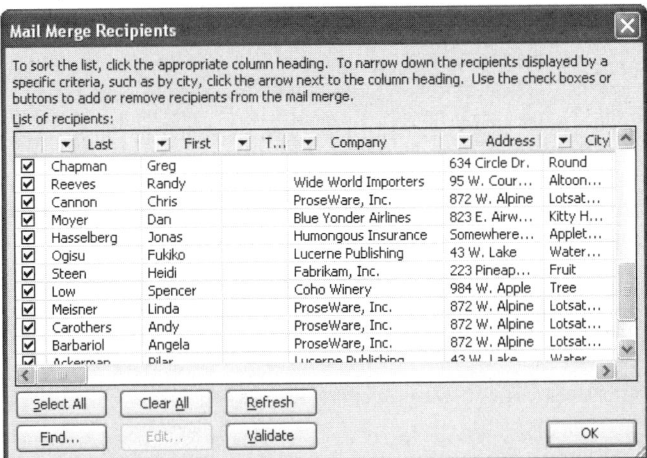

Figure 28-3. Select contacts to include in the mail merge from this dialog box.

8 Select the contacts you want to use to populate the mail merge document. You can use the following methods:

- Click Select All to select all contacts (the default).
- Clear the check boxes next to the names of those you do not want to include in the mail merge.
- Click Clear All and then select individual contacts.

> **Tip** If you want to create a mailing list that is a subset of your Contacts folder, you can filter the contacts list with a custom view and then use the custom view to perform a mail merge from Outlook. See "Performing a Mail Merge from Outlook" on page 726 for details.

9 Click OK.

10 Click Next: Write Your Letter.

11 Click Address Block to open the Insert Address Block dialog box (see Figure 28-4).

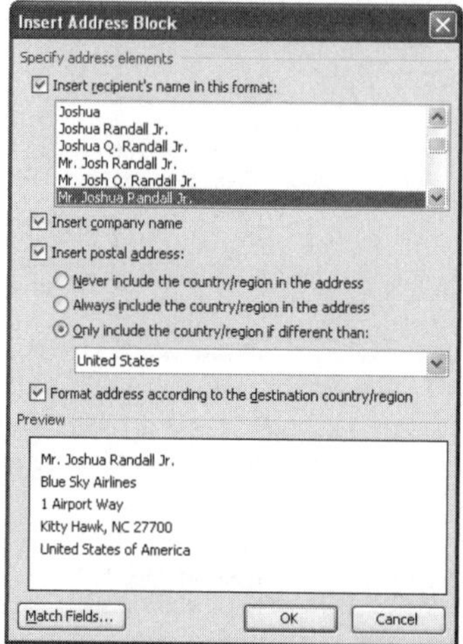

Figure 28-4. Set the address block field in this dialog box.

12 Using the options in this dialog box, specify the address fields and format you want to include in your letter. Click OK and then start writing your letter.

13 Click Next: Preview Your Letters to see how the Outlook contact data looks in your letter. Figure 28-5 shows an example.

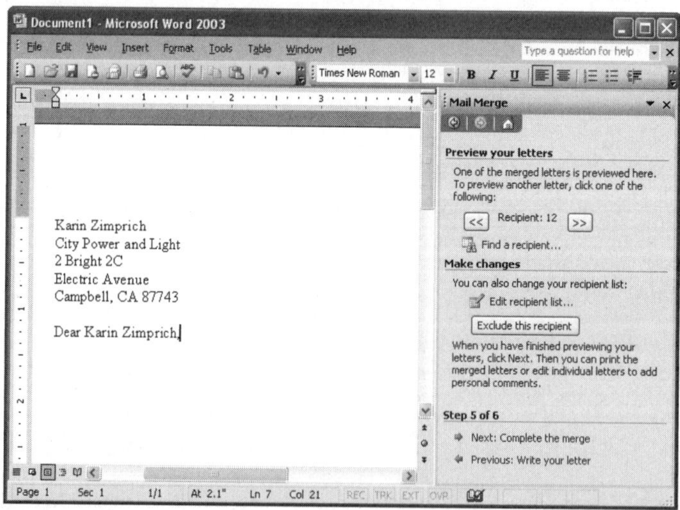

Figure 28-5. The address and salutation data in this letter came from an Outlook Contacts folder.

14 In the task pane, click Next: Complete The Merge to finish.

15 Finish editing your letter or print it.

For detailed information about performing mail merges in Word, as well as using other Word features, see *Microsoft Office Word 2003 Inside Out*, by Mary Millhollon and Katherine Murray (Microsoft Press, 2003).

Filtering Contacts in or out of the Merge

When you perform a mail merge from Word, you can use selection criteria to determine which of the contacts are included in the mail merge set. For example, assume you want to send a letter to all of your contacts who have addresses in California and last names that begin with the letter R.

In the Mail Merge Recipients dialog box shown previously in Figure 28-3, each column includes a drop-down button next to the column heading. To specify selection criteria based on a particular column, click the drop-down button and choose one of the following commands:

- **All** Do not filter based on the selected column.
- **Blanks** Include only those contacts for which the selected field is blank. For example, choose this option under the E-Mail Address column to include all contacts who do not have an e-mail address in their contact record.
- **Nonblanks** Include only those contacts for which the selected field is not blank. For example, select this option under the Last field to include only those contacts whose Last Name field is not blank.
- **Advanced** Click this button to open the Filter And Sort dialog box, explained next.

If you click Advanced to open the Filter And Sort dialog box, shown in Figure 28-6, you can specify more complex selection criteria. In the following example we'll include those contacts whose last names start with R and whose State value equals California:

1. In the Mail Merge Recipients dialog box, click the drop-down button beside the Last field.
2. From the first Field drop-down list, choose Last, then choose Greater Than, and enter Q in the Compare To field.
3. From the second Field drop-down list, choose Last, then choose Less Than, and enter S in the Compare To field.

4. Select State from the third Field drop-down list, choose Equal To from the Comparison drop-down list, and enter CA in the Compare To field. The dialog box should look similar to the one shown in Figure 28-6.

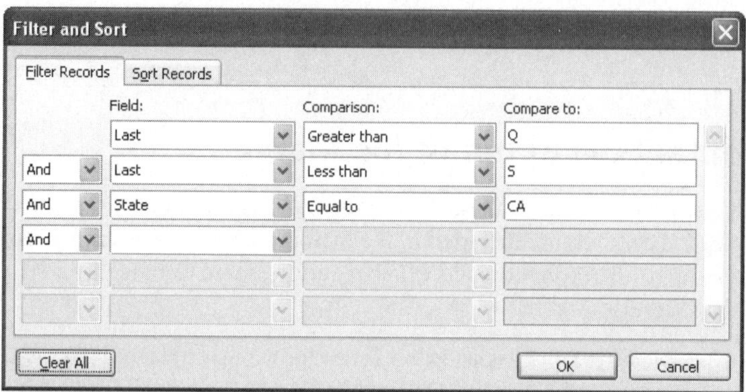

Figure 28-6. These settings will select all contacts whose names start with R and whose addresses are in California.

5. Click OK to close the Filter And Sort dialog box. After a few moments, the Mail Merge Recipients list shows only those contacts whose last name begins with R and whose State value is listed as CA.

As you might have guessed from Figure 28-6, you can select OR instead of AND in the dialog box for a particular criteria. For example, you would use OR for the third criteria (step 4) to cause Outlook to include contacts in the mail merge if their names started with R or they lived in California. A contact would also be included if both criteria were met.

Performing a Mail Merge from Outlook

As the previous sections illustrated, it's easy to perform a mail merge from Word and pull contact information from Outlook. You can also filter the contacts to include only those that suit your needs.

You can also perform a mail merge from Outlook. Starting from Outlook gives you a few advantages:

- **More control over contacts to be included** You can merge all of the contacts in the current view of the Contacts folder, or merge only those contacts you have selected in the folder.
- **Control over which fields to include** You can include all contact fields or only those fields that are visible in the current folder view.
- **Capability to save the contacts for later use** Outlook gives you the option of saving the contacts to a Word document to use for future reference or for future mail merges from Word.

To begin a mail merge from Outlook, choose Tools, Mail Merge to open the Mail Merge Contacts dialog box. As Figure 28-7 illustrates, Outlook offers two options to control which contacts are included in the merge:

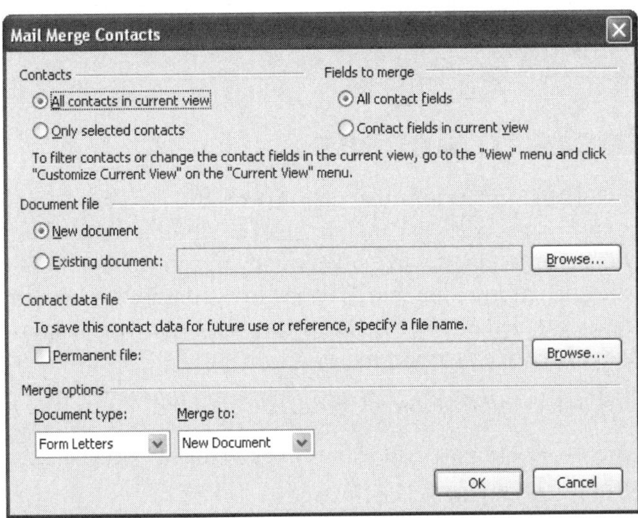

Figure 28-7. Use the Mail Merge Contacts dialog box to choose which contacts and fields to include in the merge.

- **All Contacts In Current View** Use this option to include all of the contacts in the view, understanding that all of the contacts in the view does not equate to all contacts. If you create a filtered view of the folder that excludes some of the contacts, those contacts will be excluded from the merge as well.
- **Only Selected Contacts** Choose this option to include only those contacts that you selected in the folder prior to choosing Tools, Mail Merge. Hold down the Ctrl key while clicking to select individual contacts, or Shift+Click to select a range of contacts.

In addition to specifying which contacts are included, you can control which fields are included, excluding those you don't need. The following two options determine which fields are included:

- **All Contact Fields** Choose this option to include all of the contact fields.
- **Contact Fields In Current View** Choose this option to include only the fields displayed in the current view. You can customize the view prior to choosing Tools, Mail Merge to filter in only specific fields.

Creating custom views to filter items in a folder is covered in detail in "Creating and Using Custom Views," page 681.

After you choose options in the Mail Merge Contacts dialog box and click OK, Outlook opens Word, prepopulating the mail merge contact list and starting the document type you have specified. To complete the mail merge, choose Tools, Letters And Mailings, Mail Merge to open the Mail Merge task pane at the wizard's step 3, in which you choose the contacts to include in the letter. You can click Edit Recipient List to verify or fine-tune the list, or click Next: Write Your Letter to move to the next step.

See the section "Using Contacts for a Mail Merge in Word" on page 721 for detailed instructions on using the Mail Merge Wizard in Word.

Exporting Contacts to Access

Another way to use Outlook contact information is to export this data to Access. This is handy if you want to use contact data in database tables or reports. You could spend your time opening individual contact entries in Outlook, copying information from the contact form, and then pasting the information into Access where you want it. However, Outlook makes the process much simpler. All you have to do is use the Import and Export Wizard and select Microsoft Access as the file to export to.

Here's how to export contact information to Access:

1. In Outlook, choose File, Import And Export to open the Import and Export Wizard.
2. Select Export To A File and then click Next.
3. On the wizard page shown in Figure 28-8, select Microsoft Access and then click Next.

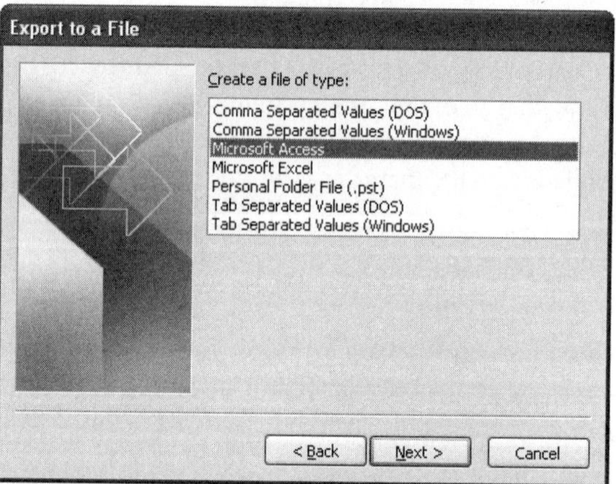

Figure 28-8. The Import and Export Wizard allows you to export to an Access file.

4. Select the folder from which to export data. In this case, select the Contacts folder (see Figure 28-9) or another folder that includes Outlook contact information. Click Next.

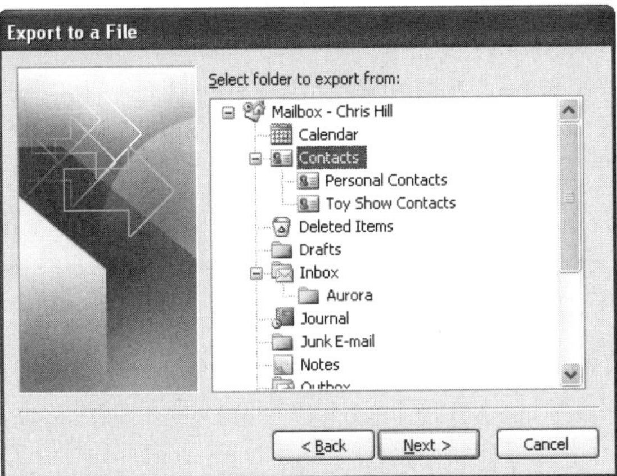

Figure 28-9. Select the folder from which you want to export.

5 Specify the folder and type a name for the export file. You can click Browse to navigate to a folder and then click OK to select that folder. When you do this, the file is given an MDB extension to denote an Access database file. Click Next.

6 Click Map Custom Fields. In this dialog box, you can add or remove field items, modifying the way the Outlook contacts list is saved in the new exported file (see Figure 28-10). Click OK when you finish.

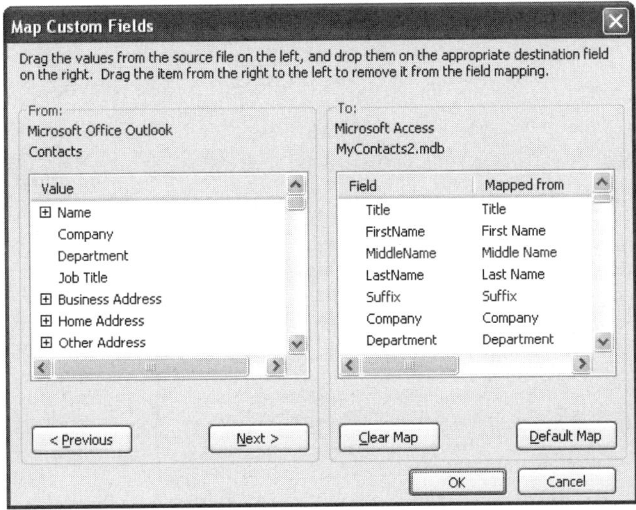

Figure 28-10. Modify field mappings in this dialog box.

7 Click Finish. Outlook exports the data from the Contacts folder and saves it in the specified file. You can now switch to Access and open the exported data as a table in that application.

For detailed information on working with Access, see *Microsoft Office Access 2003 Inside Out*, by John L. Viescas (Microsoft Press, 2003).

Importing Contacts from Access

Suppose you've collected and stored contacts in an Access database but now want to use them in Outlook. You can simply import the data to Outlook using the Import and Export Wizard. During the import process, Outlook can check to see whether duplicate entries are being added to your contacts list and can then create, ignore, or replace them.

Troubleshooting

After replacing a duplicate entry in Outlook, you find you've lost data

Before you choose to allow Outlook to replace duplicate entries, you should make sure that the items really are duplicates. Entries might erroneously appear to be duplicates if, for example, you have two contacts whose names are the same. For that reason, you might want to allow Outlook to create duplicate entries and then, after the import process is finished, go into the Outlook Contacts folder and manually remove any true duplicates.

Before you begin, make sure that the database you want to import is closed in Access. If it's not, you'll receive an error message when Outlook tries to find the data source.

Then follow these steps to import the data:

1. Switch to Outlook and choose File, Import And Export to open the Import and Export Wizard.
2. Select Import From Another Program Or File and then click Next.
3. Select Microsoft Access and click Next.
4. In the File To Import box (see Figure 28-11), specify the Access file (MDB) that you want to import.

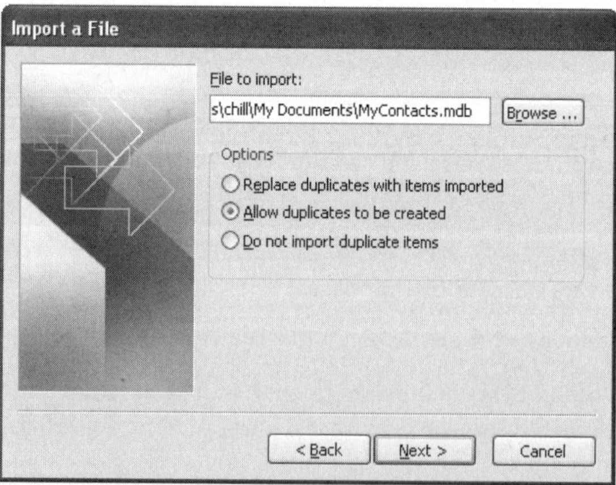

Figure 28-11. Specify the Access file to import and how Outlook should handle duplicates during the import process.

5. Specify how you want Outlook to handle duplicates, and then click Next.
6. Select the folder in which you want the imported data to be placed, such as the Contacts folder, and then click Next.
7. Click Map Custom Fields. In this dialog box, you can add or remove field items, modifying the way the Outlook contacts list is saved in the new imported file. Click OK when you finish.
8. Click Finish to start the import process.

Exporting Contacts to Excel

You might also find it useful to export Outlook contact information to Excel worksheets. In Excel, you can include the data in a spreadsheet of names and addresses for a contact management sheet, sort contact data in various ways, or perform other spreadsheet tasks with the data. Again, you simply use the Import and Export Wizard to create this Excel file.

Here's how to export contact information to Excel:

1. In Outlook, choose File, Import And Export to open the Import and Export Wizard.
2. Select Export To A File and then click Next.
3. Select Microsoft Excel and then click Next.
4. Select the folder from which to export data. In this case, select the Contacts folder or another folder that includes Outlook contact information. Click Next.
5. Specify the folder and type a name for the export file. You can click Browse to navigate to a folder and then click OK to select that folder. When you do this, the file is given an XLS file extension to denote an Excel worksheet file. Click Next.
6. Click Map Custom Fields. In this dialog box, you can add or remove field items, modifying the way the Outlook contacts list is saved in the new exported file. Click OK when you finish.
7. Click Finish. Outlook exports the data from the Contacts folder and saves it in the specified file.

Tip **Share data with others**
Another reason to export contact information is that you might need to share this data with others who do not use Outlook but do use Excel. Simply export the data to an Excel worksheet, open the worksheet, and modify or edit any column information. Then save the file and send it to the other users.

For detailed information on working with Excel, see *Microsoft Office Excel 2003 Inside Out*, by Mark Dodge and Craig Stinson (Microsoft Press, 2003).

Importing Contacts from Excel

You import contact information from an Excel worksheet the same way you import from an Access database. Suppose your coworker wants to send you contact information but is not running Outlook. Ask the coworker to save the data in an Excel worksheet and send that file to you. You can then use the Import and Export Wizard to import the new contact information into Outlook.

Before you begin the process, make sure that the worksheet you want to import is closed in Excel. If it's not, you'll receive an error message when Outlook tries to find the data source.

Then follow these steps to import the data:

1. Switch to Outlook and choose File, Import And Export to open the Import and Export Wizard.
2. Select Import From Another Program Or File and then click Next.
3. Select Microsoft Excel and then click Next.
4. In the File To Import box, specify the Excel file (XLS) that you want to import.
5. Specify how you want Outlook to handle duplicates and then click Next.
6. Select the folder in which you want the imported data to be placed, such as the Contacts folder, and then click Next.
7. Click Map Custom Fields. In this dialog box, you can add or remove field items, modifying the way the Outlook contacts list is saved in the new imported file. Click OK when you finish.
8. Click Finish to start the import process.You might want to review your contacts to ensure that the data was imported the way you need it. If it wasn't, modify it as necessary in Outlook.

Exporting Tasks to Office Applications

You can use the Import and Export Wizard to export other Outlook items. For example, you might want to export tasks to a Word or Excel file to view past or future assignments in a table format that can be easily edited or in a spreadsheet.You can then use this data in business correspondence, historical documents (such as a travel itinerary), event planning, work assignments, or presentations.

Follow these steps to export tasks to an Excel file:

1. In Outlook, choose File, Import And Export to open the Import and Export Wizard.
2. Select Export To A File and then click Next.
3. Select Microsoft Excel and then click Next.
4. Select the folder from which to export data. In this case, choose the Tasks folder or another folder that includes Outlook tasks. Click Next.

5 Specify the folder and type a name for the export file. You can click Browse to navigate to a folder and then click OK to select that folder. When you do this, the file is given an XLS file extension to denote an Excel worksheet file. Click Next.

6 Click Map Custom Fields. In this dialog box, you can add or remove field items, modifying the way Outlook task items are saved in the new imported file. Click OK when you finish.

7 Click Finish to start the import process and open the Set Date Range dialog box (see Figure 28-12).

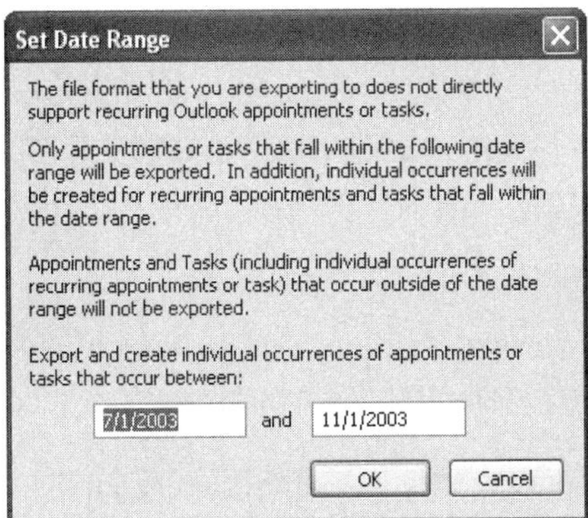

Figure 28-12. You might need to change the date range to include all the tasks you want to export.

8 Specify the date range for exported tasks. Also, some types of tasks are not directly exported or included, such as recurring tasks with recurrences that fall outside the date range you set. Modify the date range as necessary to include the tasks you want exported.

9 Click OK to start the export process. When it's finished, you can open the worksheet to review your tasks in Excel.

Using Notes in Other Applications

Outlook notes are great when you need to create electronic "sticky" notes as a reminder of things to do in a document or project or of messages to send out. However, you are limited in how you can store information in notes and how you can use that information in other documents.

One way to reuse the information you've placed in notes is to export the Notes folder and use that file in another application. Suppose you have several notes that you want to archive and then remove from the Notes folder. Simply export the Notes folder to a tab-separated file and open the file in Word, creating a document that contains the information.

Here's how to export the file:

1. In Outlook, choose File, Import And Export to open the Import and Export Wizard.
2. Select Export To A File and then click Next.
3. Select Tab-Separated Value (Windows) and then click Next.
4. Select the folder from which to export data. In this case, select the Notes folder or another folder that includes Outlook notes. Click Next.
5. Specify the folder and type a name for the export file. You can click Browse to navigate to a folder and then click OK to select that folder. When you do this, the file is given a TXT extension to denote a text file (which you can open in Word). Click Next.
6. Click Map Custom Fields. In this dialog box, you can add or remove field items, modifying the way Outlook note items are saved in the new imported file. For example, you might want to remove the Note Color field because this field exports as a numeric value. Click OK when you finish.
7. Click Finish to begin the export process.

Open the file in Word to see how the Notes file is displayed. In the example shown in Figure 28-13, the tab-separated items are converted from text to a table using the Word table feature.

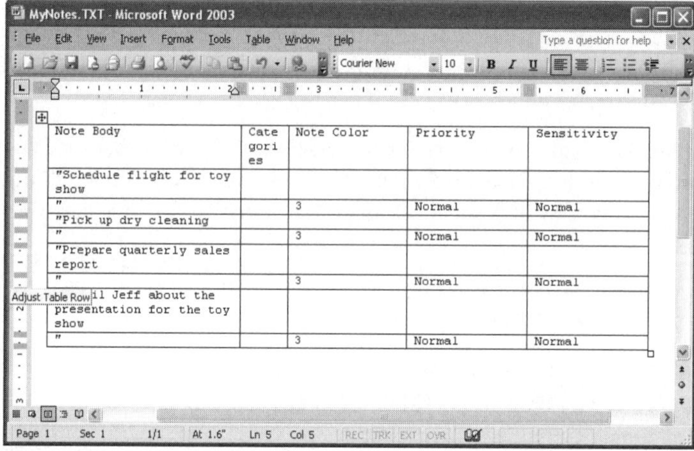

Figure 28-13. Your notes can be viewed in other Office applications, such as Word.

Chapter 29

Delegating Responsibilities to an Assistant

Microsoft Office Outlook 2003, when used with Microsoft Exchange Server, provides a handful of features that allow you to delegate certain responsibilities to an assistant. For example, you might want your assistant to manage your schedule, setting up appointments, meetings, and other events for you. Perhaps you want your assistant to send e-mail messages on your behalf.

This chapter explains how to delegate access to your schedule, e-mail messages, and other Outlook data, granting an assistant the ability to perform tasks in Outlook on your behalf. This chapter also explains how to access folders for which you've been granted delegate access.

For detailed information on other ways to share information through Outlook and public folders, see Chapter 38, "Sharing Information with Others."

Delegation Overview

Why delegate? You could simply give assistants your logon credentials and allow them to access your Exchange Server mailbox through a separate profile on their systems. The disadvantage to that approach is that your assistants then have access to all your Outlook data. By using Outlook's delegation features, however, you can selectively restrict an assistant's access to your data.

You have two ways of delegating access in Outlook. First, you can specify individuals as delegates for your account, which gives them send-on-behalf-of privileges. This means the delegated individuals can perform such tasks as sending e-mail messages and meeting requests for you. When an assistant sends a meeting request on your behalf, the request appears to the recipients to have come from you. You can also specify that delegates should receive copies of meeting-related messages that are sent to you, such as meeting invitations. This is a necessity if you want an assistant to be able to handle your calendar.

> **Note** When a message is sent on your behalf, the recipient sees these words in the From box:
>
> *<delegate>* on behalf of *<owner>*
>
> where *<delegate>* and *<owner>* are replaced by the appropriate names. This designation appears in the header of the message form when the recipient opens the message but doesn't appear in the header in the Inbox. The Inbox shows the message as coming from the owner, not the delegate.

The second way you can delegate access is to configure permissions for individual folders, granting various levels of access within the folders as needed. This does not give other users send-on-behalf-of privileges but does give them access to the folder and its contents. The tasks they can perform in the folder are subject to the permission levels you grant them.

Assigning Delegates and Working as an Assistant

You can assign multiple delegates so that more than one individual can access your data with send-on-behalf-of privileges. You might have an assistant who manages your schedule and therefore has delegate access to your calendar and another delegate—your supervisor—who manages other aspects of your work day and therefore has access to your Tasks folder. In most cases, however, you'll probably want to assign only one delegate.

Adding and Removing Delegates

You can add, remove, and configure delegates for all your Outlook folders through the same interface.

Follow these steps to delegate access to one or more of your Outlook folders:

1. Choose Tools, Options to open the Options dialog box.
2. Click the Delegates tab (see Figure 29-1).

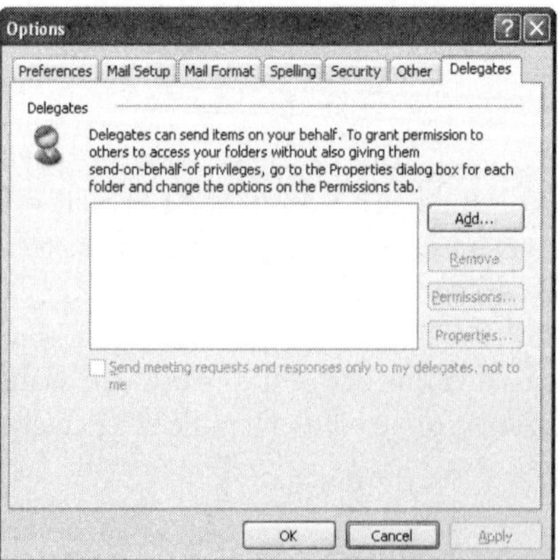

Figure 29-1. The Delegates tab shows the current delegates and lets you add, remove, and configure delegates.

3 Click Add to open the Add Users dialog box.

4 Select one or more users and click Add.

5 Click OK. Outlook displays the Delegate Permissions dialog box (see Figure 29-2).

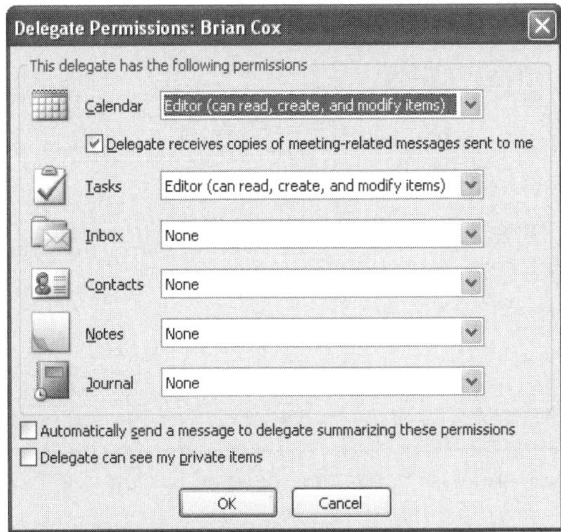

Figure 29-2. Configure delegate permissions in this dialog box.

6 For each folder, select the level of access you want to give the delegate based on the following list:

- **None** The delegate has no access to the selected folder.
- **Reviewer** The delegate can read existing items in the folder but can't add, delete, or modify items. Essentially, this level gives the delegate read-only permission for the folder.
- **Author** The delegate can read existing items and create new ones but can't modify or delete items.
- **Editor** The delegate can read existing items, create new ones, and modify existing ones, including deleting them.

7 Set the other options in the dialog box using the following list as a guide:

- **Delegate Receives Copies Of Meeting-Related Messages Sent To Me** Sends copies of all meeting-related messages to the delegate.
- **Automatically Send A Message To Delegate Summarizing These Permissions** Sends an e-mail message to the delegate informing him or her of the access permissions you've assigned in your Outlook folders (see Figure 29-3).
- **Delegate Can See My Private Items** Allows the delegate to view items you've marked as private. Clear this option to hide your private items.

8 Click OK to close the Delegate Permissions dialog box.

9 Add and configure other delegates as you want, and then click OK.

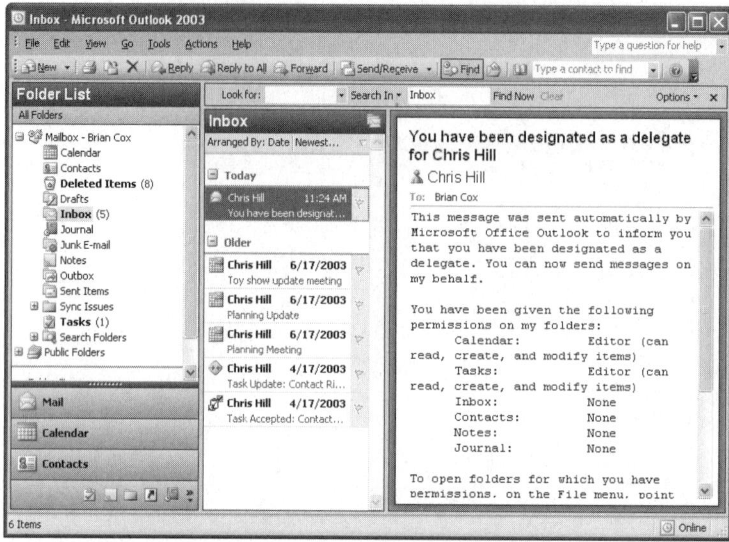

Figure 29-3. Outlook sends a message to delegates informing them of their access privileges.

If you need to modify the permissions for a delegate, open the Delegates tab, select the delegate in the list, and click Permissions to open the Delegate Permissions dialog box. Then adjust the settings as needed, just as you do when you add a delegate. If you need to remove a delegate, select the delegate on the Delegates tab and click Remove.

> **Tip** If the Permissions button appears dimmed or you are unable to assign delegate permissions for some other reason, the problem could be that you have designated a local PST as the default delivery location for your profile. Make sure you configure your profile to deliver mail to your Exchange Server mailbox instead.

Taking Yourself out of the Meeting Request Loop

If your assistant has full responsibility for managing your calendar, you might want all meeting request messages to go to the assistant rather than to you. That way, meeting request messages won't clog your Inbox.

Taking yourself out of the request loop is easy. Here's how:

1. With any folder open, choose Tools, Options.
2. Click the Delegates tab.
3. Select the option Send Meeting Requests And Responses Only To My Delegates, Not To Me.
4. Click OK.

Note This option appears dimmed if you haven't assigned a delegate.

Opening Folders Delegated to You

If you are acting as a delegate for another person, you can open the folders to which you've been given delegate access and use them as if they were your own folders, subject to the permissions applied by the owner. For example, suppose that you've been given delegate access to your manager's schedule. You can open his or her Calendar folder and create appointments, generate meeting requests, and perform the same tasks you can perform in your own Calendar folder. However, you might find a few restrictions. For example, you won't be able to view the contents of personal items unless your manager has configured permissions to give you that ability.

Follow these steps to open another person's folder:

1. Open Outlook with your own profile.
2. Choose File, Open, Other User's Folder to display the Open Other User's Folder dialog box (see Figure 29-4).

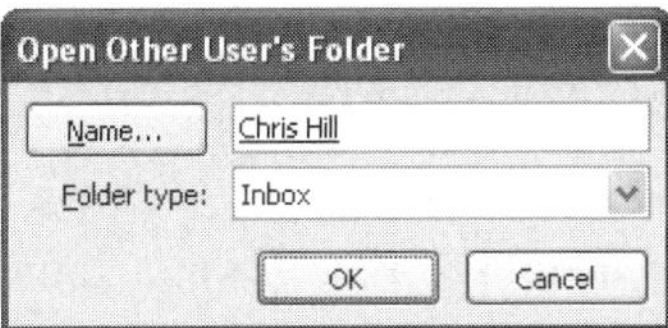

Figure 29-4. Use the Open Other User's Folder dialog box to open another person's Outlook folder.

3. Type the person's name or click Name to browse the address list, and select a name.
4. In the Folder Type drop-down list, select the folder you want to open, and then click OK. Outlook generates an error message if you don't have the necessary permissions for the folder; otherwise, the folder opens in a new window.

Depending on the permissions set for the other person's folder, you might be able to open the folder but not see anything in it. If someone grants you Folder Visible permission, you can open the folder but not necessarily view its contents. For example, if you are granted Folder Visible permission for a Calendar folder, you can view the other person's calendar. If you are granted Folder Visible permission for the Inbox folder, you can open the folder, but you can't see any headers. Obviously, this latter scenario isn't useful, so you might need to fine-tune the permissions to get the effect you need.

Tip When you click File, Open, the menu lists other users' folders that you've recently opened. You can select a folder from the list to open it.

When you've finished working with another person's folder, close it as you would any other window.

Scheduling on Behalf of Another Person

If you've been given delegate privileges for another person's calendar, you can schedule meetings and other appointments on behalf of that person.

To do so, follow these steps:

1. Open Outlook with your own profile.
2. Choose File, Open and open the other person's Calendar folder.
3. In the other person's Calendar folder, create the meeting request, appointment, or other item as you normally would for your own calendar.

As mentioned, the recipient of a meeting request sees the message as coming from the calendar's owner, not the delegate. When the recipient opens the message, however, the header indicates that the message was sent by the delegate on behalf of the owner. Responses to the meeting request come back to the delegate and a copy goes to the owner, unless the owner has removed himself or herself from the meeting request loop.

For details about how to have meeting request messages go to the delegate rather than to the owner, see "Taking Yourself out of the Meeting Request Loop," page 738.

Sending E-Mail on Behalf of Another Person

If you've been given delegate permission for another person's Inbox, you can send messages on behalf of that person. For example, as someone's assistant, you might need to send notices, requests for comments, report reminders, or similar messages.

To send a message on behalf of another person, follow these steps:

1. Open Outlook with your own profile.
2. Start a new message. If the From box isn't displayed, choose View, From Field.
3. In the From box, type the name of the person on whose behalf you're sending the message.
4. Complete the message as you would any other, and then send it.

Inside Out

Choosing an editor

Microsoft recommends that you use Microsoft Word as your e-mail editor and even set it as the default editor. However, in this instance, Outlook actually works better as the editor. With Word as your editor, you can't display the From box directly. Instead, you must configure Outlook as your e-mail editor, display the From box, and then switch back to Word as your editor. The From box will then appear in Word.

Granting Access to Folders

You can configure your folders to provide varying levels of access to other users according to the types of tasks those users need to perform within the folders. For example, you might grant access to your Contacts folder to allow others to see and use your contacts list.

Granting permissions for folders is different from granting delegate access. Users with delegate access to your folders can send messages on your behalf, as explained in earlier sections. Users with access permissions for your folders do not have that ability. Use access permissions for your folders when you want to grant others certain levels of access to your folders but not the ability to send messages on your behalf.

Configuring Access Permissions

Several levels of permissions control what a user can and cannot do in your folders. The permissions include the following:

- **Create Items** Users can post items to the folder.
- **Read Items** Users can read items in the folder.
- **Create Subfolders** Users can create additional folders inside the folder.
- **Folder Owner** The owner has all permissions for the folder.
- **Folder Contact** The folder contact receives automated messages from the folder such as replication conflict messages, requests from users for additional permissions, and other changes to the folder status.
- **Folder Visible** Users can see the folder.
- **Edit Items** Users can edit all items or only those items they own.
- **Delete Items** Users can delete all items or only those items they own.

Outlook groups these permissions into several predefined levels as follows:

- **Owner** The owner has all permissions and can edit and delete all items, including those he or she doesn't own.
- **Publishing Editor** The Publishing Editor has all permissions and can edit and delete all items but does not own the folder.
- **Editor** Users are granted all permissions except the ability to create subfolders or act as the folder's owner. Editors can edit and delete all items.
- **Publishing Author** Users are granted all permissions except the ability to edit or delete items belonging to others and the ability to act as the folder's owner.
- **Author** This level is the same as Publishing Author except Authors can't create subfolders.
- **Nonediting Author** Users can create and read items and delete items they own, but they can't delete others' items or create subfolders.

- **Reviewer** Users can view items but can't modify or delete items or create subfolders.
- **Contributor** Users can create items but not view or modify existing ones.
- **None** The folder is visible but users can't read, create, or modify any items in the folder.

Follow these steps to grant permissions for a specific folder:

1. Open Outlook, open the folder list, right-click the folder for which you want to set permissions, and then choose Properties.
2. Click the Permissions tab (see Figure 29-5).

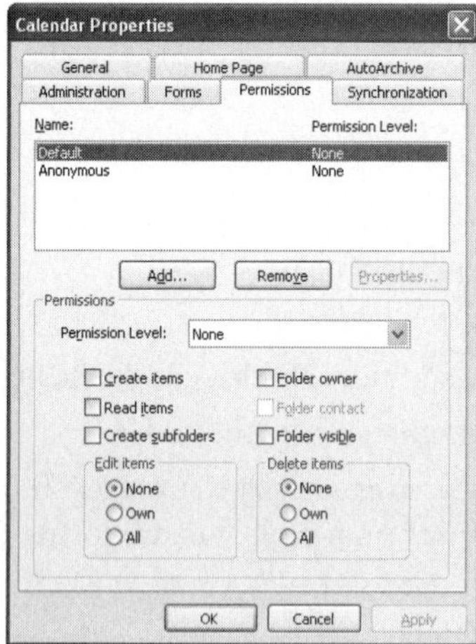

Figure 29-5. Use the Permissions tab to configure access permissions for the folder.

3. Click Default, and then set the permissions you want users to have if they are not explicitly assigned permissions (if their names don't appear in the Name list).
4. Click Add to add a user with explicit permissions. Select the name from the Add Users list, click Add, and then click OK.
5. In the Name list, select the user you just added and set permissions as you want.
6. Click OK to close the folder's dialog box.

As you can see in Figure 29-5, you can remove users to remove their explicit permissions. Just select the user and click Remove.

To view (but not modify) a user's address book properties, select the user and click Properties (see Figure 29-6). If you want, you can add the user to your Personal Address Book.

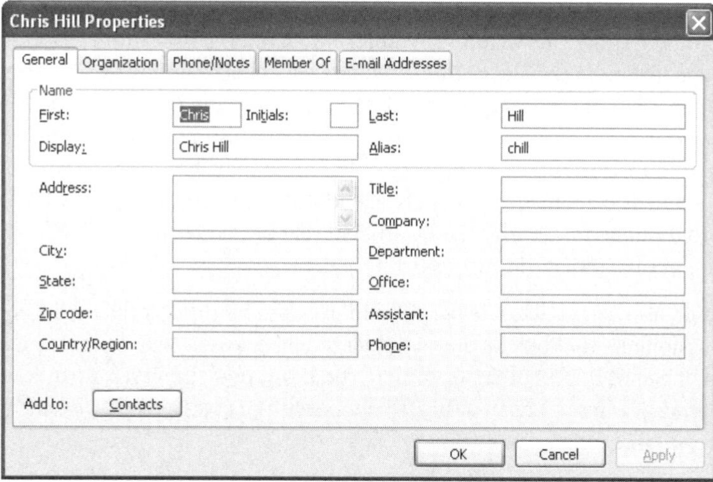

Figure 29-6. You can view a user's address book properties.

Accessing Other Users' Folders

After you've been granted the necessary permissions for another user's folder, you can open the folder and perform actions according to your permissions. For example, if you have only read permission, you can read items but not add new ones. If you've been granted create permission, you can create items.

To open another user's folder, choose File, Open, Other User's Folder. Specify the user's name and the folder you want to open, and then click OK.

For more information on opening and using another person's folder, see "Opening Folders Delegated to You," page 739.

Configuring Delegate Permissions in Exchange Server

The previous sections explained how to configure delegate permissions from Outlook. In some situations, however, it's more practical to set permissions from Exchange Server. You can actually set two delegate-related permissions: Send As and Send on Behalf. This section of the chapter explains the difference between the two and how to set them in Exchange Server.

Understanding the Send As and Send on Behalf Permissions

There are two separate permissions you can configure on an Exchange Server mailbox or folder that grant other users the ability to send mail through that mailbox. Each has a different purpose and effect on the outgoing message.

When a user who has Send As permission in a mailbox sends a message through that mailbox, the From field shows the mailbox owner as the sender. For example, let's say that you send a message through the Sales mailbox, which is a global mailbox for the Sales department. The From field of the resulting message comes from the Display Name field of the account that owns the mailbox, which in this example we assume is Tailspin Sales. Your name doesn't appear in the From field at all, and replies are directed to the Tailspin Sales e-mail address. The same is true if you grant a user Send As permission in a public folder. The user can send as that public folder, and the From field reflects the Display Name field and e-mail address of the public folder, not the sender.

Send on Behalf, also called delegate permission, works a bit differently. If you grant Send on Behalf permission in a mailbox or public folder to a given user, that delegated user can send messages on behalf of that mailbox or folder. The From field, however, reads *<user>* on behalf of *<owner>*, where *<user>* is the user who sent the message and *<owner>* is the mailbox owner (or public folder).

In Outlook, the From field in the Inbox message header shows the owner's name, but the InfoBar in the Reading Pane and the From field in the message form itself show *<user>* on behalf of *<owner>*. If the recipient is using Outlook Express, however, he or she doesn't see that the message was sent on behalf of the mailbox or folder owner. Instead, the message header in the Inbox and the Reading Pane, as well as the message form itself, shows the mailbox owner or folder as the sender, with no indication that the message was sent on behalf of someone else.

So what's really going on? If you look at the message properties of a delegate-sent message from Outlook Express and click the Details tab, you'll see that the From field in the Internet headers is set to the mailbox owner or public folder. The Sender field is set to the delegate's name and address. In effect, Send on Behalf sets the Sender field for the message, and Send As does not. Therefore, what the recipient actually sees for the From field depends on how the intervening mail server and mail client treat the From and Sender fields.

If you want a message to appear to Outlook users as if it were sent on behalf of someone else, grant the user Send on Behalf permission for the mailbox or public folder. If you want the message to appear to be from the mailbox owner or public folder, grant the user Send As permission instead. Keep in mind that if you grant both Send on Behalf and Send As permissions for a user in a given mailbox or public folder, the Send on Behalf permission is the one that affects what Outlook users see regarding the message sender. Messages will appear to be sent on behalf of the mailbox owner or public folder, even though the user also has Send As permission.

If you don't use public folders in your organization and everyone has exclusive access to their mailboxes, Send As and Send on Behalf permissions are essentially useless to you, at least the way you are currently using Exchange Server. However, these permissions have some important uses.

For example, a manager might need to delegate access to his or her mailbox to an assistant to enable that assistant to schedule meetings, monitor and respond to e-mail, or manage the owner's mailbox in other ways. Or let's assume your sales department wants to start sending out broadcast messages to customers and receiving sales inquiries. You can set up a common mailbox called Sales and grant Send on Behalf or Send As permission to everyone in the sales department so they can send and receive messages through that mailbox. You could use a public folder instead of a mailbox, if you preferred. Using a public folder is a better option when you want to simplify access to the messages. All users with the necessary permissions in the public folder can see them from Outlook without opening a separate mailbox.

Regardless of the reason for using these permissions, whether you grant Send As or Send on Behalf permission to a particular user or group depends on how you want the message received. If you want the recipient to see that the message has been sent by a delegate, use Send on Behalf. If you don't want the recipient to know that the message was sent by a delegate, use the Send As permission.

Granting Send As Permission for a Mailbox

You use the Active Directory Users and Computers console to grant Send As permission for users in your Exchange Server organization. First, open the console and choose View, Advanced Features to turn on the display of advanced features in the console. Then, decide whether you will grant Send As permission using an account or a group. If using a group, create and populate the group.

Next, open the account of the user who owns the mailbox. In the user's account properties, click the Security tab (see Figure 29-7). If the user or group is not already included in the Name list, click Add and add the user account or group. Back on the Security tab, select the user or group to which you want to grant Send As permission, then scroll through the Permissions list to locate Send As (see Figure 29-8). Place a check in the Allow column for the Send As permission and click OK.

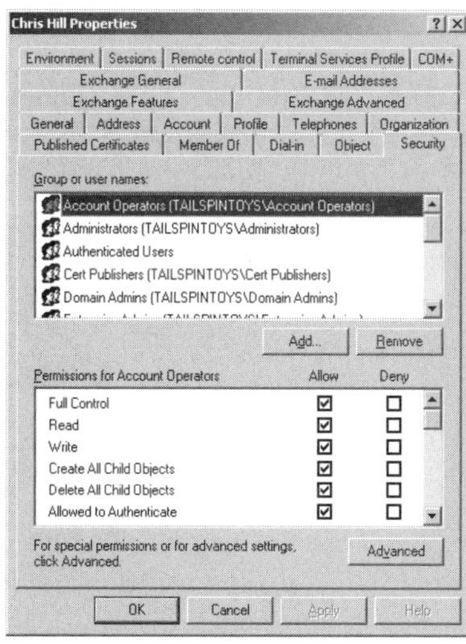

Figure 29-7. Add a delegate with the Security tab.

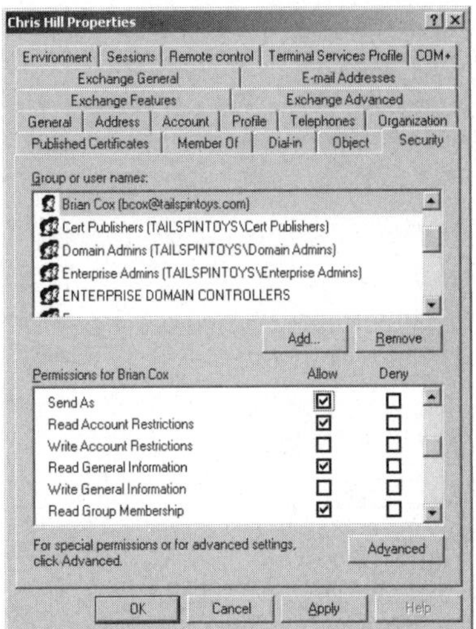

Figure 29-8. Enable the Send As permission for the delegate.

Granting Send As Permission for a Public Folder

You use the Exchange System Manager console, not Active Directory Users and Computers, to configure Send As permission for a public folder. In Exchange System Manager, expand the Folders branch, right-click the public folder, and choose Properties. Click the Permissions tab, then click Directory Rights. On the Directory Rights tab, add and select the user, scroll through the Permissions list and place a check in the Allow column beside Send As, and click OK. Close the Properties dialog box for the public folder.

You have one additional step to take. You need to configure the folder's properties to display it in the Global Address List (GAL) so users can select it from their Address Book when addressing the message. Open Exchange System Manager and expand the Public Folders branch to locate the public folder. Right-click the folder and choose Properties, then click the Exchange Advanced tab. Clear the Hide From Exchange Address Lists option and click OK. Users will need to refresh their offline address books by performing a full Send/Receive on the Exchange Server account. In Outlook 2003, choosing Tools, Send/Receive, Download Address Book accomplishes the refresh. If you prefer not to list the public folder in the GAL, users can add the public folder address to their Contacts or Personal Address Book instead.

Using Send As Permission

After the changes have propagated in the domain, the users to whom you granted Send As permission can start sending messages through the target mailbox or public folder. Open Outlook and open a new mail message. Choose View, From Field to display the From field in the message form. Click From and select the user or public folder, then select the recipient, add a subject and message body, and send the message on its way.

Granting Send on Behalf Permission in Exchange Server

How you grant Send on Behalf permission depends on whether you're delegating a mailbox or a public folder. You can grant Send on Behalf permission for a mailbox or public folder with Active Directory Users and Computers, but can grant Send on Behalf permission only to a mailbox with Outlook. Use Exchange System Manager to grant Send on Behalf permission for a public folder.

Granting Send on Behalf for a Mailbox

To grant Send on Behalf permission using the Active Directory Users and Computers console, open the mailbox owner's account and click the Exchange General tab. Click Delivery Options, click Add, select the user, and click OK. Add other delegates as needed and close the account properties.

Note If you need to configure additional delegate permissions for individual mailbox folders, you need to use Outlook instead of the Active Directory Users and Computers console to grant delegate permissions. See "Adding and Removing Delegates," page 736, for details.

Grant Send on Behalf for a Public Folder

To grant Send on Behalf permission in a public folder, open Exchange System Manager and open the properties for the public folder. Click the Exchange General tab and then click Delivery Options to open the Delivery Options dialog box, shown in Figure 29-9. Click Add, select the users, and click OK, then click OK again. Close the Properties dialog box for the folder.

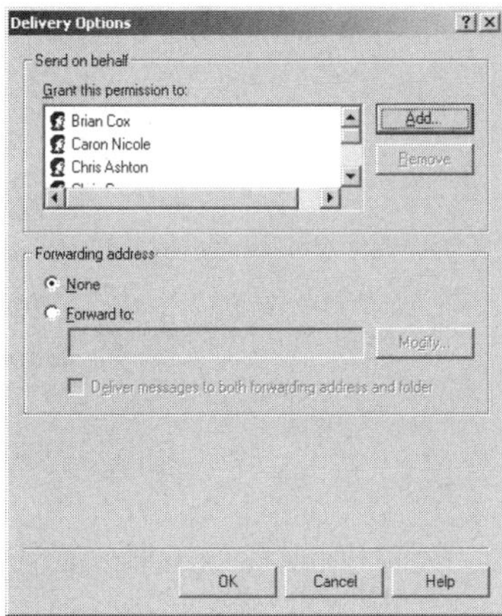

Figure 29-9. Use the Delivery Options dialog box to grant Send on Behalf permission for a public folder.

Granting Send on Behalf Privileges to a Distribution List

In some situations, you might want to grant a distribution list Send on Behalf privileges. For example, you might want all members of the sales department to be able to broadcast messages to customers about promotions. Or perhaps a small team is working on a project and needs to funnel messages through a specific mailbox to communicate with others about the project. Granting delegate permission to the distribution group gives members the ability to send messages on behalf of the specified mailbox. You could grant delegate permissions to individual users, but using the distribution list to assign permissions takes less time. To allow a distribution list to send on behalf of a mailbox, you first need to set up the distribution group. Then you can grant users delegate permissions for that group as needed.

Follow these steps:

1. In the GAL, create the distribution list, making sure to assign it an appropriate e-mail address.

For a discussion of setting up distribution lists in Outlook, see "Creating Distribution Lists," page 136.

2. Open Outlook, and log on to the mailbox for which you want to grant delegate access.
3. Choose Tools, Options.
4. Click the Delegates tab.
5. Click Add.
6. Select the distribution list and then click Add.
7. Click OK.
8. Configure delegate permissions for the Inbox to either Author or Editor. Fine-tune the permissions as necessary, and then click OK.
9. Click OK to close the Options dialog box.

Using Send on Behalf

The process for using Send on Behalf is essentially the same as for the Send As permission. In Outlook, open a new message form and with the From field displayed, click From and select the user or public folder on whose behalf you want to send the message. Finish composing and addressing the message and send it.

Troubleshooting Permissions

One problem you might experience after granting Send As and Send on Behalf permissions is that a particular user always ends up sending on behalf of the mailbox or public folder, even though he or she has Send As permission. The Send on Behalf permission in effect takes precedence because it sets the Sender field, which Outlook interprets as meaning the message was sent on behalf of the mailbox owner. If you don't want this behavior for the user, remove the user from the Delegates tab (which removes Send on Behalf permission). If you want a user to appear as the sender of a message without any mention of delegation, remove the user as a delegate.

Another potential problem can arise if you have multiple domains in your organization. A user (or you) might grant delegate access with Outlook to an Inbox, only to find that the delegated user doesn't show up on the Delivery Options tab of the mailbox owner's account properties. The crux of the matter is that you are using a global catalog server in a domain other than the one in which your account resides. The items for your domain in that global catalog are read-only, which prevents you from changing properties.

You can overcome the problem by moving the mailbox to the same domain or by changing the global catalog used by Exchange Server. To achieve the latter, open Exchange System Manager, right-click the server in question, and choose Properties. Clear the Automatically Discover Servers option, then click Add to add a global catalog. Optionally, you can try changing the global catalog at the client. Change the registry value HKEY_CURRENT_USER\Software\Microsoft\Windows NT\CurrentVersion\Windows Messaging Subsystem\Profiles\<*ProfileName*>\dca740c8c042101ab4b908002b2fe182 to point to the desired global catalog. You'll find more information about this issue in MicrosoftTechNet article 329622.

If you're using Microsoft Exchange Server 5.5 and try to delegate access for a mailbox to a distribution list, the members of that list might receive an error message stating that they don't have send-on-behalf-of permission for the mailbox. Microsoft offers a correction for this problem in the 5.5.2654.8 version of Store.exe. Obtain the fix from Microsoft's Web site at *http://www.microsoft.com/downloads/release.asp?ReleaseID=17142*.

Another problem you might run across is the inability to assign Send on Behalf privileges to a distribution group through the Exchange Server Administrator. This occurs because the distribution group doesn't appear in the address list when you attempt to select a delegate. This is by design. To assign the delegates, use Outlook instead, as described in the previous section.

Finally, users who access a mailbox with Microsoft Outlook Web Access do not gain write access to a mailbox even if you grant delegate permissions on a given folder to that user. You can give users the ability to send through another mailbox with Outlook Web Access by assigning them as mailbox owners. Open the Active Directory Users and Computers console and display advanced features. Open the account properties for the mailbox owner and click the Exchange Advanced tab, then click Mailbox Rights. Add the delegate user or group and grant Full Control permission to that user or group.

Chapter 30

Managing Folders, Data, and Archiving

Like any system, Microsoft Office Outlook 2003 can become overloaded with messages, contact information, appointments, and other data. If you can't manage all this data, you'll be lost each time you try to find a particular item. Outlook helps you manage information by providing folders for storing your data. You also can create your own folders, move data between folders, and set folder properties.

This chapter focuses on managing your Outlook folders and their contents. You'll learn how to create new folders to store e-mail messages, contact information, and other files. You'll also learn how to set up Outlook folders to use Web views so that you can display Web pages inside folders. In addition, you'll find out what it takes to archive your data, both manually when you want to archive data on the spot and automatically using AutoArchive.

Understanding Outlook Folders

Outlook folders are similar to folders you use in Windows Explorer or My Computer. You use Outlook folders to store items you work with, such as e-mail messages and attachments, contact entries, journal entries, tasks, appointments, and notes. Outlook includes default folders for each type of item—for example, the Calendar, Contacts, Journal, Inbox, and Tasks folders. Along with these item-type folders are other default folders, such as Deleted Items, Drafts, and Outbox.

These folders are all part of your personal folders, so they are private. If you are running Outlook with Microsoft Exchange Server, others on your network to whom you've assigned rights can view and manage items stored in these folders if you make the folders public. In addition, your Exchange Server administrator can set up public folders that appear in your folder list but are stored on the Exchange Server. You and others who have rights to these public folders will see a Public Folders icon in your folder list. If you have the correct rights, you can create and delete these public folders, store and manage items in them, and see content added to them by other users.

Working with the Folder List

If you move between folders frequently, you might want to navigate by using a combination of the Navigation Pane and the folder list. The Navigation Pane gives you quick access to the Outlook folders that the majority of people use most often. However, you might use different Outlook folders, or want to access certain file system folders from Outlook. For example, suppose that you have an Exchange Server account but also use a set of personal folders to store personal messages and contacts or other data. Because Outlook doesn't automatically add shortcuts on the Navigation Pane for your other folders, the best way to access these folders is usually through the folder list (see Figure 30-1).

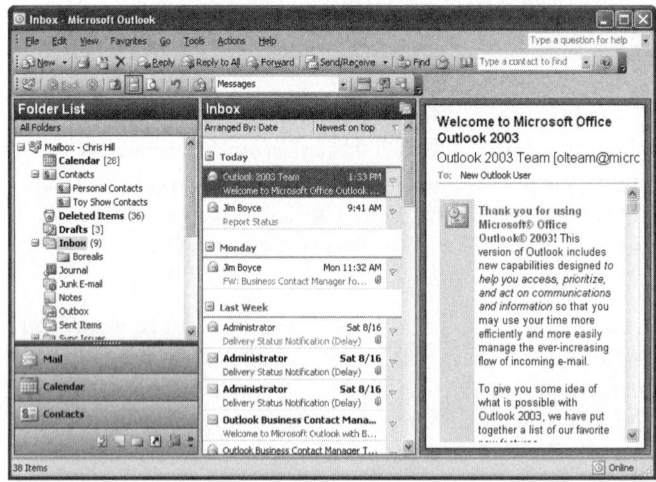

Figure 30-1. Use the folder list to move between folders not listed on the Navigation Pane or to see which folders are included in a given store.

You can display the folder list in two ways:

- Choose Go, Folder List.
- Click the Folder List button at the bottom of the Navigation Pane.

The folder list's behavior has changed from previous versions of Outlook. The folder list no longer automatically hides itself after you select a folder from it. In Outlook 2003, the folder list remains in the Navigation Pane until you click one of the Outlook folder buttons in the Navigation Pane below the folder list. Clicking a folder in the folder list itself does not cause the folder list to disappear.

> **Tip** You can right-click a folder in the folder list to display its shortcut menu, which gives you access to specific actions you can perform on the folder. Many of these actions, such as opening and deleting folders, are explained in the following sections.

Using and Managing Folders

When you perform an action in Outlook, you do so inside a folder. Outlook provides a handful of actions you can perform with folders to change their behavior, location, appearance, and so on, as described in the following sections.

Using a Folder

When you're ready to work with information in Outlook, you first go to the folder in which that information is stored. For example, to read a new e-mail message downloaded to your Inbox folder, you must open the Inbox folder and then select the message to read. To open a folder, click its button in the Navigation Pane or click the folder name in the folder list.

When you open the folder, its contents are displayed in the main Outlook window. To see the contents of a particular folder item, you must open it, using one of these methods:

- Double-click the item in the main Outlook window.
- Right-click the item and choose Open.
- Click the item and press Enter.

Depending on the type of folder you open, the Reading Pane might be available. The Reading Pane displays the contents of the currently selected item without requiring you to open a separate window for the folder item. The Reading Pane is handy because it provides a quick view and can help keep your desktop tidier. To display the Reading Pane, choose View, Reading Pane, and select Right or Bottom, or simply click the Reading Pane button on the Advanced toolbar.

By default, the Reading Pane appears in the right half of the main Outlook window, as shown in Figure 30-2. You can resize this pane by dragging the edge. To see an item in the Reading Pane, simply select the item in the folder.

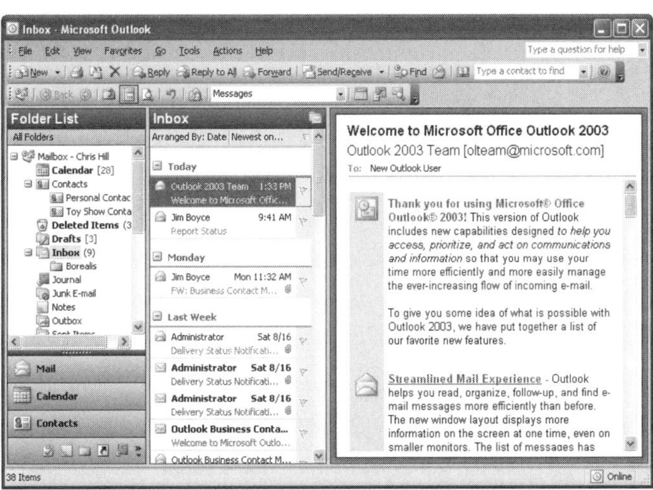

Figure 30-2. You can view the contents of a folder item in the Reading Pane.

For more information about working with the Reading Pane, see "Working with the Standard Outlook Views," page 56.

Note Only one item can be open in the Reading Pane at any given time. If you want to open additional items, you must double-click them to display them in separate windows.

Creating a Folder

As you know, Outlook provides a basic set of folders in which you can store certain types of data, such as the Contacts folder for storing contact information. As you use Outlook more, you'll want to add other folders to organize your data. For example, you might add other message folders to store particular kinds of messages.

Each Outlook folder you add has a specific *type* based on the type of data it stores. For example, an e-mail message folder differs from a contacts folder because the former stores messages and the latter stores contact entries. Similarly, the Calendar folder stores appointments and events, and the Notes folder stores notes. When you add a folder, you specify the folder type. You also specify the name of the folder and its location.

Follow these steps to create a folder:

1. Take one of the following actions to display the Create New Folder dialog box, shown in Figure 30-3:
   - Choose File, New, Folder.
   - Choose File, Folder, New Folder.
   - Right-click a folder in the folder list and choose New Folder.
   - Press Ctrl+Shift+E.
   - Click the arrow beside the New button on the Standard toolbar and choose Folder.

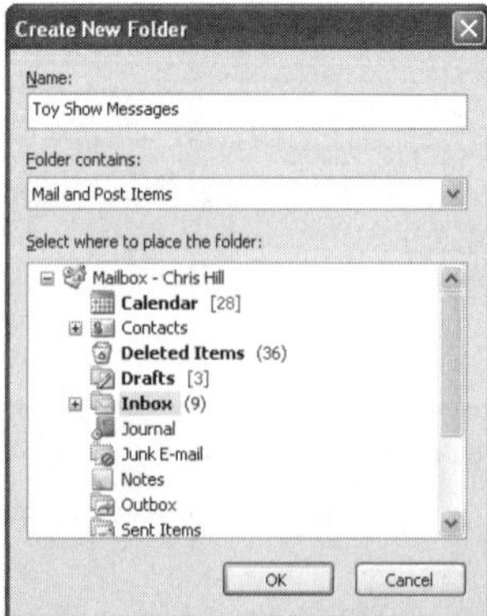

Figure 30-3. Use the Create New Folder dialog box to specify folder type, location, and other properties of the new folder.

2 In the Name box, type a name for the folder.
3 In the Folder Contains drop-down list, choose the type of item you want to store in this new folder.
4 In the Select Where To Place The Folder list, select the location for the new folder.
5 Click OK.

Adding a Folder Shortcut to the Navigation Pane

If you have a frequently used folder that isn't listed in the Navigation Pane, you can create a shortcut to the folder in the Shortcuts area of the Navigation Pane, as explained here:

1 Click the Shortcuts button at the bottom of the Navigation Pane.
2 In the Shortcuts pane, click Add New Shortcut to display the Add To Navigation Pane dialog box, shown in Figure 30-4.

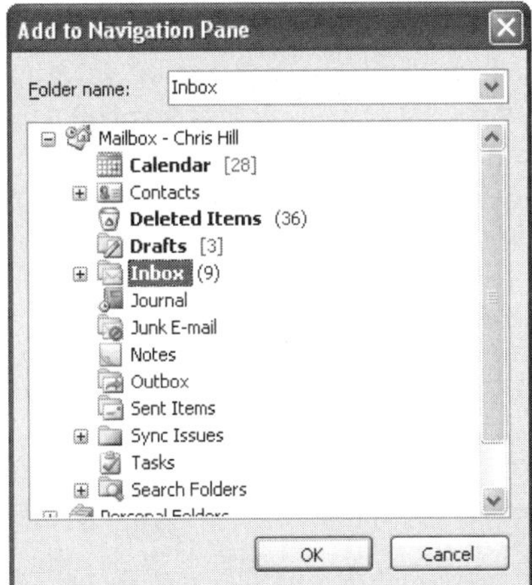

Figure 30-4. Add folders to the Shortcuts pane with the Add To Navigation Pane dialog box.

3 Select a folder from the list and click OK.

You can also create your own shortcut groups. Click the Add New Group shortcut. Outlook creates a new shortcut and highlights the name so you can change it. Type a new name and press Enter. You can easily move shortcuts from one group to another simply by dragging them.

Note You can drag folders, documents, and Web shortcuts to a group in the Shortcuts pane to quickly create shortcuts to those items. If you have several URLs in your Favorites folder that you want to copy to Outlook's shortcuts, open the Favorites folder and drag them to an Outlook shortcut group.

When you want to remove a shortcut, right-click it, choose Delete Shortcut, and then click Yes.

Note When you remove a folder shortcut from the Navigation Pane, you remove only the shortcut. You do not remove the folder from Outlook, nor do you delete the folder's contents. For information on deleting a folder and its contents, see "Deleting a Folder," page 759.

If you decide that a folder shortcut should be renamed, follow these steps:

1. Right-click the folder shortcut you want to rename.
2. Choose Rename Shortcut.
3. Type a new name and press Enter.

Note When you rename the folder shortcut, the folder name in the folder list does not change; only the shortcut name changes.

NEW FEATURE!

Working with Favorite Folders

A new feature in Outlook 2003 is the inclusion of a favorite folders area in the Navigation Pane for each of the Outlook folder types. When you click the Mail button in the Navigation Pane, for example, Outlook displays a favorite folders list at the top of the Navigation Pane. This list, by default, includes four of the most commonly used mail folders: the Inbox and Sent Items mail folders, and the Unread Mail and For Follow Up search folders (see Figure 30-5).

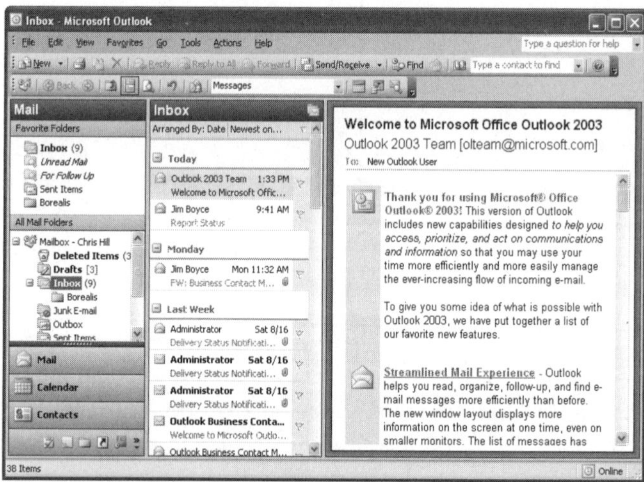

Figure 30-5. Use Favorite Folders to quickly open frequently used folders.

The naming convention isn't consistent across Outlook folder types for the favorite folder list, however. The favorites areas for the other folders are named My Calendars, My Contacts, My Tasks, My Journals, and My Notes. All but My Calendars appear at the top of the Navigation Pane when you open the folder. My Calendars appears below the date navigator in the Navigation Pane when you open the Calendar folder.

You can easily add and remove folders to their respective favorites lists. For example, if you use a separate folder for your personal contacts, you might add it to the My Contacts list to make it readily available without the need to open the folder list. To add a folder to its favorites list, open the folder list, right-click the folder, and choose Add To Favorite Folders (for a mail folder) or choose Add To My <*folder*>, where <*folder*> is the folder type, such as Contacts. To remove an item from its favorites list, right-click the folder in the folder list or in the favorites list and choose Remove From Favorite Folders or Remove From My <*folder*>, where <*folder*> is the folder type.

You can also change the order of favorite folders in the list. Right-click the folder in the list and choose Move Up In List or Move Down In List, or simply drag the folder to the desired location in the list.

Renaming a Folder

Sometimes you need to change a folder's name, perhaps as a result of project modifications or a company name change. Unfortunately, you can't rename the default folders created by Outlook. You can, however, change the name of folders you create. To rename a folder, begin with one of these actions:

- Open the folder list, right-click the folder, and choose Rename.
- Select the folder and then click the name to highlight it.
- Select the folder and choose File, Folder, Rename.

After taking one of these actions, simply type the new name and press Enter to have the change take effect.

Another way to change a folder's name is through its Properties dialog box (see Figure 30-6), which you can display by right-clicking the folder in the folder list and choosing Properties. On the General tab, type a new name in the top box. Click OK to save the name and to return to the folder list.

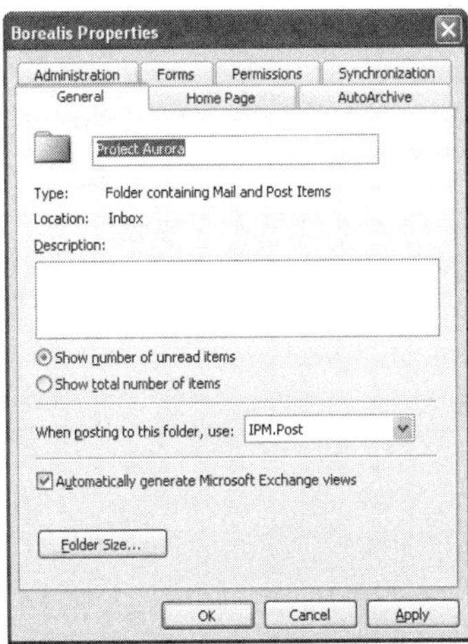

Figure 30-6. You can change a folder's name in its Properties dialog box.

Note When you change a folder's name, shortcuts to the folder on the Navigation Pane are updated to reflect the change.

Copying and Moving a Folder

Occasionally, you might need to move or copy a folder from one location to another. For example, suppose that you've created some message folders in your Inbox to organize messages, but now you want to move those folders to a folder other than the Inbox. Or maybe you want to copy the Contacts folder from your Exchange Server mailbox to a set of personal folders.

Moving or copying folders is easy. Open the folder list, right-click the folder you want to move or copy, and choose either Move or Copy from the shortcut menu. Outlook displays a Move Folder dialog box (see Figure 30-7) or a Copy Folder dialog box. Select the folder in which you want to store the moved or copied folder and click OK, or choose New to create a new folder in which to store the moved or copied folder.

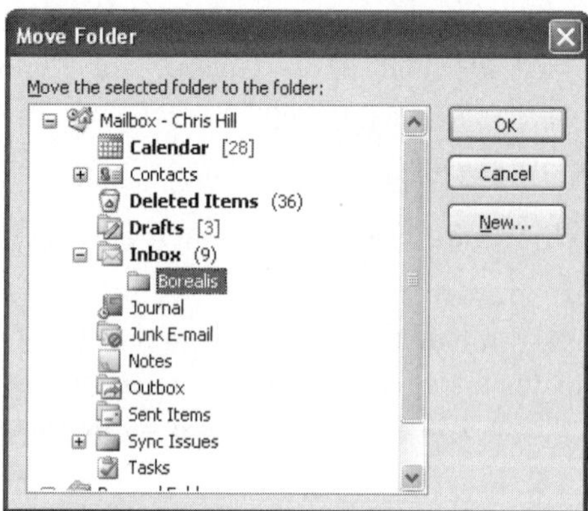

Figure 30-7. To move a folder, select its new location in this dialog box.

Another way to move a folder is to drag it to a new location. You can copy a folder using a similar technique; just hold down the Ctrl key while dragging.

You can move one type of folder so that it becomes a subfolder of another type of folder. For example, suppose that you receive e-mail messages containing contact information. You can store these messages in a folder called, say, Contact Info. You then can store the Contact Info folder as a subfolder of Contacts. The type of data you can store in the subfolder is the type you originally established for that folder. (For example, when a message-type folder becomes a subfolder of a contacts-type folder, neither folder changes its type.)

If you want to move or copy a folder to the root of the folder store, move or copy the folder to the topmost folder in the list (such as Personal Folders). If you use the Edit, Cut or Edit, Copy commands to move or copy, select the topmost folder and choose Edit, Paste.

> **Tip** **Send a link to a public folder**
> When you're working with public folders, you might want to send another user a link to a folder rather than moving or copying the folder. To send the link, open the folder list, right-click the folder, and choose Send Link To This Folder. Outlook starts a new message containing a link to the folder. Address the message and send it as you would any other message. Note, however, that recipients outside of your Exchange Server organization will not be able to open the link to view the folder.

Deleting a Folder

You can delete an Outlook folder the same way you delete a folder in Windows Explorer or My Computer. When you delete an Outlook folder, it's removed from the folder list and placed in the Deleted Items folder. This way, if you decide you want the folder back, you can retrieve it from the Deleted Items folder.

When you delete a folder, you delete the contents of the folder as well. The contents move with the folder to the Deleted Items folder and can be retrieved along with the folder later. You also can retrieve individual items from the Deleted Items folder, even if those items were deleted as part of a folder deletion. For example, if you delete a message folder named Project Alpha containing three messages, you can retrieve one, two, or all three messages individually without retrieving the Project Alpha folder. To retrieve a folder from the Deleted Items folder, click Deleted Items and select the folder to retrieve. Move that folder from the Deleted Items folder to its original location or to another location.

Although you can't delete any of the default folders (the ones Outlook provides), you can delete folders you've added.

To do so, follow these steps:

1. Make sure the folder doesn't contain any data you need to keep or any data that you have not archived or backed up.
2. Open the folder list, right-click the folder, and choose Delete.
3. Click Yes to confirm the deletion or No to cancel.

> **Tip** **Automatically delete folders of a specific date**
> Outlook can automatically remove items in a folder that match a specified date. If Outlook is configured to empty the Deleted Items folder on a certain date or whenever you quit the program, however, you might lose important items that you accidentally or prematurely sent to that folder. To see the deletion date of a folder, right-click the folder and choose Properties. On the AutoArchive tab, if the Archive This Folder Using These Settings option is selected, look to see whether the Permanently Delete Old Items option is also selected. If it is, the time in the Clean Out Old Items Older Than option specifies how much time you have to retrieve an item from that folder. Don't assume that the folder you deleted last year will still be around today.

Setting Folder Properties

Folders have several properties that control the way they appear and function, as well as others that control archiving, administration, and other activities. To view or set these properties, open the folder list, right-click the folder, and choose Properties to open a Properties dialog box for the folder. The following sections explain the options on each of the tabs in this dialog box.

Configuring General Folder Properties

You can use the General tab (see Figure 30-8) to locate information about a folder, name the folder, add a descriptive comment, and set other properties, as described in the following list:

Figure 30-8. Use the General tab of a folder's Properties dialog box to view information about the folder and set a few general properties.

- **Name** In the top box, specify the name for the folder as you want it to appear in Outlook.
- **Type** This read-only property specifies the type of content the folder contains.
- **Location** This read-only property specifies the location in the folder hierarchy for the selected folder.
- **Description** Use this box to type an optional description of the folder. The description appears only in the folder's Properties dialog box.

- **Show Number Of Unread Items** Use this option with message folders to cause Outlook to display, in the folder list and favorite folders list, the number of unread messages in the folder. Outlook displays the folder name in bold if the item contains unread messages and includes the number of items in parentheses to the right of the folder name.

NEW FEATURE!

- **Show Total Number Of Items** Use this option with all folder types to show the total number of items in the folder. Outlook shows the folder name in bold if it contains items and displays the total number of items in parentheses to the right of the folder name. This option can be particularly useful with search folders to show the total number of items that match the search folder's criteria.
- **When Posting To This Folder, Use** This drop-down list includes two selections. One is the default type of item you can store in the folder, such as Contact for a contacts folder. The other is Forms. If you select Forms in the list, Outlook opens the Choose Form dialog box (see Figure 30-9). Here you can select the form that the folder should use for new items added to the folder. For example, you might want to use the appointment form for a calendar folder.

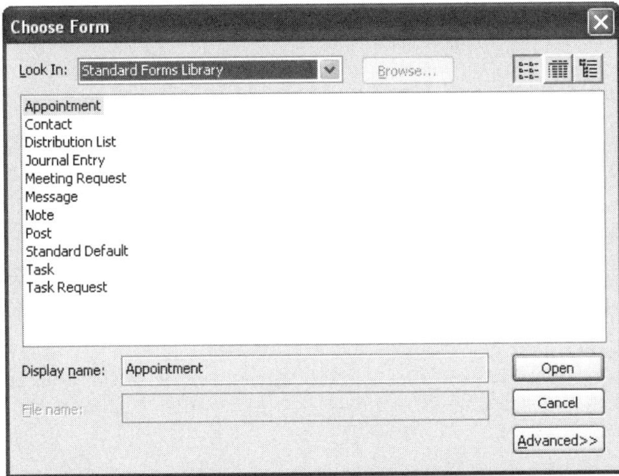

Figure 30-9. Specify the type of form to be used by the folder.

- **Automatically Generate Microsoft Exchange Views** Select this check box to have Outlook create views of public folders so that Microsoft Exchange Server users can view the folders.
- **Folder Size** Click this button to view information about the amount of space a folder and its subfolders use.

Configuring Properties for a Contacts Folder

When configuring properties for a contacts folder, you can set the following address book options on the Outlook Address Book tab:

- **Show This Folder As An E-Mail Address Book** Select this option to have Outlook display contacts in a way that lets you select e-mail addresses from the Address Book dialog box.
- **Name Of The Address Book** You can specify the address book name.

You can also specify options for the items linked to a contact in the Contacts folder by using the Activities tab of the folder's Contacts Properties dialog box (see Figure 30-10), as listed here:

Figure 30-10. Use this tab to set the default view that appears on the Activities tab of a contact form in the folder.

- **Folder Groups** You can select the group of folders that might contain activities related to contacts.
- **Copy, Modify, Reset, New buttons** Click the appropriate button to add groups to or modify groups in the Folder Groups list.
- **Default Activities View** You can select the default view that appears on the Activities tab of a contact form when you open a contact entry.

Configuring AutoArchive Properties for a Folder

Outlook's AutoArchive feature automatically archives items after a specified period, which can help you avoid having folders cluttered with old messages, tasks, and so on. You configure archival properties on the AutoArchive tab of a folder's Properties dialog box. For details, see "Configuring the Automatic Archiving of Items," page 775.

Configuring Administration Properties for a Folder

Outlook provides options for setting administration properties for each folder. To change these properties for a public folder, you must have owner permissions for that folder. In addition, for all but the Initial View On Folder option, you must be running Outlook with Exchange Server. The following options are available on the Administration tab:

- **Initial View On Folder** You can specify the view you see when you open a folder. Your choices are Normal, Group By Form, Group By Subject, Group By Conversation, and Unread By Conversation. The default view is Normal.
- **Drag/Drop Posting Is A** This option lets you specify an item's format when you drag the item to a public folder.

- **Add Folder Address To** You can choose to have Outlook add the folder address to your Personal Address Book. You can then send e-mail directly to the folder.
- **This Folder Is Available To** You can specify the users who can access the folder. You can select all users who have access permissions, or you can limit access to the owner.
- **Folder Assistant** While working online, you can modify processing rules for new items posted to the public folder.
- **Moderated Folder** This option allows you to select moderators for this moderated folder.
- **Folder Path** You can specify the location of the folder.

Configuring Form Properties for a Folder

Outlook items are based on forms, which standardize how information is distributed to other users and stored in Outlook. One example of a form is the contact form Outlook provides when you create a new contact entry.

For more information on forms, see Chapter 3, "Working in and Configuring Outlook," and Chapter 24, "Designing and Using Forms."

On the Forms tab of the Properties dialog box, you can set or view the following form properties for a folder:

- **Forms Associated With This Folder** This item shows a list of forms in the Folder Forms Library associated with the folder.
- **Manage** You can specify a form that you want to move to the Folder Forms Library, thereby listing it in the Forms Associated With This Folder list. You also can click Manage to set up a new form in the Folder Forms Library.
- **Description** Add a description of a form you select in the Forms Associated With This Folder list. You can change the description by clicking Manage, selecting Properties in the Forms Manager dialog box, and then changing the Comments box in the Form Properties dialog box. Click OK twice to save your changes.
- **Allow These Forms In This Folder** You can specify the types of forms you allow in the folder. (The folder must be a public folder.) You can specify that only forms from this list be allowed in the folder; that only forms from this list as well as standard forms be allowed in the folder; or that any form be allowed in the folder. If you select the second option, forms such as messages, tasks, and even documents (for example, Microsoft Word files or Microsoft Excel worksheets) can be stored in the folder.

Note If you run Outlook with Exchange Server, your folders might have public folders set up by system administrators or others who have folder creation privileges. In that case, you can administer permissions properties for these folders using the Permissions tab. For information on folder permissions, see "Granting Access to Folders," page 741.

Using Web Views with Folders

The popularity of the Internet and its usefulness to businesses and individuals make it almost imperative that software include features for accessing the World Wide Web. Outlook offers such features, providing ways for users to access the Web without switching to a different program. This section describes how you can access the Web by specifying a Web page as a home page for a folder.

Why Use Web Views?

When you assign a Web page as a home page for a folder, you make it convenient and easy to access intranet or Internet resources. The primary reason to use a Web view in a folder is to access a Web site or intranet resource without leaving Outlook. As shown in Figure 30-11, you can open a folder that includes a Web page as a home page and then access another page from there. You no longer have to start a separate Web browser, such as Microsoft Internet Explorer, to open the Web page.

Figure 30-11. You can view a Web page without leaving Outlook.

Assigning a Web Page to a Folder

You can assign a Web page to any folder in your folder list.

To assign a Web page, follow these steps:

1. Right-click a folder in the folder list and choose Properties.
2. Click the Home Page tab (see Figure 30-12).

3 Set Web page view properties as necessary, using the following options:

- **Show Home Page By Default For This Folder** Select this check box if you want Outlook to display the Web page rather than the existing default folder view.
- **Address** Specify the URL of a local or remote HTML page or another Internet resource, such as an FTP site.
- **Browse** Click to browse for a URL.
- **Restore Defaults** Click to restore the default settings (no Web page).

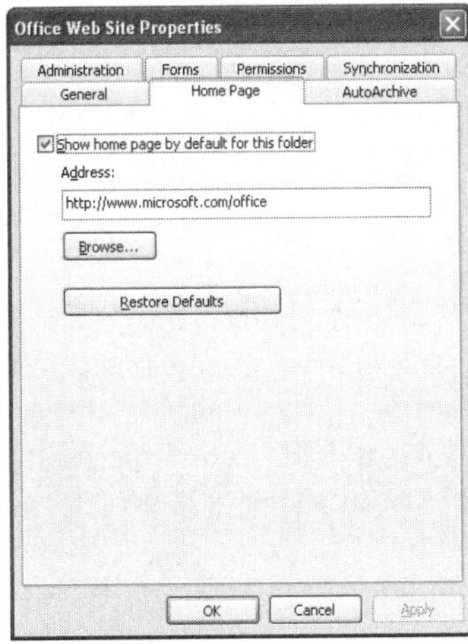

Figure 30-12. Specify a Web page view for a folder using this dialog box.

4 Type the URL (Internet or local address) for the Web page you want to display. You also can click Browse and select a Web page from the Find Web Files dialog box. Click OK after selecting a page to return to the Home Page tab.

5 Click OK.

> **Note** Once you set a Web view for a folder, you cannot switch between the Web view and normal view (that is, a folder view without a Web page showing) unless you clear the Show Home Page By Default For This Folder check box.

Removing a Web Page from a Folder

After a while, you might tire of using a Web view in a folder, or the Web page might become obsolete.

To remove a Web page from a folder, follow these steps:

1 Right-click the folder in the folder list and choose Properties.

2 Click the Home Page tab.

3 Clear the Show Home Page By Default For This Folder check box.

4 Click OK.

Using a Folder's Web Page

Each time you open a folder with a Web page view, Outlook displays the specified Web page according to the Home Page options you selected. If the Web page includes hyperlinks, you can click them to navigate to other pages or sites. In addition, you can type a different URL in the Address box in Outlook and press Enter to display a new Web page inside the Outlook folder.

> **Tip** **Create shortcuts to Web pages**
> It's a bit more difficult to create shortcuts to Web pages in the Outlook 2003 Navigation Pane than it was in the Outlook 2002 Outlook Bar. An alternative to creating shortcuts is to create Outlook folders and then assign them a home page. This method has the advantage of making the pages available from the folder list—just click on the folder in the folder list to navigate to the associated Web page or FTP folder.

Using Multiple Personal Folders

Items you create and receive in Outlook are stored in personal folder (PST) files. The default location for PST files is \Documents And Settings\<*user*>\Local Settings\Application Data\Microsoft\Outlook. On systems that were upgraded from Microsoft Windows NT, the user profiles still reside in the \Winnt\Profiles folder. Therefore on these systems, Outlook places the storage files by default in \%systemroot%\Profiles\<*user*>\Local Settings\Application Data\Microsoft\Outlook, with %systemroot% typically being \Winnt.

If you don't use Outlook with Exchange Server, you use personal folders for storing your Outlook information and data. (With Exchange Server, your messages, calendar, and other items are stored centrally on the server, although you can use PSTs in conjunction with an Exchange Server account.)

You can create multiple personal folders to help you organize your data. For example, you can store e-mail messages associated with a project or a client in one folder and store other messages and items in a more general folder. Another useful way to set up multiple PST files is to use one for archiving. This can help you back up your data more consistently, and Outlook can prompt you at different intervals to ensure that your archive is up-to-date. Outlook even includes the Archive.pst file in which you can archive items.

> **Note** As Outlook copies items to the archive file, it removes them from their original location.

You can also use a PST file to share information with other users on your network. The users must have read/write permissions to open the file.

After you create a PST file, it appears in the folder list automatically. You can add it to a Shortcuts group in the Navigation Pane just as you can with any other folders. You then can access the PST file simply by clicking its shortcut.

For information about adding a folder shortcut, see "Adding a Folder Shortcut to the Navigation Pane," page 755.

Adding a Personal Folder

A personal folder can have any name you give it. By default, the names take the form Personal Folder(1).pst, Personal Folder(2).pst, and so on. At the top of the folder list, you can see the name of the active personal folder, which by default appears as Personal Folders.

To add a personal folder, follow these steps:

1. Choose File, New, Outlook Data File to open the New Outlook Data File dialog box, shown in Figure 30-13.
2. Select Office Outlook Personal Folders File (.pst) if you will not be using the PST with an earlier version of Outlook. Choose Outlook 97-2002 Personal Folders File (.pst) if you need to use the PST with an earlier version of Outlook.

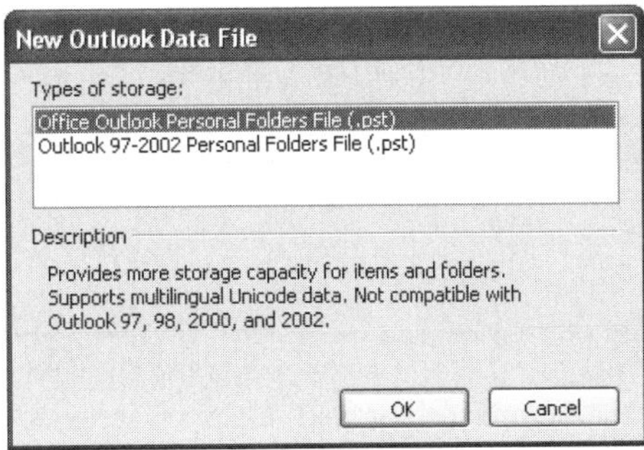

Figure 30-13. Click a Personal Folders File (.pst) option to create a personal folder.

3. Click OK. The Create Or Open Outlook Data File dialog box appears.
4. In the File Name box, type a name for the new personal folders file.
5. Click OK. The Create Microsoft Personal Folders dialog box appears (see Figure 30-14).

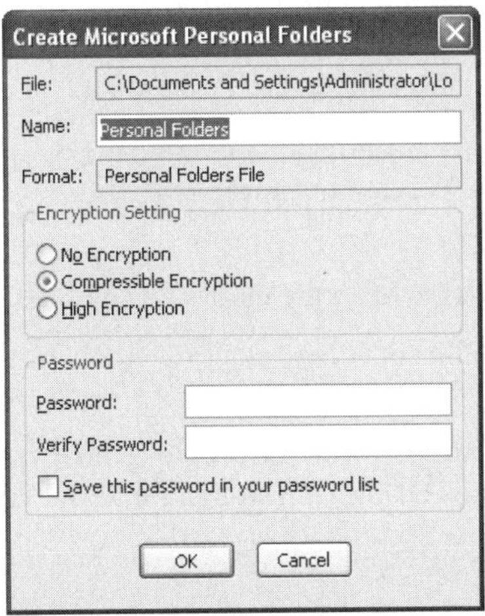

Figure 30-14. Use the Create Microsoft Personal Folders dialog box to set the PST's properties.

6. In the Name box, type a name for the folder. This name appears in the folder list after you create the folder.
7. For the Encryption setting, select the type of encryption you want for this folder. When you encrypt your folder, you ensure that other programs can't read it. Select No Encryption if you don't want to encode your personal folder. Compressible Encryption, which is the default setting, encrypts the personal folder file so that the file can be compressed. Best Encryption sets up the personal folder so that it has the tightest encryption possible.
8. If you want to protect your PST file further, type a password in the Password box and retype it in the Verify Password box. Each time Outlook starts, you'll be prompted to enter this password to access your PST file. If you want, you can save the password in your password list so that Outlook can retrieve the password when it starts.

Tip If you want to limit who can access your PST file, you should not save your Outlook password in the password list.

9. Click OK.
10. The new personal folders item appears in the folder list.

Note After you remove items from a PST file, the file size of the PST file is not reduced. To reduce the size, you must use the Compact command. To do this, choose Files, Data File Management and select your PST file in the Outlook Data Files dialog box. Choose Settings and then click Compact Now in the Personal Folders dialog box.

Removing a Personal Folder

If you no longer need a PST file, you can remove it from the folder list, which removes it from your profile. Removing a set of personal folders from your profile does not delete the PST file—it remains intact and you can add it back to the profile or add it to a different profile, if needed.

When you are ready to delete a PST file, you cannot simply delete it from the folders list; instead, you must follow these steps:

1. Choose File, Data File Management to open the Outlook Data Files dialog box.
2. Select the PST file you want to remove.
3. Click Remove.
4. When prompted about removing the PST file, click Yes to remove it or No to cancel. If you click Yes, Outlook removes the PST file from your profile and from the folder list, but does not delete it.
5. Click Close.

> **Tip** You can also remove a set of personal folders through the folder list. Right-click Personal Folders in the list and choose Close. Note that the command name reflects the name of the folders, so if you named your folder My Personal Stuff, the command reads Close "My Personal Stuff."

Managing Data

As you use Outlook, you'll find that folders will become full of messages, appointments, and other items. One way to manage this data is to copy or move it between folders so that the data is organized according to how you work. In addition, you need to make sure your data is backed up and archived properly in case you accidentally delete data or a system failure occurs.

In this section, you'll learn how to copy and move data between folders, how to archive data automatically and manually, and how to restore data in case of a crash or a reinstallation of Outlook.

Copying and Moving Data Between Folders

Occasionally, you might need to move or copy data from one location to another. For example, perhaps you've received an e-mail message from a client connected with a project you're managing. Instead of keeping that message in the Inbox folder, where it might get lost with all the other messages you receive every day, you can move it to a folder devoted to that particular project.

To move data to another folder, follow these steps:

1. Open the folder list and click the folder that includes the message or other item you want to move.
2. After the folder opens, right-click the message or other item and choose Move To Folder to open the Move Items dialog box (see Figure 30-15).

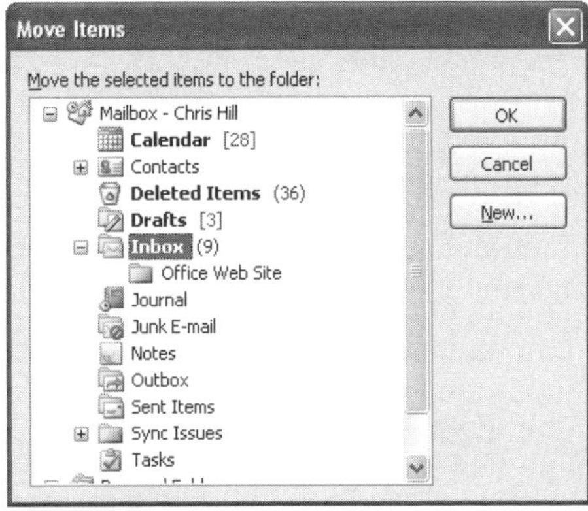

Figure 30-15. Use the Move Items dialog box to move data to a different location.

3. Select an existing folder and click OK, or click New to create a folder in which to store the moved data.
4. Click OK. The data is moved to the selected location.

> **Tip** Choose Edit, Undo Move if you need to move the item back to its original location. This command is effective only immediately after you've performed the move and before you do anything else.

Another way to move data is to select it in the folder and drag it to a new location. Similarly, you can copy data by holding down the Ctrl key while you drag.

Storing Items in Personal Folders or Mailbox Branch

If you move an item to the root of the data store by choosing Personal Folders or Mailbox in the folder list, Outlook dutifully moves the item to the root of your mail store. If the destination was a secondary set of personal folders, you can view the items simply by clicking the Personal Folders branch in the folder list.

However, Outlook displays the Outlook Today view when you click the primary Personal Folders or Mailbox branch in the folder list, effectively hiding any items stored there. You can perform a search to locate and display the items, but an easier method is to simply turn off the Outlook Today page temporarily (or permanently if you never use it).

Open the folder list, right-click Personal Folders or Mailbox, depending on your account type, and choose Properties. Click the Home Page tab, clear the Show Home Page By Default For This Folder check box, and click OK. You can now view and work with the items that are located in the root of your mail store. To restore the Outlook Today view, select the Show Home Page By Default For This Folder check box.

Archiving Your Data Automatically

Over time you will likely want to move some of your Outlook items to a separate location because you no longer need them, but don't want to delete them. For example, perhaps you want to keep a copy of all of the messages in your Sent Items folder so you can refer to them later if needed, but you don't want them to stay in Sent Items. In these situations you can use Outlook's AutoArchive feature to move out those old items.

The Outlook AutoArchive feature archives data automatically according to settings you configure for each folder or all your folders. You might want to archive every day if you receive new data that you don't want to take the chance of losing overnight. Or you might want to set AutoArchive to run once a week.

To set up a folder to automatically archive using the default AutoArchive settings, follow these steps:

1. Right-click a folder in the folder list and choose Properties, then click the AutoArchive tab.
2. Select Archive Items In This Folder Using The Default Settings (see Figure 30-16).

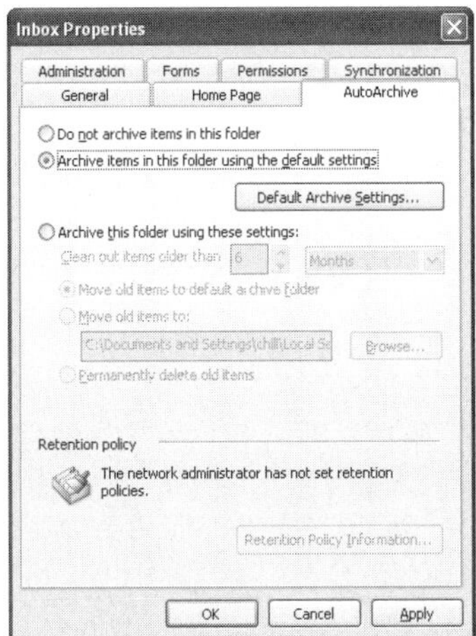

Figure 30-16. Use the AutoArchive feature to archive the data in your folders.

3. Click OK.
4. Repeat these steps for each folder you want to archive.

By default, Outlook starts AutoArchive every 14 days and archives your data in the selected folder to the Archive.pst personal folders file.

For information about changing the default AutoArchive settings, see "Configuring the Automatic Archiving of Items," page 775.

You can also specify custom AutoArchive settings for a folder. Open the properties for the folder, click the AutoArchive tab, and choose the Archive This Folder Using These Settings option. Then, specify settings on the AutoArchive tab as desired for the folder. See the section "Configuring the Automatic Archiving of Items," page 775, for details about each of the available settings.

Archiving Your Data Manually

You can archive data not only automatically but also manually—for example, before leaving on vacation or when you need to move your files to a new machine.

To archive data manually, perform these steps:

1. Choose File, Archive.

2 Select one of the following options in the Archive dialog box (see Figure 30-17):

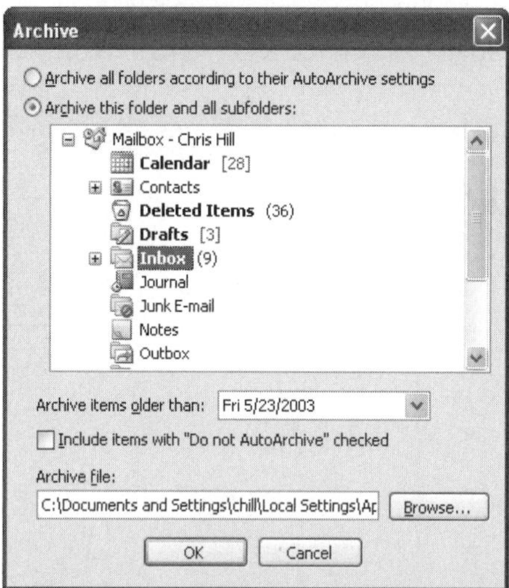

Figure 30-17. Select the way you want to archive data in all or selected folders.

- **Archive All Folders According To Their AutoArchive Settings** Use this option to archive all folders using preset AutoArchive settings. When you select this option, the remaining options in this dialog box become unavailable. Go to step 7.
- **Archive This Folder And All Subfolders** Select this option if you want to archive individual folders and their subfolders. Go to step 3.

3 Select the folder you want to archive. If the folder includes subfolders, those folders are archived as well.

4 In the Archive Items Older Than drop-down list, specify the latest date from which Outlook should start archiving data. For instance, if you want to archive data older than today's date, select that date. Otherwise, all your data in the selected folder will not be archived.

5 If you have specified that a folder should not be archived automatically (see "Configuring the Automatic Archiving of Items," page 775, for more information on this setting), but you want to archive this folder now, select the Include Items With "Do Not AutoArchive" Checked check box.

6 To change the personal folders file that will store your archive, click Browse and then choose the file and folder where the archive will be stored. You also can type the path and file name in the Archive File box if you know this information.

7 Click OK.

Outlook begins archiving your data. If the folder contains a large amount of data, archiving might take several minutes (or hours, depending on the speed of your computer and other factors). You can watch the status of the archiving by looking at the right side of Outlook's status bar. When the process has finished, the Archive.pst file (or whichever archive file you specified in step 6) will contain the data Outlook just archived.

Restoring Data After a Crash or a Reinstallation

Suppose you've worked on a project for six months and you've been diligent about archiving messages and other items from the project. You come into work one day and find that your system has crashed and Outlook has lost all your data. You need the archived data to get back all your lost information and continue working. How do you get it back?

You can restore data from an archive file in two ways: drag items from a PST file to a folder, or import a PST file.

The following steps show you how to drag data from a PST file:

1. After restoring your computer and, if necessary, reinstalling Outlook, choose File, Open, Outlook Data File to open the Open Outlook Data File dialog box (see Figure 30-18).

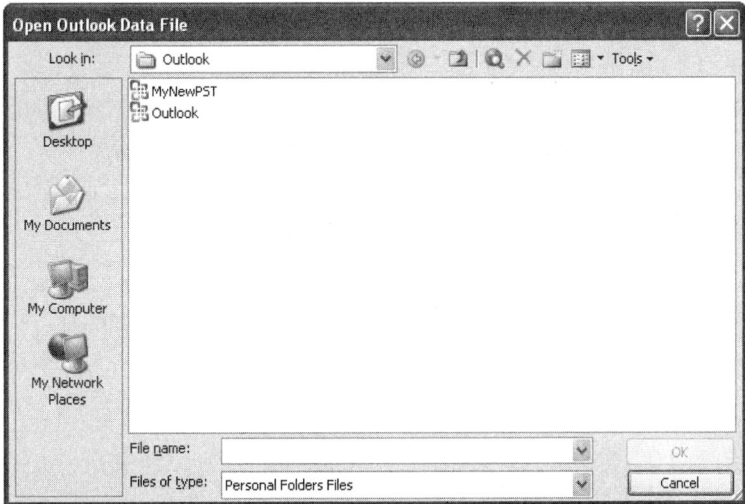

Figure 30-18. Select the PST file that contains the data you want to restore.

2. Select the file that contains the archived items you want to restore.
3. Click OK. The archive folder (named Archive Folders by default) now appears in your folder list.
4. Click the plus sign (+) next to Archive Folders (or the name you've given this folder) to expand the folder. Expand subsequent folders if necessary until your data is in the right pane.
5. Drag the folder or item to the original folder in which the data was stored.
6. Continue dragging items until they all are restored.

To restore items by importing a PST file, follow these steps:

1. Choose File, Import And Export to open the Import and Export Wizard.
2. Select Import From Another Program Or File and click Next.
3. Select Personal Folder File (.pst) and click Next.
4. On the Import Personal Folders wizard page (see Figure 30-19), type the name of the file you want to import in the File To Import box, or click Browse to locate the file using the Open Personal Folders dialog box.

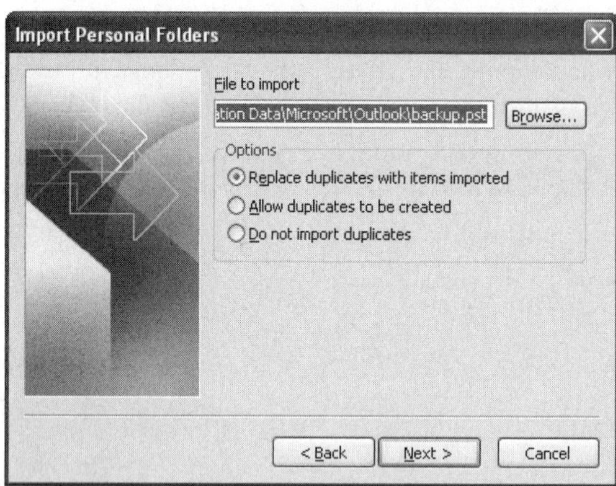

Figure 30-19. Specify the name of the file you want to import.

5. Select one of the following import options pertaining to duplicate data:
   - To replace duplicate items that might be in your folders during import, select Replace Duplicates With Items Imported.
   - To create duplicate items, select Allow Duplicates To Be Created.
   - To prevent Outlook from creating duplicates or writing over existing data, select Do Not Import Duplicates.
6. Click Next.
7. Select the folder from which you want to import data.
8. If the archived folder includes subfolders you want to import as well, select the Include Subfolders option.
9. To filter data, click Filter. You can filter by using search strings, Structured Query Language (SQL), and other advanced querying methods. Click OK after filling out your filter information.

10 Select one of the following destination options:

- **Import Items Into The Current Folder** Select this option to import data to the current folder—that is, the folder currently selected.
- **Import Items Into The Same Folder In** Choose this option to import data into the destination folder of the same name as the source folder (such as from the Inbox to the Inbox) Then, in the drop-down list under this last option, select the destination personal folders or mailbox.

11 Click Finish.

Outlook displays a window showing you the progress of the import process. The archive folder appears in the folder list (if the folder list is open), but it is removed when the operation is completed.

Configuring the Automatic Archiving of Items

Outlook provides several ways to configure and manage your data-archiving settings. For example, suppose that you want Outlook to run AutoArchive every day, but you want to be prompted before it starts. You can configure AutoArchive to do just that. In addition, you might want to delete old items after a specific date (say, after a message sits in the Inbox for six months). This section shows you how to configure AutoArchive to handle many of your archiving needs.

To set AutoArchive options, choose Tools, Options, click the Other tab, and click AutoArchive to open the AutoArchive dialog box. The following sections explain the options you'll find in the AutoArchive dialog box.

Run AutoArchive Every *n* Days

Outlook allows you to run AutoArchive on a per-day cycle. For example, if you want to run it each day, set it to run every 1 day. To archive every other day, set AutoArchive to run every 2 days, and so on.

> **Note** Outlook has different aging periods for different types of items. Calendar, Notes, Journal, Drafts, and Inbox folders have a default of six months. Outbox is three months, and Sent Items and Deleted Items are two months. Contacts folders do not have an AutoArchive option, so you must manually archive them.

To set the length of time between AutoArchive sessions, set the Run AutoArchive Every *n* Days option (see Figure 30-20) to the number of days you want between archiving sessions. The number you enter must be between 1 and 60.

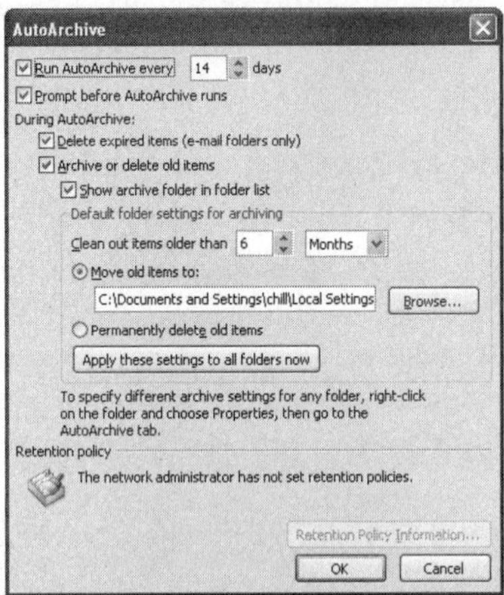

Figure 30-20. Set up Outlook to run AutoArchive at specified intervals.

Prompt Before AutoArchive Runs

You can have Outlook display a message before it starts an AutoArchive session. The message includes a Cancel button to let you cancel the AutoArchive for that day.

To activate this option, select the Prompt Before AutoArchive Runs check box in the AutoArchive dialog box.

Delete Expired Items

In your message folders, AutoArchive can delete messages if they are older than a specified amount of time. To set this option, select the Delete Expired Items check box. Also make sure that the Archive Or Delete Old Items check box is selected.

In the Default Folder Settings For Archiving area, set the amount of time you want to pass before AutoArchive automatically deletes e-mail messages. The default is six months, but you can set this to as high as 60 months or as low as one day.

Archive or Delete Old Items

If you want AutoArchive to archive or delete old Outlook items, select the Archive Or Delete Old Items check box. Then set the amount of time that should elapse before old items are archived or deleted. Again, the default is six months, but you can set it to as high as 60 months or as low as one day.

Show Archive Folder in Folder List

If you want Outlook to display your archive folder in the folder list, select the Show Archive Folder In Folder List check box. You might want to select this check box if you think you'd like to be able to see which items have been archived. Also, you might find that some items are removed from your working folders (such as Inbox or Calendar) before you want them removed. By showing the archive folder in the folder list, you can quickly and easily move items back to a working folder.

Specify How Archived Items Are Handled

In the Default Folder Settings For Archiving area, you can set the number of days that should pass before e-mail messages or other items are archived or deleted (see the previous two sections).

In addition, this area includes options for the way old items are handled. With the Move Old Items To option, you can specify a PST file to which Outlook should move archived items. Click Browse to identify a different location and the PST file in which you want to store archives.

On the other hand, if you want to delete archived items, select Permanently Delete Old Items and Outlook will delete items during the AutoArchive sessions. This option is probably not a good choice if you want to retain information for long periods of time.

Apply Settings to All Folders

If you want these AutoArchive settings to apply to all your folders, click Apply These Settings To All Folders Now. Any settings you establish for individual folders (see the next section) are not overridden by the default settings in the AutoArchive dialog box.

AutoArchive Settings for Individual Folders

When you configure AutoArchive settings, you can use the default settings just described, or you can specify options for individual folders.

To take the latter approach, open the Properties dialog box for the folder, click the Auto-Archive tab, and click Archive This Folder Using These Settings. Then set the following options:

- **Do Not Archive Items In This Folder** Specify that the current folder should not be archived.
- **Archive This Folder Using These Settings** Direct Outlook to archive items in the folder based on the custom settings you specify in the dialog box.
- **Clean Out Items Older Than *n*** This option lets you specify the number of days, weeks, or months that should pass before AutoArchive removes items in the selected folder.
- **Move Old Items To Default Archive Folder** You can have Outlook move old items to the folder specified for default AutoArchive settings.

- **Move Old Items To** This option lets you specify a different folder in which to archive old items. Click Browse to locate a different folder or file.
- **Permanently Delete Old Items** You can direct Outlook to delete items in this folder during archiving.

Setting Retention Policy

Your system administrator might enforce company retention policies for your mailbox. If you are running Outlook with Exchange Server, your administrator can set retention polices that you can't override with AutoArchive settings. For example, your company might require that all e-mail messages be saved and archived to backup tapes or disks and then retained for seven years. As much as you try, you can't change these settings without having the appropriate permissions. To view retention policy settings, click Retention Policy Information on the AutoArchive tab.

Note See Chapter 36, "Supporting Outlook Under Exchange Server," for more details on using retention policies.

Chapter 31

Finding and Organizing Data

Although some people use Microsoft Office Outlook 2003 only for e-mail, the majority of people use all the personal information manager (PIM) features the program has to offer. Because a PIM is only as good as its ability to help you search for and organize data, Outlook offers a solid selection of features to help you do just that.

This chapter shows you how to perform simple and advanced searches to locate data. You'll learn how to search using the Find A Contact tool, the Find Bar, and the Advanced Find dialog box. The chapter also explores various ways you can organize your Outlook data, for example, by creating additional folders for storing specific types of messages.

Using the Find A Contact Tool to Search for Contacts

If you're like most Outlook users, your Contacts folder will grow to contain a lot of contact entries—typically, too many to allow you to browse through the folder when you need to quickly find a particular contact. You're also likely to encounter situations in which, for example, you need to locate contact information but can't remember the person's last name. Fortunately, Outlook makes it easy to locate contact data, providing the Find A Contact box for searching right on the Standard toolbar (see Figure 31-1).

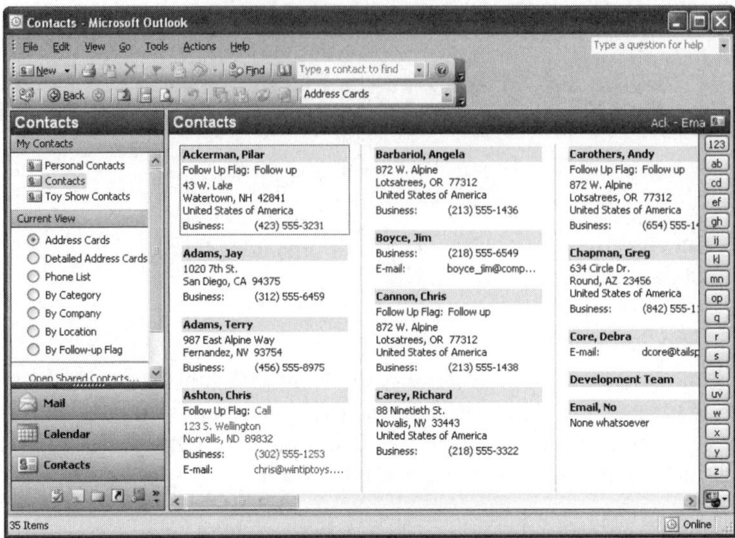

Figure 31-1. The Find A Contact box allows you to find a contact entry quickly.

To locate a contact, click the Find A Contact box on the Standard toolbar, type the search criteria (such as a first name, last name, or company), and press Enter. If Outlook finds only one contact that matches the search criteria, it opens the contact entry for that person. Otherwise, Outlook displays the Choose Contact dialog box (see Figure 31-2), from which you select the contact entry to open.

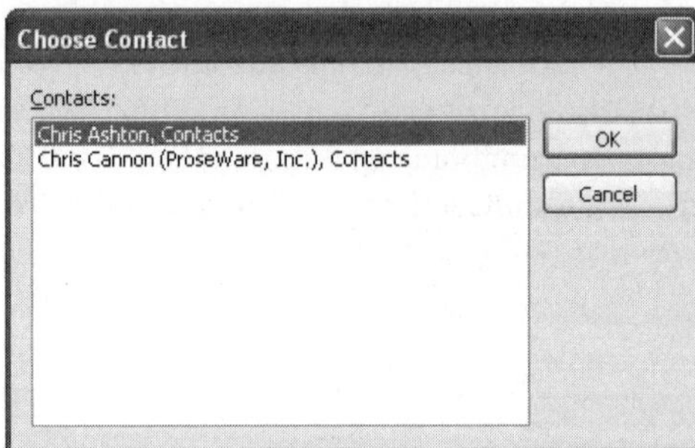

Figure 31-2. Select a contact when Outlook finds more than one that fits your search.

Tip Find A Contact is useful when you need to perform a quick search for a contact based on a limited amount of data. To locate contacts and other Outlook items based on multiple search conditions, see "Using Advanced Find," page 783.

Using the Find Bar

The Find A Contact feature searches only the Contacts folder. When you're looking for messages or other Outlook items (including contacts), you can use the Find Bar (see Figure 31-3). The Find Bar lets you quickly search the current folder, all mail folders, the Inbox, and the Sent Items folder. It also provides a Choose Folder command you can use to select any other folder to include in the search. To display the Find Bar, choose Tools, Find, Find.

> **Tip** Choose Tools, Find, Find to hide the Find Bar. You also can press Ctrl+E to show or hide the Find Bar.

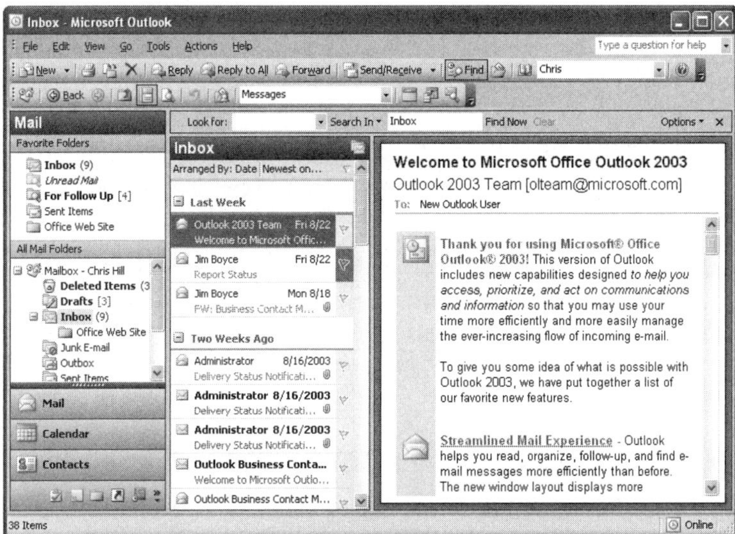

Figure 31-3. Use the Find Bar to perform simple searches of all Outlook items.

Using the Find Bar is easy. In the Look For box, type the data you want to find, such as a name, e-mail subject, or keyword contained in the item. Click Search In to specify where you want to search. The first item in the list is always the current folder. The complete list of options is as follows:

- **Current Folder** The first item in the list is the current folder. Choose this option to search through the folder currently opened in Outlook.
- **All Mail Folders** Search the Drafts, Inbox, Outbox, and Sent Items folders.
- **Mail I Received** Search the Inbox.
- **Mail I Sent** Search the Sent Items folder.
- **Mailbox/Personal Folders** Search all folders in the current mail store.

- **Choose Folders** Display the Select Folder(s) dialog box, shown in Figure 31-4, from which you can select multiple folders.

Figure 31-4. You can search multiple folders by selecting them in the Select Folder(s) dialog box.

After you specify the search data and location, you can click Options on the Find Bar to specify that you want to search all text in each message. Clear this option if you want to search only headers. When you're ready to start the search, click Find Now. Outlook organizes the current view to show the results of the search (see Figure 31-5). Click Clear to restore the previous view.

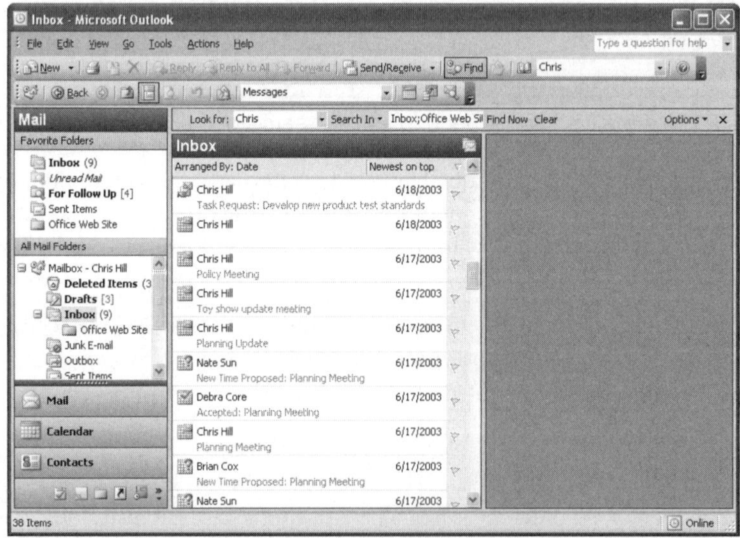

Figure 31-5. Outlook displays the results of the search so that you can select and view the items you need.

Using Advanced Find

In addition to the Find A Contact tool and the Find Bar, Outlook provides an Advanced Find feature for performing advanced searches that require specifying multiple search conditions.

The Advanced Find Dialog Box

Choose Tools, Advanced Find or press Ctrl+Shift+F to open the Advanced Find dialog box (see Figure 31-6). You can use this dialog box to search for any type of Outlook item using multiple search conditions.

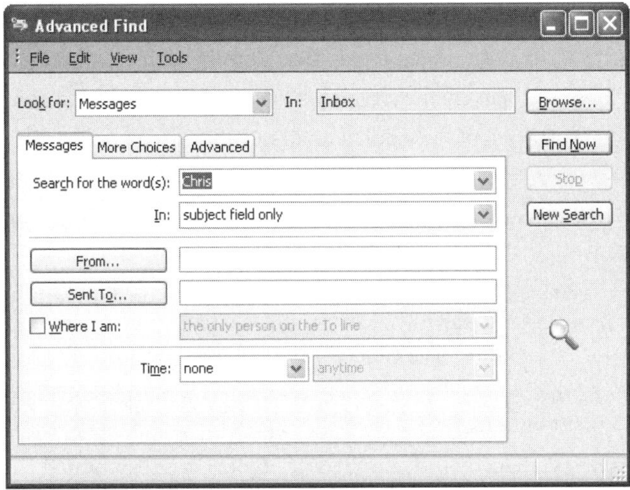

Figure 31-6. Use the Advanced Find dialog box when you need to search using multiple conditions.

The options provided in the Advanced Find dialog box change depending on the type of item you select in the Look For drop-down list. If you select Contacts, for example, the options change to provide specialized search criteria for contacts, such as restricting the search to a name, company, or address. Selecting Messages in the drop-down list changes the options so that you can search the subject field of messages, search the subject and message body, or specify other search criteria specific to messages.

> **Note** When you select a different item type in the Look For drop-down list, Outlook clears the current search and starts a new one. Outlook does, however, prompt you to confirm that you want to clear the current search.

On the Messages tab of the Advanced Find dialog box (refer to Figure 31-6), you specify the primary search criteria. The following list summarizes all the available options (although not all options appear at all times):

- **Search For The Word(s)** Specify the word, words, or phrase for which you want to search. You can type words individually or include quotes around a phrase to search for the entire phrase. You also can select from a previous set of search words.
- **In** Specify the location in the Outlook item where you want to search, such as only the subject of a message. The options available in this list vary according to the type of item you select in the Look For drop-down list.
- **From** Specify the name of the person who sent you the message. Type the name or click From to browse the address book for the name.
- **Organized By** Specify the person who generated the meeting request.
- **Sent To** For messages, specify the recipients to whom the message was sent.
- **Attendees** Specify the people scheduled to attend a meeting.
- **E-Mail** Browse the address book to search for contacts by their e-mail addresses.
- **Time** Specify the creation or modification time, the start or end time, or other time properties specific to the type of item for which you are searching.
- **Named** Specify the file name of the item for which you're searching. You can specify a single file name or use wildcards to match multiple items. The Named box appears if you select Files or Files (Outlook/Exchange) in the Look For drop-down list.
- **Of Type** Choose the type of file for which to search when using the Files or Files (Outlook/Exchange) options.
- **Journal Entry Types** Specify the journal entry type when searching the journal for items.
- **Contact** Browse for a contact associated with an item for which you're searching.
- **Where I Am** When searching for messages, specify that you are the only person on the To line, on the To line with others, or on the Cc line with others.
- **Status** Search for tasks based on their status. You can select Doesn't Matter, Not Started, In Progress, or Completed.

Specifying Advanced Search Criteria

You use the More Choices tab of the Advanced Find dialog box (see Figure 31-7) to specify additional search conditions to refine the search.

Figure 31-7. Use the More Choices tab to refine the search.

The options on the More Choices tab are the following:

- **Categories** Specify the category or categories associated with the items for which you are searching. You can type the categories separated by commas or click Categories to open the Categories dialog box and select categories.
- **Only Items That Are** Search for items by their read status (read or unread).
- **Only Items With** Search for items by their attachment status (one or more attachments or no attachments).
- **Whose Importance Is** Specify the importance (High, Normal, or Low) of the items for which you are searching.
- **Only Items Which** Specify the flag status of the items for which you are searching.
- **Match Case** Direct Outlook to match the case of the text you entered as the search criteria with the case of matching text. Clear this check box to make the search case-insensitive.
- **Size** Specify the size criteria for the items in your search. You can select one of several options to define the size range in which the item must fall to match the search.

The More Choices tab is the same for all Outlook items except the Files search item. With Files selected in the Look For drop-down list, the More Choices tab is limited to Match Case, Size, and this additional option:

- **Match All Word Forms** Outlook searches for all word forms of the text you specified for the search. For example, entering **play** would cause Outlook to search for play, playing, played, plays, and other word forms of play. Clear this check box to search for only the words specified on the Files tab.

You can use the Advanced tab (see Figure 31-8) of the Advanced Find dialog box to create more complex searches. On this tab, select the fields to include in the search as well as the search conditions for each field. You can build a list of multiple fields.

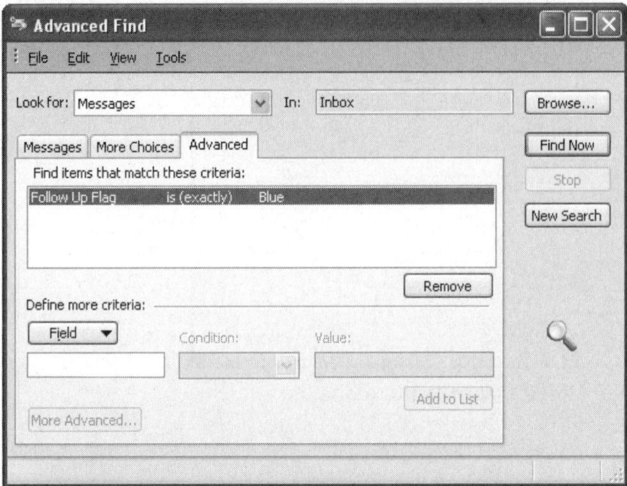

Figure 31-8. On the Advanced tab, select the fields to search and their search criteria.

Organizing Data

Searching for data and organizing data usually go hand in hand. One of the main motivations for organizing your data is that you want to be able to find it easily. Even with perfect organization, however, you'll still need to perform searches now and then because of the sheer amount of data that might be involved. Outlook provides several ways to organize your data. Whereas other chapters focus on specific ways to organize your Outlook items, this section provides an overview of ways you can organize certain types of items and points you to the appropriate chapters for additional information.

Organizing Your E-Mail

E-mail messages probably make up the bulk of your Outlook data. For that reason, organizing your messages can be a challenge. Outlook offers several features that will help you organize your messages so that you can find and work with them effectively and efficiently.

Search Folders

Search folders, which are explained in detail in Chapter 8, "Filtering, Organizing, and Using Automatic Responses," are the best means in Outlook 2003 to quickly organize messages without moving those messages around to different folders. A search folder looks and acts like a folder, but it's really a special type of view that displays in a virtual folder view all messages that fit the search condition for the search folder. Search folders offer two main benefits:

they can search multiple folders, and they organize messages without requiring that the messages be moved from their current folder.

See "Finding and Organizing Messages With Search Folders," page 215, to learn more about search folders.

Using Folders

Another great way to organize your e-mail messages is to separate them in different folders. For example, if you deal with several projects, consider creating a folder for each project and moving each message to its respective folder. You can create the folders as subfolders of your Inbox or place them elsewhere, depending on your preferences. You might even create a folder outside the Inbox called Projects and create subfolders for each project under that folder.

For more information on creating and managing folders, see Chapter 30, "Managing Folders, Data, and Archiving."

Using Rules

Rules are one of the best tools you have in Outlook for organizing messages. You can apply rules to selectively process messages—moving, deleting, copying, and performing other actions on the messages based on the sender, the recipient, the account, and a host of other message properties. You can use rules in combination with folders to organize your e-mail messages. In the multiple projects example described in the previous section, for example, you might use rules to automatically move messages for specific projects to their respective folders. You can apply rules to messages when they arrive in the Inbox or any time you need to rearrange or organize.

For a detailed discussion of rules, see "Processing Messages Automatically," page 224.

Using Colors

Outlook uses color to help organize your e-mail messages. If you create rules to apply certain colors to specified e-mail messages, the color can provide a visual indicator of the sender, the subject, the priority, or other properties of the message. In this way, you can see at a glance whether a particular message meets certain criteria. You can also use automatic formatting in a view to apply color.

Using Views

Views give you another important way to organize your Outlook data. The default views organize specific folders using the most common criteria. You can customize Outlook Today view using HTML to provide different or additional levels of organization. You can also create custom views of any Outlook folder to organize your data to suit your preferences.

For more information on customizing, see "Customizing Outlook Today View," page 673, and "Creating and Using Custom Views," page 681.

Using the Organize Pane

You can organize your Inbox and other folders manually, or you can use the Ways To Organize area, or the organize pane, which gives you quick access to some of the organizational features Outlook provides. Open a folder and choose Tools, Organize to view the organize pane (see Figure 31-9). Using this feature to organize your e-mail folders is relatively easy.

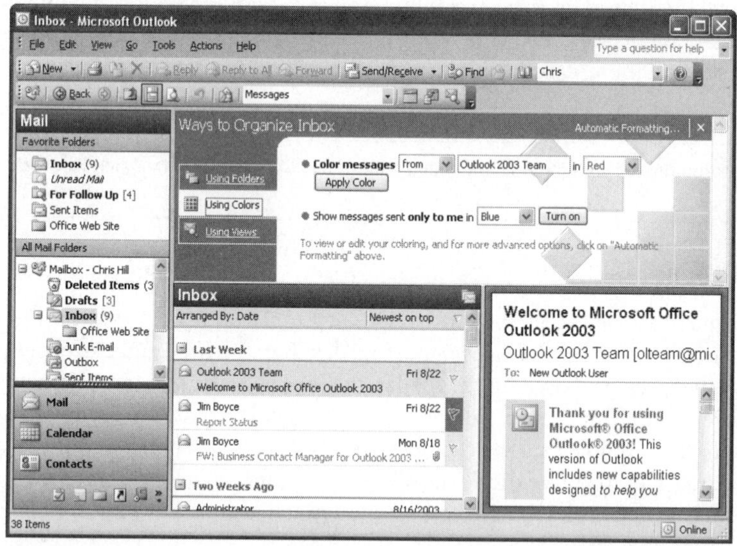

Figure 31-9. Use the organize pane to create rules and organize your message folder in other ways.

The organize pane gives you four options for organizing the current folder. Clicking the link for a particular option changes the options displayed in the organize pane. The following list explains the types of actions you can perform with each option (not all options appear in every folder):

- **Using Folders** Move selected messages to other folders.
- **Using Colors** Color messages sent to or from an individual. You can also specify that messages sent only to you are displayed in a specific color.
- **Using Categories** Add categories to selected items and create new categories.
- **Using Views** Select from several predefined views.

You'll find additional information on the organize pane in Chapter 8, "Filtering, Organizing, and Using Automatic Responses."

Organizing Your Calendar

You can use the organize pane in your Calendar folder (see Figure 31-10) to organize items in your calendar.

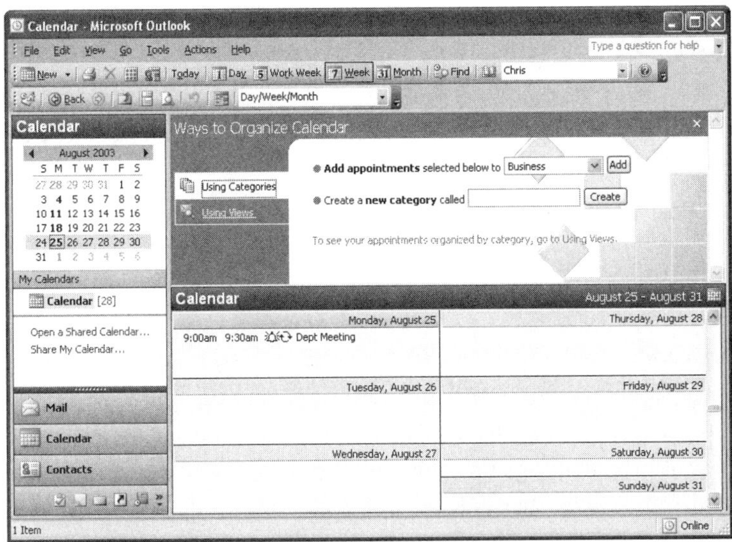

Figure 31-10. Use the organize pane in the Calendar folder to apply categories to calendar items and select a view.

To assign categories to calendar items, click the Using Categories link. Select the items, and then select the category you want in the drop-down list. You can also use the organize pane to create a category.

> **For a detailed discussion of categories, including how to modify the Master Category List and how to share categories with others, see Chapter 4, "Using Categories and Types."**

You can change the calendar view from the organize pane, which allows you to switch to a view that organizes your data the way you want. To change your view, click the Using Views link in the organize pane and then select an existing view from a list. (This provides the same functionality as choosing View, Current View, followed by the view you want to use.)

Within the Calendar folder, color labels offer another means of organizing your schedule data. You can assign any of 10 different labels to items on your calendar to help you quickly identify them. Each label has its own color, so when you assign a label to an item it appears in that color on the calendar. Outlook provides a set of predefined labels (such as Birthday, Anniversary, and Phone Call), but you can modify the labels to suit your needs.

To assign a label to an item, right-click the item on the calendar, choose Label, and then select the label to assign. To specify your own text for each label color, right-click an item, choose Label, and then choose Edit Labels.

Note Customize a view to use automatic formatting that applies colors based on the contents of an item's subject. For example, you can have Outlook automatically assign the Birthday label to all events in the Calendar folder that include *Birthday* in the subject.

Organizing Contacts, Tasks, and Notes

Like your other Outlook folders, the Contacts, Tasks, and Notes folders have an organize pane that you can use to organize your contacts, tasks, and notes. The organize pane gives you three options for organizing contacts and tasks:

- **Using Folders** Use this option to move selected items to another folder, which you can select from a drop-down list in the organize pane (refer to Figure 31-9).
- **Using Categories** Click this link to assign selected items to one or more categories and create new categories.
- **Using Views** Click this link to select a view. This is the same as choosing View, Current View, followed by the view you want to use.

The Notes folder provides only the Using Folders and Using Views options and does not let you specify categories in its organize pane. You can assign categories to a note, however, by right-clicking the note and choosing Categories.

Chapter 32

Data Security and Virus Protection

If you use Microsoft Office Outlook 2003 on a daily basis to manage e-mail, appointments, and contacts, losing the information you've stored in Outlook could cause significant problems. Outlook data can be lost in a number of ways, from accidental deletion to file corruption to hard disk failure. In addition, a user who purchases a new computer might leave behind information when transferring data information to the new machine.

This chapter discusses two different but complementary processes: using the backup and restore process to protect your Outlook information store, and moving information from one place to another using the Import And Export Wizard. Both processes involve creating copies of your data, but the methods used to create these copies—and the way you use the copies—are quite different.

This chapter also examines virus protection for both the server and workstation to help you understand how to protect yourself and your network from e-mail-borne viruses. Outlook provides features itself to protect against viruses in attachments, and there are several steps you can and should take to add other forms of virus protection.

Backing Up and Restoring Data

An important part of working with a computer system is ensuring that you protect any critical data against loss.You protect your data by making a *backup*, a copy of the information that you can store on another disk or on a backup tape. In the event of a critical failure, you can then use this copy to replace or restore any lost information.

Outlook stores information in two primary ways: in a personal folder or within a a Microsoft Exchange Server mailbox, which resides in a shared database on the Exchange server. With an Exchange Server mailbox, your message store is located on the server. The network administrator is generally responsible for backing up the server, and with it the Exchange Server database that contains all the users' information.

If you don't use Exchange Server, Outlook stores your data in a PST file, a set of personal folders. In this scenario, each user has his or her own PST file or even multiple personal folder files. PST files can be located either on the local hard disk of your computer or in a home directory on the server. Although server-based PST files and local PST files are identical from a functional standpoint, they aren't identical from a backup perspective. Generally, the network administrator regularly backs up server-based user home directories, so if the PST files are in your home directory, you shouldn't have to do backups on your own (although you can, of course). While you should not have to do backups if your data is stored on a server, it is usually a good idea to check with the network administrator to make sure your data is backed up.

With local message stores, however, normal network backup strategies do not apply. Most networks don't back up every hard disk on every machine. It simply isn't efficient. Similarly, if you're a home user, you probably don't have a server to which you can save data or a network administrator to watch over the server. In such cases, you need to take steps on your own to protect your data. Individual backup and restore scenarios apply to these kinds of cases.

Note Archive files are simply additional sets of personal folders. Users who archive their messages for later reference should also back up these archive files. For more information on archiving, see Chapter 30, "Managing Folders, Data, and Archiving."

Backing Up Your Outlook Data

Three primary options are available for backing up Outlook data:

- Exporting some or all information to a backup PST file
- Copying the PST file to another disk
- Using a backup program to save a copy of the PST file to tape, another hard disk, a Zip drive, or CD-R/CD-RW

Table 32-1 lists the features available in each backup option.

Table 32-1. Backup Options in Outlook

Backup Type	Export	Copy	Backup
Complete backup	Yes	Yes	Yes
Partial backup	Yes	No	No
Automated backup	No	Yes	Yes
Media-supported backup	Disk	Disk	Disk, tape

The process of exporting information is discussed later in the chapter. The following sections focus on the use of backup programs and PST copies.

Backing Up Your Personal Folders

If you store your Outlook data in one or more sets of personal folders, the data resides in a PST file. This file is usually located on your local hard disk, but could also be stored on a shared network folder. The first step in backing up your personal folders is to determine where the file is located.

If you are not sure whether you use an Exchange Server account, follow these steps to check your e-mail settings:

1. Open the Mail icon in Control Panel, or right-click the Outlook icon on the Start menu and choose Properties.
2. In the Mail Setup dialog box, click Show Profiles, choose your profile, and click Properties. Then click E-Mail Accounts to start the E-Mail Accounts wizard.
3. Choose View Or Change Existing E-Mail Accounts and click Next.

If the E-Mail Accounts list includes only Microsoft Exchange Server, then your Outlook data is stored in your Exchange Server mailbox on the server and you need to talk to your Exchange Server administrator about backups, or use the Export method explained in "Exporting Data," page 800. If the e-mail account list shows an Exchange Server account along with other accounts, look in the Deliver New E-Mail To The Following Location drop-down list. This drop-down list shows where incoming mail is delivered. If it specifies a mailbox, your incoming mail is delivered to your Exchange Server mailbox. If it references a set of personal folders, your incoming mail is stored in a PST.

If the account list shows more than one e-mail account, it's possible that your Outlook data is stored in more than one set of personal folders. For example, IMAP and HTTP accounts store their data in their own PST files. If you want to back up everything in this situation, you need to back up multiple PST files.

To determine if you are using more than one PST file, choose File, Data File Management to open the Outlook Data Files dialog box shown in Figure 32-1. The path and file name for the PST are generally long, so it's unlikely that you will be able to read it all. Click the vertical bar at the right of the Filename column and drag it to the right until you can view the entire path. Or, simply click Open Folder, which opens the folder where the PST is stored and highlights it in the folder.

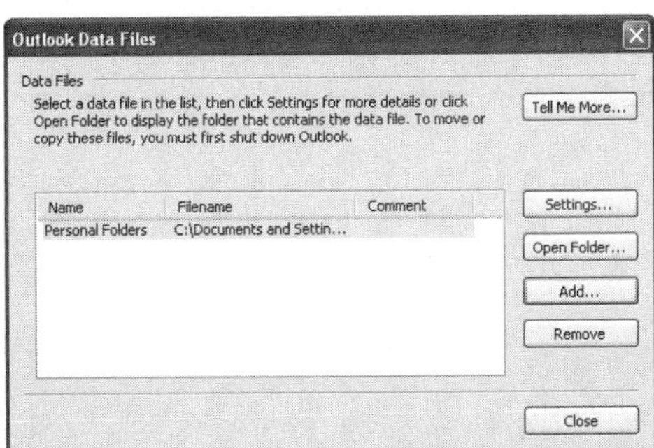

Figure 32-1. The Outlook Data Files dialog box lists message stores in use.

After you have verified that the message store is not being backed up elsewhere and is stored in a PST file, you need to choose which kind of backup to do. Both of the following methods work well, and each has its advantages. Back up each of the PSTs listed in the Outlook Data Files dialog box using one of these methods.

Backing Up Using File Copy

Personal folders or archive files can be extremely large—often hundreds of megabytes—so simply saving a PST file to a floppy disk isn't an option anymore. As files have grown, though, so have the methods available for moving them around. Any of the following options would be acceptable to use with a file backup method:

- Recordable (CD-R) or Rewritable (CD-RW) CD drive
- Zip drive or some other large-capacity storage disk
- Network server drive
- A drive on another computer on the network
- A separate hard disk in the machine where the PST is stored

Not all options are created equal, however. Using a CD-R is an expensive option because you must burn another disk each time you run a backup. The CD-RW option works well, but you add the expense of buying the CD-RW drive and media. Zip, Jaz, and similar drives all work well but are also an expense. If your computer is on a network, the best option is to copy the PST to the network server. This serves two purposes. First, the file will be duplicated to another spot on the network. Second, the administrator is probably backing up the server drives, so the file will also be saved to a backup tape during the next backup.

Inside Out

Check network backup policies

Be certain to check with your network administrator about the recommended policy for backing up PST files in your organization. If, for example, PST files are not allowed on your network because of resource allocation, you'll want to know this and choose another backup method, rather than copying your PST file to the network only to find it deleted the next week. Remember that whatever the merits of a particular backup method, it's critical that your IT staff support it.

If you are saving to a CD-R or CD-RW, you can use the CD burner's interface to copy the file. If you're using a Zip (or similar) drive or a network location, simply drag the file to your chosen backup location. Make sure to close Outlook before starting the backup copy process.

Inside Out

Don't move the PST file

When copying, be careful not to accidentally *move* the PST file instead. If you move it, you'll find no message store when you reopen Outlook. If you do accidentally move your PST, you simply need to copy the file back to the correct location. To avoid this potential problem, automate the copy. After checking with your administrator, see "Scheduling Automatic Backups," page 798.

Backing Up Using Microsoft's Backup Utility

If you prefer to use a graphic backup option or if you have access to a tape backup unit, this second method is for you. Both Microsoft Windows 2000 and Microsoft Windows XP include a Backup application in System Tools. You can use this application to identify files for archiving, and it offers the following enhancements over a standard file copy:

- Allows simple setup of a backup plan by using wizards
- Has options for verifying the backup
- Has built-in restore and scheduling options

To use the Windows Backup tool, open Backup by choosing Start, All Programs, Accessories, System Tools. In Figure 32-2, the PST file is selected for backup and will be saved in the Backup.bkf file. The location of the backup file is specified in the lower left portion of the window.

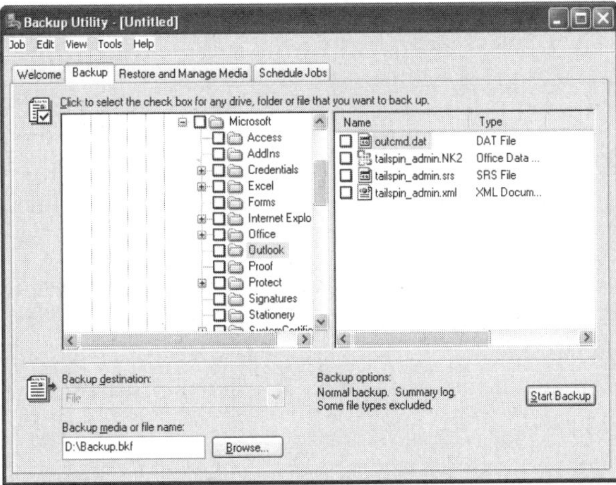

Figure 32-2. You can back up a file using the Backup tool in Windows.

Caution Having the backup file in the same directory or on the same hard disk as the PST file is a horrible backup strategy. If the drive becomes corrupted or the directory in which the PST file is saved is deleted, both the message store and its backup would be lost. Always save the BKF file to another disk drive or to tape.

To start the backup, click Start Backup. You'll need to specify a number of options, including whether to verify the backup. When the process is finished, a dialog box similar to the one shown in Figure 32-3 appears. From this dialog box, you can view a report that records any events—and, more important, any errors—that might have occurred during the backup process.

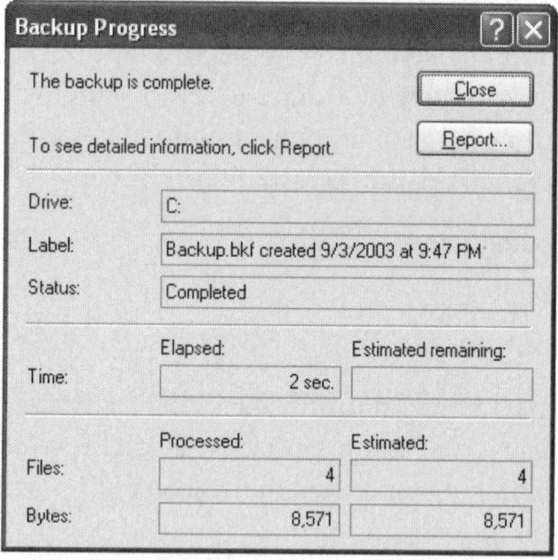

Figure 32-3. The backup process generates a summary report.

Restoring Your Data

Anyone who works with computers long enough will eventually experience a critical error. A drive will become corrupted, a virus will get through your virus software's protection, or you'll accidentally delete something you need. This is the point when all the time and trouble you've invested in backing up your data will pay dividends.

Depending on how you created your backup file, you will have one of two options: you can simply recopy your backup PST file from the backup location where you copied it, or you can run the Backup utility and use the Restore tab to bring back the missing file or files. From there, you can select the backup file that contains the PST and then determine which files to restore and where to put them.

Note By default, the Backup utility restores a file to its original location. This is generally the best choice, because if the PST file isn't restored to the proper location, Outlook won't be able to find it.

Whichever method you use, be certain to carefully check the drive for errors and viruses before you restore your data. You don't want to restore the file only to see it destroyed again a few hours later.

Tip **Familiarize yourself with the restore process**
It's important to be familiar with the restore process before a disaster-recovery process is underway. You should occasionally try restoring your backed-up PST file to another computer to verify that your backups work. This will help to ensure that the restore process will work and that you know how to perform the necessary tasks.

Troubleshooting

You're having problems with a restore operation

Problems with a restore operation can come from several sources. One of the first things to check is whether you are in fact logged on as the correct account, especially if you're supporting another user. When you're connecting to the Exchange Server or bringing back information from an offline folder (OST) file, you'll need to provide the user's credentials or, preferably, be logged on as the user. When you restore a PST file, you'll also need access to the directory to which the file needs to be restored (such as the user's home directory).

Corrupted backups can present additional problems during a restore operation. What if the saved copies of your information are bad? In this situation, the best option is to try to find a saved copy of the PST that is not corrupt. Most companies keep archived backup tapes for weeks or even months. You might lose some recent information if you have to do this, but losing a week of data is better than losing it all.

Another option for dealing with a corrupted backup is to run the Inbox Repair Tool (Scanpst.exe). This tool, which is included with Microsoft Office and is stored by default in C:\Program Files\Common Files\System\Mapi\1033, can be used to remove corruption from PST files. The problem with the Inbox Repair Tool, however, is that it works by simply deleting any portions of the PST file that are corrupt. Therefore, when you reopen the PST file, information will be missing.

If you have the choice of restoring from an older backup or using Scanpst.exe, it's probably preferable to choose the older backup. Both methods leave you with missing information, but at least with the older backup you know the period of time that's missing. Using Scanpst.exe puts you in the unpleasant situation of knowing that data is missing but not knowing exactly what has disappeared.

Note You can use the Scanost.exe application, located in the same folder as Scanpst.exe, to scan offline store (OST) files.

Scheduling Automatic Backups

The Microsoft Backup utility has built-in support for automating backups. If you're planning to automate the backup process, you'll almost certainly want to leverage the advantages of this tool. The Backup utility uses *jobs* to schedule tasks. A job is a set of commands and a schedule for executing those commands.

> **Note** You must have appropriate rights to schedule backups. Groups that have this access are Administrators, Power Users, and Backup Operators.

To create a new backup job, open Backup and start the Backup Wizard. Select the files you want to back up and the backup file in which you want to place them. While in the wizard, you can click Advanced to see additional options, including Type Of Backup and When To Back Up.

With Outlook personal folders, selecting the type of backup—Normal, Copy, Incremental, Differential, or Daily—isn't critical. Although these types vary in terms of which files they back up, depending on when the files were modified, none of them allows you to back up only the changes to a particular file. If the file has changed at all, the entire file is backed up. Because a set of personal folders is held in a single file regardless of its size, you must back up the entire file or nothing. In most cases, if you're scheduling only the backup of the PST file, you can simply use the default type of backup (Normal).

The most important option for scheduling the job is specifying when to back up. You can choose to run the backup immediately or schedule it for later. If you select Later, you can enter a name for the backup job and click Set Schedule to open the Schedule Job Options dialog box, shown in Figure 32-4.

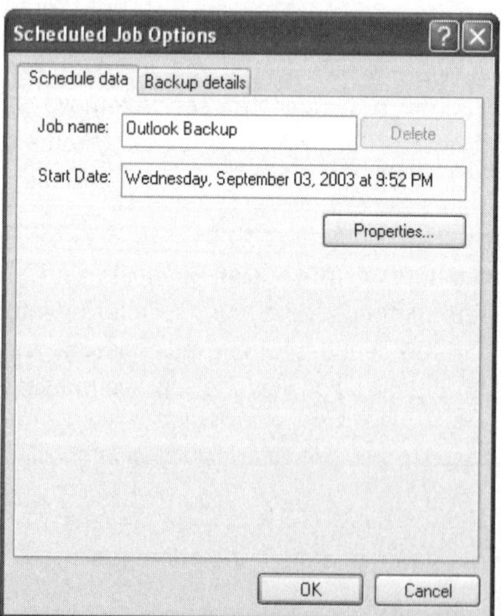

Figure 32-4. You can schedule backups to occur automatically.

You can schedule backups to occur as often as needed. Remember that frequent backups will allow you to recover more completely from a problem. If you back up the PST file weekly, you could lose up to seven days of data if the message store is lost. If you back up the PST nightly, you risk losing only one day.

After you complete the schedule, make sure that sufficient room is available for the backup. Change tapes or free up drive space as needed. Check occasionally to ensure that the scheduled task is running properly and that the backups are good.

Note Microsoft offers an Outlook-specific add-on that automates Outlook backups. Point your Web browser to *http://office.microsoft.com/downloads/2002/pfbackup.aspx* for more information on this Outlook add-in. Although this add-on was designed for Outlook 2002, it does work with Outlook 2003.

Using the Offline Folders Option

If you use an Exchange Server account and want to have a backup of your message store available locally, one possible option is to use offline folders. Offline folders allow you to access your message store when you're away from the office. To use offline folders, you must create an offline folder (OST) file, which is stored on the local drive of your computer. If you configure the Exchange Server account to use Cached Exchange Mode, Outlook creates an OST for you automatically and stores your data in that OST.

In a sense, OST files provide backup in reverse: instead of saving data to a server to back it up, the offline process saves the information from the server to the workstation. Although offline folders don't offer a standard backup, an occasional synchronization to an offline store is an easy way to create a second copy of Outlook data. (With Cached Exchange Mode, Outlook always works from the OST file and synchronizes with the Exchange Server mailbox automatically.) If the Exchange Server mailbox is lost, you need only open Outlook and choose to work offline to access the lost data. At that point, you can export the data to a PST file to create a backup, as explained in the following section.

For more information on setting up and using offline folders, see "Using Offline Folders," page 926.

Backing Up Additional Outlook Data

You should consider including some other items in your regular Outlook backup scheme in addition to your mailbox and personal folders. The following list identifies these additional items:

- **Outcmd.dat** This file stores customized toolbar and menu settings.
- **<*profile*>.xml** This file stores customized Navigation Pane settings (additional shortcuts and shortcut groups).

- ***<profile>*.nk2** This file stores nicknames for AutoComplete (shortcut names for e-mail addresses you have typed in the recipient fields).
- ***<name>*.srs** This file stores send/receive groups. Replace *<name>* with the name of the send/receive group.

> **Note** The .DAT, .XML, .NK2, and .SRS files are all located by default in the Application Data\Microsoft\Outlook folder of the user's profile, such as \Documents and Settings\Jim\Application Data\Microsoft\Outlook. In Outlook 2002, the Outlook Bar customization settings are stored in *<profile>*.fav; in Outlook 2003, the *<profile>*.xml file replaces *<profile>*.fav.

In addition to backing up these files on a regular basis, you should also back up your signature files, if you use signatures in Outlook. Signature files are stored in the \Documents and Settings*<user>*\Application Data\Microsoft\Signatures folder, where *<user>* is your Windows logon name. Outlook creates three files for each signature, one each in TXT, HTM, and RTF format. For example, if you create a signature named Knowledge, Outlook creates the files Knowledge.txt, Knowledge.htm, and Knowledge.rtf. The simplest way to back up all your signatures is to back up the entire folder.

> **Note** If you use Microsoft Word as your e-mail editor, your signatures are stored in Word's Normal.dot template file. Back up this file along with your other Outlook files.

Exporting Data

The previous section discussed ways to create a duplicate copy of your message store for disaster-recovery purposes. You might also want to make copies of part or all of the message store for use in other applications. You can do this by using the export process, in which you save information to a different PST file or transform data for use in Microsoft Access, Microsoft Word, or other programs. (The reverse process, importing data, is covered in the next section.) Table 32-2 shows the file types and formats that are available for export or import with Outlook 2003.

Table 32-2. Supported Export and Import Options

Application	Import	Export
Microsoft Schedule+ 7.*x*	Yes	No
Microsoft Schedule+ Interchange	Yes	No
Microsoft personal folder file	Yes	Yes
Microsoft Exchange Personal Address Book	Yes	Yes
Microsoft Outlook Express 4.*x*, 5.*x*, and 6.*x*	Yes	No
ACT! 3.0, 4.0, or 2000 for Windows	Yes	No

Table 32-2. Supported Export and Import Options

Application	Import	Export
Eudora Pro and Light (2.*x*, 3.*x*, and 4.*x*)	Yes	No
Netscape Mail 2.02, 3.0, or 3.01	Yes	No
Netscape Messenger 4.0	Yes	No
Lotus Organizer 4.*x* and 5.*x*	Yes	No
Comma-separated values (MS-DOS)	Yes	Yes
Comma-separated values (Windows)	Yes	Yes
Tab-separated values (MS-DOS)	Yes	Yes
Tab-separated values (Windows)	Yes	Yes
iCalendar	Yes	No
vCalendar	Yes	No
vCard	Yes	No
Microsoft Access	Yes	Yes
Microsoft Excel	Yes	Yes
Microsoft FoxPro	Yes	Yes
DBASE	Yes	Yes

The export process in Outlook is extremely straightforward. It allows you to use a wizard to send copies of information from the Outlook message store. This section looks at three export options in some depth: exporting messages, exporting addresses, and exporting data to a file.

Exporting Outlook Data to a PST

You can copy messages and other items into a new or existing set of personal folders. Unlike backing up, this option lets you choose which items you want to export and which you want to exclude. You can use this method whether your mail is stored in an Exchange Server mailbox or in a set of personal folders.

You might already know how to use the AutoArchive feature to move messages out of your message store and into a long-term storage location in another PST file. You can use the Import And Export Wizard to export messages to a file. Using the Import And Export Wizard to export messages works in a similar way to AutoArchive; the major difference is that when messages in the store are exported, they aren't removed; instead, they are copied, as they are during backup.

For information about using AutoArchive, see "Archiving Your Data Automatically," page 770.

To export some or all of your Outlook data, follow these steps:

1. Choose File, Import And Export to start the Import And Export Wizard, as shown in Figure 32-5.

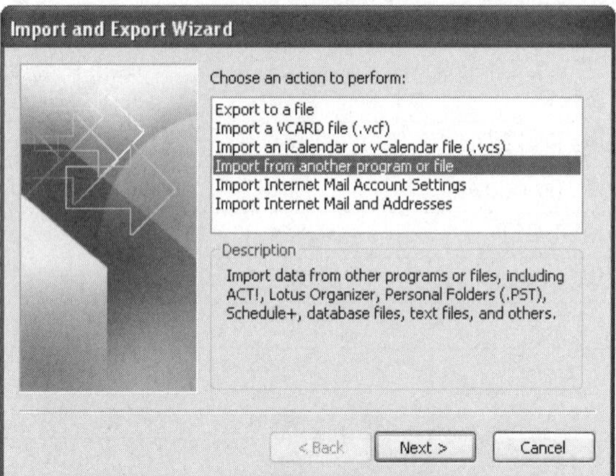

Figure 32-5. Use the Import And Export Wizard to export data to a file.

2. Select Export To A File and click Next.
3. The options available on the next page break down into four basic types: text files, databases, spreadsheets, and a personal folder file. Figure 32-6 shows most of the formats available for exporting. Although you can export your messages in any of these formats, you'll probably find PST files the most useful. For this example, select Personal Folder File (.pst) and click Next.

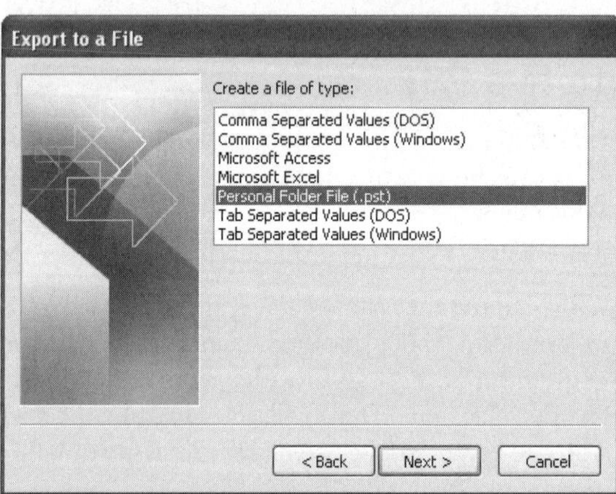

Figure 32-6. You can choose one of these file types for exporting.

4. On the Export Personal Folders page, select the folder you want to export.To include subfolders of the selected folder, select the Include Subfolders option. To export all of your Outlook data, choose the Mailbox or Personal Folders branch and select the Include Subfolders option.

Note It isn't easy to export just a selection of folders. If you want to export only the Inbox and the Sent Items folders, for example, you must run the export twice: once for the Inbox and then again for Sent Items, specifying the same backup PST location each time.

5 If you want to specify a filter, click Filter. Figure 32-7 shows the Filter dialog box. By using a filter, you can specify that only certain items are exported. This option could be useful, for example, if you need to send all correspondence with representatives of Wingtip Toys to a new sales representative who will be dealing with that firm. You could export the relevant messages to a PST file that you could send to the new rep, who could then import them. After you've specified any needed filters, click OK to close the Filter dialog box and return to the wizard page. Then click Next.

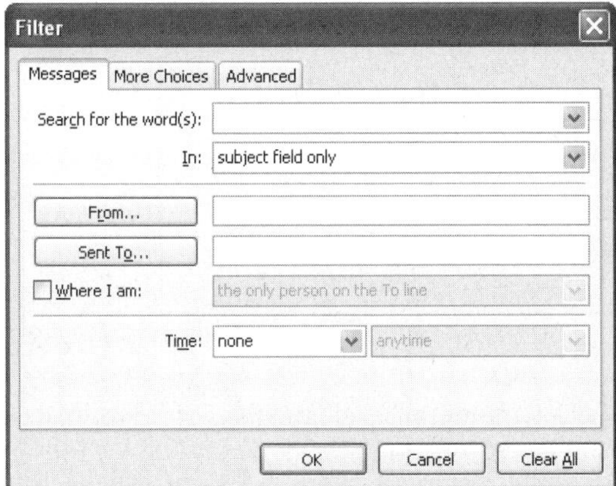

Figure 32-7. Use the Filter Dialog box to export only those messages that fit certain criteria.

6 On the final wizard page, specify the location where you want to save exported information and specify how duplicate items should be handled. If no export file exists, specify the path and name of the file to be created. If an export file does exist, browse to the file you want to use. When you click Finish, the wizard creates the personal folders file (if it is new), runs the export, and then closes the file.

Exporting Addresses

You can also export address lists out of Outlook for use elsewhere. Exporting addresses is similar to exporting messages: you use the same Import And Export Wizard. The difference is that addresses are sometimes exported to a database or a spreadsheet to allow easier access to phone numbers, addresses, and other information.

To export the address list to Access, for example, first start the Import And Export Wizard. Select Export To A File, and then select Microsoft Access. The wizard will prompt you to select the Contacts folder and to provide a name for the Access database that will be created for the exported addresses.

The primary difference between exporting to a personal folder file and exporting to a database lies in mapping out the fields for the database itself. From the wizard, you can click Map Custom Fields to open the Map Custom Fields dialog box, shown in Figure 32-8. Choosing only needed fields reduces the size of the database and allows a quicker export.

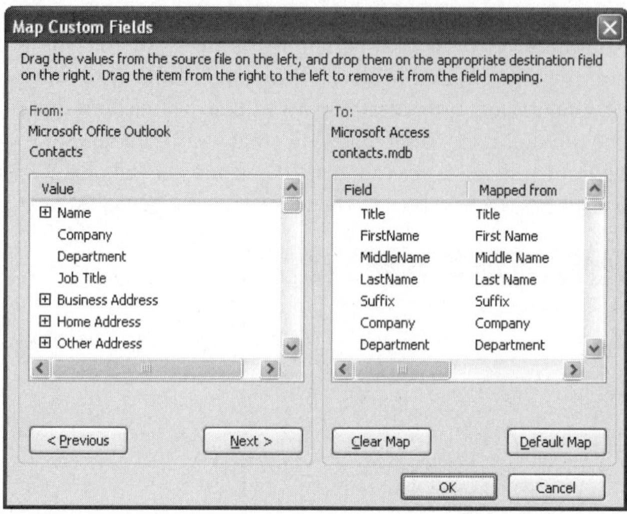

Figure 32-8. Use this dialog box to map fields for export into an Access database.

After you've finished the field mapping, click OK and then click Finish to create the new database file and export the contact information into it.

Note When you're exporting to a database, you don't have a filter option. Therefore, if you're exporting only certain records, you should create a subfolder. You can place all the contacts to be exported in that folder, which is then the target of the export.

Exporting Data to a File

Occasionally, data in PST format simply isn't usable for a particular task. Outlook gives you a number of options for other export formats, such as Excel, Access, or various text file formats. For example, if you need to export information from Outlook into a third-party software package, or if you want to use the information in any capacity for which a direct export path is not available, your best option might be to export the needed information to a basic text file, either tab-delimited or comma-delimited. Figure 32-9 shows how contacts are distilled into text fields during this sort of export.

Contacts.csv - Notepad

File Edit Format View Help


```
"Title","First Name","Middle Name","Last Name","Suffix","Company","Department","Job Title","Bus
nder","Government ID Number","Hobby","Home Address PO Box","Initials","Internet Free Busy","Key
"","No","","Email","","","","","",,,"None","whatsoever","","United States of America",,,,,,,,,
"","Debra","","Core","","","","",,,,,,,,,,,,,,,,,,,,,,,,,,,,,,,,,,,,,,"dcore","0/0/00",,,"0/
"","Jim","","Boyce","","Jim Boyce, Inc.","","President",,,,,,,,,,,,,,,,,,,,,,,,"(218) 555-6549"
"","Terry","","Adams","","","","","987 East Alpine Way",,,"Fernandez","NV","93754",,,,,,,,,,,,
",,,,"Normal","False",,,"Normal"
"","Jay","","Adams","","","","","1020 7th St.",,,"San Diego","CA","94375",,,,,,,,,,,,,,,,,"(31
"","Bill",,"Zumwalde",,"","","",,,,,,,,,,,,,,,,,,,,,,,,,,,,,,,,,,,"","0/0/00",,,"0/0/00",
"","Chris",,"Ashton",,"","","","123 S. Wellington",,,"Norvallis","ND","89832",,,,,,,,,,,,,,,,,
",,,,"Normal","False",,,"Normal"
"","Pilar","","Ackerman","","Lucerne Publishing","","Publisher","43 W. Lake",,,"Watertown","NH"
"","Karin","","Zimprich","","City Power and Light","","Service Manager","2 Bright 2C□Electric A
"","Kelly","","Focht","","Alpine Ski House","","Support Manager","1 Dunn St.",,,"Hoople","IN","
"","Jeremy","","Lostter","","Litware, Inc.","","Developer","774 Main",,,"Los Angeles","NH","883
"","Toby","","Nixon","","Northwind Traders","","President","The Place",,,"Metropolis","MD","214
"","Jeff","D.","Henshaw","","Northwind Traders","","Designer","99 D Street",,,"Eff","ID","34467
"","Jim","","Hance","","Northwind Traders","","VP Marketing","86 Dove St.",,,"Birds","CO","2833
"","Kevin","","Verboort","","Blue Yonder Airlines","","Chief of Pilots","777 Fantasy Lane",,,"T
"","John","","Wood","","Wide World Importers","","President","645 Deep St.",,,"Seventh Level","
"","Clair","","Hector","","Trey Research","","Graphic Artist","22 Weedy Place",,,"Cut the Grass
"","Karan","","Khanna","","Wingtip Toys","","Engineer","992383 Too Long St.",,,"Short Harbor","
"","Greg","","Chapman","","","","Freelance Writer","634 Circle Dr.",,,"Round","AZ","23456","Uni
"","Randy","","Reeves","","Wide World Importers","","Vice President","95 W. Court St.",,,"Altoo
"","Chris","","Cannon","","Proseware, Inc.","","Developer","872 W. Alpine",,,"Lotsatrees","OR",
"","Dan","","Moyer","","Blue Yonder Airlines","","Assistant","823 E. Airway Road",,,"Kitty Hawk
"","Jonas","","Hasselberg","","Humongous Insurance","","Sales Manager","Somewhere West of Here"
"","Richard","","Carey","","Fabrikam, Inc.","","Manager","88 Ninetieth St.",,,"Novalis","NV","3
"","Fukiko","","Ogisu","","Lucerne Publishing","","President","43 W. Lake",,,"Watertown","NH","
"","Heidi","","Steen","","Fabrikam, Inc.","","Vice President","223 Pineapple Ct.",,,"Fruit","SD
"","Spencer","","Low","","Coho Winery","","Marketing","984 W. Apple",,,"Tree","MN","42334","Uni
",,,,"Normal","False",,,"Normal"
"","Linda","","Meisner","","Proseware, Inc.","","Developer","872 W. Alpine",,,"Lotsatrees","OR"
"","Andy","","Carothers","","Proseware, Inc.","","President","872 W. Alpine",,,"Lotsatrees","OR
"","Angela","","Barbariol","","Proseware, Inc.","","Marketing Manager","872 W. Alpine",,,"Lotsa
```


Figure 32-9. This contact information has been exported into a basic text file.

Importing Data

Data transfer is a two-way street, of course, and any discussion of how to take information out of Outlook would be incomplete without a discussion of how to bring information back in as well. As mentioned earlier, far more options are available for bringing information in than for sending information out.

Importing Data to Outlook

The process of importing data into your Outlook message store is the same regardless of whether you're importing information into a personal folder or an Exchange Server mailbox. You begin the process by identifying exactly what type of information you want to import and whether Outlook can properly access and import the data.

The next sections examine some examples of importing information into Outlook. To begin the import process for any of the examples discussed in these sections, use the Import And Export Wizard.

Importing Internet Mail Account Settings

When upgrading an e-mail system to Outlook, you can often save time and avoid configuration problems by importing the Internet mail settings from the previous system. This process does not bring over any messages or addresses; it simply transfers any existing Internet e-mail account information to the current Outlook profile. This option works only if the computer on which Outlook is installed had previously been using a different e-mail client, such as Outlook Express or Eudora.

The wizard itself is very straightforward, taking you through all the steps of verifying and reestablishing the account. Fields are filled with information taken from the detected settings; you can modify them as needed during the import process. After you have imported the information, the new service will often require you to exit, log off, and restart Outlook before it will be active. At that point, you should be able to receive and send Internet e-mail through Outlook.

Importing Internet Mail and Addresses

In addition to importing Internet e-mail configuration settings, as just discussed, the other step involved in migrating e-mail data to Outlook is to bring in any address lists or saved messages that were stored in the previous system. To import an existing message store, follow these steps:

1. Choose File, Import And Export. When the wizard starts, select Import Internet Mail And Addresses and click Next.
2. Specify the program from which you are migrating the data. After you select the application, you must specify what to import: messages, addresses, or both. Then click Next.

> **Note** No filters are available during this process. You can import rules only with Outlook Express.

3. Specify how Outlook should handle duplicates. The default entry, Allow Duplicates To Be Created, can create a bit of cleanup work (deleting the duplicate entries that might be created for certain contacts), but it guards against accidental information loss from overwriting the wrong contact entry.
4. Click Finish. The wizard runs the import and then displays the Import Summary dialog box. If the import has gone well, you'll see an indication that all the messages have been imported. If you see that only a portion of the total messages have been imported, you'll know that a problem occurred and not all the information was transferred.

Importing a vCard File

One of the handiest ways to share contact information is by using vCards. When you receive a vCard from someone, you can import the card into your Contacts folder for later use. Start the Import And Export Wizard, select Import A vCard File (.vcf), and click Next. Browse to the directory where you saved the VCF file, select the file, and click Open. The file will be imported as a new contact entry in your Contacts folder.

For details about using vCards to share contact information, see "Sharing Contacts with vCards," page 420.

Tip If you receive the VCF file as an e-mail attachment, you can double-click the VCF file icon to import the card into your Contacts folder.

Importing an iCalendar or a vCalendar File

Numerous options, including iCalendar and vCalendar files, are available to users who want to share calendar information. Although they're used for much the same purpose, iCalendar and vCalendar work in different ways.

You use iCalendar to send calendar information out across the Web to anyone using an iCalendar-compatible system. Users who receive an iCalendar meeting invitation simply accept or decline the meeting, and the information is automatically entered into their calendars. An import process is generally not necessary.

In contrast, you use vCalendar files much as you use vCards: they allow you to create a meeting and send it out as an attachment to other attendees. Attendees can then double-click the attachment or use the import process to bring this meeting into their schedules. If necessary, users can also import iCalendar meetings the same way.

Note The file name extension used for vCalendar files is VCS; iCalendar files use an ICS extension.

Importing from Another Program File

You've now seen most of the common import options. However, you'll also occasionally encounter situations in which you might need to import other types of information, such as third-party data, text files, and so on. Perhaps the most important of these other possibilities is importing information from another PST file. This could involve bringing back information from an archive, restoring lost messages from a backup, or even completing the process in the example discussed earlier, in which you need to give a new sales rep copies of all messages sent to or received from Wingtip Toys. If three or four other employees had all exported messages to PST files, the easiest option for the new rep would be to import them back into his or her own message store for easy access.

The following steps describe the process of importing from an existing PST file. Keep in mind that other file import options are similar, although the particular data and formatting of each file will dictate certain changes in the import process.

To import from an existing PST file, perform the following steps:

1. Start the Import And Export Wizard. Select Import From Another Program Or File and click Next.
2. In the list of file types, select Personal Folder File (.pst).

3 Browse to the PST file you want to import. (If you want to import multiple PST files, you must import each one separately.) Specify how to handle duplicates on the same page and click Next.

Tip As mentioned earlier, allowing Outlook to create duplicates minimizes the risk of overwriting data, but it does increase the size of the store. If you're importing a number of PST files that might have overlapping data (if many recipients were copied on the same messages, for example), it's often better to avoid importing duplicates.

4 On the wizard page shown in Figure 32-10, select the folders to import—either the entire store or only a particular folder or set of folders.

Figure 32-10. Select the folder on the Import Personal Folders page.

5 The wizard allows you to filter the data you're importing the same way you filter exported data. Click Filter to open the Filter dialog box and add any filters you need.

6 Specify the folder into which the data should be imported.

7 Click Finish to begin the import.

Note Our fictional sales rep could create a subfolder called Wingtip under the Inbox and then select that folder before starting the Import And Export Wizard. Note that by choosing to import only from the PST file's Inbox and selecting Import Items Into The Current Folder, the sales rep could bring all the messages from the PST file into his or her message store without flooding the Inbox with old Wingtip information. Creating subfolders for importing and exporting can be a good way to keep track of where information is coming from and what you are sending out.

Providing Virus Protection

Hardware and software failures are by no means the only source of anguish for the average user or administrator. Viruses and worms have become major problems for system administrators and users alike. When a major virus or worm outbreak hits, companies grind to a halt, systems shut down, systems administrators turn off mail servers, and general chaos ensues.

The effects of a particularly virulent virus or worm can be devastating for a company. It can bring your mail servers to a quick halt because of the load it imposes on them with the sheer amount of traffic it generates. Bandwidth, both local and across wide area network (WAN) links, is affected as multiple copies of infected messages flood the network. Files can become infected, rendering them unusable and subjecting users to reinfection. This means you must recover the files from backups, making an adequate backup strategy even more important than usual.

One often overlooked effect that viruses have on a company is the public relations nightmare they can create. How would your customers react if they received a flood of infected messages from your users that brought their mail servers to a screeching halt and damaged their production files? Forget for a moment the ire of your customers' system administrators. Could your company survive the ill will generated by such a catastrophe?

My guess is that it would not. Therefore, developing and implementing an effective virus protection strategy is as important—perhaps more so—than developing a backup strategy. When you examine your antivirus needs, approach the problem from two angles: protecting against outside infection and preventing an outgoing flood of infected messages. You can approach the former through either client-side or server-side solutions, but the latter typically requires a server-side solution.

Implementing Server-Side Solutions

Whether or not your organization uses Exchange Server, your first line of defense against viruses and worms should reside between your local area network (LAN) and the Internet. Many antivirus solution vendors offer server-side products that monitor traffic coming from the Internet and detect and block viruses in real time. One such product is WebShield from Network Associates (*http://www.nai.com*). WebShield is part of Network Associates' Total Virus Defense product, which also includes client antivirus software and GroupShield Exchange, an antivirus solution for Exchange Server. Another solution that filters viruses before they get to your network is Panda Software's Panda Antivirus for Firewalls, which works in conjunction with any firewall that supports Content Vectoring Protocol (CVP) to allow the firewall and the antivirus product to interact. You should also consider Symantec's Norton AntiVirus for Firewalls, which supports firewalls from several vendors.

Stopping viruses before they get into your LAN is a great goal, but even the best products sometimes miss. If your organization uses Exchange Server, you should also consider installing an Exchange-based antivirus solution. Network Associates offers GroupShield Exchange, and Panda Software offers Panda Antivirus for MS Exchange Server. A third solution is Norton AntiVirus for Microsoft Exchange. Each of these applications works at the application programming interface (API) level with Exchange Server to provide real-time virus detection and removal/quarantine. Other companies also offer antivirus solutions for Exchange Server.

In addition to scrubbing network and Exchange Server traffic for viruses, you also should implement a solution that provides real-time virus detection for your network's file servers. These solutions scan the server for infected files as files are added or modified. For example, a remote user might upload a file containing a virus to your FTP server. If local users open the file, their systems become infected and the virus begins to spread across your LAN. Catching and removing the virus as soon as the file is uploaded to the FTP server is the ideal solution.

Consider all these points as you evaluate server-side antivirus products. Some might be more important to you than others, so prioritize them and then choose an antivirus suite that best suits your needs and priorities.

Implementing Client-Side Solutions

In addition to blocking viruses and worms at the server, you should also provide antivirus protection at each workstation, particularly if your server-side virus detection is limited. Even if you do provide a full suite of detection services at the server, client-side protection is a vital piece of any antivirus strategy. For example, suppose that your server provides Web-based virus filtering, scanning all network traffic coming from the Internet. Because of traffic load, the server misses a virus in a downloaded file. A user opens the file, infects his or her system, and the worm begins replicating across the LAN. If the user has a client-side antivirus solution in place, the worm is blocked before it can do any damage.

Use the following criteria to evaluate client-side antivirus solutions:

- **Are frequent updates available?** In a given day, several new viruses appear. Your antivirus solution is only as good as your virus definition files are current. Choose a solution that offers daily or (at most) weekly virus definition updates.
- **Can updates be scheduled for automatic execution?** The average user doesn't back up documents on a regular basis, much less worry about whether antivirus definition files are up-to-date. For that reason, it's important that the client-side antivirus solution you choose provide automatic, scheduled updates.
- **Does the product scan a variety of file types?** Make sure the product you choose can scan not only executables and other application files but also Microsoft Office documents for macro viruses.

For details on setting options in Outlook that can prevent infection through macro-borne viruses, see "Setting Macro Security," page 716, and "Protecting Against Office Macro Viruses," page 324. You'll find several client-side antivirus products on the market. Some popular ones include Symantec's Norton AntiVirus (*http://www.symantec.com*), Network Associates' VirusScan (*http://www.nai.com*), and Panda's Antivirus for Servers and Desktops. Many other products are available that offer comparable features.

Configuring Blocked Attachments

Attachment blocking is an important feature in Outlook 2003 to help prevent viruses from infecting systems. Outlook can block certain types of attachments, preventing users from opening attached files that could infect their systems—for example, a JavaScript file, which could execute malicious code on a user's system to damage or steal data. Outlook blocks many other types of files as well. Chapter 10, "Securing Your System, Messages, and Identity," provides a complete discussion of Outlook's attachment blocking feature from the user's perspective; see "Protecting Against Viruses in Attachments," page 320. This chapter, in contrast, focuses on how to configure attachment blocking at both the server and the client.

Outlook and Exchange Server provide two levels of attachment blocking. Level 1 attachments (see Table 32-3) cannot be opened by the user. You can view the message itself, but Outlook disables the elements in the interface that would otherwise allow you to open or save the attachment to disk. Chapter 10 offers a couple of ways to work around this restriction. Figure 32-11 shows how Outlook handles a Level 1 blocked attachment.

Table 32-3. Level 1 Attachments

File Extension	Description
ADE	Microsoft Access project extension
ADP	Microsoft Access project
APP	Microsoft FoxPro-generated application
BAS	Microsoft Visual Basic class module
BAT	Batch file
CHM	Compiled HTML Help file
CMD	Microsoft Windows NT/Windows 2000 command script
COM	Microsoft MS-DOS program
CPL	Control Panel extension
CRT	Security certificate
CSH	UNIX shell script
EXE	Program
FXP	Microsoft FoxPro file
HLP	Help file
HTA	HTML program
INF	Setup Information File
INS	Internet Naming Service
ISP	Internet Communication settings
JS	Microsoft JScript file
JSE	Microsoft JScript Encoded Script file
KSH	UNIX shell script

Table 32-3. Level 1 Attachments

File Extension	Description
LNK	Shortcut
MDA	Microsoft Access add-in program
MDB	Microsoft Access program
MDE	Microsoft Access MDE database
MDT	Microsoft Access file
MDW	Microsoft Access file
MDZ	Microsoft Access wizard program
MSC	Microsoft Common Console document
MSI	Microsoft Windows Installer package
MSP	Microsoft Windows Installer patch
MST	Microsoft Visual Test source files
OPS	FoxPro file
PCD	Photo CD image or Microsoft VisualTest compiled script
PIF	Shortcut to MS-DOS program
PRF	Microsoft Outlook profile settings
PRG	FoxPro program source file
REG	Registration entries
SCF	Windows Explorer command file
SCR	Screen saver
SCT	Microsoft Windows Script Component
SHB	Document shortcut
SHS	Shell Scrap Object
URL	Internet shortcut
VB	Microsoft VBScript file
VBE	Microsoft VBScript Encoded script file
VBS	Microsoft VBScript file
WSC	Microsoft Windows Script Component
WSF	Microsoft Windows Script file
WSH	Windows Script Host settings file
XSL	XML file potentially containing script

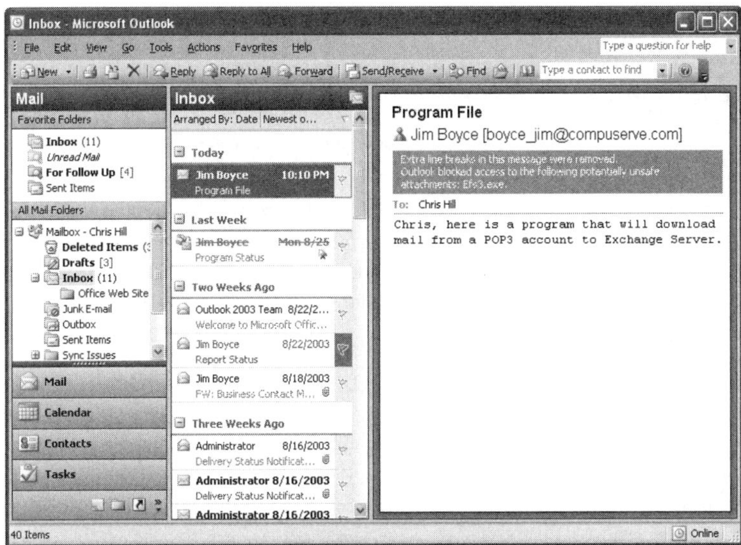

Figure 32-11. Outlook displays a message indicating the attachment is blocked and cannot be opened.

For information about how to work around the restrictions on Level 1 attachments, see "Level 1 Attachments," page 320.

Although you cannot open Level 2 attachments directly in Outlook, you can save them to disk and open them outside Outlook. You can configure Level 2 attachments only at the Exchange Server level, making them applicable only to Exchange Server accounts and not to external POP3, IMAP, or HTTP-based accounts. However, you can make modifications to the client's registry to change the Level 1 list (explained later in this chapter), and these modifications do affect non–Exchange Server accounts. Removing a file type from the Level 1 list lowers that file type to Level 2, which forces the user to save the attachment to disk before opening it.

> **Note** The Level 2 attachment list is empty by default.

Inside Out

Keeping systems safe

Apparently Microsoft's theory for Level 2 attachments is that the user has a client-side antivirus solution in place that will scan the file automatically as soon as the user saves the file to disk. Or perhaps the theory is that you can rely on the user to manually perform a virus check on the file. Neither of these scenarios is a sure bet by any means. Even if the user has antivirus software installed, it might be disabled or have an outdated virus definition file. That's why it's important to provide virus protection at the network and server levels to prevent viruses from reaching the user at all.

It's also important to educate users about the potential damage that can be caused by viruses and worms. Too often these infect systems through user ignorance—users receive an attachment from a known recipient, assume that it's safe (if they even consider that the file could be infected), and open the file. The result is an infected system and potentially an infected network.

Configuring Attachments in Exchange Server

You can configure attachment blocking in two locations: at the Exchange Server or at the user's workstation. Configuring attachment blocking at the server is the most effective and efficient; it gives you, as an administrator, control over attachment security. It also allows you to tailor security by groups within your Windows domains.

Before you can configure attachment security in Exchange Server, you must install the Outlook Security Features Administrative Package (AdminPak), which is included on the Microsoft Office 2003 Resource Kit CD.

Note You must use a computer running Windows 2000 or later to customize the security settings on Exchange Server. This computer need not be the server but can be a workstation.

The first task is to extract the files from the installation file:

1. On a system running Windows 2000 or later, insert the Office 2003 Resource Kit CD and install the Resource Kit. If you prefer not to install the entire Resource Kit, search the CD for the file Admnpack.exe.
2. Create a folder on the local computer to contain the template files. (The steps outlined here assume that you're creating a folder named AdminPak for the files.)
3. Open the folder \Program Files\ OrkTools\Ork11\Tools\Outlook Administrator Pack.
4. Double-click the file Admpack.exe and extract it to the folder created in step 2. The following sections continue the process.

Installing the Trusted Code Control

After you extract the files to the server, the next step is to install the Trusted Code control so that Exchange Server will allow the security template you use to set security options to function without conflicting with the security features embedded in Exchange Server.

Follow these steps to install the Trusted Code control:

1. Log on as Administrator to the Windows 2000 or later computer you're going to use to manage Exchange Server attachment security.
2. Copy the file Hashctl.dll from the AdminPak folder to the *%systemroot%*\System32 folder (typically \Winnt\System32).
3. Choose Start, Run and enter the following command in the Run dialog box:

   regsvr32 hashctl.dll
4. Click OK or press Enter. Then click OK in the resulting informational dialog box.
5. Copy the file Comdlg32.ocx from the AdminPak folder to the *%systemroot%*\System32 folder. Click Yes when prompted to replace the existing file.
6. Choose Start, Run and enter the following command in the Run dialog box:

   regsvr32 comdlg32.ocx
7. Click OK or press Enter. Then click OK in the resulting informational dialog box.

Creating a Public Folder to Contain Custom Security Settings

Before you can customize security settings for Exchange Server, you must create a public folder to contain the custom settings. Set the folder's access control lists (ACLs) so that all users who need custom security settings have read access to the folder. Only users who will have administrative permission to change security settings on a global basis should be given Write, Edit, or Delete permissions for the folder.

Note The following procedure assumes that you're creating the public folder in Exchange 2000 Server. The procedure is similar for Exchange Server 2003. You can also create the folder in Outlook. Just right-click the All Public Folders branch in the folder list and choose New Folder to open the Create New Folder dialog box.

Follow these steps to create and configure the public folder:

1. Open Exchange System Manager and expand the Administrative Group. Then expand the Folders\Public Folders branch.
2. Right-click Public Folders and choose New, Public Folder to open the Properties dialog box shown in Figure 32-12.

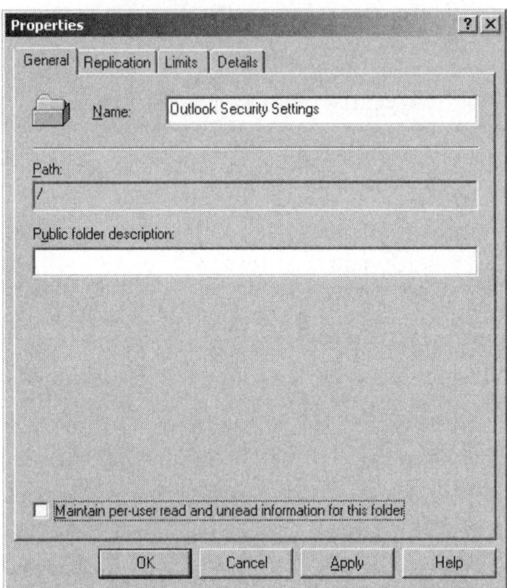

Figure 32-12. Use this Properties dialog box to specify the properties for the new public folder.

3 In the Name box on the General page, type **Outlook Security Settings**. Alternatively, you can type **Outlook 10 Security Settings** for the name, if you prefer, but you must use one of these two.

> **Note** Although you might expect otherwise, Outlook 2003 does not recognize a public folder named Outlook 11 Security Settings for security management, at least in the initial release of the product.

4 If needed, enter a description for the folder in the Public Folder Description box.

5 Click OK to create the folder.

6 Right-click the folder you just created and choose Properties. Click the Permissions tab.

7 Click Client Permissions to open the Client Permissions dialog box, shown in Figure 32-13.

8 Select Default, clear the Create Items check box, and verify that the Read Items and Folder Visible check boxes are selected.

9 Select Anonymous and select None in the Roles drop-down list.

10 If you want to grant other users or groups the ability to modify security settings, click Add and select a user or group. Click OK and then configure that user's or group's permissions as Owner by selecting Owner in the Roles drop-down list.

11 Click OK to close the Client Permissions dialog box, and then click OK to close the Properties dialog box for the folder.

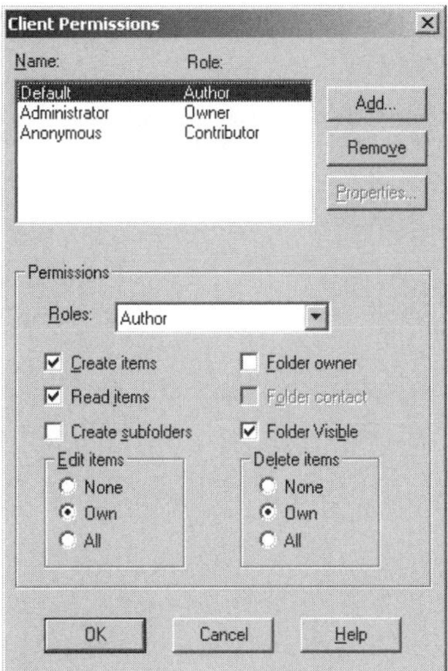

Figure 32-13. Configure ACLs for the folder in the Client Permissions dialog box.

Outlook stores the settings in the public folder when you create custom security settings (explained in the following section). When a user opens Outlook, the program checks the public folder for custom security settings and looks for settings that apply to that user. If it finds such settings, Outlook uses those settings for the current session.

Creating Custom Security Settings

After you set up the public folder, you can create custom security settings if you've been given the necessary permissions for that folder (see the previous section). You create security settings using the SecuritySettings.oft template supplied with the AdminPak.

Here's how to open the template:

1. Open Outlook and click the arrow beside the New button on the Standard toolbar. Select Choose Form to open the Choose Form dialog box.
2. In the Look In drop-down list, select User Templates In File System.
3. Click Browse and open the AdminPak folder. Click OK.
4. Select OutlookSecurity in the template list and click OK.
5. When Outlook prompts you to select a folder, select the Outlook Security Settings public folder.

6 Outlook then displays the Default Security Settings form, shown in Figure 32-14.

7 Choose Tools, Forms, Publish Form.

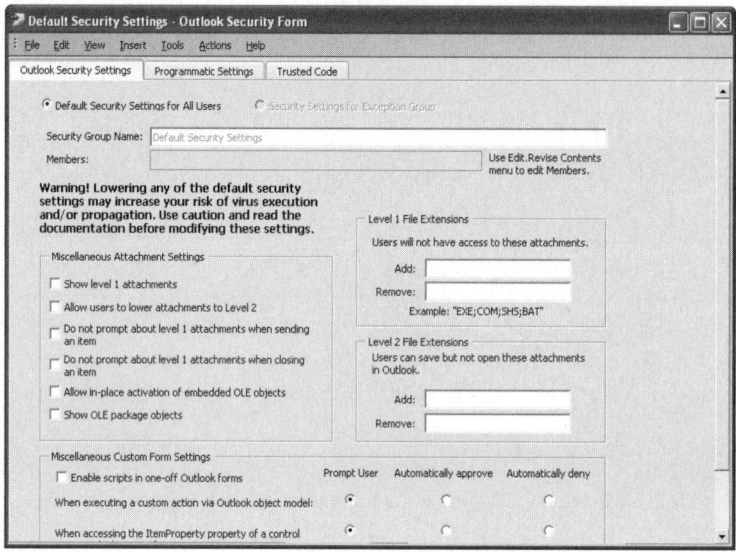

Figure 32-14. Create custom settings on the Default Security Settings form.

8 In the Publish Form As dialog box, select the Outlook Security Settings public folder.

9 Type **Outlook Security Form** in the Display Name and Form Name boxes and click Publish.

10 Scroll to the bottom of the form and click Close to close the Default Security Settings form. When you're prompted to save changes, click No.

Troubleshooting

Close button doesn't work

If the Close toolbar button does not close the form (a bug in the form), click the Close button (X) in the upper right corner of the form. To fix the form, follow these steps:

1 Choose Tools, Form, Design a Form.

2 Choose the Outlook Security Form from the Outlook Security Settings public folder.

3 With the form open in design view, choose Form, View Code to open the Script Editor.

4 Locate the line in the cmdClose_Click procedure that reads Item Close(2) and change it to Item.Close 2.

5 Close the Script Editor and in the form, choose Tools, Forms, Publish Form As. Select the Outlook Security Form in the Outlook Security Settings public folder and click Publish.

6 Close the form and click No when prompted to save changes.

The Close button should now function properly.

Next create a set of security settings to use as the default for all users who do not have their own custom settings. In most cases, you should leave the security settings at their defaults, making only minor modifications as needed, and then create custom forms for specific users or groups.

Follow these steps to create the default settings:

1. In Outlook, click the arrow beside the New button on the Standard toolbar and select Choose Form.
2. In the Choose Form dialog box, open the Outlook Security Settings public folder. Choose the security template and then click Open.
3. On the Outlook Security Settings tab (refer to Figure 32-14), verify that Default Security Settings For All Users is selected, make modifications to settings as needed (explained later), scroll to the bottom of the form, and click Close.
4. Click Yes when prompted to save changes.

Now that you have a set of default security settings, you can begin creating custom settings for individuals and groups. Choose File, New, Choose Form. From the Outlook Security Forms public folder, open the Outlook Security Form. On the Default Security Settings tab, select Security Settings For Exception Group. Then configure settings on the form using the following list as a guide:

- **Security Group Name** Specify a name for this group of settings. For example, you might use the name Unrestricted Level 1 Access for a group of settings that allows full access to Level 1 attachments.
- **Members** Type member names separated by semicolons. In Exchange 2000 Server and Exchange Server 2003, you can enter the name of a distribution list or a security group rather than individual names. If a user is added to more than one security group, the most recently created group takes precedence. Press Ctrl+K to resolve typed names to valid addresses. If any name remains without an underline, check it for spelling errors.

Note You cannot use Exchange Server 5.5 distribution lists to specify security members.

Tip **Add member names more easily**

The security form doesn't include a button that lets you browse the Global Address List and select members for the group. If you need to add several members, open a message form as if you were composing a new e-mail message and click the button beside the To box. Select users from the address list as needed, and close the Select Names dialog box. Highlight all the names in the To box, press Ctrl+C to copy them to the clipboard, and then click in the Members box on the security form and press Ctrl+V to paste the list in the box.

- **Show Level 1 Attachments** Select this check box to allow the group to open Level 1 attachments.

- **Allow Users To Lower Attachments To Level 2** Select this check box to allow the group to demote Level 1 attachments to Level 2, which lets a user save the attachments to disk and then open them.
- **Do Not Prompt About Level 1 Attachments When Sending An Item** This check box disables the warning that normally appears when a user tries to send a Level 1 attachment. The warning explains that the attachment could cause a virus infection and that the recipient might not receive the attachment (because of attachment blocking on the recipient's server).To disable this message for users who are posting Level 1 attachments to a public folder, you must also select the following check box.
- **Do Not Prompt About Level 1 Attachments When Closing An Item** This check box disables the warning that normally appears when the user closes a message, appointment, or other item that contains a Level 1 attachment. See the previous option regarding posting to a public folder.
- **Allow In-Place Activation Of Embedded OLE Objects** Select this check box to allow the group to open embedded OLE objects (such as Excel spreadsheets, Access databases, and other documents) by double-clicking the object's icon.

> **Note** Users can always open embedded OLE objects if Microsoft Word is their e-mail editor, regardless of how this option is set.

- **Show OLE Package Objects** Select this check box to show embedded OLE objects in e-mail messages. Hiding the objects prevents the user from opening them.
- **Level 1 File Extensions** Use this group of controls to modify the Level 1 attachment list. Type the file extensions of the attachments (without the period) and separate multiple file types with semicolons. Use the Add field to add to the list and the Remove field to remove from the list.
- **Level 2 File Extensions** Use this group of controls to modify the Level 2 attachment list. Type the file extensions of the attachments, separated by semicolons. Use the Add box to add to the list and the Remove box to remove from the list.
- **Enable Scripts In One-Off Outlook Forms** Selecting this check box allows scripts to be executed if the script and the form layout are contained in the message.
- **When Executing A Custom Action Via Outlook Object Model** This setting determines the action Outlook takes if a program attempts to execute a task using the Outlook object model. For example, a virus could incorporate a script that uses the Outlook object model to reply to a message and attach itself to that message, bypassing Outlook's security safeguards. Select Prompt User to have Outlook prompt the user to allow or deny the action. Select Automatically Approve to allow the program to execute the task without prompting the user. Select Automatically Deny to prevent the program from executing the task without prompting the user.
- **When Accessing the ItemProperty Property Of A Control On An Outlook Custom Form** This setting determines the action Outlook takes if a user adds a control to a custom Outlook form and binds that control to any address information fields (To or From, for example). Select Prompt User to have Outlook ask the user to allow or deny

access to the address fields when the message is received. Select Automatically Approve to allow access without prompting the user. Select Automatically Deny to deny access without prompting the user.

Troubleshooting

You added an alias to a security form, but the settings are not applied to that user

If you open an existing security form and add a member to the group without changing any other settings, the change might not be applied properly for that user. To ensure that the setting takes effect, make at least one other change to the form. If you don't want any permanent changes applied to the form, simply modify a setting and then set it back to its original state. For example, select a check box and then clear it. Then close the form and click Yes to save changes.

After you configure the settings as needed, close the form and save changes. Exchange Server then prompts you to supply authentication information if you are logged on with an account that does not have the necessary permissions in the folder. Enter account credentials that have Administrative permissions for the public folder. Outlook then saves the item in the folder using the name you specified on the form as the Security Group Name (see Figure 32-15).

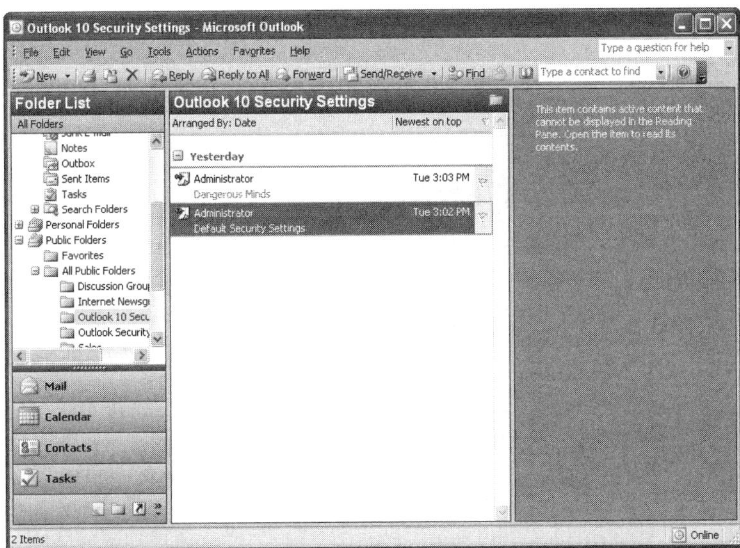

Figure 32-15. Outlook stores security settings as messages in the Outlook Security Settings public folder.

Troubleshooting

A group of security settings doesn't work

When you save a group of security settings, Exchange Server prompts you for authentication credentials with the permissions necessary to create the security settings. If you enter incorrect credentials, such as the wrong user name or password, Exchange Server creates the form, but the security settings will not work. You can't simply edit the form and repair the problem. Instead, you must delete the form and create a new one, this time using the correct authentication credentials.

Note If you receive an error that the access levels and security settings can't be saved when you try to save changes to a security form, close Outlook, change your Exchange Server account settings in your profile so it is not using Cached Exchange Mode. Restart Outlook with the Exchange Server online and make the changes to the security form settings. This problem can also occur if you log on with a local administrator account that matches the administrator credentials in the domain. To avoid the problem, log on with a domain account with administrator privileges.

Modifying Security Settings

You can easily modify security settings after you create a group. Open Outlook with an account that has the permissions necessary to make changes in the folder, and then open the Outlook Security Settings public folder. Double-click the form to open it. Make changes as needed, close the form, and click Yes to save the changes.

Configuring Clients for Custom Security

Simply creating security settings doesn't mean that they will automatically be in effect for users. You must configure Outlook on each user's computer to look to Exchange Server for custom security settings. You do so by modifying settings in the user's registry. Although you can make these changes on a case-by-case basis, doing so isn't usually practical, particularly if you need to change the registries of several hundred (or more) users.

Note If you deploy Outlook using system policies, the Outlk11.adm file administrative template automatically passes customized security settings to users when they log on. Otherwise, you must modify users' registries using the methods described in this section. The Microsoft Office 2003 Resource Kit offers a detailed explanation of how to deploy Office with system policies. You enable custom security settings on a user's computer by adding a value to the user's registry and setting it according to your public folder configuration and security requirements. You can create this value manually, either at the user's computer or by remotely editing the registry. However, it's much more practical to customize the registry through the user's logon script or by placing a registry script on a server and having the user double-click the script to incorporate the registry change.

First you need to create the registry script, as described here:

1. On a system where Outlook 2003 is installed, choose Start, Run and type **regedit** in the Run dialog box to open the Registry Editor.
2. Open the registry key HKEY_CURRENT_USER\Software\Policies\Microsoft\Security. If the key does not exist, create it.
3. Create a new DWORD value in the key and name it CheckAdminSettings.
4. Set the value of CheckAdminSettings to one of the following:

> **Note** If this key is not present on the user's system, Outlook uses the default security settings.

- 0 Use the default security settings.
- 1 Search for applicable security settings in the Outlook Security Settings public folder.
- 2 Search for applicable security settings in the Outlook 10 Security Settings public folder.
- **Any other value** Use the default security settings.

5. Choose Registry, Export Registry File to open the Export Registry File dialog box. Enter a name for the REG file, specify a path, and click Save.

> **Note** If you plan to distribute the registry file via e-mail or across the LAN, place the REG file in a share on a network server that is accessible to the users. Create separate folders under the root of the share, and use NTFS permissions to control access to the folders if you need to distribute different REG files to different users.

6. Notify your users of the availability of the custom security settings. Instruct them to add the registry settings by using the REG file, or apply the change for them automatically by using logon scripts.

If you choose not to incorporate the registry change through the users' logon scripts, you can place the REG file on a network server or send the users a shortcut to the file on the server. They can then follow the shortcut in the message to open the REG file and apply it. The registry settings are applied automatically when a user opens the REG file.

Troubleshooting

Users don't receive the REG file in e-mail

To broadcast the REG file to users through e-mail, you must insert a link to the REG file, not the REG file itself. REG files are included in the default Level 1 attachment list and are therefore blocked by Outlook. So you must save the REG file to a shared folder on a network server, compose a message to the users, and enter the Universal Naming Convention (UNC) path to the REG file in the body of the message. As an alternative, you could place the REG file in a public folder and insert a shortcut to the file in the message.

Configuring Attachment Blocking Directly in Outlook

The previous sections explained how to configure attachment blocking for Exchange Server users. Non–Exchange Server users can also control attachment blocking, although the method for modifying the attachment list is different. So if you use Outlook in a workgroup or on a stand-alone computer without Exchange Server, you can still control which attachments Outlook prevents you from opening. You simply have fewer options for controlling and applying security settings.

Note If you modify the registry settings that affect the Level 1 list, you must restart Outlook for the changes to take effect.

Removing File Types from the Level 1 List

To change the Level 1 attachment list, you must modify a registry setting on your local computer. You can remove file types from the list, as well as add them. To apply the changes across multiple computers, distribute a registry script file. You can distribute this file through a logon script, place it on a network share for users to access, or send users a message containing a shortcut to the file.

Follow these steps to create the necessary registry settings and optionally export them as a REG file for other users:

1. On a system with Outlook 2003 installed, choose Start, Run and type **regedit** in the Run dialog box.
2. In the Registry Editor, open the key HKEY_CURRENT_USER\Software\Microsoft\Office\11.0\Outlook\Security.
3. In that key, add a string value named Level1Remove.
4. Set the value of Level1Remove to include the file extensions of those files you want removed from the Level 1 attachment list, separated by semicolons. The following example removes Microsoft Installer (MSI) files and Help (HLP) files from the list:

   msi;hlp

5 If you want to share the customized registry with other users, choose Registry, Export Registry File. Then select a location for the REG file and click Save. Distribute the REG file to the other users as described previously.

Adding File Types to the Level 1 List

Outlook is aggressive about which attachments it blocks, but you might want to add other attachment types to the Level 1 list so Outlook will block them. To add file types to the Level 1 list, add the registry value HKEY_CURRENT_USER\Software\Microsoft\Office\11.0\Outlook\Security\Level1Add. Set the value of Level1Add to include the file extensions you want added to the Level 1 list. You can add multiple file types separated by semicolons. See the previous section for tips on propagating the change to other users.

Enabling Applications to Send E-Mail with Outlook

Some applications interact with Outlook, most typically accessing the address book to address and send a message. In most cases, these applications will generate a security warning dialog box. The warning is built into Outlook to help you identify when unauthorized applications are attempting to access your Outlook data. For example, a worm that propagates itself by e-mail would likely generate the warning.

See "Signing Your Macros to Avoid Security Warnings," page 717, to learn how to add a digital signature to your macros so they don't generate a security warning.

The section "Configuring Attachments in Exchange Server," page 814, explained how Exchange Server administrators can use the Outlook Security Settings public folder to deploy security settings for Outlook users. That section covered how to configure attachment blocking. You can also use the security form to configure the behavior of specific types of applications in relation to the security features in Outlook 2003, as well as specify DLLs that should be explicitly trusted and allowed to run without generating a security warning.

If you have not already added the Outlook Security Settings public folder or configured a computer to manage security settings, see "Configuring Attachments in Exchange Server," page 814 to learn how.

Configuring Programmatic Settings

To configure the settings that determine how Outlook security features handle various types of applications, follow these steps:

1. Open the Outlook Security Settings public folder and either open an existing policy item or create a new one.
2. If you are creating a new form, enter a policy name in the Security Group Name field.
3. Add members to the Members field and press Crtl+K to resolve the names.

4 Click the Programmatic Settings tab, shown in Figure 32-16.

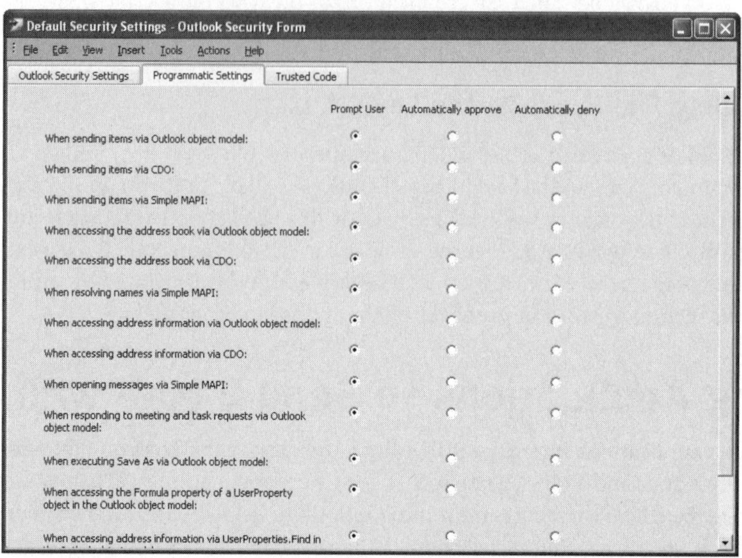

Figure 32-16. Use the Programmatic Settings tab to configure how Outlook handles general applications that try to access Outlook data.

5 Configure settings on the Programmatic Settings tab using the following list as a guide:

- **When Sending Items Via Outlook Object Model** Specifies the action Outlook takes when an application tries to send mail programmatically with the Outlook object model.
- **When Sending Items Via CDO** Specifies the action Outlook takes when an application tries to send mail programmatically with CDO.
- **When Sending Items Via Simple MAPI** Specifies the action Outlook takes when an application tries to send mail programmatically with Simple MAPI.
- **When Accessing The Address Book Via Outlook Object Model** Specifies the action Outlook takes when an application tries to access an address book with the Outlook object model.
- **When Accessing The Address Book Via CDO** Specifies the action Outlook takes when an application tries to access an address book with CDO.
- **When Resolving Names Via Simple MAPI** Specifies the action Outlook takes when an application tries to access an address book with Simple MAPI.
- **When Accessing Address Information Via Outlook Object Model** Specifies the action Outlook takes when an application tries to access a recipient field, such as To or Cc, with the Outlook object model.

- **When Accessing Address Information Via CDO** Specifies the action Outlook takes when an application tries to access a recipient field, such as To or Cc, with CDO.
- **When Opening Messages Via Simple MAPI** Specifies the action Outlook takes when an application tries to access a recipient field, such as To or Cc, with Simple MAPI.
- **When Responding To Meeting And Task Requests Via Outlook Object Model** Specifies the action Outlook takes when an application tries to send mail programmatically by using the Respond method on task and meeting requests.
- **When Executing Save As Via Outlook Object Model** Specifies the action Outlook takes when an application tries to programmatically use the Save As command to save an item.
- **When Accessing The Formula Property Of A UserProperty Object In The Outlook Object Model** Specifies the action Outlook takes if a user has added a Combination or Formula custom field to a custom form and bound it to an Address Information field. Blocking access can prevent an application from indirectly retrieving the value of the Address Information field through its Value property.
- **When Accessing Address Information Via UserProperties.Find In The Outlook Object Model** Specifies the action Outlook takes when an application tries to search mail folders for address information using the Outlook object model.

Part of the battle in getting an application past the Outlook security prompts is understanding what method it is using to access your Outlook data. If you're not sure, you can simply change one setting, test, and if the change doesn't enable the application to bypass the security prompts, change a different one. This trial-and-error method isn't the most direct, but it won't take much time to test each of the possibilities. Remember that you must save the form and restart Outlook for the changes to take effect.

Trusting Applications

In addition to (or an alternative to) configuring security settings to allow various types of applications to bypass the Outlook security prompts, you can also identify specific applications that can bypass the Outlook security prompts. These applications must be specifically written to use the Outlook security trust model.

To add a trusted application, follow these steps:

1. Copy, to a location accessible to the workstation where you will be modifying the Outlook security settings, the DLL or other executable file that loads the application to be trusted.

2 Open the Outlook security form for the target user group and click the Trusted Code tab, shown in Figure 32-17.

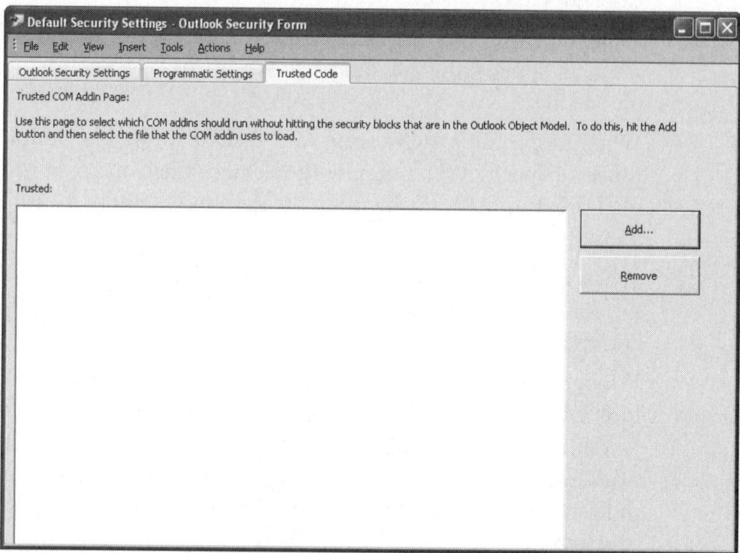

Figure 32-17. Use the Trusted Code tab to add specific trusted applications.

3 Click Add, browse to and select the DLL or executable, and click OK.

4 Repeat the process for any other applications you want to add to the trust list, then close the security form and save changes.

For additional information about creating trusted COM add-ins, see Microsoft Knowledge Base article 327657.

Part 7

Using Outlook with Exchange Server

Chapter 33

Deploying and Managing Outlook in a Network

A number of network configuration and architecture factors come into play when you set up client and server computers running Microsoft Office Outlook 2003 and Microsoft Exchange Server. Although it's true that you can get Outlook and Exchange Server to work in almost any environment, taking the time to understand the vast number of architectural considerations will make setup and deployment a lot easier. This chapter outlines some of these best practices; more information is available in the Exchange-related and Outlook-related white papers on Microsoft's MSDN Web site, *http://msdn.microsoft.com.*

Using Roaming Profiles

Using a roaming profile gives your desktop a consistent look and feel, no matter which workstation you're using. Normally, your user profile contains cookies, Favorites, and History from Microsoft Internet Explorer; the Application Data directory; files stored in personal folders; and the Send To and Start menu contents. In addition, when you use Outlook without Exchange Server, the personal folders (PST) file containing Outlook data is stored in the Application Data directory. If you configure a roaming profile, all this data follows you to each computer you use.

Note Don't confuse the term *roaming profile* with an Outlook profile. The two are not synonymous. The former stores your working environment in Microsoft Windows XP or Microsoft Windows 2000, and the latter stores your Outlook settings.

The process of configuring a roaming profile is similar in Windows XP and Windows 2000. You must store the roaming profile in a network share (such as \\<*server*>\profiles), and it should appear in directories named after the user name.

If you have an existing profile, you can configure a roaming profile by following these steps:

1 In Control Panel, double-click the System icon, and then click the User Profiles tab if you are running Windows 2000. In Windows XP, click the Advanced tab and then click

Settings in the User Profiles group to open the User Profiles dialog box, shown in Figure 33-1.

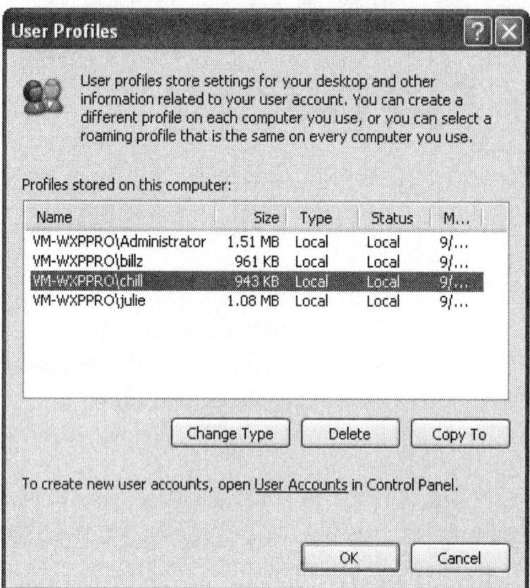

Figure 33-1. You can use the User Profiles dialog box to copy a local user profile to a shared network location, where you can use it as a roaming profile.

2 Select the profile you want to use as a roaming profile, and then click CopyTo.

3 In the Copy Profile To box, enter the directory to which the profile should be copied, such as *server**profiles**username*, and click OK to copy. The profile should now be stored in that directory.

> **Note** The hidden Local Settings folder, which is a part of the user profile and which Outlook uses as the default location for PST files, does not copy when you copy a profile. You should copy this folder manually to the location specified in step 3 to ensure that your existing PSTs are backed up. You will need to configure your Outlook profiles to point to the server for the PSTs. Or, copy the PSTs to a backup location, log on with the new profile, and import the data from the old PSTs to the new ones that Outlook will create.

4 To assign the roaming profile to a user in Microsoft Windows 2000 Server or Microsoft Windows Server 2003, open Active Directory Users And Computers and select the user. Then right-click and choose Properties. Or, for Microsoft Windows NT, open the User Manager For Domains tool, select the user, and choose User, Properties.

5 In Windows 2000 Server, click the Profile tab, and enter the profile location in the Profile Path box. This path should be *<server>**profiles**%username%*, which will automatically use the user name as the directory name (and assumes the profiles are stored in a folder named Profiles). Click OK. Or, for Windows NT, click Profile and enter the path to the profile, such as *<server>**profiles**%username%*, in the User Profile Path box.

If you copied an existing profile to the specified directory (as described here), that profile is used the next time the user logs on; otherwise, a new default profile is created based on the default user profile maintained by Windows. Figure 33-2 shows the Profile tab with a user profile path assigned.

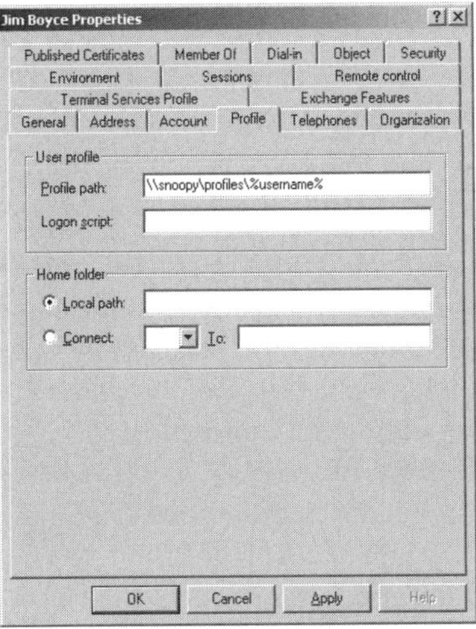

Figure 33-2. Use the Profile tab to assign a path to a roaming profile.

Troubleshooting

Logon is slow after you set up a roaming profile

You should notice very little difference in logon time with a newly created roaming profile, as compared to the time required to log on without a roaming profile. As you work with a profile over time, however, logon time invariably starts to increase. The reason for this is the size of the profile—Windows must copy your profile folders and their data from the server to the workstation each time you log on. As the number of cookies, cached Web pages, and items in your Outlook PST file (if you use one) increases, logon time increases because more and more data must be copied from the server.

You can reduce logon time by preventing certain folders from being copied with the profile. For example, you might not need to include your Temporary Internet Files folder, Cookies folder, or Favorites folder in the roaming profile. To exclude folders, open the Registry Editor and open HKEY_CURRENT_USER/Software/Microsoft/Windows NT/CurrentVersion/Winlogon. Set the value of ExcludeProfileDirs to include the directories you want to exclude from the profile; use a semicolon to separate multiple folders, such as Favorites;Temporary Internet Files;Cookies. Add other folders as needed to prevent them from being copied across the network during logon. Note, however, that certain functions won't be available if you exclude folders. For example, you won't see your favorites when you browse the Internet from a remote computer.

Configuring Folders and Permissions

One primary reason for providing users with a data-storage location on the network is to reduce the amount of data transferred with a roaming profile. Rather than including a user's PST file in a roaming profile and having it copied across the network each time the user logs on, you can place that PST on a network share where the user can access it from any location on the local area network.

In most cases, you can have two types of shared storage: a private directory that only the user can access (a *home directory*) and a public directory that everyone can access. The public directory can contain software for distribution along with other files that users want to share.

How you set up a home directory depends on the server's operating system and the operating system used by each client. You have some additional flexibility in assigning home folders for Outlook 2003 users because they will be running Windows 2000 or later rather than Windows 9*x*, Windows Me, or Windows NT. This additional flexibility comes from the way in which Windows 2000 and Windows XP handle Universal Naming Convention (UNC) paths. Other Windows platforms support UNC paths in the form *<server>**<share>*, where *<server>* is the name of the server and *<share>* is the name of the folder share point. On systems that are running Windows 2000 or later, you can specify a UNC path in the form *<server>**<share>**<folder1>**<folder2>*, where *<folder1>* is a subfolder of *<share>* and *<folder2>* is a subfolder of *<folder1>*. Non–Windows 2000 platforms support paths only in the form *<server>**<share>*.

Because you can specify these longer UNC paths with Windows 2000 and Windows XP, you can share a folder as the parent folder for all user home folders and use that folder as the share name when assigning a home folder, rather than sharing each user's home folder separately. For example, suppose that you create a folder on server srv1 named Users and share that as \\srv1\Users. When you specify the user's home folder in the user account properties, you can specify \\SRV1\Users*<userfolder>*, where *<userfolder>* is the user's home folder under the Users share point. You do not have to share *<userfolder>* separately. This is a major administrative improvement over Windows NT. You don't even have to create the folder yourself—Windows 2000 or Windows 2003 creates it automatically, as you'll learn in the next section.

> **Note** From an administrative perspective, it isn't practical to host user folders on a file allocation table (FAT) volume. You really need to use NTFS to ensure adequate security for each user's folder. This section assumes that you're setting up your user folders on an NTFS volume.

Before you begin creating user folders, determine which operating systems your users are running. If they all use Windows 2000 or later, you can use the procedure explained in the following section. If you need to support Windows NT, Windows 9*x*, or Windows Me clients, however, you'll need to make one change: rather than assigning the path *<server>*\Users*<username>* for the home folder, you must create individual shares, one per user, and specify that share name for the user's home folder. For example, if you need to assign a home directory to the user jboyce, create a folder named Jboyce under the Users folder and share that as jboyce. Then specify \\<*server*>\jboyce as the user's home directory. (For the complete procedure, see "Setting Up a Home Folder in Windows NT Server," page 837.)

Note Keep in mind that Outlook 2003 requires Windows 2000 or later as the client platform. References in this chapter to earlier versions of Windows clients apply to those users who are running earlier versions of Outlook.

Share Permissions vs. NTFS Permissions

Share permissions, which you set on the Sharing tab of the folder's Properties dialog box when you share a folder, control who can access the share from the network. NTFS permissions, which you set on the Security tab, control who can access the folder itself, both locally and from the network. (NTFS permissions also require NTFS as the file system rather than FAT.) Users who have no share permissions for a folder can't see the share in Network Neighborhood. Users who have share permissions but no NTFS permissions can see the shared folder but receive an access-denied error message if they try to open the folder. Share permissions, then, act as the first line of defense against unauthorized access, and NTFS permissions allow you to apply a more granular level of security.

Setting Up a Home Folder in Windows 2000 Server and Windows Server 2003

If all your client computers run Windows 2000 or later, follow these steps in Windows 2000 Server or Windows Server 2003 to assign a home folder to a user:

1. Decide the server and path where the user's folder will reside and create the folder. I recommend creating a folder named \Users.
2. Right-click the folder and choose Sharing to open the Sharing tab of the folder's Properties dialog box. Select Share This Folder and enter **Users** as the share name.
3. Click OK to share the folder.
4. Right-click the Users folder and choose Properties. Then click the Security tab.
5. Clear the Allow Inheritable Permissions From Parent To Propagate To This Object check box. Click Remove when prompted.
6. Click Add. Locate and select Administrators in the Select Users, Computers Or Groups dialog box, and click Add. Then click OK.

7 Read & Execute, List Folder Contents, and Read permissions are now assigned to the Administrators group. Select Full Control in the Allow column and click OK to apply the permission changes (see Figure 33-3).

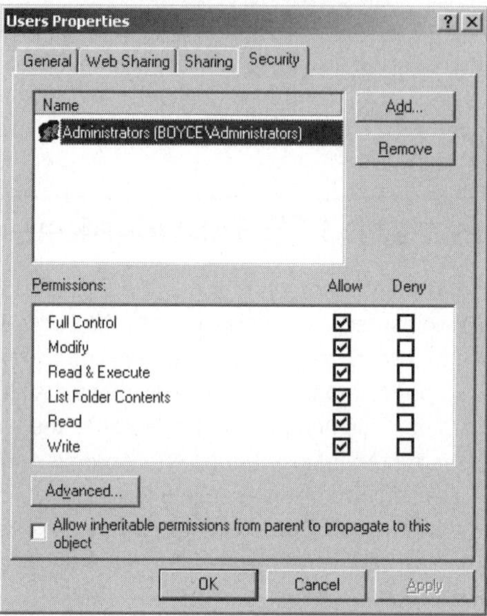

Figure 33-3. Use the Security tab to configure folder permissions.

8 Open the Active Directory Users And Computers console, right-click a user account, and choose Properties. Then click the Profile tab.

9 On the Profile tab (see Figure 33-4), select the Connect option and then select a drive letter in the drop-down list. Windows Server assigns this drive letter to the user's home folder when the user logs on.

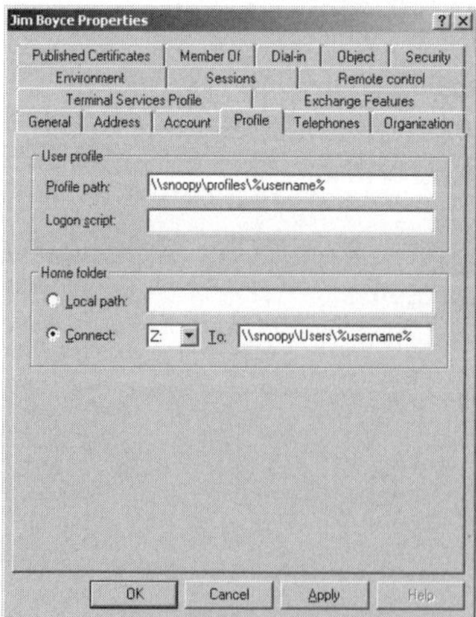

Figure 33-4. Use the Profile tab to specify the user's home directory.

10 In the To box, enter \\<***server***>\Users\<***username***>, where <*server*> is the name of the server where you created and shared the Users folder and <*username*> is the user's logon name.

11 Click OK to close the Properties dialog box. Windows Server creates the user's home folder in the specified location and grants the user full control.

> **Tip** If you can't remember the user's logon name, enter \\<*server*>\Users\%*username*% for the home folder. Windows 2000 Server converts the %*username*% variable to the user's logon name and creates the appropriate folder.

Setting Up a Home Folder in Windows NT Server

Windows NT Server requires a slightly different procedure than Windows 2000 Server or Windows Server 2003 because of the differences in how the two systems apply security. The following procedure assumes that your client computers run Windows NT and must have the home folder specified in the form \\<*server*>\<*username*>, where <*username*> is the name of the user's home folder share point. If you have Windows 2000 or later clients that authenticate in the Windows NT Server domain, you can specify the home folder for these users in the form \\<*server*>\<*sharepoint*>\<*folder*>, where <*folder*> is the user's home directory folder under the <*sharepoint*> shared folder. (See the previous section for details on using these extended UNC paths for Windows 2000 or later clients.)

Follow these steps to assign home folders in Windows NT Server:

1 Decide where user folders will be stored, log on as Administrator, and create the parent folder (such as \Users). You do not need to share this folder.

2 Right-click the folder you just created and choose Properties. Click the Security tab, and click Permissions to open the Directory Permissions dialog box (see Figure 33-5).

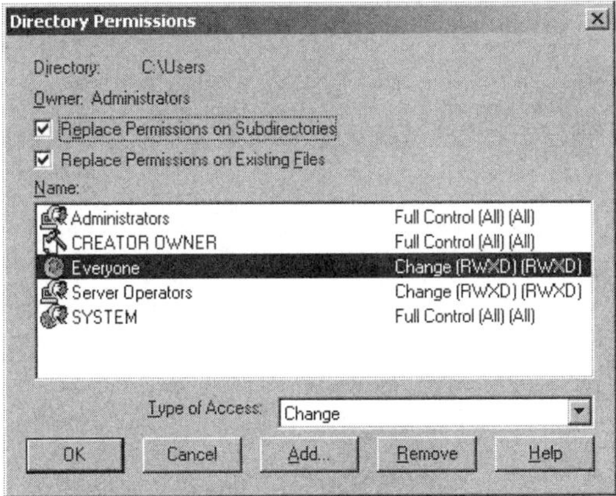

Figure 33-5. Use the Directory Permissions dialog box to configure access.

> **Note** If you specify a home folder in the form \\\\<*server*>\\<*sharepoint*>\\<*folder*> for a Windows NT, Windows 9x, or Windows Me user, that user will receive the folder \\\\<*server*>\\<*sharepoint*> as a home folder rather than the correct one.

3. Verify that the Administrators group has full control, and select the Everyone group. Click Remove and then click OK.
4. Create folders in the \Users folder, one per user, giving each a name that matches the user's logon name.
5. Right-click the folder and choose Properties. Then grant the user's account full control.
6. Share the user's folder using a share name that matches the user's account name. Repeat for the other users' folders.
7. In Windows NT Server, open User Manager For Domains and select the user. Choose User, Properties and then click Profile to open the User Environment Profile dialog box. Alternatively, you can double-click the user and then click Profile.
8. Select Connect (see Figure 33-6), select a drive letter (the default is Z), and enter the path to the home directory. Enter a path in the form \\\\<*server*>\\<*share*>, where <*server*> is the computer sharing the folder and <*share*> is the user's home directory share name. You can use %*username*% in place of the actual folder name and let Windows NT Server replace it with the user name, if you prefer.

Figure 33-6. Use the User Environment Profile dialog box to specify the home directory path.

9. Click OK to close the User Environment Profile dialog box and then close the user's Properties dialog box.

Troubleshooting

Home directories don't work for Windows 9x clients

You might have realized by trial and error that you can't assign home directories for Windows 9x and Windows Me clients the same way you assign them for Windows NT or Windows 2000 users. Windows 9x and Windows Me will not recognize drive mapping on the Profile tab of the user's Properties dialog box. Instead, you must perform the mapping by using the user's logon script. The following sample script will map drive Z to the share \\srv1\jboyce:

```
NET USE Z: \\SRV1\JBOYCE
```

When Multiple Users Share One Computer

Windows 2000 and Windows XP are both full multiuser operating systems, so local profiles are handled automatically. Users receive a profile directory the first time they log on to a system, and their settings are stored in that directory. Any number of users can log in and have profiles, and they will each see their own desktop when they are on that system.

Data security is an important factor to consider when multiple users use a computer. When using a workstation (Windows 2000 or Windows XP) with a hard disk formatted with NTFS, you can set permissions for files so that other users who log in to that computer cannot access those files. By default, only the user and the Administrators group can access the user's profile directory on the local computer (where most documents and settings are saved). You might, however, want to add a folder to store other data on the hard disk and set security for that folder. To configure security for a folder, right-click it, choose Properties, and then click the Security tab, which displays who has access to the folder. By default, the folder will inherit the permissions of the folder in which it was created. In most cases, this is full access for everyone. You can add and remove users from the list and set their access level. In Windows 2000 Server and Windows Server 2003, you must clear the Allow Inheritable Permissions From The Parent To Propagate To This Object check box, and then click Remove when prompted to remove any inherited permissions.

Customizing Outlook and Office Setup

Chapters 1 and 2 discuss single Outlook/Office installations, and the appendix on page 1069 briefly discusses deployment methods for installing Outlook for multiple users on a network. This section focuses on tools included with the Office 2003 Resource Kit that simplify Office installation for a large number of users.

Deploying Outlook with the Custom Installation Wizard

The Custom Installation Wizard included with the Office 2003 Resource Kit (see Figure 33-7) enables you to create Windows Installer transform (MST) that provide custom installation options when installing Microsoft Office 2003. You can preconfigure many options for Setup with the Custom Installation Wizard, including the following:

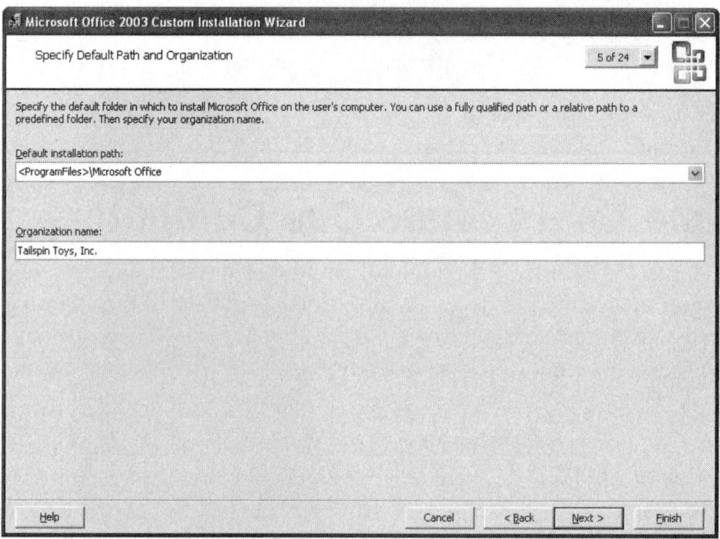

Figure 33-7. Customize Office and Outlook installation with the Custom Installation Wizard.

- Default installation location
- Organization name
- Whether Setup removes earlier versions of specific applications
- Which applications are installed and installation methods such as Run From Network, Installed On First Use, or Not Available
- Enter the Product Key for installation and accept the terms of the license agreement to bypass these steps in Setup
- Import Office settings from an existing OPS file, which you can create with the Profile Wizard, another Office 2003 Resource Kit component
- Whether to migrate users' existing Office settings
- Specify a broad range of application options and settings
- Add or remove files for the installation process, such as copying custom templates, forms, or other files
- Add or remove specific registry entries during Setup

- Specify shortcuts created during installation and where the shortcuts are created
- Specify additional application installation shares on the network
- Configure security settings such as macro security level, trust for add-ins, and ActiveX initialization
- Include other commands or programs to execute during Setup
- Specify Outlook profile settings, including creating a new profile, using an existing profile, or using a common profile you define with the Custom Installation Wizard, complete with preconfigured account settings (see the following section)
- Convert user's existing Personal Address Book to an Outlook Address Book
- Specify default e-mail editor and message format
- Configure send/receive groups and settings
- Set various Setup variables that control the way Setup functions and the messages it displays

See the Setup.htm file in the root of the Office 2003 CD to learn about the function and purpose of each of the Setup variables you can modify with the Custom Installation Wizard.

You can use the MST file that results from using the Custom Installation Wizard in a couple of ways to provide customized Outlook and Office Setup. First, Setup supports several command-line options that you can use when installing Office. You can specify an MST file in the Setup command when the user runs Setup from an administrative installation share on a network file server. See the Setup.htm file included in the root of the Office 2003 CD to learn about the /t switch, which enables you to specify an MST file during installation.

Another way to use an MST to customize Setup is when you deploy applications with group policy. When you publish or assign an application in a group policy object, one of the properties you can specify is an MST file that you have created with the Custom Installation Wizard. For more details on deploying Office with group policy, see the section "Deploying Office and Outlook with Group Policy," page 844.

Creating Outlook and Office Profiles for Users

In the previous section you learned that you can create a custom Outlook profile with the Custom Installation Wizard and have Setup deploy those profile settings during installation (see Figure 33-8).

Microsoft Office 2003 Custom Installation Wizard
Outlook: Customize Default Profile
17 of 24
Customize Outlook profile information.
Use existing profile: If no profile exists, Outlook prompts the user to create one when Outlook is first run.
Modify Profile: Define changes to make to the existing default profile. If a default profile does not exist, Outlook creates a new one using your customizations.
New Profile: Customize a new default profile. Outlook uses this profile as the default profile for all users.
Profile name: Default
Apply PRF: Outlook applies profile changes specified in your customized PRF file.
Apply the following profile (PRF file):
Browse...
Help
Cancel
< Back
Next >
Finish

Figure 33-8. Create Outlook profiles with the Custom Installation Wizard.

If you choose the New Profile option, specify a profile name, and click Next, the Custom Installation Wizard presents additional pages that enable you to configure Exchange Server account settings for the profile (see Figure 33-9) and add other e-mail accounts to the profile (see Figure 33-10).

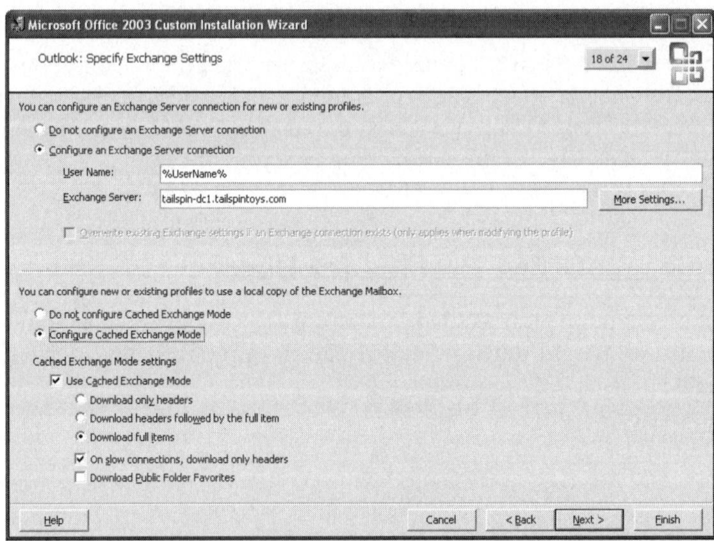

Figure 33-9. Configure Exchange Server account settings with the Custom Installation Wizard.

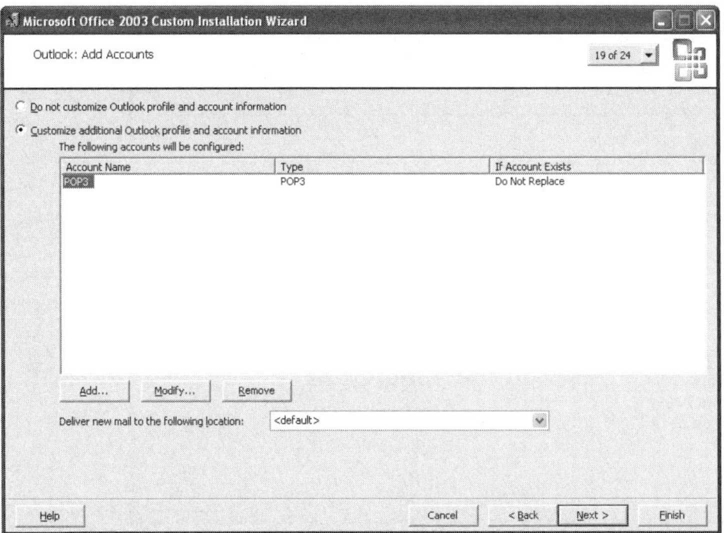

Figure 33-10. Add other e-mail accounts to the default profile with the Custom Installation Wizard.

Each user's account settings will be different, and the Custom Installation Wizard takes that into account. When you configure an Exchange Server account, for example, you don't specify the user's account name in the User Name field. Instead, the Custom Installation Wizard automatically uses %*UserName*%, which causes the user's logon account name to be used during Setup when the profile is created. Likewise, when you create POP3 account settings in the profile, you can use the %*UserName*% variable in the User Name field to specify the user's POP3 logon name. You can use %*UserName*%@*domain* for the E-Mail Address field, replacing *domain* with the user's e-mail domain, such as %*UserName*%@boyce.us.

When you finish specifying profile settings, Outlook saves the profile as a file with the name you specified for the profile and the PRF file extension. You can use this PRF file to customize other MST files you create with the Custom Installation Wizard. Choose the Apply PRF option on the Outlook: Customize Default Profile page of the Custom Installation Wizard and select the existing PRF file.

In addition to creating Outlook profiles with the Custom Installation Wizard, you can also use the Profile Wizard included with the Office 2003 Resource Kit to create a file that stores the settings and options for other Office applications as well as Microsoft Project, Microsoft Visio, and others (see Figure 33-11).

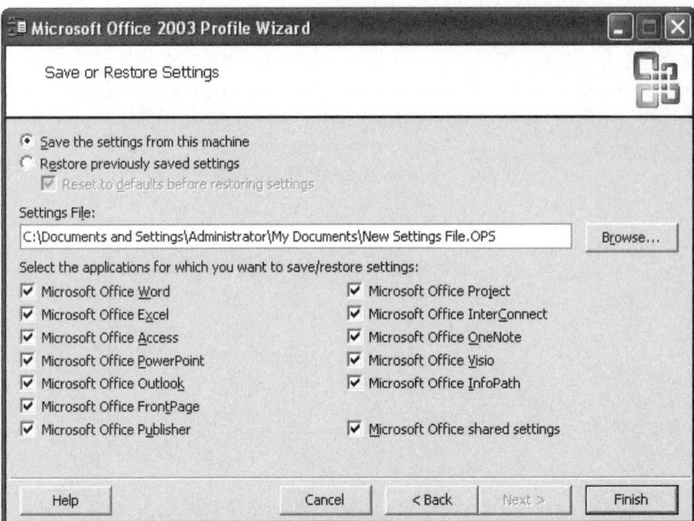

Figure 33-11. Use the Profile Wizard to capture and deploy Office application settings.

The primary purpose for the Profile Wizard is to save existing settings from a computer for use on another computer, or to import settings from another computer. You might be creating the profile to deploy to many other users to give them a consistent work environment, or use the Profile Wizard to back up a user's existing settings to restore them when the user upgrades or moves to a different system.

To capture settings, run the Profile Wizard on the computer where you want to capture the application settings for the installed applications. Select Save The Settings From This Machine, choose the applications for which you want to save settings, specify a path and file for the OPS file, and click Finish. If you are importing the settings from a previously saved OPS file, run the Profile Wizard, choose Restore Previously Saved Settings, select the OPS file, and select the applications for which you want to restore settings.

Note If you want the application settings restored to their default values before you apply the settings from the OPS file, choose Reset To Defaults Before Restoring Settings. Using this option will ensure that all options not configured within the OPS file are set back to their default settings.

Deploying Office and Outlook with Group Policy

When you need to roll out Office or Outlook to many users and want to automate the process, group policy is an excellent option. Group policy is supported by Windows 2000 or later and requires Windows 2000 Server or Windows Server 2003 with Active Directory, as well as client domain membership, to deploy. If your network fits these requirements, you can deploy Office applications through group policy.

You can make applications available to users through group policy either by publishing or by assigning the applications. When you publish an application, the application shows up in the Add New Programs area of the Add Or Remove Programs window, as shown in Figure 33-12. Publishing the application makes it available to the user for easy installation but does not automatically install it when the user logs on or attempts to open an Office document.

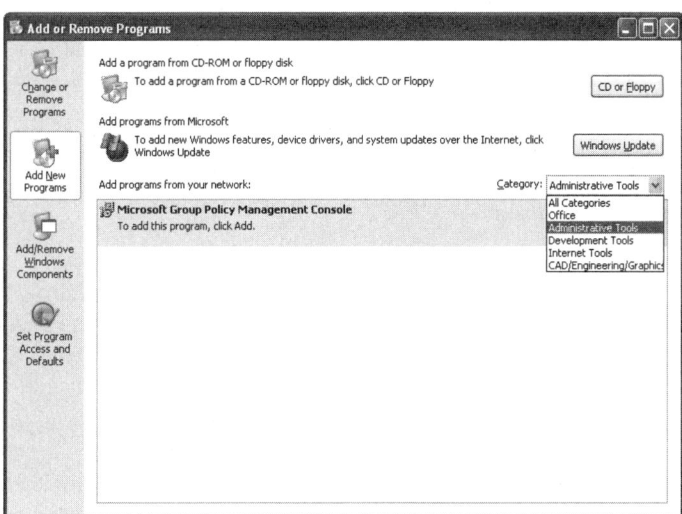

Figure 33-12. Published applications appear in the user's Add Or Remove Programs window.

> **Note** You can create categories to organize applications that you publish through group policy. These categories appear in the Add Or Remove Programs window as shown in Figure 33-12. See the section "Creating the Group Policy Object," page 847, to learn how to create these categories.

When you assign an application, that application appears in the user's Start menu as if it were already installed. When the user tries to start an application from the Start menu or attempts to open an Office document, Setup performs a just-in-time installation of the application automatically, just as it does if you install an application locally with the Installed On First Use option.

In general, you should publish those applications that you want to make available to the users who fall under the scope of the group policy object (GPO) where the application is published, and assign those applications that are required. For example, if Outlook is required but Excel is not, assign Outlook and Word (for use as the e-mail editor) and publish Excel.

Preparing the Package

Deploying an application with group policy requires that the application be installed from a Windows Installer (MSI) file. If the application is not supplied as an MSI file, you must use a *packaging application* to create the Installer package. There are a handful of third-party applications that you can use to create new Installer packages or repackage existing ones, among them WinINSTALL (*www.ondemandsoftware.com*), InstallShield (*www.installshield.com*), Wise for Windows Installer (*www.wise.com*), and Microsoft's own Visual Studio Installer (*http://msdn.microsoft.com/vstudio/downloads/tools/vsi11/default.aspx*). Each of the packaging applications has its strengths and weaknesses, and you'll no doubt have your own preferences. For that reason, I don't cover packaging applications in this chapter. If you don't already have a packager of choice, take the time to download the evaluation copies and test each to find the one that best suits your needs.

If you will be customizing the installation process, you need to create a transform, or MST file. See the section "Deploying Outlook with the Custom Installation Wizard," page 840 to learn how to create an MST with the Custom Installation Wizard. The section "Creating the Group Policy Object," page 847, explains how to add the MST to the policy object.

Setting Up Distribution Shares

After you have the Installer package for the application and any required MST files, you're ready to create the distribution share for the application. The application's files need to be made available on a network share that is accessible to all users who fall under the scope of the group policy. You don't need any special network services in place other than standard file-sharing services, but you should take into account the number of users who will be accessing the installation share at any given time and size the server accordingly. Also take into account available network bandwidth and the number of applications you will be deploying with group policy.

To set up the share, create a main folder on the server, then create individual folders under it to hold each application (for example, one for Office, one for OneNote, and another for Visio). Share the main folder and assign permissions as necessary on the application folders to grant read access to the files. You can use compression on NTFS volumes to reduce disk usage for these folders.

A good option to consider if you need to ensure high availability for the installation files is to host them on Distributed File System (Dfs) roots. Set up multiple application installation shares on different servers, and use the File Replication Service (FRS) included with Windows 2000 Server and Windows Server 2003 to replicate files between servers. Then, create a Dfs root that hosts each of the share replicas. Users will see these replicas as a single folder, but Dfs will redirect users to a different folder if a server goes offline, ensuring that the installation files are always available when needed.

> **Note** Windows Server 2003's Dfs provides smart redirection that directs clients to Dfs replicas based on site metrics. The result is that users access replicas that are relatively close to them in the network.

Creating the Group Policy Object

With the application shares and Installer packages in place, you're ready to start creating the GPOs that will deploy the applications. Your first step should be to analyze your existing domain structure to determine if you need to create additional organizational units (OUs) to accommodate application deployment, or if you need to adjust existing OU membership to do so. For example, one scenario is that you need to deploy applications on a department-by-department basis. If you already have OUs in the domain that mirror your department structure, you're all set. If not, consider creating OUs that organize the domain by department. You can then create GPOs for each OU to deploy the applications users in each department need.

Follow these steps to create the GPO:

1. Open the Active Directory Users And Computers console on the server, locate the container where you will apply the GPO, right-click the container, and choose Properties.
2. Click the Group Policy tab, then create a new GPO or select an existing GPO and click Edit.
3. The Software Settings\Software Installation policy branch, located in both the Computer Configuration and User Configuration branches, is the creation point for application deployment packages. Use the Computer Configuration branch to deploy based on computer membership in the GPO, and use the User Configuration branch to deploy based on user membership in the GPO.

Note You can only assign applications through the Computer Configuration branch, not publish them. If you need to publish the application, create or modify the GPO in the User Configuration branch.

4. Right-click the Software Installation branch and choose Properties. The General tab lets you set the default application package location, the default deployment type (publish or assign), and user interface options. Click the Categories tab, click Add, and add the application categories under which you want to publish applications.
5. Right-click the Software Installation branch and choose New, Package. In the Open dialog box, specify the path to the package file, as shown in Figure 33-13. In almost every case you should use a UNC path to ensure that users will be able to access the share. Use an absolute path only if the user's local drive mapping to the share will always be the same as the server's local drive letter.

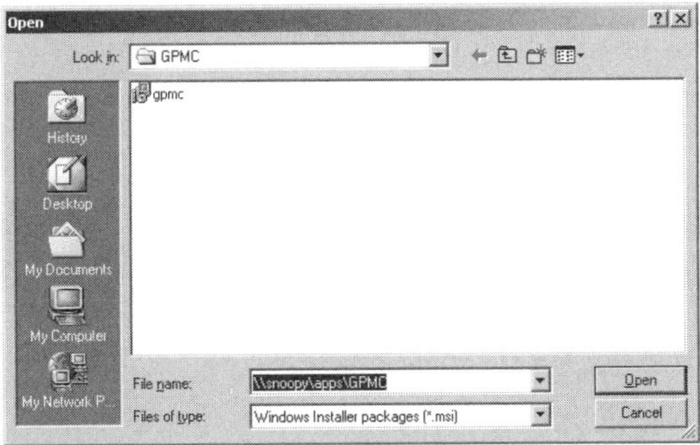

Figure 33-13. Specify a UNC path to the Installer files.

6 You can choose one of three options: Published, Assigned, or Advanced Published Or Assigned. Choose either Published or Assigned if you don't need to add transforms, configure upgrade packages, or set other advanced options when you create the policy. Choose Advanced Published Or Assigned if you do need to configure these options.

> **Note** You can change most of the options for a package after you create the policy, regardless of which option you choose here. To edit the policy, just double-click the package in the GPO to open its property sheet, which is the same one that the wizard displays if you choose the Advanced option.

7 Set properties for the package based on the following information.

The General tab shows general information about the application and publisher. The only property you can change here is the package name as it will appear in the Group Policy console.

Use the Deployment tab, shown in Figure 33-14, to specify the deployment type and other deployment options, including the following:

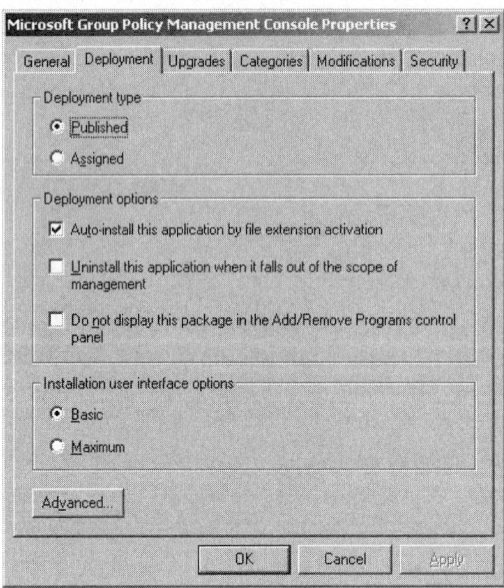

Figure 33-14. Use the Deployment tab to configure the package.

- **Auto-Install This Application By File Extension Activation** Install the application automatically when the user attempts to open a document type that requires the application.
- **Uninstall This Application When It Falls Out Of The Scope Of Management** Remove the application from the user's system when the GPO no longer applies to the user, such as when the user moves to a different department and therefore falls under the scope of a different GPO.

- **Do Not Display This Package In The Add/Remove Programs Control Panel** Prevent the application from appearing in the Add/Remove Programs list.
- **Basic** Display only basic installation information during application installation.
- **Maximum** Display all setup information during application installation.
- **Advanced** Configure the application to ignore language when deploying and to remove previous versions of the application if it was not installed by group policy–based installation.

Use the Upgrades tab to specify other packages in the current or other GPO for which this one is an upgrade. You can make the upgrade optional or mandatory, and specify whether the application should remove the existing version first or simply install over it as an upgrade.

Use the Categories tab to specify the categories in which the application will be listed in the users' Add Or Remove Programs window. Choose an existing category and click Select to add it to the Selected Categories list for the application. You can add multiple categories for an application to list it under more than one category as needed.

You can click the Modifications tab and add transform files to the package when you create the policy. You can specify multiple transforms and control the order in which the transforms are applied.

Finally, use the Security tab to configure permissions for the package policy. For example, you might have a small subset of users who fall under the scope of the GPO for whom you don't want the application installed. Simply remove the Read permission for these users to prevent the policy from applying to them.

With the policies in place, you're ready to perform a test installation. Log on in the domain with an account that falls under the scope of the policy. Check published applications as well as assigned applications to make sure they deploy properly.

> **Note** When you've worked out any kinks, consider two additional features you can implement to enhance application deployment. Remote Installation Services (RIS) enables Windows 2000 or later to be installed automatically across the network. Group policy–based folder redirection enables administrators to redirect a user's folders to a server. When combined with group policy–based application deployment, these additional features make for a relatively painless disaster-recovery mechanism and significantly reduce administrative overhead for deploying new systems and upgrades. You'll find more information about RIS at *http://www.microsoft.com/windowsserver2003/default.mspx*. See the following section for details on redirecting folders with group policy.

Group Policy Considerations for Outlook and Office

In Windows 2000 Server and Windows Server 2003 with Active Directory, group policies allow you to configure settings at the site, domain, OU, or local workstation level. Group policies are similar to system policies created with the System Policy Editor in Windows NT 4.0, although group policies provide much more power and flexibility. You can apply group policies to Windows 2000 or later clients only. Windows 9*x*, Windows Me, and Windows NT do not support group policies (although they do support system policies).

> **Note** This section is not intended as complete coverage of group policies or how to manage them. Rather, it points you to a few policies you might need to apply for Outlook users.

Follow these steps to view and edit group policies:

1. Open the Active Directory Users And Computers console.
2. Right-click the domain or OU for which you want to set policies and select Properties.
3. In the Properties dialog box, click the Group Policy tab.
4. Select the policy to edit (the default policy in this case) and click Edit. This opens the Group Policy console, from which you can change the policies.

> **Note** For more information on setting and creating group policies, take a look at *Microsoft Windows 2000 Resource Kit* (Microsoft Press, 2000) or go to *mspress.microsoft.com* for other books with more in-depth information on this topic.

Although it's beyond the scope of this book to discuss creating and applying new group policies, the following sections explain some of the policy settings you might want to modify for your Outlook users.

> **Note** The following discussion assumes that you want to apply group policies at the domain or OU level. Use the Active Directory Sites And Services console to apply group policy at the site level, or use the Local Security Policy console to apply policies to the local computer.

Setting Default Programs Through Policy

The Programs policy, which is the first policy that applies to Outlook, defines the default programs for e-mail, contacts, and scheduling.

To change default programs, follow these steps:

1. Open User Configuration/Windows Settings/Internet Explorer Maintenance in the Group Policy console. Double-click the Programs policy in the right pane.
2. When you're prompted to import the current settings of Internet Explorer to this system, click Import The Current Program Settings.

3 Click Modify Settings. In the resulting dialog box, you can change the default applications for e-mail, newsgroups, contacts, and calendar. Make any changes you want.

4 Click OK and then click OK again to apply the policy. The settings you just configured will now be the default for all users in the selected domain or OU.

Redirecting Folders Through Policies

Another change you might want to make is to apply group policies to redirect folders. These policies allow you to specify where to store folders that are normally stored in the profile directory, such as My Documents and the desktop. You can configure these folders so that applications have a consistent look and feel for all users or to lock down certain features. You can also redirect the My Documents folder to a network location so that it can be backed up more easily and so that it's always available, no matter where the user is logged in.

To configure folder redirection through group policies, open the Active Directory Users And Computers console, right-click the OU or domain, and choose Properties. Click the Group Policy tab, select the policy you want to edit, and click Edit. You'll find the folder redirection policies under the User Configuration/Windows Settings/Folder Redirection branch (see Figure 33-15). Right-click the folder you want to redirect and choose Properties to open the Properties dialog box for the folder. Figure 33-16 shows the Properties dialog box for the desktop folder.

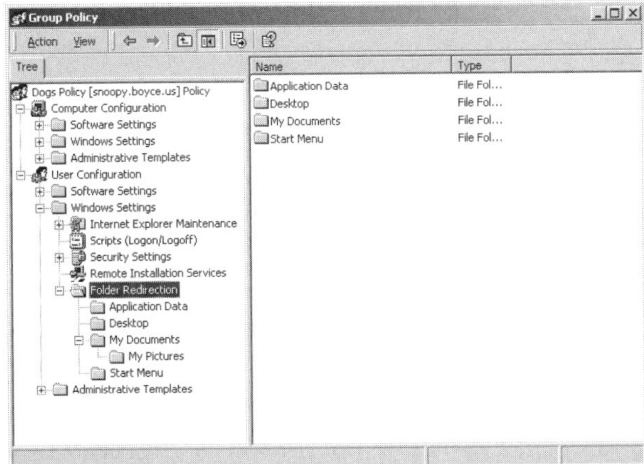

Figure 33-15. Folder redirection policies are located under the User Configuration/Windows Settings/Folder Redirection branch.

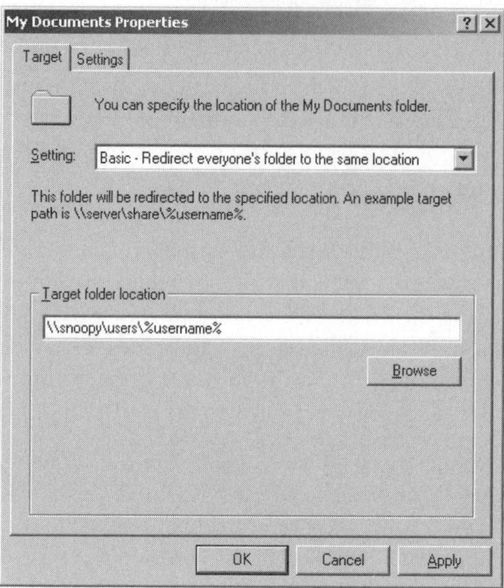

Figure 33-16. Use the folder's Properties dialog box to define its redirection policy.

In the Setting drop-down list on the Target tab, select the type of policy you want to apply:

- **No Administrative Policy Specified** Folders will not be redirected through policy at this level, but they could be redirected by group policy at higher levels (such as at the domain or site level).
- **Basic – Redirect Everyone's Folder To The Same Location** Folders for all users will be redirected to the same location.
- **Advanced – Specify Locations For Various User Groups** Folders will be redirected on a per-group basis.

If you select Basic, you then specify the path in the Target Folder Location box. If you select Advanced, the Security Group Membership list appears on the Target tab, and you can click Add to add groups and specify their folder redirection path.

On the Settings tab (see Figure 33-17), you can specify additional options that determine how the folder is redirected and how users access it. The following list summarizes these options:

- **Grant The User Exclusive Rights To <*folder*>** The user has exclusive rights to the folder and all other users, including administrators, have no rights in the folder.
- **Move The Contents Of <*folder*> To The New Location** Windows 2000 copies the contents of the user's current folder to the redirected folder.
- **Leave The Folder In The New Location When Policy Is Removed** The folder remains redirected even if the policy is later removed.

- **Redirect The Folder Back To The Local Userprofile Location When Policy Is Removed** The folder is moved back to its original location as defined by the user's profile.

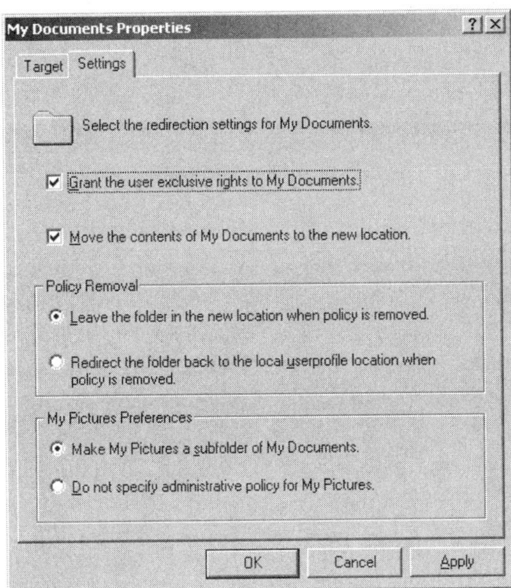

Figure 33-17. Use the Settings tab to set other redirection properties.

Resource Kit Tools for Controlling Office Group Policies

Although there are relatively few policies built into Windows 2000 Server and Windows Server 2003 to control Office and Outlook, you can add many others from the Office 2003 Resource Kit to give you the capability to control a wide range of application features and options through group policy. Controlling applications in this way is one of the best ways to simplify security and other administrative issues for Outlook and Office users.

Follow these steps to configure group policies for Office and Outlook:

1. Open the GPO where you want to configure the policies. See the section "Creating the Group Policy Object," page 847, if you're not sure how to open the GPO.
2. Right-click the Administrative Templates container and choose Add/Remove Templates to open the Add/Remove Templates dialog box.
3. Click Add and browse to the *%systemroot%*\Inf folder of a computer where the Office 2003 Resource Kit is installed.
4. You'll find several ADM files in the folder with 11 in the title, such as Outlk11.adm. Select all of the templates you want to add and click Open, then click Close in the Add/Remove Templates dialog box.

5 When you return to the Group Policy Editor, you'll find several additional policy branches in the Administrative Templates branch (see Figure 33-18).

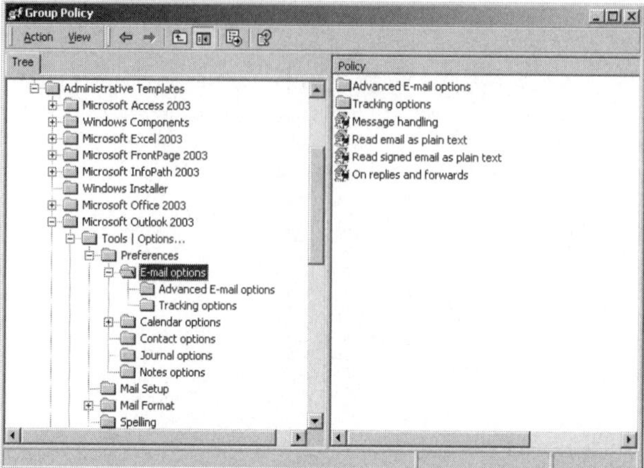

Figure 33-18. You can add many Office and related administrative templates to control group policy.

6 At this point you add policies as you would any other. Open the branch that contains the policy you want to configure, double-click the policy, and set it as needed.

Chapter 34

Configuring the Exchange Server Client

Although you can use Microsoft Office Outlook 2003 with other types of mail servers, you derive the greatest benefit when you use Outlook with Microsoft Exchange Server. Added benefits include the Out Of Office Assistant, the ability to recall messages, the ability to delegate functions to an assistant, the use of server-side message rules, and many other collaboration features.

You can connect to Exchange Server using any of several protocols, including POP3, NNTP, IMAP, and even HTTP. This means two things: you can connect to an Exchange Server using e-mail clients other than Outlook (Microsoft Outlook Express or Eudora, for example), and you can use a service provider other than the Exchange Server client within Outlook to connect to the server. To get all the benefits afforded by the combination of Outlook and Exchange Server, however, you must use the Exchange Server client provided with Outlook.

This chapter explains how to add the Exchange Server client to an Outlook profile and configure its settings.

For detailed information on adding other service providers to an Outlook profile, see Chapter 2, "Advanced Setup Tasks." You'll find additional information on setting up Internet e-mail accounts in Chapter 6, "Using Internet Mail."

Outlook as an Exchange Server Client

The Microsoft Exchange Server service in Outlook allows you to use Outlook as a client for Exchange Server. Of all the services supported by Outlook, Exchange Server offers the broadest range of functionality, providing excellent support for collaboration, information sharing, group scheduling, and more.

The remaining chapters in Part 7, "Using Outlook with Exchange Server," cover a broad range of topics to help you use Outlook effectively as an Exchange Server client.

Setting up an Exchange Server account in Outlook isn't difficult but does require several steps, as follows:

1. In the Outlook 2003 Startup Wizard, move to the Server Type page. To reach the Server Type page if your profile already includes a mail account, right-click the Outlook icon on the Start menu and choose Properties. Then click E-Mail Accounts, click Add A New E-Mail Account, and click Next.
2. Select Microsoft Exchange Server and then click Next.
3. On the Exchange Server Settings page, specify the following information:
   - **Microsoft Exchange Server** Specify the NetBIOS or Domain Name Service (DNS) name of your Exchange Server or its IP address. You don't have to include a double backslash (\\) before the server name.
   - **Use Cached Exchange Mode** Choose this option to have Outlook create a locally cached copy of your entire Exchange Server mailbox on your local computer. Outlook creates an offline folder store file (OST) in which to store the mailbox and works from that cached copy, handling synchronization issues automatically.
   - **User Name** Specify the name of your mailbox on the server. You can specify your logon account name or mailbox name. For example, my logon account is jboyce and my mailbox is Jim Boyce.
   - **Check Name** After you enter your logon or mailbox name, click Check Name to check the specified account information against the information on the server. If you specify your logon name, clicking Check Name automatically changes the user name to your mailbox name. Outlook indicates a successful check by underlining the user name.
4. Click More Settings to open the Microsoft Exchange Server dialog box (see Figure 34-1).
5. Configure the options in the dialog box according to the information in the following sections.

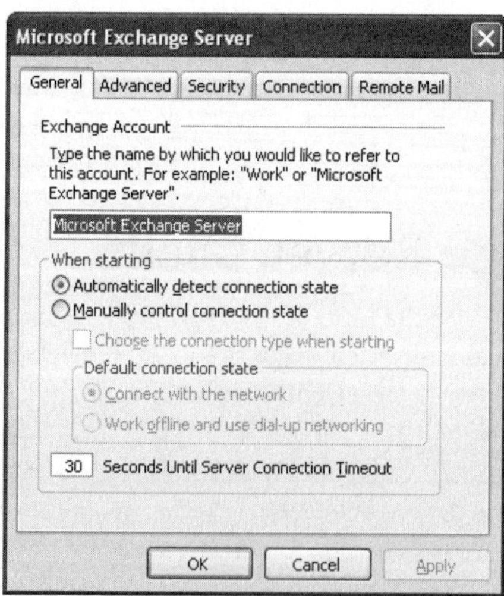

Figure 34-1. Use the Microsoft Exchange Server dialog box to configure additional options.

Configuring General Properties

You use the General tab of the Microsoft Exchange Server dialog box (refer back to Figure 34-1) to configure the account name, the connection state, and other general settings, as follows:

- **Exchange Account** Specify the name under which the account appears in your Outlook configuration. This name has no bearing on the Exchange Server name or your account name. For example, you might name the account Office E-Mail, Work Account, or Microsoft Exchange Server.
- **Automatically Detect Connection State** Direct Outlook to detect the connection state (offline or online) at startup and choose the appropriate state. Use this option if your computer is connected to the network all the time. Use this option also if you're setting up an Exchange Server account on a notebook computer under a profile you use when the notebook is connected to the network.
- **Manually Control Connection State** Control the connection state at startup. Use this option if you're setting up an Exchange Server account on a computer that is sometimes disconnected from the network (a notebook computer, for example) or that always accesses the Exchange Server remotely. See the following three options for more information.
- **Choose The Connection Type When Starting** Choose which method Outlook uses to connect to the Exchange Server at startup. If this check box is selected, Outlook prompts you each time it starts, asking whether you want to connect to the network or work offline. Clear this check box if you want Outlook to make that determination.
- **Connect With The Network** Connect to your Exchange Server through the network rather than initiating a dial-up connection. Use this option if your computer is hard-wired to the network or always online, such as with a Digital Subscriber Line (DSL), cable modem, or other persistent remote connection.
- **Work Offline And Use Dial-Up Networking** Use Dial-Up Networking to connect to the Exchange Server. Specify the connection options on the Connection tab.

For information about setting connection options, see "Configuring Connection Properties," page 861.

- **Seconds Until Server Connection Timeout** Specify the timeout for connection attempts to the Exchange Server. If you are working remotely over a slow connection, increase this value to give Outlook more time to establish the connection to the server.

Increase TCP Timeout for Shared Connections

If you use Internet Connection Sharing (ICS) or demand-dial router connections, you've no doubt had your client computer time out while waiting for the ICS or demand-dial router to establish a connection. This can cause a remote connection to the Exchange Server to fail.

TCP sets a retransmission timer when it attempts the first data transmission for a connection, with an initial retransmission timeout value of 3 seconds. TCP doubles the retransmission timeout value for each subsequent connection attempt, and by default attempts retransmission two times. The first attempt is made at 3 seconds, the second at 3 + 6 seconds, and the third at 3 + 6 + 12 seconds, for a maximum timeout of 21 seconds. Increasing the initial retransmission timer to 5 seconds results in a total maximum timeout of 5 + 10 + 20, or 35 seconds.

For Microsoft Windows 2000 and Microsoft Windows XP clients, the initial TCP retransmission timeout is defined by the registry value HKEY_LOCAL_MACHINE\System\CurrentControlSet\Services\Tcpip\Parameters\InitialRtt. The InitialRtt value is a REG_DWORD with a valid range from 0 to 65535 and specifies the timeout in milliseconds.

The number of connection attempts is defined by the registry setting HKEY_LOCAL_MACHINE\System\CurrentControlSet\Services\Tcpip\Parameters\TcpMaxDataRetransmissions. The TcpMaxDataRetransmissions value is also a REG_DWORD with a valid range of 0 to 65535.

Configuring Advanced Properties

You use the Advanced tab of the Microsoft Exchange Server dialog box (see Figure 34-2) to configure additional mailboxes to open as well as security and offline processing settings. Why use additional mailboxes? You might own two mailboxes on the server and need access to both of them. For example, if you are the system administrator, you probably have your own account and need to manage it as well as the Administrator account. Or perhaps you've been delegated as an assistant for a set of mailboxes and need to access them to manage someone's schedule. The Advanced tab is where you add additional mailboxes that you own or for which you've been granted delegate access.

The options on the Advanced tab follow:

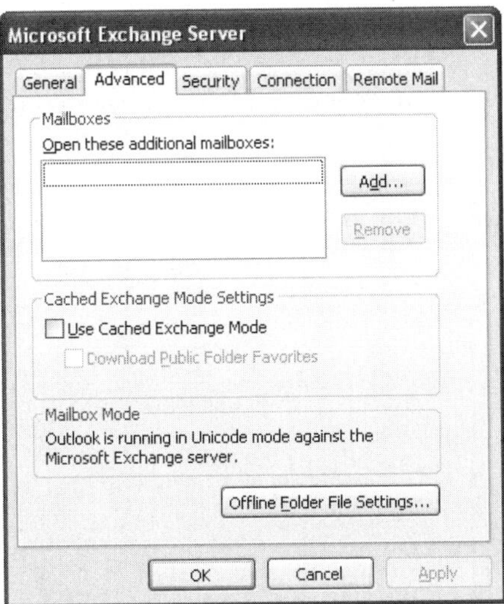

Figure 34-2. Use the Advanced tab to configure additional, Cached Exchange Mode, and offline file settings.

- **Open These Additional Mailboxes** Define the set of mailboxes you want Outlook to open. These can be mailboxes that you own or for which you've been granted delegate access.
- **Use Cached Exchange Mode** Have Outlook create and work from a locally cached copy of your mailbox. This setting corresponds to the Use Cached Exchange Mode setting on the Exchange Server Settings page of the E-Mail Accounts Wizard.
- **Download Public Folder Favorites** Select this check box if you want Outlook to cache the public folders you have added to the Favorites folder in the Public Folders branch. Before selecting this check box, consider how much replication traffic you will experience if the folders in your Favorites contain a large number of posts and are very active folders.
- **Offline Folder File Settings** Set up an OST file to use as your data cache while working offline. You need to use an OST file only if the account is configured to store your data in your Exchange Server mailbox. If your primary data file is a personal folders (PST) file, or if you don't work offline, you don't need an OST file.

> **Note** To learn how to configure personal folder files and offline storage using OST files, see "Controlling Where Outlook Stores Exchange Server Messages and Data," page 865.

Configuring Security Properties

The security settings that were located on the Advanced tab in Outlook 2002 have moved to their own Security tab in Outlook 2003 (see Figure 34-3). These settings control whether Outlook encrypts data between the client computer and the server and how authentication is handled.

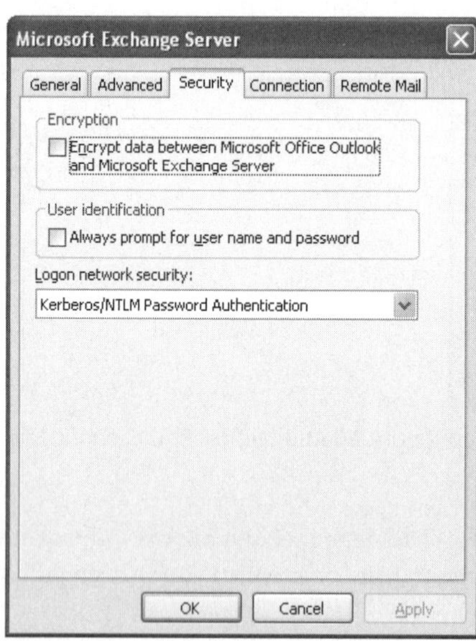

Figure 34-3. Use the Security tab to configure security settings.

- **Encrypt Data Between Microsoft Office Outlook And Microsoft Exchange Server** Determine whether Outlook uses encryption to secure transmission between your system and the server. Select this check box to enable encryption for greater security.
- **Always Prompt For User Name And Password** Select this check box if you want Outlook to prompt you for your logon credentials each time it needs to connect to the server. This is useful if you are concerned that others who have access to your computer might be accessing your mailbox.
- **Logon Network Security** Specify the type of authentication to use when connecting to Exchange Server. The Password Authentication option causes Exchange Server to use NT LAN Manager (NTLM) challenge/response to authenticate on the server using your current logon account credentials. This is the standard authentication mechanism in NT domains. Kerberos Password Authentication is the default authentication mechanism for Windows 2000 and Microsoft Windows 2003 domains. You can choose either of these or choose the Kerberos/NTLM Password Authentication option to have Outlook attempt both.

Configuring Connection Properties

The Connection tab of the Microsoft Exchange Server dialog box (see Figure 34-4) allows you to specify how your computer connects to Exchange Server. You can connect through the local area network (LAN), through Dial-Up Networking, or through a third-party dialer such as the one included with Microsoft Internet Explorer. The LAN connection option applies if you're connecting over a hard-wired connection—for example, when your computer is connected to the same network as the server. You should also use the LAN option if you connect to the server over a shared dial-up connection hosted by another computer.

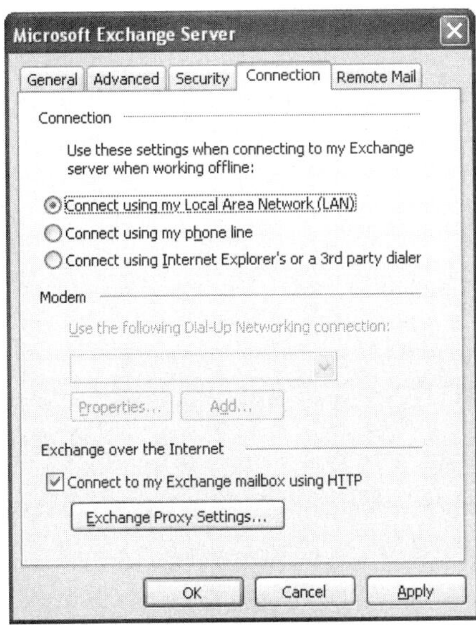

Figure 34-4. Use the Connection tab to specify how Outlook connects to Exchange Server.

Click Connect Using My Phone Line to use an existing Dial-Up Networking connection or to create a new dial-up connection. Select the desired connection from the drop-down list, and then click Properties if you need to modify the dial-up connection. Click Add if you need to add a dial-up connection.

If you want to connect to the Internet or your remote network using the dialer included with Internet Explorer or a dialer included with a third-party dial-up client, click Connect Using Internet Explorer's Or A 3rd Party Dialer.

The Exchange Over The Internet group of controls lets you configure Outlook to connect to Exchange Server using HTTP. The capability to use HTTP to connect to a remote Exchange Server provides an additional connection option for Outlook users and can drastically reduce administrative overhead. Administrators no longer need to provide virtual private network (VPN) access to the network or configure VPN client software for users to access Exchange Server from remote locations. HTTP access also provides native access to the Exchange Server as an alternative to Outlook Web Access for users.

This chapter explains client configuration topics for using remote procedure calls (RPC) over HTTP. See "Configuring RPC Over HTTP," page 1061, for details on configuring Exchange Server to support RPC over HTTP.

The Connect To My Exchange Mailbox Using HTTP check box, if selected, causes Outlook to connect to the Exchange Server using the HTTP protocol. To configure additional settings, click Exchange Proxy Settings to open the Exchange Proxy Settings dialog box shown in Figure 34-5.

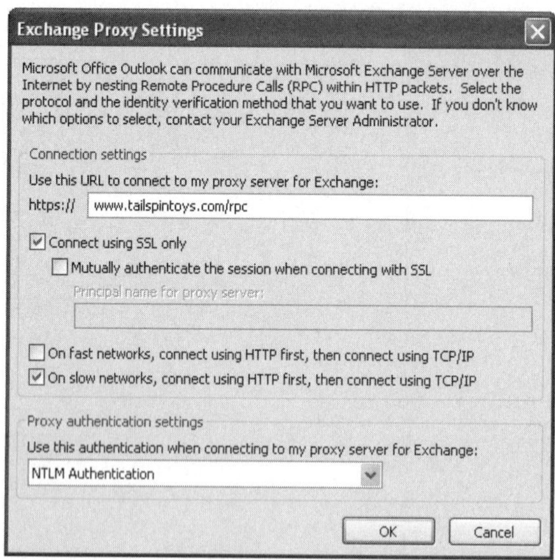

Figure 34-5. Specify settings for the HTTP connection on the Exchange Proxy Settings dialog box.

Configure settings using the following list as a guide:

- **Use This URL To Connect To My Proxy Server For Exchange** Specify the URL that serves as the access point for the server. The default is <*server*>/RPC, where <*server*> is the Web address of the Exchange front-end server. An example is: *httpmail.boyce.us/rpc*. Omit the *http://* or *https://* prefix.
- **Connect Using SSL Only** Select this check box to connect to the server using Secure Sockets Layer (SSL). Note that Outlook changes the URL prefix to *https://* for the URL (see previous option).

- **Mutually Authenticate The Session When Connecting With SSL** Perform two-way authentication with the server when connecting using SSL.
- **Principal Name For Proxy Server** Specify the principal name for the remote proxy server for SSL authentication.
- **On Fast Networks, Connect Using HTTP First, Then Connect Using TCP/IP** When Outlook senses a fast connection to the server, attempt HTTP first and then fall back to TCP/IP if HTTP fails.
- **On Slow Networks, Connect Using HTTP First, Then Connect Using TCP/IP** When Outlook senses a slow connection to the server, attempt HTTP first and then fall back to TCP/IP if HTTP fails.
- **Use This Authentication When Connecting To My Proxy Server For Exchange** Select the authentication method to use to authenticate on the remote Exchange Server. Choose the type of authentication required by the front-end server.

Verifying Connection Status

After you have finished configuring Outlook 2003 to use HTTP to connect to your Exchange Server, you can verify the type of connection it is using. Hold down the Ctrl key, right-click the Outlook icon in the system tray, and choose Connection Status to open the Exchange Server Connection Status dialog box shown in Figure 34-6.

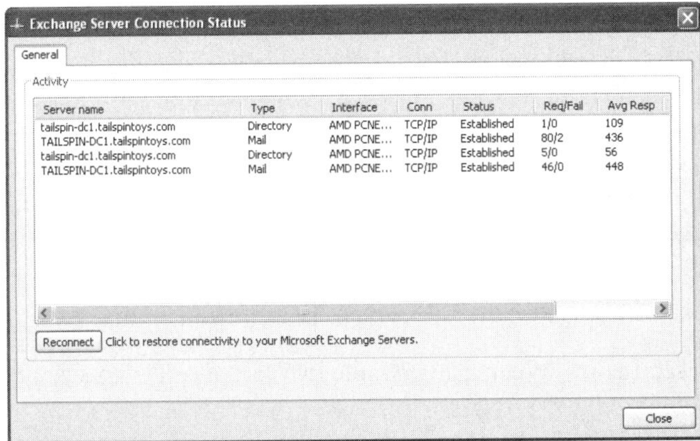

Figure 34-6. Determine the connection type with the Exchange Server Connection Status dialog box.

Configuring Remote Mail Properties

You can use the Remote Mail tab of the Microsoft Exchange Server dialog box (see Figure 34-7) to configure how Outlook processes messages for your Exchange Server account through remote mail.

Figure 34-7. Use the Remote Mail tab to configure how Outlook processes messages through remote mail.

With remote mail you can download message headers without downloading the message body or attachments, which allows you to review messages without downloading them. This is particularly useful if you have a message with a very large attachment waiting for download and you have a slow connection to the server. Being able to preview messages through remote mail and optionally delete messages without downloading them is also useful when you have a corrupted message in your message store that is preventing you from downloading your messages normally.

The following list explains the options on the Remote Mail tab:

- **Process Marked Items** When using remote mail, retrieve all items you have marked for download.
- **Retrieve Items That Meet The Following Conditions** When using remote mail, retrieve only items that meet the conditions defined by the specified filter (see the following item).
- **Filter** Click to open the Filter dialog box in which you specify conditions the message must meet for Outlook to download it from the server.

For detailed information about remote mail with non-Exchange Server accounts, see Chapter 11, "Processing Messages Selectively." See Chapter 37, "Working Offline and Remotely," for details on using remote mail with Exchange Server accounts.

Controlling Where Outlook Stores Exchange Server Messages and Data

When you create an Exchange Server account, Outlook defaults to storing your data in your Exchange Server mailbox. However, you can add a PST file to store your data, including Calendar, Contacts, e-mail folders, and other folders. This capability is different from using an OST file as an offline cache. You should understand the ramifications of changing your storage location before doing so.

For information about the default folder location where Outlook stores files under each operating system, see "How Outlook Stores Data," page 11.

If you maintain your data on the Exchange Server, chances are good that the Exchange Server system administrator backs up your data on a regular basis. Your local system, however, might not be backed up as frequently, if at all, unless you perform the backup yourself or your workstation is included in a regular network backup strategy. Therefore, if you use a PST file to store your data and that file becomes corrupted or lost, you could lose all your e-mail, contacts, and other information unless you have a recent backup.

Note If you add an Exchange Server account to a profile that already contains a POP3 account, Outlook uses the current store location defined by the profile for Exchange Server. This means your data is stored in the local PST file rather than in your Exchange Server mailbox. Therefore, you should check and perhaps change the location after adding the Exchange Server account.

The best solution is to use your Exchange Server mailbox as the primary storage location and use the OST file—either with Cached Exchange Mode or without—for offline storage. This strategy not only allows your data to be backed up easily by the Exchange Server system administrator, but also gives you the ability to work offline. Plus, your offline data store can act as a backup for your online store. Perhaps most important, however, is that other users will be able to access your calendar, contacts, and other information more easily (subject to the permissions you set) than if your store were located on your local computer or in a network share.

Tip **Reconfigure your storage location**

If you use other accounts in the same profile as Exchange Server, you might want to reconfigure the location where messages from your other accounts are stored. Also, you might want to use message rules to automatically move messages between folders and stores. For detailed help on setting up and using rules, see "Using Rules to Move Messages Between Accounts," page 240.

If you decide that you want to change the location where Outlook stores your data—either to point it to a local file or to restore your Exchange Server mailbox as the location—you can do so by changing the properties for your account.

Follow these steps to configure the storage location for your data:

1. If Outlook is open, choose Tools, E-Mail Accounts to open the E-Mail Accounts Wizard. If Outlook is not open, right-click the Outlook icon on the Start menu and choose Properties, and then click E-Mail Accounts.
2. Select View Or Change Existing E-Mail Accounts and click Next.
3. If you don't need to create the other PST file (it already exists), go to step 7. Otherwise, click New Outlook Data File.
4. Click Add, select the type of store file to create, and click OK.
5. Specify the name and location for the file and click OK.
6. In the Create Microsoft Personal Folders dialog box (see Figure 34-8), specify properties based on the following list:

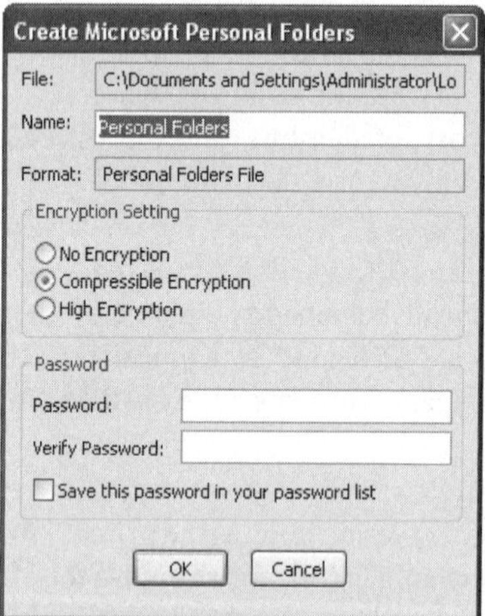

Figure 34-8. Specify settings for the PST file.

- **Name** Specify the name under which you want the folders to appear in Outlook. This is not the file name for the store file, but you can use the same name for both if you want.
- **Encryption Setting** Specify the encryption level for the folder file. Click No Encryption if you don't want Outlook to encrypt your PST file. Click Compressible Encryption if you want Outlook to encrypt the file with a format that allows compression to conserve space. Note, however, that Outlook does not compress the file. Instead, you must use the compression capabilities offered by your operating system (such as NTFS compression) or by a third-party application. Choose High Encryption for highest security. PST files formatted using High Encryption can be compressed but not as efficiently as those that use Compressible Encryption.
- **Password** Specify an optional password to protect your PST file from access by others.

- **Save This Password In Your Password List** Save the password for your PST file in your local password cache, eliminating the need for you to enter the password each time you open the PST file. Clear this check box if you want Outlook to prompt you each time (which provides greater security).

> **Tip** **Take security precautions**
> It's possible for others to gain access to your PST file and bypass the optional password, even if your data file is configured to use compression. For best security, keep your sensitive data on the Exchange Server rather than in a PST file. Or use NTFS permissions to secure the folder where your PST file is located, granting applicable permissions only to users who need access to that folder or your PST file.

7. Click OK to create the file.
8. Click Close to close the Outlook Data Files dialog box.
9. In the Deliver New E-Mail To The Following Location drop-down list, select the location where you want your data stored. Your Exchange Server mailbox appears in the list as Mailbox—<*name*>, where <*name*> is the name of your Exchange Server mailbox.
10. Click Finish to complete the change. Outlook informs you that you've changed the default location for mail delivery as well as the storage location for your other standard Outlook folders.
11. Click OK and restart Outlook for the change to take effect.

Chapter 35

Messaging with Exchange Server

This chapter focuses on some common messaging topics related specifically to Microsoft Exchange Server, such as recalling sent messages, setting messages to expire, and working with the Global Address List (GAL). This chapter also covers voting, which is another feature that relies on Exchange Server. The discussion assumes that you're using Microsoft Office Outlook 2003 for messaging with Exchange Server. Other chapters cover many topics that are more specifically applicable to Outlook's messaging capabilities. For example, see Chapter 7, "Sending and Receiving Messages," to learn about message composition, replies, and using send/receive groups to synchronize your Exchange Server mailbox.

Sending Messages

When you send messages in Outlook while connected to Exchange Server, you have more options than you do when you use a regular Internet mail account—for example, you have the ability to recall messages, and you have access to a GAL.

To send a new message, you have three choices:

- In the Inbox or another message folder, click the New toolbar button.
- Choose File, New, Mail Message.
- Click the arrow beside the New toolbar button and choose Mail Message.

Whichever method you use, a new message form opens, as shown in Figure 35-1.

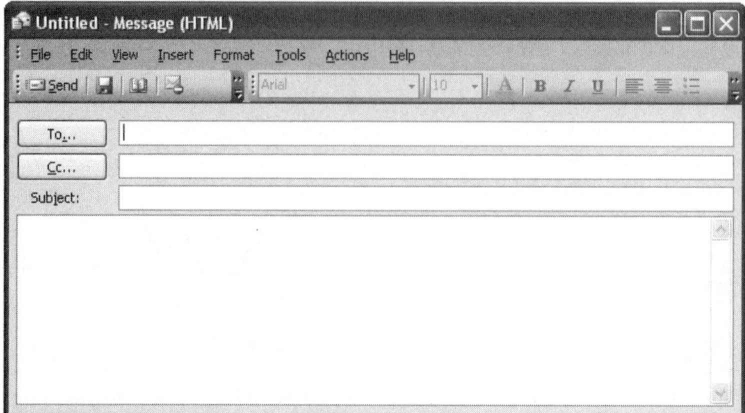

Figure 35-1. Write a message and choose the options for this message using the standard message form.

Addressing Messages

You can designate the recipients of your message in two ways. The first method is to click To or Cc to open the Select Names dialog box (see Figure 35-2). By default, the GAL is displayed.

Figure 35-2. The Select Names dialog box displays the available address books.

The GAL contains all users in the entire organization, except those who are explicitly hidden. An Exchange administrator can define other address lists in Exchange System Manager to filter addresses by any criteria, such as location.

To add a message recipient, select the recipient from the list on the left and then click To, Cc, or Bcc. Clicking Advanced and choosing Properties will display the recipient's properties so that you can verify his or her contact information.

One of the most useful features of the Select Names dialog box is the Find feature. Click Advanced and choose Find to open the Find dialog box, shown in Figure 35-3. You can search the address book by any of the criteria shown, such as Title, Company, or Department. The ability to search the address book is most useful when you have a large organization and no address lists are defined.

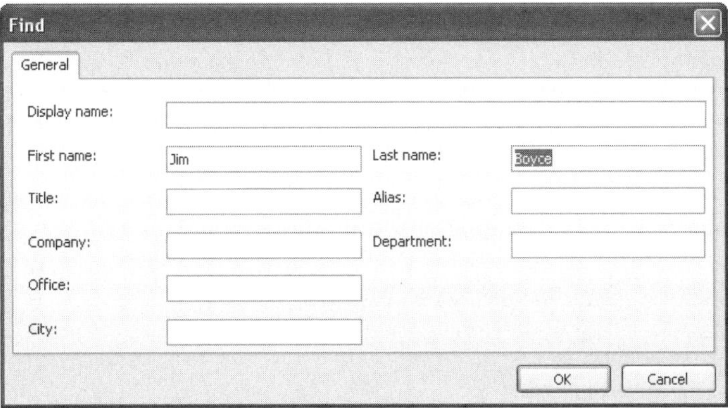

Figure 35-3. You can search the address list for recipients matching specific criteria.

The second way to add recipients to a message is the simplest: type the recipient's name or alias in the To or Cc box on the message form. An Exchange alias is another way of referring to an account. In most cases, an alias is the same as a user's Windows user name.

> **Tip** **Cut your typing time**
> You don't have to type the complete name or alias in the To or Cc box, as long as the part of the name you type is unique. For example, if only one name in the address book matches *Bob*, you can type **Bob** as the recipient, even if the recipient's name is Bob Smith and the alias is *bob.smith*. If the recipient's name is Robert Smith and the alias is *bob.smith*, you can type either **Rob** or **bob**—both will resolve to Robert Smith.

Checking Names

As soon as you finish typing a recipient's name and move the cursor out of the box, Outlook checks the name. If the name is not unique or can't be found, it is underlined in red. When this occurs, you'll need to manually check the name.

You can also check a recipient's name by clicking Check Names on the message toolbar or by pressing Ctrl+K. When a problem arises, a dialog box opens and indicates whether the name is not unique or not found. When the name is not unique, all matches are displayed so that you can make a selection.

> **Tip** If the name you typed is causing a problem, check the spelling of the name. This sounds simple enough, but a small mistake can prevent the name from being resolved. You might need to use the GAL or another address list to find the correct name.

Setting Message Importance and Sensitivity

When you set the level of importance for a message, an icon indicating the level is displayed by default in the mailbox folder of the message recipients (although they can remove the Importance field from the display). By default, messages are sent with normal importance and display no icon. Messages designated with a high importance level have a red exclamation mark, and messages with low importance are displayed with a blue down arrow.

You can set the importance level (or priority level) of a message in two ways. You can click either the red exclamation mark or the blue down arrow on the message toolbar (refer to Figure 35-1 on page 870). If you click either button again, the message returns to normal importance. Or, if Microsoft Word is not your e-mail editor, in the message you can choose View, Options or click Options to open the Message Options dialog box (see Figure 35-4). Then make your selection in the Importance drop-down list.

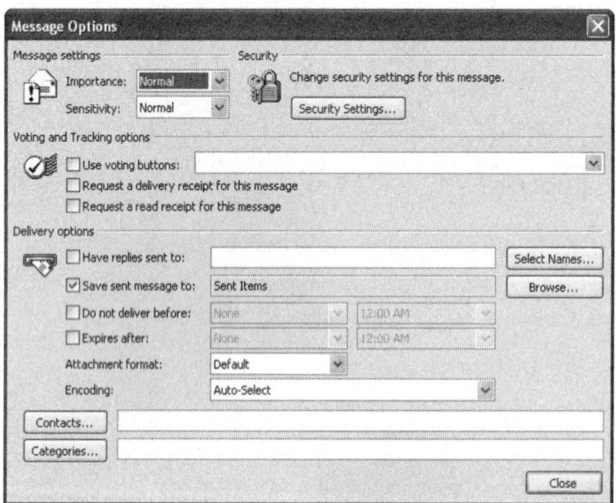

Figure 35-4. Set the importance and sensitivity in the Message Settings area of the Message Options dialog box.

Inside Out

Using importance levels

Changing the importance level of a message does more than simply change the way the message is displayed to the recipient. Many types of mail transports such as X.400 use the message importance level as a metric for determining the routing of messages. Messages with high importance are given a higher priority in the queue and are sent before low-importance messages. (Actually, the process is more complex than that, but the intricacies of mail routing are beyond the scope of this book.) It is poor etiquette to send all your messages with high priority set, however; if you overuse the setting, recipients will start to ignore the importance settings completely.

Message sensitivity, like message importance, appears as a flag on the message that the recipient sees. By default, message sensitivity is not shown in Outlook's message folder views. (You can add it to the view, of course, by choosing View, Arrange By, Current View, Customize Current View and using the Show Fields dialog box.) However, if the message sensitivity is not set to Normal (the default), Outlook does display the sensitivity level when the message is opened or viewed in the Reading Pane. You can set one of four levels of sensitivity—Normal, Personal, Private, or Confidential—in the Sensitivity drop-down list in the Message Options dialog box (see Figure 35-4).

Redirecting Replies

If for some reason you don't want to receive the reply to your message, you can have the reply sent to someone else.

To redirect a reply, follow these steps:

1. With the message form open, choose View, Options or click the Options button on the message toolbar to open the Message Options dialog box.
2. Select the Have Replies SentTo check box, and your name (the sender) is added as a recipient in the text box.
3. Delete your name from the box and either type each recipient's name (separated by semicolons) or click Select Names to select the names from the address book. Select each name in the list, click Reply To, and then click OK to have Outlook add those names to the Have Replies Sent To box. Click Close to save these options.

Each recipient listed in the Have Replies Sent To box receives any replies to the selected message. Figure 35-5 shows the Message Options dialog box with redirected replies.

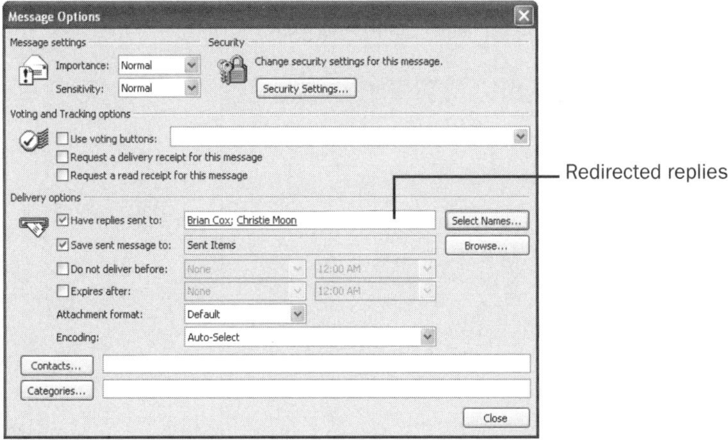

Figure 35-5. Replies to your message will now be sent not to you but to the listed recipients.

Chapter 35

Using Delivery and Read Receipts

Delivery and read receipts are useful tracking features. The delivery receipt is sent to you when the message is delivered. The read receipt is sent when the message's status changes from unread to read. (This status can change automatically in the Reading Pane, when the recipient opens the message, or when the recipient right-clicks the message and chooses Mark As Read.) Delivery and read receipts are not supported on all mail clients. Most mail clients that do support them allow the recipient to choose not to send receipts, so you can't always rely on these receipts to confirm what you need to know. Figure 35-6 shows an example of a delivery receipt.

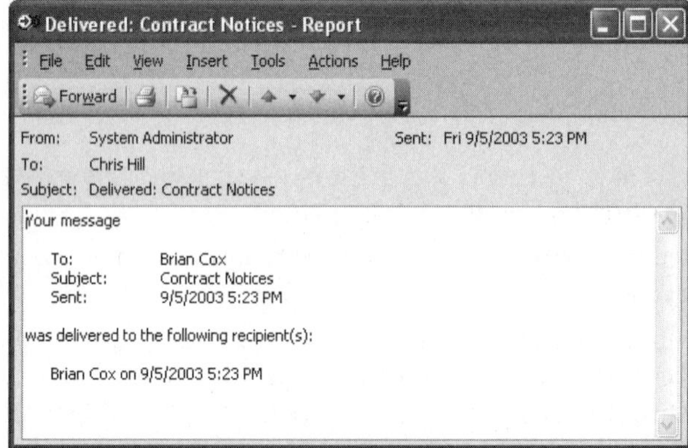

Figure 35-6. Delivery receipts are returned when requested.

To set a delivery receipt, a read receipt, or both for a message, follow these steps:

1 In the message form, choose View, Options or click the Options toolbar button to open the Message Options dialog box (see Figure 35-7).

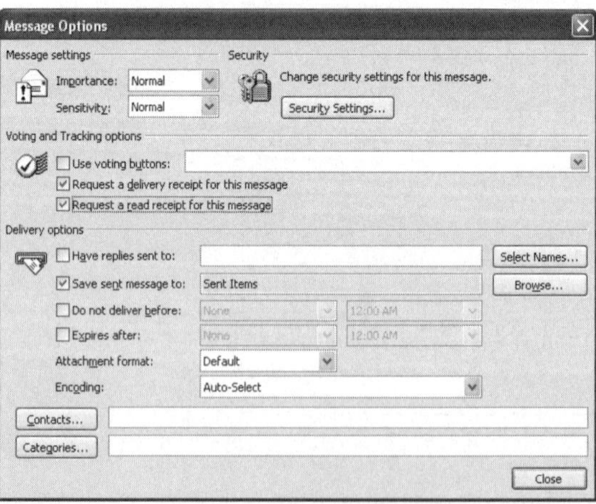

Figure 35-7. You can request receipts in the Message Options dialog box.

2. Select the Request A Delivery Receipt For This Message check box, the Request A Read Receipt For This Message check box, or both.
3. Click Close.

You can set up your mail to request delivery and read receipts by default for each message you send out.

To do so, follow these steps:

1. Choose Tools, Options to open the Options dialog box.
2. On the Preferences tab, click E-Mail Options. Then click Tracking Options to open the Tracking Options dialog box.
3. In the For All Messages I Send, Request option, select Read Receipt, Delivery Receipt, or both.
4. Click OK three times to close the three dialog boxes.

Tip In the Tracking Options dialog box, you can prevent Outlook from sending out read receipts to the senders of messages you receive. You can also direct Outlook to move any receipts to a specified folder.

Saving Messages

By default, Outlook saves messages you send by placing copies of the messages in the Sent Items folder. New outgoing messages are also saved to the Drafts folder every three minutes. You can change the defaults for both of these behaviors. You can also, of course, override these defaults for a specific message when necessary.

To change these default message behaviors for saving drafts and saving sent items, follow these steps:

1. Create your message.
2. Choose View, Options or click the Options toolbar button to open the Message Options dialog box.
3. To change the folder where the sent message is saved, click Browse and select the folder you want to use. Or, if you don't want to save the sent message, clear the Save Sent Message To check box.
4. Click OK to close the Message Options dialog box.

To specify how new unsent messages should be automatically saved, follow these steps:

1. Choose Tools, Options.
2. On the Preferences tab, click E-Mail Options, and then click Advanced E-Mail Options.
3. Select the folder in which unsent items should be saved, turn AutoSave on or off, and set the AutoSave interval.
4. Click OK to close each of the dialog boxes.

Controlling When Messages Are Delivered

When a message is sent, it is delivered immediately by default.You can, however, delay message delivery until a specified time. To do so, choose View, Options or click the Options toolbar button to open the Message Options dialog box. Select the Do Not Deliver Before check box and then set the date and time using the drop-down lists. Because delayed sending is a feature of Exchange Server, you can close Outlook as soon as you click Send—the message will wait in your Outbox on the server until the delivery time arrives.

Setting Messages to Expire

Just as you can delay the delivery of a message, you can also set a message to expire. The message expires and is removed from the recipient's mailbox after a specified period of time whether or not it has been read. You might want to have a message expire if its contents become stale after a certain amount of time or if you want to ensure that the message is deleted. To set this option, open the Message Options dialog box, select the Expires After check box, and then set a date and time. The message will no longer be available to the recipient after that time.

> **Note** The capability to set a message to expire is not a security feature, but simply causes the message to be deleted after the specified period. Use Information Rights Management, covered in Chapter 10, "Securing Your System, Messages, and Identity," to prevent messages from being forwarded, copied, or printed.

Linking a Contact Item to a Message

When sending an e-mail to a friend or colleague, it's sometimes useful to link contact information to provide a reference to the message as well as a way to sort and filter the message. For example, sales representatives who share information about client relations might want to provide a way of sorting this information. To link a contact item to a message, open the Message Options dialog box and click Contacts. Select the contact to link and then click OK. The recipient can now view the contact information in the Message Options dialog box for the received message or in a message view if that view displays the contacts field.

Assigning a Category to a Message

You assign a category to a message by clicking Categories in the Message Options dialog box. You can use the Master Category List to assign any relevant categories to the message. These categories can be used for sorting, grouping, and filtering messages.

For complete information about assigning and working with categories, see Chapter 4, "Using Categories and Types."

Recalling a Sent Message Before It's Read

There are many reasons why you might want to recall a message. For example, perhaps the message contains a mistake or is now obsolete. You can recall a message you have sent as long as the recipient has not read it and the message is still stored on an Exchange Server. Messages sent to recipients using other mail servers cannot be recalled.

To recall a sent message, double-click the message in the Sent Items folder to open it. Choose Action, Recall This Message to open the dialog box shown in Figure 35-8. Select whether you want to simply delete all unread copies of the message or delete them and replace them with another message. You can also receive a response reporting the success or failure of each recall attempt.

Caution For a number of reasons, sometimes unread messages cannot be recalled.

Figure 35-8. This dialog box is displayed when you attempt to recall a message.

Copying Global Addresses to Your Contacts Folder

You can easily copy addresses from the GAL to your Contacts folder by following these steps:

1. Choose Tools, Address Book.
2. Click the address you want to add to your Contacts folder.
3. Choose File, Add To Contacts or click the Add To Contacts toolbar button. The entry from the GAL opens in a contact form.
4. Make any necessary changes.
5. Click Save And Close. The contact information is now in your Contacts folder.

Voting in Outlook

Another feature in Outlook that takes advantage of Exchange Server is voting. Outlook's voting feature is useful when you want to solicit input from a group of message recipients. Perhaps you are looking for approval on a proposal, holding an informal election in your organization, or just want to get the group's input on an issue.

With the voting feature, you solicit and tally votes from the group. Outlook provides predefined voting responses, but you can also create your own. In this section, you'll learn how to include voting buttons on messages, tally returned votes, and configure voting options.

Here's how voting works in general: You create a message containing the question or document on which the group will be voting. Next, you add voting buttons to the message. Then you send the message. Recipients cast their vote by clicking the appropriate button. Outlook prompts them to confirm the vote and then sends the reply message back to you.

Sending a Message for a Vote

Sending a message for a vote is simple. In fact, as long as you want to use one of Outlook's default set of voting options, the process takes only a few clicks.

Using the Default Voting Responses

Use the following steps to create a message and add voting buttons to it:

1. Open Outlook and start a new message or open an existing message from your Drafts folder.
2. Click the Options toolbar button to open the Message Options dialog box.
3. In the Voting And Tracking Options area, select the Use Voting Buttons check box. In the drop-down list, select the group of voting buttons you want to include (see Figure 35-9).

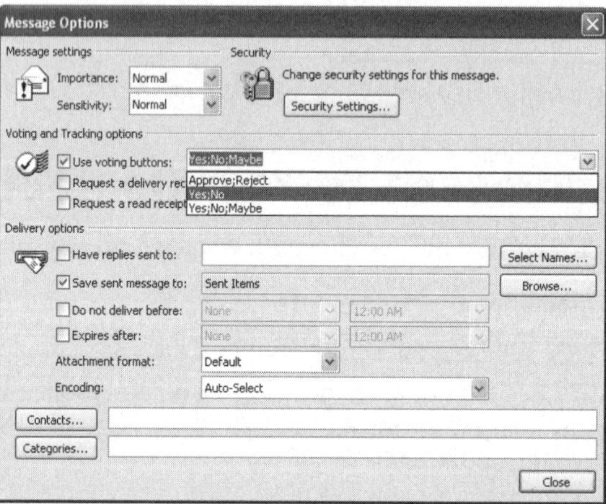

Figure 35-9. You select voting buttons in the Message Options dialog box.

4. Click Close.
5. Make any final changes to the message, including adding an attachment or configuring message options such as importance level.
6. Click Send to send the message.

Using Custom Responses

Outlook doesn't limit you to the default sets of voting options (such as Accept/Reject). You can create your own set that includes the responses you need for any situation. For example, suppose you're planning a company appreciation banquet and need to finalize the menu. You want to give everyone a choice of entree and collect those responses for the caterer. What better way to do it than electronically through Outlook?

Here's how:

1 Compose your message.
2 Click Options to open the Message Options dialog box.
3 Select the UseVoting Buttons check box.
4 Click the text portion of the Use Voting Buttons drop-down list, making sure to highlight the existing text. Type your custom vote options separated by semicolons, as shown in Figure 35-10.

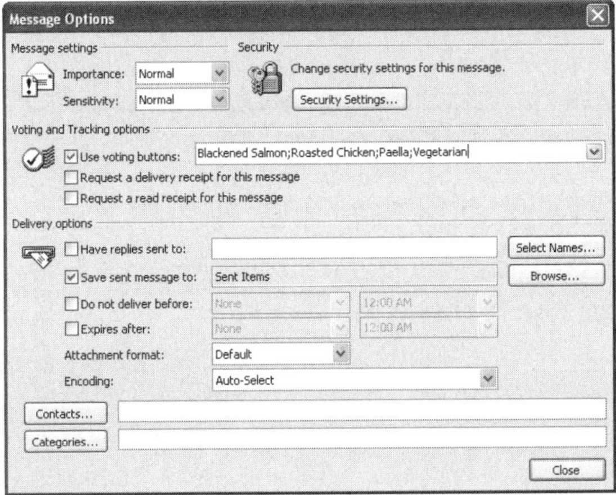

Figure 35-10. You can create custom vote responses.

5 Click Close.
6 Make any final adjustments to the message as needed.
7 Click Send.

Casting Your Vote

When you receive a message that includes voting buttons, the response buttons appear on the message form between the header and the toolbar (see Figure 35-11). In addition, Outlook displays a message in the Reading Pane, if it's open, to prompt you to vote (see Figure 35-12).

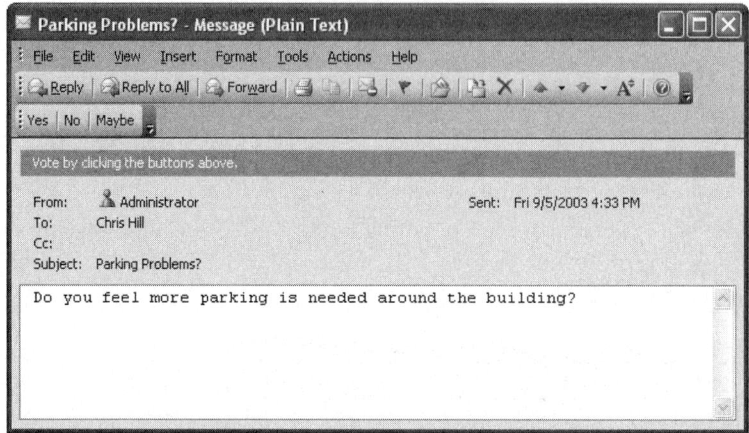

Figure 35-11. Click a button on the message form to vote.

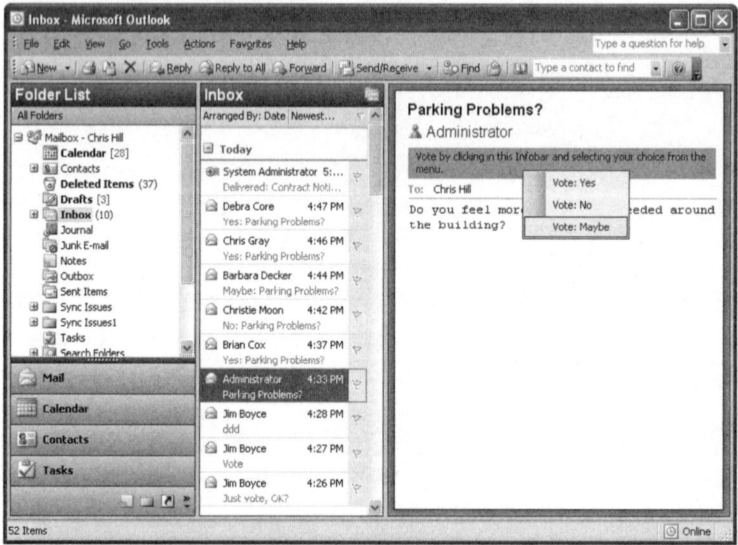

Figure 35-12. The Reading Pane shows a message prompting you to vote.

Tip Want to vote without opening the message? Simply right-click the message header and choose your vote response from the shortcut menu. Or, if the Reading Pane is open, click the InfoBar in the Reading Pane and cast your vote from the shortcut menu.

Voting is easy: just click a button to cast your vote. Outlook displays a simple dialog box asking whether you want to send the vote now or edit your response. To send the message without modification, select Send The Response Now. To cast your vote and open the message as a reply so that you can include text in your response, select Edit The Response Before Sending.

> **Tip** Outlook doesn't automatically close the message window when you cast a vote, which makes it easy to accidentally vote more than once. You must close the message window manually.

When you cast a vote, Outlook changes the subject of the message to include your vote. For example, if the original subject is Choose An Entree and you click the Blackened Salmon button, the subject of the reply returned to the sender is Blackened Salmon: Choose An Entree.

Viewing and Sorting Votes

Votes come back to you in the form of messages. You can view the vote summary in a few ways. If the Reading Pane is displayed, you can click the message header, then click the summary message in the InfoBar, and choose View Voting Responses as shown in Figure 35-13. Or you can open the Sent Items folder, open the original message, and click the Tracking tab. Either method displays the Tracking tab, shown in Figure 35-14.

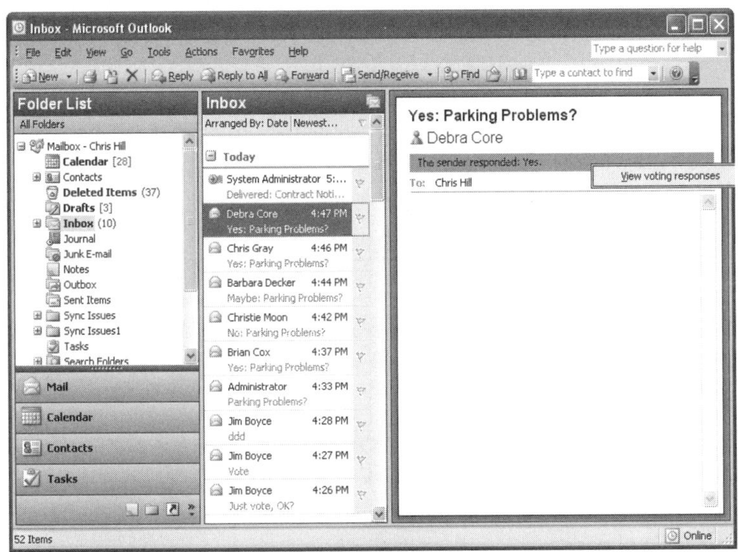

Figure 35-13. Click the summary message in the InfoBar to display the Tracking tab.

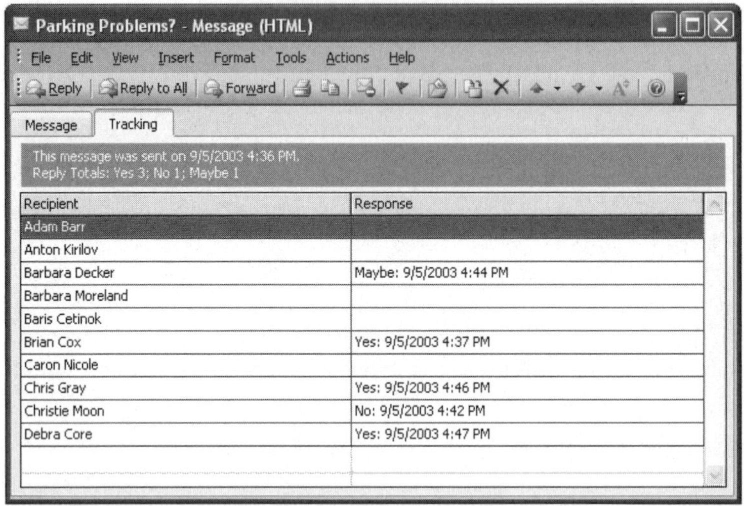

Figure 35-14. Open the message from the Sent Items folder as an alternative way to access the Tracking tab.

Inside Out

Voting suggestions

Don't rely on Outlook as a voting tool for crucial questions. It is an acceptable tool, however, for such issues as choosing entrees and polling for parking problems. Also understand that although you can vote more than once, only your first vote is recorded. This can be confusing if you aren't expecting that behavior; also, note that the voting buttons are not removed after you vote.

The Tracking tab summarizes the votes, with individual responses displayed one per line. The responses are also totaled in the InfoBar. If you want a printout of the vote responses, print the messages with the Tracking tab open.

Unfortunately, Outlook doesn't give you a way to sort the vote tally. You can, however, copy the data to Microsoft Excel to sort it.

To copy voting data to Excel, follow these steps:

1. Select the rows you want to copy. (Select a row and hold down the Shift key to select contiguous responses, or hold down the Ctrl key to select noncontiguous ones.)
2. Press Ctrl+C to copy the data to the clipboard.
3. Open Excel.
4. Select a cell in Excel and then press Ctrl+V to paste the data.
5. Choose Data, Sort to open the Sort dialog box and then click OK to accept the default settings and sort the spreadsheet.

Setting Options for Voting

You can configure a handful of options in Outlook to configure how Outlook handles voting. To configure these settings, follow these steps:

1. Open Outlook and choose Tools, Options.
2. On the Preferences tab, click E-Mail Options.
3. Click Tracking Options to open the Tracking Options dialog box (see Figure 35-15). The Tracking Options dialog box includes the following options that relate to voting:

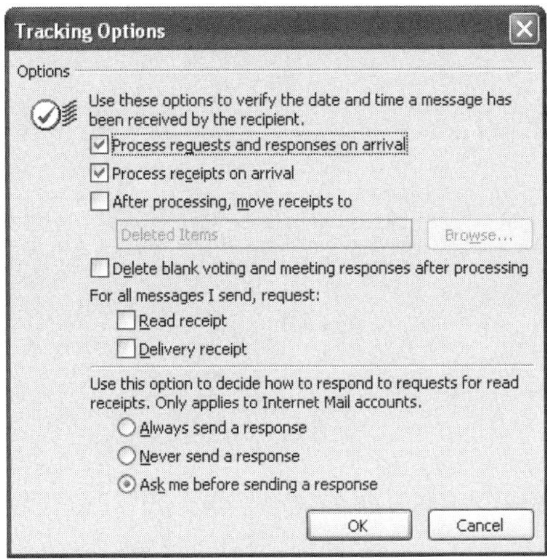

Figure 35-15. Use the Tracking Options dialog box to configure voting options.

- **Process Requests And Responses On Arrival** Outlook processes and tallies responses when they arrive. If you clear this check box, you must open each response to have Outlook tally it.
- **Delete Blank Voting And Meeting Responses After Processing** Outlook deletes voting responses that have no additional comments added to them.

4. Select the options you want to use and click OK to close theTracking Options dialog box. Then click OK twice more to close the E-Mail Options dialog box and the Options dialog box.

Troubleshooting

Votes aren't being automatically tallied

Outlook's ability to automatically tally votes without the user having to open each message might not be apparent at first. It can take several minutes even on a completely idle system for Outlook to process the messages. If you need to process them more quickly, select all the responses, right-click the selection, and choose Open Selected Items to open them all at once. Keep in mind, however, that you'll end up with an open message form for each response, which you'll then have to close.

Chapter 36

Supporting Outlook Under Exchange Server

By itself, Microsoft Office Outlook 2003 is an excellent information manager and e-mail client. When you use Outlook as a client for Microsoft Exchange Server, several features become available to you that make Outlook even better. Outlook is the client of choice for Exchange Server because of its integration with Exchange.

One of the greatest advantages of using Outlook with Exchange Server is data integrity. Instead of being stored on a local computer in a file, data is stored on the server in a fully transactional database. Transactions are logged before being committed to the database so that, in the event of a system failure, you can re-create any lost transactions from the logs. You can back up the database to retain the data of all users, ensuring that it is safe despite either workstation or server failures.

Another major advantage of using Outlook with Exchange Server is single-instance storage. Single-instance storage is used by Exchange Server when it receives a large file destined for multiple users. The file is stored in the database only once and referenced in each message to which it is attached. This reduces disk storage requirements for the database, which can be a significant savings if you have a large user base.

This chapter offers a look at some of the most common management tasks you're likely to perform in support of Outlook users under Microsoft Exchange Server 5.5, Microsoft Exchange 2000 Server, and Microsoft Exchange Server 2003. In addition to learning about client options for Exchange Server, you'll also learn about mailbox management tasks, such as creating mailboxes, setting delivery options, and setting storage limits. The chapter also covers several other management topics, including configuring alternate recipients for a mailbox, forwarding messages automatically, archiving messages, enabling Instant Messaging, and managing address lists.

Understanding Client Options for Exchange Server

You have several options when it comes to client applications for Exchange Server, including Outlook, Microsoft Outlook Web Access, Microsoft Outlook Express, and any other client that supports the SMTP and POP3 protocols. This section presents a quick overview of these client applications.

Outlook

Outlook is optimized for use with Exchange Server. No other client can provide the functionality that Outlook does, although Outlook Web Access comes close. Outlook is designed to fully integrate with Exchange Server, and it supports all of Exchange Server's collaboration features, including advanced meeting requests with automatic resource booking and sharing of free/busy times. Another advantage of using Outlook with Exchange Server is that instead of downloading mail from the server, as a POP3 client would, Exchange Server pushes the mail to the client as soon as the mail is received.

Troubleshooting

You can't connect Outlook to an Exchange Server

If you're unable to connect Outlook to an Exchange Server, check your firewall settings. It's possible to open ports on your firewall if your server is running Exchange Server 5.5 (see Microsoft Knowledge Base article Q176466 for details), but Exchange 2000 Server requires a large number of open ports—so many, in fact, that this solution is not feasible. Using a virtual private network (VPN) is a far better solution than opening firewall ports, because data is sent encrypted and eavesdropping is much more difficult. Or, install the RPC over HTTP component for Exchange Server 2003 and configure your network and servers to allow users to connect to the server with HTTP.

Outlook Web Access

Using Internet Information Services (IIS), Outlook Web Access lets users access Exchange Server mailboxes from anywhere on the Internet (if the server is publicly accessible) via a Web browser. Microsoft Internet Explorer 5 or later is recommended for use with Outlook Web Access, as it fully supports Dynamic HTML (DHTML) and Extensible Markup Language (XML). Other supported browsers include Internet Explorer 5 for Macintosh, Internet Explorer 4, and Netscape Navigator 4, although the functionality of these browsers is more limited. Outlook Web Access provides the most functionality of all client options except Outlook, offering scheduling, meeting, and collaboration capabilities.

For detailed information on Outlook Web Access, see Chapter 41, "Accessing Messages Through a Web Browser."

Outlook Express

Outlook Express provides only e-mail services and lacks most of the other information management and collaboration features of Outlook. Outlook Express downloads mail from the Exchange Server to the local system using POP3 or IMAP and sends mail using SMTP. Outlook Express can download meeting requests, but it displays the meeting request information as text in the body of the message; you can't respond to the request as you can in Outlook.

Other Mail Clients

Other mail clients, such as Netscape Messenger and Eudora, also work with Exchange Server if you configure the Exchange Server to support POP3 or IMAP and use these protocols with the mail client. Some packages can even interact with the calendar and contact features of Exchange Server by using the iCalendar and vCalendar formats for calendar items and the vCard format for contact items.

Managing User Mailboxes

Exchange 2000 Server and Exchange Server 2003 differ from Exchange 5.5 in administration. Because Exchange 2000 Server and Exchange Server 2003 are fully integrated with Active Directory, most user administration is performed from the Active Directory Users And Computers console. With Exchange Server 5.5, the Exchange Administrator is used for administration.

Managing Mailboxes in Exchange 2000 Server and Exchange Server 2003

You add user mailboxes at the same time that you add the user accounts in the Active Directory. Exchange 2000 Server and Exchange Server 2003 are fully integrated with Active Directory; there is no distinction between the user account and the mailbox (as there is in Exchange Server 5.5).

To manage user mailboxes in Exchange 2000 Server or Exchange Server 2003, open the Active Directory Users And Computers console from the Administrative Tools menu. If you're the system administrator, you'll want to have all options available to you, so be sure to select the Advanced Features on the View menu. Figure 36-1 shows the Active Directory Users And Computers console.

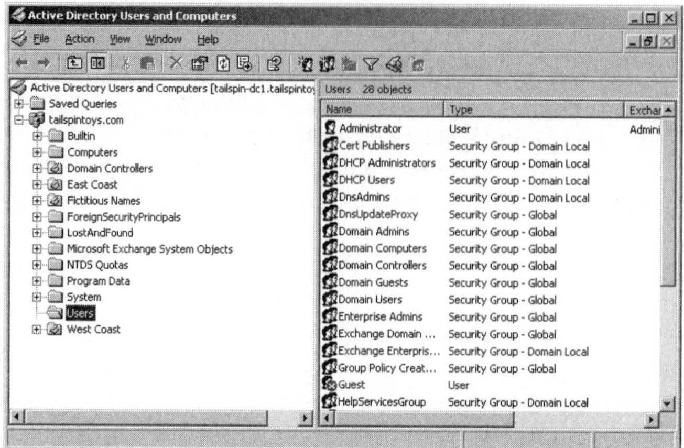

Figure 36-1. Use the Active Directory Users And Computers console to configure mailbox settings for Exchange 2000 Server and Exchange Server 2003.

To configure a user's mailbox, right-click the user, choose Properties, and click the Exchange General tab in the Properties dialog box (see Figure 36-2). This tab contains the basic configuration options for the mailbox, described in the following discussion.

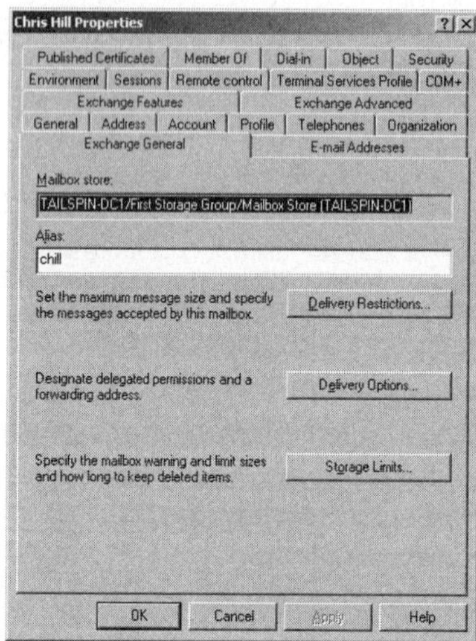

Figure 36-2. Use the Exchange General tab to view and set general configuration options for the mailbox.

The Mailbox Store box displays the database where the user data is kept (in Lightweight Directory Access Protocol [LDAP] form). In the Alias box, you can set the user's mailbox alias and e-mail address. The mailbox alias is usually set to the user name by default. Under most conditions, the SMTP address of a mailbox is *<alias>*@*<server>*. The alias is also another way of referring to the mailbox in Outlook.

Supporting Outlook Under Exchange Server

Click Delivery Restrictions on the Exchange General tab to open the Delivery Restrictions dialog box (see Figure 36-3), where you can specify restrictions on incoming and outgoing messages.

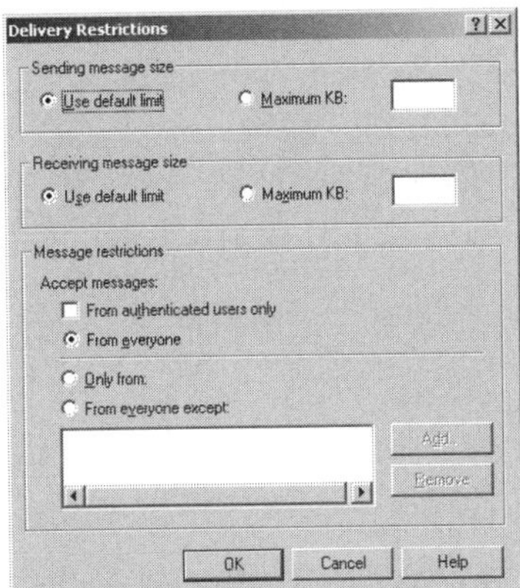

Figure 36-3. Use the Delivery Restrictions dialog box to set restrictions on incoming and outgoing messages.

The Sending Message Size and Receiving Message Size settings control the maximum allowed size (in KB) of outgoing and incoming messages. By default, the limits apply to all users in Exchange System Manager. The Accept Messages settings control who can send messages to this mailbox. You can choose to accept messages only from specified users (a deny-all-except method) or to accept messages from all users except those specified, which is useful for blocking mail from nuisance users. By default, all messages are accepted.

Clicking Delivery Options on the Exchange General tab opens the Delivery Options dialog box (see Figure 36-4), where you can configure mail delivery to and from this mailbox.

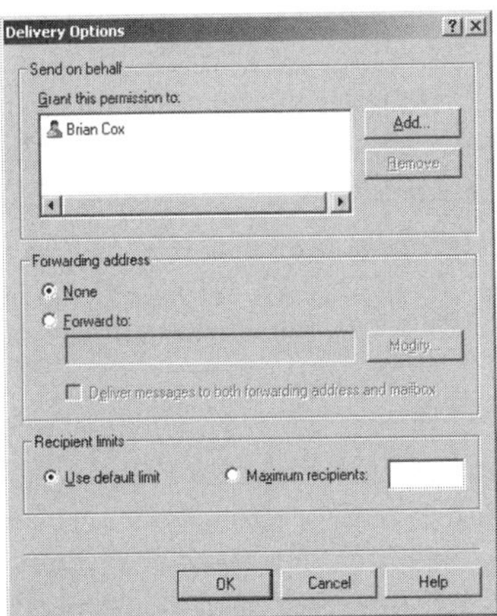

Figure 36-4. Use the Delivery Options dialog box to configure mail delivery to and from the mailbox.

The Send On Behalf option lets you specify other users who will be able to send messages on behalf of the user whose mailbox you're configuring. Add those specified users to the Grant This Permission To box. (A message sent on behalf of another user will indicate who sent it and on whose behalf.) Use the Recipient Limits option to set the maximum number of recipients to whom a message can be sent. Exchange Server by default uses the global limits set in Exchange System Manager (as explained later in this section).

For information about mail forwarding options, see "Configuring Alternate Recipients," page 897.

Clicking Storage Limits on the Exchange General tab opens the Storage Limits dialog box, which lets you control the mailbox storage space limits (see Figure 36-5).

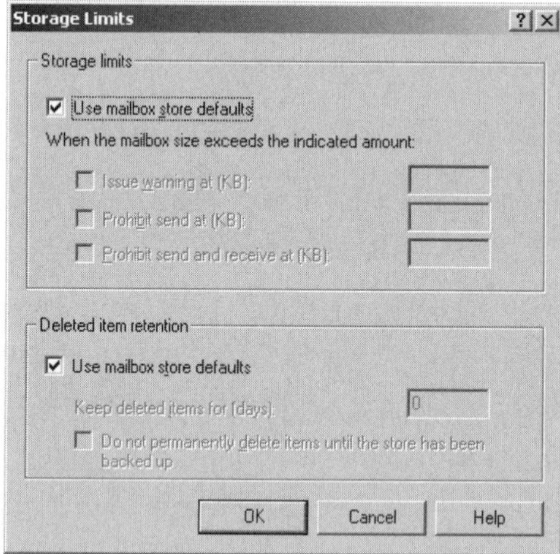

Figure 36-5. Use the Storage Limits dialog box to set the size limits and deleted item retention options for the mailbox.

The Storage Limits options define the amount of storage space (in KB) that a mailbox can use. If the mailbox exceeds the limit specified in Issue Warning At (KB), the user receives a notification that the mailbox has reached its size limit. If the mailbox exceeds the Prohibit Send At (KB) limit, the user can't send messages until the size of the mailbox is reduced. If the Prohibit Send And Receive At (KB) limit is exceeded, the user can't send or receive messages.

> **Caution** Use the Prohibit Send And Receive At limit only as a last resort, because it causes incoming mail to bounce.

The Deleted Item Retention options in the Storage Limits dialog box let you choose how to handle deleted items. Exchange Server allows you to retain deleted items even after you empty the Deleted Items folder. In the Keep Deleted Items For (Days) box, you can specify the number of days that deleted items are kept. Selecting the Do Not Permanently Delete Items Until The Store Has Been Backed Up check box retains deleted items until the next backup of the mailbox store. This way, you can recover deleted items from backups without keeping them on the server any longer than necessary. By default, both sets of Storage Limit options are set to the global limits configured in Exchange System Manager (as explained later in this section).

Next, return to the Properties dialog box and click the E-Mail Addresses tab. This tab displays the e-mail addresses associated with the mailbox, as shown in Figure 36-6.

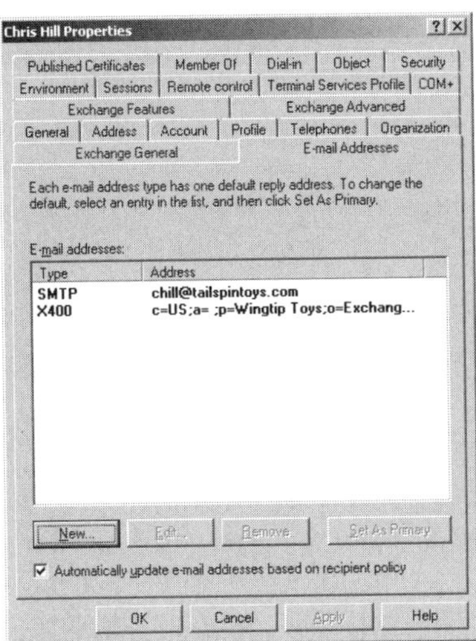

Figure 36-6. The E-Mail Addresses tab displays the existing addresses for the mailbox and lets you add, remove, and edit addresses.

The addresses currently assigned to the mailbox include an SMTP address and an X.400 address, which are automatically generated when you create the mailbox. From this tab, you can add new addresses or change existing addresses for the mailbox—for example, you might want to add SMTP aliases. To add an address, click New. Exchange Server displays a list of the address types you can add. In this case, you should add only SMTP or X.400 addresses because the connectors for other mail system types (such as Microsoft Mail) are not installed. Select the address type, click OK, and then specify the address. Click OK to add the new address to the mailbox.

If you select the Automatically Update E-Mail Addresses Based On Recipient Policy check box on the E-Mail Addresses tab, the addresses for this mailbox will change when the recipient policy changes. The recipient policy controls how the e-mail addresses are formatted when you create them. In the example shown in Figure 36-6, the format is *<firstname>.<lastname>@<domain>* for SMTP addresses. This check box is selected by default, thereby simplifying the task of globally changing the format of e-mail addresses, which was nearly impossible with earlier versions of Exchange Server. Also in the Properties dialog box, the Exchange Advanced tab (see Figure 36-7) is used to configure advanced options, which are necessary only in specific cases.

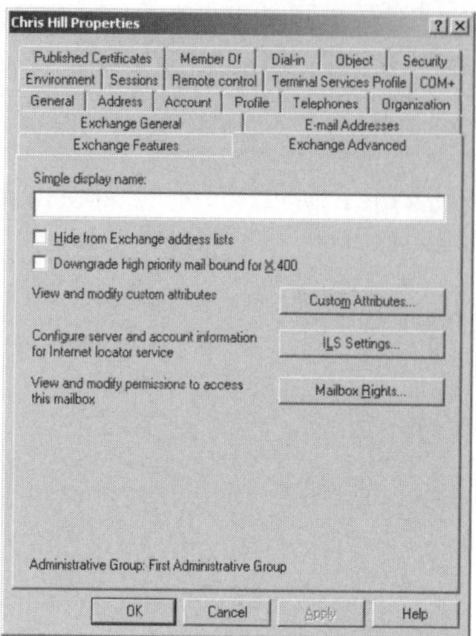

Figure 36-7. Use the Exchange Advanced tab to set special options.

In the Simple Display Name box on the Exchange Advanced tab, you can specify a display name that will be used in case a system is not capable of displaying the default display name. For example, if the normal display name uses Chinese characters, the simple display name might be in English characters.

When selected, the Hide From Exchange Address Lists check box prevents the user from being displayed in any Exchange Server address lists. Selecting the Downgrade High Priority Mail Bound For X.400 check box removes the high priority flag from a message if it is traversing an X.400 connection. This feature causes messages to conform to the original 1984 X.400 standard. Clicking Custom Attributes on this tab allows you to set values for any of Exchange Server's 15 custom attributes, which are extra fields you can use for virtually any purpose. Custom applications that use Outlook and Exchange Server can also use custom attributes.

Clicking the Protocol Settings button on the Exchange Advanced tab (Windows 2000 Server only) opens the Protocols dialog box, which displays the protocols you can use to access the mailbox. By selecting a protocol and then clicking Settings, you can configure the protocol as well as enable or disable it for the mailbox. (HTTP has no configuration settings; you can only enable or disable it.) You can set the message encoding type and options as well as the character set for the protocol. By default, these settings are configured globally (for all mailboxes) from Exchange System Manager and can be changed by the Exchange administrator.

Note You enable and configure protocol settings in Windows Server 2003 on the Exchange Features tab.

Clicking ILS Settings on the Exchange Advanced tab allows you to configure an Internet Locator Service (ILS) server and account for the mailbox. An ILS server is essentially a server that stores address information about Internet users.

Clicking Mailbox Rights opens a Permissions dialog box for the mailbox, which lets you (as an administrator) assign rights to the mailbox to other users. Normally the mailbox owner assigns these rights by using delegates in Outlook, but an administrator can force mailbox rights by using this dialog box. This is necessary only when you're assigning the rights to a resource mailbox to the resource administrator.

You can also use Exchange System Manager to manage user mailboxes. Figure 36-8 shows the default Exchange System Manager window.

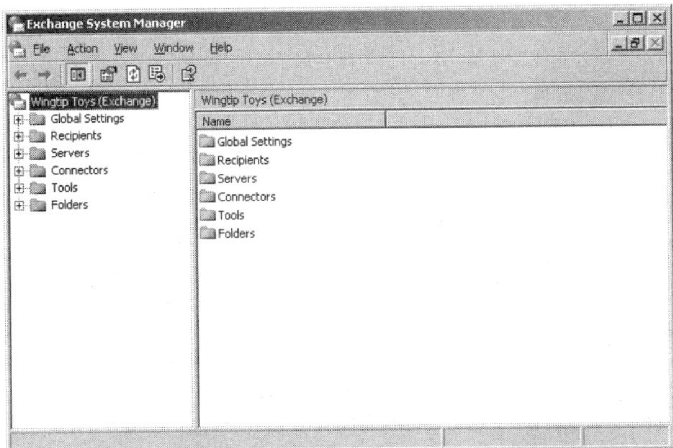

Figure 36-8. You can use Exchange System Manager to manage user mailboxes.

You can use Exchange System Manager to set the default message size limits and the maximum number of recipients. Double-click Global Settings in the left pane, right-click Message Delivery, and choose Properties. Click the Defaults tab to set the default size limits and maximum number of recipients for messages. These defaults apply to all users unless they have been overridden, as previously discussed.

To use Exchange System Manager to manage mailbox size and deleted item retention defaults, follow these steps:

1. Double-click the organization in which the server resides to expand the tree if needed.
2. Double-click Servers in the left pane, and then double-click the server for which you want to set defaults.
3. Double-click the storage group that contains the mailbox store you want to configure.
4. Right-click the mailbox store and choose Properties.
5. Click the Limits tab and set the default mailbox size limits and deleted item retention options, as discussed earlier. These settings apply to all users in the selected mailbox store.

Managing Mailboxes in Exchange Server 5.5

User mailboxes are created at the same time as user accounts in Exchange Server 5.5 and Microsoft Windows NT Server 4.0, unless the administrator chooses otherwise. Mailboxes and user accounts in these systems are logically separate entities, however. You use the Microsoft Exchange Administrator, shown in Figure 36-9, to manage these mailboxes.

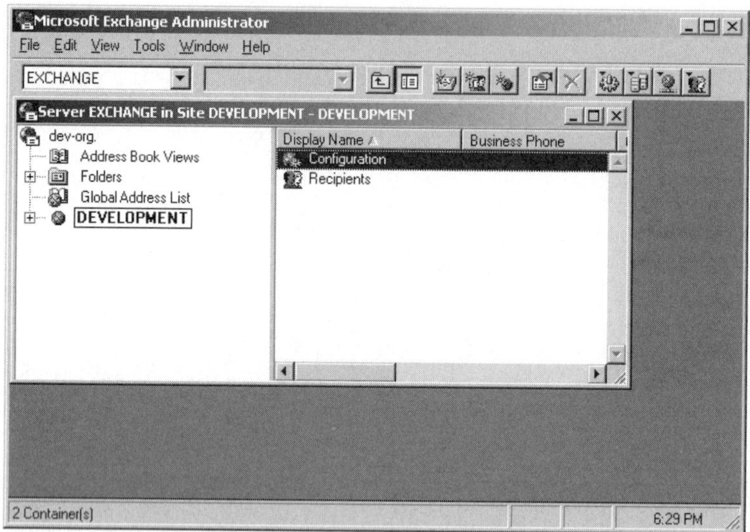

Figure 36-9. Use the Microsoft Exchange Administrator to manage user mailboxes.

To begin managing user mailboxes on a system running Exchange Server 5.5, follow these steps:

1. Choose Start, Programs, Microsoft Exchange, Microsoft Exchange Administrator. The Exchange Server organization name (dev-org. in this example) appears at the root of the tree in the left pane.
2. Double-click the site (Development in this example), double-click Configuration, and then double-click Servers.
3. Double-click the server name (Exchange in this example) and click Server Recipients. All recipients on the selected server are displayed in the right pane.
4. Double-click a user to display that user's Properties dialog box.

Figure 36-10 shows the General tab of the Properties dialog box. Use this tab to set general information such as the user's name, address, and organizational information. In the Name group, the Display setting controls how the mailbox appears in address lists. The alias is another way to reference the mailbox. The Primary Windows NT Account button and the accompanying text box are the most important part of the General tab. They let you specify the user account that owns the mailbox. Unless other permissions are set for the mailbox, only the specified account and the service account under which Exchange Server runs can log in to the mailbox.

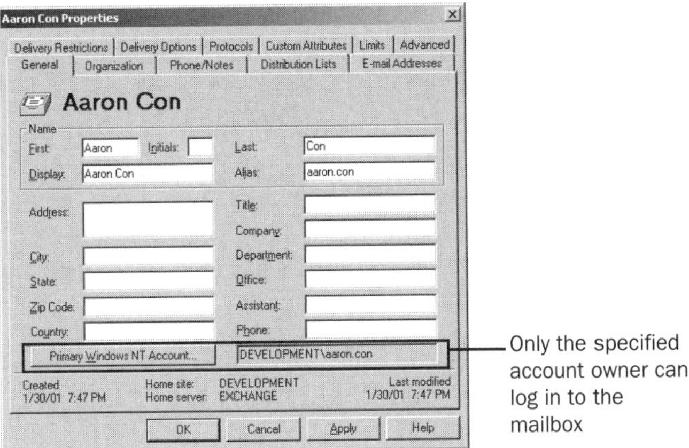

Figure 36-10. Use the General tab to configure identification information and specify the mailbox owner.

Use the Organization tab of the Properties dialog box to specify which users report directly to the current user or to set the user's manager. Setting the user's manager causes the user to show up as a direct report; specifying another user as a direct report causes the current user to show up as that user's manager. Use the Phone/Notes tab to specify the user's phone numbers and to add any relevant notes. On the Distribution Lists tab, you can add the user to distribution lists; it also lists the mailbox's membership. To add the user to distribution lists, click Modify and select the lists. The E-Mail Addresses tab functions in exactly the same manner as it does in Exchange 2000 Server and Exchange Server 2003 (described in the previous section).

Figure 36-11 shows the Delivery Restrictions tab. Delivery restrictions in Exchange Server 5.5 work similarly to those in Exchange 2000 Server and Exchange Server 2003, but they don't work on a deny-all-except or accept-all-except list; instead, two separate lists are used to obtain the same result.

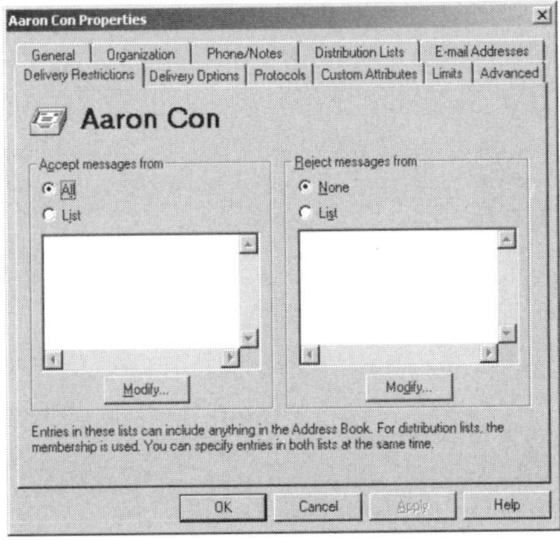

Figure 36-11. Use the Delivery Restrictions tab to set limits on who can send messages to the mailbox.

You can use the Delivery Options tab for two purposes: to configure alternate recipients (discussed in the following section) and to grant send-on-behalf-of privileges to other users. The Protocols tab functions the same way it does in Exchange 2000 Server and Exchange Server 2003: the protocol settings you specify override the global protocol defaults.

The Custom Attributes tab is also used the same way it's used in Exchange 2000 Server and Exchange Server 2003, except that 10 custom attributes are available instead of 15. Figure 36-12 shows the Limits tab of the Properties dialog box for a user in Exchange Server 5.5. Once again, the features found on the Limits tab are functionally identical to corresponding features found in Exchange 2000 Server and Exchange Server 2003.

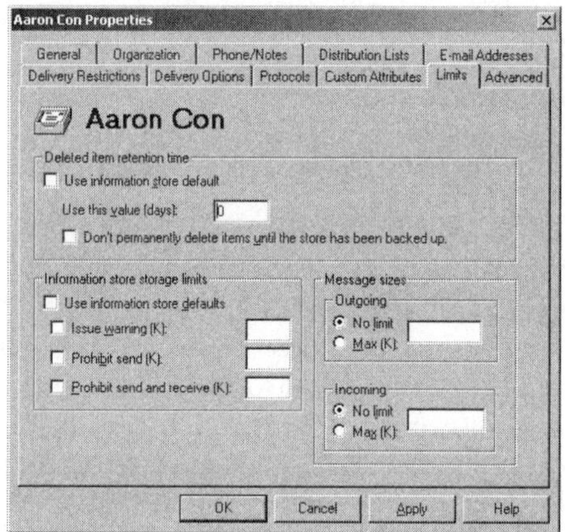

Figure 36-12. Use the Limits tab to set limits on incoming and outgoing message size and to configure deleted item retention and mailbox size.

Figure 36-13 shows the Advanced tab of the Properties dialog box. On this tab, you can specify the options listed next.

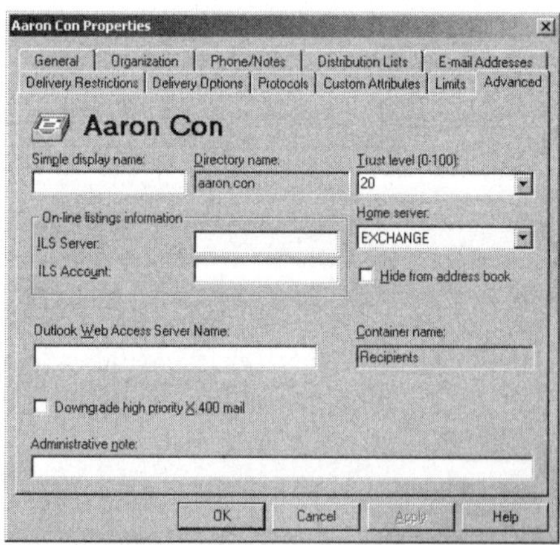

Figure 36-13. Use the Advanced tab to set advanced miscellaneous settings for the mailbox.

- **Simple Display Name** Sets a name that will be used when a client system is not capable of displaying the default display name. For example, if the normal display name uses Chinese characters, the simple display name might be in English characters.
- **Directory Name** Displays the mailbox name used for mail routing.
- **Trust Level** Controls the replication of mailbox information during directory synchronization with other systems. If the mailbox trust level is greater than the container trust level, mailbox information is not replicated.
- **ILS Server and ILS Account** Specifies an ILS server and account for the mailbox. The ILS server is used to publicly store information about the mailbox.
- **Home Server** Specifies the server with the information store that will hold the mailbox. This is a useful feature for organizations that have multiple servers in a site, because having the mailbox on a local server will decrease access time.
- **Hide From Address Book** Prevents the mailbox from appearing in any address lists.
- **Outlook Web Access Server Name** Specifies which server running Outlook Web Access should be used with this mailbox if it is different from the default Web access server.
- **Downgrade High Priority X.400 Mail** Sends High priority X.400 messages with Normal priority for compatibility reasons.
- **Container Name** Displays the name of the container that stores the mailbox in the Exchange directory store.
- **Administrative Note** Provides a descriptive note that can be viewed only with Exchange Administrator.

Configuring Alternate Recipients

Alternate recipients are recipients who receive all mail sent to a mailbox, either instead of or in addition to the mailbox user.

Specifying Recipients in Exchange 2000 Server and Exchange Server 2003

To specify alternate recipients in Exchange 2000 Server or Exchange Server 2003, follow these steps:

1. Open Active Directory Users And Computers and select the Users container under your domain. Right-click the user and choose Properties.
2. Click the Exchange General tab, and then click Delivery Options.
3. In the Delivery Options dialog box, click Forward To. Click Modify to specify the user to whom the messages will be forwarded, and then click OK.
4. If you want the messages to go to both the original and alternate recipients, select the Deliver Messages To Both Forwarding Address And Mailbox check box. Click OK.

Figure 36-14 shows an example of the Delivery Options dialog box with an alternate recipient configured.

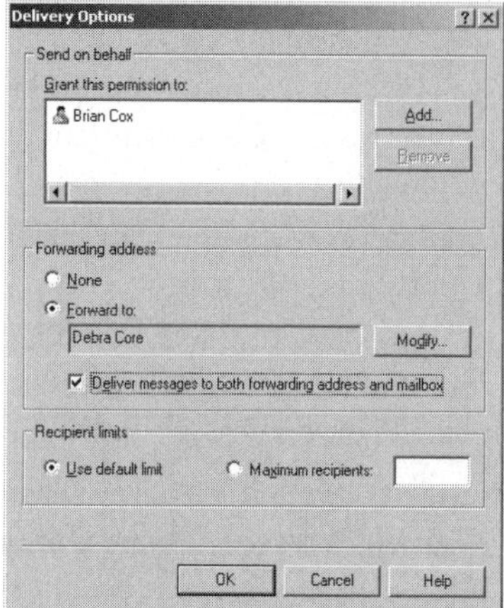

Figure 36-14. You can specify alternate recipients in the Delivery Options dialog box.

Specifying Recipients in Exchange Server 5.5

To specify an alternate recipient in Exchange Server 5.5, follow these steps:

1. Open Exchange Administrator.
2. Double-click the site, double-click Configuration, double-click Servers, double-click the server name, and then click Server Recipients.
3. Double-click a user to open that user's Properties dialog box. Click the Delivery Options tab.
4. Click Alternate Recipient, and then click Modify to select a user. Select the user from the address book and click OK.
5. If you want the messages to go to both the original and alternate recipients, select the Deliver Messages To Both Recipient And Alternate Recipient check box. Click OK.

Forwarding Messages to Users' Internet Mail Accounts

Forwarding mail to Internet mail accounts is similar to configuring an alternate recipient, except that the alternate recipient in this case must have an Internet mail address. A problem arises, however, because you cannot specify an Internet mail address as the alternate recipient—you must specify an Exchange Server mail recipient. To solve this problem, you can create *mail-enabled contacts* in Exchange 2000 Server and Exchange Server 2003, and *custom recipients* in Exchange Server 5.5.

Creating Mail-Enabled Contacts in Exchange 2000 Server and Exchange Server 2003

To create a mail-enabled contact in Exchange 2000 Server or Exchange Server 2003, follow these steps:

1. Open Active Directory Users And Computers.
2. In the left pane, right-click the container to which you want to add the contact, and choose New, Contact.
3. Enter the contact's name information, as shown in Figure 36-15. This information should be unique to the user. If this is a user's home account, specify it as such. Click Next.

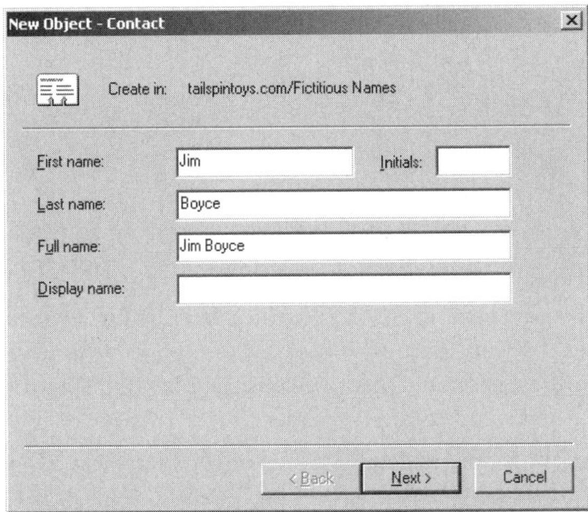

Figure 36-15. Specifying the name details is the first step in creating a mail-enabled contact.

4. Specify the e-mail address of the contact to make the contact mail-enabled. (First ensure that the alias is unique.)You can click Modify to specify an address. Select the address type from the list and click OK. Then enter the address and click OK.
5. Click Next to continue. A summary page of the contact information is displayed. Click Finish to create the contact.

To add the contact as an alternate recipient, follow these steps:

1. Open the user's Properties dialog box in the Active Directory Users And Computers console.
2. On the Exchange General tab, click Delivery Options.
3. Click Forward To, and then click Modify to add the new contact.
4. When you've added the contact, click OK twice to close the Delivery Options and the Properties dialog boxes. Messages to that mailbox will now be forwarded to the contact.

Creating Custom Recipients in Exchange Server 5.5

The process for forwarding messages to an Internet mail account in Exchange Server 5.5 is similar to the process in Exchange 2000 Server and Exchange Server 2003, except that you create a custom recipient instead of a mail-enabled contact.

To create a custom recipient in Exchange Server 5.5, follow these steps:

1. Open Exchange Administrator, select the site in the left pane, and click Recipients.
2. Choose File, New Custom Recipient. Select an e-mail address type, as shown in Figure 36-16.

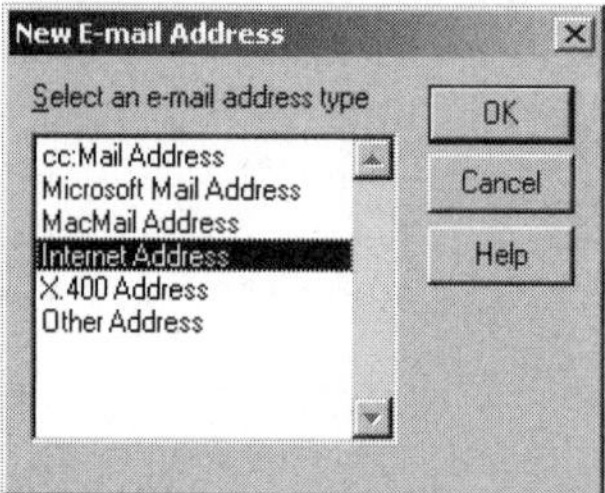

Figure 36-16. When creating a custom recipient, you must first specify the mail address type.

3. Enter the e-mail address and click OK. The Properties dialog box for a custom recipient appears. The tabs available are a subset of those available for a regular mailbox. Enter a name for the custom recipient and ensure that the display name and alias are unique. Click OK to save the custom recipient.
4. To set the forwarding, open the Properties dialog box for the mailbox and click the Delivery Restrictions tab.
5. Click List and click Modify to add the recipient. Choose the newly created custom recipient from the address book and click OK.
6. Click OK (or Apply) to close the Properties dialog box. All messages to the mailbox will now be forwarded to the custom recipient.

Archiving (Journaling) All Messages

Message archiving (known as *journaling* in Exchange Server 5.5) is the retention of all incoming and outgoing messages. In Exchange Server 5.5, message journaling is available only for mail that passes through the Mail Transfer Agent (MTA), whereas message archiving in Exchange 2000 Server and Exchange Server 2003 is more granular: messages to or from a specific message store are archived. Some organizations use message journaling to enforce employee terms of service or to discover malicious activity.

Note Before you begin archiving and reading the mail of employees in your organization, you would do well to consult your corporate lawyer. Many administrators go so far as to have management put in writing the order to read users' mail, to ensure that they cannot be blamed if an employee files suit against the company.

Archiving in Exchange 2000 Server and Exchange Server 2003

In Exchange 2000 Server or Exchange Server 2003, message archiving is done on a per-mailbox-store basis.

To archive messages for a particular store, follow these steps:

1. Open Exchange System Manager. In the left pane, navigate to the mailbox store for which you want to archive messages (see Figure 36-17).

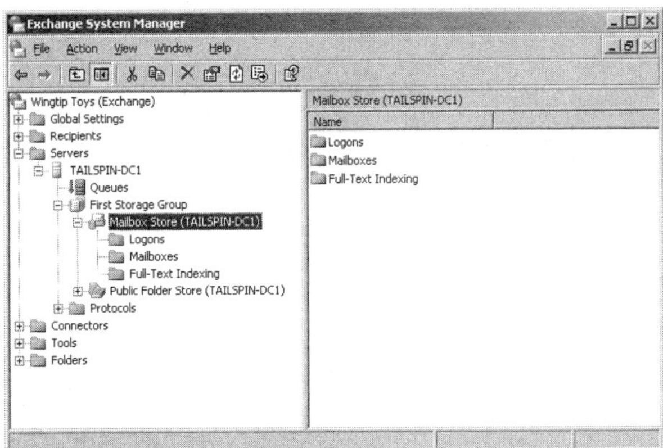

Figure 36-17. Use Exchange System Manager to set up message archiving for specific mailbox stores.

2. Right-click the mailbox store and choose Properties.
3. On the General tab of the store's Properties dialog box, select the Archive All Messages Sent Or Received By Mailboxes On This Store check box to enable message archiving.
4. Click Browse to select a mailbox or distribution list from the address list. This mailbox (or list) will receive all the archived messages.

It's useful to create a mailbox specifically for message archiving. You could also use the Administrator mailbox—the Administrator account shouldn't be in use in a secure Windows network—because that mailbox receives a relatively high volume of mail, especially if you have a large user base. If you use a separate mailbox, it's useful to grant access to all users who need access so that they can open the mailbox in Outlook while logged on as themselves. Figure 36-18 shows the General tab of the store's Properties dialog box with message archiving enabled.

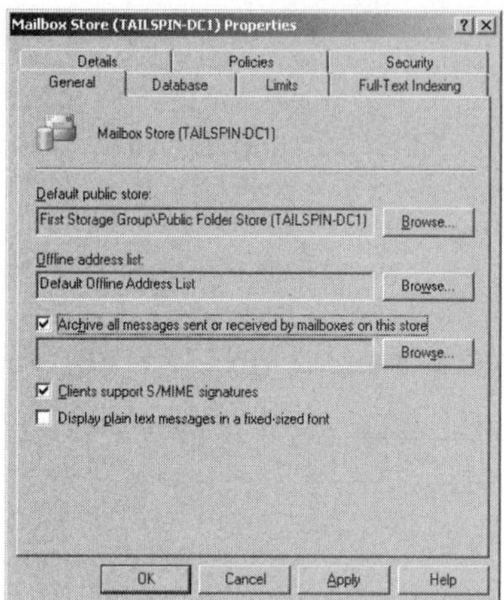

Figure 36-18. In this example, the Administrator mailbox will receive the archived mail.

Journaling in Exchange Server 5.5

Message journaling in Exchange Server 5.5 is performed for every message that is transferred over the MTA. It's much more complex to implement than archiving in Exchange 2000 Server or Exchange Server 2003. Each server must be running at least Exchange Server 5.5 Service Pack 1 or later. To implement message journaling in Exchange Server 5.5, follow these steps:

1 Determine the distinguished name of the recipient who will receive the journaled mail. A distinguished name uniquely identifies an object and its location. The recipient might be a mailbox, a custom recipient, or a public folder. To determine the distinguished name, you must run the Exchange Administrator in raw mode.

Caution Running the Exchange Administrator in raw mode is dangerous because this mode exposes all the directory schema attributes that make up individual objects. Never change any settings unless directed to do so by a Microsoft support engineer.

2 To open the Exchange Administrator in raw mode, open a command prompt and type **<*x*>:\exchsrvr\bin\admin /r**, where <*x*> is the drive on which Exchange Server is installed.

3 Locate the recipient who will receive journaled messages, select that recipient, and choose File, Raw Properties.

4 Select Obj-Dist-Name in the Object Attributes list. The distinguished name of an object will be displayed in the Attribute Value box, as shown in Figure 36-19. Make a note of the distinguished name.

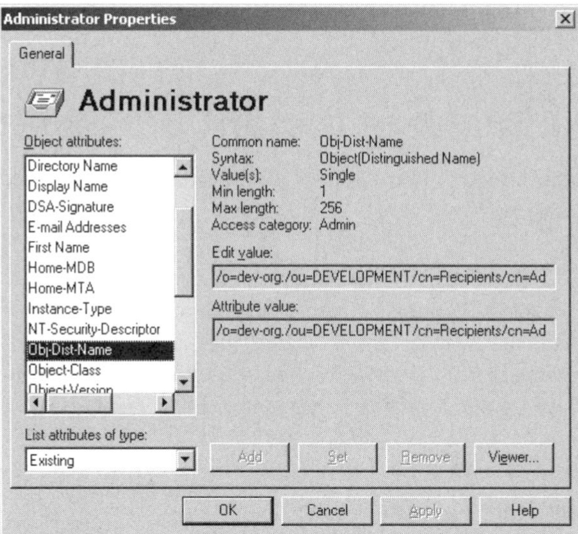

Figure 36-19. View the distinguished name in the Attribute Value box.

5 In the registry, specify this distinguished name as the recipient for journaled messages. Open the Registry Editor and locate the key HKEY_LOCAL_MACHINE\SYSTEM\CurrentControlSet\Services\MSExchangeMTA\Parameters. Add the string value *Journal Recipient Name* to that key, and set the value to the distinguished name noted in step 4.

6 By default, message journaling is performed at the organization level.To change message journaling to the site or server level, set a DWORD value named *Per-Site Journal Required* to HKEY_LOCAL_MACHINE\SYSTEM\CurrentControlSet\Services\MSExchangeMTA\Parameters. A value of 0 specifies organization-level message journaling, a value of 1 specifies site-level message journaling, and a value of 2 specifies server-level message journaling.

7 Ensure that all private information store messages are routed through the Exchange Server MTA—they are normally delivered without the MTA if the sender and receiver are on the same information store. Also ensure that Internet Mail Service (IMS) messages are routed through the private information store. This must be done on any server on which you are performing message journaling—for example, each server in the site if you are journaling on a per-site basis, or only on an individual server if you are journaling on a per-server basis.

8 To route all private information store messages through the MTA, set a DWORD value of 1 named *No Local Delivery* in HKEY_LOCAL_MACHINE\SYSTEM\CurrentControlSet\Services\MSExchangeIS\ParametersSystem. To route all IMS mail through the private information store, set a DWORD value of 1 named *RerouteViaStore* in HKEY_LOCAL_MACHINE\SYSTEM\CurrentControlSet\Services\MSExchangeIMC\Parameters. This must be done on each server running IMS if there is more than one. (A site often has more than one IMS for redundancy.)

Message journaling should now be enabled and all messages routed through the MTA should be sent to the specified recipient.

Configuring and Enabling Instant Messaging

Exchange 2000 Server provides an Instant Messaging feature that is essentially a private version of the MSN Messenger Service. This feature must be enabled on both a global basis and a per-user basis.

Note Exchange Server 2003 does not include the instant messaging component. Microsoft Live Communications Server 2003 takes the place of the instant messaging functionality in Exchange 2000 Server for Exchange Server 2003 environments. For more information about Live Communications Server, see *www.microsoft.com/office/preview/livecomm/default.asp*.

To enable Instant Messaging in Exchange 2000 Server, follow these steps:

1 Ensure that the Microsoft Exchange Instant Messaging Service is installed. Instant Messaging is optional when you install Exchange. You can install it later, as shown in Figure 36-20, but the Exchange services will be stopped during the installation process.

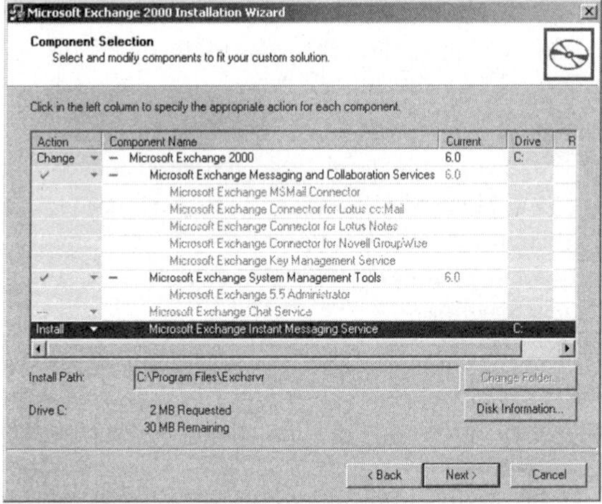

Figure 36-20. Instant Messaging is an option when Exchange Server is initially installed; you can add it later from the Exchange Server CD.

2 Open Exchange System Manager. Double-click Servers in the left pane, and then select the server on which you want to create the Instant Messaging virtual server. Click Protocols, and then click Instant Messaging (RVP).

3 Right-click in the right pane and choose New, Instant Messaging Virtual Server to start the New Instant Messaging Virtual Server Wizard. Click Next.

4 Specify the required display name for the new virtual server. Click Next.

5 Specify an existing IIS Web site to enable for Instant Messaging and click Next. You can use the default Web site, but each Instant Messaging virtual server you create in the future must have a unique site. Click Next.

6 Specify the required DNS name for the virtual server. By default, the server name is specified, but you can set it to anything you choose. Click Next.

7 Select the Allow This Server To Host User Accounts check box, shown in Figure 36-21, to make the new virtual server a home server. Click Next.

8 Click Finish to close the wizard.

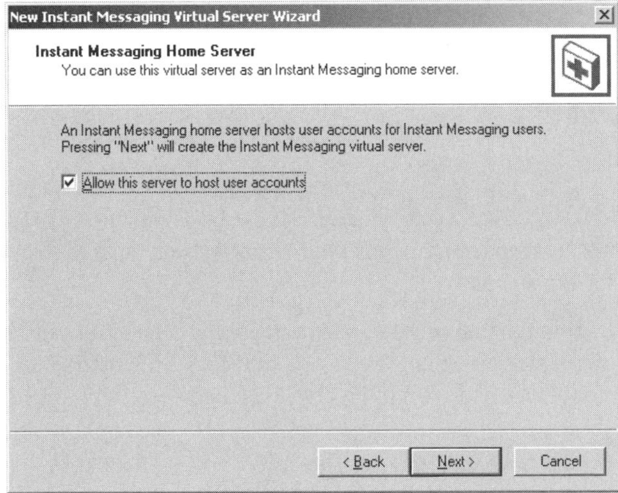

Figure 36-21. Only Instant Messaging home servers can host users.

Figure 36-22 shows the new Instant Messaging virtual server in Exchange System Manager.

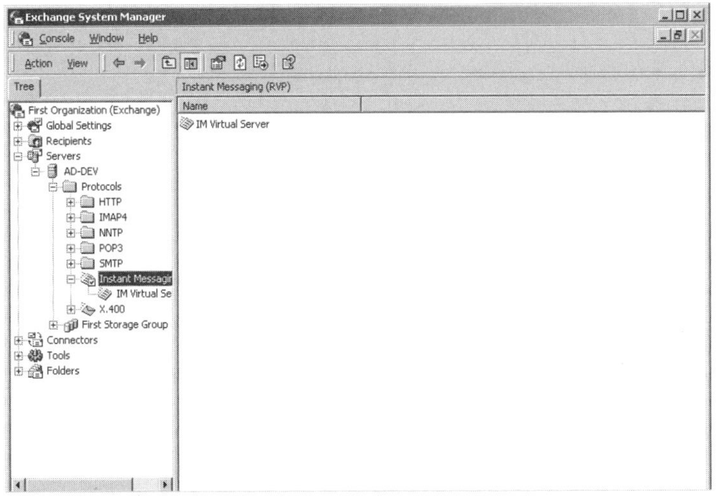

Figure 36-22. A new Instant Messaging virtual server has been created.

To enable the Instant Messaging feature for specific users, follow these steps:

1. Open the Active Directory Users And Computers console.
2. Right-click the user for whom you want to enable Instant Messaging, and choose Properties. Click the Exchange Features tab.
3. Click Instant Messaging, and then click Enable. You must specify the Instant Messaging home server and domain name, as shown in Figure 36-23.

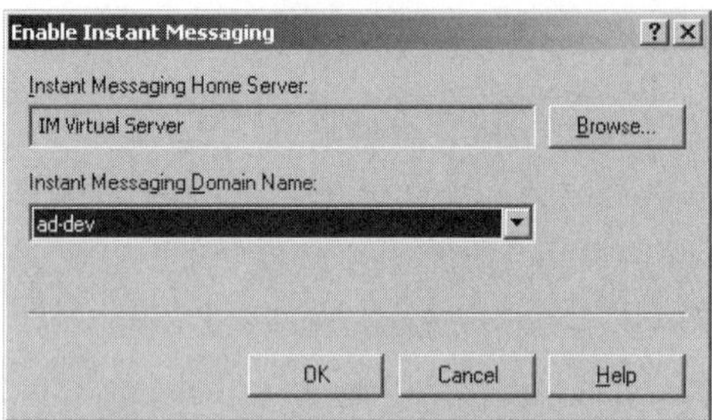

Figure 36-23. When enabling Instant Messaging, you must specify the home server and domain name.

4. Select the domain name you assigned to the newly created Instant Messaging virtual server—this is the default in most cases—and click Browse to select an Instant Messaging home server, as shown in Figure 36-24.

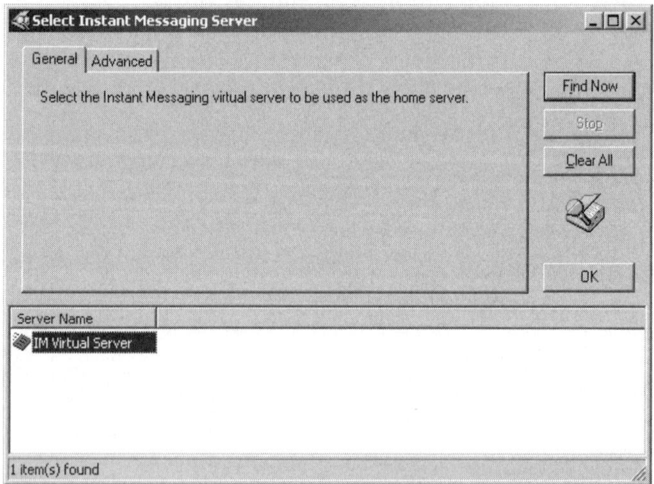

Figure 36-24. Select an available Instant Messaging home server.

5. Select the newly created Instant Messaging virtual server from the list and click OK. Click OK to close the Enable Instant Messaging window.

Figure 36-25 shows the user's Properties dialog box with Instant Messaging enabled.

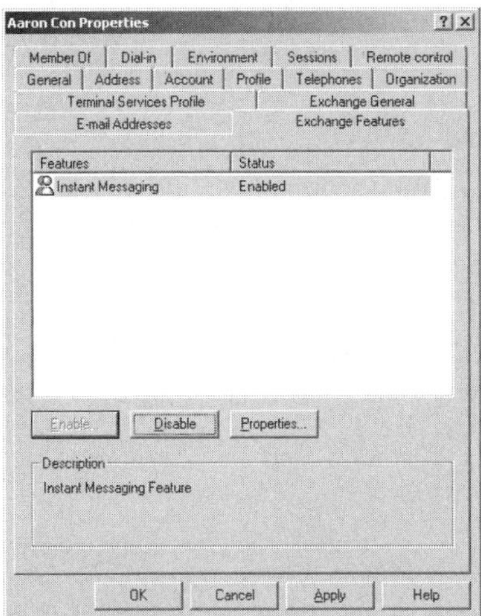

Figure 36-25. Instant Messaging has been enabled for this user.

To enable Instant Messaging for a group of users, follow these steps:

1. Select all users for whom you want to enable Instant Messaging. Right-click the selection and choose Exchange Tasks.
2. Click Next. Select Enable Instant Messaging from the list of tasks, and then click Next.
3. Specify the home server and domain name, and click Next. The next page of the wizard shows the progress of the task, and then a summary page displays the results.
4. Click Finish to close the summary.

Managing Exchange Server Address Lists

Exchange Server creates a Global Address List (GAL) in which all mail-enabled users and groups are listed. You can also create additional address lists, and manage the existing GAL. This section of the chapter explores a handful of address list management tasks.

Adding External Addresses to the GAL

All *mail-enabled* users and groups—those who have a mailbox and have been assigned an address—are placed in the GAL. If you want to add others, such as those outside the organization, to the GAL, you must make them mail-enabled contacts. (Mail-enabled contacts are the equivalent of Custom Recipients in Exchange Server 5.5.)

To create a mail-enabled contact, follow these steps:

1. In the Active Directory Users And Computers console, right-click the container to which the contact should be added (usually the Users container), and then choose New, Contact.
2. Enter the contact name information and click Next.
3. On the wizard page shown in Figure 36-26, click Modify to add an e-mail address associated with the contact.

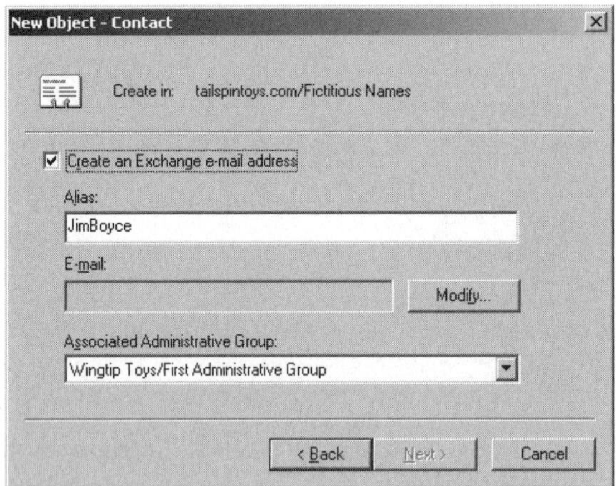

Figure 36-26. If you add an Exchange Server e-mail address for a contact external to the organization, that contact appears in the GAL.

4. Select the address type, which is usually SMTP unless other Exchange Server connectors are installed, and specify the address. Click OK.
5. Click Next and then click Finish to create the mail-enabled contact. After a few moments, the new mail-enabled contact appears in the GAL.

Restricting Access to the GAL

If you're an administrator, you can set access to the GAL. You might want to do this if you provide specific address lists for groups of users and want to restrict them from seeing users in the entire organization.

To restrict access to the GAL, follow these steps:

1. Open Exchange System Manager and navigate to Recipients, All Global Address Lists.
2. Right-click Default Global Address List and choose Properties.
3. Click the Security tab. The security settings for the various users and groups are listed on this tab.
4. By default, the Authenticated Users group has List Contents permission. Click to remove this permission, thus removing access to the GAL for all users except those for whom access is explicitly granted.

Creating and Security Custom Address Lists

You can create additional address lists on an Exchange Server to organize mail-enabled users into various categories. For example, if you have several large departments in your company, you might create individual address lists for them. Or, perhaps you want to create multiple alphabetical lists based on recipients' last names. Whatever the case, it's easy to create other address lists and apply security settings to control who can use them.

To create a new address list, follow these steps:

1. Open Exchange System Manager and expand the Recipients container.
2. Right-click All Address Lists and choose New, Address List.
3. Enter a name for the address list in the Create Exchange Address List dialog box (see Figure 36-27).

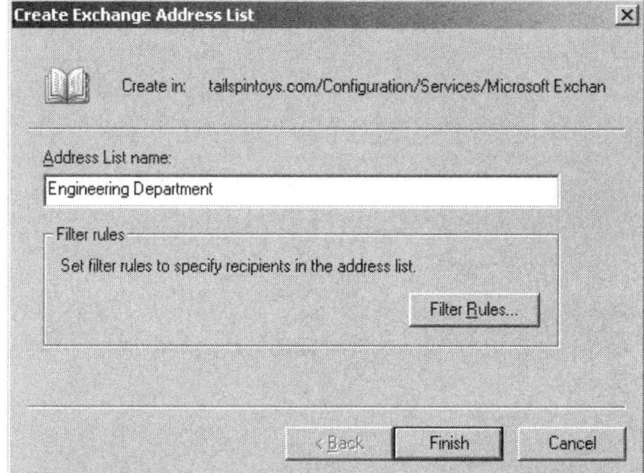

Figure 36-27. Enter a name for the address list.

4. Click Filter Rules to open the Find Exchange Recipients dialog box shown in Figure 36-28.

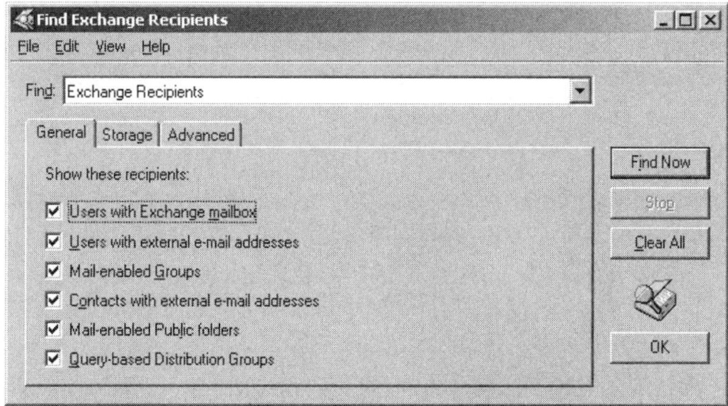

Figure 36-28. Use the Find Exchange Recipients dialog box to specify a filter for the address list.

Chapter 36

5 On the General tab, choose the options that determine which Exchange objects will be included in the address list.

6 Click the Storage tab, shown in Figure 36-29, and select the location where the mailboxes to be included in the address list reside.

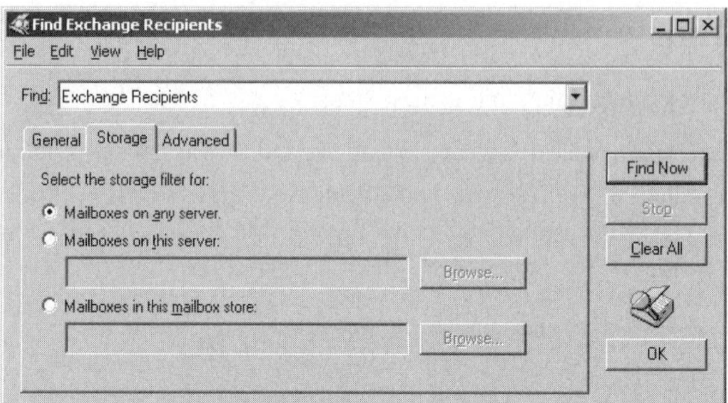

Figure 36-29. Choose which mailbox stores will be included in the address list.

7 Click the Advanced tab (see Figure 36-30), click Field, and choose a field that you want to use as a search condition for the address list. For example, choose Contact, Department if you are building an address list for a particular department.

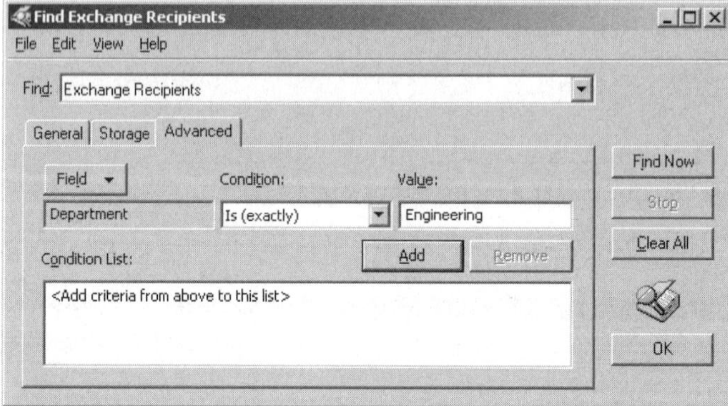

Figure 36-30. Choose the conditions that will define the address list.

8 In the Condition drop-down list, choose a condition, such as Starts With or Is (Exactly), that specifies the logic for the condition.

9 Click in the Value field and type the text for the condition, such as the department name.

10 Click Add, then repeat steps 7 through 9 to add other conditions as needed. When you have specified all the necessary conditions for the address list, click OK.

11 Click Finish to create the address list.

12 Right-click the address list you just created and choose Properties, then click Preview to open the Address List Preview dialog box to test the address list. Close the dialog box and the properties for the address list when you're satisfied with the results.

If a custom address list that you have created contains addresses to which only some of your users should have access, you can configure permissions on the address lists to control the ability to view them. Right-click the address list and choose Properties, then click the Security tab. Add and remove permissions as necessary, granting Read permission (which also grants other permissions automatically) to those groups who need access. Remove permissions to deny access to other groups as needed.

Creating Distribution Lists

You create distribution lists in Exchange 2000 Server and Exchange Server 2003 by assigning e-mail addresses to security groups or by creating special groups called *distribution groups* that aren't used for security purposes. The easiest way to establish e-mail distribution to a group of users is to assign an e-mail address to a security group. It's preferable to assign the e-mail address to a universal group because the address will then be effective across the entire organization; global and local groups, in contrast, are limited in scope. It is possible, however, to assign addresses to global and local groups, and this might even be advantageous if you have only one domain or if you want to limit the scope of the distribution list.

> **Note** There are some significant replication issues to consider if you are using universal groups and are not using Windows Server 2003 in native mode. Take replication into account when you are deciding whether to use universal groups. See *Microsoft Exchange Server 2003 Administrator's Companion* (Microsoft Press, 2003) for more details.

To create a distribution list by assigning an e-mail address to a security group, follow these steps:

1. Open the Active Directory Users And Computers console and locate the group to which you want to assign an address.
2. Right-click the group and choose Exchange Tasks to start the ExchangeTask Wizard.
3. On the Available Tasks page (see Figure 36-31), select Establish An E-Mail Address and click Next.

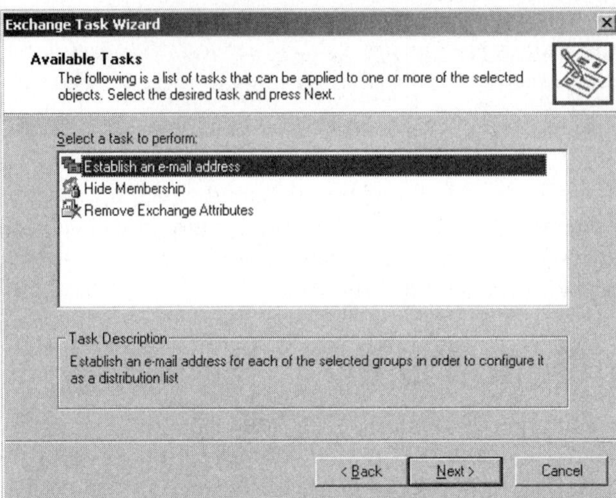

Figure 36-31. Select from the list of available Exchange tasks.

4 Assign an alias to the group and select the Associated Administrative Group in which the group will reside, as shown in Figure 36-32.

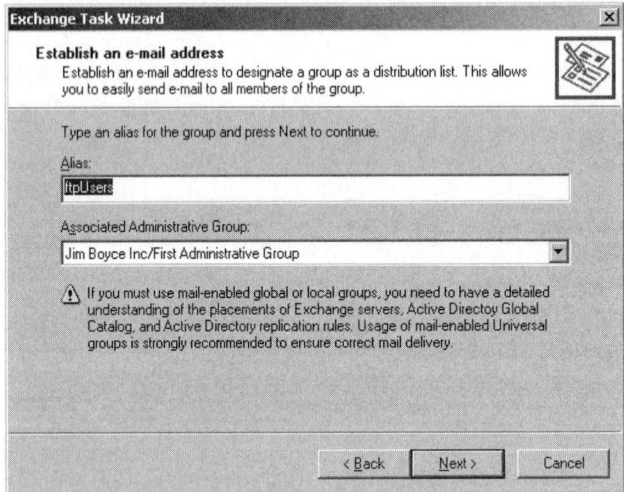

Figure 36-32. You must assign an alias to the group.

5 Click Next. The last page in the wizard displays a task summary showing the results of the operation. The distribution group should now appear in the GAL, and you should be able to send mail to it.

Troubleshooting

You can't create universal security groups

When you install Windows 2000 Server, one of the decisions you must make is whether domain controllers need to support Windows NT servers and domain controllers. If you do have Windows NT servers and domains that access applications within the Windows 2000 domain, your Windows 2000 domains must operate in *mixed mode*.

You can't create universal security groups in a mixed mode domain, however. Instead, you must change your domains to *native mode*, which supports only Windows 2000 domain authentication. This means you must upgrade your existing Windows NT domains to Windows 2000 and Active Directory.

The second method of configuring mail distribution is through a distribution group. A distribution group offers advantages over a distribution list because you can assign an owner to the group who has the ability to control group membership.

To create a new distribution group, follow these steps:

1. Navigate to the Users container in the left pane of the Active Directory Users And Computers console, right-click the Users container, and then choose New, Group.
2. Specify the group name and select Distribution in the Group Type box (see Figure 36-33). You can set the Group Scope option to Domain Local, Global, or Universal, but universal distribution groups are preferable because they're more tolerant of the architecture of large Active Directory implementations. You can have problems with mail delivery if you use local or global groups and the Active Directory infrastructure isn't distributed properly.

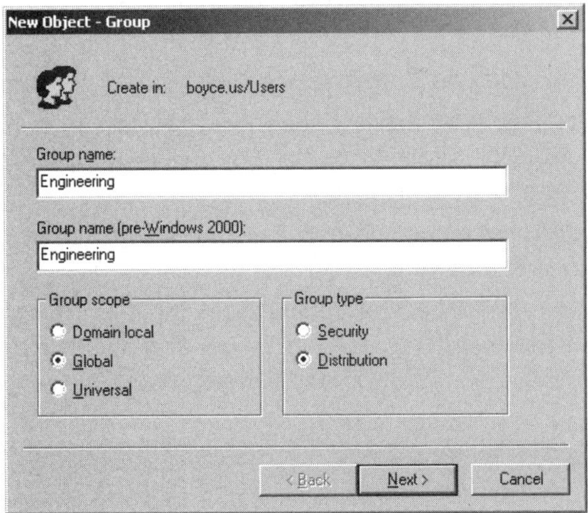

Figure 36-33. You must specify the new group's name, scope, and type.

3. Specify the group's Exchange alias and the Administrative Group where it will reside, as shown in Figure 36-34.

Figure 36-34. You must specify an Exchange alias for the new group.

4. A summary window displays the configuration options you have chosen. Click Finish to create the group. The group should now appear in the GAL and be able to accept e-mail.

Next it's time to populate the group with users. You can delegate the authority for populating a group and controlling group membership to a user. This eases the strain on administrators because they don't have to add and remove users every time a change occurs.

To populate a group with users, follow these steps:

1. Open the Active Directory Users And Computers console and locate the distribution group.
2. Right-click the group, choose Properties, and then click the Managed By tab.
3. Click Change, and then select the user who will manage the group and click OK. Click OK again to close the Properties dialog box. The user assigned as the manager can now open Outlook and the address book.
4. Right-click the distribution group and choose Properties. The Properties dialog box shows the members of the group.
5. Click Modify Members. In the Distribution List Membership dialog box, you can change the group membership (see Figure 36-35). From this dialog box, you can add members, remove members, and view their properties.

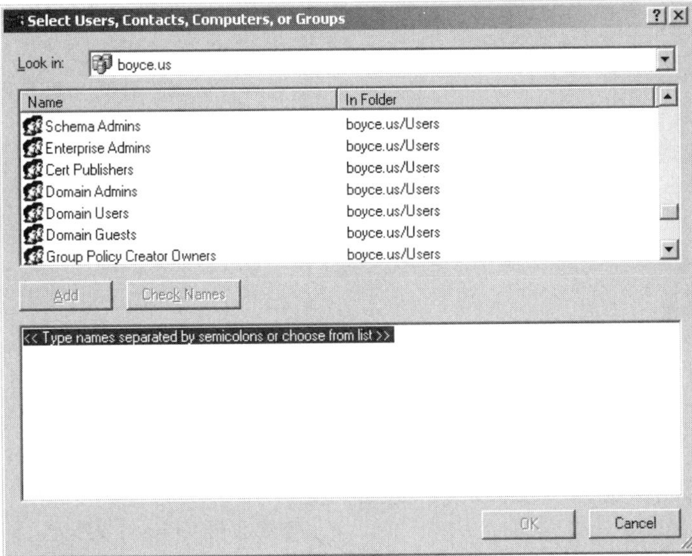

Figure 36-35. Use this dialog box to change the membership of the group.

Creating Public Folders

Public folders are useful for sharing information and collaboration in Exchange Server and Outlook. They provide a central place to store information, such as tasks for an entire group. You can use Exchange System Manager to create public folders, but they're easier to create using Outlook. An administrator must create public folders, unless the permissions on the Public Folders container in Exchange System Manager have been changed.

Follow these steps to create a public folder:

1. Open the folder list in Outlook.
2. Navigate to Public Folders, All Public Folders.
3. Right-click All Public Folders and choose New Folder.
4. Give the new folder a name and assign it a type, as shown in Figure 36-36.
5. Click OK to create the new folder.

Figure 36-36. Assign a name and a type to a new public folder.

The new folder should now be accessible to everyone. By default, everyone is assigned Author permission. If you want to restrict access, you can change the permissions for the folder. To do so, right-click the newly created folder, choose Properties, and then click the Permissions tab. You can assign permissions to the users who require them, but if you assign owner permission to users, they will be able to delete the folder and change its permissions.

For detailed information about creating and managing public folders, see "Setting Up Public Folders," page 943.

Chapter 37

Working Offline and Remotely

Microsoft Office Outlook 2003 provides several features that allow you to work offline (while you are not connected to your mail server) as well as from a remote location. Using the offline feature and Outlook's offline storage, which contains copies of all the folders and items in your Microsoft Exchange Server mailbox, you can work with contacts, messages, and other items stored in your mailbox without being connected to the server (except to perform periodic synchronizations). You can create and delete items, add folders, and make other changes while offline; Outlook synchronizes those changes the next time you connect to the server and perform a send/receive operation.

The primary feature in Outlook that supports remote use is remote mail, which lets you process message headers without downloading the message bodies. You can preview message headers, delete messages from the server without downloading them, and perform other selective processing. You can perform similar tasks with POP3, IMAP, and HTTP accounts, but only Exchange Server accounts can take advantage of the filters and other options provided through send/receive groups.

> **Note** This chapter focuses on the offline and remote features in Outlook used in conjunction with Exchange Server. If you are looking for ways to work offline and remotely using other types of e-mail servers and accounts, see Chapter 11, "Processing Messages Selectively."

Offline vs. Remote

Offline use and remote use are two separate issues in Outlook. When you work offline, your computer is not connected to the Exchange Server. This usually means you're working on a computer that uses a dial-up connection to the server or on a portable computer that you connect to the server through a docking station or a wireless access point on the local area network (LAN). You can be working offline even while your computer is connected to the LAN when the Exchange Server is down for maintenance.

You can perform most of the same functions offline that you perform when you're connected to the server. You can create messages, contacts, and other Outlook items, schedule meetings, and carry out other common Outlook tasks. The items you create and the changes you make to your folders and their contents, however, are made to the offline store, rather than to your Exchange Server mailbox store. When you reconnect to the server, Outlook synchronizes the offline store with the mailbox store. Any items that arrived in the mailbox while you were working offline are added to your offline store when Outlook performs the synchronization. This behavior is the same whether you use Cached Exchange Mode and work from a locally cached copy of your mailbox, or simply add an offline store (OST) file to your profile—the main difference is in how Outlook synchronizes the online and offline mailboxes.

In contrast, working remotely generally means working with Outlook from a location other than the LAN on which the Exchange Server is located. For example, you might dial in to your LAN with a modem, connect to it through the Internet, or even connect through a demand-dial connection between two offices. Whatever your location, you can be working either offline or online when you work remotely. The only consideration is whether or not you are connected to the server. If you are not connected to the server, you are working offline and remotely. If you are connected to the server, you are simply working remotely.

With Outlook's remote mail feature, you can read message headers without downloading the message itself. Remote mail is useful when you receive a very large message in your mailbox and don't want to download it, when your mailbox contains a corrupted message that is preventing you from downloading other messages, or when your mailbox contains a message infected by a worm or virus. You can connect with remote mail, delete the message without reading or downloading it, and continue processing the other messages normally.

Establishing a Remote LAN Connection

To work remotely, you need to establish a remote connection to the server. How you accomplish this depends on the connection options available on your LAN and how the network administrator configured the LAN. The following are the most common methods for establishing a remote LAN connection:

- **Dial up to a Remote Access Services server on the LAN** In this scenario, the LAN includes a Remote Access Services (RAS) server that allows clients to dial in to the network using a modem or other device (such as an Integrated Services Digital Network [ISDN] connection). The RAS server could be the Exchange Server or another server on the network, depending on the size of the organization and the load on the Exchange Server. Depending on the configuration of the RAS server, dial-up clients might have access to the network or only to the Exchange Server.
- **Connect through a virtual private network connection from the Internet** If your Exchange Server is connected to the Internet and your LAN includes a virtual private network (VPN) server, one of the best options for retrieving e-mail messages is to create a VPN connection to the LAN and then connect to the Exchange Server. A VPN server allows clients to establish secure connections to the network through a public network such as the Internet.
- **Use a demand-dial connection between two networks** If you have two or more offices, those offices might connect using a demand-dial connection. The connection might take place over a standard dial-up line or use ISDN or another communication

method. The demand-dial interface allows the two routers that connect the offices to establish the connection when a client requests it, such as when you connect to synchronize your Outlook data.

- **Use HTTP to connect to the server** Outlook 2003 adds support for HTTP as a communications protocol when used with Exchange Server 2003, enabling you to connect to your Exchange Server remotely (such as from the Internet) without using a VPN connection.

> **Note** You can connect to an Exchange Server through the Internet without configuring Outlook 2003 to use HTTP. However, doing so requires that you open several ports on the firewall that, for security reasons, really should not be opened. For that reason, I don't recommend or explain this method in this chapter.

Using Dial-Up and VPN Servers

If your network includes a dial-up server, you need to create a dial-up connection to the server to access your Exchange Server mailbox remotely. The process of setting up a dial-up connection is much the same regardless of the operating system you use on your client computer, although some minor differences do exist. Creating a connection to a network dial-up server is much the same as creating a connection to the Internet.

You can use Microsoft Windows NT Server, Microsoft Windows 2000 Server, or Microsoft Windows Server 2003 to provide dial-up access to the LAN as well as VPN connectivity. All three platforms include RAS and VPN server features and support multiple concurrent connections. You can also use Microsoft Windows NT Workstation, Microsoft Windows 2000 Professional, or Microsoft Windows XP Professional as your dial-up server, but they support only one connection at a time. Microsoft Windows 95 and Microsoft Windows 98 both include dial-up server capability, but they allow you to connect only to the dial-up computer and do not provide the pass-through access to the network that Windows NT and Windows 2000 provide. For example, you can't dial in to a Windows 9*x* dial-up server and through that connection gain access to servers or other computers on the dial-up computer's LAN. You can access resources only on the Windows 9*x* dial-up computer.

> **Tip** **Don't compromise your network's security**
> If your network doesn't currently include an RAS server, but your workstation includes a modem and your computer is running Windows NT Workstation, Windows 2000 Professional, or Windows XP Professional, you might be considering setting up your computer as an RAS server to provide access to your LAN and Exchange Server. Although this is possible, you should avoid doing so, particularly if you are not the network administrator. Adding a dial-up server—even one that accepts only one incoming connection at a time—poses security risks for your computer and the network. It also raises several configuration issues that can be answered only in the context of the entire network, not just your single computer (such as how the server will assign an IP address to clients).

Because this book focuses specifically on Outlook and its integration with Exchange Server, all the details of how to set up an RAS or VPN server aren't covered. You are, however, pointed in the right direction for more information.

Windows NT RRAS

In Windows NT, Routing and Remote Access Service (RRAS) lets you set up a dial-up server and a VPN server. Note that RRAS is not the same as Remote Access Service (RAS), which is included with Windows NT Server.

If you don't have RRAS installed on your computer, you can download it from Microsoft's Web site at *http://www.microsoft.com/NTServer/nts/downloads/winfeatures/rras/rrasdown.asp*. The file for Intel-based systems is Mpri386.exe. To install RRAS, you need Windows NT Server with Service Pack 3 or later. If the RAS service included with Windows NT is currently installed, remove it and restart the server. Then double-click the Mpri386.exe file to start the installation process.

Note If you are running Windows NT Server on an Alpha platform, use the Alpha version of RRAS, available at Microsoft's Web site.

If you intend to set up a VPN server, you first need to add the Point-to-Point Tunneling Protocol (PPTP) to the server. To do so, right-click Network Neighborhood and choose Properties. Click the Protocols tab and click Add. Select Point-to-Point Tunneling Protocol, and click OK to add the PPTP protocol.

Then, whether you're setting up the server for remote access or a VPN, you must configure the properties for the server on the Services tab of the Network dialog box. Select Routing And Remote Access Service and click Properties to start the configuration process. RRAS adds a management tool to the Administrative Tools folder so that you can manage RRAS.

You also need to configure the properties for each user to allow or deny dial-up access. By default, all users are denied dial-up access. Open User Manager from the Administrative Tools folder on the Start menu, open the user's account, and click Dialin to configure the dial-in permission for the user. Repeat the process for any other users to whom you want to grant dial-up access.

Windows 2000 and Windows 2003 RRAS

When you install Windows 2000 or Windows 2003, Setup installs Routing and Remote Access Service automatically, so you don't need to add it. However, you do need to enable and configure the service.

Note This section explains the steps for enabling and configuring RRAS on a Windows 2000 Server. The process is very similar on Windows Server 2003.

To do so, follow these steps:

1. Choose Start, Programs, Administrative Tools, Routing And Remote Access to open the RRAS console.
2. In the console, expand the branch in the left pane to locate the server, right-click the server, and choose Configure And Enable Routing And Remote Access to start the Routing And Remote Access Server Setup Wizard.
3. On the wizard page, specify the type of RRAS server you want to configure, either Remote Access Server or Virtual Private Network (see Figure 37-1).

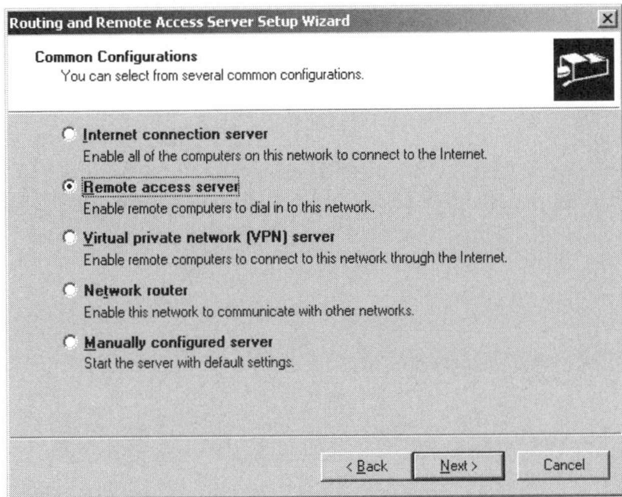

Figure 37-1. Select the type of RRAS server you want to configure.

4. Click Next and follow the wizard's prompts to configure the server. The wizard prompts you for the following information:
   - **Protocols** Specify the protocols to be supported, which must already be installed on the RRAS server. All installed protocols are enabled for RRAS by default, but you can disable specific protocols after the wizard finishes.
   - **Network interface** The wizard prompts for the network interface to assign to remote clients, which determines where the addresses and other access properties come from. If addresses will be allocated through Dynamic Host Configuration Protocol (DHCP) in a multihomed server (one with multiple network interfaces), select the network interface where the DHCP server is located.
   - **IP address assignment** You can assign addresses through DHCP (see the preceding option) or from a static address pool. If you choose a static pool, the wizard prompts you for the range of addresses to use.
   - **Remote Authentication Dial-In User Service (RADIUS)** You can configure the RRAS server to use RADIUS for authentication and accounting. You specify the IP address or host name for the primary and alternate RADIUS servers, along with the RADIUS shared secret, which is essentially a password the RRAS

server uses to authenticate its right to access the RADIUS servers. Windows 2000 includes a RADIUS server called Internet Authentication Service (IAS) that you can use for RRAS and other applications requiring RADIUS authentication. You can also use any other RADIUS server.

5 Click Finish to initiate the configuration process.

Tip **Configure RRAS for multiple functions**
Although the wizard prompts you to select one type of RRAS server, you can configure the server to perform one or more of the listed functions (such as remote access and VPN). Configure the server using the wizard, and then configure the other properties through the RRAS console. For example, you might configure the server for remote access and then add VPN ports to allow the server to function as a remote access and a VPN server.

After you configure RRAS and start the service, you can manage it through the RRAS console, shown in Figure 37-2. Initially, you should focus on three areas of the console. The Ports node lets you configure dial-up ports, including adding additional VPN ports and modems. Use the Remote Access Clients node to view connected clients and, if needed, disconnect clients. Use the Remote Access Policies branch to create the remote access policies that you want to apply for your dial-up users.

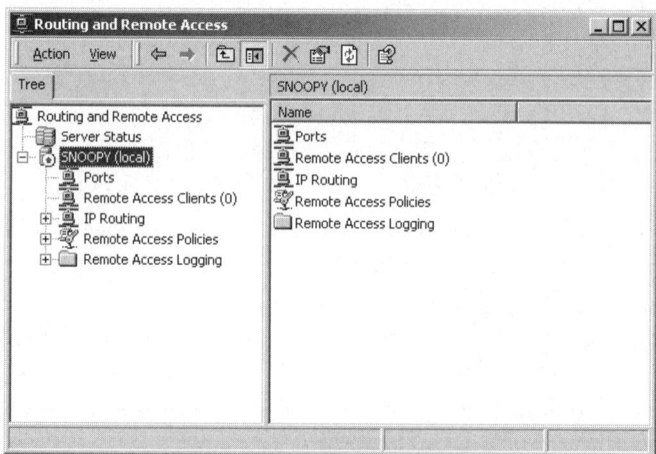

Figure 37-2. Use the RRAS console to manage your RRAS server.

At a minimum, you need to modify the Allow Access If Dial-In Permission Is Enabled policy so that users with dial-in permission in their accounts or in their group policy can connect. The policy is configured to deny access by default. To change the policy, double-click it to open its Properties dialog box (see Figure 37-3). Select Grant Remote Access Permission and click OK.

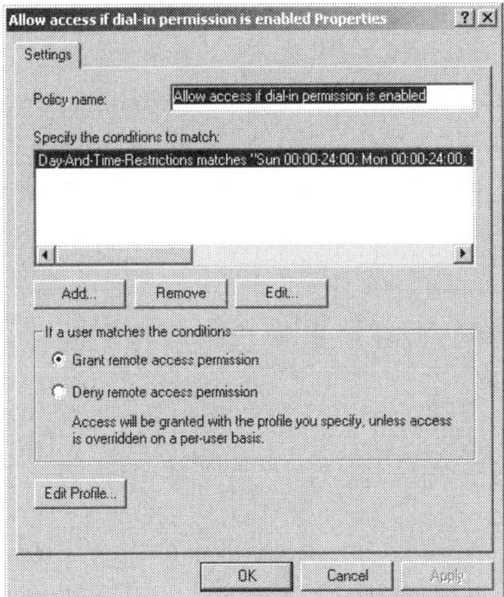

Figure 37-3. Configure the default remote access policy to allow access or create additional policies as needed.

Using HTTP to Connect

Using HTTP as the communications protocol for your Exchange Server is a very useful remote access method that eliminates the need for you to run VPN software on your client computer. It also eliminates the need for the network administrator to support those VPN connections. Most networks already have port 80 open for HTTP and port 443 open for secure HTTP (HTTPS) through Secure Sockets Layer (SSL), so providing HTTP-based access to Exchange Server only requires some setup on the Exchange Server and configuring Outlook 2003 to use HTTP.

Note HTTP-based access to Exchange Server requires Exchange Server 2003 and Outlook 2003.

Chapter 34, "Configuring the Exchange Server Client," explains how to configure the Exchange Server client for Outlook, including setting up the account to use HTTP (page 861) and configuring the server, so that information isn't repeated here. Beyond those steps, there is really nothing else to do to start using HTTP to access your mailbox. However, here is some advice:

- **Use Cached Exchange Mode and synchronize from the LAN at least once** To reduce the load on the server and the amount of bandwidth you will use connecting to the server, consider using Cached Exchange Mode, which creates a locally cached copy of your mailbox on your computer. Before connecting remotely, connect to the server on your LAN and allow Outlook to synchronize the cache with your mailbox. By synchronizing from the LAN rather than a remote connection, you will likely decrease the amount of time required to complete the synchronization.

- **Use RPC and TCP/IP when connected locally to the network** The default settings for using HTTP in Outlook 2003 to connect to your Exchange Server cause Outlook to attempt a connection with RPC over TCP/IP for a fast connection before it attempts to use HTTP. Leave this setting at its default to provide better performance when you connect to the server from your LAN. Change this setting only if your Exchange Server requires an HTTP connection to the server.

Working Offline with Outlook and Exchange Server

There are a few specific issues and settings you need to consider when working with Outlook offline. This section explains how to configure Outlook's startup mode and offline folders and how to use an offline address book.

Configuring Startup Options

When you start Outlook, it attempts by default to determine the online or offline status of the server. If the server is unavailable and Outlook is configured with an OST file, Outlook starts in offline mode and uses the offline folder specified in your profile for displaying existing items and storing new items (such as e-mail messages) before synchronizing with Exchange Server. With Cached Exchange Mode enabled, Outlook automatically uses the local cache (stored in an OST file) and attempts to synchronize the cached copy with your Exchange Server mailbox if a server connection is available. If you've configured autodial in your operating system, Outlook dials the connection to the Internet service provider (ISP) or RAS server. However, you might want to exercise more control over Outlook's startup mode and when it connects. For example, you might prefer to have Outlook start in offline mode so that you can compose messages or perform other tasks before you connect and synchronize with the server.

You configure startup options by setting the properties for the Exchange Server account in your profile, as outlined here:

1. Right-click the Outlook icon on the Start menu and choose Properties (or double-click the Mail icon in Control Panel).
2. If you don't use multiple profiles, skip to step 3. If you use multiple profiles, click Show Profiles. Select the profile you want to change and then click Properties.
3. Click E-Mail Accounts, select View Or Change Existing E-Mail Accounts, and then click Next.
4. Select the Exchange Server account and then click Change.

5 Click More Settings and then click the General tab (see Figure 37-4.)

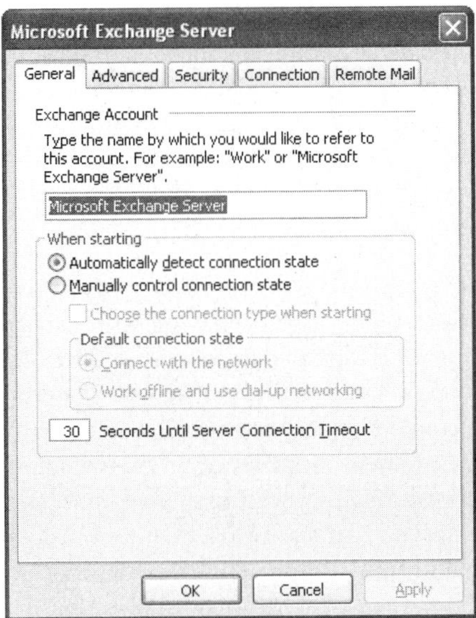

Figure 37-4. Use the General tab to configure startup options for Outlook.

6 Configure the following settings:

- **Automatically Detect Connection State** Outlook detects the connection state at startup and enters online or offline mode accordingly.
- **Manually Control Connection State** You control the connection state when Outlook starts. The following three options work in combination with this option.
- **Choose The Connection Type When Starting** Outlook prompts you to select the connection state when it starts. This allows you to select between online and offline states.
- **Connect With The Network** Connect through your local LAN to Exchange Server. You can use this option if you connect to the Internet through a dedicated connection such as a cable modem or a Digital Subscriber Line (DSL) connection.
- **Work Offline And Use Dial-Up Networking** Start in an offline state and use Dial-Up Networking to connect to Exchange Server. On the Connection tab, specify the dial-up connection you want to use.
- **Seconds Until Server Connection Timeout** Specify the timeout, in seconds, for the server. Outlook attempts a connection for the specified amount of time; if Outlook is unable to establish a connection in the specified period, it times out. You might want to increase this setting if you connect to the Internet through a shared dial-up connection hosted by another computer on your LAN.

Tip **Increase TCP/IP timeout**
You might want to change your TCP/IP timeout values if you change the Seconds Until Server Connection Timeout option in Outlook. Increasing the TCP/IP timeout increases the length of time that your computer waits for TCP/IP connections to succeed before timing out. See the sidebar "Increase TCP Timeout for Shared Connections," page 858, for details on configuring the TCP/IP timeout.

Using Offline Folders

Although you don't have to use offline folders when you work with Exchange Server over a remote connection, you do need a set of offline folders to work offline. If you haven't set up offline folders and can't connect to the remote server, Outlook can't start. One of your first tasks after you create your dial-up connection and configure your Exchange Server account should be to configure a set of offline folders. Note, however, that you don't have to accomplish this step if you configure Outlook to use Cached Exchange Mode for your Exchange Server account—when you enable Cached Exchange Mode, Outlook automatically creates an offline store for you. See Chapter 34 for more information on enabling Cached Exchange Mode.

Note The OST file does not appear as a separate set of folders in Outlook. In effect, Outlook uses it transparently when your computer is offline.

You can associate one set of offline folders with the Exchange Server account in your profile. The offline file has an OST file extension and stores a copy of all the folders and items in your Exchange Server mailbox. Outlook synchronizes the data between the two. For example, suppose that you create an e-mail message and a new contact item while working offline. The message goes in the Outbox folder of the offline store, and the new contact item goes in the Contacts folder of the offline store. When you next connect to the server and perform a synchronization, Outlook moves the message in the local Outbox to the Outbox folder on your Exchange Server, and the message then gets delivered. Outlook also copies the new contact item in your local Contacts folder to the Contacts folder stored on the Exchange Server. Any additional changes, including those at the server (such as new e-mail messages waiting to be delivered), are copied to your local offline folders.

An OST file, like a personal folders (PST) file, contains Outlook folders and items. One difference, however, is that you can have only one OST file, but you can have multiple PST files. Also, Outlook synchronizes the offline store with your Exchange Server automatically but does not provide automatic synchronization for PST files.

For more information on adding PST files to a profile, see "Adding Other Data Stores," page 48.

Follow these steps to configure offline storage with an OST file:

1. If Outlook is running, choose Tools, E-Mail Accounts. Otherwise, right-click the Outlook icon on the Start menu, choose Properties, and then click E-Mail Settings.
2. Select View Or Change Existing E-Mail Accounts and click Next.
3. Select the Exchange Server account and click Change.
4. Click More Settings and then click the Advanced tab.
5. Click Offline Folder File Settings to open the dialog box shown in Figure 37-5.

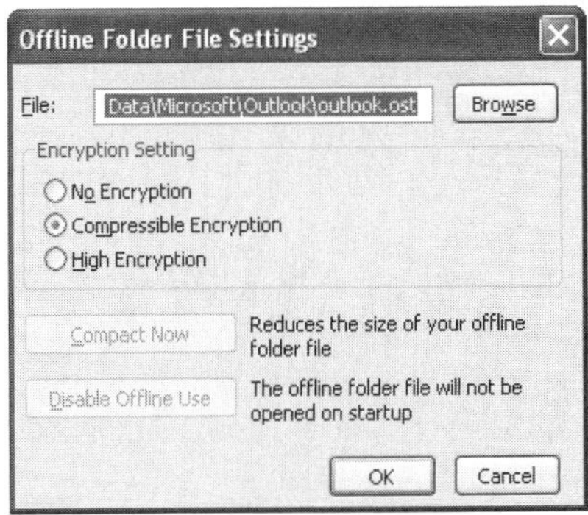

Figure 37-5. Specify the file name and other settings for the OST file.

6. In the File box, specify a path and name for the OST file.
7. Select an encryption setting and click OK.
8. On the Advanced tab, verify that the Enable Offline Use option is selected and click OK.
9. Click Next and then click Finish.

Synchronizing with the Exchange Server Mailbox

After you add an OST file to your profile, you need to synchronize the file with your Exchange Server mailbox at least once before you can work offline.

Follow these steps to synchronize your offline folders:

1. Connect to the remote network where your Exchange Server is located using the Internet, a dial-up connection to a remote access server on the remote LAN, or other means (such as ISDN, cable modem, or DSL). A LAN connection will give you the best performance for the initial synchronization.
2. Open Outlook.
3. Choose Tools, Send/Receive, Microsoft Exchange Server. Outlook then synchronizes with the Exchange Server.

> **Note** If you specified a name for the account other than the default Microsoft Exchange Server, select that account name on the Send/Receive menu. You'll find the account name on the General tab of the account's Properties dialog box.

Synchronizing with Send/Receive Groups

The preceding section explained how to synchronize your offline folders and your Exchange Server mailbox. Sometimes, though, you might not want to synchronize all folders each time you perform a send/receive operation. You can use send/receive groups to define the actions that Outlook takes when sending and receiving. For example, you might want to create a send/receive group that sends only mail waiting in your local Outbox and doesn't retrieve waiting messages from the server.

For a detailed discussion of send/receive groups, see "Controlling Synchronization and Send/Receive Times," page 184.

Using an Offline Address Book

Whether you're composing messages offline or creating tasks to assign to others, chances are good that you want access to your Exchange Server address book so that you can address messages to other users in your organization. If the Global Address List (GAL) doesn't change very often on the server (if, for example, employee turnover at your company is low), you can get by with downloading the offline address book infrequently. Otherwise, you'll need to update the offline address book more often.

> **Tip** **Download additional address lists**
>
> You can download additional address lists from the server if the Exchange Server administrator has created additional address books and given you the necessary permissions to access them. Additional address books give you quick access to addresses that are sorted using different criteria than the GAL uses or access to other addresses not shown in the GAL (such as external contacts). See "Managing Exchange Server Address Lists," page 907, to learn more about creating additional address lists.

To download the address book manually whenever you want an update, follow these steps:

1. Choose Tools, Send/Receive, Download Address Book to open the Offline Address Book dialog box (see Figure 37-6).
2. Select options as needed from the following:
   - **Download Changes Since Last Send/Receive** Download only changes made since the last time you performed a send/receive operation. Clear this check box to download the entire address list.
   - **Full Details** Download all address information, including phone, fax, and office location. You must select this option if you want to send encrypted messages, because you need the users' digital signatures.
   - **No Details** Download only e-mail addresses and no additional address book details.

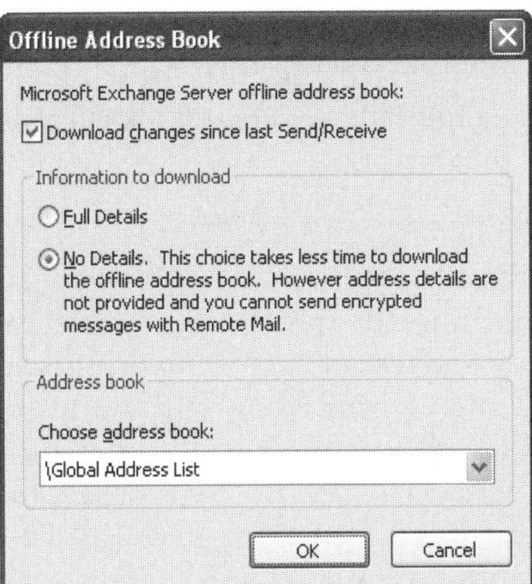

Figure 37-6. Use the Offline Address Book dialog box to specify options for downloading the offline address book.

3 Click OK to download the address book.

In addition to performing manual offline address book updates, you also can configure a send/receive group to download the address book.

Follow these steps to do so:

1 In Outlook, choose Tools, Send/Receive, Send/Receive Settings, Define Send/Receive Groups.
2 Select the send/receive group in which you want to configure the address book download, and then click Edit.
3 On the Accounts bar, select your Exchange Server account (see Figure 37-7).

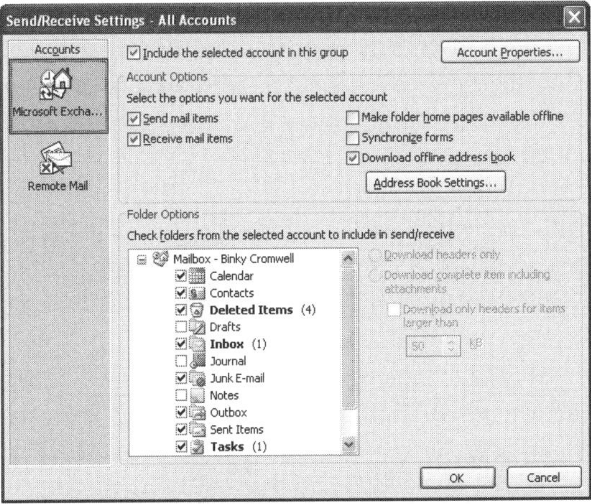

Figure 37-7. You can configure automatic offline address book synchronization.

4. Select the Download Offline Address Book check box, and then click Address Book Settings to open the Offline Address Book dialog box.
5. Configure settings as necessary in the Offline Address Book dialog box (discussed in the preceding set of steps) and then click OK.
6. Click OK to close the Send/Receive Settings dialog box.

Each time you synchronize folders using the send/receive group, Outlook downloads the offline address book according to the settings you specified. You probably won't want to configure this option for the default All Accounts send/receive group unless you have a fast connection to the server and your offline address book changes frequently. One option is to create a send/receive group that downloads only the offline address book and does not process any other folders. However, this is essentially the same as choosing Tools, Send/Receive, Download Address Book. Consider how often you need to download the address book and work that task into your send/receive groups as you see fit.

Using Remote Mail

Outlook's remote mail feature lets you manage your messages without downloading them from the server. With remote mail, you connect to the e-mail server, download the headers for new messages, and disconnect. You can take your time reviewing the message headers to decide which ones you want to download, which ones you want to delete without reading, and which ones can remain on the server for later. Then you can connect again and download the messages you've marked to retrieve, leaving the others on the server or deleting them, depending on how you marked the message headers.

To learn how to work with headers using remote mail, see "Working with Message Headers," page 331.

Remote mail is useful when you have a message with a very large attachment waiting on the server, and you want to retrieve only your most critical messages without spending the time or connect charges to download the attachment. You can connect with remote mail and select the messages for downloading, leaving the one with the large attachment on the server for when you have more time or are back in the office and can download it across the network or through a broadband Internet connection.

> **Note** If you are looking to configure how Outlook handles synchronization with Cached Exchange Mode and Exchange Server 2003—and are not specifically interested in using remote mail—see the section "Configuring Cached Exchange Mode Synchronization," page 938.

Remote mail is also useful when a corrupt message in your mailbox might prevent Outlook from downloading your messages. You can connect with remote mail, delete the problem message without attempting to download it, and then continue working normally.

Note The remote mail feature, strictly defined, works only with Exchange Server accounts; but Outlook also provides features similar to remote mail for POP3, IMAP, and HTTP accounts. For details on performing selective processing for other types of accounts, see "Understanding Remote Mail Options," page 329.

Unless you are using Outlook 2003 in combination with Exchange Server 2003, remote mail is available with Exchange Server only when you are working offline. The commands that would otherwise enable you to download headers and work with other remote mail features are unavailable when Outlook is working in online mode. You can use remote mail with any version of Exchange Server—it does not require Exchange Server 2003. However, Outlook behaves differently with remote mail if you are connecting to Exchange Server 2003, as the next section explains.

Using Remote Mail Preview with Exchange Server 2003

Figure 37-8 shows the Inbox of an Exchange 2000 Server mailbox. The icon in the selected message header is different from those of the other messages that have already been downloaded. The icon indicates that the header has been downloaded but the message body has not. Clicking on the header shows a message in the Reading Pane that the message has not yet been downloaded. Outlook does not offer a preview of the message.

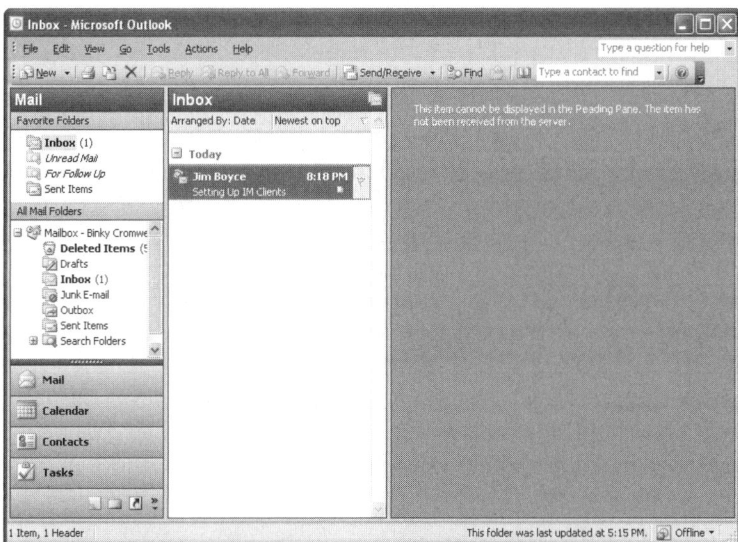

Figure 37-8. Remote mail does not provide a message preview when connecting to Exchange 2000 Server or Exchange Server 5.*x*.

When you connect to an Exchange Server 2003 mailbox, however, Outlook does provide a message preview, as shown in Figure 37-9. Outlook displays the first few lines of the message in the Reading Pane and adds a Mark This Message For Download button in the Reading

Pane. You can click the button to mark the message for download. The button changes to Unmark This Message For Download when you mark the message.

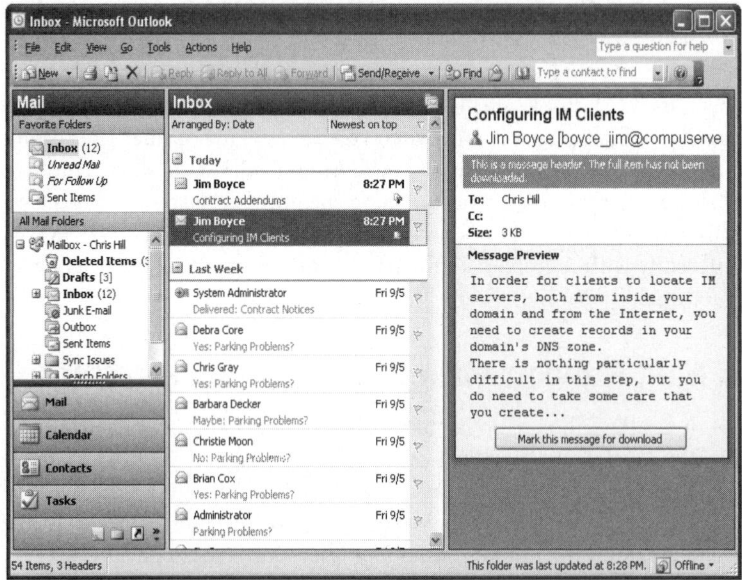

Figure 37-9. Outlook 2003 provides a preview of a message with remote mail when connected to an Exchange Server 2003 mailbox.

Remote Mail vs. Offline Folders

Remote mail and offline folders fulfill two different functions. Offline folders let you synchronize your local offline folders with your Exchange Server mailbox, allowing you to work offline. Remote mail lets you manage headers remotely without downloading their associated messages. You'll probably use both at one time or another. In fact, to use remote mail, you must either use an offline folder (OST with or without Cached Exchange Mode) or configure your mail for delivery to a set of personal folders.

Note You can achieve much the same effect with send/receive groups that you can with remote mail. For example, you can configure a send/receive group to download only message headers and not message bodies and then perform a send/receive operation on that group to retrieve the message headers. To accomplish this selective downloading for an Exchange Server account with send/receive groups, however, you must be connecting to an Exchange Server 2003 account. Outlook 2003 by default downloads full items for Exchange Server 5.5 and Exchange 2000 Server accounts.

Configuring Your System for Remote Mail

You must configure your Exchange Server account for offline use and add an offline folder file to your configuration, or you must add a PST file to the configuration and configure it as the delivery store for mail. In most cases, you probably don't want to use a PST file to store your Exchange Server messages, preferring to leave them on the Exchange Server. For Exchange Server accounts, therefore, an offline file, either with or without Cached Exchange Mode, is the way to go.

To learn how to enable Cached Exchange Mode as an alternative to the method described here, see "Outlook as an Exchange Server Client," page 855.

Follow these steps to configure your Exchange Server account for offline use without Cached Exchange Mode:

1. If Outlook is running, choose Tools, E-Mail Accounts. Otherwise, right-click the Outlook icon on the Start menu, choose Properties, and then click E-Mail Accounts.
2. Select View Or Change Existing E-Mail Accounts and click Next.
3. Select the Exchange Server account and click Change.
4. Click More Settings and then click the Advanced tab.
5. Click Offline Folder File Settings to open the Offline Folder File Settings dialog box (shown earlier in Figure 37-5 on page 927).
6. Accept the default file path and name, type a new one, or click Browse to locate and select a file.
7. Select one of the following options and then click OK:
   - **No Encryption** Slightly faster performance but less security.
   - **Compressible Encryption** Moderate performance and increased security with the ability to compress the data file for storage efficiency.
   - **High Encryption** Trades performance for optimum security. The OST file cannot be compressed, but you gain better encryption for increased security.
8. If you did not specify an existing OST file, Outlook prompts you to create one. Click Yes to create the file.
9. Make sure the Enable Offline Use option is selected, and then click OK to close the Microsoft Exchange Server dialog box.
10. Click Next and then click Finish.

Before you can work offline, you must first synchronize the OST file with your Exchange Server mailbox. Generally, you can do so by simply connecting to Exchange Server and performing a full send/receive operation.

Downloading Message Headers

When processing messages selectively, you first download the message headers and then decide what actions you want to perform with each message, based on its header.

Downloading message headers for an account is easy: In Outlook, open the Inbox and choose Tools, Send/Receive, Download Headers In This Folder. Or, if you have more than one account, you can choose Tools, Send/Receive, Microsoft Exchange Server Only, Download Inbox Headers.

Outlook then performs a send/receive operation but downloads only headers from the specified folder. If you are working from a dial-up connection and want to save on connect charges, you can disconnect the dial-up connection and review your messages offline to decide what action to take on each.

The icon for a message header with an associated message that has not been downloaded is the standard envelope icon, just as it is for downloaded but unread messages. However, Outlook also includes an icon in the Header Status column of the Inbox to indicate that the message has not yet been downloaded. Figure 37-9 shows examples of the icons that Outlook uses to indicate downloaded headers and messages marked for download.

You'll find the commands for marking and unmarking messages in the Send/Receive menu (choose Tools, Send/Receive). When you have finished marking messages as needed, choose Tools, Send/Receive, Process Marked Headers In This Folder to process the headers only in the current folder, or choose Process All Marked Headers to process marked headers in all folders.

If you need more details on working with message headers, see "Working with Message Headers," page 331.

Forcing Remote Mail for a LAN Connection

As I indicated earlier in this chapter, remote mail is available only when Outlook is working offline, unless you are using Outlook 2003 in combination with Exchange Server 2003. In most situations you won't need to use remote mail when working with a LAN connection, but remote mail can still be useful with a LAN. For example, you might have a corrupted message in your Inbox that you would like to delete.

To force remote mail for a LAN connection when you are using Cached Exchange Mode and Exchange 2000 Server or earlier, simply place Outlook in an offline state. Click the Online indicator in the status bar and choose Work Offline to place Outlook in offline mode. When you are finished using remote mail and want to place Outlook in online mode again, click the Disconnected indicator in the status bar and choose Work Offline again to return to online status.

Follow these steps if you want Outlook to start up in an offline state:

1. Open the properties for the Exchange Server account in your profile and click More Settings.
2. On the General tab, choose Manually Control Connection State, then choose the Work Offline And Use Dial-Up Networking option.

3 Click OK, Next, Finish, OK, and then restart Outlook, which will start in offline mode with remote mail features available.

Processing Headers with Send/Receive Groups

Rather than working with message headers manually, as explained in this chapter, you might prefer to process them automatically by configuring remote mail options in a send/receive group. This section explains how.

Remote mail provides options that you can use to control how it handles the downloading of items, among other processes. Although you can add remote mail to any send/receive group, it's good practice to set up a separate send/receive group just for remote mail. That way, you can process messages through remote mail by simply synchronizing folders with that particular send/receive group.

The way you configure header processing for Exchange Server accounts depends on whether the mailbox is hosted on Exchange Server 2003.

Configuring Header Processing for Exchange 2000 or Earlier Versions

To configure message processing options for a mailbox hosted on Exchange 2000 Server or an earlier version, follow these steps:

1 Choose Tools, Send/Receive, Send/Receive Settings, Define Send/Receive Groups to open the Send/Receive Groups dialog box (see Figure 37-10).

For more information on controlling message processing with send/receive groups, see "Controlling Synchronization and Send/Receive Times," page 184.

2 Click New.

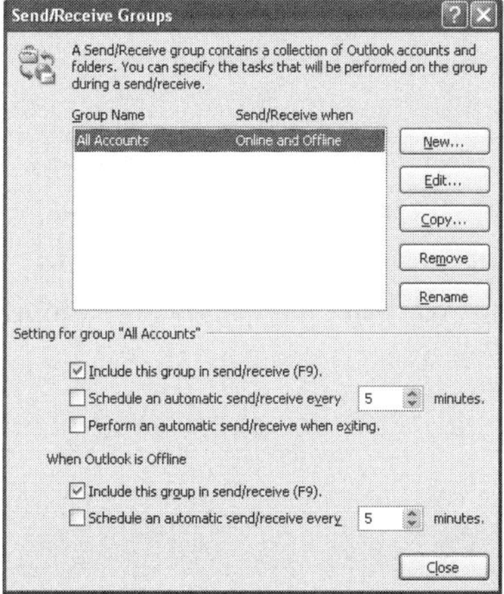

Figure 37-10. Use the Send/Receive Groups dialog box to configure how Outlook processes your accounts.

3 Specify Remote Mail as the name of the new send/receive group. Outlook opens the Send/Receive Settings dialog box for the group (see Figure 37-11).

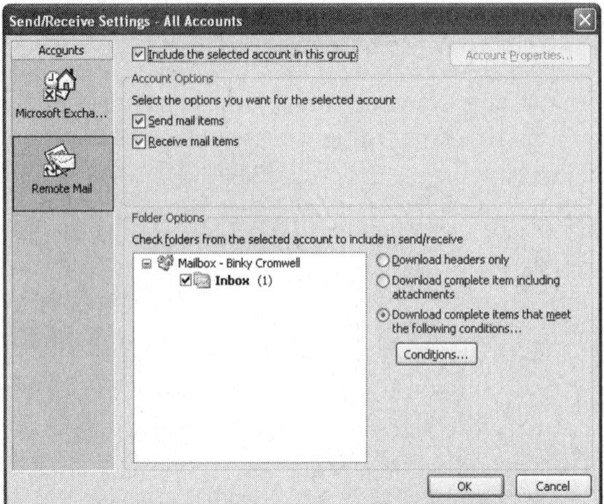

Figure 37-11. Use the Send/Receive Settings dialog box to configure options for Remote Mail.

4 On the Accounts bar, select Remote Mail.

5 Select the Include The Selected Account In This Group to activate the options in the dialog box for the account. The Remote Mail account is the only account that should be active for this send/receive group. If others are active, select them on the Accounts bar and clear the Include The Selected Account In This Group check box. Inactive accounts have a red X on their icons.

6 Configure the following settings:

- **Send Mail Items** Outlook sends outgoing messages when you process this send/receive group.
- **Receive Mail Items** Outlook retrieves messages when processing this send/receive group. See the following settings for information on how to restrict what Outlook retrieves.
- **Download Headers Only** Download message headers only.
- **Download Complete Item Including Attachments** Download headers, message bodies, and attachments (a standard receive operation).
- **Download Complete Items That Meet The Following Conditions** Selectively process messages using filters, as explained next, in step 7.

7 If you selected the last option, click Conditions to open the Filter dialog box (see Figure 37-12), which allows you to set up conditions that messages must meet to be processed. Click Advanced to open the Advanced dialog box (see Figure 37-13). Using both dialog boxes, you can define filters that download messages based on size, sender, recipient, attachments, importance, and many other conditions. Configure the options as needed and close the dialog boxes.

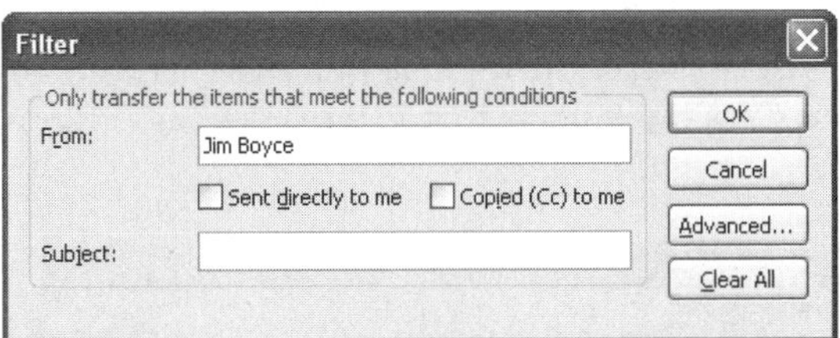

Figure 37-12. You can specify simple filters to control the downloading of messages.

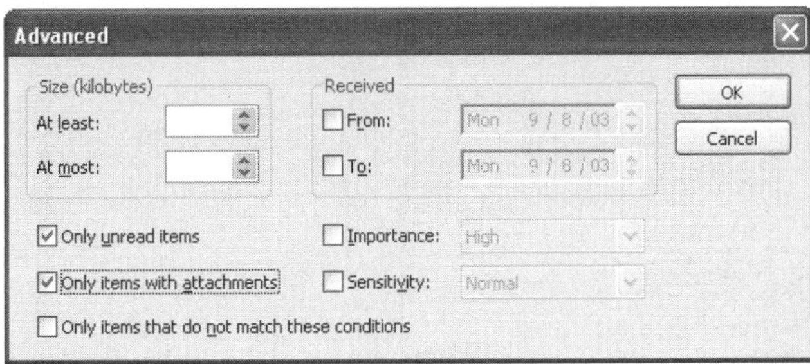

Figure 37-13. You can also create more advanced, complex filters for downloading messages.

8 Click OK to close the Advanced dialog box, and click Close to close the Send/Receive Settings dialog box.

Configuring Header Processing for Exchange Server 2003

When you configure a send/receive group for Exchange Server 2003, the options are somewhat different but the process is similar:

1 Choose Tools, Send/Receive, Send/Receive Settings, Define Send/Receive Groups.

2 Create a new group or edit an existing one.

3 In the Send/Receive Settings dialog box for the group, select the Exchange Server account in the Accounts list.

4 Click a folder in the folder list, then configure the options for the folder, choosing between Download Headers Only, Download Complete Item Including Attachment, or Download Only Headers For Items Larger Than. See the previous section for an explanation of these options.

Configuring Cached Exchange Mode Synchronization

In most respects, most of the remote mail features are the same regardless of the remote Exchange Server type. When you are using Outlook 2003 with Exchange Server 2003 and Cached Exchange Mode, however, you can control the way Outlook downloads messages or headers without placing Outlook in offline mode. Outlook makes additional commands available from the status bar when you are working with an Exchange Server 2003 account in Cached Exchange Mode. Click the Outlook icon in the status bar to access the commands shown in Figure 37-14.

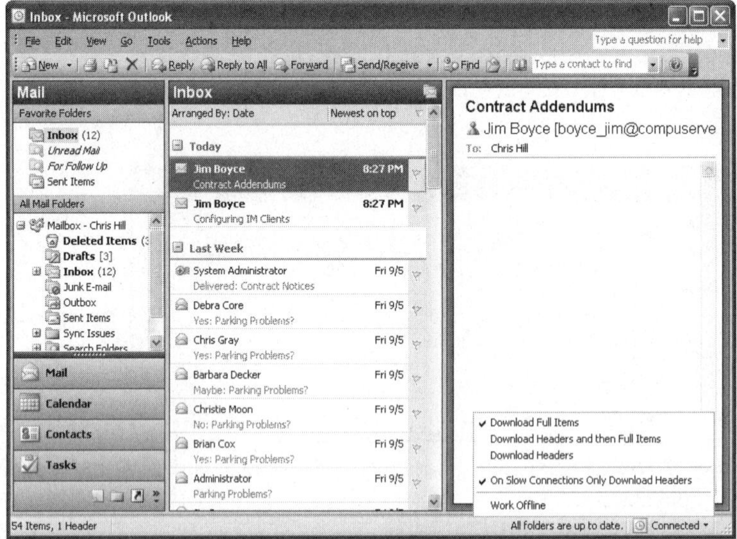

Figure 37-14. Control synchronization settings for Cached Exchange Mode from the status bar.

The commands available by clicking the status bar include the following:

- **Download Full Items** Download headers, bodies, and attachments when synchronizing the local cache with the remote mailbox.
- **Download Headers And Then Full Items** Download headers first, and after all headers are downloaded, begin downloading message bodies and attachments.
- **Download Headers** Download only headers without message bodies or attachments.
- **On Slow Connections Only Download Headers** If Outlook detects a slow connection, only download headers. If this option is not selected, Outlook uses the setting you specified (see the previous three options) regardless of the connection speed.
- **Work Offline** Place Outlook in offline mode. Also choose this command when offline to place Outlook in online mode.

Part 8

Collaboration and Mobility

Chapter 38

Sharing Information with Others

Microsoft Office Outlook 2003 has several features that allow you to share data with other users. You can share personal folder files, allow other users to access folders in your Microsoft Exchange Server mailbox, use public folders to post messages and shared files, and use the Network News Transfer Protocol (NNTP) service in Exchange Server to set up a news server for sharing information.

This chapter examines many of these features and explains how to configure and use them to share information with others. The chapter also looks at security features that help you share your data but still protect it, ensuring that other users can access only the data you want them to see.

Sharing Overview

You have several options for sharing data in Outlook. The first is to configure delegate access for a folder, which gives another user—whom you designate as your delegate—access to that folder. When you assign a delegate for a folder, you specify the level of permission the delegate has in the folder, which determines the actions he or she can take with the folder and its items. For example, you might let a delegate view your existing calendar items and create new ones but prevent the delegate from viewing items marked as private. In addition, you can grant the delegate not only access to the folder but also send-on-behalf-of privileges for that folder, which means the delegated user can send messages on your behalf—for example, the delegate could send meeting request messages under your name.

For a detailed explanation of delegation, see Chapter 29, "Delegating Responsibilities to an Assistant."

Another option for sharing data is your ability to grant permissions for a private folder, allowing other users to access the folder contents and perform other actions in the folder. This is similar to assigning delegate access for a folder, except that it does not give the other users send-on-behalf-of privileges for the folder. Depending on the permissions you assign, users can, for example, view items, create new items, or create subfolders.

For information about granting permissions for a folder, see "Granting Access to Folders," page 741.

The third data-sharing option is to use public folders, which are stored on your Exchange Server. As you can with private folders, you can configure permissions for public folders that you create, controlling the actions others can take in the folders. You might use public folders to share documents or other files, post messages for review or comment by your coworkers, share contacts, or share other types of data. You can create public folders by using Outlook, or the Exchange Server administrator can create public folders by using Exchange System Manager.

This chapter focuses on using public folders to share data. The following section explains how to create and configure public folders through Outlook. Later sections of the chapter explain how to use public folders, create a message board, manage public folders, and use the NNTP service to configure a news server.

Sharing a Common PST with the Briefcase

Exchange Server offers several features to enable you to share information with others. If you use Outlook without Exchange Server, however, your options for sharing Outlook data are more limited. You can't simply place a personal folders (PST) file on a network server and have multiple people add it to their profiles. However, you can share a PST if you use the Windows Briefcase to share it.

The Briefcase is a Windows feature that enables you to synchronize a copy of a file with its original. Many people use the Briefcase to synchronize files between their file server and their notebook computer. You can use it to share a single PST with others. The original PST continues to reside on the network server and others make copies of it in their Windows Briefcases. They use the PST from their own Briefcase, synchronizing changes periodically between their Briefcase and the shared network copy. In this way, changes made to the PST by individual users are synchronized into the original, and these changes are then synchronized to everyone else's Briefcase copy when they perform a synchronization.

Note Changes by one user can overwrite the changes of another user when the shared copy is synchronized.

Follow these steps to share a PST with the Briefcase:

1. Close Outlook and copy the PST you want to share to a network location where everyone who needs to use it can access it, or export your own Outlook data to a new PST in that location.
2. Configure permissions on the folder and file to grant read permission to everyone who needs to view the contents, and grant full control for those users who need to be able to update the contents of the PST with their own changes.
3. On a computer where the PST needs to be used, right-click the desktop and choose New, Briefcase to create a new Briefcase. You can rename the Briefcase, for example naming it SharedPST, to help you remember what is stored in it.

4. Open the shared network folder containing the PST and drag it to the Briefcase to create a sync copy.
5. Open Outlook and choose File, Open, Outlook Data File.
6. Navigate to the Briefcase and open the PST file from it.
7. When you need to synchronize changes that you have made, close Outlook and open the Briefcase from the desktop. If there are other files in your Briefcase, click the PST and choose Briefcase, Update Selection. Otherwise, simply choose Briefcase, Update All.

Setting Up Public Folders

Public folders reside on the Exchange Server, where other users can access them. The primary function of public folders is to allow you to share messages, contacts, documents, and other items. Exchange Server also uses public folders to provide the folder structure for newsgroups, in which you can read and post messages. Although you can't set up a news server through Outlook, you can create public folders that function much the way a news server does and that even allow you to moderate the discussion.

When you view the folder list in Outlook, you'll probably see two subfolders listed under the Public Folders branch: Favorites and All Public Folders, shown in Figure 38-1. The Favorites folder, discussed later in this chapter, gives you quick access to public folders you use often. The All Public Folders branch shows the folders available on the server. All Public Folders by default includes only the Internet Newsgroups folder, but other folders will also appear if other users have created them by using Outlook or if the Exchange Server administrator has created them by using Exchange System Manager.

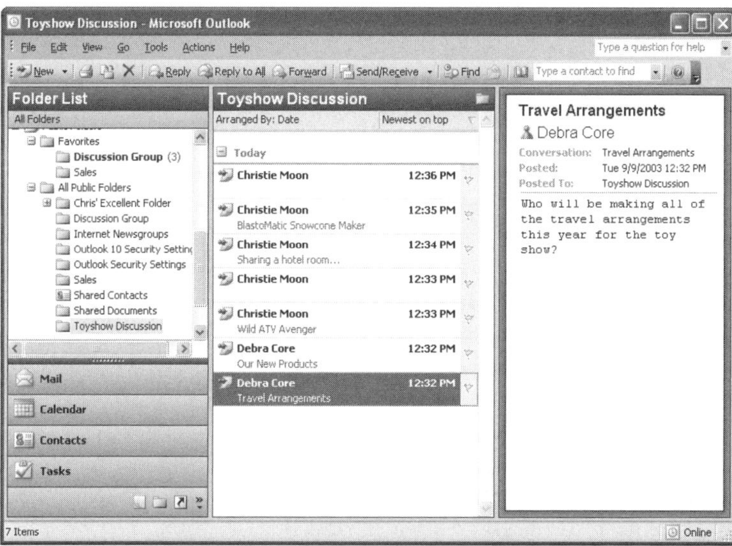

Figure 38-1. Public folders appear in Outlook under the Public Folders branch.

Creating a Public Folder

If you have the necessary permissions on the server, you can use Outlook to create public folders. The Exchange Server administrator configures permissions on the server to allow or deny individuals or groups the ability to create public folders. This section assumes that you've been given the appropriate permissions to create folders.

To learn how to configure permissions on Exchange Server to control users' ability to create public folders in a message store, see "Controlling the Ability to Create Public Folders in Exchange Server 5.5," page 962, or "Controlling the Ability to Create Public Folders in Exchange 2000 Server and Exchange Server 2003," page 971.

Follow these steps to create a public folder:

1. Open Outlook. If the folder list is not currently displayed, click the Folder List button in the Navigation Pane.
2. Expand the Public Folders branch, right-click the folder in which you want to create the new public folder, and choose New Folder to open the Create New Folder dialog box, shown in Figure 38-2.

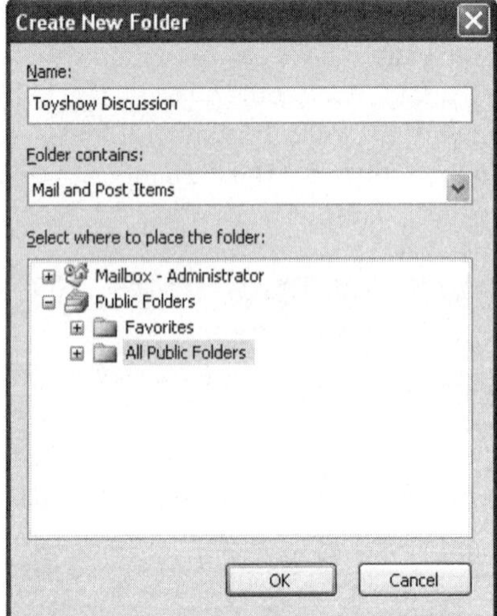

Figure 38-2. You can specify a different location for the new folder in the Create New Folder dialog box.

3. Type a name for the folder in the Name box, and then select the folder type in the Folder Contains drop-down list.
4. The folder type determines the type of items that you can create in the folder. For example, to create a folder for sharing messages, select Mail And Post Items, or select Contact Items to create a shared folder for contacts.
5. To change the location where the folder will be created, select a new parent folder in the Select Where To Place The Folder list. Then click OK to create the folder.

Configuring Folder Properties

After you create a folder, you'll want to configure its properties, including the permissions to control access. To configure a public folder's properties, right-click the folder and choose Properties. The following sections explain the options you can set on each tab of the folder's Properties dialog box.

Setting General Properties

Use the General tab (see Figure 38-3) to specify the folder's name, add a description, specify the default form for posting to the folder, configure Exchange views, and view the size of the folder.

Figure 38-3. Use the General tab to configure basic folder properties.

The General tab includes the following properties:

- **Name** Use the text box at the top of the General tab to specify the name for the public folder. (To rename the folder later on, right-click it in the folder list and choose Rename.)
- **Description** Enter an optional description for the folder in this text box. This description does not appear in Outlook when users browse the public folder list; it does appear if the user opens the Properties dialog box for the folder.
- **When Posting To This Folder, Use** Use this drop-down list to select the form to use for adding new items to the folder. Outlook by default uses a specific form based on the folder type. If you want to use a different form, select Forms in the drop-down list to display the Choose Form dialog box (see Figure 38-4), where you can select the form.

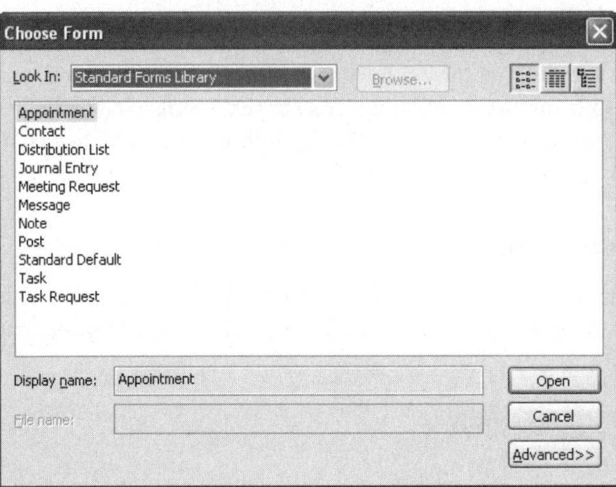

Figure 38-4. Use the Choose Form dialog box to select the form for posting new items to the public folder.

- **Automatically Generate Microsoft Exchange Views** Select this check box if Microsoft Exchange client users also connect to the server and need access to the public folder. You can clear this check box if only Outlook clients connect to the server or require access to the public folder.
- **Folder Size** Click this button to view the current size of the folder (the amount of space used by the folder's contents).

Note The General tab also shows two additional controls for a public folder: Show Number Of Unread Items and Show Total Number Of Items. You can't change these options for a public folder, even if you created the folder and have full control over it. These read-only options appear because Outlook uses the same dialog box for public folders as it does for Outlook folders, where these options can be changed.

Defining a Folder Home Page

Use the Home Page tab of the folder's Properties dialog box to assign a Web page to the folder. Enter the URL for the page in the Address box, and then select the option Show Home Page By Default For This Folder. When the user opens the folder, the specified page will open in the folder window.

Inside Out

Viewing the associated Web page

In Outlook 2002 and 2003, the only way to view the Web page associated with a folder is to set it as the default view on the Home Page tab. In previous versions, you could open a folder to view it normally and then select the Web page from the View menu. The new behavior forces you to either use a Web page for the folder or use the standard view. This can be inconvenient as you can't switch between the two views without changing the properties for the folder, and it can limit the usefulness of assigning a Web page to a folder.

Configuring Administration Properties

The Administration tab (see Figure 38-5) provides several options that let you determine how the folder displays information, specify which users have access to the folder, and affect many other behaviors.

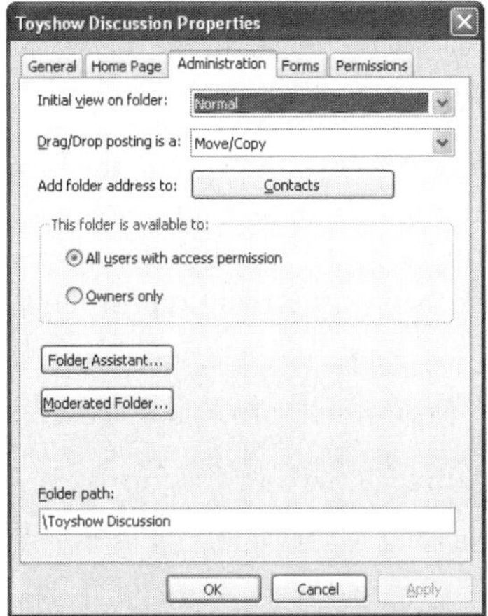

Figure 38-5. Use the Administration tab to control a wide range of options for the folder.

The Administration tab includes the following options:

- **Initial View On Folder** Use this drop-down list to define the way the folder's contents are displayed to the user by default. When the folder is open, the user can change the view by using the View menu.
- **Drag/Drop Posting Is A** This option determines how Outlook handles items that users drag to the folder. If you select Move/Copy, the item takes on the same properties as the original item. A message, for example, appears to be from the person who sent it or created it originally, and the subject remains unchanged. If you select Forward, Outlook modifies the item to indicate that it has been forwarded, and the item's sender is changed to indicate the person who placed the item in the folder.

- **Add Folder Address To** Click this button to add the folder to your Personal Address Book. Then you can easily post messages to the folder by selecting it from the address book.
- **This Folder Is Available To** This group allows you to control which users have access to the folder. Select All Users With Access Permission to allow all users who have the appropriate permissions for the folder to access the folder. Select Owners Only to limit access to only those users who are designated as the folder owners. Select Owners Only whenever you need to make changes to the folder and want to prevent users from posting items to the folder while you're working on it. Those who are not owners receive a message indicating that the folder is currently unavailable if they attempt to access it when the Owners Only option is in effect.
- **Folder Assistant** Click this button to open the Folder Assistant, which allows you to apply rules to the folder. For details, see "Applying Rules to Folders," page 951.
- **Moderated Folder** Click this button to set up a moderated folder. For details, see "Setting Up a Moderated Message Board," page 954.
- **Folder Path** This box specifies the path to the folder. You can change the folder location by entering a different path.

Setting Up Forms

The Forms tab of the folder's Properties dialog box allows you to specify the forms that people can use when posting items to the folder. You might want to limit posting to a specific form. For example, suppose that you're using a public folder to solicit survey responses and you've created a form for the survey. You would probably want to limit postings to only those responders who used the correct survey form.

The following three options on the Forms tab control which forms can be used:

- **Only Forms Listed Above** Select this option to allow only the forms explicitly associated with the folder to be used for posting. These forms are listed in the Forms Associated With This Folder list.
- **Forms Listed Above And The Standard Forms** Select this option to allow the use of Outlook standard forms in addition to the forms in the associated list.
- **Any Form** Select this option to allow the use of any form to post items to the folder.

You can add other forms and associate them with a folder when necessary. For example, perhaps you've created a special form to use to obtain survey responses. On the Forms tab, click Manage to open the Forms Manager dialog box, shown in Figure 38-6. You use the Forms Manager to select a forms library, install forms, configure their properties, copy forms between libraries, and associate forms with the folder.

For a complete discussion of creating custom forms, see Chapter 24, "Designing and Using Forms."

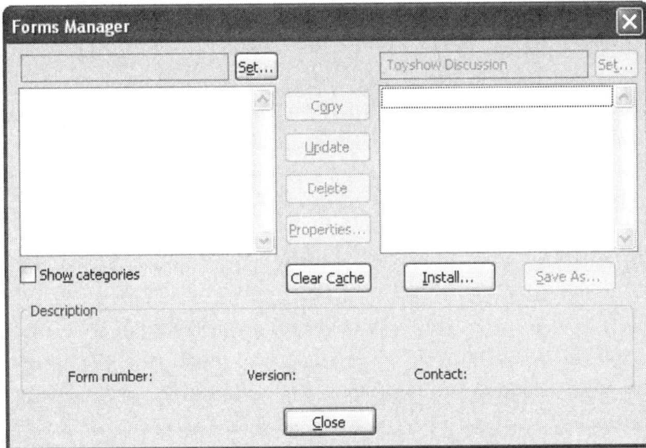

Figure 38-6. Use the Forms Manager to associate forms with a public folder.

Setting Permissions on Public Folders

You can control which users have access to public folders and the actions they can take in a folder by setting permissions for the folders. You do so on the Permissions tab of the folder's Properties dialog box, shown in Figure 38-7.

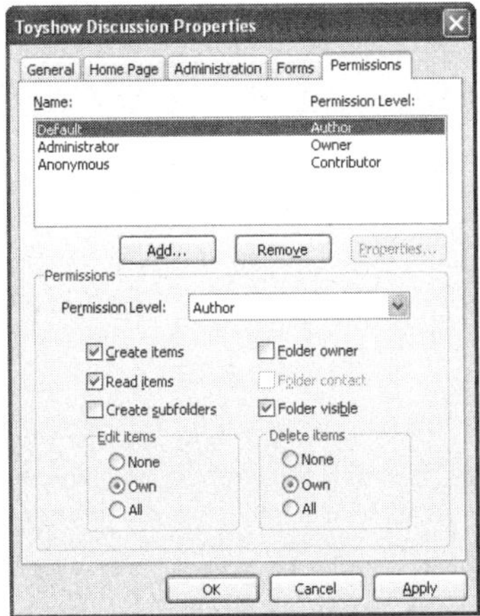

Figure 38-7. Use the Permissions tab to control the actions users can perform in a public folder.

> **Note** A Summary tab replaces the Permissions tab if another user created the folder. The Summary tab allows you to view permissions for the folder but doesn't let you change them.

Each folder includes three permission groups by default: Default, Anonymous, and <*owner*>, where *owner* is the person who created the folder. The Default permission group applies to all authenticated users for whom an explicit permission has not been defined. Default is assigned Author permission initially, letting authenticated users create new items, read existing items, view the folder, and edit and delete items that they own.

The Anonymous permission group controls access by users who connect to the server anonymously—for example, through a Web browser (including through Microsoft Outlook Web Access). Anonymous users by default have only the ability to create new items in the folder; they cannot view it or make other modifications. For users to access a public folder anonymously, the Exchange Server administrator must configure permissions on the server to allow anonymous access. The Anonymous permission group lets you specify the types of access that anonymous users have in public folders that you create.

To learn how to configure anonymous access, see "Controlling Anonymous Access to Public Folders in Exchange Server 5.5," page 963, and "Controlling Anonymous Access to Public Folders in Exchange 2000 Server and Exchange Server 2003," page 966.

The third permission group, which appears by default, is for the person who created the folder (typically, you). The owner has full permissions in the folder and can create items, view items, create subfolders, and edit and delete items, including items owned by other users. You can give other users full control of a folder by granting them Owner permissions.

You can assign permissions to individual users or to distribution groups. When you click Add on the Permissions tab, Outlook displays the Add Users dialog box, shown in Figure 38-8. The Name list includes users from the Global Address List as well as mail-enabled security and distribution groups.

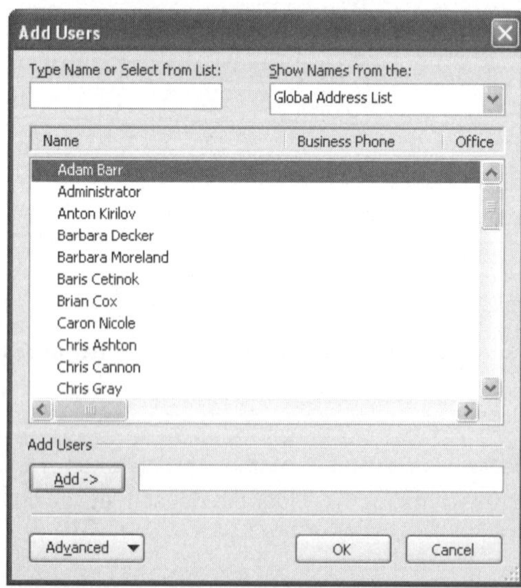

Figure 38-8. Use the Add Users dialog box to add permissions for users and groups.

Tip **Use security groups for messaging in Exchange 2000 Server, Exchange Server 2003**
In Exchange Server 5.5, you can use only distribution groups for messaging; security groups, therefore, do not appear in the Add Users dialog box. In Exchange 2000 Server and Exchange Server 2003, however, you can also use mail-enabled security groups to send and receive messages. This means that mail-enabled security groups do show up in the Add Users dialog box when you configure properties for public folders on a server running Exchange 2000 Server or Exchange Server 2003. Security groups that are not mail-enabled don't appear in the list. Outlook shows mail-enabled groups regardless of their type (domain local, global, or universal). For a discussion of creating distribution groups in Exchange Server, see "Creating Distribution Lists," page 911.

You configure and add permissions for public folders the same way you configure permissions for private folders. To learn about setting permissions, see "Configuring Access Permissions," page 741.

Applying Rules to Folders

Another aspect of setting up a public folder is creating rules that apply to items when they arrive in the folder. Rules help you perform actions automatically in the folder. For example, perhaps you want all messages posted to a public folder to be forwarded to a specific e-mail address. Or maybe you want to delete messages that come from specific senders or that have certain text in the subject field. Maybe you want messages with attachments to be moved to a different folder. Whatever the case, you can use rules to perform the action automatically, the same way you can use rules to automatically process messages that come into your Inbox.

For a complete discussion of creating and using rules to process the Inbox and other private folders, see "Processing Messages Automatically," page 224.

You configure rules for a public folder by using the Properties dialog box for the folder. Click the Administration tab, and then click Folder Assistant to open the Folder Assistant dialog box, shown in Figure 38-9.

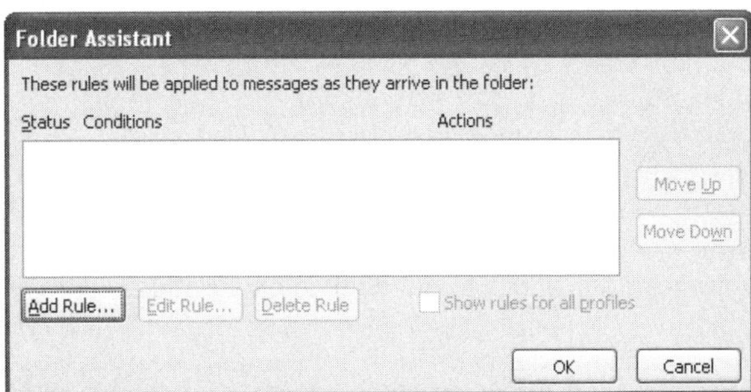

Figure 38-9. The Folder Assistant dialog box lists rules currently assigned to the folder.

In addition to listing currently assigned rules, the Folder Assistant dialog box lets you modify, delete, and add rules. Click Add Rule to display the Edit Rule dialog box when you want to add a rule (see Figure 38-10). The options available are similar to the options for creating a rule by using the Rules Wizard. You can click Advanced to set additional advanced conditions for the rule, as shown in Figure 38-11.

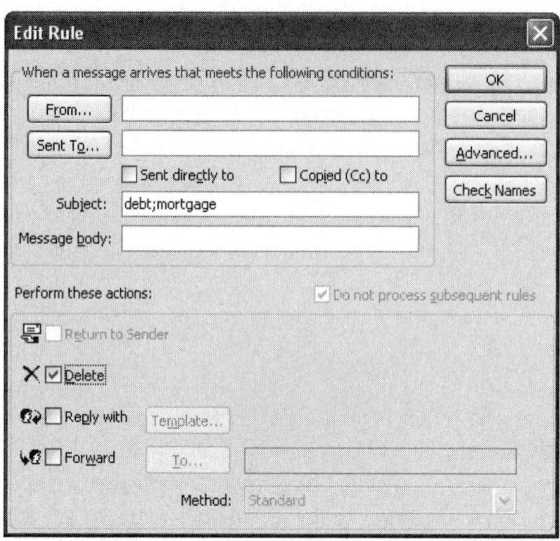

Figure 38-10. Use the Edit Rule dialog box to define conditions and actions for the folder rule.

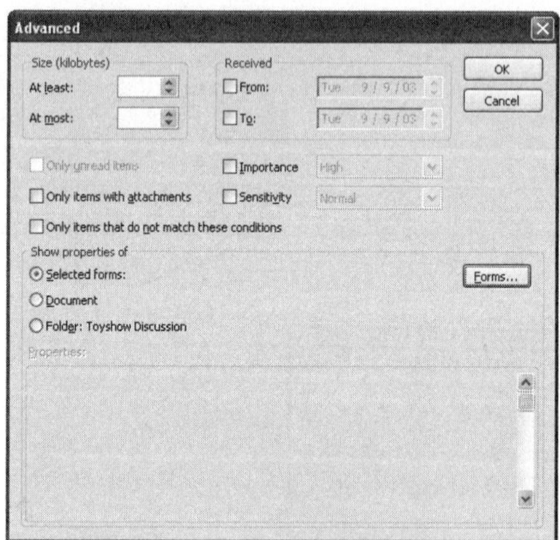

Figure 38-11. Use the Advanced dialog box to set additional conditions for the rule.

This chapter does not cover creating folder rules in depth because the process is similar to creating message rules with the Rules Wizard, discussed in detail in an earlier chapter. If you need help building folder rules, review Chapter 8, "Filtering, Organizing, and Using Automatic Responses."

Setting Up a Message Board

You can use public folders to set up a message board that allows others to post and reply to messages. This is similar to using a news server, although the end result is slightly different. You use Outlook or Outlook Web Access to follow a conversation thread, rather than using a newsreader such as Microsoft Outlook Express. In addition, the message board looks and functions like a mail folder; it doesn't organize messages by conversation thread by default, as a newsreader does. However, you can change the folder's view to organize the messages by conversation thread (see Figure 38-12), which gives you much the same effect. The advantage over a news server is that the message board does not require an administrator for setup or maintenance.

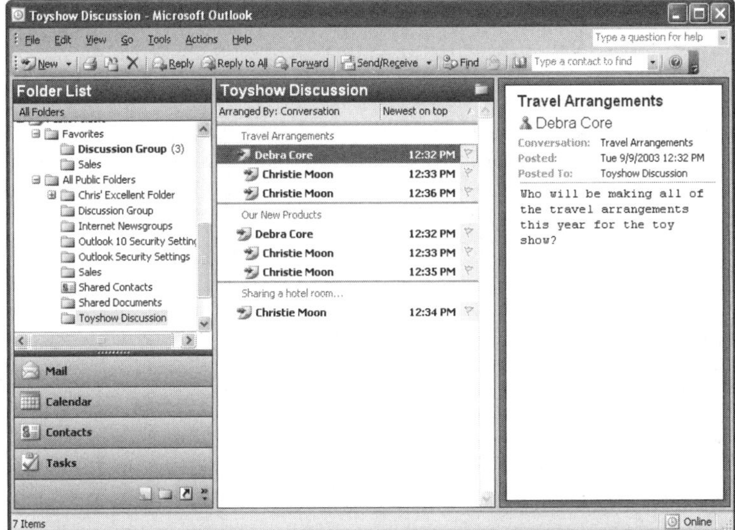

Figure 38-12. You can organize messages in a public folder by subject.

A message board can be either moderated or unmoderated. In an *unmoderated* board, any user can post a message directly to the board, depending on his or her permissions in the public folder. No one controls what messages are posted to the board. With a *moderated* message board, messages are sent to a designated moderator, who decides whether to post the messages.

Setting Up an Unmoderated Message Board

An unmoderated message board is pretty much a free-for-all. As mentioned, anyone with access to the folder can post any message. However, you can control access to the folder through the folder's permissions, thereby limiting who can post messages.

Follow these steps to create an unmoderated message board:

1. Open Outlook, and expand the Public Folders branch.

2 Right-click the folder where you want to create the new folder and choose New Folder.

3 In the Create New Folder dialog box, specify the name and folder type, change the location if needed, and click OK.

4 Right-click the newly created folder and choose Properties. Click the Permissions tab.

5 On the Permissions tab, set the permissions for Default and Anonymous to control the actions users can perform with messages in the folder.

6 Use the Permissions section to configure the folder permission. If you don't want participants to be able to edit or delete the messages they post, select Create Items, Read Items, and Folder Visible; set Edit Items and Delete Items to None; and then click OK.

Setting Up a Moderated Message Board

One additional step is required when setting up a moderated message board—you must specify the moderator.

Follow the steps outlined in the previous section for creating an unmoderated message board, and then follow these additional steps to configure the board as moderated:

1 In Outlook, right-click the public folder and choose Properties.

2 Click the Administration tab, and then click Moderated Folder to display the Moderated Folder dialog box, shown in Figure 38-13.

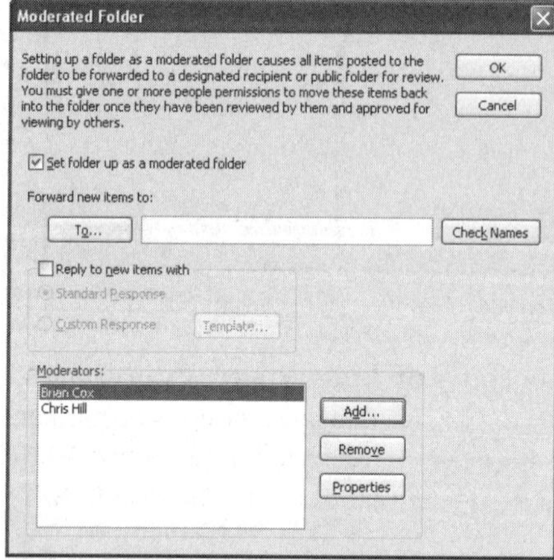

Figure 38-13. You can add multiple moderators to a folder.

3 Select the Set Folder Up As A Moderated Folder check box to configure the folder as a moderated folder. (Clear this check box to make the folder unmoderated.)

4 Configure additional options, using the following list as a guide:

- **Forward New Items To** Specify the addresses of the moderator (or moderators) who will receive new messages for posting consideration. You also can specify the name of another public folder where the moderators will place the messages for review.

- **Reply To New Items With** Select this check box to have a reply sent automatically to participants when they post a message. Clear this check box if you don't want a reply sent.
- **Standard Response** Use this option to have a standard reply sent to participants when they post a message.
- **Custom Response** Select this option to create your own message template, which is used to reply to participants when they post messages.
- **Moderators** Use the options in this group to specify which users are designated as moderators. You must list the moderators here even if you've already entered their names in the Forward New Items To box (which specifies only that copies be sent to the designated addresses).

Tip You can have copies of posted messages sent to people who are not moderators. Just add their addresses in the Forward New Items To box, but don't add them to the Moderators list.

Acting as a Moderator

If you've been designated as a moderator, you can review messages before you post them to the folder. Depending on how the folder is configured, the messages are either placed in a holding folder or sent to your Inbox. To review the messages, open the folder where they're located (or your Inbox) and read them. If you find them acceptable for posting, open the folder list and simply drag the message to the appropriate posting folder.

Tip **Configure drag-and-drop posting**
The setting Drag/Drop Posting on the Administration tab of the folder's Properties dialog box determines what happens when you drag messages to the folder. Select Move/Copy if you want the message to retain its existing subject and sender. Select Forward if you want the message to appear to be forwarded from you. The former option is probably the one you want to use for moderated public folders.

Working with Public Folders

Working with public folders isn't as difficult as you might think. This section of the chapter brings you up to speed on navigating, posting in, and using public folders after they are set up.

Navigating Public Folders

As mentioned, Public Folders by default includes an All Public Folders branch. This branch serves as the root for all public folders on the server. Navigating public folders is just like navigating your private folders. Expand All Public Folders, and then select the folder you want to view. The folder's contents appear in the folder pane.

Posting Information

You post information to a public folder in much the same way you add items to a private folder. Open the folders list and navigate to the public folder you want to use. Click New on the toolbar to use the default form for the folder. You can also click the drop-down arrow beside New to create a different type of item. Outlook opens the specified form, and you fill it out just as you would for a private folder. Figure 38-14 shows the default form for posting messages to a public folder.

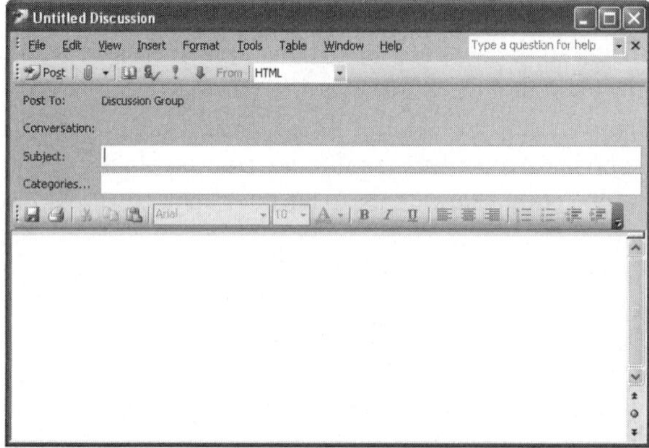

Figure 38-14. Outlook provides a simple form for posting messages to a public folder.

After you enter the information on the form, you can post your message in the following ways:

- To save the item to the folder without closing the form, choose File, Save or click the Save button on the toolbar.
- To post the message and close the form, click the Post button on the toolbar, choose File, Post, or press Ctrl+Enter. The message then appears in the public folder, and the form closes.

Replying to Posts in a Public Folder

When viewing messages posted to a public folder, you have three options for responding to the post: you can reply to the folder, reply to the sender, or forward the message.

Replying to the Folder

Replying to the folder is just like replying to an e-mail message except the reply is simply posted to the public folder. To reply, right-click the message and choose Post Reply To Folder. Outlook opens the message form shown in Figure 38-15. This form is similar to one you would use to reply to an e-mail message. Add your comments and click Post to post your reply to the folder.

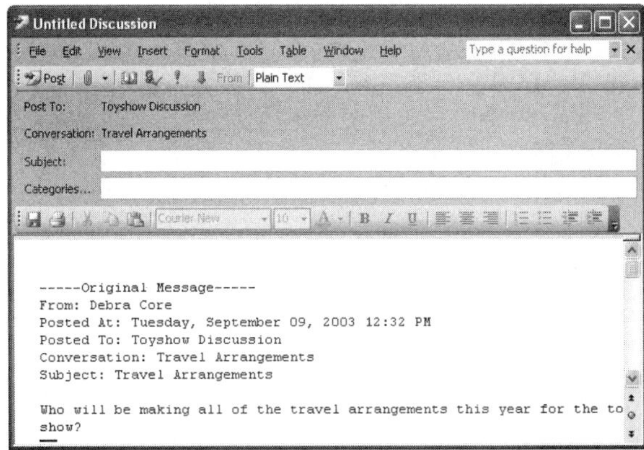

Figure 38-15. Post replies to a message in a public folder by using a form much like an e-mail message form.

Replying to the Sender

When you post a reply to the folder, the reply is placed directly in the folder rather than being sent to the person who originated the message you're replying to. If you prefer, you can send your reply to the originator rather than posting it in the folder. The message then goes out as a regular e-mail reply to the originator's e-mail address. To reply to a post in this way, right-click the message and choose Reply or click the Reply button on the toolbar.

Forwarding Messages

In addition to replying directly to a message's originator or posting replies to the folder, you can also forward the message to others. This works exactly the same way as forwarding a message from your Inbox or from another folder. Right-click the message and choose Forward, or click the Forward button on the toolbar.

Using the Favorites Folder

The Favorites folder under the Public Folders branch is not the same as the Favorites folder in your operating system. The latter contains shortcuts to frequently used Web sites, allowing you to access those sites quickly and easily. The Favorites folder under the Public Folders branch allows you to create shortcuts to public folders that you use frequently. This isn't an important feature if you deal with only a handful of public folders, but it can be a real time-saver if you work with Internet newsgroups on your server through Outlook or if your server contains numerous folders. Don't struggle to find the one folder you want among many in the folder list; simply place the folder in your Favorites folder and access it from there.

Adding folders to Favorites is easy—just drag the folder to the Favorites folder, and Outlook creates a shortcut to the folder. When you want to use the folder, open it from the Favorites folder rather than from Public Folders.

If you want more control over the addition of the folder to the Favorites branch, right-click a public folder and choose Add To Favorites to open the Add To Favorites dialog box. Click Options to expand the dialog box as shown in Figure 38-16.

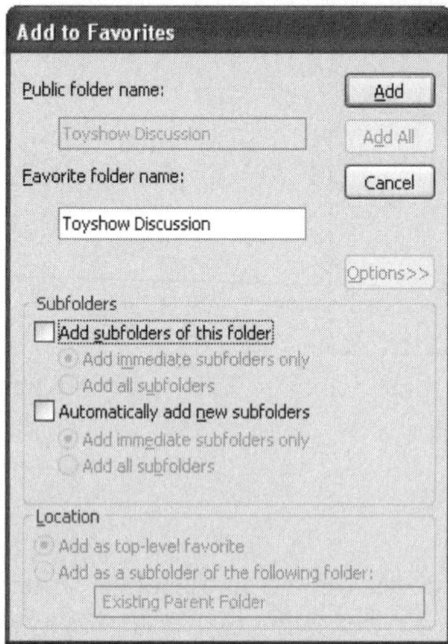

Figure 38-16. Use the Add To Favorites dialog box to set additional options when placing a public folder in Favorites.

Use the following options to control how the folder appears in the Favorites folder and set default options for Favorites:

- **Favorite Folder Name** Specify the name as you want it to appear in the Favorites branch.
- **Add Subfolders Of This Folder** Select this check box to add the public folder's subfolders to the Favorites branch as well. Choose the Add Immediate Subfolders Only option to add only the first level of child folders; choose Add All Subfolders to add all subfolders to Favorites.
- **Automatically Add New Subfolders** Select this check box to automatically add new subfolders to Favorites as they are created in the selected public folder. Choose Add Immediate Subfolders Only to add only the first level of child folders; choose Add All Subfolders to add all subfolders regardless of their relative position within the public folder.
- **Add As Top-Level Favorite** Create the entry for the folder at the root of the Favorites folder.
- **Add As A Subfolder Of The Following Folder** Create the entry for the folder as a subfolder of the specified existing folder in the Favorites branch.

Sharing Documents and Other Files Through Public Folders

You can use public folders to share files, messages, and other Outlook items. For example, you might place common documents such as policies, procedures, contracts, and databases in a public folder to allow coworkers to use them.

You have two main options for sharing files through public folders: using attachments or placing the files directly in the folder. The method you choose depends completely on how you want others to access the files and whether you want to attach a message to a particular file. For example, you might use an attachment when you need to include instructions or other information about using the file. When added information isn't necessary, simply place the file in the folder.

To use an attachment, create a new post as you would without an attachment. With the form still open, click the paper clip icon on the toolbar, select the file to attach, and then click Post. To place a file directly in a public folder, open Outlook and then open the public folder in which you want to place the file. Locate the file in Microsoft Windows Explorer, and simply drag the file to the folder.

Tip **Send a file from an application**

You can send a document from an Office application to a public folder. Open the application and choose File, Send To, Exchange Folder. The application displays a Send To Exchange Folder dialog box where you select the folder in which you want to place the file. You must have Outlook configured as the default application for e-mail to allow the application to send the document to the folder.

Using Public Folders Offline

One of Outlook's strengths is that it gives you the ability to work offline. For example, you can work from home or use a portable computer while on the road, connecting to the server only when you need to synchronize folders. In addition to working with your Outlook folders offline, you can work with public folders offline.

Outlook 2003 gives you two ways to cache public folders depending on whether you use Cached Exchange Mode or an offline store without Cached Exchange Mode. The following sections explain these options.

Synchronizing Public Folders with Cached Exchange Mode

By default, Outlook does not cache the contents of the public folders listed in your Favorites folder when you use Cached Exchange Mode to maintain a local copy of your Exchange Server mailbox. You can cache these folders if you want their contents to be available to you offline, but doing so could result in lots of replication traffic and a large cache file if the public folders contain lots of items. If you are sure that caching the folders will not result in a bloated cache file or excessive replication, follow these steps to configure Cached Exchange Mode to cache the contents of the public folders in your Favorites folder:

1. Choose Tools, E-Mail Accounts, click Next, select the Exchange Server account, and click Change.
2. Click More Settings, then click the Advanced tab.

3 Select the Download Public Folder Favorites check box (see Figure 38-17), and then click OK. Click OK when prompted that you must restart Outlook to make the change take effect, then click Next, Finish.

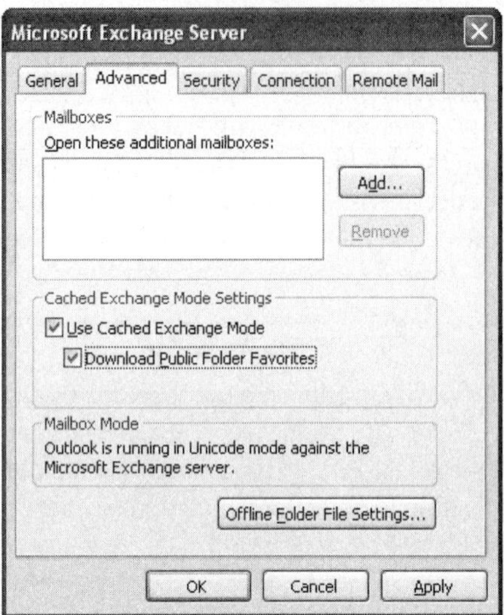

Figure 38-17. Configure Outlook to download public folders in your Favorites folder.

4 Close and restart Outlook, which begins downloading the contents of your Favorites public folders.

Synchronizing Public Folders with Send/Receive Groups

In versions of Outlook prior to Outlook 2002, you configured public folders for offline use by setting the properties for the folder. In Outlook 2002 and Outlook 2003, you can configure a folder for offline use by using the Send/Receive Groups dialog box (discussed shortly). You can have the folders synchronize each time you perform a send/receive operation through your primary send/receive group, or you can create a group specifically for synchronizing your public folders and synchronize them separately from your mailbox folders.

Note Unless you have configured Outlook to use Cached Exchange Mode, you need to set up an offline store before you can use any Exchange Server folders offline. For details on configuring an offline store, see "Working Offline with Outlook and Exchange Server," page 924.

Follow these steps to set up a send/receive group to synchronize public folders:

1 Begin by adding a public folder to your Favorites list, as explained in "Using the Favorites Folder," page 957.

2 Open Outlook and choose Tools, Send/Receive, Send/Receive Settings, Define Send/Receive Groups.

3. In the Send/Receive Groups dialog box, select the existing group you want to use to synchronize public folders or create a new group specifically for synchronization.
4. Click Edit. In the Send/Receive Settings dialog box, select Include Account In This Send/Receive Group and then scroll through the Check Folders list and expand the Public Folders branch.
5. Expand Favorites and select the folders you want Outlook to make available offline.
6. Choose Download Headers Only if you want Outlook to only cache headers, or choose Download Complete Item Including Attachments if you want the header, body, and any attachments cached.
7. Click OK, and then click Close to return to Outlook.
8. Perform a send/receive operation with the send/receive group to synchronize the public folders with your offline store.

Troubleshooting

Your public folders aren't available offline

If you've configured a send/receive group to synchronize your public folders for offline use, but the folders aren't accessible when you're working offline, make sure you've synchronized the folders at least once with the server. As is the case with your other Outlook folders, you can't work offline until you synchronize the folders at least once.

Managing Public Folders

As you learned earlier in this chapter, you can create public folders on an Exchange Server through Outlook, depending on your permissions on the server. You also can modify the properties of folders for which you have Owner permission. In addition, administrators can manage public folders through Exchange Server. This section explores some of the most common administration tasks you might need to perform as an administrator of public folders in Exchange Server.

Note This section is not intended to cover all aspects of either Exchange Server management or public folders. Instead, it focuses on some of the most common administrative issues you'll face with public folders. In addition, the chapter itself focuses primarily on Exchange 2000 Server and Exchange Server 2003 rather than Exchange Server 5.5. For a complete discussion of Exchange 2000 Server management, refer to *Microsoft Exchange 2000 Server Administrator's Companion*, by Walter J. Glenn and Bill English (Microsoft Press, 2000). See *Microsoft Exchange Server 2003 Administrator's Companion*, by Walter J. Glenn and Bill English (Microsoft Press, 2003), for details on Exchange Server 2003.

Managing Public Folders in Exchange Server 5.5

Most management tasks for public folders in Exchange Server 5.5 are most easily accomplished through Outlook, as explained in previous sections. You can create public folders, view their contents, add and modify items, and perform other actions, depending on the permissions you've been assigned for a particular folder. One action you'll likely want to perform with the Exchange Administrator is to configure the ability to create public folders.

Controlling the Ability to Create Public Folders in Exchange Server 5.5

By default, Exchange Server 5.5 allows all users to create top-level public folders. In most cases, you'll probably want to impose some restrictions to narrow the list of users who can create folders.

Follow these steps to restrict who can create public folders:

1. Open the Exchange Administrator, expand the Site, and select the Configuration container.
2. In the right pane, double-click Information Store Site Configuration to display its Properties dialog box and then click the Top Level Folder Creation tab, shown in Figure 38-18.

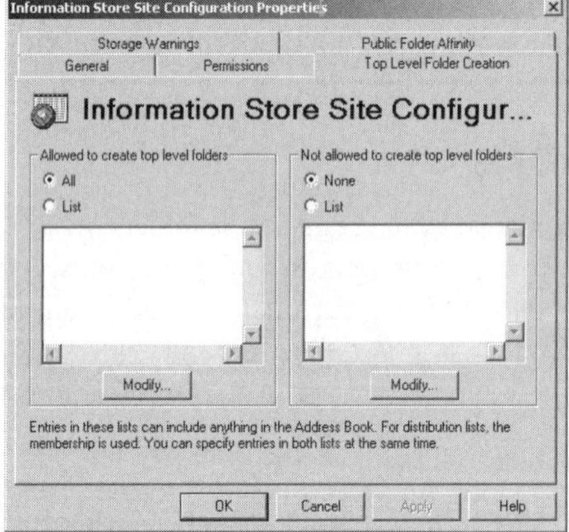

Figure 38-18. Use the Top Level Folder Creation tab to control users' ability to create public folders in the store.

3. If you want to specify explicitly which users and groups can create public folders, click List in the Allowed To Create Top Level Folders group and then click Modify to specify the users or groups who can create public folders. Click OK when you're satisfied with the list.
4. If you want to specify explicitly which users cannot create public folders, thereby allowing all others to do so, click List in the Not Allowed To Create Top Level Folders group, and then click Modify. Build the list and click OK.
5. Click OK to close the Information Store Site Configuration Properties dialog box.

Controlling Anonymous Access to Public Folders in Exchange Server 5.5

You can control anonymous access to public folders in Exchange Server 5.5 either at the server level or at the organizational level. Each server uses the defaults defined at the organizational level unless you specify otherwise. You need to configure anonymous access—either allowing or preventing it—through HTTP, IMAP, and NNTP.

> **Note** The procedure described here takes you through all the configuration changes that affect anonymous access through various protocols. You might not want to make all these changes, however, depending on your network's configuration, the types of data you need to make available, and how your users need to access that data. Take some time to examine these issues to determine how anonymous access fits—or does not fit—into your enterprise.

Follow these steps to configure anonymous access default settings at the organizational level:

1. Open the Exchange Administrator.
2. Expand the Configuration container and click the Protocols object.
3. Double-click HTTP in the right pane to open the HTTP (Web) Site Settings Properties dialog box.
4. On the General tab (see Figure 38-19), select or clear the Allow Anonymous Users To Access The Anonymous Public Folders check box. This allows or denies anonymous access through the Web to public folders published by the server on the Internet.

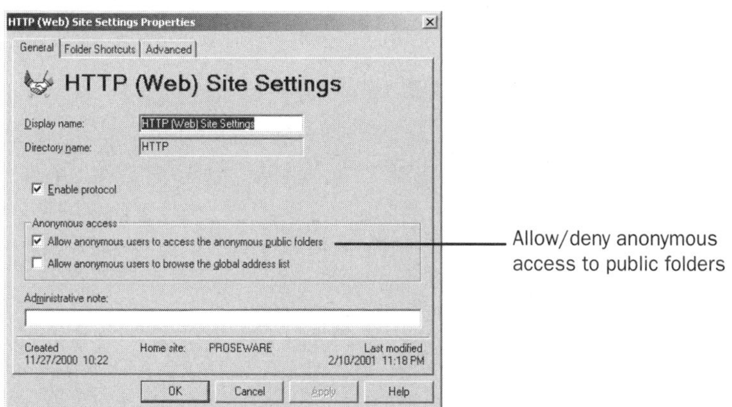

Figure 38-19. Configure anonymous access for HTTP-based access in the HTTP protocol's Properties dialog box.

5. Click OK, and then double-click IMAP to open the IMAP (Mail) Site Defaults Properties dialog box.
6. On the General tab (see Figure 38-20), clear the Include All Public Folders When A Folder List Is Requested check box if you want to prevent anonymous access. This prevents public folders from being included in response to a client's request to list folders on the server.

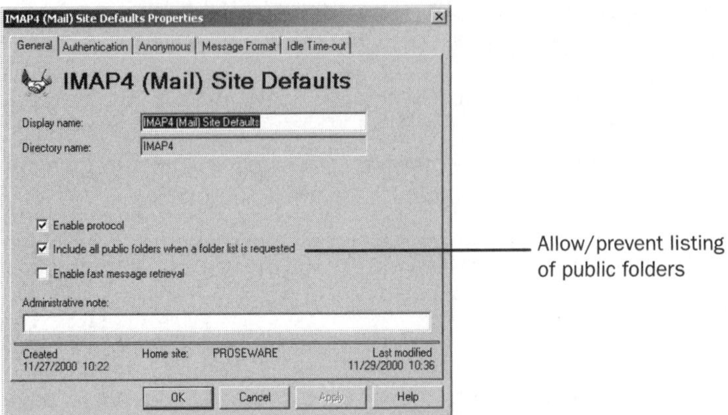

Figure 38-20. Configure anonymous access through IMAP in the IMAP protocol's Properties dialog box.

7. Click the Anonymous tab in the Properties dialog box and clear the Allow Anonymous Access check box if you want to prevent anonymous access to the folders. If you want to allow anonymous access, select this check box and specify the anonymous account name in the IMAP4 Anonymous Account box.
8. Click OK. Then double-click NNTP to open the NNTP (News) Site Defaults Properties dialog box.
9. Click the Anonymous tab (see Figure 38-21), and select the Allow Anonymous Access check box to allow anonymous access. Clear the check box to prevent anonymous access.

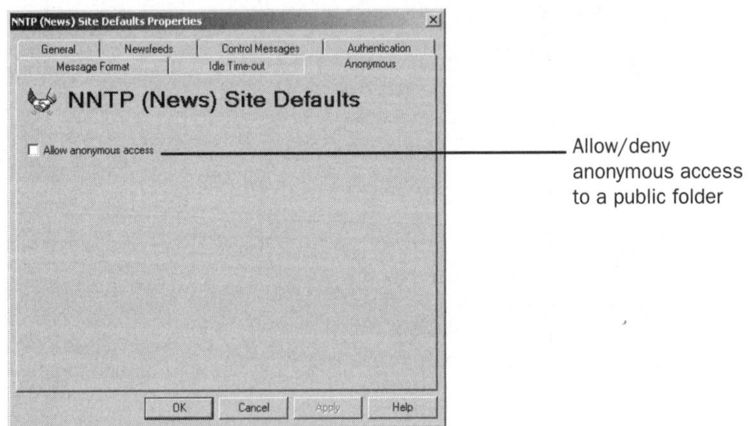

Figure 38-21. Use the Anonymous tab to allow or prevent anonymous access.

10 Click OK. You can also configure anonymous access at the server level rather than at the organizational level. For example, you might want to allow anonymous access on one server for public use but prevent anonymous access on all others where confidential information is stored. In the Exchange Administrator, expand the Configuration container, and then expand the Servers container. Expand the server you want to configure and click the Protocols object. In the right pane, double-click IMAP4 or NNTP to configure the properties for those two protocols. The options are the same as those you configure at the organizational level.

Setting Client Permissions in Exchange Server 5.5

In addition to configuring protocols, you might also want to configure permissions for anonymous users on specific folders.

Follow these steps to configure public folder permissions under Exchange Server 5.5:

1 Open the Exchange Administrator, and expand the Folders\Public Folders branch.

2 Select the public folder for which you want to configure properties. Choose File, Properties or press Alt+Enter to open the folder's Properties dialog box.

3 On the General tab, click Client Permissions to display the Client Permissions dialog box (see Figure 38-22).

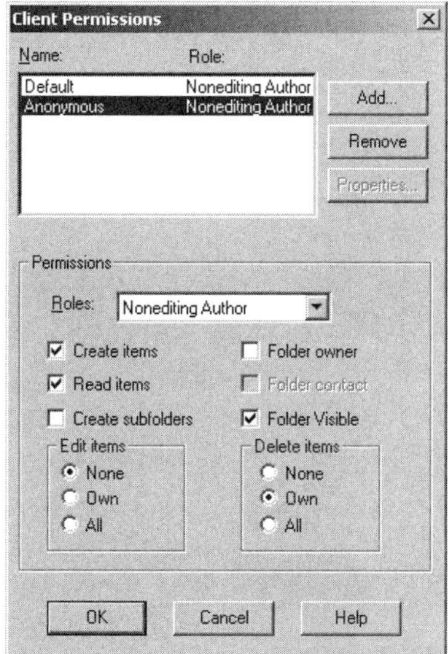

Figure 38-22. Use the Client Permissions dialog box to control the actions anonymous users can take in a public folder.

4 Select Anonymous in the Name list, and then use the Roles drop-down list and other options in the dialog box to specify the actions that anonymous users can perform in the folder.

5 Click OK to close the Client Permissions dialog box, and then click OK to close the folder's Properties dialog box. Repeat the process for other folders as needed.

Managing Public Folders in Exchange 2000 Server and Exchange Server 2003

Although you can manage some aspects of public folders through Outlook, you have much broader control through Exchange System Manager with Exchange 2000 Server and Exchange Server 2003. For example, you can apply storage limits, decide how the folder should appear in the address list, and configure many other properties not available through Outlook. The following sections discuss some of the most common administrative tasks you might want to perform on public folders in Exchange 2000 Server or Exchange Server 2003.

Controlling Anonymous Access to Public Folders in Exchange 2000 Server and Exchange Server 2003

One of the administrative tasks you might want to perform in Exchange Server is to control anonymous access to public folders through various protocols such as HTTP, IMAP, and NNTP.

Note The procedure described here takes you through all the configuration changes that affect anonymous access using various protocols. Which of these changes you make depends on how your users need to access data, your network's configuration, and the types of data you need to make available. Examine these issues in detail to determine what changes you need to make to control anonymous access.

Follow these steps to configure anonymous access in Exchange 2000 Server or Exchange Server 2003:

1. Open Exchange System Manager, and expand the Administrative Group where the server in question is located. Expand the Protocols container under the server.
2. Expand the HTTP container, and expand the Exchange Virtual Server container under it. Right-click the Public virtual directory and choose Properties.
3. In the Public Properties dialog box, click the Access tab and click Authentication to open the Authentication Methods dialog box (see Figure 38-23).

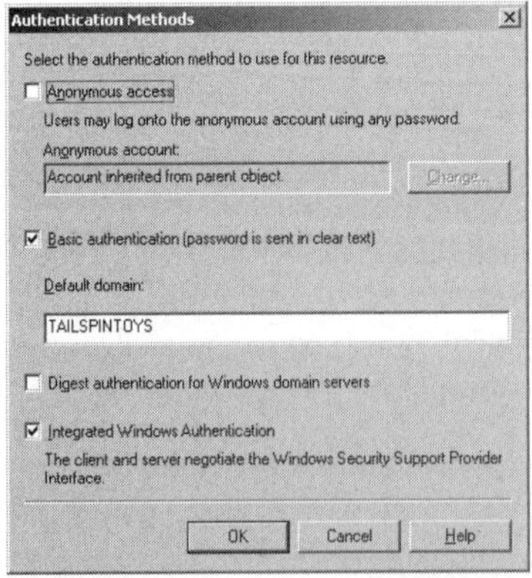

Figure 38-23. Use the Authentication Methods dialog box to allow or prevent anonymous access through HTTP.

4 If you want to allow anonymous access to public folders through HTTP (clients access the folders through a Web browser), select the Anonymous Access check box and then click in the Anonymous Account box and type the account name to use for anonymous access. Typically, the account name is IUSR_<*computer*>, where *computer* is the server name.

5 Click OK to close the Authentication Methods dialog box. Then click OK again to close the Public Properties dialog box.

6 Expand the IMAP4 container, right-click the virtual server, and choose Properties to open the IMAP4 Properties dialog box for the server. On the General tab (see Figure 38-24), select or clear the Include All Public Folders When A Folder List Is Requested check box to either list or not list public folders for IMAP clients.

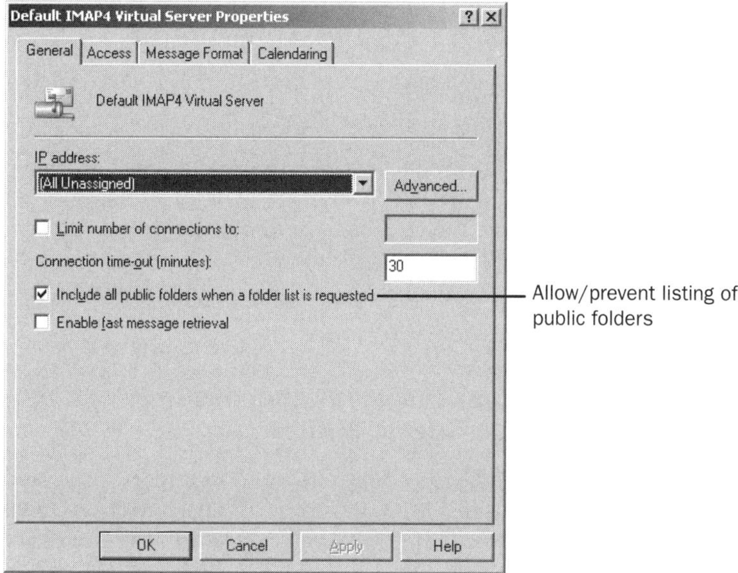

Figure 38-24. Use the General tab of the IMAP protocol's Properties dialog box to control listing of public folders for IMAP clients.

7 Click OK and expand the NNTP container. Right-click the NNTP virtual server and choose Properties.

8 Click the Access tab and click Authentication to open the Authentication Methods dialog box (see Figure 38-25).

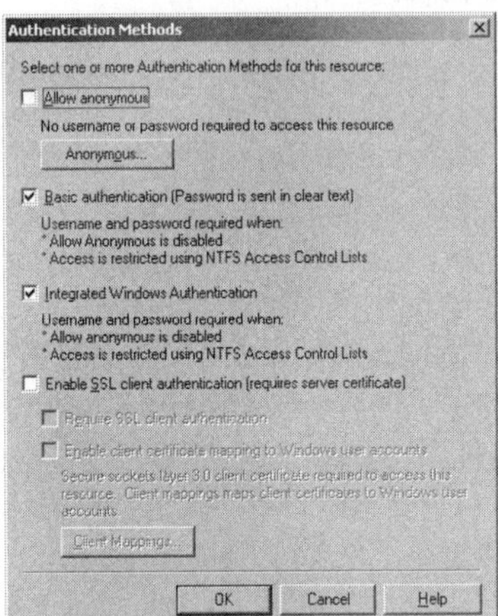

Figure 38-25. Use the Authentication Methods dialog box to allow or deny anonymous access.

9. Select or clear the Allow Anonymous check box to allow or deny anonymous access to the folders through NNTP. If you allow anonymous access, click Anonymous and choose the user account to be used to gain access to resources when an anonymous connection is made. Then click OK.
10. Click OK to close the Authentication Methods dialog box. Then click OK to close the virtual server's Properties dialog box.

Changing Address List Display Properties in Exchange 2000 Server and Exchange Server 2003

You can configure public folders to appear in the Global Address List (and in other address lists you create and make available on the server), which allows users to select a folder as the destination when sending or posting a message. By default, Exchange 2000 Server and Exchange Server 2003 hide public folders from the address lists. If you want a folder to appear in the address lists, you must configure one of the folder's properties accordingly.

Follow these steps to properly configure a folder's properties:

1. Open Exchange System Manager and configure it to display Administrative Groups (if it doesn't already).

Tip To display Administrative Groups in Exchange System Manager, right-click Organization and choose Properties. Select Display Administrative Groups and click OK.

2. Expand the Folders container, right-click the public folder, and choose Properties. Click the Exchange Advanced tab, shown in Figure 38-26.
3. In the Simple Display Name box, enter the alias name you want Exchange Server to use for the folder in address lists. For example, you might specify an alias of Support Tools for a public folder named support.tools.common.

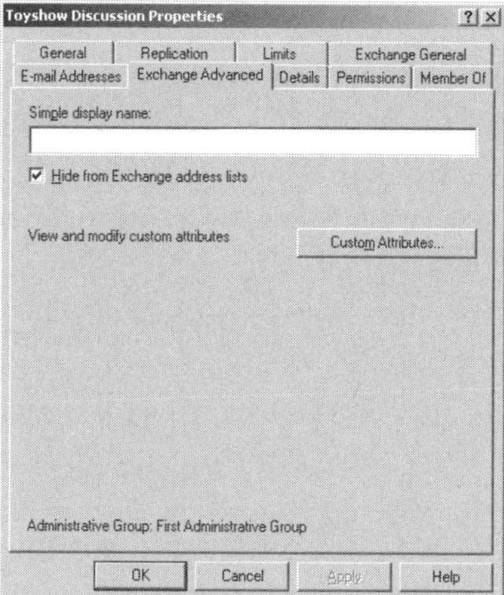

Figure 38-26. Use the Exchange Advanced tab to configure address book behavior for public folders.

4 If you want to hide the folder from the address lists, select the Hide From Exchange Address Lists check box. Clear this check box to have the folder appear in address lists.

5 Click OK to close the Properties dialog box.

Setting Folder Limits in Exchange 2000 Server and Exchange Server 2003

You can configure limits on a public folder to control the size of the folder and its contents. The folder can use the store's default limits (this is the default setting), or you can specify limits specifically for the folder. Four settings control folder limits. To view them, right-click the folder in Exchange System Manager, choose Properties, and then click the Limits tab, shown in Figure 38-27.

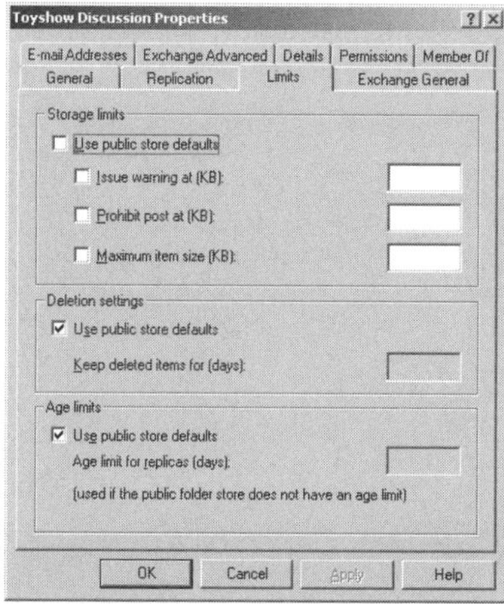

Figure 38-27. Use the Limits tab to configure storage limits for the folder.

The following settings control public folder limits:

- **Use Public Store Defaults** Select this check box to use the limit settings assigned at the store level. Clear this check box to set individual limits for the folder.
- **Issue Warning At (KB)** Use this check box to specify the size, in kilobytes, that the folder should reach before Exchange Server issues a warning to the administrator. You can specify a value from 0 to 2,097,151.
- **Prohibit Post At (KB)** When the folder reaches the size that you specify with this option, users can no longer post items to the folder.
- **Maximum Item Size (KB)** This option lets you specify a maximum size for each posted item.

> **Tip** If you allow public folders to use the public store defaults, a single folder can use all available disk space within a store. It's a good idea to assign individual limits to "space-hogging" folders.

You also can use the options in the Deletion Settings group to set the amount of time that deleted items remain in the folder before they are permanently deleted. You can configure the folder to use the store's default or specify an individual setting for the folder. Another option you can configure is the length of time that replicated items can remain in the folder before they are deleted.

Setting Client Permissions in Exchange 2000 Server and Exchange Server 2003

Outlook lets you configure folder permissions to control the actions that users can perform in a folder. You can also configure those options through Exchange System Manager. Right-click the folder, choose Properties, and then click the Permissions tab. Click Client Permissions to display the Client Permissions dialog box, shown in Figure 38-28. This dialog box is essentially identical to the one offered by Outlook for setting client permissions. For details on configuring these permissions, see "Setting Permissions on Public Folders," page 949.

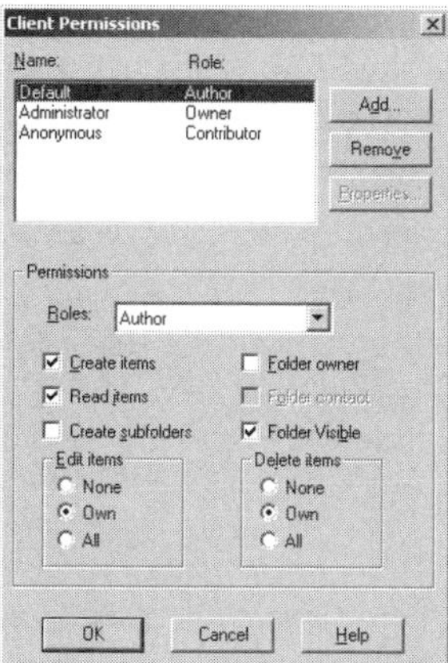

Figure 38-28. You can configure client access permissions through Exchange System Manager.

Controlling the Ability to Create Public Folders in Exchange 2000 Server and Exchange Server 2003

Although, as an administrator, you can configure the ability to create public folders through Outlook, you might prefer to do so through Exchange instead. For example, you might need to refine the permissions to allow or deny other actions as well, which is not possible through Outlook.

Follow these steps to configure the ability to create public folders and set other permissions:

1. Open Exchange System Manager, display Administrative Groups, right-click the Folders/Public Folders branch, and choose Properties.
2. Click the Security tab, shown in Figure 38-29.

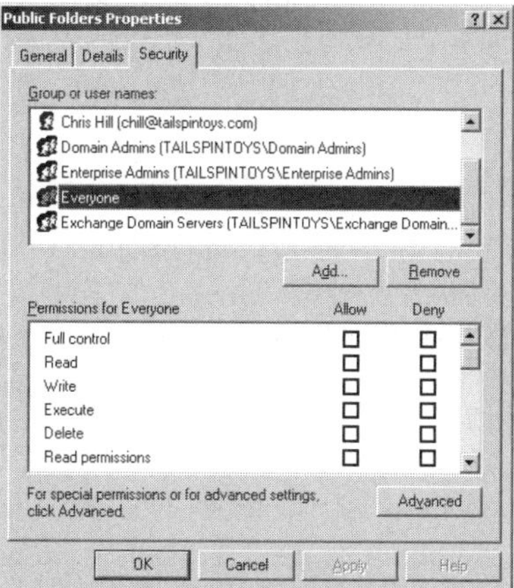

Figure 38-29. Use the Security tab to allow or deny the ability to create public folders.

3. Select the Everyone group and configure Create Public Folder and CreateTop Level Public Folder permissions. Generally, you'll want to remove these permissions from the Everyone group and assign the permissions through other security groups as needed, unless you want all users to be able to create public folders.
4. Click Advanced and review the security settings for the Everyone group, adjusting as needed to suit your security requirements.
5. Click OK to close the Advanced Control Settings For Public Folders dialog box. Then click OK again to close Public Folders Properties dialog box.

Managing a Newsgroup Server

You can use Exchange Server 5.5, Exchange 2000 Server, and Exchange Server 2003 to host Internet newsgroups, allowing users to participate in public discussions, to access files and support data, and to communicate with others across the Internet. The ability to host newsgroups is integrated into each of these Exchange Server platforms. This section focuses primarily on configuring newsgroups in Exchange 2000 Server. The process is similar to that of Exchange Server 5.5 and Exchange Server 2003.

> **Note** In Exchange Server 2003, the NTTP service is disabled by default. Basic and Integrated Windows Authentication are enabled for the NNTP service, but anonymous authentication is disabled. For additional differences between Exchange Server 2003 and Exchange 2000 Server, see Microsoft Knowledge Base article 818474 at *http://support.microsoft.com/default.aspx?scid=kb;en-us;818474*.

You can use Exchange Server to create a news server to host your own newsgroups, or you can configure it to pull a newsfeed from a public news server to provide a complete set or a subset of the public Internet newsgroups, depending on your needs. For example, suppose that you want to set up a news server to provide technical support information exchange with your customers. By using Exchange Server to host your newsgroups, you allow your customers to access messages through the Internet using a newsreader; your in-house staff can access messages through Outlook.

If you want, you can also create newsgroups in the NNTP service and not associate them with Exchange Server public folders. As a result, local users won't have access to the newsgroups through Outlook, but they can view the newsgroups using an NNTP newsreader such as Outlook Express, depending on their permissions on the virtual server. Because this book focuses on Outlook, however, this chapter assumes that you want to integrate the two.

> **Note** This chapter focuses on configuring a news server to host your own newsgroups. For a discussion of configuring a news server to pull public news feeds, see *Internet Information Services (IIS) 6 Resource Kit* (Microsoft Press, 2003). Most of the process is the same, with the exception that you must also set up a newsfeed from a public news server.

NNTP + Outlook = Internet Newsgroups

If you've browsed your folder list in Outlook, you've no doubt come across the Public Folders/Internet Newsgroups branch. Exchange Server uses this public folder to expose newsgroups to Outlook users, giving users the ability to read and post messages, and, depending on their permissions, to create additional newsgroups. Public folders do not by themselves provide for a news server, however. Exchange Server uses the NNTP service included with Microsoft Windows 2000 Server and Microsoft Windows Server 2003 to provide the back-end functionality. Local Outlook users can connect to the server and view the newsgroups through the Public Folders/Internet Newsgroups branch; remote users can connect to the server using Outlook Express or another newsreader to read and post messages.

When you install Exchange 2000 Server, Setup adds the NNTP service and configures a default NNTP virtual server, configuring it to respond on all unassigned IP addresses. (The installation process for Exchange Server 2003 requires that you first add NNTP yourself prior to running Exchange Server Setup.) Setup also creates a default virtual directory that points to the Public Folders/Internet Newsgroups public folder. The result is that new newsgroups and messages are stored in the Public Folders/Internet Newsgroups folder, including those added by remote users through the NNTP service. A user browsing the Public Folders/Internet Newsgroups branch through Outlook sees a given set of folders, as shown in Figure 38-30. When a remote user connects to the server through a newsreader such as Outlook Express, that user sees that same set of newsgroups, as shown in Figure 38-31. By pointing the default virtual directory for the NNTP server to the Public Folders/Internet Newsgroups public folder, Exchange Server provides two different views of the same data, each applicable to a particular type of user.

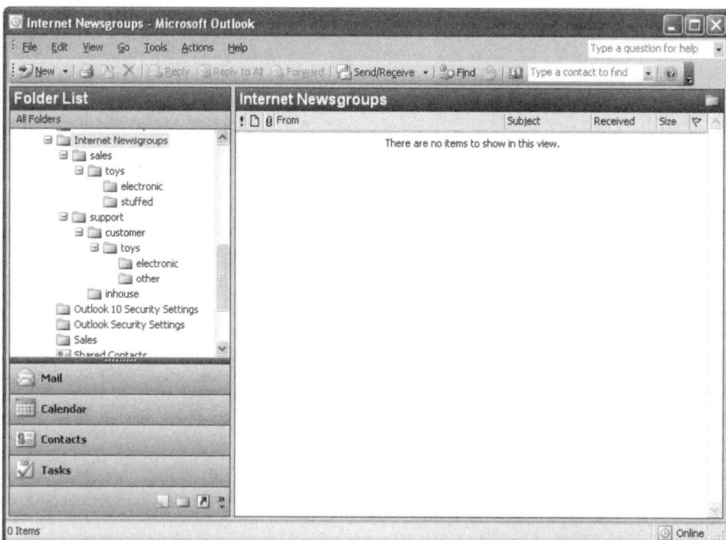

Figure 38-30. Newsgroups appear under the Public Folders/Internet Newsgroups branch in Outlook.

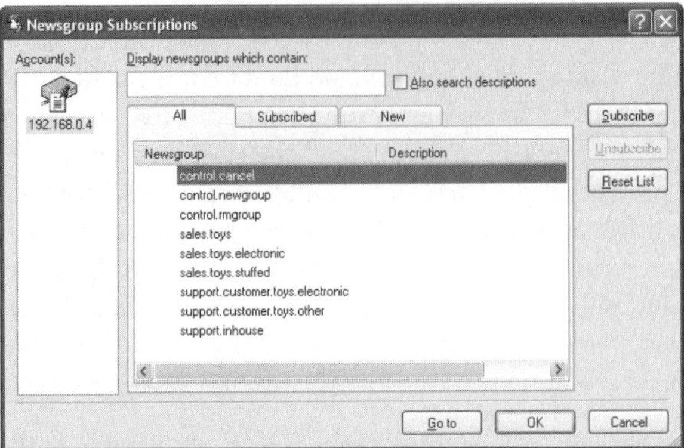

Figure 38-31. The same newsgroups appear when a user connects through a newsreader such as Outlook Express.

Troubleshooting

You can't get newsgroup access through Outlook

Many users complain that Outlook doesn't include a dedicated newsreader, but instead requires that you use an external newsreader such as Outlook Express to work with newsgroups. Although you can't use Outlook to connect to an external news server (unless it's an Exchange Server), you can use it to read public newsgroups if they are hosted on your Exchange Server. Network administrators can address these users' complaints by configuring a local Exchange Server to pull a newsfeed from a public news server. As a result, users have access to public newsgroups through Outlook. An added bonus is that the administrator can control the newsgroups that are pulled from the remote server, restricting the groups that appear on the local server.

Configuring NNTP Server Properties

Because Exchange Server Setup automatically creates a default NNTP virtual server when you install Exchange 2000 Server and points the default virtual directory to the Public Folders/Internet Newsgroups branch, this folder is the root for newsgroups on the server.

You'll probably want to adjust a few properties if you're setting up your own news server. The following sections explain many common setting adjustments.

Note The following sections don't cover all the NNTP service properties, although the procedures included here give you access to all the properties.

Configuring Server IP Address, Ports, and Connection Limits

The NNTP virtual server by default is configured to respond on all unassigned IP addresses on the server. This means that the server responds to NNTP requests that come in for IP addresses for which no other NNTP virtual server is explicitly configured on the server. If multiple IP addresses are bound to your server, you might prefer to assign a specific IP address to the server to simplify administration or DNS configuration. You also might want to configure connection limits and timeouts for the server, limiting the number of users who can connect concurrently and setting a timeout period that, when reached, will disconnect idle users.

You configure these properties on the General tab of the Properties dialog box for the virtual server, as follows:

1. Open Exchange System Manager, open the Administrative Group in which the server resides, and then expand the server's Protocols/NNTP branch.
2. Right-click the Default NNTP Virtual Server branch and choose Properties to open the General tab, shown in Figure 38-32.

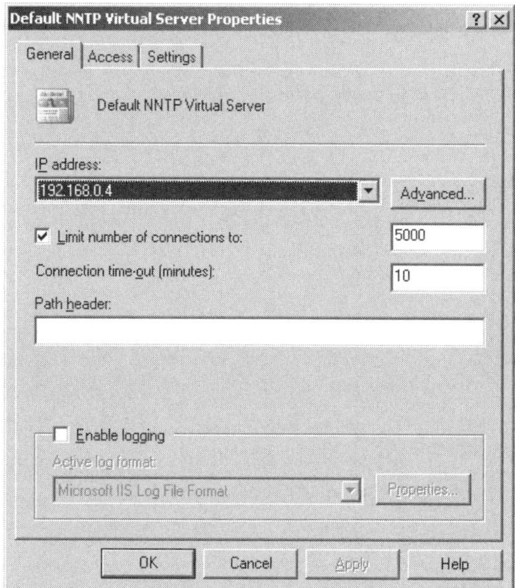

Figure 38-32. Configure address, connection limits, and timeouts on the General tab.

3. In the IP Address drop-down list, select the IP address on which you want the virtual NNTP server to respond.
4. Select the Limit Number Of ConnectionsTo check box if you want to impose a limit on the number of concurrent users, and then enter a value in the associated text box. The default is 5,000 users.

5 Use the Connection Time-Out box to specify the number of minutes after which idle users are disconnected. Click OK to close the Properties dialog box.

The NNTP server uses the standard TCP port 119 and Secure Sockets Layer (SSL) port 563 by default, but you can change those port settings if you have a special deployment topology that requires it. With the General tab open, click Advanced to edit the port assignments.

Preventing Anonymous Access

The Exchange 2000 Server NNTP service by default allows anonymous connections to the news server. This might not be a problem for you if you're setting up a news server for public access. You'll probably want to prevent anonymous access for a private news server, however. Follow these steps to prevent anonymous access for a private server:

Note Anonymous access is disabled by default for NNTP virtual servers under Exchange Server 2003.

1 Open Exchange System Manager and open the server's Protocols/NNTP branch.
2 Right-click the Default NNTP Virtual Server branch and choose Properties. Then click the Access tab.
3 Click Authentication to display the Authentication Methods dialog box, shown in Figure 38-33.

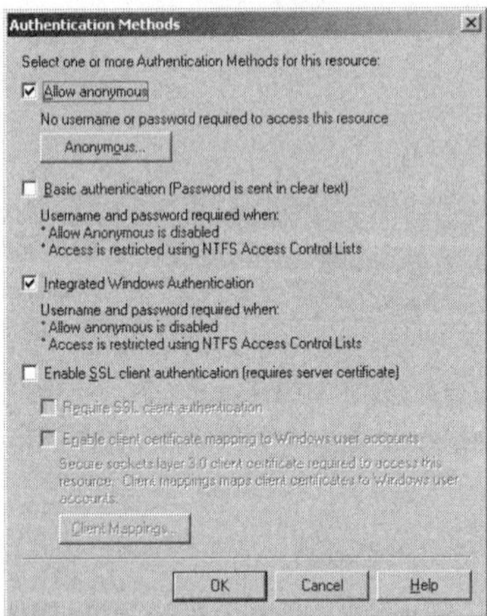

Figure 38-33. Control anonymous access and other authentication options in the Authentication Methods dialog box.

4 Clear the Allow Anonymous check box, configure other authentication options as needed, and click OK. Close the server's Properties dialog box.

Tip Use the Settings tab to impose limits on posting size, to allow feed posting from other servers, and to configure additional options for the virtual server.

Creating Newsgroups

You can create newsgroups in two locations on the server: in the Public Folders/Internet Newsgroups folder or under the NNTP virtual server. The server treats the Public Folders/Internet Newsgroups folder as the root for the newsgroup list because it associates the default virtual directory for the server with that folder. When you add other folders under that folder, they appear as newsgroups to users connecting through either Outlook or an NNTP newsreader. In addition, newsgroups you add directly under the NNTP service appear under the root of the news server. Figure 38-34 illustrates an example. Users see the same unified hierarchy regardless of whether they browse the news server using Outlook or using an NNTP newsreader.

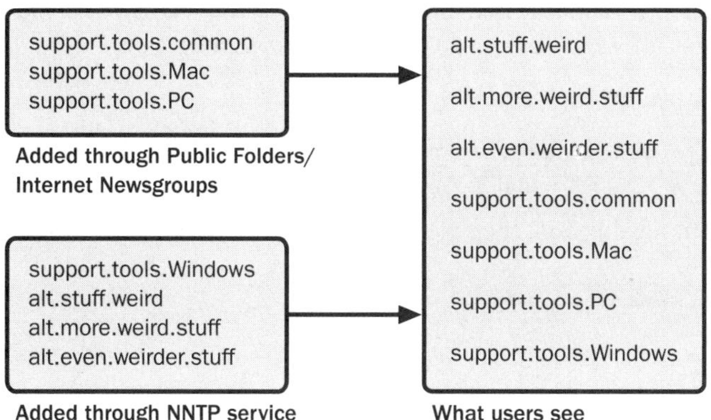

Figure 38-34. Exchange combines the two newsgroup structures into a single hierarchy for users.

You can create newsgroup folders in the Public Folders/Internet Newsgroups folder just as you can in any other public folder.

Follow these steps to create newsgroups through the NNTP service:

1. Open Exchange System Manager, expand the server's Protocols/NNTP branch, and expand the Default NNTP Virtual Server branch.
2. Click the Newsgroups node to view the existing newsgroups. Right-click Virtual Directories and choose New, Newsgroup to start the New Newsgroup Wizard.
3. On the wizard page, type the name for the newsgroup using dotted format, such as support.tools.common, and then click Next.
4. Enter an optional description and pretty name for the newsgroup and click Finish.

> **Tip** Use pretty names
>
> Some news clients can use a *list prettynames* command to view the newsgroup list using the assigned pretty name rather than the default name. The pretty name is another alias for the newsgroup that can be displayed by clients. For example, you might use Common Support Tools as the pretty name for support.tools.common. You can leave these fields blank if you prefer.

Setting Up Moderated Newsgroups

New newsgroups that you add to a virtual server are unmoderated by default. You can easily configure a newsgroup to be moderated, however, which causes all new posts to be sent to a designated moderator for review before posting in the newsgroup.

Follow these steps to set up a moderated newsgroup:

1. Open Exchange System Manager, expand the server's Protocols/NNTP branch, right-click the Default NNTP Virtual Server branch, and choose Properties.
2. In the Properties dialog box, click the Settings tab, shown in Figure 38-35.

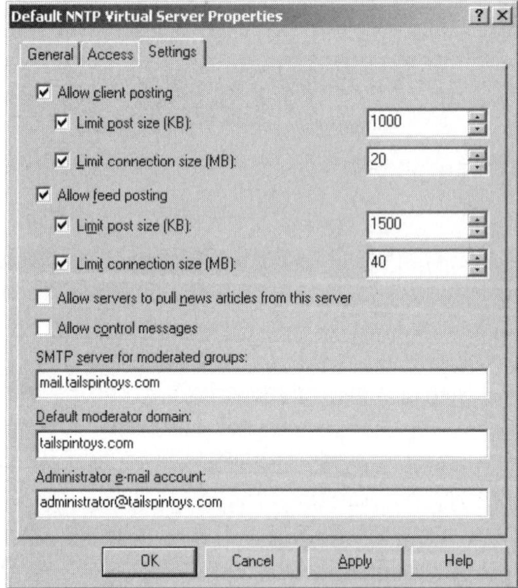

Figure 38-35. Configure the moderator's default domain and SMTP server on the Settings tab.

3. In the SMTP Server For Moderated Groups box, type the SMTP server to which posts should be sent for review by the moderator.

4 In the Default Moderator Domain box, specify the domain in which the moderator's account resides. You can leave this box blank if you specify the full e-mail address for the moderator in step 7.

5 Click OK to close the Properties dialog box, and then click the Newsgroups node.

6 Create the newsgroup or open the Properties dialog box for an existing newsgroup and select the Moderated check box, as shown in Figure 38-36.

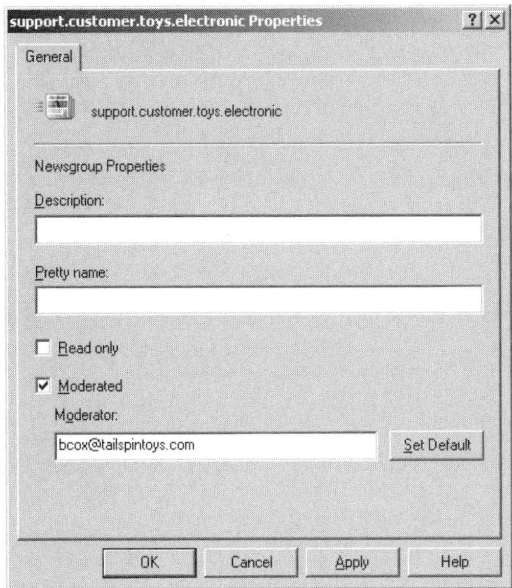

Figure 38-36. Designate the newsgroup as moderated and identify the moderator.

7 In the Moderator box, enter the e-mail address of the moderator. If you prefer, you can specify only the user name, and Exchange Server will combine it with the domain specified in step 4 to determine where to direct messages for review.

8 Click OK to close the Properties dialog box.

Chapter 39

Managing Windows SharePoint Services

Microsoft Windows SharePoint Services is a workgroup-class, Web-based portal product that can be used for collaboration, including document management for a team or workgroup within an organization. Each team requiring this collaboration functionality will typically have their own SharePoint site that they can use to share documents, have threaded discussions, share lists of important information, and more.

This chapter explains what Windows SharePoint Services is, how it works, and how it relates to Microsoft SharePoint Portal Server. SharePoint Portal Server is an enterprise-class portal product from Microsoft that uses Windows SharePoint Services but adds another layer to connect multiple SharePoint sites into a single organization-wide site.

This chapter also explains the installation process for Windows SharePoint Services, including the required prerequisites. As it is Web based, it must be installed on a Web server that must be running Microsoft Windows Server 2003 with Microsoft Internet Information Services. It also explains the basic administration of a SharePoint site, including the initial site setup and managing users, data, and sites.

Windows SharePoint Services Overview

Microsoft provides a product called Windows SharePoint Services (formerly SharePoint Team Services) that can be used as a collaboration portal for work teams within an organization. A *portal* is used to provide a unified, Web-based front end for disparate data. In fact, this is precisely what Windows SharePoint Services does. It provides a Web-based interface to data typically shared within a team, such as contacts, Web links, documents, events, and surveys. Windows SharePoint Services even provide a discussion board that can be used for threaded discussions within the team. Discussion boards provide a cleaner way to have electronic discussions with other team members as opposed to the traditional method of sending e-mail messages back and forth with every team member on the message's To: or CC: list.

One of the biggest advantages to using Windows SharePoint Services, and the reason it's discussed in this book, is that it fully integrates with Microsoft Office 2003. For example, documents on a SharePoint site can be created, viewed, and edited in Microsoft Word. Similarly, contact lists can be imported to and exported from Microsoft Outlook to the SharePoint site. The integration between Microsoft Office and Windows SharePoint Services is covered in detail in Chapter 40, "Collaboration with Outlook and Windows SharePoint Services."

Differences Between Windows SharePoint Services and SharePoint Portal Server

Windows SharePoint Services is a very feature-rich engine for building workgroup-sized portal sites used for team collaboration. Microsoft SharePoint Portal Server is essentially a scaled-up version of Windows SharePoint Services used for building enterprise-class portals. Essentially, SharePoint Portal Server allows you to build a number of team collaboration sites similar to Windows SharePoint Services, but it also allows you to link them together to form an end-to-end portal to all of the data within the organization. A smaller organization would typically use a few Windows SharePoint Services sites, one for each team, whereas a larger organization with more teams would typically implement SharePoint Portal Server. Any organization requiring a high level of data integration across teams should consider SharePoint Portal Server.

SharePoint Portal Server provides tools to organize and manage the individual SharePoint sites created for each team. In addition, SharePoint Portal Server can also form an integrated front end for all applications in an organization, including those from both Microsoft and other developers. Portals are slowly gaining ground in corporations, especially as more and more applications are moving to multitiered models with Web-based front ends. A portal creates a single point of entry into all of the applications in the enterprise.

You might notice that the functionality provided by Windows SharePoint Services and SharePoint Portal Server is similar to that of an intranet (a network of Web pages within an organization). Whereas intranets are typically used for disseminating static information, portals add the ability to access dynamic data through applications and allow users to update data in real time. It appears that many companies will be moving from simple intranets to full portals to simplify access to business data. This simplification allows users to work more efficiently as they have all the information and applications they need close at hand.

Understanding the Windows SharePoint Services Security Model

Windows SharePoint Services has a number of features to ensure the security of data stored in SharePoint sites. These security features mimic the standard security features implemented in most applications and include user and group security and connection security.

User and Group Security

Windows SharePoint Services implements user and group security to keep individual SharePoint sites secure. Each site needs only to be accessible to the associated team and should not be accessible to anyone else in case the data on the site is sensitive or confidential.

User accounts can be either local user accounts on a server or domain user accounts stored in Microsoft Active Directory service. These accounts are associated with a site and given access to the site. User authentication is taken care of by Microsoft Internet Information Services (IIS) and any user authentication methods provided by IIS can be used, such as basic authentication or Secure Sockets Layer (SSL). In addition, Windows SharePoint Services uses groups called *site groups* to determine what access each user has.

A site group is essentially a set of permissions. A user placed in a site group inherits all of the permissions associated with that group. Windows SharePoint Services includes a number of site groups by default, including Administrator, Contributor, and Reader, each with a specific set of permissions. Users in the Contributor site group can add content to the SharePoint site, whereas users in the Reader group can only view existing content on the site.

Connection Security

In addition to the user and group security provided by Windows SharePoint Services, a number of connection security features are implemented to avoid leaking confidential information on the network. The most important connection security feature that you can implement is SSL. SSL allows you to encrypt the data going to and from the Windows SharePoint Services site. Without SSL, data is sent over the network in plain text and a skilled attacker could intercept and read the data. SSL encryption ensures that even if the attacker intercepts the data, it is very difficult to decrypt and is therefore useless. SSL is especially important on the Windows SharePoint Services administrative port, which is used to perform advanced administration tasks on the site.

The other connection security feature that you should ensure is in place is Microsoft SQL Server security. SQL Server allows you to use either Windows integrated authentication or SQL Server authentication. Windows integrated authentication should always be used to ensure the security of the data in your database. Using SQL Server authentication requires that you specify the authentication information in the site configuration, whereas Windows integrated authentication allows you to keep your authentication information secret. An attacker who gains the authentication information for your SQL Server database has free reign over your data and can read or change it at will.

Installing Windows SharePoint Services

Windows SharePoint Services must be installed on a Windows Server 2003 system. Before you begin installing, you need to ensure a number of important components are in place. You can then install and configure Windows SharePoint Services.

Preparing for Windows SharePoint Services Installation

Windows SharePoint Services has several prerequisites before installation. First and foremost, it must be installed on a system running Microsoft Windows Server 2003; earlier versions of Windows are not supported.

> **Tip** **Use SharePoint Team Services**
> If you do not or cannot use Windows Server 2003, the previous version of Windows SharePoint Services, called Microsoft SharePoint Team Services, is included with Microsoft FrontPage 2002 and Microsoft Office XP Developer Edition. It is capable of being installed on a server running Microsoft Windows 2000 Server or even a Microsoft Windows 2000 Professional system.

Once you verify that you are using Windows Server 2003, you then need to ensure that the proper components are installed. Windows SharePoint Services requires the World Wide Web (WWW) component of IIS as well as the ASP.NET component. In addition, the WWW component installs a few other required components that are not installed by default in Windows Server 2003 for security reasons.

Follow these steps to install the required components:

1. Select Start, Control Panel, Add Or Remove Programs.
2. Click the Add/Remove Windows Components icon on the left side of the Add Or Remove Programs dialog box.
3. In the Windows Components Wizard, click Application Server but do not select the check box. Click Details.
4. Click Internet Information Services in the Application Server dialog box, again without selecting the check box, and click Details.
5. In the Internet Information Services (IIS) dialog box that appears, scroll down the list and select theWorld WideWeb Service check box as shown in Figure 39-1, then click OK. Some other components will be selected automatically. These other components are required for the World Wide Web Service to function.

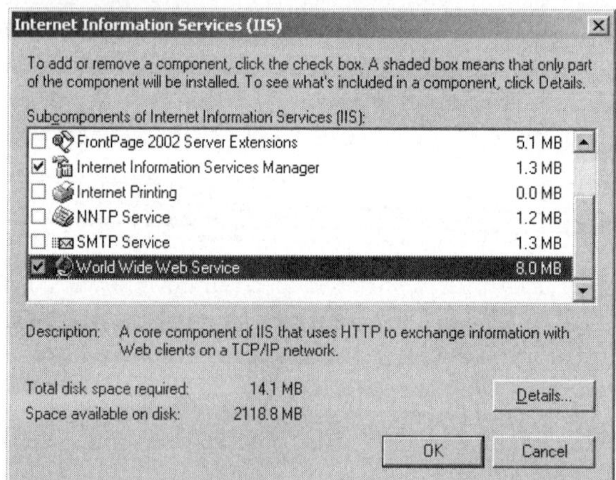

Figure 39-1. Select the World Wide Web Service check box to install the WWW component of Internet Information Services.

6 In the Application Server dialog box, select the ASP.NET check box. The Application Server dialog box should now have the ASP.NET and Enable Network COM+ Access components checked and the Internet Information Services (IIS) component checked with a gray check box as shown in Figure 39-2. The gray check box indicates that not all of the subcomponents of IIS are selected. Click OK.

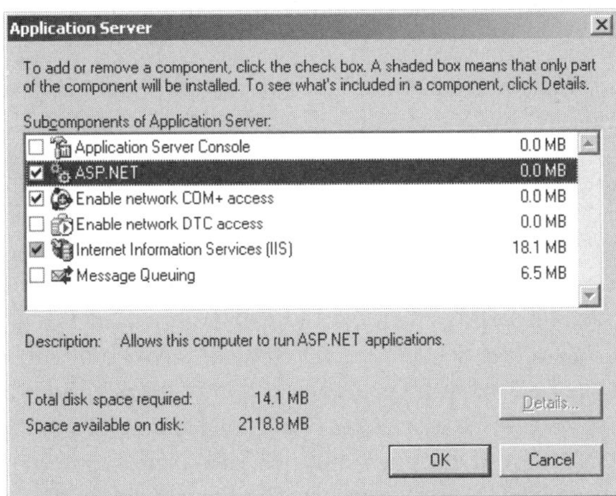

Figure 39-2. Once you have selected the required components, the ASP.NET and Enable Network COM+ Access check boxes will be selected and the Internet Information Services (IIS) check box will be gray and selected.

7 The Windows Components Wizard will now have the Application Server component selected with a gray check box. Click Next to continue the installation process.

8 The selected components will now be installed by the Windows Components Wizard. You might be prompted to insert your Windows Server 2003 CD during this process so that the wizard can copy the required files to your system.

9 Once the selected components are installed, click Finish to close the Windows Components Wizard.

With Windows SharePoint Services, the FrontPage 2002 Server Extensions must not be running on port 80. This is only a potential problem if IIS was already installed on your system either manually or through an upgrade of your system from Windows 2000 Server. If you followed the preceding steps to install IIS, you don't need to worry about the FrontPage Extensions. The simplest way to ensure that the extensions are not running on port 80 is to ensure that they are not installed in the Internet Information Services (IIS) screen of the Windows Components Wizard. If you need the FrontPage Server Extensions running on another port, you must configure this on a per-site basis, which is outside the scope of this book.

Now that the prerequisites for Windows SharePoint Services have been installed, you can move on to the next section, which outlines the installation process for Windows SharePoint Services itself.

Installing Windows SharePoint Services

The installation process for Windows SharePoint Services is a very simple, mostly hands-off procedure. Once you've completed the preliminary steps outlined in the previous section, you can begin the installation. To install Windows SharePoint Services, follow these steps:

1. Run the Windows SharePoint Services setup program in the Windows SharePoint Services folder.
2. Read the license agreement shown in the first step of the Setup wizard. Select the I Accept The Terms In The License Agreement check box and click Next to continue.
3. You have two options when installing Windows SharePoint Services, as shown in Figure 39-3:
   - **Typical Installation** The typical Windows SharePoint Services installation installs the Microsoft SQL Server Desktop Engine (MSDE) and Windows SharePoint Server and configures the default IIS Web site for Windows SharePoint Services. This is the most common Windows SharePoint Services installation type and can be used when you don't have any specific requirements for your site. This option will overwrite any data currently in your default IIS Web site. Using WSS with MSDE using the Typical Installation option is somewhat limited in that the MSDE must reside on the same server as the IIS server and the MSDE is only a basic database engine.
   - **Server Farm** This option installs Windows SharePoint Services but does not configure a database engine or an IIS Web site for use with Windows SharePoint Services. The Server Farm requires you to install and configure a database and configure a Web site manually. Although this is a much more complicated process, it allows you to run a larger, more scalable, and more robust Windows SharePoint Services site. The Server Farm option allows you to run multiple front-end Web servers pointing to a single back-end database, thus distributing the load and allowing more simultaneous users.
4. Select an option and click Next. Configuring Windows SharePoint Services when the Server Farm option is selected is covered in the Setting Up and Configuring Windows SharePoint Services Sites section later in this chapter. Selecting Typical Installation means no further configuration is necessary.
5. A summary of your selections is shown in this step of the wizard. Once you click Install, Windows SharePoint Services will be installed and your default IIS Web site will be configured automatically. Click Install to continue.
6. The installation progress is shown as Windows SharePoint Services is installed.

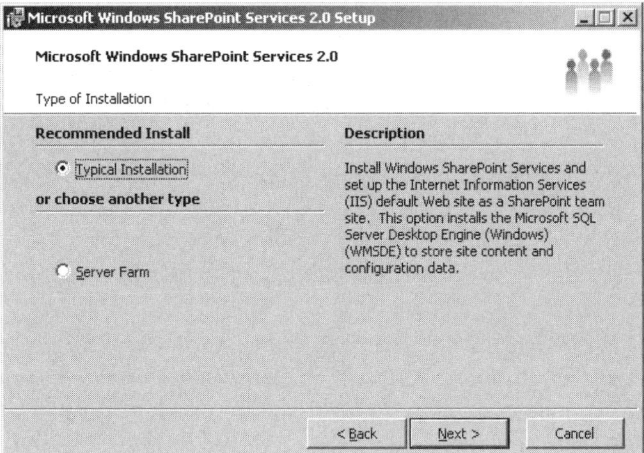

Figure 39-3. You can install Windows SharePoint Services using a Typical Installation, which installs and configures all required components automatically, or Server Farm, which requires you to install and configure the database and IIS Web site manually.

Once Windows SharePoint Services has been completely installed, the Windows SharePoint Services Team Web Site Home page opens, as shown in Figure 39-4, if you selected theTypical Installation option. If you selected Server Farm, you still need to configure your system for Windows SharePoint Services and the Windows SharePoint Services Central Administration site opens to the Configure Administrative Virtual Server page, as discussed in the section "Setting Up and Configuring Windows SharePoint Services Sites."

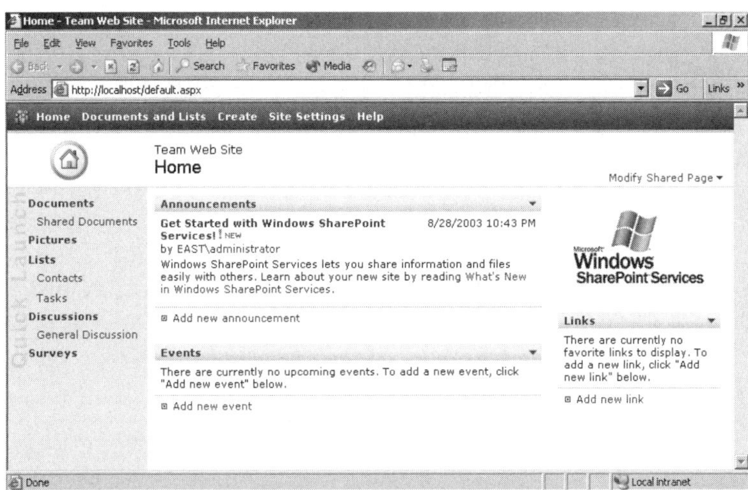

Figure 39-4. If you selected Typical Installation during the install process, the Team Web Site Home page opens once the installation completes.

Administering Windows SharePoint Services

Once Windows SharePoint Services is installed, you can begin to configure it to fit your environment. Configuration of Windows SharePoint Services includes the Windows SharePoint Services site configuration and user and group configuration. Windows SharePoint Services configuration is done from two different tools. Most basic configuration is done from the Site Settings page within the site you are configuring. The Site Settings page is opened by clicking the Site Settings link at the top of any page in the Windows SharePoint Services site. The Site Settings page is used for user and group administration, site and workspace configuration, and customization.

The second tool used to configure Windows SharePoint Services is the Windows SharePoint Services Central Administration Web site. This site can be opened by selecting SharePoint Central Administration from the Start, Administrative Tools menu. The Central Administration page is used to configure virtual servers for Windows SharePoint Services, configure security settings for the entire SharePoint installation, configure the SharePoint server settings such as e-mail and database server connections, and configure advanced site-wide components such as full-text searching, usage analysis, and quotas.

Setting Up and Configuring Windows SharePoint Services Sites

The first Windows SharePoint Services site is created automatically during installation if you selected the Typical Installation option rather than the Server Farm option. In that case you don't need to do much in the way of server configuration. You should configure the server's e-mail settings, however, as outlined in the section "E-Mail Configuration."

If you selected the Server Farm option during installation, you need to configure the application pool and configuration database for the Windows SharePoint Services site, then extend an IIS virtual Web site. The installation of Microsoft SQL Server is not covered here. See *http://www.microsoft.com/sql/techinfo/productdoc/2000/default.asp* for more information on installing SQL Server, including the MSDN Books Online with the full installation documentation.

When you complete the installation of Windows SharePoint Services with the Server Farm option selected, the Windows SharePoint Services Central Administration site opens to the Configure Administrative Virtual Server page, shown in Figure 39-5. If you closed the window, you can also open this page by selecting SharePoint Central Administration from the Start, Administrative Tools menu. If you haven't configured the Administrative Virtual Server, the Central Administration site opens to this page automatically.

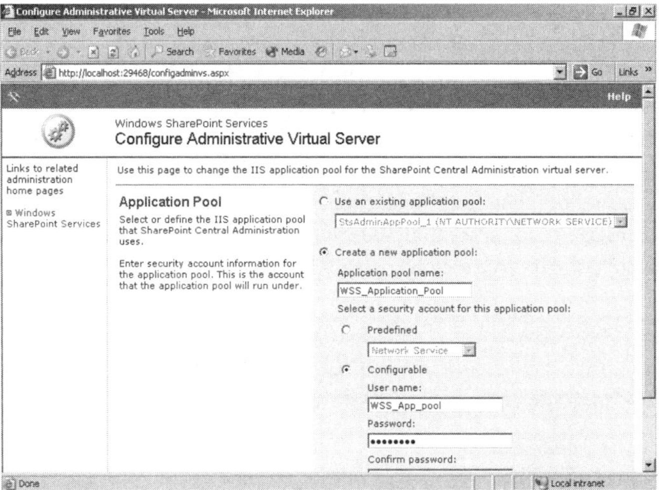

Figure 39-5. The first step in the Windows SharePoint Services site configuration for a site installed with the Server Farm option is to configure the Administrative Virtual Server.

The Configure Administrative Virtual Server page is used to configure an application pool for the SharePoint Central Administration site. This application pool is used to run the scripts that configure the Windows SharePoint Services site. Specify a name for the new application pool, then specify a user name and password for the account under which the application pool will run. This should be an account specifically created for the Windows SharePoint Services application pool. Ensure this account has the required rights in Active Directory or the Local Security Policy tool to log on as a service. Click OK to save your changes. You will now be prompted by the Application Pool Changed page in the Central Administration site to restart IIS and make the changes take effect. Click Start, All Programs, Accessories, Command Prompt to open a command prompt window. Type the command **iisreset** and press Enter. Once the restart is complete, type **exit** and press Enter to close the Command Prompt window. Go back to the Application Pool Changed page in your Web browser and click OK.

Database Configuration

Windows SharePoint Services uses two types of database: a single configuration database for the entire Windows SharePoint Services installation, and individual content databases for each Windows SharePoint Services virtual site. The configuration database contains site-wide configuration information in one central database. The content databases store the actual Windows SharePoint Services site content, such as shared documents and lists.

The next step, shown in Figure 39-6, is to specify the configuration database that will be used for Windows SharePoint Services. This database should not exist within the database server; the creation and configuration of the database is done automatically by Windows SharePoint Services. Before you do this, ensure that the user specified in the previous step has been added in SQL Server Enterprise Manager with the Database Creator and Security Administrator permissions. Specify the database server that will contain the configuration database and a name for the configuration database itself. Set the connection security and specify a user name and password if you are using SQL authentication. However, using SQL authentication is not recommended, as it sends the user name and password over the network in clear text, which leaves it vulnerable to sniffing. You can also select the Connect To Existing Configuration Database check box, which is typically used when you have multiple front-end Web servers and one database server. The first Web server would have this option disabled and the configuration database would be created automatically, and subsequent Web servers would enable this option to connect to the newly created database.

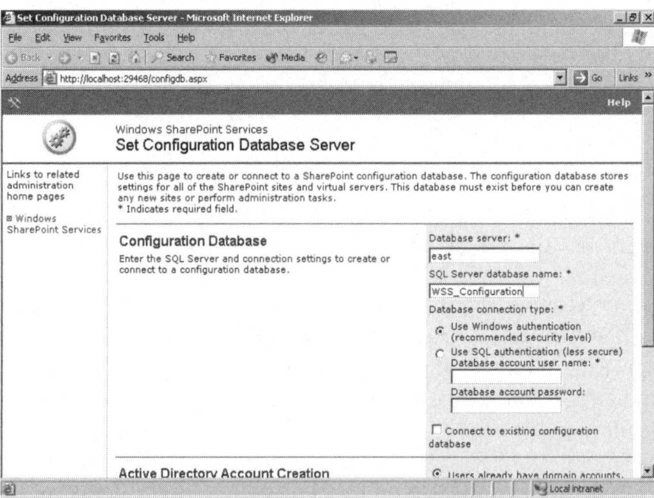

Figure 39-6. Once the application pool is configured, you must configure and create the configuration database for the Windows SharePoint Services server.

At the bottom of the Set Configuration Database Server page is the Active Directory Account Creation option. This option allows you to specify whether user accounts are created in Active Directory or existing domain accounts are used. This option is not very clear in its purpose. If the users connecting to your Windows SharePoint Services site are internal to your network and already have user accounts in your Windows domain, you should use the Users Already Have Domain Accounts option. The Automatically Create Active Directory Accounts For Users Of This Site option is used when the users accessing the Windows SharePoint Services site will access from outside your Windows domain. In this case they will have Active Directory user accounts created for them when they are added to the Windows SharePoint Services site. If you do select this second option to create the Active Directory accounts, specify the domain name and organizational unit in which the accounts will be created.

Once you have specified all of the required information, click OK and the configuration database will be created. Once the configuration database is in place, you are taken to the Windows SharePoint Server Central Administration page, where you can continue configuring Windows SharePoint Services by extending a virtual Web site.

Extending a Virtual Server

Now that your application pool and configuration database are configured and created, you need to add an actual Windows SharePoint Services site to your server. From the Windows SharePoint Server Central Administration page shown in Figure 39-7, click the Extend Or Upgrade Virtual Server link. The Central Administration page is shown by default after you complete the configuration database setup as in the previous section, but you can also open it by clicking Start, Administrative Tools, SharePoint Central Administration.

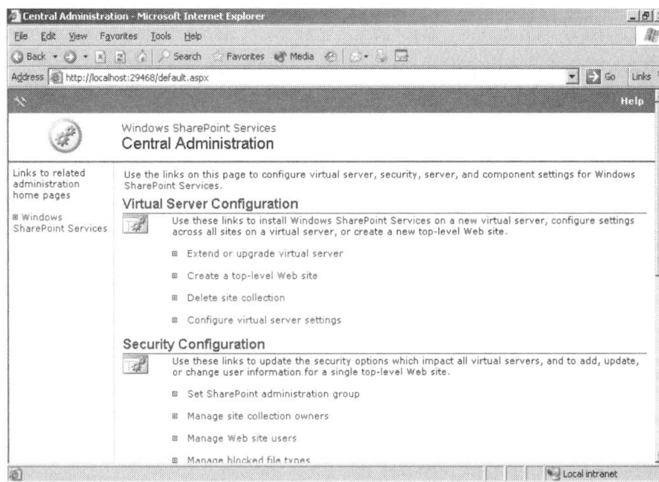

Figure 39-7. The SharePoint Central Administration page is the main tool used to configure server-wide Windows SharePoint Services settings.

When you click the Extend Or Upgrade Virtual Server link, the Virtual Server List is displayed, as shown in Figure 39-8. This page shows a list of all virtual Web servers configured on your IIS server that are not currently extended for use with Windows SharePoint Services. Click Complete List to see both the virtual servers that are extended for use with Windows SharePoint Services and those that are not. To extend a virtual server, click the virtual server name in the list. In this example, WSS Site #1 will be extended.

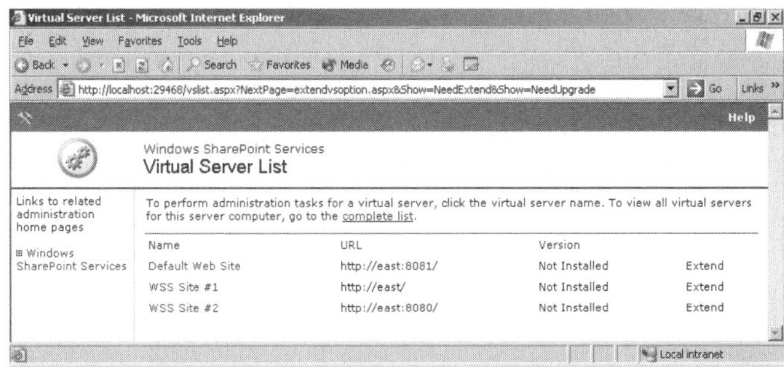

Figure 39-8. The Virtual Server List shows the IIS virtual Web servers that are not configured for use with Windows SharePoint Services.

Once you click the name of the virtual server you want to extend, the Extend Virtual Server page shown in Figure 39-9 is displayed. You have two options for extending the virtual server:

- **Extend And Create A Content Database** This option extends the virtual server for use with Windows SharePoint Services and creates a new content database for the site.
- **Extend And Map To Another Virtual Server** This option extends the virtual server for use with Windows SharePoint Services but does not create a new content database. Instead, it maps the site to another virtual server. This option is used when you have more than one front-end Web server. The first Web server is extended using the option to create a content database and subsequent servers are mapped to that content database using the Extend And Map To Another Virtual Server option.

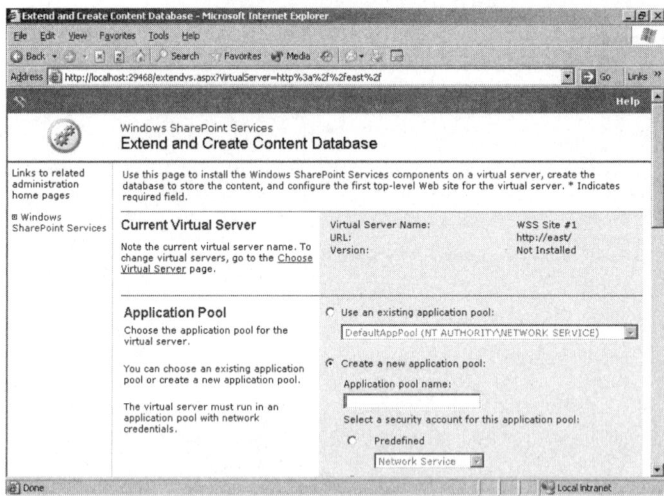

Figure 39-9. The Extend Virtual Server page is the first step in extending a virtual server for use with Windows SharePoint Services.

Creating a Stand-Alone Web Server or the First Server in a Group Whether you are extending a stand-alone Web server or the first server in a group of front-end Web servers, click the Extend And Create A Content Database option. The Extend And Create Content Database page appears, as shown in Figure 39-10. The first step is to configure the application pool that will be used with this site. You can use the existing Windows SharePoint Services application pool created earlier by selecting Use An Existing Application Pool and selecting that application pool from the list. If you are concerned about security or performance, you can create an application pool for this site by selecting Create A New Application Pool and specifying an application pool name, account, and password.

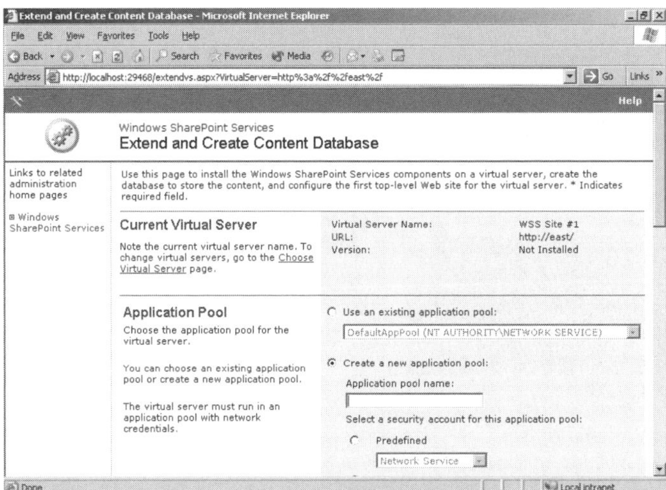

Figure 39-10. Extending a Windows SharePoint Services site and creating a new content database is done on the Extend And Create Content Database page.

Next, specify the site owner user account and e-mail address. The site owner is the user that has full control over the site when it is created. This user will have the sole responsibility for adding access to the site for other users, although he or she can delegate administrative privileges to other users.

The Database Information section is used to configure the content database, although no configuration is necessary by default. With the Use Default Content Database Server check box selected, the database will be placed on the same database server on which the configuration database resides, and the database name will be generated automatically. You can clear the check box and specify a different database server and a specific database name.

You can set a custom URL for your site if required. By default, the Windows SharePoint Services site is placed at http://URL/ but by specifying something else for this option the site will be placed at http://URL/*custom_url* where *custom_url* is the text you type in this box. You can also select a quota template to use if any have been defined, which limits the amount of space a user can fill on the site, and you can also specify the language for the Windows SharePoint Services site.

Once you have finished specifying configuration options, click OK. The site is extended and you are taken to a page notifying you that the configuration is complete. Click the URL for the new site and it opens in a new window. The site owner must log into the site and set the site template as shown in Figure 39-11. Select a template and click OK. In most cases the Team Site template is a good start. Once this is complete, the new site opens in the new browser window. You can close this window and click OK in the Virtual Server Successfully Extended page that should still be open to return to the Virtual Server Settings page.

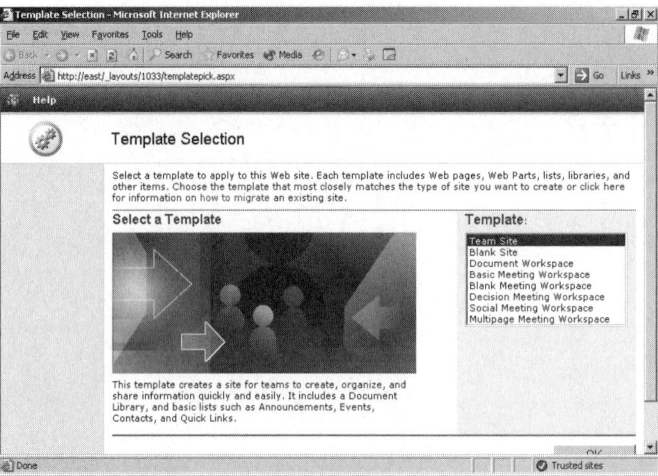

Figure 39-11. When a new site is extended the site owner must log in and select a template for the site.

Mapping a Virtual Server to an Existing Database If you have extended a virtual server and created a content database on one system and you want to add another Web server to the Windows SharePoint Services site, click Extend And Map To Another Virtual Server on the Extend Virtual Server page to open the Extend And Map To Another Virtual Server page shown in Figure 39-12.

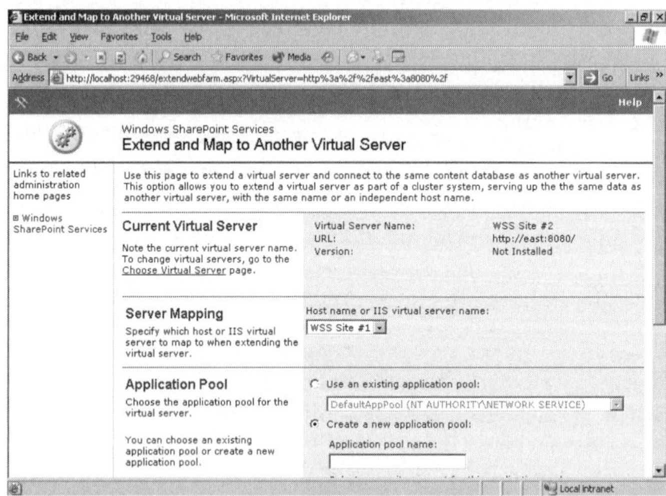

Figure 39-12. The Extend And Map To Another Virtual Server page is used when the content database for the virtual server you are creating already exists.

Select the host name of the virtual server to which you want to map your site from the Host Name Or IIS Virtual Server Name drop-down list. Configure the application pool as explained earlier. Click OK and the server will be extended and you will be taken to the Virtual Server Settings page.

Tip **Set up multiple front-end servers**
Typically, the process for setting up multiple front-end Web servers follows these steps:

1. Install the database server.
2. Install Windows SharePoint Services on the first Web server with the Server Farm installation setting and configure Windows SharePoint Services to use the database server for its configuration database.
3. Extend a virtual server on the first Web server with the content database on the database server from step 1.
4. Install Windows SharePoint Services on the second Web server with the Server Farm installation setting and configure Windows SharePoint Services to use the same configuration database as the first Web server by selecting the Connect To Existing Configuration Database option.
5. Extend a virtual server on the second Web server by using the Extend And Map To An Existing Web Server option and mapping it to the site extended on the first Web server.

Repeat steps 4 and 5 for each subsequent front-end Web server.

E-Mail Configuration

The last step when configuring Windows SharePoint Services is to configure the e-mail settings so that Windows SharePoint Services can send notification e-mail messages to users. E-mail configuration starts from the Windows SharePoint Services Central Administration page. Select SharePoint Central Administration from the Start, Administrative Tools menu, or, if you already have the Central Administration tool open, click the Windows SharePoint Services link in the left-hand column to return to the home page. In the Server Configuration section of the Central Administration page, click Configure Default E-Mail Server Settings. The Configure E-Mail Server Settings page opens, as shown in Figure 39-13.

Note The e-mail server settings must be configured for the alerting features in Windows SharePoint Services to function.

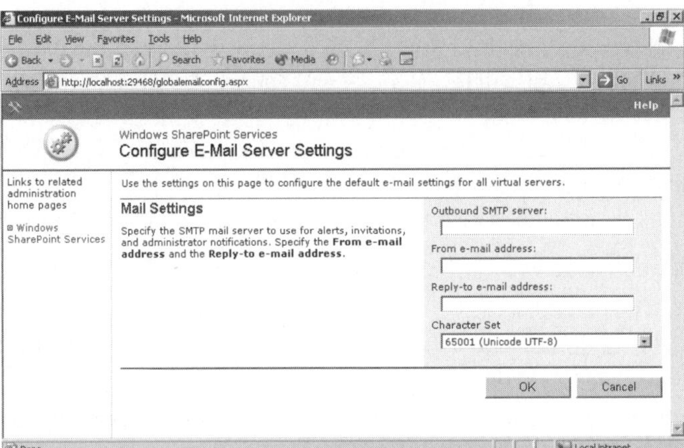

Figure 39-13. The Configure E-Mail Server Settings page is used to set the e-mail server that will be used by Windows SharePoint Services to send notification messages to users.

Specify the outgoing Simple Mail Transfer Protocol (SMTP) server, the From address and Reply-to address for the outgoing e-mail messages, and the character set that should be used for the messages. The From and Reply-to addresses are those that will be placed in every outgoing message. At least the Reply-to address should be a real e-mail address in case a user replies to a notification message. You might want to make these the e-mail address of the site owner or an address such as wss-admin@domain.tld, which is an alias for the site owner. Once you have configured these settings, click OK to save your changes and you are returned to the Windows SharePoint Services Central Administration page.

Managing Users

Once your Windows SharePoint Services site is configured, you need to add users so they can access the site. If you manually extended a Windows SharePoint Services site by following the steps in the last section, you set the site owner manually. If you installed using theTypical Installation setting, the site owner will be set to the user who installed Windows SharePoint Services. The site owner is the user who must begin managing users.

There are two concepts you need to understand when managing users:

- **Users** Users in Windows SharePoint Services are linked to Windows user accounts. Once a user is added to the Windows SharePoint Services site, he or she has access to the Windows SharePoint Services site with a specific privilege level set by the administrator.
- **Site Groups** Site groups are groups of users with specific permissions. A site group is essentially a collection of permissions that can be assigned as a group. When users are placed in a site group, they are assigned all of the permissions associated with the group. A number of site groups exist by default, such as the Reader site group, which can view but not add or modify data, and the Administrator site group, which has full access to the site.

To begin working with users and groups, open the Windows SharePoint Services site to manage in a Web browser. The address is typically *http://localhost* if you are using the default virtual server for your site and you are on the Windows SharePoint Services server itself. Click the Site Settings link at the top of the site, then click the Manage Users link in the Administration section of the Site Settings page. You are then at the Manage Users page shown in Figure 39-14.

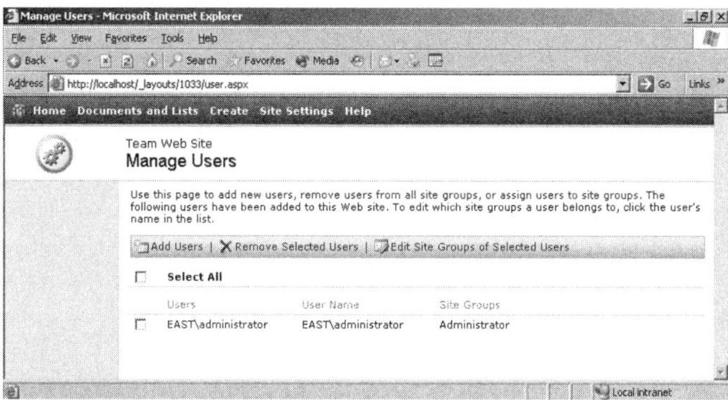

Figure 39-14. The Manage Users page shows a list of existing users in the site and is used to add and remove users and set their site group membership.

Adding Users

Adding a user to your Windows SharePoint Services site allows that user to access and work with the data in the site. Adding a user is a simple process:

1. Click Add Users on the Manage Users page.
2. In the first Add Users page, shown in Figure 39-15, specify the users to add in the Users box. You can specify users by e-mail address, user name, or cross-site group name, and the entries must be separated by semicolons.

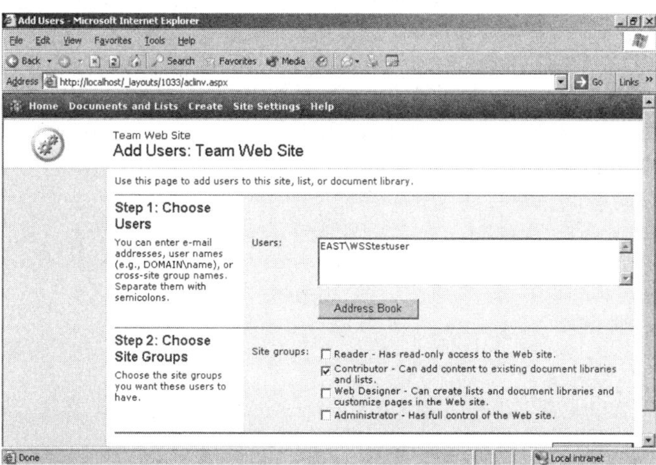

Figure 39-15. The first Add Users page allows you to specify the users to add and their site group membership.

3 Select the site groups to which the specified users should belong from the choices provided. Any custom site groups you create will be shown in this list as well.

4 Click Next.

5 The second Add Users page shown in Figure 39-16 shows a list of the users being added in the Confirm Users section. If you specified the user by e-mail address, you must specify the user's associated local or domain user account in the User Name box. If you specified the user by user name, you must specify that user's e-mail address. Every user you add must have both a user account and an e-mail address specified. The Display Name box is used to define how the user is identified when he or she posts information to the site.

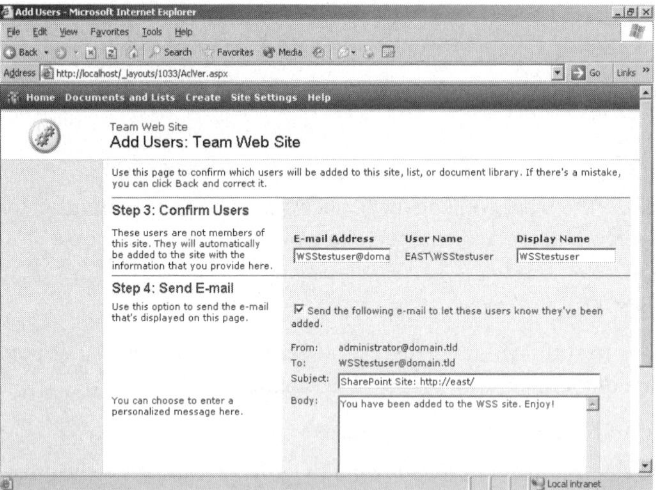

Figure 39-16. The second Add Users page is used to specify the user names or e-mail addresses for those not specified and send a notification e-mail to the users.

6 You can send the specified users an e-mail message welcoming them to the site and providing them with the site URL. Select the Send The Following E-Mail To Let These Users Know They've Been Added check box, then specify a message in the Body box. You can also change the default Subject line if you need to. Below the Body box is the text that is automatically appended to the body of the message, including the URL for the site and the user's level of access.

7 Click Finish to add the users. Once the users have been added you are returned to the Manage Users page.

Deleting and Modifying Users

Deleting a user from Windows SharePoint Services is simple from the Manage Users page. Select the check box next to the user you want to delete from the site and click Remove Selected Users. You are prompted to verify the deletion; click OK and the user will be deleted.

Modifying the site group membership of a user is equally simple. Select the check box next to the user to edit and click Edit Site Groups Of Selected Users to open the Edit Site Group Membership page shown in Figure 39-17. Change the user's site group membership as required and click OK to save your changes.

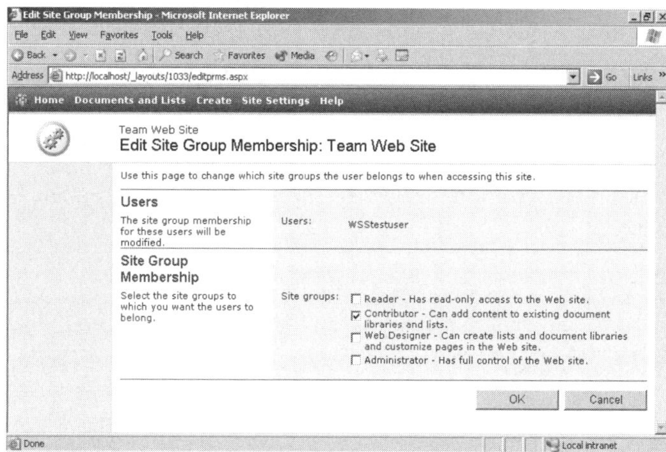

Figure 39-17. You can change a user's site group membership on the Edit Site Group Membership page.

You can delete or edit multiple users in one step by selecting the check box next to each user to edit or delete.

Customizing Site Groups

Four site groups are provided by default—Reader, Contributor, Web Designer, and Administrator—but you can create new site groups and edit the permissions associated with site groups if you want custom site groups with permission sets not reflected in the predefined groups. To add a site group, follow these steps:

1. Click Site Settings at the top of the Windows SharePoint Services page.
2. Click Go To Site Administration in the Administration section of the Site Settings page.
3. Click Manage Site Groups in the Users And Permissions section of theTop-Level Site Administration page to open the Manage Site Groups page shown in Figure 39-18.

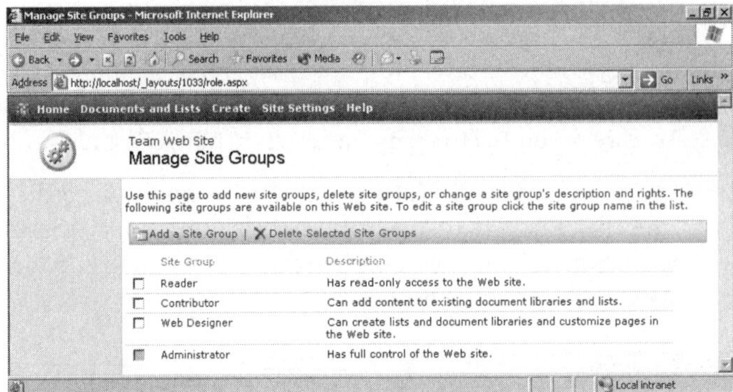

Figure 39-18. The Manage Site Groups page is used to add, remove, and modify site groups.

4 Click Add A Site Group.

5 Specify a name and description for the new site group on the Add A Site Group page shown in Figure 39-19.

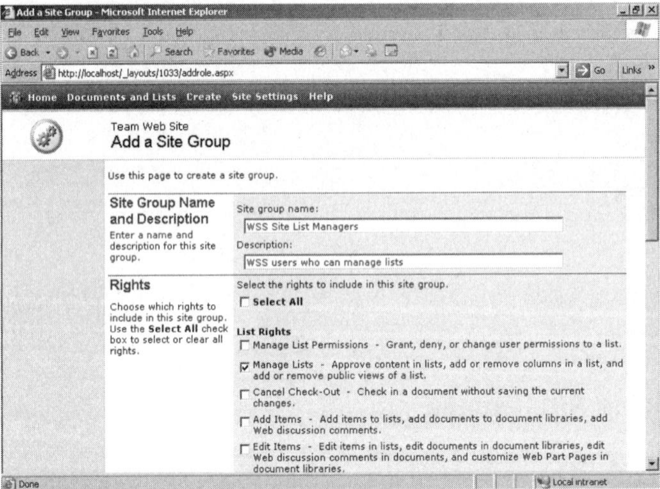

Figure 39-19. The Add A Site Group page allows you to specify the new site group's name and the permissions associated with the group.

6 Select the rights that the site group should have from the list. Note that as you select certain permissions, others are selected automatically. A user cannot have the Manage Lists permission without the View Items permission, for example, so View Items is selected when you select Manage Lists.

7 Click Create Site Group to create the group.

You are then returned to the Manage Site Groups page where you can see the newly created site group. Removing and modifying site groups is as simple as deleting and modifying users, as described in the previous section. To delete a group or groups, select the check box next to each group to delete, click Delete Selected Site Groups, confirm the deletion by clicking OK, and the group is deleted.

To edit the permissions assigned to a group, click the group name to open the Members page for the list, then click Edit Site Group Permissions. Change the permissions as required and click Submit. You can also copy the permissions in the site group from this page by clicking Copy Site Group at the bottom of the page.You can then give the copied site group a new name and description, change the permissions as needed, and click Create Site Group to create the new copied group.

> **Tip** **Copy a site group**
> Copying a site group is useful when you need a new group with permissions that are close to those of an existing group but not identical. This allows you to avoid selecting each permission individually for the new group. Copying the existing group and making the few required changes is much simpler.

Configuring Anonymous Access

The final user configuration you might wish to make is anonymous access to the site. The Anonymous Access Configuration page allows you to configure whether anonymous users can access the site and also whether authenticated users not added to the site can view the site.

To configure anonymous access, follow these steps:

1. Click Site Settings at the top of the Windows SharePoint Services page.
2. Click Go To Site Administration in the Administration section of the Site Settings page.
3. Click Manage Anonymous Access in the Users And Permissions section of the Top-Level Site Administration page to open the Change Anonymous Access Settings page shown in Figure 39-20.

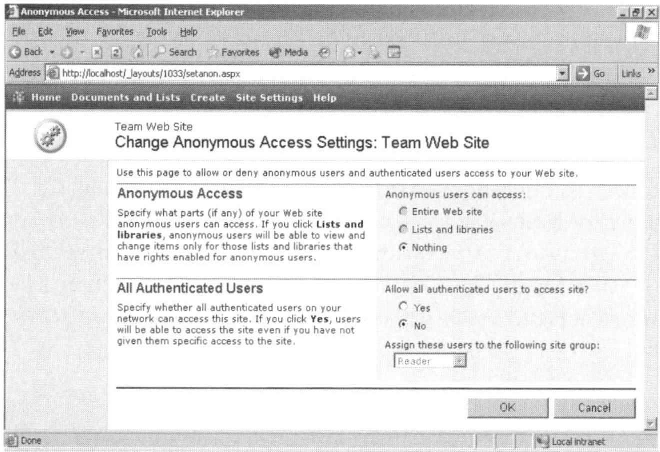

Figure 39-20. The Change Anonymous Access Settings page allows you to control what anonymous and authenticated users can view on your site.

4 Select the access level for anonymous users: EntireWeb Site, Lists And Libraries, or Nothing (the default).

Note If you enable anonymous access in the Windows SharePoint Services configuration, anonymous access must also be enabled in the IIS configuration for the virtual Web server.

5 Select whether all authenticated users should be able to access the site. Authenticated users refers to users who are logged in to the local system or domain but are not associated with the Windows SharePoint Services site in the Manage Users page.

6 Set the permissions that should be assigned to the authenticated users automatically. This is typically only set to Reader, but if you set it to Contributor then users can contribute to the site without the effort of adding every user in the Manage Users page. In a small environment this might be optimal.

7 Click OK to save your changes.

Site Customization

You might want to customize your site to provide a less generic experience for your users. You can customize the site title and description, set a theme, customize site content, and customize the Windows SharePoint Services site home page.

To customize the site title and description, click Site Settings at the top of the Windows SharePoint Services site. Click Change Site Title And Description in the Customization section of the Site Settings page. Set the title and description for the site in the appropriate boxes and click OK to save your changes.

To customize the theme of your site, click Apply Theme To Site in the Customization section of the Site Settings page to open the Apply Theme To Web Site page. A *theme* is a collection of backgrounds, colors, and graphics that customizes the look and feel of your site. Select a theme from the list provided and look at the preview on the left. Once you find a theme you like, click Apply to apply the theme to the site.

Customizing Site Content

A more detailed customization for the site is content customization. Certain content is included in the site by default, such as Contacts, Events, and Links, but content customization allows you to customize the existing content and add new content to the site. On the Site Settings page, click Modify Site Content in the Customization section. The Modify Site Content page shown in Figure 39-21 shows the existing content in the site as well as a Create New Content link.

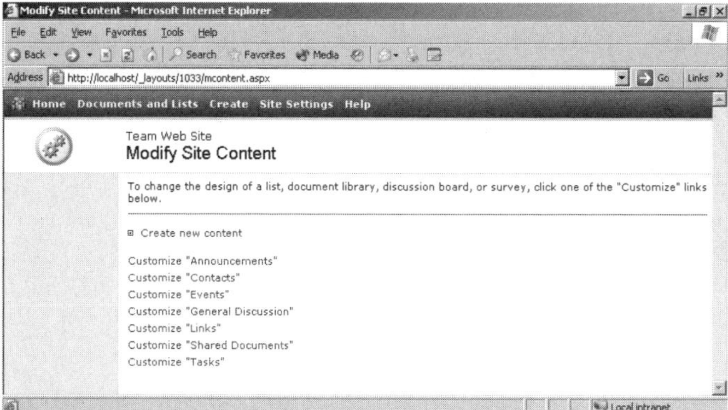

Figure 39-21. The Modify Site Content page is used to add new content and customize existing content in your site.

Click one of the Customize links for existing content to customize that specific item. Clicking Customize Announcements results in the Customize Announcements page shown in Figure 39-22. This page allows you to set general options for the content by clicking Change General Settings, saving the settings as a template, changing permissions, or deleting the content. In addition, you can add, remove, and modify the columns associated with the content and add, remove, or edit the views associated with the content. The columns outline the fields available for data entry for the content and views allow you to create filtered versions of the content that are easily accessible.

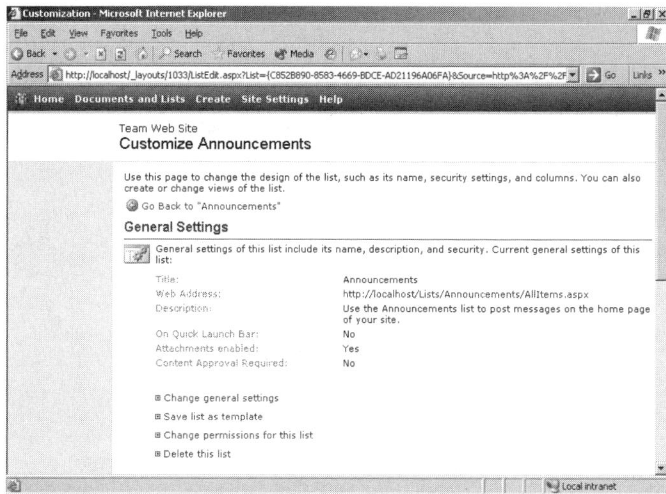

Figure 39-22. The Customize page allows you to customize general settings, columns, and views available for the content.

If you click Create New Content on the Modify Site Content page you are taken to the Create Page page shown in Figure 39-23. This page allows you to create a new type of custom content for your site.

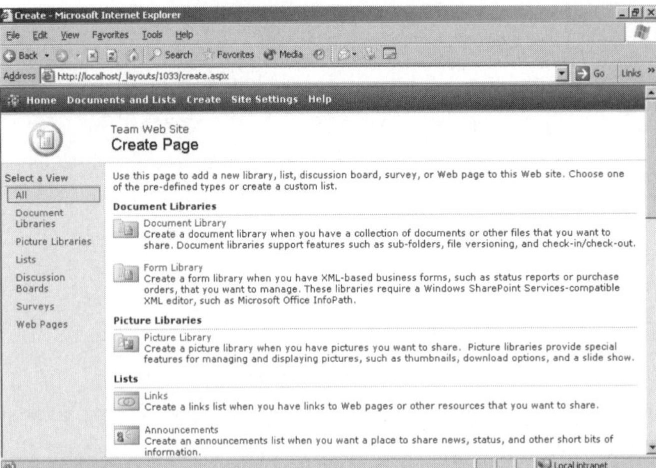

Figure 39-23. Create Page allows you to create totally custom content pages for your site.

On the Create Page page, select the type of content you want to add to your site. A number of predefined content types are listed, such as document and picture libraries and lists. You can also create totally custom blank lists, import lists from spreadsheets, and create custom Web pages that are not content driven like most Windows SharePoint Services pages.

Once you select the type of content to add, the steps differ based on the content type you selected. In most cases you assign a name and description for the content and decide whether or not you want the content shown on the Quick Launch bar as shown in Figure 39-24. You then fill in any other required information and click Create. The new content is added to your site.

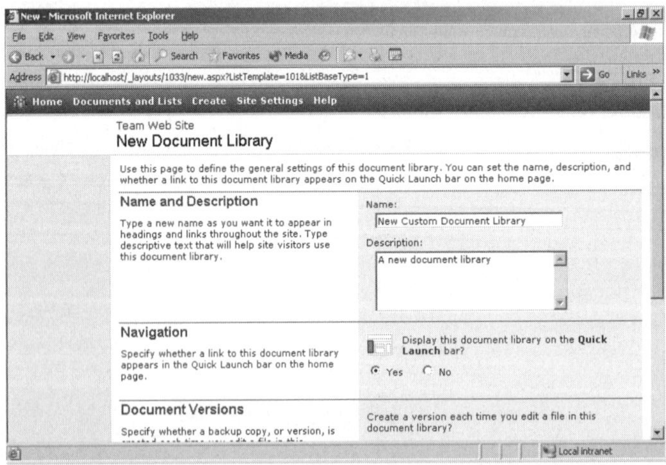

Figure 39-24. The steps for creating new content differ for different content types, but you typically specify a name, description, and whether or not the content will be listed on the Quick Launch bar.

Customizing the Site Home Page

On the Site Settings page, click Customize Home Page in the Customization section. The Home page shown in Figure 39-25 allows you to customize the look of the site's home page.

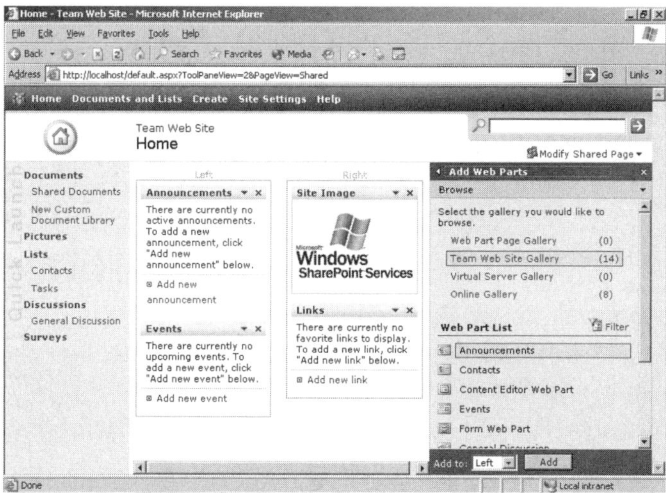

Figure 39-25. The Home page allows you to customize the look of the site home page.

In the middle of the Home page are the home page columns, left and right. You can move the existing Web parts around by clicking and dragging, and you can remove them by clicking the close icon. You can add Web parts to the page by selecting a gallery in the top of the Add Web Parts pane on the right side of the page. Drag a Web part from the bottom of the Add Web Parts pane to your home page.

> **Tip** Web parts are components that you can add to your Windows SharePoint Services site. They include both components from within the Windows SharePoint Services site itself, such as lists and discussion boards, and external components from the Internet.

Once you are finished customizing your home page, you don't need to do anything to save your changes. You can simply click the Home link at the top of the Windows SharePoint Services page to see your new home page.

Configuring Self-Service Site Creation

Self-service site creation allows your users in the Administrator site group to create Windows SharePoint Services sites beneath your main Windows SharePoint Services site. These subsites are complete Windows SharePoint Services sites, identical to the Windows SharePoint Services site you created earlier in the chapter. Self-service creation of sites is used so that Windows SharePoint Services administrators can create new sites without having to be in the Administrators group in the domain or on the local system, and without going through the process of adding a new virtual Web server to IIS and extending it for use with Windows

SharePoint Services. Self-service site creation is typically useful in very large environments because the server administrator does not need to create Windows SharePoint Services sites, and that authority can be delegated to the Windows SharePoint Services site administrators.

Configuring Self-Service Site Creation on the Virtual Server

Configuring self-service site creation is done through the SharePoint Central Administration page, following this procedure:

1. Open the SharePoint Central Administration page by selecting SharePoint Central Administration from the Start, Administrative Tools menu.
2. Click Configure Virtual Server Settings in the Virtual Server Configuration section of the Central Administration page.
3. Click the name of the virtual server containing the Windows SharePoint Services site you want to configure for self-service configuration.
4. Click Configure Self-Service Site Creation in the Automated Web Site Collection Management section of the Virtual Site Settings page.
5. Select the On option for Self-Service Site Creation on the Configure Self-Service Site Creation page shown in Figure 39-26.

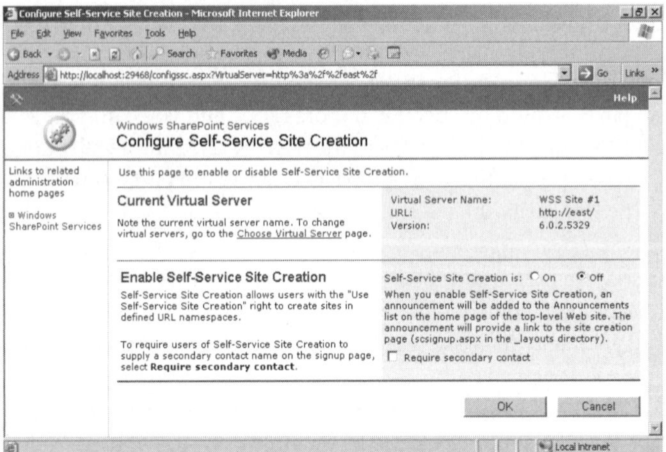

Figure 39-26. The Configure Self-Service Site Creation page is used to enable or disable self-service creation.

6. You can indicate whether a secondary contact must be specified for the newly created site when self-service creation is used. This secondary contact is a user who has some authority over the site in addition to the user who creates the site. This is useful so that the server administration has more than one person to contact with questions regarding the site. This feature is also used with automatic site deletion and site use confirmation.
7. Click OK to save your changes and enable self-service site creation for the virtual site.

Using Self-Service Site Configuration

When self-service site creation is enabled for a site, an announcement is shown in the Announcements section of the site Home page, as shown in Figure 39-27.

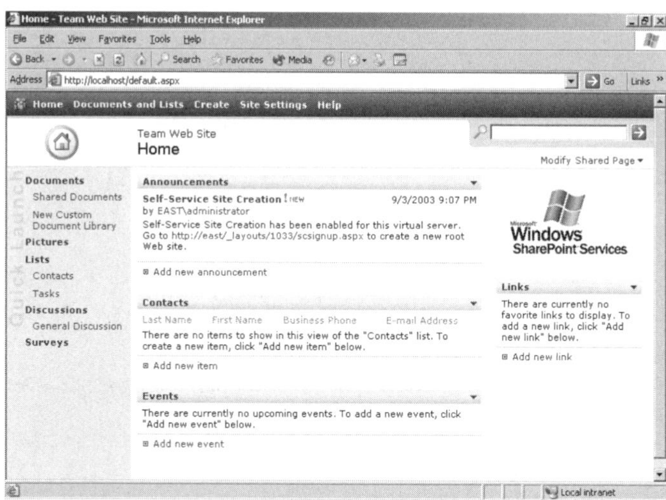

Figure 39-27. When self-service site creation is enabled, an announcement is shown on the site Home page.

> **Note** Only Windows SharePoint Services site users in the Administrators site group or any site group with the Use Self-Service Site Creation permission can add sites using self-service site creation.

To create a new site, follow these steps:

1. Click the signup link in the self-service site creation announcement.
2. On the New SharePoint Site page, shown in Figure 39-28, specify a name and description for the new site.

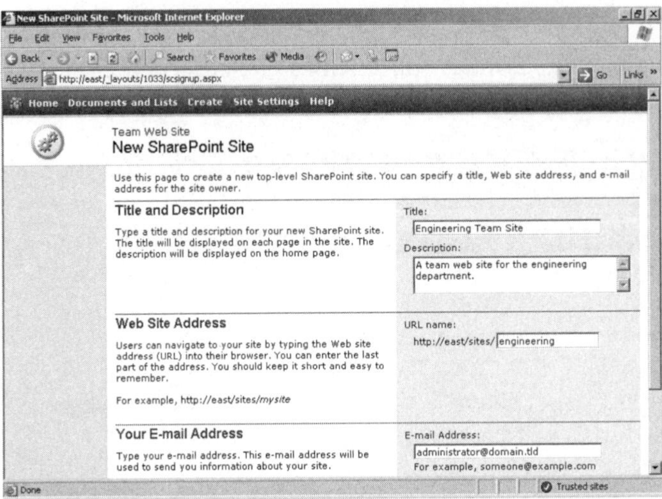

Figure 39-28. Self-service site creation is done through the New SharePoint Site page.

3 Assign an address to the new site in the URL Name box.
4 Specify your e-mail address in the E-Mail Address box.
5 Finally, specify a secondary user account and e-mail address if the secondary contact option was enabled when self-service site creation was enabled.
6 Click Create.
7 Select the template to use for the site and click OK. The template defines what content is created on the site by default. Selecting each template in the list shows a description of the content created with that template. Team Site is the most commonly used template.

Once you click OK in the last step, you are taken to the new site. The new site can be configured in the same way as any other site using the steps outlined earlier in this chapter. Users can reach the site through the URL specified in the URL box during the site creation process.

Chapter 40

Collaboration with Outlook and Windows SharePoint Services

Microsoft Windows SharePoint Services is a collaboration tool used to build Web sites for team members to share data such as contacts and documents. One of the biggest advantages to Windows SharePoint Services other than the fact that it allows team members to share information and collaborate easily, is that it fully integrates with Microsoft Office. Windows SharePoint Services allows you to share documents created with Office applications, and even lets you share contacts stored in Microsoft Office Outlook 2003 with other team members.

Understanding Windows SharePoint Services Collaboration

Chapter 39, "Managing Windows SharePoint Services," outlined what Windows SharePoint Services is and how to install and configure it. Windows SharePoint Services is a Web-based tool, but it also provides integration with Microsoft Office applications. Windows SharePoint Services provides a number of collaboration features, including the following:

- **Document sharing** Document sharing allows you to store documents on the SharePoint site, which can then be accessed by other team members. This is useful for sharing project-related documents, for example, or any other document that other team members might need access to. In addition to simple document storage, document sharing provides version control tools such as document check-in and check-out, so that a document is not accidentally modified by more than one user at a time.
- **Picture libraries** Picture libraries are similar to document libraries in that they store pictures that can be shared among team members. This is basically a photo album feature.
- **Lists** Lists are formatted lists of information. The list format can vary based on the type of information being stored. A number of lists are predefined, such as Announcements, which are displayed on the main SharePoint Home page; Contacts, which holds

contact information; and Links, which can contain links to Web pages. The Events list is a special list type:

- **Team calendar** The Events list is a calendar that can contain events relating to your team or project. The team members can then reference the calendar for important dates instead of having to maintain their own personal calendar.

- **Discussion boards** Discussion boards allow team members to have threaded discussions on specific subjects. Discussion boards are useful to replace e-mail exchanges when more than two people are involved, as those involved can place comments and replies directly in the appropriate thread rather than exchanging a large number of e-mail messages.
- **Surveys** Surveys are simply a method of polling other team members for information.

As stated earlier, one of the key features of Windows SharePoint Services is its ability to integrate with Microsoft Office applications. The features in Windows SharePoint Services that integrate with Microsoft Office include document sharing, which can be done from almost any Office application; lists, which can be synchronized with Microsoft Excel or Microsoft Access files; and calendars (events lists), contacts lists, and alerts, which can be linked into Outlook. In addition, Microsoft FrontPage can be used to edit and customize the Windows SharePoint Services pages. This chapter focuses mainly on the integration of SharePoint and Outlook. SharePoint and Outlook have the tightest integration, as they are both collaboration tools, although each has a different focus.

Setting Up Alerts

Alerts (formerly called subscriptions in the earlier version of WSS, called SharePoint Team Services) are used when you want to be notified when content on the SharePoint site changes. Alerts are sent through e-mail. Setting up an alert is simple with these steps:

1. Locate the content for which you want to configure the alert. This can be virtually anything on the SharePoint site.
2. You can be alerted on either an entire library of items, or a specific item. As you can see in Figure 40-1, there are two places to select Alert Me. Clicking Alert Me in the left column of the page creates an alert for the entire library, so you will be notified when anything in the library changes. Selecting Alert Me from the item's drop-down box means you will be alerted only when that item is changed. Select one of the two Alert Me selections.
3. The New Alert page, shown in Figure 40-2, displays the e-mail address to which alerts will be sent. From this page, select the types of changes you want to be alerted to. Some of the options shown in the figure are not available if you are configuring an alert for a specific item. You can be alerted to all changes; item additions, changes, or deletions; or updates to discussions involving the selected item or library.
4. Select the frequency for alerts from this item or library. The default setting sends an alert message every time the alert is triggered. You can also elect to receive only a daily

or weekly summary of alerts. These options are useful if the item or library for which you are configuring the alert changes often.

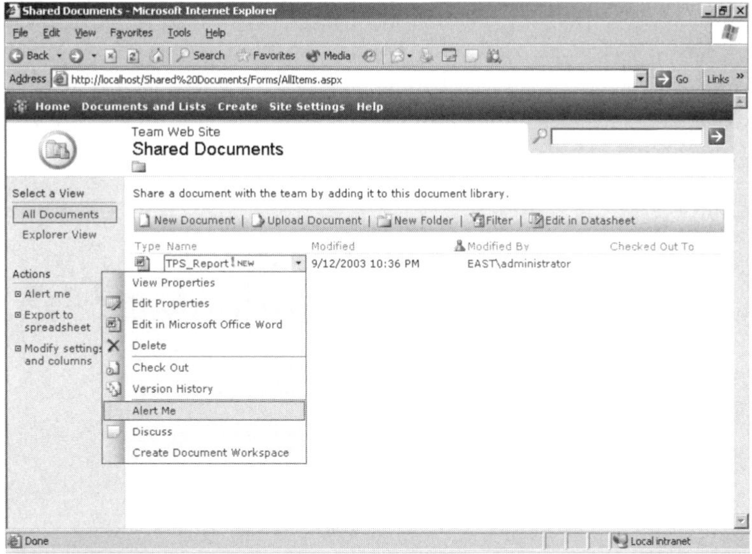

Figure 40-1. There are two Alert Me options, one for the entire library and one for the specific item.

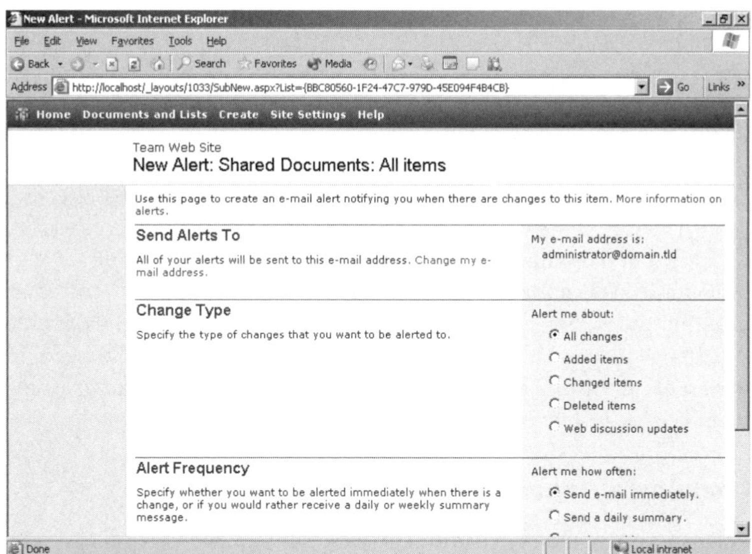

Figure 40-2. The New Alert page is used to configure the alert.

5 Click OK and the alert will be configured.

Once you have created an alert, you will be notified each time the alert criteria set on the New Alert page is met. It is possible to see a list of all of the alerts you have configured on the site by clicking Site Settings at the top of any Windows SharePoint Services page and clicking My Alerts On This Site in the Manage My Information section of the Site Settings page. The My Alerts On This Site page, shown in Figure 40-3, shows all of the alerts you have configured on the site. You can delete an alert by selecting the check box next to the alert you want to delete and clicking Delete Selected Alerts. It is also possible to add an alert for a list or document library (although not individual items) on the My Alerts On This Site page. Click Add Alert, select the library or list for the alert, and click Next. Set the options on the New Alert page as discussed earlier in this section.

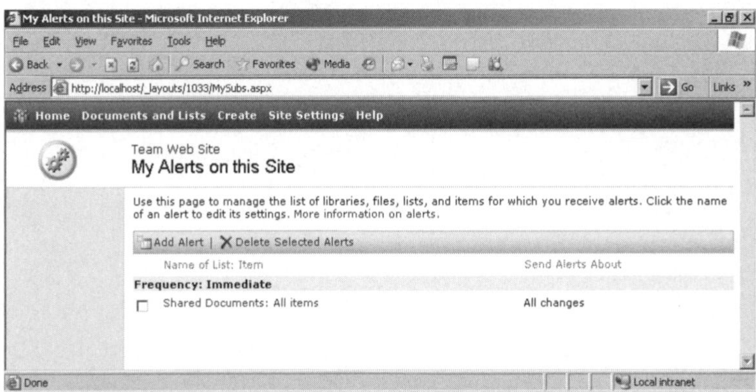

Figure 40-3. You can see all alerts you have configured on the site on the My Alerts On This Site page, which is accessible from the Site Settings page.

Working with Shared Documents

Document sharing is simple with Windows SharePoint Services and can be done in one of two ways. If you have an existing Microsoft Office document, it is an easy process to add it to a document library in Windows SharePoint Services. If you don't already have a document created, you can create it directly in the Windows SharePoint Services site. When you create a document in the Windows SharePoint Services site, the appropriate application opens automatically. When the document is saved, it is placed in the site automatically. In addition to creating and adding documents to the Windows SharePoint Services site, there are a number of things you can do with existing documents in Windows SharePoint Services. You can edit or remove existing documents, and features such as document version history, check-out, and check-in allow simple version control.

Uploading a Document

To upload a document to a document library, follow these steps:

1. Locate and open the document library either from the Quick Launch bar on the left side of the Windows SharePoint Services home page or by clicking Documents And Lists at the top of any Windows SharePoint Services page and selecting the document library.
2. Once in the document library, click Upload Document.

3 On the Upload Document page shown in Figure 40-4, click Browse, locate the file to upload, and click Open. You can also click Upload Multiple Files to open a Windows Explorer–style browser from which you can select multiple files to upload.

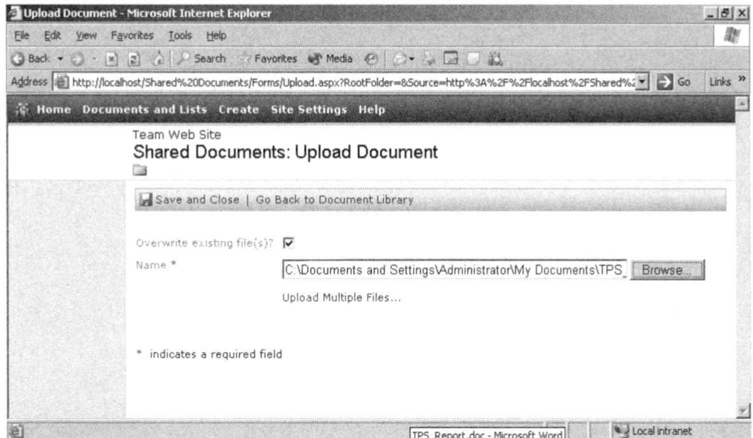

Figure 40-4. The Upload Document page is used to upload files to the document library.

4 Existing files with the same name as the file or files being uploaded are overwritten by default. If you do not want to overwrite any existing files, clear the Overwrite Existing File(s) check box.

5 Once you have specified or selected the files to upload, click Save And Close. The uploaded document will be shown in the document library.

You will now be able to see the uploaded file listed in the document library.

Creating a Document from the Site

In addition to the previous method of uploading an existing document to the document library, you can also create a new document directly from the document library site. The new document is created using the document template associated with the document library. By default, the Microsoft Word Document Template is associated with the Shared Documents library that is created when Windows SharePoint Services is installed. The Document Template setting is configured when a new document library is created and you can set it for an existing library by clicking Modify Settings And Columns in the left bar of the Document Library page, then clicking Change General Settings To create a new document, follow these steps:

1 Open the document library in which you want to create the new document.

2 Click New Document.

3 The Microsoft Office application associated with the document template specified for the selected document library will open automatically.

4 Create and edit your document as needed.

5 Select Save As from the File menu.

6 The Save As location defaults to the document library from which you clicked New Document, as shown in Figure 40-5. Specify a name for the new document in the File Name box.

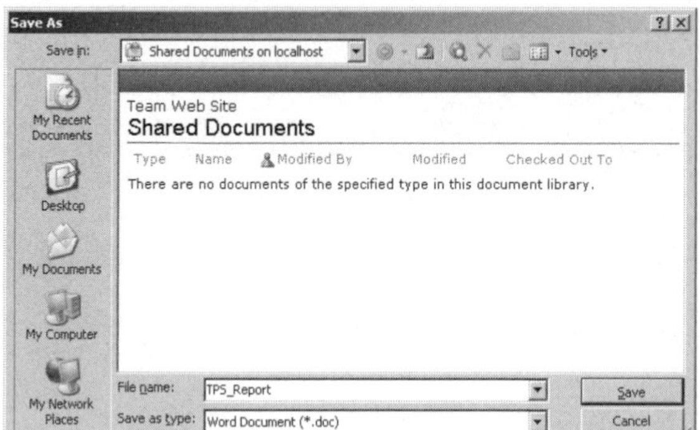

Figure 40-5. When you select Save As in the Office application launched when you clicked New Document, the location for the file defaults to the document library you were working in.

7 Click Save and your document will be saved directly to the document library.

Your newly created document will now be shown in the document library.

Working with Existing Documents and Version Control

Document options for each item in a document library are found in the item's drop-down box. Hover your mouse over a document name and a drop-down button will appear. When you click the button the Item drop-down menu appears. This menu was shown earlier in Figure 40-1. From this menu you can edit the document (clicking the document name also has this effect); edit the document properties, which include the name and a descriptive title for the document; and delete the document from the library.

The key features in a shared document library, however, are the version control features. In Windows SharePoint Services these include the ability to check a document in and out as well as view its version history. When you check a document out, other users can no longer edit the document until you return it to the document library by checking it in.

To check a document out, simply select Check Out from the Item drop-down box. The Checked Out By column will switch to your user name. Checking a document back in to the document library can be done in one of two ways. The first method is used when you open a checked-out document in the appropriate application. When you close the application having saved any changes, the Check In dialog box is displayed, as shown in Figure 40-6. You have three options: you can check the document in, leave it checked out, or discard any changes made to the document since you checked it out and undo the check-out process completely. If you select the Check In File option and click OK, the Check In Comments dialog box opens. Enter comments for the revision of the file (such as what changes were made) for version history purposes and click OK. Once the document library page is updated, the document will no longer show a user name in the Checked Out To column.

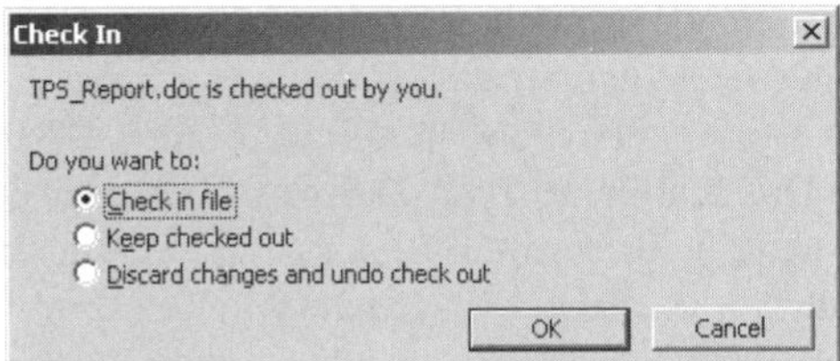

Figure 40-6. The Check In dialog box is used to automatically check a document in once you are finished editing it in an Office application.

The second method of checking a document in is usually used if no changes have been made to the document or if changes were made but the Keep Checked Out option was selected in the Check In dialog box displayed when the application used to edit the document was closed. To manually check a document in, select Check In from the Item drop-down box. The Check In page shown in Figure 40-7 is displayed. Select a check-in option, either to check in the document, check in any changes but leave the document checked out, or discard any changes made since the check out. Enter any comments for the version history and click OK. The document is then checked in.

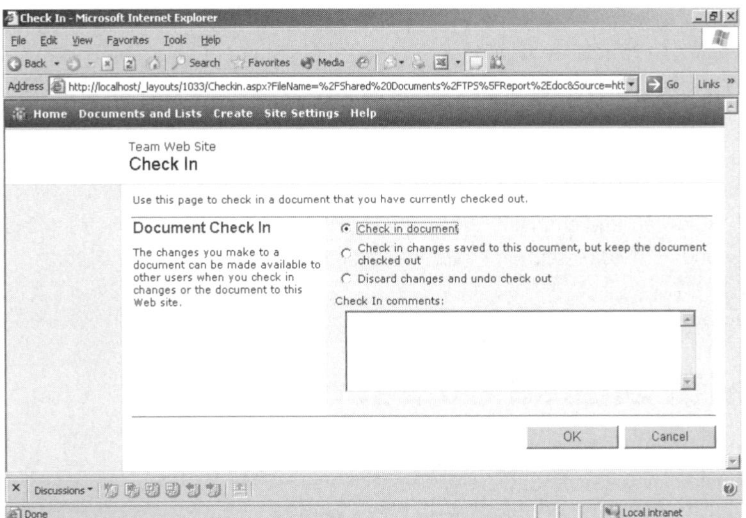

Figure 40-7. The Check In page is used to manually check a document in.

> **Tip** Force the check-in of a document
>
> A user in the Administrator site group can force the check-in of a document even if another user has it checked out. This can be useful if a user checks a document out and forgets to check it back in, and then leaves for the day, for example. An administrator can forcibly check the document back in so other users can work with it. Changes made while the document was checked out might be lost in this case.

In the document library, select Version History from the Item drop-down box for a document. If version history is enabled for the document library, every time a document is checked in, it will be shown in the version history shown in Figure 40-8. You can view each version of the document by clicking the Modified Date And Time, and you can even restore a document to an old version by hovering over the date and time for the version to restore, clicking the drop-down icon, and selecting Restore. You can also delete old versions from this drop-down menu.

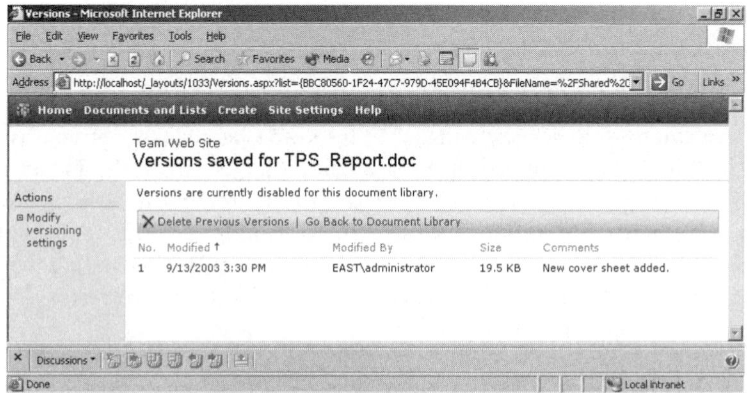

Figure 40-8. The Versions Saved page shows the document's version history and can be used to restore old versions of the document.

> **Tip** Enable version history
>
> Version history can be enabled from the version history page by clicking Modify Versioning Settings on the left and changing the Document Versions setting to Yes. It can also be set from the document library general settings and can be set when a new document library is created.

Working with Shared Contacts

Windows SharePoint Services provides lists that can be used to share a variety of information. One of the defined list types is contacts, which is used to store contact information in a way similar to the contacts folder in Microsoft Outlook.

Viewing Contacts on a Windows SharePoint Services Site

To view contacts on a Windows SharePoint Services site, click Documents And Lists at the top of any Windows SharePoint Services page. The contact lists are in the Lists section of the page. By default, a list called Contacts is created when Windows SharePoint Services is installed. You might have more lists of contacts in your site. Click a contact list name to view the list. Figure 40-9 shows a contact list. From this list you can add, edit, and delete contacts. An Item drop-down box is available for contacts if you hover your mouse cursor over the last name of a specific contact.

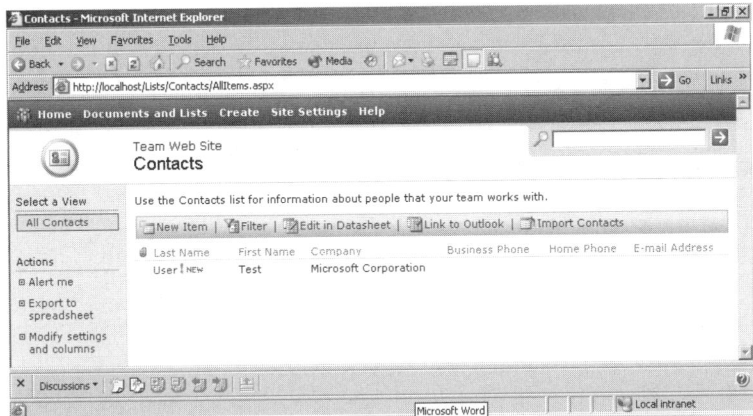

Figure 40-9. A contact list shows the contact information in the familiar SharePoint layout.

Linking Windows SharePoint Services Contact Lists to Outlook

If you use contacts in your Windows SharePoint Services team site a lot, it might be a lot of effort to open the team site every time you need a contact. Windows SharePoint Services and Outlook provide a method of linking a contact list from Windows SharePoint Services directly into Outlook so that the contacts in the Windows SharePoint Services site show up as a contacts folder in Outlook. However, contact lists linked from Windows SharePoint Services into Outlook cannot be edited, only read. To add, edit, or delete contacts in a linkeds folder you must do this directly in the SharePoint site.

To link a contact list in Windows SharePoint Services into Outlook, open the contact list and click Link To Outlook. Outlook will open if it is not already open and the dialog box shown in Figure 40-10 might appear. This dialog box notifies you that a SharePoint site is attempting to link to Outlook and that the site is not trusted by default. Ensure that the site URL in the dialog box is correct and click Yes.

Note The dialog box notifying you that SharePoint is attempting to link to Outlook appears so that rogue SharePoint sites cannot link into Outlook without your knowledge or permission.

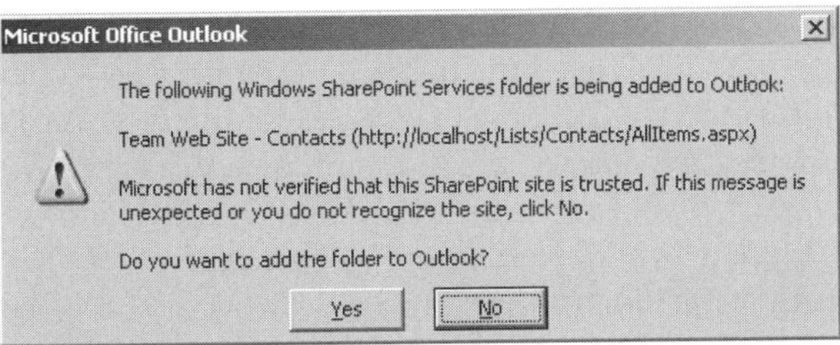

Figure 40-10. When you attempt to link a SharePoint contact list to Outlook a dialog box appears, allowing you to verify that the SharePoint site is trusted before the link is created.

Once you click Yes in this dialog box, the contact list is linked into Outlook, as shown in Figure 40-11. As you can see, you now have two contact folders in outlook, Contacts and Team Web Site – Contacts. You can open the new contacts folder linked from Windows SharePoint Services and view contacts, but you cannot add, edit, or delete contacts.

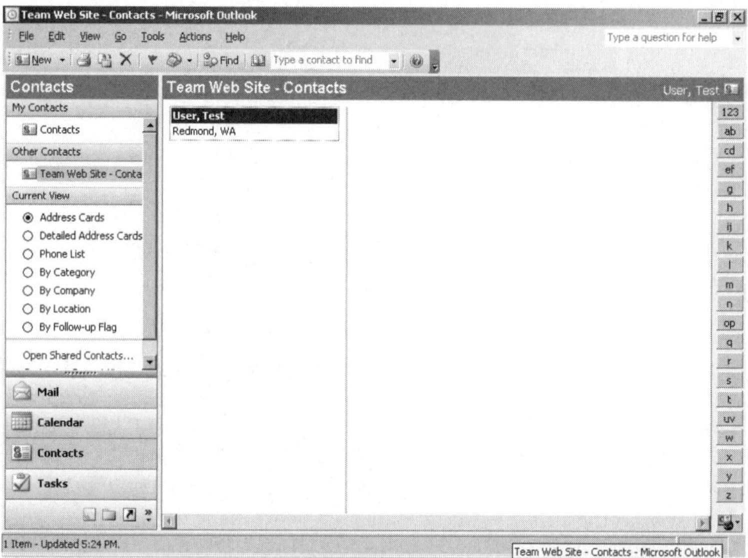

Figure 40-11. The new contact folder linked from Windows SharePoint Services is shown in Outlook.

Note The name in the Team Web Site – Contacts folder preceding the dash is the name of the SharePoint site, and following the dash is the name of the contact list within the SharePoint site. If the name of the linked contact list in Windows SharePoint Services was Project Contacts, for example, the linked folder in Outlook would be calledTeam Web Site – Project Contacts.

Copying Contacts from Windows SharePoint Services to Outlook

Linking contacts from Windows SharePoint Services to Outlook is useful if you need read-only access to an entire contact list stored in a SharePoint site, but it is also possible to copy contacts from SharePoint to Outlook. This is useful if you need only a few contacts from Windows SharePoint Services in Outlook for use on a regular basis, if you need the contacts stored in a single contacts folder in Outlook, or if you want to be able to edit the contacts. Note that if you edit the contact your changes are not reflected in the Windows SharePoint Services contact list as the two copies of the contact are independent. See the next section on how to copy the contact back to Windows SharePoint Services.

The process for copying a contact from Windows SharePoint Services to Outlook is surprisingly simple. Windows SharePoint Services has the ability to export and import contacts to and from contact lists on a SharePoint site in vCard (.VCF) format. To copy a contact from Windows SharePoint Services to Outlook, follow these steps:

1. Open the contact list in the SharePoint site from which to copy the contact.
2. Find the contact to copy, hover your mouse cursor over the Last Name, click the drop-down icon, and click Export Contact.
3. You will typically see the Internet Explorer File Download dialog box, prompting you to open or save the file. Click Open.
4. The contact opens in Outlook, as shown in Figure 40-12. Enter any additional information you want saved with the contact in the contact form and click Save And Close to save the contact in your Outlook Contacts folder.

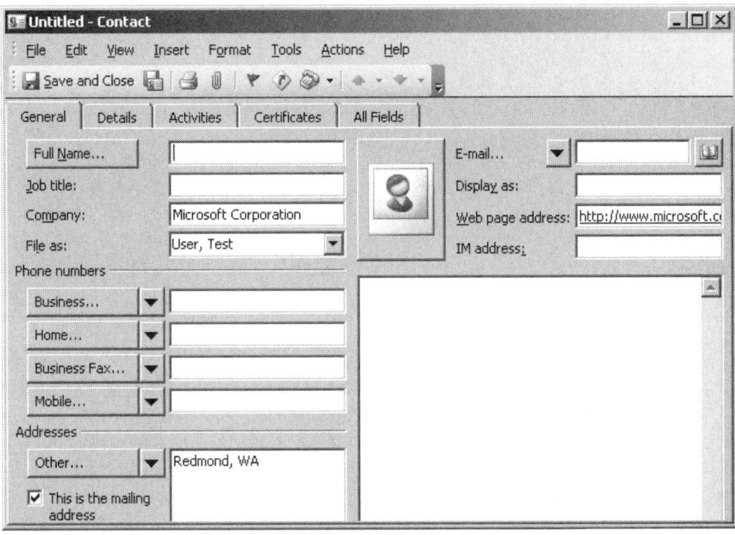

Figure 40-12. When you export a contact from the SharePoint site, the contact information opens in the Outlook contact form and you can save it to your Contacts folder.

Copying Contacts from Outlook to Windows SharePoint Services

The previous two sections covered how to get your contacts from Windows SharePoint Services into Outlook, but the ability to move Outlook contacts into Windows SharePoint Services is just as useful. If you are creating a Web site for your team, for example, and need to get a number of contacts from each team member's Contacts folder in Outlook into the Windows SharePoint Services contact list, using the Import Contacts feature is much easier than adding each one by hand. To copy contacts from Outlook to a SharePoint site, follow these steps:

1. In the SharePoint site, open the contact list into which you want to import contacts.
2. Click Import Contacts.

3. From the Select Users To Import dialog box shown in Figure 40-13, first select the Outlook contacts folder containing the contact to import from the Show Names From The drop-down list. The Contacts folder is selected by default.

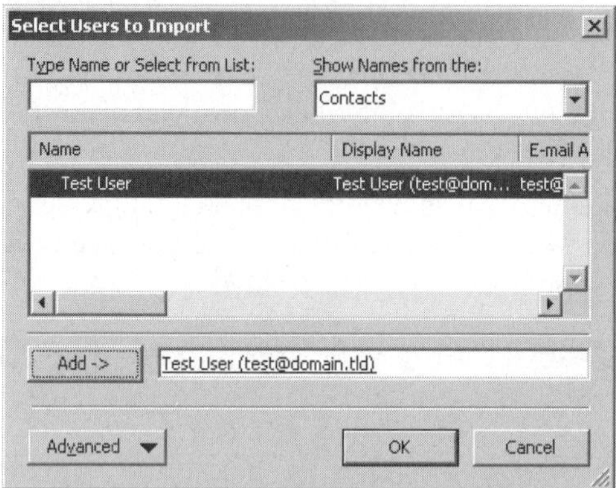

Figure 40-13. The Select Users To Import dialog box is used to select the contacts to import from Outlook.

4. Select a contact from the list.
5. Click Add.
6. Click OK.
7. When the Microsoft Office Outlook dialog box shown in Figure 40-14 is displayed, click Yes to allow access to the Outlook data. This dialog box appears to warn you that someone is trying to access your data. If you will be adding more contacts from Outlook, selecting the Allow Access For check box and selecting a time interval prevents this dialog box from being displayed again for the length of time selected.

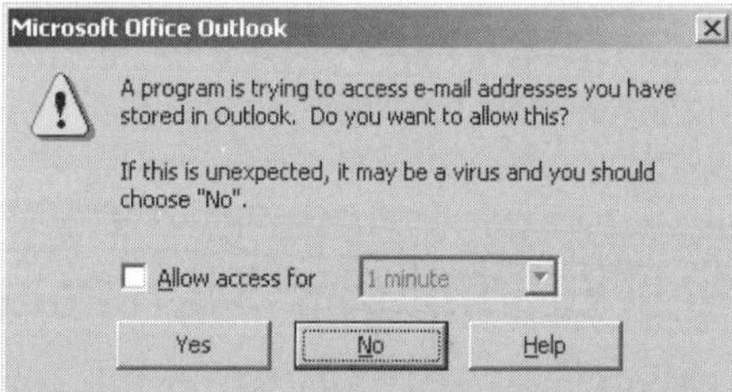

Figure 40-14. When someone tries to access your data stored in Outlook, such as when importing contacts into Windows SharePoint Services, you are notified and can grant or deny access.

Note Contacts stored in Outlook must have an associated e-mail address or they will not appear in the Select Users To Import dialog box.

The contact will now be shown in the contact list in the SharePoint site.

Linking a Team Calendar to Outlook

Just like contacts discussed in the previous section, an event list (sometimes called a team calendar) can be linked to Outlook. An events list in a SharePoint site is a calendar used to maintain important events that is shared among the team using the site. A list called Events is created by default when Windows SharePoint Services is installed. Click Documents And Lists at the top of any Windows SharePoint Services page, then click Events in the Lists section of the Documents And Lists page.

There are three ways to view events: the All Events view, the Calendar, and the Current Events view. These views are selected from the bar on the left side of the Events list. The All Events view shows a listing of events, and the Calendar shows events in a traditional calendar format.

The view you select has no effect on linking to Outlook. When an events list is linked to Outlook, it is shown in the Outlook calendar format. To link an events list to Outlook, follow these steps:

1. Open the events list you want to link to Outlook. The list called Events is created by default in a new Windows SharePoint Services site.
2. Click Link To Outlook.
3. A dialog box is displayed, warning you that a SharePoint folder is being added to Outlook. Click Yes to add the folder. This is the same dialog box shown earlier in Figure 40-10.

When the calendar is linked to Outlook, it is displayed as shown in Figure 40-15. You can see the new calendar listed in the Navigation Pane on the left. As with linked contact lists, linked event lists are read-only in Outlook. To add, edit, or delete events you must work within the SharePoint site.

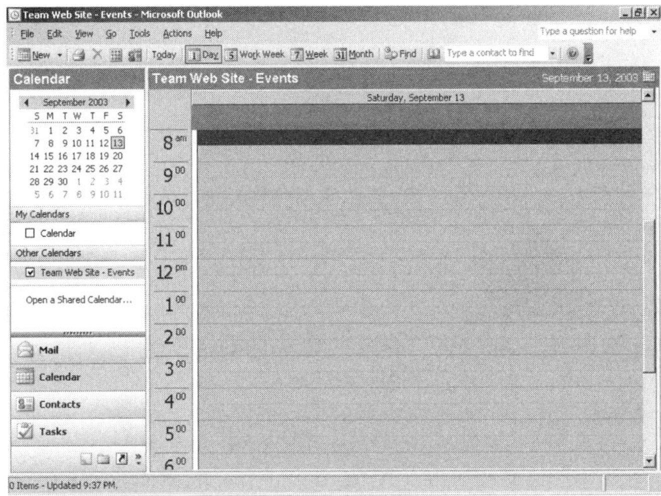

Figure 40-15. The calendar linked from the SharePoint site is shown in Microsoft Outlook.

Configuring Alerts in Outlook

Alerts were covered earlier in the chapter in the section "Setting Up Alerts." Whereas alerts in Windows SharePoint Services are sent through e-mail messages, Outlook includes integration that allows for the simple management of alert messages from a SharePoint site. The Manage Alerts tab of the Rules And Alerts dialog box provides links directly into the correct SharePoint site pages for alert management, as you will see.

First, configure an alert manually in the SharePoint site. The alert notification will be sent to you through e-mail and will appear in your Inbox. Ensure that a mail folder is open and select Rules And Alerts from the Tools menu. Click the Manage Alerts tab, shown in Figure 40-16.

Note You must configure the first alert manually in the SharePoint site because when an alert is processed by Outlook, the site is "trusted" and you can then manage alerts from the Rules And Alerts dialog box. It is possible to manage alerts without first configuring an alert through the SharePoint site if an administrator adds the site as a trusted domain for alerts.

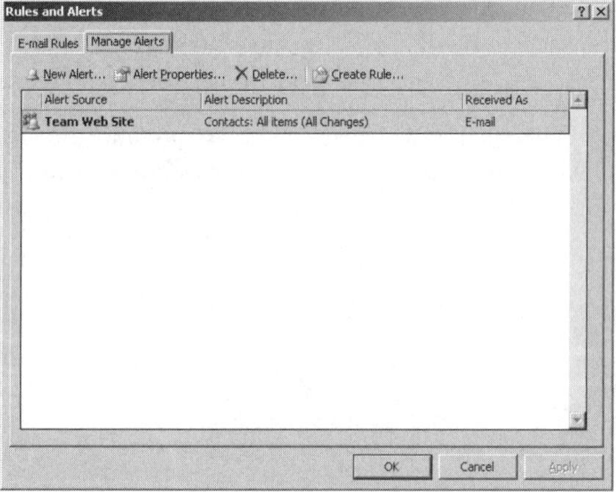

Figure 40-16. The Manage Alerts tab of the Rules And Alerts dialog box is used to manage SharePoint alerts directly from within Outlook.

Adding Alerts from Outlook

You can now work with your alerts directly within your Outlook client. To add a new alert, follow these steps:

1. Click New Alert in the Manage Alerts tab of the Rules And Alerts dialog box.
2. Expand Sites Currently Sending Me Alerts in the New Alert dialog box.
3. Select the SharePoint site from the list, as shown in Figure 40-17, and click Open.

Figure 40-17. Select the SharePoint site in which to create the new alert from the list in the New Alert dialog box.

4 The New Alert page in the SharePoint site opens automatically in a Web browser, as shown in Figure 40-18. Select the list or document library for which to set the alert and click Next.

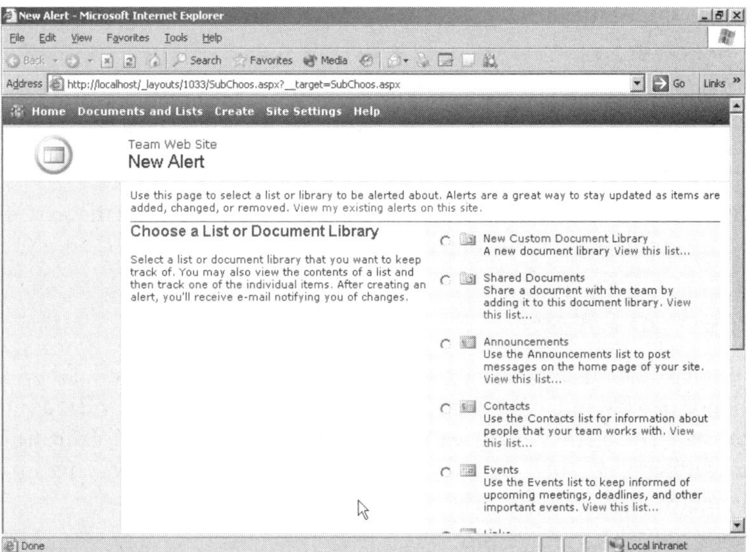

Figure 40-18. The New Alert page in the SharePoint site opens when you select the site from the list in the New Alert dialog box and click Open.

5 Set the alert type and frequency as discussed in the earlier section "Setting Up Alerts."

6 Click OK to set the alert.

You are then taken to the My Alerts On This Site page in the SharePoint site to review your alerts, but you can close your Web browser. The new alert is shown in the Manage Alerts tab of the Rules And Alerts dialog box.

Editing and Deleting Alerts from Outlook

In addition to adding alerts directly from within Outlook, you can edit existing alerts by following these steps:

1. Select the alert you want to edit on the Manage Alerts tab in the Rules And Alerts dialog box and click Alert Properties.
2. The Alert Properties dialog box opens, as shown in Figure 40-19. This dialog box shows the alert source as a clickable link to the home page of the SharePoint site and includes a link to the main alerts management page in SharePoint. Click Modify Alert to edit the alert.

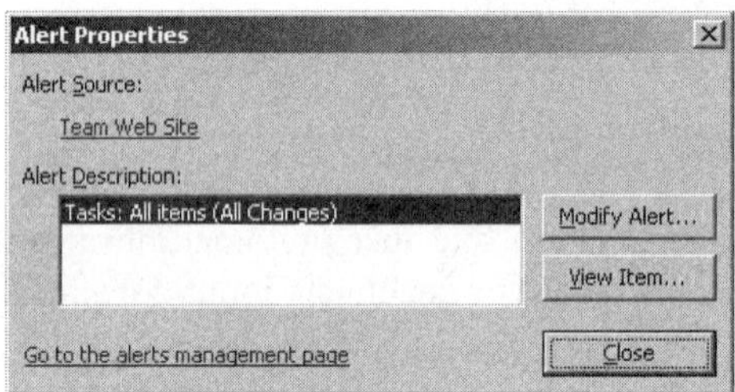

Figure 40-19. The Alert Properties dialog box is used to edit existing alerts from Outlook.

3. The Edit Alert page in the SharePoint site opens in the Web browser. Make any changes you need on the Edit Alert page and click OK. You can also click Delete to remove the alert.

You can also remove alerts on the Manage Alerts tab by selecting the alert and clicking Delete. You are prompted to verify the deletion, and the alert is removed once you click Yes.

Rules Based on Alerts

If you have a lot of alerts configured in a SharePoint site (or multiple sites) they can fill your mailbox quickly and distract from other messages. Outlook provides a simple way to create rules based on alerts. As you learned in Chapter 8, "Filtering, Organizing, and Using Automatic Responses," rules are used to process messages when they arrive in your mailbox. To configure a rule based on an alert, follow these steps:

1. Select the alert for which to configure a rule on the Manage Alerts tab of the Rules And Alerts dialog box.
2. Click Create Rule.
3. The Create Rule dialog opens, as shown in Figure 40-20. Select what Outlook should do when it receives the selected alert. You can have Outlook display the alert in the New Item Alert window, play a sound, and move the message to a new folder.

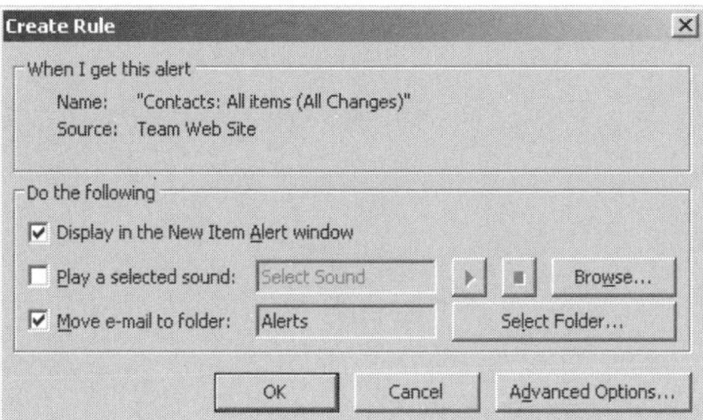

Figure 40-20. The Create Rule dialog box is used to create a rule based on an alert.

4 You can click Advanced Options to open the Rules Wizard and go into more detailed configuration for the rule. Use of the Rules Wizard is explained in Chapter 8. In most cases, this is not necessary for a basic alert.

5 Click OK to create the rule.

When the rule is created, the Success dialog box, shown in Figure 40-21, is displayed. You are notified that the rule is a client-side rule and given the option to run the rule against your mailbox immediately to catch any messages that fit the rule criteria.

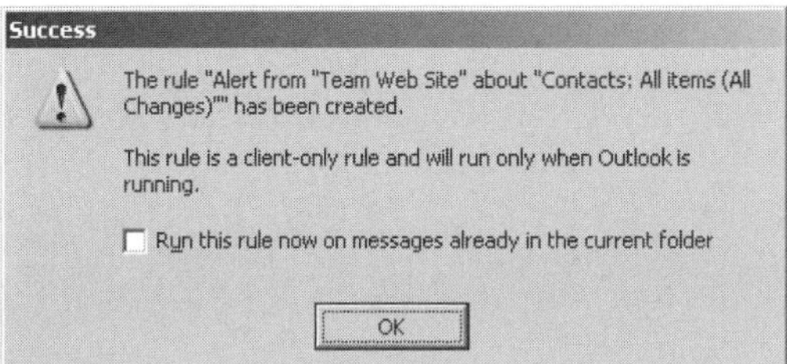

Figure 40-21. When the rule based on an alert is created, the Success dialog box is shown.

After you click OK in the Success dialog box, you can see the newly created rule by clicking the E-Mail Rules tab of the Rules And Alerts dialog box, which is already open.

Chapter 41

Accessing Messages Through a Web Browser

Microsoft introduced Outlook Web Access in Microsoft Exchange Server 5.0 so that clients could access their Exchange Server mailboxes through a Web browser. Outlook Web Access is also included in Microsoft Exchange Server 5.5. In addition, Microsoft has made significant improvements in Outlook Web Access in both Microsoft Exchange 2000 Server and Microsoft Exchange Server 2003 to provide support for a larger number of users, better performance, and improved functionality for clients. The latest version of Outlook Web Access in Exchange Server 2003 provides most of the functionality of the Microsoft Office Outlook 2003 client.

This chapter explores Outlook Web Access and explains how to configure it under Exchange Server 5.5, Exchange 2000 Server, and Exchange Server 2003. In addition to learning how to configure Outlook Web Access, you'll also learn why it can be an important feature to implement and how to best put it to work for you.

The chapter doesn't provide an exhaustive look at Outlook Web Access technology or deployment, but rather serves to explain common configuration and management tasks associated with Outlook Web Access. Although you'll find information about Exchange Server 5.5 and Outlook Web Access, the discussion focuses primarily on Exchange 2000 Server and Exchange Server 2003 because of the added benefits these platforms offer.

Overview of Outlook Web Access

With Outlook Web Access and a Web browser, users can send and receive messages, view and modify their calendars, and perform most of the other tasks available through Outlook or an Exchange Server client. Exchange 2000 Server and Exchange Server 2003 provide some additional features not included in Exchange Server 5.5. Outlook Web Access itself added some of these features; others are available in combination with Microsoft Internet Explorer 5.0 or later.

Outlook provides full access to an Exchange Server mailbox. Although Outlook Web Access isn't intended as a replacement for Outlook, it is useful for roaming users who want to access the most common mailbox features when they don't have access to their personal Outlook installation. Linux, UNIX, and Macintosh users can also benefit from Outlook Web Access by accessing Exchange Server mailboxes and participating in workgroup messaging and scheduling. In addition, Outlook Web Access can save the administrative overhead, support, and licensing costs associated with deploying Outlook to users who don't need all that Outlook has to offer. These users can use a free Web browser to access many functions provided by Exchange Server.

Outlook Web Access Features

Because e-mail is the primary function of Exchange Server and Outlook, Outlook Web Access supports e-mail access. Users can view message headers and read messages (see Figure 41-1) as well as send, reply to, forward, and delete messages. This last capability—deleting messages—might seem commonplace, but it is a useful feature. If your mailbox contains a very large attachment or a corrupted message that is preventing you from viewing your messages in Outlook, you can use Outlook Web Access to delete the message without downloading or reading it. Just open your mailbox in your Web browser, select the message header, and delete the message.

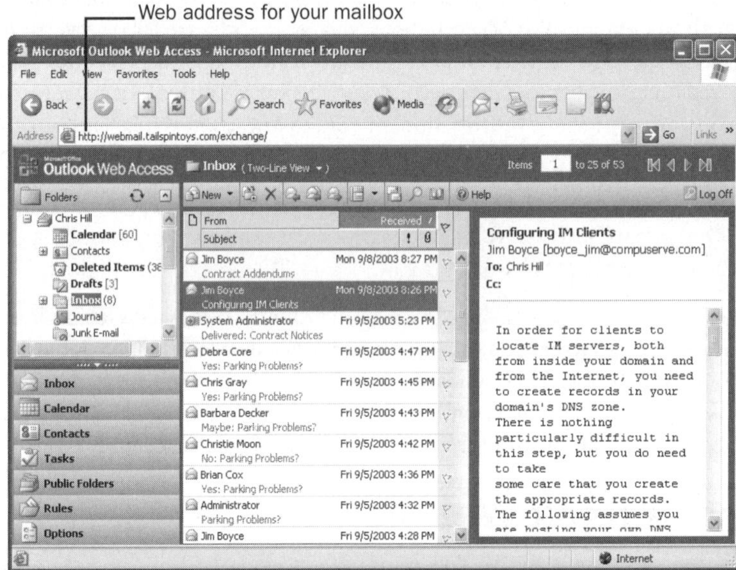

Figure 41-1. Using Outlook Web Access, you can access your Inbox through a Web browser.

> **Tip** Use remote mail for selective download
> You can use the Outlook remote mail feature to download only message headers and not message bodies. For details on using remote mail with Exchange Server, see "Using Remote Mail," page 930. For details on using remote mail with other types of e-mail servers, see "Understanding Remote Mail Options," page 329.

Exchange 2000 Server and Exchange Server 2003 offer a few additional features for messaging with Outlook Web Access. For example, Outlook Web Access in these versions of Exchange Server support Hypertext Markup Language (HTML)-based messages as well as rich-text messages. You also can access embedded objects in messages, another feature not supported by Exchange Server 5.*x*.

As mentioned earlier, you're not limited to just messaging—you can also access your Calendar folder through Outlook Web Access. You can view and modify existing items and create appointments (see Figure 41-2). You can't perform all of the same scheduling tasks through Outlook Web Access that you can with Outlook, but the ability to view your schedule and add appointments is useful, particularly when you're working from a remote location or a system without Outlook installed.

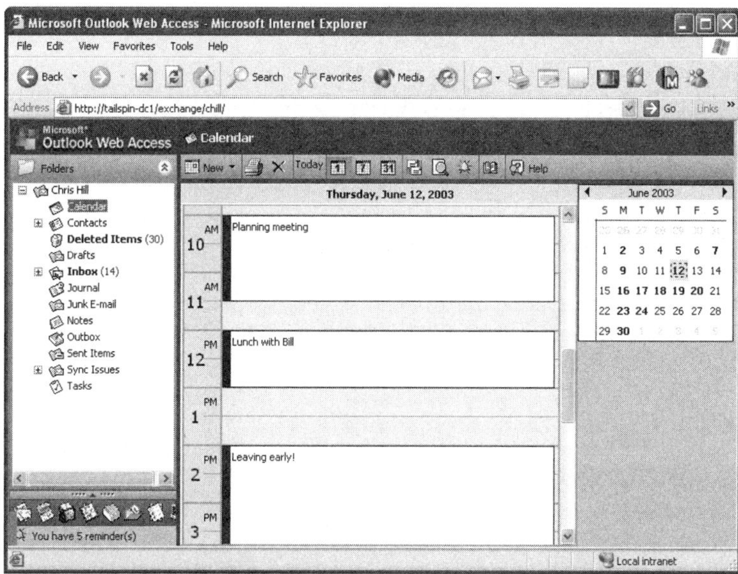

Figure 41-2. Use Outlook Web Access to manage your schedule as well as your e-mail messages.

Contacts are another type of item you can manage through Outlook Web Access. You can view and modify existing contact items and add new ones (see Figure 41-3). Other features in Outlook Web Access in Exchange 2000 Server and Exchange Server 2003 include support for ActiveX objects, named URLs for objects rather than globally unique identifiers (GUIDs), multimedia messages, and public folders containing contact and calendar items.

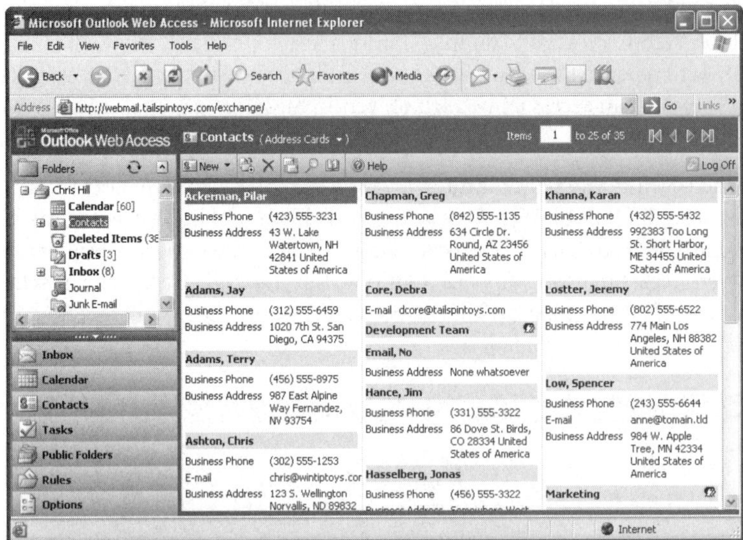

Figure 41-3. You can also work with your Contacts folder through Outlook Web Access.

Exchange Server 2003 adds new features for Outlook Web Access that are not included in Exchange 2000 Server. For example, the Outlook Web Access interface more closely matches the Outlook 2003 interface, and Outlook Web Access also adds spell checking, access to task lists, Secure Multipurpose Internet Mail Extensions (S/MIME) support, and HTML content blocking.

For all its usefulness, Outlook Web Access has some limitations, but these limitations depend on the version of Exchange Server you are using. For example, you can access your Tasks folder with Outlook Web Access in Exchange 2000 Server, but you can't create tasks. With Outlook Web Access in Exchange Server 2003, however, you can create tasks. Likewise, you can view the Journal folder with Outlook Web Access 2000, but you can't add journal entries. With Outlook Web Access in Exchange Server 2003 you can view journal entries and post messages to the Journal folder, but you cannot create new journal items. You can't use your mailbox offline through Outlook Web Access as you can through Outlook and an offline folder (OST) file. Unlike Outlook, Outlook Web Access doesn't support timed delivery and expiration for messages. However, Outlook Web Access in Exchange Server 2003 supports reminders (as does Outlook Web Access in Exchange 2000 Server), adds a spell checker, and includes the capability to define message rules for Outlook Web Access.

Web Browser Options

To access your mailbox through Outlook Web Access, you can use any Web browser that supports JavaScript and HTML version 3.2 or later, including Microsoft Internet Explorer 4.0 or later and Netscape 4.0 or later. Some features, however, rely on Internet Explorer 5.*x*, including drag-and-drop editing, shortcut menus, and native Kerberos authentication. In addition, browsers that support Dynamic HTML (DHTML) and Extensible Markup Language (XML) offer a richer set of features than those that do not. For example, Internet Explorer 5.*x* offers an interface for Outlook Web Access that is much closer to the native Outlook client, including a folder tree for navigating and managing folders as well as a Reading Pane.

> **Note** Kerberos authentication allows users to access multiple resources across the enterprise with a single set of user credentials, a capability Microsoft refers to as *single sign-on*.

Outlook Web Access Architecture

Active Server Pages (ASP) provide communication between the client and Exchange Server 5.*x*. Thus, when you access a mailbox on the Exchange Server through Outlook Web Access, your target URL is an ASP on the server. The server then uses Messaging Application Programming Interface (MAPI) to handle messaging requests generated through that page. Because the primary components of Outlook Web Access are the ASP files that allow the client to generate messaging requests through the Web, Outlook Web Access functions primarily as a Web site hosted under Internet Information Services (IIS), the Web service included with Microsoft Windows 2000 and Windows Server 2003. The site uses ASP to process client requests and then uses HTTP to communicate with the Exchange Server. The server uses MAPI to manipulate the message store. The combination of ASP and MAPI imposes a performance overhead that limits Outlook Web Access's capabilities in Exchange Server 5.*x* and reduces the number of users a server can support through Outlook Web Access.

Exchange 2000 Server and Exchange Server 2003 use a different architecture that improves performance and thereby increases the number of users a server can support. Outlook Web Access in these two platforms relies on HTML and DHTML rather than ASP. The user's browser still uses HTTP to connect to the site, but IIS simply passes the request to the Exchange Server and transmits replies back to the client. Therefore, although Outlook Web Access requires some IIS configuration, it's now integrated in Exchange as part of the Web Store.

The Web Store provides a single store for multiple data elements, including e-mail messages, documents, and Web pages, and supports important features such as offline and remote client access. It supports multiple protocols, including HTTP, WebDAV, and XML, giving developers several options for building applications that integrate with the Web Store. The Web Store doesn't exist exclusively for the benefit of Outlook Web Access. Instead, it offers a richer set of features and capabilities for storing and accessing data through means other than just Outlook.

Authentication Options

Outlook Web Access in Exchange 2000 Server provides three options for authentication:

- **Basic** Use clear text and simple challenge/response to authenticate access. This option offers the broadest client support but also offers the least security because passwords are transmitted as clear text.

- **Integrated Windows** Use the native Windows authentication method for the client's operating system. On systems running Windows 2000, for example, Internet Explorer uses Kerberos to authenticate on the server. Other Windows platforms, including Windows 9*x*, Windows NT, and Windows Me, use NTLM challenge/response rather than Kerberos. Integrated Windows authentication provides better security than basic authentication because passwords are encrypted. The client doesn't need to enter authentication credentials because the browser uses the client's Windows logon credentials to authenticate on the Outlook Web Access server.

Note Windows NT LAN Manager (NTLM) challenge/response authentication is the default authentication mechanism in Windows platforms earlier than Windows 2000.

- **Anonymous** Use anonymous access for public folders in the Exchange Server store. This option can simplify administration.

Exchange Server 2003 adds some additional options because of additions in IIS 6.0 in Windows Server 2003:

- **Digest Authentication** This authentication method works only with Active Directory accounts. It offers the benefit of sending passwords as a hash rather than in plain text. However, in order to use digest authentication, you must configure the Active Directory to allow reversible encryption, which reduces security. See the Active Directory online documentation for Windows 2000 Server and Windows Server 2003 for more detailed information on reversible encryption.
- **.NET Passport Authentication** This method allows users to authenticate with their Microsoft Passports.

In addition to these authentication methods, Outlook Web Access supports the use of Secure Sockets Layer (SSL) to provide additional security for remote connections.

Topology Considerations for Deploying Outlook Web Access

If you host only one Exchange 2000 Server or Exchange Server 2003 computer, you have few considerations for deploying the server. If you have multiple servers, however, you need to think about how you will structure your Exchange Server environment. You should use a front-end–back-end server scheme if possible when you provide access to your Exchange Servers through HTTP (Outlook Web Access), IMAP, or POP3 to users on the Internet. The front-end server sits on the Internet, either outside the firewall or inside a perimeter firewall, and accepts requests from clients on the Internet. The front-end server uses Lightweight Directory Access Protocol (LDAP) to query Active Directory on the domain controller for the location of the requested resource (a mailbox, for example) and passes the request to the appropriate back-end server.

A front-end server is a specially configured Exchange 2000 Server or Exchange Server 2003 server. A back-end server is a normal Exchange Server that handles requests from the front-end server just as it does from other clients. Any server not configured as a front-end server acts by default as a back-end server. Figure 41-4 illustrates a sample front-end–back-end configuration.

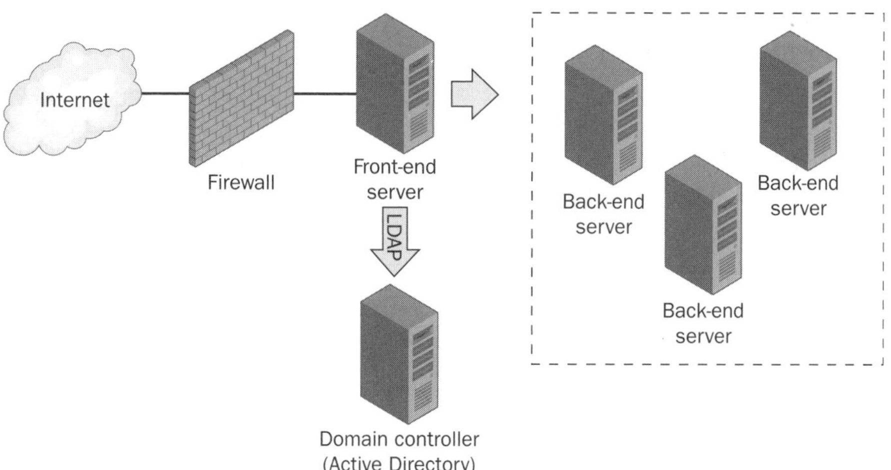

Figure 41-4. A typical front-end–back-end configuration for Exchange Server and Outlook Web Access.

An advantage to using a front-end–back-end topology is that you expose only one namespace to the Internet. Because the front-end server functions as the point of entry for your back-end Exchange Servers, clients don't need to know that other servers exist. Without a front-end server, each user must know the name of the server hosting his or her mailbox and enter the appropriate URL, such as *http://mail2.tailspintoys.com*. You make it much easier to expand and rearrange the back-end server configuration without affecting your users by providing a front-end server as the entry point to the Exchange Server network. Users can simply connect to *http://mail.tailspintoys.com* and gain access to their accounts, regardless of where the accounts reside on the network. You can set up multiple front-end servers when you have a high volume of traffic through the front-end server.

Front-end servers also offer a performance advantage when you need to use SSL to provide additional security between the client and the server. The front-end server can be configured for SSL and perform the associated encryption and decryption, removing that load from the back-end servers. This frees up additional processor time for the back-end servers to process messaging requests from clients.

Another important reason to use a front-end server is that it gives you the ability to place the back-end servers behind a firewall. The front-end server doesn't expose the mail system to intrusion because it hosts no mailboxes. You can considerably reduce the risk of denial-of-service attacks on your back-end servers by configuring the front-end server to perform authentication before relaying requests to the back-end servers.

When a request comes in to a front-end server, the server uses LDAP to query Active Directory to determine the location of the requested data. The front-end server then passes the request to the appropriate back-end server using HTTP port 80. SSL and encryption are never used between the front-end and back-end servers because the front-end server always uses port 80. This is true even when clients are using SSL for their connection with the front-end server. This also means that back-end servers must listen on port 80 and can't use a nonstandard port.

Clients must connect directly to servers with nonstandard ports, specifying the appropriate port number in the URL.

The front-end server acts as a proxy between the client and the back-end servers. The back-end servers handle the traffic from the front-end server just as they handle any other HTTP traffic, sending responses to the front-end server, which forwards them to the clients. Clients never know that the server processing their requests is different from the one they specified in the URL.

A front-end–back-end topology offers two options for authentication. The client can authenticate on the front-end server, which provides implicit authentication on the back-end server. Or the client can use explicit logon at the back-end server. In the former, clients specify the URL of the front-end server but don't include their account name in the URL (such as *http://mail.tailspintoys.com*). In the latter, clients add their account name, such as *http://mail.tailspintoys.com/jboyce*.

Explicit logon is useful when you need to access a mailbox you don't own but for which you have access permissions. When you use explicit logon, the front-end server extracts the user portion of the URL and combines it with the Simple Mail Transfer Protocol (SMTP) domain name to construct a fully qualified STMP address. The front-end server looks up the address in Active Directory and forwards the request to the back-end server for the user based on the information it finds in Active Directory.

As you begin planning how you will deploy and manage your Exchange Servers in light of Outlook Web Access, keep the front-end–back-end topology requirements in mind. Decide which strategy—including the placement of front-end servers in relationship to firewalls—makes the most sense for your organization.

Configuring Outlook Web Access in Exchange Server 5.5

By default, Outlook Web Access is not installed when you install Exchange Server 5.5. Instead, you must select it during installation. If you've already installed Exchange Server but didn't install Outlook Web Access, perform a backup of your Exchange Server system (just for good measure), and then run Setup again to add Outlook Web Access. Installation is simply a matter of selecting Outlook Web Access in the components list.

> **Note** Before you install Outlook Web Access for Exchange Server 5.5, make sure you've installed IIS 4.0 or later. Outlook Web Access for Exchange 2000 Server requires IIS 5.0.

Setup adds Outlook Web Access to the default Web site as a virtual directory named Exchange when you install Outlook Web Access in Exchange Server 5.5. You configure many of the properties for Outlook Web Access through the IIS console, but others are configured through the Exchange Administrator. The following sections explain how to configure various properties for Outlook Web Access in Exchange Server 5.5. They are intended to provide a primer to the most common configuration tasks rather than complete coverage of Outlook Web Access administration.

Enabling and Disabling Outlook Web Access Globally in Exchange Server 5.5

By default, Setup enables Outlook Web Access. If you want to prevent Exchange Server from responding to HTTP requests, however, you can disable the HTTP protocol.

Follow these steps to enable or disable the HTTP protocol in Exchange Server:

1. Open the Exchange Administrator, and then expand the site in which you want to configure Outlook Web Access.
2. Click the Protocols branch.
3. In the right pane, double-click HTTP (Web) Site Settings to open the dialog box shown in Figure 41-5.

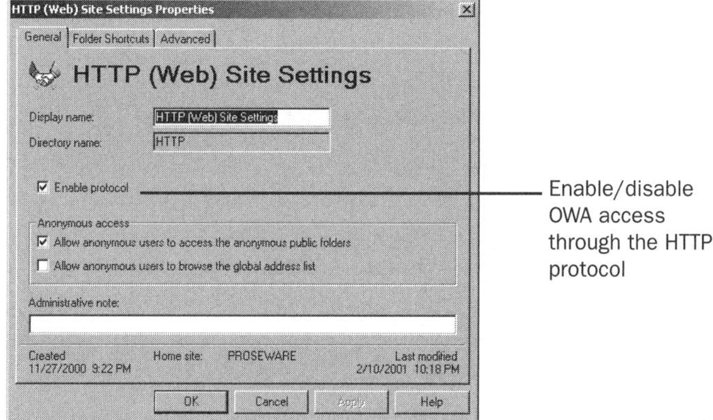

Figure 41-5. Use the HTTP (Web) Site Settings Properties dialog box to enable or disable HTTP.

4. Select the Enable Protocol check box to enable Outlook Web Access, or clear the check box to disable it.
5. Click OK.

Enabling and Disabling Outlook Web Access for Individual Users in Exchange Server 5.5

You can enable or disable Outlook Web Access not only at the site level but also for specific mailboxes.

You do this by enabling or disabling the HTTP protocol for the mailbox, as described here:

1. Open the Exchange Administrator, and then open the Recipients container.
2. Double-click the mailbox for which you want to configure Outlook Web Access, to open the mailbox's Properties dialog box.

3 Click the Protocols tab (see Figure 41-6).

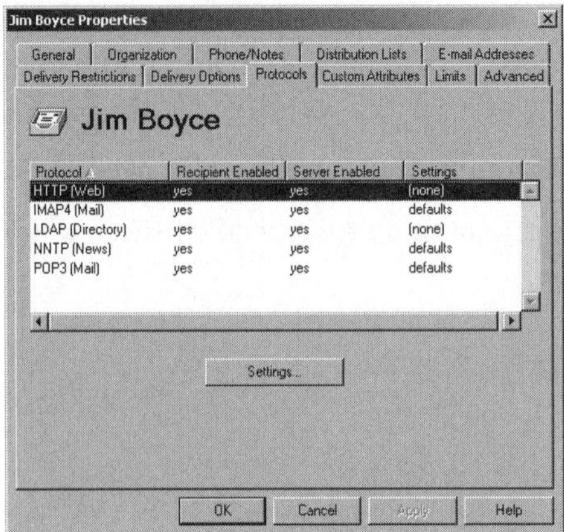

Figure 41-6. You can configure protocols for individual mailboxes to control the types of access the user has to the mailbox.

4 Select HTTP and then click Settings.

5 Select Enable HTTP For This Recipient to enable Outlook Web Access for the user, or clear the option to disable Outlook Web Access.

6 Click OK, and then close the mailbox's Properties dialog box.

Controlling Anonymous Access to Public Folders in Exchange Server 5.5

You can configure Exchange Server to allow anonymous access to public folders, which is useful if you post public messages or data to the folders. You might want to deny anonymous access, however, if the data in the public folders is for internal use only.

Follow these steps to allow or deny anonymous access to public folders:

1 Open the Exchange Administrator, open the site, and click the Protocols branch at the site level.

2 In the right pane, double-click HTTP.

3 Select the Allow Anonymous UsersTo Access The Anonymous Public Folders option to allow access, or clear the option to deny access.

4 Click OK to close the dialog box.

Publishing Public Folders in Exchange Server 5.5

You can publish Exchange Server public folders for anonymous access by users who connect to the Exchange Server through a Web browser.

You do this by creating folder shortcuts through the Exchange Administrator, as follows:

1. Open the Exchange Administrator, open the site, and click the Protocols object at the site level.
2. In the right pane, double-click HTTP.
3. Click the Folder Shortcuts tab (see Figure 41-7).

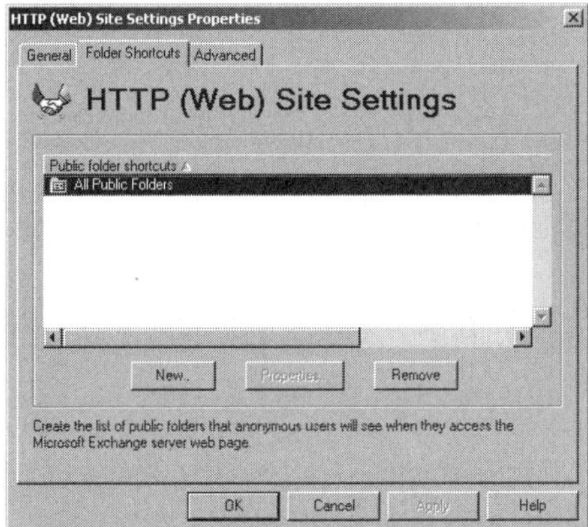

Figure 41-7. Use the Folder Shortcuts tab to publish public folders.

4. Click New, select the folder for which you want to create the shortcut, and then click OK.
5. Click OK to close the HTTP (Web) Site Settings Properties dialog box.

Configuring the Global Address List in Exchange Server 5.5

You can configure the Global Address List (GAL) to allow or deny anonymous access and also configure the number of addresses that the GAL returns.

Follow these steps to configure the address list:

1. Open the Exchange Administrator, open the site, and click the Protocols object at the site level.
2. In the right pane, double-click HTTP.
3. Click the General tab.
4. Select the Allow Anonymous Users To Browse The Global Address List option to allow anonymous access, or clear the option to prevent it.

5 Click the Advanced tab (see Figure 41-8).

6 Specify a maximum number of entries to be returned or select No Limit, and click OK.

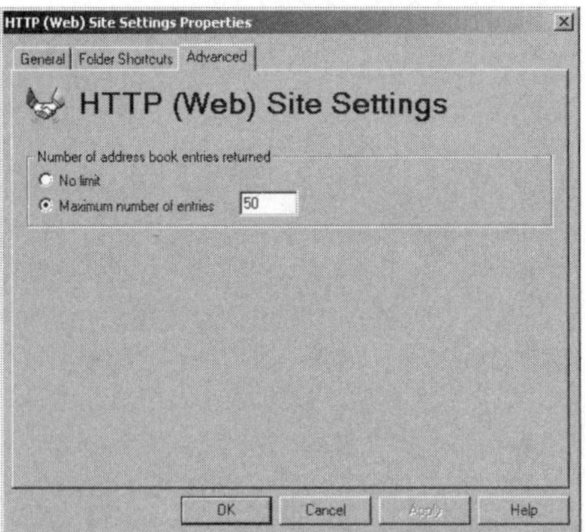

Figure 41-8. Use the Advanced tab to specify options for the address list.

Configuring Outlook Web Access in Exchange 2000 Server and Exchange Server 2003

You configure Outlook Web Access in Exchange 2000 Server using the Exchange System Manager console and the Active Directory Users And Computers console. Although you can also configure certain aspects of Outlook Web Access through the Internet Information Services Manager console, these changes are overwritten by changes you make through Exchange System Manager. You should work with Active Directory Users And Computers and Exchange System Manager for most configuration tasks, using the IIS Manager console only for tasks not available elsewhere. Typical configuration tasks include specifying which users can access their mailboxes through Outlook Web Access, which authentication methods to allow, and which public folders are exposed to clients.

Enabling and Disabling Outlook Web Access Globally in Exchange 2000 Server and Exchange Server 2003

Unlike the situation in Exchange Server 5.5, Outlook Web Access is enabled or disabled for a given virtual server through the properties of that server in IIS. You have two primary means for disabling Outlook Web Access on a global basis: remove the Exchange virtual directories or configure security for them to prevent access by all or by most, depending on your needs. For example, you might deny access to a virtual directory to all but a specific range of IP addresses.

Inside Out

Working with virtual directories

I don't recommend removing the virtual directories because getting them back again and functioning can be difficult. Instead, simply deny access to the virtual directories for all IP addresses. This has the same result as removing the virtual directories—no one can get to them, and therefore no one can use Outlook Web Access on the virtual server. If you decide later to implement Outlook Web Access, all you need to do is change the restrictions and possibly tweak authentication.

Follow these steps to configure security for the Exchange virtual directories:

1 From the Administrative folder, open the IIS Manager console.

2 Expand the Default Web Site entry, right-click the Exchange virtual directory, and choose Properties.

3 Click the Directory Security tab (see Figure 41-9).

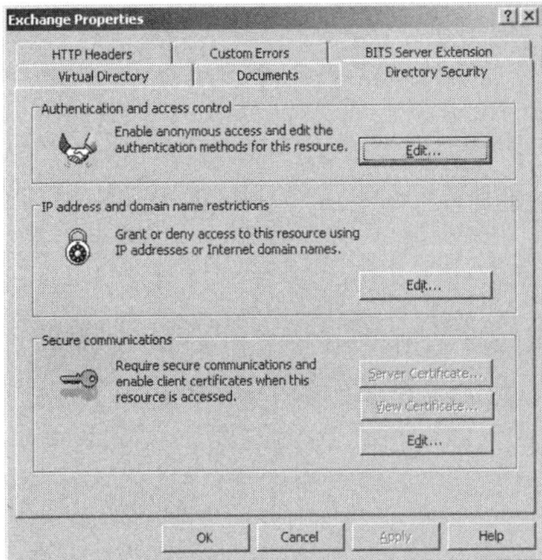

Figure 41-9. You control security and access for the virtual directory on the Directory Security tab.

4 In the IP Address And Domain Name Restrictions group, click Edit to display the IP Address And Domain Name Restrictions dialog box (see Figure 41-10).

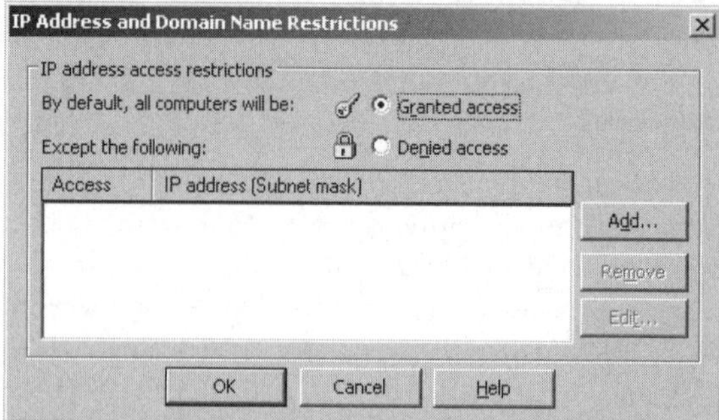

Figure 41-10. To disable Outlook Web Access, deny all users access to the virtual directory.

5 Select the Denied Access option to deny access to all, effectively disabling Outlook Web Access. Alternatively, if you want to allow access by specific addresses or domains, click Add to display the Grant Access dialog box (see Figure 41-11). You can grant access based on the individual IP address, the subnet (group of computers), or the client's domain name.

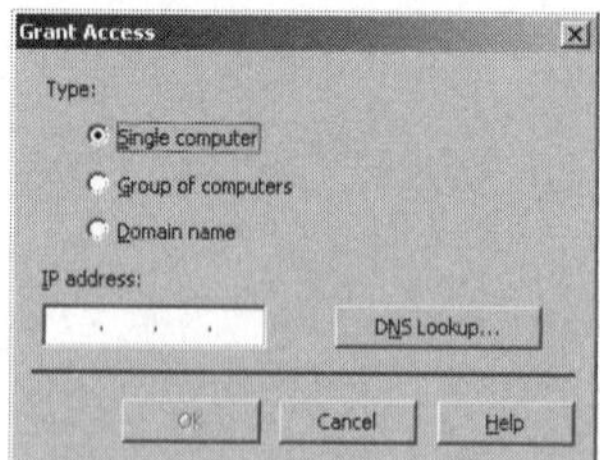

Figure 41-11. You can grant selective access to the virtual directory.

6 Close all dialog boxes and return to the IIS Manager console.

7 Repeat these steps on the Public and Exadmin virtual directories if you need to restrict access to those as well.

Inside Out

Granting or denying access based on domain name

Granting or denying access based on domain name requires a reverse Domain Name System (DNS) lookup for each client, which can impose a lot of overhead on the server and generate a ton of network traffic. It also requires that you configure host records in DNS for each host. Although this is made simpler by the ability of Windows 2000 and Microsoft Windows XP to automatically register host names in DNS, it can still be difficult to set up and administer, particularly when you must support earlier Windows clients (such as Windows NT and Windows 9x). I recommend that you use this method only if your server can handle the load.

Enabling and Disabling Outlook Web Access for Individual Users in Exchange 2000 Server

Outlook Web Access is enabled for all users by default when Setup installs Exchange 2000 Server and Exchange Server 2003. You might want to limit the users who can use Outlook Web Access, however, for security, performance, or other reasons.

You configure Outlook Web Access access in Exchange 2000 Server through the Active Directory Users And Computers console as follows:

1. Open the console and choose View, Advanced Features.
2. Expand the Users branch (or other container where the account is located) and double-click the user for whom you want to deny access.
3. Click the Exchange Advanced tab (see Figure 41-12).

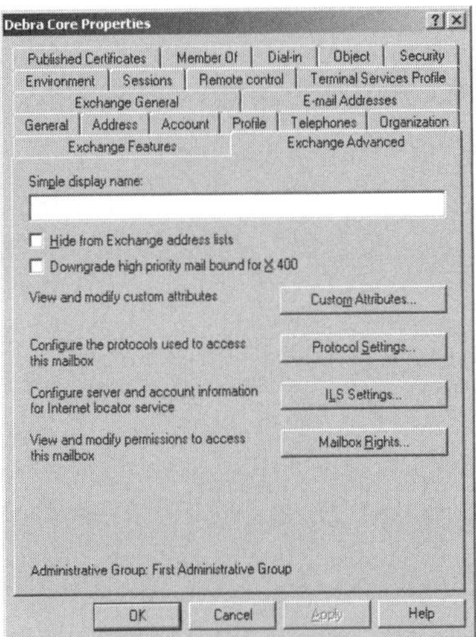

Figure 41-12. Configure protocols for individual accounts on the Exchange Advanced tab.

4. Click Protocol Settings to open the Protocols dialog box.
5. Select HTTP and then click Settings.
6. Clear the Enable For Mailbox option and click OK.
7. Click OK to close the Protocols dialog box, and then configure any other settings as needed for the user.
8. Close the user's Properties dialog box.

Troubleshooting

Public, Exchange, and Exadmin virtual directories display the Stop icon

If the Public, Exchange, and Exadmin virtual directories show a Stop icon in the IIS Manager console (indicating an error), try stopping and then restarting the Default Web Site. This problem seems to occur when IIS can't find the paths referenced by the virtual directories, which results from the Exchange services not being fully started before the site starts up. This could point to a server that needs tuning or simply to a lack of sufficient hardware to handle the job.

Enabling and Disabling Outlook Web Access for Individual Users in Exchange Server 2003

As with Exchange 2000 Server, you enable or disable Exchange Server 2003 Outlook Web Access through a user's account properties. However, the steps are slightly different, as follows:

1. Open the Active Directory Users And Computers console, then open the Properties dialog box for the user account.
2. Click the Exchange Features tab (see Figure 41-13), click Outlook Web Access, and click either Enable or Disable.

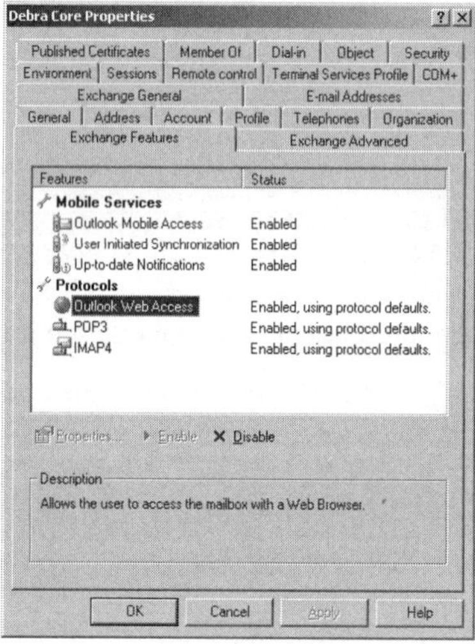

Figure 41-13. Configure protocols for individual accounts on the Exchange Features tab.

3. Close the Properties dialog box for the user account.

Controlling Anonymous Access to Public Folders in Exchange 2000 Server and Exchange Server 2003

Exchange 2000 Server and Exchange Server 2003 create a virtual directory named Public under the Default Web Site to provide access to public folders through the Web. You can configure the properties for the Public virtual directory to control whether users have anonymous or authenticated access to the folders. Providing anonymous access through the virtual directory's security settings, however, doesn't necessarily grant anonymous access to the folder. You can configure properties for the folder through Exchange System Manager to further refine access.

> **Tip** To access public folders through the Web, point your browser to *http://*<server>*/public*, where <server> is the DNS name or IP address of the server hosting the virtual directory.

Follow these steps to allow or deny anonymous access to public folders:

1. From the Administrative Tools folder, open the IIS Manager console.
2. Expand the Default Web Site entry, right-click the Public virtual directory, and choose Properties.
3. Click the Directory Security tab.
4. In the Anonymous Access And Authentication group (in Exchange Server 2003, Authentication And Access Control), click Edit to display the Authentication Methods dialog box (see Figure 41-14).

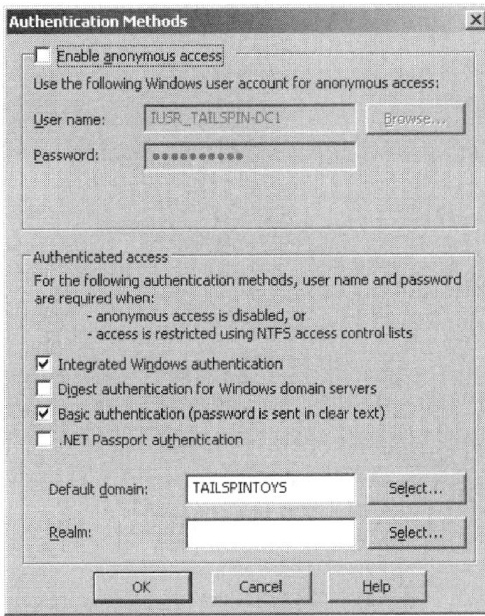

Figure 41-14. Use the Authentication Methods dialog box to allow or deny anonymous access.

5. Select the Anonymous Access check box (or the Enable Anonymous Access check box in Exchange Server 2003) to allow anonymous access to the virtual directory, or clear this check box to deny anonymous access.
6. Click OK and then close the dialog box for the virtual directory.

As mentioned, you can further control access to public folders by configuring their security settings in Exchange System Manager.

Here's how to configure these settings:

1. Open Exchange System Manager and then open the Administrative Group containing the public folder or folders you want to configure.
2. Right-click the folder branch or a specific folder (depending on the level at which you want to set security) and choose Properties.
3. Click the Security tab.
4. Configure security for individuals and groups as needed, and then click OK.
5. Repeat the process for other public folders as needed.

Configuring a Front-End Server in Exchange 2000 Server and Exchange Server 2003

If you're using a front-end–back-end topology to configure the front-end server, you need to change one setting, as explained here:

1. Open Exchange System Manager and locate the server in the Servers branch under the server's Administrative Group.
2. Right-click the server and choose Properties.
3. Click the General tab.
4. Select the This Is A Front-End Server option and then click OK.
5. To have the change take effect, restart the Exchange and IIS services or restart the server.

Back-end servers handle requests from the front-end server just as they handle any other request, so you do not need to configure the back-end server.

When you designate an Exchange Server as a front-end server, you are directing the server to forward all HTTP, POP3, and IMAP4 traffic to the back-end servers. The front-end server can still host an information store and user mailboxes, but these mailboxes are accessible only through MAPI. You can't access the front-end server's store with any of these protocols because the server forwards all HTTP, POP3, and IMAP4 traffic.

Using Outlook Web Access

After you install and configure Outlook Web Access on the server, users can begin accessing their mailboxes through their Web browsers rather than (or in conjunction with) Outlook. This section explains how to connect to the Exchange Server and use Outlook Web Access to access your mailbox.

Note This section assumes you are connecting to Exchange Server 2003 with Outlook Web Access. If you have an earlier version of Exchange Server, the features available to you will be slightly different.

Connecting to the Server

Typically, you connect to the Exchange Server through the URL *http://*<server>*/exchange*, where <server> is the DNS name, IP address, or NetBIOS name of the server. (The NetBIOS option is applicable only on an intranet or when you use WINS or Lmhosts to map the NetBIOS name to the server's IP address.) This URL isn't set in stone. The system administrator might have changed the virtual directory name for security purposes. Or, the proper URL might be in the form *http://*<mail.domain.tld>, where <mail> is a host name on the network and <domain.tld> is your server's domain name. Check with the system administrator if you're not sure what URL to use to connect to the Exchange Server.

Note Windows Internet Naming Service (WINS) maps NetBIOS names (computer names) to IP addresses, performing a service similar to that provided by DNS (although DNS maps host names, not NetBIOS names). You can use an Lmhosts file to perform NetBIOS name-to-address mapping without a WINS server, just as you can use a Hosts file to perform host name-to-address mapping without a DNS server.

Depending on the server's authentication settings, you might be prompted to log on. Enter your user name and password for the Exchange Server account. If the account resides in a different domain from the one in which the server resides, enter the account name in the form *<domain>**<account>*, where *<domain>* is the logon domain and *<account>* is the user account.

When you connect to your mailbox, you should see a page similar to the one shown in Figure 41-15 for Exchange Server 2003. Earlier versions of Exchange Server will show a somewhat different interface, as shown in Figure 41-16 (Outlook Web Access 5.5 is considerably different). Outlook Web Access opens your Inbox by default, but you can switch to other folders as needed. The left pane functions much as the Navigation Pane does in Outlook 2003 (or in the case of Exchange 2000 Server or Exchange Server 5.5, like the Outlook Bar in Outlook 2002 or earlier), and you can select folders from it. (Throughout this chapter, I'll refer to the left pane as the Navigation Pane for simplicity.) The right pane changes to show the folder's contents.

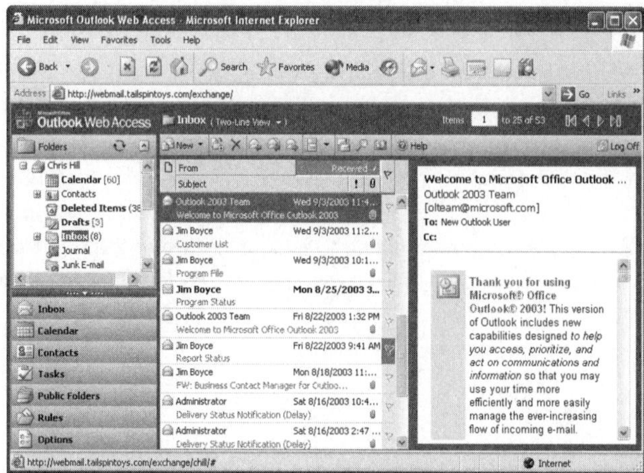

Figure 41-15. This is a typical look at a mailbox in Outlook Web Access 2003.

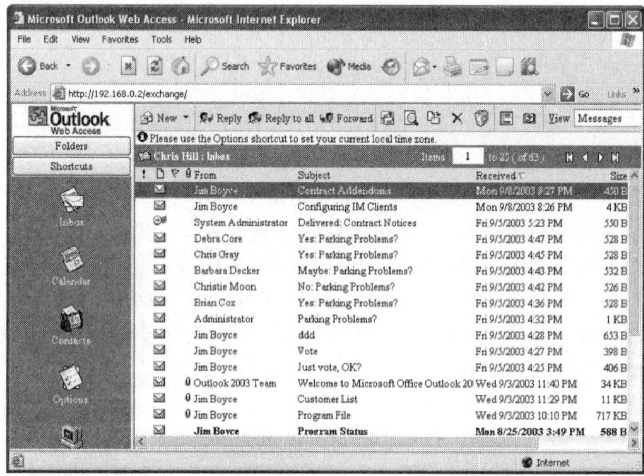

Figure 41-16. This is a typical look at a mailbox in Outlook Web Access 2000.

Note The interface for Outlook Web Access changed slightly between Exchange Server 5.5 and Exchange 2000 Server, and even more so from Exchange 2000 Server to Exchange Server 2003. The following sections assume that you're using Outlook Web Access to access Exchange Server 2003, but the procedures are similar for Outlook Web Access with Exchange Server 5.5 and Exchange 2000 Server. Also note that some features are not available with Outlook Web Access and Exchange Server 5.5 or with versions of Internet Explorer earlier than 5.0. Certain other features, such as rules, are only available with Exchange Server 2003.

Sending and Receiving Messages

Outlook Web Access automatically shows your current messages when you connect. To read a message, double-click its header to display a window similar to the one shown in Figure 41-17.

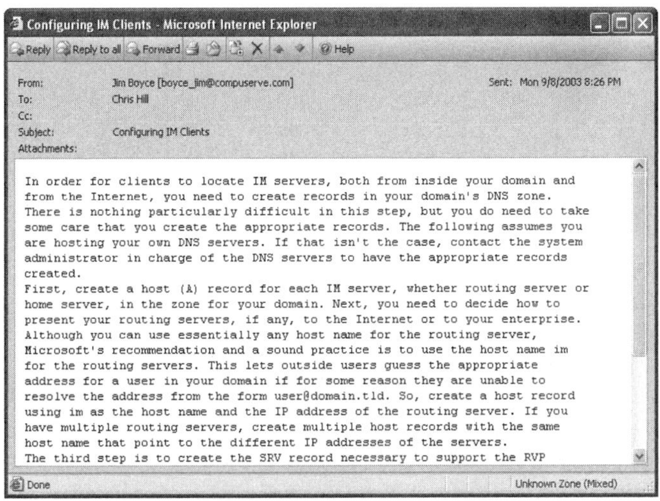

Figure 41-17. Outlook Web Access displays messages in a separate window.

> **Tip** Preview and read messages
> Each message in Outlook Web Access 5.5 acts like a hyperlink. You can click once on a message to open it. Select the check box beside a message to select the message without opening it. Click a message in Outlook Web Access 2003 to preview it in the Reading Pane, or double-click a message in either Outlook Web Access 2000 or Outlook Web Access 2003 to open it in a separate window.

As in Outlook, you can reply to or forward e-mail messages. Simply click Reply or Reply To All to reply to a message, or click Forward to forward a message. Outlook Web Access opens the form shown in Figure 41-18. Add additional addresses as needed and type your text. If you want to add an attachment, click the Add Attachment toolbar button. Outlook Web Access opens the window shown in Figure 41-19 so that you can add one or more attachments to the message.

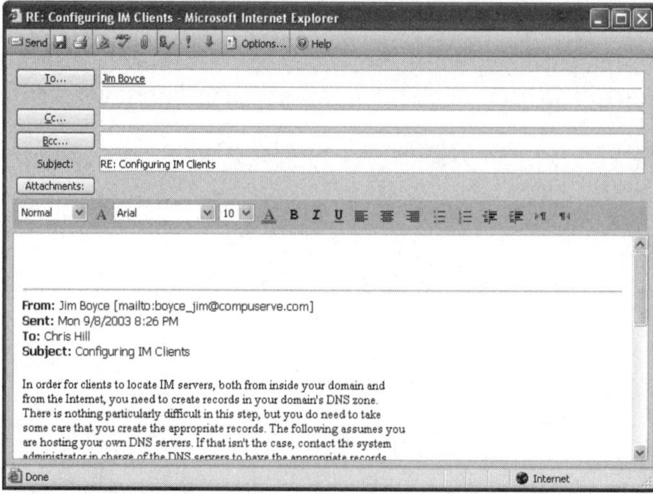

Figure 41-18. This is the Outlook Web Access form generated for a reply.

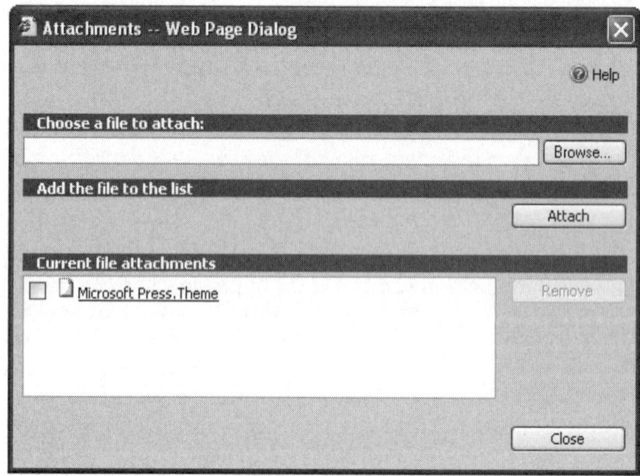

Figure 41-19. Outlook Web Access allows you to add attachments to e-mail messages.

When you want to create a message, click the New toolbar button (refer to Figure 41-15). Outlook Web Access opens a form similar to the one shown previously in Figure 41-18. You can specify addresses, attachments, body text, and other message properties.

> **Tip** To check for new messages, click the Check For New Messages toolbar button.

You can set a handful of options for a new message by clicking the Options toolbar button with the new message form open. These options correspond to options you have in Outlook (see Figure 41-20).

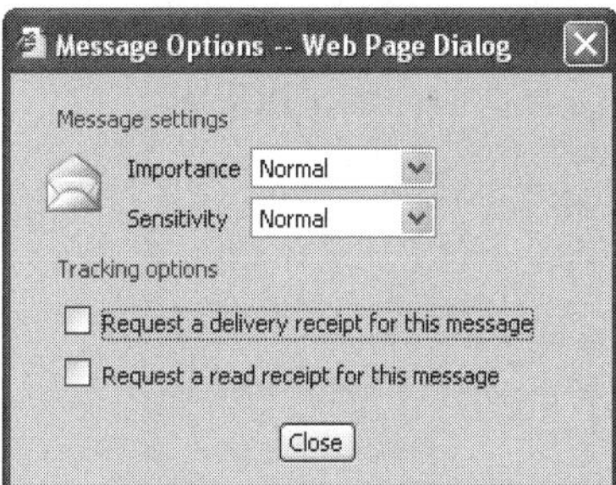

Figure 41-20. Configure message options, such as Importance.

> **Tip** Page through the Inbox
> If you maintain a lot of messages in your Inbox, they probably won't all fit on one page. Outlook Web Access displays the number of pages in your Inbox at the top of the window to the right of the toolbar. You can type a page number or use the arrow buttons to page through the Inbox.

Sorting Messages

Outlook Web Access by default displays messages sorted by date and time received.You can sort the messages by other properties as well. To do so, select an option from the View drop-down list on the Outlook Web Access toolbar (refer to Figure 41-15). You can display only unread messages; sort by sender, subject, sent to, or conversation thread; or view only unread messages by conversation thread. Outlook Web Access also provides a Two-Line View option that is very similar to the default Inbox view in Outlook 2003.

Copying and Moving Messages

The combination of Internet Explorer 5.*x* and Exchange 2000 Server or later allows you to copy and move messages by dragging in Outlook Web Access. Open the folder containing the messages you want to copy or move. Click the Show/Hide Folders button in the left pane to open the folder list (as shown in Figure 41-21). To move messages, drag them from the right pane to the destination folder in the folder list. If you want to copy the messages rather than moving them, hold down the Ctrl key while dragging.

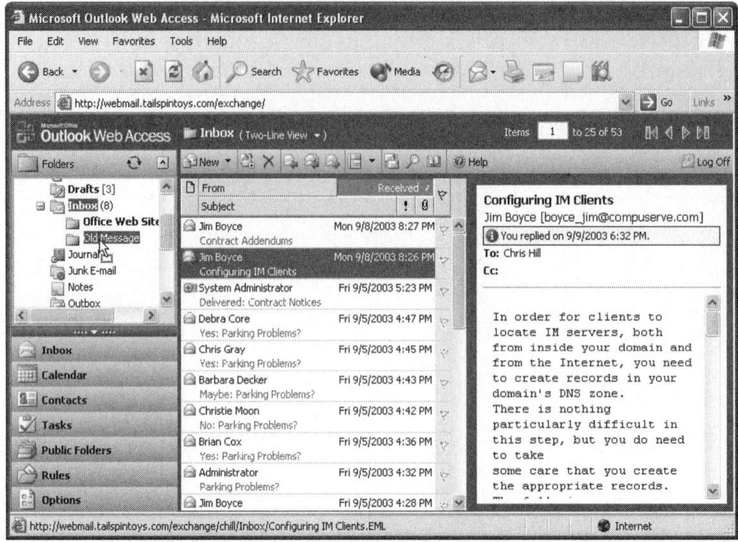

Figure 41-21. Drag messages to the folder list to copy or move them.

> **Tip** You can click the Move/Copy toolbar button to copy or move selected messages.

Deleting Messages

Deleting messages in Outlook Web Access is a good way to clean out your mailbox when you don't have Outlook handy. It's also particularly useful for deleting large or corrupted messages that would otherwise prevent Outlook from downloading your messages normally.

To delete messages in Outlook Web Access, just select the messages and click the Delete toolbar button. Outlook Web Access moves the messages to the Deleted Items folder.

> **Tip** To delete in Outlook Web Access 5.5, place a check mark beside the messages you want to delete and click the Delete Marked Items toolbar button. Outlook Web Access deletes the messages and refreshes the page.

Working with Other Folders

As mentioned, Outlook Web Access does not limit you to working only with your Inbox. You can work with your Calendar, Contacts, and other Outlook folders as well as with other message folders. In short, all folders stored in your mailbox, as well as public folders, are available.

Selecting a Different Folder

When you select a different folder in the Navigation Pane, Outlook Web Access displays the contents of the selected folder in the right pane. Click the Show/Hide Folders button in the Navigation Pane to display the folder list, which you can use to select folders other than those shown in the Navigation Pane.

Tip In Outlook Web Access 5.5, you can select folders from the folder list that appears between the left and right panes for all folders except the Calendar folder. Click the Up One Folder icon above the folder name to move to the parent folder in Calendar.

Creating New Folders

You can create new folders in Outlook Web Access, subject to your permissions on the server, by following these steps:

1. Click the arrow beside the New toolbar button.
2. Choose Folder to open the Create New Folder dialog box (see Figure 41-22).

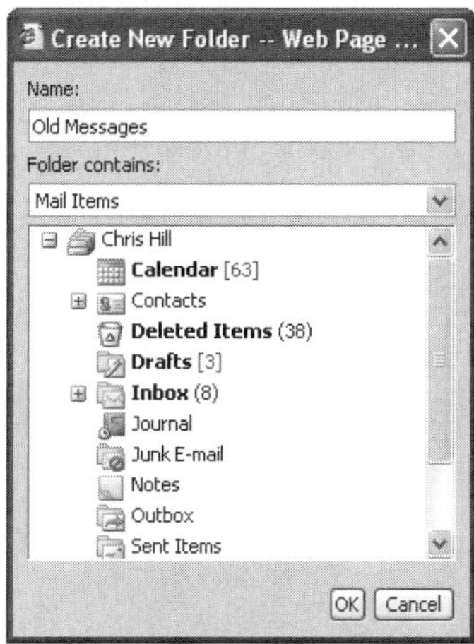

Figure 41-22. Use the Create New Folder dialog box to create a folder in Outlook Web Access.

3. In the Name box, specify a name for the folder.
4. In the Folder Contains drop-down list, select the type of folder.
5. Select the parent folder in the folder list.
6. Click OK to create the folder.

Note Outlook Web Access 5.5 limits you to creating seven public folders for messages.

Copying, Moving, Renaming, and Deleting Folders

While in Outlook Web Access, you can copy, move, and delete folders in your Exchange Server mailbox. To perform either of the first two actions, display the folder in the Navigation Pane, right-click it, and choose either Copy or Move. Outlook Web Access displays a dialog box containing a folder list in which you can select the destination folder.

To rename a folder, right-click the folder in the Navigation Pane and choose Rename. If you want to delete the folder, right-click it and choose Delete.

Working with Calendar, Contacts, and Other Items

In addition to working with the Inbox or other message folders, you can also manage your schedule, tasks, contacts list, and other items and folders on the Exchange Server.

Calendar Folder

To manage your schedule, click the Calendar icon in the Navigation Pane. Outlook Web Access updates the right pane to display your Calendar folder. Click the toolbar buttons to choose between Day, Week, or Month view. The page also includes a Date Navigator similar to the one in Outlook, which you can use to select dates (see Figure 41-23).

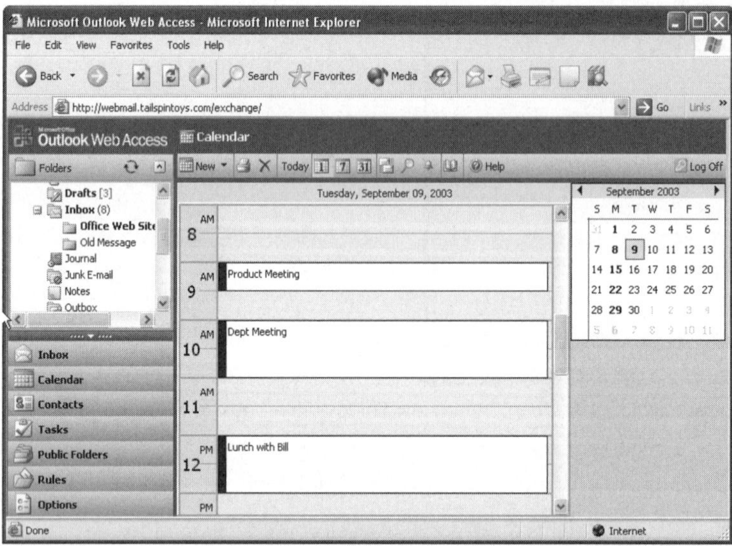

Figure 41-23. You can view and modify your schedule in Outlook Web Access.

Click the New toolbar button or click the arrow beside New and choose Appointment to display an appointment form similar to the one in Outlook. Use the appointment form to specify the title, the time, and other properties for an appointment, just as you would in Outlook.

Contacts Folder

You can also view and manage contacts in Outlook Web Access. Click the Contacts icon in the Navigation Pane to display the Contacts folder (see Figure 41-24). The default view is Address Cards, similar to the default view in Outlook. You can choose a different view in the View drop-down list.

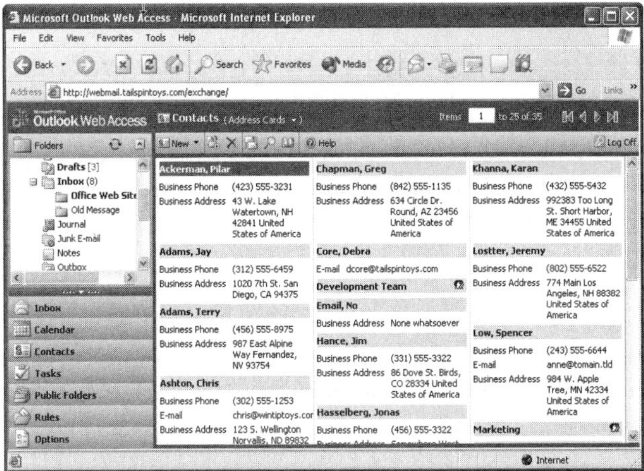

Figure 41-24. You can view and manage the Contacts folder in Outlook Web Access.

Simply double-click a contact entry in the list to open a form that contains detailed information for that contact. Click New on the toolbar to open the form shown in Figure 41-25, which you can use to create new contact entries. Click Save And Close to save a new contact entry or to save changes to an existing contact entry.

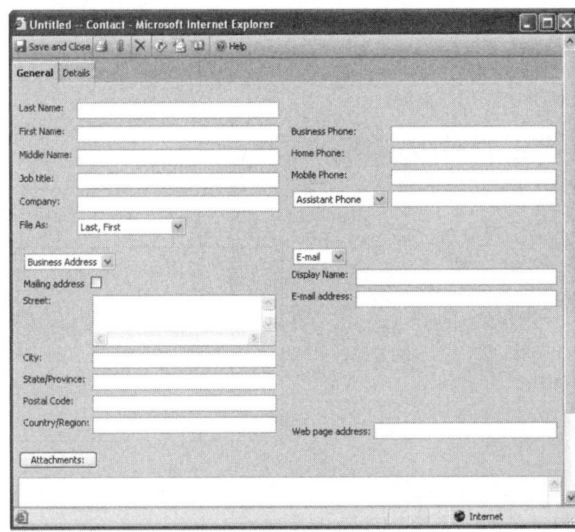

Figure 41-25. The form for creating contact entries in Outlook Web Access is similar to the contact form in Outlook.

Other Folders

In Outlook Web Access, as in Outlook, you can work with the Journal, Tasks, Notes, and other folders in your Exchange Server mailbox. Outlook Web Access 2003 allows you to create messages, contact items, distribution lists, appointments, tasks, and folders. You can view but not create items in the Journal folder. Earlier versions of Outlook Web Access restrict you to creating messages, contact items, and appointments.

Configuring the Out Of Office Assistant in Outlook Web Access

The Out Of Office Assistant automatically responds to messages when you are out of the office. The Out Of Office Assistant functions essentially as a server-side rule, replying to messages as they arrive in your Inbox. Although you usually configure the Out Of Office Assistant in Outlook, you can also configure it in Outlook Web Access.

For details on using the Out Of Office Assistant, see "Using the Out Of Office Assistant," page 253.

To configure the Out Of Office Assistant in Outlook Web Access, connect to the server using your Web browser and click Options at the bottom of the Navigation Pane to view the Options page (see Figure 41-26), where the Out Of Office Assistant properties appear. To turn on the Out Of Office Assistant, select I'm Currently Out Of The Office. In the AutoReply box, type the message that you want the Exchange Server to send as a reply to messages that arrive in your Inbox. Click Save to save the changes. When you want to turn off the Out Of Office Assistant, open the Options page again and select I'm Currently In The Office.

Note In Outlook Web Access 2000, click the Shortcuts group on the Outlook Bar and then click Options to open the Options page.

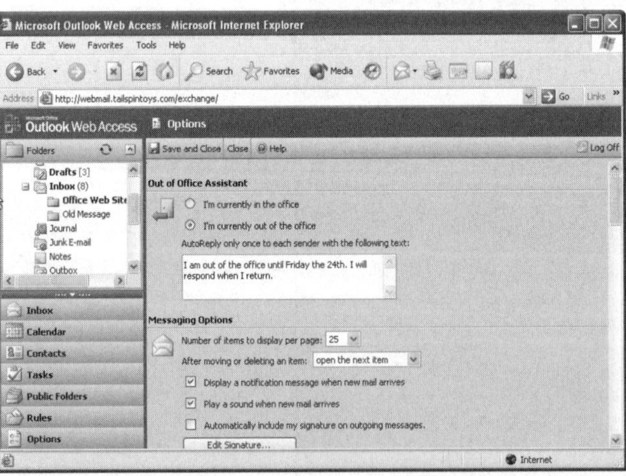

Figure 41-26. Configure the Out Of Office Assistant on the Options page.

Configuring Time, Calendar, and Other Options for Outlook Web Access

You can also use the Outlook Web Access Options page (see Figure 41-27) to set many other options for Outlook Web Access (in addition to the Out Of Office Assistant, as just discussed). You can configure date and time options, calendar options, and contact options as well as change your password. You can configure reminders, set up a signature for outgoing messages, set spelling options, and configure many additional options, all of which are essentially the same as those available in Outlook and covered elsewhere in this book. You can also download the Exchange Multimedia Control, an ActiveX control that provides support for multimedia messages.

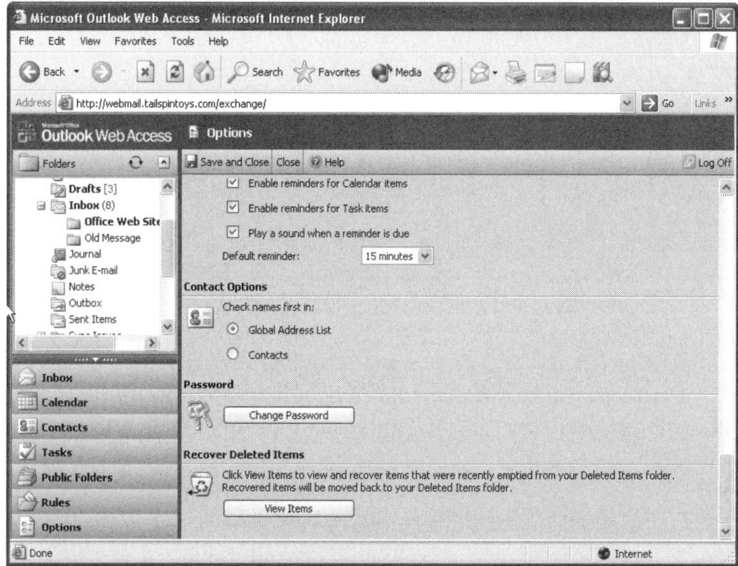

Figure 41-27. Use the Options page to configure additional Outlook Web Access options.

You can also use the Recover Deleted Items area of the Options page to recover items that you have deleted from your Deleted Items folder but are still held on the server through its retention policy. Click View Items to view and recover one or more deleted items.

Using Rules with Outlook Web Access 2003

Outlook Web Access 2003 adds a new feature that many users will find indispensable—access to rules. You can now view and modify existing rules and create new ones. You can't modify all rules with Outlook Web Access, however; only those rules that use Outlook Web Access's limited set of conditions and actions can be edited (even if they were created in Outlook). All others require Outlook to modify.

To work with rules in Outlook Web Access, click the Rules button in the Navigation Pane. Outlook Web Access displays your existing rules in the right pane, as shown in Figure 41-28.

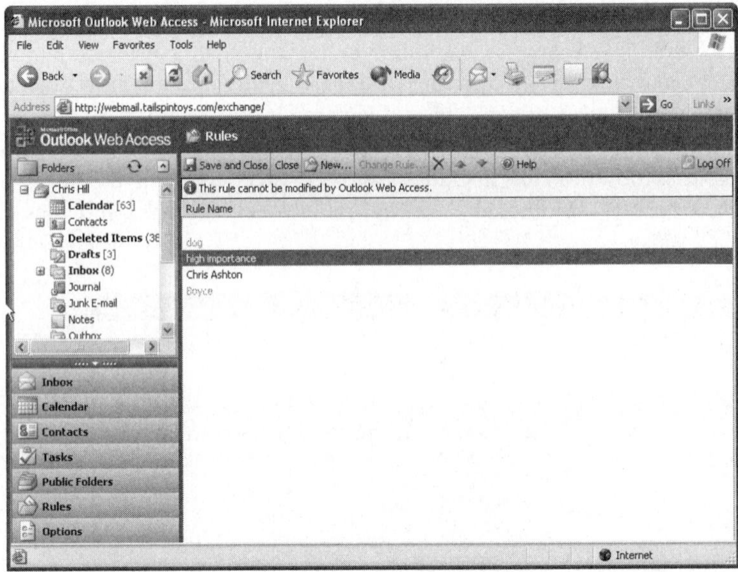

Figure 41-28. You can view and manage rules in Outlook Web Access 2003.

To create a new rule, click the New button on the toolbar to open the Edit Rule dialog box. As Figure 41-29 illustrates, you have fewer conditions and actions available to you when you create a rule in Outlook Web Access than in Outlook, but the ones that are available are the most frequently used.

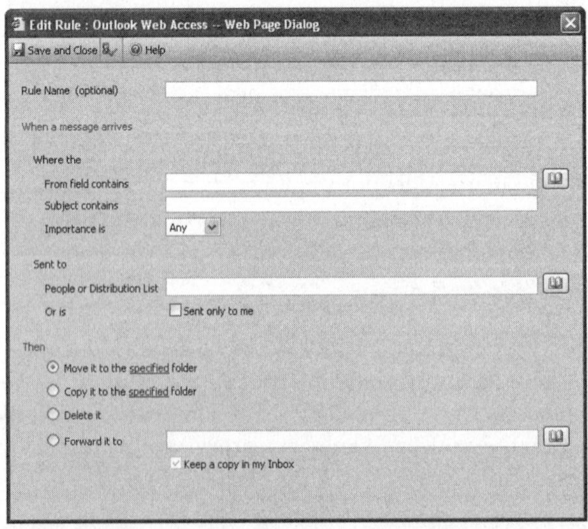

Figure 41-29. Create a new rule with Outlook Web Access.

Note The conditions and actions available for new rules are generally self-explanatory. If you need more information on creating rules, see "Processing Messages Automatically," page 224.

If you need to modify a rule, click the rule in the list and click Change Rule on the toolbar. Outlook Web Access opens the same Edit Rule dialog box shown previously in Figure 41-29. Make changes as needed and click Save And Close to save the changes.

Note You can click the Check Names button on the toolbar or press Ctrl+K to check names against the address book.

Although you can only edit a limited number of rules based on their conditions and actions, you can rearrange the order of all rules. Just click a rule in the list and then click either the Move Up or Move Down button on the toolbar to move the rule up or down in the list. Rules are processed in the order specified in the list, and changing the rule order changes the way messages are processed. See Chapter 8, "Filtering, Organizing, and Using Automatic Responses," for more information on rule order and message processing.

Chapter 42

Mobility with Outlook and Exchange Server 2003

Microsoft Exchange Server 2003 is a very powerful collaboration and e-mail server, especially when combined with Microsoft Office Outlook 2003. Many applications, such as Exchange Server, were created when high-speed Internet connections to the home were uncommon and accessing office computer systems while working from home and on the road was also not common practice.

Why Mobility Is Important

In modern offices the requirement for mobility has increased dramatically with the introduction of technologies such as high-speed broadband Internet connections to the home and the proliferation of wireless Internet connections in several forms. Employee expectations have changed with these technologies, especially among those who are frequently out of the office on business, such as sales teams and executives. These users expect that they will be able to access their e-mail and other collaboration information no matter where they are currently located.

Along with the expectation that they can access their mail, mobile users are looking for more functionality while on the road than simple mail access. With Outlook 2003 and Exchange 2003 providing full collaboration functionality as outlined elsewhere in this book, simple Web mail is not enough to satisfy their requirements. Most mobile users now want full access to all of these features from outside the office, too.

Mobility features are important for a number of reasons. However, the driving force behind the implementation of all mobility features and products is that they increase the speed of doing business. Most businesses are in existence to provide some kind of product to customers, and in many cases there are competing businesses trying to win the same customers over to their product. A business that can respond quickly to customer requests and demands has a huge advantage and that advantage can win customers. Mobility solutions, especially those integrated with collaboration products such as Outlook and Exchange, provide this speed and allow employees to conduct business from disparate locations.

Overview of Mobility Features in Exchange Server 2003

Exchange Server 2003 has been redesigned to vastly improve mobility features over earlier versions of Microsoft Exchange. Features that were included with a separate product, Mobile Information Server, in Exchange 2000 Server are now included with Exchange Server 2003. A number of new features have been added to Exchange Server 2003, and features existing in earlier versions have been improved.

Mobility features in Exchange 2003 fit into four main categories:

- **Offline support** Outlook has the ability to work in offline mode. Offline mode provides the ability to work within Outlook when not connected to your home Exchange Server. This allows access to existing information within Outlook while users are traveling or out of the office but does not allow new information to be updated from the server.
- **RPC over HTTP** Remote procedure calls (RPC) over HTTP is a method of providing access to your Exchange Server to remote clients without requiring any kind of virtual private network (VPN) connection. RPC over HTTP allows clients to connect using Outlook directly over the Internet using a publicly accessible port. The one caveat with RPC over HTTP is that the port is exposed on the Internet.
- **Web access** Microsoft has provided Outlook Web Access with several versions of Microsoft Exchange, but the main complaint has traditionally been that the Outlook Web Access interface does not match that of Microsoft Outlook, and that a number of Outlook features do not exist in Outlook Web Access. The version of Outlook Web Access included with Exchange Server 2003 addresses both of those concerns by more closely resembling the Outlook interface and including a number of important Outlook features.
- **Mobile device support** Mobile devices such as personal digital assistants (PDAs) with wireless network access and mobile phones with PDA-type interfaces have become somewhat ubiquitous in many organizations, especially among mobile staff. These devices provide portability because they are much smaller than laptop computers, and they provide much of the functionality of larger systems. Exchange Server 2003 provides a number of tools to integrate with Pocket PC and SmartPhone devices. Traditionally, handheld devices have only had the capacity to synchronize with an existing application, such as synchronizing mail from Outlook on a laptop or desktop with a PDA. Now Exchange Server 2003 has the capability to work with handheld devices in real time rather than relying on synchronization, using these features:
  - **Exchange ActiveSync** Enabled by default, Exchange ActiveSync is used to synchronize data from an Exchange mailbox to a handheld PocketPC or SmartPhone device running Pocket Outlook.

- **Outlook Mobile Access** Outlook Mobile Access, not enabled by default, is used to provide Exchange mailbox access to devices that are Internet capable but are not PocketPC or SmartPhone devices with Pocket Outlook. Although a separate product from Outlook Web Access, Outlook Mobile Access is similar to Outlook Web Access in that it provides browser-based access to an Exchange mailbox. Whereas Outlook Web Access runs on Web browsers on full-size computers, Outlook Mobile Access runs on Wireless Access Protocol (WAP) browsers on mobile devices.

Configuring Exchange Server for Mobile Users

Exchange Server 2003 doesn't need much configuration for mobility, as Outlook Web Access and Exchange ActiveSync are configured and enabled by default and they have few settings that can be changed. RPC over HTTP and Outlook Mobile Access must be manually configured.

Configuring RPC over HTTP

RPC over HTTP must run on a server running Microsoft Windows Server 2003. Configuring RPC over HTTP is complex and has several steps. You first need to configure the RPC Proxy server on your Exchange server, configure the RPC Proxy, configure the Global Catalog server, and configure Internet Information Services (IIS).

> **Note** Before you configure RPC over HTTP, make sure you understand the security implications. It is possible to expose your private data to security risks from Internet attackers using this feature, although Secure Sockets Layer (SSL) is used for these connections. You need SSL properly configured on your server with a server certificate for RPC over HTTP to function.

To configure RPC over HTTP, follow these steps:

1. Select Add Or Remove Programs from the Start, Control Panel menu on the Exchange Server.
2. Click Add/Remove Windows Components.
3. Select Networking Services from the list in the Windows Components Wizard and click Details.

4 Select the RPC over HTTP Proxy component, as shown in Figure 42-1.

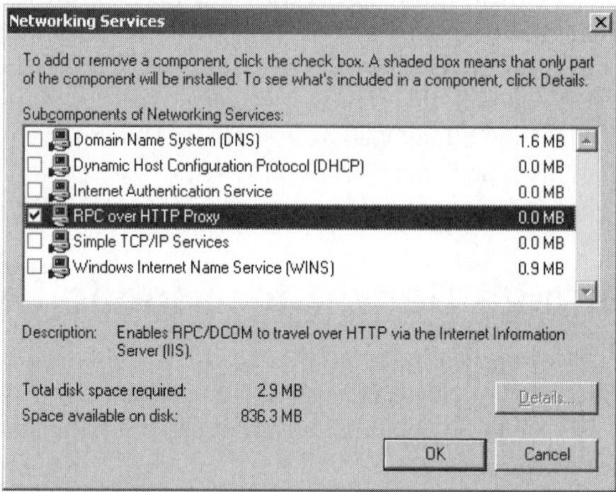

Figure 42-1. Select the RPC over HTTP Proxy component in the Networking Services dialog box.

5 Click OK.

6 Click Next in the Windows Components Wizard.

7 Insert your Windows Server 2003 CD if required and click Finish when the Windows Components Wizard completes, then close the Add Or Remove Programs dialog box.

8 On the same system, open the Registry Editor by clicking Start, Run, typing **regedit**, and clicking OK.

9 Locate and select the registry key HKEY_LOCAL_MACHINE\Software\Microsoft\Rpc\RpcProxy\ValidPorts and select Modify from the Edit menu.

10 Replace the value date with *east*:**593;***east.entdomain.tld*:**593;***east*:**6001-6002;***east.entdomain.tld*:**6001-6002;***east*:**6004;***east.entdomain.tld*:**6004;***west-dc*:**593;***west-dc.entdomain.tld*:**593;***west-dc*:**6004;***west-dc.entdomain.tld*:**6004** replacing *east* with the name of your Exchange server, *west-dc* with the name of your Global Catalog server, and *entdomain.tld* with your domain name.

11 Click OK, then close the Registry Editor.

12 You can now configure IIS for RPC over HTTP. On the same system open the IIS Manager from the Start, Administrative Tools menu.

13 In the left pane of the IIS Manager snap-in, expand the server object, Web Sites, and Default Web Site, right-click the RPC object and select Properties.

14 Click the Directory Security tab and click Edit in the Authentication And Access Control section of this tab.

15. Select the Basic Authentication check box in the Authenticated Access section of the Authentication Methods dialog box shown in Figure 42-2.

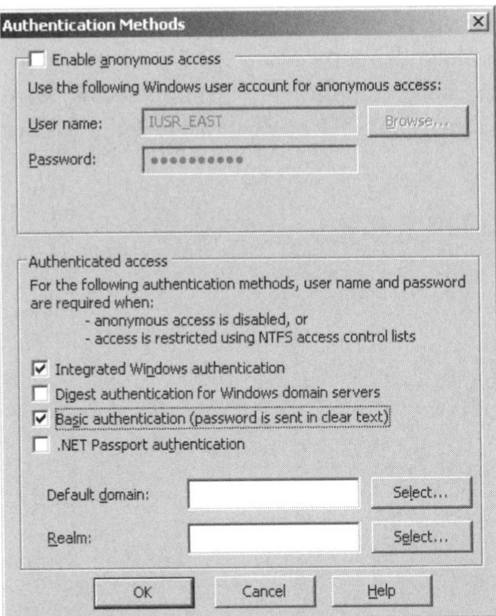

Figure 42-2. Select the Basic Authentication check box to allow plain-text authentication of RPC over HTTP connections.

16. Click OK.
17. Click OK again to close the RPC Properties dialog box, then close the IIS Manager snap-in.

The following steps need to be done on the Global Catalog server for your domain:

1. Click Start, Run, type **regedit**, and click OK to open the Registry Editor.
2. Select the HKEY_LOCAL_MACHINE\SYSTEM\CurrentControlSet\Services\NTDS\Parameters key.
3. Select New, Multi-String Value from the Edit menu.
4. Type the new value **NSPI interface protocol sequences.**
5. Select Modify from the Edit menu.
6. Enter **ncacn_http:6004** in the Value text box.
7. Click OK, then close the Registry Editor.

Your RPC over HTTP proxy server is now configured. Users must be able to access the SSL port for the default Web server over the Internet. See the section "Configuring Outlook for RPC over HTTP" later in the chapter for information on configuring Outlook to use the new connection.

Exchange ActiveSync and Outlook Mobile Access

Exchange ActiveSync and Outlook Mobile Access are both configured with Exchange System Manager. To configure them, ensure you have administration rights to the Exchange server then open Exchange System Manager from the Start, All Programs, Microsoft Exchange menu. Expand the Global Services object in the left pane of Exchange System Manager, right-click Mobile Services, and select Properties. The Mobile Services Properties dialog box opens, as shown in Figure 42-3.

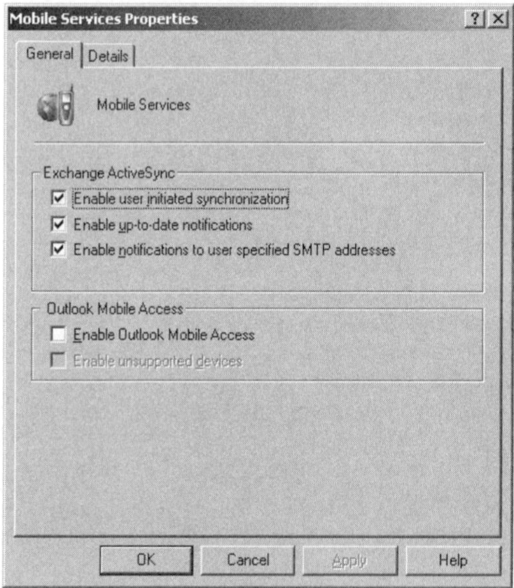

Figure 42-3. The Mobile Services Properties dialog box is used to configure Exchange ActiveSync and Outlook Mobile Access.

As you can see, Exchange ActiveSync is enabled by default. There are three available settings for ActiveSync:

- **Enable User Initiated Synchronization** The most basic setting for Exchange Active-Sync turns the feature on or off.
- **Enable Up-To-Date Notifications** Up-to-date notifications are sent from the Exchange Server to the mobile device to automatically trigger synchronization from the server side. This way the mobile device is always synchronized.
- **Enable Notifications To User Specified SMTP Addresses** This option is used to trigger up-to-date synchronization when it is not supported by the device or carrier. Instead, notifications are sent over SMTP, which triggers the synchronization.

Outlook Mobile Access is less commonly used and is disabled by default. Outlook Mobile Access has two available settings:

- **Enable Outlook Mobile Access** This option turns Outlook Mobile Access on or off.
- **Enable unsupported devices** Allows the use of mobile devices not in the list of supported devices provided by Microsoft.

> **Tip** Outlook Mobile Access is accessed by pointing the mobile device's Web browser to *http://server.domain.tld/oma*, where *server.domain.tld* is the name of your Exchange Server.

Using Mobility Features

The mobility features provided with Exchange, apart from RPC over HTTP, do not require much in the way of configuration on the client side. In addition, they are quite simple to use.

Using Outlook Web Access

Outlook Web Access is installed and configured by default on your Exchange Server. Configuration and use of Outlook Web Access is covered in detail in Chapter 41, "Accessing Messages Through a Web Browser."

Configuring Outlook for RPC over HTTP

If you've configured RPC over HTTP as covered earlier in this chapter, you need to do some special configuration to the Outlook client to make the client use the new connection. This can be done when creating a new Exchange Server connection in Outlook or it can be done for an existing connection. When creating a new connection, specify the Exchange Server name and user name on the Exchange Server Settings page of the E-Mail Accounts Wizard, then click More Settings. For an existing connection, open the E-Mail Accounts Wizard from the Tools menu in Outlook, view existing accounts, select the existing Exchange connection, and click Change. Click More Settings on the Exchange Server Settings page.

Click the Connection tab in the Microsoft Exchange Server dialog box. Select the Connect To My Exchange Mailbox Using HTTP check box as shown in Figure 42-4.

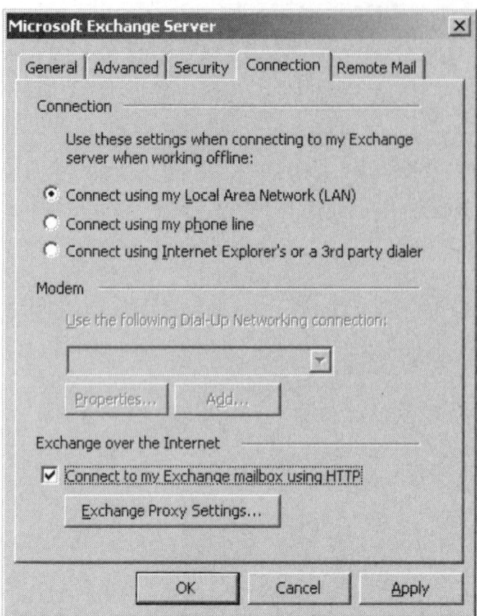

Figure 42-4. Selecting the Connect To My Exchange Mailbox Using HTTP check box enables RPC over HTTP from the client side.

On the Connection tab of the Microsoft Exchange Server dialog box, click Exchange Proxy Settings. Specify the fully qualified name of the Exchange Server on which you installed the RPC Proxy earlier in the Use This URL To Connect To My Proxy Server For Exchange box. Ensure that the Connect Using SSL Only check box is selected and select the Mutually Authenticate The Session When Connecting With SSL check box. Specify the fully qualified name of the RPC server prefixed with msstd: in the Principal Name For Proxy Server box. Select Basic Authentication from the Use This Authentication When Connecting To My Proxy Server For Exchange drop-down box. Finally, you can select the On Fast Networks, Connect Using HTTP First, Then Connect Using TCP/IP check box if you always want to use RPC over HTTP. The default behavior is to only use RPC over HTTP on slow connections such as Internet connections. RPC over HTTP is used on fast connections when the Exchange Server cannot be contacted from the Outlook client computer, such as when there is a firewall blocking the Exchange ports. As most firewalls allow HTTP (port 80) out, HTTP over RPC will work on almost any network. The Exchange Proxy Settings dialog box should now look like in the one shown in Figure 42-5.

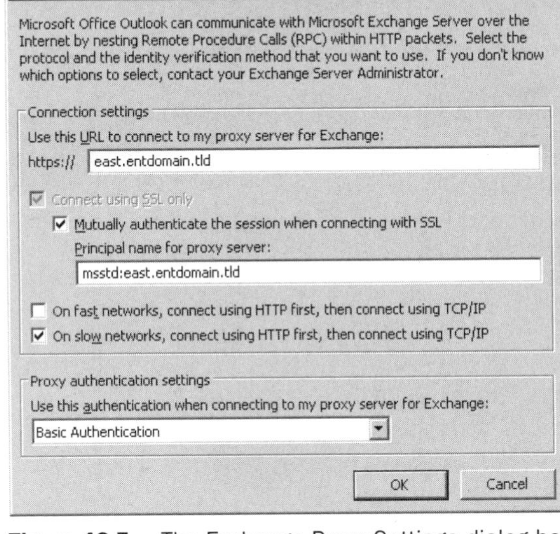

Figure 42-5. The Exchange Proxy Settings dialog box is shown here fully configured for RPC over HTTP.

Click OK to close the Exchange Proxy Settings dialog box. Click OK again to close the Microsoft Exchange Server dialog box, and click Next to finish the E-Mail Accounts Wizard. If Outlook was running while you made these changes, you need to restart Outlook for the changes to take effect.You are then using RPC over HTTP.

Synchronization Issues

Due to the way in which Outlook stores items, both locally and on the server, it uses synchronization between the client and server. The client copy is kept for mobility so that the Outlook user can work while not connected to the network, and the server copy is kept for resiliency and so that the user can work with the items from another computer or from Outlook Web Access.

Due to the synchronization process, conflicts can occur. These conflicts can come from a number of sources, including both address books and items. Microsoft Outlook maintains logs of the synchronization process and these logs can be used to troubleshoot synchronization issues. To view the synchronization logs, from the Go menu, select Folder List. Click Sync Issues, as shown in Figure 42-6.

> **Tip** In older versions of Outlook and Exchange, synchronization logs are kept in the Deleted Items folder.

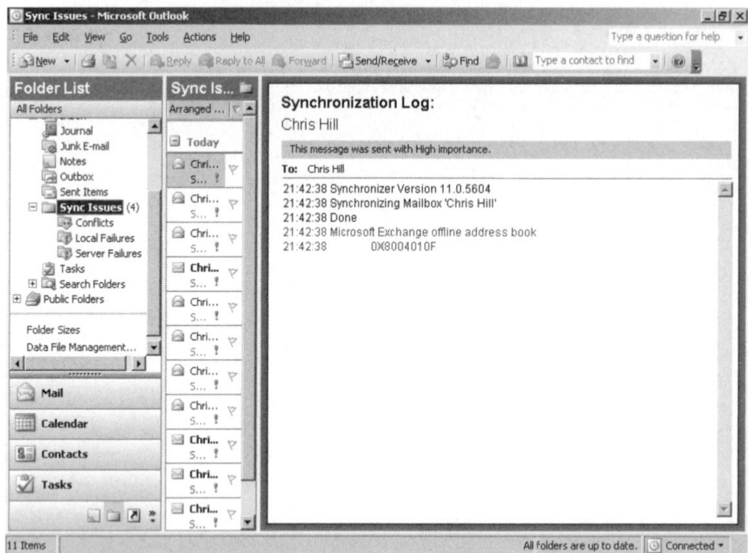

Figure 42-6. The Sync Issues folder stores synchronization logs for Outlook and Exchange.

The logs in the Sync Issues folder track the synchronization progress and any associated errors. When there are synchronization conflicts, the original item is marked as a conflict. The conflicting item that cannot be synchronized is placed in the Conflicts subfolder under Sync Issues. If you see an item marked as a conflict, check the Conflicts folder for the conflicting item and the logs in the Sync Issues folder and you might be able to troubleshoot the problem.

In addition to Sync Issues and Conflicts, there are two other folders for synchronization problems. When a synchronization fails and is not a conflict, the item that could not be synchronized is placed in either the Local Failures or Server Failures subfolder under the Sync Issues folder. Items that could not be sent to the server are placed in the Local Failures folder, and items that could not be synchronized from the server are placed in the Server Failures folder. Again, with the Sync Issues logs and these folders, you should be able to determine why the item cannot synchronize.

Appendix

Installing and Updating Outlook

You install Microsoft Office Outlook 2003 either locally from a CD-ROM or network share or remotely through a number of methods. This appendix explores these methods, offering a brief overview of each and offering resources for more information.

Installing Locally

To install Outlook locally, locate and run Setup.exe from the install medium. If the CD-ROM is used and AutoRun is enabled, setup should start automatically when you insert the Office 2003 CD-ROM. The first step in installing an Office application is to enter your product key (see Figure A-1) and click Next. After that you enter your user name, organization, and initials, and then click Next. Accept the license agreement and then click Next to continue.

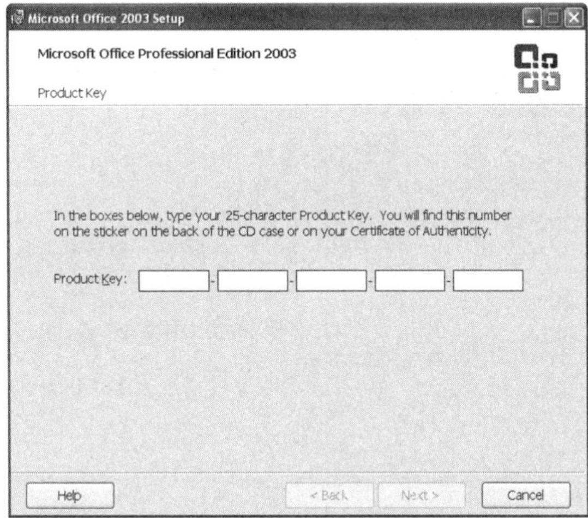

Figure A-1. You'll find the 25-character product key on the CD-ROM case.

Figure A-2 shows the next window in the installation process. To install Outlook (or Office) with the default options in the directory shown, select Typical Install. You can also select Complete Install to install all available options, select Minimal Install to install just what is required for the program to function, or select Custom Install to install only the options you want. Click Next to continue.

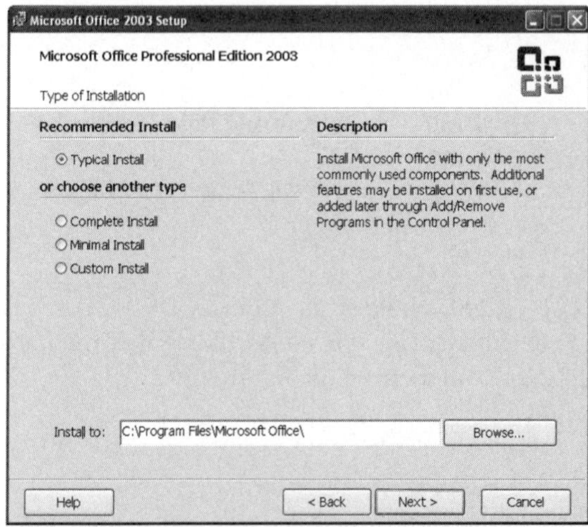

Figure A-2. You can choose the type of installation you want or select a target directory.

If you choose the Custom Install option and click Next, Setup displays the dialog box shown in Figure A-3. Choose the applications you want to install and click Next to install those applications with the typical options. You can also choose the options to install for each application by selecting the Choose Advanced Customization Of Applications check box and clicking Next to continue.

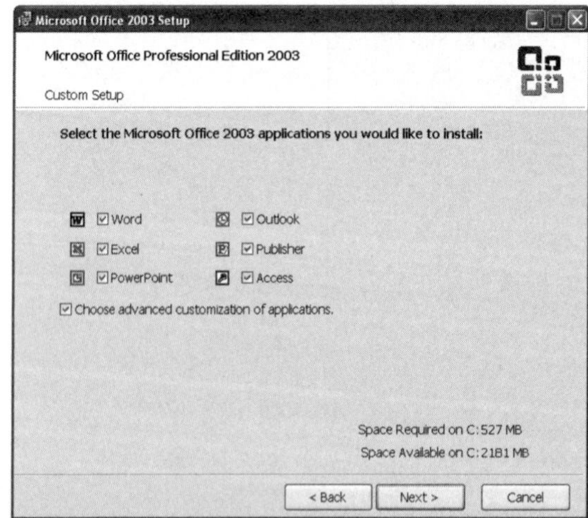

Figure A-3. If you selected Custom Install in the previous window (shown in Figure A-2), you must now select the applications you would like to install.

Figure A-4 shows the window displayed when you select the Choose Advanced Customization of Applications check box. You can expand any of the selections and select or clear specific options. For most options, there are a number of installation choices. Choosing Run From My Computer installs the option locally. If you choose Not Available, the option will not be installed. If you choose Installed On First Use, the option will be installed the first time it is used. The installation media (network or CD-ROM) must be available at that time.

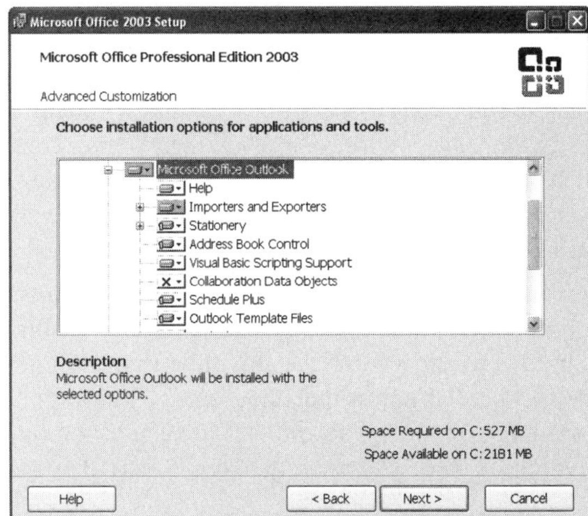

Figure A-4. If you selected the detailed installation option in the last window, this window is displayed. You can choose the options and whether they will be installed now, installed on first use, or not available.

Figure A-5 shows a summary of the options selected through the installation process. Clicking Install installs the applications shown in the summary.

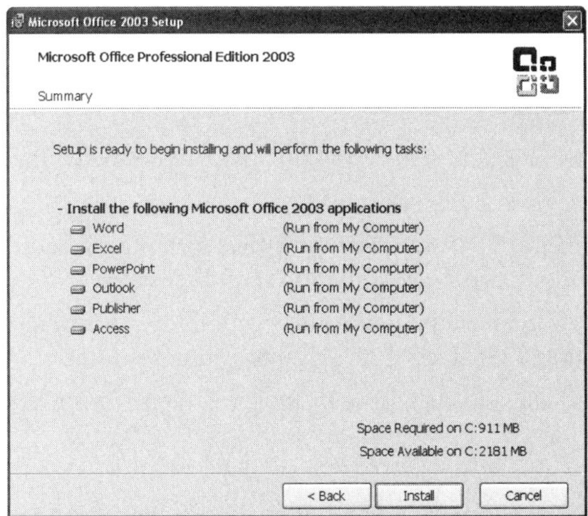

Figure A-5. This screen presents a summary of the selected installation options; clicking Install begins the installation process.

Setup Command-Line Options

You can choose from many options when running the Office Setup.exe file from the command line. A detailed outline of these options can be found in the *Microsoft Office 2003 Resource Kit* toolbox in a file called Setupref.doc. Only a summary of the available commands is provided here:

- Select /i <*msifile*> to run setup using the specified MSI file. Select /a <*msifile*> to create an administrative installation point using the specified MSI file. Select /f{option} <*msifile*> to repair the installation of Office on the system. The available options are listed in the Setupref.doc file. You must run /j{option} <*msifile*> from an administrative installation point, and it will advertise Office on the system. Office components are installed the first time they're run. Select /x <*msifile*> to remove Office, but the specified MSI file must be the same as the MSI file used to install Office. For all these options, the MSI file must be in the same directory as the Setup.exe file.
- Select /q{option} to set the user interface level for the install. The default when the /q switch is omitted in the option is *f* for full interaction. The other available options are *r* for reduced where no input is required but full status and progress indicators are shown, *b* for basic where only basic progress indicators are shown, and *n* for none, in which no interface is shown. Specifying /q with no option defaults to none. Adding a plus sign (+) to the *n* or *b* option displays a message when the install is complete (for example, /qn+).
- Select /l{options} logfile to log the installation to the specified file. See the Setupref.doc file for a complete list of available options. Select /settings filename to specify the customized INI file that setup will use. Select /wait to keep the Setup.exe process running while the installer finishes. Normally, the Setup.exe process calls the installer and terminates.

The last options that can be specified from the command line are public properties. Values for public properties are specified on the command line in the form *property=value.*

Automated Installations

You can provide users with an automatic installation of Office. To do so, use the following steps:

1. Create an administrative installation point for Office by running Setup.exe /a <*msifile*>. The <*msifile*> must be the MSI file you want to install.
2. At the prompt, type your organization name, the location for the administrative installation point, and the product key. Click Next to continue.
3. Accept the license agreement, and click Install. Office will then be installed to the specified location.

The next step is to run the installation. The automated installation method does not install Office to the local computer; it simply advertises the applications that are installed on their first use from the administrative installation point. You can also apply transforms (MST files) created with the Custom Installation Wizard included with the *Microsoft Office 2003 Resource Kit* to customize the installation.

To advertise the Office applications, run Setup.exe /jm <*msifile*> /t <*mstfile*> /qn to advertise to all users on the local computer. You can substitute /ju for /jm if you want to advertise only to the current user, and the transform (/t <*mstfile*>) is optional. Because /qn is specified, no user interface is shown. /qb is also an acceptable option, and only basic progress and status information will be shown. With the /j option, you can also add /settings <*inifile*> to use an INI file created by the Setup INI Customization Wizard included with the *Microsoft Office 2003 Resource Kit*. Both the Custom Installation Wizard and the Setup INI Customization Wizard are covered in more detail in Article 4, "Office 2003 Resource Kit," on the companion CD.

One advantage to using an automated installation is that it can be done from a login script so that every user receives the advertised applications. This leads us to the next section on remote installation.

Remote and Push Installation Options

As specified in the last section, remote installation can be performed from a login script by using the Setup.exe /j option to advertise the Office applications. Transforms and setup INI files can be specified to customize the installation. A section could be added to the login script that checks to see whether the process has already been done (by checking for the existence of a file or directory) and if not, runs the setup program with no user interaction.

The login script method of remote installation is not the most elegant solution. Without careful testing and supervision, the process can fail. A better method of installing Office (and many other applications) remotely is by using Microsoft Systems Management Server (SMS) or group policy with Microsoft Windows 2000 Server or Microsoft Windows Server 2003. Both these systems provide similar services for the remote installation of software. Group policy provides two ways to deploy the software to users, and these are covered in Chapter 33, "Deploying and Managing Outlook in a Network." SMS takes a different approach and builds software packages that are installed on the client systems regardless of user intervention. Another advantage to SMS is that it is meant to be highly scalable to very large networks and provides many more management features than remote software installation.

Updating Outlook and Office

You update Outlook and Office from the Microsoft Office Web site at *http://office.microsoft.com* (see Figure A-6).

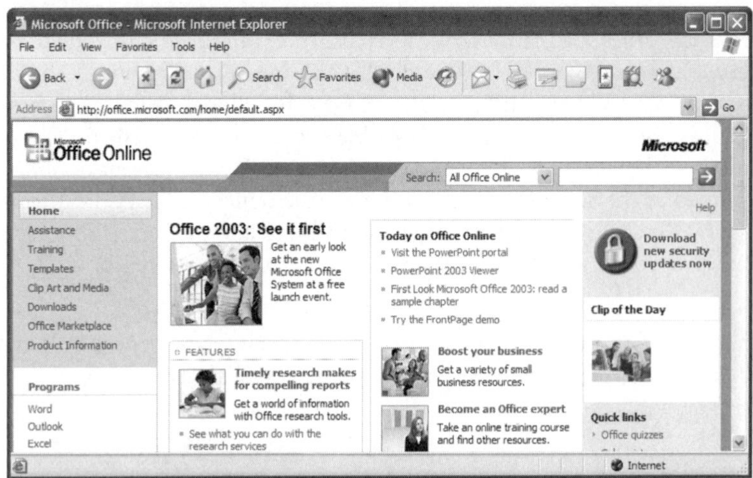

Figure A-6. Visit the Microsoft Office Web site to download and install updates and fixes for Office applications.

Click the Downloads link and then click Check For Updates to search for updates. The Microsoft Office site determines which updates you require. You can then choose which ones you want to download and install. The updates are grouped based on their importance. Critical updates are first, followed by recommended updates. Critical updates encompass issues such as security fixes, and recommended updates are small bug fixes and feature additions.

Index to Troubleshooting Topics

Note: Page numbers beginning with A denote troubleshooting tips on the companion CD.

Index

Note: Page numbers beginning with A denote articles on the companion CD.

N

Q

R

X

Z

About the Author

Jim Boyce has been a farmhand, an engineering technician and production planner for a large shipyard, and a UNIX system administrator. He also spent seven years as a senior instructor for Texas State Technical College, where he taught electromechanical design, basic drafting, CAD, and programming. He has owned and managed an Internet service business that provided Internet access and Web development services. Jim is now an independent consultant on a broad range of technologies and services.

Jim has authored or contributed to more than 50 books on computer-related topics. He specializes in operating systems and business productivity applications and has written extensively about Office, Windows 9*x*, Windows NT, Windows 2000, and Windows Server 2003. He is a former contributing editor of *Windows Magazine* and a frequent contributor to several publications and Web sites. Jim currently writes the Windows 2000 Professional and Windows 2000 Server TechMail Tips for techrepublic.com and frequently writes features for the site. He also contributes regularly to OfficeLetter.com. You'll find Jim's own Web site at *http://www.boyce.us.*

A native of Texas, Jim now lives in Minnesota with his wife, Julie. They are the biological parents of one daughter and have adopted five siblings from Russia—four boys and a girl—now ages 6 through 14. They are also the proud grandparents of two wonderful grandsons. Jim is a licensed private pilot and certified golf addict.

Proof of Purchase

Use this page as proof of purchase if participating in a promotion or rebate offer on this title. Proof of purchase must be used in conjunction with other proof(s) of payment such as your dated sales receipt—see offer details.

Microsoft® Office Outlook® 2003 Inside Out

0-7356-1514-4

CUSTOMER NAME

Microsoft Press, PO Box 97017, Redmond, WA 98073-9830